THE OXFORD HANDBOOK OF

PRODUCTIVITY ANALYSIS

THE OXFORD HANDBOOK OF

PRODUCTIVITY ANALYSIS

Edited by

EMILI GRIFELL-TATJÉ, C. A. KNOX LOVELL,

and

ROBIN C. SICKLES

OXFORD
UNIVERSITY PRESS

OXFORD
UNIVERSITY PRESS

Oxford University Press is a department of the University of Oxford. It furthers
the University's objective of excellence in research, scholarship, and education
by publishing worldwide. Oxford is a registered trade mark of Oxford University
Press in the UK and certain other countries.

Published in the United States of America by Oxford University Press
198 Madison Avenue, New York, NY 10016, United States of America.

Library of Congress Cataloging-in-Publication Data
Names: Grifell-Tatjé, E. (Emili), editor. | Lovell, C. A. Knox, editor. | Sickles, Robin, editor.
Title: The Oxford handbook of productivity analysis /
edited by Emili Grifell-Tatjé, C.A. Knox Lovell, and Robin C. Sickles.
Description: New York, NY : Oxford University Press, [2018] | Includes index.
Identifiers: LCCN 2017049559 | ISBN 9780190226718 (hardcover : alk. paper) |
ISBN 9780190226732 (epub)
Subjects: LCSH: Industrial productivity. |
Industrial productivity—Measurement.
Classification: LCC HD56 .O95 2018 | DDC 658.5—dc23
LC record available at https://lccn.loc.gov/2017049559

1 3 5 7 9 8 6 4 2

Printed by Sheridan Books, Inc., United States of America

Contents

PART III MICROECONOMIC STUDIES

PART IV MACROECONOMIC STUDIES

Contributors

Per J. Agrell, *Université Catholique de Louvain*

Oleg Badunenko, *University of Portsmouth*

Natarajan Balasubramanian, *Syracuse University*

Bert M. Balk, *Rotterdam School of Management, Erasmus University*

Eric J. Bartelsman, *Vrije Universiteit Amsterdam*

Mary J. Benner, *University of Minnesota*

Peter Bogetoft, *Copenhagen Business School*

Bruno Cassiman, *IESE Business School, University of Navarra*

Laurens Cherchye, *Katholieke Universiteit Leuven*

Jan De Loecker, *Princeton University*

Bram De Rock, *Université Libre de Bruxelles*

W. Erwin Diewert, *University of British Columbia*

Lucy P. Eldridge, *US Department of Labor*

Antonio Estache, *Université Libre de Bruxelles*

Rolf Färe, *Oregon State University*

Shainaz Firfiray, *University of Warwick*

Finn R. Førsund, *University of Oslo*

Kevin J. Fox, *University of New South Wales*

Roberto Garcia-Castro, *IESE Business School, University of Navarra*

Elena Golovko, *Tilburg University*

Luis R. Gómez-Mejía, *Arizona State University*

Emili Grifell-Tatjé, *Universitat Autònoma de Barcelona*

Shawna Grosskopf, *Oregon State University*

Daniel J. Henderson, *University of Alabama*

Robert Inklaar, *University of Groningen*

Dale W. Jorgenson, *Harvard University*

Martin Larraza-Kintana, *Universidad Pública de Navarra*

Mathieu Lefebvre, *Université de Strasbourg*

Marvin B. Lieberman, *Anderson School of Management, UCLA*

C. A. Knox Lovell, *University of Queensland*

Dimitris Margaritis, *University of Auckland*

Sergio Perelman, *Université de Liège*

Pierre Pestieau, *Université de Liège*

Hak K. Pyo, *Seoul National University*

Joan Enric Ricart, *IESE Business School, University of Navarra*

R. Robert Russell, *University of California, Riverside*

Robin C. Sickles, *Rice University*

Chris Sparks, *US Department of Labor*

Jay Stewart, *US Department of Labor*

Marcel P. Timmer, *University of Groningen*

Johannes Van Biesebroeck, *Katholieke Universiteit Leuven*

Marijn Verschelde, *IÉSEG School of Management*

William L. Weber, *Southeast Missouri State University*

Zoltan Wolf, *CES, US Census Bureau*

Xianjia Ye, *University of Groningen*

Valentin Zelenyuk, *University of Queensland*

Kim Zieschang, *University of Queensland*

THE OXFORD HANDBOOK OF

PRODUCTIVITY ANALYSIS

PART I

EDITORS' INTRODUCTION

CHAPTER 1

··

OVERVIEW OF PRODUCTIVITY ANALYSIS

History, Issues, and Perspectives

··

EMILI GRIFELL-TATJÉ, C. A. KNOX LOVELL,
AND ROBIN C. SICKLES

1.1. INTRODUCTION

OUR objective in this chapter is to provide an overview of some important aspects of productivity analysis, many of which are addressed in subsequent chapters in this *Handbook*.

In section 1.2 we stress the economic significance of productivity growth. In subsections 1.2.1 and 1.2.2 we focus on the impact of productivity growth on business financial performance and on the growth of the aggregate economy, the two being linked by the fact that successful businesses grow, and their expansion drives growth in the aggregate economy. At each level, productivity growth has been a historically important driver of performance, although its degree of importance has varied with trends in other potential drivers and with external circumstances. In subsection 1.2.3 we assume that aggregate productivity growth occurs and ask whether this is sufficient for an improvement in economic welfare, a much broader concept than that of economic output such as gross domestic product (GDP). This leads us into the literature directed at the increasingly popular but stubbornly elusive concepts of social progress and inclusive growth.

In section 1.3 we explore definition, quantification, and implementation, the procedures through which productivity measures are obtained. In subsection 1.3.1 we define alternative measures of productivity and its rate of change, suggesting some properties that these measures might be asked to satisfy. In subsection 1.3.2 we review two approaches to quantifying productivity change: one, which we call *calculation*, based exclusively on quantity and price data, and the other, which we call *estimation*, based on quantity and price data augmented by economic theory. In subsection 1.3.3 we consider some implementation issues confronting statistical agencies responsible for constructing and disseminating productivity and related measures of economic activity.

In section 1.4 we introduce productivity dispersion among producers. Dispersion matters because aggregate productivity is inversely correlated with the extent of disaggregate dispersion. In subsection 1.4.1 we review the evidence, which shows productivity dispersion to be widespread. In subsection 1.4.2 we introduce productivity dynamics, which considers two possible consequences of productivity dispersion. In one scenario, market forces generate a reallocation of resources away from productivity laggards toward productivity leaders that narrows dispersion and raises aggregate productivity. In the other scenario, barriers to the working of market forces or other factors allow dispersion to persist.

In section 1.5 we consider some forces, both internal and external to business, which contribute to productivity and its dispersion. In subsection 1.5.1 we consider technology-based drivers, for which we need information on the underlying production technology. We define productivity change in terms of the technology, and we decompose productivity change into its technology-based drivers, historically the most significant of which has been technical progress, which is inferred from outward shifts in production technology. In subsection 1.5.2 we analyze organizational and institutional drivers, the former being internal to the business and the latter being external to the business. The organizational drivers revolve around management and its practices, including human resource practices, and technology adoption strategies. The institutional drivers include various features of the business's operating environment that can enhance, as well as impede, productivity. Many of these drivers, such as the regulatory environment, are amenable to public policy intervention.

The lengthy list of references that follows is meant to serve as a readers' guide to the topics we discuss, and to encourage interdisciplinary reading.

1.2. The Significance of Productivity Growth

1.2.1. The Microeconomic Significance of Productivity Growth

Productivity growth enhances business financial performance, but its contribution is concealed by conventional financial statements expressed in current prices. This motivated Davis (1955), writing during a period of sharply rising price levels following World War II, to develop a common-price accounting framework, which he called "productivity accounting." This framework, in conjunction with the conventional current-price accounting framework, enabled him to isolate the contribution of productivity change from that of price change to business profit change, and it can be extended to alternative indicators of business financial performance.

Kendrick and Creamer (1961) and Kendrick (1984, 52) stressed the microeconomic significance of productivity growth, with Kendrick claiming that "... over the long run, probably the most important factor influencing profit margins is the relative rate of productivity advance. . . . In the short run, the effects of productivity trends may be obscured." The short-run phenomena include price movements, as Davis noted, and both Kendrick and Creamer, and Kendrick, used a variant of Davis's productivity accounting to separate the impacts of productivity advance from those of price changes. Much later, in his survey of the determinants of productivity, Syverson (2011, 327) embellished Kendrick's claim, referring to what he called a "robust" finding in the literature, namely that "... higher productivity producers are more likely to survive than their less efficient industry competitors ..." and consequently productivity "... is quite literally a matter of survival for businesses."

However, as Davis and Kendrick noted, productivity change is not the only driver of change in business financial performance, particularly in the proverbial short run; price change matters as well, as minerals companies around the world have learned, to their joy and despair, since the year 2000. Davis (1955), Eldor and Sudit (1981), and Miller (1984) developed models capable of decomposing change in business financial performance into the separate impacts of quantity changes and price changes, and to quantifiable changes in the operating environment as well.

Grifell-Tatjé and Lovell (2015) provide a theory-based approach to identifying the sources of change in business financial performance, an approach they summarize and extend in Chapter 9 of this *Handbook*. They first decompose profit change into quantity change and price change components. They then decompose the quantity change component into a productivity effect and a quantity margin, or replication, effect, and they decompose the price change component into a price recovery effect and a price margin, or inflation, effect. This identifies four distinct drivers of business financial performance. While the subject of this *Handbook* is productivity, a rich literature, highlighted perhaps by Winter and Szulanski (2001), stresses the significance of expansion through replication as a business strategy that has become the main driver of the financial performance of businesses such as Walmart, Starbucks, and fast food chains. Garcia-Castro, Ricart, Lieberman, and Balasubramanian illustrate the value of the replication effect for Southwest Airlines in Chapter 10 of this volume, although their replication effect differs analytically from that of Grifell-Tatjé and Lovell.

However, if profit is treated as the return to capital and expensed, as in national income accounting and in the investigation of the sources of US productivity growth by Jorgenson and Griliches (1967), and at the individual business level as advocated by Davis (1955), Kendrick and Creamer (1961), and Eldor and Sudit (1981), then the two margin effects disappear, leaving just two drivers of financial performance, productivity change and price recovery change, and replication is not an issue.

Lawrence, Diewert, and Fox (2006) develop an alternative analytical framework within which to analyze the impact of productivity change on change in business financial performance. They express business profit change in ratio form, and decompose it into the product of three components: productivity change, price recovery change, and change in the size of the business. Their analytical framework distinguishes primary inputs from intermediate inputs, defines business size in terms of its primary inputs, and treats profit as gross operating surplus, the difference between revenue and intermediate input expense. They apply their framework to the financial performance of Telstra, Australia's largest telecommunications provider, over the 1984–1994 decade, and find productivity growth to have been the sole driver of growth in Telstra's gross operating surplus, which was depressed by declines in the real prices of its telecommunication services. The fact that the productivity effect and the price effect work in opposite directions is not an uncommon finding, especially in extractive industries during boom and bust cycles; Topp, Soames, Parham, and Bloch (2008) recount the Australian mining experience.

From an analytical perspective, and assuming fixed prices, productivity growth leads either to an increase in output (and therefore revenue) per unit of input (and therefore cost), or to a reduction in input use (and therefore cost) per unit of output (and therefore revenue). In either case, productivity growth is lucrative, on several indicators: it increases unit revenue or it reduces unit cost; it increases profit and it increases profitability, the ratio of revenue to cost. Particularly when outputs are not under management control, it is appropriate to explore the impact of productivity change exclusively on cost or unit cost. An example is provided by the financial performance of regulated utilities that face exogenous demand and are allotted by the regulator a share of the profit they generate from cost-reducing productivity improvements.

In Chapter 15 of this *Handbook*, Cherchye, De Rock, Estache, and Verschelde trace the evolution of the use of frontier-based techniques in the analysis, and incentive-based regulation, of the performance of infrastructure industries. They provide a list of seven infrastructure industries that have been subjected to various forms of frontier-based incentive regulation in 21 countries. Of special interest is the attention they pay to the policy arenas within which incentive regulation has developed; the interaction among academics, regulators, operators, and policymakers has a long and continuing history. Against this background they propose a structural approach to performance measurement in regulated industries based on Economic objectives of the participating agents, the structure of production Technology, and Challenges associated with information asymmetry (ETC). No component of ETC is known, of course, and each must be specified by the analyst, presumably constrained by the prerequisites enumerated by Agrell and Bogetoft in Chapter 16 of this volume.

Agrell and Bogetoft survey theory and techniques, predominantly frontier-based, used in regulatory benchmarking. They begin with a demanding list of prerequisites for regulatory benchmarking, a list that is relevant not just to regulatory benchmarking but to virtually all empirical economic analysis. They continue with an equally demanding list of elements underpinning the use of frontier techniques in regulatory benchmarking. In their dynamic yardstick model, the regulator compensates a regulated firm under evaluation with a lump sum payment minus actual cost plus a fraction of the frontier-based estimated cost savings, the latter defined as the difference between a cost norm calculated from a super-efficiency cost-frontier model based on all regulated firms, excluding the regulated firm under evaluation and the regulated firm's actual cost. The authors illustrate the workings of their models with several samples of European transmission and distribution system operators.[1]

Productivity growth also increases such commonly used financial performance indicators as return on assets (ROA) and return on equity. This extension is important because these two financial performance indicators feature prominently in the business press reporting of corporate financial performance. They also serve extensively in the academic literature, both as dependent variables in regressions attempting to identify significant drivers of business financial performance, such as ownership and governance structure, and also as independent variables in regressions attempting to quantify the impact of business financial performance on firm growth. Illustrating the latter line of research, Coad (2007) and Bottazzi, Secchi, and Tamagni (2008) provide empirical evidence bearing on the evolutionary principle of "growth of the fitter," derived from the works of Schumpeter (1942), Alchian (1950), and Nelson and Winter (1982). The principle posits that relatively fit firms, being defined as being either more productive or more profitable than less fit firms, subsequently exhibit faster growth, thereby increasing their market share at the expense of less fit firms. Empirical support for both versions of the hypothesis is weak.

1.2.2. The Macroeconomic Significance of Productivity Growth

Microeconomic productivity growth aggregates to macroeconomic productivity growth. Fabricant (1961, xxxv) stressed the macroeconomic importance of productivity growth in stating that "[h]igher productivity is a means to better levels of economic well-being . . ." and that productivity ". . . affects costs, prices, profits, output, employment and investment, and thus plays a part in business fluctuations, in inflation, and in the rise and decline of industries." Kendrick (1961, 3) concurred, claiming that productivity growth has generated ". . . a large gain in the plane of living . . ." and an increase in ". . . the quality and variety of goods . . . while increasing provision was made for future growth. . . ."

Many scholars have studied the contribution of productivity growth to *output* growth. Schmookler (1952) attributed "about half" of growth in US output to productivity growth ("increased efficiency of resource use") over the period 1869–1938.[2] Kendrick (1961) attributed "about half" of growth in US output to productivity growth over the period 1899–1957. Denison (1962, 1974) attributed less than half of growth in US output to productivity growth over the periods 1929–1957 and 1950–1962. Something else has been driving US output growth, namely, input growth. The role of input growth in the studies cited in the preceding is apparent; in other studies it has been open to debate. The most-studied example may be the East Asian Miracle, in which rapid output growth in the regional economies since 1960 was, or was not, due primarily to rapid input growth, rather than impressive productivity growth. Hsieh (2002) and Felipe and McCombie (2017) summarize the debate, with the former focusing on the use of quantities or prices, and the latter focusing on the use of values related through an accounting identity, rather than quantities related through technological relationships, and concluding that the debate was "much ado about nothing."

Studies of the contribution of productivity growth to growth in *output per person* are also numerous. The relevance of output per person is emphasized by Gordon (2016), who interprets output per person as "the most accessible," though still flawed, definition of the standard of living. We return to the flaws in section 1.4. Gordon examines trends in output per person in the United States through the very long period 1890–2014. For the period 1890–1920, Gordon finds productivity growth to have accounted for approximately one-fourth of growth in output per person. This ratio tripled during the 1920–1970 period that he calls the "Great Leap Forward," and declined to approximately one-third during the 1970–2014 period, which led him to conclude that some inventions are more important than others. Crafts and O'Rourke (2013) study a number of countries over the very long period 1870–2007 and find two growth spurts, the larger, their 1950–1973 "Golden Age," roughly coinciding with the second half of Gordon's "Great Leap Forward," and the smaller during 1990–2007. Bergeaud, Cette, and Lecat (2016) also find two productivity waves over the very long period 1890–2012 in a sample of 13 advanced economies, the larger generally coinciding with Gordon's "Great Leap Forward" during 1920–1970 and the smaller occurring after 1995 and primarily in the United States. Both Gordon (2016) and Bergeaud, Cette, and Lecat (2016) emphasize that their respective larger productivity waves occurred long after the innovations that created them, such as the internal combustion engine, the assembly line, and electric light and power.

Their emphasis on lags recalls David's (1990) reaction, from the perspective of an economic historian, to Solow's (1987) famous "productivity paradox": avoid the "pitfall of unrealistic impatience," because it takes time for innovations, general-purpose technologies in particular, to diffuse through economies. Nonetheless, van Ark (2016, 4) reminds us that the productivity paradox is alive and well in the new digital economy, although he heeds the warnings of the economic historians by noting that we have not yet progressed from the installation phase to the deployment phase, ". . . when the new technological paradigm will have been widely diffused and will have become common practice across organizations, enabling its full potential in terms of economic and business growth, productivity, and profitability." Diffusion has become a recurring theme in much of the productivity literature.

In his "biography" of productivity, Hulten (2001) tracks output per person and total factor productivity (TFP) in the United States from 1779 to 1997. He finds a very different historical pattern, with the contribution of productivity growth to growth in output per person having varied widely by decade, with contributions ranging from

6.2% (1949–1959) to 161.7% (1859–1869). Earlier studies include Abramovitz (1956), who attributed 87% of growth in output per person in the United States to productivity growth from the 1869–1878 decade to the 1944–1953 decade, a share exactly the same as the more celebrated share calculated by Solow (1957) for growth in output per unit of labor (rather than per person, and the distinction can be economically significant) over the 1909–1949 period. The other driver of growth in output per person in these studies has been capital deepening, an increase in the capital intensity of production, although its role has been far smaller than that of input growth in studies of output growth.

One way to increase the role of input growth is to expand the list of inputs, perhaps by decomposing existing inputs. This is one approach followed in the new growth literature initiated by Romer (1986), Lucas (1988), and Mankiw, Romer, and Weil (1992), to name three of the more influential contributions. Romer emphasizes knowledge gained from an endogenous research technology, and the externalities associated with such knowledge. Lucas emphasizes human capital accumulated through education and learning by doing, and the externalities it creates. Mankiw, Romer, and Weil retain the elements of Solow's neoclassical growth model, and also emphasize human capital accumulation and the externalities it generates. Somewhat later, Hall and Jones (1999) augment physical and human capital with a host of endogenous institutions and government policies. Easterly and Levine (2001) stress the primacy of productivity growth over factor accumulation, and also emphasize the role of national policies and truly exogenous factors such as economic geography as potential growth determinants. Each of these factors, from human capital to national policies, continues to influence empirical studies of economic growth, and each appears in various chapters in the *Handbook*.

The cost-reducing impact of resource-saving improvements in technology mentioned in subsection 1.2.1 also aggregates to the macroeconomic level, where it has been used to analyze competitiveness among nations. The Organisation for Economic Co-operation and Development (OECD)[3] views a country's unit labor cost as ". . . a broad measure of (international) price competitiveness." Unit labor cost, the ratio of labor compensation to output, can be converted to the ratio of the wage rate to labor productivity. This conversion demonstrates that a country's competitiveness is dampened by increases in labor's wage (which may also be influenced by exchange rate movements) and enhanced by increases in labor productivity. Even within the European Union, with no exchange rate effect to complicate matters, competitiveness varies. German unit labor cost remained unchanged between 2001 and 2014 because increases in labor productivity compensated for increases in labor compensation per hour worked. Italian unit labor cost, on the other hand, increased by 2.3% per annum because labor productivity remained unchanged.[4] This labor-oriented concept of competitiveness extends easily to unit cost and multifactor productivity, although difficulties in measuring capital hamper its widespread application.

There is an alternative approach to evaluating the contribution of productivity change to change in a country's real income, with an analytical framework that inspired the framework developed by Lawrence, Diewert, and Fox (2006) for evaluating the contribution of productivity change to change in business financial performance that we discuss in subsection 1.2.1. Based on the principle that an increase in a country's terms of trade (the ratio of an index of its export prices to an index of its import prices) should have a qualitatively similar impact on its real income as an increase in its productivity, Diewert and Morrison (1986) developed an analytical framework in which change in a country's real income is decomposed into the product of the value of productivity change, the value of terms of trade change, which in principle becomes more important as countries open up to international trade, and the value of primary input change. Diewert (2014) applies this model to aggregate US data over 1987–2011, and finds productivity growth and increases in primary inputs to have been the main drivers of growth in real income, with changes in the terms of trade contributing virtually nothing.

1.2.3. The Significance of Productivity Growth for Social Economic Progress

Baumol, Blackman, and Wolff (1989, 9–10) claim that "[i]n terms of human welfare, there is nothing that matters as much *in the long run*" as productivity (emphasis in the original). Prefacing their brief survey of the long run, they stress that "... the magnitude of the changes [in living standards] is so great that they resist comprehension." Notice that they write broadly of human welfare and living standards, not narrowly of some measure of national income, or even of national income per capita.

Productivity growth increases aggregate output, but what is its impact on broader measures of national well-being that might incorporate leisure, environmental quality, or the distribution of the national income as well as its magnitude? This question was the subject of a lively debate that occurred subsequent to the Great Depression concerning what constituted "economic progress." One group, led by Ayres (1944), defined economic progress narrowly as productivity-driven output growth. The other group, including Clark (1940) and Davis (1947), defined economic progress more broadly to augment productivity-driven output growth with rapid re-employment of resources (primarily labor) displaced by resource-saving productivity improvements, a minimum inequality in the distribution of the income created by productivity growth, the imposition of minimal social costs, and various other criteria. *The Economist* (2016b) provides a good historical introduction to "the machinery question," which refers to productivity growth that displaces labor by machinery, and which it traces back to the nineteenth-century writings of David Ricardo.

The subject of economic progress resurfaced in the 1970s with the Nordhaus and Tobin (1972) "measure of economic welfare," which adjusts aggregate output for environmental and other impacts, and has resurfaced again recently, most notably in the writings of Stiglitz, Sen, and Fitoussi (2009) on social progress, the OECD (2014, 2016a) on inclusive growth, and Gordon (2016, Chapters 1 and 18) on the conceptual gap between conventional measures of aggregate output and the standard of living, and the "headwinds" threatening to expand the gap in the near future. Both concepts include the impacts of productivity growth on leisure, the environment, and income inequality, as well as on output. The basic idea is unchanged: the contribution of productivity growth to output, which is measurable, can exceed or fall short of its contribution to some measure of national well-being, which is far more difficult to measure. We call change in this measure of national well-being *social economic progress*, combining the early concept of economic progress with the recent concept of social progress.[5]

In Chapter 23 of this volume, Pyo explores the complex relationships linking productivity growth and economic development, which he distinguishes from both economic growth and inclusive growth, although it has much in common with the latter concept. The distinction turns largely on the impact of productivity growth on inequality in the distributions of income and wealth, and on the extent of poverty. Although productivity, distribution, and poverty are empirically correlated, the strength of the correlation is contextual, and causality is difficult to establish. In addition, inequality and poverty are also influenced by geography, demography, and the quality of institutional arrangements such as the security of property rights, barriers to investment in physical and human capital, access to credit, and the structure (and efficacy) of the tax system. Pyo provides a detailed survey of theoretical developments and empirical evidence on the productivity–development connection.

Whatever the name, the challenge is to develop business and public policies that counter Gordon's headwinds. Banks (2015), Hsieh (2015), and the OECD (2015a, 2015b) propose a suite of public policies to promote productivity. The list is long and unsurprising, including labor and product market reforms that would lower barriers to entry and exit; promoting business investment in research and development (R&D), information and communications technology (ICT), and other forms of knowledge-based capital; promoting reforms to the financial sector that would increase access to, and reduce the cost of, capital; promoting investment in public infrastructure; lowering tariff and nontariff barriers to promote cross-border trade and investment; promoting the transfer of resources from public to private ownership; and adopting policies that would encourage the transfer of resources from the informal sector to the formal sector, particularly in poor countries where the informal sector is large. The OECD (2015a, 2015b) also recognizes that some pro-growth policies have unintended adverse consequences for the environment and economic equality, to which we now turn.

1.2.3.1. *The Environment*

When the environment is involved, two issues arise in relation to productivity growth. Both issues involve the question: Productivity growth increases national income, but if it has adverse environmental impacts, what is its contribution to social economic progress?

First, suppose production activity has adverse environmental impacts, such as air and water pollution, and the natural environment serves as a receptacle for the disposal of pollutants, perhaps but not necessarily because disposal is free, or priced beneath marginal abatement cost. Productivity measures that exclude these impacts generally differ from measures that incorporate them. On what grounds do we prefer one to the other? And how might environmental impacts be incorporated into a holistic model of productivity change? Several writers, from Førsund (2009) and Lauwers (2009) through Dakpo, Jeanneaux, and Latruffe (2016) and the studies contained in Kumbhakar and Malikov (2018), critically survey existing models and find them lacking for their neglect of the materials balance condition, which states, in Førsund's words in Chapter 8 of this volume, that "[i]f all the material inputs into an activity are not embedded in the products the activity is set up to deliver, then the difference must be contained in residuals discharged to the environment." Dakpo, Jeanneaux, and Latruffe develop a model that incorporates the generation of residuals in a way that respects the materials balance condition, and facilitates productivity measurement incorporating residuals.

In Chapter 8, Førsund surveys the literature devoted to incorporating environmental impacts in productivity modeling, critically evaluating the standard approach based on the concept of weak disposability of residuals and sketching a new approach that dispenses with the weak disposability assumption. The preferred new approach is influenced by the work of Ragnar Frisch (1965) and is still being developed. Its four key features are the following: (i) a decomposition of the output vector into intended outputs and residuals that may pollute the environment; (ii) a decomposition of the input vector into non-materials inputs used to produce the intended outputs and materials inputs that contribute to the production of the intended outputs and also are responsible for generation of the residuals; (iii) satisfaction of the materials balance condition defined earlier; and (iv) a multi-equation system derived from a pair of linked production technologies, one for the intended outputs and the other for the residuals.

After developing the model, Førsund surveys alternative regulatory approaches to environmental impacts. In this context he dismisses as "Panglossian" the Porter (1991) hypothesis, which states, loosely, that sufficiently strict environmental regulation may induce polluting firms to innovate to such an extent that pollution diminishes and, simultaneously, profit increases, making environmental regulation a win-win strategy. Albrizio, Kozluk, and Zipperer (2017) provide empirical evidence bearing on the impacts of environmental regulation on productivity. They use data from 19 OECD countries during 1990–2010 to develop an index of environmental policy stringency, which they relate to multifactor productivity at three levels of aggregation: economy, industry, and firm. At the economy level they find a negative announcement effect that is offset within three years of the imposition of more stringent environmental regulations. At the industry level they find a temporary productivity boost from an increase in regulatory stringency for technologically advanced country-industry pairs, with the effect diminishing with declining levels of advancement. At the firm level, the focus of the Porter hypothesis, they find that only the most technologically advanced firms enjoy a productivity boost from more stringent environmental regulations; the less productive third of all firms experience productivity declines.

Second, suppose natural resources such as coal, petroleum, or natural gas are used as inputs in the production process. A number of issues have been raised concerning natural resource depletion, including (i) developing environmental accounts that would incorporate natural resource stocks, including land and sub-soil assets, that would support environmental productivity accounting; (ii) modeling and measuring the impacts of changes in natural resource stocks on estimates of productivity change; and (iii) addressing the intergenerational issue of whether these stocks are being depleted in some optimal sense. The first issue is addressed by Førsund in Chapter 8; by Nordhaus and Kokkelenberg (1999), who trace the history to date of national income and product accounts, augmented national accounts, and integrated accounts in the United States; and by Bartelmus (2014), who refers to conventional measures of aggregate output as "environmentally and socially blind," and who relates progress, or lack thereof, in the development of an integrated System for Environmental and Economic Accounting (SEEA) at the United Nations. Bartelmus (2015) continues by noting that SEEA incorporates the interaction between the economy and natural resource depletion, and bemoans the current lack of a system of accounts that incorporates the interaction between the economy and both natural resource depletion and environmental degradation.

The second issue is addressed by Topp and Kulys (2014), who show that declines in quality-adjusted stocks of (renewable and nonrenewable) natural resources reduce estimated rates of productivity growth when the resource is both an input to and the output of a production activity. Examples include fishing and mining, in which, as resource depletion makes constant quality stocks more difficult to access, additional amounts of other inputs are required to produce a given amount of fish or mineral output, and measured productivity declines. Brandt, Schreyer, and Zipperer (2017) use a standard growth accounting framework to show that, when natural capital is not included among the inputs, input growth is under- (over-)estimated by the traditional measure when the natural input grows faster (slower) than the included inputs, and consequently productivity growth is biased upward (downward). They illustrate their analysis with data from the OECD Productivity Database, augmented with natural capital data sourced from the World Bank.

The third issue is ongoing, and recalls the famous 1980 wager, made in the wake of the "Limits to Growth" movement, between biologist Paul Ehrlich and economist Julian Simon on whether the real price of a bundle of resources would rise or fall between 1980 and 1990. The real price of the bundle of resources fell, and Simon won the bet.

1.2.3.2. *Inequality*

The second prominent strand in the economic progress and inclusive growth literature concerns the distribution of the fruits of productivity growth. The general question remains: Productivity growth increases national income, but if it increases inequality in the distribution of income, what is its impact on social economic progress?

Gini coefficients have increased around the world, leading to the hypothesis that productivity growth exacerbates inequality in the distribution of income. Credible evidence must distinguish between correlation and causation, and OECD (2014, 2015b, 2016a) appears to assert causation, identifying several drivers of rising income inequality, the most important being (i) skill-biased technical progress that has caused increasing dispersion in wages and salaries and displacement of less-skilled labor; (ii) regulatory reforms that have increased product and labor market flexibility also have contributed to increased wage inequality; and (iii) rising shares of nonwage income from capital have increased income inequality. Before exploring these three drivers, however, it is worth noting that the OECD[6] also believes that productivity growth has slowed since the global financial crisis (GFC), while inequality of income and opportunity has been growing. This admittedly short-term trend suggests a negative correlation between the two, which in turn offers cause for optimism if productivity growth reverts to trend. Nonetheless, the McKinsey Global Institute (2016), in a study of 25 advanced economies, find that two-thirds of households were in segments of the income distribution whose real incomes were flat or declined in the decade to 2014, and conclude that today's younger generation is at risk of ending up poorer than their parents. They suggest enactment of government tax and regulatory and welfare policies, but they also recommend business policies aimed at increasing productivity and growth, and reducing inequality. Recommended business policies include adoption of existing best practices and pursuit of technological and operational innovations that expand best practices.[7]

Rising Gini coefficients are a cause for concern, but they need to be interpreted carefully. We have noted that the OECD has documented rising Gini coefficients within OECD economies. Lakner and Milanovic (2016) also document rising Gini coefficients within each of five world regions, with three more regions having incomplete data. However, they also find a declining global Gini coefficient, the ostensible conflict being attributable to the rapid growth of per capita incomes in still-low-income China and India.

Capital-skill complementarity exists, as Griliches (1969) pointed out long ago, and it is by no means a recent phenomenon, as Goldin and Katz (1998) have demonstrated. In addition, improvements in technology tend to be biased, using capital and skilled labor and saving less-skilled labor, as demonstrated by Krussell, Ohanian, Ríos-Rull, and Violante (2000). This combination of bias and complementarity motivates the first driver of rising income inequality mentioned in the previous paragraph. Brynjolfsson and McAfee (2014) express optimism for skilled labor but pessimism for less-skilled labor. Frey and Osborne (2013) paint a gloomy picture, predicting that computerization will put at risk of displacement nearly half of US employment, the half performing manual and/or routine tasks, a prediction that has earned them the moniker "techno-pessimists." Autor (2015) and Mokyr, Vickers, and Ziebarth (2015) review the history of automation, unemployment, and re-employment, and take a different view. While automation, through computerization, robotics, and artificial intelligence, does displace labor, it also complements labor, eventually raising output, the demand for (different types of) labor, and employment. Autor usefully distinguishes jobs from tasks, noting that while manual and routine tasks disappear, many jobs that require multiple tasks that cannot easily be unbundled survive. The OECD (2016a) traces the second driver to the fact that labor market liberalization creates nonstandard forms of work having relatively low wages and benefits, thereby putting upward pressure on inequality. *The Economist*

(2016a) emphasizes the third driver, arguing that the productivity dividend is being hoarded, ending up as business retained earnings rather than being invested in growth- and employment- boosting activities, an observation that is repeated frequently.

In a fascinating juxtaposition of rock & roll and economics, Krueger (2013)[8] provides a wealth of secondary information on income distribution in the music industry and in the US economy. He views the music industry as a microcosm of the economy, buffeted by technological changes, scale, luck, and an erosion of social norms, which compress prices and incomes, all of which have contributed to an increasingly skewed artist income distribution. As for the economy, he finds (i) all family income quintiles experienced over 2% annual growth during 1920–1979, but only the top quintile experienced over 1% annual growth during 1979–2011, and the bottom quintile experienced a decline; (ii) the share of income earned by the top 1% has roughly tripled, to 18%, since 1970; (iii) the ratio of CEO to average worker compensation has increased tenfold, to over 200-to-1, since 1970; and (iv) profitable companies pay all employees well, janitors as well as managers, suggesting that growing inequality originates between companies rather than within them. He concludes by expressing concern that rising inequality may have adverse consequences for future economic growth.

Song, Price, Guvenen, Bloom, and Wachter (2015) develop an analytical framework that enables them to decompose wage dispersion into between-firm and within-firm wage components. Their empirical findings, obtained from a matched employer-employee data set covering all US firms during 1978–2012, reinforce Krueger's final point; rising aggregate wage inequality is due exclusively to increasing inter-firm wage dispersion, since within-firm wage dispersion has been stable. The authors do not take the obvious next step of inquiring whether firms paying higher wages are also more productive. Doing so might shed light on the productivity dispersion literature we discuss in section 1.4.

In Chapter 9 of this volume, Grifell-Tatjé and Lovell adopt a standard growth accounting framework for measuring productivity change, the mirror image of which is a framework for analyzing the distribution of the value created by productivity change. Productivity growth creates value, which is distributed to consumers (in the form of product price reductions), to labor and other input suppliers (in the form of increased remuneration), and to the business itself (in the form of increased profit, which management allocates to interest, taxes, depreciation, amortization (ITDA) and retained earnings). Product price reductions and input price increase spur growth, as does business investment arising from profit increases. Distribution of the fruits of productivity growth was the principal concern of Vincent (1968), the French public institution CERC (Centre d'Études des Revenus et des Coûts) (1969), and other prominent French scholars who studied distribution at French public firms such as Electricité de France. Grifell-Tatjé and Lovell (2015) survey the extensive French literature. This growth accounting framework supports an analysis of the impacts of price changes on the functional distribution of income, which in turn forms the basis of an analysis of trends in the inequality of the functional distribution of income that can address the drivers identified by OECD and the hoarding issue raised by *The Economist*.

We conclude the discussion of income distribution by acknowledging that the income distribution dual to the productivity model characterizes the *functional* distribution of income among groups who perform a productive service that contributes to value creation, whereas much of the income inequality evidence pertains to the *size* distribution of income among groups of individuals, income deciles for example, regardless of what, if any, function they perform. The US Bureau of Labor Statistics (BLS)[9] reports that labor's share of value added in the US private business sector has declined from 0.67 to 0.62 from 1987 to 2014, a decline of nearly 7%, which documents a declining labor share in the functional distribution of income, but says very little about rising inequality in the size distribution of income in the United States. At the other extreme, the OECD (2014, 2016a, 2016b) provides extensive documentation of rising inequality in the size distribution of income in most OECD countries using a Gini coefficient based on "equivalised household disposable income," which, conversely, says very little about trends in the functional distribution of income within countries. Garvy (1954) attempted to reconcile the differences between the two concepts of income distribution, and Fixler and Johnson (2014) search for evidence on the size distribution of income in the US national accounts. Additional research that would reduce, or at least clarify, the gap between the two measures of income distribution would enlighten the inequality debate.

1.3. PRODUCTIVITY MEASUREMENT

Evaluating the significance of productivity growth, as in section 1.2, requires defining productivity and then quantifying it, which in most instances can be achieved in either of two quite different ways. We consider how to define productivity in subsection 1.3.1, and we consider two approaches to quantification of productivity change in subsection 1.3.2. In subection 1.3.3 we consider how productivity measurement is implemented by statistical agencies, and we discuss two important measurement problems that must be addressed.

1.3.1. Definitions

In general, productivity is defined as a ratio of output to input Y/X, with Y an output aggregator and X an input aggregator. An index of productivity change can be expressed as the ratio of an output quantity index Y^{t+1}/Y^t to an input quantity index X^{t+1}/X^t, with t a time indicator, or as a rate of growth $G_{Y/X} = G_Y - G_X$, with G a growth rate. Setting $X = X(L)$ generates a popular partial productivity measure $Y/X(L)$, with $X(L)$ either a scalar (e.g., hours worked) or a scalar-valued aggregate of various characteristics of labor. Setting $X = X(K, L)$ in a value added context or $X = X(K, L, E, M, S)$ in a gross output context generates a pair of multifactor productivity (MFP) measures $Y/X(K, L)$

and $Y/X(K, L, E, M, S)$. In each case, an index of productivity change is defined as in the preceding. Balk (2009) and OECD (2001a) explore the relative merits of the value added and gross output MFP indices. As Eldridge, Sparks, and Stewart note in Chapter 3 of this *Handbook*, the BLS publishes KLEMS-based MFP tables for US manufacturing and non-manufacturing sectors and industries for the period 1987–2014.[10]

In Chapter 20 of this volume, Jorgenson provides an introduction to the World KLEMS Initiative and its regional components for making international productivity comparisons at the industry level. Jorgenson relates the history of the Initiative, and provides details on the KLEMS framework for productivity measurement, including procedures for developing constant quality indices of the primary labor and capital inputs. A critical component of the Initiative, not relevant to intra-country data construction exercises, is the use of purchasing power parities, as distinct from market exchange rates, to link international currencies. He provides an empirical application of the Initiative with an industry-level productivity comparison of Japan and the United States. Inklaar uses the EU KLEMS database in his study of productivity and convergence in Chapter 22 of this volume.

MFP measures are generally preferred to partial productivity measures, but there are exceptions to the general rule. The most prominent exception occurs when labor is the only measurable input comparable across producers, as is frequently the case with international comparisons. A second exception occurs when the focus is on inequality in the size distribution of income, in which case labor productivity may be the relevant productivity indicator. These two exceptions intersect in OECD (2016b), in which declining labor productivity growth rates are contrasted with rising labor income inequality in both OECD and non-OECD countries.

Firfiray, Larraza-Kintana, and Gómez-Mejía offer a third exception in Chapter 11. They study family-controlled firms, in which non-economic objectives are important. These objectives include an emotional attachment to the firm, a desire to maintain control of the firm, and a desire to hand the firm down to future generations, a practice that Caselli and Genaioli (2013) call "dynastic management"; these objectives are collectively referred to as the protection of socioemotional wealth (SEW). The authors develop a framework in which SEW protection may be a significant factor explaining differences in labor productivity between family and nonfamily firms, and among family firms of varying sizes. They hypothesize that varying SEW priorities lead to variations in leadership styles, capital investment decisions, the role of nonfamily managers, and human resource management (HRM) practices, which combine to generate labor productivity dispersion; on productivity dispersion, see also subsection 1.4.1, and on HRM practices see also subsection 1.5.2.

Grifell-Tatjé and Lovell (2004) offer another motivation for using labor productivity. Following the cooperative literature inspired by the Illyrian firm of Ward (1958) and the Soviet collective farm of Domar (1966), they analyze the dividend-maximizing behavior of Spanish cooperative financial institutions. The dividend each employee receives consists of a wage plus the share of each employee in profit after taxes and interest. Change in the dividend decomposes into the product of labor productivity change, input deepening change, and price changes, making labor productivity change a driver of change in cooperative financial performance.

Bryan (2007, 1) proposes an intriguing indirect motivation for the use of labor productivity. He notes that the most valuable assets a firm has are not tangible physical assets but intangible assets such as ". . . the knowledge, relationships, reputations and other intangibles created by talented people and represented by investments in such activities as R&D, marketing and training." Unlike most writers on intangible capital, Bryan treats this asset as a component of the labor input, rather than of the capital input. This motivates him to propose replacing the popular return on (tangible physical) assets financial indicator with return on employees, because talent embedded in a company's employees is the ultimate profit driver. It is easy to show, using a modified duPont triangle approach, that profit per employee can be expressed as the product of the conventional profit margin on revenue and the revenue productivity of labor. For more on revenue productivity, see section 1.4.

The standard MFP concept can be extended to the concept of dynamic productivity. The essential difference is that in a standard productivity model, resources available in a period are used exclusively to produce final outputs in that period, whether or not the productive capacity of those resources is fully utilized, whereas a dynamic productivity model allows a reallocation of resources through time, with some resources available in a period being withheld from current production and made available for use in producing final outputs in a subsequent period. Another feature of a dynamic productivity model is its incorporation of intermediate inputs; produced outputs in a period can be consumed as final output, as in a standard productivity model, or saved and used as intermediate inputs in a subsequent period. A third feature of a dynamic productivity model is its property of time substitution, which allows firms to choose when to begin and cease production, and how intensely to produce; for example, technical progress encourages firms to delay production. The definition of productivity change remains unchanged as $G_{Y/X} = G_Y - G_X$, although the contents of Y and X are modified to incorporate the elements of dynamic productivity.

In Chapter 5 of this volume, Färe, Grosskopf, Margaritis, and Weber build on previous work of Shephard and Färe (1980), and Färe and Grosskopf (1996), to develop a dynamic production technology and to define standard and dynamic performance measures that allow for reallocation of resources through time. They derive a dynamic productivity index, decompose it into measures of dynamic efficiency change and dynamic technical change, and relate dynamic efficiency change to standard efficiency change. They provide an empirical application to 33 OECD countries over the period 1990–2011. A comparison of dynamic and standard productivity indices shows slightly faster dynamic productivity growth, due to faster dynamic technical progress. The authors refer to related research, to which additional empirical work would add value.

1.3.2. Quantification

Once productivity is defined, it must be quantified, which requires specification of functional forms in two quite different contexts. In one context, quantities and prices are observed, and we require a functional form that combines them. In the other context, economic theory constrains the behavior of quantities, or of quantities and prices, and we require a functional form that also incorporates the constraints imposed by theory.

1.3.2.1. *Calculation*

One approach to quantification is through *calculation*, which involves the use of market prices, or proxies for them, to weight individual output and input quantity changes in the calculation of aggregate output and input quantity indices. This procedure generates price-based *empirical* productivity indices (the most popular being the asymmetric Laspeyres and Paasche indices, and the symmetric Edgeworth-Marshall, Fisher, and Törnqvist indices). Mills (1932), Fabricant (1940), Kendrick (1961), and many others have calculated productivity change using quantities and prices to construct empirical indices of output, input, and productivity. Mills used Fisher indices, while Fabricant and Kendrick used Edgeworth-Marshall indices.

In Chapter 2 of this *Handbook*, Balk explores empirical quantity and price indices, so named because they can be calculated directly from observable quantities and prices. He specifies a set of desirable properties that empirical quantity and price indices should satisfy, including non-negativity, monotonicity, homogeneity, and units-invariance. He uses quantity and price indices to decompose change in profitability, the ratio of revenue to cost, into the product of an MFP index Y/X and a price recovery index P/W, and he relates this decomposition of profitability change to growth accounting techniques. He discusses the relationship between gross output and value added productivity indices, he relates partial productivity indices to MFP indices, and he discusses aggregation of productivity indices over producers.

Empirical index numbers are expressed in ratio form, and are employed throughout the *Handbook*. However, Bennet (1920) demonstrated that it is also possible to express quantity change, price change, and productivity change in difference form as quantity, price, and productivity indicators. Bennet's indicators can be expressed as the difference analogue to Fisher's indices. In Chapter 2, Balk specifies a set of desirable properties that empirical quantity and price indicators should satisfy, analogous to those that empirical quantity and price indices should satisfy; Balk (2008) provides details. He then uses quantity and price indicators to decompose change in profit, the difference between revenue and cost, into the sum of a productivity indicator and a price recovery indicator. In Chapter 9 of this volume, Grifell-Tatjé and Lovell relate productivity indicators, expressed in difference form as value changes, to productivity indices, expressed in ratio form as pure numbers. This relationship has the virtue of translating an index of productivity change to its contribution to a firm's bottom line, as Davis (1955) first showed.

1.3.2.2. *Estimation*

An alternative way of quantifying productivity growth is through *estimation* of some underlying technological relationship involving quantity and/or price data, which generates estimates of *theoretical* productivity indices and indicators. Estimation relies heavily on developments in economic theory that suggest particular functions to be estimated, and their properties to be imposed or tested, typically monotonicity, curvature, and homogeneity. Estimation can be based on either econometric techniques popular in economics or mathematical programming techniques popular in management science, and both techniques are utilized in the *Handbook*. Thus scholars have estimated functional forms for production functions and dual-value functions such as cost, revenue, and profit functions to obtain estimates of theoretical indices of output, input, and productivity. Each of these functions can be extended to frontiers that bound, rather than intersect, the data, thereby providing an additional potential source of productivity change or variation, namely change or variation in the efficiency with which any assumed economic objective is pursued. The econometric approach to frontiers, known as stochastic frontier analysis (SFA), was pioneered by Aigner, Lovell, and Schmidt (1977) and Meeusen and van den Broeck (1977), and the mathematical programming approach, known as data envelopment analysis (DEA), was pioneered by Charnes, Cooper, and Rhodes (1978). Sickles and Zelenyuk (forthcoming) develop a frontier framework for productivity measurement and estimation using both SFA and DEA methodologies and their extensions, and for both primal and dual approaches.

In Chapter 4 of this volume, Russell explores theoretical productivity indices, so named because they are defined on well-behaved but unobserved production technology and must therefore be estimated. He discusses the properties that a well-behaved technology satisfies, defines Shephard's (1953, 1970) distance functions on the technology, and enumerates properties satisfied by distance functions, including monotonicity and homogeneity. He uses distance functions to define the technical efficiency of production, and to define technical efficiency change and technical change, the product of which can be interpreted as a theoretical index of productivity change. He defines and decomposes two different productivity indices named after the Swedish statistician Sten Malmquist. He also defines and decomposes a dual, cost-based, productivity index, which has the virtue of allowing change in allocative, as well as technical, inefficiency to be a driver of productivity change.

Productivity growth, whether calculated or estimated, accounts for a variable share of economic growth. Debates among researchers on the primary sources of economic growth and development have often been centered on two basic explanations rooted in the decomposition of economic growth sources: factor-accumulation and productivity-growth components. Kim and Lau (1994), Young (1992, 1995) and Krugman (1994), among others, pointed out that rapid economic growth in the emerging areas of the world such as East Asia was largely explained by the mobilization of resources. Alternative explanations to the neoclassical growth model explain economic growth not only in terms of intensive and extensive utilization of input factors, but also due to factors that impact the degree to which countries can appropriate the productivity potential of world technical innovations. Factors such as governmental industrial policies, trade liberalization policies, and political, religious, and cultural institutions are often viewed as central to the ability of countries to catch up with a shifting world production possibilities frontier.

Exogenous productivity growth was the prevailing modeling assumption until the endogenous growth model put forth by Romer (1986) took hold in the late 1980s. The sources of the endogenous growth, often expressed in a reduced form equation that shifts the production function over time, were typically spillovers of one sort or another. For example, if R is such a variable or set of variables, then the production function can be written as $Y = A(R)f(K, L, R)$. The various possible sources of the spillover differentiate much of the endogenous growth literature, at least at the macroeconomic level. For example, Arrow (1962) emphasized learning by doing. For Romer (1986) the endogeneity came from the stock of research and development. For Lucas (1988) it was the stock of human capital. A major source of post–World War II economic growth has been innovation in the form of technological change.

There is, however, another interpretation for the reduced-form endogenous technology term in the modern productivity model, specifically the presence of inefficiency. Suppose one defines the endogenous factor in productivity growth as simply a country's or firm's differential ability to loosen the constraints on the utilization of the existing world technology. With this interpretation of endogenous productivity effects, Sickles and Cigerli (2009) show that TFP growth is determined by the efficiency with which the existing technology (inclusive of innovations) is utilized.

Production spillovers have important implications for economic growth and for its management. If any type of investment whose gains are not internalized by private agents impacts long-run growth, then there is no unique long-run growth path and thus no so-called golden rule. From a public policy perspective, spillovers provide a clear role for government intervention. Government intervention may take many forms if investment is too low from society's perspective. Investment tax credits or R&D grants are two traditional forms of government intervention. However, government intervention may also take the form of relaxing constraints on businesses via deregulatory reforms, reduced red tape, private-sector market reforms, or any other aspect of the institutional and political mechanism established in a country and its markets that increase $A(R)$ in the production function. The latter set of external effects can be summed up as governmental actions that reduce constraints, or efficiency-enhancing investments. If one examines the new growth paradigm more closely, it must be recognized that it is indistinguishable empirically from the stochastic frontier model wherein A is an efficiency term. A substantial engine of economic growth has been efficiency change. As pointed out by Abramovitz (1986), Dowrick and Nguyen (1989), and Nelson and Wright (1992), among many others, the major sources of country growth differentials in the developed countries after World War II can be explained by the neoclassical growth model amended to include such endogenous factors as knowledge spillovers, technological diffusion, and convergence to a best-practice production process (Smolny 2000). The "new growth theory" implicitly recognizes the role of efficiency in production. One set of papers that provides an explicit efficiency interpretation of this growth process is Hultberg, Nadiri, Sickles, and Hultberg (1999), Ahn, Good, and Sickles (2000), and Hultberg, Nadiri, and Sickles (2004), who introduce inefficiency into the growth process. Of course the standard neoclassical model without explicit treatment of efficiency has been used by many authors in examining growth and convergence.

Endogenous growth also has been addressed using formal spatial econometric specifications based on both average production/cost models as well as frontier production/cost models. Models that extend the multiplicative spillover effects by expanding $A(R)$ by framing production in a spatial autoregressive setting in order to address network effects or trade flows among countries have been formulated by Ertur and Koch (2007) and Behrens, Ertur, and Koch (2012). More general stochastic frontier treatments that do not force efficiency on the productive units, whether they are countries, states, or firms, have been introduced by Druska and Horrace (2004) in the cross-sectional setting, and for the panel model in a series of papers by Glass, Kenjegalieva, and Paez-Farrell (2013), Glass, Kenjegalieva, and Sickles (2016a, 2016b), and Han, Ryu, and Sickles (2016).

1.3.3. Implementation

Statistical agencies around the world *implement* the measurement of productivity and related economic variables. They have their choice of calculation or estimation approaches, and they make budget-constrained choices concerning what approach(es) to use, what variables to include, and what sectors of the economy to cover.

In Chapter 3 of the *Handbook*, Eldridge, Sparks, and Stewart discuss how labor productivity and MFP indices are constructed at the BLS.[11] The BLS also publishes related data on labor compensation, unit labor costs, and labor's share, and is engaged in a number of projects designed to expand its range of data products, as outlined in Chapter 3. The OECD (2001a) covers similar ground in much greater detail, and also provides links to a number of national statistical agencies that provide similar services.[12]

Long ago, Denison (1962, 1974) pointed to a factor that confronts implementation of productivity measurement, namely variation in the quality of inputs. He decomposed growth of the labor input into several sources, including hours worked, the age-sex composition, and educational attainment, and he decomposed growth in the capital input into inventories, structures and dwellings. These adjustments previewed those currently employed at the BLS, which decomposes growth in the labor input into hours and a composition effect (accounting for age, education, and gender), and decomposes growth in the capital input into productive capital stock and a composition effect (accounting for the contributions of information processing equipment, R&D, all other intellectual property products and all other capital services). Over the 1987–2015 period in the US private business and nonfarm business sectors, the two composition effects account for about 40% of total input growth.[13] Eldridge, Sparks, and Stewart show the contributions of the two composition effects to labor productivity growth in the private business sector over the 1987–2014 period and several subperiods. Eldridge, Sparks, and Stewart explain the two quality-adjustment procedures employed by the BLS, and the

OECD (2001a) devotes two chapters to the adjustment of labor and capital inputs for variation in various measures of quality.

Bushnell and Wolfram (2009) provide an empirical example based on the performance of the operators of five US power plants, demonstrating the importance of variation in the quality of a single key employee, the plant operator, for power plant performance. The plant operator is responsible for the monitoring and control of the combustion process, an integral element of the conversion of potential energy in fuel into electrical energy that also includes processing and monitoring of emissions and other waste products. Using hourly data on fuel burned and power output for individual plant operators, they find a statistically significant positive "operator effect" on fuel efficiency, the ratio of electricity output to fuel input, and they calculate that if all operators at these five plants improved to best practice, fuel cost savings of $3.5 million per year could be achieved. This operator effect is analogous to the "good captain hypothesis" explored by Alvarez and Schmidt (2006) and Wolff, Squires, and Guillotreau (2013) for captains of Spanish and French fishing vessels. This hypothesis asserts that differences in catches among vessels are due to differences in the skill of skippers, rather than to luck and other factors such as weather. Although the analytical framework varies across the three studies, in each study variation in labor quality is not accounted for prior to the empirical exercise. Rather, since quality is difficult or impossible to measure, it is inferred from empirical findings. Power-plant operator and fishing-vessel skipper performance provide ex post measures of variation in the quality of a crucial input.

The quality issue is equally relevant on the output side, as Fabricant (1940, 1961) emphasized. The BLS accounts for quality change in outputs in a number of ways, as described in Chapter 3.[14] The importance of accurate output measurement was highlighted by the Boskin Commission Report (Boskin et al. 1996), which argued that the US rate of inflation had been overestimated, and consequently the rate of real output growth had been underestimated, by 0.6% per annum prior to 1996 due to a failure to incorporate new outputs and improvements in the quality of existing outputs in a timely fashion. The qualitative impact this has on productivity measurement is clear, and to imagine the quantitative impact, try compounding 0.6% per annum over a generation. Output measurement accounting for quality change was the main focus of the contributions to the Griliches (1992) volume, each of which focused on a segment of the growing service sector. The general finding of these studies mimics that of the Boskin Commission Report: the inability to fully account for quality change in continuing products and the introduction of new goods leads to an understatement of output growth and productivity growth.

In some sectors, output measurement is notoriously difficult. Griliches (1994) lamented the fact that these "unmeasurable" sectors were growing, which made productivity measurement increasingly difficult. Indeed outputs in these sectors are difficult to define, much less measure. Education, health care, financial services, the judiciary (Peyrache and Zago 2016), tax agencies (Alm and Duncan 2014), the provision of public safety (Carrington, Puthucheary, Rose and Yaisawarng 1997), and municipal solid waste collection and disposal (Pérez-López, Prior, Zafra-Gómez, and Plata-Díaz 2016) are prominent examples, most of which occur in the public, or non-market, segment of the economy. In these sectors the definition of the service being provided is unclear, and quality concerns loom large. The Atkinson Report (2005) and Schreyer (2012) explore various measurement options.

Zieschang discusses productivity measurement in sectors with hard-to-measure output in Chapter 6. He follows the OECD to define these sectors to include high technology industries, real estate, and services, which in turn include distributive services, financial services, health care, and education. He cites three central elements of these sectors: difficulties defining the characteristics associated with outputs, a scarcity of information on the production and accumulation of intellectual property assets, and a lack of sufficiently frequent transactions to permit market valuation. He then uses a capacity utilization function to develop a Fisher-perspective quality-adjusted MFP index that is conditioned on these elements, and he discusses some properties of this index. He then develops a translog approximation, which is exact under certain conditions. He also discusses issues raised by new and disappearing products, and changes in the scope of output, intermediate input, and primary services.

Diewert discusses productivity measurement in the public sector in Chapter 7, with a micro orientation toward individual service providers. He analyzes three scenarios: (i) neither output quantities nor output prices are available; (ii) output quantity information is available but output price information is not; and (iii) both output quantity and output price information are available. In the first scenario he proposes to set output growth equal to input growth, in which case productivity growth is zero by construction. In the second scenario he proposes to value outputs either at their unit costs of production, which confronts a difficult cost allocation challenge, or at purchasers' valuations, which he interprets as quality adjustment factors. Both output valuation options allow for non-zero productivity change. In the rare third scenario conventional productivity measurement techniques are applicable. He devotes most of his attention to the first and second scenarios, in which conventional techniques cannot be applied, and ingenuity is required. In this context he places particular emphasis on the challenges confronting productivity measurement in the education, health care, infrastructure, distribution, and public transportation sectors.

In Chapter 17 Lefebvre, Perelman, and Pestieau adopt both micro and macro orientations toward public-sector performance assessment. At the micro level they contrast output, input, and exogenous data that are available for productivity measurement with "ideal" data in rail transport, waste collection, secondary education, and health care. Unsurprisingly, they find available data to be deficient, particularly for their lack of quality information and their failure to incorporate institutional features. At the macro level, they discuss the evaluation of the performance of 28 European welfare states and their evolution through time. The welfare state is a subset of the public sector, with its performance evaluated by indicators of poverty, inequality, unemployment, early school leavers, and life expectancy. Performance is defined as a function of these five indicators, without regard for welfare spending, so that performance coincides with a quantity index of outcomes only. The authors construct three performance indices, one based on simple unweighted aggregation of scaled indicators used in the original Human Development Report, and a pair of "benefit of the doubt" indices obtained from variants of DEA, in which countries are evaluated on the basis of their ability to maximize the provision of the five welfare-enhancing indicators. They use these indices to estimate change in welfare outcome through time, which grows slightly faster prior to the GFC than after it, and which they use to allocate performance change to improvements in best practice and to catching up, respectively, an exercise related to the "distance to frontier" literature we discuss in subsection 1.4.2. They continue by conducting a test of the cross-country convergence hypothesis, with convergence referring to welfare outcome performance rather than productivity performance, as Inklaar discusses in Chapter 22. They reject the welfare outcome convergence hypothesis.

When public sector output quantities are available but output prices are not, one strategy suggested by the Atkinson Report, and reiterated by Diewert in Chapter 7, is to use unit costs of production as proxies for output prices. Grifell-Tatjé and Lovell (2008) study productivity and financial performance at the US Postal Service (USPS) over the period 1972–2004. The USPS reports revenue and an output quantity index, and cost and input quantity indices, which Grifell-Tatjé and Lovell use to construct implicit output and input price indices; as there is a single output quantity index, the cost allocation problem is avoided. They also estimate an efficient unit cost index as an alternative to the implicit output price index to test if the implicit output price index reflects (diminishing) monopoly power. They find the difference between the two proxies to have been small and statistically insignificant over the period 1972–2004.

There is another scenario in which unit costs have been used to weight outputs, namely in the private sector when output prices are available but are thought to be distorted, by market power or cross-subsidization, for example. Caves, Christensen, and Swanson (1980) used the neoclassical growth accounting framework to contrast two estimates of US railroad productivity growth during 1951–1974: (i) the conventional approach based on growth in outputs weighted by observed revenue shares that reflect cross-subsidization of passenger service by freight service; and (ii) growth in outputs weighted by estimated cost shares that reflect the structure of production technology. They found, exactly as economic theory predicts, that the replacement of observed revenue share weights with estimated cost share weights reduced the estimated rate of productivity growth from 3.6% per annum to 1.5% per annum.

Ironically, a decade after Griliches (1994) lamented the growing "unmeasurable" sector and the publication of the Boskin Commission Report (1996) on difficulties in output measurement, Corrado, Haltiwanger, and Sichel (2005) argued that the fraction of capital that is difficult to measure, accounted for by intangible capital rather than physical capital, which itself is difficult enough to measure, also was growing through time, and also makes accurate productivity measurement increasingly difficult. Measurement difficulties have led the national accounts to treat expenditure on most components of intangible capital as an intermediate expense rather than as investment, which Corrado, Haltiwanger, and Sichel note has potentially serious implications for empirical analyses of business performance and the sources of aggregate economic growth.

Corrado, Hulten, and Sichel (2005) identify three categories of intangible capital: business investment in computerized information (computer software), innovative property (scientific and non-scientific R&D), and economic competencies (brand equity and firm-specific resources such as organizational capital). Well-established complementarities among various types of intangible capital, and between them and various types of labor skills, mean that organizational capital and skilled labor tend to be bundled in successful businesses, making productivity measurement even more challenging. Nonetheless Corrado, Hulten, and Sichel (2009) accept the challenge by constructing time series data for intangible capital and its three categories, and estimating their contributions to labor productivity growth in the US nonfarm business sector. They find intangible capital deepening to have accounted for about one-quarter of the 1.63% annual labor productivity growth during 1973–1995, and to have accounted for the same share of the much more rapid 3.09% annual labor productivity growth during the subsequent 1995–2003 period. Corrado and Hulten (2014) find similar results for US private industry over the longer 1980–2011 period, with intangible capital deepening accounting for 27% of labor productivity growth.

Niebel, O'Mahoney, and Saam (2017) adopt a similar approach to estimating the contribution of "new intangibles" to sectoral labor productivity growth in the European Union during 1995–2007. Their new intangible assets are distinct from ICT assets, and include scientific R&D, firm-specific human capital, and expenditure on market research and advertising, among other components. Their data exhibit considerable variation in the contribution of new intangible assets to labor productivity growth across sectors and countries. Their econometric growth accounting exercise generates statistically significant elasticities of new intangibles on the order of 0.12–0.18, with these estimated elasticities exceeding their factor shares, suggesting the potential for productivity-enhancing resource reallocation.

1.4. Productivity Dispersion

Productivity dispersion originates at the individual firm, or even plant, level. Its analysis can be traced back to Schultz (1964, 1975), who studied the ability to rectify disequilibria, departures from satisfaction of first-order optimization conditions. A popular measure of dispersion is a "productivity gap," expressed as a ratio or a difference, between best and worst performance, or between 90th and 10th deciles, or the interquartile range. Another popular measure is the second moment of the productivity distribution. Productivity dispersion is important because it constrains aggregate productivity; in a widely cited illustration, Hsieh and Klenow (2009) calculate that if productivity dispersion in China and India were reduced to that found in the United States, aggregate productivity would increase by 30%–50% in China and by 40%–60% in India. Much of the literature is devoted to the identification of the sources of productivity dispersion and the promulgation of policies aimed at its reduction.

In Chapter 18 of the *Handbook*, Bartelsman and Wolf survey alternative measures of productivity dispersion and discuss statistical and economic issues involved in measuring it. They distinguish the preferred physical MFP measure (TFPQ) from the more common revenue factor productivity measure (TFPR) imposed by the data constraint, and they discuss sources and consequences of divergence between the two measures. The problem is that TFPQ (when establishment-level output prices are observed) is an empirical productivity index, but TFPR (when establishment-level output prices are unobserved, and are replaced by an industry output price index common to all producers) is not an empirical index number but often is the only available measure. Revenue productivity is a value rather than a physical concept, which can lead to erroneous inferences about productivity and its dispersion if individual producer prices vary. They also discuss a range of statistical issues that arise in estimating productivity and its dispersion, including endogeneity of input choice and how to deal with it, the use of cost elasticities in growth accounting methods when first-order conditions are violated, the use of stochastic frontier techniques, and how to reduce sensitivity to ubiquitous measurement error. They also provide new evidence of productivity dispersion derived from US and European data. They find similarly large interquartile ranges in the United States and Europe, and less dispersion in gross-output productivity measures than in value-added productivity measures. They attribute much of the observed productivity dispersion to country and industry fixed effects. The productivity dispersion literature is not alone in searching for institutional and other factors behind country, industry, and time fixed effects. The entire productivity literature is, typically of necessity, inundated with unobserved heterogeneity controls, and consequently so is this chapter. Their replacement with variables reflecting the institutional and other sources of these effects would add considerable insight to empirical studies of productivity and its dispersion.

The distinction between TFPQ and TFPR arises frequently in the large sample segment of the productivity dispersion literature. Collard-Wexler and De Loecker (2015) show that dispersion and reallocation findings can be extremely sensitive to whether or not one controls for establishment-level price variation, which they suggest would signal variation in mark-ups reflecting market power rather than variation in productivity. They, and Andrews, Criscuolo, and Gal (2016), employ a mark-up correction developed by De Loecker and Warzynski (2012) to convert estimates of TFPR to estimates of TFPQ. Andrews, Criscuolo, and Gal (2016) find differential mark-ups to have accounted for a small portion of the rising productivity gap between frontier and laggard firms in the OECD since 2000. A similar consideration (and an analogous correction) arises on the input side, although the input side remains less frequently studied. De Loecker, Goldberg, Khandelwal, and Pavcnik (2016) develop an analogous framework for correcting for input price variation in a context in which trade reform influences mark-ups through both output and input tariff reductions. Bartelsman and Wolf refer to the issue in Chapter 18.[15]

Price variation need not reflect variation in market power. Another possibility, frequently discussed in the management literature, is that price variation may reflect variation in the willingness to pay of consumers for customized products, which in turn reflects the business strategy of the seller(s). Niche markets are common, with mobile telephones a prominent recent example highlighted in *The Economist* (2016c). The willingness-to-pay approach to business strategy was introduced by Brandenburger and Stuart (1996), with the difference between consumers' willingness to pay and sellers' opportunity cost providing a measure of the value created by businesses and its distribution, a subject we discuss in subsection 1.2.3. From this broad perspective based on business strategy, it is not surprising to find evidence of productivity dispersion. Business seeks profit-driven survival, to which end alternative business strategies generate varying productivities. It would be useful to confine an investigation into productivity dispersion to businesses following similar strategies, since then observed productivity dispersion would reflect varying success in implementing similar strategies, and would signal varying financial performance. This is essentially the approach followed in the productivity convergence literature, with convergence being either unconditional or conditioned on country-specific variables, as exemplified by Rodrick (2013). In this case, conditioning would be on variables characterizing alternative business strategies.

However it is measured and whatever its sources, evidence of productivity dispersion has accumulated for over a century, leading Syverson (2011) to characterize inter-plant and inter-firm productivity gaps as "ubiquitous, large and persistent." We survey this evidence in subsection 1.4.1. In subsection 1.4.2 we explore productivity dynamics, the intertemporal behavior of productivity dispersion. In some circumstances, market forces lead to a *reallocation* of resources that reduce productivity dispersion, while in others dispersion can be long-lasting, or *persistent*, and even increase.

1.4.1. Evidence

The BLS began publishing its *Monthly Labor Review* in 1915. Early issues contained numerous empirical studies of (usually labor) productivity dispersion at the plant and company levels. In one study covering 11 sawmills and five production processes, Squires (1917) found inter-plant labor productivity gaps within narrowly defined processes (e.g., tree felling and log-making) in excess of 5 to 1, and unit labor cost gaps ranging from 4 to 1 to 12 to 1. Stewart (1922, 3), US commissioner of labor statistics at the time, summarized numerous similar inter-plant studies across a range of industries and reported comparable dispersion in labor productivity. He concluded by pondering, reasonably, "One asks how a mine that gets but 30.1 pounds per man per day can exist as against a mine securing 371 pounds per day, but with this economic problem we have nothing to do at this time." Much of the current research on productivity dispersion is aimed at investigating precisely this economic problem.

Summarizing several studies across a wide range of industries dating from the 1930s and 1940s, Salter (1960) found similarly large variation in labor productivity, part of which he attributed to "delay in the utilisation of new techniques," as measured by variation in plant construction date. This vintage effect is a component of the quality of the capital input we mention in subsection 1.3.3, but it is difficult to quantify and its variation is frequently, and unfortunately, missing from lists of potential sources of productivity dispersion.

For a decade during the 1950s and 1960s, the European Productivity Agency published *Productivity Measurement Review*. The *Review* contained numerous studies of inter-plant and inter-firm comparisons, usually of labor productivity or its reciprocal, with substantial productivity dispersion being the norm and high/low gaps of 5 to 1 not infrequent. Some studies reported the impact of productivity dispersion on unit labor cost or unit cost, and occasionally on operating ratios such as ROA, demonstrating once again the impact of productivity on business financial performance.

Recent evidence on productivity dispersion comes in two complementary forms: large sample evidence, popular in economics, and focused sample evidence, popular in industrial relations and human resource management. The latter approach, also known as insider econometrics, has three steps: (i) interview managers, workers, and others in a firm or firms; (ii) gather relevant data; and (iii) conduct an econometric investigation to test hypotheses of the factors that generate behavior reflected in the data. The focused sample approach complements the large sample approach in two ways: (i) it contains precise measures of dependent and independent variables of interest, including management practices, and (ii) it contains detailed controls for sources of heterogeneity, many of which are unobserved in large sample studies. Shaw (2009) provides a valuable introduction to the focused sample approach, and Ichniowski and Shaw (2012) provide a comprehensive overview.

Productivity dispersion has been documented in many large sample studies, including but not limited to Foster, Haltiwanger, and Krizan (2001) [US manufacturing plants in Census of Manufactures years 1977, 1982, 1987 and 1992; US automotive repair shops, 1987–1992]; Eslava, Haltiwanger, Kugler, and Kugler (2004, 2010) [Colombian manufacturing plants, 1982–1998]; Foster, Haltiwanger, and Syverson (2008) [US manufacturing plants in five Census of Manufactures years]; Bartelsman, Haltiwanger, and Scarpetta (2009, 2013) [establishment-level data across several countries and varying time periods]; Midrigan and Xu (2014) [South Korean manufacturing establishments, 1991–1999]; Asker, Collard-Wexler, and De Loecker (2014) [nine firm-level data sets spanning 40 countries and varying time periods]; and Collard-Wexler and De Loecker (2015) [US steel plants, 1963–2002]. The motivations and issues considered vary widely across studies, but the unanimous finding is one of substantial productivity dispersion whenever and wherever one looks.

Productivity dispersion has been documented in many focused sample studies as well, including Ichniowski, Shaw, and Prennushi (1997) [complementarities among human resource practices at steel production lines]; Lazear (2000) [piece rate pay and hourly pay at a firm that installs windshields in cars]; Bartel, Ichniowski, and Shaw (2004) [complementarities among ICT and HRM practices at US valve-making plants]; and Bartel, Ichniowski, Shaw, and Correa (2009) [more complementarities at US and UK valve-making plants]. The last two studies are illustrative of the focused sample approach and its emphasis on the use of specific ICT and HRM practices. Valve-making consists of three sequential processes—setup time, run time, and inspection time—and requires three types of computer-based technology and three types of HR practices. Findings indicate that (i) some technologies significantly raise productivity (reduced time) in some processes and not in others; (ii) some HR practices significantly raise productivity in some processes and not in others; (iii) complementarities exist between some IT and HR indicator pairs; and (iv) increases in the use of IT increases the demand for skilled labor (computer skills, programming skills, and engineering skills). In sharp, and useful, contrast to the first finding, Bartel, Ichniowski and Shaw (2004) show that a conventional econometric productivity analysis of the same US valve-making plants based on Census of Manufactures data shows aggregate capital to have no effect on aggregate output (value of shipments less change in inventories), thereby illustrating a virtue of focused-sample studies. We return to focused sample studies in Section 1.5.2, where we consider HRM practices as productivity drivers.

In Chapter 10 Garcia-Castro, Ricart, Lieberman, and Balasubramanian provide a somewhat different approach to a focused sample study in which they develop a value-creation and value-capture business model and apply it to the disruptive low-cost no-frills business model of Southwest Airlines, a popular subject of management research, perhaps second only to Toyota.[16] Their model, based on Lieberman, Garcia-Castro, and Balasubramanian (2017), is structurally similar to that of Grifell-Tatjé and Lovell in Chapter 9, although terminology differs and content differs in one important way. Their value capture, or price, effect reflects changes in buyers' willingness to pay and suppliers' opportunity costs. Their value creation, or quantity, effect consists of an innovation, or productivity, effect, but no replication, or margin, effect, because they expense profit; see our discussion in subsection 1.2.1. Thus the contribution of replication, which plays such an important role at Southwest Airlines through expansion achieved by adding new routes, occurs outside rather than within their analytical framework. Although replication does not increase productivity at Southwest Airlines, it can lead to an increase in industry productivity if it occurs at the expense of less productive carriers, which provides a link to the reallocation literature we discuss in subsection 1.4.2. In their evaluation of the performance of Southwest Airlines, they find replication to have been the dominant, albeit declining, source of value creation, and they find it has increased market share relative to that of the legacy carriers, thereby raising industry productivity. Not surprisingly in light of its business model, they also find growth in value created to have been captured primarily by customers initially, and eventually by employees. They conclude by discussing some changes that Southwest Airlines has been making to its "aging" business model.

Focused sample studies can be thought of as successors to business histories that were once so popular and so influential. Since businesses generate productivity growth or decline, and create or destroy value, it is unfortunate that productivity analysts spend so little time studying, and learning from, business history. To provide a few examples, classic and modern: (i) Tarbell (1904) chronicled the rise of the Standard Oil Company, which soon thereafter the US Supreme Court found in violation of the Sherman Antitrust Act; (ii) Chandler (1962) chronicled the development of organizational structures at duPont, General Motors, and the Standard Oil Company (New Jersey) (a creation of the Supreme Court's 1911 decision) over a century ago; (iii) in a book widely ignored in the new management practices literature that we explore in subsection 1.5.2, Sloan (1964) chronicled the management practices he developed while CEO of General Motors for nearly a quarter of a century; (iv) the studies collected in Temin (1991) catalogue the uses of information to address organizational problems in largely nineteenth-century businesses; (v) Helper and Henderson (2014) trace the decline of General Motors from 1980 to its bankruptcy in 2009 to its deficient productivity and its inflexible management practices, particularly to its management of relational contracts with its suppliers and employees; and (vi) Brea-Solís, Casadesus-Masanell, and Grifell-Tatjé (2015) study the financial performance of Walmart, contending that Walmart's business model did not change over a 36-year study period, but variation in the way it was implemented under successive CEOs generated variation in productivity and profit.

1.4.2. Productivity Dynamics

Productivity dispersion leads, or might be expected to lead, to a reallocation of resources away from less productive units to more productive units, thereby raising aggregate productivity. This is an old expectation, voiced by Stewart (1922) and explored by Denison (1962, 1974). However evidence suggests that some gaps are stubbornly persistent. The intertemporal nature of this expectation has spawned the phrase "productivity dynamics" to characterize the study of changes in productivity dispersion through time. Warning: productivity dynamics is a different concept from that of dynamic productivity introduced by Färe, Grosskopf, Margaritis, and Weber in Chapter 5.

The microeconomic branch of this literature explores firm productivity dynamics that incorporate entry, exit, and reallocation among incumbents. Industry productivity can increase if market shares of more productive incumbent firms increase at the expense of those of less productive incumbent firms. Industry productivity also can increase, even without an increase in the productivity of any incumbent firm, if productivity levels of new entrants exceed those of incumbent firms, or if productivity levels of incumbent firms exceed those of exiting firms.

The macroeconomic branch explores what might be called country productivity dynamics, covering a wide range of topics such as the process of catching up, forging ahead and falling behind (Abramovitz 1986); international productivity convergence or divergence (Baumol 1986; Bernard and Jones 1996a) and whether it is unconditional or conditional, depending on institutions and other country- and time-specific factors (Rodrick 2013); the significance of natural resource endowments, distance to the equator, and other features of geography (Hall and Jones 1999); and the rhetorical question of why are we so rich and they so poor? (Landes 1990). Wolff (2013) surveys the macroeconomic literature, with an emphasis on the convergence hypothesis.

The productivity convergence literature addresses two recurring issues. The first issue is convergence of productivity to what? One measure is provided by a time series of the standard deviation of individual country productivity levels about the mean productivity level of all countries in the sample (σ-convergence, in the jargon). This measure reveals whether country productivities are converging to a common path, which could result from catching up by laggards or falling behind by leaders, or a combination of the two. Another measure is provided by the coefficient of a regression of productivity growth rates on their initial values (β-convergence). This measure reveals whether countries with relatively high initial productivities tend to grow relatively slowly, and conversely. Inklaar and Diewert (2016) propose a third measure of convergence, a time series of the ratio of actual world productivity, defined as a share-weighted average of individual country productivity levels, to frontier productivity, defined as the maximum productivity level over all countries and all years up to the current year (E-convergence). This measure reveals whether country productivities are converging to (catching up with) best practice in the sample; it combines the flavor of Debreu's (1951) coefficient of resource utilization with that of the sequential Malmquist productivity index of Tulkens and Vanden Eeckaut (1995), Shestalova (2003), and Oh, Oh, and Lee (2017), although frontier productivity has been defined in other ways, as we discuss in the following.

The second issue concerns the identification of those sectors of the economy that are driving or constraining convergence, since identification can direct policies toward the right sectors. Empirical findings have varied with countries, sectors, time periods, currency conversion procedures, and the general quality of data. Using the first convergence measure, Inklaar and Timmer (2009) find support for the finding of Bernard and Jones (1996a) of both labor productivity and TFP σ-convergence in market services, but not in manufacturing, among a sample of advanced OECD countries since 1970. Inklaar and Diewert (2016) study productivity convergence across 38 economies from 1995 to 2011, distinguishing between traded goods and nontraded goods sectors. They find evidence of σ-productivity convergence (especially in the traded sector), but in combination with E-divergence, the latter attributed in part to a compositional shift caused by the growth of China and India.

As markets worldwide become less regulated, it becomes increasingly possible and timely to establish the presence of an empirical relationship between convergence, or changes in the relative position countries find themselves in relative to the world frontier, and market forces compelling countries and agents therein to economize. The foundation for the theory of dynamic adjustment that can be broadened into convergence or efficiency analysis has been established utilizing an axiomatic approach by Silva and Stefanou (2003), who laid out a set theoretic approach that was then extended in Silva and Stefanou (2007). Elaboration on the foundation for an adjustment-cost framework by switching to the dynamic directional distance function approach allowed Silva, Lansink, and Stefanou (2015) to deal with an even broader characterization of efficiency and productivity notions. Building on the Luenberger-based approach (using the dynamic directional distance function), Stefanou and his colleagues develop the relationship between the primal and dual forms of productivity (Lansink, Stefanou, and Serra, 2015). Econometrically implementable frameworks for the dynamic adjustment model that address asymmetric dynamic adjustment appear in the review by Hamermesh and Pfann (1996). Specification and estimation of asymmetric adjustment rates for quasi-fixed factors of production, similar in spirit to the Sickles and Streitweiser (1998) model, are found in Chang and Stefanou (1988), while Luh and Stefanou (1991) provide the modeling setup for estimating productivity growth within a dynamic adjustment framework. Previous efforts to estimate productivity growth in a dynamic adjustment model essentially ignored the adjustment/disequilibrium component of the productivity decomposition.

Tests of convergence originating in the economic growth literature (Baumol 1986), determine whether or not there is a closing of the gap between inefficient and efficient firms over time. One approach regresses the firms' average growth rates in technical efficiency on the log of the carriers' efficiency scores at the beginning of the sample period. A negative coefficient indicates β-convergence. In other words, the higher a firm's initial level of efficiency, the slower that level should grow. This phenomenon is the result of the public good–nature of technology, which causes spillover effects from leaders to followers as the laggards learn from the innovators and play "catch-up." One can also utilize a more sophisticated approach involving the Malmquist productivity index procedure. This method, based on the geometric mean of two Malmquist indices, can account for changes in both technical efficiency (catching up) and changes in frontier technology (innovation). In a study of industrialized countries, Färe, Grosskopf, Norris, and Zhang (1994) note that this decomposition allows for a more comprehensive measure of productivity growth convergence since earlier endeavors failed to distinguish between these two components. Badunenko, Henderson, and Zelenyuk apply this framework to macroeconomic data in Chapter 24, and an application to microeconomic data of the sort used by Andrews, Criscuolo, and Gal (2015, 2016) is a logical extension. Whereas our earlier comparisons of the different methods of calculating technical efficiency necessitated an intertemporal production set, the Malmquist index requires the contemporaneous version. Thus, due to rank considerations, only the DEA approach can be used to calculate the index.

The existence of a technology gap may present an additional source of growth, but if nations differ in ability to adopt and absorb new knowledge, then country institutional heterogeneity must also be examined. If follower nations exhibit both a technology gap and a low absorption capacity, then technology's influence on productivity growth will be ambiguous. The importance of technology transfer has been explored previously. For example, Hultberg, Nadiri, Sickles, and Hultberg (1999) show that technology gaps relative to the United States significantly contribute to follower nations' aggregate productivity growth in the postwar period. It has also been shown that growth is affected by country heterogeneity, which in turn is highly correlated with various institutional variables. Theoretical studies also point to the importance of openness in accelerating the rate of technology transfer or technology adoption (Parente and Prescott 1993). Bernard and Jones (1996a, 1996b) use a model of TFP that includes the productivity differential within a sector from that of the most productive country. Their results are, again, that manufacturing has not contributed significantly to the overall convergence in OECD countries. Cameron, Proudman, and Redding (1999) expand on the Bernard and Jones model to include a term that is comparable to our efficiency term. They look carefully at even more disaggregated data in terms of openness and technology transfers, but only consider the relationship between United Kingdom and the United States. Their results are that the technology gap to the United States plays an important role in UK technology advancement.

In Chapter 22, Inklaar surveys the convergence literature and conducts three wide-ranging empirical investigations into the σ-convergence hypothesis. In the first he uses the EU KLEMS database to quantify and to examine the sources of trans-Atlantic productivity convergence (actually, divergence). He finds the source to have been in the ICT-producing sector, in which productivity has grown faster in the United States than in the EU-10. In the second investigation he traces the industry origins of changes in productivity dispersion for a broader set of countries. He finds that productivity convergence has been almost entirely driven by convergence in manufacturing. In the third investigation he examines the extent to which trends in productivity dispersion can be explained by several drivers of productivity change, one of which is a measure of distance to frontier. The other explanatory variables are related to R&D expenditure, the role of high-tech labor and capital, foreign direct investment, and market competition. He finds proximity to the frontier to dampen productivity growth and most of the remaining explanatory variables to enhance productivity growth, though not always significantly. However, the impacts of the remaining explanatory variables do not vary depending on distance to the frontier, suggesting that, for this data set, they do not have an impact on convergence.

A variant on the identification of the sectors of the economy that drive or constrain convergence is the identification of the geographic regions of the economy that drive or constrain economic activity in general, convergence in particular. Gennaioli, La Porta, Lopez-de-Silanes, and Shliefer (2013, 2014) study over 1,500 subnational regions from a large number of countries over varying time periods, exploring the influence of geography, natural resource endowments, institutions, human capital, and culture on regional productivity and development. They characterize regional convergence as "slow" and "puzzling," although they find regional convergence faster in richer countries and in countries with better-regulated capital markets and lower trade barriers.

Dispersion, whether inter-firm or inter-regional, reduces the aggregate value of whatever is dispersed. Hsieh and Moretti (2015) apply a spatial equilibrium model to data on 220 US metropolitan areas. This enables them to infer rising inter-city productivity dispersion from rising inter-city wage dispersion, which they attribute to increasing housing supply constraints that limit the ability of workers to reallocate to cities with higher wages and, presumably, higher productivity. They estimate that lowering these constraints to those of the median city would lead to a spatial reallocation of labor that would increase US GDP by 9.5%.

Nordhaus (2006) provides insight into the potential value added for productivity research of having detailed spatial data on economic activity. He introduces the G-Econ database (http://gecon.yale.edu) to test a variety of hypotheses concerning the impact of geography on economic activity, including the geographic impacts of global warming on output, which he finds to be larger than previously estimated.

1.4.2.1. *Reallocation*

One of many approaches to the analysis of reallocation is based on a productivity change decomposition proposed by Balk (2003), who reviews the approach in Chapter 2. In this approach, aggregate productivity change is decomposed into four sources: entry of new firms, exit of old firms, productivity change in continuing firms, and redistribution of market shares among continuing firms. If entering firms have above-average productivities, or if exiting firms have below-average productivities, or if the productivities of continuing firms increase, or if market shares of continuing firms are redistributed away from less productive firms toward more productive firms, aggregate productivity increases. One definition of the contribution of reallocation is the sum of entry of new firms, exit of old firms, and redistribution of market shares among continuing firms. As Balk notes, competing decompositions exist, but this is Balk's preferred decomposition, and it nicely characterizes the reallocation mechanism and its potential to enhance aggregate productivity. Among the competing decompositions, perhaps the most popular is that of Olley and Pakes (1996), whose decomposition contains an additional "cross" component that captures the covariance between changes in incumbents' productivity and changes in their market share, the objective being to determine whether firms experiencing productivity growth (decline) gain (lose) market share.

Empirical evidence of the workings of the reallocation mechanism is widespread and, generally speaking, encouraging; as one would expect, reallocation makes a positive contribution to aggregate productivity growth. A brief summary of three studies illustrates the empirical relevance of the reallocation mechanism.

The OECD (2001b) reports findings for several European countries over the 1985–1994 decade. In eight countries, aggregate labor productivity growth has been due primarily to labor productivity growth within continuing establishments, with the role of reallocation being small and variable across countries. However, in five countries, aggregate MFP growth has been due primarily to reallocation, driven by both net entry and redistribution. Foster, Haltiwanger, and Krizan (2006) report findings for a large number of establishments in the US retail trade sector for three census years. The data exhibit large and stable interquartile dispersion in labor productivity across establishments. Nearly all labor productivity growth is attributable to net entry, making reallocation the driving force behind aggregate labor productivity growth. The richness of their data allows the authors to decompose entry into entry by new firms and entry by continuing firms (opening additional establishments), and to decompose exit into exit by firms leaving the sector and exit by continuing firms (closing establishments). The main contributors to net entry were continuing firms opening new establishments and exiting firms leaving the sector altogether. Conditional on survival, they find substantial persistence in terms of relative productivity rankings. Foster, Haltiwanger, and Syverson (2008) report findings for a large number of US establishments in seven-digit manufacturing product categories in five census years. The primary drivers of MFP growth have been growth by continuing establishments, followed by net entry, with reallocation explaining between one-fourth and one-third of aggregate productivity growth.

Two frontier-based approaches to the investigation of productivity dynamics, re-allocation, and convergence have emerged, although there appears to be no cross-fertilization between the two literatures.

One frontier-based approach uses macroeconomic data, frequently sourced from the Penn World Tables (PWT), and its analytical foundation is provided by one of the two Malmquist productivity indices we discuss in subsection 1.3.2. This approach seems to have originated with Kumar and Russell (2002), who use PWT data on output, capital, and labor from 57 countries over 1965–1990 to estimate a Malmquist productivity index. An assumption of constant returns to scale enables them to estimate labor productivity change and decompose it into the contributions of catching up, technical change, and capital deepening. They attribute most of the aggregate productivity growth to capital deepening, with technical progress and catch-up together accounting for about 20% of the total. They find evidence of convergence to the global frontier, but no evidence of convergence of developing countries to developed countries. They also find a trend in the labor productivity distribution from unimodal to bimodal to be due entirely to the effect of capital deepening.

In Chapter 24, Badunenko, Henderson, and Zelenyuk use updated PWT data covering various countries during varying time periods to extend this Malmquist-based global frontier approach to productivity dynamics and convergence. In one extension they follow the new growth theory by incorporating human capital change as an additional driver of labor productivity change. In another they incorporate a financial development change indicator. Throughout they focus on the sources and convergence of labor productivity growth, using statistical methods to test various hypotheses. They also provide a comprehensive literature survey of the new growth theory and of the Malmquist-based global frontier approach to productivity dynamics and convergence.

An alternative frontier-based approach uses microeconomic data, is based on a distinction between "frontier" firms and "laggard" firms, and examines trends in productivity gaps between the two categories of firm. In this approach, forging ahead by frontier firms and catching up by laggard firms both raise aggregate productivity, but have the opposite effects on productivity gaps. The framework is enriched by the existence of two frontiers, a national frontier and a global frontier. The approach is reminiscent of the macroeconomic "catching up, forging ahead and falling behind" thesis of Abramovitz (1986). It is also conceptually similar to the Malmquist productivity index approach, but analytically very different.

The construction of national and global frontiers is crucial to the approach. Rather than use econometric or mathematical programming techniques to construct frontiers, this literature defines national frontier firms loosely as "best in nation." Thus Iacovone and Crespi (2010) define national frontier firms as those in the top quartile of the domestic productivity distribution, and the global frontier as an ill-defined envelope of the best national frontiers. Andrews, Criscuolo, and Gal (2015, 2016) define national and global frontiers in both absolute and percent terms, with fixed and variable number of frontier firms, and report little difference in findings. Bartelsman, Dobbeleare, and

Peters (2015) define frontier firms as belonging to the upper quantiles of the relevant productivity distribution.

Empirical evidence obtained from the frontier model of reallocation is relatively scant, but encouraging. Bartelsman, Dobbeleare, and Peters (2015) study a large sample of firms in Germany and the Netherlands over 2000–2008 and report findings across a range of industries. A common but not unanimous finding is one of positive complementarity between both investment in human capital and investment in product innovation and proximity to the frontier. Andrews, Criscuolo, and Gal (2015) study firms belonging to two-digit industries for 23 OECD countries over 2001–2009. They find firms at the global productivity frontier to be on average more productive, larger, more export-oriented, and more profitable than nonfrontier firms, productivity being measured as both labor productivity and MFP. Moreover, they find productivity gaps widening through time. This raises the (unanswered) question of why frontier technologies do not diffuse more rapidly, both from global frontier firms to national frontier firms, and from national frontier firms to domestic laggard firms. Among positive findings, gaps between national and global frontiers vary with educational quality, product and labor market regulations, the quality of markets for risk capital, and the extent of R&D collaboration, each of which is subject to public policy influence. Andrews, Criscuolo, and Gal (2016) apply the frontier model to analyze the recent global productivity slowdown, using the OECD-Orbis data base.[17] They find increasing productivity among global frontier firms, and increasing divergence between frontier and nonfrontier firms, in both manufacturing and services, even after including various controls. This leads them to attribute the global productivity slowdown to a slowdown in the diffusion process. They note that diffusion has been slowest in sectors where pro-competitive market reforms have been least extensive, and they also consider the roles of adjustment costs of adopting new technologies, rising entry barriers, and declining contestability of markets in slowing the diffusion process.

OECD (2015b, 2016a) and Berlingieri, Blanchenay, and Criscuolo (2017) provide details of the distance to the frontier approach and additional findings, and OECD (2015b, 2016a) discusses the role of public policy directed toward raising aggregate productivity growth, in large part by enhancing diffusion. As Andrews, Criscuolo, and Gal (2015) note, this literature is "very small." Its growth is to be encouraged, particularly if it incorporates some of the analytical advances appearing in the frontier and Malmquist literature.

The concept of distance to the frontier has been adopted by the World Bank as an essential component of its evaluation of the performance of economies in its annual *Doing Business* reports. The 2017 report covers 190 economies, using 41 indicators for 10 topics, each topic representing a dimension of the cost of doing business (e.g., starting a business, getting credit). Economies receive normalized scores for each indicator within a topic, which are then averaged to create 10 topic scores. Topic scores are then averaged to obtain aggregate "ease of doing business" scores. Distance to frontier is measured as the difference between an economy's score and the best score attained since a given year.

Finally, economies are ranked according to their distance to frontier scores, for each topic and for the aggregate ease of doing business.[18]

This unweighted averaging approach to the construction of composite indicators is widespread but controversial. Cherchye, Moesen, Rogge, and Van Puyenbroeck (2007) criticize the approach and propose a DEA-based "benefit of the doubt" alternative that allows countries to attach different weights to indicators. Underlying data are available at www.doingbusiness.org, and enable one to employ frontier techniques to aggregate indicators into topics, and to aggregate topics into an ease of doing business index, and then to use Malmquist productivity indices to construct annual best-practice frontiers and to measure performance variation across economies and performance change through time. Lefebvre, Perelman, and Pestieau use the benefit-of-the-doubt approach in their evaluation of the welfare performance of the public sector in 28 EU economies in Chapter 17.

1.4.2.2. *Persistence*

The evidence cited in the preceding that reallocation raises aggregate productivity is compelling, and provides evidence of market forces at work. However, this evidence also shows that reallocation does not eliminate productivity dispersion, suggesting the presence of barriers to the working of market forces. The primary finding in this regard is that, conditional on survival, substantial productivity dispersion persists through varying lengths of time. Persistence is measured by assigning units to productivity quantiles through time, which requires long panels. If units remain in the same productivity quantile, or perhaps move no further than to an adjacent productivity quantile, persistence of productivity dispersion is inferred. Andrews, Criscuolo, and Gal (2015) attribute persistence in the OECD to slow diffusion of new global frontier technologies to laggard firms. OECD (2016a) cites a particular example: the uptake of cloud computing in OECD countries has been low, particularly among small firms. OECD (2016a) also emphasizes within-country spatial productivity dispersion, and a slowdown in convergence.

This combination of productivity-enhancing reallocation and productivity-constraining persistence prompts a search for the sources of persistence. Banerjee and Moll (2010) mention four potential sources: (i) finance constraints, either inadequate access to financing or adequate access at exorbitant interest rates; (ii) firms of varying productivity self-select into the formal (and taxed) and informal sectors; (iii) political connections enable low-productivity firms to survive; and (iv) a regulatory environment that discriminates against large firms. We discuss some of these sources in subsection 1.5.2.

Gibbons and Henderson (2012a, 2012b) suggest another reason why best practices do not diffuse more readily. Their explanation is that many management practices are not based on formal contracts, but on relational contracts involving "... a shared understanding of each party's role in and rewards from achieving cooperation." These contracts are hard to build and change, causing slow diffusion and persistent productivity gaps. They illustrate with three examples, the "fair" bonus system at

Lincoln Electric, the employee-operated andon cord on the assembly line at Toyota, and the pro-publication philosophy at Merck. Helper and Henderson (2014) apply the relational contract concept to the search for explanations for the decline of General Motors.

Yet another possible source of persistence is that business models vary across firms, with some pursuing a financial objective by emphasizing productivity, and others pursuing the same or a different financial objective by pursuing replication, a strategy emphasized by Garcia-Castro, Ricart, Lieberman, and Balasubramanian in Chapter 10. Variation in the quality of management practices, which we discuss in subsection 1.5.2, is another likely source.

1.5. Productivity Drivers

Productivity varies across plants and firms and through time, but not randomly. Productivity dispersion has sources, or drivers. It is important to identify drivers in order to adopt business strategies and public policies designed to reduce dispersion and increase aggregate productivity. Two quite different approaches to the identification of drivers of productivity dispersion have developed in the literature, and have been used in two quite different contexts.

1.5.1. Technology-Based Drivers

One approach to the identification of the forces driving productivity change is technology-based, specifies two or more drivers, and is typically, although not necessarily, applied to the estimation and decomposition of productivity change through time.

In this approach, productivity change is decomposed into technical change (a shift in the best-practice frontier, perhaps caused by the introduction of a new form of ICT) and efficiency change (a movement toward or away from the best-practice frontier, perhaps caused by the diffusion of the new form of ICT). The concept of a best-practice frontier is an essential component of the technology-based approach, but this frontier is typically unobserved, and must be estimated. The search for technology-based drivers thus fits into the "Estimation" part of subsection 1.3.2.

If best-practice technology is represented by a production frontier, efficiency change is technical efficiency change. Data requirements are relatively undemanding: output quantities and input quantities for a panel of production units. Analysis is based on distance functions that provide the basis for either of two Malmquist (1953) productivity indices that Russell analyzes in Chapter 4. The Malmquist productivity index proposed by Caves, Christensen, and Diewert (1982) is more popular than the Malmquist productivity index anticipated by Hicks (1961) and Moorsteen (1961), and subsequently proposed by Diewert (1992) and Bjurek (1996), although the latter index has more desirable properties. O'Donnell (2012) demonstrates that the Malmquist productivity index proposed by Diewert and Bjurek is a "multiplicatively complete" productivity index because it can be expressed as the ratio of a well-behaved output quantity index to a well-behaved input quantity index, with good behavior requiring the indices to be non-negative, nondecreasing and homogeneous of degree one. He also shows that a multiplicatively complete productivity index can be exhaustively decomposed into the product of three drivers. He illustrates by decomposing the Diewert-Bjurek productivity index into the product of (i) technical change that measures a shift in the production frontier; (ii) technical efficiency change that measures movements toward or away from the production frontier; and (iii) scale-mix efficiency change that measures movements along the production frontier associated with changes in the input mix, the output mix, and the scale of production. However, since the Malmquist productivity index proposed by Caves, Christensen, and Diewert cannot be expressed as the ratio of an output quantity index to an input quantity index without imposing severe restrictions on the structure of technology, it is not generally multiplicatively complete and cannot be exhaustively decomposed into the product of three drivers.

If best-practice technology is represented by a cost (or revenue) frontier, efficiency change is cost (or revenue) efficiency change, and it is complemented by technical change measuring a shift in the cost (or revenue) frontier and scale-mix change that measures movements along the cost (or revenue) frontier. Data requirements are somewhat more demanding: output quantities, input prices, and expenditure on inputs for estimation of a cost frontier, and input quantities, output prices and revenue from outputs for estimation of a revenue frontier, as Russell shows in Chapter 4. Grifell-Tatjé and Lovell (2013) propose several analyses of business performance based on the concept of a cost frontier, one of which generalizes cost variance analysis in management accounting.

Additional options are available, corresponding to alternative specifications of objectives of and constraints facing firms. In one appealing specification, management is given a budget and told to spend it wisely, a specification that can be traced back to Shephard (1974) and thought of as combining primal and dual approaches. Wise expenditure might be directed toward maximizing output or revenue or ROA. In this case, an output quantity index is based on changes in output quantities as usual, and use of revenue or ROA requires constructing an implicit output price index as well. However, an indirect input quantity index is based on changes in budget-deflated input prices, since input quantities are endogenous choice variables constrained by the exogenous budget and input prices. An indirect productivity index is the ratio of an output quantity index to an indirect input quantity index. The analytical details of (cost or revenue) indirect productivity measurement are available in Färe and Grosskopf (1994). Potential applications are numerous, particularly in the provision of public services such as education, in which agencies receive operating budgets and are expected to maximize outputs such as educational outcomes; Grosskopf, Hayes, Taylor, and Weber (1997) provide an application to public schools. Johnson (1975, 1978) recounts a private sector example, in which managements at duPont and General Motors allocated funds across product lines with an objective of maximizing the return on these funds.

In Chapter 19, Diewert and Fox combine the analytical framework of Shephard (1974) with the analytical framework of Lawrence, Diewert, and Fox (2006), which we mention in section 1.2, to develop a macroeconomic decomposition of value-added growth into an extended set of drivers. They define a cost-constrained value-added function as the maximum value added that can be obtained from a flexible primary input budget. They then develop an analytical decomposition of growth in cost-constrained value added into the product of six drivers: (i) growth in cost-constrained value added efficiency; (ii) growth in net output prices; (iii) growth in primary input quantities; (iv) growth in primary input prices; (v) technical change; and (vi) scale economies. They illustrate their decomposition with data from the corporate and non-corporate nonfinancial sectors of the US economy over the period 1960–2014. Among their findings is a decline in value-added efficiency during recessionary periods when output declines but quasi-fixed inputs cannot be adjusted optimally. They conclude by considering a pair of procedure for aggregating the two decompositions to the entire nonfinancial sector, a top-down approach and a bottom-up approach, which they implement.

1.5.2. Organizational and Institutional Drivers

An alternative approach to the identification of the factors driving productivity change is based on the productivity dispersion analysis in section 1.4, and is typically, although not necessarily, applied to an investigation of the sources of productivity variation across producers. Drivers are sorted into two types: organizational factors that originate within the firm and are in principle under management control, and institutional or structural features that are external to the firm and presumably are beyond management control but subject to public policy. We review a few of the more prominent drivers of each type, with an acknowledgement that many of the organizational drivers are strongly correlated, and all could be labeled management practices.

1.5.2.1. *Organizational Drivers*

1.5.2.1.1. *Management Practices*

The distinguished management consultant Peter Drucker (1954, 71) asserted that "... the only thing that differentiates one business from another in any given field is the quality of its management on all levels. And the only way to measure this crucial factor is through a measurement of productivity that shows how well resources are utilized and how much they yield."

In a global research agenda stretching over the past decade, Bloom, Van Reenen, and colleagues have developed the World Management Survey (WMS).[19] The survey currently contains data on management practices from over 11,000 firms, primarily in manufacturing but also in retail trade, health care, and education, in 34 countries through four different survey waves from 2004 to 2014. Data include quality indices (normalized and ranked from one for worst practice to five for best practice) for 18 management practices in three categories: monitoring, target setting, and people management. Aggregating these quality indices provides an empirical measure of Drucker's management quality (although recall our reference to benefit of the doubt weighting in subsection 1.4.2). It also enhances the likelihood of discovering the previously missing input in productivity studies noted by Hoch (1955), who called it "entrepreneurial capacity," and by Mundlak (1961) and Massell (1967), who called its omission "management bias."

More significantly, the WMS data enable one to test hypotheses concerning the drivers of management quality and, in turn, the impact of management quality on various indicators of firm performance. It is dangerous to summarize what is by now a large and rapidly growing body of work, but a few findings are common to the vast majority of studies: (i) there is large cross-country variation, and even larger within-country dispersion, in the quality of management practices; (ii) product market competition is an important driver of the quality of management practices; (iii) ownership matters, with the quality of management practices higher in the private sector than in the public sector, higher in multinational firms than in domestic firms, and higher in professionally managed family firms than in family-managed family firms, particularly primogeniture family firms; (iv) the quality of management practices is positively associated with a range of measures of firm performance, including productivity, profitability as measured by return on capital employed, sales and sales growth, market value as measured by Tobin's Q, and the probability of survival; and (v) at least a quarter of country productivity gaps with the United States are accounted for by gaps in the quality of management practices. Among the more recent studies based on the WMS, each of which provides references to earlier studies, are Bloom, Genakos, Sadun, and Van Reenen (2012), Bloom, Lemos, Sadun, Scur, and Van Reenen (2014), and Bloom, Sadun and Van Reenen (2016).

The WMS contains limited information on American firms. However, Bloom, Brynjolfsson, Foster, Jarmin, Patnaik, Saporta-Eksten, and Van Reenen (2014) report findings based on a recent Management and Organizational Practices Survey (MOPS) of over 30,000 US manufacturing establishments conducted by the US Census Bureau. Their findings complement those based on the WMS, and include (i) enormous dispersion in the quality of management practices; (ii) high correlations between the quality of management practices and firm size, firm location, firm export status, firm employee education, and the intensity of ICT use; and (iii) a high correlation between the quality of management practices and firm performance as measured by productivity (labor productivity and MFP), profitability (operating profit divided by sales), employment growth, and innovation (R&D and patent intensity). In Chapter 12, Benner expresses reservations about the impact of management practices on innovation, suggesting that they may promote relatively minor process innovation at the expense of potentially major product innovation.

The evidence from both surveys is compelling: management matters, for productivity, for financial performance, and for survival. The evidence also identifies several drivers of the quality of management practices, some such as ICT adoption and the use of incentives being organizational in nature, and others such as product market competition and the regulatory environment being institutional in nature.

We have mentioned earlier the old notion of management as the missing input. This may have prompted Bloom, Lemos, Sadun, Scur, and Van Reenen (2014) and Bloom, Sadun, and Van Reenen (2016) to consider two alternative views of management, one with management as design from organizational economics, and the other with management as intangible capital, as an input in production technology. With their preferred view of management as intangible capital, they write $Y = F(A, K, L, M)$, in which M is management. Treating intangible capital as a separate input in the production technology is subtly different from treating it as a part of K (Corrado, Hulten, and Sichel 2005) or as a part of L (Bryan 2007). However, the once missing input is no longer missing, and although the interpretation of M is clear, it remains a composite indicator subject to the same concerns we express in subsection 1.4.2 in relation to the construction of distance to the frontier indicators used by the OECD and the World Bank.

1.5.2.1.2. *Human Resource Management Practices*

Human resource management (HRM) practices vary across firms and countries, as does productivity, which prompts a search for a relationship, and perhaps causality. HRM practices are similar to the people management component of management practices, but we treat the topic separately for three reasons: (i) an independent literature exists, (ii) much of its empirical content consists of focused sample studies rather than large sample studies found in the management practices literature; and (iii) large sample studies rarely isolate the impact of the people management component of management practices on productivity.

In an early focused sample study, Ichniowski, Shaw, and Prennushi (1997) study 36 homogeneous steel production lines at 17 companies over several months. In their panel, both HRM practices and productivity vary widely. Consistent with economic theory (e.g., Milgrom and Roberts 1990, 1995), they find that clusters of innovative work practices, including incentive pay, teams, flexible job assignments, employment security, and training, have a significant positive effect on productivity, while changes in individual practices have little or no impact on productivity. They also find that clusters of innovative work practices raise product quality. Finally, they find support for two explanations for the failure of best HRM practices to diffuse more widely: slow diffusion of knowledge about the performance of HRM systems, and both pecuniary and nonpecuniary barriers to change at older lines.

Lazear (2000) reports the findings of his study of a large auto glass company in which workers install auto windshields, and which gradually changed its compensation from hourly wages to piece-rate pay. Based on a sample of 3,000 workers over a 19-month period, he finds (i) the switch to piece-rate pay led to a 44% gain in output per worker; (ii) the company shared the productivity gains with workers in the form of a 10% increase in pay; (iii) the variance in worker productivity increased due to the incentive provided to ambitious workers; and (iv) company earnings increased, although this may have been caused by other factors in addition to the productivity increase.

Several focused sample studies find complementarities, not just among HRM practices, but between them and the adoption of various information technologies. Bartel, Ichniowski and Shaw (2004, 2007) find complementarities between HRM practices and computer-based information technologies to increase productivity in terms of reducing setup time, run time, and inspection time at US valve-making plants, and Bartel, Ichniowski, Shaw, and Correra (2009) report similar findings at a larger sample of US and UK valve-making plants. Note the association of productivity with time.

In a study of 629 Spanish manufacturing plants, Bayo-Moriones and Huerta-Arribas (2002) attempt to identify determinants of the adoption of production incentives for manual workers. Among the determinants they consider are product market conditions, plant characteristics, work organization, and unions. They find recent increases in product market competition and public ownership to significantly reduce the probability of adoption. They also find the way work is organized, expressed in terms of the number of tasks per job and the share of manual workers in autonomous work teams, and the extent of union influence over workers, to significantly increase the probability of adoption. The extent of plant automation and the magnitude of recent technical changes have no significant impact on the probability of adoption. The authors do not attempt to identify complementarities, and they do not explore the impact of the adoption of production incentives on productivity, but if such incentives tend to raise productivity, then they have uncovered some indirect influences on productivity.

In a related study of over 800 Spanish manufacturing plants over six years, Bayo-Moriones, Galdon-Sanchez, and Martinez-de-Morentin (2013) ask whether pay-for-performance practices are likely to be adopted for six occupations, ranging from top executives to sales and production workers. They find sales workers and top executives to be the occupations most likely to adopt such practices, although the nature of pay-for-performance practices varies across occupations. Such practices are less likely to be adopted for production and administrative workers. The idea of adoption of a common pay-for-performance program across all occupations is rejected.

Although studies of the impact of HRM practices on productivity are predominantly focused sample studies, a few large sample studies have been conducted. In one such study, which incorporates many attributes of a focused sample study, Black and Lynch (2004) use the Educational Quality of the Workforce National Employers Survey administered by the US Bureau of the Census to construct 1996 cross-section and 1993/1996 panel data sets at the individual establishment level. They find that the use of high-performance work practices such as self-managed teams, re-engineering, incentive pay, profit sharing, and employee voice, in conjunction with the adoption of information technologies, including the share of equipment less than four years old and the proportion of non-managers using computers, positively impacts labor productivity. Unlike many other studies, they are unable to detect any significant complementarities in the cross section and just one in the panel, between unionization and employee voice, as hypothesized by Freeman and Medoff (1984).

To the extent that HRM practices can be separated from other management practices, it is expected that good HRM practices enhance producer performance. To the extent that complementarities exist, the impact is magnified. However, there is compelling evidence that many findings are contextual rather than general.

1.5.2.1.3. *Adoption of New Technology*

Even before Salter analyzed vintage effects, Griliches (1957) documented the slow and variable rate of adoption of a new (and currently controversial) agricultural technology, hybrid seed corn, which he attributed to varying profitability of adoption. More generally, David (1990) and Crafts (2004) offer economic historians' responses to Solow's "productivity paradox" by providing a broad historical perspective on diffusion lags in the adoption of general-purpose technologies and their consequent delayed impact on productivity. Draca, Sadun, and Van Reenen (2007) summarize what even then was a voluminous literature, breaking it down into macroeconomic studies, industry-level studies, and firm-level studies. Their interpretation of the literature is that it reveals a positive and significant association (but not causality) of ICT with productivity, primarily at the firm level, and largely through complementarities with labor skills and organizational capital, the role of which we discuss in subsection 1.3.3.

In Chapter 12, Benner adopts an interdisciplinary approach to propose a managerial resolution to the productivity paradox, a resolution whose roots go back at least to the work of Abernathy (1978). Following Adler, Benner, Brunner, MacDuffie, Osono, Staats, Takeuchi, Tushman, and Winter (2009) and Benner and Tushman (2015), she contends that popular incremental process innovations such as Six Sigma and ISO 9000 convey marginal near-term productivity gains, but at the expense of uncertain but more substantial longer-term productivity gains that might have resulted from successful product innovations. In this view, the opportunity cost of the resources allocated to the adoption of "process management practices" that yield improvements to the existing technology is the possibility of developing an innovative new technology. To the extent that management practices, including HRM practices, can be associated with process innovation, Benner's analysis bears directly, and critically, on the management practices literature we summarize in the preceding. The pursuit of best management practices appears to raise productivity, but at a potentially high cost; by directing attention away from product innovation, it may preclude the discovery of a radical new product. To paraphrase Gordon (2016), some innovations are more important than others.

Benner also provides a useful link to the reallocation literature we survey in subsection 1.4.2 by suggesting that incumbents tend to pursue process innovations, while potential entrants are more likely to pursue product innovations, some successfully. Or, as she puts it so eloquently, ". . . as a firm engages in concerted efforts to produce Blackberries more efficiently, it is actually less likely to create the iPhone. . . ."

Following up on the product-process innovation distinction, Hall (2011) and Mohnen and Hall (2013) survey the empirical evidence, which suggests that product innovation exerts a statistically significant positive impact on revenue productivity, but process innovation, while it tends to improve business financial performance, has an ambiguous effect on revenue productivity. These incomplete findings have encouraged further research. Product innovation can increase revenue productivity in either of two ways, by increasing output quantities or output prices, and identification is a challenge. Process innovation has an ambiguous effect on revenue productivity, perhaps because it is not intended to raise revenue productivity, but rather is aimed at improving productive efficiency, the impact showing up as an improvement in cost productivity through a reduction in input use.

In Chapter 13, Cassiman and Golovko apply the distinction between product innovation and process innovation to explore the complex linkage among the participation of firms in international trade, their innovation activity, and their productivity. They hypothesize that product (but not process) innovation raises productivity and induces firms to self-select into exporting and, eventually, foreign direct investment. They also explore the reverse hypothesis of learning by exporting, which can result from intense competition in foreign markets and from knowledge spillovers from foreign buyers, suppliers, and competitors. This learning can lead to further increases in innovative activity and productivity. As a logical extension, they explore the hypothesis that product innovation and exporting activities are complementary determinants of future productivity growth. After exploring the learning by importing relationship, they explore export–import complementarities on product innovation and productivity. They illustrate these relationships with a large panel of small and medium-sized Spanish manufacturing firms in 20 industries during 1991–2009, and find a "complex dynamic" relating exporting, importing, innovation, and productivity.

In a large sample study, Bloom, Brynjolfsson, Foster, Jarmin, Patnaik, Saporta-Eksten, and Van Reenen (2014) relate the use of information technology (IT) to business performance, with management practices providing the intermediate link. Using MOPS, they find three measures of IT usage (IT investment, IT investment per worker, and percent of sales delivered over electronic networks) to be positively correlated with the quality of management practices, which in turn is positively correlated with a variety of business performance indicators. Along similar lines in a pair of focused sample studies Bartel, Ichniowski, and Shaw (2007) and Bartel, Ichniowski, Shaw, and Correa (2009) find strong complementarities between human resource practices and the adoption of new information technologies in enhancing productivity growth. In light of the findings on product versus process innovations, it is worth noting that in each of these studies the technologies being adopted are process, rather than product, technologies.

Raymond, Mairesse, Mohnen, and Palm (2015) explore the R&D-to-innovation-to-productivity relationships in a pair of unbalanced panels of Dutch and French manufacturing firms from three waves of the Community Innovation Survey. They find evidence of a lagged positive impact of R&D on innovation, a positive impact of innovation on labor productivity, ambiguous evidence of persistence in innovation, and strong evidence of persistence in productivity. They also find numerous differences in the relationships between the Netherlands and France.

Bos, van Lamoen, and Sanders (2016) also use the Community Innovation Survey, limited to Dutch manufacturing firms, to extend previous work of Mairesse and Mohnen (2002) by specifying and estimating a knowledge production frontier. In their production technology, the innovation output is sales from new or improved products, their innovation inputs consist of a knowledge stock of accumulated innovation expenditures and research labor engaged in R&D activities, and they control for other inputs, cooperation with other institutions, and government funding. They find their innovation inputs to be jointly significant drivers of innovation output, but most of the inter-firm variation in innovation output is unexplained by innovation inputs and controls, and is ascribed to inter-firm variation in innovation efficiency (or innovativeness, or productivity) in the conversion of innovation inputs to innovation output. The finding of innovation inefficiency justifies the extension of the Mairesse and Mohnen knowledge-production function to a knowledge-production frontier, and the finding of innovativeness dispersion is consistent with the widespread finding of productivity dispersion we survey in subsection 1.4.1.

Statistics Netherlands (2015) contains a number of firm-level studies exploring various linkages between ICT and productivity. In one study of the impact of ICT capital on sales per worker, ICT capital is disaggregated into eight components. Another distinguishes among product innovation, process innovation, and organizational innovation, and incorporates e-commerce intensity. A third examines the impact of ICT intensity on industry dynamics. Yet another examines the role of ICT in global value chains, distinguishing among ICT-producing firms, ICT-using firms, and non-ICT firms. Findings vary across studies, but a general conclusion is that ICT use enhances productivity, although findings can be sensitive to the definition of productivity, some types of ICT have greater impact than others, and the impact of ICT investment may depend on simultaneous investment in organizational changes.

It is apparent that adoption of new ICT investment increases productivity, especially if it is combined with complementary HRM practices. The finding seems subject to two unresolved concerns, however, one involving the distinction between product and process innovation, and the other involving the efficiency with which innovation is adopted and incorporated into business practices.

1.5.2.1.4. *Downsizing*

Global food giant Nestlé SA has embarked on a "Cost and Capital Discipline" program, which it claims has reduced operating cost by CHF1.6 billion in 2014 and 2015 through waste reduction and the leveraging of size and complexity, with an objective of improving return on invested capital.[20]

Businesses frequently make similar cost-cutting pronouncements, typically in conjunction with quarterly earnings announcements, the objective being to increase competitiveness. It is possible to cut costs in several ways, through the introduction of new resource-saving technology, by reducing waste, by right-sizing, and by recontracting with suppliers to gain lower input prices. Only the first two strategies are certain to increase productivity, although the third might. Theory suggests that all four are likely to enhance business financial performance, but the empirical evidence is inconclusive.

Attitudes toward cost-cutting vary. *The Economist* (2016a) complains that cost-cutting announcements rarely are followed by plans to pass the resulting gains on to consumers or employees, thereby exacerbating inequality in the distribution of income. Economists approve of improvements in technology, waste reduction, and right-sizing as components of optimizing behavior, although empirical evidence on their effects, particularly on productivity, is surprisingly mixed. In their study of a sample of US manufacturing plants, Baily, Bartelsman, and Haltiwanger (1996) find productivity gains among plants that increase employment, as well as among plants that reduce employment. In their study of a sample of German firms, Goesaert, Heinz, and Vanormelingen (2015) find that, subsequent to downsizing, both productivity and profitability are largely unchanged, both among downsizing firms responding to a business downturn and, surprisingly, among waste-reducing firms attempting to increase efficiency. In their provocatively titled study of US manufacturing firms, Guthrie and Datta (2008) find downsizing to be negatively correlated with firm profitability, particularly (and unsurprisingly) in growing and R&D-intensive industries. Gandolfi and Hansson (2011) survey the management literature on the causes and consequences of downsizing, and conclude that it has negligible to adverse effects on business financial and organizational outcomes, and largely adverse human impacts, on executioners, victims, and survivors, particularly if downsizing involves shrinking job-training budgets.

Perhaps the evidence on the consequences of downsizing is mixed at best because cost-cutting can have adverse unintended consequences within the firm. Fisher and White (2000) adopt a social network view of the firm to show how inefficient cost-cutting can deplete organizational capital, erase organizational memory, and reduce organizational performance, an argument that is easy to support with anecdotal evidence. Schenkel and Teigland (2017) survey the organizational downsizing literature and develop an analytical framework that integrates the concepts of downsizing, social capital, dynamic capabilities, and business performance and competitiveness. Usefully for our purposes, they discuss how ICT capital can be employed to reduce the negative impacts of downsizing.

1.5.2.1.5. *Offshore Outsourcing and Global Value Chains*

Presumably businesses engage in offshore outsourcing to reduce production costs, thereby enhancing their financial performance. If the cost reduction takes the form of an input price reduction, it is likely that offshore outsourcing has no impact on business productivity. Although most of the literature on offshore outsourcing examines its impact on domestic employment, and almost none examines its impact on financial performance, a few studies examine its impact on productivity, and the evidence is mixed. Olsen (2006) surveys the extant literature at aggregate and plant levels, using both labor productivity and MFP, and finds no clear pattern of how the practice affects productivity, with much depending on sector and firm specifics. He does find modest support for a positive productivity effect, depending on what is outsourced (materials inputs or services inputs, the MS in KLEMS), who is doing the outsourcing (manufacturing or service businesses), and a host of controls for heterogeneity. Amiti and Wei (2009) find a significant positive effect of service offshoring, and a smaller insignificant positive effect of materials offshoring, on both MFP and labor productivity in US manufacturing industries during 1992–2000. Bournakis, Vecchi, and Venturini (2018) examine the productivity impacts of offshore outsourcing in high-tech and low-tech industries in eight OECD countries during 1990–2005. As in previous studies, they find weak support for productivity-enhancing offshore outsourcing, with results varying by industry and whether materials or services are outsourced. Interestingly, they also find some indirect support for Benner's conjecture in Chapter 12: they find little support for the impact of offshore outsourcing on R&D activities, which they attribute to business' myopic behavior, and ". . . which focuses more on short-term cost gains rather than on restructuring and diverting resources towards more innovative activities."

Offshore outsourcing can be an end in itself or, increasingly, it can be a link in a larger global value chain (GVC). To illustrate, an example of a GVC is the iPod, which prior to its discontinuation was designed in the United States, assembled in China by Taiwanese companies using more than 100 components manufactured around the world, with logistics handled in Hong Kong.[21] Reijnders, Timmer, and Ye (2016) and Timmer and Ye in Chapter 21 examine alternative characteristics of GVCs. General findings are similar in both advanced and emerging economies, and include (i) increasing fragmentation of production; (ii) a strong bias to technical change that favors capital (particularly ICT capital) and high-skill labor; (iii) increasing specialization; and declining low-skill labor value-added shares. These findings within GVCs are consistent with domestic findings of capital-skill complementarity reinforced by skill-biased technical change we discuss in subsection 1.2.3 in the context of growing inequality.

In Chapter 21, Timmer and Ye show how to analyze production, technical change and its bias, factor demand elasticities and their cost shares, and productivity change in GVCs, illustrating their methodology using a KLEMS approach and the World Input-Output Database. They provide two empirical applications, one to the GVC of German automobiles and the other to 240 manufacturing GVCs, both during 1995–2007. In the former application they are able to allocate GVC productivity growth of 0.99% to the German automobile industry itself (0.73%) and to other industries in the GVC (0.26%). In the latter application they find, consistent with non-GVC studies, strong complementarity between capital and high-skill labor. They also attribute growing cost shares of capital and high-skill labor, and declining cost shares of low- and medium-skill labor, primarily to biased technical change, with input price effects being small. This decomposition of changes in cost shares into driving sources is important in its own right, and has widespread potential applicability.

Recent evidence suggests that offshoring is a two-way street, with reshoring, the practice of returning production to the home country, becoming more common. De Backer, Menon, Desnoyers-James, and Moussiegt (2016) summarize the economic factors at work and survey the evidence. The factors favoring reshoring include an eroding offshore cost advantage, increasing supply risk in longer and more complex GVCs, the need to be close to markets, lagging domestic innovation, and endangered intellectual property. However, they find limited impacts on the home country of reshoring to date, with the major finding being that reshoring leads to a large increase in investment in high-tech capital and a small increase in employment, with most of that being of high-skill labor. Many home country jobs that were offshored are gone forever.

Adidas, a German sporting goods firm, provides an excellent recent example. It has outsourced the manufacture of sport shoes, primarily to Asian countries, for many years. However, growing labor shortages and rising labor costs, in conjunction with GVCs that can take up to 18 months from design to delivery, have prompted Adidas to reshore production to Germany. Reshoring will exploit advanced technology (including robotic cutting, 3D printing, and computerized knitting) to shorten the supply chain to less than a week, with a potentially large impact on productivity; once again, productivity is measured in terms of time to completion.[22]

Not all production fragmentation involves offshoring, with or without reshoring. Using data from the 2007 US Census of Manufactures, Fort (2017) finds a positive relationship between a firm's use of ICT and its decision to fragment production, either offshore or domestically. She also finds domestic fragmentation to be far more prevalent than offshoring, a finding she attributes to complementarities between ICT and worker skill, which is generally higher in the United States than in countries to which US firms tend to offshore services.

1.5.2.2. *Institutional Drivers*

We know that some business practices enhance productivity, but what institutional features enhance or retard their adoption and diffusion?

The work of North (1990), co-recipient of the 1993 Nobel Prize in Economic Sciences "for having renewed research in economic history by applying economic theory and quantitative methods in order to explain economic and institutional change" (The Royal Swedish Academy of Sciences 1993). has inspired research into the impact of policies and institutions, including public infrastructure, on economic performance, including private productivity. Hall and Jones (1999) argue that ". . . the primary, fundamental determinant of a country's long-run economic performance is its social infrastructure," consisting of institutions and government policies. The challenge, of course, is to define and construct an index of social infrastructure. They construct such an index, and show that it exerts positive impacts on a variety of indicators of economic performance, including capital accumulation, educational attainment, and productivity, and therefore on per capita income. Easterly and Levine (2001) also emphasize the role of policies, such as legal systems, property rights, infrastructure, regulations, and taxes, that influence both factor accumulation and productivity, and they note that policy differences do not have to be large to matter, since "[s]mall differences can have dramatic long run implications." More recently, Ègert (2016) examines the effect variation in the quality of institutions, essentially the rule of law and law enforcement, on productivity, using a panel of OECD countries. He shows that higher quality institutions amplify the productivity-enhancing impact of R&D spending, although why R&D spending should provide the conduit is left unexplained. Hopenhayn (2014) provides an analytical framework for investigating the impact of institutions on economic performance, and surveys some of the more prominent institutions that retard performance. We touch on some of these institutional features in the following.

1.5.2.2.1. *Competition*

Perhaps the most prominent finding to emerge from Bloom and Van Reenen (2007) and their subsequent studies is the importance of product market competition as a determinant of the quality of management practices, and thus of the economic and financial performance of firms. This finding is robust to alternative measures of product market competition, including domestic competition, international competition, and competition as perceived by management.

Van Reenen (2011, 306), quoting Adam Smith ("Monopoly . . . is a great enemy to good management"), discusses the common finding that increased product market competition raises aggregate productivity growth, and a less common finding that it does so without substantially reducing productivity dispersion, to which we refer in section 1.4. He also claims that "[p]erhaps the most common form of a competition shock is from trade liberalization" (314). The OECD (2015b, 48) lists three channels through which trade exposure raises productivity: (i) trade openness increases competition, which promotes the productivity-enhancing reallocation we discuss in subsection 1.4.2; (ii) trade and foreign direct investment promote knowledge flows among global suppliers and customers, and within multinational firms, enhancing productivity convergence toward global frontiers; and (iii) trade openness increases effective market sizes, which raises potential productivity gains and profits from adoption of foreign technologies. The empirical literature investigating these channels is voluminous. To cite one recent example, Eslava, Haltiwanger, Kugler, and Kugler (2013) examine the impact of trade liberalization that reduced both the average level and the inter-industry variation in effective tariffs, on manufacturing plant productivity in Colombia during 1982–1998. They find liberalization to have increased exit, raised productivity within continuing plants, and improved resource allocation among continuing plants, all of which combined to raise aggregate productivity. The data constraint prevents them from considering nontariff barriers or the impact of tariff reform on entry.

In Chapter 14, De Loecker and Van Biesebroeck survey the recent literature. They consider a range of approaches to estimate the impact of changes in international competition, perhaps but not exclusively through reduced tariff barriers, on productivity. A vast empirical literature suggests that trade liberalization raises aggregate productivity in two ways that overlap with the three channels identified by the OECD (2015b): (i) by raising the minimum level of productivity necessary for survival, and (ii) by reallocating resources toward more productive firms. However, three related themes pervade their discussion. One is yet another warning of the danger in using deflated revenue as an output indicator when measuring productivity, a danger we first encountered in subsection 1.4.1. A second is the difficulty in separating the impacts of increased competition on output quantities and output prices, and the development of strategies for decomposing revenue productivity change into a mark-up change component and a productivity change component. They develop three such strategies, borrowed from the theoretical industrial organization and international trade literatures. The third theme is that, while trade liberalization, by enlarging the relevant market, has the potential to increase competition, and hence productivity, whether it actually has this effect is contextual.

1.5.2.2.2. *Regulation*

Regulation can affect productivity in three ways: (i) regulation in an industry can affect productivity in the same industry, (ii) regulation in an industry can affect productivity in other industries using the product of the regulated industry as an input, and (iii) labor market regulation can affect productivity in industries employing regulated labor. In each case, the regulatory impact can take either of two forms: it can lower the mean or increase the dispersion of the productivity distribution.

Andrews and Cingano (2014) construct a sample of over 800 country-industry observations across 21 OECD countries in 2005, with an objective of exploring the impact of cross-country variation in product market, labor market, and credit market regulations on cross-country productivity distributions. They find positive relationships between productivity dispersion among existing producers and each of employment protection legislation, product market regulations, and restrictions on foreign direct investment. However, credit market imperfections work differently, lowering the mean of the productivity distribution rather than increasing its dispersion, implying that financial frictions influence entry decisions rather than the productivity distribution of incumbent producers. They conclude that reducing product and labor market entry barriers in each country to the lowest levels observed in the European Union would reduce misallocation by half and increase aggregate labor productivity by 15%.

Égert and Wanner (2016) describe the OECD's suite of indicators of anti-competitive regulation in the economy, REGIMPACT. Components include an economy-wide product market regulation indicator, seven network industry regulation indicators, four professional services regulation indicators, and a retail trade regulation indicator. Each of these indicators varies widely across OECD countries, and all decline through time— two features that make them useful in studies of the impact of cross-country variation in regulation on cross-country productivity distributions. Across a range of regressions, REGIMPACT has a statistically significant negative impact on labor productivity, and a negative impact that is frequently statistically significant on MFP. Each of the following studies uses this database.

Bourlès, Cette, Lopez, Mairesse, and Nicoletti (2013) use REGIMPACT to examine the indirect impact of regulation in one industry on the productivity of industries using that industry's product. Based on a panel of 20 industries in 15 OECD countries over a 24-year period, they find strong evidence that upstream regulation retards downstream productivity. Additionally, using the distance to the frontier concept, they find the adverse impact to be greatest for firms closest to the global frontier, creating a catch-up effect for laggard firms. Égert (2016) adds two additional potential productivity drivers, innovation intensity and trade openness, to a similar panel. He finds a negative impact of labor market regulations and positive impacts of innovation intensity and trade openness, and complementarity between labor and product market regulations. Cette, Lopez, and Mairesse (2016) study another similar panel, examining the impacts of product and labor market regulations on productivity in downstream industries. They find potential long-term productivity gains on the order of 2.5% and 1.9%, respectively, if all countries adopted "lightest-practice" regulations, defined as the mean of the three lowest regulatory burdens in their sample. In a subsequent study Cette, Lopez, and Mairesse (2017) examine the impact of upstream regulatory burden indicators on downstream MFP in 15 OECD countries, and they find a statistically significant negative impact. They also find a mostly significant negative impact of upstream regulatory burden on downstream investment in ICT and R&D capital.

Empirical findings across a wide range of data sets are consistent, with one another and with the predictions of economic theory. Anti-competitive product and labor market regulations, and constraints on access to or the cost of capital, all have adverse consequences for productivity, either direct or indirect, by affecting either the mean or the dispersion of the productivity distribution. Evidence on the negative impact of upstream regulation on downstream productivity is particularly compelling.

1.5.2.2.3. *Financial Frictions and Credit Constraints*

Midrigan and Xu (2014) study financial frictions such as borrowing constraints, arguing that they reduce aggregate productivity through two channels: (i) they distort entry and technology adoption decisions, reducing the productivity of those producers, and (ii) they generate different rates of return to capital across producers, causing misallocation and further reducing productivity. Using establishment data from Korea, with its well-developed financial system, and China and Columbia, both with less-developed financial systems, they find the first channel to be more important than the second, reinforcing the finding of Andrews and Cingano (2014). They attribute the relatively small misallocation effect among incumbents to the ability of financially constrained but nonetheless more productive incumbents to exploit retained earnings as a source of capital. Moll (2014) also emphasizes the ability of accumulated internal funds to moderate capital misallocation caused by financial frictions. Banerjee and Duflo (2014) trace the persistent misallocation of capital among borrowing firms in India to the withdrawal and subsequent reimposition of credit constraints, although their focus is on profits rather than productivity, and they also find the extent of misallocation to be sensitive to the ability to self-finance.

Ferrando and Ruggieri (2015) argue that the impact of financial frictions on a firm's productivity depends on its financial structure. They use the Amadeus database[23] to construct a sample of over 5 million firm-year observations across nine sectors in eight Euro-area countries during 1995–2011, a period that includes the GFC. They construct a synthetic indicator of firm financial constraint as a function of financial leverage, debt burden, cash holdings, and firm controls. They find significant negative impacts of their financial constraint indicator on labor productivity across most sectors and countries, with the impacts being most severe in "innovative" industries. Fernandes and Ferreira (2017) examine the impact of tightening financing constraints caused by the GFC on firm employment decisions, using Portuguese linked employer–employee data during 2000–2012. They construct a similar indicator of firm financial constraint as a function of external finance dependence, asset tangibility, importance of trade credit, reliance on short-term debt, and a firm size-age index. Firm employment decisions are expressed as the share of workers hired on short-term contracts. Their main finding is that, subsequent to the crisis, firms with above-median financial constraint increased the share of short-term hires in total hires. The authors also suggest that this decision has productivity implications, since relatively constrained firms prefer the flexibility of short-term contracts to the higher productivity associated with permanent contracts. To test this conjecture, they regress labor productivity on the share of short-term workers and a host of firm controls, and they find a statistically negative impact.

Caselli and Gennaioli (2013) follow Burkhart, Panunzi, and Shliefer (2003) by linking institutional failures such as financial frictions with ownership. We have noted the finding of Bloom and Van Reenen (2007), repeated in many subsequent studies, that family-owned firms having a family CEO chosen by primogeniture have much lower quality of management practices than other firms, and consequently underperform other firms on a range of economic and financial indicators. Caselli and Gennaioli do not rely on primogeniture, but they do study the intergenerational transfer of management in family firms, a practice they call "dynastic management," and Firfiray, Larraza-Kintana, and Gómez-Mejia call the "protection of socioemotional wealth" in Chapter 11. They argue that financial frictions hinder the market for corporate control by deterring lending and investment, restricting financing opportunities to both talented outsiders and talented descendants, who would otherwise invest more in the family firm than their less talented siblings. As a result, poorly functioning financial institutions reward less talented descendants, thereby adversely affecting productivity in dynastic family firms, which predominate in developing countries.

Financial constraints plague global supply chains, and have motivated the growth of a non-bank "fintech" industry designed to relax these constraints. Nonetheless, *The Economist* (2017) reports that the vast majority of global supply chains lack an adequate financing program, which, by raising transaction costs, reduces their productivity.

Financial constraints also influence modes of production. Using a large panel of US manufacturing plants, Andersen (2017) finds that credit constraints distort the asset mix toward tangible assets that can serve as collateral. This in turn leads to a quantitatively large and statistically significant increase in pollution emissions, an effect that is pronounced in industries that rely on external financing.

Unlike other studies, Blancard, Boussemart, Briec, and Kerstens (2006) use the frontier techniques we mention in subsection 1.3.2 to estimate the impact of credit constraints on the financial performance of a sample of French farmers. They find financially unconstrained farmers (whose credit constraint is not binding) to be larger, more efficient, and more successful financially than those having binding credit constraints.

Their use of frontier techniques also enables them to estimate shadow prices of the constraints.

1.5.2.2.4. *Costs of Doing Business*

We have discussed regulation and finance constraints, both of which impose costs that reduce business productivity. There are other costs of doing business, and an associated literature examining the mechanisms through which these costs influence productivity.

The World Bank's Doing Business project was initiated in 2002 and provides objective measures of business regulations and their enforcement. The 2017 edition includes 11 indicators, each with several components, most of which are available for most of 190 economies. The 11 indicators measure the (money and time) costs of starting a business, dealing with construction permits, getting electricity, registering property, getting credit, protecting minority investors, paying taxes, trading across borders, enforcing contracts, resolving insolvency, and labor market regulation.

Barseghyan (2008) uses the World Bank's Cost of Doing Business data set to examine the impact of cross-country variation in entry costs on productivity. He regresses output per worker and TFP on an entry cost indicator, including all official fees that must be paid to complete legal procedures for starting a business, and incorporates a number of institutional controls. He finds that higher entry costs significantly reduce labor productivity, primarily by reducing its MFP component. Moscoso Boedo and Mukoyama (2012) also use the Cost of Doing Business data set, and they add exit costs, consisting of the cost of advance notice requirements, severance payments and penalties due when terminating a worker, to their entry cost indicator, consisting of the monetary and time costs of starting and licensing a business. Both costs and their components vary dramatically across countries, and both reduce productivity. Entry costs lower productivity by keeping low-productivity establishments in business, and exit costs lower productivity by dampening the reallocation of labor from low-productivity to high-productivity establishments. The authors calculate that raising the two costs from their US levels to those of the average low-income countries reduces aggregate GDP by as much as one-third.

Industrial policies that keep low-productivity firms in business, and discourage more productive firms from investing, have led to the "zombie firm" phenomenon. Caballero, Hoshi, and Kashyap (2008) study the phenomenon during the Japanese macroeconomic stagnation of the 1990s. They define zombie firms as potentially receiving subsidized bank credit, and they focus on credit misallocation resulting from zombie lending, which they attribute to relationship banking and regulatory forbearance, both of which keep zombie firms from exiting. In a large sample of Japanese firms, they find an increase in the share of zombies in an industry to be associated with a decline in investment and employment growth for non-zombies, and a widening productivity gap between non-zombies and zombies. Adalet McGowan, Andrews, and Millot (2017) define zombie firms as being at least 10 years old with an interest coverage ratio (the ratio of operating income to interest expense) of less than one for the preceding three years. In a large sample of OECD firms, they find (i) zombie firms to have increased in number and market share since 2000; (ii) the increasing survival of zombie firms congests markets, restricting exit, constraining the growth of more productive incumbent firms and raising barriers to entry for new firms; (iii) resources devoted to zombie firms reduce productivity-enhancing resource allocation that constrains investment and employment in more productive firms; and (iv) an increased productivity gap between zombie firms and more productive firms; all of which lead to (v) reduced potential output through two channels, business investment and MFP growth. Their primary policy prescription is to reduce credit and other barriers to the exit of zombie firms.

Complementarities can be positive, as with combinations of HR practices and types of ICT adoption, but they can be negative as well. Bergoeing, Loayza, and Piguillem (2016) contend that entry barriers and exit barriers are complements; each imposes costs, and they reinforce each other's negative impact on productivity. They use the Cost of Doing Business data set to estimate the impact of these barriers on the gap between US and developing country per capita output. They find entry and exit barriers to account for roughly half of the gap between the United States and the median developing country, half of which is accounted for by complementarities. The policy implication is that removal, or lowering, of both entry and exit barriers have a greater productivity impact than removing or lowering either of them separately.

Entry costs and other costs of doing business have a second depressing effect on productivity. Several writers have documented that high costs of doing business divert business from the formal sector to the informal sector, where productivity is lower than in the formal sector, due in part to the small size and inefficiencies of enterprises in the informal sector. D'Erasmo and Moscoso Boedo (2012) argue that high costs of doing business reduce aggregate MFP by encouraging the growth of the informal sector, where firms tend to be small and less productive than their formal-sector counterparts. This misallocation of capital reduces aggregate MFP; based on World Bank Cost of Doing Business data, they calculate this reduction to be "up to 25%." La Porta and Shleifer (2014) emphasize the fundamental differences between firms in the formal and informal sectors, arguing that informal firms are long-lived and rarely move to the formal sector, and that informality is reduced only by economic development.

1.5.2.2.5. *Home Production*

Becker's (1965) analysis of household time allocation was in large part responsible for his receipt of the 1992 Nobel Prize in Economic Sciences for ". . . having extended the domain of microeconomic analysis to a wide range of human behaviour and interaction, including non-market behaviour" (Royal Swedish Academy of Sciences 1992). We know that much non-market economic activity, home production in particular, is not captured by the national accounts. For our purposes, the relevant questions are how to measure the productivity of home production and whether incorporation of home production into the national accounts would have an impact on aggregate productivity, and then on social economic progress, as we discuss in subsection 1.2.3.

The OECD (2002, Annex 2) defines household production for own use as comprising ". . . those activities that are carried out by household unincorporated enterprises that are not involved in market production. By definition, such enterprises are excluded from the informal sector" (which is engaged in market production). Bridgman (2016) summarizes the efforts of the US Bureau of Economic Analysis to construct satellite accounts that estimate the value of household production. These accounts suggest that including home production raises GDP by 37% in 1965 and by 23% in 2014, the decline being attributable to increasing female labor force participation. Poissonnier and Roy (2015) report on the development of a satellite household account for France. Their findings suggest that incorporating household production in the national accounts would increase GDP by a third while reducing its rate of growth, and increase disposable income by half. They also conduct sensitivity analyses of various methodological issues, including the use of gross or net wages, and minimum or living wages, to value household labor.

The OECD (2011) provides preliminary estimates of the value of household production of non-market services, with the ultimate objective of comparing material well-being across countries. Among their many findings, they conclude that national estimates are acutely sensitive to the valuation of household labor using replacement cost or opportunity cost methodologies, although international comparisons are not. Schreyer and Diewert (2014) apply Becker's household time allocation model to determine the conditions under which the replacement cost or opportunity cost approaches are the appropriate way to value household labor, and they develop a cost of living index for Becker's full income and full consumption (of market goods, work at home, hired labor services, and leisure). This leads them to an international comparison of GDP growth rates with, and without, household production included. They characterize the differences as "not-insignificant." Their work constitutes an important analytical step toward household productivity measurement, although much more analytical and empirical work is needed.

NOTES

1. Blázquez-Gómez and Grifell-Tatjé (2011) find the Spanish regulator to have exhibited a pro-industry, anti-consumer bias during the 1988–1998 period, with the estimated value of the intended fraction having been outside [0, 1] for the majority of electricity distribution companies.
2. Here and henceforth we refer to all aggregate output measures such as GDP and GNP as "output," except when a precise definition is necessary.
3. https://data.oecd.org/lprdty/unit-labour-costs.htm (accessed October 24, 2016).
4. http://stats.oecd.org/# (accessed October 24, 2016).
5. For more on social economic progress, see Grifell-Tatjé, Lovell, and Turon (2016).
6. http://www.oecdobserver.org/news/fullstory.php/aid/5548/The_productivity_and_equality_nexus.html (accessed October 24, 2016)
7. This example is one of many suggesting potential complementarities between academics and consultancies such as the McKinsey Global Institute. Lewis (2004) provides a readable account of the Institute's forays into the measurement of productivity and its determinants, at both firm and country levels.

8. Alan B. Krueger served as chairman of President Obama's Council of Economic Advisors from 2011 to 2013.
9. http://www.bls.gov/mfp/data.htm (accessed October 24, 2016).
10. http://www.bls.gov/mfp/mprdload.htm (accessed October 24, 2016).
11. See also www.bls.gov/bls/productivity.htm (accessed October 24, 2016).
12. See http://www.oecd.org/economy (accessed October 24, 2016).
13. See http://www.bls.gov/news.release/pdf/prod3.pdf (accessed October 24, 2016).
14. See also www.bls.gov/ppi/qualityadjustment.pdf (accessed October 24, 2016).
15. Haltiwanger (2016) provides a critical overview of the TFPQ/TFPR literature.
16. A December 30, 2016, Google Scholar search for "the Toyota production system" turned up about 257,000 results.
17. http://www.bvdinfo.com/en-gb/our-products/company-information/international-products/orbis (accessed January 4, 2017).
18. This brief summary masks many details, which are available at www.doingbusiness.org/data/distance-to-frontier (accessed November 22, 2016).
19. http://worldmanagementsurvey.org (accessed November 1, 2016).
20. http://www.nestle.com/asset-library/documents/library/presentations/investors_events/investor-seminar-2016/nis-2016-14.pdf (accessed January 31, 2017).
21. Timmer, Erumban, Los, Stehrer, and de Vries (2014) attribute this example to Dedrick, Kraemer, and Linden (2010), who also estimate how profit is distributed along the GVC.
22. www.adidas-group.com//en/group/stories-copy/specialty/adidas-future-manufacturing/
23. http://www.bvdinfo.com/en-gb/our-products/company-information/international-products/amadeus (accessed January 4, 2017).

References

Abernathy, W. J. 1978. *The Productivity Dilemma*. Baltimore, MD: Johns Hopkins University Press.

Abramovitz, M. 1986. "Catching Up, Forging Ahead, and Falling Behind." *Journal of Economic History* 46: 385–406.

Adalet McGowan, M., D. Andrews, and V. Millot. 2017. "The Walking Dead? Zombie Firms and Productivity Performance in OECD Countries." OECD Economics Department Working Papers No. 1372. www.oecd.org/eco/The-Walking-Dead-Zombie-Firms-and-Productivity-Performance-in-OECD-Countries.pdf.

Adler, P., M. J. Benner, D. Brunner, P. MacDuffie, E. Osono, B. Staats, H. Takeuchi, M. L. Tushman, and S. G. Winter. 2009. "Perspectives on the Productivity Dilemma." *Journal of Operations Management* 27: 99–113.

Ahn, S. C., D. Good, and R. C. Sickles. 2000. "Estimation of Long-Run Inefficiency Levels: A Dynamic Frontier Approach." *Econometric Reviews* 19: 461–92.

Aigner, D., C. A. K. Lovell, and P. Schmidt. 1977. "Formulation and Estimation of Stochastic Frontier Production Function Models." *Journal of Econometrics* 6: 21–37.

Albrizio, S., T. Kozluk, and V. Zipperer. 2017. "Environmental Policies and Productivity Growth: Evidence across Industries and Firms." *Journal of Environmental Economics and Management* 81: 209–226.

Alchian, A. 1950. "Uncertainty, Evolution and Economic Theory." *Journal of Political Economy* 58: 211–222.

Alm, J., and D. Duncan. 2014. "Estimating Tax Agency Efficiency." *Public Budgeting & Finance* 34: 92–110.

Alvarez, A., and P. Schmidt. 2006. "Is Skill More Important Than Luck in Explaining Fish Catches?" *Journal of Productivity Analysis* 26: 15–25.

Amiti, M., and S.-J. Wei. 2009. "Service Offshoring and Productivity: Evidence from the US." *The World Economy* 33: 203–220.

Andersen, D. C. 2017. "Do Credit Constraints Favor Dirty Production? Theory and Plant-Level Evidence." *Journal of Environmental Economics and Management* 84: 189–208.

Andrews, D., and F. Cingano. 2014. "Public Policy and Resource Allocation: Evidence from Firms in OECD Countries." *Economic Policy* 29: 253–296.

Andrews, D., C. Criscuolo, and P. N. Gal. 2015. "Frontier Firms, Technology Diffusion and Public Policy: Micro Evidence from OECD Countries." OECD Productivity Working Papers No. 02. http://www.oecd-ilibrary.org/economics/frontier-firms-technology-diffusion-and-public-policy_5jrql2q2jj7b-en.

Andrews, D., C. Criscuolo, and P. N. Gal. 2016. "The Best versus the Rest: The Global Productivity Slowdown, Divergence across Firms and the Role of Public Policy." OECD Productivity Working Papers No. 05. http://www.oecd-ilibrary.org/economics/the-best-versus-the-rest_63629cc9-en.

Arrow, K. J. 1962. "The Economic Implications of Learning by Doing." *Review of Economic Studies* 29: 155–173.

Asker, J., A. Collard-Wexler, and J. De Loecker. 2014. "Dynamic Inputs and Resource (Mis) Allocation." *Journal of Political Economy* 122: 1013–1063.

Atkinson, T. 2005. "Measurement of Government Output and Productivity for the National Accounts." Atkinson Review: Final Report, HMSO. http://web.ons.gov.uk/ons/search/index.html?newquery=atkinson+report.

Autor, D. H. 2015. "Why Are There Still So Many Jobs? The History and Future of Workplace Automation." *Journal of Economic Perspectives* 29: 3–30.

Ayres, C. E. 1944. *The Theory of Economic Progress.* Chapel Hill: University of North Carolina Press.

Baily, M. N., E. J. Bartelsman, and J. Haltiwanger. 1996. "Downsizing and Productivity Growth: Myth or Reality?" *Small Business Economics* 8: 259–278.

Balk, B. M. 2003. "The Residual: On Monitoring and Benchmarking Firms, Industries and Economies with Respect to Productivity." *Journal of Productivity Analysis* 20: 5–48.

Balk, B. M. 2008. *Price and Quantity Index Numbers: Models for Measuring Aggregate Change and Difference.* New York: Cambridge University Press.

Balk, B. M. 2009. "On the Relation between Gross Output- and Value Added-Based Productivity Measures: The Importance of the Domar Factor." *Macroeconomic Dynamics* 13(Suppl 2): 241–267.

Banerjee, A. V., and E. Duflo. 2014. "Do Firms Want to Borrow More? Testing Credit Constraints Using a Directed Lending Program." *Review of Economic Studies* 81: 572–607.

Banerjee, A. V., and B. Moll. 2010. "Why Does Misallocation Persist?" *American Economic Journal: Macroeconomics* 2: 189–206.

Banks, G. 2015. "Institutions to Promote Pro-Productivity Policies." OECD Productivity Working Papers No. 01. http://www.oecd-ilibrary.org/economics/institutions-to-promote-pro-productivity-policies_5jrql2tsvh41-en.

Barseghyan, L. 2008. "Entry Costs and Cross-Country Differences in Productivity and Output." *Journal of Economic Growth* 13: 145–167.

Bartel, A., C. Ichniowski, and K. Shaw. 2004. "Using 'Insider Econometrics' to Study Productivity." *American Economic Review* 94: 217–223.

Bartel, A., C. Ichniowski, and K. Shaw. 2007. "How Does Information Technology Affect Productivity? Plant-Level Comparisons of Product Innovation, Process Improvement and Worker Skills." *Quarterly Journal of Economics* 122: 1721–1758.

Bartel, A., C. Ichniowski, K. L. Shaw, and R. Correa. 2009. "International Differences in the Adoption and Impact of New Information Technologies and New HR Practices: The Valve-Making Industry in the United States and United Kingdom." In *International Differences in the Business Practices and Productivity of Firms*, edited by R. B. Freeman and K. L. Shaw, Chapter 2, 59–78. Chicago: University of Chicago Press.

Bartelmus, P. 2014. "Environmental-Economic Accounting: Progress and Digression in the SEEA Revisions." *Review of Income and Wealth* 60: 887–904.

Bartelmus, P. 2015. "Do We Need Ecosystem Accounts?" *Ecological Economics* 118: 292–298.

Bartelsman, E., S. Dobbelaere, and B. Peters. 2015. "Allocation of Human Capital and Innovation at the Frontier: Firm-Level Evidence on Germany and the Netherlands." *Industrial and Corporate Change* 24: 875–949.

Bartelsman, E., J. Haltiwanger, and S. Scarpetta. 2009. "Measuring and Analyzing Cross-Country Differences in Firm Dynamics." In *Producer Dynamics: New Evidence from Micro Data* edited by T. Dunne, J. B. Jensen, and M. J. Roberts, Chapter 1, 15–76. Chicago: University of Chicago Press.

Bartelsman, E., J. Haltiwanger, and S. Scarpetta. 2013. "Cross-Country Differences in Productivity: The Role of Allocation and Selection." *American Economic Review* 103: 305–334.

Baumol, W. J. 1986. "Productivity Growth, Convergence, and Welfare: What the Long-Run Data Show." *American Economic Review* 76: 1072–1085.

Baumol, W. J., S. A. B. Blackman, and E. N. Wolff. 1989. *Productivity and American Leadership: The Long View.* Cambridge, MA: MIT Press.

Bayo-Moriones, A., J. E. Galdon-Sanchez, and S. Martinez-de-Morentin. 2013. "The Diffusion of Pay for Performance across Occupations." *ILR Review* 66: 1115–1148.

Bayo-Moriones, A., and E. Huerta-Arribas. 2002. "The Adoption of Production Incentives in Spain." *British Journal of Industrial Relations* 40: 709–724.

Becker, G. S. 1965. "A Theory of the Allocation of Time." *Economic Journal* 75: 493–517.

Behrens, K., C. Ertur, and W. Koch. 2012. "'Dual Gravity': Using Spatial Econometrics to Control for Multilateral Resistance." *Journal of Applied Econometrics* 27: 773–794.

Benner, M. J., and M. Tushman. 2015. "Reflections on the 2013 Decade Award—'Exploitation Exploration and Process Management: The Productivity Dilemma Revisited' Ten Years Later." *Academy of Management Review* 40: 497–514.

Bennet, T. L. 1920. "The Theory of Measurement of Changes in Cost of Living." *Journal of the Royal Statistical Society* 83: 455–462.

Bergeaud, A., G. Cette, and R. Lecat. 2016. "Productivity Trends in Advanced Countries between 1890 and 2012." *Review of Income and Wealth* 62: 420–444.

Bergoeing, R., N. V. Loayza, and F. Piguillem. 2016. "The Whole Is Greater Than the Sum of Its Parts: Complementary Reforms to Address Microeconomic Distortions." *World Bank Economic Review* 30: 268–305.

Berlingieri, G., P. Blanchenay, and C. Criscuolo. 2017. "The Great Divergence(s)." OECD STI Policy Paper #39.

Bernard, A. B., and C. I. Jones. 1996a. "Comparing Apples to Oranges: Productivity Convergence and Measurement across Industries and Countries." *American Economic Review* 86: 1216–1238.

Bernard, A. B., and C. I. Jones. 1996b. "Productivity across Industries and Countries: Time Series Theory and Evidence." *Review of Economics and Statistics* 78: 135–46.

Bjurek, H. 1996. "The Malmquist Total Factor Productivity Index." *Scandinavian Journal of Economics* 98: 303–313.

Black, S. E., and L. M. Lynch. 2004. "What's Driving the New Economy? The Benefits of Workplace Innovation." *Economic Journal* 114: F97–F116.

Blancard, S., J.-P. Boussemart, W. Briec, and K. Kerstens. 2006. "Short- and Long-Run Credit Constraints in French Agriculture: A Directional Distance Function Framework Using Expenditure-Constrained Profit Functions." *American Journal of Agricultural Economics* 88: 351–364.

Blázquez-Gómez, L., and E. Grifell-Tatjé. 2011. "Evaluating the Regulator: Winners and Losers in the Regulation of Spanish Electricity Distribution." *Energy Economics* 33: 807–815.

Bloom, N., E. Brynjolfsson, L. Foster, R. Jarmin, M. Patnaik, I. Saporta-Eksten, and J. Van Reenen. 2014. "IT and Management in America." CEP Discussion Paper No 1258, Centre for Economic Performance, London School of Economics and Political Science. http://cep.lse.ac.uk/pubs/download/dp1258.pdf.

Bloom, N., C. Genakos, R. Sadun, and J. Van Reenen. 2012. "Management Practices Across Firms and Countries." *Academy of Management Perspectives* 26: 12–33.

Bloom, N., R. Lemos, R. Sadun, D. Scur, and J. Van Reenen. 2014. "The New Empirical Economics of Management." *Journal of the European Economic Association* 12: 835–876.

Bloom, N., R. Sadun, and J. Van Reenen. 2016. "Management as a Technology?" National Bureau of Economic Research. http://www.nber.org/papers/w22327.pdf.

Bloom, N., and J. Van Reenen. 2007. "Measuring and Explaining Management Practices Across Firms and Countries." *Quarterly Journal of Economics* 122: 1351–1408.

Bos, J. W. B., R. C. R. van Lamoen, and M. W. J. L. Sanders. 2016. "Producing Innovations: Determinants of Innovativity and Efficiency." In *Advances in Efficiency and Productivity*, edited by J. Aparicio, C. A. K. Lovell, and J. T. Pastor, Chapter 10, 227–248. New York: Springer.

Boskin, M. J., E. Dulberger, R. Gordon, Z. Griliches, and D. Jorgenson. 1996. "Towards a More Accurate Measure of the Cost of Living." *Final Report to the US Senate Finance Committee.* https://www.ssa.gov/history/reports/boskinrpt.html.

Bottazzi, G., A. Secchi, and F. Tamagni. 2008. "Productivity, Profitability and Financial Performance." *Industrial and Corporate Change* 17: 711–751.

Bourlès, R., G. Cette, J. Lopez, J. Mairesse, and G. Nicoletti. 2013. "Do Product Market Regulations in Upstream Sectors Curb Productivity Growth? Panel Data Evidence for OECD Countries." *Review of Economics and Statistics* 95: 1750–1768.

Bournakis, I., M. Vecchi, and F. Venturini. 2018. "Off-Shoring, Specialization and R&D." *Review of Income and Wealth*, 64: 26–51. doi:10.1111.roiw.12239.

Brandenburger, A. M., and H. W. Stuart, Jr. 1996. "Value-Based Business Strategy." *Journal of Economics and Management Strategy* 5: 5–24.

Brandt, N., P. Schreyer, and V. Zipperer. 2017. "Productivity Measurement with Natural Capital." *Review of Income and Wealth* 63: S7–S21.

Brea-Solís, H., R. Casadesus-Masanell, and E. Grifell-Tatjé. 2015. "Business Model Evaluation: Quantifying Walmart's Sources of Advantage." *Strategic Entrepreneurship Journal* 9: 12–33.

Bridgman, B. 2016. "Accounting for Household Production in the National Accounts: An Update, 1965–2014." *Survey of Current Business* 96: 1–5.

Bryan, L. L. 2007. "The New Metrics of Corporate Performance: Profit per Employee." *McKinsey Quarterly*. http://www.mckinsey.com/business-functions/strategy-and-corporate-finance/our-insights/the-new-metrics-of-corporate-performance-profit-per-employee.

Brynjolfsson, E., and A. McAfee. 2014. *The Second Machine Age: Work, Progress and Prosperity in a Time of Brilliant Technologies*. New York: W. W. Norton.

Burkhart, M., F. Panunzi, and A. Shleifer. 2003. "Family Firms." *Journal of Finance* 58: 2167–2201.

Bushnell, J. B., and C. Wolfram. 2009. "The Guy at the Controls: Labor Quality and Power Plant Efficiency." In *International Differences in the Business Practices and Productivity of Firms*, edited by R. B. Freeman and K. L. Shaw, Chapter 3, 79–102. Chicago: University of Chicago Press.

Caballero, R., T. Hoshi, and A. K. Kashyap. 2008. "Zombie Lending and Depressed Restructuring in Japan." *American Economic Review* 98: 1943–1977.

Cameron, G., J. Proudman, and S. Redding. 1999. "Productivity Convergence and International Openness." In *Openness and Growth*, edited by J. Proudman and S. Redding, 221–260. London: Bank of England.

Carrington, R., N. Puthucheary, D. Rose, and S. Yaisawarng. 1997. "Performance Measurement in Government Service Provision: The Case of Police Services in New South Wales." *Journal of Productivity Analysis* 8: 415–430.

Caselli, F., and N. Gennaioli. 2013. "Dynastic Management." *Economic Inquiry* 51: 971–996.

Caves, D. W., L. R. Christensen, and W. E. Diewert. 1982. "The Economic Theory of Index Numbers and the Measurement of Input, Output, and Productivity." *Econometrica* 50: 1393–1414.

Caves, D. W., L. R. Christensen, and J. A. Swanson. 1980. "Productivity in U.S. Railroads, 1951–1974." *Bell Journal of Economics* 11: 166–181.

CERC (Centre d'Études des Revenus et des Coûts). 1969. " 'Surplus de productivité globale' et 'Comptes de surplus.' " Documents du Centre d'Études des Revenus et des Coûts, No. 1, 1er trimestre. Paris: CERC.

Cette, G., J. Lopez, and J. Mairesse. 2016. "Market Regulations, Prices and Productivity." *American Economic Review* 106: 104–108.

Cette, G., J. Lopez, and J. Mairesse. 2017. "Upstream Product Market Regulations, ICT, R&D and Productivity." *Review of Income and Wealth* 63: S68–S89.

Chandler, A. D. 1962. *Strategy and Structure: Chapters on the History of the Industrial Enterprise*. Cambridge, MA: MIT Press.

Chang, C.-C., and S. E. Stefanou. 1988. "Specification and Estimation of Asymmetric Adjustment Rates for Quasi-Fixed Factors of Production." *Journal of Economic Dynamics and Control* 12: 145–51.

Charnes, A., W. W. Cooper, and E. Rhodes. 1978. "Measuring the Efficiency of Decision-Making Units." *European Journal of Operational Research* 2: 429–444.

Cherchye, L., W. Moesen, N. Rogge, and T. Van Puyenbroeck. 2007. "An Introduction to 'Benefit of the Doubt' Composite Indicators." *Social Indicators Research* 82: 111–145.

Clark, C. 1940. *The Conditions of Economic Progress*. London: Macmillan.

Coad, A. 2007. "Testing the Principle of 'Growth of the Fitter': The Relationship Between Profits and Firm Growth." *Structural Change and Economic Dynamics* 18: 370–386.

Collard-Wexler, A., and J. De Loecker. 2015. "Reallocation and Technology: Evidence from the US Steel Industry." *American Economic Review* 105: 131–171.

Corrado, C., J. Haltiwanger, and D. Sichel. 2005. "Introduction." In *Measuring Capital in the New Economy*, edited by C. Corrado, J. Haltiwanger, and D. Sichel, 1–10. Chicago: University of Chicago Press.

Corrado, C., and C. Hulten. 2014. "Innovation Accounting." In *Measuring Economic Sustainability and Progress*, edited by D. W. Jorgenson, S. Landefeld, and P. Schreyer, Chapter 18, 595–628. Chicago: University of Chicago Press.

Corrado, C., C. Hulten, and D. Sichel. 2005. "Measuring Capital and Technology: An Expanded Framework." In *Measuring Capital in the New Economy*, edited by C. Corrado, J. Haltiwanger, and D. Sichel, Chapter 1, 11–46. Chicago: University of Chicago Press.

Corrado, C., C. Hulten, and D. Sichel. 2009. "Intangible Capital and U.S. Economic Growth." *Review of Income and Wealth* 55: 661–685.

Crafts, N. 2004. "Steam as a General Purpose Technology: A Growth Accounting Perspective." *Economic Journal* 114: 338–351.

Crafts, N., and K. O'Rourke. 2013. "Twentieth Century Growth." Oxford University Economic and Social History Series 117. http://www.economics.ox.ac.uk/materials/papers/12884/Crafts%20O'Rourke%20117.pdf.

Dakpo, K. H., P. Jeanneaux, and L. Latruffe. 2016. "Modelling Pollution-Generating Technologies in Performance Benchmarking: Recent Developments, Limits and Future Prospects in the Nonparametric Framework." *European Journal of Operational Research* 250: 347–359.

David, P. A. 1990. "The Dynamo and the Computer: An Historical Perspective on the Modern Productivity Paradox." *American Economic Review* 80: 355–361.

Davis, H. S. 1947. *The Industrial Study of Economic Progress*. Philadelphia: University of Pennsylvania Press.

Davis, H. S. 1955. *Productivity Accounting*. Philadelphia: University of Pennsylvania Press.

De Backer, K., C. Menon, I. Desnoyers-James, and L. Moussiegt. 2016. "Reshoring: Myth or Reality?" OECD Science, Technology and Industry Policy Papers No. 27. http://dx.doi.org/10.1787/5jm56frbm38s-en.

Debreu, G. 1951. "The Coefficient of Resource Utilization." *Econometrica* 19: 273–292.

Dedrick, J., K. L. Kraemer, and G. Linden. 2010. "Who Profits from Innovation in Global Value Chains? A Study of the iPod and Notebook PCs." *Industrial and Corporate Change* 19: 81–116.

De Loecker, J., P. K. Goldberg, A. K. Khandelwal, and N. Pavcnik. 2016. "Prices, Markups and Trade Reform." *Econometrica* 84: 445–510.

De Loecker, J., and F. Warzynski. 2012. "Markups and Firm-Level Export Status." *American Economic Review* 102: 2437–2471.

Denison, E. F. 1962. *The Sources of Economic Growth in the United States and the Alternatives Before Us*. Supplementary Paper No. 13, Committee for Economic Development.

Denison, E. F. 1974. *Accounting for United States Economic Growth 1929–1969*. Washington, DC: The Brookings Institution.

D'Erasmo, P. N., and H. J. Moscoso Boedo. 2012. "Financial Structure, Informality and Development." *Journal of Monetary Economics* 59: 286–302.

Diewert, W. E. 1992. "Fisher Ideal Output, Input and Productivity Indexes Revisited." *Journal of Productivity Analysis* 3: 211–248.

Diewert, W. E. 2014. "US TFP Growth and the Contribution of Changes in Export and Import Prices to Real Income Growth." *Journal of Productivity Analysis* 41: 19–39.

Diewert, W. E., and C. J. Morrison. 1986. "Adjusting Output and Productivity Indexes for Changes in the Terms of Trade." *Economic Journal* 96: 659–679.

Domar, E. D. 1966. "The Soviet Collective Farm as a Producer Cooperative." *American Economic Review* 56: 734–757.

Dowrick, S., and D.-T. Nguyen. 1989. "OECD Comparative Economic Growth 1950–85: Catch-up and Convergence." *American Economic Review* 79: 1010–1030.

Draca, M., R. Sadun, and J. Van Reenen. 2007. "Productivity and ICTs: A Review of the Evidence." In *The Oxford Handbook of Information and Communication Technologies*, edited by R. Mansell, C. Avgerou, D. Quah, and R. Silverstone, Chapter 5, 100–147. Oxford: Oxford University Press.

Drucker, P. F. 1954. *The Practice of Management*. New York: Harper & Row.

Druska, V., and W. C. Horrace. 2004. "Generalized Moments Estimation for Spatial Panel Data: Indonesian Rice Farming." *American Journal of Agricultural Economics* 86: 185–198.

Easterly, W., and R. Levine. 2001. "It's Not Factor Accumulation: Stylized Facts and Growth Models." *World Bank Economic Review* 15: 177–219.

Economist. 2016a. "The Problem with Profits" and "Too Much of a Good Thing." *The Economist*, March 26. http://www.economist.com/printedition/2016-03-26.

Economist. 2016b. "Special Report: Artificial Intelligence." *The Economist*, June 25. http://www.economist.com/printedition/2016-06-25.

Economist. 2016c. "A Sea of Black Mirrors: The Niche in Phones That Are Different." *The Economist*, November 5. http://www.economist.com/printedition/2016-11-05.

Economist. 2017. "Every Little Helps." *The Economist*, January 14. http://economist.com/printedition/2017-01-14.

Égert, B. 2016. "Regulation, Institutions and Productivity: New Macroeconomic Evidence from OECD Countries." *American Economic Review* 106: 109–113.

Égert, B., and I. Wanner. 2016. "Regulations in Services Sectors and Their Impact on Downstream Industries: The OECD 2013 Regimpact Indicator." OECD Economics Department Working Papers No. 1303. http://dx.doi.org/10.1787/5jlwz7kz39q8-en.

Eldor, D., and E. Sudit. 1981. "Productivity-Based Financial Net Income Analysis." *Omega* 9: 605–611.

Ertur, C., and W. W. Koch. 2007. "Growth, Technological Interdependence and Spatial Externalities: Theory and Evidence." *Journal of Applied Econometrics* 22: 1033–1062.

Eslava, M., J. Haltiwanger, A. Kugler, and M. Kugler. 2004. "The Effects of Structural Reforms on Productivity and Profitability Enhancing Reallocation: Evidence from Colombia." *Journal of Development Economics* 75: 333–371.

Eslava, M., J. Haltiwanger, A. Kugler, and M. Kugler. 2010. "Factor Adjustments after Deregulation: Panel Evidence From Colombian Plants." *Review of Economics and Statistics* 92: 378–391.

Eslava, M., J. Haltiwanger, A. Kugler, and M. Kugler. 2013. "Trade and Market Selection: Evidence from Manufacturing Plants in Colombia." *Review of Economic Dynamics* 16: 135–158.

Fabricant, S. 1940. *The Output of Manufacturing Industries, 1899–1937*. New York: National Bureau of Economic Research. http://www.nber.org/chapters/c6435.

Fabricant, S. 1961. "Basic Facts on Productivity Change." In *Productivity Trends in the United States*, edited by J. W. Kendrick, xxxv–lii. Princeton, NJ: Princeton University Press. Also issued as National Bureau of Economic Research Occasional Paper 63, http://papers.nber.org/books/fabr59-1.

Färe, R., and S. Grosskopf. 1994. *Cost and Revenue Constrained Production*. New York: Springer-Verlag.

Färe, R., and S. Grosskopf .1996. *Intertemporal Production Frontiers: With Dynamic DEA*. Boston: Kluwer Academic.

Felipe, J., and J. McCombie. 2017. "The Debate about the Sources of Growth in East Asia after a Quarter of a Century: *Much Ado about Nothing*." Asian Development Bank Economics

Working Paper Series No. 512, Manila, Philippines. https://www.adb.org/publications/debate-sources-growth-east-asia.

Fernandes, A. P., and P. Ferreira. 2017. "Financing Constraints and Fixed-Term Employment: Evidence from the 2008-9 Financial Crisis." *European Economic Review* 92: 215–238.

Ferrando, A., and A. Ruggieri. 2015. "Financial Constraints and Productivity: Evidence from Euro Area Companies." European Central Bank Working Paper No. 1823. http://www.ecb.europa.eu/pub/pdf/scpwps/ecbwp1823.en.pdf.

Fisher, S. R., and M. A. White. 2000. "Downsizing in a Learning Organization: Are There Hidden Costs?" *Academy of Management Review* 25: 244–251.

Fixler, D., and D. S. Johnson. 2014. "Accounting for the Distribution of Income in the US National Accounts." In *Measuring Economic Sustainability and Progress*, edited by D. W. Jorgenson, J. S. Landefeld, and P. Schreyer, Chapter 8, 213–244. Chicago: University of Chicago Press.

Førsund, F. R. 2009. "Good Modelling of Bad Outputs: Pollution and Multiple-Output Production." *International Review of Environmental and Resource Economics* 3: 1–38.

Fort, T. C. 2017. "Technology and Production Fragmentation: Domestic versus Foreign Sourcing." *Review of Economic Studies* 84: 650–687.

Foster, L., J. Haltiwanger, and C. J. Krizan. 2001. "Aggregate Productivity Growth: Lessons from Microeconomic Evidence." In *New Developments in Productivity Analysis*, edited by C. R. Hulten, E. R. Dean, and M. J. Harper, Chapter 8, 303–372. Chicago: University of Chicago Press.

Foster, L., J. Haltiwanger, and C. J. Krizan. 2006. "Market Selection, Reallocation, and Restructuring in the U.S. Retail Trade Sector in the 1990s." *Review of Economics and Statistics* 88: 748–758.

Foster, L., J. Haltiwanger, and C. Syverson. 2008. "Reallocation, Firm Turnover, and Efficiency: Selection on Productivity or Profitability?" *American Economic Review* 98: 394–425.

Freeman, R., and J. Medoff. 1984. *What Do Unions Do?* New York: Basic Books.

Frey, C. B., and M. A. Osborne. 2013. "The Future of Employment: How Susceptible Are Jobs to Computerisation?" http://www.oxfordmartin.ox.ac.uk/downloads/academic/The_Future_of_Employment.pdf.

Frisch, R. 1965. *Theory of Production*. Dordrecht: D. Reidel.

Gandolfi, F., and M. Hansson. 2011. "Causes and Consequences of Downsizing: Towards an Integrative Framework." *Journal of Management & Organization* 17: 498–521.

Garvy, G. 1954. "Functional and Size Distributions of Income and Their Meaning." *American Economic Review* 44: 236–253.

Gennaioli, N., R. La Porta, F. Lopez-de-Silanes, and A. Shleifer. 2013. "Human Capital and Regional Development." *Quarterly Journal of Economics* 128: 105–164.

Gennaioli, N., R. La Porta, F. Lopez-de-Silanes, and A. Shleifer. 2014. "Growth in Regions." *Journal of Economic Growth* 19: 259–309.

Gibbons, R., and R. Henderson. 2012a. "What Do Managers Do? Exploring Persistent Performance Differences among Seemingly Similar Enterprises." In *The Handbook of Organizational Economics*, edited by R. Gibbons and J. Roberts, Chapter 17, 680–731. Princeton, NJ: Princeton University Press.

Gibbons, R., and R. Henderson. 2012b. "Relational Contracts and Organizational Capabilities." *Organization Science* 23: 1350–1364.

Glass, A., K. Kenjegalieva, and J. Paez-Farrell. 2013. "Productivity Growth Decomposition Using a Spatial Autoregressive Frontier Model." *Economics Letters* 119: 291–295.

Glass, A. J., K. Kenjegalieva, and R. C. Sickles. 2016a. "Returns to Scale and Curvature in the Presence of Spillovers: Evidence from European Countries." *Oxford Economic Papers* 68: 40–63.

Glass, A. J., K. Kenjegalieva, and R. C. Sickles. 2016b. "A Spatial Autoregressive Stochastic Frontier Model for Panel Data with Asymmetric Efficiency Spillovers." *Journal of Econometrics* 190: 289–300.

Goesaert, T., M. Heinz, and S. Vanormelingen. 2015. "Downsizing and Firm Performance: Evidence from German Firm Data." *Industrial and Corporate Change* 24: 1443–1472.

Goldin, C., and L. F. Katz. 1998. "The Origins of Technology-Skill Complementarity." *Quarterly Journal of Economics* 113: 693–732.

Gordon, R. J. 2016. *The Rise and Fall of American Growth: The U.S. Standard of Living since the Civil War*. Princeton, NJ: Princeton University Press.

Grifell-Tatjé, E., and C. A. K. Lovell. 2004. "Decomposing the Dividend." *Journal of Comparative Economics* 32: 500–518.

Grifell-Tatjé, E., and C. A. K. Lovell. 2008. "Productivity at the Post: Its Drivers and Its Distribution." *Journal of Regulatory Economics* 33: 133–158.

Grifell-Tatjé, E., and C. A. K. Lovell. 2013. "Advances in Cost Frontier Analysis of the Firm." In *The Oxford Handbook of Managerial Economics*, edited by C. R. Thomas and W. F. Shughart II, Chapter 4, 66–88. New York: Oxford University Press.

Grifell-Tatjé, E., and C. A. K. Lovell. 2015. *Productivity Accounting: The Economics of Business Performance*. New York: Cambridge University Press.

Grifell-Tatjé, E., C. A. K. Lovell, and P. Turon. 2016. "Social Economic Progress and the Analysis of Business Behaviour." Working Paper.

Griliches, Z. 1957. "Hybrid Corn: An Exploration in the Economics of Technological Change." *Econometrica* 25: 501–522.

Griliches, Z. 1969. "Capital-Skill Complementarity." *Review of Economics & Statistics* 51: 465–468.

Griliches, Z. 1992. *Output Measurement in the Service Sectors*. Chicago: University of Chicago Press.

Griliches, Z. 1994. "Productivity, R&D, and the Data Constraint." *American Economic Review* 84: 1–23.

Grosskopf, S., K. J. Hayes, L. L. Taylor, and W. L. Weber. 1997. "Budget-Constrained Frontier Measures of Fiscal Equality and Efficiency in Schooling." *Review of Economics and Statistics* 79: 116–124.

Guthrie, J. P., and D. K. Datta. 2008. "Dumb and Dumber: The Impact of Downsizing on Firm Performance as Moderated by Industry Conditions." *Organization Science* 19: 108–123.

Hall, B. 2011. "Innovation and Productivity." *Nordic Economic Policy Review* 2: 167–204.

Hall, R. E., and C. I. Jones. 1999. "Why Do Some Countries Produce So Much More Output Per Worker Than Others?" *Quarterly Journal of Economics* 114: 83–116.

Haltiwanger, J. 2016. "Firm Dynamics and Productivity: TFPQ, TFPR and Demand Side Factors." *Economía* 17. http://www.cid.harvard.edu/Economia/contents.htm.

Hamermesh, D. S., and G. A. Pfann. 1996. "Adjustment Costs in Factor Demand." *Journal of Economic Literature* 34: 1264–1292.

Han, J., D. Ryu, and R. C. Sickles. 2016. "How to Measure Spillover Effects of Public Capital Stock: A Spatial Autoregressive Stochastic Frontier Model." *Advances in Econometrics* 37: 259–294.

Helper, S., and R. Henderso.n 2014. "Management Practices, Relational Contracts, and the Decline of General Motors." *Journal of Economic Perspectives* 28: 49–72.

Hicks, J. R. 1961. "Measurement of Capital in Relation to the Measurement of Economic Aggregates." In *The Theory of Capital*, edited by F. A. Lutz and D. C. Hague, 18–31. London: Macmillan.

Hoch, I. 1955. "Estimation of Production Function Parameters and Testing for Efficiency." *Econometrica* 23: 325–326.

Hopenhayn, H. A. 2014. "Firms, Misallocation and Aggregate Productivity: A Review." *Annual Review of Economics* 6: 735–770.

Hsieh, C.-T. 2002. "What Explains the Industrial Revolution in East Asia? Evidence from the Factor Markets." *American Economic Review* 92: 502–526.

Hsieh, C.-T. 2015. "Policies for Productivity Growth." OECD Productivity Working Papers No. 03. http://www.oecd-ilibrary.org/economics/policies-for-productivity-growth_5jrp1f5rddtc-en.

Hsieh, C.-T., and P. J. Klenow. 2009. "Misallocation and Manufacturing TFP in China and India." *Quarterly Journal of Economics* 124: 1403–1448.

Hsieh, C.-T., and E. Moretti. 2015. "Why Do Cities Matter? Local Growth and Aggregate Growth." National Bureau of Economic Research Working Paper 21154. http://www.nber.org/papers/w21154.

Hultberg, P. T., M. I. Nadiri, and R. C. Sickles. 2004. "Cross-Country Catch-up in the Manufacturing Sector: Impacts of Heterogeneity on Convergence and Technology Adoption." *Empirical Economics* 29: 753–68.

Hultberg, P. T., M. I. Nadiri, R. C. Sickles and P. T. Hultberg. 1999. "An International Comparison of Technology Adoption and Efficiency: A Dynamic Panel Model." *Annales d'Économie et de Statistique* 55–56: 449–474.

Hulten, C. R. 2001. "Total Factor Productivity: A Short Biography." In *New Developments in Productivity Analysis*, edited by C. R. Hulten, E. R. Dean, and M. J. Harper, Chapter 1, 1–53. Chicago: University of Chicago Press.

Iacovone, L., and G. A. Crespi. 2010. "Catching up with the Technological Frontier: Micro-Level Evidence on Growth and Convergence." *Industrial and Corporate Change* 19: 2073–2096.

Ichniowski, C., and K. Shaw. 2012. "Insider Econometrics." In *The Handbook of Organizational Economics*, edited by R. Gibbons and J. Roberts, Chapter 7, 263–311. Princeton, NJ: Princeton University Press.

Ichniowski, C., K. Shaw, and G. Prennushi. 1997. "The Effects of Human Resource Management Practices on Productivity: A Study of Steel Finishing Lines." *American Economic Review* 87: 291–313.

Inklaar, R., and W. E. Diewert. 2016. "Measuring Industry Productivity and Cross-Country Convergence." *Journal of Econometrics* 191: 426–433.

Inklaar, R., and M. P. Timmer. 2009. "Productivity Convergence across Industries and Countries: The Importance of Theory-Based Measurement." *Macroeconomic Dynamics* 13 (Suppl 2): 218–240.

Johnson, H. T. 1975. "Management Accounting in an Early Integrated Industrial: E. I. duPont de Nemours Powder Company, 1903–1912." *Business History Review* 49: 184–204.

Johnson, H. T. 1978. "Management Accounting in an Early Multidivisional Organization: General Motors in the 1920s." *Business History Review* 52: 490–517.

Jorgenson, D. W., and Z. Griliches. 1967. "The Explanation of Productivity Change." *Review of Economic Studies* 34: 249–283.

Kendrick, J. W. 1961. *Productivity Trends in the United States*. Princeton, NJ: Princeton University Press.

Kendrick, J. W. 1984. *Improving Company Productivity: Handbook with Case Studies*. Baltimore, MD: Johns Hopkins University Press.

Kendrick, J. W., and D. Creamer. 1961. *Measuring Company Productivity: Handbook with Case Studies*. Studies in Business Economics 74. New York: The Conference Board.

Kim, J.-I., and L. J. Lau. 1994. "The Sources of Economic Growth of the East Asian Newly Industrialized Countries." *Journal of the Japanese and International Economies* 8: 235–71.

Krueger, A. B. 2013. "Land of Hope and Dreams: Rock and Roll, Economics and Rebuilding the Middle Class." www.whitehouse.gov/sites/default/files/docs/hope_and_dreams_-_final.pdf.

Krugman, P. 1994. "The Myth of Asia's Miracle." *Foreign Affairs* 73: 62–78.

Krussell, P., L. E. Ohanian, J.-V. Ríos-Rull, and G. L. Violante. 2000. "Capital-Skill Complementarity and Inequality: A Macroeconomic Analysis." *Econometrica* 68: 1029–1053.

Kumar, S., and R. R. Russell. 2002. "Technological Change, Technological Catch-up, and Capital Deepening: Relative Contributions to Growth and Convergence," *American Economic Review* 92: 527–548.

Kumbhakar, S. C., and E. Malikov. 2018. "Good Modeling of Bad Outputs: Editors' Introduction." *Empirical Economics* 54: 1–6. http://dx.doi.rg/10.1007/s00181-017-1231-8.

Lakner, C., and B. Milanovic. 2016. "Global Income Distribution: From the Fall of the Berlin Wall to the Great Recession." *World Bank Economic Review* 30: 203–232.

Landes, D. S. (.1990. "Why Are We So Rich and They So Poor?" *American Economic Review* 80: 1–13.

Lansink, A. O., S. E. Stefanou, and T. Serra. 2015. "Primal and Dual Dynamic Luenberger Productivity Indicators." *European Journal of Operational Research* 241, 555–563.

La Porta, R., and A. Shleifer. 2014. "Informality and Development." *Journal of Economic Perspectives* 28: 109–126.

Lauwers, L. 2009. "Justifying the Incorporation of the Materials Balance Principle into Frontier-Based Eco-Efficiency Models." *Ecological Economics* 68: 1605–1614.

Lawrence, D., W. E. Diewert, and K. J. Fox. 2006. "The Contributions of Productivity, Price Change and Firm Size to Profitability." *Journal of Productivity Analysis* 26: 1–13.

Lazear, E. 2000. "Performance Pay and Productivity." *American Economic Review* 90: 1346–1361.

Lewis, W. W. 2004. *The Power of Productivity*. Chicago: University of Chicago Press.

Lieberman, M. B., R. Garcia-Castro, and N. Balasubramanian. 2017. "Measuring Value Creation and Appropriation in Firms: The VCA Model." *Strategic Management Journal* 38: 1193–1211.

Lucas, R. E., Jr. 1988. "On the Mechanics of Economic Development." *Journal of Monetary Economics* 22: 3–42.

Luh, Y.-H., and S. E. Stefanou. 1991. "Productivity Growth in US Agriculture under Dynamic Adjustment." *American Journal of Agricultural Economics* 73: 1116–25.

Mairesse, J., and P. Mohnen. 2002. "Accounting for Innovation and Measuring Innovativeness: An Illustrative Framework and an Application." *American Economic Review* 92: 226–230.

Malmquist, S. 1953. "Index Numbers and Indifference Surfaces." *Trabajos de Estadistica* 4: 209–242.

Mankiw, N. G., D. Rome, and D. N. Weil. 1992. "A Contribution to the Empirics of Economic Growth." *Quarterly Journal of Economics* 107: 407–437.

Massell, B. F. 1967. "Elimination of Management Bias from Production Functions Fitted to Cross-Section Data: A Model and an Application to African Agriculture." *Econometrica* 35: 495–508.

McKinsey Global Institute. 2016. "Poorer Than Their Parents? A New Perspective on Income Inequality."   http://www.mckinsey.com/global-themes/employment-and-growth/poorer-than-their-parents-a-new-perspective-on-income-inequality.

Meeusen, W., and J. van den Broeck. 1977. "Efficiency Estimation from Cobb-Douglas Production Functions with Composed Error." *International Economic Review* 18: 435–444.

Midrigan, V., and D. Y. Xu. 2014. "Finance and Misallocation: Evidence from Plant-Level Data." *American Economic Review* 104: 422–458.

Milgrom, P., and J. Roberts. 1990. "The Economics of Modern Manufacturing." *American Economic Review* 80: 511–528.

Milgrom, P., and J. Roberts. 1995. "Complementarities and Fit: Strategy, Structure and Organizational Change in Manufacturing." *Journal of Accounting and Economics* 19: 179–208.

Miller, D. M. 1984. "Profitability = Productivity + Price Recovery." *Harvard Business Review* 62: 145–153.

Mills, F. C. 1932. *Economic Tendencies in the United States: Aspects of Pre-War and Post-War Changes*. Cambridge, MA: National Bureau of Economic Research. http://papers.nber.org/books/mill32-1.

Mohnen, P., and B. H. Hall. 2013. "Innovation and Productivity: An Update." *Eurasian Business Review* 3: 47–65.

Mokyr, J., C. Vickers, and N. L. Ziebarth. 2015. "The History of Technological Anxiety and the Future of Economic Growth: Is This Time Different?" *Journal of Economic Perspectives* 29: 31–50.

Moll, B. 2014. "Productivity Losses from Financial Frictions: Can Self-Financing Undo Capital Misallocation?" *American Economic Review* 104: 3186–3221.

Moorsteen, R. H. 1961. "On Measuring Productive Potential and Relative Efficiency." *Quarterly Journal of Economics* 75: 451–467.

Moscoso Boedo, H. J., and T. Mukoyama. 2012. "Evaluating the Effects of Entry Regulations and Firing Costs on International Income Differences." *Journal of Economic Growth* 17: 143–170.

Mundlak, Y. 1961. "Empirical Production Function Free of Management Bias." *Journal of Farm Economics* 43: 44–56.

Nelson, R. R., and S. G. Winter. 1982. *An Evolutionary Theory of Economic Change*. Cambridge, MA: Harvard University Press.

Nelson, R. R., and G. Wright. 1992. "The Rise and Fall of American Technological Leadership: The Postwar Era in Historical Perspective." *Journal of Economic Literature* 30: 1931–64.

Niebel, T., M. O'Mahoney, and M. Saam. 2017. "The Contribution of Intangible Assets to Sectoral Productivity Growth in the EU." *Review of Income and Wealth* 63: S49–S67.

Nordhaus, W. D. 2006. "Geography and Macroeconomics: New Data and New Findings." *Proceedings of the National Academy of Sciences* 103: 3510–3517.

Nordhaus, W. D., and E. C. Kokkelenberg. 1999. *Nature's Numbers: Expanding the National Accounts to Include the Environment*. Washington, DC: National Academy Press.

Nordhaus, W. D., and J. Tobin. 1972. "Is Growth Obsolete?" In *Economic Research: Retrospect and Prospect*, Vol. 5: *Economic Growth* edited by William D. Nordhaus and James Tobin, Chapter 1, 1–80. Cambridge, MA: National Bureau of Economic Research http://www.nber.org/chapters/c7620.

North, D. C. 1990. *Institutions, Institutional Change and Economic Performance*. Cambridge: Cambridge University Press.

O'Donnell, C. J. 2012. "An Aggregate Quantity Framework for Measuring and Decomposing Productivity Change." *Journal of Productivity Analysis* 38: 255–272.

OECD. 2001a. *Measuring Productivity: OECD Manual*. http://www.oecd.org/std/productivity-stats/2352458.pdf

OECD. 2001b. "Productivity and Firm Dynamics: Evidence from Microdata." In *OECD Economic Outlook* 69: Chapter 7, 209–223. www.oecd.org/eco/outlook/2079019.pdf.

OECD. 2002. *Measuring the Non-Observed Economy: A Handbook*. https://www.oecd.org/std/na/1963116.pdf.

OECD. 2011. "Incorporating Estimates of Household Production of Non-Market Services into International Comparisons of Material Well-Being." www.oecd.org/officialdocuments/publicdisplaydocumentpdf/?cote=std/doc(2011)7&doclanguage=en.

OECD. 2014. "All on Board. Making Inclusive Growth Happen." http://www.oecd.org/inclusive-growth/All-on-Board-Making-Inclusive-Growth-Happen.pdf.

OECD. 2015a. *Economic Policy Reforms: Going For Growth*. http://www.oecd-ilibrary.org/economics/economic-policy-reforms-2015_growth-2015-en.

OECD. 2015b. *The Future of Productivity*. http://www.oecd-ilibrary.org/economics/the-future-of-productivity_9789264248533-en.

OECD. 2016a. *The Productivity–Inclusiveness Nexus*. Meeting of the OECD Council at Ministerial Level, Paris, June 1–2. https://www.oecd.org/global-forum-productivity/library/The-Productivity-Inclusiveness-Nexus-Preliminary.pdf.

OECD. 2016b. "Promoting Productivity and Equality: A Twin Challenge." In *OECD Economic Outlook* 2016(1), Chapter 2. http://www.oecd.org/eco/outlook/OECD-Economic-Outlook-June-2016-promoting-productivity-and-equality.pdf.

Oh, Y., D.-h. Oh, and J. D. Lee. Forthcoming. "A Sequential Global Malmquist Productivity Index: Productivity Growth Index for Unbalanced Panel Data Considering the Progressive Nature of Technology." *Empirical Economics* 52: 1651–1674. http://dx.doi.rg/10.1007/s00181-016-1104-6.

Olley, S. G., and A. Pakes. 1996. "The Dynamics of Productivity in the Telecommunications Equipment Industry." *Econometrica* 64: 1263–1297.

Olsen, K. B. 2006. "Productivity Impacts of Offshoring and Outsourcing: A Review," OECD Science, Technology and Industry Working Papers, 2006/01. http://dx.doi.org/10.1787/685237388034.

Parente, S. L., and E. C. Prescott. 1993. "Changes in the Wealth of Nations." *Federal Reserve Bank of Minneapolis Quarterly Review* 17: 3–16.

Pérez-López, G., D. Prior, J. L. Zafra-Gómez, and A. M. Plata-Díaz. 2016. "Cost Efficiency in Municipal Solid Waste Service Delivery. Alternative Management Forms in Relation to Local Population Size." *European Journal of Operational Research* 255: 583–592.

Peyrache, A., and A. Zago. 2016. "Large Courts, Small Justice! The Inefficiency and the Optimal Structure of the Italian Justice Sector." *Omega* 64: 42–56.

Poissonnier, A., and D. Roy. 2017. "Household Satellite Account for France: Methodological Issues on the Assessment of Domestic Production." *Review of Income and Wealth*, 63: 353–377. doi: 10.1111/roiw.12216.

Porter, M. E. 1991. "America's Green Strategy." *Scientific American* (April): 168.

Raymond, W., J. Mairesse, P. Mohnen, and F. Palm. 2015. "Dynamic Models of R&D, Innovation and Productivity: Panel Data Evidence from Dutch and French Manufacturing." *European Economic Review* 78: 285–306.

Reijnders, L. S. M., M. P. Timmer, and X. Ye. 2016. "Offshoring, Biased Technical Change and Labor Demand: New Evidence from Global Value Chains." GGDC Research Memorandum 164, Groningen Growth and Development Centre, University of Groningen. http://www.ggdc.net/publications/memorandum/gd164.pdf.

Rodrick, D. 2013. "Unconditional Convergence in Manufacturing." *Quarterly Journal of Economics* 128: 165–204.

Romer, P. M. 1986. "Increasing Returns and Long-Run Growth." *Journal of Political Economy* 94: 1002–1037.

Royal Swedish Academy of Sciences. 1992. "Press Release." https://www.nobelprize.org/nobel_prizes/economic-sciences/laureates/1992/press.html

Royal Swedish Academy of Sciences. 1993. "Press Release." https://www.nobelprize.org/nobel_prizes/economic-sciences/laureates/1993/press.html

Salter, W. E. G. 1960. *Productivity and Technical Change*. Cambridge: Cambridge University Press.

Schenkel, A., and R. Teigland. 2017. "Why Doesn't Downsizing Deliver? A Multi-Level Model Integrating Downsizing, Social Capital, Dynamic Capabilities and Firm Performance." *International Journal of Human Resource Management* 28: 1065–1107.

Schmookler, J. 1952. "The Changing Efficiency of the American Economy, 1869–1938." *Review of Economics and Statistics* 34: 214–231.

Schreyer, P. 2012. "Output, Outcome and Quality Adjustment in Measuring Health and Education Services." *Review of Income and Wealth* 58: 257–278.

Schreyer, P., and W. E. Diewert. 2014. "Household Production, Leisure and Living Standards." In *Measuring Economic Sustainability and Progress*, edited by D. W. Jorgenson, J. S. Landefeld, and P. Schreyer, Chapter 4, 89–114. Chicago: University of Chicago Press.

Schultz, T. W. 1964. *Transforming Traditional Agriculture*. New Haven, CT: Yale University Press.

Schultz, T. W. 1975. "The Value of the Ability to Deal with Disequilibria." *Journal of Economic Literature* 13: 827–846.

Schumpeter, J. A. 1942. *Capitalism, Socialism and Democracy*. New York: Harper & Row.

Shaw, K. 2009. "Insider Econometrics: A Roadmap with Stops along the Way." *Labour Economics* 16: 607–617.

Shephard, R. W. 1953. *Cost and Production Functions*. Princeton, NJ: Princeton University Press.

Shephard, R. W. 1970. *Theory of Cost and Production Functions*. Princeton, NJ: Princeton University Press.

Shephard, R. W. 1974. *Indirect Production Functions*. Meisenheim Am Glan: Verlag Anton Hain.

Shephard, R. W., and R. Färe. 1980. *Dynamic Theory of Production Correspondences*. Cambridge, MA: Oelgeschlager, Gunn and Hain Publishers.

Shestalova, V. 2003. "Sequential Malmquist Indices of Productivity Growth: An Application to OECD Industrial Activities." *Journal of Productivity Analysis* 19: 211–226.

Sickles, R. C., and B. Cigerli. 2009. "Krugman and Young Revisited: A Survey of the Sources of Productivity Growth in a World with Less Constraints." *Seoul Journal of Economics* 22: 29–54.

Sickles, R. C., and M. L. Streitwieser. 1998. "An Analysis of Technology, Productivity and Regulatory Distortion in the Interstate Natural Gas Transmission Industry: 1977–1985." *Journal of Applied Econometrics* 13: 377–95.

Sickles, R. C., and V. Zelenyuk. Forthcoming. *Measurement of Productivity and Efficiency: Theory and Practice*. New York: Cambridge University Press.

Silva, E., A. O. Lansink and S. E. Stefanou. 2015. "The Adjustment-Cost Model of the Firm: Duality and Productive Efficiency." *International Journal of Production Economics* 168: 245–256.

Silva, E., and S. E. Stefanou. 2003. "Nonparametric Dynamic Production Analysis and the Theory of Cost." *Journal of Productivity Analysis* 19: 5–32.

Silva, E., and S. E. Stefanou. 2007. "Dynamic Efficiency Measurement: Theory and Application." *American Journal of Agricultural Economics* 89: 398–419.

Sloan, A. P. 1964. *My Years with General Motors*. Garden City, NY: Doubleday.

Smolny, W. 2000. "Sources of Productivity Growth: An Empirical Analysis with German Sectoral Data." *Applied Economics* 32: 305–14.

Solow, R. M. 1957. "Technical Change and the Aggregate Production Function." *Review of Economics and Statistics* 39: 312–320.

Solow, R. M. 1987. "We'd Better Watch Out." *New York Times*, 36. July 12.

Song, J., D. J. Price, F. Guvenen, N. Bloom, and T. von Wachter. 2015. "Firming Up Inequality." National Bureau of Economic Research Working Paper 21199. http://www.nber.org/papers/w21199.

Squires, B. M. 1917. "Productivity and Cost of Labor in the Lumber Industry." *Monthly Labor Review* 5: 66–79.

Statistics Netherlands. 2015. *ICT and Economic Growth*. http://www.cbs.nl/en-GB/menu/themas/macro-economie/publicaties/publicaties/archief/2015/2015-ict-and-economic-growth-pub.htm.

Stewart, E. 1922. "Efficiency of American Labor." *Monthly Labor Review* 15: 1–12.

Stiglitz, J. E., A. Sen, and J-P Fitoussi. 2009. "The Measurement of Economic Performance and Social Progress Revisited." OFCE Centre de recherché en économie de sciences Po. Working Paper 2009-33 (December). www.ofce.sciences-po.fr/pdf/dtravail/WP2009-33.pdf

Syverson, C. 2011. "What Determines Productivity?" *Journal of Economic Literature* 49: 326–365.

Tarbell, I. M. 1904. *The History of the Standard Oil Company*. New York: McClure, Phillips.

Temin, P. (ed.). 1991. *Inside the Business Enterprise: Historical Perspectives on the Use of Information*. Chicago: University of Chicago Press.

Timmer, M. P., A. A. Erumban, B. Los, R. Stehrer, and G. J. de Vries. 2014. "Slicing Up Global Value Chains." *Journal of Economic Perspectives* 28: 99–118.

Topp, V., and T. Kulys. 2014. "On Productivity: The Influence of Natural Resource Inputs." *International Productivity Monitor* 27: 64–78.

Topp, V., L. Soames, D. Parham and H. Bloch. 2008: "Productivity in the Mining Industry: Measurement and Interpretation." Productivity Commission Staff Working Paper. www.pc.gov.au/research/staffworkingpaper/mining-productivity.

Tulkens, H., and P. Vanden Eeckaut. 1995. "Nonparametric Efficiency, Progress and Regress Measures for Panel Data: Methodological Aspects." *European Journal of Operational Research* 80: 474–499.

van Ark, B. 2016. "The Productivity Paradox of the New Digital Economy." *International Productivity Monitor* 31: 3–18.

Van Reenen, J. 2011. "Does Competition Raise Productivity Through Improving Management Quality?" *International Journal of Industrial Organization* 29: 306–316.

Vincent, A. L. A. 1968. *La Mesure de la productivité*. Paris: Dunod.

Ward, B. 1958. "The Firm in Illyria: Market Syndicalism." *American Economic Review* 48: 566–589.

Winter, S. G., and G. Szulanski. 2001. "Replication as Strategy." *Organization Science* 12: 730–743.

Wolff, E. N. (2013), *Productivity Convergence: Theory and Evidence*. New York: Cambridge University Press.

Wolff, F.-C., D. Squires, and P. Guillotreau. 2013. "The Firm's Management in Production: Management, Firm, and Time Effects in an Indian Ocean Tuna Fishery." *American Journal of Agricultural Economics* 95: 547–567.

Young, A. 1992. "A Tale of Two Cities: Factor Accumulation and Technical Change in Hong Kong and Singapore." *NBER Macroeconomics Annual 1992*: 13–54.

Young, A. 1995. "The Tyranny of Numbers: Confronting the Statistical Realities of the East Asian Growth Experience." *Quarterly Journal of Economics* 110: 641–680.

PART II

THE FOUNDATIONS OF PRODUCTIVITY ANALYSIS

CHAPTER 2

....

EMPIRICAL PRODUCTIVITY INDICES AND INDICATORS

....

BERT M. BALK

2.1. INTRODUCTION

THROUGH its activities a firm creates value, and this has more dimensions than only the monetary.[1] Accordingly, there is a multitude of perspectives coming from a multitude of stakeholders from which firm performance can be assessed (see Harrison and Wicks 2013). Marr (2012), for instance, discusses 75 measures, covering financial, customer, marketing and sales, operational processes and supply chain, employee, and corporate social responsibility perspectives. In this chapter, however, our attention will be restricted to economic performance measures such as profit, profitability, profit margin, productivity, price recovery, and their interlinkages.

Though these concepts are primarily defined for actual economic agents such as plants or firms, they can easily be extended to industries, industrial sectors, or economies. This brings us to the realm of national accounts.

What may the reader expect? In section 2.2 we begin by defining the key concepts: profit (revenue minus total cost), profitability (revenue divided by total cost), and two margins (profit-cost and profit-revenue). As the building blocks of these concepts are values, and we are interested in change through time, section 2.3 is devoted to the difference between direct and chained indices and indicators. The next question to consider is how to decompose value change into price and quantity components. Thus, section 2.4 provides a brief survey of index number theory, basically concentrating on price indices, the practice of deflation, and the practically important subject of two-stage indices.

After all these preparations, section 2.5 turns to the heart of the matter, namely the definition of total factor productivity (TFP) and total price recovery *indices* as the two components of profitability change. Section 2.6 discusses the relation between our definition and the practices of growth accounting and production function estimation. In the extended online version of this chapter, the closely related problem of the decomposition of a margin change is discussed. Section 2.7, finally, discusses the relation between total and partial productivity indices.

Profit change is another key area. Since profit change is measured as a difference, indicators come into play—indicators being the difference-type counterparts from indices, which are ratio-type measures. Section 2.8 briefly reviews the theory, after which section 2.9—which can be considered as the correlate of section 2.5—defines TFP and total price recovery *indicators*. In the extended online version of this chapter, the fundamental equivalence of the two approaches, the multiplicative based on indices and the additive based on indicators, is demonstrated.

In sections 2.2–2.9 the discussion is cast in terms of the so-called KLEMS-Y input–output model, where Y stands for physical output (goods and services). An important alternative is the KL-VA model, where value added serves as output. Value-added-based profitability change and its decomposition in price and quantity components is discussed in sections 2.10 and 2.11. For a discussion of the decomposition of value added change as such, the reader is referred to the extended online version of this chapter.

Sections 2.2–2.11 basically consider the case of a single production unit moving through time. Section 2.12 continues by considering a dynamic ensemble of production units, and the relation between aggregate and subaggregate, or individual, measures of productivity change. The main results available in the literature are reviewed in two subsections, devoted to the top-down and the bottom-up approach, respectively.

Section 2.13 recapitulates the main characteristics of the approach outlined in this chapter. Summarizing, this chapter shows what can be done with data alone, in particular (observable) nominal value data and (constructed) price index numbers (or, deflators).

2.2. NOTATION AND KEY CONCEPTS

We consider a single production unit through time and will later consider the comparison of multiple production units at a given point of time (a so-called cross-sectional or spatial comparison). This production unit may be a plant, a firm, an industry, an industrial sector, or even (the measurable part of) an entire economy. The unit is considered to be consolidated; that is, all within-unit transactions are netted out. At the output side of this unit we distinguish M items (goods and services), each with their unit price (as received by the production unit) p_m^t and quantity y_m^t, where $m = 1, \ldots, M$, and $t = 0, 1, \ldots, T$ denotes an accounting period (say, a year). Similarly, at the input side we distinguish N items (goods, services, and assets), each with their unit price (as paid by the production unit) w_n^t and quantity x_n^t, where $n = 1, \ldots, N$.

Usually the input-side items are allocated to a few broadly defined classes:[2] capital K, labor L, energy E, materials M, services S. Thus, we are primarily discussing the so-called KLEMS-Y input–output model.[3]

To avoid notational clutter, simple vector notation will be used throughout this chapter. All the prices and quantities are assumed to be positive, unless stated otherwise. The *ex post* accounting point of view will be used; that is, quantities and monetary values of the so-called flow variables (output Y, and *LEMS* inputs) are realized values, complete knowledge of which becomes available after the accounting period has expired. Similarly, the cost of capital input K is calculated *ex post*. This is consistent with official statistical practice.

The unit's revenue, that is, the value of its output, during the accounting period t is defined as

$$R^t \equiv p^t \cdot y^t \equiv \sum_{m=1}^{M} p_m^t y_m^t, \tag{2.1}$$

whereas its (total) production cost is defined as

$$C^t \equiv w^t \cdot x^t \equiv \sum_{n=1}^{N} w_n^t x_n^t. \tag{2.2}$$

Given positive prices and quantities, it will always be the case that $R^t > 0$ and $C^t > 0$.

The unit's *profit* (including taxes on production) is then given by its revenue minus its cost;[4] that is,

$$\Pi^t \equiv R^t - C^t = p^t \cdot y^t - w^t \cdot x^t. \tag{2.3}$$

The unit's (gross-output based) *profitability* (also including taxes on production) is defined as its revenue divided by its cost; that is,

$$\Upsilon^t \equiv R^t / C^t = p^t \cdot y^t / w^t \cdot x^t. \tag{2.4}$$

Profit and profitability are similar financial performance concepts. The profitability concept seems to have been introduced by the economist Georgescu-Roegen in 1951. Whereas profit is a difference, profitability is a ratio. Profit can be positive, zero, or negative. Profitability is always positive, but can be greater than one, equal to one, or less than one. Since profitability is independent of the size of the production unit, for comparative purposes, profitability is a more natural measure than profit.

The fundamental equivalence of the two concepts is expressed by the following relation:

$$\frac{\Pi^t}{\ln \Upsilon^t} = LM(R^t, C^t) \quad (\Pi^t \neq 0, \Upsilon^t \neq 1), \tag{2.5}$$

where $LM(a, b)$ denotes the logarithmic mean.[5]

The next two performance concepts are margins. The first is the *profit-cost margin* of the production unit, defined as profit over cost,

$$\mu^t \equiv \frac{\Pi^t}{C^t}. \tag{2.6}$$

The relation between profit-cost margin and profitability is then given by

$$\mu^t = \Upsilon^t - 1; \tag{2.7}$$

that is, the profit-cost margin is the profitability expressed as a percentage (which is usually published as $\mu^t \times 100\%$). But what precisely does this mean?

To get a clue, consider first the single-output case; that is, $M = 1$. Then the production unit's profitability reduces to

$$\Upsilon^t = p^t y^t / C^t = p^t / \left(C^t / y^t \right); \tag{2.8}$$

that is, price over cost per unit. Put otherwise, the profit-cost margin μ^t is then the *markup* of price over unit cost.

For the general, multi-output case, suppose that the cost can be allocated to the various outputs; that is, $C^t = \sum_{m=1}^{M} C_m^t$, where C_m^t is the cost for producing y_m^t units of output m ($m = 1, \ldots, M$). Then the unit's profitability can be decomposed as

$$\Upsilon^t = \frac{\sum_{m=1}^{M} p_m^t y_m^t}{\sum_{m=1}^{M} C_m^t} = \sum_{m=1}^{M} \frac{C_m^t}{C^t} \frac{p_m^t}{C_m^t / y_m^t}. \tag{2.9}$$

Thus profitability is a cost-share weighted mean of output-specific price over unit-cost relatives. Put otherwise, the profit-cost margin is a cost-share weighted mean of output-specific markups,

$$\mu^t = \sum_{m=1}^{M} \frac{C_m^t}{C^t} \mu_m^t, \tag{2.10}$$

where $\mu_m^t \equiv p_m^t / (C_m^t / y_m^t)$ ($m = 1, \ldots, M$).

The second margin is the *profit-revenue margin*, defined as profit over revenue,[6]

$$v^t \equiv \frac{\Pi^t}{R^t}. \tag{2.11}$$

This margin plays an important role in the duPont triangle, a management accounting system developed at duPont and General Motors early in the twentieth century (see Grifell-Tatjé and Lovell 2014). The relation between profit-revenue margin and profitability is given by

$$v^t = 1 - 1 / \Upsilon^t. \tag{2.12}$$

The profit-revenue margin is the percentage of revenue that is considered as profit (and usually published as $v^t \times 100\%$).

The two margin concepts are connected by the profitability concept. Connecting the three definitions yields

$$\Upsilon^t = \mu^t / v^t; \tag{2.13}$$

that is, profitability equals profit-cost margin divided by profit-revenue margin.

Notice that the two margin concepts share with profit the property of being positive, zero, or negative.

2.3. Measuring Change

As said, we are primarily concerned with the performance of our production unit through time. That is, we want to compare revenue, cost, profit, or profitability of a certain period t to an earlier period t' where t, $t' = 0, 1, \ldots, T$. The key to the index number approach is that the availability of detailed data makes it possible to decompose any value change into two components: a price component and a quantity component. Now change can basically be measured in two ways: multiplicatively as a ratio and additively as a difference. The first leads to indices and the second to indicators. Let us consider indices first and take revenue as an example.[7]

2.3.1. Indices

Let the periods t and t' be adjacent; that is, $t' = t - 1$. Given the price and quantity data and using the economic statistician's toolkit, the ratio R^t / R^{t-1} can be decomposed into two parts,

$$\frac{R^t}{R^{t-1}} = P(p^t, y^t, p^{t-1}, y^{t-1}) Q(p^t, y^t, p^{t-1}, y^{t-1}), \tag{2.14}$$

where $P(.)$ is a bilateral price index and $Q(.)$ is a bilateral quantity index, the precise definitions of which will be postponed to the next section.

When the periods t and t' are non-adjacent, that is, when $t' = t - s$ with $1 < s \leq t$, then there are two options. The first is to use a set of bilateral indices to decompose the ratio R^t / R^{t-s}; that is,

$$\frac{R^t}{R^{t-s}} = P(p^t, y^t, p^{t-s}, y^{t-s}) Q(p^t, y^t, p^{t-s}, y^{t-s}). \tag{2.15}$$

The second is to decompose the ratio R^t/R^{t-s} first as a multiplicative chain of adjacent-period ratios,

$$\frac{R^t}{R^{t-s}} = \prod_{s'=t-s+1}^{t} \frac{R^{s'}}{R^{s'-1}}, \tag{2.16}$$

and then to decompose each of these adjacent-period ratios like expression (2.14),

$$\frac{R^{s'}}{R^{s'-1}} = P(p^{s'}, y^{s'}, p^{s'-1}, y^{s'-1})Q(p^{s'}, y^{s'}, p^{s'-1}, y^{s'-1}) \quad \left(s' = t-s+1, ..., t\right). \tag{2.17}$$

Substituting expression (2.17) into (2.16) and rearranging delivers as an alternative decomposition of the ratio R^t/R^{t-s} the more complicated expression

$$\frac{R^t}{R^{t-s}} = \prod_{s'=t-s+1}^{t} P(p^{s'}, y^{s'}, p^{s'-1}, y^{s'-1}) \times \prod_{s'=t-s+1}^{t} Q(p^{s'}, y^{s'}, p^{s'-1}, y^{s'-1}). \tag{2.18}$$

The first factor at the right-hand side of this expression is called a chained price index, and the second factor is called a chained quantity index. It is important to observe that in general, on the same data, the decompositions (2.15) and (2.18) deliver different outcomes. The first decomposition is in terms of direct indices. A direct index is a bilateral index; that is, a function depending only on the data of the two periods t and $t-s$. The second decomposition is in terms of chained indices. A chained index is a multilateral index; that is, a function that does not only depend on the data of the two periods being compared, t and $t-s$ respectively, but also on the data of all the intervening periods.

2.3.2. Indicators

Let the periods t and t' be adjacent; that is, $t' = t-1$. Given the price and quantity data and using the economic statistician's toolkit, the difference $R^t - R^{t-1}$ can be decomposed into two parts,

$$R^t - R^{t-1} = \mathcal{P}(p^t, y^t, p^{t-1}, y^{t-1}) + \mathcal{Q}(p^t, y^t, p^{t-1}, y^{t-1}), \tag{2.19}$$

where $\mathcal{P}(.)$ is a bilateral price indicator and $\mathcal{Q}(.)$ is a bilateral quantity indicator, the precise definitions of which are provided in a later section of the chapter. Of course, a difference such as $R^t - R^{t-1}$ only makes sense when the two money amounts involved are deflated by some general inflation measure (such as the headline Consumer Price Index, or CPI), or when the two periods are so close that deflation is deemed unnecessary. In the remainder of this subsection, when discussing difference measures, either of the two situations is tacitly presupposed.

When the periods t and t' are non-adjacent, that is, when $t' = t - s$ with $1 < s \le t$, then there are two options. The first is to use a set of bilateral indicators to decompose the difference $R^t - R^{t-s}$; that is,

$$R^t - R^{t-s} = \mathcal{P}(p^t, y^t, p^{t-s}, y^{t-s}) + \mathcal{Q}(p^t, y^t, p^{t-s}, y^{t-s}). \qquad (2.20)$$

The second is to decompose the difference $R^t - R^{t-s}$ first as an additive chain of adjacent-period differences,

$$R^t - R^{t-s} = \sum_{s'=t-s+1}^{t} (R^{s'} - R^{s'-1}), \qquad (2.21)$$

and then to decompose each of these adjacent-period differences like expression (2.19),

$$R^{s'} - R^{s'-1} = \mathcal{P}(p^{s'}, y^{s'}, p^{s'-1}, y^{s'-1}) + \mathcal{Q}(p^{s'}, y^{s'}, p^{s'-1}, y^{s'-1}) \quad \left(s' = t-s+1, \dots, t\right). \quad (2.22)$$

Substituting expression (2.22) into (2.21) and rearranging delivers as an alternative decomposition of the difference $R^t - R^{t-s}$ the more complicated expression

$$R^t - R^{t-s} = \sum_{s'=t-s+1}^{t} \mathcal{P}(p^{s'}, y^{s'}, p^{s'-1}, y^{s'-1}) + \sum_{s'=t-s+1}^{t} \mathcal{Q}(p^{s'}, y^{s'}, p^{s'-1}, y^{s'-1}). \quad (2.23)$$

The first factor at the right-hand side of this expression is called a chained price indicator, and the second factor is called a chained quantity indicator. It is important to observe that in general, on the same data, the decompositions (2.20) and (2.23) deliver different outcomes. The first decomposition is in terms of direct indicators. A direct indicator is a bilateral function, depending only on the data of the two periods t and $t - s$. The second decomposition is in terms of chained indicators. A chained indicator is a multilateral function, depending on the data of the two periods being compared, t and $t - s$ respectively, and on the data of all the intervening periods.

2.3.3. Conclusion

From the preceding two subsections, it is clear that there is no loss of generality when in the remainder of this survey we consider only the comparison of adjacent periods. To simplify notation, the two periods we consider are $t = 1$ (which will be called the comparison period) and $t' = 0$ (which will be called the base period).

2.4. INDICES

In this section we consider an aggregate consisting of M items (goods and services) with (unit) prices going from p_m^0 to p_m^1 and quantities going from y_m^0 to y_m^1 ($m = 1, \dots, M$). The first subsection reviews price indices, the second subsection reviews quantity indices, and the third subsection reviews the concept of two-stage indices.

It is important to note that, though stated in terms of output, the theory surveyed in this section is equally applicable to other situations after appropriate modification of the number of items and the interpretation of the variables.

2.4.1. Price Indices

Formally, a *bilateral price index* is a positive, continuously differentiable function $P(p^1, y^1, p^0, y^0): \Re_{++}^{4M} \to \Re_{++}$ that, except in extreme situations, correctly indicates any increase or decrease of the elements of the *price* vectors p^1 or p^0, conditional on the quantity vectors y^1 and y^0. Likewise, a *bilateral quantity index* is a positive, continuously differentiable function of the same variables $Q(p^1, y^1, p^0, y^0): \Re_{++}^{4M} \to \Re_{++}$ that, except in extreme situations, correctly indicates any increase or decrease of the elements of the *quantity* vectors y^1 or y^0, conditional on the price vectors p^1 and p^0. The number M is called the dimension of the price or quantity index.

These two definitions are deliberately kept pretty vague, to accommodate official and unofficial practice. Over the last century, index number theory has delivered much more precise statements in the form of axioms and/or tests, but it was soon discovered that no index satisfies simultaneously all those requirements.

The basic requirements on price and quantity indices comprise the following:

1. that they exhibit the desired monotonicity properties globally; that is, $P(p^1, y^1, p^0, y^0)$ is nondecreasing in p^1 and nonincreasing in p^0, and $Q(p^1, y^1, p^0, y^0)$ is nondecreasing in y^1 and nonincreasing in y^0;
2. that $P(p^1, y^1, p^0, y^0)$ is linearly homogeneous in p^1 and $Q(p^1, y^1, p^0, y^0)$ is linearly homogeneous in y^1;
3. that they satisfy the Identity Test; that is, $P(p^0, y^1, p^0, y^0) = 1$ and $Q(p^1, y^0, p^0, y^0) = 1$;
4. that $P(p^1, y^1, p^0, y^0)$ is homogeneous of degree 0 in (p^1, p^0), and $Q(p^1, y^1, p^0, y^0)$ is homogeneous of degree 0 in (y^1, y^0);
5. that they are invariant to changes in the units of measurement of the items.

The reader is referred to Balk (2008, 56–61) for the formalization and an extensive discussion of these and other requirements. Though $P(p^1, y^1, p^0, y^0)$ and $Q(p^1, y^1, p^0, y^0)$ are both defined as functions of $4M$ variables, it appears that any such function that is invariant to changes in the units of measurement can be written as a function of only $3M$ variables, namely the price relatives p_m^1 / p_m^0 or the quantity relatives y_m^1 / y_m^0, the comparison period values $v_m^1 \equiv p_m^1 y_m^1$, and the base period values $v_m^0 \equiv p_m^0 y_m^0$ $(m = 1, \ldots, M)$. This feature appears to be very useful in practice, especially when M is large. Price and quantity indices can then be *estimated* from samples of items for which price or quantity relatives are observed and for which population value information is available.

We review the most important functional forms, starting with price indices. The Laspeyres price index is conventionally defined as a function of prices and quantities,

$$P^L(p^1, y^1, p^0, y^0) \equiv p^1 \cdot y^0 / p^0 \cdot y^0,$$

but notice that this index can be written as a function of price relatives and (base period) values or value shares,

$$P^L(p^1, y^1, p^0, y^0) = \sum_{m=1}^{M}(p_m^1/p_m^0)v_m^0 \Big/ \sum_{m=1}^{M}v_m^0 = \sum_{m=1}^{M}s_m^0(p_m^1/p_m^0),$$

where $s_m^0 \equiv v_m^0/\Sigma_{m=1}^{M}v_m^0$ $(m=1, \ldots, M)$ are base period value shares. Put otherwise, the Laspeyres price index is a weighted *arithmetic* mean of price relatives, using base period value shares as weights.

Similarly, the Paasche price index, conventionally defined as

$$P^P(p^1, y^1, p^0, y^0) \equiv p^1 \cdot y^1/p^0 \cdot y^1,$$

can be written as a function of price relatives and (comparison period) values or value shares,

$$P^P(p^1, y^1, p^0, y^0) = \left(\sum_{m=1}^{M}(p_m^0/p_m^1)v_m^1 \Big/ \sum_{m=1}^{M}v_m^1\right)^{-1} = \left(\sum_{m=1}^{M}s_m^1(p_m^1/p_m^0)^{-1}\right)^{-1},$$

where $s_m^1 \equiv v_m^1/\Sigma_{m=1}^{M}v_m^1$ $(m=1, \ldots, M)$ are comparison period value shares. Thus the Paasche price index is a weighted *harmonic* mean of price relatives, using comparison period value shares as weights.

Both indices are by definition asymmetric: the Laspeyres index compares prices by means of base-period quantities, whereas the Paasche index does this by means of comparison-period quantities. A symmetric alternative is provided by the Marshall-Edgeworth index, which uses the (arithmetic) mean of base and comparison period quantities as instrument for comparing prices; that is,

$$P^{ME}(p^1, y^1, p^0, y^0) \equiv p^1 \cdot (y^0 + y^1)/ p^0 \cdot (y^0 + y^1).$$

A little bit of manipulation reveals that this index can be written as a function of values, Laspeyres, and Paasche indices,

$$P^{ME}(p^1, y^1, p^0, y^0) = \frac{p^0 \cdot y^0 P^L(p^1, y^1, p^0, y^0) + p^1 \cdot y^1}{p^0 \cdot y^0 + p^1 \cdot y^1 / P^P(p^1, y^1, p^0, y^0)}.$$

A different symmetric index is the Fisher price index, defined as the geometric mean of the Laspeyres and Paasche indices:

$$P^F(p^1, y^1, p^0, y^0) \equiv \left[P^L(.)P^P(.)\right]^{1/2} = \left[\frac{\sum_{m=1}^{M} s_m^0 (p_m^1 / p_m^0)}{\sum_{m=1}^{M} s_m^1 (p_m^1 / p_m^0)^{-1}}\right]^{1/2}.$$

The Geometric Laspeyres price index is defined as the base period value-share weighted *geometric* mean of the price relatives,

$$P^{GL}(p^1, y^1, p^0, y^0) \equiv \prod_{m=1}^{M} (p_m^1 / p_m^0)^{s_m^0}.$$

It is a mathematical fact that $P^{GL}(p^1, y^1, p^0, y^0) \leq P^L(p^1, y^1, p^0, y^0)$ and that the difference between these two index numbers depends on the variance of the price relatives p_m^1 / p_m^0 $(m = 1, \ldots, M)$. The Geometric Paasche price index is the alternative, using comparison period value shares as weights,

$$P^{GP}(p^1, y^1, p^0, y^0) \equiv \prod_{m=1}^{M} (p_m^1 / p_m^0)^{s_m^1}.$$

Due to the same mathematical theorem, it is the case that $P^{GP}(p^1, y^1, p^0, y^0) \geq P^P(p^1, y^1, p^0, y^0)$. Notice the difference between this and the previous inequality.

The geometric mean of the Geometric Laspeyres and Paasche price indices is known as the Törnqvist price index,

$$P^T(p^1, y^1, p^0, y^0) \equiv \left[P^{GL}(.)P^{GP}(.)\right]^{1/2} = \prod_{m=1}^{M} (p_m^1 / p_m^0)^{(s_m^0 + s_m^1)/2}.$$

Since the Marshall-Edgeworth, Fisher, and Törnqvist price indices are symmetric with respect to weights, they satisfy the Time Reversal Test requiring that $P(p^0, y^0, p^1, y^1) = 1 / P(p^1, y^1, p^0, y^0)$.[8]

Whether, at the same data, $P^T(.) \geq P^F(.)$ or $P^T(.) \leq P^F(.)$ is an empirical question. As Diewert (1978, Theorem 5) has shown, at any point where $p^1 = p^0$ and $y^1 = y^0$ the indices $P^T(.)$ and $P^F(.)$ differentially approximate each other to the second order.

To facilitate a comparison of Fisher and Törnqvist price indices, Balk (2008, section 4.2.3) showed that the Fisher price index can be expressed in geometric mean form as

$$\ln P^F(p^1, y^1, p^0, y^0) = (1/2)\sum_{m=1}^{M}\left[\frac{s_m^0 LM(p_m^1 / p_m^0, P^L(.))}{\sum_{m=1}^{M} s_m^0 LM(p_m^1 / p_m^0, P^L(.))}\right.$$
$$\left. + \frac{s_m^{01} LM(p_m^1 / p_m^0, P^P(.))}{\sum_{m=1}^{M} s_m^{01} LM(p_m^1 / p_m^0, P^P(.))}\right]\ln(p_m^1 / p_m^0), \tag{2.24}$$

where $s_m^{01} \equiv p_m^0 y_m^1 / p^0 \cdot y^1$ $(m = 1, ..., M)$. This then can be compared to a similar expression for the Törnqvist price index,

$$\ln P^T(p^1, y^1, p^0, y^0) = (1/2) \sum_{m=1}^{M} \left[s_m^0 + s_m^1 \right] \ln(p_m^1 / p_m^0). \tag{2.25}$$

It is clear that the difference between the two indices depends on the variance of the price relatives p_m^1 / p_m^0 $(m = 1, ..., M)$.

2.4.2. Deflation

Rather than providing a similarly structured review of the main quantity indices, we will pursue what happens when a value ratio is deflated by a price index—that is, when the quantity index is defined by

$$Q(p^1, y^1, p^0, y^0) \equiv \frac{p^1 \cdot y^1}{p^0 \cdot y^0} \Big/ P(p^1, y^1, p^0, y^0). \tag{2.26}$$

Notice that this is equivalent to stating that $P(.)$ and $Q(.)$ satisfy the Product Test. Let us review the earlier examples.

As one checks easily, deflating a value ratio by a Laspeyres price index delivers a Paasche quantity index,

$$Q^P(p^1, y^1, p^0, y^0) \equiv p^1 \cdot y^1 / p^1 \cdot y^0 = \left(\sum_{m=1}^{M} s_m^1 (y_m^1 / y_m^0)^{-1} \right)^{-1}.$$

Similarly, deflating a value ratio by a Paasche price index delivers a Laspeyres quantity index,

$$Q^L(p^1, y^1, p^0, y^0) \equiv p^0 \cdot y^1 / p^0 \cdot y^0 = \sum_{m=1}^{M} s_m^0 (y_m^1 / y_m^0).$$

It follows then quickly that deflating a value ratio by a Fisher price index delivers a Fisher quantity index,

$$Q^F(p^1, y^1, p^0, y^0) \equiv \left[Q^L(.) Q^P(.) \right]^{1/2} = \left[\frac{\Sigma_{m=1}^{M} s_m^0 (y_m^1 / y_m^0)}{\Sigma_{m=1}^{M} s_m^1 (y_m^1 / y_m^0)^{-1}} \right]^{1/2}.$$

Fisher indices are examples of so-called ideal indices; that is, they satisfy the Product Test and have the same functional form (after interchanging prices and quantities, of course).

Deflating a value ratio by a Marshall-Edgeworth price index delivers

$$\frac{1+Q^L(p^1,y^1,p^0,y^0)}{1+1/Q^P(p^1,y^1,p^0,y^0)};$$

an expression that is not linearly homogeneous in comparison period quantities (see also Balk 2008, 83).

Deflating a value ratio by a Geometric Laspeyres price index delivers an expression that cannot be simplified:

$$\frac{p^1\cdot y^1}{p^0\cdot y^0}\Bigg/\prod_{m=1}^{M}(p_m^1/p_m^0)^{s_m^0}.$$

As one easily checks, this expression does not satisfy one of the fundamental requirements for a quantity index, namely that such an index satisfies the Identity Test. Similarly, deflating a value ratio by a Geometric Paasche price index delivers an expression that does not satisfy the Identity Test, and *a fortiori* the same holds when a value ratio is deflated by a Törnqvist price index. In particular, it is important to notice that the Törnqvist indices are not ideal; that is,

$$\frac{p^1\cdot y^1}{p^0\cdot y^0}\Bigg/P^T(p^1,y^1,p^0,y^0)\neq Q^T(p^1,y^1,p^0,y^0)\equiv\prod_{m=1}^{M}(y_m^1/y_m^0)^{(s_m^0+s_m^1)/2},$$

though in practice the discrepancy often may be negligible. Notice that the Törnqvist quantity index $Q^T(p^1,y^1,p^0,y^0)$ does satisfy the Identity Test.

Do there exist price and quantity indices of the geometric mean form that are ideal? The answer appears to be positive. Sato-Vartia indices are defined as

$$P^{SV}(p^1,y^1,p^0,y^0)\equiv\prod_{m=1}^{M}(p_m^1/p_m^0)^{\phi_m}$$

$$Q^{SV}(p^1,y^1,p^0,y^0)\equiv\prod_{m=1}^{M}(y_m^1/y_m^0)^{\phi_m},$$

where $\phi_m\equiv LM(s_m^0,s_m^1)/\sum_{m=1}^{M}LM(s_m^0,s_m^1)$ $(m=1,...,M)$. The Sato-Vartia indices are, like the Törnqvist indices, geometric means. The difference is in the weights: a Törnqvist index weighs the individual price or quantity relatives with arithmetic mean value shares, whereas a Sato-Vartia index weighs with (normalized) logarithmic mean shares. It is a straightforward exercise to check that $P^{SV}(p^1,y^1,p^0,y^0)\times Q^{SV}(p^1,y^1,p^0,y^0)=p^1\cdot y^1/p^0\cdot y^0$.

2.4.3. Two-Stage Indices

The number of items distinguished in a particular aggregate (M) may be very large. To accommodate this, (detailed) classifications are used, by which all the items are allocated to hierarchically organized (sub-)aggregates. The calculation of price and/or quantity indices then proceeds in stages. Theoretically, it suffices to distinguish only two stages. At the first stage, one calculates indices for all the subaggregates at a certain level; at the second stage, these subaggregate indices are combined to aggregate indices. Let us be more precise.

Let the aggregate under consideration, comprising all the M items, be partitioned arbitrarily into K disjunct subaggregates A_k,

$$A \equiv \{1, \ldots, M\} = \cup_{k=1}^{K} A_k, \ A_k \cap A_{k'} = \emptyset \quad (k \neq k').$$

Each subaggregate consists of a number of items. Let $M_k \geq 1$ denote the number of items contained in A_k $(k = 1, \ldots, K)$. Obviously $M = \Sigma_{k=1}^{K} M_k$. Let $(p_k^1, y_k^1, p_k^0, y_k^0)$ be the subvector of (p^1, y^1, p^0, y^0) corresponding to the subaggregate A_k. Recall that $v_m^t \equiv p_m^t y_m^t$ is the value of item m at period t. Then $V_k^t \equiv \Sigma_{m \in A_k} v_m^t$ $(k = 1, \ldots, K)$ is the value of subaggregate A_k at period t, and $V^t \equiv \Sigma_{m \in A} v_m^t = \Sigma_{k=1}^{K} V_k^t$ is the value of the aggregate A at period t.

Let $P(.), P^{(1)}(.), \ldots, P^{(K)}(.)$ be price indices of dimension $K, M_1, \ldots, M_K$, respectively, that satisfy the basic requirements. Recall that any such price index can be written as a function of price relatives and base and comparison period item values. Now we replace in $P(.)$ the price relatives by subaggregate price indices and the item values by subaggregate values. Then the price index defined by

$$P^*(p^1, y^1, p^0, y^0) \equiv P(P^{(k)}(p_k^1, y_k^1, p_k^0, y_k^0), V_k^1, V_k^0; k = 1, \ldots, K) \quad (2.27)$$

is of dimension M and also satisfies the basic requirements. The index $P^*(.)$ is called a *two-stage price index*. The first stage refers to the indices $P^{(k)}(.)$ for the subaggregates A_k $(k = 1, \ldots, K)$. The second stage refers to the index $P(.)$ that is applied to the subindices $P^{(k)}(.)$ $(k = 1, \ldots, K)$. A two-stage index such as defined by expression (2.27) closely corresponds to the calculation practice at statistical agencies. All the subindices are then usually of the same functional form, for instance, Laspeyres or Paasche indices. The aggregate, second-stage index may or may not be of the same functional form. This could be, for instance, a Fisher index.

If the functional forms of the subindices $P^{(k)}(.)$ $(k = 1, \ldots, K)$ and the aggregate index $P(.)$ are the same, then $P^*(.)$ is called a two-stage $P(.)$-index. Continuing our example, the two-stage Laspeyres price index reads

$$P^{*L}(p^1, y^1, p^0, y^0) \equiv \sum_{k=1}^{K} P^L(p_k^1, y_k^1, p_k^0, y_k^0) V_k^0 \Big/ \sum_{k=1}^{K} V_k^0,$$

and, by inserting the various definitions, one easily checks that the two-stage and the single-stage Laspeyres price indices coincide:

$$P^{*L}(p^1, y^1, p^0, y^0) = \sum_{k=1}^{K} \frac{p_k^1 \cdot y_k^0}{V_k^0} \frac{V_k^0}{V^0} = \frac{\Sigma_{k=1}^{K} \Sigma_{m \in A_k} p_m^1 y_m^0}{V^0} = P^L(p^1, y^1, p^0, y^0).$$

This, however, is the exception rather than the rule. For most indices, two-stage and single-stage variants do not coincide. Indices for which two-stage and single-stage variants coincide are called *consistent in aggregation* (CIA). Though the Fisher price index is not CIA, fortunately single-stage and two-stage Fisher indices appear to be close approximations of each other (as shown by Diewert 1978, Appendix 2).

Two-stage quantity indices are defined similarly. Thus, let $Q(.)$, $Q^{(1)}(.)$, ..., $Q^{(K)}(.)$ be quantity indices of dimension $K, M_1, ..., M_K$, respectively, that satisfy the basic requirements. Then the quantity index defined by

$$Q^*(p^1, y^1, p^0, y^0) \equiv Q(Q^{(k)}(p^1_k, y^1_k, p^0_k, y^0_k), V^1_k, V^0_k; k = 1, ..., K) \qquad (2.28)$$

is of dimension M and also satisfies the basic requirements. The index $Q^*(.)$ is called a *two-stage quantity index*. If the functional forms of the subindices $Q^{(k)}(.)$ $(k = 1, ..., K)$ and the aggregate index $Q(.)$ are the same, then $Q^*(.)$ is called a *two-stage $Q(.)$-index*.

It is important to observe that not any two-stage construct satisfies the basic requirements, even if the constituent parts do. Consider, for instance,

$$Q^T\left((V^1_k / V^0_k) / P^{T(k)}(p^1_k, y^1_k, p^0_k, y^0_k), V^1_k, V^0_k; k = 1, ..., K\right).$$

At the first stage, subaggregate quantity indices are calculated as value ratios deflated by Törnqvist price indices. At the second stage, these quantity indices are aggregated by means of the Törnqvist quantity index. It is a straightforward exercise to check that the entire construct does not satisfy the Identity Test.

2.5. Decomposing a Profitability Ratio

We now return to our main topic. The development over time of profitability is, rather naturally, measured by the ratio Υ^1 / Υ^0. How to decompose this into a price and a quantity component? By noticing that

$$\frac{\Upsilon^1}{\Upsilon^0} = \frac{R^1 / C^1}{R^0 / C^0} = \frac{R^1 / R^0}{C^1 / C^0} \qquad (2.29)$$

we see that the question reduces to the question of how to decompose the revenue ratio R^1 / R^0 and the cost ratio C^1 / C^0 into two parts. The revenue ratio has been discussed extensively in the previous section. Thus there exist price and quantity indices $P(.)$ and $Q(.)$ such that

$$\frac{R^1}{R^0} = P(p^1, y^1, p^0, y^0) Q(p^1, y^1, p^0, y^0)$$
$$\equiv P_R(1, 0) Q_R(1, 0), \qquad (2.30)$$

where the second line serves to define our shorthand notation. The cost ratio is structurally the same as the revenue ratio. Thus there exist also price and quantity indices $P(.)$ and $Q(.)$ such that the cost ratio can be decomposed as

$$\frac{C^1}{C^0} = P(w^1, x^1, w^0, x^0)Q(w^1, x^1, w^0, x^0)$$
$$\equiv P_C(1, 0)Q_C(1, 0).$$

(2.31)

All these price and quantity indices may or may not exhibit the same functional form. Ideally, they all satisfy the basic requirements. Notice that the dimensions of the indices in expressions (2.30) and (2.31) will usually be different. The subscripts R and C are used because, as will appear later, there are more output and input concepts.

Using the two relations (2.30) and (2.31), the profitability ratio can be decomposed as

$$\frac{\Upsilon^1}{\Upsilon^0} = \frac{P_R(1,0)}{P_C(1,0)}\frac{Q_R(1,0)}{Q_C(1,0)}.$$

(2.32)

This is the fundamental equation of the KLEMS-Y model, and basic for much of what follows.

The *TFP index*, for period 1 relative to period 0, is now defined by

$$ITFPROD(1,0) \equiv \frac{Q_R(1,0)}{Q_C(1,0)}.$$

(2.33)

Thus $ITFPROD(1,0)$ is the real or quantity component of the profitability ratio. Put otherwise, it is the ratio of an output quantity index and an input quantity index; $ITFPROD(1,0)$ is the factor with which the output quantities on average have changed relative to the factor with which the input quantities on average have changed. If the ratio of these factors is larger (smaller) than 1, there is said to be productivity increase (decrease).[9]

Notice that $ITFPROD(1,0)$ is a function of all the output and input prices and quantities; that is $ITFPROD(1,0) = ITFPROD(p^1, y^1, w^1, x^1, p^0, y^0, w^0, x^0)$. Its properties follow from those of the output and input quantity indices $Q(p^1, y^1, p^0, y^0)$ and $Q(w^1, x^1, w^0, x^0)$. In particular,

- in the single-input–single-output case ($N = M = 1$) the TFP index reduces to $ITFPROD(1,0) = \frac{y^1 / y^0}{x^1 / x^0} = \frac{y^1 / x^1}{y^0 / x^0}$; that is, the ratio of the productivities in the two periods compared;
- $ITFPROD(1,0)$ exhibits the desired monotonicity properties: nondecreasing in y^1, nonincreasing in x^1, nonincreasing in y^0, nondecreasing in x^0;

- *ITFPROD*(1,0) exhibits proportionality in input and output quantities; that is, $ITFPROD(p^1, \mu y^0, w^1, \lambda x^0, p^0, y^0, w^0, x^0) = \mu / \lambda (\lambda, \mu > 0)$.

Notice also that, again using expressions (2.30) and (2.31), there appear to be three other, equivalent representations of the TFP index, namely

$$ITFPROD(1,0) = \frac{(R^1 / R^0) / P_R(1,0)}{(C^1 / C^0) / P_C(1,0)} \tag{2.34}$$

$$= \frac{(R^1 / R^0) / P_R(1,0)}{Q_C(1,0)} \tag{2.35}$$

$$= \frac{Q_R(1,0)}{(C^1 / C^0) / P_C(1,0)}. \tag{2.36}$$

Put in words, we are seeing here, respectively, a deflated revenue index divided by a deflated cost index, a deflated revenue index divided by an input quantity index, and an output quantity index divided by a deflated cost index.

The other part of the profitability ratio decomposition (2.32) is called *total price recovery (TPR) index*:

$$ITPR(1,0) \equiv \frac{P_R(1,0)}{P_C(1,0)}. \tag{2.37}$$

This index measures the extent to which input price change is recovered by output price change.

Now, if revenue change equals cost change, $R^1 / R^0 = C^1 / C^0$ (for which zero profit in the two periods is a sufficient condition), then it follows that

$$ITFPROD(1,0) = 1 / ITPR(1,0); \tag{2.38}$$

that is, the TFP index is equal to the inverse of the TPR index. Thus, zero profit does not imply zero productivity growth; it only implies that productivity growth is compensated by price recovery. In general, however, the *dual* productivity index $1 / ITPR(1,0)$ will differ from the *primal* one, $ITFPROD(1,0)$.

A non-market unit is characterized by the fact that there is no revenue, which limits the usefulness of expressions (2.32)–(2.36). But if there is some prices-free output quantity index $Q(y^1, y^0)$, then the TFP index, for period 1 relative to period 0, is naturally defined by $Q(y^1, y^0) / Q_C(1,0)$. An alternative expression is obtained by replacing the input quantity index by the deflated cost index, $Q(y^1, y^0) / [(C^1 / C^0) / P_C(1,0)]$. In the single-output case (that is, $M = 1$) this reduces to an index of unit cost divided by an input price index, $[(y^1 / C^1) / (y^0 / C^0)] / P_C(1,0)]$.

2.6. Growth Accounting and Production Functions

2.6.1. Growth Accounting

The foregoing definitions are already sufficient to provide examples of simple but useful analysis. First, reconsider relation (2.35), and rewrite this as

$$R^1 / R^0 = ITFPROD(1,0) \times Q_C(1,0) \times P_R(1,0). \tag{2.39}$$

Taking logarithms, one obtains

$$\ln(R^1 / R^0) = \ln ITFPROD(1,0) + \ln Q_C(1,0) + \ln P_R(1,0). \tag{2.40}$$

This relation, implemented with Fisher and Törnqvist indices, was used by Dumagan and Ball (2009) for an analysis of the US agricultural sector.

Further, revenue change through time is only interesting insofar as it differs from general inflation. Hence, it makes sense to deflate the revenue ratio, R^1 / R^0, by a general inflation measure such as the (headline) CPI. Doing this, the previous equation can be written as

$$\ln\left(\frac{R^1 / R^0}{CPI^1 / CPI^0}\right) = \ln ITFPROD(1,0) + \ln Q_C(1,0) + \ln\left(\frac{P_R(1,0)}{CPI^1 / CPI^0}\right). \tag{2.41}$$

Lawrence, Diewert, and Fox (2006) basically used this relation to decompose "real" revenue change into three factors: productivity change, input quantity change (which can be interpreted as measuring change of the production unit's size), and "real" output price change, respectively.

Our second example follows from rearranging expression (2.36) and taking logarithms. This delivers the following relation:

$$\ln(C^1 / C^0) = \ln P_C(1,0) + \ln Q_R(1,0) - \ln ITFPROD(1,0). \tag{2.42}$$

This relation was also used by Dumagan and Ball (2009).[10] A further rearrangement gives

$$\ln\left(\frac{C^1 / C^0}{Q_R(1,0)}\right) = \ln P_C(1,0) - \ln ITFPROD(1,0). \tag{2.43}$$

We see here that the growth rate of average cost can be decomposed into two factors, namely the growth rate of input prices and a residual that is the negative of TFP growth. Put otherwise, in the case of stable input prices, the growth rate of average cost is equal to minus the TFP growth rate.

Our third example follows from rearranging expression (2.34) as

$$ITFPROD(1,0) = \frac{1+\mu^1}{1+\mu^0} \frac{1}{P_R(1,0)} P_C(1,0), \tag{2.44}$$

where the profit-cost margin μ^t was defined by expression (2.6). Expression (2.44) can be read as picturing the distribution of the fruits of productivity increase: to the owner(s) of the production unit as the profit-cost margin increase, or to the customers as output prices decrease, or to the suppliers (including employees) as input prices (including wages) increase.

Taking logarithms and rearranging a bit delivers the following relation:

$$\ln P_R(1,0) = \ln\left(\frac{1+\mu^1}{1+\mu^0}\right) + \ln P_C(1,0) - \ln ITFPROD(1,0), \tag{2.45}$$

This relation analyses output price change as resulting from three factors: change of the profit-cost margin, input price change, and, with a negative sign, TFP change. This relation may be used for regulatory purposes. For example, if the profit-cost margin is not allowed to grow, then output prices may on average rise as input prices do, but adjusted by the percentage of TFP growth.

All these are examples of what is called *growth accounting*. The relation between index number techniques and growth accounting techniques can, more generally, be seen as follows. Recall the generic definition of the TFP index in expression (2.33), and rewrite this expression as follows:

$$Q_R(1,0) = ITFPROD(1,0) \times Q_C(1,0). \tag{2.46}$$

Taking logarithms, this multiplicative expression can be rewritten as an additive one,

$$\ln Q_R(1,0) = \ln ITFPROD(1,0) + \ln Q_C(1,0). \tag{2.47}$$

For index numbers in the neighborhood of 1, the logarithms thereof approximate percentages, and the last expression can thus be interpreted as saying that the percentage change of output volume equals the percentage change of input volume plus the percentage change of TFP.

Growth accounting economists like to work with equations expressing output volume growth in terms of input volume growth plus a residual that is interpreted as TFP growth, thereby suggesting that the last two factors cause the first. However, TFP change cannot be considered as an independent factor since it is *defined* as output quantity change minus input quantity change. Put otherwise, a growth accounting table is nothing but an alternative way of presenting TFP growth and its contributing factors. And decomposition does not at all imply something about causality.

2.6.2. Production Functions

The identity in expression (2.46) is formulated in terms of indices. Economists, however, usually prefer working with levels. To transform the identity, we multiply both sides by base period revenue R^0,

$$R^0 Q_R(1,0) = ITFPROD(1,0) \times (R^0/C^0) \times C^0 Q_C(1,0). \qquad (2.48)$$

Now the Product Test, expression (2.26), tells us that base period value times quantity index equals comparion period value divided by (deflated by) price index. Thus expression (2.48) can be rewritten as

$$R^1 / P_R(1,0) = ITFPROD(1,0) \times (R^0/C^0) \times C^1 / P_C(1,0). \qquad (2.49)$$

These two equations are identities with two degrees of freedom each. Choosing particular functional forms for the price indices $P_R(1,0)$ and $P_C(1,0)$, or the quantity indices $Q_R(1,0)$ and $Q_C(1,0)$, fixes the outcome of the TFP index $ITFPROD(1,0)$.

Consider as a special case the input quantity index

$$Q_C(1,0) \equiv \prod_{k \in \mathcal{K}} Q_k(1,0)^{\alpha_k} \text{ where all } \alpha_k > 0 \text{ and } \sum_{k \in \mathcal{K}} \alpha_k = 1. \qquad (2.50)$$

This is a two-stage quantity index. The first stage consists of subindices $Q_k(1,0)$ for the input classes $k \in \mathcal{K} \equiv \{K, L, E, M, S\}$. The second stage combines (aggregates) these subindices with help of a (generalized) Cobb-Douglas function. Substituting expression (2.50) into expression (2.48) delivers

$$R^0 Q_R(1,0) = ITFPROD(1,0) \times \frac{R^0}{C^0} \times \frac{C^0}{\prod_{k \in \mathcal{K}} (C_k^0)^{\alpha_k}} \times \prod_{k \in \mathcal{K}} (C_k^0 Q_k(1,0))^{\alpha_k}, \qquad (2.51)$$

which, again due to the Product Test, can also be written as

$$R^1 / P_R(1,0) = ITFPROD(1,0) \times \frac{R^0}{C^0} \times \frac{C^0}{\prod_{k \in \mathcal{K}} (C_k^0)^{\alpha_k}} \times \prod_{k \in \mathcal{K}} (C_k^1 / P_k(1,0))^{\alpha_k}. \qquad (2.52)$$

Now this is beginning to look familiar. The left-hand side of this equation is called real output; that is, deflated revenue. Similarly, $C_k^1/P_k(1,0)$ is real input (that is, deflated cost) of class $k \in \mathcal{K}$. Given suitable price indices, these are all measurable magnitudes. Next, $ITFPROD(1,0)$ is interpreted as technological change. Recall that $R^0/C^0 = \Upsilon^0 = 1 + \mu^0$. If real output can be considered as a single output, then μ^0 is the base period markup. Finally, the term $C^0/\prod_{k \in \mathcal{K}} (C_k^0)^{\alpha_k}$ is a remainder. Actually, it is the reciprocal of the weighted geometric mean of the cost shares of the input classes C_k^0/C^0 ($k \in \mathcal{K}$) (recall that $C^0 = \Sigma_{k \in \mathcal{K}} C_k^0$).

Thus, summing up, for any production unit, real output is related to aggregate real input, TFP change, and a constant covering base period markup and nonlinearity. The coefficients α_k of the Cobb-Douglas function are as yet unspecified. Specifying them would immediately determine TFP change. Now what basically happens in production-function estimation is that these coefficients are *estimated* from a sample of production units. The procedure can be stylized as follows in a number of steps:

- For a (balanced) panel of production units, say from a specific industry, real output and real inputs are given (whereby the use of specific deflators is presupposed).
- TFP change is seen as consisting of two components, one industry-specific and the other production-unit-specific (idiosyncratic); the second component is usually considered as (random) noise.
- The coefficients α_k are assumed to be the same for all the production units and must be estimated.

Transforming expression (2.52) into logarithmic form, we obtain

$$\ln(R^1 / P_R(1,0)) = \ln ITFPROD(1,0) + \ln \alpha_0 + \sum_{k \in \mathcal{K}} \alpha_k \ln(C_k^1 / P_k(1,0)), \qquad (2.53)$$

where $\alpha_0 \equiv R^0 / \Pi_{k \in \mathcal{K}} (C_k^0)^{\alpha_k}$. This is the typical form of a Cobb-Douglas "production function."[11] Notice that this form deviates from that usually shown in textbooks and research articles. Conventionally, the Cobb-Douglas production function, like any other such function, is stated in terms of quantities. However, in most if not all realistic multiple-input multiple-output settings, quantities of inputs and outputs are *not* given. The best one can hope for is obtaining good proxies for real values. Put otherwise, there are only data to estimate equations such as given by expression (2.53).[12]

This and the previous expressions in a way condense all the outputs, the number M of which can be very large, into a single variable. Suppose that we are interested in a special set of outputs, say A, and let B denote the remainder. Let the aggregate output quantity index $Q_R(1,0)$ be a two-stage index of the Cobb-Douglas form, $Q_R(1,0) = Q_A(1,0)^\beta Q_B(1,0)^{1-\beta}$, where $0 < \beta < 1$ and $Q_A(1,0)$ and $Q_B(1,0)$ are suitable quantity indices for the subaggregates A and B, respectively. Then

$$R^0 Q_R(1,0) = \frac{R^0}{(R_A^0)^\beta (R_B^0)^{1-\beta}} (R_A^0 Q_A(1,0))^\beta (R_B^0 Q_B(1,0))^{1-\beta} \qquad (2.54)$$

or, due to the Product Test,

$$R^1 / P_R(1,0) = \frac{R^0}{(R_A^0)^\beta (R_B^0)^{1-\beta}} (R_A^1 / P_A(1,0))^\beta (R_B^1 / P_B(1,0))^{1-\beta}, \qquad (2.55)$$

or, in logarithms,

$$\ln(R^1 / P_R(1,0)) = \ln \gamma + \beta \ln(R_A^1 / P_A(1,0)) + (1-\beta)\ln(R_B^1 / P_B(1,0)), \tag{2.56}$$

where $\gamma \equiv R^0 / (R_A^0)^\beta (R_B^0)^{1-\beta}$. Substituting now expression (2.56) into expression (2.53), and rearranging a bit, delivers

$$\ln(R_A^1 / P_A(1,0)) = (1/\beta)\ln ITFPROD(1,0) + (1/\beta)\ln(\alpha_0 / \gamma) \tag{2.57}$$

$$+ \sum_{k \in K}(\alpha_k / \beta)\ln(C_k^1 / P_k(1,0)) - ((1-\beta)/\beta)\ln(R_B^1 / P_B(1,0))$$

Here we see the logarithm of real output of subaggregate A expressed as a linear function of TFP change, a constant, and a weighted sum of all the logarithmic real inputs minus the logarithmic real output of the remainder subaggregate B. Expression (2.57) corresponds to the "production function" estimated by Dhyne et al. (2014). Notice, however, that the parameters in this expression are interrelated, unlike the parameters in expression (2.53).

2.7. PARTIAL PRODUCTIVITY MEASURES

The distinguishing feature of a TFP index, such as in the KLEMS-Y model $ITFPROD(1,0)$, is that all the (classes of) inputs are taken into account. To define partial productivity indices, first some additional notation is necessary.

Recall that all the items at the input side of our production unit are supposedly allocated to the following five, mutually disjunct, classes: capital (K), labor (L), energy (E), materials (M), and services (S). The entire input price and quantity vectors can then be partitioned as $w^t = (w_K^t, w_L^t, w_E^t, w_M^t, w_S^t)$ and $x^t = (x_K^t, x_L^t, x_E^t, x_M^t, x_S^t)$, respectively. Energy, materials, and services together form the category of intermediate inputs—that is, inputs which are acquired from other production units or imported. Capital and labor are called *primary inputs*. Consistent with this distinction, the price and quantity vectors can also be partitioned as $w^t = (w_{KL}^t, w_{EMS}^t)$ and $x^t = (x_{KL}^t, x_{EMS}^t)$, or as $w^t = (w_K^t, w_L^t, w_{EMS}^t)$ and $x^t = (x_K^t, x_L^t, x_{EMS}^t)$.

Since monetary values are additive, total production cost can be decomposed in a number of ways, such as

$$C^t = \sum_{n \in K} w_n^t x_n^t + \sum_{n \in L} w_n^t x_n^t + \sum_{n \in E} w_n^t x_n^t + \sum_{n \in M} w_n^t x_n^t + \sum_{n \in S} w_n^t x_n^t$$

$$\equiv C_K^t + C_L^t + C_E^t + C_M^t + C_S^t$$

$$\equiv C_K^t + C_L^t + C_{EMS}^t \tag{2.58}$$

$$\equiv C_{KL}^t + C_{EMS}^t.$$

Based on the last line, total production cost change can be decomposed as

$$\frac{C^1}{C^0} = \frac{C_{KL}^0}{C^0}\frac{C_{KL}^1}{C_{KL}^0} + \frac{C_{EMS}^0}{C^0}\frac{C_{EMS}^1}{C_{EMS}^0},$$ (2.59)

but also as

$$\frac{C^1}{C^0} = \left(\frac{C_{KL}^1}{C^1}\left(\frac{C_{KL}^1}{C_{KL}^0}\right)^{-1} + \frac{C_{EMS}^1}{C^1}\left(\frac{C_{EMS}^1}{C_{EMS}^0}\right)^{-1}\right)^{-1},$$ (2.60)

and then each ratio can be decomposed further. For instance, the labor-cost ratio can be decomposed as

$$\frac{C_L^1}{C_L^0} = P(w_L^1, x_L^1, w_L^0, x_L^0)Q(w_L^1, x_L^1, w_L^0, x_L^0)$$
$$\equiv P_L(1,0)Q_L(1,0),$$ (2.61)

for some pair of price and quantity indices.

The *labor productivity index* for period 1 relative to period 0 is defined by

$$ILPROD(1,0) \equiv \frac{Q_R(1,0)}{Q_L(1,0)};$$ (2.62)

that is, the ratio of an output quantity index to a labor input quantity index. Multiplying both sides of this definition by $P_R(1,0)/P_L(1,0)$, using expressions (2.61), (2.30) and (2.29), and rearranging a bit delivers the following expression:

$$\frac{P_L(1,0)}{P_R(1,0)} = ILPROD(1,0) \times \frac{C_L^1/C^1}{C_L^0/C^0} \times \frac{\Upsilon^0}{\Upsilon^1}.$$ (2.63)

It is interesting to look somewhat closer at the various components of this expression. First, the ratio $P_L(1,0)/P_R(1,0)$ is usually called the real wage index. Its inverse is the counterpart of the total price recovery index, defined by expression (2.37). Second, C_L^t/C^t ($t = 0,1$) is the period t labor cost share, the share of labor cost in total input cost. Third, Υ^0/Υ^1 is the inverse profitability ratio.

The practical usefulness of expression (2.63) lies in the conclusion that if profitability and the labor cost share remain constant, then real wage development must be proportional to labor productivity development.

Notice that in expression (2.62) labor is not considered as a homogeneous commodity. The class L consists of several types of labor, each with their quantities x_n^t (say, hours worked) and prices w_n^t (say, wage per hour). Conventionally, however, labor is considered as homogeneous, so that the quantities x_n^t can be added up. Let $L^t \equiv \Sigma_{n \in L} x_n^t$ denote the total labor input of our production unit (say, measured in hours worked of whatever type) during period t ($t = 0$, 1). Then the *simple labor productivity index* for period 1 relative to period 0 is defined by

$$ISLPROD(1,0) \equiv \frac{Q_R(1,0)}{L^1 / L^0}. \tag{2.64}$$

Formally, L^1 / L^0 is a simple sum or Dutot quantity index. The ratio of the two labor productivity indices,

$$LQUAL(1,0) \equiv \frac{ISLPROD(1,0)}{ILPROD(1,0)} = \frac{Q_L(1,0)}{L^1 / L^0}, \tag{2.65}$$

is said to measure the shift in "labor quality"; actually this ratio measures the shift in the composition of labor input. To see this, let the labor input quantity index be defined as some weighted mean of the quantity relatives of the labor types; that is, $Q_L(1,0) \equiv \sum_{n \in L} s_n x_n^1 / x_n^0$ with $\sum_{n \in L} s_n = 1$. Then it appears that

$$LQUAL(1,0) = \sum_{n \in L} s_n \left(\frac{x_n^1 / L^1}{x_n^0 / L^0} \right). \tag{2.66}$$

Now x_n^t / L^t is the share of the hours worked by type $n \in L$ in the total number of hours worked during period t, and $LQUAL(1,0)$ measures the aggregate shift of those shares from period 0 to period 1. Put otherwise, $LQUAL(1,0)$ measures the reallocation of labor input.

The *capital productivity index* is defined as

$$IKPROD(1,0) \equiv \frac{Q_R(1,0)}{Q_K(1,0)}, \tag{2.67}$$

where $Q_K(1,0)$ satisfies the equality $C_K^1/C_K^0 = P_K(1,0)Q_K(1,0)$. The other partial productivity indices $IkPROD(1,0)$ for $k = E, M, S$ are defined similarly. The ratio of labor and capital productivity indices,

$$\frac{ILPROD(1,0)}{IKPROD(1,0)} = \frac{Q_K(1,0)}{Q_L(1,0)}, \tag{2.68}$$

is called the *index of capital deepening*. Loosely speaking, this index measures the change of the quantity of capital input per unit of labor input.

The relation between total factor (*ITFPROD*) and partial (*IkPROD*) productivity indices is not always simple. Let, for example, the total input quantity index $Q_C(1,0)$ be a two-stage index in which the second stage is a Fisher index,

$$Q_C(1,0) \equiv Q^F(Q_k(1,0), C_k^1, C_k^0; k = K, L, E, M, S) \tag{2.69}$$

and all the first-stage indices $Q_k(1,0)$ are left unspecified. It is straightforward to check that then

$$ITFPROD(1,0) = \frac{Q_R(1,0)}{Q_C(1,0)}$$

$$= \frac{Q_R(1,0)}{\left(\Sigma_k Q_k(1,0) C_k^0 / C^0\right)^{1/2} \left(\Sigma_k Q_k(1,0)^{-1} C_k^1 / C^1\right)^{-1/2}}$$

$$= \left(\Sigma_k \frac{Q_k(1,0)}{Q_R(1,0)} \frac{C_k^0}{C^0}\right)^{-1/2} \left(\Sigma_k \frac{Q_R(1,0)}{Q_k(1,0)} \frac{C_k^1}{C^1}\right)^{1/2}$$

$$= \left(\frac{\Sigma_k C_k^0 (IkPROD(1,0))^{-1}}{C^0}\right)^{-1/2} \left(\frac{\Sigma_k C_k^1 IkPROD(1,0)}{C^1}\right)^{1/2}, \tag{2.70}$$

thus the TFP index is not a particularly simple function of the partial productivity indices. The first bracket shows a base-period-cost-share weighted harmonic mean, whereas the second bracket shows a comparison-period-cost-share weighted arithmetic mean.

If instead as second-stage total input quantity index the Cobb-Douglas functional form, defined by expression (2.50), were chosen, then it appears that

$$\ln ITFPROD(1,0) = \sum_k \alpha_k \ln IkPROD(1,0). \tag{2.71}$$

This is a very simple relation between TFP change and partial productivity change. Notice, however, that this simplicity comes at a cost. Definition (2.50) implies for the relation between aggregate and subaggregate input price indices that

$$P_C(1,0) = \prod_k P_k(1,0)^{\alpha_k} \frac{C^1 / C^0}{\prod_k (C_k^1 / C_k^0)^{\alpha_k}}. \tag{2.72}$$

Such an index does not necessarily satisfy the fundamental Identity Test; that is, if all the prices in period 1 are the same as in period 0, then $P_C(1,0)$ does not necessarily deliver as outcome 1.

Though data requirements at the output side are the same, a partial productivity index needs less input data than a TFP index. For instance, for a labor productivity index, one only needs (more or less detailed) labor cost data. Partial productivity indices are useful for specific analytical purposes, but they don't tell the whole story of productivity change. In an interesting assessment of the strengths and weaknesses of the various tools, Murray (2016, 124) concludes that "a complete understanding of productivity growth is best achieved by examining TFP and partial productivity measures together."

2.8. Indicators

Let us now turn to profit and its development through time.[13] This is naturally measured by the difference $\Pi^1 - \Pi^0$. Recall that such a difference only makes sense when the two money amounts involved, profit from period 0 and profit from period 1, are deflated by some general inflation measure (such as the headline CPI), or when the two periods are so close that deflation is deemed unnecessary. In the remainder of this chapter, when discussing difference measures, either of the two situations is tacitly presupposed.

How does one decompose the profit difference into a price and a quantity component? By noticing that

$$\Pi^1 - \Pi^0 = (R^1 - R^0) - (C^1 - C^0), \tag{2.73}$$

we see that the question reduces to the question of how to decompose revenue change $R^1 - R^0$ and cost change $C^1 - C^0$ into two parts. This is where indicators come into play. Let us again take revenue as example.

Formally, a *bilateral price indicator* is a continuously differentiable function $\mathcal{P}(p^1, y^1, p^0, y^0) : \Re_{++}^{4M} \to \Re$ that, except in extreme situations, correctly indicates any increase or decrease of the elements of the *price* vectors p^1 or p^0, conditional on the quantity vectors y^1 and y^0. Likewise, a *bilateral quantity indicator* is a continuously differentiable function of the same variables, $\mathcal{Q}(p^1, y^1, p^0, y^0) : \Re_{++}^{4M} \to \Re$, that, except in extreme situations, correctly indicates any increase or decrease of the elements of the *quantity* vectors y^1 or y^0, conditional on the price vectors p^1 and p^0. The number M is called the dimension of the price or quantity indicator. Notice that both functions may take on negative or zero values.

The basic requirements on price and quantity indicators are analogous to those for indices and comprise the following:

1. that they exhibit the desired monotonicity properties globally;
2. that they satisfy the (analogue of the) Identity Test; that is, $\mathcal{P}(p^0, y^1, p^0, y^0) = 0$ and $\mathcal{Q}(p^1, y^0, p^0, y^0) = 0$;
3. that they are homogeneous of degree 1 in prices (quantities, respectively);
4. that they are invariant to changes in the units of measurement of the items.

The reader is referred to Balk (2008, 126–129) for the formalization and an extensive discussion of these and other requirements.

Though $\mathcal{P}(p^1, y^1, p^0, y^0)$ and $\mathcal{Q}(p^1, y^1, p^0, y^0)$ are defined as functions of $4M$ variables, it appears that any such function that is invariant to changes in the units of measurement can be written as a function of only $3M$ variables, namely the price relatives

p_m^1 / p_m^0 or the quantity relatives y_m^1 / y_m^0, the comparison period values $v_m^1 \equiv p_m^1 y_m^1$, and the base period values $v_m^0 \equiv p_m^0 y_m^0$ $(m = 1, \ldots, M)$. The interesting point to notice here is that differences $p_m^1 - p_m^0$ or $y_m^1 - y_m^0$ are not necessary for the computation of $\mathcal{P}(p^1, y^1, p^0, y^0)$ or $\mathcal{Q}(p^1, y^1, p^0, y^0)$.

Also, here some simple examples might be more useful than formal definitions. The Laspeyres price indicator as function of prices and quantities is defined as

$$\mathcal{P}^L(p^1, y^1, p^0, y^0) \equiv (p^1 - p^0) \cdot y^0.$$

This indicator can be written as a function of individual price relatives and (base period) values, but also as a function of the Laspeyres price index and aggregate base period value,

$$\mathcal{P}^L(p^1, y^1, p^0, y^0) = \sum_{m=1}^{M} (p_m^1 / p_m^0 - 1) v_m^0 = \left(P^L(p^1, y^1, p^0, y^0) - 1 \right) V^0,$$

where we recall that $V^0 \equiv \sum_{m=1}^{M} v_m^0$. Similarly, the Paasche price indicator

$$\mathcal{P}^P(p^1, y^1, p^0, y^0) \equiv (p^1 - p^0) \cdot y^1$$

can be written as a function of individual price relatives and (comparison period) values, and as a function of the Paasche price index and aggregate comparison period value,

$$\mathcal{P}^P(p^1, y^1, p^0, y^0) = \sum_{m=1}^{M} (1 - p_m^0 / p_m^1) v_m^1 = \left(1 - 1 / P^P(p^1, y^1, p^0, y^0) \right) V^1,$$

where $V^1 \equiv \sum_{m=1}^{M} v_m^1$. Notice the reciprocals here. Finally, the Bennet price indicator is defined as

$$\mathcal{P}^B(p^1, y^1, p^0, y^0) \equiv (1/2)(p^1 - p^0) \cdot (y^0 + y^1),$$

which is the arithmetic mean of $\mathcal{P}^L(p^1, y^1, p^0, y^0)$ and $\mathcal{P}^P(p^1, y^1, p^0, y^0)$. One immediately verifies that

$$\mathcal{P}^B(p^1, y^1, p^0, y^0) = (1/2) \left[\sum_{m=1}^{M} (p_m^1 / p_m^0 - 1) v_m^0 + \sum_{m=1}^{M} (1 - p_m^0 / p_m^1) v_m^1 \right]$$
$$= (1/2) \left[\left(P^L(p^1, y^1, p^0, y^0) - 1 \right) V^0 + \left(1 - 1 / P^P(p^1, y^1, p^0, y^0) \right) V^1 \right].$$

Notice that the Bennet indicator is symmetric in the two periods, and hence satisfies the (analogue of the) Time Reversal Test. The Bennet indicator is the analogue of the Marshall-Edgeworth index as well as the Fisher index.

The analogue of the Product Test requires that price indicator plus quantity indicator equals the value difference. Put otherwise, the analogue of deflation is subtraction, and one easily checks that the following relations hold:

$$V^1 - V^0 - \mathcal{P}^L(p^1, y^1, p^0, y^0) = \mathcal{Q}^P(p^1, y^1, p^0, y^0)$$

$$V^1 - V^0 - \mathcal{P}^P(p^1, y^1, p^0, y^0) = \mathcal{Q}^L(p^1, y^1, p^0, y^0)$$

$$V^1 - V^0 - \mathcal{P}^B(p^1, y^1, p^0, y^0) = \mathcal{Q}^B(p^1, y^1, p^0, y^0),$$

where $\mathcal{Q}^P(.), \mathcal{Q}^L(.)$, and $\mathcal{Q}^B(.)$ are the Paasche, Laspeyres, and Bennet quantity indicators, respectively. The last equation expresses that the Bennet indicators are ideal; that is, they satisfy the analogue of the Product Test and have the same functional form.

Finally, a noteworthy feature of price and quantity indicators is that, due to their additive structure, aggregation is not an issue. Put otherwise, indicators are always *consistent in aggregation*.

2.9. DECOMPOSING A PROFIT DIFFERENCE

Continuing now from expression (2.73), we select pairs of price and quantity indicators such that

$$\begin{aligned} R^1 - R^0 &= \mathcal{P}(p^1, y^1, p^0, y^0) + \mathcal{Q}(p^1, y^1, p^0, y^0) \\ &\equiv \mathcal{P}_R(1,0) + \mathcal{Q}_R(1,0), \end{aligned} \tag{2.74}$$

and similarly,

$$\begin{aligned} C^1 - C^0 &= \mathcal{P}(w^1, x^1, w^0, x^0) + \mathcal{Q}(w^1, x^1, w^0, x^0) \\ &\equiv \mathcal{P}_C(1,0) + \mathcal{Q}_C(1,0). \end{aligned} \tag{2.75}$$

Notice that the dimension of the indicators in these two decompositions is generally different. Also the functional form of the indicators may or may not be the same.

The profit difference can then be written as

$$\begin{aligned} \Pi^1 - \Pi^0 \\ &= \mathcal{P}_R(1,0) + \mathcal{Q}_R(1,0) - [\mathcal{P}_C(1,0) + \mathcal{Q}_C(1,0)] \\ &= \mathcal{P}_R(1,0) - \mathcal{P}_C(1,0) + \mathcal{Q}_R(1,0) - \mathcal{Q}_C(1,0). \end{aligned} \tag{2.76}$$

The first two terms at the right-hand side of the last equality sign provide the price component, whereas the last two terms provide the quantity component of the profit difference. Thus, based on this decomposition, the *TFP indicator* is defined by

$$DTFPROD(1,0) \equiv \mathcal{Q}_R(1,0) - \mathcal{Q}_C(1,0); \qquad (2.77)$$

that is, output quantity indicator minus input quantity indicator. Notice that productivity change is now measured as an amount of money. An amount greater (less) than 0 indicates productivity increase (decrease).[14]

The equivalent expressions for difference-type TFP change are

$$DTFPROD(1,0) = [R^1 - R^0 - \mathcal{P}_R(1,0)] - [C^1 - C^0 - \mathcal{P}_C(1,0)] \qquad (2.78)$$

$$= [R^1 - R^0 - \mathcal{P}_R(1,0)] - \mathcal{Q}_C(1,0) \qquad (2.79)$$

$$= \mathcal{Q}_R(1,0) - [C^1 - C^0 - \mathcal{P}_C(1,0)], \qquad (2.80)$$

which can be useful in different situations.

The *total price recovery (TPR) indicator* is defined as

$$DTPR(1,0) \equiv \mathcal{P}_R(1,0) - \mathcal{P}_C(1,0). \qquad (2.81)$$

This is also an amount of money. It is clear that $\Pi^1 - \Pi^0 = DTFPROD(1,0) + DTPR(1,0)$, and that, if $\Pi^1 = \Pi^0$ then

$$DTFPROD(1,0) = -DTPR(1,0). \qquad (2.82)$$

For a non-market production unit, a productivity indicator is difficult to define. Though one might be able to construe some output quantity indicator, it is hard to see how, in the absence of output prices, such an indicator could be given a money dimension.

Can we also define partial productivity *indicators*? Given a set of indicators, the labor-cost difference between periods 0 and 1 is decomposed as

$$\begin{aligned} C_L^1 - C_L^0 &= \mathcal{P}(w_L^1, x_L^1, w_L^0, x_L^0) + \mathcal{Q}(w_L^1, x_L^1, w_L^0, x_L^0) \\ &\equiv \mathcal{P}_L(1,0) + \mathcal{Q}_L(1,0). \end{aligned} \qquad (2.83)$$

In the same way one can decompose the capital, energy, materials, and services cost difference. However, since costs are additive, it turns out that the TFP indicator can be written as

$$DTFPROD(1,0) = \mathcal{Q}_R(1,0) - \sum_{k=K,L,E,M,S} \mathcal{Q}_k(1,0). \qquad (2.84)$$

By definition, the left-hand side measures real profit change. The right-hand side provides the contributing factors. The contribution of category k to real profit change is simply measured by the amount $\mathcal{Q}_k(1,0)$. A positive amount, which means that the aggregate quantity of input category k has increased, means a negative contribution to real profit change.

Ball et al. (2015) called $Q_R(1,0) - Q_E(1,0)$ a partial energy productivity indicator. However, notice that summing all those partial indicators, $\Sigma_{k=K,L,E,M,S}(Q_R(1,0) - Q_k(1,0))$, does not lead to the overall indicator, $DTFPROD(1,0)$, which makes the interpretation of such partial indicators difficult.

In the extended online version of this chapter, the equivalence of the multiplicative and additive models is discussed. First, it is shown that, given that the profitability ratio can be decomposed into two factors, $\Upsilon^1 / \Upsilon^0 = ITFPROD(1,0) \times ITPR(1,0)$, the profit difference $\Pi^1 - \Pi^0$ decomposes into *four* factors, namely a productivity effect, a price recovery effect, and two margin effects. The existence of these margin effects "makes the difference-based model of profit change richer than the ratio-based model of profitability change," according to Grifell-Tatjé and Lovell (2015, 201).

However, it is also shown that, given that the profit difference can be decomposed into two factors, $\Pi^1 - \Pi^0 = DTFPROD(1,0) + DTPR(1,0)$, the profitability ratio Υ^1 / Υ^0 decomposes into *four* factors, namely a productivity effect, a price recovery effect, and two margin effects.

The overall conclusion, then, is that the two models, the multiplicative model based on profitability and the additive model based on profit, are completely equivalent.

2.10. THE KL-VA MODEL (1)

There are alternatives to the KLEMS-Y input–output model. The most prominent of these models, widely employed by economists, uses value added (VA) as its output concept. The production unit's *value added (VA)* is defined as its revenue minus the costs of energy, materials, and services; that is,

$$VA^t \equiv R^t - C^t_{EMS}$$
$$= p^t \cdot y^t - w^t_{EMS} \cdot x^t_{EMS}. \tag{2.85}$$

The value-added concept subtracts the total cost of intermediate inputs from the revenue obtained, and in doing so essentially conceives the production unit as producing value added (that is, money) from the two primary input categories, capital and labor. It is assumed that $VA^t > 0$.[15]

The fundamental accounting relation of our production unit was given by expression (2.3) as $C^t + \Pi^t = R^t$. Subtracting from the left- and the right-hand side intermediate inputs cost C^t_{EMS}, using expressions (2.58) and (2.85), this accounting relation transforms into $C^t_{KL} + \Pi^t = VA^t$. Thus the same production unit can be described by two different accounting relations, featuring different input and output concepts.

Although gross output, represented by the quantity vector y^t, is the natural output concept, the value-added concept is important when one wants to aggregate single units to larger entities. Gross output consists of deliveries to final demand and intermediate destinations. The split between these two output categories depends very much on the level of aggregation. Value added is immune to this problem. It enables one to compare (units belonging to) different industries. From a welfare-theoretic point of view, the value-added concept is important because value added can be conceived as the income (from production) that flows into society.

In the KL-VA input–output model, it is natural to define *(value-added-based) profitability* as the ratio of value added to primary inputs cost,

$$\Gamma_{VA}^{t} \equiv VA^{t} / C_{KL}^{t}, \tag{2.86}$$

and the natural starting point for defining a productivity index is to consider the development of this ratio through time. Since

$$\frac{\Gamma_{VA}^{1}}{\Gamma_{VA}^{0}} = \frac{VA^{1} / VA^{0}}{C_{KL}^{1} / C_{KL}^{0}}, \tag{2.87}$$

we need a decomposition of the value-added ratio and a decomposition of the primary inputs cost ratio.

The question of how to decompose a value-added ratio into a price and a quantity component cannot be answered unequivocally. There are several options here, the technical details of which are discussed in the extended online version of this chapter. It is there shown that

- single deflation is simple, leads to a quantity index that is always positive, but this index may be biased;
- double deflation by a Fisher index leads to a quantity index that is unbiased but may not always be well defined;
- double deflation by a Montgomery-Vartia index leads to a quantity index that is always well defined but fails the Equality Test.

Thus, there is no theoretically entirely satisfactory solution to the problem of decomposing a value-added ratio into a price index and a quantity index.

2.11. THE KL-VA MODEL (2)

Suppose now that a practically satisfactory decomposition of the value-added ratio is available; that is,

$$\frac{VA^{1}}{VA^{0}} = P_{VA}(1,0)Q_{VA}(1,0), \tag{2.88}$$

and that, by employing some pair of price and quantity indices, the primary inputs cost ratio is decomposed as

$$\frac{C_{KL}^1}{C_{KL}^0} = P(w_{KL}^1, x_{KL}^1, w_{KL}^0, x_{KL}^0)\, Q(w_{KL}^1, x_{KL}^1, w_{KL}^0, x_{KL}^0)$$

$$\equiv P_{KL}(1,0)\, Q_{KL}(1,0). \tag{2.89}$$

The *value-added-based TFP index* for period 1 relative to period 0 is then defined as

$$ITFPROD_{VA}(1,0) \equiv \frac{Q_{VA}(1,0)}{Q_{KL}(1,0)}. \tag{2.90}$$

This index measures the "quantity" change of value added relative to the quantity change of primary inputs, or, can be seen as the index of real value added relative to the index of real primary inputs.

As observed in section 2.11, profit in the KL-VA model is the same as profit in the KLEMS-Y model, and this also applies to profit differences and their price and quantity components. One easily checks that

$$DTFPROD_{VA}(1,0) \equiv Q_{VA}(1,0) - Q_{KL}(1,0)$$

$$= Q_R(1,0) - Q_C(1,0) \tag{2.91}$$

$$= DTFPROD(1,0);$$

that is, the productivity indicators are the same in the two models. This, however, does not hold for the productivity *indices*. One usually finds that $ITFPROD_{VA}(1,0) \neq ITFPROD(1,0)$. Balk (2009) showed that if profit is zero in both periods, that is, $R^t = C^t$ ($t = 0,1$), then, for certain two-stage indices that are second-order differential approximations to Fisher indices,

$$\ln ITFPROD_{VA}(1,0) = D(1,0)\ln ITFPROD(1,0), \tag{2.92}$$

where $D(1,0) \geq 1$ is the (mean) Domar-factor (= ratio of revenue over value added). Usually expression (2.92) is, in a continuous-time setting, derived under a set of strong neoclassical assumptions (see, for instance, Gollop 1979; Jorgenson et al. 2005, 298; Schreyer 2001, 143), so that this equation seems to be some deep economic-theoretical result. From the foregoing it may be concluded, however, that the inequality of the value-added-based productivity index and the gross-output-based productivity index is only due to the mathematics of ratios and differences. There is no underlying economic phenomenon, which does not mean that there cannot be given an economic interpretation to equation (2.92).

The *value-added-based labor productivity index* for period 1 relative to period 0 is defined as

$$ILPROD_{VA}(1,0) \equiv \frac{Q_{VA}(1,0)}{Q_L(1,0)}, \tag{2.93}$$

where $Q_L(1,0)$ was defined by expression (2.61). The index defined by expression (2.93) measures the "quantity" change of value added relative to the quantity change of labor input; or, this expression can be seen as the index of real value added relative to the index of real labor input.

Recall that the labor quantity index $Q_L(1,0)$ is here defined as acting on the prices and quantities of all the types of labor that are being distinguished. Suppose that the units of measurement of the various types are in some sense the same; that is, the quantities of all the types are measured in hours, or in full-time equivalent jobs, or in some other common unit. The *simple value-added-based labor productivity index*, defined as

$$ISLPROD_{VA}(1,0) \equiv \frac{Q_{VA}(1,0)}{L^1 / L^0}, \tag{2.94}$$

can then be interpreted as an index of real value added per unit of labor. Recall that $L^t \equiv \Sigma_{n \in L} x_n^t$ ($t = 0,1$). The simple value-added-based labor productivity index frequently figures at the left-hand side (thus, as *explanandum*) in a growth accounting equation. However, for deriving such a relation, nothing spectacular is needed, as will now be shown.

Consider the definition of the value-added-based TFP index, expression (2.90), and rewrite this as

$$Q_{VA}(1,0) = ITFPROD_{VA}(1,0) \times Q_{KL}(1,0). \tag{2.95}$$

Dividing both sides of this equation by the Dutot labor quantity index L^1 / L^0, applying definitions (2.65) and (2.94), one obtains

$$ISLPROD_{VA}(1,0) = ITFPROD_{VA}(1,0) \times \frac{Q_{KL}(1,0)}{Q_L(1,0)} \times LQUAL(1,0). \tag{2.96}$$

Taking logarithms and, on the assumption that all the index numbers are in the neighborhood of 1, interpreting these as percentages, the last equation can be read as the following: (simple) labor productivity growth equals TFP growth plus "capital deepening" plus "labor quality" growth.[16] Again, productivity change is measured as a residual and, thus, the three factors at the right-hand side of the previous equation can in no way be regarded as causal factors.

If, continuing the example of section 2.6.2, the primary inputs quantity index were defined as a two-stage index of the form

$$Q_{KL}(1,0) \equiv Q_K(1,0)^\alpha Q_L(1,0)^{1-\alpha} \quad (0 < \alpha < 1), \tag{2.97}$$

where any reader will recognize the simple Cobb-Douglas form, then the index of "capital deepening" reduces to the particularly simple form

$$\frac{Q_{KL}(1,0)}{Q_L(1,0)} = \left[\frac{Q_K(1,0)}{Q_L(1,0)} \right]^\alpha. \tag{2.98}$$

As mentioned earlier, the "labor quality" index, $LQUAL(1,0)$, basically measures compositional shift or structural change among the various labor input types, since it is a ratio of two quantity indices.

2.12. AGGREGATION

In the previous sections we considered the measurement of productivity change for a single, consolidated production unit. This section continues by considering an ensemble of such units, and the relation between aggregate and subaggregate (or individual) measures of productivity change. The theory surveyed here is applicable to a variety of situations, such as (1) a firm consisting of a number of plants, (2) an industry consisting of a number of firms, or (3) an economy or, more precisely, the commercial sector of an economy consisting of a number of industries.

On an intuitive level, the relation between aggregate and subaggregate, or individual, measures of productivity change is not too difficult to understand. Productivity is output quantity divided by input quantity and, thus, productivity change is output quantity change divided by input quantity change. Any aggregate is somehow the sum of its parts, which in the present context implies that aggregate productivity is somehow a weighted mean of subaggregate (or individual) productivities, where the weights somehow express the "importance" of the subaggregates, or individual units, making up the aggregate. Hence, there are two, independent, factors responsible for aggregate productivity change: (1) productivity change at subaggregate, or individual, level; and (2) change of the "importance" of the subaggregate, or individual, units.

Coming down to practice, things are rapidly becoming complicated. First, firms produce and use multiple commodities, which brings input and output prices into play. Quantities of different commodities cannot be added, but must be aggregated by means of prices. Through time, prices are also changing, which implies that we cannot simply talk about aggregate prices and quantities, but must talk about price and quantity index numbers. Moreover, aggregation rules are not unique anymore. Second, firms and industries deliver to each other, which implies that the "simple" addition of production units easily leads to a form of double-counting of outputs and inputs. Third, especially when we are dealing with firms or plants, an important fact to take into account is the dynamics of growth, decline, birth, and death of production units.

Let $\mathcal{K}$ denote an ensemble of consolidated production units. For each unit k and time period t the KL-VA accounting identity in nominal values reads

$$C_{KL}^{kt} + \Pi^{kt} = VA^{kt} \quad (k \in \mathcal{K}), \qquad (2.99)$$

where we recall that by assumption $VA^{kt} > 0$ for all production units and time periods considered.

The KL-VA model is chosen because capital input, labor input, and value added are specific for each production unit. Hence, adding the relations (2.99) over all the units,

$$\sum_{k\in\mathcal{K}} C_{KL}^{kt} + \sum_{k\in\mathcal{K}} \Pi^{kt} = \sum_{k\in\mathcal{K}} VA^{kt}, \tag{2.100}$$

avoids the possibility of double-counting and delivers the same relation for the ensemble $\mathcal{K}$ considered as a consolidated production unit:

$$C_{KL}^{\mathcal{K}t} + \Pi^{\mathcal{K}t} = VA^{\mathcal{K}t}, \tag{2.101}$$

with $C_{KL}^{\mathcal{K}t} \equiv \Sigma_{k\in\mathcal{K}} C_{KL}^{kt}$, $\Pi^{\mathcal{K}t} \equiv \Sigma_{k\in\mathcal{K}} \Pi^{kt}$, and $VA^{\mathcal{K}t} = \Sigma_{k\in\mathcal{K}} VA^{kt}$.

The ensemble we consider is dynamic; that is, its composition changes through time. Thus, wherever necessary, we must add a superscript t to $\mathcal{K}$.

For any two time periods compared, whether adjacent or not, a distinction must then be made between continuing, exiting, and entering production units. In particular,

$$\mathcal{K}^0 = \mathcal{C}^{01} \cup \mathcal{X}^0 \tag{2.102}$$

$$\mathcal{K}^1 = \mathcal{C}^{01} \cup \mathcal{N}^1, \tag{2.103}$$

where $\mathcal{C}^{01}$ denotes the subset of continuing units (active in both periods), $\mathcal{X}^0$ the subset of exiting units (active in the base period only), and $\mathcal{N}^1$ the subset of entering units (active in the comparison period only).[17] The sets $\mathcal{C}^{01}$ and $\mathcal{X}^0$ are disjunct, as are $\mathcal{C}^{01}$ and $\mathcal{N}^1$.

It is important to observe that in any application the distinction between continuing, entering, and exiting production units depends on the length of the time periods being compared, and on the time span between these periods. Of course, when the production units studied form a balanced panel, then the sets $\mathcal{X}^0$ and $\mathcal{N}^1$ are empty. The same holds for the case where the production units are industries.

2.12.1. Top-Down

We first consider TFP indices. For the static case— $\mathcal{X}^0$ and $\mathcal{N}^1$ empty, so that $\mathcal{K}^0 = \mathcal{K}^1 = \mathcal{K}$— Balk (2015) studied the relation between the aggregate TFP index $ITFPROD_{VA}^{\mathcal{K}}(1,0)$ and the subaggregate (individual or industrial) TFP indices $ITFPROD_{VA}^{k}(1,0)$ $(k \in \mathcal{K})$, all the indices defined according to expression (2.90). Out of a number of alternatives, he recommended[18]

$$\begin{aligned}
\ln ITFPROD_{VA}^{\mathcal{K}}(1,0) = &\sum_{k\in\mathcal{K}} \psi^k \ln ITFPROD_{VA}^{k}(1,0) \\
&+ \sum_{k\in\mathcal{K}} \psi^k \left(\ln\left(\frac{P_{VA}^k(1,0)}{P_{VA}^{\mathcal{K}}(1,0)} \right) - \ln\left(\frac{P_{KL}^k(1,0)}{P_{KL}^{\mathcal{K}}(1,0)} \right) \right) \\
&+ \sum_{k\in\mathcal{K}} \psi^k \ln\left(\frac{C_{KL}^{k1}/C_{KL}^{k0}}{C_{KL}^{\mathcal{K}1}/C_{KL}^{\mathcal{K}0}} \right),
\end{aligned} \tag{2.104}$$

where

$$\psi^k \equiv \frac{LM\left(\dfrac{VA^{k1}}{VA^{\mathcal{K}1}}, \dfrac{VA^{k0}}{VA^{\mathcal{K}0}}\right)}{\sum\limits_{k\in\mathcal{K}} LM\left(\dfrac{VA^{k1}}{VA^{\mathcal{K}1}}, \dfrac{VA^{k0}}{VA^{\mathcal{K}0}}\right)} \quad (k \in \mathcal{K})$$

is the (logarithmic) mean share of production unit k's value added in aggregate value added.

There occur three main terms at the right-hand side of expression (2.104). The first is a weighted mean of unit-specific TFP changes. The second is the aggregate effect of differential price change at the output and input side of the production units. The third can be interpreted as the aggregate effect of relative size change, where the size of a unit is measured by its primary-input cost share.

If there is no differential price change, then the second term at the right-hand side vanishes.[19] Moreover, if for all units $k \in \mathcal{K}$ and time periods $t = 0,1$ value added equals primary input cost, $VA^{kt} = C_{KL}^{kt}$, or profit $\Pi^{kt} = 0$, then $C_{KL}^{kt} / C_{KL}^{\mathcal{K}t} = VA^{kt} / VA^{\mathcal{K}t}$ $(t = 0,1)$, and by using the definition of the logarithmic mean, one easily checks that also the third term vanishes.

Under these two conditions, expression (2.104) reduces to

$$\ln ITFPROD_{VA}^{\mathcal{K}}(1,0) = \sum_{k\in\mathcal{K}} \psi^k \ln ITFPROD_{VA}^{k}(1,0). \tag{2.105}$$

For the dynamic case— $\mathcal{X}^0$ and $\mathcal{N}^1$ non-empty—the decomposition in expression (2.104) must be extended. For the details the reader is referred to Balk (2015, ex. [79]).

For aggregate and subaggregate simple labor productivity indices, Balk (2014) and Dumagan and Balk (2016) derived the following relation for the static case:[20]

$$\ln ISLPROD_{VA}^{\mathcal{K}}(1,0) = \sum_{k\in\mathcal{K}} \psi^k \ln ISLPROD_{VA}^{k}(1,0)$$
$$+ \sum_{k\in\mathcal{K}} \psi^k \ln\left(\frac{P_{VA}^{k}(1,0)}{P_{VA}^{\mathcal{K}}(1,0)}\right) + \sum_{k\in\mathcal{K}} \psi^k \ln\left(\frac{L^{k1}/L^{\mathcal{K}1}}{L^{k0}/L^{\mathcal{K}0}}\right), \tag{2.106}$$

where $ISLPROD_{VA}^{\mathcal{K}}(1,0)$ and $ISLPROD_{VA}^{k}(1,0)$ $(k \in \mathcal{K})$ were defined according to expression (2.94). The first term at the right-hand side of the equality sign is a weighted mean of unit-specific simple labor productivity changes. The second term is a weighted mean of individual relative output price changes $P_{VA}^{k}(1,0) / P_{VA}^{\mathcal{K}}(1,0)$ $((k \in \mathcal{K}))$. The third term measures labor reallocation.

2.12.2. Bottom-Up

The bottom-up approach, as surveyed by Balk (2016), has two main characteristics. The first is that one freely talks about levels, of input, output, or productivity. The second is that one does not care too much about the interpretation of aggregate input, output, or productivity levels.

Let us first turn to the concept of level. For each production unit $k \in \mathcal{K}^t$ *real value added* is (ideally) defined as

$$RVA^k(t,b) \equiv VA^{kt} / P_{VA}^k(t,b);$$

(2.107)

that is, nominal value added at period t divided by (or, as one says, deflated by) a production-unit-k-specific value-added based price index for period t relative to a certain reference period b, where period b may or may not precede period o. Notice that this definition tacitly assumes that production unit k, existing in period t, also existed or still exists in period b; otherwise, deflation by a production-unit-k-specific index would be impossible. When production unit k does not exist in period b, then for deflation some substitute index must be used.

It is good to realize that, by using the Product Test for value-added-based price and quantity indices, $RVA^k(t,b) = VA^{kb}Q_{VA}^k(t,b)$. Put otherwise, real value added is a (normalized) quantity index.

Like real value added, *real primary, or capital-and-labor, input,* relative to reference period b, is (ideally) defined as deflated primary input cost,

$$X_{KL}^k(t,b) \equiv C_{KL}^{kt} / P_{KL}^k(t,b),$$

(2.108)

and *real labor input,* relative to reference period b, is (ideally) defined as deflated labor cost,

$$X_L^k(t,b) \equiv C_L^{kt} / P_L^k(t,b).$$

(2.109)

Using the foregoing building blocks, the *value-added-based TFP level* of production unit k at period t is defined as real value added divided by real primary input,

$$TFPROD_{VA}^k(t,b) \equiv \frac{RVA^k(t,b)}{X_{KL}^k(t,b)}.$$

(2.110)

Notice that numerator and denominator are expressed in the same price level, namely that of period b. Thus $TFPROD_{VA}^k(t,b)$ is a dimensionless variable.

Likewise, the *value-added-based labor productivity level* of unit k at period t is defined as real value added divided by real labor input,

$$LPROD_{VA}^k(t,b) \equiv \frac{RVA^k(t,b)}{X_L^k(t,b)}.$$

(2.111)

This is also a dimensionless variable.

Finally, the *simple value-added-based labor productivity level* of unit k at period t is defined by

$$SLPROD_{VA}^k(t,b) \equiv \frac{RVA^k(t,b)}{L^{kt}}.$$

(2.112)

Notice that this level does have a dimension, namely money-of-period-b per unit of labor (say, hour of whatever type of work).

Now, let $PROD^{kt}$ denote (the logarithm or inverse of) total factor productivity $TFPROD^k_{VA}(t,b)$, labor productivity $LPROD^k_{VA}(t,b)$, or simple labor productivity $SLPROD^k_{VA}(t,b)$, then the bottom-up approach is concerned with the decomposition of

$$PROD^1 - PROD^0 \equiv \sum_{k \in \mathcal{K}^1} \theta^{k1} PROD^{k1} - \sum_{k \in \mathcal{K}^0} \theta^{k0} PROD^{k0}, \qquad (2.113)$$

where the period-specific weights, measuring the relative size (importance) of the production units, add up to 1; that is, $\Sigma_{k \in \mathcal{K}^0} \theta^{k0} = \Sigma_{k \in \mathcal{K}^1} \theta^{k1} = 1$.

Balk's (2016) survey revealed the existence of a large number of decompositions, scattered through the literature. Because of its symmetry and its natural benchmarks for exiting and entering production units, the Diewert-Fox (2010) decomposition was preferred. This decomposition reads

$$PROD^1 - PROD^0$$

$$= \left(\sum_{k \in \mathcal{N}^1} \theta^{k1} \right) \left(PROD^{\mathcal{N}^1} - PROD^{\mathcal{C}^{01}1} \right)$$

$$+ \sum_{k \in \mathcal{C}^{01}} \frac{\tilde{\theta}^{k0} + \tilde{\theta}^{k1}}{2} \left(PROD^{k1} - PROD^{k0} \right) \qquad (2.114)$$

$$+ \sum_{k \in \mathcal{C}^{01}} (\tilde{\theta}^{k1} - \tilde{\theta}^{k0}) \left(\frac{PROD^{k0} + PROD^{k1}}{2} - a \right)$$

$$- \left(\sum_{k \in \mathcal{X}^0} \theta^{k0} \right) \left(PROD^{\mathcal{X}^0} - PROD^{\mathcal{C}^{01}0} \right),$$

where $PROD^{\mathcal{X}^0} \equiv \Sigma_{k \in \mathcal{X}^0} \theta^{k0} PROD^{k0} / \Sigma_{k \in \mathcal{X}^0} \theta^{k0}$ is the mean productivity level of the exiting units; $PROD^{\mathcal{N}^1} \equiv \Sigma_{k \in \mathcal{N}^1} \theta^{k1} PROD^{k1} / \Sigma_{k \in \mathcal{N}^1} \theta^{k1}$ is the mean productivity level of the entering units; and $PROD^{\mathcal{C}^{01}t} \equiv \Sigma_{k \in \mathcal{C}^{01}} \theta^{kt} PROD^{kt} / \Sigma_{k \in \mathcal{C}^{01}} \theta^{kt}$ is the aggregate productivity level of the continuing production units at period t ($t = 0,1$); the relative size of continuing units is defined by $\tilde{\theta}^{kt} \equiv \theta^{kt} / \Sigma_{k \in \mathcal{C}^{01}} \theta^{kt}$ ($k \in \mathcal{C}^{01}$; $t = 0,1$); and a is an arbitrary scalar.

The first right-hand side term of expression (2.114) refers to the entering production units. As we see, its magnitude is determined by the period 1 share of the entrants and the productivity gap with the continuing units. The last right-hand side term refers to the exiting production units. The magnitude of this term depends on the share of the exiters and the productivity gap with the continuing units. The second and third term refer to the continuing production units. These units may contribute positively in two ways: if their productivity levels on average increase, or if the units with mean productivity levels above (or below) the scalar a increase (or decrease) in relative size.

Notice that the third term is the only place where an arbitrary scalar a can be inserted, since the relative weights of the continuing production units add up to 1 in both periods.

Though the term itself is invariant to the actual magnitude of a, the unit-specific components $(\tilde{\theta}^{k1} - \tilde{\theta}^{k0})((PROD^{k0} + PROD^{k1})/2 - a)$ are not.

The Diewert-Fox decomposition (2.114) bears a strong resemblance to the decomposition proposed decades ago by Griliches and Regev (1995), which has found many applications. The last decomposition reads:

$$
PROD^1 - PROD^0
$$

$$
= \left(\sum_{k \in \mathcal{N}^1} \theta^{k1} \right) \left(PROD^{\mathcal{N}^1} - a \right)
$$

$$
+ \sum_{k \in \mathcal{C}^{01}} \frac{\theta^{k0} + \theta^{k1}}{2} \left(PROD^{k1} - PROD^{k0} \right) \qquad (2.115)
$$

$$
+ \sum_{k \in \mathcal{C}^{01}} (\theta^{k1} - \theta^{k0}) \left(\frac{PROD^{k0} + PROD^{k1}}{2} - a \right)
$$

$$
- \left(\sum_{k \in \mathcal{X}^0} \theta^{k0} \right) \left(PROD^{\mathcal{X}^0} - a \right).
$$

With respect to the scalar a there are several options available in the literature. A rather natural choice is $a = (PROD^0 + PROD^1)/2$, the overall two-period mean aggregate productivity level. Then, entering units contribute positively to aggregate productivity change if their mean productivity level is above this overall mean. Exiting units contribute positively if their mean productivity level is below the overall mean. Continuing units can contribute positively in two ways: if their productivity level increases, or if the units with productivity levels above (below) the overall mean increase (decrease) in relative size.

As we see, the single benchmark in the Griliches-Regev decomposition is replaced by a threefold benchmark in the Diewert-Fox decomposition. If there are no exiting or entering units, that is, $\mathcal{K}^0 = \mathcal{K}^1 = \mathcal{C}^{01}$, then both decompositions reduce to

$$
PROD^1 - PROD^0 = \sum_{k \in \mathcal{C}^{01}} \frac{\theta^{k0} + \theta^{k1}}{2} \left(PROD^{k1} - PROD^{k0} \right)
$$

$$
+ \sum_{k \in \mathcal{C}^{01}} (\theta^{k1} - \theta^{k0}) \left(\frac{PROD^{k0} + PROD^{k1}}{2} - a \right),
$$

where we recognize a Bennet-type decomposition.

The question of which weights θ^{kt} are appropriate, when a choice has been made as to the productivity levels $PROD^{kt}$ ($k \in \mathcal{K}^t$), has received some attention in the literature. Given that somehow $PROD^{kt}$ is output divided by input, should θ^{kt} be output- or input-based? And how is this related to the type of mean—arithmetic, geometric, or harmonic? The literature does not provide us with definitive answers. Indeed, as long as one stays in the bottom-up framework, it is unlikely that a convincing answer can be obtained. This is the point where the bottom-up view must connect with the top-down view. For details the reader is referred to Balk (2018).

2.13. Concluding Remarks

The World Confederation of Productivity Science at its website (www.wcps.info) once defined productivity as "the single ratio of output to input—improving productivity means getting the most out for the least put in. It is important to companies, to nations (since it is a major determinant of national competitiveness) and to the world." Basically this chapter reviews the empirical implementation of this "single ratio" concept. It has been shown that there are a number of alternative, non-competing measurement objectives; that one can distinguish between total or partial measures; and that there is choice with respect to functional forms.

It is useful to recapitulate the main characteristics of the approach outlined in the foregoing:

- We did not make any of the usual neoclassical structural and behavioral assumptions; in particular, we did not assume the existence of production functions or a certain kind of optimizing behavior of the production units. Nevertheless, the approach advocated here is able to deliver the same results as the neoclassical approach; for example, it appears that for a table in which output growth is decomposed into the contributions of TFP change and input growth, the neoclassical assumptions are neither necessary nor do they contribute anything to our understanding of what productivity precisely is.
- To get insight into the "drivers" of productivity change at the lowest level of aggregation, appropriate theoretical instruments as well as additional data must be invoked. This, however, brings us outside the area of empirical measurement of productivity change as such.
- The data required here are in the first place nominal value data extracted from the annual *ex post* profit/loss accounts of a production unit. The extent to which the various cost categories are covered (capital, labor, energy, materials, services) determines whether one can compile total factor, multi-factor, or partial productivity indices.
- For the various monetary flows considered, at the input and output sides of a production unit, we need bespoke deflators. As shown, for example, deflating nominal value added by a revenue-based price index is likely to generate a picture of output growth contaminated by price effects. Similarly, deflating input or output nominal value changes of individual production units by industry-level price indices is likely to generate bias.

- Though nominal values can be observed "as a whole," the price indices serving as deflators are functions of all the detailed price and quantity data constituting the monetary flows. In practice, such price indices are compiled from samples of relative price and value data. Put otherwise, any deflator tacitly comes with a certain (sampling) inaccuracy—a fact hardly acknowledged in discussions of particular numerical outcomes.
- It should also be noted that there is a certain freedom in the choice of functional form for the deflators. One should be aware, however, that any choice at the "price side" has implications for the "quantity side."
- As a matter of convenience, the theory reviewed here is cast in terms of time: a production unit or an ensemble of such units is moving from one period to the next. With a little bit of imagination, the theory can be modified to be applicable to cross-sectional comparisons. Of course, there are some limitations here: a plant or firm cannot be at different locations at the same time. For industries, however, international comparisons are feasible, provided that the underlying data are comparable.
- The theory reviewed here assumes that at the (physical) output side, market prices are available. It is possible, however, to extend the theory by including unpriced bad outputs with negative shadow prices.

Notes

1. An extended version of this chapter is available at SSRN: http://ssrn.com/abstract=2776956. This chapter is not an intellectual history of the subject. The references are not intended as originality claims but serve to direct the reader to quickly available sources for further reading or for details that had to be omitted due to space limitations.
2. The precise definitions of these classes are beyond the scope of this chapter.
3. Other input–output models are discussed in Balk (2010). For an empirical comparison the reader is referred to Vancauteren et al. (2012).
4. It is not so simple to link this definition to the various profit concepts discussed by Marr (2012). The closest comes his concept of "economic value added," since the (user) cost of (tangible and intangible) capital assets is included in C^t. Marr's "pretax profit" (EBT or EBITDA) corresponds to revenue minus the cost of labor, energy, materials, and services, $R^t - C^t_{LEMS}$, a concept Balk (2010) called cash flow, CF^t. Marr's "net profit" then equals cash flow minus tax on production. Our definition of profit includes cost and revenue of raising and maintaining financial capital. See Diewert (2014) for an attempt to disentangle these components.
5. For any two strictly positive real numbers a and b, their logarithmic mean is defined by $LM(a, b) = (a - b) / \ln(a / b)$ if $a \neq b$ and $LM(a, a) = a$. It has the following properties: (1) $\min(a, b) \leq LM(a, b) \leq \max(a, b)$; (2) $LM(a,b)$ is continuous; (3) $LM(\lambda a, \lambda b) = \lambda LM(a,b)$ $(\lambda > 0)$; (4) $LM(a,b) = LM(b,a)$; (5) $(ab)^{1/2} \leq LM(a,b) \leq (a + b) / 2$; (6) $LM(a,1)$ is concave. See Balk (2008, 134–136) for details.
6. Marr (2012) distinguishes here between three concepts: "net profit margin" (based on cash flow minus tax on production); "gross profit margin" (where C^t_{LEMS} covers only the direct costs of production and distribution of goods and services); and "operating profit margin" (where R^t and C^t_{LEMS} cover only regular operations of the production unit).

7. The revenue growth rate is the 6th of the 75 key performance indicators discussed by Marr (2012).

8. Under extreme conditions the monotonicity properties of geometric mean indices break down; see Balk (2008, 72).

9. This approach follows Diewert (1992), Diewert and Nakamura (2003), and Balk (2003). Notice that the productivity concept introduced here is purely descriptive. As components of productivity change may be distinguished between technological change, efficiency change, scale effects, and input/output-mix effects; economic research has unearthed a large number of underlying drivers. Chapter 4 of this *Handbook* discusses a narrower concept of productivity.

10. But note that it is not necessary to assume that $R^t = C^t$ $(t = 0,1)$, as Dumagan and Ball did.

11. Gordon (2016), for instance, employs a Cobb-Douglas function with $\alpha_K = 0.3$ and $\alpha_L = 0.7$.

12. This point was also forcefully made by Felipe and McCombie (2013).

13. The extended online version of this chapter contains a section on the profit-revenue and profit-cost margin ratios.

14. This approach follows Balk (2003).

15. An early advocate of the value-added output concept was Burns (1930). Specifically, he favored net value added (see Balk 2010 for the definition). Burns was aware of the possibility that for very narrowly defined production units and small time periods, value added may become non-positive.

16. This decomposition repeatedly turns up in the (labor productivity) growth accounting literature, a recent example being Muntean (2014). This author used an endogenous rate of return for capital, so that profit $\Pi^t = 0$. Though the neoclassical growth accounting theory was invoked, this theory neither proved necessary—since all the empirical results remained within the confines of the approach sketched here—nor helpful in understanding the "sources" of TFP change.

17. The definition of "active" should of course be made precise in any empirical application on microdata to ascertain that exit of a certain production unit is due to quitting business and not due to, for example, obtaining a new name, merging with another unit, splitting into two or more units, falling below the observation threshold; likewise for entry.

18. See Diewert (2016) for the asymmetric, base period weighted, variant which is known as the Generalized Exactly Additive Decomposition (GEAD). Calver and Murray (2016) provide an interesting application on Canadian data.

19. If there is differential price change at the output side but not at the input side, then the GEAD reduces to the so-called CSLS decomposition. See Calver and Murray (2016) for an example of the dramatic differences occurring between these two decomposition methods when there does exist differential price change.

20. See Diewert (2016) for the asymmetric, base period weighted variant, also known as the GEAD.

References

Balk, B. M. 2003. "The Residual: On Monitoring and Benchmarking Firms, Industries, and Economies with Respect to Productivity." *Journal of Productivity Analysis* 20: 5–47. Reprinted in *National Accounting and Economic Growth*, edited by John M. Hartwick. The International Library of Critical Writings in Economics No. 313. Cheltenham, UK; Northampton, MA: Edward Elgar, 2016.

Balk, B. M. 2008. *Price and Quantity Index Numbers: Models for Measuring Aggregate Change and Difference*. New York: Cambridge University Press.

Balk, B. M. 2009. "On the Relationship Between Gross-Output and Value-Added Based Productivity Measures: The Importance of the Domar Factor." *Macroeconomic Dynamics* 13(S2): 241–267.

Balk, B. M. 2010. "An Assumption-Free Framework for Measuring Productivity Change." *The Review of Income and Wealth* 56(Special Issue 1): S224–S256. Reprinted in *National Accounting and Economic Growth*, edited by John M. Hartwick. The International Library of Critical Writings in Economics No. 313. Cheltenham, UK; Northampton, MA: Edward Elgar, 2016.

Balk, B. M. 2014. "Dissecting Aggregate Output and Labour Productivity Change." *Journal of Productivity Analysis* 42: 35–43.

Balk, B. M. 2015. "Measuring and Relating Aggregate and Subaggregate Total Factor Productivity Change Without Neoclassical Assumptions." *Statistica Neerlandica* 69: 21–48.

Balk, B. M. 2016. "The Dynamics of Productivity Change: A Review of the Bottom-Up Approach." In *Productivity and Efficiency Analysis*, edited by W. H. Greene, L. Khalaf, R. C. Sickles, M. Veall and M.-C. Voia, 15–49. Proceedings in Business and Economics. Cham, Switzerland: Springer International.

Balk, B. M. 2018. "Aggregate Productivity and Productivity of the Aggregate: Connecting the Bottom-Up and Top-Down Approaches." In *Productivity and Inequality*, edited by W. H. Greene, L. Khalaf, P. Makdissi, R. C. Sickles, M. Veall and M.-C. Voia, 119–141. Proceedings in Business and Economics. Cham, Switzerland: Springer International..

Ball, V. E., R. Färe, S. Grosskopf, and D. Margaritis. 2015. "The Role of Energy Productivity in U.S. Agriculture." *Energy Economics* 49: 460–471.

Burns, A. F. 1930. "The Measurement of the Physical Volume of Production." *Quarterly Journal of Economics* 44: 242–262.

Calver, M., and A. Murray. 2016. "Decomposing Multifactor Productivity Growth in Canada by Industry and Province, 1997–2014." *International Productivity Monitor* 31: 88–112. Center for the Study of Living Standards, Ontario, Canada.

Dhyne, E., A. Petrin, V. Smeets, and F. Warzynski. 2014. "Import Competition, Productivity and Multi-Product Firms." Working Paper Research No. 268 National Bank of Belgium, Brussels.

Diewert, W. E. 1978. "Superlative Index Numbers and Consistency in Aggregation." *Econometrica* 46: 883–900.

Diewert, W. E. 1992. "The Measurement of Productivity." *Bulletin of Economic Research* 44: 163–198.

Diewert, W. E. 2014. "The Treatment of Financial Transactions in the SNA: A User Cost Approach." *Eurona* 1: 73–89.

Diewert, W. E. 2016. "Decompositions of Productivity Growth into Sectoral Effects: Some Puzzles Explained." In *Productivity and Efficiency Analysis*, edited by W. H. Greene, L. Khalaf, R. C. Sickles, M. Veall, and M.-C. Voia, 1–14. Proceedings in Business and Economics. Cham, Switzerland: Springer International.

Diewert, W. E., and K. J. Fox. 2010. "On Measuring the Contribution of Entering and Exiting Firms to Aggregate Productivity Growth." In *Price and Productivity Measurement*, Vol. 6: *Index Number Theory*, edited by W. E. Diewert, B. M. Balk, D. Fixler, K. J. Fox, and A. O. Nakamura, 41–66. Vancouver: Trafford Press. www.vancouvervolumes.com, www.indexmeasures.com.

Revised version of Discussion Paper No. 05-02, Department of Economics, University of British Columbia, Vancouver, 2005.

Diewert, W. E., and A. O. Nakamura. 2003. "Index Number Concepts, Measures and Decompositions of Productivity Growth." *Journal of Productivity Analysis* 19: 127–159.

Dumagan, J. C., and B. M. Balk. 2016. "Dissecting Aggregate Output and Labour Productivity Change: A Postscript on the Role of Relative Prices." *Journal of Productivity Analysis* 45: 117–119.

Dumagan, J. C., and V. E. Ball. 2009. "Decomposing Growth in Revenues and Costs into Price, Quantity and Total Factor Productivity Contributions." *Applied Economics* 41(23): 2943–2953.

Felipe, J., and J. S. L. McCombie. 2013. *The Aggregate Production Function and the Measurement of Technical Change: "Not Even Wrong."* Cheltenham, UK; Northhampton, MA: Edward Elgar.

Gollop, F. M. 1979. "Accounting for Intermediate Input: The Link Between Sectoral and Aggregate Measures of Productivity Growth." In *Measurement and Interpretation of Productivity*, edited by A. Rees, 318–333. Report of the Panel to Review Productivity Statistics, Committee on National Statistics, Assembly of Behavioral and Social Sciences, National Research Council. Washington, DC: National Academy of Sciences.

Gordon, R. J. 2016. *The Rise and Fall of American Growth: The U.S. Standard of Living since the Civil War*. Princeton, NJ: Princeton University Press.

Grifell-Tatjé, E., and C. A. K. Lovell. 2014. "Productivity, Price Recovery, Capacity Constraints and Their Financial Consequences." *Journal of Productivity Analysis* 41: 3–17.

Grifell-Tatjé, E., and C. A. K. Lovell. 2015. *Productivity Accounting: The Economics of Business Performance*. New York: Cambridge University Press.

Griliches, Z., and H. Regev. 1995. "Firm Productivity in Israeli Industry, 1979–1988." *Journal of Econometrics* 65: 175–203.

Harrison, J. S., and A. C. Wicks. 2013. "Stakeholder Theory, Value and Firm Performance." *Business Ethics Quarterly* 23: 97–124.

Jorgenson, D. W., M. S. Ho, and K. J. Stiroh. 2005. *Productivity*, Vol. 3: *Information Technology and the American Growth Resurgence*. Cambridge, MA: MIT Press.

Lawrence, D., W. E. Diewert, and K. J. Fox. 2006. "The Contributions of Productivity, Price Changes and Firm Size to Profitability." *Journal of Productivity Analysis* 26: 1–13.

Marr, B. 2012. *Key Performance Indicators: The 75 Measures Every Manager Needs to Know*. Harlow, UK: Pearson.

Muntean, T. 2014. "Intangible Assets and Their Contribution to Labour Productivity Growth in Ontario." *International Productivity Monitor* 27: 22–39. Center for the Study of Living Standards, Ontario, Canada.

Murray, A. 2016. "Partial versus Total Factor Productivity Measures: An Assessment of their Strengths and Weaknesses." *International Productivity Monitor* 31: 113–126. Center for the Study of Living Standards, Ontario, Canada.

Schreyer, P. 2001. *Measuring Productivity: Measurement of Aggregate and Industry-Level Productivity Growth*. Paris: OECD.

Vancauteren, M., E. Veldhuizen, and B. M. Balk. 2012. "Measures of Productivity Change: Which Outcome Do You Want?" Paper presented at the 32nd General Conference of the IARIW, Boston, MA, August 5–11. www.iariw.org.

CHAPTER 3

....

THE US BUREAU
OF LABOR STATISTICS
PRODUCTIVITY PROGRAM

....

LUCY P. ELDRIDGE, CHRIS SPARKS,
AND JAY STEWART[1]

3.1. INTRODUCTION

THE Bureau of Labor Statistics (BLS) at the US Department of Labor produces the official productivity statistics for the US economy.[2] The BLS productivity measurement program has evolved over time, reflecting changes in available source data, improvements in methodology, and the demands of data users for new data products. The BLS's studies of output per hour in individual industries began in the 1920s, and these early measures related output to the number of workers. The productivity program expanded to about 50 industries in the 1930s and 1940s with a focus on the manufacturing sector. Since then, the BLS industry productivity program has evolved from publishing occasional industry-specific studies to the regular publication of annual measures of labor productivity for manufacturing and service providing industries. Labor productivity data for the aggregate economy were first published in 1959, following the 1954 development of real gross national product (GNP) from the National Income and Product Accounts (NIPA) at the US Department of Commerce. The BLS began publishing quarterly measures of labor productivity growth in 1976. In 1983, the BLS developed and began publishing a broader measure of productivity, multifactor productivity (MFP), which is also referred to as total factor productivity (TFP).[3] A major part of this effort was developing the methodology for estimating capital input from investment and other data.

Today, the BLS continues to produce productivity statistics for major sectors of the US economy and individual industries. The BLS also publishes a number of related measures that shed light on the elements of productivity growth, including output and implicit price deflators for output, employment, hours worked, unit labor costs, real and nominal hourly compensation, and unit non-labor payments. Labor's share is another measure that can be constructed from these pieces, although it is not included in the productivity news releases.

In constructing measures of labor and multifactor productivity, the BLS combines data from a number of sources, makes adjustments to ensure consistency, and removes known sources of bias specific to productivity measurement. The basic components of its productivity measures are output, labor inputs, capital inputs, and intermediate inputs. In the following, we describe how the BLS constructs these components and estimates productivity growth, and we discuss some of the measurement issues that the BLS faces going forward.

The rest of this chapter is laid out as follows. In section 3.2, we describe the industry and sector coverage of the BLS's productivity measures, and explain why certain sectors are excluded. Section 3.3 describes the growth accounting framework that the BLS uses to construct its labor and multifactor productivity measures. Section 3.4 describes the BLS's output concepts. BLS methodologies for constructing labor, capital and other inputs are described in sections 3.5, 3.6, and 3.7. Section 3.8 discusses other measures that the BLS produces, and we wrap up the chapter with a look at ongoing projects in section 3.9.[4]

3.2. INDUSTRY AND SECTOR COVERAGE

Ideally, BLS productivity statistics would measure productivity for the US economy at the most aggregate level of domestic output, gross domestic product (GDP).[5] However, the real output of general government, private households, and nonprofit institutions are estimated using data on labor compensation and other inputs, which implies little or no productivity growth for these sectors. The output of general government is measured as the sum of the compensation of general government employees and the consumption of general government fixed capital, which is a proxy for the capital services derived from general government assets. The output of the private household sector is measured as the compensation of paid employees of private households plus the rental value of owner-occupied housing; and the output of nonprofit institutions serving individuals is measured as the compensation paid to their employees plus the rental value of buildings and equipment owned and used by these institutions. The trends in output measured using compensation data will, by construction, move with inputs and thus will tend to imply little or no labor productivity growth.[6] Therefore, to get a more accurate picture of productivity growth, the BLS focuses on the business sector, which excludes these activities and constitutes about 74% of GDP.

The BLS produces quarterly and annual labor productivity measures for the business, nonfarm business, and nonfinancial corporate sectors.[7] Excluding the farm sector, which is small in the United States, reduces the volatility of labor productivity.

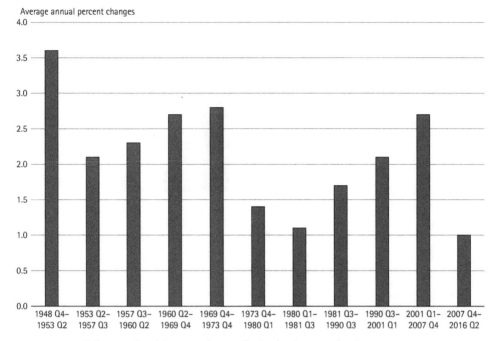

Average annual percent changes

FIGURE 3.1. Labor productivity growth rates during business cycles since 1947.

Source: US Bureau of Labor Statistics.

Output for the nonfinancial corporate sector is equal to that of the business sector less the output of financial corporations and unincorporated businesses.[8] The BLS also produces quarterly and annual measures of labor productivity for manufacturing, and durable and nondurable manufacturing.[9,10]

The labor productivity series for the business and nonfarm business sectors extend from 1947 onward, for nonfinancial corporations from 1958 onward, and for manufacturing (total, durable, and nondurable sectors) from 1987 onward. Figure 3.1 shows productivity growth from the fourth quarter of 1948 through the second quarter of 2016. Here you can see the high productivity growth of the postwar period and the 1960s. These periods contrast with the low productivity growth of the 1970s and the even-lower growth since the Great Recession.

The BLS also produces annual labor productivity measures for all three- and four-digit North American Industry Classification System (NAICS) industries in manufacturing, wholesale, and retail trade and for a variety of industries in mining and the services-providing sector.[11] Figure 3.2 shows the distribution of industry productivity growth rates for the four-digit industries for which the BLS publishes estimates. Here we can see how the period after the Great Recession contrasts with earlier periods that also include recessions—productivity growth is negative for a large fraction of industries.

In addition to labor productivity, the BLS produces annual MFP measures for the private business sector, the private nonfarm business sector, manufacturing sectors, all three- and four-digit NAICS manufacturing industries, roughly two-digit

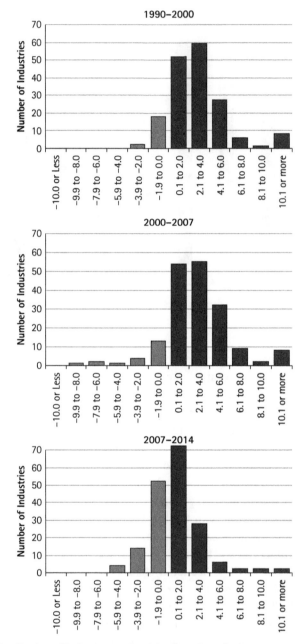

FIGURE 3.2. Distribution of industry productivity for selected years.

Source: US Bureau of Labor Statistics.

Table 3.1 Summary of BLS Productivity Measures and Coverage

	Frequency	Sectors (Start Year)	Industries	Output Concept
Labor Productivity	Quarterly Annual	Business (1947) Nonfarm business (1947) Nonfinancial corporations (1958)		Value added
	Annual	Manufacturing (1987) Durable (1987) Nondurable (1987)	All three- and four-digit NAICS industries in manufacturing, wholesale, and retail trade; selected industries in mining and service-producing (1987)	Sectoral Output
Multifactor Productivity	Annual	Private business sector (1987) Private nonfarm business (1987) Manufacturing (1987)		Value added
	Annual		All three- and four-digit NAICS manufacturing industries and two service-sector industries (1987)	Sectoral Output

non-manufacturing industries,[12] and the total economy, as well as for the three-digit air transportation industry and the six-digit line-haul railroads industry. The BLS restricts its coverage to the private business sector for its aggregate MFP measures because the appropriate capital data are not available for the government sector. In particular, subsidies account for a large fraction of government capital income, which makes it impossible to estimate the requisite rental prices and cost-share weights. The MFP measures for the private business and private nonfarm business sectors, and the total economy are calculated as value-added output per unit of combined labor and capital input, while the manufacturing and industry measures are calculated as sectoral output per unit of combined capital (K), labor (L), energy (E), materials (M), and purchased business services (S) inputs: KLEMS. Table 3.1 summarizes the different BLS productivity measures, and helps illustrate how they are related.

3.2.1. Preliminary Annual Estimates

Major sector labor productivity measures are published shortly after the end of the reference quarter but, due to source data availability, there can be a considerable lag in the publication of MFP data and the industry-level labor productivity measures. To meet data users' demand for timely data, the BLS produces preliminary estimates based on a simplified methodology.

For private business and private nonfarm business sector MFP, output and hours data are available, shortly after the end of the reference year. But the data required for the capital measures are not available until long after the end of the reference year. The simplified methodology uses fewer more-aggregated asset categories than the final published estimates, and a simpler methodology for estimating rental prices. Final estimates are published when complete data become available.

Preliminary estimates of industry-level labor productivity growth for selected manufacturing, mining, and service industries are available within five months after the end of the reference period. As time passes, more and better data are available for generating preliminary estimates. Therefore, the BLS must balance the cost to users of delaying publication with the advantages of having better data to generate preliminary estimates.

3.3. Labor and Multifactor Productivity

Quarterly labor productivity growth, which is designated by the US government as a Principal Federal Economic Indicator (PFEI), is calculated as the percentage growth in value-added output less the percentage growth in hours worked:

$$\dot{LP}^{VA} = \frac{\dot{Q}^{VA}}{Q^{VA}} - \frac{\dot{H}}{H}, \tag{3.1}$$

where Q is output and H is hours, and the dot notation indicates the first derivative with respect to time. This is a simple and easy-to-calculate productivity measure, but it does not tell the whole story. To provide a more complete picture, the BLS publishes estimates of MFP growth, which also accounts for capital and changes in the composition of the labor force. The BLS estimates MFP growth using a growth accounting framework that assumes Hicks-neutral technical change and constant returns to scale (see Solow 1957):

$$\dot{MFP}^{VA} = \frac{\dot{Q}^{VA}}{Q^{VA}} - s_K^{VA} \frac{\dot{K}}{K} - s_L^{VA} \frac{\dot{L}}{L}, \tag{3.2}$$

where K is capital input, L is labor input, and s_K^{VA} and s_L^{VA} are cost share weights. Labor input can be broken down into the growth in hours (H) and labor composition (LC), which accounts for changes in the demographic composition of the labor force. Expanding equation (3.2), we have:

$$MF\dot{P}^{VA} = \frac{\dot{Q}^{VA}}{Q^{VA}} - s_K^{VA}\frac{\dot{K}}{K} - s_L^{VA}\left(\frac{\dot{H}}{H} + \frac{\dot{LC}}{LC}\right) = \frac{\dot{Q}^{VA}}{Q^{VA}} - s_K^{VA}\frac{\dot{K}}{K} - s_L^{VA}\frac{\dot{H}}{H} - s_L^{VA}\frac{\dot{LC}}{LC} \quad (3.2')$$

The MFP measure was originally created to explain labor productivity growth and, by rearranging terms in equation (3.2'), we can see the relationship between labor and multifactor productivity:

$$L\dot{P}^{VA} = \frac{\dot{Q}^{VA}}{Q^{VA}} - \frac{\dot{H}}{H} = MF\dot{P}^{VA} + s_K^{VA}\left(\frac{\dot{K}}{K} - \frac{\dot{H}}{H}\right) + s_L^{VA}\frac{\dot{LC}}{LC} \quad (3.3)$$

Thus, value-added labor productivity growth is equal to MFP growth plus the growth in the capital-to-labor ratio (capital intensity) weighted by capital's share of cost plus the growth in labor composition weighted by labor's share of cost.

Table 3.2 shows how MFP growth has varied over time and its relationship to labor productivity. Over a given time period, the average logarithmic growth rate of capital intensity, labor composition, and MFP will sum to the average logarithmic growth rate

Table 3.2 **Labor Productivity and the Contributions of Capital Intensity, Labor Composition, and Multifactor Productivity to Labor Productivity in the Private Nonfarm Business and Private Business Sectors for Selected Periods, 1987–2014**

Compound Annual Growth Rates

Private nonfarm business	1987–2014	1987–1990	1990–1995	1995–2000	2000–2007	2007–2014	2013–2014
Labor productivity	2.0	1.6	1.6	2.9	2.6	1.2	0.7
Contribution of capital intensity	0.8	0.7	0.6	1.2	1.0	0.6	-0.1
Contribution of information-processing equipment	0.3	0.3	0.3	0.6	0.3	0.1	0.0
Contribution of research and development	0.1	0.1	0.1	0.1	0.1	0.1	0.0
Contribution of all other intellectual property products	0.2	0.2	0.4	0.4	-0.1	0.1	0.1
Contribution of all other capital services	0.2	0.1	-0.1	0.1	0.7	0.2	-0.3
Contribution of labor composition	0.3	0.2	0.5	0.2	0.2	0.3	0.1
Multifactor productivity	0.9	0.7	0.5	1.5	1.4	0.4	0.7
Contribution of R&D to multifactor productivity	0.2	0.2	0.2	0.2	0.2	0.1	0.1

of labor productivity. To illustrate, the strong growth in labor productivity in the 1995–2000 and 2000–2007 periods can be mainly attributed to strong growth in capital intensity and MFP. The contribution of labor composition was relatively small, and not very different from other time periods.

3.4. Output Concepts and Industry Productivity

Productivity estimates can be computed using any one of three output concepts: gross output, sectoral output, or value-added output.[13] Gross output is the total output produced by an industry or sector, while value-added output is equal to gross output less all intermediate inputs used in production. Sectoral output lies between gross output and value-added output and is equal to gross output less only those intermediate inputs that are produced within that industry or sector; intermediate inputs used in production from outside the industry are not removed. Thus, sectoral output represents the value of output leaving the sector or industry.[14] For detailed industries, sectoral output is very close to gross output because very few industry outputs are used as intermediate inputs in the same industry. Going from detailed industries to more-aggregated industries and major sectors, sectoral output converges toward value-added output. For the total economy, value-added and sectoral output are the same except for imported intermediate inputs.[15]

Different output concepts are useful for answering different questions.[16] Value-added labor productivity more closely reflects an industry's ability to translate labor hours into final income, while sectoral-output-based labor productivity measures the efficiency with which an industry transforms labor hours into output.[17] The BLS uses value-added output for its major sector labor and multifactor productivity measures. For industry-level productivity measures, the BLS calculates both labor and multifactor productivity using sectoral output within a KLEMS framework so that the MFP measures can be used to explain labor productivity growth. Although the volume of intrasectoral transactions does not materially affect KLEMS MFP calculations, it does affect labor productivity because intermediate inputs that are produced within the industry would be double-counted if a gross output concept were used. Specifically, the intermediate input would show up twice in output—once as an intermediate output and once as part of the final output that is sold outside the industry—but the hours used to produce the intermediate input are counted only once.

By using the sectoral output concept for both, it is easier to see the relationship between labor productivity and MFP. Starting with MFP, we have:

$$\dot{MFP}^{SO} = \frac{\dot{Q}^{SO}}{Q^{SO}} - s_K^{SO}\frac{\dot{K}}{K} - s_L^{SO}\left(\frac{\dot{H}}{H} + \frac{\dot{LC}}{LC}\right) - s_E^{SO}\frac{\dot{E}}{E} - s_{M_{-i}}^{SO}\frac{\dot{M}_{-i}}{M_{-i}} - s_S^{SO}\frac{\dot{S}}{S}, \qquad (3.4)$$

where E denotes energy, M_{-i} denotes materials purchased from outside industry i, and S denotes purchased services. This is the standard KLEMS model, but materials exclude those that are produced in the industry. Rearranging equation (3.4), sectoral-output-based labor productivity is:

$$
\begin{aligned}
\dot{LP}^{SO} &= \frac{\dot{Q}^{SO}}{Q^{SO}} - \frac{\dot{H}}{H} \\
&= \dot{MFP}^{SO} + s_K^{SO}\left(\frac{\dot{K}}{K} - \frac{\dot{H}}{H}\right) + s_E^{SO}\left(\frac{\dot{E}}{E} - \frac{\dot{H}}{H}\right) + s_{M_{-i}}^{SO}\left(\frac{\dot{M}_{-i}}{M_{-i}} - \frac{\dot{H}}{H}\right) \\
&\quad + s_S^{SO}\left(\frac{\dot{S}}{S} - \frac{\dot{H}}{H}\right) + s_L^{SO}\frac{\dot{LC}}{LC}
\end{aligned}
\tag{3.5}
$$

Under both output concepts, value-added and sectoral, changes in labor productivity can be due to technological progress, increased capital intensity, greater economies of scale, improved management techniques, and changes in the skills of the labor force.[18] The key difference between the two concepts is that sectoral-output-based labor productivity includes the effects of substituting other inputs (EMS) for labor, whereas value-added labor productivity does not.[19] Sectoral-output-based labor productivity will therefore grow with increased outsourcing of labor and purchases of intermediate inputs. But if these purchased intermediate inputs are subtracted from the value of output, as with value-added output, they can no longer be a source of productivity growth.[20] Thus, outsourcing of labor has a smaller effect on industry-level value-added labor productivity, because the substitution of purchased services for labor reduces both output and labor input.[21]

3.4.1. Output Data

The BLS gets its output data from the US Bureau of Economic Analysis (BEA) and the US Census Bureau. The real value-added output used for business-sector productivity measures come from the BEA's NIPAs. BEA calculates business-sector output (business, nonfarm business, private business, and private nonfarm business) by removing from GDP the gross product of general government, private households, and nonprofit institutions.

Output measures for the manufacturing sectors and industries begin with value of industry shipments from the US Census Bureau. These gross output data are then adjusted to remove transactions that occur between establishments within the sector or industry, and to account for resales and changes in inventories. Intrasectoral transactions are calculated using delivered-costs data from the US Census Bureau's Materials Consumed by Kind table, which includes detailed data on the products that are purchased by industries for use in the manufacturing process. The BLS adjusts the delivered costs using BEA input–output tables to remove the difference between the price the producer receives and the price that the consuming establishment pays. BEA Import Matrixes are then used to remove imported materials so that only domestically produced products are included in the intrasectoral adjustment. In years where the Census does not publish the Materials Consumed by Kind table, the BLS uses value-of-shipments and cost-of-materials data from the Annual Survey of Manufactures to estimate intrasectoral transactions.

The BLS produces labor productivity measures for non-manufacturing industries only if output can be defined and measured in a way that is independent from labor input measures. For those non-manufacturing industries, the output measures are constructed primarily using data from the economic censuses and annual surveys of the US Census Bureau together with information on price changes from the BLS.[22] Real output is most often derived by deflating nominal sales or values of production using BLS price indexes and removing intra-industry transactions, but for a few industries, such as education, commercial banking, line-haul railroads, and industries in the mining sector, it is measured by "physical" quantities of output.[23] For NIPA-level non-manufacturing industries, for which the BLS publishes MFP measures, sectoral output is estimated using BEA gross output estimates and intrasectoral transaction data based on the BEA input–output use tables—specifically, the use tables before redefinitions.[24]

In order to publish quarterly estimates of labor productivity for manufacturing, the BLS estimates sectoral output by adjusting annual manufacturing output data using a quarterly reference series and a quadratic minimization formula.[25] The quarterly reference series is constructed from the Federal Reserve Board monthly Indexes of Industrial Production. Due to a lag in the availability of the annual benchmark data, quarterly and annual manufacturing output measures are estimated by extrapolation based on the changes in the Indexes of Industrial Production.

3.5. LABOR INPUT

For labor productivity, labor input is measured as total hours worked. This is a straightforward concept, but it treats every hour the same, regardless of the labor force's experience and education. For MFP, a more comprehensive measure of labor input is used. Specifically, the MFP labor input measure accounts for changes in the composition of the labor force in a way that gives greater weight to more highly paid (and presumably more experienced and higher skilled) labor hours. In the following, we describe how the BLS estimates hours worked and calculates its labor composition index.[26]

3.5.1. Hours Worked

Total hours worked includes all time available for production and excludes paid vacations and other forms of leave, which are viewed as benefits.[27] This definition of hours worked is consistent with the International Labour Organization–United Nations (ILO-UN) resolution on measuring working time.

The BLS productivity program uses data from three BLS surveys to construct its estimate of work hours: the Current Employment Statistics survey (CES), the Current Population Survey (CPS), and the National Compensation Survey (NCS).[28] The CES is a monthly payroll survey that collects data on employment and hours paid from a sample of about 623,000 worksites.[29] The CPS is a monthly survey of approximately 60,000 households that collects data on employment status, hours worked, and demographic characteristics.[30] The NCS is a quarterly survey of 28,900 occupations from a sample of 6,900 establishments that collects data on hours worked and paid leave.[31]

The BLS uses the CES as its main source of hours data, because industry classifications in establishment surveys are more consistent with those used in the surveys that collect output data and because the CES's large sample size permits considerable industry detail. However, the CES hours data are hours *paid* and, until 2006, covered only production (in goods-producing industries) and nonsupervisory (in services-providing industries) employees.[32,33] Hereafter, we will refer to these workers as production workers. In contrast, the CPS collects data on hours *worked* by all workers, but does not use industry classifications that are completely consistent with those in the output data sources.[34] Moreover, the small sample size of the CPS limits the amount of industry detail. The CPS is used to estimate hours for nonproduction workers. The NCS is used to convert CES production worker hours to an hours-worked basis.

The BLS begins by taking published estimates of average weekly hours paid by production workers from the CES, and adjusting them from an hours-paid to an hours-worked basis using a ratio estimated from the NCS.[35] This adjustment ensures that changes in vacation, holiday, and sick pay do not affect hours growth. More formally, hours worked by production workers is given by:

$$HOURS_{PW} = AWH_{PW}^{CES} \times hwhp_{PW}^{NCS} \times EMP_{PW}^{CES} \times 52 \qquad (3.6)$$

where AWH is average weekly hours, *hwhp* is the hours-worked-to-hours-paid ratio, and EMP is employment. Superscripts indicate the survey, and subscripts indicate the worker category.

Note that production worker hours, as calculated in equation (3.6), do not capture off-the-clock hours. Off-the-clock work is not an issue for hourly paid workers, who comprise about 70% of production workers. But it may be an issue for the 30% of production workers who are not paid hourly. Employers are not required to keep records for these workers and, for this reason, CES respondents are instructed to report standard workweeks. This means that changes in off-the-clock hours worked by non-hourly-paid production workers are not captured.

To estimate nonproduction worker hours, the BLS constructs a ratio of nonproduction worker average weekly hours to production worker average weekly hours using data from the CPS and then multiplies the NCS-adjusted production worker hours by that ratio.[36] Note that this CPS-ratio adjustment does capture off-the-clock work for nonproduction workers. Hours worked by nonproduction workers are calculated as follows:

$$HOURS_{NPW} = \left(AWH_{PW}^{CES} \times hwhp_{PW}^{NCS}\right) \times \frac{AWH_{NPW}^{CPS}}{AWH_{PW}^{CPS}} \times EMP_{NPW}^{CES} \times 52 \qquad (3.7)$$

Total hours worked for all employees is equal to the sum of production worker hours and nonproduction worker hours.[37] Total hours for all workers are equal to total employee hours plus the hours worked by farm workers, the unincorporated self-employed, and unpaid family workers, all of which are estimated using hours-worked data from the CPS.[38]

3.5.1.1. *Hours Research at the Bureau of Labor Statistics*

It is worth noting that the BLS differs from statistical agencies in many other countries in that it builds its estimates of hours worked from three different data sources, with data from the monthly establishment survey being the primary source. It has been documented that the two primary BLS hours series differ in level and trend (Abraham, Spletzer, and Stewart 1998, 1999; Frazis and Stewart 2010). The BLS has conducted a significant amount of research to evaluate the quality of its hours data.[39]

Several studies examine the quality of hours reports from the CPS. Frazis and Stewart (2004, 2009, 2010) examined the claim that respondents in household surveys such as the CPS tend to overstate their hours worked. They compared hours data from the CPS to hours data from the American Time Use Survey (ATUS) and found that hours are correctly stated on average, although some groups overstate hours while other groups understate hours. They also found that multiple job holding is understated in the CPS and hours worked on second jobs are overstated (Frazis and Stewart, 2009). The net effect is that total hours worked on second jobs is slightly understated in the CPS. They also found that people tend to work more hours during CPS reference weeks compared with nonreference weeks.[40]

Eldridge and Pabilonia (2010) use data from the CPS and the ATUS to examine whether off-the-clock work done at home is counted. They find that workers who bring work home tend to work less at the office, but work more hours overall. They find that there may be a small downward bias (less than 1%) in the official level of hours worked, but this does not affect growth rates.

Frazis and Stewart (2010) investigated the differences in level and trend between the CPS and the CES. Their approach was to simulate the CES data using data from the CPS. They found that virtually all of the difference in level could be accounted for by differences in coverage (all workers in the CPS vs. production/nonsupervisory workers in the CES), the treatment of multiple job holders (counted once in the CPS vs. multiple times in the CES), and the hours concept (hours worked in the CPS vs. hours paid in the CES). The difference in trends was harder to reconcile. Frazis and Stewart investigated a number of possible explanations but were only able to explain about one-third to one-half of the divergence in trend. They did, however, identify three industries that accounted for a large portion of the divergence: retail trade, leisure and hospitality, and business and professional services.

3.5.2. Labor Composition

The labor composition term in the MFP equation (3.2′) accounts for changes in the demographic composition of the labor force and is a rough proxy for labor quality.[41] The BLS labor composition index accounts for the effect of shifts in the age, education, and gender composition of the workforce on the efficiency of labor.

The demographic information required for labor composition calculations are available only in household surveys, such as the CPS. The BLS uses the CPS Outgoing Rotation Group (ORG) data, which has information on workers' hours and earnings, as well as a wealth of demographic information. In addition, ORG data files have a large enough sample to allow the labor composition adjustment to be calculated at the three-digit industry level.[42,43]

The BLS divides the CPS sample into gender × age category × education level worker groups, and computes the year-to-year growth in hours for each group. These growth rates are Törnqvist aggregated into a measure of total labor input growth, where the weight for each group is its share of total labor compensation:[44]

$$\Delta Labor\ Input_t = \sum_j \frac{1}{2}\left(s_{jt} + s_{j,t-1}\right) \times \Delta HOURS_{jt}, \tag{3.8}$$

where

$$s_{jt} = \frac{\overline{\overline{w}}_{jt} \times HOURS_{jt}}{\sum_j \overline{\overline{w}}_{jt} \times HOURS_{jt}}, \tag{3.9}$$

and $\overline{\overline{w}}_{jt}$ is the median wage of workers in worker group j in year t. Theoretically, the mean wage is more appropriate, but the BLS uses medians because some groups have only a few observations, and medians are not as sensitive to outliers. The change in labor composition is calculated as follows:

$$\Delta Labor\ Composition_t = \Delta Labor\ Input_t - \Delta Total\ Hours_t \tag{3.10}$$

Note that the second term, the (unweighted) change in total hours, is also calculated using the CPS ORG data to be consistent with the data used to calculate labor input. The labor composition index is calculated by chaining the annual growth rates back to the base period.

3.6. Capital Inputs

The BLS estimates of capital input cover a wide range of asset types, including fixed business equipment, structures, artistic originals, research and development, own-account software, inventories, and land.[45] Financial assets are excluded from capital input measures, as are owner-occupied residential structures. The BLS, like other statistical agencies, estimates capital inputs by first estimating the productive capital stock using the perpetual inventory method and then estimating the rental price of capital.[46] The BLS calculates capital stocks and rental prices for 90 asset types in 60 NIPA-level NAICS industries (and 29 assets for 86 4-digit manufacturing industries).

3.6.1. The Productive Capital Stock

The productive capital stock is measured as the sum of past investments net of deterioration. Past investments are assumed to decline in productive capacity according to an *age-efficiency function*, $\lambda(a,\Omega)$—where a is the age of the asset and Ω is its maximum service life—that represents the proportion of the investment's original productive capacity that remains at age a. Letting K_t denote the (net) productive capital stock of an asset in year t and I_{t-a} denote investment expenditures in year $t-a$ (that is, $t-a$ is the vintage of the asset), the productive capital stock for a group of identical assets that have a maximum service life of Ω is given by:[47]

$$K_t = \sum_{a=0}^{\Omega} \lambda(a,\Omega) I_{t-a} \qquad (3.11)$$

The BLS assumes a hyperbolic age-efficiency function, which is given by:

$$\lambda(a,\Omega) = \frac{(\Omega - a)}{(\Omega - \beta a)} \quad \text{if } a < \Omega \qquad (3.12)$$

$$\lambda(a,\Omega) = 0 \qquad \qquad \text{if } a \geq \Omega$$

where $\beta \leq 1$ is a shape parameter and $\lambda(\cdot)$ is concave, linear, or convex in age, depending on whether $\beta \gtreqless 0$ ($\beta = 1$ implies one-hoss shay[48]). The BLS assumes $\beta = 0.75$ for structures and $\beta = 0.5$ for equipment.[49]

The age-efficiency function accounts for three avenues by which the productive capacity of a group of assets can decline. First, assets become physically less productive when used or require more "down time" for maintenance or repairs. The second avenue is through obsolescence. The third is through failure. With all three of these avenues, one would expect the age-efficiency function for an individual asset to be concave with respect to age. Thus, even a group of one-hoss-shay assets would have a concave age-efficiency function due to failure and obsolescence.

The age-efficiency function in equation (3.12) assumes that all assets in the group have identical maximum service lives. However, the investment data that the BLS receive from BEA are for asset categories that contain assets that are similar, but likely have different maximum service lives.[50] Within an asset category, maximum service lives can differ because the assets are heterogeneous or because the assets are used differently. Therefore, within an asset category, the BLS assumes a distribution of maximum service lives for each type of asset and computes a cohort age-efficiency function that is a weighted average of the deterioration functions of the individual asset types.[51]

The cohort age-efficiency function for an asset category with mean service life of $\bar{\Omega}$ is given by

$$\bar{\lambda}(a,\bar{\Omega}) = \int_{\Omega^{min}}^{\Omega^{max}} \tilde{\phi}(a,k) \cdot \lambda(a,k) \, dk \qquad (3.13)$$

where the limits of the integral are the upper and lower bounds of the distribution of service lives, and $\Omega^{min} = 0.02\bar{\Omega}$ and $\Omega^{max} = 1.98\bar{\Omega}$.

The BLS assumes that $\tilde{\phi}(\cdot)$ is a modified truncated normal distribution with mean $\bar{\Omega}$ and $\sigma = 0.49\bar{\Omega}$. It is derived by truncating the normal distribution at ±2 standard deviations ($\bar{\Omega} \pm 0.98\bar{\Omega}$), shifting the density function downward so that it equals zero at the upper and lower bounds of the distribution, and then inflating the density function proportionately so that the final modified density, $\tilde{\phi}(\cdot)$, integrates to 1.

The final capital stock for each industry × asset-category combination is estimated by substituting equation (3.13) for the age-efficiency function in equation (3.11):

$$K_t = \sum_{a=0}^{\Omega^{max}} \bar{\lambda}(a,\bar{\Omega}) I_{t-a} \qquad (3.14)$$

Note that the upper limit of the summation differs from that in equation (3.11). In equation (3.11), maximum service life refers to homogeneous assets with a maximum service life of Ω. But in equation (3.14), the maximum service life is the maximum of the longest-lived asset in the asset category, Ω^{max}.

3.6.2. The Rental Price of Capital

Conceptually, the rental price, or *user cost*, of capital is the opportunity cost of holding and using it for a period of time. The equilibrium rental price is equal to the forgone earnings of money invested in the asset plus the decline in the asset's value. In its simplest form, the rental price for a period is set to the price of the asset multiplied by the sum of the depreciation rate and the appropriate rate of return:

$$c_t = p_t \left(r_t + d_t \right),$$ (3.15)

where c_t is the rental price for period t, p_t is the price of the asset, r_t is the rate of return, and d_t is the rate of depreciation.

The equation that the BLS uses to construct rental prices of capital is somewhat more complicated because it also accounts for inflation in the price of new assets and the effects of taxes. The BLS equation is given by:

$$c_{ijt} = \frac{\left(1 - u_t z_t - e_t\right)\left(P_{j,t-1} r_{it} + P_{j,t-1} d_{ijt} - \Delta P_{j,t-1}\right)}{1 - u_t} + P_{j,t-1} x_t$$ (3.16)

where:

u_t is the corporate income tax rate;
z_t is the present value of \$1 of the depreciation deduction;
e_t is the effective rate of the investment tax credit (zero since 1979);
r_t is the nominal industry-specific internal rate of return on capital;
d_{ijt} is the average rate of economic depreciation of asset j in industry i;
$P_{j,t-1}$ is the asset-specific (for asset category j) deflator for new capital goods;
$\Delta P_{j,t-1}$ is the revaluation of assets due to inflation in new goods prices (asset category j);
x_t is the rate of indirect taxes.

Rental prices are computed separately for each asset category × industry combination. Data are available, or easily calculated, for all of the variables in equation (3.16) except the internal rate of return, r.[52]

3.6.2.1. *Wealth Stock and Depreciation*

The BLS calculates the wealth stock in order to estimate depreciation. The wealth stock differs from the productive capital stock in that it measures the financial value of the capital stock, rather than its productive capacity. Analogously, depreciation differs from deterioration in that it measures the decline in the financial value of the capital stock, rather than the decline in its productive capacity. However, the two measures are linked through the age-efficiency function. The main difference between the productive capital stock and the wealth stock is that the productive stock is a point-in-time measure (the current productive capacity of past investments), whereas the wealth stock is a forward-looking measure (the discounted value of the remaining productive capacity of the productive capital stock).

The wealth stock is equal to the age-adjusted price of the asset multiplied by real investment summed over all asset cohorts that have positive productive capacity at time t:

$$W_t = \sum_{\tau=t}^{2t} p\left(\tau - t, \bar{\Omega}\right) \cdot I_{2t-\tau} \tag{3.17}$$

where $p\left(\tau - t, \bar{\Omega}\right)$ is the price of a $(\tau-t)$-year-old asset (group) that has an average maximum service life of $\bar{\Omega}$. The age-price function is derived from the cohort age-efficiency function and is equal to the discounted value of the remaining productive capacity of the asset divided by the discounted value of the productive capacity of the asset over its entire service life:

$$p\left(a, \bar{\Omega}\right) = \frac{\sum_{\alpha=a}^{2\bar{L}+1} \bar{\lambda}\left(\alpha, \bar{\Omega}\right) \cdot \left(1-\rho\right)^{\alpha-a}}{\sum_{\alpha=0}^{2\bar{L}+1} \bar{\lambda}\left(\alpha, \bar{\Omega}\right)\left(1-\rho\right)^{\alpha}} \tag{3.18}$$

where $\bar{\lambda}(a, \bar{\Omega})$ is the cohort age-efficiency function (3.13), and ρ is the real discount rate, which is assumed to be 4% per year. The age-price function declines over time from 1, when the asset is new, to 0 at the end of its service life. It declines more quickly than the age-efficiency function, because the financial value of an asset declines—due to decreased remaining service life—even if its productive capacity does not.

3.6.2.2. The Internal Rate of Return

The internal rate of return is calculated by setting capital income (which is available from BEA) equal to the product of the capital stock (from equation (3.14) and the rental price of capital (defined in equation (3.16)):

$$Y_{it} \equiv K_{it} c_{it}, \tag{3.19}$$

where Y_{it} is nominal capital income in industry i and K_{it} is the productive capital stock in industry i. Substituting equation (3.16) for c_t and arranging terms, the internal rate of return is:

$$r_{it} = \frac{Y_{it} - x K_{it} P_{i,t-1} - K_{it} \left(P_{i,t-1} d_{it} - \Delta P_{i,t-1}\right)\left(1 - u_t z_t - e_t\right) / \left(1 - u_t\right)}{K_{it} P_{i,t-1}\left(1 - u_t z_t - e_t\right) / \left(1 - u_t\right)} \tag{3.20}$$

where $P_{i,t-1}$ is the industry level price deflator:

$$P_{i,t-1} = \sum_{j \in J_i} \frac{K_{ij,t-1}}{\sum_{j \in J_i} K_{ij,t-1}} \cdot \frac{I_{ij,t-1}^N}{I_{ij,t-1}^R} = \sum_{j \in J_i} \frac{K_{ij,t-1}}{K_{i,t-1}} P_{j,t-1} \tag{3.21}$$

where J_i is the set of asset categories in industry i.[53]

In about one-third of industries the BLS uses an external rate of return, which is calculated as the capital-stock-weighted average of the industry internal rates of return (including the negative rates). The external rate of return is used: when the internal rate is negative, when the change in the rental price is abnormally large, when the capital composition adjustment is abnormally large, or when capital income is negative. Negative internal rates of return are the most common reason for using the external rate.

Note that capital income is available only for the corporate sector. For the non-corporate sector, the published data are for proprietors' income, which includes capital income and proprietors' labor compensation. The BLS estimates non-corporate capital income using data on proprietors' income, average wages of wage and salary workers, and the non-corporate capital stock. The BLS computes independent estimates of proprietors' labor compensation and capital income, sums these two components, and then inflates or deflates this sum so that it equals proprietors' income. These independent estimates are generated by assuming that proprietors earn the same hourly wage as wage and salary workers (for labor compensation) and that non-corporate capital earns the same rate of return as corporate capital (for capital income).

3.6.2.3. *Capital Input and Capital Composition*

The BLS assumes that the growth in capital inputs is approximately proportional to the growth of the productive capital stock. Capital input growth is calculated as a Törnqvist index, similar to MFP labor input as described in equation (3.8)—except that it is the Törnqvist aggregation of productive capital stock growth rates weighted by each asset × industry combination's share of total capital cost (averaged over both years).[54]

The contribution of capital inputs to output growth can be decomposed into the contributions of changes in the capital stock and changes in the composition ("quality") of the capital stock. The growth in capital input is calculated as described above. The effect of capital composition on output growth is simply the growth in capital input minus the growth in the (unweighted) capital stock. This decomposition is exactly analogous to the decomposition of labor input into changes in hours worked and changes in the composition of the workforce.[55]

3.7. ENERGY, MATERIALS, AND PURCHASED BUSINESS SERVICES

As the focus narrows to more specific industries that use sectoral output instead of value-added output, intermediate inputs (energy, materials, and purchased business services) take on a more visible role in productivity measurement and analysis. Manufacturing industry nominal values of materials, fuels, and electricity, as well as quantities of electricity consumed are obtained from the Annual Survey of Manufacturers and the economic censuses of the Census Bureau. Purchased business services are estimated using benchmark input–output tables and other annual industry data from the BEA. Prices of material and service inputs are based on the BLS price programs, the NIPAs, and the US Department of Agriculture. Prices of energy for manufacturing industries are obtained from economic censuses and annual surveys of the Census Bureau, as well as data from the Manufacturing Energy Consumption Survey of the Energy Information Administration, US Department of Energy.

For NIPA-level non-manufacturing industries, intermediate inputs (energy, materials, and purchased business services) are obtained from BEA's annual industry accounts. For air transportation, nominal values of cost of materials, services, fuels, and electricity are obtained from the Bureau of Transportation Statistics, US Department of Transportation, and are deflated with cost indexes from Airlines for America. For line-haul railroads, nominal values and price indexes are obtained from the Surface Transportation Board of the US Department of Transportation, and are supplemented with data from AMTRAK and other sources.

Total intermediate inputs are calculated as a Törnqvist aggregation of these three input classes. In addition, purchased materials and services are adjusted to exclude transactions between establishments in the same industry or sector to maintain consistency with the sectoral output concept.

3.8. Other Measures

In addition to the productivity measures described in the preceding, the BLS produces several related measures: labor compensation, unit labor costs, and labor share. These are not productivity measures per se, but they shed light on the BLS's productivity statistics by showing the relationship between productivity and compensation.

3.8.1. Labor Compensation

The BLS real hourly compensation data for the aggregate sectors of the US economy are based on data published by BEA as part of the national income accounts. These quarterly data include direct payments to labor—wages and salaries (including executive compensation), commissions, tips, bonuses, and payments in kind representing income to the recipients—and supplements to these direct payments. Supplements consist of vacation and holiday pay, all other types of paid leave, employer contributions to funds for social insurance, private pension and health and welfare plans, compensation for injuries, and so on.[56]

The BEA's source data come from the BLS and the Census Bureau. For service-providing, mining, and utility industries, labor compensation is derived using annual wage data from the Quarterly Census of Employment and Wages (QCEW) published by the BLS, along with data on employer costs for fringe benefits from the Census Bureau and the BEA. For manufacturing industries, annual payroll and fringe benefit data from the Census Bureau are used.

The BEA compensation measures cover only wage and salary workers, which means that the BLS must estimate the labor compensation of proprietors. Hourly compensation for proprietors is assumed to be the same as that of the average employee in that sector; this measure is multiplied by the hours worked by proprietors in each sector to arrive at proprietors' total labor compensation.

The BLS productivity program's labor compensation series is one of the most comprehensive wage series covering the private business sector. All private business sector workers are covered, and the measure includes virtually every form of compensation. Compared to other BLS earnings series (the production/nonsupervisory series from the Current Employment Statistics survey and an all-worker series from the Current Population Survey), the Labor Compensation series exhibits significantly stronger growth over the last 50 or so years, with the divergence becoming even greater starting in the late 1990s. Champagne, Kurmann, and Stewart (2015) compare these series and find that the main reason for the faster growth of the labor compensation series is the inclusion of non-wage compensation, which has grown in importance over the last few decades.

3.8.2. Unit Labor Costs

Unit labor costs measure the cost of labor required to produce one unit of output. This measure can be derived by dividing an index of nominal labor compensation by an index of real industry output, or directly by dividing nominal compensation per hour by real output per hour. As such, unit labor cost measures describe the relationship between hourly compensation and labor productivity, and can be used as an indicator of inflationary pressure on producers. Increases in hourly compensation increase unit labor costs, while increases in labor productivity increases lower unit labor costs.

3.8.3. Labor Share

Labor share is the portion of output that goes to labor, and is defined as nominal compensation divided by nominal output. Labor share relates the output of the private business sector to the compensation received by all workers in the private business sector, and tells us whether productivity growth has translated into higher incomes for labor. It also gives an indication of how competitive labor markets are—in a competitive labor market we would expect wages to rise with productivity. The decline in labor share over the last couple of decades has received a lot of attention in the popular press. The BLS does not publish data on labor share in its quarterly news release, although it is easily calculated from the data that are published.[57]

A paper by Elsby, Hobijn, and Şahin (2013) has taken issue with the BLS's labor share measure, specifically how the BLS estimates proprietors' labor compensation. As noted earlier, proprietors' labor compensation is estimated under the assumption that proprietors earn the same wage as all wage and salary workers, which can result in proprietors' labor compensation exceeding proprietors' income, implying a negative return to capital (this happened in the 1980s—see Elsby et al. 2013). Elsby et al. prefer the approach to estimating proprietors' labor compensation used in the BLS's MFP statistics (described earlier). Unfortunately, the capital data needed to estimate proprietors' capital income are available only with a substantial lag. The BLS is looking into ways of developing preliminary estimates of proprietors' capital income that can be used until the final data become available.

3.8.3.1. *The Compensation Gap*

Related to labor share is the compensation gap, which is equal to the difference between real output per hour (labor productivity) and real hourly compensation. This measure differs from labor share in that hourly compensation is deflated using the Consumer Price Index, while output per hour is deflated using an output price index. Thus, some of the gap is due to differences in the price indexes used. Figure 3.3 shows the growth rates of real hourly compensation, labor productivity, and the wage gap. The compensation gap has been growing since the 1960s, although there has been significant variation in the growth rates over time.[58]

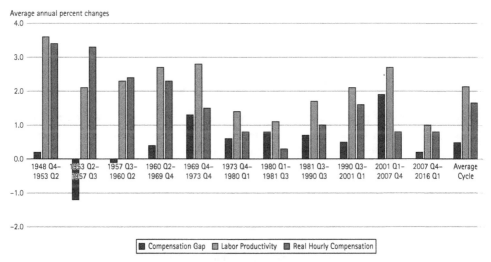

FIGURE 3.3. Compensation gap, labor productivity, and real hourly compensation.

Source: US Bureau of Labor Statistics.

3.9. Ongoing Efforts

The BLS is continually seeking ways to improve the quality of its existing data products by incorporating newly available data sources and developing improvements in methodology. And to meet ever-increasing customer demands for yet more timely data, the BLS is working to expand its data products and to speed up the production of existing products. Currently, the BLS is working on several projects to improve and expand its productivity measures. We describe a few of them in the following.

3.9.1. Improved Data on Asset Service Lives

The BLS currently receives data on depreciation rates and service lives from the BEA.[59] The BEA's data on depreciation rates come from a variety of sources, which include studies by Hulten and Wykoff (1981a, 1981b), studies from the 1970s by the Office of Industrial Economics of the US Department of the US Treasury, and studies from the 1980s and 1990s by the Office of Tax Analysis of the Department of the Treasury.[60] It is clear from the dates of these sources that the service lives used in BEA and BLS calculations are based on very old data.

The BLS is currently exploring ways of improving data on asset service lives by first looking for existing data, such as data from trade associations and surveys conducted by other countries. The most promising of these, from the BLS's perspective, is the survey conducted by Statistics Canada. The main difficulty with using these data is that the asset categories are not the same. In some cases the Statistics Canada classifications are more detailed, and in others they are more aggregated. The BLS has research underway to develop and evaluate new estimates of capital asset service lives using data from Statistics Canada.

3.9.2. Establishment-Level Productivity Statistics

The BLS currently publishes estimates of productivity growth at a fairly detailed industry level, which allows one to examine the contributions of individual industries to aggregate productivity growth. Because the BLS uses aggregate, industry-level data, it is not possible to look beyond detailed industries. However, there is a large literature that shows that examining within-industry variation can provide important insights into aggregate productivity growth. (see Syverson 2011 for a nice summary).

These studies have found that there is significant intra-industry dispersion in productivity (both labor productivity and MFP), and that high-productivity establishments are more likely to survive and grow compared with low-productivity establishments. A significant portion of aggregate productivity growth can be attributed to the reallocation of resources through entry and exit, but also among existing establishments as a result of resources being directed away from low-productivity establishments toward those with higher productivity.[61]

The BLS is currently working with the Census Bureau's Center for Economic Studies on a project to produce two new data products: a data set that researchers can use to study productivity at the establishment level, and a periodic news release that examines the dispersion of productivity across establishments within various manufacturing industries.

The project's initial findings, which are summarized in Cunningham et al. (2018), indicate that, in addition to considerable dispersion within industries, there is also considerable "dispersion in dispersion." That is, there is considerable variation, both between industries and within industries over time, in the amount of within-industry dispersion. Cunningham et al, also find that micro-level dynamics can account for a significant portion of industry productivity growth in official productivity statistics.

3.9.3. Output Concepts

Multifactor productivity can be measured using one of three different output concepts: gross output, sectoral output, or value-added output. As noted earlier, gross output is the total output produced by an industry or sector, while value-added output is equal to gross output less all intermediate inputs used in production. The BLS uses value-added output in constructing productivity measures for major sectors of the US economy. However, for industry productivity measurement the BLS prefers sectoral output.[62]

To illustrate the impact of output and input choices on productivity measurement, BLS research is underway to estimate multifactor productivity and industry contributions to aggregate multifactor productivity using these three different, but related, definitions of output. This study will examine the relationship between MFP growth rates calculated using the three output concepts, as well as the different conclusions about industry contributions to aggregate productivity implied by each framework.

3.9.4. Expanded Industry Coverage

As noted earlier, the BLS productivity program produces estimates for detailed industries. However, there is significantly less coverage of detailed industries in the services sector due to difficulties defining output in a way that is independent from measures of labor input (see Table 3.1).[63] For detailed services industries, the BLS uses deflated revenues when they are available, and uses direct measures of output when good revenue data and deflators are not available. The BLS is continually undertaking research to expand coverage in hard-to-measure industries and most recently introduced the following new series:

Construction: the BLS began publishing productivity measures for four construction industries in 2017. These measures use deflated revenues as the output measure, but they take advantage of newly-available price deflators that are a significant improvement over those that were previously available. The methodology and results are described in Sveikauskas, Rowe, Mildenberger, Price, and Young (2015, 2016, and 2018).

Education: the BLS introduced productivity measures for primary and secondary schools in 2017. For this industry, output cannot be measured using deflated revenues, because most schools are public.[64] For this reason, the BLS measures output as school enrollment adjusted for quality using standardized test scores (Powers 2016a). The BLS has also constructed some experimental series that account for other types of school output, such as transportation and food services, and that account for the difference between disabled and nondisabled students (Powers 2016b).

Commercial banking: the BLS revised its output and productivity measures for the commercial banking industry in 2012 (see Royster 2012). The previous BLS measure counted the different transactions, and aggregated them into a total output measure using employment-based weights. The new measure is a hybrid that uses a combination of deflated revenues (for fee-based services) and "physical" counts (for non-fee-based services). The new measure accounts for a wider range of bank services and uses revenue-based share weights (rather than the employment-based weights). This new measure better captures the broad range of services provided by the commercial banking industry.

3.9.5. Improved Measure of Proprietors' Labor Compensation

As noted earlier, the BLS assumes that proprietors earn the same hourly wage as wage-and-salary workers. The main drawback to this approach is that it treats the proprietors' return to capital as a residual, which can be negative. The BLS is conducting research to address this issue. Because the data on proprietors' capital income are not available until long after the end of the reference period, BLS would need to generate preliminary estimates of proprietor's labor compensation using data from prior periods.

As with other BLS data products, the estimates would be revised as new data become available, and final estimates would not be available until the official MFP (and capital) data are published.

3.9.6. Improved Estimates of Nonproduction and Supervisory Hours

The BLS introduced the CES all-employee hours series in 2006. However, the fact that the CES form instructs respondents to report the standard workweek for salaried employees is problematic for productivity measurement. Hourly workers are paid for every hour they work, that is not necessarily the case for salaried workers. Thus, the CES hours data may miss some cyclical variation in hours worked by salaried workers.[65]

The BLS's nonproduction-to-production worker ratio in equation (3.7) captures some of this variation. But, it implicitly assumes that production/nonsupervisory workers in the CES are paid for every hour they work. In fact, analysis of CPS data indicates that about 30% of production workers are not paid by the hour. The BLS is researching the possibility of adjusting the production-worker hours to account for off-the-clock work by non-hourly workers. As part of this research, BLS is looking into the possibility of using the CES all-employee hours data (adjusted to account for paid time off and off-the-clock work).

Notes

1. Disclaimer: Any views expressed in this chapter are ours and do not necessarily reflect those of the BLS.
2. The United States has a decentralized statistical system that consists a number of statistical agencies housed in different executive departments of the US government, and the Federal Reserve Board. The Bureau of Labor Statistics is housed in the Department of Labor, and produces data related to the labor force, including employment, unemployment, price, compensation, and productivity statistics. Much of this introduction draws from Dean and Harper (2001), which is a detailed description of the evolution of the BLS productivity program. BLS productivity data can be found at http://www.bls.gov/bls/productivity.htm
3. MFP is a broader measure of productivity in which an index of output is divided by an index of combined inputs—capital, labor, and, for more detailed industries, energy, materials, and purchased services.
4. For more information on the BLS methods, see "Technical Information about the BLS Major Sector Productivity and Cost Measures," February 2008, http://www.bls.gov/lpc/lpcmethods.pdf.
5. As a result of interest from data users, the BLS produces quarterly labor productivity measures and annual multifactor productivity measures for the total economy, but they are known to be downward biased and are therefore not included in the press releases. See "A Guide to the National Income and Product Accounts of the United States," http://www.bea.gov/national/pdf/nipaguid.pdf for a description of output measures.
6. Note that measured labor productivity growth can still be positive if, for example, the composition of the labor force shifts toward more skilled (i.e., higher-paid) workers or if these sectors become more capital intensive.
7. To facilitate comparisons across various time periods, quarterly estimates are expressed as annualized levels, and quarterly growth rates are expressed as annual growth rates using the following formula: $g_t = \left(\dfrac{X_t}{X_{t-1}}\right)^4 - 1$.
8. These include depository institutions, nondepository institutions, security and commodity brokers, insurance carriers, regulated investment offices, small business offices, and real estate investment trusts.
9. The press release includes quarterly and annual indexes, and percentage changes, for output per hour and related measures, such as unit labor costs, real and current dollar compensation per hour, and unit nonlabor payments. See http://www.bls.gov/lpc/home.htm.

10. BLS has looked into publishing quarterly estimates of labor productivity by industry, but the series is fairly volatile and BLS is not publishing these data at this time. See Eldridge (2016).

11. Industry measures produced include levels, annual indexes, and percentage changes for output per hour, output per employee, output, implicit price deflators for output, employment, hours of employees, labor compensation, and unit labor costs. Separate news releases are issued for selected services (http://www.bls.gov/news.release/prin2.nro.htm), manufacturing (http://www.bls.gov/news.release/prin.nro.htm), and trade (http://www.bls.gov/news.release/prin1.nro.htm).

12. In order to have a complete industry accounting of the private business sector, estimates of MFP for nonmanufacturing industries corresponding to the NIPA level are prepared with available data. For several industries, there are concerns about the quality of the measures, and therefore the nonmanufacturing measures are not included in official BLS news releases.

13. Internationally, value-added labor productivity is by far the most frequently computed productivity statistic. See OECD (2001). This measure is easy to calculate and accounts for all factors of production except capital and labor composition.

14. For more discussion, see Gullickson (1995).

15. For more information on how imports affect productivity measures, see Eldridge and Harper (2010).

16. The BLS is conducting research on the feasibility of constructing new productivity measures using alternative output concepts.

17. For a complete discussion to the advantages and disadvantages of the gross and value-added output concepts, see OECD (2001), Chapter 3, 23–33.

18. Note that for four-digit NAICS industries, it is not possible to account for labor composition.

19. See Dean, Harper, and Sherwood (1996).

20. If technical change within an industry does not affect all factors of production but operates primarily on the primary inputs, then value-added approach is preferable (OECD 2001, 28).

21. Thus, labor productivity measures using value-added are less sensitive to outsourcing than sectoral output labor productivity, although the reverse is true when measuring multifactor productivity. Multifactor productivity measured using a sectoral output concept is less sensitive to outsourcing than value-added based measures.

22. See Gullickson (1995).

23. See Chapter 11 of *BLS Handbook of Methods* for more information on industry measures.

24. Output and the corresponding inputs for these particular nonmanufacturing industries are difficult to measure and can produce productivity measures of inconsistent quality. Multifactor productivity is estimated for these industries because of interest from data users; however, data users are alerted to be cautious when interpreting these data.

25. This is also known as an RAS procedure. See Denton (1971). The Denton proportional first difference method preserves the pattern of growth in quarterly indicator series by minimizing the proportional period-to-period change while meeting the average annual level constraints.

26. Labor composition indexes are only calculated for major sector and NIPA-industry MFP data—labor composition indexes are not calculated for four-digit NIACS industries due to source data limitations.

27. Hours worked also include paid time for traveling between job sites, coffee breaks, and machine downtime. They also include time spent on maintenance activities.

28. Many countries use household data to estimate labor productivity, mainly because establishment data are not available. Some studies have examined how labor productivity growth would differ if CPS data were used exclusively. See Ramey (2012), Cociuba et al. (2012), and Burda et al. (2013), who also look at ATUS data.

29. For more information on the CES, see http://www.bls.gov/ces/.

30. For more information on the CPS, see http://www.bls.gov/cps/.

31. For more information on the NCS, see http://www.bls.gov/ncs/.

32. The CES all-employee hours series begins in March 2006, and BLS is currently evaluating whether to start using this new series.

33. In goods-producing industries, workers are divided into production and nonproduction workers. Nonproduction workers include professional, specialty, and technical workers; executive, administrative, and managerial workers; sales workers, and administrative support workers, including clerical. In service-providing industries, workers are divided into supervisory and nonsupervisory workers. Supervisory workers include all executives and managerial workers.

34. The Census Bureau's industry codes, which are used in the CPS, have become more consistent with the NAICS codes used in the establishment survey.

35. The BLS major-sector productivity program uses annual hours-worked to hours-paid ratios at the three-digit industry level in manufacturing and more aggregate data outside of manufacturing. The quarterly series is estimated using a Denton procedure. Industry level data below the three-digit level are constructed using the three-digit ratios wherever possible.

36. This methodology for estimating nonproduction/supervisory hours was introduced in August 2004. See Eldridge, Manser, and Otto (2004).

37. For major sectors, hours worked by employees are calculated at the three-digit NAICS industry level; for detailed industries, employee data are constructed at a more detailed level. Seasonally adjusted monthly data from the CES are used to construct quarterly averages of employment and average weekly hours. National Compensation Survey data are used at the three-digit level where available.

38. The published quarterly labor productivity statistics aggregate employee hours from 14 major industry groups and then adds aggregate hours worked by self-employed and unpaid family worker hours. For quarterly measures, this ratio is constructed by pooling three months of data, seasonally adjusted using an X-12-ARIMA program. The BLS performs indirect seasonal adjustment (seasonally adjusting the components of the hours calculation rather than the final value), which is preferred when component series are suspected of having distinct seasonal patterns. Given the limited observations for some industry groups, the CPS data are seasonally adjusted quarterly rather than monthly.

39. See Stewart (2014) for a longer discussion of the issues and a summary of the relevant research.

40. This should not be too surprising, because the reference week (the week that includes the 12th of the month) was chosen to avoid holidays.

41. The BLS only constructs labor composition estimates for the multifactor productivity measures for the private business sectors, manufacturing sector, three-digit manufacturing industries, and NIPA nonmanufacturing industries.

42. Households in the CPS are surveyed for four consecutive months, are out of the survey for eight months, and then resurveyed for four additional months. Earnings data are collected only in months-in-sample 4 and 8, which are referred to as the outgoing rotations.

43. The BLS recently switched from using the March Annual Social and Economic (ASEC) Supplement to using the ORG data. The main advantages of the ORG data are (1) a much larger sample size (two to three times the size of the ASEC sample depending on the year), and (2) better concordance between earnings and workers' industry classification. The main disadvantages are (1) there are no earnings data on second jobs, and (2) there are no earnings data on self-employed workers. The productivity program assumes that self-employed workers and workers on second jobs have the same hourly wage as demographically similar wage and salary workers on their main jobs. Although the ASEC data are more comprehensive in that they include data on earnings and hours from all jobs, including self-employment, the ASEC only collects industry data for the longest job held in the previous year, which means that some earnings and hours are not attributed to the correct industry when the individual held more than one job during the year. To further increase sample size, BLS will start using the entire CPS (that is, adding months in sample 1–3 and 5–7) to estimate changes in hours worked.

44. Additional information concerning data sources and methods of measuring labor composition can be found in Zoghi (2010).

45. Data on investments in physical assets are obtained from BEA. See Bureau of Labor Statistics [2009], Multifactor Productivity Trends, 2007, News Release, US Department of Labor, #09-0302 (March 25).

46. Land and inventories capital inputs are also calculated using productive stocks and estimated rental prices. However, land and inventories stock are estimated directly, rather than via the perpetual inventory method, and rental prices do not have a depreciation term.

47. BEA and many academic studies assume geometric deterioration, where the rate of deterioration is constant over time. This simplifies calculations, because this deterioration rate can be applied to the entire stock of capital, so there is no need to keep track of assets' vintages. However, Harper (1982, 1999) concluded that this assumption was unrealistic in many cases because assets' productivity tend to decline slowly at first and more rapidly as they approach the end of their service lives.

48. A one-hoss shay asset functions the same until the end of its service life, at which time it fails (from the Oliver Wendell Holmes, Sr. poem "The Deacon's Masterpiece or the Wonderful One-Hoss Shay").

49. These values were chosen because they are close to values estimated by Hulten and Wykoff (1981a) using actual data.

50. The BEA provides the BLS with information on service lives and depreciation rates. The BLS does not use the BEA service lives. Instead, the BLS estimates services lives so that, when used in conjunction with the hyperbolic age-efficiency function, they are consistent with the BEA's depreciation rates.

51. Because average maximum service lives are estimates and there are no data about individual asset types within categories, the distribution can also be viewed as accounting for the uncertainty, as well as heterogeneity.

52. Depreciation is calculated as the change in wealth stock minus the current year's investment. The depreciation rate is equal to depreciation divided by the wealth stock, although in practice the BLS uses the productive capital stock because it is less volatile than the wealth stock. The present value of $1 of tax depreciation allowance is calculated using equations from Hall and Jorgenson (1967), and the deflator is calculated from the real and nominal investment data the BLS gets from the BEA. Use of the internal rate of return is

necessary because of the assumption of perfect competition, which requires that profits be zero in equilibrium.

53. Note that equation (3.16) is defined for an industry × asset combination, whereas the rental price in equation (3.19) is defined for an industry only. Since capital income is available only at the industry level, equation (3.16) is modified using equation (3.21) so that the rental price used in the derivation of equation (3.20) is defined at the industry level.

54. This description glosses over many details. The Törnqvist aggregation is done in two steps, with the BEA asset categories being aggregated into seven asset groups for each industry (equipment, structures, land, rental residential capital, inventories, intellectual property products, and "all assets"). These asset group × industry combinations are then combined using the Törnqvist formula to arrive at the required intermediate and final aggregates.

55. Capital input can also be decomposed by type of asset, as in Table 3.1, which shows the portion of capital input attributable to each type of asset.

56. The data are adjusted from a cash basis to an accrual basis, so that the reference period is consistent with the output data.

57. See Giandrea and Sprague (2017) for a description of how the BLS measures labor's share.

58. For more on the compensation gap, see Fleck, Glaser, and Sprague (2011).

59. The BLS cannot use the BEA depreciation and service life data directly, because the BLS and BEA assume different age-efficiency functions. The BEA assumes a constant (geometric) rate of depreciation/deterioration, whereas the BLS's hyperbolic function assumes that the rate of deterioration increases as the asset ages. To account for this difference, the BLS recalculates average maximum asset service lives ($\overline{Q}$) so that the average deterioration rate is close to the BEA's constant rate. The resulting BLS estimates of service lives tend to be a little longer than those of the BEA.

60. BEA obtains service lives from these sources, and calculates depreciation rates (Fraumeni 1997; Giandrea 2015).

61. This line of research uses data from the ASM or data from other countries (for example, see Andrews, 2015). The US data reside at the Census Bureau, and access is restricted (this restriction also applies to BLS employees)—they can be used only for approved projects. This is major drawback of the decentralized US statistical system. It is very difficult for the different statistical agencies to share data.

62. For more discussion, see Gullickson (1995).

63. MFP measures are available for all NIPA-level services-providing industries in response to data users' demand. However, data users are cautioned that output and the corresponding inputs for nonmanufacturing industries are often difficult to measure and can produce productivity measures of inconsistent quality. Data users should be cautious when interpreting these data.

64. The BEA output measure for this industry is generated from data on labor compensation and other inputs.

65. Aaronson and Figura (2010) find evidence of this.

References

Aaronson, Stephanie, and Andrew Figura. 2010. "How Biased are Measures of Cyclical Movements in Productivity and Hours?" *Review of Income and Wealth* 56(3): 539–558.

Abraham, Katharine G., James R. Spletzer, and Jay C. Stewart. 1998. "Divergent Trends in Alternative Wage Series." In *Labor Statistics Measurement Issues*, edited by John Haltiwanger, Marilyn Manser, and Robert Topel, 293–325. Chicago: University of Chicago Press.

Abraham, Katharine G., James R. Spletzer, and Jay C. Stewart. 1999. "Why Do Different Wage Series Tell Different Stories?" *American Economic Review Papers and Proceedings* 89(2): 34–39.

Andrews, Dan, Chiara Criscuolo, and Peter N. Gal. 2015. *The Global Productivity Slowdown, Technology Divergence and Public Policy: A Firm Level Perspective.* Paris: OECD.

Burda, Michael C., Daniel S. Hamermesh, and Jay Stewart. 2013. "Cyclical Variation in Labor Hours and Productivity Using the ATUS." *American Economic Review Papers & Proceedings* 103(3): 99–104.

Champagne, Julien, Andre Kurmann, and Jay Stewart. 2015. "Reconciling the Divergence in Aggregate U.S. Wage Series." *Labour Economics* 49, December: 27–41.

Cociuba, Simona E., Edward C. Prescott, and Alexander Ueberfeldt. 2012. "U.S. Hours and Productivity Using CPS Hours Worked Data: 1947-III to 2011-IV." Unpublished manuscript.

Cunningham, Cindy, Lucia Foster, Cheryl Grim, John Haltiwanger, Sabrina Wulff Pabilonia, Jay Stewart, Zoltan Wolf. 2018. "Dispersion in Dispersion: Measuring Establishment-Level Differences in Productivity." Working Paper 18–25, Center for Economic Studies, US Census Bureau.

Dean, Edwin R., Michael J Harper, and Mark S Sherwood. 1996. "Productivity Measurement with Changing Weight Indices of Outputs and Inputs." In *Industry Productivity: International Comparisons and Measurement Issues,* edited by Bart van Ark, 183–215. Paris: OECD.

Dean, Edwin R., and Michael J Harper. 2001. "The BLS Productivity Measurement Program." In *New Developments in Productivity Analysis,* edited by Charles R. Hulten, Edwin R. Dean, and Michael J. Harper, 55–84. Chicago: University of Chicago Press.

Denton, Frank T. 1971. "Adjustment of Monthly or Quarterly Series to Annual Totals: An Approach Based on Quadratic Minimization." *Journal of the American Statistical Association* 66 (333): 99–102.

Eldridge, Lucy P. 2016. "Measuring Quarterly Labor Productivity by Industry." *Monthly Labor Review.* http://www.bls.gov/opub/mlr/2016/article/measuring-quarterly-labor-productivity-by-industry.htm.

Eldridge, Lucy P., and Michael J. Harper. 2010. "Effects of Imported Intermediate Inputs on Productivity." *Monthly Labor Review* 133(6): 3–15.

Eldridge, Lucy P., Marilyn E. Manser, and Phyllis F. Otto. 2004. "Alternative Measures of Supervisory Employee Hours and Productivity Growth." *Monthly Labor Review* 127(4): 9–28.

Eldridge, Lucy P., and Sabrina Pabilonia. 2010. "Bringing Work Home: Implications for BLS Productivity Measures." *Monthly Labor Review* 133(12): 18–35.

Elsby, Michael W. L., Bart Hobijn, and Aysegul Şahin. 2013. "The Decline of the U.S. Labor Share." *Brookings Papers on Economic Activity* 44(2): 1–63.

Fleck, Susan, John Glaser, and Shawn Sprague. 2011. "The Compensation-Productivity Gap: A Visual Essay. *Monthly Labor Review* 134(1): 57–69.

Fraumeni, Barbara. 1997. "The Measurement of Depreciation in the U.S. National Income and Product Accounts." *Survey of Current Business* (July): 7–23.

Frazis, Harley, and Jay Stewart. 2004. "What Can Time Use Data Tell Us about Hours of Work?" *Monthly Labor Review* 127(12): 3–9.

Frazis, Harley, and Jay Stewart. 2009. "Comparing Hours Worked per Job in the Current Population Survey and the American Time Use Survey." *Social Indicators Research* 93(1): 191–195.

Frazis, Harley, and Jay Stewart. 2010. "Why Do BLS Hours Series Tell Different Stories about Trends in Hours Worked?" In *Labor in the New Economy,* edited by Katharine G. Abraham,

James R. Spletzer, and Michael J. Harper, 343–372. NBER Studies in Income and Wealth. Chicago: University of Chicago Press.

Giandrea, Michael, and Shawn Sprague. 2017. "Estimating Labor Share." *Monthly Labor Review*, February. https://www.bls.gov/opub/mlr/2017/article/estimating-the-us-labor-share.htm

Giandrea, Michael. 2015. "Estimation of Asset Service Lives by the Bureau of Labor Statistics." Internal BLS report.

Gullickson, William. 1995. "Measurement of Productivity Growth in U.S. Manufacturing." *Monthly Labor Review* 118(7): 13–28.

Hall, R. E., and Dale W. Jorgenson. 1967. "Tax Policy and Investment Behavior." *American Economic Review* 57(3): 391–414.

Harper, Michael J. 1982. "The Measurement of Productive Capital Stock, Capital Wealth, and Capital Services." BLS Working Paper 128, June.

Harper, Michael J. 1999. "Estimating Capital Inputs for Productivity Measurement: An Overview of U.S. Concepts and Methods." *International Statistical Review* 67(3): 327–337.

Hulten, Charles R., and Frank C. Wykoff. 1981a. "The Estimation of Economic Depreciation Using Vintage Asset Prices." *Journal of Econometrics* 15: 367–396.

Hulten, Charles R., and Frank C. Wykoff. 1981b. "The Measurement of Economic Depreciation." In *Depreciation, Inflation, and the Taxation of Income from Capital*, edited by Charles R. Hulten, 81–125. Urban Institute Press, Washington, DC.

OECD. 2001. *Measuring Productivity: Measurement of Aggregate and Industry-Level Productivity Growth*. Paris: OECD.

Powers, Susan G. 2016a. "Labor Productivity Growth in Elementary and Secondary School Services: 1989–2012." *Monthly Labor Review*, June. http://www.bls.gov/opub/mlr/2016/article/labor-productivity-growth-in-elementary-and-secondary-school-services.htm.

Powers, Susan G. 2016b. "Heterogeneous Education Outputs in Public School Elementary and Secondary Education Output Measures: Disabled and Non-Disabled Students." *Monthly Labor Review*, September. https://www.bls.gov/opub/mlr/2016/article/heterogeneous-education-output-measures-for-public-school-students-with-and-without-disabilities.htm

Ramey, Valerie. 2012. "The Impact of Hours Measures on the Trend and Cycle Behavior of U.S. Labor Productivity." Unpublished paper, University of California, San Diego.

Royster, Sara E. 2012. "Improved Measures of Commercial Banking Output and Productivity." *Monthly Labor Review* 135(7): 3–17.

Solow, Robert M. 1957. "Technical Change and the Aggregate Production Function." *Review of Economics and Statistics* 39(3): 312–320.

Stewart, Jay. 2014. "The Importance and Challenges of Measuring Work Hours." *IZA World of Labor*. http://wol.iza.org/articles/importance-and-challenges-of-measuring-work-hours/long.

Sveikauskas, Leo, Samuel Rowe, James Mildenberger, Jennifer Price, and Arthur Young. 2015. "Productivity Growth in Construction." BLS Working Paper 478.

Sveikauskas, Leo, Samuel Rowe, James Mildenberger, Jennifer Price, and Arthur Young. 2016. "Productivity Growth in Construction." *Journal of Construction Engineering and Management*. 142(10). http://ascelibrary.org/doi/abs/10.1061/%28ASCE%29CO.1943-7862.0001138.

Sveikauskas, Leo, Samuel Rowe, James Mildenberger, Jennifer Price, and Arthur Young. 2018. "*Measuring* Productivity Growth in Construction." *Monthly Labor Review*. https://www.bls.gov/opub/mlr/2018/article/measuring-productivity-growth-in-construction.htm

Syverson, Chad. 2011. "What Determines Productivity?" *Journal of Economic Literature* 49(2): 326–365.

US Bureau of Labor Statistics. "Chapter 11: Industry Productivity Measures," BLS Handbook of Methods. https://www.bls.gov/opub/hom/pdf/homch11.pdf

Zoghi, Cynthia. 2010. "Measuring Labor Composition: A Comparison of Alternate Methodologies." In *Labor in the New Economy*, edited by Katharine G. Abraham, James R. Spletzer, and Michael J. Harper, 457–485. NBER Studies in Income and Wealth. Chicago: University of Chicago Press.

CHAPTER 4

THEORETICAL PRODUCTIVITY INDICES

R. ROBERT RUSSELL

4.1. INTRODUCTION: SOLOW TECHNICAL CHANGE

THIS chapter focuses on *theoretical* productivity indices, defined for the purpose at hand as indices predicated on the assumption that the technology is known and nonstochastic but unspecified (e.g., nonparameterized).[1] See Chapter 2 of this *Handbook* for a thorough discussion of more expansive notions of nonstochastic productivity indices.

I begin, in this introductory section, with a preview of the chapter, motivating the contents with a retrospective look at Solow's (1957) seminal contribution to the measurement of technical change, the genesis of today's analysis of productivity comparisons (across production units as well as time).

A (mostly inconsequential) generalization of Solow's setup[2] is as follows:

$$y^t = f^t(x^t) \quad \forall\, t,$$

where, for observation t, $y^t \in \mathbf{R}_+$ is the scalar output quantity, $x^t \in \mathbf{R}_+^n$ is an input quantity vector, and $f^t \colon \mathbf{R}_+^n \to \mathbf{R}_+$ is the production function.

The nomenclature of the chapter adheres to Solow's context in which t is a time index, but the results apply equally to cross-sectional analysis, where t is an index assigned to different economic units (e.g., firms or national economies).

For expositional purposes only, Solow considered the special case of neutral technological change:

$$y^t = a^t f(x^t) \quad \forall\, t, \tag{4.1}$$

where a^t is a scalar indicator of the state of technology and $f : \mathbf{R}_+^n \to \mathbf{R}_+$ is a stationary (reference) production function. Additionally, $a^t = y^t / f(x^t)$ has come to be interpreted as *total factor productivity* at observation t, where $f(x^t)$ is the (aggregate) total factor input at observation t.

Solow's definition of technical change from a base period b to a current period c, under the assumption of neutral technological change, is given simply by the relative productivity states, a^c / a^b. The Solow productivity index under neutrality, $\Pi^{SN} : \mathbf{R}_+^{2(n+1)} \to \mathbf{R}_+$, is then obtained by substitution from (4.1):[3]

$$\Pi^{SN}(x^b, x^c, y^b, y^c) := \frac{a^c}{a^b} = \frac{y^c / f(x^c)}{y^b / f(x^b)}. \tag{4.2}$$

The last term in (4.2) underscores the interpretation of Solow's technical change index, under the assumption of neutral technological change, as an index of total-factor productivity change.

Another evocative interpretation of Solow technical change is obtained by multiplying top and bottom of a^c / a^b by $f(x^b)$ to obtain

$$\Pi^{SN}(x^b, x^c, y^b, y^c) := \frac{a^c f(x^b)}{a^b f(x^b)} = \frac{f^c(x^b)}{y^b}. \tag{4.3}$$

The last term indicates that Solow technical change is given by the ratio of (a) the maximal (frontier) output that can be produced with the base-period input vector using the current-period technology to (b) the (frontier) output produced in the base period. While the last equality in (4.3) holds only under the assumption of neutral technology change, the last term is a natural definition of technological change for the general case of (possibly) non-neutral technological change.

Under neutrality, the proportional shift of the frontier is identical across input vectors; under non-neutrality, when the frontier shift is input dependent, the last term in (4.3) measures the shift in the frontier specifically at the base-period input vector. In fact, as Solow did not assume neutrality in his calculations, his index was actually *defined* by

$$\Pi^{Sb}(x^b, x^c, y^b, y^c) := \frac{f^c(x^b)}{y^b}, \tag{4.4}$$

which is input-quantity dependent and indicates how much more can be produced with the base-period input vector using the current-period technology (rather than the base-period technology).

While Solow measured technological change at the base-period input quantity (using the current-period technology), he could just as well have measured it at the current-period input vector (using the base-period technology):

$$\Pi^{Sc}(x^b, x^c, y^b, y^c) := \frac{y^c}{f^b(x^c)}. \tag{4.5}$$

The indices in (4.4) and (4.5) are identical if and only if technological change is neutral; that is, if and only if the production function is given by (4.1).

The indices (4.4) and (4.5) are special cases—owing to the restriction to a single output—of the widely employed (output-oriented) *Malmquist productivity indices* formulated by Caves, Christensen, and Diewert (1982) (CCD). Generalization of (4.4) and (4.5) to multiple outputs requires an aggregation rule to obtain a measure of the change in "output." The aggregation rule employed by CCD is the Malmquist (1953) output distance (gauge) function (independently formulated by Shephard 1953). In this context, it serves essentially as a measure of the "radial distance" from an output vector to a future or past technology frontier in output space (i.e., a production possibility frontier) for a fixed input, much as, for example, $y^c / f^b(x^c)$ is a proportional measure of the distance from current-period output to the base-period production frontier at the current-period input vector x^c.

Measuring technological change in the region of ⟨input, output⟩ space at which the economic unit is operating has intuitive appeal, but there seems to be no compelling criterion to choose between using the current-period technology and the base-period quantities (4.4) or using the base-period technology and the current-period quantities (4.5). Diewert (1992a) therefore suggests adoption of the Fisher "ideal" index number formulation—namely, taking the geometric average of the two indices. In the single-output case, the *Malmquist "ideal" output-based productivity index* is

$$\Pi^{MI}(x^b, x^c, y^b, y^c) = \left(\frac{f^c(x^b)}{y^b} \right)^{1/2} \left(\frac{y^c}{f^b(x^c)} \right)^{1/2}.$$

As the preceding nomenclature suggests, Diewert also formulated *input-based* Malmquist and Malmquist "ideal" indices. These formulations employ the Malmquist-Shephard input-oriented distance function, a radial measure of the distance of an input vector from a base-period or current-period frontier in input space (i.e., an isoquant).

The CCD-Diewert development of the various Malmquist productivity indices in the general case of multiple outputs and multiple inputs is described in section 4.3 (following presentation of some preliminaries in section 4.2).

Suppose we multiply top and bottom of the indices in (4.4) and (4.5) by $y^c = f^c(x^c)$ and $y^b = f^b(x^b)$, respectively, to obtain

$$\Pi^{Sb}(x^b, x^c, y^b, y^c) = \frac{y^c / y^b}{f^c(x^c) / f^c(x^b)} \tag{4.6}$$

and

$$\Pi^{Sc}(y^c, y^b, x^c, x^b) = \frac{y^c / y^b}{f^b(x^b) / f^b(x^c)}. \tag{4.7}$$

Thus, the Solow index can also be interpreted as a measure of the change in output divided by a measure of the change in an aggregate input, where the input aggregation rule is the current-period production function in (4.6) and the base-period production function in (4.7).[4]

Following up on a suggestion of Diewert (1992a), Bjurek (1996) exploited the CCD theory of Malmquist indices of aggregate input and output change (based respectively on Malmquist-Shephard input and output distance functions) to develop multiple-output (as well as multiple-input) productivity indices analogous to (4.6) and (4.7).[5] Diewert attributed the ideas behind this index formulation to Moorsteen (1961) and (maybe) Hicks (1961), and the *Hicks-Moorsteen productivity index* assignation has stuck. These indices are exposited in section 4.4.

The CCD and Bjurek papers are essential to understanding most of today's research on multiple-output productivity, and the remainder of this chapter covers extensions and refinements of the Malmquist and Hicks-Moorsteen indices. The possibility of technological inefficiency—production below the frontier—is implicit in the CCD-Bjurek framework, since the Malmquist-Shephard input and output distance functions serve as measures of inefficiency as well as shifts in the production frontier. Exploiting this dual use of the distance functions, Färe, Grosskopf, Norris, and Zhang (1994) decompose the Malmquist index into two components: technological change (shifts in the production frontier) and efficiency change (movements toward or away from the frontier). This decomposition is discussed in section 4.5.

Much—perhaps most—of the theoretical research on productivity indices in recent years has been directed at the incorporation of additional decomposition components, like scale effects and input- or output-mix effects; this literature is also reviewed in section 4.5.

The Malmquist and Hicks-Moorsteen indices, owing to their radial structure, are not applicable to the measurement of productivity in the full space of inputs and outputs.[6] Section 4.6 describes two nonradial indices: the hyperbolic index and the (Luenberger 1992) directional-distance index.

Dual productivity indices (employing cost and revenue functions) and aggregation of productivity indices across economic units are discussed in sections 4.7 and 4.8, respectively.

In the concluding comments in section 4.9, I take liberties—for the most part resisted in earlier sections—to offer some evaluative comments, particularly with respect to the comparison of the Malmquist and Hicks-Moorsteen approaches.

4.2. Preliminaries: Technological Change and Productivity Indices

4.2.1. Technologies

Although I frequently refer to the unit of analysis as a "firm," the theory is applicable to any type of economic unit, even an aggregate (national) economy. The firm produces a vector of outputs $y \in \mathbf{R}_+^m$ using a vector of inputs $x \in \mathbf{R}_+^n$. To avoid the nuisance of dealing with null vectors, some of our functions map from production space with the origins of input and output space expunged:[7] $\dot{\mathbf{R}}_+^{n+m} = \mathbf{R}_+^n \setminus \{0^{[n]}\} \times \mathbf{R}_+^m \setminus \{0^{[m]}\} =: \dot{\mathbf{R}}_+^n \times \dot{\mathbf{R}}_+^m$.

The firm's production is constrained by a (known) technology—the set of technologically feasible production vectors,

$$T = \left\{ \langle x, y \rangle \in \mathbf{R}_+^{n+m} \mid x \text{ can produce } y \right\}.$$

Given the technology T, the output-possibility set for input vector x is[8]

$$P(x, T) = \left\{ y \in \mathbf{R}_+^m \mid \langle x, y \rangle \in T \right\}$$

and the input-requirement set for output vector y is

$$L(y, T) = \left\{ x \in \mathbf{R}_+^n \mid \langle x, y \rangle \in T \right\}.$$

Clearly, $\langle x, y \rangle \in T \Leftrightarrow x \in L(y, T) \Leftrightarrow y \in P(x, T)$.

We restrict the set of technologies, denoted $\mathcal{T}$, to those that are closed and satisfy free input disposability ($L(y, T) + \mathbf{R}_+^n = L(y, T)$ for all $y \in \mathbf{R}_+^m$) and free output disposability ($P(x, T) = \left(P(x, T) - \dot{\mathbf{R}}_+^m \right) \cap \mathbf{R}_+^m$ for all $x \in \mathbf{R}_+^n$). As T is closed for all $T \in \mathcal{T}$, so are the slices, $L(y, T)$ and $P(x, T)$, for all $\langle x, y \rangle \in \mathbf{R}_+^{n+m}$.

The isoquant for output $y \in \dot{\mathbf{R}}_+^m$ is given by

$$I(y, T) = \{ x \in L(y, T) \mid \lambda x \notin L(y) \; \forall \; \lambda < 1 \},$$

and the production possibility surface for input $x \in \mathbf{R}_+^n$ is

$$\Gamma(x, T) = \{ y \in P(x, T) \mid \lambda y \notin P(x) \; \forall \; \lambda > 1 \}.$$

4.2.2. Distance Functions

An essential building block of multiple-output (and, of course, multiple-input) productivity analysis is the "distance function," independently introduced into the economics literature,[9] in different contexts and with different objectives, by Debreu (1951), Malmquist (1953), and Shephard (1953). Malmquist's context is the closest to the thrust of this chapter (even though his objective was the construction of consumer cost-of-living indices rather than productivity indices).

The input distance function, $D_I : \mathbf{N} \times \mathcal{T} \to \mathbf{R}_{++}$, maps from a subset of production space, $\mathbf{N} = \left\{ \langle x, y \rangle \in \dot{\mathbf{R}}_+^{n+m} \mid L(y, T) \neq \varnothing \right\}$, and the set of allowable technologies into the positive real line and is defined by

$$D_I(x, y, T) = \max \left\{ \lambda > 0 \mid x / \lambda \in L(y, T) \right\}.$$

Thus, the input distance function is defined as the maximal (proportional) radial contraction (or minimal radial expansion) of a given input vector consistent with technological feasibility of production of a given output vector.[10] Thus, the input distance function can be characterized as a notion of "radial distance" of an input-quantity vector from the frontier of the technology (the isoquant in input space)—a characterization that, as we shall see, is evocative in the construction of productivity indices.

With our (parsimonious) restrictions on the technology (closedness and free input disposability), D_I is well-defined, homogeneous of degree one and nondecreasing in x, and nonincreasing in y for all $\langle x, y, T \rangle \in \mathbf{N} \times T$. Moreover, $x \in L(y, T) \Leftrightarrow D_I(y, x, T) \geq 1$, and $x \in I(y, T) \Leftrightarrow D_I(x, y, T) = 1$, so that, for any $y \in \dot{\mathbf{R}}_+^m$, $L(y, T)$ is recovered from D_I by

$$L(y, T) = \{ x \in \mathbf{R}_+^n \mid D_I(x, y, T) \geq 1 \}$$

and $I(y, T)$ is recovered from D_I by

$$I(y, T) = \{ x \in \mathbf{R}_+^n \mid D_I(x, y, T) = 1 \}.$$

Thus, the input distance function also serves as a functional representation of the technology.

The output distance function, $D_O : \mathbf{N} \times T \to \mathbf{R}_+$, is similarly defined by

$$D_O(x, y, T) = \min \{ \lambda > 0 \mid y / \lambda \in P(x, T) \};$$

that is, as the minimal (proportional) radial contraction (or maximal radial expansion) of a given output vector consistent with technological feasibility of production for a given input vector. Thus, the output distance function is the "radial distance" of an output-quantity vector from the frontier of the technology (the production possibility surface in output space).[11]

With our restrictions on the technology (closedness, free output disposability, and boundedness of $P(x, T)$), D_O is well-defined, homogeneous of degree one and nondecreasing in y, and nonincreasing in x for all $\langle x, y \rangle \in \dot{\mathbf{R}}_+^{n+m}$. Moreover, $y \in P(x, T) \Leftrightarrow D_O(x, y, T) \leq 1$, so that, for any $x \in \dot{\mathbf{R}}_+^n$, $P(x, T)$ is recovered by

$$P(x, T) = \{ y \in \mathbf{R}_+^m \mid D_O(x, y, T) \leq 1 \}$$

and $\Gamma(x, T)$ is recovered by

$$\Gamma(x, T) = \{ y \in \mathbf{R}_+^m \mid D_O(x, y, T) = 1 \},$$

indicating that the output distance function is a functional representation of the technology.

Finally, it is easy to see that each of these distance functions is independent of units of measurement.[12]

4.2.3. Technological Efficiency

A firm is input inefficient at time t if $D_I(x^t, y^t, T^t) > 1$ and output inefficient if $D_O(x^t, y^t, T^t) < 1$. Moreover, with restriction of the distance-function domains to feasible production vectors $\langle x^t, y^t \rangle \in T^t$, $1/D_I(x^t, y^t, T^t) =: E_I(x^t, y^t, T^t)$ and $D_O(x^t, y^t, T^t) =: E_O(x^t, y^t, T^t)$ are, respectively, *(Debreu-Farrell) input and output efficiency indices* (Debreu 1951; Farrell 1957). Each measures the radial distance of the quantity vector from the frontier and, for technologically feasible production vectors, maps into the $(0,1]$ interval.

4.2.4. Technological Change

The essence of technological comparisons across periods (or across production units) is the comparison of production possibilities, as reflected by production possibility sets or input requirement sets, under counterfactual assumptions about input availability or output requirement.

The production possibility set at the *current-period* input vector using the *base-period* technology is $P(x^c, T^b)$, and the production possibility set at the base-period input vector using the current-period technology is $P(x^b, T^c)$. The corresponding production possibility surfaces are $\Gamma(x^c, T^b)$ and $\Gamma(x^b, T^c)$.

If

$$P(x^c, T^b) \subset P^c(x^c, T^c) \quad \wedge \quad \Gamma(x^c, T^b) \cap \Gamma(x^c, T^c) = \varnothing, \tag{4.8}$$

we say that, measuring qualitatively in output space and normalizing on the current-period input vector, the technology of the economic unit unambiguously (globally) improved between b and c. This normalization is arbitrary, and we could just as well normalize on the base-period input vector, in which case the technology of the economic unit unambiguously improved if

$$P(x^b, T^b) \subset P(x^b, T^c) \quad \wedge \quad \Gamma(x^b, T^b) \cap \Gamma(x^b, T^c) = \varnothing. \tag{4.9}$$

(These characterizations of unambiguous technological improvement can similarly be expressed in terms of [shrinking] input requirement sets at stipulated output vectors.)

These criteria for global technological change are overly strong: a more reasonable requirement is to normalize on the output quantity vector as well—that is, to require only that the production possibility set expand in a neighborhood of the output quantity vector, y^c in (4.8) or y^b in (4.9). This is the approach adopted by CCD in their pathbreaking analysis of productivity measurement, entailing quantitative as well as qualitative measurement using the output distance function as a measure of the radial distance of an output vector in one period from the production possibility surface of the technology in the other period.

The qualitative characterization of technological change in input space is analogous. The input requirement set at the *current-period* output vector using the *base-period* technology is $L(y^c, T^b)$, and the input requirement set at the base-period output vector using the current-period technology is $L(y^b,T^c)$. The corresponding isoquants are $I(y^c,T^b)$ and $I(y^b,T^c)$.

Under alternative normalizations, the technology of the economic unit unambiguously (globally) improves between b and c if $L(y^c,T^c) \subset L(y^c,T^b)$ or $L(y^b,T^c) \subset L(y^b,T^b)$. More reasonably, we can say that there has been technological progress (in the appropriate normalization) if the input requirement set expands (toward the origin) in a neighborhood of x^c or, alternatively, x^b.

4.2.5. Productivity Indices

At the most abstract, generic (even austere) level, the definition of a multiple-output productivity index is a mapping, $\Pi : \mathbf{R}_+^{2(n+m)} \to \mathbf{R}_{++}$, with image $\Pi\left(x^b,x^c,y^b,y^c\right)$. Without some imposed structure or required set of properties, however, this concept is close to vacuous. The two main approaches to adding structure are the axiomatic, or test, approach (requiring that the index satisfy certain properties, like monotonicity) and the economic approach (tying the index to economic or technological constructs). (These approaches are complementary.)

The desirable properties of productivity indices include the following:[13]

(I) *Identity:* $\langle x^b,y^b \rangle = \langle x^c,y^c \rangle \Rightarrow \Pi(x^b,x^c,y^b,y^c)=1$.

(M) *Monotonicity:* Productivity is nondecreasing in current-period output and base-period inputs and nonincreasing in current-period inputs and base-period outputs:

$$\langle x^b,-x^c,-y^b,y^c \rangle \geq \langle \hat{x}^b,-\hat{x}^c,-\hat{y}^b,\hat{y}^c \rangle$$
$$\Rightarrow \Pi(x^b,x^c,y^b,y^c) \geq \Pi(\hat{x}^b,\hat{x}^c,\hat{y}^b,\hat{y}^c).$$

(UI) *Invariance with respect to units of measurement (commensurability):*

$$\Pi\left(x^b K_x,x^c K_x,y^b K_y,y^c K_y\right) = \Pi\left(x^b,x^c,y^b,y^c\right),$$

for arbitrary $n \times n$ and $m \times m$ positive diagonal (unit transformation) matrices, K_x and K_y.

(P) *Proportionality:* Π is homogeneous of degree 1 in y^c and homogeneous of degree –1 in x^c (hence homogeneous of degree zero in $\langle x^c,y^c \rangle$).

(T) *Transitivity:* For any three periods, $b,c,$ and d, the product of the measured productivity changes from period b to period c and from period c to period d is equal to the productivity change from period b to period d:

$$\Pi\left(x^b,x^c,y^b,y^c\right) \cdot \Pi\left(x^c,x^d,y^c,y^d\right) = \Pi\left(x^b,x^d,y^b,y^d\right).^{14}$$

Linkage to technological or economic concepts requires a more constructive approach. To this end, we expand the domain to encompass the space of technologies T.[15] The extended productivity index (in a slight abuse of notation), $\Pi : \mathbf{R}_{+}^{2(n+m)} \times T^2 \to \mathbf{R}_{++}$, now has the image $\Pi\left(x^b, x^c, y^b, y^c, T^b, T^c\right)$. In many specific cases, the index is invariant with respect to changes in some quantity vectors or one of the technologies.

Application of the preceding axioms to indices with the enhanced domain is straightforward. (One could add axioms related to the technologies, but this approach, to my knowledge, has not been explored.)

4.3. Malmquist Productivity Indices

Caves, Christensen, and Diewert (1982) (CCD) imposed structure by a natural linkage to the technology using the distance function as a representation of the technology and as a notion of distance from a quantity vector in one period to a technological frontier in another. They proposed four basic productivity indices predicated on alternative normalizations with respect to the choice of the base period or the current period for the reference technology and for the production vector. These indices are defined as follows (where the relation $\underset{\text{eff}}{=}$ holds only under the assumption of technological efficiency):[16]

Output-based, technology b-based Malmquist productivity index:

$$\Pi_O^M\left(x^b, x^c, y^b, y^c, T^b\right) = \frac{D_O(x^c, y^c, T^b)}{D_O\left(x^b, y^b, T^b\right)} \underset{\text{eff}}{=} D_O(x^c, y^c, T^b)$$

$$= \min\left\{\lambda > 0 \mid y^c / \lambda \in P(x^c, T^b)\right\} =: \bar{\Pi}_O^M(x^c, y^c, T^b).$$
(4.10)

Output-based, technology c-based Malmquist productivity index:

$$\Pi_O^M\left(x^b, x^c, y^b, y^c, T^c\right) = \frac{D_O\left(x^c, y^c, T^c\right)}{D_O\left(x^b, y^b, T^c\right)} \underset{\text{eff}}{=} \frac{1}{D_O\left(x^b, y^b, T^c\right)}$$

$$= \left(\min\left\{\lambda > 0 \mid y^b / \lambda \in P(x^b, T^c)\right\}\right)^{-1} =: \bar{\Pi}_O^M(x^b, y^b, T^c).$$
(4.11)

Input-based, technology b-based Malmquist productivity index:

$$\Pi_I^M\left(x^b, x^c, y^b, y^c, T^b\right) = \frac{D_I(x^b, y^b, T^b)}{D_I(x^c, y^c, T^b)} \underset{\text{eff}}{=} \frac{1}{D_I(x^c, y^c, T^b)}$$

$$= \left(\max\left\{\lambda > 0 \mid x^c / \lambda \in L(y^c, T^b)\right\}\right)^{-1} =: \bar{\Pi}_I^M(x^c, y^c, T^b).$$
(4.12)

Input-based, technology c-based Malmquist productivity index:

$$\Pi_I^M\left(x^b,x^c,y^b,y^c,T^c\right)=\frac{D_I\left(x^b,y^b,T^c\right)}{D_I\left(x^c,y^c,T^c\right)}\overset{\text{eff}}{=}D_I\left(x^b,y^b,T^c\right)$$

(4.13)

$$=\max\left\{\lambda>0\,|\,x^b\,/\,\lambda\in L(y^b,T^c)\right\}=:\bar{\Pi}_I^M(x^b,y^b,T^c).$$

Thus, each of these productivity indices is defined, in the first instance, as a ratio of radial distances to an (input or output) frontier for base-period and current-period quantities and for a common technology.[17] Under the assumption that production units operate (efficiently) on the production frontier, $D_O(x^b,y^b,T^b)=D_I(x^b,y^b,T^b)=1$ for $t=b,c$, so that the indices simplify to single distance functions evaluated at a mixture of a production vector for one period and a technology for the other period.

The (output-based) productivity index normalized on the base-period technology, defined in (4.10), measures the maximal radial contraction of the current-period output vector needed to place the contracted vector in the production possible set for current-period input, using the base-period technology. Of course, if $y^c\in P(x^c,T^b)$, it must be expanded radially to the frontier. Clearly, $\bar{\Pi}_O^M\left(x^c,y^c,T^b\right)>1$ if and only if there is technological progress—expansion of the frontier—in the neighborhood of the current-period production vector; conversely, $\bar{\Pi}_O^M\left(x^c,y^c,T^b\right)<1$ if and only if the frontier of the production possibility set has receded in this neighborhood, evincing technological retardation. Note that this index, under technological efficiency, is precisely a generalization to multiple outputs (and to nonhomothetic technologies) of Solow's measure of technical progress in the scalar-output case (equation (4.5)).[18]

The calculation of the (output-based) productivity index normalized on the current-period technology in (4.11) generates the inverse of the minimal expansion of the base-period output vector required to reach the frontier of the current-period production possibility set for base-period input vector. $\bar{\Pi}_O^M\left(x^b,y^b,T^c\right)>1$ if and only if there has been expansion of the frontier of production possibility set in the neighborhood of the base-period production vector and $\bar{\Pi}_O^M\left(x^b,y^b,T^c\right)<1$ if and only if the frontier of the production possibility set has receded in this neighborhood. This index is a generalization of the scalar-output measure of technological change in (4.4).[19]

The (input-based) productivity index normalized on the base-period technology, defined in (4.12), measures the inverse of the maximal radial expansion of the current-period input vector needed to place the expanded vector in the input-requirement set for current-period output, using the base-period technology. Clearly, $\bar{\Pi}_I^M\left(x^c,y^c,T^b\right)>1$ if and only if there is technological progress—expansion of the isoquant toward the origin—in the neighborhood of the current-period production vector. This index is an alternative generalization of the scalar-output measure of technological change in (4.5).[20]

Interpretation of the (input-based) productivity index normalized on the current-period technology, defined in (4.13) is similar, and again $\bar{\Pi}_I^M\left(x^b,y^b,T^c\right)>1$ if and only if technological progress has lowered the isoquant in the neighborhood of base-period quantities.

These four indices, in general, provide different implications about productivity change, even possibly about the direction of change. The delineations among them are arbitrary enough to suggest that there is unlikely to be a compelling criterion for choosing any one. One suggestion, inspired by Irving Fisher's recommendation for dealing with arbitrary normalizations in the construction of index numbers, is to take geometric averages over current-period and base-period constructions. He referred to these confluences as "ideal" indices. In this spirit, Diewert (1992a) suggested "Fisher-ideal" indices for input-oriented and for output-oriented productivity indices; they are defined as follows: *Malmquist "ideal" output-based productivity index:*

$$\Pi_O^{MI}\left(x^b,x^c,y^b,y^c,T^b,T^c\right)=\left(\Pi_O^M\left(x^b,x^c,y^b,y^c,T^b\right)\cdot\Pi_O^M\left(x^b,x^c,y^b,y^c,T^c\right)\right)^{1/2}$$

$$\stackrel{\text{eff}}{\equiv}\left(\frac{D_O\left(x^c,y^c,T^b\right)}{D_O\left(x^b,y^b,T^c\right)}\right)^{1/2} \tag{4.14}$$

Malmquist "ideal" input-based productivity index:

$$\Pi_I^{MI}\left(x^b,x^c,y^b,y^c,T^b,T^c\right)=\left(\Pi_I^M\left(x^b,x^c,y^b,y^c,T^b\right)\cdot\Pi_I^M\left(x^b,x^c,y^b,y^c,T^c\right)\right)^{1/2}$$

$$\stackrel{\text{eff}}{\equiv}\left(\frac{D_I\left(x^b,y^b,T^c\right)}{D_I(x^c,y^c,T^b)}\right)^{1/2}. \tag{4.15}$$

The properties of the input and output distance functions, described earlier, endow each of these indices with the identity (*I*), monotonicity (*M*), and unit-invariance (*UI*) properties. On the other hand, these indices satisfy neither proportionality (*P*) nor transitivity (*T*) on their domains.[21] In the next section I describe an index that does satisfy proportionality (though not transitivity).

4.4. Hicks-Moorsteen Indices

Recall from equation (4.2) that Solow technical change for a single output can be interpreted as a ratio of total factor productivity in two periods. The various Malmquist indices are indisputably measures of technological change—that is, shifts in the frontier of the technology—but in general they do not have the interpretation as ratios of aggregate productivity in the two periods. Nor can they be interpreted in general as ratios of (aggregate) output change to (aggregate) input change, unlike the Solow single-output index in the form given by identity (4.6) or (4.7).

Building on the construction in CCD (and following a suggestion of Diewert 1992a), Bjurek (1996) developed multiple-output indices analogous to (4.6) and (4.7). The key building blocks for these indices are essentially Malmquist distance functions evaluated at intertemporal mixtures of production vectors (base-period input vector and current-period output vector, or vice versa). Define the *Malmquist quantity indices* as follows (where, again, the last equation in each case holds only under the assumption that firms operate on the technological frontier):

Technology b-based Malmquist output index:

$$Q_O^M\left(x^b,y^b,x^c,y^c,T^b\right)=\frac{D_O(x^b,y^c,T^b)}{D_O(x^b,y^b,T^b)}\overset{\text{eff}}{=}D_O(x^b,y^c,T^b). \tag{4.16}$$

Technology c-based Malmquist output index:

$$Q_O^M\left(x^b,y^b,x^c,y^c,T^c\right)=\frac{D_O\left(x^c,y^c,T^c\right)}{D_O\left(x^c,y^b,T^c\right)}\overset{\text{eff}}{=}\frac{1}{D_O\left(x^c,y^b,T^c\right)}. \tag{4.17}$$

Technology b-based Malmquist input index:

$$Q_I^M\left(x^b,y^b,x^c,y^c,T^b\right)=\frac{D_I\left(x^c,y^b,T^b\right)}{D_I\left(x^b,y^b,T^b\right)}\overset{\text{eff}}{=}D_I\left(x^c,y^b,T^b\right). \tag{4.18}$$

Technology c-based Malmquist input index:

$$Q_I^M\left(x^b,y^b,x^c,y^c,T^c\right)=\frac{D_I\left(x^c,y^c,T^c\right)}{D_I\left(x^b,y^c,T^c\right)}\overset{\text{eff}}{=}\frac{1}{D_I\left(x^b,y^c,T^c\right)}. \tag{4.19}$$

Identity (4.16) yields a measure of the (aggregate) output change between the base period b and the current period c. Specifically, it is the radial reduction of current-period output required to place the contracted output vector in the production possibility set for base-period input vector using the base-period technology. As such, it can be interpreted as the radial distance of the current-period output vector from the base-period production possibility set. Obviously, $Q_O(x^b,y^b,x^c,y^c,T^b)>1$ if (and only if) $y^c\notin P(x^b,T^b)$ (i.e., the current-period output vector lies above the production possibility surface for base-period technology and input vector), in which case we say that output increased.

Identity (4.17), on the other hand, yields the maximal expansion of the base-period output vector consistent with the expanded output vector remaining in the production possibility set for current-period input vector using the current-period technology. As such, it is a measure of the radial distance of the base-period output vector from the current-period technological frontier. Clearly, $Q_O(x^b,y^b,x^c,y^c,T^c)>1$ if and only if y^b is below the current-period output frontier, in which case we say that output increased.

The input indices in (4.18) and (4.19) have analogous interpretations, in terms of radial distances of input vectors in one period to isoquants of the alternative period.

The *Hicks-Moorsteen productivity indices* can now be defined as the ratios of output changes to input changes, normalized alternatively on base-period and current-period technologies:

$$\Pi^{HM}\left(x^b,x^c,y^b,y^c,T^b\right)=\frac{Q_O^M\left(x^b,x^c,y^b,y^c,T^b\right)}{Q_I^M\left(x^b,x^c,y^b,y^c,T^b\right)}\overset{\text{eff}}{=}\frac{D_O\left(x^b,y^c,T^b\right)}{D_I\left(x^c,y^b,T^b\right)} \tag{4.20}$$

and

$$\Pi^{HM}\left(x^b,x^c,y^b,y^c,T^c\right)=\frac{Q_O^M\left(x^b,x^c,y^b,y^c,T^c\right)}{Q_I^M\left(x^b,x^c,y^b,y^c,T^c\right)}\overset{\text{eff}}{=}\frac{D_I\left(x^b,y^c,T^c\right)}{D_O\left(x^c,y^b,T^c\right)}. \tag{4.21}$$

The Hicks-Moorsteen index can also be interpreted as a multiple-output generalization of the total-factor-productivity version of the Solow index, equation (4.2). Rewrite, for example, the first equality in (4.20) as

$$\Pi^{HM}\left(x^b,x^c,y^b,y^c,T^b\right)=\frac{D_O\left(x^b,y^c,T^b\right)/D_I\left(x^c,y^b,T^b\right)}{D_O\left(x^b,y^b,T^b\right)/D_I\left(x^b,y^b,T^b\right)}. \tag{4.22}$$

The numerator is interpreted as the period-c ratio of a (static) output quantity index normalized on base-period input quantity and technology to an input quantity index normalized on base-period input quantity vector and technology. The denominator is similarly interpreted as an aggregate output–input ratio in the base period b.

Finally, in the absence of a compelling criterion for choosing between the base-period and current-period normalizations, Bjurek suggests the "Fisher ideal" amalgamation to obtain the *Hicks-Moorsteen "ideal" productivity index*:

$$\Pi^{HMI}\left(x^b,x^c,y^b,y^c,T^b,T^c\right)=\frac{Q_O^I\left(x^b,x^c,y^b,y^c,T^b,T^c\right)}{Q_I^I\left(x^b,x^c,y^b,y^c,T^b,T^c\right)}, \tag{4.23}$$

where

$$Q_O^I\left(x^b,x^c,y^b,y^c,T^b,T^c\right)=\left(Q_O^M\left(x^b,x^c,y^b,y^c,T^b\right)\cdot Q_O^M\left(x^b,x^c,y^b,y^c,T^c\right)\right)^{1/2}$$

and

$$Q_I^I\left(x^b,x^c,y^b,y^c,T^b,T^c\right)=\left(Q_I^M\left(x^b,x^c,y^b,y^c,T^b\right)\cdot Q_I^M\left(x^b,x^c,y^b,y^c,T^c\right)\right)^{1/2}$$

are *Fisher "ideal" quantity indices*.

A comparison of the Malmquist and Hicks-Moorsteen indices is instructive. In a nutshell, as first emphasized by Grifell-Tatjé and Lovell (1995), the former is a measure of *technological change* (shift in the production frontier), while the latter is a (broader) measure of the change in *total-factor productivity* (incorporating the effects of movement along the frontier as well as the shift of the frontier). Maintaining technological efficiency, each of the four Malmquist indices, (4.10)–(4.13), measures productivity as the radial shift of the frontier (in either input or output space) in the neighborhood of a *given production vector*. The Hicks-Moorsteen indices, (4.20) and (4.21), on the other hand, incorporate the effects of changes in the production vector—most notably, scale effects[22]—as well as shifts in the technological frontier.

This comparison suggests that the difference between the two types of indices vanishes if productivity is invariant with respect to shifts of the production vector along the surface of the technology. Indeed, this fact has been proved by Färe, Grosskopf, and Roos (1996). A straightforward generalization of their finding is as follows: if and only if, for all t, the technology satisfies (a) input and output homotheticity (isoquants and production possibility surfaces are radial transformations of one another)[23] and (b) constant returns to scale $(D_O(\lambda x^b, y^b, T^b) = (1/\lambda) \cdot D_O(x^b, y^b, T^b)$ for all $\langle x^b, y^b \rangle \in T^b)$, the four Malmquist indices, (4.10)–(4.13), and the two Hicks-Moorsteen indices, (4.20) and (4.21), are identical (cf. Balk 1998, 112–114).

4.5. Decompositions of Productivity Growth

4.5.1. Inefficiency and Technological Change

Recall that CCD initially defined the four (output- and input-based, technology-based) Malmquist indices as ratios of distance functions. But under the assumption that production units operate (efficiently) on the production frontier, the indices simplify to the expressions to the right of the relation $\overset{\text{eff}}{=}$ in (4.10)–(4.13). Färe, Grosskopf, Norris, and Zhang (1994) (FGNZ) elaborated on the CCD framework by allowing firms to operate inefficiently, below the production possibility surface for the extant input vector or above the isoquant for the extant output vector.

The acknowledgment that economic units might operate less than fully efficiently opens up the possibility of decomposing the Malmquist index into two components: changes in the technology (shifts of the frontier) and changes in efficiency (radial distance from the frontier). FGNZ executed this idea by rewriting the initial identity in (4.10)–(4.13) in terms of efficiency indices (see subsection 4.2.3) as follows:

$$\Pi_O^M\left(x^b, x^c, y^b, y^c, T^b\right) = \frac{D_O\left(x^c, y^c, T^b\right)}{D_O\left(x^c, y^c, T^c\right)} \frac{E_O\left(x^c, y^c, T^c\right)}{E_O\left(x^b, y^b, T^b\right)}, \tag{4.24}$$

$$\Pi_O^M\left(x^b, x^c, y^b, y^c, T^c\right) = \frac{D_O(x^b, y^b, T^b)}{D_O\left(x^b, y^b, T^c\right)} \frac{E_O\left(x^c, y^c, T^c\right)}{E_O(x^b, y^b, T^b)}, \tag{4.25}$$

$$\Pi_I^M\left(x^b,x^c,y^b,y^c,T^b\right)=\frac{D_I\left(x^c,y^c,T^c\right)}{D_I(x^c,y^c,T^b)}\frac{E_I\left(x^c,y^c,T^c\right)}{E_I(x^b,y^b,T^b)},\tag{4.26}$$

and

$$\Pi_I^M\left(x^b,x^c,y^b,y^c,T^c\right)=\frac{D_I\left(x^b,y^b,T^c\right)}{D_I\left(x^b,y^b,T^b\right)}\frac{E_I\left(x^c,y^c,T^c\right)}{E_I(x^b,y^b,T^b)}.\tag{4.27}$$

In each case, the Malmquist index allowing for the possibility of inefficient production is the multiple of two indices: the two ratios on the right-hand sides. The first ratio is an index of technical change: the radial shift, in either input space or output space, of the production frontier in the neighborhood of either the base-period or the current-period production vector. The second is an index of the change in efficiency, oriented alternatively to output space or input space.

As in the case of efficient production, the output-oriented and input-oriented Malmquist "ideal" indices are defined as the geometric means taken over the indices normalized on the base period and the current period:

$$\Pi_O^{MI}\left(x^b,x^c,y^b,y^c,T^b,T^c\right)$$
$$=\left(\Pi_O^M\left(x^b,x^c,y^b,y^c,T^b\right)\cdot\Pi_O^M\left(x^b,x^c,y^b,y^c,T^c\right)\right)^{1/2}$$
$$=\left(\frac{D_O\left(x^c,y^c,T^b\right)}{D_O\left(x^c,y^c,T^c\right)}\cdot\frac{D_O(x^b,y^b,T^b)}{D_O\left(x^b,y^b,T^c\right)}\right)^{1/2}\frac{E_O\left(x^c,y^c,T^c\right)}{E_O\left(x^b,y^b,T^b\right)}$$

and

$$\Pi_I^{MI}\left(x^b,x^c,y^b,y^c,T^b,T^c\right)$$
$$=\left(\Pi_I^M\left(x^b,x^c,y^b,y^c,T^b\right)\cdot\Pi_I^M\left(x^b,x^c,y^b,y^c,T^c\right)\right)^{1/2}$$
$$=\left(\frac{D_I\left(x^c,y^c,T^c\right)}{D_I(x^c,y^c,T^b)}\cdot\frac{D_I\left(x^b,y^b,T^c\right)}{D_I\left(x^b,y^b,T^b\right)}\right)^{1/2}\frac{E_I\left(x^c,y^c,T^c\right)}{E_I(x^b,y^b,T^b)}.$$

Thus, as originally formulated, the CCD indices capture efficiency change as well as technological change, and FGNZ capitalized on this formulation to implement a binary decomposition of productivity change into these two components. The success of this decomposition, particularly in empirical studies, provided an impetus to refine the decomposition into additional contributing factors. These efforts are summarized in the next subsection.

4.5.2. Returns to Scale and Output Mix

As noted earlier, the Malmquist productivity index does not encompass the effects of returns to scale (RTS) as quantities change. Thus, it is not surprising that efforts to incorporate RTS into the decomposition of the Malmquist index[24] led instead to revisions of the index itself.

The first of these revisions is a "Malmquist index" defined, not on the actual technology, but instead on a virtual constant-returns-to-scale (CRS) technology, a conical envelopment of the actual technology. Among the many papers directed at this issue, perhaps the "constructive" approach—starting with individual components of a productivity index and then aggregating over these components to construct a consistent overall productivity index—best illustrates this progression. A good example is the contribution of Balk (2001), who referred to it as the "bottom-up" approach (as opposed to the "top-down" approach begun by FGNZ).

Define the conical envelopment of the technology T by

$$C(T) = \{\langle \lambda x, \lambda y \rangle \in \dot{\mathbf{R}}_+^{n+m} \mid \langle x, y \rangle \in T \wedge \lambda > 0\}$$

and restrict the set of allowable technologies to those for which $C(T)$ is a proper subset of $\mathbf{R}_+^{n+m}$ (thus excluding, e.g., technologies with globally increasing returns to scale and Cobb-Douglas-like technologies where some marginal product goes to infinity as the quantity goes to zero). The cone $C(T)$ is a virtual technology—informally, the "smallest" CRS technology containing T.

Roughly speaking, scale efficiency at a point in production space is measured as the "proportional distance" from the actual technological frontier to the conical (envelopment) technological frontier in either input or output space. I stick here to the output notion; the alternative approach in input space can be found in Balk (2001).

Output scale efficiency is thus defined as the ratio of output efficiency defined on the virtual technology divided by output efficiency defined on the true technology:

$$S_O(x, y, T) = \frac{E_O(x, y, C(T))}{E_O(x, y, T)} = \frac{D_O(x, y, C(T))}{D_O(x, y, T)}.$$

Note that $S_O(x, y, T) \leq 1$ and, if the technology satisfies constant returns to scale, $C(T) = T$ and $S(x, y, T) = 1$.

As in the case of the FGNZ decomposition of Malmquist productivity change into technical change and technological efficiency components, there exists more than one path of quantity and technological change along which to measure these components. Again in the face of space constraints, I consider only the path of, first, quantity changes along the base-period technological frontier and, then, shift of the frontier at current-level quantities. (Technological efficiency change is path independent.)

The returns-to-scale index for a change in the input quantity vector from x^b to x^c is the resultant change in the gap between the actual and conical production frontiers:

$$SI_O(x^b, x^c, y^b, T^b) = \frac{S_O(x^c, y^b, T^b)}{S_O(x^b, y^b, T^b)} = \frac{D_O(x^c, y^b, C(T^b)) / D_O(x^c, y^b, T^b)}{D_O(x^b, y^b, C(T^b)) / D_O(x^b, y^b, T^b)}. \quad (4.28)$$

Interchanging the SW and NE part of the last term yields the interpretation of the index as a measure of the expansion (or contraction) of the *virtual* (conical) production possibility frontier along a ray through y^b resulting from the change in the input vector divided by a measure of the expansion (or contraction) of the *actual* production possibility frontier along a ray through y^b for the same change in the input vector.

As Balk (2001) perspicaciously pointed out, (4.28) does not tell the whole story: as the input vector changes from x^b to x^c, the ray through the output vector also shifts to pass through y^c (unless the technology satisfies output homotheticity). This shift also changes the level of scale efficiency, $S_O(x,y,T)$.[25] Balk refers to this change as the *output-mix effect* and measures it as follows:

$$M_O(x^c, y^c, y^b, T^b) = \frac{D_O(x^c, y^c, C(T^b)) / D_O(x^c, y^c, T^b)}{D_O(x^c, y^b, C(T^b)) / D_O(x^c, y^b, T^b)}.$$

Combining the returns-to-scale and output-mix effects with the FGNZ technological and efficiency change indices in (4.24),

$$TC_O(x^c, y^c, T^b, T^c) := \frac{D_O(x^c, y^c, T^b)}{D_O(x^c, y^c, T^c)}$$

and

$$EC_O(x^b, x^c, y^b, y^c, T^b, T^c) := \frac{D_O(x^c, y^c, T^c)}{D_O(x^b, y^b, T^b)},$$

we obtain, after some cancellation of terms, the overall productivity index,

$$TC_O(x^c, y^c, T^b, T^c) \cdot EC_O(x^b, x^c, y^b, y^c, T^b, T^c)$$
$$\cdot SI_O(x^b, x^c, y^b, T^b) \cdot M_O(x^c, y^c, y^b, T^b) = \frac{D_O(x^c, y^c, C(T^b))}{D_O(x^b, y^b, C(T^b))}.$$

Thus, the four components aggregate to a Malmquist index defined on the virtual (conical) technology $C(T)$ rather than the actual technology T.

The conical-envelopment approach to incorporating returns to scale into the Malmquist index has come under some criticism in recent years. I noted earlier the problem of the index not being defined for all technologies in T. In addition, measuring technological change essentially by comparing "maximal average product" in two different periods, which has little if any economic significance, leaves much to be desired.

An alternative bottoms-up approach is that of Peyrache (2014). Following up on suggestions by Lovell (2003), Peyrache constructed a discrete approximation to the differential returns-to-scale coefficient evaluated at $\hat{y} = y / D_O(x,y,T)$ (a radial projection of y to the output possibility surface):

$$\epsilon(x,\hat{y}) = \frac{\partial \ln D_O(\lambda x, \hat{y}, T)^{-1}}{\partial \ln \lambda}\bigg|_{\lambda=1}.$$

Distinguishing between an approximation from below and from above (owing to possible nondifferentiability), Peyrache arrives at the following alternative indices measuring the contribution of returns to scale:

$$R(x^b, x^c, y^c, T^b) = \frac{D_O(x^b, \hat{y}^c, T^b) / D_O(x^c, \hat{y}^c, T^b)}{D_I(x^c, \hat{y}^c, T^b) / D_I(x^b, \hat{y}^c, T^b)}$$

and

$$R(x^b, x^c, y^b, T^b) = \frac{D_O(x^b, \hat{y}^b, T^b) / D_O(x^c, \hat{y}^b, T^b)}{D_I(x^c, \hat{y}^b, T^b) / D_I(x^b, \hat{y}^b, T^b)}.$$

In each case, the denominator is an input quantity index normalized on the frontier point $\hat{y}^b$ or $\hat{y}^c$. The numerator in each case is a measure of the radial expansion (or contraction if the value is less then 1) of the production possibility frontier along the ray through $\hat{y}^b$—equivalently, through y^b (owing to the first-degree homogeneity of D_O in y)—as the input vector changes from x^b to x^c.[26] Thus, in each case, the returns-to-scale index is a discrete measure of the aggregate increase in frontier output along a ray through the projected period-t frontier point, $\hat{y}^b$ or $\hat{y}^c$, as input quantities change between time b and time c.

Peyrache then defines his *radial productivity index*, Π_{RPI}, as the composition of the Malmquist output-oriented, technology-b-based productivity index (4.10)—which does not include scale effects—and the matching returns-to-scale index. Some manipulation, exploitating first-degree homogeneity of D_O in y, yields the following:

$$\Pi_{RPI}^c(x^b, x^c, y^b, y^c, T^b) = \Pi_O^M(x^b, x^c, y^b, y^c, T^b) \cdot R(x^b, x^c, y^c, T^b)$$

$$= \frac{D_O(x^b, y^c, T^b) / D_O(x^b, y^b, T^b)}{D_I(x^c, \hat{y}^c, T^b) / D_I(x^b, \hat{y}^c, T^b)} \qquad (4.29)$$

and

$$\Pi_{RPI}^b(x^b, x^c, y^b, y^c, T^b) = \Pi_O^M(x^c, x^c, y^b, y^c, T^b) \cdot R(x^b, x^c, y^b, T^b)$$

$$= \frac{D_O(x^c, y^c, T^b) / D_O(x^c, y^b, T^b)}{D_I(x^c, \hat{y}^b, T^b) / D_I(x^b, \hat{y}^b, T^b)}. \qquad (4.30)$$

The first index (4.29) normalizes on the current-period output ray, while the second (4.30) normalizes on the base-period output ray. As $\Pi_O^M(x^c, x^c, y^b, y^c, T^b)$ decomposes into a technological change component and an efficiency component, (4.29) and (4.30) yield tripartite decompositions of *RPI* productivity changes.

4.6. Nonradial Indices and Indicators

The orientation of the Malmquist productivity index to either input space or output space poses a quandary—which orientation to use when. An approach to circumvention of this quandary is the (singular) measurement of productivity in the full ⟨input, output⟩ space (commonly referred to as "graph space"). Measurement in this space cannot follow a radial path to a (current- or base-period) frontier, since outputs must be expanded and inputs must be contracted. The most natural extension of the Malmquist index to this space is the hyperbolic index, a multiplicative expansion of output and contraction of input to a (current- or base-period) frontier of graph space. An alternative is the directional distance indicator, an *additive* expansion of output and contraction of input in a stipulated direction to a current- or base-period frontier of graph space.[27] These functions are discussed in the next two subsections.

4.6.1. Hyperbolic Indices

As noted earlier, the distance-function components of Malmquist and Hicks-Moorsteen productivity indices are essentially equivalent to (simple transformations of) Debreu-Farrell technological efficiency indices. Extension of efficiency indices to ⟨input, output⟩ space is a precursor of extension of productivity indices to this space. This extension begins with the Färe, Grosskopf, and Lovell (1985) extension of the Debreu-Farrell efficiency index to ⟨input, output⟩ space:

$$E^H(x, y, T) = \min\{\lambda > 0 \,|\, \langle \lambda x, y / \lambda \rangle \in T\}.$$

As the path of the production vector to the frontier (as λ shrinks to its minimal level) is hyperbolic, Färe, Grosskopf, and Lovell refer to this index as the *hyperbolic efficiency index*. It maps (technologically feasible) production vectors and technologies into the $(0,1]$ interval and is nonincreasing in x and nondecreasing in y.

Analogously to the use of the Debreu-Farrell efficiency index to formulate the Malmquist index in input or output space, the hyperbolic efficiency index can be used to construct a "hyperbolic" productivity index in ⟨input, output⟩ space:

Technology b-based hyperbolic Malmquist index:

$$\Pi^H\left(x^b, x^c, y^b, y^c, T^b, T^c\right) = \frac{E^H\left(x^c, y^c, T^b\right)}{E^H\left(x^b, y^b, T^b\right)} \overset{\text{eff}}{=} E^H\left(x^c, y^c, T^b\right). \qquad (4.31)$$

Technology c-based hyperbolic Malmquist index:

$$\Pi^H\left(x^b, x^c, y^b, y^c, T^b, T^c\right) = \frac{E^H\left(x^c, y^c, T^c\right)}{E^H\left(x^b, y^b, T^c\right)} \overset{\text{eff}}{=} \frac{1}{E^H\left(x^b, y^b, T^c\right)}. \qquad (4.32)$$

Under the assumption of technologically efficient operation, this index measures productivity change as the "hyperbolic distance" from the current-period production vector to the base-period technology frontier or, alternatively, as the inverse of the hyperbolic distance from the base-period production vector to the current-period technological frontier. The index takes a value greater than one if and only if the technology frontier shifts upward in the hyperbolic direction in the neighborhood of the indicated production vector and hence is fundamentally a measure of technological change, analogously to the Malmquist index under the assumption of technological efficiency. These indices satisfy the identity (I), monotonicity (M), and unit-invariance (UI) properties, but fail to satisfy proportionality (P) or transitivity (T).

The middle terms in (4.31) and (4.32) reflect the possibility of technological inefficiency: for example, $E^H(x^b, y^b, T^b) < 1$ in (4.31) renders this term greater than the third term. Multiplication of top and bottom of these two terms by $E^H(x^c, y^c, T^c)$ and $E^H(x^b, y^b, T^b)$, respectively, yields decompositions of productivity change into indices of technical change and efficiency change:

$$\Pi^H(x^b, x^c, y^b, y^c, T^b, T^c) = \frac{E^H(x^c, y^c, T^b)}{E^H(x^c, y^c, T^c)} \frac{E^H(x^c, y^c, T^c)}{E^H(x^b, y^b, T^b)} \tag{4.33}$$

and

$$\Pi^H(x^b, x^c, y^b, y^c, T^b, T^c) = \frac{E^H(x^b, y^b, T^b)}{E^H(x^b, y^b, T^c)} \frac{E^H(x^c, y^c, T^c)}{E^H(x^b, y^b, T^b)}. \tag{4.34}$$

The first term on the right of each equation reflects technological change, measured in the hyperbolic direction and normalized alternatively on current-period and base-period production, while the second terms in each case reflect the change in efficiency. The hyperbolic Malmquist index was proposed and implemented by Zofio and Lovell (2001).

4.6.2. Luenberger (Directional Distance) Indicators

The dominant nonradial formulation, however, has been the *Luenberger productivity indicator*, adapted from the shortage function of Luenberger (1992) to the measurement of productivity by Chambers (1996).[28] In the economics literature, Luenberger's concept has typically gone by the more evocative name, *directional distance function* (DDF). The DDF is defined by

$$\vec{D}(x, y, T, g) = \max\left\{ \lambda \big| \langle x - \lambda g_x, y + \lambda g_y \rangle \in T \right\},$$

where $g = \langle g_x, g_y \rangle \in \mathbf{R}_+^{n+m}$. This function measures the feasible $\langle$contraction, expansion$\rangle$ of $\langle$input, output$\rangle$ quantities in the direction g and maps into $\mathbf{R}_+$.

Given our assumptions about the technology, the DDF is well-defined, nondecreasing in x, and nonincreasing in y for all $\langle x, y, T \rangle \in \mathbf{N} \times T$. As g lies in the same coordinate space as the production vector, the DDF is also independent of units of measurement. Moreover, $\vec{D}(x, y, T, g) \geq 0$ if and only if $\langle x, y \rangle \in T$, so that the DDF is a functional representation of the technology, and $\vec{D}(x, y, T, g) = 0$ if and only if $\langle x, y \rangle$ is contained in the frontier of T.

In contrast to the Debreu-Farrell-Malmquist distance function, which measures distance in ratio form, the DDF measures distance in terms of vector differences (as multiples of the direction vector g). Consequently, while the radial distance function has invariance properties with respect to certain rescaling of the data (owing to the homogeneity conditions), the DDF is invariant under transformations of the origin.

The *Luenberger productivity indicator* is defined as the arithmetic average of differences of directional distances from production vectors in periods b and c to a common technology (b or c):

$$
\begin{aligned}
\Pi_L(x^b, x^c, y^b, y^c, T^b, T^c) &= \frac{1}{2}\Big(\vec{D}(x^b, y^b, T^c, g) - \vec{D}(x^c, y^c, T^c, g) \\
&\quad + \vec{D}(x^b, y^b, T^b, g) - \vec{D}(x^c, y^c, T^b, g)\Big) \\
&=: \frac{1}{2}\Big(\overline{\Pi}_L^c(x^b, x^c, y^b, y^c, T^c) \\
&\quad + \overline{\Pi}_L^b(x^b, x^c, y^b, y^c, T^b)\Big);
\end{aligned}
\tag{4.35}
$$

that is, as the arithmetic average of a technology c-based Luenberger indicator and a technology b-based Luenberger indicator. Input-oriented and output-oriented Luenberger indicators are generated by setting $g_y = 0$ or $g_x = 0$.

The nomenclature *indicator*, as opposed to *index*, has been adopted to draw a distinction between difference-based measures like the Luenberger indicator and ratio-based measures like the Malmquist and Hicks-Moorsteen indices. For theoretical comparisons of ratio-based and difference-based measures, see Chambers (1998, 2002) and Diewert (2005). See Boussemart, Briec, Kerstens, and Poutineau (2003) for empirical comparisons of the two approaches to productivity measurement.

Analogously to the multiplicative decomposition of the Malmquist index (4.24)–(4.27), the Luenberger indicator (4.35) can be additively decomposed as follows:

$$
\begin{aligned}
\Pi_L(x^b, x^c, y^b, y^c, T^b, T^c) &= \Big[\vec{D}(x^b, y^b, T^b, g) - \vec{D}(x^c, y^c, T^c, g)\Big] \\
&\quad + \frac{1}{2}\Big(\vec{D}(x^c, y^c, T^c, g) - \vec{D}(x^c, y^c, T^b, g) \\
&\quad + \vec{D}(x^b, y^b, T^c, g) - \vec{D}(x^b, y^b, T^b, g)\Big),
\end{aligned}
\tag{4.36}
$$

where the first term (in brackets) is efficiency change and the second term is technological change. This indicator satisfies properties analogous to those of the hyperbolic index.

Briec (1997) proposed a variation of the directional distance function by using the definition of $\vec{D}$ with the direction $g = \langle x, y \rangle$ and thereby specifying a specific distance measure rather than a class of measures parameterized by g. The *proportional directional distance function*, defined by

$$\vec{D}_p(x, y, T) = \max\left\{\lambda \mid \left\langle(1-\lambda)x, (1+\lambda)y\right\rangle \in T\right\},$$

maps into the [0, 1] interval. Replacing the directional distance function in (4.36) with this function yields a *proportional Luenberger productivity indicator*. Note that this indicator, roughly speaking, is an additive analog of the hyperbolic index.

4.7. DUAL PRODUCTIVITY INDICES

The Farrell technological efficiency index lies at the core of the decomposition of productivity indices in section 4.5. Farrell, however, was interested in a broader concept, encompassing *allocative* as well as technological efficiency. While the latter notion is a measure of the excess cost (above the minimum) attributable to operating below the production frontier (above the isoquant), the former is a measure of the extra cost accrued by operating at an inefficient point on the frontier, given input prices. Thus, examination of allocative efficiency, unlike technological efficiency, necessarily entails information about prices and economic units' adjustments to price changes. A thorough examination of economic efficiency would expand considerably the scope of this chapter beyond the common notion of productivity as a technological phenomenon. Nevertheless, the recent introduction of notions of dual productivity indices suggests that a brief discussion is called for.

The cost function, $C : \mathbf{R}_{++}^n \times \mathbf{R}_+^m \times \mathcal{T} \to \mathbf{R}_+$, dual to the input distance function, is defined by

$$C(p, y, T) = \min_x\{p \cdot x \mid \langle x, y\rangle \in T\}$$
$$= \min_x\{p \cdot x \mid D_I(x, y, T) \geq 1\},$$

where, of course, p is the input price vector. Under the CCD assumption of technological efficiency, the obvious candidate for a cost-based productivity index is simply the ratio of minimal costs in two situations normalized on particular output and price vectors: $C(y^t, p^t, T^b) / C(y^t, p^t, T^c)$, $t = b$ or c, and of course the geometric average of the two.

Assume the possibility of inefficient production. Cost efficiency is defined and decomposed into allocative and technological efficiency as follows:[29]

$$CE(p, x, y, T) := \frac{C(p, y, T)}{p \cdot x} = \frac{C(p, y, T)}{p \cdot x / D_I(x, y, T)} \cdot \frac{1}{D_I(x, y, T)} \tag{4.37}$$
$$=: AE_I(p, x, y, T) \cdot E_I(x, y, T).$$

Recall that the Malmquist "ideal" (input-oriented) efficiency index (equation (4.15) can be written as

$$\Pi_I^{MI}(x^b,x^c,y^b,y^c,T^b,T^c)=\left(\frac{E_I(x^c,y^c,T^b)}{E_I(x^b,y^b,T^b)}\frac{E_I(x^c,y^c,T^c)}{E_I(x^b,y^b,T^c)}\right)^{1/2}. \tag{4.38}$$

The dual to this index, first formulated by Balk (1998, 67–70) (and recently re-examined by Zelenyuk 2006), is the Malmquist ideal *cost-based productivity index*, a geometric average of cost-based productivity indices normalized on technologies b and c:

$$C\Pi^M(p^b,p^c,x^b,x^c,y^b,y^c,T^b,T^c)=\left(\frac{CE(p^c,x^c,y^c,T^b)}{CE(p^b,x^b,y^b,T^b)}\frac{CE(p^c,x^c,y^c,T^c)}{CE(x^b,y^b,p^b,T^c)}\right)^{1/2} \tag{4.39}$$

$$=:\left(C\Pi_b^M(p^b,p^c,x^b,x^c,y^b,y^c,T^b)\,C\Pi_c^M(p^b,p^c,x^b,x^c,y^b,y^c,T^c)\right)^{1/2}.$$

To obtain some intuition about this index, consider the case of no technological or allocative inefficiency in either period. In this case, $CE(p^b,x^b,y^b,T^b)=1$ and the cost-based productivity index normalized on technology b simplifies to

$$C\Pi_b^M(p^b,p^c,x^b,x^c,y^b,y^c,T^b)=CE(p^c,x^c,y^c,T^b)=\frac{C(p^c,y^c,T^b)}{p^c\cdot x^c}.$$

If $T^b\subset T^c$ and $\Gamma(T^b)\cap\Gamma(T^c)=\varnothing$ (reflecting global technological improvement), $CE(p^c,x^c,y^c,T^b)>1$, indicating increased cost-based productivity (under the assumption of technological efficiency). Also, if there is allocative or technological inefficiency in period b, $CE(p^b,x^b,y^b,T^b)<1$, providing additional fillip to the increase in measured productivity. The technology-c based index $C\Pi_c^M(p^c,p^b,x^c,x^c,y^b,y^c,T^c)$ can be similarly deconstructed.

Revenue-based "Malmquist" indices are analogously derived using the revenue function (dual to the output distance function),

$$R(r,x,T)=\max_y\{r\cdot y\,|\,\langle x,y\rangle\in T\}=\max_y\{r\cdot y\,|\,D_O(x,y,T)\le 1\},$$

(where $r\in\mathbf{R}_{++}^m$ is the output price vector) and revenue-efficiency indices analogous to the cost-efficiency indices (4.37) (see Balk 1998, 107–112; Zelenyuk 2006 for details).

4.8. Aggregation of Productivity Indices

Productivity measurement is carried out at many levels of aggregation—for example, at the firm level, the industry/sector level, and the economy-wide level. Some efforts have been made to establish conditions for consistent aggregation across these units of observation.

Index the individual economic units by $k = 1,\ldots,K$, so that the profiles of input vectors, output vectors, and technologies in period t are $\langle x_1^t,\ldots,x_K^t \rangle$, $\langle y_1^t,\ldots,y_K^t \rangle$, and $\langle T_1^t,\ldots,T_K^t \rangle$. The aggregate technology in period t is the Minkowski sum, $\bar{T}^t = \Sigma_k T_k^t$. Denote the aggregate production vector in period t by $\langle \bar{x}^t, \bar{y}^t \rangle := \langle \Sigma_k x_k^t, \Sigma_k y_k^t \rangle \in T^t$.

The strongest form of consistent aggregation, often referred to as "exact aggregation," is the existence of a productivity index Π and an aggregation rule Ξ such that

$$\Pi(\bar{x}^b, \bar{x}^c, \bar{y}^b, \bar{y}^c, \bar{T}^b, \bar{T}^c)$$
$$= \Xi\left(\Pi(x_1^b, x_1^c, y_1^b, y_1^c, T_1^b, T_1^c), \ldots, \Pi(x_K^b, x_K^c, y_K^b, y_K^c, T_K^b, T_K^c) \right). \tag{4.40}$$

To my knowledge, sufficient conditions (restrictions on the productivity index Π and the aggregation rule Ξ) for this strong form of aggregation have not been proved, and given related results in Blackorby and Russell (1999), tolerable sufficient conditions are highly unlikely to exist: they showed that, substituting efficiency indices for productivity indices, (4.40) holds only if production functions are highly linear (entailing linear isoquants and linear production possibility surfaces) and congruent across economic units.

Limited aggregation results have been established for dual productivity indices, owing to the well-known (Koopmans 1957) principle of interchangeability of set summation and optimization: for example,

$$\tilde{C}\left(p, \sum_k L^k(y^k) \right) = \sum_k C(p, L^k(y^k)).$$

This fact, combined with (4.37), yields

$$\widetilde{CE}\left(p, x, \sum_k L^k(y^k) \right) = \sum_k CE\left(p, L(y^k) \right) \times S^k\left(p, x^k \right). \tag{4.41}$$

where $S^k(p, x^k) = p \cdot x^k / p \cdot \Sigma_k x^k$ is the kth unit's share of aggregate cost. A suitable elaboration of (4.41) to encompass multiple periods and substitution into (4.39) yields a cost-based aggregate productivity index.

While this aggregation result has some power, since the aggregate index depends only on the aggregate technology, rather than the profile of technologies, it does not satisfy aggregation consistency, since aggregate cost efficiency, and hence aggregate productivity, depends on the entire distribution of both input and output quantities. Given the Koopmans interchangeability principle, this exercise yields little more than a simple summation: the aggregate economic unit really plays no specific role in the analysis.[30]

4.9. Concluding Remarks: Malmquist versus Hicks-Moorsteen Redux

The Malmquist and Hicks-Moorsteen indices, developed respectively by Caves, Christensen, and Diewert (1982) and Bjurek (1996), persist to this day as the foundation of much of the pure theory of technology-based productivity indices. While the building blocks for both are Malmquist-Shephard distance functions, the two edifices are conceptually very different and give the same answer only under very restrictive conditions.

Consequently, there has been some discussion (and even a little controversy) in the literature about which is the appropriate measure—or even which is the one correct measure—of productivity change. Some of the discussion is almost semantic, revolving around the "appropriate" definition of *productivity*. On the one hand, some make the valid point that the common understanding of productivity is *total-factor productivity*—an aggregate output quantity divided by aggregate input quantity—in which case a productivity index should be an output index divided by an input index.[31] The Hicks-Moorsteen index has this property and, unlike the Malmquist index, incorporates the effects of returns to scale (as well as input and output mix effects) into the measurement of productivity.

Consider, on the other hand, a comparison of the "productivity" of a firm in two periods b and c, and suppose that the production possibility surface of a firm at time c is above that at time b at all input quantities but, owing to diminishing returns to scale and a lower output in period c, total factor productivity at c is lower than that at b. It seems natural to say that the firm is more productive at time c, and that the lower total factor productivity at time c, when prices are different, is simply the result of optimizing behavior and hence does not reflect lower productivity of the firm. (If the technology at time b is not a proper subset of that at c, it is natural to compare the two in the neighborhood of production in period b or c, or at the mean of the two.)

It seems to me that there is not a "correct" choice between the Malmquist and Hicks-Moorsteen indices: the choice may depend on the context of the productivity question (and the proclivities of the researcher), and the important thing is to be cognizant of the differences and take them into account in analyses, particularly in the interpretation of results.

From a purely axiomatic point of view, however, the Hicks-Moorsteen index would seem to have the upper hand, since it satisfies the proportionality condition (P) in addition to the conditions satisfied by the Malmquist index. (Both fail the transitivity test (T).[32])

While it is tempting to differentiate between the Malmquist index and the Hicks-Moorsteen index by renaming the former as an *index of technological change*, reserving the term *productivity index* for the latter, this would be misleading when we take into account the possibility of technologically inefficient production (production below the technological frontier): in this case, the Malmquist index incorporates the effects of a change in technological efficiency as well as technological change (as does the Hicks-Moorsteen index).

While Malmquist indices decompose cleanly into technological and efficiency components, decomposition of the Hicks-Moorsteen index and further decomposition of the Malmquist index (into scale and mix effects) have been fraught with difficulties, though creative efforts have generated some interesting results.

Another nice attribute of Malmquist indices is that they can be extended quite naturally to measurement in the full ⟨input, output⟩ space. (The Hicks-Moorsteen index, by way of contrast, is a hybrid of separate measurements in input space and in output space.) The most natural extension is the hyperbolic index of technological change, a fairly straightforward generalization of the hyperbolic efficiency index. For reasons that escape me, this index has not flourished. In fact, several other technological efficiency indices in ⟨input, output⟩ space could be used to construct technology-based productivity indices.[33]

As noted earlier, the dominant nonradial productivity measure is based on the directional distance function. The DDF is actually a *class* of functions parameterized by the directional vector g. The discretion that this parameterization yields to the researcher is a double-edged sword. On the one hand, it opens up the possibility of incorporating a weighting scheme for inputs and outputs that reflects legitimate policy objectives. On the other hand, too much discretion can impose an unwanted burden on the researcher or, heaven forbid, can make productivity measurement subject to the specious whims of the researcher. Empirical researchers have commonly disposed of this burden by setting the direction g equal to the unit vector. Although the DDF *formally* satisfies unit invariance (*UI*), when conjoined with this convention in the selection of g, it violates (*UI*) *in practice*.

Two other strands of research on theoretical productivity indices, dual indices and aggregation of indices, in my view have not yet led to important theoretical breakthroughs. Technological productivity is an important component of economic efficiency, but I think it is useful to maintain a distinction between purely internal productivity considerations and market-oriented considerations. It is possible to derive quasi-aggregation results if some (optimal) reallocation of inputs or outputs among production units is incorporated into the analysis, but this approach really circumvents the aggregation problem by effectively converting the separate decision-making units into single decisions-making units.

To summarize, it seems to me that theoretical developments since the trailblazing CCD and Bjurek papers, while impressive, are not as important as the rich set of applications based on their indices. These applications are described in several chapters of this volume.

NOTES

1. The chapter was substantially improved by a thorough perusal of a first draft by Bert Balk and Knox Lovell. It has also benefited from comments by Chris O'Donnell, Rolf Färe, Valentin Zelenyuk, and Oleg Badunenko.

2. Allowing for more than two inputs *is* inconsequential; eschewing Solow's assumption of first-degree homogeneity (constant returns to scale) of the production function is not inconsequential but is nevertheless innocuous for most of our discussion.

3. $A := B$ means the relation defines A, and $A =: B$ means the relation defines B.

4. Solow's assumption of first-degree homogeneity of the production function is not needed for any of the foregoing concepts to be well defined, but without it (4.6) and (4.7) fail to satisfy the proportionality property described in subsection 4.2.5. (The Hicks-Moorsteen generalization of the Solow index does satisfy this property, but the Malmquist index does not unless the technology satisfies constant returns to scale.)

5. And (4.2) as well.

6. Nor are they appropriate for productivity measurement in input or output space in the presence of "bads" like pollution; see Chapter 8 of this volume.

7. This problem can be dealt with in other ways (see footnote 12 in Russell 1998), but given the unimportance of the shutdown condition, I think the simple approach of purging the null vector from the domain is best.

8. It is not standard in the literature to make explicit the dependence of the input-requirement and production-possibility sets on the specification of the technology, but it is convenient to do so when we contemplate productivity changes in the face of changes in the technology over time or differences of the technology among production units.

9. Mathematicians refer to it as the "gauge function"; "distance function" is a distinctive (and different) concept in real analysis.

10. The input distance function in the Solow setup is given by $D_I^S(x, y) = \max\{\lambda > 0 \mid y \leq f(x / \lambda)\}$. If f is homogenous of degree 1, $D_I^S(x, y) = f(x)/y$.

11. The output distance function in the Solow setup is given by $D_O^S(x, y, T) = \min\{\lambda > 0 \mid y / \lambda \leq f(x)\} = y/f(x)$.

12. For proofs, discussions, and illustrations of the properties of input and output distance functions, see Färe and Primont (1995) and Russell (1998).

13. For thorough examinations of properties of productivity indices, see Diewert (1992b) and Balk (1998).

14. This condition is equivalent to *circularity*, $\Pi(x^b, x^c, y^b, y^c) \cdot \Pi(x^c, x^d, y^c, y^d) \cdot \Pi(x^d, x^b, y^d, y^b) = 1$, if (and only if) the identity condition holds, but the two conditions are typically used interchangeably under the implicit assumption that the latter condition holds.

15. Dependence on economic variables, like prices, is briefly discussed in subsection 4.7.

16. Comprehension of the concepts discussed throughout this chapter would be enhanced by drawing the diagrams that take up too much space to include in this survey. For diagrammatic expositions of many of these concepts, see Russell (1998).

17. I follow convention in normalizing on either the base-period or current-period technology, but the Malmquist indices could in principle be defined with respect to any technology in T. Cf. note 21.

18. Use note 11 to obtain $D_O(x^c, y^c, T^b) = y^c / f^b(x^c)$.

19. Use note 11 to obtain $1 / D_O(x^b, y^b, T^c) = f^c(x^b)/y^b$.

20. Use note 10 to obtain $1 / D_I(x^c, y^c, T^b) = y^c / f^b(x^c)$.

21. See Färe and Grosskopf (1996). Input-oriented (output-oriented) Malmquist indices satisfy (*P*) if the distance function is homogeneous of degree -1 in output quantities (homogeneous of degree -1 in input quantities). To get around the nontransitivity problem, Berg, Førsund, and Jansen (1992) and Pastor and Lovell (2005), following a suggestion of Diewert (1987), propose indices defined on a particular technology (the first-period

technology or the union of all technologies). This approach is critiqued by Balk and Althin (1996), who then propose a more elaborate construction to impose transitivity.

22. But also output mix effects; see Balk (2001) and the discussion of the decomposition of a productivity change into its separate components in section 4.5.

23. Färe and Primont (1995, 69–72) showed that this property, which they called *inverse homotheticity*, is equivalent to $D_O(x, y, T) = D_O(\bar{x}, y, T) / \Psi(D_I(x, \bar{y}, T))$ for an arbitrary $\langle \bar{x}, \bar{y} \rangle \in \dot{\mathbf{R}}_+^{n+m}$ and for some strictly monotonic function Ψ.

24. See Färe, Grosskopf, Norris, and Zhang (1994), Ray and Desli (1997), Grifell-Tatjé and Lovell (1999), and Wheelock and Wilson (1999). These contributions are reviewed by Balk (2001), Grosskopf (2003), and Zofio (2007).

25. Note that, since $S_O(x, y, T)$ is homogeneous of degree zero in y, its value depends on y only through the location of the ray through y.

26. Bert Balk points out (in a private communication) that the numerators can also be characterized as dual input indices.

27. Note that the Hicks-Moorsteen index does not measure productivity change along a stipulated path in graph space; rather, it is an amalgamation of separate measurements along radial paths to a frontier in input space and output space.

28. See also Chambers, Chung, and Färe (1996), Chambers, Färe, and Grosskopf (1996), Färe and Grosskopf (1996), Balk (1998), and Chambers (1998, 2002). A precursor of this literature is Diewert (1983), where a directional distance function is introduced to measure waste in production.

29. Note that $x / D_I(x, y, T) \in I(y)$ is the maximally contracted input vector.

30. Weaker aggregation conditions have been explored by Zelenyuk (2006) and Balk (2016).

31. This position has been most ardently argued by O'Donnell (2012), who goes on to develop an array of such ("multiplicatively complete") indices and proposed decompositions. In contrast to most of the theoretical literature on multiple-output productivity indices, however, O'Donnell's notion of total-factor productivity indices comprises "mechanistic" aggregate outputs and inputs—that is, aggregates that are not necessarily integral to the specification of the technology.

32. But see note 21.

33. See Russell and Schworm (2011) for descriptions and evaluations of these efficiency indices.

References

Balk, B. M. 1998. *Industrial Price, Quantity, and Productivity Indices: The Micro-Economic Theory and an Application*. Boston: Kluwer Academic.

Balk, B. M. 2001. "Scale Efficiency and Productivity Change." *Journal of Productivity Analysis* 15: 159–183.

Balk, B. M. 2016. "Various Approaches to the Aggregation of Economic Productivity Indices." *Pacific Economic Review* 21: 445–463.

Balk, B. M., and R. Althin. 1996. "A New, Transitive Productivity Index." *Journal of Productivity Analysis* 7: 19–27.

Berg, A., F. R. Førsund, and E. S. Jansen. 1992. "Malmquist Indexes of Productivity Growth during the Deregulation of Norwegian Banking." *Scandinavian Journal of Economics* 94 (Supplement): S211–S228.

Bjurek, H. 1996. "The Malmquist Total Factor Productivity Index." *Scandinavian Journal of Economics* 98: 303–313.

Blackorby, C., and R. R. Russell. 1999. "Aggregation of Efficiency Indexes." *Journal of Productivity Analysis* 12: 5–20.

Boussemart, J.-P., W. Briec, K. Kerstens, and J.-C. Poutineau. 2003. "Luenberger and Malmquist Productivity Indices: Theoretical Comparisions and Empirical Illustration." *Bulletin of Economic Research* 55: 391–405.

Briec, W. 1997. "A Graph-Type Extension of Farrell Technical Efficiency Measure." *Journal of Productivity Analysis* 8: 95–110.

Caves, D. W., L. R. Christensen, and W. E. Diewert. 1982. "The Economic Theory of Index Numbers and the Measurement of Input, Output, and Productivity." *Econometrica* 50: 1393–1414.

Chambers, R. G. 1996. "A New Look at Input, Output, Technical Change and Productivity Measurement." University of Maryland Working Paper.

Chambers, R. G. 1998. "Input and Output Indicators." In *Index Numbers: Essays in Honor of Sten Malmquist*, edited by R. Färe, S. Grosskopf, and R. R. Russell, 241–271. Boston: Kluwer Academic.

Chambers, R. G. 2002. "Exact Nonradial Input, Output, and Productivity Measurement." *Economic Theory* 20: 751–765.

Chambers, R. G., Y. Chung, and R. Färe. 1996. "Benefit and Distance Functions." *Journal of Economic Theory* 70: 407–419.

Chambers, R., R. Färe, and S. Grosskopf. 1996. "Productivity Growth in APEC Countries." *Pacific Economic Review* 1: 181–190.

Debreu, G. 1951. "The Coefficient of Resource Utilization." *Econometrica* 19: 273–292.

Diewert, W. E. 1983. "The Measurement of Waste within the Production Sector of an Open Economy." *Scandinavian Journal of Economics* 85: 159–179.

Diewert, W. E. 1987. "Index Numbers." In *The New Palgrave Dictionary of Economics*, edited by J. Eatwell, M. Milgate, and P. Newman, 767–780. London: Palgrave Macmillan.

Diewert, W. E. 1992a. "Fisher Ideal Output, Input, and Productivity Indexes Revisited." *Journal of Productivity Analysis* 3: 211–248.

Diewert, W. E. 1992b. "The Measurement of Productivity." *Bulletin of Economic Research* 44: 163–198.

Diewert, W. E. 2005. "Index Number Theory Using Differences Rather Than Ratios." *American Journal of Economics and Sociology* 64: 311–360.

Färe, R., and S. Grosskopf. 1996. *Intertemporal Production Frontiers: With Dynamic DEA*. Boston: Kluwer Academic.

Färe, R., S. Grosskopf, and C. A. K. Lovell. 1985. *The Measurement of Efficiency of Production*. Boston: Kluwer-Nijhoff.

Färe, R., S. Grosskopf, M. Norris, and Z. Zhang. 1994. "Productivity Growth, Technical Progress, and Efficiency Change in Industrialized Countries." *American Economic Review* 84: 66–83.

Färe, R., S. Grosskopf, and P. Roos. 1996. "On Two Definitions of Productivity." *Economics Letters* 53: 269–274.

Färe, R., S. Grosskopf, and R. R. Russell (eds.). 1998. *Index Numbers: Essays in Honor of Sten Malmquist*. Boston: Kluwer Academic.

Färe, R., and D. Primont. 1995. *Multi-Output Production and Duality: Theory and Applications*. Boston: Kluwer Academic.

Farrell, M. J. 1957. "The Measurement of Productive Efficiency." *Journal of the Royal Statistical Society, Series A* 120: 253–290.

Grifell-Tatjé, E., and C. A. K. Lovell. 1995. "A Note on the Malmquist Productivity Index." *Economics Letters* 47: 169–175.

Grifell-Tatjé, E., and C. A. K. Lovell. 1999. "A Generalized Malmquist Productivity Index." *Sociedad de Estadística e Investigación Operativa TOP* 7: 81–101.

Grosskopf, S. 2003. "Some Remarks on Productivity and Its Decompositions." *Journal of Productivity Analysis* 20: 459–474.

Hicks, J. R. 1961. "Measurement of Capital in Relation to the Measurement of Economic Aggregates." In *The Theory of Capital*, edited by F. A. Lutz and D. C. Hague, 18–31. London: Macmillan.

Koopmans, T. J. 1957. *Three Essays on the State of Economic Analysis.* New York: McGraw-Hill.

Lovell, C. A. K. 2003. "The Decomposition of Malmquist Productivity Indexes." *Journal of Productivity Analysis* 20: 437–458.

Luenberger, D. G. 1992. "Benefit Functions and Duality." *Journal of Mathematical Economics* 21: 115–145.

Malmquist, S. 1953. "Index Numbers and Indifference Curves." *Trabajos de Estadística* 4: 209–242.

Moorsteen, R. H. 1961. "On Measuring Productive Potential and Relative Efficiency." *Quarterly Journal of Economics* 75: 451–467.

O'Donnell, C. 2012. "An Aggregate Quantity Framework for Measuring and Decomposing Productivity Change." *Journal of Productivity Analysis* 38: 255–272.

Pastor, J. T., and C. A. K. Lovell. 2005. "A Global Malmquist Productivity Index." *Economics Letters* 88: 266–271.

Peyrache, A. 2014. "Hicks–Moorsteen Versus Malmquist: A Connection by Means of a Radial Productivity Index." *Journal of Productivity Analysis* 41: 187–200.

Ray, S. C., and E. Desli. 1997. "Productivity Growth, Technical Progress, and Efficiency Change in Industrialized Countries: Comment." *American Economic Review* 87: 1033–1039.

Russell, R. R. 1998. "Distance Functions in Consumer and Producer Theory." In *Index Numbers: Essays in Honor of Sten Malmquist*, edited by R. Färe, S. Grosskopf, and R. R. Russell, 7–90. Boston: Kluwer Academic.

Russell, R. R., and W. Schworm. 2011. "Properties of Inefficiency Indexes on ⟨Input, Output⟩ Space." *Journal of Productivity Analysis* 36: 143–156.

Shephard, R. W. 1953. *Cost and Production Functions.* Princeton, NJ: Princeton University Press.

Solow, R. M. 1957. "Technical Change and the Aggregate Production Function." *Review of Economics and Statistics* 39: 312–320.

Wheelock, D. C., and P. W. Wilson. 1999. "Technical Progress, Inefficiency, and Productivity Changes in U.S. Banking, 1984–1993." *Journal of Money, Credit, and Banking* 31: 212–234.

Zelenyuk, V. 2006. "Aggregation of Malmquist Productivity Indexes." *European Journal of Operational Research* 174: 1076–1086.

Zofio, J. L. 2007. "Malmquist Productivity Index Decompositions: A Unifying Framework." *Applied Economics* 39: 2371–2387.

Zofio, J. L., and C. A. K. Lovell. 2001. "Graph Efficiency and Productivity Measures: An Application to US Agriculture." *Applied Economics* 33: 1433–1442.

CHAPTER 5

···

DYNAMIC EFFICIENCY
AND PRODUCTIVITY

···

ROLF FÄRE, SHAWNA GROSSKOPF,
DIMITRIS MARGARITIS, AND WILLIAM L. WEBER

5.1. Introduction

THE measurement of productivity change using linear programming methods has its roots in the Malmquist productivity index, introduced as a theoretical index by Caves, Christensen, and Diewert (1982), hereafter CCD. They showed that this index, defined directly on technology through distance functions, can be expressed as a Törnqvist productivity index by applying Diewert's (1976) quadratic lemma.[1] This link provided both index theoretic and production theoretic underpinnings to the Törnqvist index. The work was generalized by Diewert (1992), Balk (1993), and Färe and Grosskopf (1992) to include a link between the Malmquist productivity index and the Fisher productivity index. Nishimizu and Page (1982) provided an empirical application using parametric frontier estimation based on work by Aigner and Chu (1968), which used linear programming techniques to estimate parametric production frontiers. Later, beginning with Färe, Grosskopf, Lindgren, and Roos (1994), the Aigner and Chu method was extended to nonparametric frontier estimation.

A 1949 conference at the Cowles Commission applied linear programming methods to analyze production decisions. Since then, a veritable industry has developed that employs what Koopmans (1951) termed *activity analysis* and is now associated with *data envelopment analysis*, hereafter DEA, to analyze performance, including efficiency and productivity. The link to estimation of performance using DEA methods is the distance function, which provides a description of technology that—unlike the classic Törnqvist and Fisher indices—does not require price data to provide a means of aggregating multiple inputs and outputs to arrive at the input and output quantity indices required to measure productivity, but does require an optimization procedure.

It also provides a measure of technical efficiency, allowing for decompositions of the productivity indices.

Most of the better-known total factor productivity (TFP) indices in this class, including Malmquist, Hicks-Moorsteen, and the Färe-Primont index recently promoted by O'Donnell (see, e.g., O'Donnell 2014), are what might be called comparative static measures of changes in productivity. Hans Bjurek (1996) proposed a Malmquist-type productivity index that was explicitly defined as ratios of distance function–based output and input quantity indices over time.

A static technology evaluates producer performance given the current level of inputs used to produce current outputs, that is how firms allocate their inputs in the current period to produce their optimal output mix. Moreover, static descriptions of the technology do not capture the effects of how current input and output use affect future production possibilities, and hence the ability of firms to enhance productivity in the long run. Given a static technology where producers use a single input to produce a single output, productivity equals the amount of output per unit of input. A productivity change index then equals the ratio of productivity in one period to productivity in a past period. When producers use multiple inputs to produce multiple outputs, distance functions can be used to aggregate inputs and outputs. In this case a simple measure of total factor productivity is the ratio of an output distance function to an input distance function, and a total factor productivity change index equals the ratio of total factor productivity over time (O'Donnell 2014).

We note that various static productivity change indices, such as the Malmquist and Hicks-Moorsteen indices, evaluate productivity change using mixed-period distance functions. The mixed-period distance functions measure the distance of current period outputs and inputs to an observed future frontier technology and the distance of future period outputs and inputs to the current frontier technology. However, these mixed-period distance functions do not constitute a dynamic problem in that current input and output decisions have no impact on future production possibilities.

Based on work by Shephard and Färe (1980), who constructed index numbers in function spaces, this chapter extends the comparative static Malmquist productivity index to a dynamic setting that allows the reallocation of resources over time so that today's resource decisions have an impact on tomorrow's production.[2] Thus, if today's decisions restrict current outputs or appear to use inputs inefficiently but augment future production, static measures give a biased estimate of productivity change and might lead one to infer a spurious causal effect.[3] We obtain the dynamic version of the Malmquist productivity index by applying distance functions to a dynamic production model, thereby mimicking the original approach taken by CCD in 1982. We also show how to estimate the dynamic distance functions using activity analysis, which follows the approach taken by Färe and Grosskopf (1996). We include an empirical illustration that compares the dynamic to the original static Malmquist productivity index.

The basic approach is to begin with the underlying dynamic technology. A characteristic of dynamic technologies is that production decisions undertaken in one period affect production possibilities in subsequent periods. Examples of dynamic technologies abound. The bank lending process typically generates a jointly produced undesirable byproduct: nonperforming loans. As banks accrue nonperforming loans, future lending opportunities are constrained unless offset by greater use of financial equity capital. In education, students typically take a sequence of courses, with knowledge gained in one course serving as an input to subsequent courses. Farmers can choose to produce grain and beef cattle as final outputs, or save some portion of the grain as seed for future crops and use some beef cattle to maintain or augment the herd size (see Färe and Whitaker in Färe and Grosskopf 1996 for an example). More generally, all firms that invest in capital expect to receive a flow of services from that capital over time, and so the timing of capital investment projects affects that flow. Generally, though, capital investment requires that some resources that might have been used to produce final outputs be diverted to produce the capital so as to enhance future production. For example, including investment as a variable to be endogenously determined as part of a dynamic optimization problem in the specification of the distance functions can be thought of as a network with intermediate products or multistage production that links to supply chain models. In fact, dynamic models based on DEA can be thought of as a type of network DEA model. This linkage allows for solving for the optimal allocation of investments over time, as for example in Bogetoft et al. (2009), which solves for the optimal mix of public and private investment over time for a panel of US states.

Developed by Färe and Grosskopf (1996), a common example of a dynamic technology accounts for producers choosing between using current inputs to produce final outputs or an intermediate product—capital investment—that can be used to enhance future production. Static models that ignore the intermediate product give a biased measure of current and future performance. Using the stock of forests as an intermediate product, Kao (2013) shows that system efficiency is overestimated when dynamic links between periods are ignored.[4] Nemoto and Goto (2003) and Sueyoshi and Sekitani (2005) measure cost efficiency in a single period by treating the past capital stock as a quasi-fixed input to the current period and the current-period capital stock as an output. Emrouznejad and Thanassoulis (2005) measure dynamic efficiency over a finite period, accounting for input used and output produced in each period, with the value of the capital stock in the final period treated as an output. Thus, two producers who begin with the same capital stock and use the same inputs and produce the same outputs in each period will have different dynamic efficiency scores if one producer has a larger final capital stock.

More recent work has specified an infinite horizon dynamic technology where firms are assumed to minimize the present value of costs of production over time by choosing an optimal amount of capital investment and other inputs across time. These models have been estimated using the present-value Hamilton-Jacobi-Bellman equation for costs. Such models have been employed by Rungsuriyawiboon and Stefanou (2007) to examine the technical and allocative efficiencies of US electric utilities; Silva and Stefanou (2003, 2007) for Pennsylvania dairy farmers; Serra, Lansink, and Stefanou (2011) for Dutch dairy farmers; Skevas, Lansink, and Stefanou (2012) for Dutch arable farms; and Kapelko, Lanskink, and Stefanou (2014) for firms in the Spanish construction industry. Lansink, Stefanou, and Serra (2015) extend the dynamic efficiency measures estimated for Dutch dairy farmers to dynamic Luenberger productivity indicators, which are based on directional distance functions. Chen and van Dalen (2010) build a dynamic model to account for the effect of past advertising expenditures (an input) on future sales (output), whereas Ang and Lansink (2014) assess dynamic profit efficiency for Belgian dairy farms.

The dynamic technology and performance measures can also be generalized to allow for identification of optimal starting points, input intensity, and stopping points, which we call the time substitution model. The time substitution model determines when a given amount of input is to be allocated across time so as to maximize output (Färe, Grosskopf, and Margaritis 2010). In these types of problems, production is optimized by producers choosing when to begin and end production and how intensively to use inputs. Technological progress makes it optimal for firms to delay production until later periods since the same inputs will produce greater outputs. In contrast, production should take place in earlier periods, when the production technology is experiencing stagnation or technological regress. At the optimum, the marginal rate of transformation between outputs and marginal rate of substitution between inputs should be the same across all periods.

One might ask why technological regress—that is, implosion of the technological frontier—can occur if outputs and inputs are measured accurately over time. In regard to observed technological regress from 1965 to 1990 among countries with low capital/labor ratios, Kumar and Russell (2002, 540) ask, "Were 'blueprints' lost?" and conclude instead that the nonparametric DEA frontier probably lies below the true but unobservable frontier at low capital/labor ratios. Pastor and Lovell (2005) measure productivity change by constructing a DEA frontier where historical input and output combinations are part of the current-period technology. As a consequence, their method attributes declines in output or increases in input usage as efficiency loss, rather than technological regress. However, there might still be instances in which technological regress occurs. When population and technological progress are endogenous, Aiya, Dalgaard, and Moav (2008) find that Malthusian population shocks can cause technological regress. Research scientists employed by for-profit firms sometimes hold tacit knowledge and face a trade-off between codifying their tacit knowledge into words, codes, and formulas versus their contractual obligations for creating new knowledge (Zucker, Darby, and Armstrong 2002). Regress might then occur when tacit knowledge exists but disappears before being passed on to other users following the death of the scientist or the firm.

In many production technologies, desirable outputs and undesirable byproducts are jointly produced. Since the goal of producers facing regulation of emissions is to simultaneously maximize desirable outputs and minimize undesirable outputs, the Shephard radial output distance function, which seeks to increase all outputs, is inappropriate. In these cases, dynamic efficiency can be estimated using directional distance functions, which allow for asymmetric scaling of goods and bads, and dynamic productivity change can be estimated using Luenberger productivity indices, which are constructed from directional distance functions. Fukuyama and Weber (2015b, 2017) build a dynamic model of the bank production process where bank managers choose the amount of excess reserves to carry over to a subsequent period in order to maximize loans and securities investments and simultaneously minimize nonperforming loans.

In section 5.2 we present the static and dynamic production possibility sets that show how inputs are transformed into outputs and how current resource decisions impact future production possibilities. We also show how those production sets can be represented using activity analysis. Section 5.3 consists of two subsections that provide measures of dynamic performance. In subsection 5.3.1 the static and dynamic distance functions are defined and the dynamic Malmquist productivity index is presented and discussed. In subsection 5.3.2 we provide an overview of the time substitution model. In section 5.4 we offer an illustration of our dynamic productivity index for a panel of 26 Organisation for Economic Co-operation and Development (OECD) countries during the period 1990–2011 and compare it to the static Malmquist productivity index. Section 5.5 concludes the chapter.

5.2. Static and Dynamic Production Models

In this section we introduce the production models relative to which we define the static and dynamic productivity indices. We denote inputs as $x = \left(x_1, \ldots, x_N\right) \in \mathfrak{R}_+^N$ and outputs by $y = \left(y_1, \ldots, y_M\right) \in \mathfrak{R}_+^M$. Then the technology may be described by the output sets

$$P\left(x\right) = \left\{y : x \text{ can produce } y\right\}, \quad x \in \mathfrak{R}_+^N. \tag{5.1}$$

We assume that the output sets satisfy the standard regularity conditions including free disposability of inputs and outputs, and convex, closed, and bounded output sets.[5] We also assume that the output sets satisfy constant returns to scale so the productivity index can be interpreted as the ratio of an index of outputs to an index of inputs between two periods or between two producers, which, in the case of a single output and a single input, equals the ratio of average products. In addition, productivity growth measures are biased when variable returns to scale are assumed and can no longer be interpreted as the ratio of average products. For instance, when producers operate in the range of increasing returns to scale and input growth occurs, productivity change is understated; when firms operate in the range of decreasing returns to scale and input growth occurs, productivity change is overstated (Grifell-Tatje and Lovell 1995). Furthermore, we decompose dynamic productivity growth into the product of an index of efficiency change and an index of technical change.

Both our static and dynamic production models consist of a sequence of output sets $P^\tau\left(x^\tau\right), \tau = 1, \ldots, T$. In the static case these are not interconnected, except by the march of time, but in our very simple dynamic model they are interconnected by intermediate products. Thus at each period τ, the output vector y^τ can be either used as final output $^f y^\tau$ for consumption in period t or as intermediate products $^i y^\tau$ so that $y^\tau = {}^f y^\tau + {}^i y^\tau$.

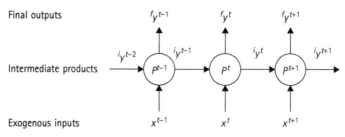

Final outputs

Intermediate products

Exogenous inputs

FIGURE 5.1. The dynamic technology.

The intermediate products can be used as inputs in a future period to augment production. In Figure 5.1 we provide an illustration.[6]

Three production sets (P^{t-1}, P^t, and P^{t+1}) are illustrated in Figure 5.1. These form a directed network, that is, a network that is connected in a specific forward direction. It may also be thought of as a discrete Ramsey (1928) model, where output at, say, period t can be used either as final output (consumption) or as input into the following period's production (investment or saving). In this simple dynamic structure, where only intermediate product links the adjacent periods, it is clear that if $^iy^\tau$ is zero for all periods so that all output y^τ is final output $^fy^\tau$, then the dynamic model collapses to the comparative static case (i.e., there is no intertemporal interaction, and today's production decisions have no further consequences and are not affected by history).

In the empirical illustration of a simple dynamic Malmquist productivity index, we will use an activity analysis or DEA formulation of the output sets. Suppose we are given a set of $k = 1, \ldots, K$ observations of inputs and outputs (x_k, y_k), then the static activity analysis model of technology in a single period is constructed from these data as[7]

$$P(x) = \left\{ (y_1, \ldots, y_M): y_m \leq \sum_{k=1}^{K} z_k y_{km}, \quad m = 1, \ldots, M, \right. \tag{5.2}$$

$$x_n \geq \sum_{k=1}^{K} z_k x_{kn}, \quad n = 1, \ldots, N,$$

$$\left. z_k \geq 0, \quad k = 1, \ldots, K \right\}.$$

Thus the technology is created from the data $(x_k, y_k), k = 1, \ldots, K$ by forming the smallest convex cone that includes the data, hence the moniker *data envelopment analysis*. This cone technology is the constant returns to scale technology and is formed from the intensity variables, z_k, $k = 1, \ldots, K$ such that no more output can be produced using no less input than a linear combination of the observed outputs and inputs.

If the observed inputs and outputs satisfy the following conditions set out by Kemeny, Morgenstern, and Thompson (1956),

(i) $\Sigma_{k=1}^{K} x_{kn} > 0$, $n = 1, \ldots, N$, each input is used by at least one k

(ii) $\Sigma_{n=1}^{N} x_{kn} > 0$, $k = 1, \ldots, K$, each k uses at least one input, n

(iii) $\Sigma_{k=1}^{K} y_{km} > 0$, $m = 1, \ldots, M$, each output is produced by at least one k

(iv) $\Sigma_{m=1}^{M} y_{km} > 0$, $k = 1, \ldots, K$, each k produces at least one output, m,

then the technology satisfies the standard regularity conditions of free disposability of inputs and outputs, and convex, closed, and bounded output sets (Färe and Primont 1995).

The dynamic activity analysis model is formed from the data $\left(x_k^\tau, y_k^\tau \right), k = 1, \ldots, K^\tau, \tau = 1, \ldots, T$. As an illustration, following Färe and Grosskopf (1996), we can write out the three-period model from Figure 5.1 as

$$P\left(x^{t-1}, x^t, x^{t+1}, {}^i y^{t-2} \right) = \left\{ \left({}^f y^{t-1}, {}^f y^t, \left({}^f y^{t+1} + {}^i y^{t+1} \right) \right) : \right. \tag{5.3}$$

$${}^f y_m^{t-1} + {}^i y_m^{t-1} \leq \sum_{k=1}^{K^{t-1}} z_k^{t-1} ({}^f y_{km}^{t-1} + {}^i y_{km}^{t-1}), \quad m = 1, \ldots, M,$$

$$x_n^{t-1} \geq \sum_{k=1}^{K^{t-1}} z_k^{t-1} x_{kn}^{t-1}, \quad n = 1, \ldots, N,$$

$${}^i y_m^{t-2} \geq \sum_{k=1}^{K^{t-1}} z_k^{t-1} ({}^i y_{km}^{t-2}), \quad m = 1, \ldots, M,$$

$$z_k^{t-1} \geq 0, \quad k = 1, \ldots, K^{t-1}$$

$${}^f y_m^t + {}^i y_m^t \leq \sum_{k=1}^{K^t} z_k^t ({}^f y_{km}^t + {}^i y_{km}^t), \quad m = 1, \ldots, M,$$

$$x_n^t \geq \sum_{k=1}^{K^t} z_k^t x_{kn}^t, \quad n = 1, \ldots, N,$$

$${}^i y_m^{t-1} \geq \sum_{k=1}^{K^t} z_k^t ({}^i y_{km}^{t-1}), \quad m = 1, \ldots, M,$$

$$z_k^t \geq 0, \quad k = 1, \ldots, K^t$$

$${}^f y_m^{t+1} + {}^i y_m^{t+1} \leq \sum_{k=1}^{K^{t+1}} z_k^{t+1} ({}^f y_{km}^{t+1} + {}^i y_{km}^{t+1}), \quad m = 1, \ldots, M,$$

$$x_n^{t+1} \geq \sum_{k=1}^{K^{t+1}} z_k^{t+1} x_{kn}^{t+1}, \quad n = 1, \ldots, N,$$

$${}^i y_m^t \geq \sum_{k=1}^{K^{t+1}} z_k^{t+1} ({}^i y_{km}^t), \quad m = 1, \ldots, M,$$

$$z_k^{t+1} \geq 0, \quad k = 1, \ldots, K^{t+1} \Big\}.$$

The three-period dynamic model of $P(.)$ gives the endogenously determined final outputs $({}^f y^{t-1}, {}^f y^t, {}^f y^{t+1})$ that can be produced in periods $t-1$, t, and $t+1$ with the exogenous inputs $(x^{t-1}, x^t, x^{t+1}, {}^i y^{t-2})$ and the endogenous intermediate products $({}^i y^{t-1}, {}^i y^t, {}^i y^{t+1})$.[8] The right-hand side of the output and input constraints form the technology by taking linear combinations of the outputs and inputs of the $k = 1, \ldots, K$ producers. The left-hand side variables are the outputs and inputs, including the intermediate products from the previous period that are feasible given the right-hand side technology. This model is consistent with that depicted in Figure 5.1, where $^i y^\tau, \tau = t-1, t, t+1$ are the intermediate products that make the model dynamic. Allowing the intensity variables, z_k^τ, to vary across periods $\tau = t-1, t, t+1$ allows each period's technology to vary. One can show (see Färe and Grosskopf, 1996) that if each technology $P^\tau(.), \tau = t-1, t, t+1$ satisfies the standard regularity conditions, then so does the associated dynamic model—for example, the three-period technology specified in the preceding. Moreover, if there are no intermediate products, $^i y^\tau$, then the dynamic model simplifies to three sequential static models. In the dynamic model, increases in the intermediate products that are produced in period τ expand the output set in the subsequent period. In section 5.3 we define Shephard (1970) distance functions for the static output set represented by (5.2) and dynamic distance functions for the dynamic output sets represented by (5.3).

5.3. Static and Dynamic Performance Measures

5.3.1. Static and Dynamic Productivity Indices

The classic definition of productivity (in level terms) is simply the ratio of output to input. This becomes complicated when there are multiple inputs and outputs; the challenge is how best to aggregate these. CCD (1982) appealed to a natural aggregator function, namely the distance function, to represent technology and provide a means of aggregating inputs and outputs. They considered their resulting Malmquist productivity index to be purely theoretical, since they considered the component distance functions to be unobservable. They used the Malmquist index to provide theoretical underpinnings for the empirical Törnqvist productivity index. The Malmquist productivity index proposed by CCD was defined using Shephard's distance functions, which can be estimated using DEA and, in contrast to the Törnqvist index, do not require price data to aggregate inputs and outputs. Here we follow Färe, Grosskopf, Lindgren, and Roos (1994) and use the index they developed based on the output distance function.[9]

We begin with technology. Let $P(x)$ be an output set. Then the associated output distance function is defined as

$$D_o(x, y) = \inf\{\theta : (y / \theta) \in P(x)\},\tag{5.4}$$

hence it is the largest feasible radial extension of the observed output vector y.

For the input-output vectors (x^t, y^t) and (x^{t+1}, y^{t+1}), CCD define two Malmquist output-oriented productivity indices, namely

$$M_o^t = D_o^t\left(x^{t+1}, y^{t+1}\right)/ D_o^t\left(x^t, y^t\right) \tag{5.5}$$

and

$$M_o^{t+1} = D_o^{t+1}\left(x^{t+1}, y^{t+1}\right)/ D_o^{t+1}\left(x^t, y^t\right) \tag{5.6}$$

where the first is defined relative to the technology in period t, $P^t(x)$, and the second is defined relative to the $t+1$ technology $P^{t+1}(x)$. One can prove (see Färe, Grosskopf, and Roos 1998), that these two indices are equal if and only if the output sets are of the form

$$P^t(x) = A(t)P(x), \tag{5.7}$$

which implies that technology and technical change are Hicks output-neutral. To avoid imposing this condition or having to arbitrarily choose one or the other of the preceding indices, Färe, Grosskopf, Lindgren, and Roos (1994) use the geometric mean of these indices as their definition of productivity change.[10] Here we adopt that approach and define the (comparative static) Malmquist productivity index as

$$M_o\left(x^t, y^t, x^{t+1}, y^{t+1}\right) = (M_o^t \cdot M_o^{t+1})^{1/2} \tag{5.8}$$

$$= \left(\frac{D_o^t\left(x^{t+1}, y^{t+1}\right)}{D_o^t\left(x^t, y^t\right)} \frac{D_o^{t+1}\left(x^{t+1}, y^{t+1}\right)}{D_o^{t+1}\left(x^t, y^t\right)}\right)^{1/2}.$$

Färe, Grosskopf, Lindgren, and Roos (1989, 1994) also show that the index can be decomposed into an efficiency change and a technical change component, namely,

$$EFFCH = D_o^{t+1}\left(x^{t+1}, y^{t+1}\right)/ D_o^t\left(x^t, y^t\right) \tag{5.9}$$

and

$$TECH = \left(\frac{D_o^t\left(x^{t+1}, y^{t+1}\right)}{D_o^{t+1}\left(x^{t+1}, y^{t+1}\right)} \frac{D_o^t\left(x^t, y^t\right)}{D_o^{t+1}\left(x^t, y^t\right)}\right)^{1/2} \tag{5.10}$$

so that

$$M_o\left(x^t, y^t, x^{t+1}, y^{t+1}\right) = EFFCH \cdot TECH. \tag{5.11}$$

The distance functions for the comparative static CCD-type Malmquist index can be estimated using an activity analysis or DEA approach. For example, we may estimate the distance functions for the period t technology defined in (5.2) as

$$\left(D_o^t\left(x^t,y^t\right)\right)^{-1} = \max \lambda \tag{5.12}$$

$$\text{s.t. } \lambda y_{km}^t \leqq \sum_{k=1}^{K} z_k^t y_{km}^t, \quad m=1,\ldots,M,$$

$$x_{kn}^t \geqq \sum_{k=1}^{K} z_k^t x_{kn}^t, \quad n=1,\ldots,N,$$

$$z_k \geqq 0, \quad k=1,\ldots,K,$$

and

$$\left(D_o^t\left(x^{t+1},y^{t+1}\right)\right)^{-1} = \max \lambda \tag{5.13}$$

$$\text{s.t. } \lambda y_{km}^{t+1} \leqq \sum_{k=1}^{K} z_k^t y_{km}^t, \quad m=1,\ldots,M$$

$$x_{kn}^{t+1} \geqq \sum_{k=1}^{K} z_k^t x_{kn}^t, \quad n=1,\ldots,N,$$

$$z_k \geqq 0, \quad k=1,\ldots,K.$$

In both sets of problems, the technology is determined by the data from period t through the convex combinations formed with the activity variables z_k. The first problem assesses data from that same period t, whereas the second problem assesses data from period $t+1$ relative to the period t technology. By interchanging $t+1$ and t in (5.13) we can have data from period t assessed relative to the period $t+1$ technology, yielding the distance function $D_o^{t+1}(x^t,y^t)$.

Before turning to the dynamic Malmquist productivity index, we note that the Färe-Primont and Hicks-Moorsteen productivity indices also are constructed from adjacent-period distance functions. However, they use the distance functions to construct Malmquist quantity indices of output and input, with the ratio forming the productivity index, which follows the classic definition of productivity as the ratio of output to input. Following O'Donnell (2014), they differ slightly with respect to specification of the distance functions. The general specification for the Färe-Primont version for the quantity indices is

$$QI = \frac{D_o\left(\mu_x,q_{it},\mu_z\right)}{D_o\left(\mu_x,q_{ks},\mu_z\right)} \tag{5.14}$$

$$XI = \frac{D_i\left(x_{it},\mu_q,\mu_z\right)}{D_i\left(x_{ks},\mu_q,\mu_z\right)} \tag{5.15}$$

where QI is the output quantity index and XI the input quantity index. The z variables are included as environmental variables (although they were not included in the original Färe-Primont specification). Following O'Donnell (2014, 190) the "μ_x,μ_q,μ_z

are arbitrary vectors that in most empirical applications would be representative of all inputs, outputs and time periods in the dataset (e.g., sample means)." The Hicks-Moorsteen productivity index is typically specified using fixed-period data for the inputs and z variables in the output quantity index and for the outputs and z variables in the input quantity index.

The dynamic Malmquist productivity index is defined—like the static Malmquist productivity index—in terms of distance functions; in this case, however, they are dynamic distance functions. Let $\Delta_o^t\left(x^t, {}^f y^t, {}^i \overline{y}\right)$ and $\Delta_o^{t+1}\left(x^{t+1}, {}^f y^{t+1}, {}^i \overline{y}\right)$ be dynamic distance functions as defined in the following, where ${}^i \overline{y}$ denotes the initial and terminal conditions for the intermediate products. Then the dynamic Malmquist productivity index is

$$\Omega_o\left(x^t, {}^f y^t, x^{t+1}, {}^f y^{t+1}, {}^i \overline{y}\right) = \left[\frac{\Delta_o^t\left(x^{t+1}, {}^f y^{t+1}, {}^i \overline{y}\right)}{\Delta_o^t\left(x^t, {}^f y^t, {}^i \overline{y}\right)} \times \frac{\Delta_o^{t+1}\left(x^{t+1}, {}^f y^{t+1}, {}^i \overline{y}\right)}{\Delta_o^{t+1}\left(x^t, {}^f y^t, {}^i \overline{y}\right)}\right]^{1/2}. \tag{5.16}$$

Recall that total outputs equal the sum of final outputs and intermediate products: $y = {}^f y + {}^i y$. Whereas the static distance functions are defined in terms of total outputs, the dynamic distance functions are defined in terms of final outputs and exclude the intermediate products that are produced and included in total output. As we noted earlier, if there are no intermediate products, then this simple dynamic index simplifies to the usual Malmquist productivity index.

For the dynamic technology represented by (5.3), the dynamic distance functions $\Delta_o^t\left(x^t, {}^f y^t, {}^i \overline{y}\right)$ and $\Delta_o^{t+1}\left(x^{t+1}, {}^f y^{t+1}, {}^i \overline{y}\right)$ are defined as

$$\Delta_o^t\left(x^t, {}^f y^t, {}^i \overline{y}\right) = 1/\lambda^{*t} \tag{5.17}$$

$$\Delta_o^{t+1}\left(x^{t+1}, {}^f y^{t+1}, {}^i \overline{y}\right) = 1/\lambda^{*t+1}$$

where λ^{*t} and λ^{*t+1} are the maximizers in the following problem

$$\max \psi^1 \lambda^1 + \ldots + \psi^t \lambda^t + \psi^{t+1} \lambda^{t+1} + \ldots + \psi^T \lambda^T \tag{5.18}$$

$$\text{s.t.} \quad \lambda^1 {}^f y^1 + {}^i y^1 \in P^1\left(x^1, {}^i \overline{y}^0\right)$$

$$\vdots$$

$$\lambda^t {}^f y^t + {}^i y^t \in P^t\left(x^t, {}^i y^{t-1}\right)$$

$$\lambda^{t+1} {}^f y^{t+1} + {}^i y^{t+1} \in P^{t+1}\left(x^{t+1}, {}^i y^t\right)$$

$$\vdots$$

$$\lambda^T {}^f y^T + {}^i \overline{y}^T \in P^T\left(x^T, {}^i y^{T-1}\right).$$

In (5.18) each λ^t is weighted by ψ^t to account for the producer's rate of time preference. If production is valued equally across all periods then one might choose, $\psi^\tau = 1$, $\tau = 1, \ldots, T$. Alternatively, given an interest rate r, the weights might be chosen as $\psi^\tau = 1/(1+r)^{\tau-1}$ so that any expansion of production in later periods is valued less than an equivalent expansion in production in earlier periods. The optimization problem (5.18) chooses an optimal amount of intermediate products in each period so as to maximize the proportional expansion (λ^t) of observed final output to the frontier of final output summed over all periods, $t = 1, \ldots, T$. The amount of intermediate product produced in period t determines the size of the output set and potential final output in period $t + 1$. Therefore, it might sometimes be optimal for the producer to forgo final outputs and instead produce the intermediate product so as to expand final output by a greater amount in the subsequent period. For example, in a two-period dynamic problem, suppose that the actual amounts of final output and intermediate product in $t = 1$ are $^f y^1 = 100$ and $^i y^1 = 10$, respectively. Given the amounts of exogenous inputs x^1 and x^2 and intermediate product from period $t = 0$, suppose that $\lambda^1 = 1.05$ and $\lambda^2 = 1.08$, with their sum equal to 2.13. In this case, total frontier output in $t = 1$ would equal $y^1 = 1.05 \times 100 + 10 = 115$. If the amount of intermediate product was chosen optimally, say $^i y^{*1} = 13$, then the amount that final output can be expanded in period 1 falls to $\lambda^1 = 1.02$ with $y^1 = 1.02 \times 100 + 13 = 115$. However, if the increase in intermediate product produced in $t = 1$ expands the output set in $t = 2$ such that $\lambda^2 \geq 1.11$ (so that $\lambda^1 + \lambda^2 \geq 2.13$) then the reallocation toward producing greater amounts of the intermediate product in $t = 1$ improves dynamic efficiency.

In (5.18) there are a total of T periods, and the initial conditions include $^i \bar{y}^0$ as the initial intermediate product vector. Transversality conditions include $^i \bar{y}^T$ as the terminal intermediate product vector. We place a "$\_$" over the exogenous initial and terminal values of the intermediate products to distinguish them from the endogenous intermediate products that are chosen in periods $t = 1, \ldots, T - 1$ as part of the optimization problem.[11] Since our model is not stochastic, the terms *exogenous* and *endogenous* have the standard meanings of determined outside and determined within the model. To simplify the notation, let $^i \bar{y} = (^i \bar{y}^0, {}^i \bar{y}^T)$. Each of the individual period technologies use intermediate products (which are variables to be solved in the optimization problem) and exogenous inputs x. While the dynamic distance functions scale only final outputs $^f y$ to the dynamic frontier, the static distance functions scale total output to the static frontier. Moreover, the dynamic distance functions $\Delta_o^t (x^t, {}^f y^t, {}^i \bar{y})$, $t = 1, \ldots, T$ are obtained by solving the dynamic optimization problem (5.18) once, whereas the distance functions defined in the static case by (5.4) must be solved T times.

As with the traditional static Malmquist productivity index, the dynamic productivity index may be decomposed into an efficiency change and a technical change component,

$$\Omega_o \left(x^t, {}^f y^t, x^{t+1}, {}^f y^{t+1}, {}^i \bar{y} \right) = \left(\frac{\Delta_o^{t+1} \left(x^{t+1}, {}^f y^{t+1}, {}^i \bar{y} \right)}{\Delta_o^t \left(x^t, {}^f y^t, {}^i \bar{y} \right)} \right)$$

$$\times \left(\frac{\Delta_o^t \left(x^{t+1}, {}^f y^{t+1}, {}^i \bar{y} \right)}{\Delta_o^{t+1} \left(x^{t+1}, {}^f y^{t+1}, {}^i \bar{y} \right)} \frac{\Delta_o^t \left(x^t, {}^f y^t, {}^i \bar{y} \right)}{\Delta_o^{t+1} \left(x^t, {}^f y^t, {}^i \bar{y} \right)} \right)^{1/2}. \tag{5.19}$$

where $DEFFCH = \dfrac{\Delta_o^{t+1}(x^{t+1},\ ^f y^{t+1},\ ^i \overline{y})}{\Delta_o^{t}(x^{t},\ ^f y^{t},\ ^i \overline{y})}$ represents dynamic efficiency change and

$DTECH = \left(\dfrac{\Delta_o^{t}(x^{t+1},\ ^f y^{t+1},\ ^i \overline{y})}{\Delta_o^{t+1}(x^{t+1},\ ^f y^{t+1},\ ^i \overline{y})} \dfrac{\Delta_o^{t}(x^{t},\ ^f y^{t},\ ^i \overline{y})}{\Delta_o^{t+1}(x^{t},\ ^f y^{t},\ ^i \overline{y})} \right)^{1/2}$ represents dynamic technical change.

To calculate each of the components of the dynamic productivity index, two mixed-period distance functions $\Delta_o^{t+1}(x^{t},\ ^f y^{t},\ ^i \overline{y})$ and $\Delta_o^{t}(x^{t+1},\ ^f y^{t+1},\ ^i \overline{y})$ must be derived. The mixed-period distance function $\Delta_o^{t+1}(x^{t},\ ^f y^{t},\ ^i \overline{y})$ measures the distance from observed quantities of final outputs in period t to the period $t+1$ technology. This function is estimated as

$$\max\ \psi^1 \lambda^1 + \ldots + \psi^t \lambda^t + \psi^{t+1} \lambda^{t+1} + \ldots + \psi^{T-1} \lambda^{T-1} \qquad (5.20)$$

$$\text{s.t.} \qquad \lambda^1\ ^f y^1 + {}^i y^1 \in P^2 \left(x^2,\ ^i \overline{y}^1 \right)$$

$$\vdots$$

$$\lambda^{t+1}\ ^f y^{t+1} + {}^i y^{t+1} \in P^{t+2} \left(x^{t+2},\ ^i y^{t+1} \right)$$

$$\vdots$$

$$\lambda^{T-1}\ ^f y^{T-1} + {}^i \overline{y}^{T-1} \in P^T \left(x^T,\ ^i y^{T-1} \right).$$

The mixed-period distance function $\Delta_o^{t}\left(x^{t+1},\ ^f y^{t+1},\ ^i \overline{y} \right)$ measures the distance from observed quantities of final outputs in period $t+1$ to the period t technology. These functions are estimated from the problem

$$\max\ \psi^2 \lambda^2 + \ldots + \psi^t \lambda^t + \psi^{t+1} \lambda^{t+1} + \ldots + \psi^T \lambda^T \qquad (5.21)$$

$$\text{s.t.} \qquad \lambda^2\ ^f y^2 + {}^i y^2 \in P^1 \left(x^1,\ ^i \overline{y}^o \right)$$

$$\vdots$$

$$\lambda^{t+1}\ ^f y^{t+1} + {}^i y^{t+1} \in P^t \left(x^t,\ ^i y^{t-1} \right)$$

$$\vdots$$

$$\lambda^T\ ^f y^T + {}^i \overline{y}^T \in P^{T-1} \left(x^{T-1},\ ^i y^{T-2} \right).$$

Problems (5.20) and (5.21) are each solved once for each decision-making unit and the $T-1$ estimates of λ^{*t} are obtained. From (5.20) the function $\Delta_o^{t+1}\left(x^t,\ ^f y^t,\ ^i \overline{y} \right) = 1/\lambda^{*t}$ and from (5.21) the function $\Delta_o^{t}\left(x^{t+1},\ ^f y^{t+1},\ ^i \overline{y} \right) = 1/\lambda^{*t+1}$.

Next we introduce the static distance functions $D_o^{t}\left(x^t, y^t \right)$ and $D_o^{t+1}\left(x^{t+1}, y^{t+1} \right)$ into the dynamic efficiency change component ($DEFFCH$) so that we can decompose it into two dynamic parts and one static part. Typically, the static distance functions do not include intermediate products as variables to be solved for in the optimization. Instead, intermediate products ($^i y$) are taken to equal zero, or they are treated as given or exogenous in the optimization. To facilitate comparisons between dynamic and static cases, we change our notation slightly and describe the static distance functions in terms of final output, ${}^{f}y^{t} = y^{t} - {}^{i}y^{t}$, as in the case of the dynamic distance functions. Intermediate products will be treated the same as the exogenous inputs from the dynamic distance function. That is, for the static distance functions the given inputs are x^{t} and ${}^{i}y^{t-1}$, where x^{t} includes the exogenous inputs in the dynamic technology. We substitute the ${}^{f}y$ terms for the y terms in the static distance functions and define efficiency change as

$$
DEFFCH = \left(\frac{\Delta_{o}^{t+1}\left(x^{t+1},\, {}^{f}y^{t+1},\, {}^{i}\overline{y}\right)}{\Delta_{o}^{t}\left(x^{t},\, {}^{f}y^{t},\, {}^{i}\overline{y}\right)} \right) \tag{5.22}
$$

$$
= \left(\frac{\left(\dfrac{\Delta_{o}^{t+1}\left(x^{t+1},\, {}^{f}y^{t+1},\, {}^{i}\overline{y}\right)}{D_{o}^{t+1}\left(x^{t+1},\, {}^{f}y^{t+1},\, {}^{i}y^{t}\right)} \right)}{\left(\dfrac{\Delta_{o}^{t}\left(x^{t},\, {}^{f}y^{t},\, {}^{i}\overline{y}\right)}{D_{o}^{t}\left(x^{t},\, {}^{f}y^{t},\, {}^{i}y^{t-1}\right)} \right)} \right) \times \left(\frac{D_{o}^{t+1}\left(x^{t+1},\, {}^{f}y^{t+1},\, {}^{i}y^{t}\right)}{D_{o}^{t}\left(x^{t},\, {}^{f}y^{t},\, {}^{i}y^{t-1}\right)} \right).
$$

The first term on the right-hand side is an index of the gain in efficiency from dynamic reallocation of the intermediate products from period t to $t+1$. The numerator equals the ratio of the distance from the dynamic frontier to the static frontier in period $t+1$, and the denominator equals the ratio of the distance from the dynamic frontier to the static frontier in period t. This index takes a value greater than one when there has been an improvement in dynamic reallocation, resulting in the static frontier moving closer to the dynamic frontier from t to $t+1$, and takes a value less than one when the static frontier moves further away from the dynamic frontier because of greater misallocation of the intermediate products between periods. The second term equals the static change in efficiency that results from a producer catching up or falling behind the static frontier. This static change in efficiency takes a value greater than one when the producer is closer to the static frontier in $t+1$ relative to the static frontier in t. The product of the two terms in (5.22) give the efficiency gain between the two periods due to the advantages of the reallocation allowed in the dynamic case relative to the static case.

One disadvantage of the dynamic specification in the preceding is that the results will depend on the initial conditions and the transversality conditions; that is, if we wish to add one more year to our analysis, we would be re-estimating productivity change for the entire time period, which could change the results for the earlier periods.[12] This problem is avoided in the traditional and sequential DEA comparative static productivity measures, which estimate productivity change for each pair of adjacent periods, but is present in the global Malmquist index (Pastor and Lovell 2005). One could avoid the end-point problem in a dynamic context by estimating (5.18) using only a subset of the entire sample period, say only three periods at a time in a horizon where there are $T > 3$ periods. The estimation would be then be done multiple times: first, data from period $t = 0, 1$, and 2 would be used allowing for reallocation of the intermediate product from $t = 1$ to $t = 2$; second, data from periods $t = 1, 2$, and 3 would be used allowing for reallocation of the intermediate product from $t = 2$ to $t = 3$; and so forth, with the final estimation using data from periods $t = T - 2$, $T - 1$, and T allowing for reallocation of the intermediate product from $t = T - 1$ to T. Of course, one can use subsets of the time series longer than three periods. However, as long as the number of periods used is less than the entire sample period $t = 0, \dots, T$ the shorter time period limits possible reallocation across time. As a practical matter, choosing a short time horizon for the dynamic specification has several advantages. First, even a short two- or three-period horizon provides information that is not available in the static model specification. Second, a two- or three-period horizon is likely being more realistic in that it limits the time frame that the decision-maker is required to optimize over. Third, a shorter horizon means that productivity estimates do not have to be continually updated as new information becomes available.

An advantage to using all available periods to estimate the dynamic distance functions is that not only can one observe the pattern of dynamic productivity change and its components, but also optimal investment spending can be compared with the history of actual investment spending. This information might enhance policymakers' ability to engage in countercyclical policy. Furthermore, the dynamic model specification can be easily extended to cases where the technology generates both desirable outputs and jointly produced undesirable outputs, such as real gross domestic product (GDP) and carbon equivalent emissions. Here, information about productivity change and the history of optimal and actual investment spending could inform policymakers about how quickly new investment spending might be expected to reduce carbon emissions. When examining resources allocated for education, knowledge of optimal and actual investments to enhance human capital might inform policymakers about the amounts of money to allocate to K–12 education, higher education, and extended learning opportunities.

5.3.2. Time Substitution

In this section we briefly outline the idea of time substitution—another type of dynamic production model—as developed by Färe, Grosskopf, and Margaritis (2010). In the dynamic optimization problem (5.18) the amount of intermediate product is chosen so as to maximize the amount of final output to be produced over all periods, given exogenous inputs available in each period. In contrast, time substitution would constrain the amount of exogenous inputs to some fixed amount, say the sum of inputs over all periods, and would choose when to begin and end production and how intensively to use those inputs so as to maximize final outputs.

Suppose that production can take place anywhere from period $t = 1$ to $t = T$. If producers have a limited amount of resources to use during the period, when should those resources be used in order to maximize total production? This question relates to the issue of time substitution, where producers choose not only the amounts of intermediate products to produce, but also when to begin production, τ, and when to end production, $\tau + \Gamma$, so as to maximize final outputs. Färe, Grosskopf, and Margaritis (2010) showed that when there are increasing returns to scale, inputs should be used intensively in a single period, and when there are decreasing returns to scale, inputs should be spread over as many periods as possible, with the proportion of inputs to use in each period equal to $1/T$. Furthermore, when technological progress occurs, it is optimal to delay production, and when technological regress occurs, it is optimal to produce sooner.

Let $\bar{x}_n = \Sigma_{t=1}^{T} x_n^t$, $n = 1, \ldots, N$ represent the amount of input available to use over all periods. The time substitution problem can be written as

$$\max \ \psi^\tau \lambda^\tau + \ldots + \psi^{\tau+\Gamma} \lambda^{\tau+\Gamma} \tag{5.23}$$

$$\text{s.t.} \ \lambda^{\tau \, f} y^\tau + {}^i y^\tau \in P^\tau \left(x^\tau, {}^i \bar{y}^{\tau-1} \right)$$

$$\lambda^{\tau+1 \, f} y^{\tau+1} + {}^i y^{\tau+1} \in P^{\tau+1} \left(x^{\tau+1}, {}^i y^\tau \right)$$

$$\vdots$$

$$\lambda^{\tau+\Gamma \, f} y^{\tau+\Gamma} + {}^i \bar{y}^{\tau+\Gamma} \in P^{\tau+\Gamma} \left(x^{\tau+\Gamma}, {}^i y^{\tau+\Gamma-1} \right)$$

$$\sum_{t=\tau}^{\tau+\Gamma} x_n^t \le \bar{x}_n, \ n = 1, \ldots, N.$$

The choice variables in the time substitution problem (5.23) are when to begin production, τ, when to end production, $\tau + \Gamma$, the amounts of inputs to use in each period, x_t, $t = \tau, \ldots, \tau + \Gamma$, and the amount of intermediate product $({}^i y^t)$ to produce in periods $t = \tau+1, \ldots, \tau+\Gamma$, with the objective of maximizing the proportional expansion of final outputs summed over all production periods. We note that $\tau = 0$ and $\Gamma = T$ are possible solutions to (5.23), but other solutions having shorter horizons with $\tau > 0$ and $\Gamma < T$ are also possible. As in the dynamic optimization problem (5.18), the producer faces a trade-off between expanding final outputs or intermediate products. Producing more intermediate products in the current period expands the output set in the subsequent period, but at a cost; fewer final outputs can be produced in the current period.

The time substitution problem is related to the Shephard indirect output distance function. Given input prices, the indirect output distance function allows inputs to be reallocated as long as they satisfy a cost constraint consistent with the status quo. Since the status quo inputs are feasible, but not necessarily optimal, a greater proportional expansion in outputs is possible relative to $D_o(x, y)^{-1}$. However, unlike the Shephard indirect output distance function, the time substitution problem (5.23) does not require one to know input prices or have a targeted cost constraint, only that the reallocated inputs be no greater than the sum of inputs across time. In terms of productivity, the sum over time of the potential final outputs produced with time substitution will be greater than the same sum without time substitution, but the total amount of inputs will be the same. However, with time substitution some periods will see more inputs used than the status quo and some periods will see lower levels of potential output produced, so that a productivity change index might be either greater or less than a static productivity index in some periods.

Färe, Grosskopf, Margaritis, and Weber (2012) use time substitution to determine when countries should reduce emissions of carbon dioxide to be in compliance with the Kyoto Treaty. Fukuyama, Weber, and Xia (2016) examine the allocation of National Science Foundation funds for nanobiotechnology research between universities and across time in another application of time substitution. Fukuyama and Weber (2015a) examine bank production decisions using time substitution. They estimate a quadratic directional output distance function and then use the parameter estimates to calculate when it would be optimal for banks to reduce nonperforming loans so long as performing loans and securities investments were not reduced and costs of production were no greater than actual costs. Färe, Grosskopf, Margaritis, and Weber (2015) use the time substitution model to examine the European Union Stability and Growth Pact and how countries in the Union might optimally meet their government budget obligations, highlighting the fact that strict adherence to rigid fiscal rules might entail large costs in terms of lost output, as evidenced by the case of Greece.

5.4. Empirical Illustration of Static and Dynamic Performance

To illustrate our method, we use pooled data taken from the Penn World Tables for 33 OECD countries during the period 1990–2011.[13] We focus on estimating dynamic productivity change, rather than the time substitution problem. Countries produce total output equal to real GDP. We ignore discounting and assume the weights for each period are $\psi^t = 1$. Total output (y) consists of an intermediate product (^iy)—real investment spending—and a final output (^fy) equal to real GDP less investment spending. Labor is a given input (x) in each period and is not reallocated between periods. In period $t = 1$, which corresponds to 1991, the producer has access to a given amount of investment spending from period 0, and this given investment spending ($^i\bar{y}^0 = {}^i\bar{y}^{1990}$) is an input to the period $t = 1$ (1991) technology. Thus, in period $t = 1$ there are two given inputs—labor and prior investment spending—that are used to produce a single total output, which equals the sum of final output and current period investment spending. In $t = 1$ (1991) to $t = T - 1$ (2010) the amount of investment is chosen as part of the optimization. This chosen investment spending becomes an input in periods $t = 2$ (1992) to $t = T$ (2011) and is used, along with labor, to produce total output, which equals the sum of final output and current investment spending. In period T (2011) investment spending is fixed to satisfy the transversality condition: ${}^{i}\overline{y}^{T} = {}^{i}\overline{y}^{2011}$. Using DEA, the optimization problem is to calculate the dynamic distance functions for country k' in the form:

$$\max \quad \lambda^{1} + \ldots + \lambda^{T} \tag{5.24}$$

$$\text{s.t.} \quad \lambda^{1}\, {}^{f}y_{k'}^{1} + {}^{i}y^{1} \leq \sum_{k=1}^{K} z_{k}^{1} y_{k}^{1}$$

$$\quad {}^{i}\overline{y}_{k'}^{0} \geq \sum_{k=1}^{K} z_{k}^{1}\, {}^{i}y_{k}^{0}$$

$$\quad x_{k'}^{1} \geq \sum_{k=1}^{K} z_{k}^{1} x_{k}^{1}$$

$$\quad z_{k}^{1} \geq 0, \quad k = 1, \ldots, K, \quad t = 1,$$

$$\lambda^{t}\, {}^{f}y_{k'}^{t} + {}^{i}y^{t} \leq \sum_{k=1}^{K} z_{k}^{t} y_{k}^{t}$$

$$\quad {}^{i}y^{t-1} \geq \sum_{k=1}^{K} z_{k}^{t}\, {}^{i}y_{k}^{t-1}$$

$$\quad x_{k'}^{2} \geq \sum_{k=1}^{K} z_{k}^{t} x_{k}^{t}$$

$$\quad z_{k}^{t} \geq 0, \quad k = 1, \ldots, K, \quad t = 2, \ldots, T-1,$$

$$\vdots$$

$$\lambda^{T}\, {}^{f}y_{k'}^{T} + {}^{i}\overline{y}_{k'}^{T} \leq \sum_{k=1}^{K} z_{k}^{T} y_{k}^{T}$$

$$\quad {}^{i}y^{T-1} \geq \sum_{k=1}^{K} z_{k}^{T}\, {}^{i}y_{k}^{T-1}$$

$$\quad x_{k'}^{T} \geq \sum_{k=1}^{K} z_{k}^{T} x_{k}^{T}$$

$$\quad z_{k}^{T} \geq 0, \quad k = 1, \ldots, K, \quad t = T.$$

The LP problem (5.24) is solved once for each of the 33 countries in our sample. In (5.24) the choice variables are λ^{t}, $t = 1, \ldots, T$, which represent the maximum feasible expansion of final outputs in each period. The solution to (5.24) provides estimates of λ^{t} for each period $t = 1, \ldots, T$ corresponding to 1991 to 2011. Dynamic efficiency equals $\Delta_{o}^{t}\left(x^{t}, {}^{f}y^{t}, {}^{i}\overline{y}^{0}\right) = 1/\lambda^{*t}$, which is a vector of length T. In addition, the intensity variables, z_{k}^{t}, $t = 1, \ldots, T$ and the amount of optimal investment $({}^{i}y^{t})$ to undertake in periods $t = 1$ to $t = T-1$ are also chosen as part of the optimization. Investment in period $t = 0$, ${}^{i}\overline{y}_{k'}^{0}$ enters as an input to the period $t = 1$ technology but is given. Similarly, investment in period $t = T$, ${}^{i}\overline{y}_{k'}^{T}$ enters the output equation but is taken as given. Problem (5.24) uses data from periods $t = 0, 1, \ldots, T$ corresponding to 1990 to 2011. We solve (5.24) one time for each of the $K = 33$ countries in our sample.

To estimate dynamic productivity change, we solve two mixed-period problems that are the DEA representations of (5.20) and (5.21). The first mixed-period problem estimates the distance from the observed outputs in period t to the technological frontier defined by the outputs and inputs in periods $t + 1$. This problem is written as

$$\max \; \lambda^1 + \ldots + \lambda^{T-1} \tag{5.25}$$

$$\text{s.t.} \quad \lambda^1 \, {}^f y_{k'}^1 + {}^i y^1 \leq \sum_{k=1}^{K} z_k^2 y_k^2$$

$$\quad {}^i \overline{y}_{k'}^0 \geq \sum_{k=1}^{K} z_k^2 \, {}^i y_k^1$$

$$\quad x_{k'}^1 \geq \sum_{k=1}^{K} z_k^2 x_k^2$$

$$\quad z_k^2 \geq 0, \quad k = 1, \ldots, K, \quad t = 1,$$

$$\lambda^t \, {}^f y_{k'}^t + {}^i y^t \leq \sum_{k=1}^{K} z_k^{t+1} y_k^{t+1}$$

$$\quad {}^i y^{t-1} \geq \sum_{k=1}^{K} z_k^{t+1} \, {}^i y_k^t$$

$$\quad x_{k'}^t \geq \sum_{k=1}^{K} z_k^{t+1} x_k^{t+1}$$

$$\quad z_k^{t+1} \geq 0, \quad k = 1, \ldots, K,$$

$$\vdots$$

$$\lambda^{T-1} \, {}^f y_{k'}^{T-1} + {}^i \overline{y}_{k'}^{T-1} \leq \sum_{k=1}^{K} z_k^T y_k^T$$

$$\quad {}^i y^{T-2} \geq \sum_{k=1}^{K} z_k^T \, {}^i y_k^{T-1}$$

$$\quad x_{k'}^{T-1} \geq \sum_{k=1}^{K} z_k^T x_k^T$$

$$\quad z_k^T \geq 0, \quad k = 1, \ldots, K.$$

The mixed-period efficiency found as part of the solution from (5.25) equals $\Delta_o^{t+1}\left(x^t, {}^f y^t, {}^i \overline{y}\right) = 1/\lambda^{*t}$.

The second mixed-period problem estimates the distance from the observed outputs in period $t + 1$ to the technological frontier defined by the outputs and inputs in periods t. This problem is written as

$$\max \quad \lambda^2 + \ldots + \lambda^T \tag{5.26}$$

$$\text{s.t.} \quad \lambda^2 \, {}^f y_{k'}^2 + {}^i y^2 \le \sum_{k=1}^{K} z_k^1 y_k^1$$

$$ {}^i \overline{y}_{k'}^1 \ge \sum_{k=1}^{K} z_k^1 \, {}^i y_k^0$$

$$x_{k'}^2 \ge \sum_{k=1}^{K} z_k^1 x_k^1$$

$$z_k^1 \ge 0, \quad k = 1, \ldots, K,$$

$$\lambda^{t+1} \, {}^f y_{k'}^{t+1} + {}^i y_k^{t+1} \le \sum_{k=1}^{K} z_k^t y_k^t$$

$$ {}^i y^t \ge \sum_{k=1}^{K} z_k^t \, {}^i y_k^{t-1}$$

$$x_{k'}^{t+1} \ge \sum_{k=1}^{K} z_k^t x_k^t$$

$$z_k^t \ge 0, \quad k = 1, \ldots, K,$$

$$\vdots$$

$$\lambda^T \, {}^f y_{k'}^T + {}^i \overline{y}_k^T \le \sum_{k=1}^{K} z_k^{T-1} y_k^{T-1}$$

$$ {}^i y^{T-1} \ge \sum_{k=1}^{K} z_k^{T-1} \, {}^i y_k^{T-2}$$

$$x_{k'}^T \ge \sum_{k=1}^{K} z_k^{T-1} x_k^{T-1}$$

$$z_k^{T-1} \ge 0, \quad k = 1, \ldots, K.$$

The mixed-period efficiency found as part of the solution from (5.26) equals $\Delta_o^t \left(x^{t+1}, \, {}^f y^{t+1}, \, {}^i \overline{y} \right) = 1 / \lambda^{*t+1}$.

Table 5.1 reports the geometric means for the dynamic and static efficiency estimates by year and the number of countries defining the frontier. In our static model specification, each country produces a final output $({}^f y^t)$ equal to real GDP less real investment spending using two inputs: labor (x^t) and prior investment spending $({}^i \overline{y}^{t-1})$. Average efficiency over all years for the dynamic model $\Delta^t \left(x, \, {}^f y, \, {}^i y^{t-1} \right) = 0.549$ is less than average efficiency for the static model $D_o^t \left(x, \, {}^f y, \, {}^i y^{t-1} \right) = 0.694$. This result indicates the greater potential for dynamic optimization to expand production by optimally choosing investment relative to the static model that takes investment as given. By year, average dynamic efficiency ranges from a low of $\Delta^t \left(x, \, {}^f y, \, {}^i \overline{y} \right) = 0.474$ in 2004 to a high of $\Delta^t \left(x, \, {}^f y, \, {}^i \overline{y} \right) = 0.747$ in 1991. Average static efficiency ranges from a low of $D_o^t \left(x, \, {}^f y, \, {}^i y^{t-1} \right) = 0.592$ in 2004 to a high of $D_o^t \left(x, \, {}^f y, \, {}^i y^{t-1} \right) = 0.762$ in 1999.

Table 5.1 Estimates of Dynamic and Static Efficiency

	Dynamic		Static	
	$\Delta^t(x^t, {}^fy^t, \overline{y})$	# on Frontier	$D_o^t(x^t, {}^fy^t, {}^iy^{t-1})$	# on Frontier
1991	0.747	6	0.722	2
1992	0.601	4	0.701	3
1993	0.567	1	0.682	2
1994	0.535	1	0.700	3
1995	0.546	1	0.706	2
1996	0.513	1	0.678	2
1997	0.544	1	0.687	1
1998	0.593	1	0.751	2
1999	0.547	1	0.762	2
2000	0.526	1	0.716	2
2001	0.478	1	0.630	1
2002	0.502	1	0.627	2
2003	0.486	1	0.632	2
2004	0.474	1	0.592	2
2005	0.492	1	0.666	2
2006	0.512	1	0.725	3
2007	0.517	1	0.748	3
2008	0.680	3	0.755	4
2009	0.532	1	0.727	3
2010	0.564	1	0.723	4
2011	0.569	1	0.651	2
Sub-periods				
1991–1996	0.585		0.698	
1997–2001	0.538		0.709	
2002–2006	0.493		0.648	
2007–2011	0.572		0.721	
All years	0.549		0.694	

The same number or more countries produce on the static frontier than produce on the dynamic frontier in every year except 1991 and 1992. This finding suggests that misspecified dynamics might be a source of bias in the estimation of technical efficiency, a finding consistent with Ahn and Sickles (2000), who found that technical efficiency follows an autoregressive process. Although not reported, Norway is on the dynamic frontier in 18 out of 21 years, and it produces on the static frontier in 20 out of 21 years. Table 5.1 also reports estimates of dynamic and static efficiency for four sub-periods. Dynamic efficiency is greatest during 1991–1996, which coincided with a global downturn, and lowest during the 2002–2006 expansion in the global economy. Static efficiency exhibits less variation between sub-periods and is highest during 2007–2011 and lowest in 2002–2006.

Table 5.2 reports the geometric means of the dynamic and static productivity indices and their components of efficiency change and technical change for each year and for four sub-periods. For the dynamic model, productivity growth is positive in 14 out of 20 years and averages 1.7% over all years. The static model gives positive

Table 5.2 Estimates of Dynamic and Static Productivity Change
(Geometric Means)

Year	Dynamic			Static		
	Malm	EFFCH	TECH	Malm	EFFCH	TECH
1991–1992	0.998	0.777	1.285	1.083	0.963	1.125
1992–1993	0.992	0.954	1.040	1.037	0.978	1.061
1993–1994	1.015	0.934	1.087	1.023	1.030	0.993
1994–1995	1.032	1.025	1.007	1.018	1.010	1.008
1995–1996	1.011	0.936	1.080	0.966	0.957	1.010
1996–1997	1.029	1.060	0.970	1.015	1.012	1.003
1997–1998	1.017	1.089	0.934	0.987	1.097	0.900
1998–1999	1.040	0.921	1.129	1.027	1.019	1.008
1999–2000	1.055	0.962	1.096	1.080	0.934	1.156
2000–2001	1.020	0.909	1.122	0.964	0.880	1.095
2001–2002	1.020	1.050	0.971	1.039	0.995	1.045
2002–2003	0.994	0.966	1.029	1.010	1.006	1.004
2003–2004	1.006	0.977	1.029	0.997	0.931	1.071
2004–2005	1.026	1.043	0.984	0.965	1.131	0.853
2005–2006	0.967	1.040	0.930	0.929	1.085	0.856
2006–2007	0.997	1.010	0.987	0.951	1.033	0.921
2007–2008	0.979	1.333	0.735	0.939	1.012	0.928
2008–2009	1.097	0.780	1.407	1.016	0.970	1.047
2009–2010	1.015	1.062	0.955	1.260	0.996	1.266
2010–2011	1.031	1.011	1.020	0.949	0.900	1.055
1991–1996	1.010	0.921	1.096	1.025	0.987	1.038
1997–2001	1.032	0.986	1.047	1.014	0.986	1.028
2002–2006	1.003	1.015	0.988	0.987	1.027	0.961
2007–2011	1.023	1.024	0.999	1.016	0.981	1.036
1991–2011	1.017	0.986	1.031	1.011	0.995	1.016

productivity growth in 10 out of 20 years and averages 1.1%. Increases in efficiency occur in 10 years for both the dynamic and the static models, but during the entire period there is a slight decline in efficiency, averaging 1.4% per year for the dynamic model and 0.5% for the static model. Positive technical progress occurs in 12 years for the dynamic model and 14 years for the static model. Average technical progress of 3.1% for the dynamic model and 1.6% for the static model more than offsets the declines in average efficiency.

From Table 5.2 we see positive productivity growth in every sub-period for the dynamic model and in three out of four sub-periods for the static model. Productivity growth during the Great Recession period of 2007–2011 averages 2.3% for the dynamic model and 1.6% for the static model. During 2007–2010 efficiency increases by 2.4% for the dynamic model with 0.1% decline in technical progress. These results are consistent with evidence reported for the United States by Fernald (2015) and Petrosky-Nadeau (2013), who suggest that crises bring about productive resource reallocation. Foster et al. (2013) note that "[e]vidence shows this high pace of reallocation is closely linked to production dynamics."

We regard these results as illustrative; the empirical specification model is very parsimonious, we ignore discounting, and there are no connections of the intermediate product to the next period's capital stock. A more sophisticated specification might result in larger differences between the comparative static and dynamic results. Nonetheless, these results illustrate what can be accomplished with dynamic productivity models, and these models can be expanded accordingly in several directions.

5.5. Conclusion

In this chapter we have focused on at least some of the efforts to move measuring efficiency and productivity in a DEA framework from a static or comparative-static approach toward a more dynamic approach. The underlying links here are the distance functions, which have been the workhorses of the pioneering work motivated by CCD (1982). Since the distance functions represent technology, the first step is to specify technology in a dynamic framework that is still amenable to DEA-type estimation. A number of scholars have addressed this topic—a few of whom we have included here, with apologies to the many we did not. Our view of a dynamic technology is one in which decisions in the current (or past) period are explicitly linked and affect later periods. This includes notions of intermediate products, investment, time substitution, supply chain, and so on, and allows for possible reallocation across periods. This structure is also familiar from the network DEA literature. We believe the advantage of this approach is in better describing production processes and in providing more information to both analysts and policymakers.

The resulting distance functions defined on these technologies we interpret as dynamic distance functions. We specify a many-period dynamic model in the spirit of

Ramsey (1928), as well as an adjacent-period model familiar from the Malmquist productivity literature, and we provide an empirical illustration for the former. Extensions of the general setup are relatively straightforward for other distance function based productivity indices, both parametric and nonparametric.

Although not explicitly included here, efficiency and productivity in the presence of good and bad outputs can also be cast in a dynamic setting; examples are cited in the introduction to the chapter. In the joint production framework, directional distance functions and Luenberger indices are appropriate building blocks. Future directions include the many refinements that have been developed in the comparative-static framework: statistical inference and possible bootstrapping, treatment of environmental variables, decompositions, and windows-type models, among many others.

Notes

1. CCD assume translog distance functions with identical second-order coefficients and input and output prices reflecting competitive outcomes.
2. This framework may also be useful in accommodating longer lags. For example, strong demand for energy and minerals from China and India in the first decade of the 2000s led Australian mining companies to begin capital expansion. Eslake (2011) attributed the decline in Australian mining sector productivity to be the result of the long lead times necessary to bring the new capital into full production.
3. Research by Pearl (2009) provides an important graphical exposition of how causal effects can be unraveled.
4. See also Kao (2013, 2014) for overviews of dynamic DEA and network DEA. We view dynamic DEA as a subset of network DEA.
5. For a survey of these conditions, see Färe and Primont (1995). Although we focus on measuring dynamic productivity using output sets, one can also measure dynamic productivity using input sets with the same regularity conditions.
6. This figure is from Färe and Grosskopf (1996).
7. This model is due to von Neumann; see Karlin (1959, 340).
8. We use the terms *exogenous* and *endogenous* in a nonstatistical sense. By exogenous we mean that those inputs are not variables, but rather data. By endogenous we mean that those factors are variables for which we solve.
9. This model is not consistent with the simple definition of productivity and productivity change as ratios of output and input quantity indices; see the discussion in O'Donnell (2012a, 2012b).
10. In a recent paper Diewert and Fox (2014) provide theoretical justification for why the geometric mean should be used in the Bjurek productivity index. Similar arguments apply to the Malmquist index.
11. Again, our use of exogenous/endogenous in this context is not statistical. Exogenous means given by observed data, and endogenous means solved for as part of the optimization problem.
12. The preceding problem is essentially a fixed base problem, which allows for transitivity but is base dependent; see Balk and Althin (1996) and Althin (2001).
13. Data and the GAMS programs used to estimate the static and dynamic models are available at http://cstl-hcb.semo.edu/wlweber.

References

Ahn, S. C., and R. Sickles. 2000. "Estimation of Long-Run Inefficiency Levels: A Dynamic Frontier Approach." *Econometric Reviews* 19: 461–492.

Aigner, D. J., and S. F. Chu. 1968. "On Estimating the Industry Production Function." *American Economic Review* 58: 226–239.

Aiyar, S., C.-J. Dalgaard, and O. Moav. 2008. "Technological Progress and Regress in Pre-industrial Times." *Journal of Economic Growth* 13(2): 125–144.

Althin, R. 2001. "Measures of Productivity Changes: Two Malmquist Index Approaches." *Journal of Productivity Analysis* 16: 108–128.

Ang, F., and A. O. Lansink. 2014. "Dynamic Profit Inefficiencies: A DEA Application to Belgian Dairy Farms." Bioeconomics Working Paper 2014/3, University of Leuven. http:// ageconsearch.umn.edu/bitstream/165693/2/BioeconWP_2014_3.pdf

Balk, B. M. 1993. "Malmquist Productivity Indexes and Fisher Ideal Indexes: Comment." *Economic Journal* 103: 680–682.

Balk, B. M., and R. Althin. 1996. "A New Transitive Productivity Index." *Journal of Productivity Analysis* 7: 19–27.

Bjurek, H. 1996. "The Malmquist Total Factor Productivity Index." *Scandinavian Journal of Economics* 98(2): 303–313.

Bogetoft, P., R. Färe, S. Grosskopf, K. Hayes, and L. Taylor. 2009. "Dynamic Network DEA: An Illustration." *Journal of the Operational Research Society of Japan* 52(2): 147–162.

Caves, D., L. Christensen, and W. E. Diewert. 1982. "The Economic Theory of Index Numbers and the Measurement of Input, Output, and Productivity." *Econometrica* 50(6): 1393–1414.

Chen, C.-M., and J. Van Dalen. 2010. "Measuring Dynamic Efficiency: Theories and an Integrated Methodology." *European Journal of Operational Research* 203: 749–760.

Diewert, W. E. 1976. "Exact and Superlative Index Numbers." *Journal of Econometrics* 4: 115–145.

Diewert, W. E. 1992. "Fisher Ideal Output, Input and Productivity Indexes Revisited." *Journal of Productivity Analysis* 3(3): 211–248.

Diewert, W. E., and K. J. Fox. 2014. "Decomposing Bjurek Productivity Indexes into Explanatory Factors." UNSW Australia Business School Research Paper No. 2014-33.

Emrouznejad, A., and E. Thanassoulis. 2005. "A Mathematical Model for Dynamic Efficiency Using Data Envelopment Analysis." *Applied Mathematics and Computation* 160(2): 363–378.

Eslake, S. 2011. "Productivity: The Lost Decade." Paper presented to the Reserve Bank of Australia Conference: The Australian Economy in the 2000s, Sydney, August. http://www. rba.gov.au/publications/confs/2011/pdf/eslake.pdf.

Färe, R, and S. Grosskopf. 1992. "Malmquist Productivity Indexes and Fisher Ideal Indexes." *The Economic Journal* 102(4): 158–160.

Färe, R., and S. Grosskopf. 1996. *Intertemporal Production Frontiers: With Dynamic DEA.* Boston: Kluwer Academic.

Färe, R., S. Grosskopf, B. Lindgren, and P. Roos. 1994. "Productivity Developments in Swedish Hospitals: A Malmquist Output Index Approach." In *Data Envelopment Analysis: Theory, Methodology and Applications*, edited by A. Charnes, W. Cooper, A. Lewin, and L. Seiford, 253–272. Boston: Kluwer Academic.

Färe, R., S. Grosskopf, and D. Margaritis. 2010. "Time Substitution with Application to DEA." *Journal of the Operational Research Society* 62(7): 1420–1422.

Färe, R., S. Grosskopf, D. Margaritis, and W. Weber. 2012. "Technological Change and Timing Reductions in Greenhouse Gas Emissions." *Journal of Productivity Analysis* 37(3): 205–216.

Färe, R., S. Grosskopf, D. Margaritis, and W. Weber. 2015. "The EU Stability and Growth Pact." In *Advances in Data Envelopment Analysis*, edited by R. Färe, S. Grosskopf, and D. Margaritis, 75–86. Singapore: World Scientific-Now Publishers Series in Business.

Färe, R., S. Grosskopf, and P. Roos. 1998. "Malmquist Productivity Indexes: A Survey of Theory and Practice." In *Index Numbers: Essays in Honour of Sten Malmquist*, edited by R. Färe, S. Grosskopf, and R. R. Russell, 127–190. Boston: Kluwer Academic.

Färe, R., and D. Primont. 1995. *Multi-Output Production and Duality: Theory and Applications.* Boston: Kluwer Academic.

Färe, R., and G. Whitaker. 1996. "Dynamic Measurement of Efficiency: An Application to Western Public Grazing." In *Intertemporal Production Frontiers: With Dynamic DEA*, edited by R. Färe and S. Grosskopf, 168–186. Boston: Kluwer Academic.

Fernald, J. G. 2015. "Productivity and Potential Output before, during and after the Great Recession." *NBER Macroeconomics Annual* 29(1): 1–51.

Foster, L., C. Grim, and J. Haltiwanger. 2013. "Reallocation in the Great Recession: Cleansing or Not?" NBER Working Paper 20427. http://www.nber.org/papers/w20427.

Fukuyama, H., and W. L. Weber. 2015a. "Nonperforming Loans in the Bank Production Technology." In *Quantitative Financial Risk Management: Theory and Practice*, edited by Constantin Zopounidis and Emilios Galariotis, 46–70. Hoboken, NJ: John Wiley & Sons.

Fukuyama, H., and W. L. Weber. 2015b. "Measuring Japanese Bank Performance: A Dynamic Network DEA Approach." *Journal of Productivity Analysis* 44(3): 249–264.

Fukuyama, H., and W. L. Weber. 2017. "Measuring Bank Performance with a Dynamic Network Luenberger Indicator." *Annals of Operations Research* 250(1): 85–104.

Fukuyama, H., W. L. Weber, and Y. Xia. 2016. "Time Substitution and Network Effects with an Application to Nanobiotechnology Policy for US Universities." *Omega* 60: 34–54.

Grifell-Tatje, E., and C. A. K. Lovell. 1995. "A Note on the Malmquist Productivity Index." *Economics Letters* 47: 169–175.

Kao, C. 2013. "Dynamic Data Envelopment Analysis: A Relational Analysis." *European Journal of Operational Research* 227(2): 325–330.

Kao, C. 2014. "Network Data Envelopment Analysis: A Review." *European Journal of Operational Research* 239(1): 1–16.

Kapelko, M., A. O. Lansink, and S. Stefanou. 2014. "Assessing Dynamic Inefficiency of the Spanish Construction Sector Pre- and Post-Financial Crisis." *European Journal of Operational Research* 237: 349–357.

Karlin, S. 1959. *Mathematical Methods and Theory of Games, Programming and Economics.* Reading, MA: Addison Wesley.

Kemeny, J. G., O. Morgenstern, and G. L. Thompson. 1956. "A Generalization of the Von Neumann Model of an Expanding Economy." *Econometrica* 24: 115–135.

Koopmans, T. C. 1951. *Activity Analysis of Production and Allocation.* Cowles Commission Monograph No. 13. New York: John Wiley & Sons.

Kumar, S., and R. R. Russell. 2002. "Technical Change, Technological Catch-Up, and Capital Deepening: Relative Contributions to Growth and Convergence." *American Economic Review* 923(3): 527–548.

Lansink, A. O., S. Stefanou, and T. Serra. 2015. "Primal and Dual Dynamic Luenberger Productivity Indicators." *European Journal of Operational Research* 241(1): 555–563.

Nemoto, J., and M. Goto. 2003. "Measurement of Dynamic Efficiency in Production: An Application of Data Envelopment Analysis to Japanese Electric Utilities." *Journal of Productivity Analysis* 19: 191–210.

Nishimizu, M., and J. M. Page. 1982. "Total Factor Productivity Growth, Technological Progress and Technical Efficiency Change: Dimensions of Productivity Change in Yugoslavia 1965–78." *Economic Journal* 92: 920–936.

O'Donnell, C. J. (2012a). "Aggregate Quantity Framework for Measuring and Decomposing Productivity Change." *Journal of Productivity Analysis* 38: 255–272.

O'Donnell, C. J. 2012b. "Nonparametric Estimation of Productivity and Profitability Change in U.S. Agriculture." *American Journal of Agricultural Economics* 94(4): 873–890.

O'Donnell, C. J. 2014. "Econometric Estimation of Distance Functions and Associated Measures of Productivity and Efficiency Change." *Journal of Productivity Analysis* 41: 187–200.

Pastor, J. T., and C. A. K. Lovell. 2005. "A Global Malmquist Productivity Index." *Economics Letters* 88(2): 266–271.

Pearl, J. 2009. *Causality: Models, Reasoning, and Inference.* Cambridge: Cambridge University Press.

Petroskey-Nadeau, N. 2013. "TFP during a Credit Crunch." *Journal of Economic Theory* 148: 1150–1178.

Ramsey, F. P. 1928). "A Mathematical Theory of Saving." *Economic Journal* 38: 543–559.

Rungsuriyawiboon, S., and S. E. Stefanou. 2007. "Dynamic Efficiency Estimation: An Application to U.S. Electric Utilities." *Journal of Business and Economic Statistics* 25(2): 226–238.

Serra, T., O. Lansink, and S. E. Stefanou. 2011. "Measurement of Dynamic Efficiency: A Directional Distance Function Parametric Approach." *American Journal of Agricultural Economics* 93(3): 756–767.

Silva, E., and S. E. Stefanou. 2003. "Nonparametric Dynamic Production Analysis and the Theory of Cost." *Journal of Productivity Analysis* 19(1): 5–32.

Silva, E., and S. E. Stefanou. 2007. "Dynamic Efficiency Measurement: Theory and Application." *American Journal of Agricultural Economics* 89(2): 398–419.

Shephard, R. W. 1970. *Theory of Cost and Production Functions.* Princeton, NJ: Princeton University Press.

Shephard, R. W., and R. Färe. 1980. *Dynamic Theory of Production Correspondences.* Cambridge, MA: Oelgeschlager, Gunn and Hain.

Skevas, T., A. O. Lansink, and S. E. Stefanou. 2012. "Measuring Technical Efficiency in the Presence of Pesticide Spillovers and Production Uncertainty: The Case of Dutch Arable Farms." *European Journal of Operational Research* 223: 550–559.

Sueyoshi, T., and K. Sekitani. 2005. "Returns to Scale in Dynamic DEA." *European Journal of Operational Research* 161: 536–544.

Zucker, L. G., M. R. Darby, and J. S. Armstrong. 2002. "Commercializing Knowledge: University Science, Knowledge Capture, and Firm Performance in Biotechnology." *Management Science* 48(1): 138–153.

CHAPTER 6

PRODUCTIVITY MEASUREMENT IN SECTORS WITH HARD-TO-MEASURE OUTPUT

KIM ZIESCHANG

6.1. INTRODUCTION

THE key challenge in measuring productivity is its inherently residual nature: productivity is output growth—including changes in output quality—over and above growth in intermediate and capital service inputs—including changes in input quality—while adjusting change in inputs for non-unitary returns to scale. Thus, using the national accounting term *volume* for the combined measure of change in quantity and quality, a key objective in compiling estimates of growth in output and intermediate consumption is to distinguish *volume* change from price change within the change in economic value aggregates, key among which is gross domestic product (GDP). Productivity thus purportedly measures the contribution of everything *but* output and input volume to evolution in the scale-adjusted output over input ratio. Everything else comprises, for example, technology, process, and environmental factors that are not embodied in the measure of output and input quality change. However, given a chosen scope of output, everything else also includes omitted inputs and measurement errors in output and input quantity and quality. This chapter is concerned with sectors having hard-to-measure output, but in measuring productivity in sectors with hard-to-measure output, we also are implicitly dealing with hard-to-measure intermediate input to the extent that those outputs are used in further production, changes in the quality of quasi fixed (capital) inputs, and correctly setting the boundary between what is an indicator of output and input quality and what is an indicator of evolution in technology, process, and environment.

The central heuristic of the theory and practice of productivity and efficiency measurement is an agricultural or manufacturing enterprise producing goods (output) with goods sourced from other producers (intermediate consumption), as well as labor and capital (primary services). Although produced (as opposed to primary) services have been part of output for the national accounts since Stone (1947), measuring the output and intermediate consumption of produced services has, as a rule, been challenged by problems with defining the volume, and even the nominal value of service outputs and inputs. As well, there have been long economics literatures on measuring both labor and (nonhuman) capital primary services, using the empirical capital services and capital accumulation paradigm defined in Jorgenson (1963).

Practically speaking, quantity is in the units of the buyer-seller contract. Goods examples are a liter of fuel, a metric ton of grain, a car, a lathe, a building. Legal and other professional services are charged by the hour or by the job, while the principal quantity metric of financial services is the account, augmented in some instances by indicators of account servicing activity, such as check clearing. The quantity variable's variations are directly reflected in a contractual pricing formula—the simplest of which being price times quantity—describing how the monetary value of the transaction between buyer and seller is determined.

Quantity metrics are necessarily associated with conditioning metrics, or characteristics, describing what constitutes each transacted unit and that collectively comprise "product quality." For example, fuel has an octane dimension; grain has species and grading dimensions; a car has quite a large number of dimensions such as size, power, interior and exterior finishes, and reliability ratings; a real estate asset is defined by building and lot size, location, quality of finishes, and local amenities/services. The value of legal services is conditioned by the reputation of the service provider in successful litigation. Financial services comprise indicators of the provision of liquidity, asset management, and insurance.

When we declare a good or service difficult to measure, we are almost always dealing with a lack of data on the characteristics metrics—quality—associated with the quantity metric, and in some cases are not clear on what information to look for in acquiring these data. When variations in conditioning metrics affect the price of a given primary quantity transaction, we characterize them as describing input, output, or process quality, thus connecting us with the economics literature on product quality measurement and its impact on volume transacted.

We can identify the following hard-to-measure sectors for productivity measurement:

- High technology industries
- Real estate
- Services, notably
  - Distributive services
  - Financial services
    - Banking
    - Insurance

- Health care
- Education

A first class of issues among these hard-to-measure cases is where the characteristics metrics on outputs and inputs are changing (i.e., "quality" is changing) between periods or places, along with quantities, in a productivity comparison. Quality change is particularly evident in service activities, but goods undergoing rapid changes in technology, such as information and communications technology (ICT) equipment, are also among well-known hard-to-measure cases of this type. Bosworth and Triplett (2007) provide a good overview of the state of play in services measurement, while Byrne, Fernald, and Reinsdorf (2016) explore issues in measuring the output of high-technology industries, and across all industries, in measuring the capital input from the accumulation of ICT equipment and intangible assets such as intellectual property.

A second element of "hardness to measure" is lack of sufficiently frequent transaction data to permit market valuation, and is particularly relevant for certain durables. A key example of this is real estate, a combination of land, improvements to land, and structures with location-specific, time-varying quality dimensions whose market prices are determined by sale transactions separated by years or decades.

A third "hardness to measure" issue is lack of information on the production and accumulation of intellectual property assets, which are relatively recent additions to national accounting standards aimed at capturing at least some of Romer's (1990) and others' "endogenous technological change."[1] These types of products may be both output and intermediate consumption in the calculation of GDP, but as underscored in Byrne et al. (2016), our overview of hard-to-measure sectors would be incomplete without also considering the human and nonhuman capital measurement problems within the denominator, input component of productivity measures.

6.2. ANALYTICS OF HARD-TO-MEASURE GOODS, SERVICES, AND ASSETS

We begin with the economic analytics of accounting for changes in quality and environmental characteristics in measuring productivity.

6.2.1. Primal Technology: Distance Functions

Distance functions are representations of production functions expressly designed to measure efficiency and productivity by looking at how much less input than we observe would be required to generate observed output, or how much more than the output we observe could be produced with observed inputs. We begin by defining the following variables:

y	the vector of output quantities
x	the vector of input quantities provided by other producers (intermediate inputs)
$K = \begin{bmatrix} K_H, K_N \end{bmatrix}'$	the vector of human (H) and nonhuman (N) capital stocks yielding primary input services
$\gamma > 0$	the vector of characteristics metrics ("quality") for outputs
$\chi > 0$	the vector of characteristics metrics ("quality") for intermediate inputs
$\kappa = \begin{bmatrix} \kappa_H, \kappa_N \end{bmatrix}' > 0$	the vector of characteristics metrics ("quality") for capital (human and nonhuman asset) stocks
$\vartheta > 0$	the vector of conditioning metrics ("characteristics" or "quality") for technology and environment.

The quality and environment variables are presumed to be defined, with little or no sacrifice of generality, so that $(\gamma, \chi, \kappa, \vartheta) > 0$. We define the primal technology as the set T of feasible $(y, x, K, \gamma, \chi, \kappa, \vartheta)$. In the interest of focusing on key points, we make the following free disposal (monotonicity) assumptions concerning technology T:

If $(y, x, K, \gamma, \chi, \kappa, \vartheta) \in T$ and $(y^0, \gamma^0) \le (y, \gamma)$ then $(y^0, x, K, \gamma^0, \chi, \kappa, \vartheta) \in T$;

If $(x, K, \chi, \kappa) \in T$ and $(x^0, K^0, \chi^0, \kappa^0) \ge (x, K, \chi, \kappa)$ then $(y, x^0, K^0, \gamma, \chi^0, \kappa^0, \vartheta) \in T$.

Thus armed, we can choose the economist's production function from an array of functional metrics on T. These functional metrics are called distance functions, and for any given technology T can be set up in various configurations, depending on the analytical focus. We will introduce three such metrics briefly—the input distance function, the output distance function, and the capacity utilization function—before narrowing detailed discussion to the third option in the remainder of the chapter.

The *input distance function* is defined[2,3]

$$d_x (y, x, K, \gamma, \chi, \kappa, \vartheta) \equiv \min \left\{ \lambda : (y, \lambda x, K, \gamma, \chi, \kappa, \vartheta) \in T \right\}.$$

$(y, x, K, \gamma, \chi, \kappa, \vartheta)$ is feasible (that is, $(y, x, K, \gamma, \chi, \kappa, \vartheta) \in T$) if and only if $d_x (y, x, K, \gamma, \chi, \kappa, \vartheta) \ge 1$. By definition d_x is positively linear homogeneous in x: $d_x (y, \lambda x, K, \gamma, \chi, \kappa, \vartheta) = \lambda d_x (y, x, K, \gamma, \chi, \kappa, \vartheta)$ for $\lambda > 0$. Given the free disposal assumptions on T, d_x is nonincreasing in (y, γ) and nondecreasing in (x, K, χ, κ).

The *output distance function* is defined as

$$d_y (y, x, K, \gamma, \chi, \kappa, \vartheta) \equiv \min \left\{ \delta : (y / \delta, x, K, \gamma, \chi, \kappa, \vartheta) \in T \right\}.$$

$(y, x, K, \gamma, \chi, \kappa, \vartheta)$ is feasible if and only if $d_y (y, x, K, \gamma, \chi, \kappa, \vartheta) \le 1$. By definition d_y is positively linear homogeneous in y: $d_y (\lambda y, x, K, \gamma, \chi, \kappa, \vartheta) = \lambda d_y (y, x, K, \gamma, \chi, \kappa, \vartheta)$

for $\lambda > 0$. Given the free disposal assumptions on T, d_y is nonincreasing in (x, K, χ, κ), nondecreasing in (y, γ).

The *capacity utilization function* is defined as

$$d_{yx}\left(y, x, K, \gamma, \chi, \kappa, \vartheta\right) \equiv \min\left\{\eta : \left(y / \eta, x / \eta, K, \gamma, \chi, \kappa, \vartheta\right) \in T\right\}.[4]$$

d_{yx} is positively linear homogeneous in (y, x): $d_{yx}\left(\lambda y, \lambda x, K, \gamma, \chi, \kappa, \vartheta\right) = \lambda d_{yx}\left(y, x, K, \gamma, \chi, \kappa, \vartheta\right)$ for $\eta > 0$. If $\left(y, x, K, \gamma, \chi, \kappa, \vartheta\right)$ is feasible, then $d_{yx}\left(y, x, K, \gamma, \chi, \kappa, \vartheta\right) \leq 1.[5]$ Given the free disposal assumptions on T, d_{yx} is nondecreasing in (y, γ) and nonincreasing in (x, K, χ, κ).

Notwithstanding our capacity utilization function moniker for the third distance function, all three production functions have a capacity utilization interpretation. Full capacity is indicated when the associated distance function is equal to 1 and the degree of less than full capacity is indicated by a distance function value less than 1.

For the input distance function, capacity is defined by a set of outputs y conditional on $(K, \gamma, \chi, \kappa, \vartheta)$. $d_x\left(y, x, K, \gamma, \chi, \kappa, \vartheta\right)^{-1}$ (the reciprocal of the input distance function) measures the utilization of inputs in producing y given $(K, \gamma, \chi, \kappa, \vartheta)$, where full capacity (efficiency) is given by $d_x\left(y, x, K, \gamma, \chi, \kappa, \vartheta\right)^{-1} = 1$ and the degree of less than full capacity is given by $d_x\left(y, x, K, \gamma, \chi, \kappa, \vartheta\right)^{-1} < 1$.

For the output distance function, capacity is defined by the degree to which production of outputs y can be feasibly scaled up conditional on $(x, K, \gamma, \chi, \kappa, \vartheta)$ (i.e., the degree to which they lie below the output frontier), where $d_y\left(y, x, K, \gamma, \chi, \kappa, \vartheta\right) = 1$ indicates full capacity and $d_y\left(y, x, K, \gamma, \chi, \kappa, \vartheta\right) < 1$ indicates the degree of less than full capacity.

For the capacity utilization function, capacity indicates the degree to which outputs and intermediate inputs (y, x) can be feasibly scaled up conditional on capital stocks and characteristics $(K, \gamma, \chi, \kappa, \vartheta)$. Our capacity utilization terminology for this distance function follows the traditional notion that capacity is set by quasi-fixed inputs, namely human and nonhuman capital stocks $K = \left[K_H, K_N\right]$, which are the sources of primary services in the national accounts, and whose compensation is value added, the sum of which over all producers in the economy is GDP from the production approach.[6] $d_{yx}\left(y, x, K, \gamma, \chi, \kappa, \vartheta\right) = 1$ thus indicates full capacity—that value added has reached what is commonly known as potential GDP—and $d_{yx}\left(y, x, K, \gamma, \chi, \kappa, \vartheta\right) < 1$ indicates the degree of less than full capacity (capital stock underutilization and GDP below potential).

6.2.2. Quality Adjusted Productivity

Applying the three production metrics to comparisons of two situations, say, $\left(y^0, x^0, K^0, \gamma^0, \chi^0, \kappa^0, \vartheta^0\right)$ and $\left(y^1, x^1, K^1, \gamma^1, \chi^1, \kappa^1, \vartheta^1\right)$, where 0 and 1 might reference distinct time periods or geographical regions or industrial activities or enterprises, produces three variants of *multifactor productivity* when comparing successive points on the production possibilities frontier of T. The input and output distance function approaches have been extensively applied in the efficiency and productivity literature, mostly for individual enterprises within industries, but we focus here only on productivity based on the third, the capacity utilization function, because of its relationship to value added and GDP. We therefore consider the following multifactor productivity index

$$
M_{y,x}^{01|s} = \frac{d_{yx}^0\left(y^s, x^s, K^s, \gamma^s, \chi^s, \kappa^s, \vartheta^0\right)}{d_{yx}^1\left(y^s, x^s, K^s, \gamma^s, \chi^s, \kappa^s, \vartheta^1\right)}
$$

where s indicates information from a reference situation (e.g., time period, locality, or type of activity/industry). $M_{y,x}^{01|s}$ measures the change in the capacity frontier for $\left(y^s, x^s\right)$ as environmental characteristics and perhaps the functional form of technology change from ϑ^0 to ϑ^1 given capital stocks K^s and the characteristics of outputs, intermediate inputs, and capital stocks $\left(\gamma^s, \chi^s, \kappa^s\right)$. $M_{y,x}^{01|s}$ throws the residual nature of productivity measurement into relief, as the measure of that part of the change in capacity utilization *not* arising from the change in output or input volume. $M_{y,x}^{01|s}$ is interpreted as follows:

- If the capacity utilization function declines in moving from technology 0 to technology 1 ($M_{y,x}^{01|s} > 1$), so that a given vector of outputs, intermediate consumptions, capital stocks, and the associated characteristics are *less* efficiently produced under technology 1, then technology 1 must be *more* productive than technology 0 (given K, there is greater capacity to expand (y, x) under technology 1 than under technology 0).
- If the capacity utilization function increases in moving from technology 0 to technology 1 ($M_{y,x}^{01|s} > 1$), so that a given vector of outputs, intermediate consumptions, and capital stocks, and the associated characteristics are *more* efficiently produced under technology 1, then technology 1 must be *less* productive than technology 0 (given K, there is less capacity to expand (y, x) under technology 1 than under technology 0).

When the reference situation s is chosen as $s = 0$, we say the productivity comparison has a *Laspeyres perspective*, inspired by the weighted linear and still widely used Laspeyres (1871) index number. When $s = 1$, we say the productivity comparison has a *Paasche perspective*, inspired by the weighted harmonic and still widely used Paasche (1874) index number. If we take the geometric mean of Laspeyres and Paasche perspective multifactor indices, we will term this a *Fisher perspective* comparison, inspired by Fisher's (1922) ideal index number, which is the geometric mean of Laspeyres and Paasche index numbers.

With these preliminaries, we can write the Fisher-perspective multifactor productivity index

$$
\bar{M}_{y,x}^{01|01} = \left[\frac{d_{yx}^0\left(y^0, x^0, K^0, \gamma^0, \chi^0, \kappa^0, \vartheta^0\right)}{d_{yx}^1\left(y^0, x^0, K^0, \gamma^0, \chi^0, \kappa^0, \vartheta^1\right)} \times \frac{d_{yx}^0\left(y^1, x^1, K^1, \gamma^1, \chi^1, \kappa^1, \vartheta^0\right)}{d_{yx}^1\left(y^1, x^1, K^1, \gamma^1, \chi^1, \kappa^1, \vartheta^1\right)}\right]^{\frac{1}{2}}. \quad (6.1)
$$

Aside from symmetry in binary comparisons (not having to choose between the Laspeyres and Paasche perspectives in a comparison by incorporating both), if there were no change in the quality characteristics $\left(\gamma^0,\chi^0,\kappa^0\right)=\left(\gamma^1,\chi^1,\kappa^1\right)$, and *under the assumption that we only observe efficient states where* $d^s_{yx}\left(y^s,x^s,K^s,\gamma^s,\chi^s,\kappa^s,\vartheta^s\right)=1$,[7] the Fisher perspective productivity index also is associated with empirically powerful and useful exact index number results. These results allow us to calculate multifactor productivity using a formula depending only on the prices and quantities for outputs, intermediate consumptions, and capital stocks $\left(y^s,x^s,K^s\right)$, by applying the Translog identity of Caves, Christensen, and Diewert (CCD) (1982). The CCD (1982) result in our capacity utilization function context is the following.

Assuming

- there is no quality change in outputs, intermediate inputs, or capital stocks so that $\left(\gamma^0,\chi^0,\kappa^0\right)=\left(\gamma^1,\chi^1,\kappa^1\right)$;
- producers maximize value added, $V \equiv p'y - v'x$ given $\left(K,\gamma,\chi,\kappa,\vartheta\right)$, where p is the given vector of basic prices[8] of outputs and v is the given vector of purchasers' prices[9] of intermediate inputs;
- producers minimize primary input cost, $C \equiv u'K$ given $\left(y,x,\gamma,\chi,\kappa,\vartheta\right)$, where $u = \rho\iota + \delta$ is the given price vector of quasi-fixed inputs (capital stocks), with ρ the enterprise cost of capital, ι is a vector of ones of same dimension as K, and δ is the vector of depreciation rates for capital stocks K; and
- for each period, location, or activity s the capacity utilization function $d^s_{yx}\left(y,x,K,\gamma,\chi,\kappa,\vartheta\right)$ has a Translog flexible functional form (the log of the capacity utilization function is quadratic in the logs of its arguments), where the coefficients second-order terms of the Translog functions do not vary from time to time;

the following Törnqvist multifactor productivity index number is exact

$$\bar{M}^{01|01}_{y,x|T} = \exp\left[\frac{1}{2}\left(w^0_y + w^1_y\right)'\left(\ln y^1 - \ln y^0\right)\right]$$
$$\times \exp\left[-\frac{1}{2}\left(w^0_x + w^1_x\right)'\left(\ln x^1 - \ln x^0\right)\right] \quad (6.2)$$
$$\times \exp\left[-\frac{1}{2}\left(\varepsilon^0_{d_{yx},K}w^0_K + \varepsilon^1_{d_{yx},K}w^1_K\right)'\left(\ln K^1 - \ln K^0\right)\right]$$

where

(a) if $\odot$ is the Hadamard or elementwise product operator on two vectors of the same dimension,[10]

$$w^s_y = p^s \odot y^s / \left(p^{s'}y^s - v^{s'}x^s\right)$$
$$w^s_x = v^s \odot x^s / \left(p^{s'}y^s - v^{s'}x^s\right)$$
$$w^s_K = u^s_K \odot K^s / u^{s'}_K K^s$$

are the vectors of, respectively, the value-added shares of outputs, the value-added shares of intermediate inputs, and the primary input cost shares of capital services; and,

(b)
$$\varepsilon^s_{d_{yx},K} = -\frac{K^{s'}\nabla_K d^s_{yx}}{y^{s'}\nabla_y d^s_{yx} + x^{s'}\nabla_x d^s_{yx}}$$

is the elasticity of outputs and intermediate consumptions $\left(y^s, x^s\right)$ with respect to the scale of quasi-fixed inputs (capital stocks) K^s conditional on the quality $\left(\gamma^s, \chi^s, \kappa^s, \vartheta^s\right)$ of output y^s, intermediate consumption x^s, capital stock κ^s, and technology/environment ϑ^s.

The nonparametric expression for the elasticity of scale $\varepsilon^s_{d_{y,x},K}$ derives as follows. Suppose λ is a scaling factor for capital stocks K^s and θ is a scaling factor for outputs and intermediate consumptions $\left(y^s, x^s\right)$ such that

$$d^s_{yx}\left(\theta y^s, \theta x^s, \lambda K^s, \gamma^s, \chi^s, \kappa^s, \vartheta^s\right) = 1.$$

We know from the maintained assumptions that value added is maximized and primary input cost is minimized that, respectively, $\theta = 1$ and $\lambda = 1$. Take the total differential of the preceding expression with respect to θ and λ and solve for $\varepsilon^s_{d_{y,x},K} = d\theta/d\lambda$ at $\lambda = 1$ as

$$\varepsilon^s_{d_{yx},K} = \frac{d\theta}{d\lambda} = -\frac{K^{s'}\nabla_K d^s_{yx}}{y^{s'}\nabla_y d^s_{yx} + x^{s'}\nabla_x d^s_{yx}}.$$

If, in addition, the enterprise is subject to eventual decreasing returns to scale[11] and also maximizing "super surplus" $p^{s'}y^s - v^{s'}x^s - u^{s'}K^s$,[12] the CCD (1982) results can be used to determine the elasticity of scale as

$$\varepsilon^s_{d_{yx},K} = \frac{u^{s'}K^s}{p^{s'}y^s - v^{s'}x^s}$$

under the assumption that we observe $\dfrac{u^{s'}K^s}{p^{s'}y^s - v^{s'}x^s} \leq 1$.[13]

However, if the characteristics $\left(\gamma^s, \chi^s, \kappa^s\right)$ change for $s = 0,1$, as they almost certainly will, to account for their impact on productivity we must know the gradients of $d_{y,x}$ with respect to $\left(\gamma^s, \chi^s, \kappa^s\right)$ to apply the CCD (1982) Translog identity.

We can obtain these gradients by estimating an assumed parametric form for $d_{y,x}$ and taking the characteristics or quality gradients of the estimated capacity utilization function. Alternatively, we can proceed to a "semi-nonparametric" result generalizing the CCD (1982) translog identity. If $\left(\gamma^s, \chi^s, \kappa^s\right)$ reliably affect the prices the producer receives for $\left(y^s, x^s, K^s\right)$ within each period/situation 0,1, then using a result from Fixler and Zieschang (1992):[14]

Under the same assumptions as the CCD (1982) translog identity, plus additionally that

- there are (presumed known) *hedonic price functions* for, respectively, outputs, intermediate inputs, and capital service inputs as $p^s = P_y^s(\gamma^s)$, $v^s = P_x^s(\chi^s)$, and $u^s = P_K^s(\kappa^s)$

the following Törnqvist quality adjusted multifactor productivity index number is exact

$$
M_{y,x|T}^{01|01} = \exp\left[\frac{1}{2}\left(w_y^0 + w_y^1\right)'\left(\ln y^1 - \ln y^0\right)\right]
$$

$$
\times \exp\left[-\frac{1}{2}\left(w_x^0 + w_x^1\right)'\left(\ln x^1 - \ln x^0\right)\right]
$$

$$
\times \exp\left[-\frac{1}{2}\left(\varepsilon_{d_{yx},K}^0 w_K^0 + \varepsilon_{d_{yx},K}^1 w_K^1\right)'\left(\ln K^1 - \ln K^0\right)\right]
$$

$$
\times \exp\left[\frac{1}{2}\left(\omega_\gamma^0 + \omega_\gamma^1\right)'\left(\ln \gamma^1 - \ln \gamma^0\right)\right]
$$

$$
\times \exp\left[-\frac{1}{2}\left(\omega_\chi^0 + \omega_\chi^1\right)'\left(\ln \chi^1 - \ln \chi^0\right)\right]
$$

$$
\times \exp\left[-\frac{1}{2}\left(\varepsilon_{d_{yx},K}^0 \omega_\kappa^0 + \varepsilon_{d_{yx},K}^1 \omega_\kappa^1\right)'\left(\ln \kappa^1 - \ln \kappa^0\right)\right] \qquad (6.3)
$$

where

$$
\omega_y^s = \nabla_{\gamma^s} P_y^s(\gamma^s)' y^s / \left(p^{s\prime} y^s - v^{s\prime} x^s\right)
$$

$$
\omega_x^s = \nabla_{\chi^s} P_x^s(\chi^s)' x^s / \left(p^{s\prime} y^s - v^{s\prime} x^s\right)
$$

$$
\omega_K^s = \nabla_{\kappa^s} P_K^s(\kappa^s)' K^s / u^{s\prime} K^s.
$$

So, *assuming we only observe efficient states*, always on the production frontier, then aside from needing to know the characteristics gradients of the hedonic functions $p^s = P_y^s(\gamma^s)$, $v^s = P_x^s(\chi^s)$, and $u^s = P_K^s(\kappa^s)$, the capacity utilization productivity index can be written as a nonparametric index number when enterprises in the economy are presumed to be maximizing super surplus. In fact, the quality varying multifactor productivity index $M_{y,x|T}^{01|01}$ of equation (6.3) is the constant quality Törnqvist multifactor productivity index $\bar{M}_{y,x}^{01|01}$ of equation (6.2) multiplied by the output-input quality adjustment factor

$$
Q_{y,x|T}^{01|01} \equiv \exp\left[\frac{1}{2}\left(\omega_\gamma^0 + \omega_\gamma^1\right)'\left(\ln \gamma^1 - \ln \gamma^0\right)\right]
$$

$$
\times \exp\left[-\frac{1}{2}\left(\omega_\chi^0 + \omega_\chi^1\right)'\left(\ln \chi^1 - \ln \chi^0\right)\right]
$$

$$
\times \exp\left[-\frac{1}{2}\left(\varepsilon_{d_{yx},K}^0 \omega_\kappa^0 + \varepsilon_{d_{yx},K}^1 \omega_\kappa^1\right)'\left(\ln \kappa^1 - \ln \kappa^0\right)\right].
$$

It also is evident from this that $Q_{y,x|T}^{01|01}$ decomposes into three quality adjustment factors:

- for output, $\exp\left[\frac{1}{2}\left(\omega_\gamma^0 + \omega_\gamma^1\right)'\left(\ln\gamma^1 - \ln\gamma^0\right)\right]$,

- for intermediate consumption, $\exp\left[-\frac{1}{2}\left(\omega_\chi^0 + \omega_\chi^1\right)'\left(\ln\chi^1 - \ln\chi^0\right)\right]$, and

- for capital stocks, $\exp\left[-\frac{1}{2}\left(\varepsilon_{d_{yx},K}^0\omega_\kappa^0 + \eta_{d_{yx},K}^1\omega_\kappa^1\right)'\left(\ln\kappa^1 - \ln\kappa^0\right)\right]$.

Thus, quality improvements in output increase, and quality improvements in intermediate inputs and capital stocks decrease, multifactor productivity.

6.2.3. Relationship to Deflation Techniques Used in Productivity Accounting

Productivity accountants typically obtain the quantities in the productivity index $M_{y,x|T}^{01|01}$ via deflation of current price monetary values from the national accounts. Thus, if the current price monetary flow for the ith output is $E_{yi}^t = p_{yi}^t y_i^t$, for the jth intermediate consumption is $E_{xj}^t = p_{xj}^t x_j^t$, and for the kth capital rental is $E_{Kk}^t = u_k^t K_k^t$, then the relative change in nominal flows also can be written as

$$\frac{E_{yi}^t}{E_{yi}^0} = \left(\frac{p_{yi}^t}{p_{yi}^0}\right)\exp\left[-\frac{1}{2}\left(\omega_{\gamma i}^0 + \omega_{\gamma i}^1\right)'\left(\ln\gamma_i^1 - \ln\gamma_i^0\right)\right]$$

$$\times\exp\left[\frac{1}{2}\left(\omega_{\gamma i}^0 + \omega_{\gamma i}^1\right)'\left(\ln\gamma_i^1 - \ln\gamma_i^0\right)\right]\left(\frac{y_i^t}{y_i^0}\right)$$

$$\frac{E_{xj}^t}{E_{xj}^0} = \left(\frac{p_{xj}^t}{p_{xj}^0}\right)\exp\left[-\frac{1}{2}\left(\omega_{\chi j}^0 + \omega_{\chi j}^1\right)'\left(\ln\chi_j^1 - \ln\chi_j^0\right)\right]$$

$$\times\exp\left[\frac{1}{2}\left(\omega_{\chi j}^0 + \omega_{\chi j}^1\right)'\left(\ln\chi_j^1 - \ln\chi_j^0\right)\right]\left(\frac{x_j^t}{x_j^0}\right)$$

$$\frac{E_{Kk}^t}{E_{Kk}^0} = \left(\frac{u_k^t}{u_k^0}\right)\exp\left[-\frac{1}{2}\left(\varepsilon_{d_{yx},K}^0\omega_{\kappa k}^0 + \varepsilon_{d_{yx},K}^1\omega_{\kappa k}^1\right)\right]'\left(\ln\kappa_k^1 - \ln\kappa_k^0\right)$$

$$\times\exp\left[\frac{1}{2}\left(\varepsilon_{d_{yx},K}^0\omega_\kappa^0 + \varepsilon_{d_{yx},K}^1\omega_\kappa^1\right)'\left(\ln\kappa^1 - \ln\kappa^0\right)\right]\left(\frac{K_k^t}{K_k^0}\right).$$

By implication, the quality-adjusted quantities in the productivity index (6.3) can be obtained by substituting for them nominal expenditures deflated by quality adjusted price indices:

$$\exp\left[\frac{1}{2}\left(\omega_{\gamma i}^0 + \omega_{\gamma i}^1\right)'\left(\ln\gamma_i^1 - \ln\gamma_i^0\right)\right]\left(\frac{y_i^t}{y_i^0}\right)$$

$$= \left(\frac{E_{yi}^t}{E_{yi}^0}\right)\Big/\left[\left(\frac{p_{yi}^t}{p_{yi}^0}\right)\exp\left[-\frac{1}{2}\left(\omega_{\gamma i}^0 + \omega_{\gamma i}^1\right)'\left(\ln\gamma_i^1 - \ln\gamma_i^0\right)\right]\right]$$

$$\exp\left[\frac{1}{2}\left(\omega_{\chi j}^0 + \omega_{\chi j}^1\right)'\left(\ln\chi_j^1 - \ln\chi_j^0\right)\right]\left(\frac{x_j^t}{x_j^0}\right)$$

$$= \left(\frac{E_{xj}^t}{E_{xj}^0}\right)\Big/\left[\left(\frac{p_{xj}^t}{p_{xj}^0}\right)\exp\left[-\frac{1}{2}\left(\omega_{\chi j}^0 + \omega_{\chi j}^1\right)'\left(\ln\chi_j^1 - \ln\chi_j^0\right)\right]\right]$$

$$\exp\left[\frac{1}{2}\left(\varepsilon_{d_{yx},Kk}^0\omega_{Kk}^0 + \varepsilon_{d_{yx},Kk}^1\omega_{Kk}^1\right)'\left(\ln\kappa_k^1 - \ln\kappa_k^0\right)\right]\left(\frac{K_k^t}{K_k^0}\right)$$

$$= \left(\frac{E_{Kk}^t}{E_{Kk}^0}\right)\Big/\left[\left(\frac{u_k^t}{u_k^0}\right)\exp\left[-\frac{1}{2}\left(\varepsilon_{d_{yx},K}^0\omega_{Kk}^0 + \varepsilon_{d_{yx},K}^1\omega_{Kk}^1\right)'\left(\ln\kappa_k^1 - \ln\kappa_k^0\right)\right]\right].$$

6.2.4. Environment Variables ϑ

In the semi-nonparametric results in the preceding, we do not include the environment variables ϑ^s in the productivity quality adjustment index number $Q_{y,x|T}^{01|01}$ because if they do not affect the hedonic price equations of the outputs, intermediate inputs, and/or capital stocks, they are subsumed into the change in technology between 0 and 1 and thus have no independent effect on the semi-nonparametric index. Of course, many hedonic evaluations assessing the economic value of environment-type variables find that these variables do affect the prices of market products.[15] We will assume that if this is the case, such environmental variables are already included in the characteristics vectors $\left(\gamma^s, \chi^s, \kappa^s\right)$. Thus ϑ^s is the vector of environmental and technology metrics whose variations do *not* affect the prices of outputs and inputs and thus are in this sense "disembodied" from those outputs and inputs.[16] Failure to include environmental variables that affect the prices of market outputs and inputs in the hedonic equations describing the relationship between prices and the price-determining characteristics of those products constitutes a misspecification that will lead to bias in the residual productivity measure of the impacts of "disembodied" factors ϑ^s.

6.2.5. Inefficiency

A discussion point concerning the preceding result is that assuming value-added maximization conditional on primary inputs (capital stocks) and primary input cost minimization conditional on output and intermediate consumption means that all observed data points (e.g., $s = 0,1$) are conditionally efficient and lying on the boundary of the technology T, but that the enterprise is not necessarily operating at efficient scale. The fully nonparametric result hinges on the further requirement that super surplus be maximized, which in turn requires nonincreasing returns to the scale of capital stocks at the observed outputs, intermediate inputs, and capital stocks. If we further examine the derivation of the implicit rental rates of capital stocks u from the cash flow equation, we are further led to the conclusion that under the assumption of super surplus maximization and price taking we will only observe unitary, constant returns to scale. Thus in the CCD (1982) nonparametric result and the Fixler and Zieschang (1992) extension, inefficiency or super-efficiency is implied, not at the observed situations, where $d_{y,x}^0 \left(y^0, x^0, K^0, \gamma^0, \chi^0, \kappa^0, \vartheta^0 \right) = 1$ and $d_{y,x}^1 \left(y^1, x^1, K^1, \gamma^1, \chi^1, \kappa^1, \vartheta^1 \right) = 1$, but only at the unobserved perturbations $d_{y,x}^1 \left(y^0, x^0, K^0, \gamma^0, \chi^0, \kappa^0, \vartheta^0 \right) \le 1$ and $d_{y,x}^0 \left(y^1, x^1, K^1, \gamma^1, \chi^1, \kappa^1, \vartheta^0 \right) \le 1$.

Efficiency, like multifactor productivity, is a fundamentally residual concept and thus is ultimately a measure of our ignorance, particularly regarding incomplete information on the characteristics variables $\left(\gamma^s, \chi^s, \kappa^s, \vartheta^s \right)$ and capital stocks K^s. For nonhuman capital stocks specifically, this pertains to high technology tangible assets and imperfectly measured intangibles, such as intellectual property[17] and goodwill and marketing assets.[18] We could therefore expect that the more comprehensively we measure the characteristics vectors, including ultimately the "disembodied" environmental characteristics, and include their effects in the productivity measure, the smaller the productivity and efficiency change we are likely to calculate. Thus, efficiency (like productivity) is not so much a concept in itself, but an indicator of the completeness of model specification.[19]

6.3. Empirical Issues in Hard-to-Measure Goods and Services

6.3.1. Parametric or Semi-Nonparametric?

Econometric estimation of a parametric functional form for the primal capacity utilization function in the productivity index (6.1) is ultimately constrained by the size of the data sets available, particularly if the functional form is flexible. The context generally will be industry-level time series data at quarterly frequency. Given the large number of variables for which parameters are needed, degrees of freedom are likely to be exhausted quickly and the reliability of estimates thereby impaired.

The semi-nonparametric index number results (6.3) for the Törnqvist index numbers presented here still require period by period hedonic estimates of some type, which usually (and least restrictively) are based on cross-sectional firm- or product-level data from given time periods, though the hedonic price equations can be estimated from industry time series under restrictive assumptions. Size of data set may be significantly larger in the cross-sectional than time-series context (but also might not be large, as in concentrated industries), and the degree-of-freedom demands of hedonic equations potentially more parsimonious, as they are often less saturated with parameters than distance functions and their value-added and cost-function duals.

Ultimately, it appears that better accounting for quality change in productivity indices will require more detailed enterprise- and/or establishment-level time series data—both time series and cross-sectional—from panel surveys.

6.3.2. Availability of Data on Key Variables

The residual nature of productivity measures, particularly multifactor productivity indices, makes them sensitive to excluded intermediate and, particularly, capital inputs, as well as inaccurate adjustments for output quality change, because of lack of data on characteristics variables, or insufficient observations to identify a hedonic model for which price on the left-hand side is dependent on many characteristics variables on the right-hand side.

Based on equation (6.3), within the Törnqvist measurement framework of this chapter, an omitted output characteristic for a given activity first drops the output factor corresponding to that quality characteristic from the index and, second, probably affects the estimated gradient(s) of the output price hedonic equation(s) $P_y^s(\gamma^s)$ with respect to other characteristics, thus affecting the weights of the other characteristics in the index. If the characteristic shows rapidly improving quality of that output, its effect on the overall productivity picture will be attenuated by the degree to which the remaining included characteristics are correlated with it. If the index pertains to a particular industrial activity, the aggregate effect of its omission on productivity at the economy-wide level may be attenuated further to the extent that that output is used as an intermediate consumption by another activity. This is evident from the negative sign on the exponents in the productivity index's quality-adjusted intermediate consumption factor:

$$\exp\left[-\frac{1}{2}\left(w_x^0 + w_x^1\right)'\left(\ln x^1 - \ln x^0\right)\right] \times \exp\left[-\frac{1}{2}\left(\omega_\chi^0 + \omega_\chi^1\right)'\left(\ln \chi^1 - \ln \chi^0\right)\right].$$

That is to say, an understatement of output and thus productivity in the given activity as a result of understatement in output quality change will result in overstatement of productivity in activities using that output as an intermediate consumption, attenuating the impact of the error on total economy productivity.

An omitted capital stock input in the multifactor productivity index for a given activity, such as an accumulating intellectual property position, will drop the input factor for that capital stock and could affect the returns to scale adjustment for all inputs in that activity (depending on how the returns to scale $\varepsilon_{d_{yx},K}^s$ is calculated). The aggregate effect on GDP is attenuated by the extent to which the output of that activity is itself accumulated as a durable capital asset (e.g., research and development [R&D] services or mineral exploration services): an understatement of the accumulation of that durable capital asset will overstate productivity change in all activities using that asset. On the other hand, if the intellectual property output is not accumulated as a nonhuman asset but instead used as an intermediate input of other activities, its exclusion understates the value added of the intellectual output and overstates the value added of sectors using the intellectual product service. As a rule, the distinction between accumulating intellectual property assets and provision of intellectual services is decided by whether intellectual services such as R&D are generated for own use (capital formation final expenditure), sold to other producers (intermediate consumption), or sold to households as consumption (consumption final expenditure).

6.3.3. When Hedonic Quality-Adjusted Productivity Becomes a "Matched Models" Index

At base, price and quantity index methodology conventionally relies on recording the prices and quantities of exactly the same collection of products over time, as in the CCD (1982)–type result of equation (6.2). This traditional approach is sometimes called a "matched models" method. Our superlative Törnqvist Index approach to multifactor, GDP productivity still captures change in the importance of available varieties of products through changes in the value-added and primary-input cost shares appearing in the exponents of equation (6.2). Index compilers then deal with cases where they lack observations on the quantities and prices of appearing or disappearing product varieties. This "lack of comparable varieties" problem seems to become less quantitatively important in a time series context as the frequency of data recording increases, because new varieties often enter and leave markets with very low market shares, depending on how powerful the price dynamics and change in market share are in the market penetration/exit period. This said, the frequency of price data recording often is limited by the cost of data acquisition, and the entering (exiting) share may not be captured soon enough (late enough). In non-time-series contexts, such as geographic (e.g., international or interregional) productivity comparisons the "lack of comparable varieties" problem remains unavoidable. The "lack of comparable varieties" issue is the "replacement" version of the "new and disappearing varieties" issue, about which more in a moment, where the introduction of a new variety or class of product with updated characteristics replaces a specific old variety or class.

The framework of this chapter accommodates the lack of comparable varieties issue. Equation (6.3) reduces to equation (6.2) if the set of varieties or classes of products is unchanged over the comparison, but their quantities and prices change. If only some items change in quality, then only those items require a quality-adjusted treatment within the quality-adjusted productivity index of equation (6.3).

6.3.4. Truly New Products, Disappearing Products, and Changes in the Scope of Output, Intermediate Inputs, and Primary Services

Equations (6.2) and (6.3) do not address changes in the scope of products—the number of varieties transacted. This is the purest form of the new and disappearing goods problem that does not imply replacement of a given existing product variety with a new one having different characteristics, but rather is the emergence of a new category of product or complete disappearance of an old category. The preferred conceptual treatment of a new or disappearing product is to impute its reservation price in the period prior to introduction or after disappearance. The reservation price is the lowest price at which just one unit of output would be produced, other things equal, or the highest price at which just one unit of intermediate or primary service input would be used, other things equal.[20]

6.3.5. Output and Intermediate Consumption Measurement Issues by Sector

Byrne et al. (2016) provide an assessment of productivity measurement issues in the US economy over three successive eras: 1978–1995, 1995–2004, and 2004–2015. The US economy is large and diversified, with significant high technology and service sectors, and thus reasonably reflects the state of multifactor productivity measurement worldwide. Their findings, overall, suggest that better measurement of product quality, as well as of intellectual property and high technology assets, would have had a mildly salutary effect on productivity trends over the last 30 years, on the order of hundredths of a percentage point. However, these improvements would not have changed the historical profile or current trend in multifactor or labor productivity. In particular, the US productivity slowdown since 2004 remains intact after plausible adjustments are made to outputs and inputs for technical progress in a variety of industries, from high technology to mining to online retailing, social media, and the sharing economy.

6.3.5.1. *High Technology Industries*

The high technology industries are principally the information and communications technology (ICT) group, comprising computers and peripherals; communications equipment; other information systems; and software.

Quality change in computers and peripherals has been studied since the mid- to late 1980s, pioneered by the US Bureau of Economic Analysis (Cole et al. 1986; Dulberger 1989). Steady improvements have been made since, though over 2005–2014 (1) import substitution has been imperfectly captured in US data as domestic production has given way to nonresident producers, and (2) quality adjustment has been much less accurate on imports than on domestic production. Byrne et al. (2016) used the computers and peripherals price index from communications equipment to deflate the nominal output of these goods.

6.3.5.2. *Construction and Real Estate Assets*

Construction output is imminently tangible and visible, and seemingly easily measurable, but for two issues. The first is that data are expensive to collect because construction happens at a constantly changing set of geographical locations with projects at various stages of completion, and multiple personal visits are usually necessary to collect project data. The second is that constructions often build custom products that are not directly comparable with each other in a given time period or with other constructions completed in the past. Thus, the "matched models" approach to measuring price and volume change does not apply, and the hedonic approach to quality adjustment must contend with a large array of product characteristics that threaten to overwhelm the available sample of projects with the need to estimate parameter coefficients for large numbers of price determining characteristics. Sveikauskas et al. (2014) provide a comprehensive state of play for productivity measurement in construction.

While there are active rental markets for property and structures capital in place, the related problem of measuring the price and volume of real estate assets in place is a still a developing field, which is partly susceptible to matched models methodology, but for staggered and infrequent property transactions that make the valuation of stocks and measurement of depreciation problematic. There is a recent set of international recommendations on measuring residential property prices (and thus via deflation the volume of the residential property stock).[21] Graf and Silver (2014) provide an overview of thinking on measuring commercial property capital.

6.3.5.3. *Services*

6.3.5.3.1. *Distributive Services*

Nominal distributive services are measured as the aggregate gross margins of retailers and wholesalers. Distributive service vendors sell marketing and display, transactions, and, more recently, logistics services to purchasers of goods as well as services. As a rule, the volume of distributive services is measured by the volume of goods and services these enterprises sell, which arguably captures aspects of the transactions and logistics services they produce. While goods and services transaction volume is perhaps not an adequate treatment of distributors' marketing and display functions, aspects of these services may be captured by scope indicators such as number of product varieties marketed. This sector has undergone significant upheaval over the last 20 years with the advent and rapid increase in market share of online retailers and wholesalers, who display their wares on video screens rather than marketing physical product samples and fulfilling purchase transactions from inventory in brick and mortar stores and showrooms. Though not totally overwhelmed, the brick and mortar retail business model has lost ground to web distribution by computerized logistics directing massive regional order-fulfillment operations and high-speed shipping modalities such as air freight and efficient local package delivery. Services have begun to enter the same web-enabled distributive modality through "gig economy" enterprises vending taxi trips and hotel stays, among other services. Arguably, very significant gains in distributive service productivity have occurred in the key sense that purchasers' shopping efficiency has been greatly enhanced by (1) not having to make trips to search physical inventories or negotiate with service providers in disparate locations, and (2) suffering little or no incremental delay (and perhaps an acceleration) in taking delivery of the selected product. By the same token, in 2015 distributive services originated about 12% of US GDP,[22] and the advent of the gig economy in particular is not thought to have had much of an impact on GDP growth.[23]

6.3.5.3.2. *Financial Services*
Measurement of financial services output and intermediate consumption remains an unsettled area, even regarding its nominal value, much less growth in its volume of output and use in intermediate consumption. The national accounts limit financial service output to units in the financial corporations institutional sector, which includes deposit-taking corporations (banks), finance companies, money market investment funds, non-money-market investment funds, and insurance and pension schemes, among others. As investment funds are the most specialized and thus the simplest of financial institutions, we begin with them before discussing output measurement issues with finance companies, banks, and insurance companies.

6.3.5.3.2.1. Investment Funds The nominal output of the portfolio-management services of investment funds is reasonably well understood as a function of the "expense ratio" published by their prospectuses. Shareholders get the return on the fund portfolio minus the product of the expense ratio with the value of (generally financial) assets under management. The expense ratio per unit of currency of assets under management can be rewritten as the difference between the rate of return on the investment portfolio and the rate of return paid out to the investment fund's shareholders. The latter, return on equity, is self-evidently the investment fund's cost of capital. So the value of services provided by an investment fund to its funders (who are generally, though not always, all equity holders) per currency unit invested is the rate of return on the fund less the cost of capital or, equivalently, the expense ratio.

6.3.5.3.2.2. Banking and Finance Companies Banking was the initial focus of service imputations at the postwar inception of national accounting standards.[24] Some of the output of banks is measured from explicitly charged fees, but the national accounts "indirectly measure" a large part of the output of banks and finance companies as a function of the spread between the income from financial assets and the expense of non-equity liabilities. The national accounts' "financial intermediation services indirectly measured"

(FISIM) output and intermediate input measure depends on a "reference rate of interest" and involves the following basic calculation:

$$\left(\text{rate of return on financial assets} - \text{reference rate of interest}\right) \times \text{financial assets}$$
$$+ \left(\text{reference rate of interest} - \text{rate of return on non-equity liabilities}\right) \times \text{non-equity liabilities}.$$

If the reference rate of interest is actually the bank's or finance company's cost of capital, then with reference to the investment fund case, FISIM's first, asset term is self-evidently an *asset-management charge* in the same vein as the "expense ratio" that investment funds charge their shareholders. If the reference rate is the cost of capital, the second, debt-liability term, applying to banks only (because of their use of deposit financing), is a *liquidity service charge.* It is the supply value of the liquidity service concept underlying Barnett's (1980) monetary service aggregates. As of the 2008 version of the national accounting standards, the financial instrument scope of the FISIM output calculation is limited to loans and deposits, which de facto means that FISIM is nearly exclusively applied to banks and finance companies.[25]

From a productivity point of view, the FISIM liquidity service charge can be broken down into deposit account servicing and liquidity service components, while asset-management FISIM can be decomposed into loan account servicing and portfolio management components. The key volume indicators for the account servicing components on both sides of the ledger is the number of accounts/contracts and number of transactions processed per account/contract.[26] Liquidity traditionally has been treated in both the economics and accounting literatures as yielding a volume of services proportional to its "real" or deflated value to the depositor. Asset-management output has been viewed similarly as proportional to the deflated value of assets under management to funders of all types, though portfolio complexity and intensity of research effort, however measured, also appear relevant. Choice of the deflators for debt liabilities and financial assets is seen related to the uses for which a depositor or borrower would spend the funds.

Recent economics literature has argued that the FISIM calculation effectively overstates the share of value added in GDP of institutions to which FISIM is applied,[27] but this critique remains under discussion. The issue revolves ultimately around what should and should not be considered inside the national accounts "production boundary." The current FISIM calculation for *assets* is essentially identical to the "expense ratio" service charge levied by investment funds on their shareholders and that national accountants recognize as an explicit payment for service. The current FISIM calculation for liabilities is a de facto link between financial production in the current national accounts and the liquidity aggregates promulgated in the Divisia aggregation literature in monetary economics.[28]

At the same time, liquidity services are the key component of FISIM that the recent critics of the established methodology would (de facto) place outside the production boundary, thus treating flows associated with it as a type of appropriation or transfer, rather than a payment for service. This contrasts with the monetary aggregation literature (initiated by Barnett 1978, 1980), which considers the demand value of liquidity as payment for a capital service. Intersecting with this connection of the established FISIM principle of national accounting to monetary aggregation theory and practice is the need to distinguish between the production orientation of the national accounts and the use orientation of the monetary aggregation literature. The national accounts attempt to measure liquidity services at their *supply* value from the enterprise *issuers* of the debt instruments (deposits, but also debt securities, loans, insurance reserves, and other payables) with which these liquidity services are associated. The monetary aggregation literature measures liquidity at its *demand* value from the point of view of debt instrument *holders*. With the supply orientation of the national accounts and the demand orientation of monetary aggregation in mind, there is a reassuring coherence between the evolved measurement practice for the financial service output of banks and finance companies and the measurement of liquidity in the monetary aggregation literature.

6.3.5.3.2.3. Insurance The official measure of current price insurance output is premiums minus claims (net premiums) on policies plus "premium supplements," the investment income that insurers earn on reserves held for policyholder claims. In 2008 national accountants revised the standards to smooth the often volatile claims component of this nominal output measure. Hornstein and Prescott (1991) proposed a volume indicator for net premiums related to number of policies in force. Their approach tracked output as an index of the premiums less claims of a set of specified policies through time, adjusted as needed using hedonic methods for changes in policyholder and other actuarial characteristics. Reece (1992) provided a reasonably detailed analysis of the price of policy services for life insurance. His approach de facto took the policy contract as the underlying output volume counter.

Beginning from first principles, insurers sell policies in risk classes based on policyholder characteristics and other factors relevant to the probability of a claim. Within a risk class, which sets the actuarial estimate of the probability of a claim, insurers set premiums as a percentage per currency unit of coverage. The price of this "vanilla insurance" per currency unit is the premium percentage minus the actuarial claim probability. Because policies are priced as percentages of the face amount insured, however, there remains a fundamentally nominal aspect to vanilla insurance—the face value of the policy.

In looking at volume metrics for "vanilla insurance," clearly there are account servicing aspects to insurance services and, within a broad class of policy, number of policies and number of claims processed should be relevant indicators for the volume of services underlying the net premiums part of national accounts insurance output. By analog with deposits and loans, however, the insured have—and insurers generally require them to have—an "insurable interest" underlying the face value of a policy, in the form of loss or impairment of a nonfinancial durable asset owned by the insured.

This can be as a result of loss of or damage to a piece of durable equipment or a structure, of a durable consumer asset such as a house or automobile, or of a human capital asset as a result of disability or death. Consequently, a further indicator of insurance service seems to be related to the face value of the policy, deflated by a price index for the insurable interest.

It is worth reconsidering what the national accounts term "premium supplements." Aside from vanilla insurance, there are two other aspects of insurance output not considered explicitly by the national accounts: liquidity and asset-management services. Like banks, insurers finance their operations not only with equity, but also debt. For banks, deposits are the key component of debt financing, and current practice associates provision of liquidity services with deposit debt. For insurers, insurance reserves are the key component of debt financing.[29] At the same time, like investment funds, finance companies, and banks, insurers manage a portfolio of financial assets that generate investment income and, like these other financial enterprises, insurers charge their funders an "expense ratio" for that service. While the national accounts exclude the liquidity and asset-management services associated with financial instruments other than deposit and loan liabilities, productivity analysts should not be proscribed from taking them into account for other types of financial instruments. This granted, the "premium supplements" component of insurance output is better characterized as the sum of the liquidity on insurance reserves that insurers generate in behalf of policyholders and the asset-management services on the total investment portfolio that insurers provide to their equity and debt funders. Volume measures for these two components of insurance output could be developed analogously to the deflation approach used for banks and finance companies for the liquidity and asset-management services they provide to their funders.

6.3.5.3.3. *Health Care*

Health-care service output measurement is straightforward in nominal terms but problematic in volume terms. Scheiner and Malinovskaya (2016) summarize the substantial health-care measurement literature by identifying two related problems with measuring the volume of health-care services: setting a classification for specific health-care services transacted within aggregate health-care expenditure relevant to disease treatment outcomes, and tracking change in the characteristics (quality) of those services once identified. The line of attack for the first problem is to reorganize expenditure and quantity indicator information from a treatment-service classified basis to a disease-classified—medical care expenditure (MCE)—basis. Having selected MCE-basis service classification, the second problem, quality measurement, has been characterized as developing treatment outcome measures by disease. The most easily accessible disease outcome data tend to be for mortality (life expectancy), while comprehensive and regularly reported data on more granular measures of health status remain to be developed or need strengthening. Outcome measurement remains an active area of research, and the quality of medical care remains an unsettled measurement area.

6.3.5.3.4. *Education*

Education delivery is measured in number of individuals completing primary, tertiary, and secondary levels of study, but these completion rates disguise a range of outcome levels in terms of what graduates actually know. The results of standardized tests of achievement may be important, if still imperfect, additional indicators of educational outcomes.[30] For example, as described by the OECD,

> [t]he Programme for International Student Assessment (PISA) is a triennial international survey which aims to evaluate education systems worldwide by testing the skills and knowledge of 15-year-old students.
>
> In 2015 over half a million students, representing 28 million 15-year-olds in 72 countries and economies, took the internationally agreed two-hour test. Students were assessed in science, mathematics, reading, collaborative problem solving and financial literacy.[31]

National average PISA scores might be used as a quality variable to standardize public and private educational effectiveness between countries. According to Cambridge International Examinations (2015, n.p.), other standardized international testing regimes include

> TIMSS (Trends in International Mathematics and Science Study), which is repeated every 4 years and tests learners of 10 and 14 years old. It is managed by the International Association for the Evaluation of Educational Achievement (IEA).
>
> PIRLS (Progress in International Reading Literacy Study), repeated every 5 years and focusing on 10 year old learners' abilities in reading, and on national policies concerning literacy.

There are several other testing regimes besides these three. PISA, TIMSS, and PIRLS have the advantage of international standardization, but no regime can yet claim universal and at least annual application, complicating the use of test scores as education service quality variables.

6.4. CONCLUDING REMARKS

Hard-to-measure sectors display chronic mismeasurement or outright omission of key outputs, intermediate consumptions, and/or capital stocks. Mismeasurement occurs if the period-to-period comparisons of given goods, services, and/or stocks are not of like items; that is, if one or more characteristics of the measured items has changed, or if the number of varieties—the scope—of the types of measured items has changed.

This discussion of sectors with "hard to measure" outputs, intermediate consumption, and capital stocks began with a fairly detailed analytical section based on the capacity utilization function, whose dual is the value-added function that underlies

GDP. We worked with the Translog aggregator and associated Törnqvist index number representations of the capacity utilization function. There are other indexing frameworks, but the Translog/Törnqvist allows exact depiction (to a second-order differential approximation) of multifactor productivity change for a general technology that decomposes into volume factors for output, intermediate consumption, and scale-adjusted capital stock quantity change. Presuming existence of a well-defined (hedonic) functional relationship between the characteristics/quality of outputs, intermediate inputs, and capital stocks in each time period, these volume factors further decompose into quantity factors and associated quality adjustment factors that allow for a changing hedonic locus through time. We characterized the multifactor productivity framework as "semi-nonparametric" because it relies on a parametric form for the hedonic relationship between the prices and associated characteristics of outputs, intermediate inputs, and capital stocks, but does not require parametric estimation of the Translog capacity utilization function.[32] Eliminating the need for estimation of technology parameters is an argument for the practicality of this framework, as a good compromise between accurate measurement of multifactor productivity, flexibility of the underlying functional form for technology, and minimal (if not zero) need for estimating structural parameters. As well, its straightforward multiplicative decompositions make it a good heuristic for the practices that economic statisticians actually use in compiling productivity statistics from accounting and other economic data.

This semi-nonparametric index number framework is not the only analytical apparatus that might be used for understanding how to chip away at the mismeasurement problem in multifactor productivity. However, it has key flexibilities while remaining reasonably simple.

We have discussed some of the restrictions of this framework. Most important, it requires efficiency at all observed levels of prices, quantities, and characteristics, a strong requirement if there is reason to suppose there is significant scale inefficiency in our observations. Allowing for inefficiency seems to require that we know more about the parametric structure of technology than superlative index numbers allow, as suggested by O'Donnell (2015). On the other hand, there is a great deal not known about the evolution of multifactor productivity that is related to unmeasured or imperfectly measured quantities of some outputs/intermediate consumptions, capital stocks, and, important, the changing characteristics or quality of these key productivity drivers. The latter may well be at least as important as disallowing scale inefficiency, and this framework fixes a spotlight on the importance of dealing with mismeasurements and omitted variables in assessing the evolution of an inherently residual concept like multifactor productivity.

We briefly considered issues in the main hard-to-measure productive activities. The cited references in that discussion contain lists of additional sources that go more deeply into the sector-specific issues. Among key frontier measurement challenges are those involving the contributions of human and environmental capital to production. Although labor services metrics are available in most countries and are accounted for in standard productivity measures, human capital assets, while likely to comprise the principal part of national wealth in many countries, are not included within the national accounts asset boundary. However, much is known about human capital, and statistical standards for including it in official output and wealth are in process.[33] Although the asset boundary of existing national accounting standards includes natural resources such as subsoil mineral assets and cultivated biological assets, the depletion of these assets is not accounted for in existing measures of net national output, where it plays a similar role to depreciation of produced capital assets. International standards have been developed to measure depletion, but official measures remain under development.[34] Beyond natural resources in measuring the contribution of natural capital to output, however, are ecosystems and the associated ecosystem services, which currently lie outside the asset boundary of the national accounts due in part to significant measurement challenges.[35] There is much being done, but there is a great deal more to be done in deciding what concepts to measure and, once decided, secularly measuring those concepts.

Notes

1. The endogenous technical progress literature aims to more fully close the specification of technology and more fully explain productivity and efficiency residuals as the resultants of the accumulation of excluded or poorly measured capital inputs, namely, nonrival and partially or fully nonexcludable knowledge assets. In recognition of the role of knowledge capital, national accounting standards have been revised (European Commission, IMF, OECD, UN, and World Bank (2008), paragraph 1.38, p. 555) to include a new class of nonfinancial asset—Intellectual property products (AN117)—including

   - Research and development (AN1171)
   - Mineral exploration and evaluation (AN1172)
   - Computer software and databases (AN1173)
   - Entertainment, literary or artistic originals (AN1174)
   - Other intellectual property products (AN1179).

   Progress since 2008 has been steady in developing data sources and statistical measures for these assets, but much remains to be done.
2. In the interest of simplicity, this chapter assumes that the various maxima and minima defining the various distance function representations of a joint production function are attainable on the technology set T , and subsume "defined in the limit" ("infimum" or "supremum") into "minimum" or "maximum." If these minima and maxima are not bounded, we say the resultant is undefined.
3. Shephard's (1953, 1970) definition of the input distance function is the reciprocal of the input distance function defined here.
4. Balk (2009) employs the capacity utilization concept.
5. However, because we do not assume the technology T is convex, the converse— if $d_{yx}(y, x, K, \gamma, \chi, \kappa, \vartheta) \leq 1$ then $(y, x, K, \gamma, \chi.\kappa, \vartheta)$ is feasible—is not necessarily true.
6. We are treating labor as a *human* capital stock, rather than a rented service, to highlight its role as a quasi-fixed factor of production like nonhuman capital. The standard national accounts presentation does not account for human capital, only the rental of it in the form of "compensation of employees." On the other hand, the presence of *nonhuman* capital

in stock form among primary inputs *does* imply here that the using enterprise owns the nonhuman asset. If the nonhuman capital asset is not owned by the enterprise, then as in the most recent, 2008 version of national accounting standards, it enters the production function of that enterprise as an intermediate consumption of rented services and thus is not in value added.

7. Observed states are indicated in equation (6.1) when the superscript on the capacity utilization function and the superscripts on all of its arguments match, as in $d^0_{yx}\left(y^0,x^0,K^0,\gamma^0,\chi^0,\kappa^0,\vartheta^0\right)$ and $d^1_{yx}\left(y^1,x^1,K^1,\gamma^1,\chi^1,\kappa^1,\vartheta^1\right)$. Non-observed states are indicated when the superscript on the capacity utilization function and/or the superscripts on its arguments differ, as in $d^0_{yx}\left(y^1,x^1,K^1,\gamma^1,\chi^1,\kappa^1,\vartheta^0\right)$ and $d^1_{yx}\left(y^0,x^0,K^0,\gamma^0,\chi^0,\kappa^0,\vartheta^1\right)$. When observed states are efficient, $d^0_{yx}\left(y^0,x^0,K^0,\gamma^0,\chi^0,\kappa^0,\vartheta^0\right)=1$ and $d^1_{yx}\left(y^1,x^1,K^1,\gamma^1,\chi^1,\kappa^1,\vartheta^1\right)=1$.

8. Basic prices in national accounts are the prices the producer receives for output; they exclude taxes on products, include subsidies on products, and exclude separately invoiced transportation and distribution margins.

9. Purchasers' prices are the prices the producer pays for input; they include taxes on products, exclude subsidies on products, and include separately invoiced trade and transportation margins.

10. If $a=\left(a_1,a_2,...,a_n\right)'$ and $b=\left(b_1,b_2,...,b_n\right)'$ their Hadamard product is $a\odot b=\left(a_1b_1,a_2b_2,...,a_nb_n\right)$.

11. Being subject to eventual decreasing returns to scale means that it is always possible to find outputs, intermediate consumptions, and capital stocks sufficiently large that

$$\varepsilon^s_{d_{yx},K}=\frac{d\theta}{d\lambda}=-\frac{K^{s'}\nabla_K d_{y,x}}{y^{s'}\nabla_y d_{y,x}+x^{s'}\nabla_x d_{y,x}}\leq 1.$$ It does not preclude increasing returns to scale $\varepsilon^s_{d_{yx},K}>1$

at lower levels of outputs and intermediate consumptions, as exemplified by S-shaped plots of the scale of outputs and intermediate consumptions against the scale of primary inputs.

12. We use the term "super surplus" to distinguish the margin $p^s{}'y^s-v^s{}'x^s-u^s{}'K^s$ from the national accounts' "operating surplus" $p^s{}'y^s-v^s{}'x^s-u^s_L K^s_L$. Neither of these is "profit" as understood in commercial or national accounting (in national accounts "profit" goes by the term "entrepreneurial income"), which includes, among other things, the income and expense from the financial instruments the enterprise owns or for which it is liable that is not attributable to a financial service flow.

13. Dealing with the elasticity of scale becomes rather slippery in application. According to CCD(1982), if $\dfrac{u^{s'}K^s}{p^{s'}y^s-v^{s'}x^s}>1$, (corresponding to negative super surplus) and/or returns to scale are known to be increasing at one or both observed states, then we have to estimate $\varepsilon^s_{d_{yx},K}$ by other means. On the other hand, when $\dfrac{u^{s'}K^s}{p^{s'}y^s-v^{s'}x^s}\leq 1$, (corresponding to nonnegative super surplus), CCD(1982) note that we can determine the elasticity of scale as $\varepsilon^s_{d_{yx},K}=\dfrac{u^{s'}K^s}{p^{s'}y^s-v^{s'}x^s}\leq 1$; that is, returns to scale are nonincreasing. Intermediate microeconomic theory associates the long run equilibrium of an enterprise varying all inputs, including quasi fixed inputs, with operating at the point of unitary returns to scale, $\varepsilon^s_{d_{yx},K}=1$. This latter case corresponds to zero super surplus (thus, we could argue that super surplus is, de facto, the "economic profit" of microeconomics). Under the assumption that

the enterprise is operating at a point of unitary returns to the scale of quasi fixed (primary) inputs K^s, or long run equilibrium, $\varepsilon^s_{d_{ys},K}$ disappears from the multifactor productivity index (6.2). Allowing for the possibility of nonunitary returns to scale in applications of this framework to accounting data would involve specific treatments of the user cost of quasi fixed capital stocks that do not imply that super surplus is zero.

14. Feenstra (1995) derived a similar, though not identical, result for quality-adjusted Törnqvist household consumption price indices.

15. This is particularly true of land assets, whose prices are most directly affected by environmental quality characteristics.

16. Jorgenson (1966) attributed the "disembodied" technical progress concept to Tinbergen (1959) and its complement—"embodied" technical progress—to Solow (1960). Hulten (1992) observed that technical change embodied in inputs (e.g., capital stocks) can be equivalently viewed as an adjustment for the quantity of inputs or to the price of those inputs.

17. On intellectual property assets, see European Commission, IMF, OECD, UN, and World Bank (2008), paragraphs 10.98–10.117, 206–207.

18. On goodwill and marketing assets, see European Commission, IMF, OECD, UN, and World Bank (2008), paragraphs 10.196–10.199, 216. Prevailing commercial and naöional accounting standards allow booking of goodwill and marketing assets only if their value has been revealed in a previous transaction, thus the "purchased goodwill and marketing assets" terminology in the aforementioned 2008 SNA reference.

19. The usefulness of productivity as a measure of ignorance, or lack thereof, in specific contexts is arguably relevant. For example, Paul Romer (2016) recently has critiqued "real business cycle" macroeconomic models by asking why fluctuations in a measure of our ignorance ("productivity shocks," which he terms "phlogiston") should be a key independent variable in a macroeconomic model.

20. On reservation prices for new and disappearing products, see Fisher and Shell (1972). Some indicative exact results for new and disappearing goods in the vein of the translog "semiparametric" results in this chapter are in a rather obscure working paper by Zieschang (1989). Lovell and Zieschang (1994) approached the reservation price problem by estimating shadow prices via linear envelopment (data envelopment analysis or DEA). See Feenstra (1995) for exact index number results for new and disappearing products when the aggregator (e.g., cost or revenue) function has constant elasticity of substitution (CES) form.

21. Eurostat, International Labour Organisation, International Monetary Fund, Organisation for Economic Cooperation and Development, United National Economic Commission for Europe, and World Bank (2013).

22. Bureau of Economic Analysis, *Annual Industry Accounts (GDP by Industry and Input-Output Accounts)*, https://bea.gov; Strassner and Wasshausen (2014).

23. As noted at the beginning of this section, Bryne et al. (2016) did not find large impacts on US GDP growth from improving measurement of the high technology sector, including web-enabled distributive services. Nakamura, Samuels, and Soloveichik (2016) reach a similar conclusion. This said, measurement in web-enabled distribution remains an unsettled area.

24. Stone (1947, 40–41) and United Nations (1953, 39).

25. European Commission, International Monetary Fund, Organisation for Economic Co-operation and Development, United Nations, and World Bank (2008). The previous,

1993 version of the same standards did not proscribe FISIM to deposits and loans, thus implicitly allowing the scope of FISIM to be all financial instruments, though it did exclude "own funds" (equity) from playing a role in FISIM production. The 1993 national accounting standards thus did not foreclose alignment of the liquidity services component of FISIM with the liquidity services recognized in the monetary aggregation literature, which includes liquidity generated not only from deposits but from almost all other forms of debt, in particular debt securities (bonds).

26. The US Bureau of Labor Statistics takes this approach to account servicing-type products in US price and productivity statistics, for example. See Royster (2012).

27. Basu, Inklaar, and Wang (2011); Colangelo and Inklaar (2012); Inklaar and Wang (2013).

28. Barnett (1978, 1980), Donovan (1978), and the large economics literature that they started.

29. See, e.g., Task Force on Financial Statistics (2013, 29, paragraph 3.3) for the financial instruments classified as debt, among which are insurance reserves.

30. Hanushek and Ettema (2016).

31. http://www.oecd.org/pisa/aboutpisa/.

32. Or the dual of the capacity utilization function, the value-added function. The value-added function is a form of restricted profit function.

33. United Nations Economic Commission for Europe Task Force on Measuring Human Capital (2016).

34. Eurostat, International Monetary Fund, Organisation for Economic Co-operation and Development, United Nations, United Nations Food and Agriculture Organisation, World Bank (2012).

35. European Commission, Organisation for Economic Co-operation and Development, United Nations, World Bank (2013).

REFERENCES

Balk, Bert M. 2009. "On the Relation Between Gross Output- and Value Added-Based Productivity Measures: The Importance of the Domar Factor." *Macroeconomic Dynamics* 13(S2) (Measurement with Theory): 241–267.

Barnett, William A. 1978. "The User Cost of Money." *Economics Letters* 1(2): 145–149.

Barnett, William A. 1980. "Economic Monetary Aggregates: An Application of Index Number and Aggregation Theory." *Journal of Econometrics* 14(1): 11–48.

Basu, Susanto, Robert Inklaar, and Christina Wang. 2011. "The Value of Risk: Measuring the Service Output of U.S. Commercial Banks." *Economic Inquiry* 49(1): 226–245.

Bosworth, Barry, and Jack Triplett. 2007. "Services Productivity in the United States; Griliches's Services Volume Reconsidered." In *Hard-to-Measure Goods and Services: Essays in Honor of Zvi Griliches*, edited by Barry Bosworth and Jack Triplett, 413–447. Chicago: Chicago University Press for National Bureau of Economic Research.

Bureau of Economic Analysis. Various quarters. *Annual Industry Accounts (GDP by Industry and Input-Output Accounts)*. https://bea.gov.

Byrne, David M., John G. Fernald, and Marshall B. Reinsdorf. 2016. "Does the United States Have a Productivity Slowdown or a Measurement Problem?" *Brookings Papers on Economic Activity* (Spring): 109–157.

Cambridge International Examinations. 2015. "International Surveys: PISA, TIMSS, PIRLS." *Education Brief* 7. http://www.cie.org.uk/images/271193-international-surveys-pisa-timss-pirls.pdf.

Cole, Rosanne, Y. C. Chen, Joan A. Barquin-Stollerman, Ellen Dulburger, Nurhan Halvacian, and James H. Hodge. 1986. "Quality-Adjusted Price Indexes for Computer Processors and Selected Peripheral Equipment." *Survey of Current Business* 66(1): 41–50.

Colangelo, Antonio, and Robert Inklaar. 2012. "Bank Output Measurement in the Euro Area: A Modified Approach." *Review of Income and Wealth*, Series 58, 1 (March): 142–165.

Donovan, Donal J. 1978. "Modeling the Demand for Liquid Assets: An Application to Canada." IMF Staff Papers 25 (December), 676–704.

Dulberger, Ellen R. 1989. "The Application of a Hedonic Model to a Quality-Adjusted Price Index for Computer Processors." In *Technology and Capital Formation*, edited by Dale W. Jorgenson and Ralph Landau. Cambridge, MA: MIT Press.

Caves, Douglas W., Laurits R. Christensen, and W. Erwin Diewert. 1982. "The Economic Theory of Index Numbers and the Measurement of Input, Output, and Productivity." *Econometrica* 50(6): 1393–1414.

European Commission, International Monetary Fund, Organsation for Economic Co-operation and Development, United Nations, United Nations Food and Agriculture Organisation, and World Bank. 2012. *System of Environmental-Economic Accounting 2012 Central Framework*. https://unstats.un.org/unsd/envaccounting/seeaRev/SEEA_CF_Final_en.pdf.

European Commission, International Monetary Fund, Organisation for Economic Co-operation and Development, United Nations, and World Bank. 1993. *System of National Accounts 1993*. New York: United Nations.

European Commission, International Monetary Fund, Organisation for Economic Co-operation and Development, United Nations, and World Bank. 2008. *System of National Accounts 2008*. New York: United Nations.

European Commission, Organisation for Economic Co-operation and Development, United Nations, and World Bank. 2013. *System of Environmental-Economic Accounting 2012 Experimental Ecosystem Accounting*. https://unstats.un.org/unsd/envaccounting/eea_white_cover.pdf.

Eurostat, International Labour Organisation, International Monetary Fund, Organisation for Economic Co-operation and Development, United National Economic Commission for Europe, and World Bank. 2013. *Handbook on Residential Property Prices Indices (RPPIs)*, http://ec.europa.eu/eurostat/documents/3859598/5925925/KS-RA-12-022-EN.PDF.

Feenstra, Robert C. 1995. "Exact Hedonic Price Indexes." *The Review of Economics and Statistics* 77(4): 634–653.

Fisher, F. M., and K. Shell. 1972. *The Economic Theory of Price Indices*. New York: Academic Press.

Fisher, Irving. 1922. *The Making of Index Numbers: A Study of Their Varieties, Tests, and Reliability*. New Haven, CT: Houghton Mifflin.

Fixler, Dennis, and Kimberly Zieschang. 1992. "Incorporating Ancillary Measures of Process and Quality Change into a Superlative Productivity Index." *Journal of Productivity Analysis* 2: 243–267.

Graf, Brian, and Mick Silver. 2014. "Commercial Property Price Indexes: Problems of Sparse Data, Spatial Spillovers, and Weighting." IMF Working Paper 14/72. https://www.imf.org/~/media/Websites/IMF/imported-full-text-pdf/external/pubs/ft/wp/2014/_wp1472.ashx.

Hanushek, Eric A., and Elizabeth Ettema. 2016. "Defining Productivity in Education: Issues and Illustrations." *The American Economist* 65(2), October 2017, 165–183.

Hornstein, Andreas, and Robert C. Prescott. 1991. "Measures of the Insurance Sector Output." *The Geneva Papers on Risk and Insurance* 16 (59): 191–206.

Hulten, Charles R. 1992. "Growth Accounting When Technical Change Is Embodied in Capital." *The American Economic Review* 82(4): 964–980.

Inklaar, Robert, and Christina Wang. 2013. "Real Output of Bank Services: What Counts Is What Banks Do, Not What They Own." *Economica*, London School of Economics and Political Science, 80(317): 96–117.

Jorgenson, Dale W. 1963. "Capital Theory and Investment Behavior." *The American Economic Review* 53(2), Papers and Proceedings of the Seventy-Fifth Annual Meeting of the American Economic Association (May): 247–259.

Jorgenson, Dale W. 1966. "The Disembodiment Hypothesis." *Journal of Political Economy* 1(Feb): 1–17.

Laspeyres, E. 1871. :Die Berechnung einer mittleren Waarenpreissteigerung." *Jahrbücher für Nationalökonomie und Statistik* 16: 296–314.

Lovell, C. A. Knox, and Kimberly Zieschang. 1994. "The Problem of New and Disappearing Commodities in the Construction of Price Indexes." In *Data Envelopment Analysis: Theory, Methodology, and Applications*, edited by Abraham Charnes, William W. Cooper, Arie Y. Lewin, and Lawrence M. Seiford, 353–367. Dordrecht: Springer.

Nakamura, L., J. Samuels, and R. Soloveichik. 2016. "Valuing 'Free' Media in GDP, 1929–2015." Paper presented at the Allied Social Science Associations meeting, January 8.

O'Donnell, C. J. 2015. "Using Information about Technologies, Markets and Firm Behaviour to Decompose a Proper Productivity Index." *Journal of Econometrics* 190: 328–340.

Paasche, H. 1874. "Über die Preisentwicklung der letzten Jahre nach den Hamburger Borsennotirungen." *Jahrbücher für Nationalökonomie und Statistik* 12: 168–178.

Reece, William S. 1992. "Output Price Indexes for the U.S. Life Insurance Industry." *The Journal of Risk and Insurance* 59(1): 104–115.

Romer, Paul M. 1990. "Endogenous Technological Change," Journal of Political Economy 98(5), Part 2: The Problem of Development: A Conference on the Institute for the Study of Free Enterprise Systems (October): S71–102.

Romer, Paul M. 2016. "The Trouble With Macroeconomics," https://paulromer.net/wp-content/uploads/2016/09/WP-Trouble.pdf.

Royster, Sara E. 2012. "Improved Measures of Commercial Banking Output and Productivity." *Monthly Labor Review* (July): 3–17.

Scheiner, Louise, and Anna Malinovskaya. 2016. "Measuring Productivity in Healthcare: An Analysis of the Literature, Hutchins Center on Fiscal and Monetary Policy." Washington, DC: Brookings Institution. https://www.brookings.edu/wp-content/uploads/2016/08/hp-lit-review_final.pdf.

Shephard, Ronald W. 1953. *Cost and Production Functions*. Princeton, NJ: Princeton University Press.

Shephard, Ronald W. 1970. *Theory of Cost and Production Functions*. Princeton, NJ: Princeton University Press.

Solow, Robert M. 1960. "Investment and Technical Progress." In *Mathematical Methods in the Social Sciences*, edited by K. J. Arrow, S. Karlin, and P. Suppes, 89–104. Stanford, CA: Stanford University Press.

Stone, Richard. 1947. "Appendix: Definition and Measurement of the National Income and Related Totals." In *Measurement of National Income and the Construction of Social Accounts: Report of the Sub-Committee on National Income Statistics of the League of Nations Committee of Statistical Experts*. http://unstats.un.org/unsd/nationalaccount/docs/1947NAreport.pdf.

Strassner, Eric, and David B. Wasshausen. 2014. "New Quarterly Gross Domestic Product by Industry Statistics." *BEA Briefing*, Bureau of Economic Analysis. https://www.bea.gov/scb/pdf/2014/05%20May/0514_gdp-by-industry.pdf.

Sveikauskas, Leo, Samuel Rowe, James Mildenberger, Jennifer Price, and Arthur Young. 2014. "Productivity Growth in Construction." BLS Working Paper 478. https://www.bls.gov/osmr/pdf/ec140090.pdf.

Task Force on Financial Statistics. 2013. *External Debt Statistics: Guide for Compilers and Users*. Washington, DC: International Monetary Fund. http://www.tffs.org/edsguide.htm.

Tinbergen, J. 1959. "On the Theory of Trend Movements." In *Jan Tinbergen Selected Papers*, edited by L. H. Klaassen, L. M. Koyck, and H. J. Witteveen, 182–221. Amsterdam: North-Holland (originally published in German as "Zur Theorie der langfristigen Wirtschaftsentwicklung," *Weltwirtschaftliches Archiv* LV(1) [1942]: 511–549).

United Nations Economic Commission for Europe Task Force on Measuring Human Capital. 2016. *Guide on Measuring Human Capital*. https://unstats.un.org/unsd/nationalaccount/consultationDocs/HumanCapitalGuide%20Global%20Consultation-v1.pdf.

Zieschang, Kimberly. 1989. "The Characteristics Approach to the Problem of New and Disappearing Goods in Price Indexes." BLS Working Paper WP-183. US Bureau of Labor Statistics. https://www.bls.gov/osmr/workpapers_catalog1992.htm#1992.

CHAPTER 7

PRODUCTIVITY MEASUREMENT IN THE PUBLIC SECTOR

W. ERWIN DIEWERT

7.1. Introduction: How Should Public-Sector Non-Market Outputs Be Valued?

In order to measure the total factor productivity (TFP) of a public-sector production unit (or establishment) using index number techniques, it is necessary to measure the prices and quantities of the outputs produced and the inputs used by that unit for two periods of time.[1] Then TFP growth can be defined as a quantity index of outputs produced, divided by a quantity index of inputs used by the establishment.[2] It is usually possible to measure the price and quantity of inputs in a fairly satisfactory manner,[3] but there are problems in measuring the prices and quantities of public-sector nonmarket outputs. Thus in this chapter, we will take a systematic look at possible methods for the valuation of non-market outputs produced by public-sector production units.

In many cases, it is difficult to determine exactly what it is that a public-sector production unit produces. In this case, we may have neither quantities nor prices for the outputs of the government service provider. However, in many cases, we can measure at least the quantities of the outputs produced by the public-sector unit but not the corresponding prices. Finally, in some cases, it may be possible to measure output quantities produced and to obtain estimates of purchaser's valuations for the missing non-market output prices. Thus the "best practice" methodology that can be used to form productivity estimates for the public-sector unit will depend to a large extent on what information on prices and quantities is available.

From the perspective of measuring the effects on the *welfare of households* of public-sector production, we suggest the following methods for valuing government outputs in the order of their desirability:

- *First best*: valuation at market prices or purchaser's valuations;
- *Second best*: valuations at producer's unit costs of production;
- *Third best*: output growth of the public-sector production unit is set equal to real input growth, and the corresponding output price growth is set equal to an index of input price growth.

Obviously, the third-best option is the least desirable option. If it is used, then productivity growth for the public-sector production unit will be nonexistent by construction. *If* there are competitive markets with no economies of scope and constant returns to scale in production, then the first- and second-best options will be roughly equivalent (i.e., the purchaser's price will be approximately equal to the long-run marginal cost of producing a unit of the commodity). However, in a non-market setting, even with no economies of scope and constant returns to scale in production, there is nothing to force the cost of producing a unit of public-sector output to equal its value to recipients of the commodity.[4] In an extreme case, the production unit could be producing nothing of value. Thus from the viewpoint of welfare economics, valuation of public-sector outputs at purchasers' valuations appears to be the preferred option.[5]

The task of this chapter is to suggest methods for measuring the TFP of a public-sector production unit that produces at least some outputs that are allocated to recipients at non-market prices (i.e., at zero prices or at highly subsidized prices that do not cover their unit costs of production). In general, the TFP level of a production unit is defined as the real output produced by the production unit at a time period divided by the real input utilized by the production unit during the same time period. There is TFP growth if real output grows more rapidly than real input. The main drivers of TFP growth are the following: (i) technical progress (i.e., at outward shift of the unit's production possibilities set); (ii) increasing returns to scale combined with input growth; and (iii) improvements in technical and allocative efficiency.[6] This volume outlines many methods for measuring TFP, but in this chapter, we will concentrate on index number methods.[7] The use of index number methods means that we will not be able to decompose the TFP growth of a public-sector production unit into the contributions of the preceding three main components of TFP growth (i.e., index number methods do not allow us to measure separately the effects of these explanatory factors; in general, all three explanatory factors will be combined into the overall TFP growth measure). However, the use of index number methods requires a methodological framework for the determination of output prices for the non-market outputs produced by the public sector. If the public-sector unit minimizes its cost of production in producing its non-market outputs, then from the viewpoint of the economic approach to productivity measurement, the "right" prices to use to value non-market outputs are the (long-run) marginal costs of producing the non-market outputs. Diewert (2012, 222–228) provided a nonparametric methodological justification for this marginal cost method of output price valuation for non-market outputs.[8] Diewert also justified the use of the Fisher (1922) index number formula to aggregate inputs and outputs using his approach. We will summarize his approach in the Appendix to this chapter. Variants of this cost-based method for valuing non-market outputs will be discussed in section 7.5.

The third-best option outlined earlier is the only option that can be used when there is little or no information on both the prices and quantities produced by a government establishment. This is the option that is recommended in the *System of National Accounts 1993* to value government production when direct information on the prices and quantities of government outputs is not available. The quantity or volume measure for establishment output that results from using this methodology can be interpreted as a *measure of real resources used* by that establishment, and as such, it is an acceptable indicator of the output produced by a government unit. This third-best option will be discussed in more detail in the following three sections. Section 7.2 introduces the method. Section 7.3 discusses how user costs should be used to value public-sector capital stock inputs. Section 7.4 addresses the problems associated with choosing an index number formula and how TFP could be measured either as gross output TFP or as value-added TFP. This section also shows that the choice of an index number formula to aggregate outputs and inputs does matter.

The second-best option for valuing public-sector outputs will be discussed in section 7.5 and the first-best option in section 7.6. Section 7.7 provides a numerical example due to Schreyer (2010, 21) that illustrates how the first-best option (from the viewpoint of welfare economics) could be used in order to value non-market outputs. This section also discusses some aspects of the problem of adjusting output quantities for quality change. Section 7.8 discusses some of the practical difficulties associated with the measurement of public-sector outputs in selected industries. Section 7.9 concludes.

7.2. THE CASE WHERE NO INFORMATION ON THE PRICES AND QUANTITIES OF NON-MARKET OUTPUTS IS AVAILABLE

The third-best option outlined earlier is the only option that can be used when there is little or no information on both the prices and quantities produced by a public-sector production unit (or there is no agreement on how to measure the outputs of the unit). For example, usually there is little information on the price and quantity of educational services produced by the public sector.[9] As was mentioned earlier, the quantity or volume measure for establishment output that results from using this methodology can be interpreted as a *measure of real resources used* by the production unit, and as such, it is an acceptable indicator of the output produced by the unit. Although this third-best option is fairly straightforward in principle (and has been extensively discussed in the national income accounting literature), there are some aspects of the method that deserve some additional discussion.

The two aspects of the third method that we will discuss in more detail in the following two sections are as follows:

- How exactly should the contribution of durable inputs used in a public-sector production unit to current period production be valued?
- How exactly should estimates for the aggregate real output produced by a non-market production unit be constructed? In particular, which index number formula should be chosen to perform the aggregation, and does the choice of formula make a difference?

7.3. THE VALUATION OF DURABLE INPUTS USED IN THE PUBLIC SECTOR

The basic tool that economists use to value the contribution of a durable input (or a capital input) to production in an accounting period is the concept of a *user cost*.

We will first explain how to construct the user cost of a capital input[10] for a durable input for which market prices exist for the same input at different ages. Consider a production unit that purchases q^t units of a durable input at the beginning of accounting period t at the price P^t. After using the services of the capital input during period t, the production unit will have $q_u^{\ t} = (1 - \delta)q^t$ units of used or depreciated capital (in constant quality units) on hand at the end of period t where δ is the one period depreciation rate for the capital good under consideration.[11] Finally, we assume that the production unit has a one period financial opportunity cost of capital at the beginning of period t (i.e., a beginning of the period nominal interest rate) equal to r^t. The gross cost of the capital input is the beginning of the period purchase cost of the capital inputs, $P^t q^t$. But this cost is offset by the revenue that could be raised by selling the depreciated capital stock value at its imputed market value at the end of the period, which is $P^{t+1}q_u^{\ t} = P^{t+1}(1-d)q^t$. But this imputed revenue is not equivalent to the cost outlay made at the beginning of the period. To make it equivalent, we need to take into account that money received at the end of the period is less valuable than money received at the beginning of the period, and so the end of period market value should be discounted by $(1 + r^t)$. Thus the *net cost of using the services of the capital input* during period t is U^t, defined as follows:[12]

$$U^t \equiv P^t - \left(1 + r^t\right)^{-1}(1 - d)P^{t+1}. \tag{7.1}$$

Define the *constant quality asset inflation rate* over period t, i^t, by the following equation:

$$1 + i^t \equiv P_K^{\ t+1} / P_K^{\ t}. \tag{7.2}$$

Substituting (7.2) into (7.1) leads to the following expression for the *ex post user cost U^t* defined by (7.1):

$$U^t \equiv P^t - \left(1+r^t\right)^{-1}\left(1-\delta\right)\left(1+i^t\right)P^t = (1+r^t)^{-1}\left[\left(1+r^t\right)-\left(1-d\right)\left(1+i^t\right)\right]P^t. \quad (7.3)$$

Rather than discounting the end-of-period value of the capital stock to the beginning of the period, it is more convenient to anti-discount costs and benefits to the end of the period. Thus the *ex post end of period user cost of a capital input*, u^t, is defined as $\left(1+r^t\right)$ times U^t:[13]

$$u^t \equiv \left(1+r^t\right)U^t = \left[\left(1+r^t\right)-\left(1-\delta\right)\left(1+i^t\right)\right]P^t = \left[r^t -i^t + \delta\left(1+i^t\right)\right]P^t. \quad (7.4)$$

Using this formula, we add the opportunity cost of tying up financial capital for one period, r^tP^t, to the beginning of the period purchase cost of the asset, P^t, to obtain a total cost of purchasing one unit of an asset and tying up financial capital for one period, which is $\left(1+r^t\right)P^t$. This total asset cost is offset by the end-of-period (imputed) benefit of the depreciated value of one unit of the purchased capital stock, $\left(1-d\right)\left(1+i^t\right)P^t$. Taking the difference of this cost and benefit leads to the user cost formula (7.4). This ex post formula for the user cost of capital defined was obtained by Christensen and Jorgenson (1969, 302) for the geometric model of depreciation.[14]

However, the derivation of the user cost of capital defined by (7.3) or (7.4) is not the end of the problems associated with valuing the cost of using a capital input over an accounting period. There are four additional issues that need to be discussed:

- Ex ante versus ex post user costs;
- How to treat specific taxes on some capital inputs such as property taxes;
- What to do if there are no market prices for used capital stocks; and
- What should be done if inappropriate user costs of capital are used.

We will address each of these problems in turn.

The problem with the user cost formulae defined by (7.3) or (7.4) is that they use the ex post or actual asset inflation rate i^t defined by (7.2). For land assets in particular, ex post asset inflation rates can at times be so large that it makes the user costs defined by (7.3) or (7.4) negative. Basically, we would like the user cost of an asset to be approximately equal to the rental price for the asset (if rental markets for the asset exist). Rental prices will rarely be negative, so obviously a negative user cost will be a poor approximation to a rental price. A way around the negative user cost problem is to replace the ex post asset inflation rate by an *anticipated asset inflation rate*. Thus suppose that at the beginning of period t, the *anticipated end of period t price for an asset of the same quality is P^{t+1^*}*. Use this price in order to define an *anticipated asset inflation rate* as $i^{t^*} \equiv \left(P^{t+1^*} / P^t\right)-1$. Now replace the ex post asset inflation rate i^t that appears in the user cost formulae (7.3) and (7.4) by their anticipated counterparts i^{t^*} and we obtain the corresponding *ex ante user costs, U^{t^*} and u^{t^*}*. Jorgenson (1989, 1996) and his coworkers[15] endorsed the use of ex post user costs, arguing that producers can perfectly anticipate future asset prices.

On the other hand, Diewert (1980, 476; 2005, 492–493), Schreyer (2001, 2009), and Hill and Hill (2003) endorsed the ex ante version for most purposes, since these ex ante user costs will tend to be smoother than their ex post counterparts, and they will generally be closer to a rental or leasing price for the asset.[16] Diewert and Fox (2016) used sectoral data on the US corporate and non-corporate financial sector to compute capital services aggregates and the resulting rates of TFP growth using both Jorgensonian and smoothed user costs that use predicted asset inflation rates.[17] They found that Jorgensonian ex ante user costs for land components were indeed negative for many years, but the use of ex ante or predicted asset inflation rates cured the problem of negative user costs and, indeed, led to much smoother user costs, as could be expected.[18] There is another solution to the problem of negative user costs if rental prices for the asset are available: take the maximum of the user cost and the corresponding market rental price as the appropriate valuation for the services of the asset during the period under consideration. The user cost valuation for the services of the asset is essentially a financial opportunity cost of using the asset, while the rental price is the opportunity cost of using the services of the asset for productive purposes, rather than renting it out for the period. Both valuations are valid opportunity costs, so the true opportunity cost of using the asset should be the maximum of these two costs. Diewert (2008) called this the *opportunity cost method* for asset services valuation.[19]

We have ignored tax complications in deriving the user cost formulae (7.3) and (7.4). Any specific capital taxes (such as property taxes on real estate assets) should be added to the user cost formula for the relevant assets.[20] Business income taxes that fall on the gross return to the asset base can be absorbed into the cost of capital, r^t, so that r^t can be interpreted as the before income tax gross return to the asset used by the production unit.[21]

The user costs (7.3) and (7.4) were derived under the assumption that there are market prices for used assets that can be used to value the asset at the end of the accounting period. However, for many *unique assets* that do not trade in each accounting period (such as real estate, intellectual property, and mining assets, and certain types of artistic assets, such as a movie), there are no end-of-period asset prices that are available. In these cases, estimates of the future discounted cash flows that the asset might generate have to be used in order to value the asset as it ages. It will usually be difficult to form these estimates.[22]

There is still a certain amount of controversy on how exactly to measure capital services in the international System of National Accounts (SNA).[23] A particular problem with the *System of National Accounts 1993* and *System of National Accounts 2008* is that capital services in the general government sector are to be measured by depreciation only; that is, there is no allowance for the opportunity cost of capital in government-sector user costs,[24] whereas as we have seen in the preceding, market-sector user costs of capital include both depreciation and the opportunity cost of capital that is tied up in holding productive assets. This omission of imputed interest cost will lead to a substantial underestimate of public-sector costs (from an opportunity cost perspective) and hence economy wide gross domestic product (GDP) will also be underestimated.[25]

The Office of National Statistics (ONS) in the United Kingdom has made a substantial effort to measure productivity in the public sector, and it recognized that the SNA-recommended treatment of capital input in the public sector is not appropriate for productivity measurement purposes. Thus the ONS treatment of capital services costs in the public sector for productivity measurement purposes is different from its SNA treatment, which follows the international guidelines. This is unfortunate because ideally, we would like the official GDP measure to coincide with the GDP measure that is used for productivity measurement purposes.

The preceding material should alert the reader to the fact that the measurement of capital services input in the public sector is not a completely straightforward exercise. Thus it is not that simple to measure the non-market output produced by a public-sector production unit by its corresponding input measure due to the fact that it is not completely straightforward to measure capital services in both the private and public sector.

7.4. Measuring Output Growth by Input Growth: Gross Output versus Value Added

If it proves to be difficult or impossible to measure non-market output quantities, then as indicated earlier, economic statisticians have generally measured the value of non-market outputs by the value of inputs used and implicitly or explicitly set the price of non-market output equal to the corresponding input price index. Atkinson (2005, 12) describes the situation in the United Kingdom prior to 1998 as follows:

> In many countries, and in the United Kingdom from the early 1960's to 1998, the output of the government sector has been measured by convention as the value equal to the total value of inputs; by extension the volume of output has been measured by the volume of inputs. This convention regarding the volume of government output is referred to below as the (output = input) convention, and is contrasted with direct measures of government output. The inputs taken into account in recent years in the United Kingdom are the compensation of employees, the procurement costs of goods and services and a charge for the consumption of fixed capital. In earlier years and in other countries, including the United States, the inputs were limited to employment.

As was noted in the previous section, the preceding conventions imply that capital services input for government-owned capital will generally be less than the corresponding capital services input if the capital services were rented or leased. In the owned case, the government user cost of capital consists only of depreciation, but in the leased case, the rental rate would cover the cost of depreciation plus the opportunity cost of the financial

capital tied up in the capital input. Atkinson (2005, 49) makes the following recommendation on this issue (and we concur with his recommendation):

> We recommend that the appropriate measure of capital input for production and
> productivity analysis is the flow of *capital services* of an asset type. This involves
> adding to the capital consumption an interest charge, with an agreed interest rate, on
> the entire owned capital.

In addition to the preceding problem, there are some subtle problems associated with
measuring public-sector outputs by their real input utilization:

- How exactly should real input be measured (i.e., which index number formula
  should be used to aggregate inputs, and does the choice of formula matter)?
- Should the output aggregate for a public-sector production unit be measured by
  its real *primary* input or by its real *gross* input (i.e., by primary plus intermediate
  inputs)?

In order to address these questions, we will calculate alternative input aggregates for
an artificial data set. In Table 7.1, we list the prices $\left(w_1^t, w_2^t\right)$ and the corresponding
quantities $\left(x_1^t, x_2^t\right)$ for two primary inputs and the prices $\left(p_1^t, p_2^t\right)$ and quantities
$\left(z_1^t, z_2^t\right)$ for two intermediate inputs for five periods, $t = 1, \ldots, 5$.

It can be seen that the price of the first primary input (labor) is slowly trending upward, while the price of the second primary input (capital services) is trending downward at a faster rate. The quantity of the first primary input is slowly trending downward,
while the quantity of the second primary input is trending upward at a rapid rate. Thus
normal substitution effects are taking place over time. The price of the first intermediate input (general imports) is trending downward, while the quantity trends upward.
Finally, the price of the second intermediate input (energy imports) is rising rapidly,
while the corresponding quantity falls. The trends in these prices and quantities are
fairly smooth.

Table 7.1 Primary and Intermediate Input Prices and Quantities

Period t	w_1^t	w_2^t	p_1^t	p_2^t	x_1^t	x_2^t	z_1^t	z_2^t
1	1.00	1.00	1.00	1.00	60	40	50	50
2	1.02	0.95	0.99	1.10	59	42	52	48
3	1.04	0.90	0.95	1.20	58	50	55	45
4	1.05	0.82	0.92	1.30	57	57	57	43
5	1.06	0.75	0.90	1.40	56	65	60	40

The most commonly used index number formulae that are used to aggregate prices and quantities are the Laspeyres, Paasche, Fisher, and Törnqvist price indexes. Once the sequence of aggregate prices has been formed using these formulae, the corresponding quantity indexes are formed by dividing the period t value for the aggregate by the corresponding price indexes. Let w^t and x^t denote the price and quantity vectors for primary inputs for $t = 1, \ldots, 5$. Then the period t *fixed base Laspeyres, Paasche, Fisher, and Törnqvist price indexes* are defined as follows for $t = 1, \ldots, 5$:[26]

$$P_L^t \equiv P_L\left(w^1, w^t, x^1, x^t\right) \equiv w^t \cdot x^1 / w^1 \cdot x^1;[27] \tag{7.5}$$

$$P_P^t \equiv P_P\left(w^1, w^t, x^1, x^t\right) \equiv w^t \cdot x^t / w^1 \cdot x^t; \tag{7.6}$$

$$P_F^t \equiv P_F\left(w^1, w^t, x^1, x^t\right) \equiv \left[P_L\left(w^1, w^t, x^1, x^t\right) P_F\left(w^1, w^t, x^1, x^t\right)\right]^{1/2}; \tag{7.7}$$

$$P_T^t \equiv P_T\left(w^1, w^t, x^1, x^t\right)\right] \equiv \exp\left[\sum_{n=1}^{N} (1/2)\left(s_n^1 + s_n^t\right)\ln\left(w_n^t / w_n^1\right)\right] \tag{7.8}$$

where $s_n^t \equiv w_n^t x_n^t / w^t \cdot x^t$ is the nth primary-input cost share in period t. The four fixed-base primary-input price indexes defined by (7.5)–(7.8) are listed in columns 2–5 of Table 7.2, using the primary-input data listed in Table 7.1. These period t fixed-base indexes are denoted by $P_{LX}^t, P_{PX}^t, P_{FX}^t$ and P_{TX}^t. It can be seen that P_{LX}^t is always greater than P_{PX}^t for $t = 2, \ldots, 5$ and the gap between the fixed-base Laspeyres and Paasche price indexes gradually becomes greater as time marches on. Since the Fisher index P_{FX}^t is the geometric mean of P_{LX}^t and P_{PX}^t, it lies between these two equally plausible fixed-basket-type price indexes. Note that the fixed-base Törnqvist price index, P_{TX}^t, is quite close to its fixed-base Fisher counterpart, P_{TX}^t.[28]

An alternative to the use of fixed-base indexes is to use *chained indexes*. Consider how a chained Laspeyres price index, say P_{LX}^{t*}, is formed. For periods 1 and 2, the chained indexes coincide with their fixed-base counterparts; that is, $P_{LX}^{1*} \equiv 1$ and $P_{LX}^{2*} \equiv P_{LX}^2 = P_L\left(w^1, w^2, x^1, x^2\right)$. The period 3 chained Laspeyres price index is defined as the period 2 chained index level, P_{LX}^{2*}, multiplied by $P_L\left(w^2, w^3, x^2, x^3\right)$, which is (one plus) the Laspeyres rate of change of input prices going from period 2 to period 3. In general, the chained Laspeyres price level in period $t+1$ is equal to the corresponding

Table 7.2 Fixed Base and Chained Laspeyres, Paasche, Fisher, and Törnqvist Primary–Input Price Indexes

Period t	P_{LX}^t	P_{PX}^t	P_{FX}^t	P_{TX}^t	P_{LX}^{t*}	P_{PX}^{t*}	P_{FX}^{t*}	P_{TX}^{t*}
1	1.00000	1.00000	1.00000	1.00000	1.00000	1.00000	1.00000	1.00000
2	0.99200	0.99089	0.99145	0.99145	0.99200	0.99089	0.99145	0.99145
3	0.98400	0.97519	0.97958	0.97963	0.98288	0.97844	0.98066	0.98067
4	0.95800	0.93500	0.94643	0.94661	0.95096	0.94314	0.94704	0.94706
5	0.93600	0.89347	0.91449	0.91492	0.92045	0.90957	0.91499	0.91502

Laspeyres price level in period t times the Laspeyres chain link going from period t to $t+1$; that is, $P_{LX}^{t+1*} \equiv P_{LX}^{t*} P_L \left(w^t, w^{t+1}, x^t, x^{t+1} \right)$. The chained Paasche, Fisher, and Törnqvist input price indexes, P_{PX}^{t*}, P_{FX}^{t*} and P_{TX}^{t*} are formed in a similar fashion, except that the Paasche, Fisher, and Törnqvist chain link formulae $P_P \left(w^t, w^{t+1}, x^t, x^{t+1} \right)$, $P_F \left(w^t, w^{t+1}, x^t, x^{t+1} \right)$, and $P_T \left(w^t, w^{t+1}, x^t, x^{t+1} \right)$ are used, instead of the Laspeyres chain link formula $P_L \left(w^t, w^{t+1}, x^t, x^{t+1} \right)$. The chained Laspeyres, Paasche, Fisher, and Törnqvist input price indexes, P_{LX}^{t*}, P_{PX}^{t*}, P_{FX}^{t*} and P_{TX}^{t*}, are listed in the last four columns of Table 7.2.

It can be seen that the use of the chained indexes dramatically reduces the spread between these four types of indexes as compared to their fixed-base counterparts. In period 5, the percentage difference between the Laspeyres and Paasche fixed-base indexes is 4.8%, but the difference between the chained Laspeyres and Paasche indexes is only 1.6%. In period 5, the percentage difference between the superlative Fisher and Törnqvist fixed-base indexes is 0.047%, but the difference between the chained Fisher and Törnqvist indexes is only 0.003%, which is negligible. Thus chaining has substantially reduced the spread between the four most popular index number formulae that are used in empirical applications. This will generally happen if annual data are used so that trends in prices and quantities are fairly smooth.[29]

The period t primary input implicit quantity indexes that correspond to the input price indexes listed in Table 7.2 can be obtained by dividing the period t aggregate input value by the corresponding period t price index.[30] The resulting implicit quantity indexes are listed in Table 7.3.

Exactly the same methodology can be used to form eight alternative price indexes for intermediate inputs using the data listed in Table 7.1. Denote the Laspeyres, Paasche, Fisher, and Törnqvist intermediate input price indexes for period t by P_{LZ}^{t}, P_{PZ}^{t}, P_{FZ}^{t} and P_{TZ}^{t} and their chained counterparts by P_{LZ}^{t*}, P_{PZ}^{t*}, P_{FZ}^{t*} and P_{TZ}^{t*}, respectively. These indexes are listed in Table 7.4.

Viewing the entries in Table 7.4, it can be seen that the fixed-base Laspeyres and Paasche intermediate input price indexes differ by almost 5% in period 5, while the Fisher and Törnqvist fixed-base indexes are virtually the same. The chained Laspeyres and Paasche intermediate input price indexes differ by about 1% in period 5, while the

Table 7.3 Fixed–Base and Chained Implicit Laspeyres, Paasche, Fisher, and Törnqvist Primary–Input Quantity Indexes

Period t	Q_{LX}^{t}	Q_{PX}^{t}	Q_{FX}^{t}	Q_{TX}^{t}	Q_{LX}^{t*}	Q_{PX}^{t*}	Q_{FX}^{t*}	Q_{TX}^{t*}
1	100.000	100.000	100.000	100.000	100.000	100.000	100.000	100.000
2	100.887	101.000	100.944	100.943	100.887	101.000	100.944	100.943
3	107.033	108.000	107.515	107.510	107.154	107.640	107.397	107.396
4	111.263	114.000	112.623	112.602	112.086	113.016	112.550	112.548
5	115.502	121.000	118.219	118.164	117.453	118.859	118.154	118.150

Table 7.4 Fixed–Base and Chained Laspeyres, Paasche, Fisher, and Törnqvist Intermediate Input Price Indexes

Period t	P_{LZ}^{t}	P_{PZ}^{t}	P_{FZ}^{t}	P_{TZ}^{t}	P_{LZ}^{t*}	P_{PZ}^{t*}	P_{FZ}^{t*}	P_{TZ}^{t*}
1	1.00000	1.00000	1.00000	1.00000	1.00000	1.00000	1.00000	1.00000
2	1.04500	1.04280	1.04390	1.04390	1.04500	1.04280	1.04390	1.04390
3	1.07500	1.06250	1.06873	1.06874	1.07226	1.06587	1.06906	1.06906
4	1.11000	1.08340	1.09662	1.09664	1.10102	1.09198	1.09649	1.09649
5	1.15000	1.10000	1.12472	1.12475	1.13313	1.12050	1.12680	1.12680

Table 7.5 Fixed–Base and Chained Implicit Laspeyres, Paasche, Fisher, and Törnqvist Aggregate Input Price Indexes

Period t	P_{LY}^{t}	P_{PY}^{t}	P_{FY}^{t}	P_{TY}^{t}	P_{LY}^{t*}	P_{PY}^{t*}	P_{FY}^{t*}	P_{TY}^{t*}
1	1.00000	1.00000	1.00000	1.00000	1.00000	1.00000	1.00000	1.00000
2	1.01850	1.01672	1.01761	1.01761	1.01850	1.01672	1.01761	1.01761
3	1.02950	1.01716	1.02331	1.02331	1.02747	1.02135	1.02441	1.02440
4	1.03400	1.00435	1.01907	1.01919	1.02470	1.01474	1.01971	1.01972
5	1.04300	0.98692	1.01457	1.01490	1.02346	1.00923	1.01632	1.01635

corresponding chained Fisher and Törnqvist indexes are exactly the same. Thus again, chaining reduces the spread between indexes for this data set.

Use the same methodology to form eight alternative aggregate input price indexes for both primary and intermediate inputs using the data listed in Table 7.1. Denote the Laspeyres, Paasche, Fisher, and Törnqvist aggregate input price indexes for period t by P_{LY}^{t}, P_{PY}^{t}, P_{FY}^{t} and P_{TY}^{t} and their chained counterparts by P_{LY}^{t*}, P_{PY}^{t*}, P_{FY}^{t*} and P_{TY}^{t*}, respectively. These indexes are listed in Table 7.5.

Viewing the entries in Table 7.5, it can be seen that the fixed-base Laspeyres and Paasche aggregate input price indexes differ by approximately 5% in period 5, while the Fisher and Törnqvist fixed-base indexes differ by 0.0003. The chained Laspeyres and Paasche intermediate input price indexes differ by about 2% in period 5, while the corresponding chained Fisher and Törnqvist indexes differ by 0.00003. Thus again, chaining reduces the spread between indexes. Also, the superlative indexes (whether they are fixed base or chained) are much closer to each other than are the corresponding Laspeyres and Paasche indexes.[31]

Once the aggregate input price indexes have been calculated, corresponding aggregate implicit input quantity or volume measures can be calculated by deflating each period's total input costs by the appropriate aggregate input price index. Thus the period t fixed-base implicit aggregate input quantity that corresponds to fixed-base Laspeyres price aggregation, Q_{LY}^{t}, is defined as follows for $t = 1, \ldots, 5$:[32]

$$Q_{LY}^{t} \equiv (w^{t} \cdot x^{t} + p^{t} \cdot z^{t})/P_{LY}^{t}. \tag{7.9}$$

The other seven aggregate implicit input quantity levels, $Q_{PY}^{t}, Q_{FY}^{t}, Q_{TY}^{t}, Q_{lY}^{t*}, Q_{PY}^{t*}, Q_{FY}^{t*}$, Q_{TY}^{t*}, are defined in an analogous manner. The eight aggregate implicit input quantity indexes are listed in Table 7.6. Note that the *value of gross output* produced during period t, say V_{Y}^{t}, is equal to the value of aggregate input used during period t; that is, we have for $t = 1, \ldots, 5$:

$$V_{Y}^{t} \equiv w^{t} \cdot x^{t} + p^{t} \cdot z^{t} = P_{LY}^{t} Q_{LY}^{t} = P_{PY}^{t} Q_{PY}^{t} = \ldots = P_{TY}^{t*} Q_{TY}^{t*} \tag{7.10}$$

Thus for each period t, the price of gross output times the corresponding quantity of gross output is equal to the nominal value of aggregate input for each of our eight pairs of gross output price and quantity indexes.

The differences between the Laspeyres and Paasche fixed-base and chained aggregate implicit input indexes grow over time and are fairly substantial by period 5, but the other four superlative indexes are reasonably close to each other.

With no actual output prices and quantities available for our imaginary public-sector production unit, we set the aggregate output price and quantity levels for period t to equal the corresponding aggregate input price and quantity levels that are listed in Tables 7.5 and 7.6. Thus if we choose to use the fixed-base Laspeyres formula to form aggregate input prices, the period t output price is set equal to P_{LY}^{t} listed in Table 7.5, and the period t aggregate output quantity is set equal to Q_{LY}^{t} listed in Table 7.6. The *period t gross output TFP level* using the fixed-base Laspeyres price index formula is defined as TFP_{LY}^{t}, equal to period t gross output using Laspeyres fixed-base price indexes divided by the period t aggregate input level using fixed base Laspeyres price indexes, which leads to the result $TFP_{LY}^{t} \equiv Q_{LY}^{t} / Q_{LY}^{t} = 1$ for each t. Using the other seven methods for aggregating inputs similarly leads to *gross output productivity levels*

Table 7.6 Fixed–Base and Chained Laspeyres, Paasche, Fisher, and Törnqvist Aggregate Implicit Input Quantity Indexes

Period t	Q_{LY}^{t}	Q_{PY}^{t}	Q_{FY}^{t}	Q_{TY}^{t}	Q_{LY}^{t*}	Q_{PY}^{t*}	Q_{FY}^{t*}	Q_{TY}^{t*}
1	200.000	200.000	200.000	200.000	200.000	200.000	200.000	200.000
2	200.648	201.000	200.824	200.824	200.648	201.000	200.824	200.824
3	205.508	208.000	206.750	206.750	205.913	207.147	206.529	206.530
4	207.863	214.000	210.909	210.883	209.749	211.808	210.776	210.773
5	209.118	221.000	214.977	214.907	213.110	216.114	214.607	214.602

that are identically unity; that is, $TFP_{PY}^{t} \equiv Q_{PY}^{t} / Q_{PY}^{t} = 1$, $TFP_{FY}^{t} \equiv Q_{FY}^{t} / Q_{FY}^{t} = 1, \ldots,$ $TFP_{TY}^{t*} \equiv Q_{TY}^{t*} / Q_{TY}^{t*} = 1$ for all t.

Instead of calculating gross output TFP levels, it is also useful to construct *value-added TFP levels*.[33] Nominal value added for a production unit for period t is defined as the value of outputs produced during period t less the value of intermediate inputs used by the production unit during period t, where an intermediate input is an input that was produced by another domestic or foreign production unit. Thus for our numerical example, *period t nominal value added V_O^{t}* is defined as follows for $t = 1, \ldots, 5$:

$$V_O^{t} \equiv V_Y^{t} - p^{t} \cdot z^{t} \tag{7.11}$$
$$= \left(w^{t} \cdot x^{t} + p^{t} \cdot z^{t} \right) - p^{t} \cdot z^{t}$$
$$= w^{t} \cdot x^{t}$$

where the second equality follows using (7.10). Thus period t nominal value added for our public-sector production unit, V_O^{t}, is equal to period t value of primary inputs used in the unit, $w^{t} \times x^{t}$, for each period t. Thus period t nominal value added V_O^{t} is unambiguously defined. But how exactly should the *price* of real value added and the corresponding *quantity or volume* be defined? We will follow the methodology that was used in the *Producer Price Index Manual*[34] and simply apply normal index number theory to the components of value added, treating all prices and output quantities as positive numbers, but changing the sign of intermediate input quantities from positive to negative.[35] Thus the *fixed-base Laspeyres, Paasche, Fisher, and Törnqvist price indexes for period t value added* are defined as follows for $t = 1, \ldots, 5$:

$$P_{LO}^{t} \equiv \left[P_{LY}^{t} Q_{LY}^{1} - p^{t} \cdot z^{1} \right] / \left[P_{LY}^{1} Q_{LY}^{1} - p^{1} \cdot z^{1} \right]; \tag{7.12}$$

$$P_{PO}^{t} \equiv \left[P_{PY}^{t} Q_{PY}^{t} - p^{t} \cdot z^{t} \right] / \left[P_{PY}^{1} Q_{PY}^{t} - p^{1} \cdot z^{t} \right]; \tag{7.13}$$

$$P_{FO}^{t} \equiv \left[P_{LO}^{t} P_{PO}^{t} \right]^{1/2}; \tag{7.14}$$

$$P_{TO}^{t} \equiv \exp \left[\begin{array}{l} (\tfrac{1}{2})\left(s_{T1}^{1} + s_{T1}^{t} \right) \ln \left(P_{TY}^{t} / P_{TY}^{1} \right) + (\tfrac{1}{2})\left(s_{T2}^{1} + s_{T2}^{t} \right) \\ \times \ln \left(p_1^{t} / p_1^{1} \right) + (\tfrac{1}{2})\left(s_{T3}^{1} + s_{T3}^{t} \right) \ln \left(p_2^{t} / p_2^{1} \right) \end{array} \right] \tag{7.15}$$

where $s_{T1}^{t} \equiv V_Y^{t} / V_O^{t}$, $s_{T2}^{t} \equiv -p_1^{t} z_1^{t} / V_O^{t}$ and $s_{T3}^{t} \equiv -p_2^{t} z_2^{t} / V_O^{t}$ for $t = 1, \ldots, 5$. Note that $s_{T1}^{t} > 0$, $s_{T2}^{t} < 0$, $s_{T3}^{t} < 0$, but these value-added "shares" sum up to one; that is, $s_{T1}^{t} + s_{T2}^{t} + s_{T3}^{t} = 1$ for $t = 1, \ldots, 5$. The value-added price indexes defined by (7.12)–(7.15) are listed in Table 7.7. The fixed-base price index formulae defined by (7.12)–(7.15) can be modified to provide the corresponding chain link price indexes, and these links can be chained together to defined the corresponding Laspeyres, Paasche, Fisher, and Törnqvist value-added chained indexes $P_{LO}^{t*}, P_{PO}^{t*}, P_{FO}^{t*}$ and P_{TO}^{t*}. These chained indexes are also listed in Table 7.7.

As usual, the Laspeyres type price indexes are higher (after period 1) than the corresponding Paasche type indexes, and the spread between the fixed-base Laspeyres and

Table 7.7 Fixed Base and Chained Laspeyres, Paasche, Fisher, and Törnqvist
Value–Added Output Price Indexes

Period t	P_{LO}^t	P_{PO}^t	P_{FO}^t	P_{TO}^t	P_{LO}^{t*}	P_{PO}^{t*}	P_{FO}^{t*}	P_{TO}^{t*}
1	1.00000	1.00000	1.00000	1.00000	1.00000	1.00000	1.00000	1.00000
2	0.99200	0.99089	0.99142	0.99144	0.99200	0.99089	0.99142	0.99144
3	0.98400	0.97519	0.97909	0.97963	0.98288	0.97844	0.98052	0.98065
4	0.95800	0.93500	0.94445	0.94662	0.95096	0.94314	0.94681	0.94705
5	0.93600	0.89347	0.90920	0.91494	0.92045	0.90957	0.91465	0.91500

Table 7.8 Fixed–Base and Chained Implicit Laspeyres, Paasche, Fisher, and
Törnqvist Indexes of Real Value Added

Period t	Q_{LO}^t	Q_{PO}^t	Q_{FO}^t	Q_{TO}^t	Q_{LO}^{t*}	Q_{PO}^{t*}	Q_{FO}^{t*}	Q_{TO}^{t*}
1	100.000	100.000	100.000	100.000	100.000	100.000	100.000	100.000
2	100.887	101.000	100.946	100.944	100.887	101.000	100.946	100.944
3	107.033	108.000	107.570	107.510	107.154	107.640	107.412	107.398
4	111.263	114.000	112.859	112.601	112.086	113.016	112.578	112.550
5	115.502	121.000	118.907	118.161	117.453	118.859	118.199	118.153

Paasche price indexes is larger than the spread between their chained counterparts. As usual, the superlative indexes are generally close to each other. Note also that the value-added price indexes listed in Table 7.7 end up below unity in period 5, whereas the gross output price indexes listed in Table 7.5 end up above unity in period 5 (except for the fixed-base Paasche index).

The period t implicit real value-added output quantities or volumes that correspond to the four fixed-base value-added price indexes defined by (7.12)–(7.15) are defined by (7.16) and the corresponding chained indexes are defined by (7.17) for $t = 1, \ldots, 5$:

$$Q_{LO}^t \equiv V_O^t / P_{LO}^t; Q_{PO}^t \equiv V_O^t / P_{PO}^t; Q_{PO}^t \equiv V_O^t / P_{PO}^t; Q_{PO}^t \equiv V_O^t / P_{PO}^t; \quad (7.16)$$

$$Q_{LO}^{t*} \equiv V_O^t / P_{PO}^{t*}; Q_{PO}^{t*} \equiv V_O^t / P_{PO}^{t*}; Q_{PO}^{t*} \equiv V_O^t / P_{PO}^{t*}; Q_{PO}^{t*} \equiv V_O^t / P_{PO}^{t*}. \quad (7.17)$$

The above implicit quantity indexes of real value added are listed in Table 7.8. The substantial difference between the fixed-base implicit Laspeyres and Paasche indexes of real value added in period 5 is noteworthy.

The primary-input quantity indexes listed in Table 7.3, along with the real value-added output indexes listed in Table 7.8, can be used to form TFP indexes by dividing period t real value added by the corresponding measure of real input. Thus the *period t value-added TFP level* using the fixed-base Laspeyres price index formula is defined as $TFP_{LO}^{t} \equiv Q_{LO}^{t}/Q_{LX}^{t}$ for each t. Using the other seven methods for aggregating inputs similarly leads to the following alternative measures of real value-added TFP for period t: $TFP_{PO}^{t} \equiv Q_{PO}^{t}/Q_{PX}^{t}; TFP_{FO}^{t} \equiv Q_{FO}^{t}/Q_{FX}^{t}; TFP_{TO}^{t} \equiv Q_{TO}^{t}/Q_{TX}^{t}; TFP_{LO}^{t*} \equiv Q_{LO}^{t*}/Q_{LX}^{t};$ $TFP_{PO}^{t*} \equiv Q_{PO}^{t*}/Q_{PX}^{t}; TFP_{FO}^{t*} \equiv Q_{FO}^{t*}/Q_{Fx}^{t}; TFP_{TO}^{t*} \equiv Q_{TO}^{t*}/Q_{TX}^{t}$. These alternative measures of value added productivity are listed in Table 7.9.[36]

Since there are no independent measures of output for our production unit, it should be the case that all TFP levels for our public-sector production unit should equal unity. Looking at Table 7.9, it can be seen that this result holds whenever Laspeyres or Paasche indexes are used. For the Fisher and Törnqvist methods of aggregation, it can be seen that this result does not hold, but it does hold to a high degree of approximation.[37]

This has been a rather lengthy discussion on how to construct price and quantity estimates for a public-sector production unit when information on the price and quantity of the unit's outputs is not available. In the end, we have seen that it does not really matter very much whether we measure the productivity of the unit on the basis of its gross output or on its value-added output: in the first case, the level of TFP is always equal to unity, and in the second case, it is either equal to unity if Laspeyres or Paasche aggregation is used or almost equal to unity if superlative index aggregation is used. Thus it would seem that the choice of index number formula is not very relevant for public-sector production units that do not have independent output measures. While this is true as far as the calculation of TFP is concerned, it is definitely relevant when measuring the size of the real value added (and gross output) of public-sector production units. From Table 7.6, it can be seen that the fixed-base Laspeyres and Paasche estimates of real gross output in period 5 were 209.1 versus 221.0, while from Table 7.8, the fixed-base Laspeyres and Paasche estimates of real value added in period 5 were 115.5 versus 121.0. These are substantial differences: the choice of index number formula does matter.

Table 7.9 Fixed–Base and Chained Laspeyres, Paasche, Fisher, and Törnqvist Indexes of Total Factor Productivity Based on Real Value Added

Period t	TFP_{LO}^{t}	TFP_{PO}^{t}	TFP_{FO}^{t}	TFP_{TO}^{t}	TFP_{LO}^{t*}	TFP_{PO}^{t*}	TFP_{FO}^{t*}	TFP_{TO}^{t*}
1	1.00000	1.00000	1.00000	1.00000	1.00000	1.00000	1.00000	1.00000
2	1.00000	1.00000	1.00003	1.00001	1.00000	1.00000	1.00003	1.00001
3	1.00000	1.00000	1.00051	1.00000	1.00000	1.00000	1.00014	1.00002
4	1.00000	1.00000	1.00210	0.99999	1.00000	1.00000	1.00025	1.00002
5	1.00000	1.00000	1.00582	0.99997	1.00000	1.00000	1.00038	1.00002

7.5. Cost-Based Methods for Valuing Public-Sector Outputs When Information on the Quantities of Non-Market Outputs Is Available

In this section, we assume that there is quantity information on the non-market outputs produced by a public-sector production unit, but there are no corresponding market prices to value the non-market outputs. The main public sectors at the national or state level where this situation arises are the health, education, and social services sectors.[38] At the municipal or local level, the same situation arises for provision of some services such as waste disposal, water, and sewage services.[39] The provision of road and highway services arises at both levels of government. The *System of National Accounts 1993* recommends valuing publicly provided services at their unit costs of production.[40] In particular, Chapter 16 in *SNA 1993* notes that if we have quantity information on the numbers of various different types of outputs produced by a public-sector production unit, then Laspeyres or Paasche indexes can be calculated using sales as values for market services and unit costs times quantities produced as values for non-market services.[41] We will indicate in the following exactly how this can be done.

We will consider the following two cases:

- Case 1: The production unit produces only one non-market output.
- Case 2: The production unit produces many non-market outputs.

Case 1 is easy to deal with if we make use of the algebra that was developed in the previous section. Thus define the period t price and quantity vectors for primary inputs by w^t and x^t and the period t price and quantity vectors for intermediate inputs by p^t and z^t as before. However, now we have information on the *quantity of output produced* by the production unit during period t, say q^t for $t = 1, \ldots, 5$. In order to apply the algebra that was developed in the previous section, we need to change the units of measurement for the single output so that output in period 1 is equal to input cost in period 1. Thus define the *normalized output* for the production unit for period t, Q^t, for $t = 1, \ldots, 5$ as follows:

$$Q^t \equiv \left[p^1 \cdot z^1 \cdot w^1 \cdot x^1 \right]\left[q^t / q^1 \right]. \tag{7.18}$$

Thus when $t = 1$, the quantity of output produced Q^1 is equal to total input cost in period 1. The corresponding period t *cost-based output price* P^t is defined as period t total cost divided by period t normalized output; that is, define P^t for $t = 1, \ldots, 5$ as follows:[42]

$$P^t \equiv (p^t \cdot z^t \cdot w^t \cdot x^t)/Q^t. \tag{7.19}$$

The Q^t and P^t defined by (7.18) and (7.19) are now independent estimates for the quantity and price of gross output produced by the public-sector production unit during period t. Thus period t *fixed-base Laspeyres and Paasche type gross output TFP* for the public-sector production unit can be defined as $TFP_{GOL}{}^t \equiv Q^t / Q_{LY}{}^t$ and $TFP_{GOP}{}^t \equiv Q^t / Q_{PY}{}^t$, respectively. The remaining 6 input indexes listed in Table 7.6 can be used to define analogous gross output TFP indexes.

Value-added TFP indexes can also be defined by adapting the algebra used in the previous section. The new fixed-base Laspeyres and Paasche value-added price indexes that are counterparts to definitions (7.12) and (7.13) in the previous section are now defined as follows:

$$P_{LO}{}^t \equiv \left[P^t Q^1 - p^t \cdot z^1 \right] / \left[P^1 Q^1 - p^1 \cdot z^1 \right]; \tag{7.20}$$

$$P_{PO}{}^t \equiv \left[P^t Q^t - p^t \cdot z^t \right] / \left[P^1 Q^t - p^1 \cdot z^t \right]. \tag{7.21}$$

Thus P^t defined by (7.19) has replaced $P_{LY}{}^t$ in (7.12), and P^t defined by (7.19) has replaced in (7.13), and Q^t defined by (7.18) has replaced $Q_{LY}{}^t$ in (7.12) and $Q_{PY}{}^t$ in (7.13) in equations (7.20) and (7.21). The remaining six value-added price indexes that are counterparts to the remaining six value-added price indexes that are listed in Table 7.7 can be defined in an analogous manner. Denote these remaining six indexes for period t by $P_{FO}{}^t$, $P_{TO}{}^t$, $P_{LO}{}^{t*}$, $P_{PO}{}^{t*}$, $P_{FO}{}^{t*}$ and $P_{TO}{}^{t*}$. The value of value added in period t, $V_O{}^t$, is still equal to the value of primary input in period t, $w^t \cdot x^t$. Now period t real value added can be defined in eight different ways by deflating $V_O{}^t$ by our new eight alternative real value-added price indexes. Thus we obtain counterparts to the eight real value-added quantity indexes that appeared in Table 7.8; that is, we have $Q_{LO}{}^t \equiv V_O{}^t / P_{LO}{}^t$; $Q_{PO}{}^t \equiv V_O{}^t / P_{PO}{}^t$; . . . , $Q_{TO}{}^{t*} \equiv V_O{}^t / P_{TO}{}^{t*}$. Finally, eight alternative measures of TFP that are counterparts to the Table 7.9 measures of TFP can be obtained by dividing the new real value-added output indexes by the corresponding primary-input quantity indexes; that is, we have $TFP_{LO}{}^t \equiv Q_{LO}{}^t / Q_{LX}{}^t$; $TFP_{PO}{}^t \equiv Q_{PO}{}^t / Q_{PX}{}^t$; . . . , $TFP_{TO}{}^{t*} \equiv Q_{TO}{}^{t*} / Q_{TX}{}^{t*}$. Now that we have independent measures of the quantity of gross non-market outputs produced by the public-sector production unit, it will no longer be the case that TFP (either on a gross output or a value-added output concept) will be identically (or approximately) equal to unity in all periods. The choice of index number formula is now important for the measurement of TFP as well as for the measurement of sectoral real output.

We will now consider the second case, where the public-sector production unit produces many outputs. Obviously, if data on the price and quantity for each input that is used to produce each output can be found, then the production activities of the public-sector unit can be decomposed into separate production functions, and the index number treatment that was explained earlier for a single output can be applied to each separate production activity. Typically, it will be difficult to allocate the fixed inputs used by the public-sector establishment to the separate activities that produce each output.[43] However, it may be possible to obtain estimates of the *fraction* of total establishment costs in a period that can be imputed to each production activity. Thus define the overall period t price and quantity vectors used by the production unit for primary inputs by w^t and x^t and the period t price and quantity vectors for intermediate inputs by p^t and z^t as before. Suppose that the unit produces K outputs and information on the quantity of each output produced by the production unit during period t is available, say $q_k^{\;t}$ for $k = 1, \ldots, K$ and $t = 1, \ldots, 5$. Suppose, in addition, that $f_k^{\;t} > 0$ is the fraction of period t total cost that can be attributed to the production of output k during period t. Approximate cost-based period t output prices for the K outputs can now be defined as follows for all t and k:

$$P_k^{\;t} \equiv f_k^{\;t}\left(p^t \cdot z^t + w^t \cdot x^t\right)/q_k^{\;t}. \tag{7.22}$$

Thus we will have period t output price and quantity vectors, $P^t \equiv \left[P_1^{\;t}, \ldots, P_K^{\;t}\right]$ and $q^t \equiv \left[q_1^{\;t}, \ldots, q_K^{\;t}\right]$, for the production unit, and normal index number theory can be used to form output aggregates,[44] which in turn can be matched up with the corresponding input aggregates to form TFP estimates.

The problem with this method for the valuation of non-market outputs is that it will generally be difficult to determine the appropriate cost fractions $f_k^{\;t}$.[45] In other words, typically it will be possible to measure establishment outputs and total cost in each period, but it will be difficult to decompose the total cost into cost components that can be allocated to each individual output so that the vector of unit costs can be calculated.

7.6. The Use of Quality-Adjusted Output Weights

In this section, we discuss the use of purchaser or recipient weights to aggregate the non-market outputs of a public-sector production unit. The basic idea is easy to explain. Consider a public-sector establishment that is producing K outputs over T periods, say $q_k^{\;t}$ for $k = 1, \ldots, K$ and $t = 1, \ldots, T$. Let $q^t \equiv \left[q_1^{\;t}, \ldots, q_K^{\;t}\right]$ be the period t vector of non-market outputs. We assume that these output quantities can be observed. Define the period t price and quantity vectors of intermediate and primary inputs by the usual p^r, w^t for prices, and z^t and x^t for quantities. The aggregation of inputs proceeds as was explained in section 7.4. The problem is how exactly can we construct a period t aggregate output price, say P^t and the corresponding aggregate gross output quantity, say Q^t?

A possible solution to the problem is to use a vector of user-based relative valuations for the K outputs.[46] Let $\omega_k > 0$ represent the *relative value to users or recipients* of output k for $k = 1, \ldots, K$ and let $\omega \equiv [\omega_1, \ldots, \omega_K]$ be the vector of weights. These weights can be regarded as *quality adjustment factors*: the higher the weight, the more recipients or users of the non-market outputs of the establishment value the particular output.[47] The period t output aggregate can be defined as the weighted sum of the individual period to output quantities using the vector ω as weights, and the corresponding period t

non-market aggregate price P^{t*} can be defined as period t total cost divided by Q^{t*}; that is, we have the following definitions for $t = 1, \ldots, T$:[48]

$$Q^{t*} \equiv \omega \cdot q^t; \tag{7.23}$$

$$P^{t*} \equiv \left[p^t \cdot z^t + w^t \cdot x^t \right] / Q^{t*}. \tag{7.24}$$

Now define the aggregate normalized period t output price and quantity by $P^t \equiv P^{t*}/P^{1*}$ and $Q^t \equiv P^{1*}Q^{t*}$ and we can apply the algebra that was developed for Case 1 in section 7.5 to the normalized output price and quantity that we have just defined.[49]

It should be noted that this method can in principle deal with the introduction of new non-market goods and services; all that is required is a valuation weight for a new commodity relative to the weights for continuing commodities.[50]

The advantage of this welfare weights method for valuing the non-market outputs of a public-sector production unit over the section 7.5 method is that the present method does not require estimates for the unit cost of production for each non-market output. Of course, the problem with the present method for valuing non-market outputs is that it will be difficult to determine the appropriate vector of output weights ω.[51] If experts cannot agree on the appropriate weights, this puts statistical agencies in a difficult position since their estimates of output and input should be *objective* and *reproducible*. In the following two sections, we will consider examples of how the use of output valuation weights could work in practice.

7.7. QUALITY CHANGE, UNIT VALUES, AND LINKING BIAS

Technical progress occurs in the public sector, just as it occurs in the private sector. When a new product appears in the private sector during a time period, statistical agencies that construct price indexes face a problem: there is no price in the previous period that can be matched to the new product. Hence, historically, statistical agencies have ignored the existence of the new product during the period when it first appears, but in the second (or later) period of its existence, the new product can be treated in the normal way in which a Laspeyres, Paasche, or other index going from one period to the next is constructed because price and quantity information on the new product is now available for two consecutive periods. Thus the new product is *linked in* to an existing index that excluded the new product. The problem with this procedure is that it can lead to biased price and quantity indexes.[52] We will illustrate the problem by analyzing an artificial example that is due to Schreyer (2010, 21).

Schreyer supposes that there is a clinic that offers treatments for eye surgery. In period 1, only a traditional treatment exists. In period 2, a laser surgery alternative is introduced that is equivalent to the traditional treatment but has a lower unit cost. His data cover three periods. Let q_1^t and q_2^t denote the number of traditional and laser treatments done in period t. Schreyer assumes that the period t total costs for performing the traditional and laser surgeries are C_1^t and C_2^t, respectively. Thus period t unit costs for the two types of treatment, c_1^t and c_2^t, are defined as $c_k^t \equiv C_k^t / q_k^t$ for $k = 1, 2$ and $t = 1, 2, 3$. These data are listed in Table 7.10. Following the cost-based methodology explained in section 7.5, the normalized unit costs for each sector can be used as prices to value the outputs of each sector. Thus the *normalized cost-based output prices* for the first sector are defined as $P_1^t \equiv c_1^t / c_1^1$ for $t = 1, 2, 3$ and the (normalized) cost-based output prices for the second sector are defined as $P_2^t \equiv c_2^t / c_2^2$ for $t = 2, 3$. The *normalized quantities* for each sector k in period t, Q_k^t, are defined as the sectoral total costs C_k^t divided by the corresponding normalized output price, P_k^t, so we have $Q_1^t \equiv C_1^t / P_1^t = q_1^t c_1^1$ for $t = 1, 2, 3$ and $Q_2^t \equiv C_2^t / P_2^t = q_2^t c_2^2$ for $t = 2, 3$. These normalized output prices and quantities are also listed in Table 7.10.

Since we are interested in productivity measurement in this survey, we will augment Schreyer's data by adding some detail on the decomposition of treatment costs into price and quantity components. For simplicity, we suppose that there is only one input that is used in each treatment, and the price of this input in period t for treatment k, w_k^t, is always equal to unity, so we have $w_k^t = 1$ for $k = 1, 2$ and $t = 1, 2, 3$. Thus the quantity of input used in treatment k for period k, x_k^t, is equal to the corresponding total cost C_k^t divided by w_k^t. Thus for $k = 1, 2$ and $t = 1, 2, 3$, we have:

$$x_k^t \equiv C_k^t / w_k^t = C_k^t. \qquad (7.25)$$

The input prices w_k^t and the corresponding input quantities $x_k^t = C_k^t$ are also listed in Table 7.10.

Period t *total cost*, C^t, is defined as the sum of the two treatment total costs; that is, we have $C^t \equiv C_1^t + C_2^t$ for $t = 1, 2, 3$. Since the sectoral input prices w_k^t are always equal to unity, it can be seen that any reasonable index number estimate for an aggregate input price will be equal to unity as well. Thus let the period t aggregate input price be defined as $W^t \equiv w_1^t = w_2^t = 1$ for $t = 1, 2, 3$. Define period t aggregate input X^t as total cost C^t divided by the period t input price index W^t, so we have $X^t \equiv C^t / W^t = x_1^t + x_2^t$ for $t = 1, 2, 3$. C^t, W^t, and X^t are listed in Table 7.11.

Table 7.10 Data for Schreyer's Laser Surgery Example

t	q_1^t	q_2^t	w_1^t	w_2^t	$C_1^t(x_1^t)$	$C_2^t(x_2^t)$	c_1^t	c_2^t	P_1^t	P_2^t	Q_1^t	Q_2^t
1	50	0	1.0	1.0	5000	0	100	—	1.0	—	5000	0
2	40	10	1.0	1.0	4000	900	100	90	1.0	1.0	4000	900
3	5	45	1.0	1.0	500	4050	100	90	1.0	1.0	500	4050

From Table 7.10, it can be seen that the normalized cost-based output prices for both treatments are equal to one for all periods, except that the output price for laser treatments in period 1, P_2^1, is missing. How should an aggregate output price be constructed, given that there is a missing price for the second commodity in period 1? Following standard statistical agency practice in past years, it is natural to use the price movements in the first commodity as the deflator for the value of both outputs in period 2. Letting P^t be the aggregate output price index, this methodology leads to the following definitions for P^t for $t = 1, 2$: $P^1 \equiv P_1^1 \equiv 1$; $P^2 \equiv P_1^2 = 1$. The output price index that takes us from period 2 to period 3 could be the Laspeyres, Paasche, Fisher, or Törnqvist index, but since both output prices remain constant over these two periods, all of these bilateral price indexes will remain constant as well. Thus the aggregate output price index will remain constant over periods 2 and 3. Putting this all together, we will have $P^t = 1$ for $t = 1$, 2, 3. The corresponding period t aggregate quantity, Q^t, is defined as aggregate cost C^t divided by P^t and thus $Q^t \equiv C^t / P^t = C^t$ for $t = 1, 2, 3$. TFP^t is defined as aggregate output Q^t divided by aggregate input X^t; that is, $TFP^t \equiv Q^t / X^t = 1$ for $t = 1, 2, 3$ since both Q^t and X^t turn out to equal aggregate period cost, C^t, for all t. Thus using the usual linking methodology to deal with new products, we end up showing that the introduction of a new more productive technology has led to no measured productivity gains. C^t, W^t, X^t, P^t, Q^t, and TFP^t are all listed in Table 7.11.

Since each treatment gives equivalent results to recipients of the treatment, an alternative measure of aggregate clinic output can be obtained by simply adding up the number of treatments. Thus we define a *utility-based measure of output* in period t, Q_u^{t*}, by performing this addition and define the corresponding *unit value price*, P_u^{t*}, by deflating total cost C^t by Q_u^{t*}. Thus for $t = 1, 2, 3$, we have:

$$Q_u^{t*} \equiv q_1^t + q_2^t; \quad P_u^{t*} \equiv C^t / Q_u^{t*}. \tag{7.26}$$

In keeping with our convention that the aggregate output and input prices should equal unity in the base period, we normalize the price series P_u^{t*} by dividing each price by the price in the base period P_u^{t*} and the quantity series Q_u^{t*} is normalized by multiplying each quantity by P_u^{t*}. Denote the resulting *normalized aggregate output price and quantity series* for period t by P_u^t and Q_u^t. For $t = 1, 2, 3$, we have the following definitions:

Table 7.11 Alternative Measures of Aggregate Output, Input, and TFP for the Schreyer Example

t	C^t	W^t	X^t	P^t	Q^t	TFP^t	Q_u^{t*}	P_u^{t*}	Q_u^t	P_u^t	TFP_u^t
1	5000	1.0	5000	1.0	5000	1.000	50	100	5000	1.00	1.000
2	4900	1.0	4900	1.0	4900	1.000	50	98	5000	0.98	1.020
3	4550	1.0	4550	1.0	4550	1.000	50	91	5000	0.91	1.099

$$P_u^t \equiv P_u^{t*} / P_u^{1*}; \quad Q_u^t \equiv Q_u^{t*} P_u^{1*} = Q_u^{t*} \left[C^1 / Q_u^{1*} \right]. \tag{7.27}$$

The utility-based output measure, Q_u^t, can now be used to define a utility-based measure of TFP that is equal to Q_u^t divided by our measure of aggregate input X^t; that is, define $TFP_u^t \equiv Q_u^t / X^t$ for $t = 1, 2, 3$. The series $P_u^{t*}, Q_u^{t*}, P_u^t, Q_u^t$ and TFP_u^t are listed in Table 7.11. Comparing TFP_u^t with our earlier measure TFP^t, it can be seen that our new measure shows that productivity increased substantially during periods 2 and 3, as compared to our old measure that showed no increase in productivity.[53]

An example of how linking bias can lead to estimates of output that have a downward bias occurred when Griliches and Cockburn (1994) discussed how statistical agencies treated the introduction of generic drugs into the marketplace. A generic drug has the same molecular composition as the corresponding brand name drug and so instead of treating the generic and brand name drug as separate products and linking in the generic to the price index for drugs when the generic drug first appears on the marketplace, it may be preferable to treat the products as being equivalent, which will lead to a higher aggregate output of drugs, as in the preceding example.[54]

Recall that the utility-oriented approach to output measurement initially measured period t aggregate output as $Q_u^{t*} = q_1^t + q_2^t$ and our final output measure Q_u^t was proportional to Q_u^{t*}. Thus it can be seen that Schreyer's model is a special case of the more general quality-adjustment model that was defined by equation (7.23) in the previous section. This equation is $Q^{t*} \equiv \omega \cdot q^t$, which in turn is equal to $\omega_1 q_1^t + w_2 q_2^t$ when there are only two outputs. Thus if we set $\omega_1 = \omega_2 = 1$, the general quality-adjustment model in the previous section reduces to the method used by Schreyer. For Schreyer's example, it was easy to determine the weights ω_1 and ω_2. In most real-life examples, it will be more difficult to determine the appropriate weights.

There is an alternative method for dealing with new goods or services that is due to Hicks (1940, 114). In the period before the new commodity appears, we could imagine (or estimate)[55] an imputed price for the new product that would just cause potential purchasers to demand zero units of it. Now match up this imputed price with the corresponding quantity (which is 0) in the period that precedes the introduction of the new good and apply normal index number theory. For Schreyer's example, since the two commodities are close to being identical, an imputed price for the laser treatment that is slightly higher than the actual period 1 price for the traditional treatment would be appropriate. From Table 7.10, we see that the price for the traditional treatment in period 1 is $c_1^1 = 100$. Thus, following Hicks's methodology, set the imputed price for the laser treatment, c_2^1, equal to 100 as well. Now go to Table 7.10 and use the output quantity data that is in the q_1^t and q_2^t columns and the corresponding price data that are in the unit cost columns c_1^t and c_2^t but replace the missing price for c_1^1 by 100. Apply normal index number theory to this new set of price and quantity data. Calculate the fixed base Laspeyres, Paasche, Fisher, and Törnqvist price indexes for each period t, $P_L^t, P_P^t, P_F^t, P_T^t$, and the corresponding quantity indexes, $Q_L^t, Q_P^t, Q_F^t, Q_T^t$, which are defined as total period t cost C^t divided by the corresponding price index for period t. These fixed-base output price and quantity indexes are listed in Table 7.12.

As usual, the superlative price indexes, P_F^t and P_T^t, are fairly close to each other and hence so are the companion superlative quantity indexes, Q_F^t and Q_T^t. The use of these superlative quantity indexes as the clinic's output measure would lead to TFP indexes that end up around 1.048 in period 3. The use of the fixed-base Laspeyres formula to aggregate output prices leads to a constant price index (i.e., $P_L^t = 1$ for all periods t); the corresponding output quantity index (listed as Q_L^t in Table 7.12) is actually a fixed-base Paasche quantity index and it takes on exactly the same values as Q^t in Table 7.11. Thus for this example, the use of the fixed-base Laspeyres formula for aggregating output prices leads to the same (downward-biased) TFP indexes that occurred when we used the linking methodology that was explained in the beginning of this section. What is striking is that the use of the fixed-base Paasche formula to aggregate output prices leads to the output price index listed as P_P^t in Table 7.12 (the corresponding output quantity index is listed as Q_L^t), and this price index is exactly equal to the utility weighted output price index P_u^t that is also listed in Table 7.11. Thus the productivity index that results from the use of P_P^t is exactly equal to the utility weights TFP index, TFP_u^t, that is listed in Table 7.11. The reason why this equality occurs is due to the fact that the output quantity index Q_P^t that corresponds to P_P^t turns out to be equal to the fixed-weight index $Q_P^t \equiv c_1^1 q_1^t + c_2^1 q_2^t = 100 q_1^t + 100 q_2^t = Q_u^t$.

The preceding analysis shows that there are at least two methods that can be used to mitigate possible bias due to the introduction of new products into the public sector: the use of utility weighting of outputs, or the use of Hicksian imputed prices to value the new product in the period before its introduction. The first method requires estimates for relative welfare or utility weights for the new product relative to existing products. The second method requires estimates for shadow prices that value the new product relative to existing products (these shadow prices are essentially proportional to utility weights) in the period prior to the introduction of the new product. At first glance, it appears that the second method is preferable, since the use of Hicksian shadow prices is consistent with normal consumer theory. Using a superlative index number formula to aggregate either prices or quantities, the resulting volume or quantity indexes can be consistent with utility-maximizing behavior on the part of users of the products, where the functional

Table 7.12 Fixed–Base Laspeyres, Paasche, Fisher, and Törnqvist Price and Quantity Indexes for the Schreyer Data with Hicksian Imputation

Period t	P_L^t	P_P^t	P_F^t	P_T^t	Q_L^t	Q_P^t	Q_F^t	Q_T^t
1	1.00000	1.00000	1.00000	1.00000	5000.000	5000.000	5000.000	5000.000
2	1.00000	0.98000	0.98995	0.99037	4900.000	5000.000	4949.747	4947.642
3	1.00000	0.91000	0.95394	0.95419	4550.000	5000.000	4769.696	4768.436

form for the underlying utility function is reasonably flexible. The use of the first method essentially assumes that purchasers of the products have linear sub-utility functions that remain constant from period to period. However, the apparent superiority of the second method rests on the assumption of utility-maximizing behavior on the part of purchasers and on the existence of market prices for the commodities under consideration. In the case of goods and services supplied by the public sector, the usual justifications for the economic approach to index number theory do not apply, and so it is not clear that the second method for mitigating new good bias is superior to the first method.

A final method that might be used to quality adjust the outputs of public-sector production units is the use of hedonic regression methods.[56] A hedonic regression model regresses the price of a product on the price-determining characteristics of the product. Once a hedonic regression has been determined, the relative value of a new product with certain characteristics can be determined relative to existing products using a hedonic regression model. Thus if a new public-sector output has a mix of characteristics that is similar to products with similar characteristics that sell in the marketplace, then the value of the new public-sector output relative to existing marketplace outputs that are similar could be determined using a hedonic regression that involves only marketed products. Thus a hedonic regression model may provide a scientific method for determining the valuation weights ω_k that made their appearance in the previous section. The problem with this suggestion is that the characteristics of the public-sector outputs may be quite different from characteristics of "similar" products that appear in the market sector; that is, there may be no such similar products. However, in some situations, such as the valuation of subsidized housing, the hedonic regression methodology may well work in a satisfactory manner.

7.8. SPECIFIC MEASUREMENT ISSUES

In this section, a few of the measurement issues that arise in measuring outputs in specific subsectors of the public sector will be discussed. The focus will be on possible methods for choosing the utility-oriented valuation weights ω_k that made their appearance in section 7.6. For a comprehensive discussion on how to measure outputs for the entire public sector, see Hill (1975) and Atkinson (2005). For a detailed discussion on how to measure education and health outputs, see Schreyer (2010, 2012a).

7.8.1. The Education Sector

Hill (1975, 48) recommended that output in the public education sector should be measured by *pupil hours of instruction* with possible quality adjustment for the number of students in the classes of instruction under consideration.[57] Hill (1975, 46) did not favor any quality adjustment for class failure rates or for class performance on test scores. He argued that the output of private driving classes is measured by fees collected and hence is proportional to the number of students taking the driving course of instruction, and he observed that there is no quality adjustment of the outputs of driving schools for subsequent failures when students take their driving tests. Hence, by analogy, there should be no adjustment for failures when students fail their classes. This argument is not convincing since it may be more reasonable to quality adjust the private-sector driving school output for student failure of the subsequent driving tests.

Atkinson (2005, 128) noted that the United Kingdom uses the number of *full-time equivalent students* as the output measure in the national accounts.[58] Atkinson (2005, 130) basically endorsed this method for measuring school outputs but noted that there should be a switch from registered pupil numbers to actual school attendance numbers, and for pupils aged 16 and over, some account of school examination success should be taken into account.

Schreyer (2010, 37) recommended (as a first step) that education output for primary and secondary education services be measured by *pupil hours*, differentiated by the level of education and possibly other characteristics. However, Schreyer (2010, 42) later indicated how pupil hours could be quality adjusted by average test results for the class under consideration:

> The target measure for the quality-adjusted volume change of education services is the change in the number of pupil hours (H) multiplied by the quality of teaching. The indicator for the quality of teaching is average scores (S) divided by the change of pupil hours per pupil (H/N). Division by H/N is necessary because pupil attainments are influenced by possible changes in the number of lessons and this influence should be eliminated to arrive at quality of one pupil hour.

Schreyer (2010, 42) went on to show that the change in the volume of educational services going from period t–1 to t for the class under consideration was equal to the following expression:

$$\text{Change in volume} = \left[H^t / H^{t-1} \right]\left[S^t / S^{t-1} \right] / \left\{ \left[H^t / N^t \right] / \left[H^{t-1} / N^{t-1} \right] \right\} \tag{7.28}$$
$$= N^t S^t / N^{t-1} S^{t-1}.$$

Thus the final Schreyer measure of output in period t for the class under consideration is proportional to $N^t S^t$, the number of students in the class, N^t, times the average class score, S^t, for a test that appropriately measures what has been learned in the class. Thus if there are K classes in scope for the educational output index where the number of pupils in class k in period t is N_k^t and the average test score for students in the class is S_k^t, then period t output is proportional to $Q^t = S_{k=1}^K S_k^t N_k^t$. This output measure fits in with the general class of quality-adjusted output measures that were discussed in section 7.6, where Q^t was proportional to $\omega \cdot q^t \equiv \Sigma_{k=1}^K \omega_k q_k^t$ or, more generally, proportional to $\omega^t \cdot q^t \equiv \Sigma_{k=1}^K \omega_k^t q_k^t$, where the vector of quality-adjustment factors ω^t can change as t changes. Thus the average test score S_k^t plays the role of a period t quality-adjustment factor ω_k^t and the number of students in class k during period t, N_k^t, plays the role of an output measure q_k^t that is not quality adjusted.

The Schreyer volume measure is a reasonable one, but it suffers from two defects:

- The tests administered in each period may not adequately reflect the actual average increase in knowledge that students have acquired going from period $t-1$ to t;
- The previously mentioned average test results do not take into account the capabilities of the class being tested.

The first problem is always a potential problem with using standardized tests to measure the increased capabilities of a class, and so caution must be used in allowing test results to be the dominant factor in measuring educational outputs.[59]

The second problem could potentially be addressed by testing students at the beginning of each class term and at the end of the class term. Suppose there are K classes in scope during a number of periods indexed by t. Suppose that the number of students in class k during period t is N_k^t for $k = 1, \ldots, K$. Suppose further that students are tested at the beginning of period t and at the end of period t on the materials to be covered in the class and that the beginning and end of period test scores for student n in class k during year t are S_{kn}^{tb} and S_{kn}^{te} for $k = 1, \ldots, K$ and $n = 1, \ldots, N_k^t \equiv N(k,t)$. Define the *beginning and end of year average test scores*, $S_{k\bullet}^{tb}$ and $S_{k\bullet}^{te}$, for class k in year t as follows:

$$S_{k\bullet}^{tb} \equiv \sum_{n=1}^{N(k,t)} S_{kn}^{tb}/N_k^t; \; S_{k\bullet}^{te} \equiv \sum_{n=1}^{N(k,t)} S_{kn}^{te}/N_k^t. \tag{7.29}$$

If we attempt to measure educational output by the increase in a student's knowledge and capabilities due to classroom teaching, then the quality-adjusted output of class k in year t, Q_k^{t*}, could be measured as being proportional to the class sum of end of period t test scores less the corresponding sum of beginning of period t test scores; i.e., we have for $k = 1, ..., K$:

$$\begin{aligned} Q_k^{t*} &\equiv \sum_{n=1}^{N(k,t)} S_{kn}^{te} - \sum_{n=1}^{N(k,t)} S_{kn}^{tb} \\ &= S_{k\bullet}^{te} N_k^t - S_{k\bullet}^{tb} N_k^t \\ &= \left[S_{k\bullet}^{te} - S_{k\bullet}^{tb} \right] N_k^t \end{aligned} \tag{7.30}$$

Now set $\omega_k^t \equiv S_{k\bullet}^{te} - S_{k\bullet}^{tb}$ and $q_k^t \equiv N_k^t$ and define (preliminary)[60] total period t output as $Q^{t*} \equiv \sum_{k=1}^{K} \omega_k^t q_k^t$. Thus we see that the number of students in class k can play the role of an unadjusted measure of class k output, and the average difference in the class test scores between the end and beginning of the year can play the role of a quality-adjustment factor.

It may be very difficult to design tests given at the beginning and end of a class that will accurately measure the effect of the teaching on increasing student knowledge and capabilities. Moreover, because the quality-adjustment factor is a difference, the resulting output volume measures could turn out to be quite volatile.[61]

Obviously, the issues surrounding the quality adjustment of educational output measures are far from settled.

7.8.2. The Health Sector

Hill (1975) has an extensive (and thoughtful) discussion of the problems associated with the measurement of health services in both the private and public sectors. Hill (1975. 33) noted that there are two general approaches to the measurement of health service outputs:

> As already explained, the appropriate measure of the output of the health industry or branch in the context of economic accounting is the treatment actually provided to consumers or patients. An alternative view is to regard medical treatment as only a means to an end, namely achieving an improvement in health, and to seek to measure the output in these terms.

Thus Hill endorsed output measures that are based on the amount of medical treatment provided to patients (such as patient days in hospitals or number of visits to general practitioners), irrespective of the outcome of such treatments. But if a particular public-sector medical treatment accomplishes nothing, does it make sense to treat the expenditures associated with the treatment as a positive output?

Thus the issues are similar to the measurement of outputs in the public education sector. Patient hours (in hospitals) or patient days replace pupil hours or pupil days as unadjusted measures of output in the hospital sector compared to measures of output in the public education sector, and number of patients treated replace number of students in classes as alternative unadjusted measures of output in the health sector as compared to the education sector. These measures do not reflect any improvements (or failures) in capabilities of patients treated or of pupils taught.

The quality-adjustment methodology that was suggested at the end of section 7.8.1 could be modified to apply to the public health sector. Instead of a test score at the beginning and end of each class, the health sector counterpart would be some measure of the capabilities of a patient before and after the medical treatment. Thus suppose the medical treatment is a hip joint replacement. Before the operation, medical experts would have to devise a "test" score that rated the capabilities of the patient to perform a range of tasks with the impaired leg on a scale of say 1 to 10, with 10 being completely "normal" and 1 being essentially immobile. After the operation with suitable recovery time, the patient would be graded again for mobility using the same scale. However, mobility is not the only issue: before and after the operation, the patient could have various degrees of pain associated with the condition. Again, the degree of pain before and after the operation could be measured on a scale of 1 to 10, but now we would have to face the issue of how to weight the two scales in an overall scale. Assuming that these "test" design issues could be adequately addressed by medical experts, the algebra surrounding equations (7.29) and (7.30) could be adapted to the medical context.[62] Obviously, there would be many difficulties associated with implementing this outcome-based methodology. Thus in the face of all the difficulties associated with implementing an outcomes methodology for health services, it may be necessary to implement Hill's preferred methodology and just measure the various services that the health sector provides without attempting to measure outcomes.

Hill (1975, 36) provided the following description of the type of hospital services that he would measure:

> For example, suppose an individual enters a hospital for treatment. In general, such treatment can be decomposed into a number of different elements. The following services may be itemized.
> (1)   The provision of food, accommodation and hotel type services.
> (2)   Nursing care.
> (3)   Medical examinations including diagnostic services such as: (i) laboratory tests; (ii) X-ray examinations; (iii) other forms of examinations such as cardiographs, etc.
> (4)   The provision of drugs and other similar remedial treatment.
> (5)   Various specialist services such as: (i) surgery; (ii) radiotherapy; (iii) physiotherapy, etc.
> The above breakdown is only intended to be illustrative.

Using this breakdown of hospital-associated services, there are still some problems associated with measuring the outputs of each of the preceding five components. The number of patient days would probably suffice for measuring outputs for category (1); the number of nurse days could suffice for (2); the number of "standard" examinations would work for (3); the number of drugs administered for (4); and either the number of "standard" interventions for category (5) or the number of hours of each type of intervention that was administered by the hospital. Of course, working out the allocation of total hospital costs to each of the five types of activity would be difficult.

If, instead of following Hill's service-oriented methodology, we followed an outcome-oriented methodology, then we would no longer measure all of the particular services listed in categories (2)–(5): the focus would be on the number of individual patient treatments for various ailments and the outcomes of the hospitalization process. However, we should still measure the "hotel" services that the hospital provides as separate outputs that should be added to the treatment outcome outputs. These food and accommodation services are substituting for the food and accommodation services that are no longer being consumed at the residences of hospital patients. The provision of hotel services for nursing homes and assisted living arrangements are very important components of the outputs of these subsectors of the public sector.

It can be seen that the measurement of public health sector outputs is an extremely difficult problem. In practice, national statistical agencies use only very rough measures of output for their public health sectors. Hill (1975, 42–43) listed how various countries measured the output of their health sectors as of 1975. For example, in the Netherlands, the output of the hospital sector was measured by the number of patient days, while the output of other health services was proportional to an index of employment in the non-hospital health sector. For the United Kingdom, the output of the hospital sector was also proportional to an index of hospital employment, the output of general practitioners was measured by the number of general practitioners, and the output of most other kinds of health services (including dental services) was measured by the number of treatments.

Atkinson (2005, 103–124) provided an extensive review of health output measurement issues in the United Kingdom. Atkinson (2005, 106) noted that prior to 2004, hospital outputs were primarily measured by patient days, while other medical outputs were primarily measured by the number of consultations for specific treatments. After 2004, the number of treatments that were recognized as separate categories was greatly increased and cost weights for each category were constructed. This constitutes a big improvement over the UK output measures that were in place in 1975, as described by Hill in the previous extract.

Schreyer (2010, 72–106) has an extensive treatment of the measurement issues surrounding health care, including references to the literature as well as a detailed description of methods used to measure health outputs in a large number of countries. Schreyer adopted a *treatment-based definition* for the outputs of the health sector as his target output concept.[63] In practical terms, using a treatment approach to measuring health sector outputs means that the hospital output measure for the treatment of a narrowly defined medical condition would not use patient days as the output measure, but would simply use the number of patients treated for the condition (assuming that average treatment outcomes remain constant from period to period). For an application of the treatment outcome approach to the problem of making international comparisons of health sector real output, see Koechlin, Konijn, Lorenzoni, and Schreyer (2015).[64]

7.8.3. The Infrastructure, Distribution, and Public Transportation Sectors

The public sector in every country provides a vast network of *roads and highways* that typically can be used free of charge to transport passengers and goods from place to place. From a utility or demander perspective, the output generated by a given stretch of homogeneous road or highway over a period of time should at least include the passenger miles traveled over the road as well as the ton miles of freight that is shipped over the road during the time period. However, even if a household or firm does not use the road in a given period, they may still value the *option* or *possibility* of using the road, and thus the road network itself could also be regarded as a valued output from the demander perspective. From the cost or supplier perspective, building the road initially is definitely a cost-determining output. If the public sector also maintains the road, then measures of the utilization of the road (such as passenger miles and ton miles generated by users of the road over the time period) will also be cost-determining outputs. Note that the network weights and the utilization weights will generally be quite different from the user and supplier perspectives. Taking the cost perspective to the valuation of public-sector outputs, the supplier cost weights will be based on the initial cost of building the road, and the resulting user costs[65] will form the network component of total road cost in period t, and the utilization cost component will be based on the sum of labor and material costs plus the maintenance and capital equipment user costs that pertain to period t.

Lawrence and Diewert (2006, 215) noted the similarity in measuring the output of a road system with measuring the output of an *electricity distributor*:

> The distributor has the responsibility of providing the "road" and keeping it in good condition but it has little, if any, control over the amount of "traffic" that goes down the road. Consequently they argue it is inappropriate to measure the output of the distributor by a volume of sales or "traffic" type measure. Rather the distributor's output should be measured by the availability of the infrastructure it has provided and the condition in which it has maintained it—essentially a supply side measure.

Lawrence and Diewert (2006, 215) go on to suggest that a comprehensive output measure for a regulated electricity distributor should consist of three components: throughput, network line capacity, and the number of customers.[66] Moreover, they followed the national accounts treatment of public-sector production and valued each of the three output components by their imputed cost of production.

Lawrence and Diewert (2006, 215) also suggested that the same methodology that treats throughput and the underlying network as separate outputs could be applied to passenger traffic on government-owned or regulated *railways and transit systems*, to *pipelines*, to *telecommunication providers*, and to *natural gas distributors*. The point is that many distribution production units have the opportunity to behave in a monopolistic manner and thus they are regulated by the government. The regulators typically force the distribution unit to provide services to all potential customers in an area at regulated prices. Hence these prices are not necessarily the prices that would be generated by unregulated markets. This fact has implications for the economic approach to the measurement of TFP that relies on exact index numbers, which in turn relies on the assumption of competitive behavior in both output and input markets.[67] While it is reasonable to assume that a regulated firm behaves competitively on input markets, it is not reasonable to assume that regulated firms behave competitively on output markets. Thus a different index number methodology that relies on the estimation of cost functions or on the estimation of unit costs to value outputs (as was explained in section 7.5) is needed to measure productivity, not only for public-sector production units, but also for regulated production units in the distribution, telecommunications, and transportation sectors.[68] Thus the unit-cost-based methodology to the measurement of public-sector production and productivity that was pioneered by Scitovsky (1967), Hill (1975), and Schreyer (2010) has a wider application to the regulated part of the private sector.

National post offices that offer nationwide mail delivery at regulated prices are another example of a production unit that produces a network availability output as well as utilization or throughput outputs. The unit-cost-based methodology for output measurement could also be applied to this sector.

7.9. Conclusion

This chapter has covered the three main classes of methods used by national income accountants to construct measures of real output for public-sector establishments that produce non-market outputs. If it is difficult or impossible to construct unambiguous measures for the quantities of non-market outputs produced by a public-sector production unit, then aggregate output is typically set equal to a measure of establishment aggregate input and the resulting TFP estimates will show no productivity gains. However, in section 7.4, we showed that measurement was not completely clear-cut in this situation; that is, we looked at the complications that arise if we want to measure the value added of the production unit versus its gross output, and the consistency between the two measures. We also showed that the choice of index number formula will, in general, make a substantial difference to the resulting measures of gross output or value-added growth of public-sector production unit.

In section 7.5, we covered the second general method for constructing aggregate output measures for the non-market outputs of a public-sector production unit. Using this methodology, the prices of non-market outputs are set equal to the unit costs of producing the outputs. Once these imputed prices have been determined, normal index number theory can be applied to construct estimates of aggregate non-market output and of TFP of the public-sector unit. Of course the practical problem with this method is that it will typically be difficult to construct suitable measures of unit cost for the non-market outputs.

In section 7.6, we covered the final general method for constructing aggregate output measures for public-sector production units. Using this approach, the non-market outputs of a public-sector establishment are aggregated together by using a vector of weights that reflect the relative value of the non-market outputs to users or recipients of the non-market outputs. The corresponding aggregate non-market output price is determined by dividing total establishment cost (less the value of market outputs) by the welfare-oriented non-market quantity index. The advantage of this method over the section 7.5 method is that it is not necessary to form estimates of the unit costs for the non-market outputs. This disadvantage of the section 7.6 method is that it will generally be difficult to determine the appropriate vector of non-market output weights.

In section 7.7, we discussed the problem of quality adjustment of non-market outputs, which boiled down to the problem of finding appropriate vectors of non-market output weights. We also discussed the problems associated with linking in new products.

In section 7.8, the problems associated with measuring non-market outputs in the education and health sectors were discussed and how the general measurement methods discussed in sections 7.5 and 7.6 could be applied to these sectors. We also noted that there were measurement problems for finding suitable prices for the outputs of regulated firms that are entirely analogous to the problems associated with finding reasonable prices for the non-market outputs of public-sector units. Regulated firms are regulated because they have some sort of monopoly power. Typically, the regulatory authorities require the regulated firms to provide uniform levels of service over regions or locations at regulated prices. Thus the quantities produced by a regulated firm are typically not the quantities that a price-taking competitive firm would provide at the prices that regulators set. Hence the same methods that are used to value the outputs of non-market producers should be used to measure aggregate output and TFP of regulated firms; that is, the regulated prices should be replaced by marginal or average unit cost prices. Thus the methods discussed in this chapter have some applicability to the measurement of TFP in regulated industries.

In section 7.3, we provided an extensive discussion on how to measure the value of capital services in the public sector. These measurement problems deserve a lot more attention than they have received in the past. Statistical agency measures of the value of capital services in the government sector do not include the imputed interest cost of the fixed capital that is used in this sector, due to national income accounting conventions. This convention has led to a very large downward bias in both the nominal and real GDP of all countries, with the bias being bigger for rich countries that generally have larger public sectors than poorer countries. The only cost associated with capital inputs used in the public sector that is allowed in the international System of National Accounts is depreciation. Thus the user costs of government buildings are vastly understated. In addition to the understatement of the costs associated with the use of structures, there is a further understatement due to the complete neglect of land-user costs for government-owned land. Because land does not depreciate, the costs associated with the land that sits under public schools and hospitals are set equal to zero, which is the ultimate understatement! If a government-owned office building were instead rented from the private sector, the explicit rent would be recognized in the SNA and this explicit rent would include the interest opportunity cost of capital that is tied up in the structure and the land plot that supports the structure.[69] The neglect of the land that roads and government-owned railways sit on also will lead to a substantial downward bias in the GDP of the public sector.

Finally, we conclude this chapter with some observations on the difficulties associated with determining the "right" prices for valuing public-sector outputs that are allocated to households at very low or zero prices. Suppose that a household has preferences over market goods and services and over non-market goods and services that are provided to it by the public sector. Denote the household consumption vectors of non-market and market commodities by y and z, respectively, and suppose that the households preferences can be represented by the utility function $f(y, z)$. Suppose that the household faces the price vector w^t for market goods and services and has "income" I^t to spend on these commodities. The various levels of government allocate the vector y^t of public goods and services to the household in period t. We assume that the vector z^t solves the following period t utility-maximization problem for the household:

$$\max\nolimits_z \left\{ f\left(y^t, z\right) : w^t \cdot z \le I^t \right\} \equiv u^t = f\left(y^t, z^t\right). \tag{7.31}$$

Thus $z^t = d\left(I^t, p^t, y^t\right)$ where d is the *household's system of conditional market demand functions for market goods and services*, conditional on (i) income spent on market commodities I^t; and (ii) the price vector for market goods and services p^t and the household's allocation of public goods, y^t. The *conditional expenditure function e* that is generated by the utility function f is defined as follows:

$$e\left(u^t, w^t, y^t\right) \equiv \min\nolimits_z \left\{ w^t \cdot z \; ; f\left(y^t, z\right) \ge u^t \right\} = w^t \cdot z^t. \tag{7.32}$$

Suppose that $e(u^t, w^t, y)$ is differentiable with respect to the components of y when $y = y^t$ and let

$$p^t \equiv \nabla_y e\left(u^t, w^t, y^t\right) \tag{7.33}$$

denote this vector of partial derivatives. Define the *household's augmented period t income, I^{t*}*, as follows:

$$I^{t*} \equiv I^t + p^t \cdot y^t. \tag{7.34}$$

Then under suitable regularity conditions, it can be shown that y^t, z^t is a solution to the following *augmented income utility maximization problem*:

$$\max\nolimits_{y,z} \left\{ f\left(y, z\right) : p^t \cdot y + w^t \cdot z \le I^{t*} \right\} \equiv u^t = f\left(y^t, z^t\right). \tag{7.35}$$

It can be seen that p^t defined by (7.33) is an appropriate vector of shadow prices that value the components of the public-sector quantity vector y^t for this household; that is, the components of p^t reflect the value of the public goods vector y^t from a household welfare perspective.

How could we calculate this vector of shadow prices in practice? It would be necessary to estimate the household's system of market demand functions, $d(I^t, p^t, y^t)$, given a time series of data on I^t, p^t, and y^t for the household. We could then use the estimated market demand functions and attempt to recover the underlying utility function, $f(y, z)$, up to a cardinalization, and then the corresponding dual expenditure function e could be recovered, and finally the welfare-oriented prices p^t could be calculated. Normal index number theory could be applied at this point.[70]

But there is a problem with the preceding methodology: we cannot fully recover the preferences of the household using this methodology![71] To show why this is the case, replace the original household utility function $f(y, z)$ by $F(y, z) \equiv f(y, z) + g(y)$ where $g(y)$ is a subutility function that is just defined over the public goods. Now assume that the household solves the following conditional utility maximization problem:

$$\max\nolimits_z \left\{ F\left(y^t, z\right) : w^t \cdot z \le I^t \right\}. \tag{7.36}$$

It can be seen that the $z^t = d(I^t, p^t, y^t)$, which was the solution to the original utility maximization problem defined by (7.31), is also a solution to the new utility maximization problem defined by (7.36). This shows that a knowledge of the household's system of conditional market demand functions is not sufficient to fully reconstruct household preferences over market and non-market goods and services,[72] and hence it will be difficult to construct prices for non-market commodities from the welfare perspective.[73]

Notes

1. W. Erwin Diewert, School of Economics, University of British Columbia, Vancouver, BC, Canada, V6T 1Z1, and the School of Economics, UNSW Sydney 2052, Australia. Email: erwin.diewert@ubc.ca. The author thanks Knox Lovell, Kevin Fox, Paul Schreyer, and Robin Sickles for helpful comments and the SSHRC of Canada and the Australian Research Council (DP150100830) for financial support. None of the above is responsible for any opinions expressed in the chapter.

2. This follows the approach pioneered by Jorgenson and Griliches (1967, 1972). For further developments of the index number approach to measuring TFP growth, see Diewert (1976, 1980, 1983, 1992a, 1992b, 2014), Caves, Christensen, and Diewert (1982a, 1982b), Diewert and Morrison (1986), Kohli (1990), Fox and Kohli (1998), Balk (1998, 2003), Schreyer (2001), Diewert and Nakamura (2003), and Inklaar and Diewert (2016).

3. However, there are some significant problems associated with the measurement of capital services inputs and we will spend some time dealing with these difficulties.

4. For a more detailed discussion of valuation principles based on purchaser versus supplier valuations, see Hill (1975, 19–20), Atkinson (2005, 88), and Schreyer (2012a, 261–266).

5. However, from the perspective of measuring the total factor productivity growth of a public-sector production unit, valuation of unpriced outputs by their marginal or unit costs is best, as we shall see later.

6. During recessions, outputs decrease more than inputs due to the short-run fixity of many inputs. Thus production units may be in the interior of their production possibilities sets at times and so movements from a technically inefficient allocation of resources toward the production frontier will improve TFP.

7. Other methods involve the estimation of cost or production functions, but typically, statistical agencies do not have the resources to undertake the required econometric estimation. Nonparametric productivity measurement methods could also be used, but unless price information is used in addition to quantity information on the inputs used and outputs produced by a production unit, these methods often do not generate reasonable estimates in the time series context that is the focus of this chapter. For the application of nonparametric methods in the cross-sectional context, see the pioneering papers by Charnes, Cooper, and Rhodes (1978) and Charnes and Cooper (1985).

8. Atkinson (2005, 88–90) advocated the use of marginal costs to value outputs in the non-market sector. Hill (1975, 19–21) advocated the use of (average) unit costs to value non-market outputs.

9. In section 8.1, we will discuss various suggested methods for estimating output prices and quantities for this sector. It will be seen that there is no general agreement on these methods.

10. A capital input is an input that contributes to production for more than one accounting period. In practice, national income accountants treat capital inputs that last less than three years as nondurable inputs.

11. For simplicity, we assume the geometric model of depreciation where the one period depreciation rate δ remains constant regardless of what the age of the asset is at the beginning of the period. For more on the geometric model of depreciation, see Jorgenson (1989, 1996).

12. This simple discrete time derivation of a user cost (as the net cost of purchasing the durable good at the beginning of the period and selling the depreciated good at an interest rate discounted price at the end of the accounting period) was developed by Diewert (1974, 504; 1980, 472–473; 1992b, 194). Simplified user cost formulae (the relationship between the rental price of a durable input to its stock price) date back to Babbage (1835, 287) and to Walras (1954, 268–269). The original version of Walras in French was published in 1874. The early industrial engineer Church (1901, 907–909) also developed a simplified user cost formula.

13. It should be noted that the user costs that are anti-discounted to the end of the period are more consistent with commercial accounting conventions than the corresponding user costs that are discounted to the beginning of the period; see Peasnell (1981).

14. Diewert (2005, 2010) and Diewert and Wei (2017) derive user cost formula for more general models of depreciation. In particular, one hoss shay or light-bulb depreciation may be a more appropriate model of depreciation in valuing the contribution of structures and long-lived infrastructure assets. Diewert (2005) also discussed in more detail user costs that are formed by discounting or anti-discounting costs and benefits to either the beginning or end of the accounting period.

15. See, in particular, Jorgenson and Griliches (1967, 1972) and Christensen and Jorgenson (1969).

16. Of course, the problem with using ex ante user costs is that there are many methods that could be used to predict asset inflation rates and these different methods could generate very different user costs. For empirical evidence on this point, see Harper, Berndt, and Wood (1989), Diewert (2005), and Schreyer (2012b).

17. The predicted asset inflation rate was set equal to the ex post geometric average inflation rate for the asset over the past 25 years.

18. While Jorgensonian user costs may not be the best for productivity measurement purposes, they are the "right" user cost concept to use when calculating sectoral ex post rates of return. Moreover, Diewert and Fox (2016a) found that even though many Jorgensonian land user costs turned out to be negative, the resulting rates of TFP growth did not differ much from the corresponding TFP growth rates using ex ante or smoothed asset inflation rates.

19. See also Diewert, Nakamura, and Nakamura (2009).

20. Thus the user cost formula (4) should be modified to $u^t \equiv (1+r^t)U^t = \left[(1+r^t)-(1-\delta)(1+i^t)+\tau^t\right]P^t = \left[r^t - i^t + \delta(1+i^t)+\tau^t\right]P^t$ where τ^t is the period t specific tax rate on one unit of the asset. This modified user cost formula assumes that the specific tax (such as a property tax in the case of a structure or a land plot) is paid at the end of the accounting period.

21. For material on the construction of user costs for more complex systems of business income taxation, see Diewert (1992b) and Jorgenson (1996).

22. For references to the literature on valuing fixed inputs as they age, see Diewert (2009), Cairns (2013), and Diewert and Fox (2016b). See Diewert and Huang (2011) for a discussion on how to value intellectual property products. Finally, for references to the literature on decomposing property values into their land and structure components, see de Haan and Diewert (2011), Diewert, de Haan, and Hendriks (2015), and Diewert and Shimizu (2015a) for residential property decompositions, Diewert and Shimizu (2017) for condominium property decompositions, and Diewert and Shimizu (2015b, 2016) and Diewert, Fox, and Shimizu (2016) for commercial property decompositions.

23. See Diewert (1980, 475–486) and Schreyer (2001, 2009).

24. The property tax component of the use cost of public-sector property input is also omitted from the SNA user cost treatment.

25. Some countries want to make their GDP as small as possible in order to minimize international transfer payments that are based on their per capita GDP. Thus the treatment of capital services for the general government sector in the System of National Accounts is at least partially a political issue rather than a pure measurement issue.

26. For further discussion on all of these indexes and their properties, see Fisher (1922) and Diewert (1978, 1992a). The US Bureau of Economic Analysis uses chained Fisher indexes to aggregate over inputs and outputs. The use of Törnqvist price and quantity indexes in productivity analysis can be traced back to Jorgenson and Griliches (1967, 1972). Justifications for the use of Törnqvist indexes based on the economic approach to index number theory can be found in Diewert (1976, 1980), Caves, Christensen, and Diewert (1982a, 1982b), Diewert and Morrison (1986), Kohli (1990), and Inklaar and Diewert (2016). Justifications for the use of Fisher indices based on the economic approach to index number theory can be found in Diewert (1992a; 2012, 222–228).

27. Notation: $w^1 \cdot x^1 \equiv \sum_{n=1}^{N} w_n^1 x_n^1$ denotes the inner product of the vectors w^1 and x^1.

28. Both of these indexes are *superlative indexes*; that is, they are exact for flexible functional forms for an underlying flexible functional form for an economic aggregator function as defined by Diewert (1976). Diewert (1978) showed that these two functional forms for an index number formula approximated each other to the accuracy of a second-order Taylor series approximation when the derivatives are evaluated at a point where the two price vectors are equal and where the two quantity vectors are equal.

29. Diewert (1978) pointed this out many years ago. However, chaining does not always work well if the data are available on a subannual basis: seasonal fluctuations and price-bouncing behavior can create a chain drift problem, which was pointed out by Szulc (1983). Ivancic, Diewert, and Fox (2011) and de Haan and van der Grient (2011) suggested adapting multilateral indexes (used to make cross-sectional comparisons) to the time series context in order to deal with the chain drift problem that generally arises when monthly or weekly data are aggregated. See also de Haan and Krsinich (2014).

30. Thus the period t fixed-base *implicit* quantity indexes that match up with the period t fixed-base Laspeyres and Paasche price indexes are $Q_{LX}^t \equiv w^t \cdot x^t / P_{LX}^t$ and $Q_{PX}^t \equiv w^t \cdot x^t / P_{PX}^t$ and so on. It should be noted that our is normally called the Paasche quantity index and our Q_{PX}^t is normally called the Laspeyres quantity index. Our notation is simplified if we label the implicit quantity index that matches up with a particular price index formula in the same way. Note that our Q_{LX}^t is less than our Q_{PX}^t for $t = 2, \ldots, 5$. This is a typical relationship between Laspeyres and Paasche price and quantity indexes (but it does not always hold).

31. Diewert (1978) found the same results using Canadian annual national accounts data and thus he advocated the use of chained superlative indexes for national accounts purposes. This is probably good advice if the data are at an annual frequency, but there is the possibility of some chain drift if quarterly data are used.

32. As mentioned earlier, our implicit Laspeyres quantity index $Q_{LY}{}^{t}$ corresponds to what is normally called a fixed-base Paasche quantity index. Cost-weighted input quantity indexes of the type defined by (7.9) have been used widely in the United Kingdom in recent years when constructing measures of non-market output quantity growth; see Atkinson (2005, 88).

33. Generally speaking, gross output TFP growth will be smaller than value-added TFP growth; see Schreyer (2001) and Diewert (2015) for explanations of this phenomenon.

34. See the IMF/Eurostat/ILO/OECD/UNECE/The World Bank (2004).

35. Justifications for this procedure that are based on the economic approach to index number theory can be found in Diewert (1976), Diewert and Morrison (1986), and Kohli (1990), who justified the use of Törnqvist indexes using the economic approach to the measurement of productivity. Diewert (1992a, 2012) justified the use of Fisher indexes using the economic approach. If the public-sector production unit sells some outputs at market prices, then these sales should become a part of the unit's intermediate input subaggregate, except that the positive signs associated with the quantities of such outputs should be replaced by negative signs.

36. Note that the TFP levels listed in Table 7.9 can also be generated by dividing the input price indexes listed in Table 7.2 by the corresponding real value-added output prices listed in Table 7.7. This result was first established by Jorgenson and Griliches (1967, 252) and is a consequence of the fact that for our example, the value of inputs is always exactly equal to the value of outputs for each period.

37. The reason why $TFP = 1$ when Laspeyres or Paasche indices are used as the method of aggregation over commodities is due to the fact that these two formulae are *consistent in aggregation*; that is, if a Laspeyres aggregate is formed by using the Laspeyres formula to aggregate two or more subaggregates and then the resulting subaggregate price and quantities are aggregated in a second stage using the Laspeyres formula again, then the resulting two stage Laspeyres indices of price and quantity are exactly equal to the corresponding Laspeyres indices of price and quantity that are constructed using a single stage of aggregation. On the other hand, the two superlative indices are not exactly consistent in aggregation, but they are approximately consistent in aggregation; see Diewert (1978) for an explanation of these results.

38. We will discuss in more detail the problems associated with measuring health and education outputs in section 7.8. The Atkinson (2005) Report on measuring government outputs in the context of the national accounts has a much more detailed discussion of the associated measurement problems.

39. Data envelopment analysis or benchmarking production units for relative performance was initiated by Farrell (1957) and Charnes, Cooper, and Rhodes (1978) and these methods have been widely applied to public-sector production units. We will not discuss these methods in this chapter since they generally do not generate reasonable output prices in the case where there are many outputs.

40. Scitovsky (1967) suggested this method for imputing prices to outputs produced by the public health sector. Hill (1975, 19–20) noted that unit costs should equal selling prices for competitive market producers and advocated the general use of unit costs to value outputs for non-market producers. Hill carried over his 1975 advice into the *System of*

National Accounts 1993 where he was a principal contributor. Schreyer (2012a) formally developed the price equals unit cost methodology to value non-market outputs in much more detail.

41. See paragraphs 16.133 and 16.134 of Eurostat, IMF, OECD, UN, and the World Bank (1993). If the public-sector production unit produces some outputs that are sold at market prices, then these outputs can be reclassified as negative intermediate inputs for our purposes; that is, these outputs would appear as negative components in the z^t vectors, while the corresponding prices would appear as positive components in the p^t vectors.

42. It can be seen that $P^1 = 1$.

43. If it is possible to estimate a period t joint cost function for the public-sector production unit, say $C^t(q, p, w)$, and this cost function is differentiable with respect to the components of the output vector q when evaluated at the period t data so that the vector of first-order partial derivatives $\nabla_q C^t(q^t, p^t, w^t) \equiv P^t$ exists, then this vector of marginal costs can serve as an appropriate vector of cost-based output prices. In addition, if the technology is subject to constant returns to scale, then the value of period t output, $P^t \cdot q^t$, will be equal to period t total cost, $C^t(q^t, p^t, w^t) = p^t \cdot z^t + w^t \cdot x^t$. This cost function based methodology for the measurement of the productivity growth of a public-sector production unit is developed in some detail in Diewert (2011, 2012, 2017).

44. The resulting gross output aggregates should be normalized so that aggregate real output equals aggregate real input in the base period.

45. Suppose that the producer's total cost function for period t, $C^t(q_1^t, \ldots, q_K^t, p^t, w^t) \equiv C^t$, has been estimated and it is differentiable with respect to the outputs, q_k. If in addition, production is subject to constant returns to scale, then the fractions f_k^t should be defined as $f_k^t \equiv \left[q_k^t \partial C^t(q_1^t, \ldots, q_K^t, p^t, w^t) / \partial q_k \right] / C^t$ for $k = 1, \ldots, K$.

46. Our suggested methodology is simply an elaboration of a methodology suggested by Schreyer (2010, 21).

47. Sections 7.7 and 7.8 suggest some methods for determining these weights, but there is no generally applicable method for choosing these welfare-oriented weights. In the concluding section of this chapter, we indicate that it is very difficult to determine these valuation weights in a rigorous fashion.

48. Suppose the welfare weights change over time. Thus let ω^1 and ω^2 be the weights for periods 1 and 2. Define $Q^{1^*} \equiv 1$ and $Q^{2^*} \equiv [\omega^1 \cdot q^2 / \omega^1 \cdot q^1]^{1/2} [\omega^2 \cdot q^2 / \omega^2 \cdot q^1]^{1/2}$. Now use (7.24) to define P^{1^*} and P^{2^*} and define the normalized prices and quantities by $P^t \equiv P^{t^*} / P^{1^*}$ and $Q^t \equiv P^{1^*} Q^{t^*}$ for $t = 1, 2$. The resulting P^t and Q^t are Fisher type aggregate prices and quantities for periods 1 and 2. Thus the methodology can be generalized to deal with changing welfare weights.

49. Note that we are forcing the aggregate price times quantity in each period to equal period t total cost; that is, we have $P^t Q^t = P^{t^*} Q^{t^*} \equiv p^t \cdot z^t + w^t \cdot x^t$ for each t. This follows the convention applied to the valuation of non-market production that is recommended by Schreyer (2010, 76): "Throughout this handbook, it is understood that the value of output of institutional units in the health care industry is measured by the observed money value of output in the case of market producers and by the sum of costs in the case of non-market producers. This follows national accounts conventions." It is not necessary to perform the normalizations of output prices and quantities to make the value of non-market output equal to the total net cost of producing the non-market outputs in period t, but if this is not done, then the non-market production unit will make a profit or loss that is more or

less arbitrary. Thus the Schreyer-Hill normalizing convention leads to a value of aggregate output that will exactly exhaust period t cost.

50. If non-market commodity 1 is not present in period 1 but is present in subsequent periods, then this implies that $q_1^1 = 0$ and for subsequent periods $t > 1$, $q_1^t > 0$. For a more explicit treatment of the new commodity problem in the non-market context, see the following section or Diewert (2012, 220–221).

51. See Atkinson (2005, 88–90) and Schreyer (2012) for nice discussions on the valuation of non-market outputs and the differences between marginal cost and final demander valuations.

52. This problem was pointed out by Griliches (1979, 97): "What happens to price indices will depend on whether they allow for the 'quality' improvements embedded in the new item or not. By and large they do not make such quality adjustments. Instead, the new product is 'linked in' at its introductory (or subsequent) price with the price indices left unchanged." Gordon (1981, 130–133) and Diewert (1996, 31; 1998, 51–54) also recognized this source of bias and suggested methods for measuring its magnitude.

53. This analysis is essentially due to Schreyer (2010, 21). Diewert (2012, 220–221) presented a similar analysis of the linking problem that came to the same conclusion.

54. Linking bias occurs not only with respect to the introduction of new products, but also when new lower-cost outlets come into existence. The resulting bias is called *outlet substitution bias* and it can occur in the public sector as well as in the private sector; see Reinsdorf (1993) and Diewert (1996, 31; 1998, 50–51) for references to the literature.

55. Hausman (1997) estimated these reservation prices econometrically for new breakfast cereals. For a diagram explaining the Hicks methodology, see Diewert (1996, 32). For additional approaches to the estimation of reservation prices, see Lovell and Zieschang (1994), Feenstra (1994), and Diewert (1998, 51–53).

56. For reviews and references to the literature on hedonic regression techniques, see Triplett (1983, 2004), de Haan (2010), de Haan and Diewert (2011), de Haan and Krsinich (2014), and Aizcorbe (2014). Diewert (2011, 180) and Schreyer (2012a, 260–266) present cost function and utility function based hedonic regression models, respectively, to adjust for quality change in the public sector. Schreyer's model is probably the more appropriate model.

57. Eurostat (2001) also recommended this measure be used by countries belonging to the European Union.

58. "The fte pupils in the four types of maintained school (nursery, primary, secondary and special schools) are added together using cost-weighting by type of school, based on total UK expenditure for that type of school. The cost weights have not been updated since 2000" (Atkinson 2005, 128). He goes on to note that there was a small quality adjustment based on exam success.

59. When measuring the output for a public school class that consists of young students, one could argue that the school is providing a day care component as well as augmenting student skills and knowledge. The day care component of school output would be proportional to student hours spent at school during the time period under consideration. With no change in school hours, student hours would be proportional to school attendance days. Determining non-arbitrary relative weights for the day care and knowledge acquisition components of school output would be problematic.

60. There is a final adjustment that makes the value of output in period t equal to total input cost, as was explained in section 7.6.

61. This potential volatility could be reduced by making the final quality-adjustment factor equal to an average of the Schreyer quality-adjustment factor that appears in (7.28) and the one that appears in (7.30), where Schreyer's S^t could be replaced by our $S_{k\bullet}^{te}$.

62. This outcome-oriented methodology is not a new idea. Consider the following quotation from Atkinson (2005, 118): "One approach would be to seek to use weights based on the value of health gain from each treatment rather than on its cost."

63. "A complete treatment refers to the pathway that an individual takes through heterogeneous institutions in the health industry in order to receive full and final treatment for a disease or condition. . . . Our target definition of health care services includes medical services to prevent a disease" (Schreyer 2010, 73). "The target definition of health care volume output proposed earlier is the number of complete treatments with specified bundles of characteristics so as to capture quality change and new products" (Schreyer 2010, 76). Schreyer goes on to explain why constructing measures of complete treatments is very difficult and hence why one might have to settle for measures of processes that are components of a complete treatment.

64. For an application of the treatment approach in the time series context, see Gu and Morin (2014).

65. Note that the land acquisition costs or opportunity costs for the road can be high. If interest is not allowed as a component of user cost, then the corresponding user cost of the land component of the road will be (mistakenly) set equal to zero and the contribution of public-sector roads to the country's GDP will be greatly undervalued. It is difficult to determine what an appropriate depreciation rate for the road bed should be, but it will probably be a very small number. The depreciation rate for the asphalt or concrete surface of the road can be relatively large, and it will be related to the utilization of the road.

66. Each customer requires a separate (costly) connection, plus each customer has a separate cost of billing.

67. The exact index number approach to measuring productivity growth can be extended to encompass some limited forms of monopolistic behavior; see Diewert and Fox (2008, 179; 2010, 75). These papers also show that in more general models of monopolistic behavior, exact index number techniques can be used to obtain very simple estimating equations where the contributions of increasing returns to scale and technical progress to productivity growth can be separately identified.

68. See Lawrence and Diewert (2006, 231–233) for an example of how the cost function approach to measuring TFP can be applied in the regulated firm context. For more general expositions of how cost functions can be utilized to measure TFP in the public and regulated sectors, see Diewert (2012) and Schreyer (2012a).

69. Many national income accountants recognize that the current treatment of government-owned capital in the SNA is not consistent with general accounting principles: "The fact that exactly the same kind of service may be provided on both a market and on a non-market basis raises an important question for this report. It is proposed as a matter of principle that the basic methodology used to measure changes in the volume of real output should always be the same irrespective whether the service is provided on a market or on a non-market basis" (Hill 1975, 19). Atkinson (2005, 49) explicitly recommended that the opportunity cost of capital be added to depreciation charges to account for the cost of capital: "We recommend that the appropriate measure of capital input for production and productivity analysis is the flow of *capital services* of an asset type. This involves adding to the capital consumption an interest charge, with an agreed interest rate, on the entire owned capital."

70. Alternatively, once f has been determined up to a cardinalization, we could use the resulting time series for u^t as our household quantity index.
71. This recovery impossibility theorem does not apply to business demanders of the outputs of a public-sector production unit; it only applies to household demanders.
72. This problem was first noticed by Pollak and Wales (1979, 219).
73. However, this task can be accomplished by making extra assumptions on the structure of the underlying preferences. Adding a time constraint to the household's budget constraint and making some separability assumptions is one way of proceeding; see Schreyer and Diewert (2014).

References

Aizcorbe, A. A. 2014. *A Practical Guide to Price Index and Hedonic Techniques*. Oxford: Oxford University Press.

Atkinson, T. 2005. *Atkinson Review: Final Report; Measurement of Government Output and Productivity for the National Accounts*. New York: Palgrave Macmillan.

Babbage, C. 1835. *On the Economy of Machinery and Manufactures*, 4th edition. London: Charles Knight.

Balk, B. M. 1998. *Industrial Price, Quantity and Productivity Indices*. Boston: Kluwer Academic.

Balk, B. M. 2003. "The Residual: On Monitoring and Benchmarking Firms, Industries and Economies with Respect to Productivity." *Journal of Productivity Analysis* 20: 5–47.

Cairns, R. D. 2013. "The Fundamental Problem of Accounting." *Canadian Journal of Economics* 46: 634–655.

Caves, D. W., L. R. Christensen, and W. E. Diewert. 1982a. "The Economic Theory of Index Numbers and the Measurement of Input, Output and Productivity." *Econometrica* 50: 1393–1414.

Caves, D. W., L. R. Christensen, and W. E. Diewert. 1982b. "Multilateral Comparisons of Output, Input and Productivity using Superlative Index Numbers." *Economic Journal* 96: 659–679.

Charnes, A., and W. W. Cooper. 1985. "Preface to Topics in Data Envelopment Analysis." *Annals of Operations Research* 2: 59–94.

Charnes, A., W. W. Cooper, and E. Rhodes. 1978. "Measuring the Efficiency of Decision Making Units." *European Journal of Operational Research* 2: 429–444.

Christensen, L. R., and D. W. Jorgenson. 1969. "The Measurement of U.S. Real Capital Input, 1929–1967." *Review of Income and Wealth* 15: 293–320.

Church, A. H. 1901. "The Proper Distribution of Establishment Charges, Parts I, II, and III." *The Engineering Magazine* 21: 508–517, 725–734, 904–912.

de Haan, J. 2010. "Hedonic Price Indexes: A Comparison of Imputation, Time Dummy and 'Re-pricing' Methods." *Journal of Economics and Statistics (Jahrbücher fur Nationalökonomie und Statistik)* 230: 772–791.

de Haan, J., and W. E. Diewert (eds.). 2011. *Residential Property Price Indices Handbook*. Luxembourg: Eurostat.

de Haan, J., and F. Krsinich. 2014. "Scanner Data and the Treatment of Quality Change in Nonrevisable Price Indexes." *Journal of Business and Economic Statistics* 32(3): 341–358.

de Haan, J., and H. A. van der Grient. 2011. "Eliminating Chain Drift in Price Indexes Based on Scanner Data." *Journal of Econometrics* 161: 36–46.

Diewert, W. E. 1974. "Intertemporal Consumer Theory and the Demand for Durables." *Econometrica* 42: 497–516.

Diewert, W. E. 1976. "Exact and Superlative Index Numbers." *Journal of Econometrics* 4: 114–145.

Diewert, W. E. 1978. "Superlative Index Numbers and Consistency in Aggregation." *Econometrica* 46: 883–900.

Diewert, W. E. 1980. "Aggregation Problems in the Measurement of Capital," In *The Measurement of Capital*, edited by D. Usher, 433–528. Chicago: University of Chicago Press.

Diewert, W. E. 1983. "The Theory of the Output Price Index and the Measurement of Real Output Change." In *Price Level Measurement*, edited by W. E. Diewert and C. Montmarquette, 1049–1113. Ottawa: Statistics Canada.

Diewert, W. E. 1992a. "Fisher Ideal Output, Input and Productivity Indexes Revisited." *Journal of Productivity Analysis* 3: 211–248.

Diewert, W. E. 1992b. "The Measurement of Productivity." *Bulletin of Economic Research* 44(3): 163–198.

Diewert, W. E. 1996. "Comments on CPI Biases." *Business Economics* 32(2): 30–35.

Diewert, W. E. 1998. "Index Number Issues in the Consumer Price Index." *Journal of Economic Perspectives* 12(1): 47–58.

Diewert, W. E. 2005. "Issues in the Measurement of Capital Services, Depreciation, Asset Price Changes and Interest Rates." In *Measuring Capital in the New Economy*, edited by C. Corrado, J. Haltiwanger and D. Sichel, 479–542. Chicago: University of Chicago Press.

Diewert, W. E. 2008. "OECD Workshop on Productivity Analysis and Measurement: Conclusions and Future Directions." In *Proceedings from the OECD Workshop on Productivity Measurement and Analysis*, 11–36. Paris: OECD.

Diewert, W. E. 2009. "The Aggregation of Capital over Vintages in a Model of Embodied Technical Progress." *Journal of Productivity Analysis* 32: 1–19.

Diewert, W. E. 2010. "User Costs versus Waiting Services and Depreciation in a Model of Production." *Journal of Economics and Statistics* 230(6): 759–771.

Diewert, W. E. 2011. "Measuring Productivity in the Public Sector: Some Conceptual Problems." *Journal of Productivity Analysis* 36: 177–191.

Diewert, W. E. 2012. "The Measurement of Productivity in the Nonmarket Sector." *Journal of Productivity Analysis* 37: 217–229.

Diewert, W. E. 2014. "US TFP Growth and the Contribution of Changes in Export and Import Prices to Real Income Growth." *Journal of Productivity Analysis* 41: 19–39.

Diewert, W. E. 2015. "Reconciling Gross Output TFP Growth with Value Added TFP Growth." *International Productivity Monitor* 29(Fall): 17–24.

Diewert, W. E. 2017. "Productivity Measurement in the Public Sector: Theory and Practice." Discussion Paper 17–01, Vancouver School of Economics, University of British Columbia.

Diewert, W. E., J. de Haan, and R. Hendriks. 2015. "Hedonic Regressions and the Decomposition of a House Price Index into Land and Structure Components." *Econometric Reviews* 34(1–2): 106–126.

Diewert, W. E., and K. J. Fox. 2008. "On the Estimation of Returns to Scale, Technical Progress and Monopolistic Markups." *Journal of Econometrics* 145: 174–193.

Diewert, W. E., and K. J. Fox. 2010. "Malmquist and Törnqvist Productivity Indexes: Returns to Scale and Technical Progress with Imperfect Competition." *Journal of Economics* 101: 73–95.

Diewert, W. E., and K. J. Fox. 2016a. "Alternative User Costs, Rates of Return and TFP Growth Rates for the US Nonfinancial Corporate and Noncorporate Business Sectors: 1960–2014." Discussion Paper 16–03, Vancouver School of Economics, University of British Columbia.

Diewert, W. E., and K. J. Fox. 2016b. "Sunk Costs and the Measurement of Commercial Property Depreciation." *Canadian Journal of Economics* 49: 1340–1366.

Diewert, W. E., K. J. Fox, and C. Shimizu. 2016. "Commercial Property Price Indexes and the System of National Accounts." *The Journal of Economic Surveys* 30: 913–943.

Diewert, W. E., and N. Huang. 2011. "Capitalizing R&D Expenditures." *Macroeconomic Dynamics* 15(4): 537–564.

Diewert, W. E., and C. J. Morrison. 1986. "Adjusting Output and Productivity Indexes for Changes in the Terms of Trade." *The Economic Journal* 96: 659–679.

Diewert, W. E., and A. O. Nakamura. 2003. "Index Number Concepts, Measures and Decompositions of Productivity Growth." *Journal of Productivity Analysis* 19: 127–159.

Diewert, W. E., A. O. Nakamura, and L. Nakamura. 2009. "The Housing Bubble and a New Approach to Accounting for Housing in a CPI." *Journal of Housing Economics* 18(3): 156–171.

Diewert, W. E., and C. Shimizu. 2015a. "Residential Property Price Indices for Tokyo." *Macroeconomic Dynamics* 19: 1659–1714.

Diewert, W. E., and C. Shimizu. 2015b. "A Conceptual Framework for Commercial Property Price Indexes." *Journal of Statistical Science and Application* 3(9–10): 131–152.

Diewert, W. E., and C. Shimizu. 2016. "Alternative Approaches to Commercial Property Price Indexes for Tokyo." *Review of Income and Wealth* 63(3): 492–519.

Diewert, W. E., and C. Shimizu. 2017. "Hedonic Regression Models for Tokyo Condominium Sales." *Regional Science and Urban Economics* 60: 300–315.

Diewert, W. E., and H. Wei. 2017. "Getting Rental Prices Right for Computers." *Review of Income and Wealth* 63(Supplement 1): S149–S168..

Eurostat. 2001. *Handbook on Price and Volume Measures in National Accounts*. Brussels: European Commission.

Eurostat, IMF, OECD, UN, and the World Bank. 1993. *System of National Accounts 1993*. New York: United Nations.

Farrell, M. J. 1957. "The Measurement of Production Efficiency." *Journal of the Royal Statistical Society, Series A* 120: 253–278.

Feenstra, R. C. 1994. "New Product Varieties and the Measurement of International Prices." *American Economic Review* 84: 157–177.

Fisher, I. 1922. *The Making of Index Numbers*. Boston: Houghton-Mifflin.

Fox, K. J., and U. Kohli. 1998. "GDP Growth, Terms of Trade Effects and Total Factor Productivity." *Journal of International Trade and Economic Development* 7: 87–110.

Griliches, Z. 1979. "Issues in Assessing the Contribution of Research and Development to Productivity Growth." *Bell Journal of Economics* 10 (Spring): 92–116.

Griliches, Z., and I. Cockburn. 1994. "Generics and New Goods in Pharmaceutical Price Indexes." *American Economic Review* 84: 1213–1232.

Gordon, R. 1981. "The Consumer Price Index: Measuring Inflation and Causing It." *The Public Interest* 63 (Spring): 112–134.

Gu, W., and S. Morin. 2014. "Experimental Measures of Output and Productivity in the Canadian Hospital Sector, 2002 to 2010." *Canadian Productivity Review*, Catalogue No. 15-206-X-No. 034. Ottawa: Statistics Canada.

Harper, M. J., E. R. Berndt, and D. O. Wood. 1989. "Rates of Return and Capital Aggregation Using Alternative Rental Prices." In *Technology and Capital Formation*, edited by D. W. Jorgenson and R. Landau, 331–372. Cambridge MA: MIT Press.

Hausman, J. 1997. "Valuation of New Goods under Perfect and Imperfect Competition." In *The Economics of New Goods*, edited by T. Bresnahan and R. Gordon, 209–237. NBER Studies in Income and Wealth, Volume 58. Chicago: University of Chicago Press.

Hicks, J. R. 1940. "The Valuation of the Social Income." *Economica* 7: 105–140.

Hill, P. 1975. *Price and Volume Measures for Non-Market Services*. Brussels: Statistical Office of the European Communities.

Hill, R. J., and T. P. Hill. 2003. "Expectations, Capital Gains and Income." *Economic Inquiry* 41: 607–619.

Inklaar, R., and W. E. Diewert. 2016. "Measuring Industry Productivity and Cross-Country Convergence." *Journal of Econometrics* 191: 426–433.

IMF/Eurostat/ILO/OECD/UNECE/The World Bank. 2004. *Producer Price Index Manual: Theory and Practice*, edited by Paul Armknecht. Washington, DC: International Monetary Fund.

Ivancic, L., W. E. Diewert, and K. J. Fox. 2011. "Scanner Data, Time Aggregation and the Construction of Price Indexes." *Journal of Econometrics* 161: 24–35.

Jorgenson, D. W. 1989. "Capital as a Factor of Production." In *Technology and Capital Formation*, edited by D. W. Jorgenson and R. Landau, 1–35. Cambridge MA: MIT Press.

Jorgenson, D. W. 1996. *Investment*, Vol.2: *Tax Policy and the Cost of Capital*. Cambridge, MA: MIT Press.

Jorgenson, D. W., and Z. Griliches. 1967. "The Explanation of Productivity Change." *The Review of Economic Studies* 34: 249–283.

Jorgenson, D. W., and Z. Griliches. 1972. "Issues in Growth Accounting: A Reply to Edward F. Denison." *Survey of Current Business* 52(4) Part II (May): 65–94.

Kohli, U. 1990. "Growth Accounting in the Open Economy: Parametric and Nonparametric Estimates." *Journal of Economic and Social Measurement* 16: 125–136.

Koechlin, F., P. Konijn, L. Lorenzoni, and P. Schreyer. 2015. "Comparing Hospitals and Health Prices and Volumes across Countries: A New Approach." *Social Indicators Research* (December): 1–22.

Lawrence, D. and W. E. Diewert. 2006. "Regulating Electricity Networks: The ABC of Setting X in New Zealand." In *Performance Measurement and Regulation of Network Utilities*, edited by T. Coelli and D. Lawrence, 207–241. Cheltenham, UK: Edward Elgar.

Lovell, C. A. K., and K. Zieschang. 1994. "The Problem of New and Disappearing Commodities in the Construction of Price Indexes." In *Data Envelopment Analysis: Theory, Methodology and Application*, edited by A. Charnes, W. W. Cooper, A. Y. Lewin and L. M. Seiford, 353–369. New York: Springer.

Peasnell, K. V. 1981. "On Capital Budgeting and Income Measurement." *Abacus* 17(1): 52–67.

Pollak, R. A., and T. J. Wales. 1979. "Welfare Comparisons and Equivalence Scales." *American Economic Review* 69(2): 216–221.

Reinsdorf, M. 1993. "The Effect of Outlet Price Differentials in the U.S. Consumer Price Index." In *Price Measurement and Their Uses*, edited by M. F. Foss, M. E. Manser, and A. H. Young, 227–254. NBER Studies in Income and Wealth, Volume 57. Chicago: University of Chicago Press.

Schreyer, P. 2001. *Measuring Productivity: Measuring Aggregate and Industry Level Productivity Growth*. Paris: OECD.

Schreyer, P. 2009. *Measuring Capital: OECD Manual 2009*, 2nd edition. Paris: OECD.

Schreyer, P. 2010. "Towards Measuring the Volume Output of Education and Health Services: A Handbook." OECD Statistics Working Paper No. 31. Paris: OECD.

Schreyer, P. 2012a. "Output, Outcome and Quality Adjustment in Measuring Health and Education Services." *The Review of Income and Wealth* 58(2): 257–278.

Schreyer, P. 2012b. "Measuring Multifactor Productivity When Rates of Return Are Endogenous." In *Price and Productivity Measurement*, Vol. 6: *Index Number Theory*, edited by W. E. Diewert, B. M. Balk, D. Fixler, K. J. Fox, and A. O. Nakamura, 13–40. Victoria: Trafford.

Schreyer, P., and W. E. Diewert. 2014. "Household Production, Leisure and Living Standards." In *Measuring Economic Sustainability and Progress*, edited by D. W. Jorgenson, J. S. Landefeld, and P. Schreyer, 89–114. Chicago: University of Chicago Press.

Scitovsky, A. A. 1967. "Changes in the Cost of Treatment of Selected Illnesses, 1951–65." *American Economic Review* 57: 1182–1195.

Szulc, B. J. (Schultz). 1983. "Linking Price Index Numbers." In *Price Level Measurement*, edited by W. E. Diewert and C. Montmarquette, 537–566. Ottawa: Statistics Canada.

Triplett, J. E. 1983. "Concepts of Quality in Input and Output Price Measures: A Resolution of the User Value and Resource Cost Debate." In *The U.S. National Income and Product Accounts: Selected Topics*, edited by M. F. Foss, 269–311. NBER Studies in Income and Wealth, Volume 47. Chicago: University of Chicago Press.

Triplett, J. E. 2004. "Handbook on Hedonic Indexes and Quality Adjustments in Price Indexes: Special Application to Information Technology Products." STI Working Paper 2004/9. Paris: OECD.

Walras, L. 1954. *Elements of Pure Economics*, a translation by W. Jaffé of the Edition Définitive (1926) of the *Eléments d'économie pure*, first edition published in 1874. Homewood, IL: Richard D. Irwin.

CHAPTER 8

....

PRODUCTIVITY MEASUREMENT AND THE ENVIRONMENT

....

FINN R. FØRSUND

8.1. INTRODUCTION

....

THE purpose of the chapter is to review and explore attempts to measure productivity when facing environmental problems caused by economic activities of production and consumption. The emphasis will be on how to include degradation of the natural environment by the discharge of pollutants from these activities. We are facing both regional and global negative effects, such as acid rain and global warming, the latter leading to sea level rise, forced human migrations, and adverse health effects, such as diseases, including malaria and the zika virus, caused by the spread of mosquitoes to new areas.

Another aspect of environmental degradation not reflected in how conventional productivity is measured is the depletion of natural resources. The value of extracting or harvesting commercial resources is entered into national accounts, but the running down of stocks is not. A problem with the national accounts is that only current market transactions are included; the valuation of resource depletion and environmental degradation of the public good aspects of Nature is absent. This chapter will focus on how to incorporate environmental degradation, but will not attempt to deal in depth with resource depletion.

Environmental problems until the late 1950s had been treated by economists as cases of externalities. The examples used had an innocent flair; Pigou (1920) used factory smoke dirtying laundry hanging to dry outdoors as a negative externality, and Meade (1952) used the interaction of bees and apple blossoms as a positive externality. The publishing of the seminal paper by Ayres and Kneese (1969) (see also Kneese et al. 1970; Kneese 1971), coining the phrase *materials balance*, heralded a new view within economics of the pervasiveness and seriousness of environmental pollution.[1] The conservation of mass and energy (based on the first law of thermodynamics) tells us that matter cannot be created, nor can it disappear. If all the material inputs into an activity are not embedded in the products the activity is set up to deliver, then the difference must be contained in residuals discharged to the environment. In other words, if we weigh the inputs employed in an activity, and weigh the products that are the purpose of activities, the difference is the residuals (taking into consideration nonpaid factors like oxygen from the air), which may turn out to be polluting the natural environment. Thus, the general feature of residuals is that they arise from the use of material inputs in a wide sense. The concept of materials balance underlines the general inevitability of residuals generation and the pervasiveness of pollution when employing material resources. The materials balance principle leads naturally to a model of production activity (by firms or consumers) based on joint production of the intended goods of the production activity and unintended products. The latter are in general termed *residuals*, but they become pollutants if their discharge to the environment leads to degradations as evaluated by consumers.

The plan of the chapter is as follows. Section 8.2 introduces briefly the conventional way of measuring productivity as adopted when using data from the national accounts. Macro issues such as dynamics of growth with pollutants, sustainability, green national product, and the extension of input—output analysis to cover pollutants are touched upon. This section introduces physical satellite accounts for resource depletion and refers to the state of the environment. The concept of an environmental damage function is defined as the willingness to forsake man-made goods in order to sustain a certain quality of the environment. This cost is a key term in environmental economics. The effect on productivity of introducing environmental costs will then be shown in principle. In Section 8.3 the micro-level model used for studying the interaction of production and generation of pollution is introduced. The key assumption is that the use of material inputs in the production of intended (desirable) goods leads simultaneously to the generation of residuals that may turn out to be polluting the natural environment. The model consists of two types of relations: a production function for the intended output, and another production function for the unintended output. This model is consistent with the materials balance discussed in detail in Subsection 8.3.2; there is no trade-off between desirable and undesirable outputs for given resources, as implied by the material balance and efficiency assumptions on technology (Førsund 2018). Technical change is defined, and end-of-pipe abatement is introduced as a separate activity. The social optimization problem using a damage function representing the evaluation of environmental degradation is set up in Section 8.4, and the impact of direct environmental regulation on productivity and profitability is shown. The Porter hypothesis of positive technology effects of environmental regulation is studied in Section 8.5. Basic regulatory instruments such as the Pigou tax and cap and trade are studied. The key statements that environmental regulation represents a pressure on firms to reduce short-term inefficiency, and in the longer run leads to innovation reducing the generation of pollutants, are discussed. The impact on productivity change is commented upon. Productivity measures assuming persistent inefficiency of some firms, compared with the contemporaneous best-practice frontier function, are discussed in Section 8.6. It is argued that the most popular model in the inefficiency literature applied to pollution from the late 1980s is based on a single-equation model that does not satisfy the materials balance, and efficiency of resources utilization. Consequently, multi-equation models should be used instead. A summary of the chapter's main results and conclusions is provided in Section 8.7, and indications of further research issues are offered.

8.2. Productivity Measures

8.2.1. Conventional Productivity Measures

Productivity may be defined in several ways and used both in a macro and micro setting.[2] The most common definition is to use some measure of production per unit of labor used as an input in the activity in question; productivity can be measured simply as Y/L where Y is the output and L the input of labor. The two output measures used based on the national accounts are value added and gross production. Value added is the difference between revenue and variable cost excluding labor and capital, and gross production is measured as shipments, sales, or revenue. Value added is the preferred measure at an aggregated level. In the national accounts it can be calculated from the supply side as defined above, or from the income side. Then value added is the sum of labor expenditures and remuneration to capital, including depreciation and return on the assets (including owner income). At an industry level or lower levels of aggregation, a multifactor measure of productivity based on gross output may be preferred. Then an index of inputs is used in the denominator. Gross output in the numerator also has to be represented by an index if there is more than one output.

We must distinguish between productivity and productivity change. The latter is the relative change in productivity from one period to another. The seminal definition of productivity change in continuous time is the Solow residual (Solow 1956), where productivity change is the same as change in technology, and is defined as the growth in output that cannot be explained by the growth of inputs.

The labor productivity measure is a partial measure. Looking at the contribution of all factors of production, a concept of multifactor productivity can be defined in the single output case as

$$TFP = \frac{Y}{F(x_K, x_L, x_E, x_M, x_S)} \tag{8.1}$$

where the $F(.)$ function is an aggregator function, having positive partial derivatives and being linear homogenous, in the typical factors x_j ($j = K, L, E, M, S$) with the subindices denoting production capital K, labor L, energy E, materials M, and services

S. In Organisation for Economic Co-operation and Development (OECD) and EU studies of production, *KLEMS* is used as a term for these factors.[3] Multifactor productivity reflects the change in output that cannot be accounted for by the change in all the inputs. The best output measure corresponding to the use of all inputs is gross output. We can aggregate the individual outputs yielding revenue using an output aggregator function. A Törnqvist index of productivity on logarithmic form uses the revenue shares as weights in a linear aggregation of outputs and cost shares to aggregate inputs, using the behavioral assumption of revenue maximization or cost minimization.

8.2.2. Extending Productivity Measures to Include the Environment

The problem of pollution as a byproduct of economic activity is a major topic in contemporary environmental economics, ranging from global warming due to generation of greenhouse gases, to deteriorations in local air, water, and land quality due to emission and discharge of a variety of polluting substances, as pointed out in Section 8.1. Other related issues both on the macro and the micro level should also be mentioned.

At the macro level the interest was focused on the dynamics of growth, including pollutants of the accumulating kind (d'Arge and Kogiku 1973; Keeler et al. 1972; Nijkamp and Paelinck 1973; Plourde 1972; Smith 1972). The Pontryagin's maximum principle was the method adapted.[4] Resource depletion was also analyzed at the aggregated level with this new mathematical tool, following up on the early work of Hotelling in the 1930s. As stated in Section 8.1, this is an environmental problem of its own, but it will not be treated here.

The interest in sustainable growth led to some specific principles for utilizing natural resources including environmental ones. Hartwick's rule (Hartwick 1977) for compensating resource depletion was to invest the resource rent. This was called *genuine savings*. Solow (1974) showed that one way to design a sustainable consumption program for an economy is to accumulate produced capital sufficiently rapidly. The pinch from the shrinking exhaustible resource stock can then be precisely countered by the services from the enlarged produced capital stock, given a sufficient degree of substitutability between produced capital and natural resources (see also Mäler 1991; Weitzman 1976 on the savings rule).

Since the construction of national accounts became common in most countries after World War II (through the work of the United Nations Statistical Division, UNSD), there has been a discussion about gross national product (GNP) (or gross domestic product; GDP) as a welfare measure (Stiglitz et al. 2009). The blossoming of environmental economics also led to a wish to have the (mis)use of environmental resources included in a welfare measure, as well as the running down of exhaustible resources. Indeed, there is also a more recent interest in having national accounts provide a measure of gross human happiness, which would be a comprehensive welfare measure that also includes environmental concerns. (However, the only country that has attempted to make a human happiness account is Bhutan.)

The term *green national product* (see, e.g., Aaheim and Nyborg 1995; Asheim 2000) has been used to refer to attempts to integrate national accounting with environmental considerations. A key concept is sustainable consumption that can be based on the Hicksian definition of sustainable income as consumption that can be had without degrading the resource base or environmental assets.

Attempts to integrate national accounts and the emission of pollutants were also tried at a more detailed level of aggregation for input–output models (Leontief 1970, 1974; Leontief and Ford 1972). An abatement sector dealing with pollutants was introduced in the papers. The fixed input–output coefficients were extended to include fixed-emission coefficients for various pollutants, calculated as emissions per unit of output. Recognizing the role of material inputs, fixed coefficients related to outputs assume that there are fixed coefficients in production in general, as there are in the input–output model. Based on data for Norway, the costs of obtaining a "greener" mix of final deliveries for a given amount of primary inputs were shown in Førsund and Strøm (1976) and Førsund (1985).

However, it turned out to be too difficult to integrate environmental issues formally and statistically in the national accounts. Instead, so-called satellite accounts for natural resources, environmental resources, and pollution emissions were established (United Nations 1993; Nordhaus and Kokkelenberg 1999). These accounts keep track of the extraction, harvesting, and development of stock of resources, and record emissions and change in various quality indicators of the natural environment.

We will limit our attention to the micro level of production, and for ease we use a firm as the term for a production unit. The effect of environmental regulation on various aspects such as productivity and profitability in the short and long run will be considered.

The point of departure of this chapter is the way of modelling the interaction between economic activity and the natural environment within environmental economics (Førsund and Strøm 1988; Perman et al. 2011). The standard productivity indices used both on the macro level and on a micro level have to be extended to include environmental concerns.

How, then, may productivity measures be extended to include environmental assets? The general approach is to express environmental considerations in measuring units compatible with the way outputs are evaluated (i.e., money). Nature provides us with a number of amenities or services: clean air and water, wildlife, biodiversity, recreational possibilities, and aesthetic experiences, among many other forms of services. However, it should be realized that it is not meaningful to ask what the value or price of such services is in an absolute sense. The point is that a valuation must be based on what we are willing to give up of man-made goods to enjoy such services at specific quality levels, rather than being based on any concept of intrinsic value.

We will narrow down our approach to investigate pollutants generated as byproduct of economic activity. A key construct in environmental economics is to use a *damage function* monetizing the degradation of the environment by discharging pollutants into Nature:

$$D(z) = D(z_1, ..., z_R), \quad \frac{\partial D}{\partial z_i} \geq 0, \quad i = 1, ..., R \tag{8.2}$$

where z is a vector of R types of pollutants. If we have $\partial D(z) / \partial z_i > 0$, the residual is called *undesirable* or a *pollutant*. This will be assumed to be the case in the following. The damage is measured as the value we are willing to give up (or demand in compensation) of produced goods, the production of which generates the pollutants as unintended products. Damage cost will be used synonymously with environmental costs.

Nature has a spatial dimension. A damage function has to be detailed a lot more before we can talk about how to estimate the damage function. A distinction has to be made between local pollution from a single source and the transport of pollutants from several sources to receptors in Nature where the damage is occurring. The latter form is called *regional pollution*. Damage depends on the location of the sources, and the impacts of the emission from each source can in principle be identified. Acid rain is a typical example, and has been subject to large-scale modelling effort at the International Institute for Applied System Analysis (IIASA) initiated by the United Nations International Economic Commission for Europe (UNECE). Acid substances are transported via air from the sources, and the place where it is deposited on the ground or vegetation may be a long way from the source, especially if high chimneys are used or flue gases are ejected using pressurized air.

Another main type of damage function is emission to the air that mixes in the atmosphere and becomes a global pollutant as climate gases, causing climate change. The type of gas is then simply summed over all sources emitting this gas. Although the damages are local, all sources contribute to these damages.

A technique developed within environmental economics is to measure the willingness to pay for preserving the present environmental qualities, or willingness to pay for an improvement. Necessary compensation demanded for accepting deterioration in environmental quality is also used. The damage function (8.2) is a theoretical construct commonly used in textbooks on environmental economics based on such willingness-to-pay concepts. Methods of estimation may be based on transport costs of visiting recreation sites, complementary equipment bought to enjoy recreation activities, or contingent valuation based on elaborated interview schemes (see, e.g., Førsund and Strøm 1988; Perman et al. 2011).

For a given level of aggregation (e.g., using the industrial classification system of national accounts) let p_i be the price and y_i the volume of desirable good i. Measuring the social gross output, the damage cost of the environmental services caused by producing the goods must now be subtracted from the revenue of desirable goods to be used in the numerator, calculating the social total factor productivity TFP_E:

$$TFP_E = \frac{\sum_i p_i y_i - D(z)}{F(x_K, x_L, x_E, x_M, x_S)} \tag{8.3}$$

In a static setting, it is obvious that the social multifactor productivity must be lower because of the reduction in the numerator, assuming no change in outputs and inputs (i.e., $TFP_E < TFP$). However, once environmental damage is included in the calculation of social gross output in a period predating period t, the productivity change may go either way:

$$\Delta TFP_E^{t,t+1} = \frac{\sum_i p_i y_i^{t+1} - D(z^{t+1})}{F\left(x_K^{t+1}, x_L^{t+1}, x_E^{t+1}, x_M^{t+1}, x_S^{t+1}\right)} \bigg/ \frac{\sum_i p_i y_i^t - D(z^t)}{F\left(x_K^t, x_L^t, x_E^t, x_M^t, x_S^t\right)} \quad \begin{matrix} > \\ = \\ < \end{matrix} 1 \qquad (8.4)$$

Prices are kept fixed in the numerator, and damage cost must also be deflated by a price index to become a volume index. The direction of productivity change depends on the development of relative terms, including environmental damage, and may increase as well as decrease. If outputs and inputs used in production change over time, the scale properties of the underlying production function will play a role. Over time it is reasonable to assume change in the volume indices due to change in output and input mixes. The damage function may also shift to show increased damage for the same level of pollution. In that case, productivity change may be negative. However, damages may go down over time due to reduced discharge of pollutants (e.g., as a result of the effort to decarbonize societies).

But we must not forget the macro effects due to resources reallocated to reduce pollution, to restore the natural environment, and resources in general used on mitigation and abatement. There are also effects of lowering investment in polluting activities, reducing their growth, which may be reducing the pace of capital accumulation, and thus cause reduced future productivity growth. Research and development (R&D) resources may be redirected to activities reducing the growth of economies.

8.3. Modelling Production and the Environment

When modelling environmental–economic interactions, it is important to capture the main features of such interactions within a model small enough not to become unmanageable by trying to incorporate numerous real-life details. Adhering to the principle of Ockham's razor as to the size of a model, we will develop such a parsimonious model based on a multi-output multi-input production model, termed *factorially determined multi-output model* in Frisch (1965).[5]

8.3.1. A Multi-Equation Model

Pollution is generically a problem with joint outputs in economic activities of production and consumption. As pointed out in Section 8.1, there is a materials balance that accounts for where the mass contained in material inputs ends up—in the desirable output or in the natural environment. If all the material inputs into an activity are not embedded in the products the activity is set up to deliver, then the difference must be contained in residuals discharged to the environment. It seems important to capture these physical realities from use of material inputs in a modelling of the interaction of economic activity and the generation of pollutants. It will then be clarifying to distinguish between input factors x_M with material content (raw materials) being affected physically by the production process and factors unchanged (not used up) by the production process, the main types of the latter being labor, capital, and external services, termed service inputs x_S. The factorially determined multi-output model seems tailor-made for capturing the simultaneous physical process of generation of residuals and the linkages to production of outputs (a unit index is suppressed for simplicity):

$$
\begin{aligned}
y &= f(x_M, x_S), f'_{x_M}, f'_{x_S} > 0 \\
z &= g(x_M, x_S), g'_{x_M} > 0, g'_{x_S} \leq 0
\end{aligned}
\tag{8.5}
$$

Here y is the desirable output that it is the purpose of setting up the activity, x_M and x_S are material inputs and service inputs, respectively, and z is the unintended residual generated simultaneously, utilizing inputs to produce outputs. The multi-equation system of Frisch consists of a production function $f(.)$ for each desirable output as a function of the same bundle of inputs, and a production function $g(.)$ for the generation of each residual as a function of the same set of inputs. This is product separation. The functions $f(.)$ and $g(.)$ are assumed to be efficient in the sense that y is maximized for a given bundle of inputs, while the residual z is minimized for the same given bundle of inputs, so equalities are used in (8.5).[6] The system of equations (8.5) is a drastic simplification of engineering realities, but still captures the most essential feature of the type of joint production of goods and residuals; the crucial connection between these two types of outputs goes through the use of material inputs. It is not the case that the desirable output in general has a fixed relationship with the undesirable one independent of the inputs. The environmental problem of generation of residuals is that emitting them to the natural environments may create negative externalities due to degradation of environmental qualities or in general creating harmful effects. As defined following Equation (8.2), residuals are then called pollutants. To keep the model as simple as possible, we consider a single desirable output y and an undesirable output z (generalizing to multi-output and multi-pollutants can be done in the Frisch model just by adding more equations, one for each variable, keeping the same inputs as arguments in all relations; see Førsund 2009). The material inputs are fossil primary energy (in the form of, e.g., coal, oil, gas, and wood), and various types of raw materials. The service inputs are those that are not used up in the production process in a material sense, remaining physically intact and providing services such as labor and capital. Electricity used as input is in our context also a service input since it does not have any mass. The production of desirable outputs and undesirable residuals occurs simultaneously and is based on the technology of multiple-output production. The separation into two types of equations does not mean that we have two technologies, but is done as a very helpful simplification of a possibly complex technology, without sacrificing key aspects of a technology such as identifying substitution between inputs, scale properties, and the connection between desirable and undesirable outputs.

The partial derivatives (the productivities) of the desirable output function are assumed to have the usual positive signs. However, concerning the production function for the undesirable output, the two types of inputs are assumed to have opposite signs: marginal increases in material inputs increase the undesirable output, while marginal increases in service inputs decrease the undesirable output. The positive partial productivity of service inputs in the desirable output production function and the negative sign in the residuals generation function can be explained by the fact that more of a service input improves the utilization of the given raw materials through better process control or increased internal recycling of waste materials.[7]

As a consequence of the typical way in which service inputs increase the output by utilizing the material inputs more efficiently, the production of pollutants will then typically decrease. Therefore, the signing of the marginal productivity in the pollutants production function is negative. However, if the output y is non-material then $g'_{x_S} = 0$.

The material inputs are *essential* in the sense that we will have no production, either of goods or pollutants, if x_M is zero:[8]

$$y = f(0, x_S) = 0, z = g(0, x_S) = 0 \qquad (8.6)$$

There will in general be substitution possibilities between material and service inputs. The rate of substitution evaluated at a point on an isoquant of the production function for the desirable output is $(-f'_{x_M} / f'_{x_S}) < 0$. This is the amount of material input that is reduced if the service input is increased with one unit, keeping output y constant. Considering several material inputs, there may be substitution possibilities between them, for example between coal and natural gas, keeping the output constant, but decreasing the generation of bads if the marginal contribution of gas to the creation of bads is smaller than the marginal contribution of coal: $g'_{x_{coal}} > g'_{x_{gas}}$ for the same heat content.

The role of service inputs in the residuals production function is crucial as to the substitution effect of decreasing a material input and increasing a service input, resulting in less generation of residuals for a constant production of the desirable output. The marginal rate of substitution is positive, $(-g'_{x_M} / g'_{x_S}) > 0$, due to the marginal productivity of service inputs being negative. This implies a special form of isoquants in the factor space and the direction of increasing residual level compared with a standard isoquant map for the output, as seen in Figure 8.1.

The isoquants for the two outputs can be shown in the same diagram because the arguments in the functions are the same (see Frisch 1965, 272; Førsund 2009, 7) for the original illustration of isoquants in the factorially determined multi-output case). The level of the residual z is increasing moving southeast (see dotted arrow pointing

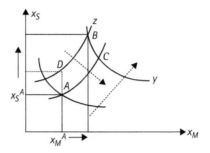

FIGURE 8.1. Isoquants for the production of y and z.

southeast) while the level of the desirable good y is increasing moving northeast (see dotted arrow pointing northeast). Going from point A to point B in input space increasing both inputs, but nonproportionally, we see that the production of the residual z has decreased while the production of output y has increased.

Going from B to C reducing the input x_S and increasing the input x_M the desirable output is constant, but the undesirable output has increased. The two types of outputs y and z are only implicitly related through being generated by the same inputs as shown by the model (8.5); there is no trade-off between y and z for given x. In the input–output space we only get one point each for y and z given a bundle of inputs x as implicitly shown by, for example, points A and B where the isoquants for the two outputs intersect.

There are obviously limits to substitution between material and service input keeping the same desirable output. Moving along the y isoquant from point A in a northwest direction, there is a limit to the amount of raw materials that can be extracted from the material input while keeping the output constant (i.e., there is a lower limit on how much the residual generation can be reduced). Another angle on this lower limit is keeping the material input constant at the level x_M^A at point A, and then see how much residuals can be reduced increasing the service input from x_S^A. Let us say point D will be the point with the minimum generation of residuals z, but then the good output has also increased. The minimum level of residual generation depends on the level of both types of inputs, as does the level of maximal good output.

8.3.2. The Materials Balance

Assuming that one or more inputs to a production process of a production unit consists of physical mass, this mass will not disappear during the production process, but, as stated previously in Section 8.1, must either be contained in the products being produced, or become residuals emitted to the external environment. Thus, for model (8.5) a materials balance exists for each production unit, and α, β, γ are coefficients converting units of inputs x and desirable outputs y and residuals z to a common mass unit:

$$\alpha x_M \equiv \beta y + \gamma z \qquad (8.7)$$

As in the earlier discussion of (8.5), we simplify for convenience by operating formally with only a single input, desirable output and residual, respectively, but generalization to multiple inputs, outputs, and residuals is a straightforward, but cumbersome extension of the number of equations and a summation over the type of each variable yielding the same pollutant. Regarding combustion processes, it is the case that substances drawn from the air like oxygen and nitrogen may combine with substances in the raw materials (e.g., creating CO_2, NO_x, SO_2, etc.). The mass balance can either reflect these both on the left-hand and right-hand side of (8.7), or the residual can be considered as the substance contained in the raw material only, like carbon or sulfur. We follow the last option. Assuming that inputs and desirable outputs are homogenous across units, the coefficients α and β must be equal for each type of input and output, and assuming that given homogenous inputs, and respectively desirable outputs, will generate homogenous undesirable outputs, the coefficient γ is also constant across units.

The parameters α, β and γ are technical unit-conversion coefficients and are not parameters of a production relation. It should therefore be realized that the materials balance is not a production function relation proper. All observations of a production activity, perfectly observed, must obey the materials balance as a physical law. That is why an identity sign is used in (8.7). It is without good meaning, for example, to differentiate (8.7) w.r.t. y and z holding x constant using (8.7) as a production relation. If (8.7) is regarded as a production technology, y cannot increase without increasing x; a given input x cannot be reallocated from producing z to produce y.

If a parametric or nonparametric efficient production function is estimated based on observations of x, y, and z, the materials balance must also hold for unobserved points obeying the production function. In this sense the materials balance puts a constraint on the efficient production function construction.[9] However, the materials balance represents another type of link between the two types of outputs and inputs than the relations representing the production technology. The materials balance does not tell us anything about the specific technology that has generated the observations of the variables in (8.7) (Førsund 2018).

Desirable outputs y cannot be produced without residuals z if the complete amount of the material content of the inputs is not contained in the outputs. This is the inevitability of generating pollutants together with the desirable product. Thermal electricity generation is an extreme case with no material content of the desirable output, implying $\beta = 0$, and then all material content of the material input ends up as waste products. The aging of a vintage wine may be an extreme example of an opposite case with zero residual. All the material content of the vintage wine is contained in the desirable output, the wine bottle; if we assume that no other material inputs are required, such as heating/cooling of the storage facility (e.g., the wine is stored in a natural cave with the right temperature). (However, the production activity is just transportation in time with chemical processes taking place within the same mass.)

The materials balance is fulfilled for any combination of inputs in the model (8.5) because of the unique correspondence between input use and outputs generated by these inputs. The same inputs determine both outputs, so we only get two single values for the outputs for a given level of inputs. Then the materials balance (8.7) being a physical law is also obeyed by definition. Therefore, in our type of model, the materials balance can be regarded as a pure accounting identity since it holds at any point in input–output space satisfying the production functions.

This is illustrated in Figure 8.1. At point A or B, the desirable output cannot be increased by reducing the undesirable output keeping inputs constant; all points giving the values in output space are intersections of isoquants in the input space. The inputs supporting point A give simultaneously the amounts of desirable and undesirable outputs given by the intersection point of the respective isoquants, and similarly at point B. Moving from A to B increases the desirable output and decreases the undesirable output, but this is happening due to an increase in material inputs and a considerable increase in service input.

Model (8.5) does not allow any transformation relationship between the desirable and undesirable outputs for a given level of inputs in the usual sense of a trade-off between the desirable and the undesirable outputs for a given bundle of inputs in a single-equation system.

8.3.3. Technical Change

There are four main methods of influencing the generation of undesirable output when keeping the same type of desirable output. Two methods can be done within a static technology, and two other methods require change in technology. Output of desirable goods may be reduced in such a way that the use of material inputs is also reduced. This is the only option at a sectoral level within a standard input–output model with fixed coefficients in production (see Subsection 8.2.2). Another way is to utilize substitution possibilities between material inputs with different marginal productivities in the residuals production function (e.g., switch from coal to natural gas in thermal generation of electricity), and between material inputs and service inputs. These substitution options are captured by our model (8.5).

A third way is to change the production technology so as to create less pollution for a constant output of desirable goods. Technology improvements that may be small-scale and introduced in the short run (e.g., a period of a year or less) may be considered variable factors.[10] But technology improvement may also need large capital investments; changing the main production processes into technologies that use fewer amounts of raw materials, or processing them in such a way that less waste of material inputs occur. Such changes will be more of a long-term character based on real capital with a long technical lifetime. This type of technical change is typical in industries using capital with embodied technology. Investment in new technology developed to use fewer raw materials or to reduce waste is needed in order to reduce generation of residuals.

Technology change, covering both short run and long run, means a simultaneous change of the functional forms $f(.)$ and $g(.)$ over time:

$$f^{t_2}(x_M, x_S) > f^{t_1}(x_M, x_S)$$
$$g^{t_2}(x_M, x_S) < g^{t_1}(x_M, x_S), \quad t_2 > t_1 \tag{8.8}$$

Technical change in the two production functions in (8.5) can be illustrated in Figure 8.1 by just changing the level labeling of the two sets of isoquants. A positive technical change of the desirable output production function means producing more for given inputs, while positive "green" technical change in the residuals production function means generating less residuals for the same input levels. Note that the unit conversion coefficients in the materials balance equation (8.7) remain the same as long as the inputs and the outputs stay the same. However, technical change may also involve using new types of inputs or redesigning products to use fewer raw materials ("dematerialization" of desirable outputs). These possibilities are not explored further here.

A fourth possibility is to install a separate facility using the residuals from (8.5) as inputs and processing them in such a way that less harmful pollutants result, for example capturing particles using electrostatic filters on smoke stacks converting an air pollution into a solid waste problem, and installing scrubbers converting emission to air to discharges to water. Such facilities are called end-of-pipe abatement in environmental economics and will be addressed in the next subsection.

8.3.4. End-of-Pipe Abatement

We will add a specific abatement process to the multi-equation model (8.5) that may need inputs distinct from inputs employed in the production process described by the equations in (8.5). End-of-pipe abatement often consists of a facility separated from the production activity. Another abatement option in the short run is to retool the processes and do small-scale changes, as mentioned earlier. This option is an alternative to integrated technological process solutions. However, it is often rather difficult to identify such activities and to identify the inputs involved. It is easier to do this with a stand-alone abatement facility in terms of inputs used and outputs produced. The residuals generated in the production process will then be channeled to a treatment facility and will be regarded as inputs in this activity. In addition, other inputs—like labor, capital, chemicals, absorbing substances, and energy—may have to be used in order to convert part of the original pollutants into outputs being abated pollutants, creating less harm (usually assumed to be zero) than the primary ones (Førsund 2009).

In the long run there may be a choice between end-of-pipe abatement and large-scale investment in new technology integrating production processes and abatement. The time horizon for environmental improvement, determined by a regulation authority, and certainty about what can be achieved may determine the choice between these two options.

Add-on abatement requires that we make a distinction between pollutants z from the production process of (8.5), renaming them primary pollutants z^P, and secondary pollutants z^S actually discharged to the environment. In Førsund (2009) a production function for end-of-pipe abatement is formulated following the single-equation format of factorially determined multi-output production of having one production function for abatement of each type of residual. Here we will use a simpler formulation by focusing on a cost function in the abated amount a that is the difference between the original generation of residuals, now termed primary residuals z^P, and the residuals emitted to the environment, termed secondary residuals z^S. The cost function can be regarded as an index for abatement inputs and is written

$$c(a) = c(z^P - z^S), \quad a = z^P - z^S, \quad c' > 0, \quad c'' > 0 \tag{8.9}$$

The abatement cost function has standard textbook properties in the abated amount.[11] We will assume that the capital costs are also included in the form of yearly costs (levelized using an annuity depending on the rate of discount and the lifetime of the equipment) making capital a variable factor. The secondary residuals are assumed to be expressed in the same units as the primary residuals. The abated amounts are generally of other forms than the primary residuals. As observed in Ayres and Kneese (1969, 283) abatement does not "destroy residuals but only alter their form." We assume that the cost of disposing of these amounts (e.g., using landfills) is included in the cost function, but that any environmental cost is zero.[12]

As to the materials balance principle, the abatement activity will add to the total mass of residuals if material inputs are used, but the point is that abatement means less mass of the harmful residual emitted to the environment: $z^S < z^P$.

In the literature, the resources of a firm are often regarded as given, and then increased abatement will imply fewer resources to produce the intended output and thereby decrease the generation of primary pollutants (Martin 1986; Murty et al. 2012). To do this requires in principle that an explicit restriction is imposed on the availability of inputs; however, this is seldom done. The situation is created by the analyst and does not necessarily reflect decisions of a firm having access to markets for inputs to given prices. If it is assumed that abatement is a separate identifiable activity (as, e.g., end-of-pipe), and inputs are sourced in competitive markets, there is no reason to assume that abatement resources are taken from the production inputs of a firm. Thus, abatement does not influence the output directly, but increases the cost of production and may then indirectly reduce output. It is closer to reality not to consider a common resource pool for the production unit.[13]

8.4. ENVIRONMENTAL CONSIDERATIONS

8.4.1. The Social Optimization Problem

In order to see how productivity can be influenced by environmental consideration, we will use our model with joint production of desirable and undesirable outputs and add end-of-pipe abatement possibilities. The approach is as simple as possible and of a partial equilibrium nature. The social planning problem is to maximize social consumer plus producer surplus, introducing a demand function on price form, $p(y)$, for the desirable output, assuming a positive output price p. (The model is still kept simple with only a single desirable output.) Fixed positive price w_j is used as "social evaluation coefficient" for input j for types M, S.

Simplifying by assuming single desirable and undesirable output as in model (8.5), a single abatement cost function in the abated amount as in (8.9), and a monetized damage function (8.2), now with a single pollutant emitted to the environment, the social planner's optimization problem, maximizing the social consumer plus producer surplus, is

$$\max \int_{u=0}^{y} p(u)du - \sum_{j=M,S} w_j x_j - c(a) - D(z^S)$$

s.t.

$$y = f(x_M, x_S), f'_{x_M}, f'_{x_S} > 0 \tag{8.10}$$
$$z^P = g(x_M, x_S), g'_{x_M} > 0, g'_{x_S} \leq 0$$
$$a = z^P - z^S$$

The first term in the objective function is the area under the demand curve from 0 to y, that is, the sum of consumers' willingness to pay for y and the revenue generated by production. The next two terms are the input and abatement costs of production. The last term is the social cost of emission of secondary pollutants. The model can straightforwardly be extended to multiple desirable and undesirable outputs, as suggested previously. When considering several units, demand functions must be adjusted according to type of demand interactions, and it must be specified whether the damage functions are unique to each unit, or the nature of interactions between damage functions must be specified if there are any (see Section 8.2). This simple model makes the fundamental trade-off between desirable output y and undesirable secondary pollutant z^S tractable, allowing for optimal allocation rules both for the two types of inputs and for abatement effort. From the objective function, we see that the abatement activity does not directly influence the generation of pollutants, but indirectly by influencing the optimal solution both for primary and secondary pollution.

Inserting the production functions for the good y and the pollutant z^P that is the primary pollutant into the objective function, and substituting for abatement a in the abatement cost function yields

$$\max \int_{u=0}^{f(x_M, x_S)} p(u)du - \sum_{j=M,S} w_j x_j - c(g(x_M, x_S) - z^S) - D(z^S) \tag{8.11}$$

There are three endogenous variables remaining in the problem: x_M, x_S, and z^S. The necessary first-order conditions for interior solutions are

$$pf'_{x_j} - w_j - c'g'_{x_j} = 0, \quad j = M, S \tag{8.12}$$
$$c' - D' = 0$$

There are three equations in the three endogenous variables. When these variables are determined, the optimal solutions for y, z^P, and a follow directly. The two first necessary conditions tell us that for each type of factor $j = M, S$, the revenue of increasing factor x_M marginally, and consequently increasing the desirable output, is equal to the unit cost of the factor plus the abatement cost of increasing factor x_M, generating primary pollutant that is abated. For services x_S negative productivities in the generation of primary pollutants imply that the last term in the first condition is positive and show the abatement cost *savings* of a marginal increase in a service input. The third condition tells us that at the optimal level of abatement (i.e., both primary and secondary pollutants are at their optimal levels), the marginal abatement cost should be equal to the marginal damage of the secondary pollutant.

We may also have a corner solution of not using abatement at all. This will be the solution if equality between marginal abatement cost and marginal damage cannot be reached, that is, $c'(z^P - z^S) > D'(z^S)$ for $z^S \in [0, z^P]$ for all z^P. Abatement is too expensive.

The two first conditions in (8.12) can be written

$$\underbrace{f'_{x_j} p}_{\substack{\text{Marginal} \\ \text{revenue}}} = \underbrace{w_j}_{\substack{\text{Unit factor} \\ \text{cost}}} + \underbrace{D'(z^S) g'_{x_j}}_{\substack{\text{Marginal damage cost} = \\ \text{marginal abatement cost}}}, \qquad j = M, S \qquad (8.13)$$

At the margin, a material input generates environmental damage cost, in addition to the input price, while a service input generates a saving of damage cost by subtracting the marginal damage from the input price. The equation shows the fundamental trade-off between the value of the man-made good and the total social cost, including the environmental damage at the margin.

In the case of a corner solution, the first-order condition will look like (8.13), but the marginal damage will be $D'(z^P)$ and both optimal desirable and undesirable outputs will be lower.

To see the impact of the relative use of inputs due to different productivities in the generation of primary pollutant, the rate of substitution between a material input and a service input is

$$\frac{f'_{x_M}}{f'_{x_S}} = \frac{w_M + D'(z^S) g'_{x_M}}{w_S + D'(z^S) g'_{x_S}} \qquad (8.14)$$

The optimal unit price on the material input faced by the decision-maker is higher than the given market price, but the opposite is the case for the service factor because the impact g'_{x_S} on cost is negative. The optimal solution implies a relative reduced use of the material input compared with a solution without a damage function and abatement cost function. As to the substitution between material inputs, the increase in the social price follows the marginal productivity in pollutant generation, thus stimulating a shift to "greener" material inputs. It is easy to see that if a material input has a social factor price that is greater than the value of the marginal product in the desirable goods production for any value of the input, then this input should not be used. In a realistic case of a technologically forced choice between, for example, coal and natural gas as primary energy source, the input with the lowest social factor price given the same level of marginal revenue will be chosen.

The social productivity measure TFP_E introduced in (8.3) for the solution to problem (8.10) and corresponding measure of productivity change are

$$TFP_E = \frac{y - D(z^S)}{F(x_M, x_S) + c(a)},$$

$$\Delta TFP_E^{t,t+1} = \frac{y^{t+1} - D(z^{S,t+1})}{F(x_M^{t+1}, x_S^{t+1}) + c(a^{t+1})} \bigg/ \frac{y^t - D(z^{S,t})}{F(x_M^t, x_S^t) + c(a^t)} \begin{array}{c} \geq \\ < \end{array} 1$$

(8.15)

The abatement cost term in the denominator represents an index for abatement resources used, and is deflated over time. This measure of productivity may increase as well as decrease over time depending on the optimal solution for each period. Technical change and change in input mix may influence the input variables, and the damage and abatement functions may change over time, the former due to preference changes and the latter due to technical changes. The optimal level of both the secondary residual in the damage function and amount of abatement may then change over time also.

The macro factors mentioned in Section 8.2—reallocation of resources to less polluting activities and mitigation and abatement effort—that may drive prices on the resources up, slowing capital accumulation and growth, are relevant for the development of productivity at the micro level in (8.15).

8.4.2. Imposing a Constraint on Emission

The social planner is a hypothetical construct to give us a frame of reference for evaluating a real world situation with private firms as decision-makers and a regulator imposing constraints on private activities. To see how productivity is influenced, we look at a firm regulated in such a way as to implement the social optimal solution to (8.10). We will investigate the effects on a private firm operating in a competitive environment of the cost burden of environmental regulation. Two typical instruments of direct control is, first, that the environment agency imposes a change in technology, most often concerning end-of-pipe abatement technology, and, second, that an upper limit z^R on the amount of the secondary pollutant emitted during a specific time period is imposed: $z^s \leq z^R$. The firm's optimization problem of private profit under an environmental constraint becomes

$$\max py - \sum_{j=M,S} w_j x_j - c(z^P - z^S)$$

s.t.
$$y = f(x_M, x_S)$$
$$z^P = g(x_M, x_S)$$
$$z^S \leq z^R$$

(8.16)

where the last inequality is the restriction on emissions of the secondary pollutant. A regulation is often expressed as restricting emission per unit of output: $z^S/y \leq z^R/y$. However, this is the same condition as in the preceding.

We assume perfect compliance and costless enforcement of the regulation.

Substituting for the output and the primary pollutant in the cost function, the Lagrangian function can be written as follows:

$$L = pf(x_M, x_S) - \sum_{j=M,S} w_j x_j - c(g(x_M, x_S) - z^S) - \lambda(z^S - z^R) \qquad (8.17)$$

The necessary first-order conditions are

$$pf'_{x_j} - w_j - c'g'_{x_j} = 0, \quad j = M, S$$
$$c' - \lambda \leq 0 \left(= 0 \text{ for } z^S > 0\right) \qquad (8.18)$$
$$\lambda \geq 0 (= 0 \text{ for } z^S < z^R)$$

Here λ is the shadow price on the emission constraint, that is, the gain (loss) in profit if the constraint is relaxed (tightened). If the constraint is not binding, we see from the complementarity slackness condition that the firm is not influenced by the environmental regulation and will not use any abatement. If the price of the desirable output cannot meet the unit cost including abatement cost at any level of the input j (assuming several inputs in group M), this input should not be used. Assuming that our input j is used in a positive amount and that the emission constraint is binding, the shadow price on the constraint takes the place of the marginal damage of the secondary pollutant in the optimal solution (comparing (8.12) and (8.18)). When the emission constraint is binding, the output of the desirable output in the optimal solution becomes smaller and cost becomes greater than in the private optimal solution without emission regulation because abatement has to be used and input substitution forced. The substitution effects between inputs triggered by the use of abatement resources shift the use of production inputs away from material inputs. The shift is stronger the higher the marginal productivity of the material input in question is in residuals production. The use of service inputs is increased. These substitution effects counter some of the reduction in output and profit, but these latter variables will inevitably decrease. Levels of service inputs may increase to higher levels than in the pre-regulation situation, but not enough to compensate the reduction in output and profit; if so, the firm would itself have imposed a subsidy on its use of service inputs in the pre-regulation case.

The private productivity development is equal to the social productivity development in (8.15), with the important exception that the environmental damage term is absent from the numerators. Due to abatement costs in the denominator, the private productivity level goes down if output and inputs remain constant. Once regulation is introduced, the development of productivity can be either positive or negative, depending on relevant factors discussed in connection with (8.15). A new element is that the regulated amount is subject to political changes over time. Stricter regulation is to be expected, strengthening, *ceteris paribus*, the case of reduced private productivity.

As stated earlier, the shadow price on the emission constraint in (8.17) shows the impact on the profit of a change of the allowed emission. Marginal abatement cost has been suggested as measure of the price on pollution (Aaheim and Nyborg 1995; Pittman 1983). In the optimal solution with a binding emission constraint, we see from (8.18) that the marginal cost of abatement equals the shadow price. However, this shadow price is not in general equal to the social price on pollution. In the optimal solution of the social model (8.10), marginal damage is equal to marginal cost, so setting a price on pollutants equal to the shadow price λ in (8.18) may either undervalue or overvalue the social marginal cost, depending on the difference between the regulated amount z^R and the optimal solution of z^S to (8.11). It is only if the allowed amount of secondary pollutants is equal to the optimal solution of the social planner's problem (8.11) that marginal abatement cost should equal marginal damage.

8.5. Efficiency and Environmental Regulation

8.5.1. The Porter Hypothesis

On the backdrop of the huge cost that climate change may inflict on us all, and other pressing environmental problems of a more regional nature, stricter and stricter environmental regulation is introduced or is planned to be introduced in the near future. The Stern Review (Stern 2006) gives estimates of mitigating and abatement costs necessary to reach global environmental targets. A worry is that environmental regulations will set back the growth of standard goods (exclusive of environmental goods) and prevent developing countries from achieving the standard of living enjoyed in developed countries. At the micro level, a strict environmental policy imposes costs on firms and leads to lower profit and activity, according to the traditional view by most economists. This is also the case for private productivity, as pointed out in the previous section, but is not necessarily the case for productivity growth.

In Porter (1991) and Porter and van der Linde (1995), a more optimistic Panglossian hypothesis, the Porter hypothesis, is put forward: strict environmental regulation may induce firms to innovate to such a degree that private profit increases, and thus strict regulation represents a win-win situation. It states that the pessimistic view stems from considering a static situation only, but that the pressure of environmental regulation induces a dynamic process of change representing retooling, process improvement, and technical change, which more than offsets the abatement costs. However, Porter and van der Linde do not present any formal mechanism supporting the cost-offset hypothesis, but refer to a few examples of successful adaptation and technical change. The Porter hypothesis and attempts to model the positive dynamics (Ambec and Barla 2002; Xepapadeas and deZeeuw 1999) and empirical studies and critique of the hypothesis (e.g., Palmer et al. 1995) are extensively reviewed in Brännlund and Lundgren (2009), Lanoie et al. (2011), and Ambec et al. (2013). The latter three references provide long lists of references to the literature on the Porter hypothesis. Notice that in the discussion of the Porter hypothesis environmental costs, the damage costs used in Sections 8.2 and 8.4, are not considered. The focus is on the possibilities of reducing emissions and the private cost of this.

8.5.2. Dynamic Effects of Environmental Regulation

Porter and van der Linde (1995) suggest two different dynamic effects. First, assuming that there is inefficiency in the utilization of resources before the introduction of environmental regulation, this inefficiency is reduced or even removed after regulation has been introduced. Second, the regulation induces new technology to be developed shifting the production function outward. This is set out in Figure 8.2, which illustrates these two effects. In the space of the desirable output (q in the figure) and emissions z, the pre-regulation position of the firm is at the inefficient point C below the initial frontier production function $f_0(z)$. The efficient point A on the frontier shows the production the firm could have had corresponding to emission z^0. After introducing regulation, the firm improves its efficiency and reduces the emissions down to z^R and increases output from q^0 to q^R at point B on the initial frontier. Then there is a shift of the frontier due to innovation after introducing regulation to $f_R(z)$ where the point E is the efficient point for the level z^R of the reduced emission. The firm continues to reduce emissions and increase output q, and profit Π moving toward the new frontier.[14] This is a neat possible illustration of the story told in Porter and van den Linde (1995) of the increased efficiency effect and the shift in technology effect, but it does not explain the mechanisms behind the moves.

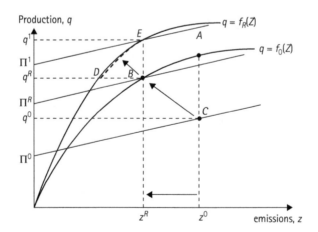

FIGURE 8.2. The Porter hypothesis.

Source: Brännlund and Lundgren (2009, Panel (b), 83).

Establishing credible dynamic mechanisms has proven to be rather difficult. Regarding inefficiency, this difficulty is underlined by the fact that there are hardly any dynamic mechanisms in the huge body of specialized literature on inefficiency explaining the reduction of inefficiency. Estimating efficiency scores based on parametric and nonparametric production functions, and indices for productivity change of the Malmquist type using technical efficiency scores, may be said to be no more than more or less advanced descriptions of implications of observed data on outputs and inputs and do not represent explanations of inefficiency. There is a general methodological problem here, namely the difficulty in explaining inefficiency based on rational decisions. One type of explanation mentioned in the early efficiency literature (see, e.g., Førsund 2010 for a review) is that the inputs may be heterogeneous (Farrell 1957 mentions capital), implying that the estimated inefficiencies are biased. Stigler (1976) goes so far, in reviewing the Leibenstein (1966) concept of X-efficiency, to state that there is no inefficiency in competitive industries, just inhomogeneous inputs, including not only capital and labor, but also management (Charnes et al. 1978 point to the latter factor as a cause of inefficiency).

Inefficiency can be rationalized if the technology in production capital and equipment is embodied (Førsund and Hjalmarsson 1974). Then, if a firm having old technology is compared with one having a new technology, it may appear as inefficient. However, with long-lived equipment, this type of inefficiency may well serve an objective of maximizing the present value of profit (Førsund 2010).

The standard critique of the Porter hypothesis builds on the following questions: Why haven't good ideas already been utilized? And why should the firms wait until environmental regulation comes along? If profitable opportunities to reduce emissions of pollutants exist, profit-maximizing firms would already be taking advantage of them (Ambec et al. 2013). Apart from pointing to limited information about possibilities and limited resources, support for the dynamics of the Porter hypothesis can be found in the theory of induced innovations of Hicks (1932). Porter and van der Linde (1995) talk about the pressure put on firms to comply with environmental regulations. The pressure in the theory of Hicks is represented by costs of inputs (i.e., resources are devoted to R&D in order to reduce costs). However, the development of technology may have deeper roots than mere cost savings. There is a path from basic research, without any cost considerations firms may have about usefulness, to applied research and to innovations within firms themselves or within equipment-producing industries. However, it is not easy to establish a dynamic mechanism for events that are stochastic by nature.[15]

We can distinguish between three types of reactions to new environmental regulation by a firm:

(1) short-run measures like better process control, small-scale re-engineering, introducing more internal recycling of waste, leading to improved efficiency of utilizing material inputs and thereby reducing pollutants,

(2) medium-term measures like investing in end-of-pipe technologies,

(3) long-term measures involving developing new technologies for the main processes saving material inputs and reducing waste products, and even developing waste products into salable products. Technologies used in material-processing industries often have embodied specific technologies so technical change can only come by investing in new technologies and scrapping old machinery and equipment.

It may be the case that a choice has to be made between investing in short-term measures or long-term measures. However, going for short-term measures may lead to less emphasis on developing new process technologies and thus may not be a socially optimal decision. Uncertainty about future regulation may imply favoring short-term measures.

The requirement for technical change to lead to increased private profit can be expressed using the relations (8.8). In addition, there may be technical change in the abatement function that we can express using the cost function (8.9):

$$c^{t_2}(z^P - z^S) < c^{t_1}(z^P - z^S), \quad t_2 > t_1 \tag{8.19}$$

The periods t_1 and t_2 may not necessarily be consecutive years, but may span a period more reasonable for technical change to take place. We will therefore consider capital as one of the factors, but without formulating any investment problem that should have to be done in a realistic setting. Let us assume that the environmental regulator set an upper limit on allowable emission, as in model (8.16), but let the firm itself determine how to obtain this level. We assume that the regulation starts in period t_1 and that the regulated amount is the same and binding in both periods. It is reasonable that it takes some time before the regulatory pressure leads to new technology being available, so the difference between t_1 and t_2 may be several years (Lanoie et al. 2008). The product price and the factor prices, respectively, are the same in both periods by assumption. The condition for the pressure to lead to increased profit is then

$$py^{t_2} - \sum_{j=M,S} w_j x_j^{t_2} - c^{t_2}(z_{t_2}^P - z^R) > py^{t_1} - \sum_{j=M,S} w_j x_j^{t_1} - c^{t_1}(z_{t_1}^P - z^R) \Rightarrow$$

$$\underbrace{p(f^{t_2}(x_M^{t_2}, x_S^{t_2}) - f^{t_1}(x_M^{t_1}, x_S^{t_1}))}_{\text{Output effect}} + \underbrace{\sum_{j=M,S} w_j(x_j^{t_1} - x_j^{t_2})}_{\text{Input effect}} \tag{8.20}$$

$$+ \underbrace{(c^{t_1}(g^{t_1}(x_M^{t_1}, x_S^{t_1}) - z^R) - c^{t_2}(g^{t_2}(x_M^{t_2}, x_S^{t_2}) - z^R))}_{\text{Abatement cost effect}} > 0$$

In period t_1 the initial output effect is negative, but input costs probably go down, but then abatement costs contribute to reducing the profit. There are three effects of technical change in period t_2: the change of the amount of output, the change in the amounts of inputs, and the change in the abatement costs. As to the latter effect, we also have a negative cost consequence due to the reduction in primary pollutant following technical change. Technical change satisfying the condition (8.20) will have a positive output effect, an uncertain input effect, and a reduction in the abatement costs because of the two technology shifts in the second period.

If the effect on profit is positive, then private productivity will also increase over time. To keep up a pressure on firms that have managed to comply with the regulation, it may be necessary to have more stringent regulation over time to keep the dynamic process going.

8.5.3. Regulation Using Economic Incentives

The type of regulation introduced can play a decisive role for the reactions of firms. Porter and van der Linde (1995) base their dynamic innovation process on well-designed environmental regulations based on economic instruments. They go strongly against using a command-and-control approach that demands that a specific technology be used. This will stifle any innovation activity of the firms exploring other solutions and may not lead to any further development of technology if the command of a specific technology to be used satisfies the required reduction in emissions. The technology imposed by the regulator is usually of the type "best available technology" (BAT) or "best available technology not entailing excessive cost" (BATNEEC). Installing end-of-pipe abatement may be cheaper and less complicated than demanding new basic process technologies, so the regulator may be biased toward imposing end-of-pipe solutions without considering the socially optimal solution in a longer time perspective. However, regulators may also give firms a certain number of years before complying if changing the process technology is the best solution. Thus, existing firms may enjoy a positive quasi-rent from "dirty" processes, biasing against new firms entering the market and having to invest in new, less polluting technology.

Jaffe and Stavins (1995) study empirically the importance of dynamic incentives of regulation for technology diffusion and find economic instruments more effective than direct regulations. The seminal economic instrument is to introduce a Pigou tax on the emitted pollutant (Pigou 1920). Using our model (8.5) extended with (8.9), the environmental regulator uses a tax on secondary pollution as the instrument giving incentive to react in both the short and the long run. Regarding the unit as a firm that maximizes profit, facing competitive markets for both output and inputs, introducing a Pigouvian tax t on secondary pollutants yields the following optimization problem:

$$\max pf(x_M, x_S) - \sum_{j=M,S} w_j x_j - c(g(x_M, x_S) - z^S) - tz^S \tag{8.21}$$

The production functions for output and pollutant from (8.5) are inserted for output and primary pollutant, respectively, and a flat unit tax t is imposed on the secondary pollutant. We assume that the firm has access to an end-of-pipe abatement technology, and we regard capital as a variable factor in the cost function as explained in connection with (8.9).

The necessary first-order conditions, assuming that abatement will be used, are

$$pf'_{x_j} - w_j - c'g'_{x_j} = 0, \quad j = M, S$$
$$c' - t = 0 \tag{8.22}$$

The optimal firm solution will be a function of the exogenous tax rate t. Going back to (8.12), we see that the firm solution will conform with the social solution if the tax rate is set equal to the marginal environmental damage in the latter optimal solution.

The choice between using and not using abatement is decided by the last condition in (8.22): if the marginal cost is higher than the unit tax for all levels of abatement, then it is optimal to set abatement equal to zero and emitting the primary pollutant with the tax levied on it, yielding the condition $pf'_{x_j} - w_j - tg'_{x_j} = 0$. Because the tax t is exogenous, we can solve these two equations for the inputs x_M and x_S. Then the solutions for the outputs y and z^P follow directly. With positive abatement, the optimal solution to problem (8.21) implies that the marginal abatement cost is set equal to the tax. We then see that we get the same solution for the inputs and the desirable and undesirable outputs in the two cases, but without the abatement being optimal to use, the emission to the environment z^P is higher than the secondary pollutant z^S in the case of the abatement facility being profitable to use. Going back to the discussion in connection with Equation (8.12), without abatement being socially optimal to use, the tax rate must be set at a higher level to realize a certain goal for environmental pollution. The relative use of factors will be changed in the same way as illustrated by (8.14), and output will be scaled down, compared with the profit-maximizing solution, without a charge levied on the pollutant and no use of abatement.

The results are based on static technologies; substitution takes place within the pre-regulation technology. According to the Porter hypothesis, the tax introduces a pressure on the firms to try to reduce the tax "punishment" in the short run by diminishing any existing polluting waste, and in a longer run adopt end-of-pipe solutions that reduce the tax burden, and develop new technologies using less raw materials that generate pollutants per unit of output.

The impact on productivity and productivity change is similar to what is described in the previous subsection. However, a new element has entered the numerator: the tax paid on the secondary pollution is deducted from the private profit. Again, the static productivity is reduced, but the productivity change may be both negative and positive according to the strength of the different factors, as discussed earlier. Now the tax amount is a new influence on the productivity change if it increases over time.

Direct regulation in the form of an upper limit on pollutant emitted to the environment should also work as a pressure to adapt and adjust the technology and to innovate basic process technologies. We see from the necessary first-order conditions (8.12) for optimal solution of model (8.11) that these conditions are of the same form as in (8.22). However, there is a difference as to the strength of the pressure because the regulated amount z^R is not necessarily the optimal amount z^{S*}, and in the case of using a tax this has to be paid in addition to the abatement costs, thus reducing the private profit below the socially optimal one.[16] With the direct regulation of this type, the firm has the same freedom as under a tax regime to develop ways of reducing the use of pollution-generating raw materials and to develop technologies either of the end-of-pipe type or of process type doing the same. For the regulator, the difference is that a known maximum amount z^R is emitted to the environment imposing such a limit, while with the tax solution the regulator may be uncertain about what will actually be realized as the emission (assuming that the regulator does not have perfect information about the firm's technology).

8.5.4. Cap and Trade

It is well known from the environmental economics literature that "cap and trade" can combine both types of instruments for a situation in which a number of sources emit the same type of pollutant or pollutants that have the same effect on the environment independent of the location of the source (e.g., greenhouse gases and their effects on global temperature). By imposing an upper limit on the total amount of emission from all firms and then introducing quotas for each firm made tradeable, the equilibrium price of quotas will act as if a tax on pollutants is introduced, as in problem (8.21).

The optimization problem for firm i ($i = 1, \ldots, N$) is now

$$\max pf_i(x_{iM}, x_{iS}) - \sum_{j=M,S} w_j x_{ij} - c_i(g_i(x_{iM}, x_{iS}) - z_i^S) + p_Q(z_i^Q - z_i^S) \qquad (8.23)$$

We have three types of endogenous variables: x_M, x_S, and z^S. The quota for firm i is z_i^Q and we assume that $z_i^Q < z_i^{S_0}$ for all firms, where $z_i^{S_0}$ is the optimal level of secondary residuals for unit i before the cap and trade regime is introduced. The total emission then goes down due to the caps. We assume that the quota price p_Q is clearing the quota market. The emission z_i^S is the optimal emission under the cap and trade regulation.

The necessary first-order conditions are

$$\begin{aligned} pf'_{ix_j} - w_j - c'_i g'_{ix_j} &= 0, \quad j = M, S \\ c'_i - p_Q &= 0, \quad i = 1, \ldots, N \end{aligned} \qquad (8.24)$$

Having obtained the solution for the endogenous variables x_M, x_S, and z^S, the solutions for y and z^P can be obtained. The first condition shows that use of material inputs will be reduced; the unit cost will go up, but the use of service inputs will go up; their unit cost is reduced. It is reasonable to assume that the firm will react with a cutback in production, thus reducing revenue and profit. As to buying or selling quotas, the crucial condition is the second one saying that marginal abatement cost should be equal to the quota price. Since the quota price is the same for all firms, the marginal abatement costs will also be the same across firms. The firms that abate, but have optimal emissions that exceed the quota, $z_i^S > z_i^Q$, have to buy additional quotas. It is possible that marginal abatement cost is higher than the quota price for zero abatement, then $z_i^P - z_i^Q$ has to be bought on the quota market. The sellers will be firms for which it is profitable to abate so much that $z_i^S < z_i^Q$. It is formally possible that marginal abatement cost is lower than the quota price for maximal abatement, that is, $a = z_i^P$ and z_i^S is zero, although observations typically show that this is not the case.

We see that all firms that abate will face the same marginal abatement cost equal to the clearing price p_Q in the market. Comparing this solution to the solution (8.24) to problem (8.23) with a tax on the emission we have that, provided that the total restriction on emissions is the same as the sum of optimal solutions for emissions when using a tax, the market clearing price is equal to the tax.

The advantage with cap and trade is that it combines three features; the certainty of regulated emissions, provides perfect compliance, and gives economic incentives or pressures to improve efficiency and develop new technologies that reduce emissions. An additional advantage is that the regulator can tighten the total amount of quotas over time as a single decision.

However, a tax on emissions and cap-and-trade may have different incentives in a dynamic setting. A tax represents a predictable form of regulation for a firm, assuming that it is not changed so frequently. But the price on emission permits may fluctuate quite a lot and represents an unpredictable factor for investment decisions related to environmental regulations.

Behind fluctuations are the business cycle, technology change, competition from firms in countries not regulating carbon emissions, and the thermal electricity generators' competition from renewable energy with its fluctuations of production. The incentives of the two different instruments may give incentives to investment in different technologies, presumably more short-term considerations in the form of end-of- pipe technologies than long-term more costly and fundamental process innovations due to uncertainties about the price. The fluctuations are illustrated in Figure 8.3, showing the price development for carbon certificates[17] within the European Union

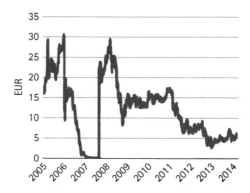

FIGURE 8.3. Volatility of the EU Emission Trading System (ETS) carbon certificate market (2005–2014).

Source: Alexandru P. Luta. The current state of the EU ETS. The Sanbag Climate Campaign, July 22, 2014. https://www.google.no/webhp?gws_rd=ssl#q=The+current+state+of+the+EU+ETS.

Emission Trading System (ETS) for 10 years. The preceding theoretical model of the quota market links marginal abatement costs to the quota price. However, estimates of abatement costs of participating firms fluctuate much less. The EU ETS has had three phases, the first phase covering the period 2005–2007, the second phase 2008–2012, and the third phase 2013–2020. The scheme started out with free quotas for about the total emissions. A positive price in spite of the total free quota is due to mismatch between firm-specific quotas and actual emissions. The fall in price during 2007 is due to earlier trades leading to a closer match between quotas and emissions, and the fact that quotas bought earlier but saved to be used later could not be transferred to Phase II.

In Phase II the total quota was reduced somewhat below the emissions, and more countries joined the system. The price started at levels similar to the start of Phase I, but then the economic recession caused by the financial crisis started to bite and reduced the output of firms within the system and the quota price plummeted. The continuing slide and low level, which has continued to date, is due to structural adjustments by firms in the participating sector, such as fuel substitution of thermal electricity generators and the increased share of renewables in electricity production.

8.5.4. Empirical Studies of the Porter Hypothesis

In the substantial literature on the Porter hypothesis, it is difficult to find general theoretical arguments on which to build mechanisms that give the results of the hypothesis. Therefore, the validity of the hypothesis may be regarded as an empirical question. There is also a rich literature trying to do this, but there is a high ratio of speculation and anecdotes to real evidence (Jaffe et al. 1995; Lanoie et al. 2008), so it is difficult to generalize the obtained results. We will not give a detailed account of empirical studies here, but will focus on the main findings.[18]

A common approach is to study separately three aspects of the Porter hypothesis; the weak version, the narrow version, and the strong version (Lanoie et al. 2011). The weak version posits that environmental regulation will stimulate innovations and technology choice to make production "greener," as measured by R&D, investment in capital, and patents. The narrow version states that flexible environmental regulation gives firms stronger incentive to innovate than command-and-control regulation prescribing specific technologies. The strong hypothesis states that properly designed regulation may induce innovations that more than compensates for the cost of compliance measured by firms' performance such as productivity and costs.

The main findings are that the weak hypothesis has some empirical support, as is the case for the narrow hypothesis, but that there is not much evidence for the strong hypothesis of increased profit due to regulatory-induced innovations.

In the studies of innovations, attention is paid to time lags between the introduction of environmental regulation and innovations. There is a transition period in most cases. Contemporaneous impact on economic performance may be negative, but can turn out positive when using lags between regulatory variables and effects (Lanoie et al. 2008).

There is a data problem in identifying the environmental cost element of process-changing investments that may have been done without regulation. The lack of accurate accounting of regulation cost that allocates the parts attributable to environmental regulation and to process changes undertaken without regulation is becoming a problem because there is an increase in process changes and product reformulations rather than installation of end-of-pipe equipment.

8.6. Productivity Measures Based on Inefficiency

An interpretation of the Porter hypothesis is that existing inefficiency (before the introduction of environmental regulation) is reduced or even eliminated as low-hanging fruits in the short run, and in the long run inefficiency seems to disappear completely, at least it is not mentioned in connection with long run. However, there is a body of literature on productivity that assumes that inefficiency may be persistent over time, the main reason being that innovation and new technology shift the frontier production function upward over time, and consequently make it harder for firms to become as efficient as current best practice. This strand of research is commonly based on the assumption that prices are not available, and the estimation of the efficiency scores is mainly based on a nonparametric frontier (for reviews of this literature, see Arabi et al. 2015; Arabi et al. 2016; Dakpo et al. 2016).

8.6.1. Single-Equation Models

Pittman (1983) extended the approach of Caves et al. (1982a) of measuring productivity, introducing translog multilateral productivity indices, to include undesirable outputs or pollutants. Shadow prices, mainly based on abatement costs, on undesirable outputs were used in calculating the output index based on revenue shares and an input index based on cost shares.

Färe et al. (1989) were not satisfied with the approach of Pittman (1983), pointing to difficulties in determining the prices of undesirable outputs. They introduced a hyperbolic efficiency measure based on estimating Farrell (1957) efficiency measures, using only quantitative information about inputs and outputs, specifying a nonparametric frontier function. This was done in order to credit producers for "their provision of desirable outputs and penalize them for their provision of undesirable outputs" (90). Undesirable outputs z were introduced in addition to the standard desirable outputs y.

The starting point is to introduce a technology using the output possibility set

$$P(x) = \{(y,z): x \geq 0 \text{ can produce } y \geq 0, z \geq 0\} \tag{8.25}$$

where y, z, and x are vectors. In order to give the technology some structure, it is common to start with properties that the set should fulfill. In order to be as general as possible, the set $P(x)$ is assumed to be convex, closed, and bounded, and is monotonic in y, z, and x; both y and x are strongly disposable, but there is a question about the disposability property of the undesirable output that will be addressed in the following. If we assume that also z is strongly disposable, an output-oriented distance function (Shephard 1953) can be used to characterize the technology:

$$D_O(y,z,x) = \min\{\theta : (y / \theta, z / \theta) \in P(x)\} \in (0,1]. \tag{8.26}$$

The point $(y / \theta, z / \theta)$ on the border of the set $P(x)$ is the largest feasible radial extension of the observed output vectors y and z for a given x vector. The distance function gives the Farrell output-oriented efficiency score for the observation (y, z) for a given x. The relation $D_O(y,z,x) = 1$ gives the implicit relation between outputs for a given vector x along the efficient border of the set. This means that we have a trade-off between outputs, that is, inputs can be reallocated to any desired mix of outputs (the assortment is maximal, in the language of Frisch 1965). If we have both desirable and undesirable outputs, this implies that resources can be reallocated away from all undesirable outputs and thus we do not have any problem with undesirable outputs. The trade-off between desirable and undesirable output y and z, respectively, must therefore be restricted in some way for the technology to lead to sensible results (Färe et al. 2013, 110; Førsund 2009). This is accomplished in Färe et al. (1989) and the literature that followed by imposing weak disposability (introduced in Shephard 1970) for y and z together:

$$(y,z) \in P(x) \text{ and } 0 \leq \theta \leq 1 \text{ imply } (\theta y, \theta z) \in P(x). \tag{8.27}$$

Furthermore, it is assumed that y cannot be produced without z also being produced; this null jointness is defined as: if $(y,z) \in P(x)$, and $z = 0$, then $y = 0$.

However, although the intention of measuring efficiency taking into account generation of pollutants is a good one, the solution using the assumption of weak disposability is not (see critique in Førsund 2009, 2018; Murty et al. 2012; Murty and Russell 2018). As pointed out in Subsection 8.3.2, the generation of pollutants stems from the use of material inputs. Then the materials balance accounts for where the mass content of the raw materials ends up; incorporated in the desirable output or as pollutants. There is physically no possibility of a technical trade-off between a desirable output and a pollutant for given amounts of inputs.[19] But such a possibility is not only allowed by the formulation (8.27), but is crucial for the modeling, using a radial or directional distance function as the single-equation model (see the many illustrations in the weak-disposability literature of such a trade-off, starting with Shephard 1970, 188).

One should be aware of the fact that a production possibility set is a very general statement to make about production possibilities until more structure is introduced. Moreover, there is nothing in a general specification saying that such a set can only be described by a single equation such as a distance function. The modelling of joint production may involve a number of equations in order to capture some essential feature of the technology, as demonstrated in Frisch (1965). The technology set may be the intersection of many subsets. This seems to be overlooked in the single-equation literature. The point is how to model the essential connection between desirable and undesirable outputs on one hand, and the inputs on the other. The simultaneous generation of both desirable and undesirable outputs transforming inputs (including at least one material one) is the essential feature. This implies that to look at a relation between the desirable and undesirable outputs for given inputs is futile; there is no transformation possibility here due to the materials balance principle and the assumption of an efficient utilization of all inputs in obtaining the desirable output (Førsund 2018).

The problem dealing with both desirable and undesirable goods when prices on the latter do not exist was addressed in Färe et al. (1989), calculating a hyperbolic index of the type

$$H(y,z,x) = \max\{\lambda : (\lambda y, \lambda^{-1}z) \in P(x)\} \tag{8.28}$$

This idea of asymmetric treatment has in the last decade been developed by estimating efficiency scores using directional distance function (Arabi et al. 2015; Arabi et al. 2016; Chung et al. 1997). The directional distance function is based on choosing a direction from an inefficient observation (adding or subtracting from the observed values) to the frontier that is not necessarily radial. For an output-oriented efficiency score, the value of the output point on the frontier is measured adding to the observed output the product of a common expansion factor and the desirable outputs, and in the case of an undesirable product to subtract the product of the expansion factor and the value of the observation of an undesirable output.

The directional output distance function is defined by

$$\vec{D}_o(x,y,z;g_y,-g_z) = \sup[\beta : y+\beta g_y, \, z-\beta g_z] \in P(x). \tag{8.29}$$

The directions g_y and g_z are usually chosen as (y, z). The minimal value of the directional distance function is zero when the unit in question is on the frontier, and it is restricted to be greater than or equal to 0. The expansion factors for desirable outputs with directions (y, z) are $(1+\beta)$ and the contraction factor for undesirable outputs is $(1-\beta)$.

However, apart from the problem that the directional distance function goes against the material balance and efficiency of production relations, as pointed out earlier, there is the special feature of imposing the same expansion of goods as the contraction of bads. This seems to be rather arbitrary. "Punishing" the generation of pollutants with the same factor as "rewarding" desirable goods is just one of many ways of implicitly weighting the two types of outputs. The fundamental definition of environmental damage we are seeking may be far from the interpretation of efficiency measures based on directional distance functions.

It may be useful for the reader to see how a Malmquist type of productivity-change index, termed Malmquist-Luenberger index (ML) in Chung et al. (1997), is set up using directional output distance functions for period t and $t+1$:[20]

$$ML_t^{t+1} = \frac{1+\vec{D}_o^t(x^t,y^t,z^t;y^t,-z^t)}{1+\vec{D}_o^t(x^{t+1},y^{t+1},z^{t+1};y^{t+1},-z^{t+1})}. \tag{8.30}$$

$ML_t^{t+1} > 1$ implies $\vec{D}_o^t > \vec{D}_o^{t+1}$, that is, that period t efficiency for the unit in question is less than the efficiency in period t +1, resulting in an increase in productivity.

The crucial point for environmental policy is a trade-off between values of goods and pollutants. However, this must be based on a trade-off between man-made desirable goods and jointly generated pollutants measured in the same unit. It is difficult to see that this can be captured by defining productivity as changes in directional distance functions with a fixed goods expansion factor and the same factor as a contraction factor of pollutants. Productivity measures consistent with real trade-offs are inevitably required by regulatory activities, carefully balancing benefits and costs (Jaffe et al. 1995).

Another weakness in the way that single-equation models based on distance function have been used is the lack of explicit modelling of abatement activities, as is done in the model in Subsection 8.3.4. Measuring abatement in the form of only lost output is taking into account only one of the ways to reduce the generation of pollutants mentioned in Subsection 8.3.3. It is standard in the environmental economics literature to model abatement as end-of-pipe, as used in Subsection 8.3.4 (see Førsund 2009, 2018). Abatement is introduced in Färe et al. (2013) as a separate activity, using the primary pollutant, shares of resources and a share of the output from the primary process as inputs producing the secondary pollutant. However, generating the two types of outputs, weak disposability is still maintained as an assumption, so this approach to estimate efficiency including abatement is problematic to accept.

8.6.2. The Multi-Equation Model and Inefficiency

The model of factorially determined multi-output production used in Section 8.3 highlights insights from environmental economics. This model can easily be generalized to include inefficient operations. The simplest way is to use the three relations (8.5) and (8.9) depicting frontier functions, obeying the materials balance (8.7), by expanding the functions involved into sets:

$$y \le f(x_M, x_S) \Rightarrow T_1 = \{(y, z, x) : y \le f(x_M, x_S)\}$$
$$z^P \ge g(x_M, x_S) \Rightarrow T_2 = \{(y, z, x) : z \ge g(x_M, x_S)\} \tag{8.31}$$
$$c^o \ge c(a) = c(z^P - z^S)$$

Following Murty et al. (2012), the production possibility set T is the intersection of the two first sets; $T = T_1 \cap T_2$. The observed cost for abatement a is c^o. The production and cost frontiers are on the right-hand side of the inequalities. Strict inequalities open for inefficient operations, while equations holding with equalities mean efficient operations. (Recall from Subsection 8.3.5 that introducing abatement activity makes it necessary to operate with two types of emission; primary pollutants and secondary pollutants.) We can distinguish between three types of efficiency measures:

(1) Efficiency in producing desirable outputs: $E_y = y^{obs} / f(x_M, x_S) \in (0, 1]$
(2) Efficiency in generating pollutants: $E_z = g(x_M, x_S) / z^{Pobs} \in (0, 1]$
(3) Efficiency in abatement cost: $E_c = c(a) / c^o \in (0, 1]$.

The index *obs* indicates the observations of the three variables, and in addition the inputs x_M, x_S, and abatement a are also the observed ones.

Productivity development can be calculated using, for example, a Malmquist productivity change index[21] based on efficiency calculations for each of the three frontiers of the equations (8.31). These equations are independent; y is not depending on z and vice versa, and abatement is an independent stage. From a policy point of view, this is the preferred information. It does not seem to make sense from a policy point of view to try to estimate a total or aggregated efficiency and productivity. Keeping the developments separate also underlines the point that to see the trade-off between desirable and undesirable goods is only something that can be achieved if the effects of pollution in the environment are made comparable with man-made goods by measuring each type of output in the same unit. It does not make much sense to try to capture a trade-off by forcing a numerical trade-off not based on real evaluation of values.

8.7. Conclusions

The main question has been how to include considerations of the natural environment when measuring productivity of production and its change over time. The natural environment provides us with services of various kinds, influencing our health and well-being in a profound way. However, many of these services are not traded in markets and also have a public good character. It may therefore be futile to search for prices of these services. What can be done for monetized evaluation is to estimate the damages inflicted on the environment as evaluated by consumers of environmental services. Concentrating on how to deal with pollution from production using material resources, estimates of damages constituting the damage function are based on the value of man-made desirable goods that we are willing to forsake in order to reduce the pollution from residuals that are generated jointly with the desirable outputs.

The guiding principle for formulating a model describing joint generation of intended and unintended outputs has been the materials balance principle. Matter cannot be created, nor can it disappear, so the matter of raw materials must either be part of the desirable outputs or end up as residuals discharged to the environment. A multi-equation model is then most suitable to capture the simultaneous generation of desirable and undesirable outputs. The choice was the factorially determined multi-output model having separate production functions for desirable outputs and residuals. This model does not allow any functional relationship between the desirable output and the undesirable one for given amounts of inputs; just a single point in output space is determined, thus obeying the materials balance.

Productivity is measured as the ratio between aggregated outputs and inputs. Outputs are either value added or gross output, and volume indices have to be constructed in the multi-output case. Inputs can be just labor, or may comprise all types in the case of multifactor productivity pursued here. Environmental concerns are then entered by forming the social gross output, subtracting damage costs from gross "economic" outputs. For constant outputs and inputs, static productivity then has to go down. However, once the adjustment is done, productivity change may be both positive or negative, depending on the time path of the different components. Within a general equilibrium framework, resources are channeled to pollution-reducing activities, thus leading to a general reduction of man-made goods, but it is still possible for productivity change incorporating damage cost to show an increase. However, capital accumulation may go down in general and may be a brake on productivity growth if not compensated sufficiently by increase in environmental qualities (i.e., a reduction in damage cost).

Generation of pollutants can be reduced in this model by substitution between inputs (e.g., fuel substitution, and using non-material inputs instead of material ones), keeping desirable output constant, and reducing the amount of desirable outputs. Another way of abatement is changing technology, which usually is possible in the long run only, but there is also an option of installing end-of-pipe facilities that can be done within a shorter time horizon. Such a facility is added to the factorially determined multi-output model (8.5). As for productivity, abatement costs represent additional inputs reducing static productivity, but again productivity change may go either way; this is an empirical question also influenced by technical change in the long run.

The Porter hypothesis postulates environmental regulation based on the "right" incentives to be a win-win situation; regulation puts pressure on firms to reduce current inefficiency and to innovate to such an extent that profit and productivity increase. However, there is not much systematic evidence for such a Panglossian view. No proper formulations of formal dynamic mechanisms have been put forward.

In the literature on inefficiency, environmental considerations have also been developed. The bulk of inefficiency modelling has used a single-equation model based on a special assumption called weak disposability, linking desirable and undesirable outputs to move proportionally at the efficient border of the production possibility set. Weak disposability (together with null jointness) blocks the reduction of pollution to zero, keeping positive amounts of desirable outputs, but no economic or engineering explanations have been put forward backing up these assumptions. The physical background for the generation of residuals when using raw materials is not commented upon at all, and the materials balance is neglected. Indeed, the weak disposability goes counter to the materials balance principle because it is based on a transformation possibility (assorted production) between the desirable and undesirable outputs for given amount of resources. However, it is impossible to decrease both desirable and undesirable outputs simultaneously for given resources remaining on the efficient part of the frontier function (or the efficient border of the production possibility set). Saying that resources are just made idle goes against the definition of an efficient border of the set, and telling a story that resources in production are reduced because they are reallocated to abatement without modelling such activity is not acceptable.

Calculations of productivity and its change have been done applying directional distance function within the weak disposability framework and using a Malmquist type of productivity measure. To make productivity of desirable goods comparable with pollutants, the expansion factor for undesirable outputs is restricted to be the same as for desirable outputs, but with a negative sign. But this is just an arbitrary way of comparing productivity growth, having nothing to do with a proper evaluation of pollutants and desirable goods; the task is to make desirable man-made goods comparable with environmental services in value terms.

The strong conclusion of this chapter is that the use of single-equation models based on the assumption of weak disposability should be at the end of its road. However, it should be stressed that it is not the assumption of weak disposability that is the main problem: the point is that a single-equation model assuming a trade-off between desirable and undesirable outputs is not compatible with the materials balance and the efficiency requirement of the (implicit) production relations at the efficient border of the production possibility set. Multi-equation models capturing essential mechanisms behind simultaneous generation of pollutants and desirable goods should be developed. The solution to the problem of incorporating pollution into productivity measures has been based on introducing an environmental damage function. However, although a neat theoretical solution, it may not be so helpful for practical calculation. Further building up of satellite accounts is needed, tracking physical changes in various types of natural environments and stocks of resources, both biological renewable ones and nonrenewable resources. An alternative to estimating damage costs is to impose physical limits on the discharge of pollutants if the physical damages are known well enough. As demonstrated with cap-and-trade schemes, setting physical limits implies that mitigation costs are revealed, thus making a trade-off between man-made goods and pollutants possible.

NOTES

1. See Mishan (1971) for a review of the earlier externalities literature, and Fisher and Peterson (1976) and Cropper and Oates (1992) for reviews of the literature covering the 1970s and 1980s.
2. See Chapters 2 (Balk), 3 (Eldridge, Sparks, and Stewart), and 4 (Russell) in this volume for more detailed accounts.
3. See Chapter 20 (Jorgenson) in this volume on the international KLEMS project.
4. The Maximum principle was published in 1956 in Russian and an English version in 1962, and the mathematical technique was applied to economic problems in the 1960s—a fast and widespread diffusion of an intellectual invention.
5. The adaptation of the Frisch multi-equation model to environmental pollution is based on the models presented in Førsund (2009, 2018).
6. In the case of inefficiency that will be introduced in Section 8.6, the functions $f(.)$ and $g(.)$ represent the efficient border of the production possibility sets and are called *frontier functions* in our setting.
7. Cf. the famous chocolate production example in Frisch (1935) discussed in Førsund (1999), of short-run substitution between labor and cocoa fat due to more intensive recycling of chocolate with moulding defects the more labor that is employed. Moulding defects decrease with a higher proportion of cocoa fat. Stricter quality control using more labor reduces the share of defective products, utilizing the raw material more efficiently.

8. One or more service inputs may also be essential, however, the point is that residuals are in general an unavoidable feature using material inputs in production. Although $y = f(x_M, 0) = 0$ we may have $z = g(x_M, 0) > 0$; for example, a fully automated thermal electricity-generating plant running in a spinning mode.

9. This theme is developed in the ecological economics literature; see, e.g., Pethig (2006).

10. Retooling or re-engineering processes, and recycling internally more waste materials, may be done within a reasonably short period, and small-scale investments like heat exchangers to recapture waste heat can reduce the amount of residuals for constant primary energy, and thus increase production (Martin 1986).

11. Factor prices of abatement inputs are not introduced because the employment of individual abatement inputs will not be studied (see Førsund 2009, 2018 for such studies).

12. This may not always be the case; there may be harmful run-offs from landfills, and the incineration of waste may create harmful gases, but these factors can in principle be entered into the analysis at some cost of extending the equation system (Førsund 2009).

13. At an aggregated or macro level, the resources used on abatement mean fewer resources to other activities, but at the micro level of a single firm operating in competitive markets, this is not a concern in a partial equilibrium analysis.

14. As opposed to the model (8.5), the pollutant is functioning as an input. This can be the case if there is a fixed relationship between the real input and the pollutant in a single desirable output and a single input and pollutant world. The pollutant is then a shadow factor to the material input, using the terminology of Frisch (1965, 22).

15. Innovations may also be directed to develop new products. As mentioned before, this is not addressed in this chapter.

16. This is a well-known result in textbooks on environmental economics (Førsund and Strøm 1988).

17. Note that it is carbon that is the physical basis in the market, not CO_2. This means that yz in (8.7) is the basis.

18. For detailed accounts, see Brännlund and Lundgren (2009), who give extensive tables of references with information on purpose and method, data, and results; Lanoie et al. (2011), who used a data set for approximately 4,200 facilities collected from seven OECD countries by postal survey in 2003; and Ambec et al. (2013), who also give an account of many empirical studies.

19. This is extensively discussed in Førsund (2009, 2018).

20. In Chung et al. (1997), the ML index is computed as the geometric mean using the technology from period t and period $t + 1$, respectively, as the base technology, following the practice in the literature set by Färe et al. (1992, 1994). However, we follow here the original Caves et al. (1982b) using the technology from period t only as the base technology. Notice that there is a problem of comparability over time if the directions for each period are taken as the observations.

21. The original popular Caves et al. (1982b) Malmquist productivity change index is not a true total factor productivity index. However, the total factor productivity index developed in Bjurek (1996) is a productivity change index, defined as a Malmquist volume index for outputs in the numerator and a Malmquist input index in the denominator and is therefore a true total factor productivity index. This index is also called the Hicks-Moorsteen index, following a suggestion in Diewert (1992).

References

Aaheim, A., and K. Nyborg. 1995. "On the Interpretation and Applicability of a "Green National Product." *Review of Income and Wealth* 41(1): 57–71.

Ambec, S., and P. Barla. 2002. "A Theoretical Foundation of the Porter Hypothesis." *Economics Letters* 75(3): 355–360.

Ambec, S., M. A. Coheny, S. Elgiez, and P. Lanoie. 2013. "The Porter Hypothesis at 20: Can Environmental Regulation Enhance Innovation and Competitiveness?" *Review of Environmental Economics and Policy* 7(1): 2–22.

Arabi, B., S. Munisamy, and A. Emrouznejad. 2015. "A New Slacks-Based Measure of Malmquist–Luenberger Index in the Presence of Undesirable Outputs." *Omega* 51(March): 29–37.

Arabi, B., M. S. Doraisamy, A. Emrouznejad, and A. Khoshroo. 2017. "Eco-Efficiency Measurement and Material Balance Principle: An Application in Power Plants Malmquist Luenberger Index." *Annals of Operations Research* 255(1–2): 221–239. doi: 10.1007/s10479-015-1970-x.

Asheim, G. B. 2000. "Green Accounting: Why and How?" *Environment and Development Economics* 5(1): 25–48.

Ayres, R. U., and A. V. Kneese. 1969. "Production, Consumption and Externalities." *American Economic Review* 59(7): 282–297.

Bjurek, H. 1996. "The Malmquist Total Factor Productivity Index." *Scandinavian Journal of Economics* 98(2): 303–313.

Brännlund, R., and T. Lundgren. 2009. "Environmental Policy Without Cost? A Review of the Porter Hypothesis." *International Review of Environmental and Resource Economics* 3(1): 75–117.

Caves, D. W., L. R. Christensen, and W. E. Diewert. 1982a. "Multilateral Comparisons of Output, Input, and Productivity Using Superlative Index Numbers." *Economic Journal* 92(365): 73–86.

Caves, D. W., L. R. Christensen, and W. E. Diewert. 1982b. "The Economic Theory of Index Numbers and the Measurement of Input, Output, and Productivity." *Econometrica* 50(6): 1393–1414.

Charnes, A., W. W. Cooper, and E. Rhodes. 1978. "Measuring the Efficiency of Decision Making Units." *European Journal of Operational Research* 2(6): 429–444.

Chung, Y. H., R. Färe, and S. Grosskopf. 1997. "Productivity and Undesirable Outputs: A Directional Distance Approach." *Journal of Environmental Management* 51(3): 229–240.

Cropper, M. L., and W. E. Oates. 1992. "Environmental Economics: A Survey." *Journal of Economic Literature* 30(2): 675–740.

d'Arge, R. C., and K. C. Kogiku. 1973. "Economic Growth and the Environment." *The Review of Economic Studies* 40(1): 61–77.

Dakpo, K. H., P. Jeanneaux, and L. Latruffe. 2016. "Modelling Pollution-Generating Technologies in Performance Benchmarking: Recent Developments, Limits and Future Prospects in the Nonparametric Framework." *European Journal of Operational Research* 250(2): 347–359.

Diewert, W. E. 1992. "Fisher Ideal Output, Input and Productivity Indexes Revisited." *Journal of Productivity Analysis* 3(3): 211–248.

Färe, R., S. Grosskopf, B. Lindgren, and P. Roos. 1992. "Productivity Changes in Swedish Pharmacies 1980–1989: A Nonparametric Malmquist Approach." *Journal of Productivity Analysis* 3(1–2): 85–101.

Färe, R., S. Grosskopf, C. A. K. Lovell, and C. Pasurka. 1989. "Multilateral Productivity Comparisons When Some Outputs Are Undesirable: A Nonparametric Approach." *Review of Economics and Statistics* 71(1): 90–98.

Färe, R., S. Grosskopf, M. Norris, and Z. Zhang. 1994. "Productivity Growth, Technical Progress and Efficiency Change in Industrialized Countries." *American Economic Review* 84(1): 66–83.

Färe, R., S. Grosskopf, and C. Pasurka. 2013. "Joint Production of Good and Bad Outputs with a Network Application." In *Encyclopedia of Energy, Natural Resources and Environmental Economics*, edited by J. Shogren, Vol. 2, 109–118. Amsterdam: Elsevier. http://dx.doi.org/ 10.1016/B978-0-12-375067-9.00134-0.

Farrell, M. J. 1957. "The Measurement of Productive Efficiency of Production." *Journal of the Royal Statistical Society, Series A*, 120(III): 253–281.

Fisher, A. C., and F. M. Peterson. 1976. "The Environment in Economics: A Survey." *Journal of Economic Literature* 14(1): 1–33.

Frisch, R. 1935. "The Principle of Substitution: An Example of Its Application in the Chocolate Industry." *Nordisk Tidskrift for Teknisk Økonomi* 1(1–2): 12–27.

Frisch, R. 1965. *Theory of Production*. Dordrecht: D. Reidel.

Førsund, F. R. 1985. "Input-Output Models, National Economic Models, and the Environment." In *Handbook of Natural Resource and Energy Economics*, Vol. I, edited by A. V. Kneese and J. L. Sweeney. Amsterdam: Elsevier Science Publishers BV. Chapter 8: 325–341.

Førsund, F. R. 1999. "On the Contribution of Ragnar Frisch to Production Theory." *Rivista Internazionale di Scienze Economiche e Commerciali (International Review of Economics and Business)* 46(1): 1–34.

Førsund, F. R. 2009. "Good Modelling of Bad Outputs: Pollution and Multiple-Output Production." *International Review of Environmental and Resource Economics* 3(1): 1–38.

Førsund, F. R. 2010. "Dynamic Efficiency Measurement." *Indian Economic Review* 45(2): 123–157. Also published as Chapter 4 in *Benchmarking for Performance Evaluation: A Frontier Production Approach*, edited by S. C. Ray, S. C. Kumbhakar, and P. Dua (2015), 187–219. London: Springer.

Førsund, F. R. 2018. "Multi-Equation Modelling of Desirable and Undesirable Outputs Satisfying the Material Balance." *Empirical Economics* 54(1), 67–99. doi: 10.1007/s00181-016-1219-016.

Førsund, F. R., and L. Hjalmarsson. 1974. "On the Measurement of Productive Efficiency." *Swedish Journal of Economics* 76(2): 141–154.

Førsund, F. R., and S. Strøm. 1976. "The Generation of Residual Flows in Norway: An Input-Output Approach." *Journal of Environmental Economics and Management* 3(2): 129–141.

Førsund, F. R., and S. Strøm. 1988. *Environmental Economics and Management: Pollution and Natural Resources*. London: Croom Helm.

Hartwick, J. M. 1977. "Intergenerational Equity and the Investment of Rents from Exhaustible Resources." *American Economic Review* 67 (5): 972–974.

Hicks, J. R. 1963 [1932]. *The Theory of Wages*, 2nd edition. London: Macmillan.

Jaffe, A. B., and R. N. Stavins. 1995. "Dynamic Incentives of Environmental Regulations: The Effects of Alternative Policy Instruments on Technology Diffusion." *Journal of Environmental Economics and Management* 29(3): S-43–S-63.

Jaffe, A. B., S. R. Peterson, and P. R. Portney. 1995. "Environmental Regulation and the Competitiveness of U.S. Manufacturing: What Does the Evidence Tell Us?" *Journal of Economic Literature* 33(1): 132–163.

Keeler, E., M. Spence, and R. Zeckhauser. 1972. "The Optimal Control of Pollution." *Journal of Economic Theory* 4(1): 19–34.

Kneese, A. V. 1971. "Background for the Economic Analysis of Environmental Pollution." *Swedish Journal of Economics* (Special issue on environmental economics) 73(1): 1–24.

Kneese, A. V., R. U. Ayres, and R. C. d'Arge. 1970. *Economics and the Environment: A Materials Balance Approach*. Baltimore, MD: Johns Hopkins University Press.

Lanoie, P., M. Patry, and R. Lajeunesse. 2008. "Environmental Regulation and Productivity: Testing the Porter Hypothesis." *Journal of Productivity Analysis* 30(2): 121–128.

Lanoie, P., J. Laurent-Lucchetti, N. Johnstone, and S. Ambec. 2011. "Environmental Policy, Innovation and Performance: New Insights on the Porter Hypothesis." *Journal of Economics and Management Strategy* 20(3): 803–842.

Leibenstein, H. 1966. "Allocative Efficiency vs. 'X-Efficiency.'" *American Economic Review* 56(3): 392–415.

Leontief, W. 1970. "Environmental Repercussions and the Economic Structure: An Input-Output Approach." *The Review of Economics and Statistics* 52(3): 262–271.

Leontief, W. 1974. "Environmental Repercussions and the Economic Structure: An Input-Output Approach: A Reply." *The Review of Economics and Statistics* 56(1): 109–110.

Leontief, W., and D. Ford. 1972. "Air Pollution and the Economic Structure: Empirical Results of Input–Output Computations." In *Input–Output Techniques*, edited by A. Brody and A. Carter, 9–30. Amsterdam; London: North-Holland.

Mäler, K.-G. 1991. "National Accounts and Environmental Resources." *Environmental and Resource Economics* 1(1): 1–15.

Martin, R. E. 1986. "Externality Regulation and the Monopoly Firm." *Journal of Public Economics* 29(3): 347–362.

Meade, J. E. 1952. "External Economies and Diseconomies in a Competitive Situation." *Economic Journal* 62 (245): 54–67.

Mishan, E. J. 1971. "The Postwar Literature on Externalities: An Interpretative Essay." *Journal of Economic Literature* 9(1): 1–28.

Murty, S. 2015. "On the Properties of an Emission-Generating Technology and Its Parametric Representation." *Economic Theory* 60(2): 243–282.

Murty, S., and R. R. Russell. 2018. "Modeling Emission-Generating Technologies: Reconciliation of Axiomatic and By-Production Approaches." *Empirical Economics* 54(1), 7–30. doi: 10.1007/s00181-016-1183-4.

Murty, S., R. R. Russell, and S. B. Levkoff. 2012. "On Modelling Pollution-Generating Technologies." *Journal of Environmental Economics and Management* 64(1): 117–135.

Nijkamp, P., and J. Paelinck. 1973. "Some Models for the Economic Evaluation of the Environment." *Regional and Urban Economics* 3(1): 33–62.

Nordhaus, W. D., and E. C. Kokkelenberg (eds.). 1999. *Nature's Numbers: Expanding the National Economic Accounts to Include the Environment*. National Research Council. Washington, DC: The National Academies Press. doi: 10.17226/6374.

Palmer, K., Oates, W. E., and P. R. Portney. 1995. "Tightening Environmental Standards: The Benefit-Cost or the No-Cost Paradigm?" *Journal of Economic Perspectives* 9(4): 119–132.

Perman, R., Y. Ma, M. Common, D. Maddison, and J. McGilvray. 2011. *Natural Resource and Environmental Economics*, 4th edition. Harlow, UK: Pearson Education.

Pethig, R. 2006. "Non-Linear Production, Abatement, Pollution and Materials Balance Reconsidered." *Journal of Environmental Economics and Management* 51(2): 185–204.

Pigou, A. C. 1920. *The Economics of Welfare*. London: Macmillan.

Pittman, R. W. 1983. "Mulitilateral Productivity Comparisons with Undesirable Outputs." *The Economic Journal* 93 (372): 883–891.

Plourde, C. G. 1972. "A Model of Waste Accumulation and Disposal." *The Canadian Journal of Economics / Revue canadienne d'Economique* 5 (1): 119–125.

Porter, M. E. 1991. "America's Green Strategy." *Scientific American* 264(4), 168.

Porter, M. E., and C. van der Linde. 1995. "Toward a New Conception of the Environment-Competitiveness Relationship." *Journal of Economic Perspectives* 9(4): 97–118.

Shephard, R. W. 1953. *Cost and Production Functions*. Princeton, NJ: Princeton University Press.

Shephard, R. W. 1970. *Theory of Cost and Production Functions*. Princeton, NJ: Princeton University Press.

Smith, V. L. 1972. "Dynamics of Waste Accumulation: Disposal versus Recycling." *The Quarterly Journal of Economics* 86(4): 600–616.

Solow, R. M. 1956. "A Contribution to the Theory of Economic Growth." *Quarterly Journal of Economics* 70(1): 65–94.

Solow, R. M. 1974. "Intergenerational Equity and Exhaustible Resources." *Review of Economic Studies: Symposium on the Economics of Exhaustible Resources* 41(5): 29–46.

Stern, N. H. 2006. *The Economics of Climate Change*. HM Treasury. http://hm-treasury.gov.uk.

Stigler, G. J. 1976. "The Xistence of X-Efficiency." *American Economic Review* 66(1): 213–216.

Stiglitz, J. E., A. Sen, and J.-P. Fitoussi. 2009. *Report by the Commission on the Measurement of Economic Performance and Social Progress*. http://graphics8.nytimes.com/packages/pdf/business/ Stiglitzreport.pdf

United Nations (UN). 1993. *System of Accounts 1993*. United Nations Department for Economic and Social Information and Policy Analysis, Statistics Division. New York: United Nations.

Weitzman, M. 1976. "On the Welfare Significance of National Product in a Dynamic Economy." *Quarterly Journal of Economics* 90(1): 156–162.

Xepapadeas, A., and A. deZeeuw. 1999. "Environmental Policy and Competitiveness: The Porter Hypothesis and the Composition of Capital." *Journal of Environmental Economics and Management* 37(2): 165–182.

PART III

MICROECONOMIC STUDIES

CHAPTER 9

··

PRODUCTIVITY AND FINANCIAL PERFORMANCE

··

EMILI GRIFELL-TATJÉ AND C. A. KNOX LOVELL

9.1. INTRODUCTION

IN this chapter we explore the complex relationship between business productivity and financial performance, and we use BHP Billiton, an Anglo-Australian global resources company headquartered in Melbourne, Australia, to illustrate key concepts.[1] The *BHP Billiton 2016 Annual Report* provides a good introduction to the material we cover in this chapter. The *Report* contains three key performance indicators that are used "to assess the financial performance of the Company . . . and to make decisions on the allocation of resources," one being underlying EBIT (earnings before interest and taxes and excluding exceptional items).[2] Figures 9.1 and 9.2 track recent trends in profit (underlying EBIT, expressed in USD) and return on assets (underlying EBIT/ total assets).

Segments of the *Report* are devoted to a discussion of the sources of profit variation, both through time and across businesses. The three primary sources are volume changes, price changes, and change in external factors such as exchange rate movements and climate change. Volume changes are attributed toproductivity change and growth. Price changes are attributed to changing market conditions in countries where commodities are consumed and produced. Importantly, the financial contribution of productivity improvements is attributed to both "sustainable productivity-led volume improvements" and "sustainable productivity-led cost efficiencies." These productivity gains are valued at more than USD 10 billion over 2013–2016, values we refer to as a *productivity bonus* throughout the chapter.

The concepts of productivity and financial performance are linked throughout the *Report*. It is apparent that BHP Billiton management understands that change in financial performance is driven by quantity changes, price changes, and change in external factors, and that productivity change creates value through its impact on both quantity

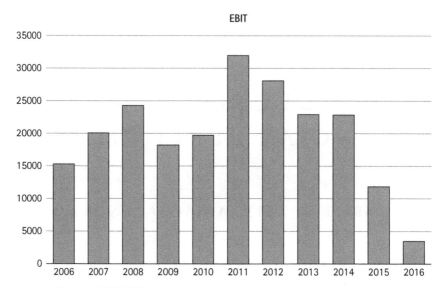

FIGURE 9.1. Profit at BHP Billiton.

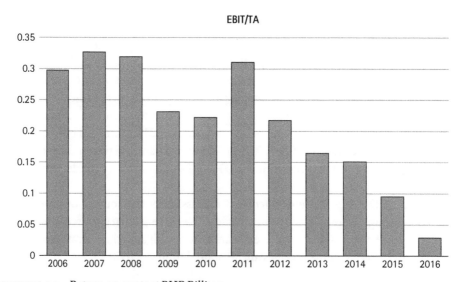

FIGURE 9.2. Return on assets at BHP Billiton.

changes and unit cost changes. In this chapter we analyze the separate impacts of quantity change and price change on three measures of financial performance.

In section 9.2 we measure financial performance with profit, whatever its precise definition, although we use EBIT. We develop an analytical framework that allows us to attribute profit change to quantity changes, a driver of which is productivity change, and price changes, a driver of which is price-recovery change. We measure productivity change with the ratio of an output quantity index to an input quantity index, and we measure price-recovery change with the ratio of an output price index to an input price index.[3]

The analytical framework has a rich history, the primary contributors being Davis (1955); Kendrick (1961, Chapter 5; 1984); Kendrick and Creamer (1961); Kendrick and Sato (1963); Vincent (1968); Courbis and Templé (1975); Houéry (1977); writers associated with the French state agency Centre d'Étude des Revenus et des Coûts (CERC, 1969); Eldor and Sudit (1981); and Miller (1984). We utilize two accounting conventions within this framework. In subsection 9.2.1 we treat profit as the difference between revenue and cost, which can be positive, zero, or negative. In subsection 9.2.2 we treat profit as a return to those who bear the risk of providing capital to the business; in the business accounts this return augments the cost of capital, and so revenue minus augmented cost is zero by construction.[4] The latter treatment also is consistent with national accounts, in which receipts and expenditures balance; this accounting identity is exploited by Jorgenson and Griliches (1967).

In section 9.3 we explore selected topics relevant to both accounting conventions, including the identification of potential drivers of productivity change, and the appropriation (or distribution) of the financial benefits of productivity change among those agents involved in its creation, among others.

In section 9.4 we measure financial performance with return on assets (ROA), and we embed the ROA analysis within a duPont triangle framework, in which change in ROA is decomposed into the product of change in profit margin and change in asset turnover. ROA is a widely acknowledged key financial performance indicator, and Kline and Hessler (1952) describe the pioneering use of ROA and its two components at duPont. In his study of management accounting at duPont, Johnson (1975, 185) describes the triangle as the use of accounting data "for management control" and to support "the allocation of new investment among competing economic activities." This assessment of ROA is strikingly similar to the assessment of EBIT at BHP Billiton. The literature linking ROA as a financial performance indicator with potential drivers of ROA is extremely diverse, although apart from the recent work of Bloom and his colleagues (e.g., Bloom and Van Reenen 2007, 2010; Bloom, Lemos, Sadun, Scur, and Van Reenen 2014), the list of potential drivers of ROA seems to have managed to exclude productivity! Our analytical framework incorporates productivity change as a driver of ROA change.

Inspired by the significance that BHP Billiton attaches to productivity-led cost reductions, in section 9.5 we measure financial performance with unit cost if we can aggregate multiple outputs into a single value, or with unit costs of individual outputs if we cannot. BHP Billiton identifies five business segments, one for each commodity it extracts and markets. The largest segment is iron ore, for which "[o]ur focus remains on producing at the lowest possible cost. . . ."[5] Nearly a century ago, Bliss (1923, 104) recommended the use of unit cost, particularly "[i]n businesses having satisfactory measures of physical volume." Gold (1971) believed information on unit cost to be essential to all areas of managerial decision-making, including the allocation of resources among product lines and pricing policies. More recently, Borenstein and Farrell (2000) have explored alternative cost-cutting strategies. Each of these scenarios fits BHP Billiton.

Section 9.6 provides a summary of the chapter and suggests some avenues for future research.[6]

We conclude this section with an introduction to our notation, which we augment in the following as necessary. A firm uses input vector $x = (x_1, \ldots, x_N) \in R_+^N$ to produce output vector $y = (y_1, \ldots, y_M) \in R_+^M$. The set of feasible (x, y) combinations is the production set $T = \{(x, y): x \text{ can produce } y\}$, whose outer boundary is a production frontier. The set of feasible x is the input set $L(y) = \{x : (x, y) \in T\} \forall y$, and the set of feasible y is the output set $P(x) = \{y : (x, y) \in T\} \forall x$. Input prices and output prices are given by the vectors $w = (w_1, \ldots, w_N) \in R_{++}^N$ and $p = (p_1, \ldots, p_M) \in R_{++}^M$. Cost is $C = w^T x = \Sigma_{n=1}^N w_n x_n \geq 0$, revenue is $R = p^T y = \Sigma_{m=1}^M p_m y_m \geq 0$, profit is $\pi = R - C \gtrless 0$, and profitability (or cost recovery) is $\Pi = R / C \gtrless 1$. Return on assets is π / A, where A is the firm's assets, and the duPont triangle decomposes ROA as $\pi / A = \pi / R \times R / A$, the product of the profit margin and asset turnover. A cost frontier is defined as $c(y, w) = \min_x \{w^T x : D_i(y, x) \geq 1\} \leq w^T x$, in which the input distance function $D_i(y, x)$ is defined as $D_i(y, x) = \max\{\phi : x / \phi \in L(y)\} \geq 1$. A revenue frontier is defined as $r(x, p) = \max_y \{p^T y : D_o(x, y) \leq 1\} \geq p^T y$, with output distance function $D_o(x, y)$ defined as $D_o(x, y) = \min\{\theta : y / \theta \in P(x)\} \leq 1$.[7]

We consider two time periods, indicated by superscripts "o" and "1." Thus profit change from base period to comparison period is $\pi^1 - \pi^0$. The superscripts also can refer to producing units, for example a benchmarking organization and a target organization, in which case "change" becomes "variance" or "deviation." Miller (1984) developed a framework similar to ours to analyze yet another difference, that between actual and anticipated comparison-period profit, and Grifell-Tatjé and Lovell (2013) apply this framework to cost variance analysis.

9.2. Decomposing Profit Change

Decomposing profit change requires a definition of profit, which varies across accounting conventions. We consider two conventions.

One accounting convention defines $\pi = R - C$, without imposing equality between the value of output and the value of input, and without associating profit with any specific input. This convention is consistent with defining the cost of capital narrowly as depreciation expense and interpreting $R - C$ as profit (EBIT), and also with defining the cost of capital more broadly as depreciation expense plus interest expense, and interpreting $R - C$ as "pure" profit (EBT). The choice between reporting interest as an expense or as a component of profit can be important empirically, but it is irrelevant analytically. Under this accounting convention, we analyze variation in $\pi = R - C$.

Another accounting convention places special emphasis on the capital input. We write $w_N x_N = w_N K$, K being the capital input and w_N being the unit cost of capital. Davis (1955) associates $w_N K$ with depreciation expense, which is consistent with BHP Billiton's use of EBIT as a measure of profit. We distinguish the cost of capital $w_N K$ from the (endogenous) return to capital, which we define as $rK = \pi$, r being the (endogenous) rate of return to capital. The return to capital must be sufficient to cover interest payments and taxes (hence EBIT), and also dividends and retained earnings to provide for future growth. Consistent with national income accounting conventions, this convention imposes equality between the value of output and the value of input by treating the return to capital as an expense, yielding augmented cost $\tilde{C} = w_1 x_1 + \cdots + w_{N-1} x_{N-1} + (w_N + r)K = \tilde{w}^T x$. Under this accounting convention, we analyze variation in $R - \tilde{C} \equiv 0.$[8]

The two conventions use the same data to analyze variation in financial performance, but they organize the data in different ways, and they yield complementary insights. We analyze variation in $R - C$ in subsection 9.2.1, and we analyze variation in $R - \tilde{C}$ in subsection 9.2.2.

9.2.1. Change in $R - C$

Under the first accounting convention, we examine change in $R - C$, one expression for which is

$$\pi^1 - \pi^0 = \left[p^{0T} \left(y^1 - y^0 \right) - w^{0T} \left(x^1 - x^0 \right) \right] + \left[y^{1T} \left(p^1 - p^0 \right) - x^{1T} \left(w^1 - w^0 \right) \right], \quad (9.1)$$

in which we use base-period prices to weight quantity changes in what we call the quantity effect, and comparison-period quantities to weight price changes in what we call the price effect.

The quantity effect decomposes in two different ways:

$$\begin{aligned}
p^{0T} \left(y^1 - y^0 \right) - w^{0T} \left(x^1 - x^0 \right) &= w^{0T} x^1 \left[\left(Y_L / X_L \right) - 1 \right] + \pi^0 \left(Y_L - 1 \right) \\
&= p^{0T} y^1 \left[1 - \left(Y_L / X_L \right)^{-1} \right] + \pi^0 \left(X_L - 1 \right),
\end{aligned} \quad (9.2)$$

in which $Y_L = p^{0T} y^1 / p^{0T} y^0$ is a Laspeyres output-quantity index, $X_L = w^{0T} x^1 / w^{0T} x^0$ is a Laspeyres input-quantity index, and $Y_L / X_L \gtrless 1$ is a Laspeyres productivity index. The first term on the right side of each equality is a productivity effect, and the second is a growth (or contraction) effect. In the first equality the productivity effect scales the rate of productivity change $[(Y_L / X_L) - 1]$ by deflated comparison-period cost $w^{0T} x^1$ to generate a productivity bonus, which measures the contribution, positive or negative, of productivity change to profit change, and which amounted to USD 0.4 billion for BHP Billiton in 2016. The growth effect scales the output growth rate $(Y_L - 1)$ by base period profit π^0 to generate what we call a *growth bonus*, which measures the contribution, again positive or negative, of output change to profit change. The growth effect evaluates the business strategy of replication, often referred to as the "McDonalds approach"

(Winter and Szulanski 2001). It is worth noting that the productivity effect can create (or destroy) value in the absence of output growth, and the growth effect can create (or destroy) value in the absence of productivity growth. Garcia-Castro, Ricart, Lieberman, and Balasubramanian emphasize this dual source of value creation in Chapter 10. The second equality is interpreted similarly, although the two effects in the second equality are not generally equal to their counterparts in the first equality.

The price effect also decomposes in two different ways:

$$
\begin{aligned}
y^{1T}(p^1 - p^0) - x^{1T}(w^1 - w^0) &= p^{0T} y^1 \left[\left(P_p / W_p \right) - 1 \right] + \pi^1 \left[1 - W_p^{-1} \right] \\
&= w^{0T} x^1 \left[1 - \left(P_p / W_p \right)^{-1} \right] + \pi^1 \left[1 - P_p^{-1} \right],
\end{aligned}
\tag{9.3}
$$

in which $P_p = y^{1T} p^1 / y^{1T} p^0$ is a Paasche output-price index, $W_p = x^{1T} w^1 / x^{1T} w^0$ is a Paasche input-price index, and $P_p / W_p \gtreqless 1$ is a Paasche price-recovery index, which measures the extent to which a producer's output price changes compensate for its input price changes.[9] The first term on the right side of each equality is a price-recovery effect, and the second is an inflation (or deflation) effect. In the first equality, the price-recovery effect scales the rate of price-recovery change $[(P_p / W_p) - 1]$ by deflated comparison-period revenue $p^{0T} y^1$ to generate a price-recovery bonus, which measures the contribution, positive or negative, of price-recovery change to profit change. The price-recovery effect can be interpreted as a financial reflection of a firm's market power. A notable application of the price-recovery effect occurs under incentive regulation, in which the regulator can constrain the ability of regulated firms to recover cost increases through price or revenue caps. Agrell and Bogetoft analyze incentive regulation in Chapter 16 of this *Handbook*. The inflation effect scales the input-price growth rate $\left[1 - W_p^{-1} \right]$ by comparison-period profit π^1 to generate an inflation bonus, which measures the contribution of input-price change to profit change. The second equality is interpreted similarly, and again the two effects in the second equality are not generally equal to their counterparts in the first equality. An empirically relevant interpretation of both inflation effects is that, assuming $\pi^1 > 0$, "a little inflation is good for business." Conversely, the inflation effects also suggest that a little deflation, such as that recently threatening the European Union, is bad for business and has induced the European Central Bank to adopt policies designed to stimulate moderate inflation.[10]

Expressions (9.2) and (9.3) provide four distinct decompositions of profit change. Each identifies productivity change and price-recovery change as potential drivers of profit change, and the choice among them depends on the objective of the analysis. Identifying the drivers of productivity change, and those of price-recovery change, requires tools from economic theory. We provide an input-oriented identification of the drivers of productivity change in section 9.3.

As a concluding observation, it is noteworthy that in its *Annual Report* BHP Billiton, although it does not explicitly follow our methodology, does decompose annual change in underlying EBIT into volume and price effects. It also decomposes the volume effect into a productivity effect and a growth effect, and it decomposes the price effect into change in sales prices and change in price-linked costs. It also reports a third component of profit change, which includes exogenous factors such as exchange rate movements, exploration and business development, and asset sales.

9.2.2. Change in $R - \tilde{C}$

Under the second accounting convention, we examine change in $R - \tilde{C}$. This change is zero by construction, but the zero change nonetheless decomposes into offsetting quantity and price effects as

$$
\begin{aligned}
\left(R^1 - R^0\right) - \left(\tilde{C}^1 - \tilde{C}^0\right) &= \left[p^{0T}\left(y^1 - y^0\right) - w^{0T}\left(x^1 - x^0\right) - r^0\left(K_0^1 - K^0\right) \right] \\
&\quad + \left[y^{1T}\left(p^1 - p^0\right) - x^{1T}\left(w^1 - w^0\right) - K_0^1\left(r^1 - r^0\right) \right] \\
&= \left[p^{0T}\left(y^1 - y^0\right) - \tilde{w}^{0T}\left(x^1 - x^0\right) \right] \\
&\quad + \left[y^{1T}\left(p^1 - p^0\right) - x^{1T}\left(\tilde{w}^1 - \tilde{w}^0\right) \right],
\end{aligned}
\tag{9.4}
$$

in which K_0^1 is comparison-period capital, valued at base-period prices. Capital is the only quantity variable measured in monetary units, and so the nominal change in capital from one period to the next combines the effects of price change with those of quantity change. We eliminate the effect of price change by using capital's real comparison period value K_0^1.[11]

Expensing the return to capital in the base period makes $p^{0T}y^0 = \tilde{w}^{0T}x^0$, which simplifies the quantity effect in expression (9.4) to

$$
\begin{aligned}
p^{0T}\left(y^1 - y^0\right) - \tilde{w}^{0T}\left(x^1 - x^0\right) &= p^{0T}y^1 - \tilde{w}^{0T}x^1 \\
&= \tilde{w}^{0T}x^1\left[\left(Y_L / \tilde{X}_L\right) - 1\right] \\
&= p^{0T}y^1\left[1 - \left(Y_L / \tilde{X}_L\right)^{-1}\right],
\end{aligned}
\tag{9.5}
$$

and so the quantity effect is a productivity effect in which $\tilde{X}_L = \tilde{w}^{0T}x^1 / \tilde{w}^{0T}x^0$ is a Laspeyres input-quantity index with price weights $\tilde{w}^0$. Under this accounting convention, there is no growth effect, even if $Y_L \neq 1$ or $\tilde{X}_L \neq 1$, because the associated value weight analogous to π^0 in expression (9.2) is $p^{0T}y^0 - \tilde{w}^{0T}x^0$, which is zero by construction. The two expressions for the productivity effect are equal, even if $Y_L / \tilde{X}_L \neq 1$, because they both equal $p^{0T}y^1 - \tilde{w}^{0T}x^1$ in the first row of expression (9.5).

Expensing the return to capital in the comparison period makes $p^{1T}y^1 = \tilde{w}^{1T}x^1$, which simplifies the price effect in expression (9.4) to

$$
\begin{aligned}
y^{1T}\left(p^1 - p^0\right) - x^{1T}\left(\tilde{w}^1 - \tilde{w}^0\right) &= -y^{1T}p^0 + x^{1T}\tilde{w}^0 \\
&= p^{0T}y^1\left[\left(P_P / \tilde{W}_P\right) - 1\right] \\
&= \tilde{w}^{0T}x^1\left[1 - \left(P_P / \tilde{W}_P\right)^{-1}\right],
\end{aligned}
\tag{9.6}
$$

and so the price effect is a price-recovery effect in which $\tilde{W}_p = x^{1T}\tilde{w}^1 / x^{1T}\tilde{w}^0$ is a Paasche input price index. Under this accounting convention, there is no inflation effect, even if $P_P \neq 1$ or $\tilde{W}_p \neq 1$, because the associated value weight analogous to π^1 in expression (9.3) is $p^{1T}y^1 - \tilde{w}^{1T}x^1$, which is zero by construction. The two expressions for the price-recovery effect are equal, even if $P_P / \tilde{W}_p \neq 1$, because they both equal $-y^{1T}p^0 + x^{1T}\tilde{w}^0$ in the first row of expression (9.6).

Under this accounting convention, special interest attaches to the return to those who provide capital to the business; Davis (1955) called them "investors." However, the return to capital is profit under a different name, since in the comparison period $p^{1T}y^1 - w^{1T}x^1 - r^1K_0^1 = 0$, $p^{1T}y^1 - w^{1T}x^1 = r^1K_0^1 = \pi^1$, and in the base period $p^{0T}y^0 - w^{0T}x^0 - r^0K^0 = 0$, $p^{0T}y^0 - w^{0T}x^0 = r^0K^0 = \pi^0$. Consequently, $r^1K_0^1 - r^0K^0 = \pi^1 - \pi^0$. Thus the following expression for change in the return to capital also provides a new expression for profit change

$$r^1K_0^1 - r^0K^0 = \left[p^{0T}\left(y^1 - y^0\right) - w^{0T}\left(x^1 - x^0\right) - r^0\left(K_0^1 - K^0\right) \right] \\ + r^0\left(K_0^1 - K^0\right) + \left[y^{1T}\left(p^1 - p^0\right) - x^{1T}\left(w^1 - w^0\right) \right], \tag{9.7}$$

and adding and subtracting $r^0\left(K_0^1 - K^0\right)$ to the right side yields

$$r^1K_0^1 - r^0K^0 = \left[p^{0T}(y^1 - y^0) - \tilde{w}^{0T}\left(x^1 - x^0\right) \right] \\ + r^0\left(K_0^1 - K^0\right) + \left[y^{1T}\left(p^1 - p^0\right) - x^{1T}\left(w^1 - w^0\right) \right]. \tag{9.8}$$

Thus, under this accounting convention, change in the return to those who provide capital to the business has three components: that portion of profit change attributable solely to productivity change (from expression (9.5)), a return to capital expansion effect $r^0\left(K_0^1 - K^0\right)$, and a price effect based on (p, w) rather than $(p, \tilde{w})$, which appears in expression (9.3). The return to capital expansion effect was introduced by Eldor and Sudit (1981), and is analogous to the growth effects $\pi^0\left(Y_L - 1\right)$ and $\pi^0\left(X_L - 1\right)$ in expression (9.2), although it collects the impact of growth in a single input, that of capital expansion.

We conclude by returning to Davis (1955), who showed that comparison-period profitability valued at base-period prices

$$\tilde{\Pi}_0^1 = y^{1T}p^0 / x^{1T}\tilde{w}^0 \\ = Y_L / \tilde{X}_L \tag{9.9}$$

is the Laspeyres productivity index appearing in expression (9.5), and that comparison-period profit valued at base-period prices

$$\tilde{\pi}_0^1 = p^{0T}y^1 - \tilde{w}^{0T}x^1 \\ = \tilde{w}^{0T}x^1\left(\tilde{\Pi}_0^1 - 1\right) \tag{9.10}$$

converts the Laspeyres productivity index in expression (9.9) to a Laspeyres productivity bonus. Since expression (9.10) is another way of expressing the second equality in expression (9.5), it confirms that, when profit is expensed, the quantity effect is a productivity effect (which we also call a *productivity bonus*). The significance of these two results is that the two financial performance indicators $\tilde{\Pi}_0^1$ and $\tilde{\pi}_0^1$, both of which can be obtained from a company's accounts, provide measures of productivity change and the productivity bonus, respectively. These two results do not hold unless profit is expensed.

9.3. Selected Topics

We briefly consider some topics relevant to both accounting conventions, and we show how the treatment of each differs between the two conventions.

9.3.1. Drivers of Productivity Change

We have attributed a portion of profit change to productivity change, but we have not explored the sources of productivity change. Doing so requires specification of an orientation, either input-conserving or output-expanding, which in turn depends on management strategy. We adopt an input-conserving orientation, in keeping with our observation in section 9.1 on the emphasis that BHP Billiton places on the cost savings arising from productivity growth. We develop two approaches.

In the first approach we begin with the first productivity effect in expression (9.2), which we rewrite, exploiting the fact that $\Pi^0 = p^{0T}y^0 / w^{0T}x^0$, as

$$w^{0T}x^1\left[(Y_L / X_L)-1\right]=\left(p^0 / \Pi^0\right)^T\left(y^1-y^0\right)-w^{0T}\left(x^1-x^0\right)$$
$$=\left(p^0 / \Pi^0\right)^T y^1 - w^{0T}x^1. \tag{9.11}$$

With the assistance of Figure 9.3, which depicts production sets in base and comparison periods, we decompose the productivity effect in expression (9.11) as

$$\begin{aligned}
&\left(p^0/\Pi^0\right)^T y^1 - w^{0T}x^1 \\
&= w^{0T}\left(x^0-x^A\right)-w^{0T}\left(x^1-x^C\right) \quad &\text{technical efficiency effect} \\
&+ w^{0T}\left(x^A-x^B\right) \quad &\text{technical change effect} \\
&+ (p^0 / \Pi^0)^T\left(y^1-y^0\right)-w^{0T}(x^C-x^B), \quad &\text{size effect}
\end{aligned} \tag{9.12}$$

in which $x^A = x^0/D_i^0\left(y^0,x^0\right)$ is a technically efficient radial contraction of observed base-period input vector x^0, $x^B = x^0/D_i^1\left(y^0, x^0\right)$ incorporates a further radial contraction of

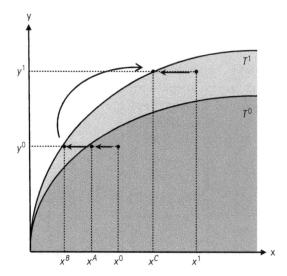

FIGURE 9.3. Identifying the drivers of productivity change.

x^0 made possible by input-saving technical progress, and $x^C = x^1/D_i^1\left(y^1, x^1\right)$ is a technically efficient radial contraction of observed comparison-period input vector x^1. If production is more technically efficient in the comparison period than in the base period, the technical efficiency effect contributes positively to productivity change. If technical change is input-saving technical progress, the technical change effect also contributes positively to productivity change. Size change can contribute to productivity change in either direction, depending on the magnitudes of $\left(y^1 - y^0\right)$ and $\left(x^C - x^B\right)$, and since y^1 and x^C are not necessarily radial expansions or contractions of y^0 and x^B, size change includes both scale and mix changes.

Decomposition (9.12) has an input-saving, cost-reducing orientation, in the sense that both technical efficiency change and technical change are measured, and valued, in an input-saving direction. It is analytically possible, and equally plausible from a managerial perspective, to adopt an output- and revenue-enhancing orientation when decomposing the productivity effect, so that both technical efficiency change and technical change are measured and valued in an output-enhancing direction.

In the second approach, originally developed by Grifell-Tatjé and Lovell (1999), we also begin with the first quantity effect in expression (9.2), but we use the entire quantity effect instead of just its productivity effect component. Continuing to use Figure 9.3, we have

$$
\begin{aligned}
p^{0T}\left(y^1 - y^0\right) &- w^{0T}\left(x^1 - x^0\right) \\
&= w^{0T}\left(x^0 - x^A\right) - w^{0T}\left(x^1 - x^C\right) && \text{technical efficiency effect} \\
&\quad + w^{0T}\left(x^A - x^B\right) && \text{technical change effect} \\
&\quad + p^{0T}\left(y^1 - y^0\right) - w^{0T}\left(x^C - x^B\right), && \text{activity effect}
\end{aligned}
\tag{9.13}
$$

in which the technical efficiency effect and the technical change effect are unchanged from expression (9.12). The activity effect collects the margin effect from the first quantity effect in expression (9.2) and the size effect in expression (9.12), and quantifies the aggregate impact on profit of efficient firm growth along the surface of T^1 in Figure 9.3. In this approach, the technical efficiency effect and the technology effect are the only drivers of productivity change, which is defined as $w^{0T}\left(x^0 - x^B\right) - w^{0T}\left(x^1 - x^C\right)$.

This strategy of decoupling the impacts of productivity change and size change on profit change can be particularly appropriate in certain situations, such as

- when one of the main components of the business model and strategy of the firm is growth. In this case, it is appropriate to distinguish the contribution of growth from that of productivity change to change in financial performance. The activity effect plays a leading role in the Brea-Solís, Casadesus-Masanell, and Grifell-Tatjé (2015) study of Walmart's sources of competitive advantage.
- when a regulator is willing to pay for improvements in productivity associated with technical efficiency change and technical change, but not for size change linked with mergers and acquisitions. De Witte and Saal (2010) distinguished the activity effect from the productivity effect in their study of regulatory impacts on the Dutch drinking water sector.

The decomposition strategy is very similar under the second accounting convention, in which $R - \tilde{C} = 0$. The productivity effect in expression (9.5) can be rewritten as

$$\tilde{w}^{0T} x^1 \left[\left(Y_L / \tilde{X}_L\right) - 1\right] = p^{0T}\left(y^1 - y^0\right) - \tilde{w}^{0T}\left(x^1 - x^0\right), \qquad (9.14)$$

and we apply the same decomposition as in expression (9.12), substituting $\tilde{w}^0$ for w^0. The size effect in expression (9.12) coincides with the activity effect in expression (9.13) since $\left(p^0 / \Pi^0\right) = p^0 / \left[p^{0T} y^0 / \tilde{w}^{0T} x^0\right] = p^0$. Consequently, under the second accounting convention, decompositions (9.12) and (9.13) coincide apart from their different input price vectors. This decomposition identifies the same input vectors x^A, x^B and x^C, but it weights output-quantity changes with p^0 rather than (p^0/Π^0) and weights input-quantity changes with $\tilde{w}^0$ rather than w^0. Implementing either procedure requires estimation of the unobserved input vectors x^A, x^B, and x^C.

9.3.2. Value Creation and Its Appropriation (or Distribution)

We consider how the productivity bonus, the value created by the production unit, is appropriated by (or distributed among) those who participate in its creation. But what value is to be distributed? The productivity effect? The quantity effect? An augmented quantity effect? The answer depends on how one views the firm as creating value.

Davis (1955) and Kendrick (1984) at the level of the individual business, and Kendrick (1961) and Kendrick and Sato (1963) at the level of the aggregate economy, viewed productivity change as the source of value creation. Kendrick (1961, 111) explained the distribution process succinctly: "If productivity advances, wage rates and capital return necessarily rise in relation to the general product price level, since this is the means whereby the fruits of productivity gains are distributed to workers and investors by the market mechanism."

Substituting the first equality in expression (9.2) into expression (9.1) and solving for the productivity effect yields an expression for the functional distribution of created value

$$w^{0T} x^1 \left[\left(Y_L / X_L \right) - 1 \right] = -y^{1T} \left(p^1 - p^0 \right) + x^{1T} \left(w^1 - w^0 \right) + \left(\pi^1 - Y_L \pi^0 \right), \qquad (9.15)$$

which shows how the productivity bonus is distributed to consumers through product price changes, to input suppliers through input price changes, and to investors who receive an income greater than, equal to, or less than profit change, depending on the value of the Laspeyres output-quantity index Y_L. Of course, some product prices can fall, consumer electronics providing a prominent example, while others rise; some input prices can rise, iron ore until 2011, while others fall; and profit can increase or decline.[12]

Expression (9.15) can provide evidence on the source(s) of increasing income inequality observed in most advanced nations (International Monetary Fund, n.d.). For example, a movement of the bonus away from input suppliers toward suppliers of capital is likely to increase inequality (OECD, 2014). In addition, disaggregating $- y^{1T} (p^1 - p^0)$ can identify consumer groups who gain or lose from product group price changes, and disaggregating $x^{1T} (w^1 - w^0)$ can identify input supplier groups who gain or lose from input-group price changes. For example, new technology generates a shift in demand away from less educated labor groups toward highly educated labor groups, which also is likely to increase inequality.

Some writers associated with CERC distribute the entire quantity effect, rather than just the productivity effect. The argument underlying this enlarged view of value creation is that growth, perhaps obtained through a strategy of replication, can also contribute to profit change. To see this, rewrite the growth effect in the first quantity effect in expression (9.2) as $\pi^0 \left(Y_L - 1 \right) = (\pi^0 / R^0) \left[p^{0T} \left(y^1 - y^0 \right) \right]$, which shows that the producing unit can create value through growth $p^{0T} (y^1 - y^0) > 0$, even in the absence of productivity gains, provided it has a positive base-period profit margin $(\pi^0 / R^0) > 0$ to build on. Under this view, the first quantity effect in expression (9.2), which includes the financial benefits of growth as well as those of productivity change, generates the following expression for the functional distribution of created value:

$$w^{0T} x^1 \left[\left(Y_L / X_L \right) - 1 \right] + \pi^0 \left(Y_L - 1 \right) = -y^{1T} \left(p^1 - p^0 \right) + x^{1T} \left(w^1 - w^0 \right) + \left(\pi^1 - \pi^0 \right), \qquad (9.16)$$

and so the quantity effect is distributed among the same claimants as the productivity effect is, but in a larger or smaller amount and in a different composition, depending on $\pi^0 \gtrless 0$ and $Y_L \gtrless 1$. In this scenario, a profitable growth strategy enables firms to distribute more than just the productivity effect. Again, some product prices can fall while others rise, some input prices can rise while others fall, and profit can increase or decrease.

Other writers associated with CERC go still further, augmenting the quantity effect to be distributed with what they call "héritages," the sum of the values of any product price increases and any input price decreases, leading to yet another expression for the functional distribution of created value:

$$w^{0T}x^1\left[\left(Y_L / X_L\right)-1\right]+\pi^0\left(Y_L - 1\right)+y^{1T}\left(p^1 - p^0\right)-x^{1T}\left(w^1 - w^0\right)-\left(\pi^1 - \pi^0\right)$$
$$p^1 > p^0 \qquad w^1 < w^0 \qquad \pi^1 < \pi^0$$
$$= -y^{1T}\left(p^1 - p^0\right)+x^{1T}\left(w^1 - w^0\right)+\left(\pi^1 - \pi^0\right) \qquad (9.17)$$
$$p^1 > p^0 \qquad w^1 > w^0 \qquad \pi^1 > \pi^0.$$

In this scenario, the productivity bonus and the growth effect are enhanced by additional revenue generated by price increases in some product markets, by cost reductions resulting from price decreases in some input markets, and by declines in any components of profit, such as taxes, dividends, or retained earnings. The number of claimants to the augmented quantity effect declines, but the amount to be distributed grows by the amount of héritages. Providers of capital continue to gain or lose. Among the applications of this approach are Grifell-Tatjé and Lovell (2008), who examined the distribution of the fruits of profit (and loss) change at the United States Postal Service over a 30-year period subsequent to its reorganization from a government department to an independent agency in 1971; Arocena, Blázquez, and Grifell-Tatjé (2011), who examined the sources of value creation and its distribution by utilities in the Spanish electric power sector prior to and subsequent to its restructuring in the late 1990s; and Estache and Grifell-Tatjé (2013), who identified distributional winners and losers among key stakeholders in a brief failed water privatization experience in Mali, one of the poorest countries in the world.

In section 9.2.2 there is no growth effect, and the productivity bonus also is distributed to consumers, suppliers, and investors [via the $(r^1 - r^0)$ component of $\left(\tilde{w}_N^1 - \tilde{w}_N^0\right)$]. In expression (9.5) the productivity bonus $p^{0T}y^1 - \tilde{w}^{0T}x^1 = p^{0T}y^1\left[1-\left(Y_L / \tilde{X}_L\right)^{-1}\right]$ is distributed by means of

$$p^{0T}y^1\left[1-\left(Y_L / \tilde{X}_L\right)^{-1}\right]=-y^{1T}\left(p^1 - p^0\right)+x^{1T}\left(w^1 - w^0\right)+K_0^1\left(r^1 - r^0\right), \qquad (9.18)$$

since the price-recovery effect is the negative of the productivity effect in expression (9.4). Just as other claimants receive their portion of the bonus through changes in the prices they receive or pay, investors receive their portion of the bonus as a change in the rate of return to the capital they provide. Among the applications of this approach are Boussemart, Butault, and Ojo (2012), who analyze the generation and distribution of productivity gains in French agriculture over a half century, and Garcia-Castro and

Aguilera (2015), who build a value creation and appropriation model similar to ours, but expressed in ratio form inspired by the Solow growth model. The latter approach is summarized and extended, with emphasis on replication gains, and applied to US airlines by Garcia-Castro et al. in Chapter 10 of this *Handbook*.

Eldor and Sudit (1981) augment the productivity bonus with the return on capital expansion effect in expression (9.8), and so under this convention the value to be distributed is

$$p^{0T} y^1 \left[1 - \left(Y_L / \tilde{X}_L \right)^{-1} \right] + r^0 \left(K_0^1 - K^0 \right) = -y^{1T} \left(p^1 - p^0 \right)$$
$$+ x^{1T} \left(w^1 - w^0 \right) + \left(r^1 K_0^1 - r^0 K^0 \right).$$

(9.19)

The qualitative difference between expressions (9.18) and (9.19) is the return to investors. In expression (9.18) investor income derives from a change in the rate of return to capital, whereas in expression (9.19) investor income derives from both a change in the rate of return to capital and a change in the real quantity of capital to which the rates are applied. The two sources of investor income constitute profit change, since $r^1 K_0^1 - r^0 K^0 = \pi^1 - \pi^0$.

9.3.3. Weights

In both subsections 9.2.1 and 9.2.2 we use base-period prices to weight quantity changes, and comparison-period quantities to weight price changes, which leads to Laspeyres quantity and productivity indices and Paasche price and price-recovery indices. It is also possible to use comparison-period prices to weight quantity changes, and base-period quantities to weight price changes, which leads to Paasche quantity and productivity indices and Laspeyres price and price-recovery indices. A third approach, inspired by Bennet (1920), uses arithmetic mean prices to weight quantity changes and arithmetic mean quantities to weight price changes, which leads to Edgeworth-Marshall quantity, productivity, price, and price-recovery indices.

Whenever base and comparison periods are far apart, or in turbulent times of rapid price and quantity change, the use of arithmetic mean prices and quantities is appealing. Adopting the accounting convention in subsection 9.2.1, profit change becomes

$$\pi^1 - \pi^0 = \left[\bar{p}^T \left(y^1 - y^0 \right) - \bar{w}^T \left(x^1 - x^0 \right) \right] + \left[\bar{y}^T \left(p^1 - p^0 \right) - \bar{x}^T \left(w^1 - w^0 \right) \right],$$

in which $\bar{p} = \frac{1}{2} \left(p^0 + p^1 \right)$ and $\bar{w} = \frac{1}{2} \left(w^0 + w^1 \right)$, and similarly for $\bar{y}$ and $\bar{x}$.

Grifell-Tatjé and Lovell (2015, 219) have shown that one of four decompositions of the quantity effect is

$$\bar{p}^T \left(y^1 - y^0 \right) - \bar{w}^T \left(x^1 - x^0 \right) = \bar{p}^T y^1 \left[1 - \left(Y_{EM} / X_{EM} \right)^{-1} \right] + \left(\bar{p}^T y^0 - \bar{w}^T x^0 \right) \left[X_{EM} - 1 \right], \quad (9.20)$$

in which $Y_{EM} = \bar{p}^T y^1 / \bar{p}^T y^0$; $X_{EM} = \bar{w}^T x^1 / \bar{w}^T x^0$ and Y_{EM} / X_{EM} are Edgeworth-Marshall output quantity, input quantity, and productivity indices. This quantity-effect decomposition into productivity and growth components is structurally similar to the second decomposition in (9.2), but it uses Bennet arithmetic mean prices to generate Edgeworth-Marshall quantity and productivity indices.

Similarly, one of four decompositions of the price effect is

$$\bar{y}^T \left(p^1 - p^0 \right) - \bar{x}^T \left(w^1 - w^0 \right) = \bar{y}^T p^0 \left[\left(P_{EM} / W_{EM} \right) - 1 \right] + \left(\bar{y}^T p^1 - \bar{x}^T w^1 \right) \left[1 - W_{EM}^{-1} \right], \quad (9.21)$$

in which $P_{EM} = \bar{y}^T p^1 / \bar{y}^T p^0$; $W_{EM} = \bar{x}^T w^1 / \bar{x}^T w^0$, and P_{EM} / W_{EM} are Edgeworth-Marshall output-price, input-price, and price-recovery indices. This decomposition is structurally similar to the first decomposition in expression (9.3), but it uses Bennet arithmetic mean quantities to generate Edgeworth-Marshall price and price-recovery indices.

An alternative way of implementing the arithmetic mean concept is to calculate the arithmetic mean of either Laspeyres quantity effect in expression (9.2) and the corresponding Paasche quantity effect to generate a Bennet type of quantity effect

$$\bar{p}^T \left(y^1 - y^0 \right) - \bar{w}^T \left(x^1 - x^0 \right) = \tfrac{1}{2} \left\{ p^{0T} y^1 \left[1 - \left(Y_L / X_L \right)^{-1} \right] + p^{1T} y^0 \left[\left(Y_P / X_P \right) - 1 \right] \right\} \\ + \tfrac{1}{2} \left[\pi^0 \left(X_L - 1 \right) + \pi^1 \left(1 - X_P^{-1} \right) \right], \quad (9.22)$$

in which the first term on the right-hand side is a productivity effect and the second is a growth effect. Similarly, the arithmetic mean of either Paasche price effect in expression (9.3) and the corresponding Laspeyres price effect generates a Bennet type of price effect

$$\bar{y}^T \left(p^1 - p^0 \right) - \bar{x}^T \left(w^1 - w^0 \right) = \tfrac{1}{2} \left\{ p^{0T} y^1 \left[\left(P_P / W_P \right) - 1 \right] + p^{1T} y^0 \left[1 - \left(P_L / W_L \right)^{-1} \right] \right\} \\ + \tfrac{1}{2} \left[\pi^1 \left(1 - W_P^{-1} \right) + \pi^0 \left(W_L - 1 \right) \right], \quad (9.23)$$

which consists of a price-recovery effect and an inflation effect.

Application of the arithmetic mean concept to the accounting convention used in subsection 9.2.2 follows similar procedures, noting that neither growth effects nor inflation effects appear in the decompositions, and replacing w with $\tilde{w}$, which in turn replaces X_L and X_P with $\tilde{X}_L$ and $\tilde{X}_P$, and W_P and W_L with $\tilde{W}_P$ and $\tilde{W}_L$. The analysis is based on the arithmetic mean of expression (9.8) and the corresponding expression having quantity effect with comparison-period price weights and price effect with base-period quantity weights, in which the productivity effect is the arithmetic mean of the Laspeyres productivity effect in expression (9.5) and the corresponding Paasche productivity effect, and the price-recovery effect is the arithmetic mean of the Paasche price-recovery effect in expression (9.6) and the corresponding Laspeyres price-recovery effect. Under this accounting convention, we lose the linkage between Bennet indicators and EM indices.

9.3.4. Missing, Subsidized, or Distorted Prices

The productivity effect is a function of prices as well as quantities. However, prices can be missing or subsidized in the non-market sector, and distorted, by discrimination or cross-subsidy, for example, in the market sector. If, for example, output prices are distorted, then it may be desirable to weight output quantities with their unit costs of production $c = (c_1, \ldots, c_M)$, $c_m = $ (expenditure on output y_m)$/y_m$, $c^T y = C = w^T x$, in the quantity effect.

In subsection 9.2.1 this procedure converts the quantity effect in expression (9.1) to

$$p^{0T}\left(y^1 - y^0\right) - w^{0T}\left(x^1 - x^0\right) = c^{0T}\left(y^1 - y^0\right) - w^{0T}\left(x^1 - x^0\right) + \left[\left(p^0 - c^0\right)^T \left(y^1 - y^0\right)\right]$$
$$= w^{0T} x^1 \left[\left(Y_L^c / X_L\right) - 1\right] + \left[\left(p^0 - c^0\right)^T \left(y^1 - y^0\right)\right] \qquad (9.24)$$
$$= c^{0T} y^1 \left[1 - \left(Y_L^c / X_L\right)^{-1}\right] + \left[\left(p^0 - c^0\right)^T \left(y^1 - y^0\right)\right],$$

in which $Y_L^C = c^{0T} y^1 / c^{0T} y^0$ is a Laspeyres output-quantity index with base-period unit cost weights in place of base-period output prices. The quantity effect decomposes into an adjusted productivity effect and an adjusted growth effect. The adjusted productivity effect $c^{0T} y^1 [1 - (Y_L^c / X_L)^{-1}]$ is a productivity bonus, free of output price distortion. The adjusted growth effect $(p^0 - c^0)^T (y^1 - y^0)$ incorporates both distorted output prices p^0 and output unit costs c^0. Products for which $p_m^0 \gtrless c_m^0$ make positive, zero, or negative contributions to the quantity effect, and hence to profit change, provided $y_m^1 > y_m^0$. The expressions for the adjusted productivity effect in the final two equalities are equal.

In subsection 9.2.2 the quantity effect is the productivity effect, and so use of unit cost output weights converts the productivity effect in (9.5) to

$$p^{0T}\left(y^1 - y^0\right) - \tilde{w}^{0T}\left(x^1 - x^0\right) = \tilde{w}^{0T} x^1 \left[\left(Y_L / \tilde{X}_L\right) - 1\right]$$
$$= c^{0T} y^1 \left[1 - \left(Y_L^c / \tilde{X}_L\right)^{-1}\right]. \qquad (9.25)$$

The first equality is unaffected. In the second equality, unit costs replace product prices in the productivity index and in the value used to scale the productivity growth rate to create an adjusted productivity bonus.[13]

9.3.5. Exchange Rates

BHP Billiton publishes its consolidated financial statements in US dollars because the majority of its revenues are earned in US dollars, although its operating costs are incurred in the currencies of those countries where its operations are located. To ensure comparability of revenue and cost data, BHP Billiton converts its operating costs to US dollars, and this introduces a new element into the price effect: exchange rate variation.

Suppose, contrary to fact but to simplify the exposition, that all operating costs are incurred and denominated in Australian dollars. Then its input price vector expressed in USD is $w^{USD} = w^{AUD} \times E$, where $E = AUD / USD$ is the exchange rate that converts AUD to USD. Expressions (9.1) and (9.3) show that price change influences profit change, and that price change has two components. Expressing the price effect in USD converts expression (9.3) to

$$y^{1T}\left(p^1 - p^0\right) - x^{1T}\left(w^{USD1} - w^{USD0}\right) = p^{0T}y^1\left[\left(P_p / W_p^{USD}\right) - 1\right] + \pi^{USD1}\left[1 - \left(W_p^{USD}\right)^{-1}\right]$$
$$= w^{USD0T}x^1\left[1 - \left(P_p / W_p^{USD}\right)^{-1}\right] + \pi^{USD1}\left[1 - P_p^{-1}\right], \quad (9.26)$$

in which

$$W_p^{USD} = \frac{x^{1T}\left(w^{AUD1} \times E^1\right)}{x^{1T}\left(w^{AUD0} \times E^0\right)},$$

and

$$\pi^{USD1} = p^{1T}y^1 - w^{USD1T}x^1 = p^{1T}y^1 - \left(w^{AUD1} \times E^1\right)^T x^1.$$

Exchange rate movements influence both components of the price effect. They influence the price-recovery effect in both equalities in expression (9.26) through their impact on W_p^{USD}. They influence the inflation effect through their impact on π^{USD1} and, in the first expression only, through their impact on W_p^{USD}. Each influence on W_p^{USD} is of the form $(w^{AUD} \times E)$, and so exchange rate movements can reinforce or counter domestic input price changes.

9.3.6. Indirect (or Dual) Productivity Measurement

Under some circumstances, productivity can be measured indirectly, by tracking price changes rather than quantity changes. Siegel (1952) first proposed the idea, and Fourastié (1957, 196_, 196_) made extensive use of indirect productivity indices, noting that price trends reflect productivity trends, and since rates of productivity change vary across sectors of the economy, sectoral price trends also vary. Fourastié's idea continues to gain adherents (Aiyar and Dalgaard 2005; Jorgenson and Griliches 1967). A strong argument in support of indirect productivity measurement is that price changes can be measured more accurately than quantity changes, especially with reference to physical capital. Fernald and Neiman (2011) provide an analytical comparison of direct and indirect productivity measurement, with an empirical application that calls into question the conventional wisdom that the primary source of the East Asian growth miracle was factor accumulation rather than productivity growth.

In subsection 9.2.1, suppose that $\pi^1 = \pi^0 = 0$. In this case, $\pi^1 - \pi^0 = 0$ and the price effect is the negative of the quantity effect. In addition, the growth effect in (9.2) and the inflation effect in (9.3) are both zero, and so the price-recovery effect is the negative of the productivity effect. Thus

$$p^{0T}y^1\left[1-\left(P_P/W_P\right)\right]=w^{0T}x^1\left[\left(W_P/P_P\right)-1\right]=w^{0T}x^1\left[\left(Y_L/X_L\right)-1\right]=p^{0T}y^1\left[1-\left(Y_L/X_L\right)^{-1}\right]$$

provide equivalent measures of the productivity bonus. It follows from the second and third measures, or from the first and fourth, that $W_P/P_P = Y_L/X_L$. Thus if profit is zero in both periods, the reciprocal of the rate of price recovery equals the rate of productivity change. The argument generalizes beyond Laspeyres and Paasche indices to Fisher indices. The $\pi^1 = \pi^0 = 0$ assumption is sufficient for existence, but not necessary. A weak necessary condition is $\Pi^1 = \Pi^0 \gtreqless 1$.

In subsection 9.2.2, the price effect is the negative of the quantity effect, and since there is no growth effect and no inflation effect, the price-recovery effect is a dual productivity effect, based on $\tilde{w}$ rather than w, so that $\tilde{W}_P/P_P = Y_L/\tilde{X}_L$. The same duality holds in subsection 9.2.1 if $\pi^1 = \pi^0 = 0$, which is easily seen in expressions (9.2) and (9.3). In both cases, this duality result also extends to Fisher indices.

9.4. Decomposing Return on Assets Change

In section 9.1 we noted the possibility of analyzing return on assets (ROA) within a duPont triangle framework, and we wrote $\text{ROA} = \pi/A = \pi/R \times R/A$. While the analysis of profit change involves quantities and prices, the analysis of ROA change involves an additional variable, the producing unit's assets. It is clear that reducing A raises asset turnover R/A and thus ROA, and financial institutions around the world have done just this in the wake of the global financial crisis. BHP Billiton reports having divested assets "that no longer fit our strategy" worth several billion US dollars since 2013. Although asset shedding raises ROA, it does so directly, rather than through quantities or prices, and so we do not incorporate the rather obvious impact on ROA of changes in assets in our analysis.[14] Our analytical framework shows how productivity change and price-recovery change influence the profit margin π/R, and hence ROA π/A.

It is useful to express change in ROA as the product of change in profit margin and change in asset turnover as

$$\frac{\pi^1/A^1}{\pi^0/A^0} = \frac{\pi^1/R^1}{\pi^0/R^0} \times \frac{R^1/A^1}{R^0/A^0}. \tag{9.27}$$

Change in profit margin occurs because quantities change and because prices change, and it is useful to separate the two sources in two ways as

$$\frac{\pi^1/R^1}{\pi^0/R^0} = \frac{\pi^1/R^1}{\pi_0^1/R_0^1} \times \frac{\pi_0^1/R_0^1}{\pi^0/R^0}$$

$$= \frac{\pi_1^0/R_1^0}{\pi^0/R^0} \times \frac{\pi^1/R^1}{\pi_1^0/R_1^0}, \tag{9.28}$$

in which $R_0^1 = p^{0T}y^1$ and $\pi_0^1 = p^{0T}y^1 - w^{0T}x^1$ are comparison-period revenue and profit evaluated at base-period prices, and $R_1^0 = p^{1T}y^0$ and $\pi_1^0 = p^{1T}y^0 - w^{1T}x^0$ are base-period revenue and profit evaluated at comparison-period prices.

In the first term in the first equality comparison period, quantities appear in numerator and denominator, but comparison-period prices appear in the numerator and base-period prices appear in the denominator. This term therefore captures the contribution of price change to profit-margin change, and it can be rewritten as

$$\frac{\pi^1/R^1}{\pi_0^1/R_0^1} = \frac{\pi^1}{R^1 - \left(\dfrac{P_P}{W_P}\right)w^{1T}x^1}. \tag{9.29}$$

Expression (9.29), which shows the contribution of (P_P/W_P) to profit-margin change, and hence to ROA change, can be compared with expression (9.3), which shows the contribution of (P_P/W_P) to the price-recovery effect, and hence to profit change, and to expression (9.6), which shows the contribution of $(P_P/\tilde{W}_P)$ to the modified price-recovery effect.

In the second term in the first equality, the opposite is true; prices are fixed at base-period values and quantities change. This term therefore captures the contribution of quantity change to profit-margin change, and it can be rewritten as

$$\frac{\pi_0^1/R_0^1}{\pi^0/R^0} = \frac{\pi_0^1}{R_0^1 - \left(\dfrac{Y_L}{X_L}\right)w^{0T}x^1}. \tag{9.30}$$

Expression (9.30), which shows the contribution of (Y_L/X_L) to profit margin change, and hence to ROA change, can be compared with expression (9.2), which shows the contribution of (Y_L/X_L) to the productivity effect, and hence to profit change, and to expression (9.5), which shows the contribution of $(Y_L/\tilde{X}_L)$ to the modified productivity effect.

Substituting expressions (9.29) and (9.30) into the first equality in expression (9.28) and substituting again into expression (9.27) generates

$$\frac{\pi^1/A^1}{\pi^0/A^0} = \frac{\pi^1}{R^1 - \left(\dfrac{P_P}{W_P}\right)w^{1T}x^1} \times \frac{\pi_0^1}{R_0^1 - \left(\dfrac{Y_L}{X_L}\right)w^{0T}x^1} \times \frac{R^1/A^1}{R^0/A^0}, \tag{9.31}$$

which attributes change in ROA to a Paasche measure of the contribution of price-recovery change to profit-margin change, a Laspeyres measure of the contribution of productivity change to profit-margin change, and change in asset turnover.

Repeating the analysis using the second equality in expression (9.28) generates a similar decomposition of ROA change, and taking the geometric mean of the two yields

$$\frac{\pi^1/A^1}{\pi^0/A^0} = \left[\frac{\pi^1}{R^1 - \left(\dfrac{P_P}{W_P}\right)w^{1T}x^1} \times \frac{\pi_1^0}{R_1^0 - \left(\dfrac{P_L}{W_L}\right)w^{1T}x^0} \right]^{1/2}$$

$$\times \left[\frac{\pi_0^1}{R_0^1 - \left(\dfrac{Y_L}{X_L}\right)w^{0T}x^1} \times \frac{\pi^1}{R^1 - \left(\dfrac{Y_P}{X_P}\right)w^{1T}x^1} \right]^{1/2} \times \frac{R^1/A^1}{R^0/A^0},$$

(9.32)

which attributes change in ROA to a geometric mean of Paasche and Laspeyres measures of the contribution of price-recovery change to profit-margin change, a geometric mean of Laspeyres and Paasche measures of the contribution of productivity change to profit-margin change, and change in asset turnover. Improvements in price recovery and productivity, and asset shedding, all raise ROA.

Grifell-Tatjé and Lovell (2014) apply the productivity change decomposition in section 9.3 to the geometric mean productivity effect in expression (9.32). They also introduce change in the rate of capacity utilization as an additional driver of change in ROA. Both the economic drivers of productivity change and change in the rate of capacity utilization influence ROA change through their impact on profit-margin change.

9.5. Decomposing Unit Cost Change

We consider unit cost as a measure of financial performance, which we motivate by noting that BHP Billiton, already one of the lowest-cost producers of iron ore, expects to reduce its unit cost by a quarter from 2015 to 2018. It claims it can reach this target through productivity gains achieved by eliminating supply chain bottlenecks, and by expanding output by nearly 30 percent. We develop an analytical framework within which these claims can be tested.

The difficulty with unit cost is defining a "unit" of output. This is not a problem in a single-product firm, for which $UC = \sum_{n=1}^{N} w_n x_n / y = w^T x / y$ in which y is a scalar, but it presents a challenge otherwise. BHP Billiton defines unit cost for each commodity it extracts, and so $UC_m = \sum_{n=1}^{N} w_n x_{nm} / y_m$, $m = 1, \ldots, M$. This requires cost allocation, which is difficult. The alternative is to define unit cost for a multiproduct producer as

$UC = \sum_{n=1}^{N} w_n x_n / Y = w^T x / Y$, in which Y is a measure of aggregate output level such as real gross output or real value added. We follow the latter approach and define unit cost as $UC = w^T x / Y = w^T z$, with $z = x / Y$ a quantity vector of input–output ratios.[15]

9.5.1. Decomposing Unit-Cost Change by Economic Driver

We begin by decomposing unit-cost change into its economic drivers, with the help of a unit-cost frontier, which we define as $uc(y, w) = c(y, w) / Y$, where $c(y,w)$ is a cost frontier and Y is aggregate output. Since $uc(y,w)$ is the minimum unit cost required to produce output vector y at input prices w, $w^T z \geq uc(y, w)$. Use of a unit cost frontier leads to the decomposition

$$w^{1T} z^1 - w^{0T} z^0 = uc^1 \left(y^1, w^1 \right) - uc^1 \left(y^1, w^0 \right) \qquad \text{input price effect}$$
$$+ \left[w^{1T} z^1 - uc^1 \left(y^1, w^1 \right) \right] - \left[w^{0T} z^0 - uc^1 \left(y^1, w^0 \right) \right] \text{productivity effect.}$$
(9.33)

The input price effect and the productivity effect are illustrated in Figure 9.4, which depicts three unit cost frontiers, a base-period frontier $uc^0(y, w^0)$, a comparison-period frontier $uc^1(y, w^1)$ and a mixed-period frontier $uc^1(y, w^0)$. All are U-shaped, reflecting the existence of increasing and decreasing returns to scale; $uc^1(y, w^0)$ lies beneath $uc^0(y, w^0)$ on the assumption that technical progress has occurred from base period to comparison period; $uc^1(y, w^1)$ lies between the two on the assumption that the cost-reducing impact of technical progress outweighs the cost-increasing impact of input price growth. Unit cost in the two periods is $w^{1T} z^1 \geq uc^1 \left(y, w^1 \right)$ and $w^{0T} z^0 \geq uc^0 \left(y, w^0 \right)$.

In expression (9.33) and in Figure 9.4, the input price effect captures the increase in $uc^1(y^1, w)$ when w increases from w^0 to w^1, and the productivity effect measures the change in $w^T z$ not attributable to the input price increase. The productivity effect decomposes as

$$\left[w^{1T} z^1 - uc^1 \left(y^1, w^1 \right) \right] - \left[w^{0T} z^0 - uc^1 \left(y^1, w^0 \right) \right]$$
$$= \left[w^{1T} z^1 - uc^1 \left(y^1, w^1 \right) \right] - \left[w^{0T} z^0 - uc^0 \left(y^0, w^0 \right) \right] \quad \text{cost efficiency effect}$$
$$+ \left[uc^1 \left(y^0, w^0 \right) - uc^0 \left(y^0, w^0 \right) \right] \qquad \text{technical change effect}$$
$$+ \left[uc^1 \left(y^1, w^0 \right) - uc^1 \left(y^0, w^0 \right) \right] \qquad \text{size effect.}$$
(9.34)

Expression (9.34) attributes the cost-reducing impact of productivity growth to three drivers: change in cost efficiency, technical change, and size change. Change in cost efficiency compares the extent to which actual unit cost exceeds minimum feasible unit cost (for the output produced and input prices paid) in comparison and base periods. The technical change effect measures by how much the minimum unit-cost frontier shifts, downward in this case, holding outputs and input prices constant at their base period values. The size effect compares minimum unit cost at comparison-period and base-period outputs, holding technology fixed at comparison period level and holding input prices fixed at base-period values. In Figure 9.4, cost efficiency has deteriorated, technical progress has shifted the minimum unit-cost frontier downward, and the exploitation of economies of size through output growth has reduced minimum unit cost along $uc^1(y, w^0)$. It is clear from expressions (9.33) and (9.34) and Figure 9.4 that these three drivers fully account for actual unit cost change.

It is instructive to compare expression (9.34), Figure 9.4, and surrounding discussion with expression (9.12), Figure 9.3, and surrounding discussion. Both are input oriented. Both attribute productivity change to technical change and size change, although they do so differently. Both also attribute productivity change to efficiency change, although one measures the impact on cost of change in technical efficiency, while the other measures the impact on unit cost of change in cost efficiency, of which technical efficiency is one component. It is also worth reiterating that BHP Billiton aims for a 25 percent reduction in the unit cost of producing iron ore through a combination of productivity improvements, which shift $uc(y, w)$ down, and expansion, which is a movement down the declining portion of uc (y, w), both of which appear as drivers of unit-cost change in expression (9.34).

9.5.2. Decomposing Unit-Cost Change by Partial Productivities

The second unit-cost change decomposition we develop is structurally similar to the cost side of the profit-change decomposition in section 9.2, with two exceptions. We replace cost change with unit-cost change, which is achieved by replacing x with z, and

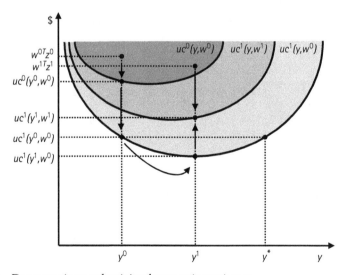

FIGURE 9.4. Decomposing productivity change using unit cost.

we disaggregate quantity and price effects into quantity and price effects for each input. This approach enables management to identify individual quantity and price changes most responsible for increases and decreases in unit cost.

Unit cost change can be written and decomposed as

$$
\begin{aligned}
w^{1T}z^1 - w^{0T}z^0 &= w^{0T}\left(z^1 - z^0\right) + z^{1T}\left(w^1 - w^0\right) \\
&= w^{0T}z^1\left(1 - Z_L^{-1}\right) + z^{1T}w^0\left(W_P - 1\right) \\
&= w^{0T}z^1\left(W_P - Z_L^{-1}\right).
\end{aligned}
\tag{9.35}
$$

The first equality states that unit-cost change has quantity-change and price-change components. The second and third equalities show that the quantity-change component is a Laspeyres input–output quantity effect, and the price-change component is a Paasche input-price effect. The input–output quantity index is $Z_L = w^{0T}z^1 / w^{0T}z^0 = (w^{0T}x^1 / w^{0T}x^0)/(Y^1 / Y^0) = X_L / Y_L$, and so $Z_L^{-1} = \left(Y^1/Y^0\right)\big/X_L = Y_L/X_L$ is a productivity index.[16] An increase in productivity $\left(Z_L^{-1} > 1\right)$ reduces unit cost, and an increase in input prices $(W_P > 1)$ raises unit cost.

Expressions (9.35) and (9.33) both decompose unit-cost change into *aggregate* productivity and price effects. Both aggregate effects in expression (9.35) decompose by variable, since the aggregate productivity effect

$$
w^{0T}\left(z^1 - z^0\right) = \Sigma\, w_n^0\left[\left(x_n^1 / Y^1\right) - \left(x_n^0 / Y^0\right)\right] = \Sigma\, w_n^0 z_n^1\left[\left(1 - \left(z_n^0 / z_n^1\right)\right)\right],
\tag{9.36}
$$

with N *partial* productivity change terms $z_n^0 / z_n^1 = \left(Y^1 / Y^0\right)/\left(x_n^1 / x_n^0\right) = \left(Y^1 / x_n^1\right)/\left(Y^0 / x_n^0\right)$, $n = 1, \ldots, N$, with weights $w_n^0 z_n^1 = w_n^0 x_n^1 / Y^1$ that measure comparison-period unit input costs valued at base-period input prices, and the aggregate price effect

$$
z^{1T}\left(w^1 - w^0\right) = \Sigma\left(x_n^1 / Y^1\right)\left[w^1 - w^0\right] = \Sigma\, w_n^0 z_n^1\left[\left(w_n^1 / w_n^0\right) - 1\right],
\tag{9.37}
$$

with N *partial* input price effects w_n^1/w_n^0, $n = 1, \ldots, N$, with the same weights.

Interest naturally centers on the labor input, for three reasons. In most if not all economies, and in most sectors, labor has a larger cost share than any other input, frequently larger than all other inputs combined. This makes unit labor cost an important determinant of unit cost and hence economic competitiveness, both among firms and among nations. And the labor input is easier to measure than most other inputs.[17] Labor's partial productivity change is, in reciprocal form,

$$
\begin{aligned}
w_\ell^0\left[\left(\ell^1 / Y^1\right) - \left(\ell^0 / Y^0\right)\right] &= \left(S_{\ell 0}^1 \times UC_0^1\right) \times \left\{1 - \left[\left(Y^1 / \ell^1\right)/\left(Y^0 / \ell^0\right)\right]\right\} \\
&= U\ell C_0^1 \times \left\{1 - \left[\left(Y^1 / \ell^1\right)/\left(Y^0 / \ell^0\right)\right]\right\},
\end{aligned}
\tag{9.38}
$$

in which ℓ indicates labor, $S_{\ell 0}^1 = w_\ell^0 \ell^1 / w^{0T}x^1$ is labor's comparison-period cost share valued at base-period input prices, $UC_0^1 = w^{0T}x^1/Y^1$ is comparison-period unit cost valued at base-period input prices, and $U\ell C_0^1 = w_\ell^0 \ell^1/Y^1$ is comparison-period unit labor cost valued at labor's base-period unit price. Thus the cost impact of a change in labor's partial productivity depends on the extent of the change and on comparison-period unit labor cost valued at labor's base-period unit price.

Labor's partial price change is

$$
\begin{aligned}
\left(\ell^1 / Y^1\right)\left[w_\ell^1 - w_\ell^0\right] &= \left(S_{\ell 0}^1 \times UC_0^1\right)\times\left[\left(w_\ell^1 / w_\ell^0\right)-1\right]\\
&= U\ell C_0^1 \times\left[\left(w_\ell^1 / w_\ell^0\right)-1\right],
\end{aligned}
\tag{9.39}
$$

and so the cost impact of a change in labor's unit price depends on the extent of the change and on the comparison-period unit labor cost valued at labor's base-period unit price.

Combining expressions (9.38) and (9.39) gives labor's net contribution to unit cost change

$$
\begin{aligned}
w_\ell^0\left[\left(\ell^1 / Y^1\right)-\left(\ell^0 / Y^0\right)\right]&+\left(\ell^1 / Y^1\right)\left(w_\ell^1 - w_\ell^0\right)\\
&= \left(S_{\ell 0}^1 \times UC_0^1\right)\times\left\{\left(w_\ell^1 / w_\ell^0\right)-\left[\left(Y^1 / \ell^1\right)/\left(Y^0 / \ell^0\right)\right]\right\}\\
&= U\ell C_0^1 \times\left\{\left(w_\ell^1 / w_\ell^0\right)-\left[\left(Y^1 / \ell^1\right)/\left(Y^0 / \ell^0\right)\right]\right\}.
\end{aligned}
\tag{9.40}
$$

Thus unit labor cost acts as a multiplier, scaling the difference between labor's wage change and its partial productivity change. Labor's net impact on unit cost change is positive, zero, or negative, according as $\left(w_\ell^1 / w_\ell^0\right) \gtrless \left(Y^1 / \ell^1\right)\big/\left(Y^0 / \ell^0\right)$.

9.6. SUMMARY AND NEW DIRECTIONS

At the outset we noted that BHP Billiton management understands that changes in its financial performance, however measured, are driven by quantity changes, price changes, and changes in external factors such as exchange rates. It also understands that it has no control over commodity prices or exchange rates, both of which have been extremely volatile since 2006.[18] In such an operating environment it explicitly recognizes that "controlling our operating costs is a key driver of our results," and its management strategy has therefore focused on improving financial performance through cost-reducing productivity growth.

We have examined the relationship between productivity change and three popular financial performance indicators—profit, return on assets, and unit cost—each of which plays a prominent role in BHP Billiton *Annual Reports*. In order to focus on productivity change, in each case we have had to separate the financial impacts of quantity change from those of price change, and then identify the financial impact of productivity change as a component of the financial impact of quantity change.

With two exceptions, the approach we have taken has been entirely empirical, based on price-dependent quantity indices and quantity-dependent price indices. These indices can be calculated from price and quantity information readily available from company reports (as we have demonstrated with BHP Billiton), trade associations, regulatory bodies, and government statistical agencies. The two exceptions involve identifying, and ultimately quantifying, the economic drivers of productivity change, an exercise that requires the assistance of economic theory. Thus productivity change decomposition (9.13) is based on production frontiers, and these frontiers are not contained in any database and must be estimated. Productivity change decomposition (9.34) is based on unit-cost frontiers, which also must be estimated. With these two exceptions, the analysis in this chapter is based exclusively on quantity and price data, and so requires no estimation.

There is an alternative approach, grounded in economic theory and based on best-practice frontiers, production, cost, revenue, profit, and profitability. The choice between production and value frontiers typically depends on the availability of relevant price information. The choice among value frontiers is usually governed by the perceived objective of the production units. In some cases, the business strategy is clear ("Every Day Low Prices" at Walmart, for example). In other cases, the business orientation is constrained by the nature of the operating environment or by a regulatory body; when product prices are exogenous, attention naturally focuses on cost control.

This alternative approach exploits theoretical quantity and productivity indices inspired by and named after Malmquist (1953), and theoretical price and price-recovery indices inspired by and named after Konüs (1939). The cost change decomposition in expressions (9.33) and (9.34) is based on Konüs indices. Diewert (2014b) and Grifell-Tatjé and Lovell (2015, 2016) combine theoretical Konüs indices with empirical Fisher indices to decompose profitability change, a size-independent alternative to profit change as a financial performance indicator.

Both approaches provide valuable information to management concerning how well the firm's business strategy is working, and on the sources of the strengths and weaknesses of the business strategy. As we noted in the introduction to this chapter, BHP Billiton has used EBIT to assess its performance and to allocate resources. The decompositions developed in this chapter can identify the sources of variation in EBIT or other financial performance indicators, both through time and across segments of the business.[19]

Much work remains to be done. As the title of this chapter suggests, our objective has been to develop analytical frameworks within which the contribution of productivity change to change in financial performance can be identified. A logical sequel is to decompose the contribution of productivity change into those of its economic drivers. We achieved this objective in expressions (9.13) and (9.34). The value of these decompositions is that they shed light on the sources of productivity change. We have paid somewhat less attention to the contribution of price-recovery change to change in financial performance, and no attention to the possible sources of price-recovery change. This is a glaring omission in the case of BHP Billiton, whose product prices and exchange rates have been so volatile. Businesses, governments, competition commissions, and regulatory agencies are keenly interested in what is also known as cost recovery, the ratio of (or the difference between) product prices and input prices, and this interest may motivate another logical sequel, a decomposition of the contribution of price-recovery change into those of its drivers.

Notes

1. Grifell-Tatjé thanks the Spanish Ministry of Science and Technology (ECO2013-46954-C3-2-R) for financial support, and Lovell thanks the University of Queensland School of Economics for financial support.
2. The 2016 Annual Report and supporting documents are available at http://www.bhpbilliton.com/investor-centre/annual-reporting-2016. Accessed March 6, 2017.
3. Kendrick (1984) has productivity and price recovery as the two ingredients of a business performance measurement system that he attributes to van Loggerenberg and Cucchiaro (1981–1982).
4. Davis (1955, 68) interprets profit as ". . . the input of risk-taking combined with the foregoing of alternative uses of the funds invested in the company's operations."
5. BHP Billiton's CEO Andrew MacKenzie, referring to unit cost, cost per tonne of iron ore, at http://www.abc.net.au/news/2015-04-22/bhp-billiton-continues-to-lift-output-cut-costs/6411594. Accessed March 7, 2017.
6. Grifell-Tatjé and Lovell (2015) provide a comprehensive survey and extension of the literature on productivity and financial performance.
7. Färe and Primont (1995) provide details on distance functions and value (cost and revenue) functions.
8. The return to capital goes by a number of names, including "investor input" (Davis 1955), "operating surplus" (OECD, http://stats.oecd.org/glossary/detail.asp?ID=1912), and "EBIT." Whatever its name, it is a return, positive or negative, to those who provide capital to the business. The rate of return is endogenous because it emerges from an accounting convention that requires $rK = \pi$, which equates the value of output with the value of input. Schreyer (2010) and Diewert (2014a) have examined productivity measurement with alternative exogenous rates of return that do not force equality; see also Balk's Chapter 2 in this volume.
9. An improvement in a firm's price recovery raises its profit. In an international trade context, the analogous concept is called the terms of trade, the ratio of an export-price index to an import-price index, and an improvement in a country's terms of trade raises its real income. Diewert and Morrison (1986) provide analytical details.
10. The inflation effect is a microeconomic counterpart to the rate of inflation in an economy, and "a little inflation is good for business" is a microeconomic counterpart to the belief in an optimal rate of inflation in an economy. Schmitt-Grohé and Uribe (2010) provide a good introduction to the huge literature on the optimal rate of inflation.
11. Ideally K_0^1 would measure a flow of capital services, but frequently it is a measure of book value. OECD (2001) has a good discussion of the measurement of capital services.

12. In principle the *functional* distribution of created value in (9.15) can be related to the *size* distribution of income, which exhibits increasing inequality in most developed countries. In practice this would seem to require disaggregation of the price vectors p and w and the scalar π, and the development of an analytical framework. Glyn (2011) asserts a linkage between the two types of distribution, but without an analytical framework or empirical evidence.

13. The System of National Accounts (Eurostat, 1993) recommends the use of unit cost output valuations in the public sector when prices are missing. Diewert (2012) discusses productivity measurement when output prices are missing, and notes that our output-quantity index Y_L^C is used in the United Kingdom. Diewert extends his (2012) work in Chapter 7 of this volume. A prominent example of missing prices concerns productivity measurement in the presence of undesirable outputs such as pollutants. Førsund analyzes this situation in Chapter 8 of this volume.

14. This assumes independence of A from x. BHP Billiton's assets include just one component, plant and equipment, that incurs depreciation and amortization expense, and so might be considered an input.

15. The term "level" is due to Eichhorn and Voeller (1976), who define a price level as a strictly increasing linearly homogeneous function $\rho\,(p)$ of a price vector p, and a price index as a function $P\left(p, p^0\right) = \rho(p)\big/\rho\left(p^0\right)$.

16. $\left(Y^1/Y^0\right) = Y_L$ assumes, following Eichhorn and Voeller (1976), that $Y^1 = p^{0T}y^1$ and $Y^0 = p^{0T}y^0$.

17. The OECD (https://stats.oecd.org/glossary/detail.asp?ID=2809) treats unit labor cost as "a reflection of cost competitiveness," and tracks unit labor cost in a variety of sectors across its member countries (http://stats.oecd.org/Index.aspx?DataSetCode=PDBI_I4#).

18. The nominal price per dry metric ton of iron ore has fluctuated widely, from USD 33 in late 2006 to a peak of USD 187 in early 2011 and a trough of USD 41 in late 2015 before recovering to USD 81 in early 2017. http://www.indexmundi.com/commodities/?commodity=iron-ore&months=120. Accessed March 3, 2017. The prices of BHP Billiton's other export products have behaved similarly. The exchange rate (AUD/USD) has exhibited similar volatility, ranging from 0.75 in 2006 to a high of 1.10 in 2011 and back down to 0.76 in early 2017.

19. After many years of using EBIT as its preferred financial performance indicator, in its 2016 *Annual Report* it prefers EBITDA (EBIT plus depreciation and amortization) because it is "... more relevant to capital-intensive industries with long-life assets."

References

Aiyar, S., and C.-J. Dalgaard. 2005. "Total Factor Productivity Revisited: A Dual Approach to Development Accounting." *IMF Staff Papers* 52: 82–102.

Arocena, P., L. Blázquez, and E. Grifell-Tatjé. 2011. "Assessing the Consequences of Industry Restructuring on Firms' Performance." *Journal of Economic Policy Reform* 14: 21–39.

Bennet, T. L. 1920. "The Theory of Measurement of Changes in Cost of Living." *Journal of the Royal Statistical Society* 83: 455–462.

Bliss, J. H. 1923. *Financial and Operating Ratios in Management*. New York: The Ronald Press.

Bloom, N., R. Lemos, R. Sadun, D. Scur, and J. Van Reenen. 2014. "The New Empirical Economics of Management." *Journal of the European Economic Association* 12: 835–876.

Bloom, N., and J. Van Reenen. 2007. "Measuring and Explaining Management Practices across Firms and Countries." *Quarterly Journal of Economics* 122: 1351–1408.

Bloom, N., and J. Van Reenen. 2010. "Why Do Management Practices Differ across Firms and Countries?" *Journal of Economic Perspectives* 24: 203–224.

Borenstein, S., and J. Farrell. 2000. "Is Cost-Cutting Evidence of X-Inefficiency?" *American Economic Review* 90: 224–27.

Boussemart, J.-P., J.-P. Butault, and O. Ojo. 2012. "Generation and Distribution of Productivity Gains in French Agriculture: Who Are the Winners and the Losers over the Last Fifty Years?" *Bulletin UASVM Horticulture* 69: 55–67.

Brea-Solís, H., R. Casadesus-Masanell, and E. Grifell-Tatjé. 2015. "Business Model Evaluation: Quantifying Walmart's Sources of Advantage." *Strategic Entrepreneurship Journal* 9: 12–33.

CERC (Centre d'Études des Revenus et des Coûts). 1969. "Surplus de productivité globale' et 'Comptes de surplus.'" Documents du Centre d'Études des Revenus et des Coûts, no. 1, 1er trimestre. Paris: CERC.

Courbis, R., and P. Templé. 1975. *La méthode des 'Comptes de surplus' et ses applications macroéconomiques*. Collections de INSEE 160, Série C. 35: 1–100.

Davis, H. S. 1955. *Productivity Accounting*. Philadelphia: University of Pennsylvania Press.

De Witte, K., and D. S. Saal. 2010. "Is a Little Sunshine All We Need? On the Impact of Sunshine Regulation on Profits, Productivity and Prices in the Dutch Drinking Water Sector." *Journal of Regulatory Economics* 37: 219–242.

Diewert, W. E. 2012. "The Measurement of Productivity in the Nonmarket Sector." *Journal of Productivity Analysis* 37: 217–229.

Diewert, W. E. 2014a. "The Treatment of Financial Transactions in the SNA: A User Cost Approach." *Eurona* 1: 73–89.

Diewert, W. E. 2014b. "Decompositions of Profitability Change Using Cost Functions." *Journal of Econometrics* 183: 58–66.

Diewert, W. E., and C. J. Morrison. 1986. "Adjusting Output and Productivity Indexes for Changes in the Terms of Trade." *Economic Journal* 96: 659–679.

Eichhorn, W., and J. Voeller. 1976. *Theory of the Price Index*. Lecture Notes in Economics and Mathematical Systems 140. Berlin: Springer-Verlag.

Eldor, D., and E. Sudit. 1981. "Productivity-Based Financial Net Income Analysis." *Omega* 9: 605–611.

Estache, A., and E. Grifell-Tatjé. 2013. "How (Un)even Was the Distribution of the Impacts of Mali's Water Privatization across Stakeholders?" *Journal of Development Studies* 49: 483–499.

Eurostat. 1993. *System of National Accounts 1993*. New York: United Nations. http://unstats.un.org/unsd/nationalaccount/docs/1993sna.pdf.

Färe, R., and D. Primont. 1995. *Multi-Output Production and Duality: Theory and Applications*. Boston: Kluwer Academic.

Fernald, J., and B. Neiman. 2011. "Growth Accounting with Misallocation: Or, Doing Less with More in Singapore." *American Economic Journal: Macroeconomics* 3: 29–74.

Fourastié, J. 1957. *Productivity, Prices and Wages*. Paris: European Productivity Agency.

Fourastié, J. 196_. *Documents pour l'histoire et la théorie des prix*, Tome I. Centre d'Études Économiques, Recherches sur l'Évolution des Prix en Période de Progrés Technique. Paris: Librairie Armand Colin.

Fourastié, J. 196_. *Documents pour l'histoire et la théorie des prix*, Tome II. Centre d'Études Économiques, Recherches sur l'Évolution des Prix en Période de Progrés Technique. Paris: Librairie Armand Colin.

Garcia-Castro, R., and R. V. Aguilera. 2015. "Incremental Value Creation and Appropriation in a World with Multiple Stakeholders." *Strategic Management Journal* 36: 137–147.

Glyn, A. 2011. "Functional Distribution and Inequality." In *The Oxford Handbook of Economic Inequality*, edited by B. Nolan, W. Salverda and T. M. Smeeding, Chapter 5, 101–126. New York: Oxford University Press.

Gold, B. 1971. *Explorations in Managerial Economics: Productivity, Costs, Technology and Growth.* New York: Basic Books.

Grifell-Tatjé, E., and C. A. K. Lovell. 1999. "Profits and Productivity." *Management Science* 45: 1177–1193.

Grifell-Tatjé, E., and C. A. K. Lovell. 2008. "Productivity at the Post: Its Drivers and Distribution." *Journal of Regulatory Economics* 33: 133–158.

Grifell-Tatjé, E., and C. A. K. Lovell. 2013. "Advances in Cost Frontier Analysis of the Firm." In *The Oxford Handbook of Managerial Economics*, edited by C. R. Thomas and W. F. Shughart II, Chapter 4, 66–88. New York: Oxford University Press.

Grifell-Tatjé, E., and C. A. K. Lovell. 2014. "Productivity, Price Recovery, Capacity Constraints and Their Financial Consequences." *Journal of Productivity Analysis* 41: 3–17.

Grifell-Tatjé, E., and C. A. K. Lovell. 2015. *Productivity Accounting: The Economics of Business Performance.* New York: Cambridge University Press.

Grifell-Tatjé, E., and C. A. K. Lovell. 2016. "Exact Relationships between Fisher Indexes and Theoretical Indexes." In *Advances in Efficiency and Productivity*, edited by J. Aparicio, C. A. K. Lovell, and J. T. Pastor, Chapter 5, 97–120. Springer International Series in Operations Research and Management Science, Volume 249. Berlin: Springer.

Houéry, N. 1977. *Mesurer la productivité: Les comptes de surplus.* Paris: Dunod.

Johnson, H. T. 1975. "Management Accounting in an Early Integrated Industrial: E. I. duPont de Nemours Powder Company, 1903–1912." *Business History Review* 49: 184–204.

International Monetary Fund. n.d. "IMF's Work on Income Inequality." http://www.imf.org/external/np/fad/inequality/index.htm

Jorgenson, D. W., and Z. Griliches. 1967. "The Explanation of Productivity Change." *Review of Economic Studies* 34: 249–283.

Kendrick, J. W. 1961. *Productivity Trends in the United States.* Princeton, NJ: Princeton University Press.

Kendrick, J. W. 1984. *Improving Company Productivity: Handbook with Case Studies.* Baltimore, MD: Johns Hopkins University Press.

Kendrick, J. W., and D. Creamer. 1961. *Measuring Company Productivity: Handbook with Case Studies.* Studies in Business Economics 74. New York: The Conference Board.

Kendrick, J. W., and R. Sato. 1963. "Factor Prices, Productivity, and Economic Growth." *American Economic Review* 53: 974–1003.

Kline, C. A., Jr., and H. L. Hessler. 1952. "The du Pont Chart System for Appraising Operating Performance." *N. A. C. A. Bulletin* (August), Section 3: 1595–1619.

Konüs, A. A. 1939. "The Problem of the True Index of the Cost of Living."*Econometrica* 7: 10–29.

Malmquist, S. 1953. "Index Numbers and Indifference Surfaces." *Trabajos de Estadistica* 4: 209–242.

Miller, D. M. 1984. "Profitability = Productivity + Price Recovery." *Harvard Business Review* 62: 145–153.

OECD. 2001. "Measuring Productivity: Measurement of Aggregate and Industry-Level Productivity Growth." http://www.oecd.org/std/productivity-stats/2352458.pdf.

OECD. 2014. "All On Board: Making Inclusive Growth Happen." http://www.oecd.org/inclusive-growth/All-on-Board-Making-Inclusive-Growth-Happen.pdf

Schmitt-Grohé, S., and M. Uribe. 2010. "The Optimal Rate of Inflation." In *Handbook of Monetary Economics*, edited by B. M. Friedman and M. Woodford, Vol. 3, Chapter 13, 653–722. Amsterdam: Elsevier.

Schreyer, P. 2010. "Measuring Multi-Factor Productivity When Rates of Return Are Exogenous." In *Price and Productivity Measurement*, Vol. 6: *Index Number Theory*, edited by W. E. Diewert, B. M. Balk, D. Fixler, K. J. Fox, and A. O. Nakamura, Chapter 2, 13–40. Bloomington, IN: Trafford Press.

Siegel, I. H. 1952. *Concepts and Measurement of Production and Productivity.* Washington, DC: US Bureau of Labor Statistics.

van Loggerenberg, B. J., and S. J. Cucchiaro. 1981–1982. "Productivity Measurement and the Bottom Line." *National Productivity Review* (Winter): 87–99.

Vincent, A. L. A. 1968. *La mesure de la productivité.* Paris: Dunod.

Winter, S. G., and G. Szulanski. 2001. "Replication as Strategy." *Organization Science* 12: 730–743.

CHAPTER 10

BUSINESS MODEL INNOVATION AND REPLICATION

Implications for the Measurement of Productivity

ROBERTO GARCIA-CASTRO, JOAN ENRIC RICART,
MARVIN B. LIEBERMAN, AND
NATARAJAN BALASUBRAMANIAN

10.1. INTRODUCTION

VALUE is created by the different players in the game.[1,2] In the most basic setup, buyers, firms, and suppliers are needed. The total value created by the interaction of a buyer, a firm, and a supplier is distributed among these different players, depending on the opportunity cost of the suppliers (SOC) and the willingness to pay of the buyers (WTP), and the relative bargaining power and ability of the players. Total value created by a transaction is the difference between this willingness to pay and opportunity costs. Competition among different buyers, firms, and suppliers determines the bounds of the value captured by each of these different players (Brandenburger and Stuart 1996; MacDonald and Ryall 2004).

A change in strategy results in a change in the value created among these players and affects the distribution of value between them. As we illustrate in this chapter, the methodology of the productivity literature allows us to break down the change in value captured and allocate it to the different players in the game based on changes in their value-creation and value-capture potential. Over time these distributions are affected by the interactions between the players and changes in the market.

In a nutshell, our approach builds on the fact that in the absence of substantial changes in willingness to pay and opportunity costs, most of the *variations* in value creation over a period are driven by productivity changes (Chen, Delmas, and Lieberman 2015; Lieberman et al. 2018; Lieberman et al. 2017).[3] It is thus possible to use productivity changes to provide some (quantitative) answers to the fundamental strategy question of how value is created and distributed in a firm. Related to our work, Grifell-Tatjé and Lovell in Chapter 9 of this *Handbook* also rely on a "productivity accounting" model to study value creation at the firm level.

10.2. STRATEGY, BUSINESS MODELS, AND PERFORMANCE

The objective of a firm's strategy is to create a sustainable competitive advantage through the development of a distinctive business model. The outcome of this strategy is reflected in the firm's enterprise value. Three different levers affect enterprise value: the profit margin, the resource utilization, and the growth of the business. The business model will directly affect the margin and resource utilization of the business. A successful business model with a higher return on invested capital will then translate into growth by the firm through replication of the business model.

The development of a new business model radically changes the value creation and value capture potential of the different players in the game and, hence, the distribution of value among the players. For example, when Southwest Airlines introduced the low-cost no-frills airline model, the value captured by Southwest was very different compared with the traditional full-service carriers. Southwest grew by improving and replicating its model. Over time, the full-service carriers responded, by imitating some parts of Southwest business model while adjusting their own. As a result, the value captured by Southwest was affected. Southwest's low-cost model initially benefited its customers. However, as the new business model matured, employees started to capture more value to the detriment of customers and other stakeholders—in the following, we provide quantitative estimates supporting these qualitative observations.

Business models capture the logic of the firm, the way it operates, and how it creates value for its stakeholders (Baden-Fuller, Demil, Lecoq, and MacMillan 2010; Casadesus-Masanell and Ricart 2010). This definition is general enough to be used in different business contexts and emphasizes the role of business models as "theories" of how a firm creates value for *all* its stakeholders, not just how value is captured by the focal firm (Zott and Amit 2013).

The business model concept is nothing new. Any business, in its inception, has to design business models to exploit the opportunities identified in the environment. Consequently, the history of the business world is full of inventions and innovations in business models. While it is an "old" concept, the business model concept is fashionable today, and probably for good reasons. One of these reasons is a definite acceleration in the presence of new business models or different ways to compete (create and capture value) popping up in many different fields. Today we are witnessing an increasing variety of simultaneous competition with different business models in multiple sectors. There is more room for innovation, and even more important, the relevant competition relies less on imitation and more on replacement (or, stated otherwise, in the use of disparate business models to address the same customer needs).

Behind this increasing variability there are obviously important changes in our competitive environment—changes that probably occur more rapidly than in the past. Without attempting to be exhaustive, it may be worth our time to consider some drivers of change. First, there are significant technological changes, and many but not all of them are associated with the Internet. A second type of change that we highlight is demographic, opening new opportunities or revealing areas that previously were harder to cover and can now be taken care of (perhaps, again, thanks to technology). A third change force is regulation—or deregulation—or the role of governments in many sectors. We can talk about globalization as the fourth change for many industries. In short, the convergence of all these factors—and probably other unidentified factors—entail a tremendous innovation potential in business models.

If the business model becomes the twenty-first century's competitive weapon, it will be important to be clear about what it is and to have an operational way of thinking about it, what we normally call "business model representation." Probably the most established business model representation is the "value chain" concept introduced by Michael Porter in 1985 in his book on competitive advantage (Porter 1985). Porter realized that companies should design their value chain idiosyncratically to gain differential positioning and thus competitive advantage. From this moment, the value chain went from being extremely useful to becoming a ball and chain, and variations on this theme began to emerge. Even Porter decided to replace the value chain concept with the activity system to make his concept more flexible (Porter 1996). Despite its many offshoots, the field of strategy converges toward the consensus that the value chain and its variations must give way to a broader, more systemic concept such as the business model.

Perhaps the most famous business model representation is Osterwalder's "Canvas" (Osterwalder and Pigneur 2010). He defines business models based on nine key components organized similarly to the value chain: value proposition, customer segments, customer relationships, channels, key activities, key resources, key partners, cost structures, and revenue streams. The various elements of the Canvas are not independent. Besides being interconnected, their representation in the figure aims to show the view of the whole, or system, that goes beyond mere description of its parts.

Amit and Zott (2001) propose a definition derived from the study of multiple online business models and that, therefore, has a clearly transactional orientation, but is also a useful tool for entrepreneurs. In its generalization, presented in the referenced article, the authors start with the activity system as the central focus of activities and add two important aspects for reflection for the design of the system's basic parameters. First, three design elements of the activity system are established: (1) the content, which identifies what activities should be carried out; (2) the structure, which determines how activities are connected and their relative importance; and (3) the ownership, which identifies who must perform each activity. Second, they identify four design themes or coherent settings for activity systems, summarized in the acronym NICE: novelty, for novel systems; lock-in, designed to capture third parties; complementarities, for those exploiting the complementarities between these activities; and efficiency, for those emphasizing transaction cost reduction. The set of tools developed by these authors is tremendously useful for discussing business models, especially in the context of the Internet (where transaction is the core element) and in the initial stages of the entrepreneurial process.

Teece (2010, 172) considers the business model as a company's "conceptual model"—as opposed to its financial model. According to him,

> A business model articulates the logic, the data, and other evidence that support a value proposition for the customer, and a viable structure of revenues and costs for the enterprise delivering that value. In short, it's about the benefit the enterprise will deliver to customers, how it will organize to do so, and how it will capture a portion of the value that it delivers.

Teece (2009) considers the business model to be a generic visualization that the competitive strategy should then spell out. According to him, there are three fundamental dynamic capabilities for a company: sensing, or the detection of opportunities; seizing, or the exploitation of such opportunities, and managing threats/transforming, or the continuous reinvention and adjustment of business. The business model is one of the fundamental elements of the seizing capacity, since it determines how the company wants to capture this business opportunity. Teece's vision of the business model strays slightly from previous representations by failing to identify its key elements, but emphasizes a key feature—design—which stems from the company or model owner.

We could continue to present alternative ways of understanding, conceptualizing, and representing the business model, but the ones outlined here are some of the best known in a literature where each author tries to give his or her own personal outlook. Overall, we would like to emphasize three ideas. First, the business model is something that a company designs. Second, the business model therefore has a high entrepreneurial component, since we are designing how we create and capture value, the essence of the entrepreneurial process. Third, the system of activities, perhaps supplemented by the design elements and themes, or "modernization" in the nine elements of the Canvas representation, is a very useful tool when it comes to identifying key aspects of the entrepreneurial design.

These representations are useful but have two main drawbacks. On the one hand, they are very static descriptions of reality. Obviously, it is the analyst's responsibility to use them properly. One or another instrument describes the model's features at a given time, whether based on activities or more processes, such as Canvas. They also describe the business model looking only at its interactions. The approach focuses on the model features and its internal consistency, but with little or no reference to the fundamental interactions.

These two features, dynamism and interactivity, led Casadesus-Masanell and Ricart (2011) to develop an alternative conception of the business model. They define a business model as "the set of choices a company makes and their consequences." The strategy defines choices (which may be political), assets (physical, where we invest), and governance structures for these policies and assets. But every choice has consequences, and these, in turn, can be classified as flexible or rigid, depending on their persistence when the effect causing them is no longer in place. The interesting thing is that choices and their aftermath create a certain dynamism and ultimately end up closing the loop: choices generate consequences, and these support the choices themselves (so that the cycle is closed). These cycles can be beneficial (which we call "virtuous") or harmful (which we describe as "vicious").

The representation of this model has two additional advantages that are worth highlighting. First, it connects perfectly with the strategy, which is to choose. Strategy is a contingent plan of choices that determine the future we want to create for this business. These choices and their impact, dynamics, and collective history make up the business model. This is the portrayal of the strategy at a given time. Or, stated differently, strategy is really the contingent and dynamic choice of the company's business model (or business unit).

Second, this representation of business models allows incorporating into the analysis the interaction with relevant participants that may affect the creation and capture of value. This can be done properly, since the interdependence between business models involves sharing consequences or the choice of one affecting the consequences of the other, and vice versa. Thus, the representation itself allows taking into account others' choices and consequences, or virtuous cycles that reinforce or contradict each other, providing a language that supports not only the business model dynamics, but also its dynamic interaction with other interdependent models.

In fact, this interaction analysis highlights a fundamental aspect of business model design: the interdependence with other models is endogenous, that is, part of the business model design is not independent. This endogeneity is a key variable in the design of a business model.

10.3. BUSINESS MODEL INNOVATION

In their attempt to link business models to value creation and appropriation, scholars generally distinguish between *innovation* and *replication* activities.

Business model renewal or *innovation* implies some redesign of the essential activities that constitute the firm's business model (Amit and Zott 2012; Casadesus-Masanell and Zhu 2013; Gambardella and McGahan 2010). By contrast, business model *replication* entails transplanting a successful model to other market segments, geographical locations, or the re-creation of a successful business model over time (Bowman and Ambrosini 2003; Jonsson and Foss 2011; Winter and Szulanski 2001). Sometimes this phenomenon is referred as the "McDonald's approach." Throughout this chapter we will refer to business model renewal or innovation simply as *innovation* activities, and to business model replication as *replication* activities.

Strategic management scholars have extensively characterized the different activities leading to business model innovation and replication—how value is created and captured, how knowledge is generated and transferred, the different mix of exploration and exploitation activities in firms, and so forth. However, the implications of replication and innovation activities for performance and value creation are less well understood. We elaborate on these implications in this chapter.

The essence of strategy is the trade-offs involved in the choices made on where we want to play and how we are going to win. As a result, there is an important difference between operating efficiency and strategy (Porter 1996). Operating efficiency calls for improving what we are doing and learning best practices, and therefore it is reflected very quickly in productivity measures. We do more with less and increase productivity.

As strategy represents trade-offs, not best practices, it is much harder to link strategy to productivity. In fact, strategy helps to defeat competing offerings because we create more value for at least some customers and we are able to appropriate part of it. In most cases, we are able to do so because we make choices different from those made by competitors, and the differential choices create trade-offs so that competitors cannot easily imitate them. That means that choices are not better in any direct way, but rather that they are different. Therefore, how can we link competitive advantage (based on trade-off choices to beat competition) with productivity and firm financial performance?

Let's start by focusing on a strategic change (or a new entrepreneurial activity). If we select a strategy that defeats competing offerings, it means that we are creating more value than these competing offerings for at least some customers. Following this line, it means either greater value created for a customer (measured by willingness to pay) at an opportunity cost that is not much higher, and therefore we create more value for some given input; or otherwise we provide similar value (willingness to pay) at a lower opportunity cost, again creating more value for the same inputs. In both cases, we increase performance relative to competing offerings. However, when we do so, this is associated with a strategy *change*.

Once we have fully implemented our strategy, if we are successful at sustaining this competitive advantage and keep creating the same value for customers at the same cost, we can increase enterprise value through growth, but we are not improving the productivity and relative financial performance of the offering any more. We can, of course, improve relative financial performance and productivity by running these activities more efficiently. We can improve productivity also by gaining greater volume or operating at a higher scale. But disruptive gains in financial performance and productivity are associated mostly with strategy change.

These considerations can be better understood by using the business model construct. The business model depicts the logic of the firm, the way the firm creates and captures value for its stakeholders. Casadesus-Masanell and Ricart (2010) define the business model as the set of managerial choices and their consequences. Defined in this way, the business model is the reflection of realized strategy. Whenever we "change" the business model (and therefore the realized strategy), we will say that there is a business model innovation.

Such innovation can be of two types—increasing willingness to pay or decreasing opportunity cost (or a combination). In both cases, we increase the value creation, and this is reflected in relative financial performance gains whenever the firm is able to appropriate part of this increased value. For instance, Cirque du Soleil (DeLong and Vijayaraghavan 2002) created an offering that was superior compared with the traditional type of circus and therefore raised willingness to pay relative to the existing circus offering. Furthermore, some key choices, such as eliminating the animals or not using stars, also decreased the associated opportunity costs. Cirque du Soleil created greater value and was able to capture part of that value, which resulted in improved relative financial performance.

Once the business model innovation is firmly in place, no new value is created (per unit); sustaining a competitive advantage keeps the differences intact. However, more value can be created by replicating the business model in other contexts (such as new geography and new clients), then creating additional value while increasing enterprise value.

To summarize the previous discussion, managers can create value in two broad ways: (1) redesigning, renewing, or upgrading the essential activities of the firm's business model and their relationships (*innovation*); and (2) using the firm's current business model to reach new customers (*replication*). The former creates value through affecting the profit margin and resource utilization in the enterprise value equation. The latter relates to the growth of the business while maintaining the relative (per unit) competitive advantage.

In the more formal analysis we present in the following, *innovation* includes all forms of business model change. Gains from innovation thus defined include disruptive transformations of a firm's business model, but also incremental improvements in operating efficiency due to technological changes in the production processes, product, or service, and organizational innovation or economies of scale in place within the firm's current business model.[4] Thus, we include in innovation not only the elements normally associated with strategic change, but also more incremental elements associated with the process of refining and improving the business model over time.

10.4. BUSINESS MODEL REPLICATION

By contrast, *replication* does not generally give rise to a firm's productivity and relative performance gains because it works as a "duplicate" of the activities performed by the firm at the same current productivity levels, which are transported to other markets or regions or over time in order to gain new customers.

However, replication does have an impact on industry-wide productivity. Industry productivity will rise in growing industries if the more productive firm captures most or all of the industry growth. In addition, replication does produce genuine productivity gains at the industry level when replication occurs at the expense of a less efficient competitor (Lieberman et al. 2018). In this last case, the industry as a whole becomes more productive, since the reduction in size of the less efficient firm frees up resources—people, capital, materials, and so on—that can be used elsewhere in the economy. We refer to this second type of replication simply as *productive replication*. Separating productive from nonproductive replication requires many assumptions and is empirically difficult, but we sketch some rough estimation toward the end of this chapter using US airline data.[5]

The distinction between innovation, replication, and productive replication, as defined in this chapter, is illustrated in Figure 10.1. Assume that there are only two firms in the industry (firm 1 and firm 2), which each produce Y_1 and Y_2, respectively, so that $Y_1 = Y_2 = 1$. To simplify, we consider only two periods ($t = 0$ and $t = 1$). The value created per unit by each firm (v_1 and v_2) is given by the difference between *customers' willingness to pay* (WTP) and *stakeholders' opportunity costs* (SOC) (Brandenburger and Stuart

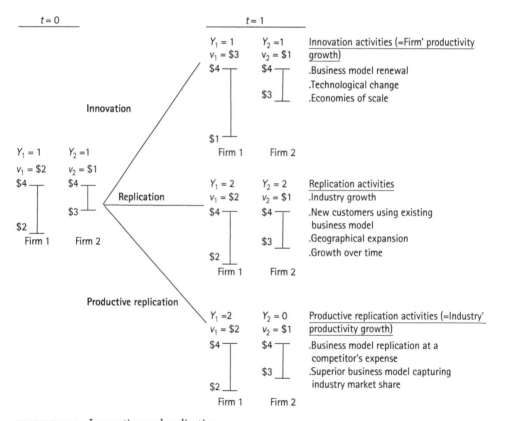

FIGURE 10.1. Innovation and replication.

1996; Garcia-Castro and Aguilera 2015; Lieberman et al. 2018). Hence, the total value created in a period by the two firms is given by $Y_1 v_1 + Y_2 v_2$. Further, assume that firm 1 has a competitive advantage over firm 2 ($v_1 > v_2$) so that firm 1 creates a value per unit (v_1) of $2 (the average difference between WTP and SOC per unit = $4 − $2) while firm 2's v_2 is only $1 ($4 − $3). As such, the total value created by the two firms in period 1 is equal to $3 ($1*\$2 + 1*\$1$).

Innovation gains are produced if, for example, firm 1's innovation activities lead to a reduction in SOC or an increase in WTP in the second period. Following the example in Figure 10.1, innovation gains total $1 (firm 1's SOC reduced from $2 to $1 in the second period). Alternatively, $1 innovation gains are also obtained if, for example, firm 1 improves the product in a way that raises the willingness to pay to $5, keeping SOC constant. Or any other combination could produce innovation gains—in the interest of simplicity, Figure 10.1 describes only the first situation. Changes in WTP and SOC per unit can be driven by factors such as changes in customers' tastes and preferences, the availability of substitutes, price changes in the factor markets, and so on. Also, innovations in the firm's business model leading to productivity improvements—such as increases in economies of scale, economies of scope, utilization rates, changes in technology, new organizational forms, process improvements, and so on—reduce the SOC per unit of output because fewer inputs are needed to produce the same output and so they generate innovation gains.

In our analysis, *innovation* is assumed to be exactly equivalent to economic gains as measured by the Value Creation and Appropriation model (VCA model) developed in the following (Lieberman et al. 2018; Lieberman et al. 2017). In the absence of changes in WTP and SOC over a period of time, innovation gains boil down to changes in firm' productivity.[6] This operationalization presents the advantage that quantitative estimates can be obtained using publicly available data, adding some precision to the discussion of how business models contribute to value creation.

Turning to replication, an increase in overall industry size in the second period permits firms to expand their activities at current levels—that is, WTP and SOC remain constant. Firm 1's growth in size by one unit creates economic gains of $2 ($\Delta Y_1 * v_1 = 1 * \$2$), but this sort of replication caused by industry growth does not represent a genuine productivity increase since WTP and SOC remain the same, and both firms' market shares remain constant (firm 2 also expanded by one unit). Firm 1's growth is fully driven by the growth in industry size—industry size grew from two to three units in the second period.

Finally, Figure 10.1 shows a case of productive replication. Assume that industry size, WTP, and SOC of firm 1 and firm 2 remain constant. If the more efficient firm 1 grows at firm 2's expense so that $Y_1 = 2$ and $Y_2 = 0$ in period 2, then the value created by the two firms increases by $1 relative to period 1. This economic gain implies an increase in overall industry productivity since a more efficient firm—that is, one with a superior business model—is replacing a less efficient competitor to produce the same total output as in period 1. By way of illustration, if the more efficient air carrier Southwest replaces an inefficient legacy carrier, Southwest's productivity will remain unaltered, but the airline industry as whole will be able to fly more passengers using fewer resources, or will be able to offer a better service to passengers while keeping the amount of resources used constant, or some combination of the two.

Innovation and replication activities are often intertwined. Firms regularly explore their business landscape, revising their core activities as they hope to foster innovation and, simultaneously, they try to reach as many customers as possible using their existing business models. At the same time, innovation and replication activities demand rather heterogeneous managerial skills to design and implement effectively. Think, for example, of the type of managers that Starbucks requires to expand and replicate its core business model worldwide, opening one coffee shop per day in different locations, compared with the management skills Amazon needed during its first years to create an entirely new business model around e-commerce and online transactions.

To summarize, business model innovation and replication are two distinctive drivers of productivity and relative firm financial performance. Innovation alters the firm's internal productivity (ratio of *firm* inputs/outputs), while productive replication modifies the industry's external productivity (ratio of *industry* inputs/outputs). Nonproductive replication captures how much a firm grows over a period of time *without altering either firm-level productivity or industry-level productivity*. Of course, very often it is difficult to separate innovation, as defined here, from replication. For instance, a company such as Mango (Ricart and Kordecka 2009), an apparel manufacturer, grows by replicating its business model in new cities around the world. But this growth is fundamental to increasing the overall economies of scale that make its business model stronger. So it also innovates in the way we have defined. However, for reasons of presentation, we do separate the different components of productivity change.

In the next section we use these distinctions to analyze the evolution of Southwest Airlines in the US airline industry.

10.5. INNOVATION AND REPLICATION IN SOUTHWEST AIRLINES: EMPIRICAL ESTIMATES

Southwest Airlines, once considered the brightest among all US air carriers (Gittell 2005; Porter 1996), recently lost some of its aura of invincibility in the industry (*Wall Street Journal* 2011). The company's productivity has started to converge toward the industry average. Air carriers' business models have started to successfully imitate Southwest's best practices, eroding part of the company's competitive edge (*Wall Street Journal* 2011, 2014a, 2014b). All this despite Southwest's robust growth over the past few years: its shares reached a record peak of $35 in September 2014. How can this be reconciled?

We contend that standard financial benchmarks hide the erosion of Southwest's competitive advantage, which is arguably better shown in the declining rate of innovation and replication in the past few years. It is likely that some of the recent changes introduced by the air carrier in its business model (Heskett and Sasser 2013) aim to avoid the decline in innovation and replication that has started to translate into a worsened bottom line.

10.5.1. Business Model Innovation in Southwest Airlines

Southwest's disruptive business model changed the rules by which air carriers operated and competed. Amid an industry once characterized by excessive regulation, bureaucracy, and poor operational efficiency, the Southwest model combined an agile, simple, low-fare customer experience with a strong internal culture based on passionate and caring customer service (Gittell 2005; Porter 1996).

One essential ingredient in Southwest's low-cost carrier (LCC) business model was the consistent implementation of mutually reinforcing activities, as shown in Figure 10.2. This figure shows the business model of Southwest by representing the value loops

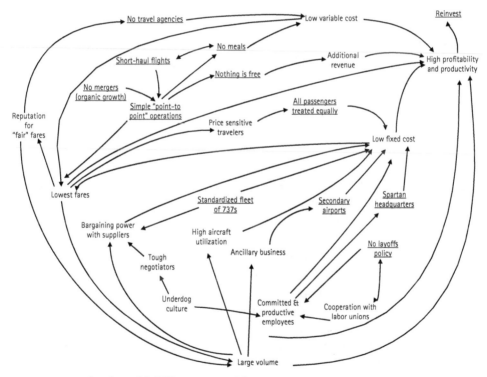

FIGURE 10.2. Southwest's LCC business model.

Source: Casadesus-Masanell and Ricart (2011).

associated with its consistent set of choices (underlined) and their consequences (Casadesus-Masanell and Ricart 2010). Southwest offered, for instance, a point-to-point, short-haul service between midsize cities and secondary airports, such as Love Field in Dallas or Hobby in Houston. The company deliberately avoided large, congested airports and did not fly great distances. It operated only standardized 737 aircraft and did not provide meals, assigned seats, or premium classes of service, all of which improved the efficiency of operations. As one can see in Figure 10.2, these and other choices resulted mainly in low fixed and variable costs, which were the basis for attracting customers with low fares and for having great profitability to keep investing in the airline's key asset choices such as aircrafts and new slots.[7]

As a consequence of its commitment to this particular set of choices and its consequences, Southwest achieved levels of operational efficiency and productivity unprecedented in the industry during the 1980s and 1990s: its aircraft spent an average of 11 hours in the air daily (compared with the industry average of eight hours); its turnaround times were 15 minutes (compared with the industry average of 35 minutes); it averaged 10.5 flights per gate (compared with the industry average of 4.5); and it was able to fly an average of 2,400 passengers per employee (compared with the industry average of 850). The LCC model put into practice by Southwest reduced its cost per available seat mile (ASM) to only 7 cents, while traditional hub-and-spoke carriers such as United, American, or Delta had a cost of more than 10 cents per ASM. Southwest leveraged its sizable lower operating costs to offer the lowest fares in the industry, stimulating demand on its routes and increasing the load factors of its aircraft. As a result, Southwest created value by the introduction of its disruptive LCC model that improved efficiency in the use of resources and stimulated demand for point-to-point flights (O'Reilly and Pfeffer, 1995).

A second aspect of the Southwest model was its outstanding customer service. Herb Kelleher, Southwest founder and CEO until 2001, was adamant about treating employees as internal customers, and he tried to make sure that the firm was a comfortable and fun place in which to work. His logic was that, if employees were engaged and satisfied, they would take care of Southwest passengers. The results of this strategy were undeniable. In the airline industry, customer service was measured by (1) on-time performance, (2) number of lost bags, and (3) number of customer complaints. If an air carrier was the best in all three categories in a single month, it won the "Triple Crown." Southwest won the Triple Crown 24 times in the early 1990s.

The benefits reaped from Southwest's LCC model were reflected in multiple performance metrics. Southwest stock earned the highest returns of any publicly traded US stock in the 1972–1992 period, with a compounded return of more than 21,000% and it was the only US air carrier to earn a profit for 40 consecutive years. While these metrics clearly indicate the above-average performance of Southwest's business model, somehow they mask how much value came from innovation and how much can be attributed to replication activities. As an alternative, next we rely on a productivity model—the VCA model—first introduced by Lieberman et al. (2017, 2018) to estimate the value created from innovation. In addition, the VCA model estimates how much of the value created in a period was captured by Southwest's various stakeholders.

10.5.2. Innovation Gains and Productivity: The VCA Model

The productivity literature in economics has evolved from a tradition of measuring labor productivity to adding other production factors, such as capital or resources used, giving way to a measure of total factor productivity (TFP). Thus, TFP models provide an account of the growth rate of a firm's output relative to the inputs utilized. Based on the TFP literature (Harberger 1998, 1999; Hulten 2001), the VCA model is a particular productivity model that relies on some assumptions, such as small changes over time, to estimate a firm's internal productivity growth using more production factors than the ones traditionally considered in the literature, labor and capital (see Lieberman et al. 2017). Moreover, the model uses accounting and other firm-related information to compute productivity gains.[8]

We assume a firm's productivity growth to be the result of a renewal and reconfiguration of activities conforming the basic business model plus improvements in operational efficiency and economies of scale. The model is based on increments rather than absolute levels. Hence WTP and SOC can be assumed away if they do not change much during the analyzed period. As such, the only inputs for the model are the relative changes in prices and amounts of factors used.

In essence, the VCA model can be written as follows:

$$
\begin{aligned}
&\left(\Delta Y/Y\right) - s_L\left(\Delta L/L\right) - s_K\left(\Delta K/K\right) - s_F\left(\Delta F/F\right) - s_M\left(\Delta M/M\right) \\
&= s_L\left(\Delta w/w\right) + s_K\left(\Delta r/r\right) + s_F\left(\Delta f/f\right) + s_M\left(\Delta m/m\right) - \left(\Delta p/p\right)
\end{aligned}
\tag{10.1}
$$

where Y is the firm's total output; p is the price of the firm's product; L is the number of employees; w is the wage rate; K is the amount of capital employed by the firm; r is the rate of return on capital; F is the amount of fuel consumed per year and f its average cost per gallon; M is the amount of materials and other purchased inputs and m their average price. The factor cost shares in the revenues for employees, capital, fuel suppliers, and other suppliers are denoted by S_L, S_K, S_F, and S_M, respectively.

The value captured by employees is denoted by $s_L\left(\Delta w/w\right)$. Similarly, $s_K\left(\Delta r/r\right)$ denotes the value appropriated by capital providers, $s_F\left(\Delta f/f\right)$ by fuel suppliers, $s_M\left(\Delta m/m\right)$ by nonfuel suppliers and $-\left(\Delta p/p\right)$ by customers. For simplicity, we use VL, VK, VF, VM, and VC to refer to $s_L\left(\Delta w/w\right)$, $s_K\left(\Delta r/r\right)$, $s_F\left(\Delta f/f\right)$, $s_M\left(\Delta m/m\right)$, and $-\left(\Delta p/p\right)$, respectively.

It is worth noticing that the return to all capital providers (r) is estimated as a residual, once the value captured by all other stakeholders has been computed. As such, unlike other related works, it does not require the firm's accounting profit to enter as an input. Grifell-Tatjé and Lovell (2015) provide a thorough discussion of how accounting profit more generally relates to productivity.

Equation (10.1) implies that productivity gains (left-hand side) have to be necessarily captured by one or more stakeholder groups (right-hand side). Productivity gains on the left-hand side are measured as increments in total output minus the increments in the inputs used in terms of quantities adjusted by their relative weights. The value captured on the right-hand side is measured as wage increases, price increments, and so on. Further, in the absence of productivity gains (the left-hand side is zero), there is no *new* value creation that can be captured by any stakeholder group, only value redistribution from one stakeholder group to another, reflected in the values on the right-hand side. This equation is equivalent to the Solow decomposition for total factor productivity used in economics (Solow 1957).

All the parameters in equation (10.1) can be computed by using the following data items: revenues, operating costs, total output, amount of materials and services purchased, number of employees, wages and benefits, and the capital employed. These data items can be obtained from *Compustat* and annual reports of the companies. We estimate Y and M using some proxies. Air carriers report their revenue passenger miles (RPM) each year, that is, the number of (fare-paying) passengers carried multiplied by distance flown. Hence, the RPM captures the total level of output (Y) for a single company in a given year. One can obtain the average RPM price (p) by dividing the firm's total revenues for the year by the RPM. All prices and costs are computed in real terms using the GDP deflator to ensure that inflationary issues do not affect our estimates.

Estimating purchased quantities and purchasing costs is often difficult using secondary data. Fortunately, in the airline industry, there are annual data on each carrier's fuel inputs and costs.[9] Thus, we separate the fuel purchased in one year (F) and its average cost (f) from all the other materials purchased (M). By doing so, we are able to isolate the most important input for these firms—the fuel component roughly accounts for 50% of a carrier's total purchased materials from suppliers (Grant, 2010).

In addition, airlines annually disclose the total number of seat miles that were available to passengers (available seat miles, or ASM). The ASM measure is computed as the aircraft miles flown multiplied by the number of seats available for passenger use. The ASM is a rough proxy for the materials and services purchased (other than fuel) because the leasing of the aircraft, insurance, food and beverages, and other transport-related expenses in a carrier tend to be a function of the number of seats flown during the year. Thus, we use the ASM to roughly estimate the remaining inputs purchased (M). The average (m) was computed by dividing the total cost of materials and services purchased, excluding fuel, by the ASM.

The VCA model results are shown in Table 10.1. Productivity growth is computed in this table using the left-hand side of equation (10.1), whereas VL, VC, VF, VM, and VK—value appropriation—correspond to the terms on the right-hand side of the same equation. Hence, total productivity growth is equal to the sum of the value captured by the various stakeholders of the firm reported in Table 10.1. For comparison purposes, we analyzed three decades (1980–1990, 1990–2000, and 2000–2010) in the evolution of Southwest Airlines. All percentage increases are computed using log differences.

Table 10.1 Southwest Airlines Productivity Growth (1980–2010)

Panel A: Basic Data

	1980	1990	2000	2010
Price indices	$ million			
GDP deflator (US)	1.00	1.47	1.79	2.21
Company data (nominal): Compustat				
Revenues	213	1,187	5,649	12,104
COGS	152	1,025	4,310	10,488
Total output (RPM)	2,024,097	9,958,940	42,215,162	78,046,967
Materials purchased (ASM)	2,969,448	16,411,115	59,909,965	98,437,000
Fuel consumed	74	282	1,013	1,437
Cost per gallon fuel	0.84	0.78	0.79	2.40
Employment	1,839	8,620	29,274	34,901
Capital employed	196	1,326	5,899	10,821
Wages and benefits	48	357	1,683	3,704

Panel B: Value Creation Analysis

		Decade ending: 1990	2000	2010
VT	Economic gains	5.9%	17.5%	26.5%
VL	Gains to employees	2.5%	4.0%	12.2%
VC	Gains to customers	26.1%	8.1%	6.3%
VF	Gains to fuel suppliers	–11.0%	–3.0%	19.2%
VM	Gains to suppliers	7.9%	–3.0%	–3.1%
VK	Gains to capital (b/tax)	–19.7%	11.4%	–8.1%

GDP: gross domestic product; COGS: cost of goods sold; RPM: revenue per mile passenger; ASM: available seat miles.

Southwest's innovation gains were of 5.9% (log increase) in the 1980–1990 period. This means that during this period the company managed to introduce improvements in its business model, some of them disruptive, such as the acquisition of Morris Air in 1992,[10] and others more incremental, such as the optimization of routes, improved load factors, and other upgrades in operational efficiency. These gains were captured mainly by customers, who enjoyed gains of 26.1% (e.g., fare reductions) during the period. Employees (2.5%) and nonfuel suppliers (7.9%) also benefited, although at a much lower rate. Fuel suppliers' value capture decreased by 11% during this period as a consequence of the oil price reduction in real terms in the 1980–1990 period. For their part, gains by Southwest's shareholders and other capital providers such as debt-holders decreased by 19.7%. This reduction does not imply that Southwest's shareholders lost money during this decade; it only means that their fraction of the total value created in the period was lower.

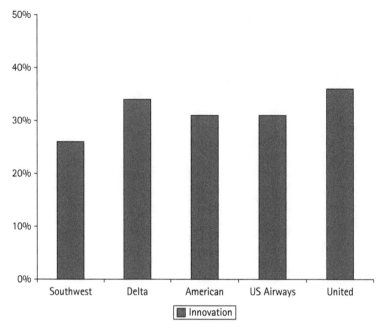

FIGURE 10.3. Innovation in the US airline industry (2000–2010).

During the next two decades, Southwest continued to produce innovation gains (17.5% in 1990–2000, and 26.5% in 2000–2010). These gains were captured mainly by employees and to a lesser extent by air passengers. Fuel suppliers increased their share in total gains due to the reversal in oil prices, which increased from $30 per barrel in the late 1990s to a maximum of $140 per barrel by 2009.

While Southwest managed to sustain its innovation gains in the 1980–2010 period, industry rivals' innovation gains were higher in all cases (Figure 10.3). Southwest's innovation gains of 26.5% over the last decade were lower than the gains obtained by Delta (34%), American (31%), US Airways (31%), and United (36%). Apparently, legacy carriers are closing the competitive gap with Southwest, probably by partially imitating Southwest's LCC business model. Even worse, it may be the case that Southwest's innovation gains in recent decades might not be entirely driven by internal changes introduced by the firm, but by industry-wide innovations that all competitors immediately adopt in their business models. Together, these results suggest that Southwest's current business model might soon be reaching some upper bound. Anecdotal evidence seems to confirm our results (*Wall Street Journal* 2011, 2014a).

10.5.3. Business Model Replication in Southwest Airlines

Despite Southwest's diminishing competitive edge against its rivals (Figure 10.3), its revenues and share price have continued to rise at a steady rate.[11] There are two main reasons for that. The first is related to Southwest's capacity to transport its basic business model to new geographical areas and market segments and over time. The second reason concerns the substantial overall industry growth in air passenger traffic from 1970 to 2010. The industry total RPM grew from 557,234 million in 1995 to 847,989 million in 2013, a 52% increase. Southwest both benefited from and stimulated this growth in demand—traffic on most routes served by Southwest increased by four times as travelers found it more convenient and cost-effective to fly with Southwest than to use alternatives such as road transportation.

Replication is closely related to the expansion rate of firms. Southwest saw its revenue grow from $213 million in 1980 to $17.7 billion in 2013, a compound annual growth rate of 14%. In 1980, the Southwest fleet consisted of 23 Boeing 737 planes; by 2013 its fleet had increased to 614 Boeing 737s and 66 Boeing 717s. On the one hand, this growth was achieved mainly by an increase over time in the number of passengers served on Southwest's traditional routes. For instance, in 1980 Southwest produced 135 million RPM per city connected. By 2010, this number had grown to 1.2 billion RPM per city.

On the other hand, in addition to adding more passengers in each market it served, Southwest put into motion an expansion plan based on controlled growth to other US regions (Figure 10.4). One major wave of growth took place in 1984, when Southwet added new flight segments to the West Coast, including three-hour connections to Los Angeles, Las Vegas, San Diego, and San Francisco, among others. In 1993, Southwet first extended its route structure to the Northeast United States with its first flight to Baltimore. Other Northeast routes followed, and by 2004 Southwet offered flights to

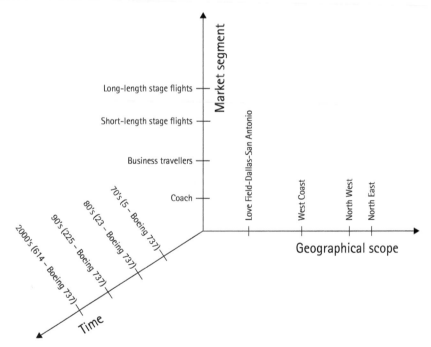

FIGURE 10.4. Replication vectors: Geographic scope, market segment, and time.

Islip in Long Island, Manchester in New Hampshire, and Pittsburgh and Philadelphia in Pennsylvania. While some of these new routes were longer than Southwest's traditional segments—for example, three or more hours—the essence of the business model remained the same: low cost and low fares, point-to-point, lean operations, and first-rate customer service. A careful hiring policy, combined with the transfer of Southwest veterans from traditional routes to Baltimore and other Northeast routes, allowed the company to transport its distinctive culture even to the East Coast. To achieve this transplantation of the business model into new regions and markets, Southwest carefully chose the less congested airports in that area to facilitate the firm's lean operations.

In Figure 10.5 we compare Southwest's growth attributed to innovation and replication. We estimate replication simply as the total percentage increase in RPM not accrued to productivity growth. For instance, Southwest's total RPM growth from 2000 to 2010 was 61% (log differences) and its productivity growth in the same period was 26% (Table 10.1). The difference between both numbers results in the growth attributed to replication of 35% shown in Figure 10.5.

Replication gains were considerably larger than innovation gains for the three decades as a result of Southwest's rapid expansion in those years. Replication gains, however, decreased by a factor of four from the 1980–1990 to the 2000–2010 period, probably reflecting the fact that the LCC model was reaching some stage of maturity. Still, Figure 10.5 evidences that the main driver for Southwest revenues and profit

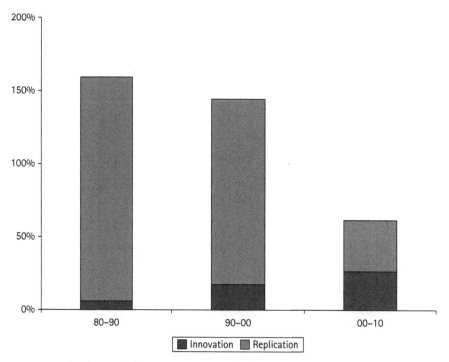

FIGURE 10.5. Southwest Airlines: Innovation and replication (1980–2010).

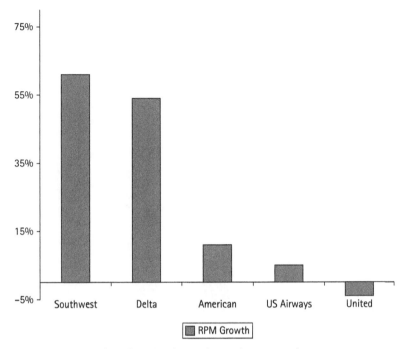

FIGURE 10.6. RPM growth in the US airline industry (2000–2010).

increases from the 1980s onward was its rapid expansion to new regions, transplanting the more efficient LCC business model it introduced when it began flying with three Boeing 737s in 1971.

Figure 10.6 compares Southwest with its main competitors' RPM growth in 2000–2010. Despite the fact that by 2010 Southwest was the fourth largest air carrier in the United States, it continued to grow at a much higher rate than any other legacy carrier. In the absence of this above-average growth, Southwest's gains would have been lower than those of legacy carriers. In fact, Southwest's innovation gains in the 2000–2010 period have been lower than its main rivals.[12]

Given the fundamental role of replication in Southwest's strategy in the 1980–2010 period, we explore next how much of that replication could be attributed to productive replication—that is, growth at the expense of less efficient competitors.

10.5.4. Estimating Productive Replication

The replication gains noted in the preceding include both productive and nonproductive replication. Productive replication requires a more efficient firm to replace a less efficient competitor. In the US airline industry, an estimation of productive replication gains requires knowledge of how much Southwest grew at the expense of its competitors. While this is generally difficult, a rough estimate can be

Table 10.2 Market Share in RPM (Southwest vs. Legacy Carriers)

	2007	2013	Dif. 2007–2013
American	138,448	128,410	(10,038)
Delta[1]	176,473	172,925	(3,549)
United[2]	198,827	178,561	(20,266)
US Airways[3]	61,255	66,160	4,905
Legacy carriers	**575,004**	**546,056**	**-28,948**
Southwet	**72,410**	**104,461**	**+32,051**
RPM legacy carriers + Southwest	647,414	650,517	
Total RPM industry	840,860	847,989	
RPM share legacy carriers + Southwest	77.0%	76.7%	

[1] Includes Northwest's RPM. Northwest merged with Delta in 2008.
[2] Includes Continental's RPM. Continental merged with United in 2012.
[3] Includes America West's RPM. America West merged with US Airways in 2007.

obtained if, for example, the industry size remains constant in a period so that the growth of a firm necessarily means that it displaces other rivals. For instance, in the 2007–2013 period the industry size remained almost constant: the total RPM in 2007 were 840,860 million, compared with 847,989 million in 2013 (see Table 10.2). At the same time, Southwest continued to grow in this period, increasing its RPM from 72,410 million to 104,461 million RPM. Southwest's increase of 32,051 million RPM was matched by an almost identical decrease of 28,948 million RPM for the legacy carriers combined (American, Delta, United, and US Airways). Hence, it is reasonable to assume that part of the growth of Southwest in this period came at the expense of these competitors.

Let v_1 and v_2 be the difference between WTP and SOC. As illustrated in Figure 10.1, the amount of productive replication will depend on the differential in value created per unit (v_1-v_2) between Southwest and the legacy carriers combined—that is, how superior the Southwest business model was in 2007 relative to those of its competitors. If we take the legacy carriers' value created per unit as a benchmark and use the industry's average value creation per unit instead of v_2, then productive replication gains can be roughly estimated as follows:

$$\left(v_1-\overline{v}\right)\Delta Y=\left(\begin{array}{c}\left(\overline{p}-p_1\right)+\left(w_1-\overline{w}\right)\left(L_1/Y_1\right)+\left(r_1-\overline{r}\right)\left(K_1/Y_1\right)\\+\left(m_1-\overline{m}\right)\left(M_1/Y_1\right)+\left(f_1-\overline{f}\right)\left(F_1/Y_1\right)\end{array}\right)\Delta Y \qquad (10.2)$$

Table 10.3 Southwest versus Legacy Carriers (2007–2013)
(Real Prices; Base = 1980)[1]

	2007		2013	
	Southwest	Legacy	Southwest	Legacy
p	0.064	0.090	0.073	0.092
w	47,338	38,327	50,739	42,392
r	0.062	0.054	0.060	0.023
f	0.802	1.062	1.558	1.278
m	0.021	0.036	0.023	0.038
Y	72,409	–	104,461	–
L	33,680	–	44,831	–
K	5,815	–	6,390	–
F	1,491	–	1,526	–
M	99,767	–	130,503	–

[1] Y, K, F and M in millions of dollars.

where $\bar{v}, \bar{p}, \bar{w}, \bar{r}, \bar{m}$ and $\bar{f}$ are the average of v, p, w, r, m and f for all legacy carriers combined (American, US Airways, Delta, and United). The intuition for (10.2) is this: the differential in productivity between the focal firm (Southwest) and the rest of competitors determines the extent of productive replication at the industry level. The higher this differential, the higher the productive replication. If the focal firm's productivity is identical to the productivity of the firms it replaces, then there is no *productive* replication. The formal derivation of equation (10.2) is provided in the Appendix to this chapter.

We use equation (10.2) to estimate Southwest's productive replication gains. Table 10.3 displays the values of all the parameters needed to estimate equation (10.2). Using this data, the total amount of productive replication in this period is about $128 million, or about a 3% increase in RPM. This estimate is obtained as follows. In the 2007–2013 period, Southwest's RPM increased by 37% (Table 10.3). Out of this increase, 18.8% can be attributed to innovation gains—productivity growth as measured by the VCA model (Table 10.4). The remainder 18.2% (37%–18.8%) can be further decomposed into replication (15.2%) and productive replication gains (3%). These three sources of value creation are depicted in Figure 10.7.

Estimates of productive replication gains are highly sensitive to the benchmark used. Under the assumption that Southwest was not replacing an average legacy carrier but a less efficient one in each segment, productive replication will be much higher (see Lieberman et al. 2018). But it is also possible that Southwest replaced carriers

Table 10.4 VCA Analysis (2007–2013), Southwest Airlines		
Productivity Growth		18.8%
VL	Gains to employees	4.5%
VC	Gains to customers	-12.7%
VF	Gains to fuel suppliers	19.1%
VM	Gains to suppliers	4.9%
VK	Gains to capital	3.0%

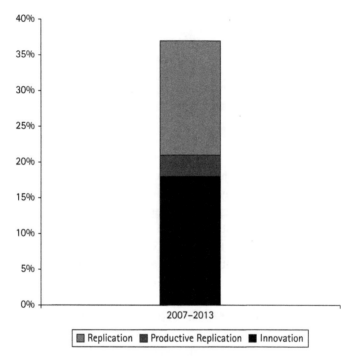

FIGURE 10.7. Productive replication in Southwest Airlines using legacy carriers' averages (2007–2013).

performing above the industry average on some selected routes and, as a result, the estimated productive replication will be lower. Thus, the rough 3% increment obtained by using industry averages is only a surrogate measure of productive replication and varies depending on the underlying assumption of which particular carriers Southwest replaced during its expansion into new routes and geographical areas.

Overall, Southwest's productive replication gains seem to be relatively small in the analyzed period. This may be attributed to legacy carriers' successful imitation of

Southwest's LCC business model, resulting in a reduced competitive disadvantage compared with the 1980–2000 period. Productive replication gains are likely to be larger for the 1980–1990 and 1990–2000 periods. Further, the amount of RPM captured by Southwest at its competitors' expense (about 32,000 million RPM), although substantial, represents less than 4% of the total industry size, suggesting that Southwest's substitution of other, less efficient carriers was limited in this period. Finally, it is possible that the amount of productive replication has been understated as a result of the assumptions required to estimate equation (10.2).

10.6. CONCLUSION

In this chapter we take advantage of current advancements in the measurement of productivity (Lieberman et al. 2018; Lieberman et al. 2017) to connect business model design and development with value creation and capture. Building on recent literature on business model innovation and replication, we propose a more fine-grained distinction between *innovation, replication,* and *productive replication,* based on the different sources of productivity growth.[13] Innovation refers to all those activities in a business model that create economic value by altering the input-to-output ratio at the firm level, leading to genuine productivity growth. By contrast, productive replication increases the value created by a firm by replacing less efficient firms in the industry, leaving the firm's productivity unaltered but upgrading the industry's overall productivity. Finally, in the absence of innovation or productive replication, a firm can create value by simply expanding its activities at the average industry growth rate.

We illustrated these ideas using the example of the low-cost air carrier Southwest Airlines. Southwest has been the subject of hundreds of academic and business press articles over the past few years. How can there possibly be anything new to say? Our contribution to understanding Southwest's value creation in the airlines industry is based on the distinction between innovation and replication activities and their implications for productivity. While the connection between Southwest's low-cost business model and innovation gains is well understood, less is known about the role of replication in its success.

The empirical results shown in this chapter confirm the intuition that Southwest's growth, once fostered by its disruptive LCC model and characterized by innovation activities, has recently begun to lose impetus. In such a context, it seems reasonable that Southwest would seek to grow via replication. However, our results also show that Southwest's growth due to replication has declined as well. This rapid decline in replication can be explained partly by the smaller growth rate of the US airline industry in the past few years, showing some signs of maturity.

In addition to connecting Southwest's business model changes with productivity measures, the empirical tools used in this chapter also permit us to explore how the fruits of productivity gains were distributed. Both Southwest customers and employees consistently benefited during the three analyzed decades. Oil suppliers' value capture fluctuated in parallel to changes in market oil prices. The decreases in Southwest's shareholders value capture in 1980–1990 and 2000–2010 reflect the fact that Southwest's outstanding financial performance in the 1970s and early 1980s is proving hard to sustain, especially given Southwest's recent lower innovation rates compared with industry peers.

Our results suggest that most of Southwest's value creation in recent years has been driven by replication activities. The relatively lower rates of innovation in Southwest's business model, if prolonged in the future, will diminish the firm's potential to sustain its competitive advantage over less efficient carriers in the coming years. Southwest has recently started to introduce some changes to its core business model, such as code-sharing agreements, a new business class, reserved places in the waiting line, experimentation at LaGuardia and other congested airports, and new acquisitions such as Airtran (Heskett and Sasser, 2013), but it remains to be seen whether all these changes will prove to be innovative enough to replace its aging LCC business model.

Beyond the specifics of Southwest's case, the concepts discussed in this chapter, together with the measurement framework based on the VCA model, can be generally used in subsequent works to provide quantitative insights of the impact that alternative strategies have on innovation and replication in firms, to explore the intertwining between these two distinctive sources of value creation, and to shed light on the connections between firm strategy (business models), value creation, and productivity.

Notes

1. The ideas developed in this chapter are based on two related, more formal works: Lieberman, Balasubramanian, and Garcia-Castro (2018) and Lieberman, Garcia-Castro, and Balasubramanian (2017). We refer the interested reader to these two papers for a more thorough treatment of innovation and replication gains.

2. The first author is indebted to the Spanish Ministry of Economy and Competitiveness (ECO2012-33018) for providing financial support.

3. Because the concept of "value" in strategy (e.g., Brandenburger and Stuart 1996) goes beyond a given firm to include suppliers and customers, it is broader than the concept of "productivity." Consider the case of coal mining, for example. The appearance of more efficient methods of transporting coal to customers (which reduces SOC), or a temporary shortage of coal substitutes (which raises WTP), increases the gap between SOC and WTP, and hence total value created. These changes in SOC *per unit of input* and WTP *per unit of output* would not affect productivity as measured within a coal-mining firm. However, the concepts of "value" and "productivity" are essentially equivalent if SOC *per unit of input* and WTP *per unit of output* remain constant over time. Under these assumptions, a firm's ability to increase "value" comes from reducing input requirements (and hence, SOC) *per unit of output*, which corresponds to a gain in productivity. Lieberman et al. (2018) discuss more broadly the precise theoretical conditions under which "productivity" is equivalent to "value" and how to deal with the measurement error that may arise whenever *changes* (per unit) in WTP and SOC are substantial.

4. Previous characterizations of business model innovation tend to focus on major renewals of a firm's business models and they typically do not include smaller upgrades in operations or economies of scale. We consider both types of innovation in our analysis. In addition, many studies require some degree of novelty, meaning new to the industry, for consideration as business model innovation. We just require a change new to the firm.

5. Given our interest in productive replication that occurs when one firm displaces a less efficient competitor, in the empirical section we chose a time period (2007–2013) when there was no overall industry growth in the US airlines industry (i.e., industry RPM remained constant).

6. Theoretically, innovation gains depend on changes in productivity, WTP and SOC. While WTP and SOC are often difficult to observe, in the empirical section we rely on the VCA model, which uses the *increments* in the total value captured by the various stakeholders of the firm as a rough proxy of changes in value creation *per unit*. One main advantage of using incremental values is that WTP and SOC can be assumed away if they do not change much over the analyzed period. Furthermore, the VCA model can be easily reformulated to use *value added* when some of the inputs and/or outputs cannot be observed using available data. Hence, innovation gains will coincide with pure productivity gains only in the particular case that changes in WTP and SOC are equal to zero—for a more thorough discussion of the relationship between productivity and value, see Lieberman et al. (2018) and Lieberman et al. (2017).

7. Of course there are other ways to represent a business model. A common alternative is to use an activity map. In this case, we also will see a lot of consistency and reinforcement among the set of activities being chosen.

8. Grifell-Tatjé and Lovell (2015) provide a useful review of the productivity literature with a special emphasis on the relationship between productivity and accounting measures of profit and profitability.

9. http://transtats.bts.gov/fuel.asp; http://web.mit.edu/airlinedata/www/default.html.

10. The acquisition of Morris Air in 1992 represents a relatively minor exception to Southwest's strategy based on internal growth.

11. The treatment of "replication" in this section is based on the growth rate of the firms. Such growth may include both productive and nonproductive replication. In the next section we provide a rough estimate of the amount of productive replication, taking advantage of the fact that there was no industry growth in the 2007-2013 period. A more technical and precise treatment of replication is provided by Lieberman et al. (2018).

12. Throughout this period, Southwest beat the competition and sustained its competitive advantage. In fact, Southwest is a good example of a firm sustaining its competitive advantage for a long period of time. Competitors had a hard time. However, this is not fully reflected in productivity gains because Southwest's competitive advantage was built earlier, in the 1970s, not in the 1980–2010 period.

13. The distinction between innovation and replication gains as drivers of value creation in an industry was introduced by Lieberman, Balasubramanian, and Garcia-Castro (2018).

References

Amit, R., and C. Zott. 2001. "Value Creation in E-Business." *Strategic Management Journal* 22(6): 493–520.

Amit, R., and C. Zott. 2012. "Creating Value Through Business Model Innovation." *MIT Sloan Management Review* 53(3): 41–49.

Baden-Fuller, C., B. Demil, X. Lecoq, X., and I. MacMillan. 2010. "Editorial." *Long Range Planning* 43: 143–145.

Bowman, C., and V. Ambrosini. 2003. "How the Resource-Based and the Dynamic Capability Views of the Firm Inform Corporate-Level Strategy." *British Journal of Management* 14(4): 289–303.

Brandenburger, A., and H. Stuart. 1996. "Value-Based Business Strategy." *Journal of Economics and Management Strategy* 5(1): 5–24.

Casadesus-Masanell, R., and J. E. Ricart. 2010. "From Strategy to Business Models and onto Tactics." *Long Range Planning* 43(2–3): 195–215.

Casadesus-Masanell, R., and J. E. Ricart. 2011. "How to Design A Winning Business Model." *Harvard Business Review* 89(1/2): 100–107.

Casadesus-Masanell, R., and F. Zhu. 2013. "Business Model Innovation and Competitive Imitation: The Case of Sponsor-Based Business Models." *Strategic Management Journal* 34(4): 464–482.

Chen, C. M., M. A. Delmas, and M. B. Lieberman. 2015. "Production Frontier Methodologies and Efficiency as a Performance Measure in Strategic Management Research." *Strategic Management Journal* 36(1): 19–36.

DeLong, T. J., and V. Vijayaraghavan. 2002. "Cirque du Soleil." *Harvard Business School Case 403-006*, July.

Gambardella, A., and McGahan, A. M. 2010. "Business-Model Innovation: General Purpose Technologies and Their Implications for Industry Structure." *Long Range Planning* 43(2–3): 262–271.

Garcia-Castro, R., and R. V. Aguilera. 2015. "Incremental Value Creation and Appropriation in a World with Multiple Stakeholders." *Strategic Management Journal* 36(1): 137–147.

Gittell, J. H. 2005. *The Southwest Airlines Way*. New York: McGraw-Hill.Grant, R. 2010. *Contemporary Strategy Analysis: Text and Cases*. Hoboken, NJ: John Wiley & Sons.

Grifell-Tatjé, E., and C. A. K. Lovell. 2015. *Productivity Accounting: The Economics of Business Performance*. New York: Cambridge University Press.

Harberger, A. C. 1998. "A Vision of the Growth Process." *American Economic Review* 88(1): 1–32.

Harberger, A. C. 1999. "Studying the Growth Process: A Primer." In *Capital Formation and Economic Growth*, edited by M. J. Boskin. Stanford, CA: Hoover Institution.

Heskett, J. L., and W. E. Sasser. 2013. "Southwest Airlines: In a Different World." *Harvard Business School Case (9-910-419)*.

Hulten, C. R. 2001. "Total Factor Productivity: A Short Biography." In *New Developments in Productivity Analysis*, edited by C. R. Hulten, E. R. Dean, and M. J. Harper. Studies in Income and Wealth, Volume 63. Chicago and London: University of Chicago Press for the National Bureau of Economic Research.

Jonsson, A., and N. J. Foss. 2011. "International Expansion Through Flexible Replication: Learning from the Internationalization Experience of IKEA." *Journal of International Business Studies* 42(9): 1079–1102.

Lieberman, M. B., N. Balasubramanian, and R. Garcia-Castro. 2018. "Toward a Dynamic Notion of Value Creation and Appropriation in Firms: The Concept and Measurement of Economic Gain." *Strategic Management Journal* 39(6): 1546–1572.

Lieberman, M. B., Garcia-Castro, R., and Balasubramanian, N. 2017. "Measuring Value Creation and Appropriation in Firms: The VCA Model." *Strategic Management Journal* 38(6): 1193–1211.

MacDonald, G., and M. D. Ryall. 2004. "How Do Value Creation and Competition Determine Whether a Firm Appropriates Value?" *Management Science* 50(10): 1319–1333.

O'Reilly, C., and J. Pfeffer. 1995. "Southwest Airlines." *Stanford Graduate School of Business, HR1A, 2005.*

Osterwalder, A., and Y. Pigneur. 2010. *Business Model Generation.* Hoboken, NJ: John Wiley & Sons.

Porter, M. E. 1985. *Competitive Advantage.* New York: Free Press.

Porter, M. E. 1996. "What Is Strategy?" *Harvard Business Review* 74(6): 61–78.

Ricart, J. E., and I. Kordecka. 2009. "Mango, Socializing Fashion." *IESE Case SM-1547-E.*

Solow, R. 1957. "Technical Change and the Aggregate Production Function." *The Review of Economics and Statistics* 39: 312–320.

Teece, D. J. 2009. *Dynamic Capabilities and Strategic Management: Organizing for Innovation and Growth.* Oxford University Press.

Teece, D. J. 2010. "Business Models, Business Strategy and Innovation." *Long Range Planning* 43: 172–194.

Wall Street Journal. 2011. "Rivals Invade Southwest's Air Space." December 16.

Wall Street Journal. 2014a. "Showing Its Age: Southwest Air Faces Grown-Up Woes." April 2.

Wall Street Journal. 2014b. "Southwest Airlines: Freer to Fly, but Also More Baggage." October 1.

Winter, S. G., and G. Szulanski. 2001. "Replication as Strategy." *Organization Science* 12(6): 730–743.

Zott, C., and R. Amit. 2013. "The Business Model: A Theoretically Anchored Robust Construct for Strategic Analysis." *Strategic Organization* 11(4): 403–411.

CHAPTER 11

··

THE LABOR PRODUCTIVITY OF FAMILY FIRMS

A Socioemotional Wealth Perspective

··

SHAINAZ FIRFIRAY, MARTIN LARRAZA-KINTANA,
AND LUIS R. GÓMEZ-MEJÍA

11.1. INTRODUCTION

IN this chapter we examine the relationship between family firms and labor productivity.[1] We focus on labor productivity for three reasons. First, it is an essential component of total factor productivity (TFP) for which recent analyses have found differences between family and nonfamily firms. Second, it is directly tied to employee attitudes and behaviors and therefore is a key indicator to look at in order to further understand people-management issues in family firms. A family firm is a firm controlled by a group of individuals related to each other by ties of blood or marriage. Family ownership is the most common type of ownership form in almost every country (Gomez-Mejia et al. 2003; La Porta et al. 1999). Further, family firms can be found in all economic sectors and size categories, and are also significantly present among publicly held firms (Gomez-Mejia et al. 2010). Because of this ubiquity, family firm research in recent years is becoming one of the classic lines of inquiry in the management and economics literature. This literature has gained momentum during the past decade, with significant contributions published in major academic journals. Lastly, and more broadly, labor productivity is a fundamental input affecting firm profitability and at a macro level it is a key determinant of economic development.

The study of family firms is not only relevant because of family firms' prevalence in the business landscape around the world. An analysis of family firms improves our understanding of how non-economic goals and priorities affect business decisions and results. Over the years, the literature on family firms has described in detail the non-economic utilities that controlling families try to obtain and preserve. These utilities—which include maintaining control of the firm, emotional attachment to the company, a sense of belonging and identification, or the value of handing the business down to future generations—are grouped under the label of socioemotional wealth (SEW) (Gomez-Mejia et al. 2007). More important, research has shown that the decision-making process in family firms is strongly driven by a desire to protect SEW, even at the expense of economic goals (Berrone et al. 2012; Gomez-Mejia et al. 2007). Because of the desire to protect SEW, the strategic decision-making process in family firms differs from that found in nonfamily firms (Berrone et al. 2010; Cruz et al. 2014; Gomez-Mejia et al. 2010).

The strong preference of family firms for alternatives that preserve their SEW may generate differences in performance, and more specifically in productivity, when compared with their nonfamily counterparts. The few studies that have tried to disentangle whether or not the presence of controlling families in firms is beneficial for firm productivity have not reached a clear consensus (Barbera and Moores 2013; Barth et al. 2005). As part of the ongoing debate, it has been suggested that perhaps family firms may show better labor productivity (i.e., the amount of output per unit of labor) than nonfamily firms, particularly when firms are small (Barbera and Moores 2013). However, this advantage in labor productivity among small family firms may vanish as they grow in size. Additionally, the literature on family firms has noted that family-controlled firms would be less likely, particularly when management is also in the hands of the family, to implement people-management practices that result in better labor productivity (e.g., Bloom and Van Reenen 2011; Cruz et al. 2011).

In light of these results, the goal of this chapter is to present a framework to further understand the impact that family ownership may have over the company's labor productivity and to reconcile the existing evidence. While labor productivity can vary with factors such as capital intensity, technology, or scale, we suggest, based on the SEW perspective (Gomez-Mejia et al. 2007, 2011), that SEW protection may be another factor that explains differences in labor productivity between family and nonfamily firms, as well as among different family firms. We acknowledge that SEW preservation is a core determinant in the decision-making process of family firms, but also that SEW has multiple dimensions or facets, such as control and influence, identification with the firm, and binding social ties (Berrone et al. 2012). Based on these ideas, we contend that controlling families may differ in the way they prioritize those dimensions of SEW, for example with some families emphasizing control, while others seek to guarantee strong social ties first. Consequently, we argue that different SEW priorities lead to differences in the way family firms manage their employees, which eventually translates into differences in labor productivity. In particular, we propose that the SEW dimensions prioritized by the controlling family affect the formation of trust, the leadership style, the presence of influential nonfamily managers in family firms, and the adoption of high performance work practices (HPWPs), all of which ultimately influence labor productivity in family firms. Underlying our argument is the notion that through its effect on trust, leadership, appointment of nonfamily managers, and people-management practices, SEW priorities affect the attitudes and behaviors of the workforce and, all else being equal, end up influencing labor productivity. Prioritization of certain SEW dimensions over others may have an influence on decisions such as capital investment, which may alter total factor productivity and eventually labor productivity. However, in this chapter we will focus on how SEW may influence people management and thus impact the attitudes and behaviors of the workforce, which are the primary indicators of resourceful labor use.

The remainder of this chapter is organized as follows. In the next section, we briefly review three literature streams that elucidate how family control of the firm may end up influencing the attitudes and behaviors of the workforce and ultimately affect the firm's labor productivity. Then, we build upon the SEW perspective of family firms to develop a set of propositions that connect SEW priorities to labor productivity. The underlying idea is that SEW priorities warrant adoption of a set of policies and behaviors among the controlling family managers that shape the behaviors and attitudes of the workforce, and these in turn affect labor productivity. Importantly, our model helps explain differences in labor productivity between family and nonfamily firms across different firm sizes, as well as differences in labor productivity among family firms. The final section summarizes the main conclusions of our approach.

11.2. LITERATURE REVIEW

In this section, we briefly review the main findings of three different and largely disconnected streams of research that help explain the theoretical framework we develop later: productivity and family control of the firm, productivity and people management, and decision-making in family firms.

11.2.1. Productivity and Family Control of the Firm

Firm-level productivity is a central variable in the study of firm performance. Because of its importance, it has been a topic of interest in many research efforts across years and disciplines (see, for example, Grifell-Tatjé and Lovell 1999; Huselid 1995; Lagakos and Waugh 2013). Despite the widespread interest in this variable, relatively few studies have attempted to explain the impact that ownership may have on firm productivity (Barbera and Moores 2013; Bloom and Van Reenen 2007, 2011; Palia and Lichtenberg 1999). These few studies converge on a common conclusion: the person at the helm matters when it comes to explaining differences in productivity levels. As noted in the introduction to this chapter, families are one of the most common types of firm owners in every country. Yet if little is known about the effect of ownership generally on firm productivity, even less is known about the impact of family control. The fairly exhaustive list of previous investigations on the subject compiled in an article by Barbera and Moores (2013) identifies only six studies. Only a few more recent studies could be added to this short list.

The studies conducted to date on the impact of family control on productivity have not reached a consensus on whether family firms are more or less productive compared to their nonfamily counterparts, or the circumstances under which family firms are more productive. Most previous studies have focused on the question of whether family firms are more or less productive than nonfamily firms. A review of the results shows that some studies report better productivity among family firms (Galve-Gorriz and Salas 2011; Sraer and Thesmar 2007), while others report worse productivity (Barth et al. 2005; Bloom et al. 2012). Differences in samples, time frames, and/or methodologies may explain this lack of consensus to a certain degree.

In this context, Barbera and Moores (2013) have suggested that family firms may exhibit better labor productivity than their nonfamily counterparts, particularly in the case of small firms. This apparent advantage in labor productivity may disappear as a firm increases in size. This relative advantage of family firms in terms of people's contribution to productivity stands in sharp contrast to another finding in the literature on family firms, which is that family-controlled firms are, in general, less likely, particularly when they are family managed, to implement more sophisticated practices that result in greater motivation and productivity among employees (Bloom et al. 2012; Bloom and Van Reenen 2007, 2011; Cruz et al. 2011). The theoretical framework we develop later in this chapter seeks to reconcile this apparent contradictory evidence.

11.2.2. Productivity and People Management

There is a long line of studies in human resource management (HRM) that have examined how HRM practices impact labor productivity. Similarly, there is also a large related stream of studies on the relationship between people management practices and firm performance as well as on employees' attitudes and behavior.

Most of the research efforts within this literature have been concerned with the question of whether a set of people management practices, often identified as high performance work practices (HPWPs), improve labor productivity independent of the context in which they were implemented, or whether their influence is contingent upon certain factors. HPWPs encompass a set of mutually reinforcing people management practices that positively impact labor productivity by enhancing ability, motivation, and the opportunity to participate (Appelbaum et al. 2000). Extensive training, rigorous selection procedures, cross-functional and cross-trained teams, information sharing, participatory mechanisms, above-market pay, and performance-based rewards are among the practices usually acknowledged as part of HPWPs. In this vein, it is also argued that the effectiveness of these practices should be greater when they are implemented as a bundle than when they are implemented in isolation (Datta et al. 2005).

Early research showed that HPWPs were indeed beneficial for labor productivity (e.g., Huselid 1995; Ichniowski et al. 1997). A comprehensive study conducted by Datta and colleagues (2005) concluded that while the impact of the implementation of HPWPs on labor productivity may vary depending on industry characteristics, it is always beneficial. A more recent meta-analysis conducted by Jiang and colleagues (2012) also pointed toward the positive influence of HPWPs on labor productivity. While these authors covered a broader range of research in their meta-analysis, they confirmed that different bundles of HPWPs positively influence employee human capital and motivation. Their impact subsequently reduces turnover rates and improves operational outcomes, including productivity, and finally firm-level financial performance (Bloom and Van Reenen 2011; Bloom et al. 2012).

Another relevant aspect concerning the effectiveness of HPWPs and their influence on labor productivity has to do with managers and their leadership style. For example, the research conducted by Bloom and associates (2007, 2011, 2012) presents managers and their actions as key drivers of firm-level productivity. Managers may vary in their leadership styles. A common classification of leadership styles in studies exploring the impact of leadership on employee behavior and performance is the transformational versus transactional dichotomy (Bass, 1985; Burns, 1978). Transactional leaders set clear goals and targets for followers and employ rewards or punishments to encourage compliance with those goals. Transformational leaders, on the other hand, create a vision to guide change through inspiration and execute change through the commitment of the members of their group. Studies on the impact of these two leadership styles have shown that transformational leadership may be more effective in generating positive employee attitudes and behaviors, and ultimately greater labor productivity (Jung and Avolio 2000; MacKenzie et al. 2001). For example, in a study of salespeople's performance, MacKenzie et al. (2001) observed that transformational leadership influences salespeople to perform above and beyond the call of duty. The impact of leadership styles on employees is often mediated by employees' trust in managers, which is another key variable that may help explain the relationship between HRM and employee attitudes and behaviors (Jung and Avolio 2000; MacKenzie et al. 2001; Zhu and Akhtar 2014).

11.2.3. Decision-Making in Family Firms

The large body of literature on family firms has always pointed toward the role that non-economic goals play in the decision-making processes and outcomes of family-controlled firms. The close association between the family and the firm spheres in this particular type of firm introduces targets in the management process that are not necessarily compatible with pure economic or efficiency goals. While non-economic goals may also be present in nonfamily firms, they are particularly noticeable in family firms. Furthermore, the literature on family firms has been able to identify and describe the non-economic goals that are most relevant to family firms. Gomez-Mejia and colleagues (2007) grouped these non-economic goals that meet the family's affective needs under the SEW label.

Importantly, Gomez-Mejia and colleagues (2007) use behavioral theory to argue that decision-making in family firms is primarily directed toward the preservation of SEW, even if this means accepting greater economic risk. They find support for this proposition in a study of Spanish olive oil mills. Other studies have confirmed the importance of SEW protection motives in the decision-making processes of family firms and have helped to consolidate the SEW perspective as one of the principal frameworks for the study of family firms (Gomez-Mejia et al. 2011).

SEW protection—and more specifically, the desire to protect one of the key dimensions of SEW, control—has also been linked with the likelihood of incorporating nonfamily executives within the firm. In certain family firms, the fear of losing control over firm operations explains the absence of nonfamily executives. This is important because the absence or presence of nonfamily executives explains part of the variation in HRM practices among family firms, with nonfamily executives bringing more advanced management practices to the firm (Bloom and Van Reenen 2011). The failure to adopt advanced management practices by family firms run by family members may be important, as its use has been linked with improved labor productivity and finally improved financial performance (Bloom et al. 2012). We will delve into the consequences of family versus outside management later on in section 11.3.3.

Recently, some studies have set out to further refine and develop the SEW perspective in an attempt to reach a better understanding of the decision-making processes in individual family firms and of the differences in such processes among family firms. In this vein, Berrone et al. (2012) argue that SEW is a multidimensional construct composed of five interrelated dimensions, which they summarized under the "FIBER" label: family control and influence (F), identification with the firm (I), binding social ties (B), emotional attachment (E), and the renewal of family bonds (R). "F" refers to the utilities family members receive from exerting control and influence over the business. "I" addresses the close identification of the family with the firm. "B" captures the reciprocal bonds seen within family businesses that are not exclusively between family members but are extended to a wider set of constituencies. Nonfamily employees often share the family's attachment to the firm via a sense of belonging, promoting stability and commitment to the firm. "E" captures the affective content of SEW and refers to the role of emotions in the family business context. Because the boundaries between the family and the corporation are somewhat blurred in family businesses, emotions permeate the organization, influencing the family business's decision-making process. Finally, "R" refers to the intention of handing the business down to future generations.

Relatedly, Miller and Le Breton-Miller (2014) differentiate between restricted and extended SEW. The former captures the emphasis on permanent job security and access to business resources for all current family members, while the latter encompasses the long-term well-being of the firm through formation of sustainable relationships with stakeholders to increase the chances of firm survival, and to ensure goodwill toward the family and its business. Different facets or dimensions of SEW may trigger different strategic responses and behaviors.

Because of the multidimensional nature of SEW, sometimes there may be a conflict among its dimensions. For example, Cruz et al. (2014) indicate that social activities may improve family image and reputation but may threaten control. These authors suggest that in order to protect their SEW endowment as much as possible, family firms may try to satisfy both goals by differentiating their approach when dealing with different groups of stakeholders. Specifically, they note that when it comes to corporate social responsibility, the way to address the conflict between competing SEW dimensions is to be more socially responsible with external stakeholders but less socially responsible with internal stakeholders—including the firm's employees—than nonfamily firms. Their analysis, based on a sample of large publicly traded European firms, confirms the latter view and finds no differences between family and nonfamily firms with regard to their social responsibility toward external stakeholders.

11.3. AN SEW FRAMEWORK OF LABOR PRODUCTIVITY IN FAMILY FIRMS

In this section, we build upon existing literature on family firms, and particularly on the SEW perspective, to link family control of the firm with labor productivity (i.e., the contribution of people to the firm's output). In line with recent developments in the family business literature, we take into consideration the multidimensional nature of SEW to propose that controlling families may prioritize certain dimensions of SEW over others, either because these dimensions conflict with others, or simply because controlling families show a personal preference for these dimensions. This prioritization, which manifests in the desire to protect primarily certain aspects of SEW, will influence a firm's decision-making and therefore will impact organizational aspects such as trust formation, leadership style, the presence of influential nonfamily managers, and the adoption of HRM practices, all of which may ultimately influence the basis of firms' labor productivity: employees' attitudes and behavior. In our model, firm size is projected as a central factor for understanding the effect of SEW priorities on labor productivity.

But before we develop the specific propositions of our model, we must consider the dimensions of SEW and their prioritization. We are going to build our arguments upon the previously described FIBER model proposed by Berrone et al. (2012). While interrelated, the five dimensions of SEW described in the FIBER model may lead to different behaviors and reactions, which may have different implications for firm management. Families seek to maximize their SEW, and it may seem logical to expect that families will look for improvements in all SEW dimensions. However, family members may also show a preference for some dimensions over others; that is, within their overall tendency to protect their SEW, they may prioritize some dimensions or aspects of SEW over others, and therefore seek to protect those dimensions first. These priorities may reflect the personal preferences and experiences of the owning family. In cases in which SEW dimensions may conflict (Cruz et al. 2014), these preferences would determine which dimension is attended to first. Since decision-making will be influenced by the SEW dimension or dimensions that are ranked higher, differences in prioritization may lead to differences in the decisions made by different family firms. Depending on the dimensions of SEW that are prioritized, family firms may experience different productivity outcomes.

We argue that two main groups of family firms can be distinguished based on which SEW dimensions of the FIBER model they rank first: those that primarily emphasize F and E versus those that put emphasis on I, B, and R. This dichotomization is in line with the proposal by Miller and Le Breton-Miller (2014) that differentiates between restricted SEW and extended SEW. While restricted priorities are highly family-centric and are at odds with the interests of nonfamily stakeholders and the firm in the long run, extended SEW priorities result in benefits that go beyond the owning family. The emphasis in protecting each of these two types of SEW may trigger different strategic responses and behaviors. For example, restricted SEW could be connected with conservatism, sparse investment, risk aversion, or family extraction of funds from the business. In contrast, extended SEW leads to investment in products and processes and continuous reinvestment in the business and its renewal. We suggest that the FIBER dimensions of family control and influence and emotional attachment (F and E) are representative of restricted SEW priorities and that the dimensions of family identification, binding social ties, and the renewal of family bonds (I, B, and R) are characteristic of extended SEW priorities.

We now move to our theoretical framework. In what follows, we first elaborate on the relationship between SEW priorities, trust, and labor productivity. Then, we connect SEW priorities with the leadership style of managers, and explore its consequences for the development of trust and ultimately for a firm's labor productivity. We then move to an analysis of the link between SEW priorities and the presence of nonfamily managers, connecting it with the adoption of HPWPs and labor productivity. Finally, and based on all the preceding arguments, we advance propositions about the relationship between SEW priorities and the firm's labor productivity. In all these cases, we observe that as a firm grows in size, focusing on certain SEW priorities may be more beneficial for a firm's labor productivity. Our model predicts, in line with existing empirical evidence (Barbera and Moores 2013), that small family firms show better levels of labor productivity than nonfamily firms of the same size. However, as firms grow in size, the labor productivity of family firms that focus on the F and E priorities of the FIBER model will be lower than that of comparable nonfamily firms, while the labor productivity of family firms emphasizing the I, B and R priorities of the FIBER model will be on par with that of nonfamily firms of similar size.

11.3.1. SEW Priorities, the Formation of Trust, and Labor Productivity

Trust, or the willingness to make oneself vulnerable to others despite uncertainty about their motives and prospective actions (Kramer 1999; Mayer et al. 1995; McAllister 1995), is often a central feature in relationships that involve the exchange of valuable resources. Trust is perceived to foster better cooperation (Messick and Brewer 1983) and richer information exchange (Uzzi 1996) than would otherwise occur.

The extant literature on trust distinguishes between cognition-based trust and affect-based trust. The central distinction between these two forms can be explained in terms of how people place trust in others—from the head (cognition-based) versus from the heart (affect-based). Cognition-based trust is based on performance-related cognitions such as competence, responsibility, reliability, and dependability. Conversely, affect-based trust refers to "emotional bonds between individuals" that are grounded upon "expressions of genuine care and concern for the welfare" of the other party (McAllister 1995). It emphasizes empathy, affiliation, and rapport on the basis of a shared regard for the other person. The distinction between cognition-based and affect-based trust brings to the fore two distinct systems of social-psychological processes. While cognition-based trust evolves from a calculative and instrumental assessment, affect-based trust emerges through empathy, rapport, and self-disclosure (Chua, Ingram, and Morris 2008).

The creation of both cognition-based and affect-based trust can enhance a firm's labor productivity. However, affect-based and cognition-based trust represent two different functions (Colquitt et al. 2012), and therefore the processes through which they affect firm productivity are different. Affect-based trust reflects a sense of social obligation to reciprocate and reinforce emotional bonds between two individuals, whereas cognition-based trust gives people a sense of confidence about the other party's decisions and actions (Mayer et al. 1995), thus reducing the sense of uncertainty and risk within a social exchange relationship (Colquitt et al. 2012). The prosocial motivation that arises through both forms of trust triggers employees' desire to expend greater effort and leads employees to engage in citizenship behaviors (Grant and Mayer 2009) that can enhance a firm's labor productivity.

Within the context of family businesses, SEW priorities in family firms may influence the development of cognition-based and affect-based trust, and ultimately labor productivity. When a family firm is small in size, it is far more likely to have a strong communitarian culture (Nicholson 2008). Such a culture lends itself well to the formation of affect-based relationships. At this stage, irrespective of the SEW priorities emphasized by the family firm, we expect a higher incidence of open communication, resource sharing, and cooperation. In small firms, it is considerably easier for family owners to convey care and consideration to a majority of employees. This behavior can help foster positive perceptions of the owning family's motives and enables the formation of affect-based trust. Affect-based trust in turn can contribute to a belief among employees that the owning family will form positive social exchange relationships with them and encourages them to invest time and effort in a way that benefits the firm (Colquitt et al. 2012; Zhu and Akhtar, 2014), thus enhancing labor productivity. Importantly, the proportion of family members who are also employees or managers of the firm is higher in smaller firms than in larger firms. Hence,

> *Proposition 1a: Employees in small family firms will show high levels of affect-based trust, which will positively contribute to a firm's labor productivity.*

However, as a firm grows in size, fostering affect-based trust will become more challenging. Larger firms are less likely to have a communitarian culture, and their family owners are less likely to share close ties with a majority of employees. Under these conditions, because it is more difficult for family owners to form personal relationships with employees, it is unlikely that family owners will be able to create an impression of care and concern for employee welfare (Miller, Minichilli, and Corbetta 2013). The proportion of family members in the workforce is also smaller in large firms.

We contend that a focus on the SEW priorities of family identification, binding social ties, and the renewal of family bonds (I, B, and R) can enable the formation of cognition-based trust. In contrast, a focus on firm control and influence and emotional attachment (F and E) is less likely to facilitate cognition-based trust as the firm grows in size. Family identification with the firm aligns the interests of family owners and a number of other stakeholders, including employees and consumers. This tendency stems from the fact that a family owner or employee experiences deep psychological gratification when his or her beliefs about the firm become self-referential or self-defining (Gomez-Mejia et al. 2007); hence, it is in his or her interest to maintain an attractive and a positive organizational identity. Family owners and managers' strong identification with the family business also leads the firm's employees to infer that the firm has qualities such as power, competence, efficiency, and moral worth (Gecas 1982) and gradually facilitates the formation of cognition-based trust. With regard to binding social ties, family firms possess unique opportunities to generate reciprocal stewardship through their time-honored relationships with family and nonfamily members. These binding ties are a source of social capital for the family firm (Arregle et al. 2007) and can facilitate positive perceptions about the firm's reliability and competence; hence, they also facilitate cognition-based trust. The desire for the renewal of family bonds encourages family owners to adopt an attitude that is less one of personal self-interest than one of stewardship (Le Breton-Miller and Miller 2009). Furthermore, it can also foster a long-term strategic perspective on the business and allows firms to mitigate the pitfalls of short-termism (Nicholson 2008). Together, these SEW priorities facilitate the formation of cognition-based trust among employees.

Further, although it is difficult for affect-based trust to emerge in a large family firm, the formation of cognition-based trust among employees can serve as a stepping-stone to the formation of affect-based trust. While cognition-based trust relies on evidence of another person's reliability and competence, affect-based trust arises from an individual's emotions and a sense of another person's feelings and intentions. Prior research suggests that affect-based trust is more enduring and generalizable over situations than cognition-based trust (Lewicki and Buncker 1996). Within a family firm setting, the experience of successful social exchange interactions that stem from cognition-based trust between nonfamily employees and family owners/managers will gradually facilitate the formation of closer personal ties between them. These ties in turn may promote the formation of affect-based trust. While this does not mean that affect-based trust necessarily follows from the formation of cognition-based trust, it has been suggested that a baseline level of cognition-based trust is a precursor to the formation of emotional attachments that are characteristic of affect-based trust. Thus, cognition-based trust may positively influence the formation of affect-based trust (McAllister 1995).

In sum, as family firms grow in size, cognition-based trust is more likely to develop in those firms that prioritize family identification (I), binding social ties (B), and the renewal of family bonds (R). Cognition-based trust may also gradually evolve into affect-based trust. Therefore, it follows that only family firms that emphasize the I, B, and R dimensions of the FIBER model would develop cognition-based trust, which would potentially lead to affect-based trust, and that both forms of trust would foster the prosocial motivations that will ultimately contribute to improved employee productivity. Hence,

> Proposition 1b: As a family firm grows in size, only family firms with a focus on the I, B, and R priorities of the FIBER model will be likely to experience both cognition-based and affect-based trust, which in turn will positively contribute to a firm's labor productivity.

11.3.2. SEW Priorities, Leadership Styles, and Labor Productivity

The SEW priorities emphasized by family firms also determine the type of leadership approach adopted by family owners and managers. An emphasis on restricted SEW priorities, such as family control and influence and emotional attachment, favors a transactional approach toward managing people. The desire to exercise authority and maintain family influence is compatible with the transactional approach for a number of reasons. First, although transactional leadership is conceptualized as an exchange of valued outcomes, scholars have observed that relationships between leaders and followers are often based on contingent rewards and reprimands. Effective transactional leaders clarify the roles that followers must play and the task requirements they must accomplish to reach their goals while fulfilling the mission of the firm (Kuhnert and Lewis 1987). Furthermore, they also monitor followers' performance and take corrective action when necessary (Howell and Avolio 1993). The weight given to performance monitoring within the transactional approach is a good fit with the owning family's desire to exercise family control and influence.

The emotional attachment dimension of SEW, which suggests that family businesses are places where the owning family's needs for belonging, affect, and intimacy are satisfied (Kepner 1983), is associated with the transactional approach for different reasons. A high level of emotional attachment among members of the owning family is often associated with job security and access to business resources for family members. However, it can give rise to asymmetric altruism, where the altruism that is extended to family employees is generally not extended to nonfamily employees, thus triggering feelings of injustice among nonfamily employees. This type of altruism may also result in nepotism, entrenchment, and family extraction of perquisites from the business. In an environment where nonfamily employees' perceptions of organizational justice are of secondary importance, the firm will likely focus on merely reaching an agreement between leaders (management) and followers (employees) concerning what the follower will receive for achieving a negotiated level of performance (Howell and Avolio 1993). Thus, we expect an emphasis on emotional attachment to be associated with a transactional approach toward managing employees.

> *Proposition 2a: In family firms, a focus on the F and E priorities of the FIBER model will be associated with a transactional leadership style in people management.*

On the other hand, the presence of extended SEW priorities such as family identification, binding social ties, and the renewal of family bonds through succession creates an environment that is conducive to a transformational leadership approach toward managing people. Transformational leadership originates within the personal values and beliefs of leaders and goes beyond an exchange of commodities between leaders and followers (Bass 1985; Kuhnert and Lewis 1987). It focuses on developing, intellectually stimulating, and inspiring followers to transcend their own self-interests for a higher collective purpose or a vision. Thus, transformational leaders center their efforts on "longer term goals and place value on developing a vision and inspiring followers to pursue the vision; change or align systems to accommodate their vision rather than work within existing systems; and coach followers to take on greater responsibility for their own development, as well as the development of others" (Howell and Avolio 1993:, 891–892). Extended SEW priorities encompass benefits that go beyond the family and include goals such as enhancing a firm's reputation with stakeholders, as well as forming sustainable relationships with partners (Berrone et al. 2012). Given these characteristics, we argue that a transformational leadership style, with its long-term and inspirational approach toward pursuing a desired vision, is a good fit for a firm that emphasizes extended SEW priorities.

> *Proposition 2b: In family firms, a focus on the I, B, and R priorities of the FIBER model will be associated with a transformational leadership style in people management.*

Differences in SEW priorities would engender differences in leadership styles, which in turn are likely to generate differences in labor productivity between firms, particularly as they grow in size. As mentioned earlier, while trust among managers and employees can be developed with relative ease in small family firms, as the firm grows in size the formation of relationships that facilitate the emergence of trust among employees becomes more challenging. However, transformational leaders who operate out of deeply held value systems are able to demonstrate confidence and motivate followers to change their existing perceptions, beliefs, and goals. Indeed, transformational leaders can arouse followers' trust in both cognitive and affective domains (Schaubroeck et al. 2011), but will do so for different reasons (Zhu and Akhtar 2014). Transformational leaders may engage in a number of impression-management activities to establish a devoted and capable image (Bass 1985). Often they may utilize written communications or public speeches to successfully convince their followers to believe in their vision. The trust arising from such a process has a cognitive element because direct social interaction may not necessarily be involved (Zhu and Akhtar 2014). These behaviors send out signals about the leaders' qualities, and followers may draw inferences about leaders' characteristics, such as integrity and ability, which leads to cognition-based trust (Dirks and Ferrin 2002).

On the other hand, the development of affect-based trust is contingent upon the formation of socioemotional relationships between leaders and followers (Dirks and Ferrin 2002). Once a certain number of interactions involving cognition-based trust have occurred between leaders and followers, the two parties may develop affect-laden relationships with each other. When that happens, followers begin to perceive transformational leaders as their role models, internalize the leaders' values and beliefs, and learn desired behaviors that are consistent with these values and beliefs (Kark et al. 2003). At this point, leaders may also show concern for followers' needs and their fulfillment. When employees perceive care and consideration from their leaders—in this case, family owners or managers—they reciprocate by developing affect-based trust toward their leaders. As previously stated, we expect that an increase in both cognition-based and affect-based trust would trigger the processes of employee motivation and prosocial behaviors that improve labor productivity.

In sum, generating trust among employees that would contribute to better labor productivity becomes more challenging as the firm grows in size. Family firms that use a transformational leadership style will be more likely to generate that trust when the firm grows larger. Taking into consideration our previous propositions about SEW priorities and leadership style, only the family firms that focus on the I, B and R priorities will be the ones that will be likely to adopt such a transformational leadership style, and therefore the ones that will be more likely to experience the positive effects that such a style may bring to labor productivity as the firm grows in size. Hence,

Proposition 2c: As a family firm grows in size, only family firms with a focus on the I, B, and R priorities of the FIBER model will be associated with a transformational leadership approach that will favor the formation of both cognition-based and affect-based trust, which in turn will positively contribute to a firm's labor productivity.

11.3.3. SEW Priorities, Nonfamily Managers, and Labor Productivity

We also expect that the dimensions of family influence and emotional attachment will have a negative impact on the appointment of nonfamily managers and adoption of HPWPs, whereas an emphasis on family identification, binding social ties, and the renewal of family bonds will be positively associated with the inclusion of nonfamily managers on the top management team and the use of HPWPs. The absence or presence of nonfamily managers generated by different SEW priorities may hold important implications for a firm's labor productivity, particularly when the firm grows larger.

Family owners' desire to maintain strong control over the firm can lead to asymmetric treatment of family versus nonfamily managers. The SEW perspective predicts that, in order to preserve SEW, family owners perceive the need to control the firm on a permanent basis (Berrone et al. 2012). Thus, they engage in strategies that empower them to retain or extend their power over the firm's operations. Often, they do this by employing family members on the top management team even though these individuals are not qualified (Chua et al. 2009). The "emotional attachment" dimension of SEW can also explain this differential treatment. Due to the type of social links family members have with their firms, family companies become the place where family owners satisfy their needs for affection and belonging (Berrone et al. 2012). The presence of family altruism fosters a set of interdependent relationships among family members that differentiates them from people outside the family (Chua et al. 2009). Thus, family altruism can cause inconsistencies in the application of organizational rules depending on whether the employee is a family or a nonfamily member. The presence of emotional attachment among family members also gives rise to a natural inclination to prioritize income and employment for family members (Levie and Lerner 2009) and to appoint more family members within the top management team. Moreover, the asymmetries in treatment that arise from an emphasis on restricted SEW priorities (i.e., control and emotional attachment) might generate agency issues such as adverse selection and opportunism. These issues could be at odds with the adoption of practices such as HPWPs (Bloom et al. 2012), which emphasize consistent application of performance standards, active employee participation in decision-making processes, and unbiased progression opportunities for all employees. Hence, family firms that emphasize the F and E dimensions of SEW are less likely to incorporate nonfamily managers, which will suppress the adoption of HPWPs. Consequently,

> *Proposition 3a: A focus on the F and E priorities of the FIBER model will hinder the presence of nonfamily executives in family firms, which in turn will hinder the adoption of HPWPs.*

On the other hand, an emphasis on extended SEW priorities facilitates the presence of nonfamily executives on the top-management teams of family firms. These

SEW priorities promote stewardship motivations, which can manifest in lifelong commitment to the firm, farsighted perspectives, assiduous management of organizational resources, and a number of competency-creating investments (Davis et al. 1997). In family firms that attach value to the family identity, family owners and managers may be more willing to do what it takes to strengthen the business (Donaldson and Davis 1991). Moreover, firms that esteem long-term social ties and encourage the renewal of family bonds through succession are particularly likely to shun "quick-fix" solutions. They are less likely than firms that emphasize restricted SEW priorities to make opportunistic decisions that may serve the family's self-interest in the short term but destroy morale and erode the firm's human capital and knowledge base in the long term (Laverty 1996). Thus, we expect such family firms to favor professionalizing the firm by appointing nonfamily executives who are hired on the basis of merit from a competitive labor pool. Competent nonfamily managers, who tend to make decisions based on logic and rational analysis, are more apt to adopt sophisticated management practices such as HPWPs than family managers (Bloom et al. 2012; Bloom and Van Reenen 2011), whose decisions are often dictated by intuition and altruism. In addition, nonfamily managers tend to focus on economic goals to increase their payoffs at the employing firm and to enhance their human capital, which improves their standing in executive labor markets (Patel and Cooper 2014). Furthermore, nonfamily managers have a more positive attitude toward change and growth (Poza, Alfred, and Maheshwari 1997) and focus consistently on practices that are likely to reap better economic rewards. Thus, we expect there to be a higher incidence of HPWPs as the number of nonfamily managers on the top-management team increases.

Proposition 3b: A focus on the I, B, and R priorities of the FIBER model will facilitate the presence of influential nonfamily executives in family firms, which in turn will facilitate the adoption of HPWPs.

As a family firm grows in size, higher productivity can be ensured through the presence of talented and engaged employees. However, scholars have recognized that there are limits to the quality of human capital in family firms because the goal of providing employment for family members to preserve key elements of SEW, such as control, leads to hiring suboptimal employees (Sirmon and Hitt 2003). Family firms can surmount these deficiencies in talent by increasing the heterogeneity of their human capital, particularly in their top management team. Hiring external managers involves changes in the firm's authority relationships, norms of legitimacy, and incentives (Gedajlovic et al. 2004), but it may also bring some important benefits for the company when it becomes larger. In complex administrative situations within large firms, the value of more formalized managerial skills and the mastery of management practices surpasses the benefits of the tacit knowledge that family members may possess (Miller et al. 2013). Hence, family members' lack of experience may put them at a disadvantage vis-à-vis outside nonfamily managers who are chosen from among a much larger pool of candidates on the basis of their competence alone (Salvato et al. 2012).

Greater heterogeneity in their top management teams would also increase family firms' stock of competing ideas, alternatives, and assumptions (Schweiger, Sandberg, and Ragan 1986; Sirmon and Hitt 2003).

Additionally, as we previously noted, nonfamily managers will have a strong incentive to professionalize the family firm through the introduction of sophisticated practices such as HPWPs so as to enhance their power and influence within the firm and reduce the amount of risk they face in a family firm context. This not only can ensure the family firm's long-term sustainability, but may also attract external talent to overcome the firm's human capital deficiencies that emerge as family firms grow larger, and enhance labor-productivity levels (Jiang et al. 2012). Hence, allowing nonfamily managers into the family firm may lead to improvements in labor productivity as the firm grows.

Within family firms that emphasize extended SEW priorities of family identification, binding social ties and renewal of family bonds, there is a strong belief that efficiency and productivity can be reinforced by bringing in professional nonfamily managers (Dyer 1989). Therefore, as the family firm grows in size, those firms that emphasize I, B, and R dimensions of SEW will show better labor-productivity levels than family firms that prioritize the F and E dimensions because nonfamily managers will face fewer obstacles to implementing sophisticated human resource practices such as HPWPs in firms with extended SEW priorities.

> *Proposition 3c: As a family firm grows in size, only firms with a focus on the I, B, and R priorities of the FIBER model will be associated with the presence of influential nonfamily executives and the implementation of HPWPs which in turn will positively contribute to a firm's labor productivity.*

This prediction is consistent with the evidence reported by Bloom and associates (2007, 2011, 2012), who note that family firms run by family members are less likely to implement advanced management practices, such as those previously described under the HPWPs label, which in turn hinders firm productivity. Our model proposes a mechanism to explain the conditions that favor or deter the presence of nonfamily executives in family firms, and its link with the adoption of advanced management practices and labor productivity.

11.3.4. SEW Priorities, Firm Size, and Labor Productivity

Our previous propositions link elements that, having been analyzed in different lines of research, have remained largely unconnected in business scholarship. In doing so, these propositions suggest a relationship between SEW priorities and firms' labor productivity that is contingent upon firm size. This association would be consistent with the limited prior empirical evidence on the impact of family firms on labor productivity.

When a family firm is small in size, irrespective of its SEW priorities, we expect it to have higher levels of labor productivity than small nonfamily firms. As stated previously, in small family firms employee trust formation is independent of the SEW priorities of the controlling family. Essentially, small size favors personal contact and exchange between different actors in the firm, and most important, between employees, managers, and owners of the company. Open communication, resource sharing, and mutual adaptation mechanisms are common in small firms, and these characteristics help build both cognitive-based and affect-based trust.

In a small family firm, family owners associate closely with their business over a prolonged period (Miller, Minichilli, and Corbetta 2013). Close ties and familiarity with a firm enhance attitudes of stewardship over a business, which signify highly valued emotional attachments to employees, customers, and other stakeholders both internal and external to the firm (Gomez-Mejia et al. 2007). The "family-like" atmosphere of such firms is likely to extend to other nonfamily workers when the firm is small enough. For example, there is evidence that family firms are more likely to offer employment protection to their workers (Bassanini et al. 2013; Block 2010), which could be considered proof that family owners protect their employees as they would do their own family and may engender a heightened sense of commitment among their workforce (Miller and LeBreton Miller 2005). Because of this, and largely independent of the SEW dimensions emphasized by the family, we expect small family firms to experience better levels of labor productivity than comparable nonfamily firms.

Proposition 4a: Labor productivity in small family firms will be higher than in comparable nonfamily firms.

However, as a firm grows in size and complexity, the factors that contributed to higher productivity when the firm was small will not have the same effect. It is at this stage, we argue, that the type of SEW priorities emphasized by the firm will either enhance or diminish labor productivity. We expect that growing family firms that emphasize family control and emotional attachment will show lower levels of labor productivity than those that emphasize other dimensions of SEW. This is because family firms that focus primarily on the former dimensions will experience lower levels of trust as the firm grows, which may hamper the firms' ability to encourage the necessary attitudes and behaviors from their employees to maintain high labor-productivity levels. This is in part due to the fact that a focus on family control and emotional attachment will lead to a transactional leadership style, which does not guarantee the appropriate levels of employee trust. In addition, we have also noted that a focus on the F and E dimensions of the FIBER model does not facilitate the presence of influential nonfamily managers in the firm. Thus, firms that emphasize these dimensions may be associated with a lower likelihood of implementing HPWPs.

Proposition 4b: As a family firm grows in size, a focus on the F and E priorities of the FIBER model will result in lower levels of labor productivity than those of comparable nonfamily firms and comparable family firms that emphasize other SEW dimensions.

On the other hand, extended SEW priorities such as family identification, binding social ties, and the renewal of family bonds foster higher labor productivity in family firms and bring it on par with that of nonfamily firms that are similar in size. It is possible that family firms that emphasize these priorities will continue to experience the superior labor-productivity levels of small family firms even as they continue to grow. In contrast to family firms that focus on restricted SEW priorities, these family firms are capable of creating and maintaining employee trust even when the size of the firm complicates the formation of close personal relationships and continuous exchange. Additionally, the managers of these family firms show a transformational leadership style that further reinforces trust formation. This, added to the presence of influential nonfamily managers and the greater likelihood of implementing HPWPs, forms the basis for higher levels of labor productivity. Therefore,

> *Proposition 4c: As a family firm grows in size, a focus on the I, B, and R priorities of the FIBER model brings family firms' levels of labor productivity on par with those of comparable nonfamily firms.*

11.4. Discussion and Conclusions

Labor productivity is the result of a combination of different factors. Employee attitudes and behaviors are central elements of that combination. In this chapter, we have argued that labor productivity in family firms may vary as a function of SEW priorities, defined as the dimensions of the family's SEW that are prioritized and attended to first. Such priorities influence the leadership style adopted by family leaders, the formation of employee trust, the presence of nonfamily managers in the firm, and the implementation of HPWPs. Together, these elements influence the attitudes and behaviors of the workforce and ultimately labor productivity.

Our model provides a mechanism to explain the impact of family ownership on firm-level productivity. More precisely, it clarifies some of the differences in labor-productivity levels observed between family firms and comparable nonfamily firms and also among family firms as a group. Specifically, as noted in the introduction to this chapter, the existing empirical evidence indicates that family and nonfamily firms may not be so different in terms of total productivity, and that the levels of labor productivity achieved by small family firms are actually superior to those obtained by comparable nonfamily firms. However, such differences in labor contributions may vanish with firm size.

In line with this evidence, our model considers how the influence of SEW priorities on labor productivity varies with size. Essentially, when family firms prioritize extended SEW dimensions (i.e., identification with the firm, binding social ties, and the renewal of family bonds), family leaders are more likely to use a transformational leadership style and to engender higher levels of cognition-based trust. Likewise, these family firms are more likely to incorporate nonfamily managers and to implement HPWPs. As the size of the firm increases, those elements are the ones that may guarantee the necessary attitudes and behaviors to keep labor productivity high. A more restricted SEW perspective (i.e., emphasis on control and emotions) is less likely to engender a positive response from employees as the firm grows and direct communication between family leaders and the larger proportion of nonfamily workforce becomes impossible. When family firms gravitate toward a leadership style that is less likely to generate trust as the firm grows, they show a lower propensity to incorporate nonfamily managers or HPWPs. As a firm grows in size, such decisions may limit the possibilities for engaging the company's workforce and achieving good labor-productivity levels.

The SEW framework stresses the links between the preferences of family owners, their decisions, and the consequences of those decisions. Our model further develops that framework by establishing, in line with other recent developments in the literature on family firms (Cruz et al. 2014; Miller and Le Breton-Miller 2014), the possibility of a categorization of SEW priorities. In particular, our model links these priorities with specific outcomes and ultimately with people's attitudes, behavior, and labor productivity. In this sense, the model further underscores the importance that the family owners' preferences may have for firm decision-making and results. While the firm's performance will clearly be influenced by forces outside the control of the firm's owners and managers, the goals and objectives that these owners and managers pursue have a bearing on the evolution of the firm.

While our focus in this chapter has been on labor productivity, our caveats and basic logic could be extended to the broader debate about the superior or inferior financial performance of family-controlled firms, and could provide insights into the factors that explain the heterogeneity of family firms. We link those differences directly with the preferences of the controlling family members. Family firms with a restricted SEW perspective would be less likely to outperform other family firms and comparable nonfamily firms, particularly as they grow in size. As explained, when the firm is small, direct contact with employees and the relatively large presence of family members in the firm may create a "family-like" atmosphere that compensates for other inefficiencies that may arise due to a restricted view of the firm's goals. However, as the firm grows in size, the relationships and leadership styles that tie the firm together tend to evaporate, and new ways of managing the workforce become necessary to remain competitive. In a growing family firm, the restricted SEW view is an impediment to the adoption of the people-management practices that are necessary to facilitate desired employee attitudes and behaviors.

Future research attempts may be directed toward empirically testing the propositions developed above. For example, it may be interesting to obtain further evidence on the labor-productivity differences, and by extension on financial performance, across family firms of different sizes. Methodologies such as the one employed by Barbera and Moores (2013) could be applied to further explore the connection between the family control of the firm and productivity levels, especially labor-productivity levels. Also, because these authors focused on small firms, it may be worthwhile to complement their findings with samples of medium-sized and large firms. Secondary data sources may be helpful for this endeavor.

But a direct test of our propositions would probably need the use of primary data sources. Survey instruments, case studies, or family stories could be instrumental in testing our propositions and may provide interesting insights. Probably the biggest challenge here, which could be extended to all research on the SEW perspective of family firms, is how to properly measure the family's SEW. While measures of other central constructs in our model, such as trust, leadership style, or HPWPs, have been developed, and even validated, in the literature, we still do not have a standard measure of SEW. There have been some attempts to measure SEW, but the path ahead is replete with methodological difficulties, and much needs to be done to build a reliable measure of a central concept of contemporary research in family firms. In this sense, the suggestions provided by Berrone et al. (2012) may be a good starting point to develop and validate a measure of SEW. This validation is not easy, though, since the identification of and access to firms and controlling families is a major barrier.

The difficulties just described involved in measuring SEW could be extended to the task of measuring the different dimensions of SEW and their relative importance for the controlling family that our framework requires. In this sense, the dichotomous categorization of SEW priorities we proposed in our model (i.e., extended versus restricted) facilitates this task. We can either ask for the relative importance the family gives to each of the two categories, or try to measure (using, for example, a 1 to 7 Likert-type scale) how important a particular dimension is to the owning family and determine whether the family favors one set of dimensions over the others.

NOTE

1. Martin Larraza-Kintana would like to acknowledge financial support from the Spanish Ministry of Economy and Competitiveness research projects ECO2013-48496-C4-2-R.

REFERENCES

Appelbaum, E., T. Bailey, P. Berg, and A. Kalleberg. 2000. *Manufacturing Advantage: Why High-Performance Work Systems Pay Off.* Ithaca, NY: Cornell University Press.

Arregle, J. L., M. A. Hitt, D. G. Sirmon, and P. Very. 2007. "The Development of Organizational Social Capital: Attributes of Family Firms." *Journal of Management Studies* 44 73–95.

Barbera, F., and K. Moores. 2013. "Firm Ownership and Productivity: A Study of Family and Non-Family SMEs." *Small Business Economics* 40: 953–976.

Barth, E., T. Gulbrandsen, and P. Schone. 2005. "Family Ownership and Productivity: The Role of Owner-Management." *Journal of Corporate Finance* 11: 107–127.

Bass, B. M. 1985. *Leadership and Performance Beyond Expectations.* New York: Free Press.

Bassanini, A., E. Caroli, A. Rebérious, and T. Breda. 2013. "Working in Family Firms: Less Paid but More Secure? Evidence from French Matched Employer-Employee Data." *Industrial and Labor Relations Review* 66: 433–466.

Berrone, P., C. Cruz, and L. R. Gómez-Mejía. 2012. "Socioemotional Wealth in Family Firms: Theoretical Dimensions, Assessment Approaches and Agenda for Future Research." *Family Business Review* 25(3): 258–279.

Berrone, P., C. Cruz, L. Gómez-Mejía, and M. Larraza-Kintana. 2010. "Socioemotional Wealth and Corporate Responses to Institutional Pressures: Do Family-Controlled Firms Pollute Less?" *Administrative Science Quarterly* 55: 82–113.

Block, J. 2010. "Family Management, Family Ownership, and Downsizing: Evidence from S&P 500 Firms." *Family Business Review* 23: 109–130.

Bloom, N., C. Genakos, R. Sadun, and J. Van Reenen. 2012. "Management Practices across Firms and Countries." *Academy of Management Perspectives* 26(1): 12– 33.

Bloom, N., and J. Van Reenen. 2007. "Measuring and Explaining Management Practices across Firms and Countries." *Quarterly Journal of Economics* 122: 1351–1408.

Bloom, N., and J. Van Reenen. 2011. "Human Resource Management and Productivity." *Handbook of Labor Economics* 4b: 1697–1767.

Burns, J. M. 1978. *Leadership*. New York: Harper & Row.

Chua, J. H., J. J. Chrisman, and E. B. Bergiel. 2009. "An Agency Theoretic Analysis of the Professionalized Family Firm." *Entrepreneurship Theory and Practice* 33: 355–372.

Chua, R. Y. J., P. Ingram, and M. W. Morris. 2008. "From the Head and the Heart: Locating Cognition- and Affect-Based Trust in Managers' Professional Networks." *Academy of Management Journal* 51: 436–452.

Colquitt, J. A., J. A. LePine, R. F. Piccolo, C. P. Zapata, and B. L. Rich. 2012. "Explaining the Justice–Performance Relationship: Trust as Exchange Deepener or Trust as Uncertainty Reducer?" *Journal of Applied Psychology* 97: 1–15.

Cruz, C., S. Firfiray, and L. R. Gome-Mejia. 2011. "Socioemotional Wealth and Human Resource Management (HMR) in Family-Controlled Firms." *Research in Personnel and Human Resources Management* 30: 159–217.

Cruz, C., M. Larraza-Kintana, L. Garces-Galdeano, and P. Berrone. 2014. "Are Family Firms Really More Socially Responsible?" *Entrepreneurship Theory and Practice* 38(6): 1295–1316.

Datta, D. K., J. P. Guthrie, and P. M. Wright. 2005. "Human Resource Management and Labor Productivity: Does Industry Matter?" *Academy of Management Journal* 48(1): 135–145.

Davis, J., R. Schoorman, and L. Donaldson. 1997. "Towards a Stewardship Theory of Management." *Academy of Management Review* 22: 20–47.

Dirks, K. T., and D. L. Ferrin. 2002. "Trust in Leadership: Meta-Analytic Findings and Implications for Organizational Research." *Journal of Applied Psychology* 87: 611–628.

Donaldson, L., and J. Davis. 1991. "Stewardship Theory or Agency Theory." *Australian Journal of Management* 16: 49–64.

Dyer, W. G., Jr. 1989. "Integrating Professional Management into a Family-Owned Business." *Family Business Review* 2: 221–235.

Galve-Gorriz, C., and V. Salas-Fumas. 2011. "Family Ownership and Firm Performance: The Net Effect of Productive Efficiency and Growth Constraints." *Innovar-Revista de Ciencias Administrativas y Sociales* 21: 155–170.

Gecas, V. 1982. "The Self-Concept." *Annual Review of Sociology* 8: 1–33.

Gedajlovic, E., M. Lubatkin, and W. Schulze. 2004. "Crossing the Threshold from Founder Management to Professional Management: A Governance Perspective." *Journal of Management Studies* 41: 899–912.

Gómez-Mejía, L. R., C. Cruz, P. Berrone, and J. De Castro. 2011. "The Bind That Ties: Socioemotional Wealth Preservation in Family Firms." *Academy of Management Annals* 5(1): 653–707.

Gómez-Mejía, L. R., K. Haynes, M. Nuñez-Nickel, K. J. L. Jacobson, and J. Moyano-Fuentes. (2007). "Socioemotional Wealth and Business Risks in Family-Controlled Firms: Evidence from Spanish Olive Oil Mills." *Administrative Science Quarterly* 52(1): 106–137.

Gomez-Mejia, L. R., M. Larraza-Kintana, and M. Makri. 2003. "The Determinants of Executive Compensation in Family-Controlled Public Corporations." *Academy of Management Journal* 46: 226–237.

Gomez-Mejia, L. R., M. Makri, and M. Larraza-Kintana. 2010. "Diversification Decisions in Family-Controlled Firms." *Journal of Management Studies* 47: 223–252.

Grant, A. M., and D. M. Mayer. 2009. "Good Soldiers and Good Actors: Prosocial and Impression Management Motives as Interactive Predictors of Affiliative Citizenship Behaviors." *Journal of Applied Psychology* 94: 900–912.

Grifell-Tatjé, E., and C. A. K. Lovell. 1999. "Profits and Productivity." *Management Science* 45: 1177–1193.

Howell, J. M., and B. J. Avolio. 1993. "Transformational Leadership, Transactional Leadership, Locus of Control, and Support for Innovation: Key Predictors of Consolidated-Business-Unit Performance." *Journal of Applied Psychology* 78: 891–902.

Huselid, M. A. 1995. "The Impact of Human Resource Management Practices on Turnover, Productivity, and Corporate Financial Performance." *Academy of Management Journal* 38: 635–672.

Ichniowski, C., K. Shaw, and G. Prennushi. 1997. "The Effects of Human Resource Management Practices on Productivity: A Study of Steel Finishing Lines." *American Economic Review* 87: 291–313.

Jiang, K., D. P. Lepak, J. Hu, and J. C. Baer. 2012. "How Does Human Resource Management Influence Organizational Outcomes? A Meta-Analytic Investigation of Mediating Mechanisms." *Academy of Management Journal* 55(6): 1264–1294.

Jung, D. I., and B. J. Avolio. 2000. "Opening the Black Box: An Experimental Investigation of the Mediating Effects of Trust and Value Congruence on Transformational and Transactional Leadership." *Journal of Organizational Behavior* 21: 949–964.

Kark, R., B. Shamir, and G. Chen. 2003. "The Two Faces of Transformational Leadership: Empowerment and Dependency." *Journal of Applied Psychology* 88: 246–255.

Kepner, E. 1983. "The Family and the Firm: A Coevolutionary Perspective." *Organizational Dynamics* 12: 57–70.

Kramer, R. M. 1999. "Trust and Distrust in Organizations: Emerging Perspectives, Enduring Questions." *Annual Review of Psychology* 50: 569–598.

Kuhnert, K. W., and P. Lewis. 1987. "Transactional and Transformational Leadership: A Constructive/Developmental Analysis." *Academy of Management Review* 12: 648–657.

Lagakos, D., and M. E. Waugh. 2013. "Selection, Agriculture, and Cross-Country Productivity Differences." *American Economic Review* 103: 948–980.

La Porta, R., F. Lopez-de-Silanes, and A. Shleifer. 1999. "Corporate Ownership around the World." *Journal of Finance* 54: 471–517.

Laverty, K. J. 1996. "Economic 'Short-Termism': The Debate, the Unresolved Issues, and Implications for Management." *Academy of Management Review* 21: 825–860.

Le Breton-Miller, I., and D. Miller. 2009. "Agency vs. stewardship in Public Family Firms: A Social Embeddedness Reconciliation." *Entrepreneurship Theory and Practice* 33: 1169–1191.

Levie, J., and M. Lerner. 2009. "Resource Mobilization and Performance in Family and Nonfamily Businesses in the United Kingdom." *Family Business Review* 22: 25–38.

Lewicki, R. J., and B. B. Buncker. 1996. "Developing and Maintaining Trust in Work Relationships." In *Trust in Organizations: Frontiers of Theory and Research*, edited by R. M. Kramer and T. R. Tyler, 114–139. Thousand Oaks, CA: Sage.

MacKenzie, S. B., P. M. Podsakoff, and G. A. Rich. 2001. "Transformational and Transactional Leadership and Salesperson Performance." *Journal of the Academy of Marketing Science* 29: 115–134.

Mayer, R. C., J. H. Davis, and F. D. Schoorman. 1995. "An Integrative Model Of Organizational Trust." *Academy of Management Review* 20: 709–734.

McAllister, D. J. 1995. "Affect- and Cognition-Based Trust as Foundations for Interpersonal Cooperation in Organizations." *Academy of Management Journal* 38: 24–59.

Messick, D., and M. Brewer. 1983. "Solving Social Dilemmas: A Review." In *Review of Personality and Social Psychology*, edited by L. Wheeler and P. Shaver, Vol. 4, 11–44. Beverly Hills, CA: Sage.

Miller, D., and I. Le Breton-Miller. 2005. *Managing for the Long Run: Lessons in Competitive Advantage from Great Family Businesses.* Cambridge, MA: Harvard Business Press.

Miller, D., and I. Le Breton-Miller. 2014. "Deconstructing Socioemotional Wealth." *Entrepreneurship Theory and Practice* 38: 713–720.

Miller, D., A. Minichilli, and G. Corbetta. 2013. "Is Family Leadership Always Beneficial?" *Strategic Management Journal* 34: 553–571.

Nicholson, N. 2008. "Evolutionary Psychology, Organizational Culture, and the Family Firm." *Academy of Management Perspectives* 22: 73–84.

Palia, D., and F. Lichtenberg. 1999. "Managerial Ownership and Firm Performance: A Re-examination Using Productivity Measurement." *Journal of Corporate Finance* 5(4): 323–339.

Patel, P., and D. Cooper. 2014. "Structural Power Equality Between Family and Non-Family TMT Members and the Performance of Family Firms." *Academy of Management Journal* 57: 1624–1649.

Poza, E. J., T. Alfred, and A. Maheshwari. 1997. "Stakeholder Perceptions of Culture and Management Practices in Family and Family Firms: A Preliminary Report." *Family Business Review* 10: 135–155.

Salvato, C., A. Minichilli, and R. Piccarreta. 2012. "Faster Route to the CEO Suite: Nepotism or Managerial Proficiency?" *Family Business Review* 25: 206–224.

Schaubroeck, J., S. S. Lam, and A. C. Peng. 2011. "Cognition-Based and Affect-Based Trust as Mediators of Leader Behavior Influences on Team Performance." *Journal of Applied Psychology* 96: 863–871.

Schweiger, D. M., W. R. Sandberg, and J. W. Ragan. 1986. "Group Approaches for Improving Strategic Decision Making: A Comparative Analysis of Dialectical Inquiry, Devil's Advocacy, and Consensus." *Academy of Management Journal* 29: 51–71.

Sirmon, D. G., and M. A. Hitt. 2003. "Managing Resources: Linking Unique Resources, Management and Wealth Creation in Family Firms." *Entrepreneurship Theory and Practice* 27: 339–358.

Sraer, D., and D. Thesmar. 2007. "Performance and Behavior of Family Firms: Evidence from the French Stock Market." *Journal of the European Economic Association* 5: 709–751.

Uzzi, B. 1996. "The Sources and Consequences of Embeddedness for the Economic Performance of Organizations: The Network Effect." *American Sociological Review* 61: 674–698.

Zhu, Y., and S. Akhtar. 2014. "How Transformational Leadership Influences Follower Helping Behavior: The Role of Trust and Prosocial Motivation." *Journal of Organizational Behavior* 35: 373–392.

CHAPTER 12

INNOVATION, MANAGEMENT
PRACTICES, AND
PRODUCTIVITY

MARY J. BENNER

12.1. INTRODUCTION

THIS chapter explores the relationships between and among innovation, management practices, and productivity—topics that have been studied in three distinct research domains with minimal conversation between them. Researchers in economics, interested in understanding the determinants of productivity largely at the macroeconomic level, have explored the influences of innovation on productivity, viewing innovation as an important driver of aggregate total factor productivity growth. A general finding from this work is that innovation at the firm level improves aggregate productivity and explains differences in productivity across industries and countries (e.g., Mohnen and Hall 2013). More recently, economists have also begun to study management practices, examining whether a specific set of "best practices" is an additional driver of differences in firm- and country-level productivity (e.g., Bloom and Van Reenan 2007). At the same time, in a separate research domain in the field of operations management, researchers have long studied the influences of management practices, such as Lean Manufacturing, Six Sigma, and ISO 9000, among others, on firm-level productivity-related outcomes. This work similarly studies how particular sets of "best practices" influence organizational outcomes, specifically focusing on the practices aimed at improving operational processes and efficiency in firms. Correspondingly, some of this research has found that the implementation of specific management practices intended to improve efficiency can indeed reduce costs and improve firm performance.

But these research streams have not generally considered whether and how these "best practices" affect firm innovation. Separately, research in management has studied the influence of management practices on innovation and has highlighted a paradox: that as organizations intentionally adopt "best practices" to improve operating processes and enhance efficiency, these activities also dampen and drive out innovation, particularly more novel innovations (Benner and Tushman 2002). Since it is the more novel forms of product innovation that are believed to explain productivity growth at the industry and country level in economics research, this creates an interesting puzzle that has not been addressed in these disparate research streams. If practices believed to improve firms' current productivity actually drive out firms' innovation in the longer term, it raises potentially important implications for firm, industry, and country productivity. Being able to produce Blackberry phones more efficiently is certainly one form of increased productivity, but it is clearly different from the potential longer-term outcomes from creating the iPhone. Prior research suggests that within-firm, undertaking the specific management practices involved in improving productivity in the products in an old technology can directly preclude the innovative activities required to create more novel innovations and future productivity growth in a new technology.

Combining these disparate streams of research—in particular, discussing how management practices not only influence productivity but also innovation—offers the potential for richer insights into the relationship between innovation, firm-level management practices undertaken to improve productivity, and productivity outcomes. In addition, this chapter also provides definitions of innovation and distinguishes among the many types of innovation that have been described in previous research, which help clarify the influences of management practices and innovation on productivity.

The chapter proceeds as follows. In section 12.2, I outline the definitions of types of innovation that have been used in past work. In sections 12.3 and 12.4, I review two separate bodies of research: the first from economics discussing the influence of innovation on productivity, and the second on the influence of management practices, including both a large body of research from the field of operations management and recent work from economics. This work discusses the influences of both innovation and specific management practices or "best practices" on improving firm-level operational efficiency or productivity. In section 12.5, I describe in more depth the paradox that has been described in prior research in management: specific management practices that are adopted as best practices intended to improve operational efficiency might at the same time dampen firm innovation. Thus, while these practices are adopted to improve productivity and efficiency, their effects on innovation likely have further—and possibly unintended—implications for productivity longer term and in the aggregate. In section 12.6, I discuss possible alternative explanations for findings from productivity research that are consistent with this paradox. In subsequent sections I further explore the implications that arise from combining insights from these disparate research streams. Finally, I develop several hypotheses and outline avenues for future research that would enhance our understanding of the important mechanisms underlying the relationships between management practices, innovation, and productivity.

12.2. INNOVATION DEFINED

It is useful to first clearly define *innovation* and the ways it has been discussed in past research. Scholars have distinguished between product and process innovation, incremental and radical innovation, new-to-the-world and new-to-the-firm innovation, the extent to which innovations serve new versus existing customers or incorporate new versus existing technologies, and in measures of innovation, innovation inputs versus innovation outputs.

The distinction between product and process innovation is particularly useful for the insights developed in this chapter. Mohnen and Hall (2013, 48), following the OECD's Oslo Manual (2005), define product innovation as "the introduction of a good or service that is new or significantly improved with respect to its characteristics or intended uses," whereas process innovation is the "implementation of a new or significantly improved production or delivery method." The important distinctions between product and process innovation have been captured in research on technological change, which describes alternating periods of a focus on product versus process innovation, driven by the dynamics of technology life cycles (Abernathy and Utterback 1978; Klepper, 1996; Tushman and Anderson 1986). Technology life cycles are typically depicted in stages, where a period of rapid product innovation, high uncertainty, and an influx of new entrants follows a major technological change—or discontinuity—in an industry. This stage is often followed by the emergence of a dominant technology standard, or a "dominant design," a reduction in the number of firms participating in the industry (often termed a "shakeout"), and a subsequent period of focus on process innovation and incremental improvements in the product. Thus, in these traditional life-cycle depictions of technological change, a focus on process innovation typically follows a period of product innovation, as firms learn to produce the dominant product design more efficiently.

In related ideas, scholars have also distinguished between incremental versus radical technological changes and innovations, broadly at the industry level and also at the firm level. Incremental innovations build on the existing industry technology (e.g., Abernathy and Utterback 1978; Benner and Tushman 2003; Henderson and Clark 1990; Tushman and Anderson 1986), while radical innovations entail a shift to a new base of knowledge or "science" underlying the products in an industry, along with an improved price/performance frontier for products enabled by the new technology (Benner and Tushman 2003; Henderson and Clark 1990). Examples of radical technological changes include the shift from silver halide film photography to digital technology in the photography industry, or the shift from mechanical escapement technology to quartz in the watch industry (Benner 2010; Landes 1983; Tripsas and Gavetti 2000). Such shifts are instances of technological substitution, where the new technology offers dramatic reductions in price, along with improved "performance" on particular technological dimensions that are important for adoption and diffusion. For example, the introduction of quartz technology in watches promised improved precision at much lower prices than the most precise watches utilizing mechanical technology. Similarly, digital technology in the photography industry promised higher resolution (measured in megapixels) at lower prices than traditional film technology. In both cases, as in many instances of technological substitution, products based on the new technology are typically not initially superior to products incorporating the existing technology, so substitution is not immediate; additional development and refinement of the new technology unfold before the promise of the new technological trajectory can be realized and substitution occurs. For example, the earliest quartz timepieces were clunky and unattractive compared to skillfully designed mechanical watches, but quartz watches soon became an attractive alternative to mechanical watches due to the relatively low cost for comparable precision (Landes 1983). Similarly, back in the early 1990s at the outset of digital photography, available digital cameras had either high resolution coupled with a very high price (16 megapixels for $25,000), or at a price targeted to individual consumers, but with very low resolution (VGA) (Benner 2010). Widespread diffusion of digital cameras (and technological substitution) generally occurred as three megapixel cameras reached a price near $300. Although industry insiders often realize that substitution will ultimately occur, the apparent inferiority of the new technology at the outset, uncertainty about the timing of change, and competition between the old and new technologies for a time creates a dilemma for incumbent firms: whether to engage in rapid incremental improvements and process innovation to compete with the new technology, or to adopt the new technology and make the corresponding investments in developing new capabilities. Research has documented the substantial improvements in the price/performance ratio of technologies on "the eve" of substitution, as producers strive to compete with a new technology. For example, mechanical watches improved substantially as quartz watches emerged (Landes 1983), and the "disposable" film cameras offered by film producers offered a dramatically improved price/performance for film technology as digital photography diffused.

Scholars have also distinguished innovations by their novelty, both relative to a particular firm's existing customers and also relative to its current technologies. For example, innovations have been characterized both by the extent to which they are aimed at a firm's (or business unit's) existing customers versus new/emerging customers, and the extent to which they incorporate a firm's current technologies versus technologies that are new to that firm or business unit (Benner and Tushman 2003). These ideas are closely related to the influential work by March (1991) and Levinthal and March (1993), which distinguishes between exploitation and exploration in organizational "search" or knowledge. "Exploitation" refers to building on and extending knowledge that is familiar to an organization, while "exploration" involves search for new knowledge in new and unfamiliar domains. These labels have been extended further, to characterizing innovation activities within firms as exploitation versus exploration (e.g., Benner and Tushman 2002; Rosenkopf and Nerkar 2001).

Finally, research further highlights the need to distinguish between innovation inputs (such as the decisions about R&D investments or capital expenditures by firms) versus outputs—the actual innovative products or processes that result from these investments (e.g., Crepon, Duguet, and Mairesse 1998).[1]

12.3. INNOVATION AND PRODUCTIVITY (FROM ECONOMICS)

Over the past few decades, economists studying productivity have looked to technological change, or innovation and research and development (R&D), to explain the "residual," that is, productivity increases or differences in productivity that are unexplained by changes in capital and labor (e.g., Solow 1957; Griliches 1979, 1996, 1998). This has prompted a rich stream of research in economics exploring the relationship between innovation and productivity (e.g., see Hall 2011; Mohnen and Hall 2013; and Syverson 2011 for reviews). The focus of this research has been on how "growth" or increases in total output, typically at the industry or country level, are influenced by firm-level innovation within those industries or countries. In this work, productivity is typically defined as the quantity of output that can be produced using a given level of inputs, and the relationship between inputs and outputs is modeled by economists using a production function, with capital and labor as the inputs. Productivity increases occur when more output is produced with a given set of inputs (or the same output with fewer inputs), and studies of productivity frequently focus on labor productivity (i.e., where the "input" under consideration is the number of employees).

The results of much of this research over several decades have shown consistent evidence that innovation, particularly product innovation, is a driver of productivity growth in industries and countries, giving rise to an important and well-understood idea that "innovation is a key factor of economic growth" (Mohnen and Hall 2013, 47). For example, Geroski (1989) found, in a study of firms in 79 industries in the United Kingdom, that innovation positively affected productivity growth rates. Crepon, Duguet, and Mairesse (1998) also found a positive relationship between innovation and firm productivity, using a measure of the "percentage share of firm innovative sales" (i.e., the percent of sales from products introduced in the most recent five years, from the French Innovation Survey). Cassiman, Golovko, and Martinez-Ros (2010) found that the positive relationship between firm productivity and exports in a sample of Spanish manufacturing firms can be explained by innovation—in particular, product innovation that is associated with productivity and that spurs small firms to enter the export market. Lentz and Mortensen (2008) also found a link between total factor productivity and product innovation, while others have found an influence of patents (Balasubramanian and Sivadasan 2011) and the number of products a firm produces (Bernard, Redding and Schott 2010) on productivity growth. Several other studies also show a positive relationship between product innovation and productivity or productivity growth (Belderbos, Carree, and Lokshin 2004; Hall, Lotti, and Mairesse 2009; Loof and Heshmati 2006).

Research in this area has traditionally relied on firm-level surveys, where product innovation and process innovation are measured with dummy variables indicating whether a firm has undertaken such activities in the past three years. In a few other studies, product innovation has been measured with a continuous variable, such as the share of total sales from new products (e.g., Crepon, Duguet, and Mairesse 1998). More recently, scholars have begun to use detailed "microdata," at the level of the establishment or firm, to better understand the drivers of productivity at both the firm level and in the aggregate (e.g., Bartelsman and Doms 2000; Foster, Haltiwanger, and Syverson 2008), and this work has similarly demonstrated links between innovation (R&D expenditures, patenting, and product innovation) and productivity (see Syverson, 2011).

Thus, the overall benefits of product innovation for increased productivity have been fairly well established in several studies that find a positive relationship between product innovation and total factor productivity. But in contrast to the consistent findings on the relationship between product innovation and productivity, the results of studies of process innovation on productivity have been more equivocal, with some scholars finding no relationship and some even finding a negative relationship between process innovation and productivity (Hall, Lotti, and Mairesse 2008; Loof and Heshmati 2006; Van Leeuwen and Klomp 2006), or a decrease in the benefits of process innovation over time (Huergo and Jaumandreu 2004). Similarly, although Cassiman et al. (2010) find that firms engaging in product innovation have greater productivity, they find no additional productivity for firms engaging in process innovation. Hall (2011:16) concludes in her review that there is an "economically significant impact of product innovation on revenue productivity and a somewhat more ambiguous impact of process innovation...."

These overall results about the influence of process innovation on productivity are puzzling, since given the typical focus of process innovation on improving efficiency, we would expect process innovation to even more directly and measurably improve productivity than product innovation. As Mohnen and Hall (2013, 51) note, "Process innovation is a priori expected to have a clearer positive effect on productivity as new processes are often introduced in order to reduce production costs by saving some of the more costly inputs (often labor)." Similarly, Cassiman et al. (2010) note, "Process innovation usually involves changes in the production process aimed at improving production efficiency, thus presumably having a direct effect on the firm's productivity. We do not observe such an effect in our data."

These scholars largely attribute this non- or negative result to measurement issues, noting that outcomes from product innovation might be more easily captured in the measures than process innovation, particularly when researchers use revenue (adjusted with price deflators to reflect "real" values) to measure productivity, rather than "real" or physical outputs. Mohnen and Hall (2013: 57) argue that market power differences might be associated with product innovation, affecting the revenue measure of output, "whereas efficiency improvements from process innovations may not show up in the revenue figures if they result in lower prices without corresponding increases in output." Cassiman et al. (2010) also note measurement issues that may explain their nonfinding: "The possible explanation could be that very often process innovation is incorporated in the capital investment. . . . As we already control for capital investment in our productivity measure (TFP), we should not expect a significant effect of process innovation on productivity measured as total factor productivity."

While these explanations may partly address why process innovation seems to have little effect on productivity (or a negative effect on productivity), the story may be a different one, not considered in this research. Later in this chapter I return to this puzzle and explore an alternative explanation from management research for the counterintuitive influence of process innovation on productivity that has not been examined by economists in studies on productivity and innovation.

12.4. Management Practices and Productivity (from Operations Management and Economics)

At the same time that researchers in economics have considered the influences of innovation on productivity growth in industries and countries, researchers in operations management have focused on how firms can—and should—improve firm-level efficiency and productivity through the implementation of specific sets of management practices. A long tradition of research in the operations management field has focused on the efficiency-enhancing effects of particular management practices (i.e., those specifically undertaken to directly improve operational processes and adhere to streamlined efficient processes). Such practices fall in the general category of "process-management practices," as they are typically focused on how firms can improve processes or procedures, by adopting best practices or streamlining and standardizing processes to make the firm more efficient. Over the last few decades, several programs focused on processes have diffused across—and have been implemented in—firms, including Total Quality Management (TQM), the Malcolm Baldrige National Quality Award, Business Process Reengineering, the International Organization for Standardization's Series 9000 program (ISO 9000), Six Sigma, Lean Manufacturing, and more recently, Lean Six Sigma (e.g., Garvin 1991; Harry and Schroeder 2000). These programs have been widely adopted by firms with the explicit intent to improve productivity and reduce costs (Linderman, Schroeder, Zaheer, and Choo 2003; Schroeder, Linderman, Liedtke, and Choo 2008; Swink and Jacobs 2012).

Research in this area often provides detailed descriptions of the elements of practices that organizations undertake, and it is often prescriptive, with these practices generally viewed as "best practice" in the research that has focused on the positive results of adopting such practices (e.g., Done, Voss, and Rytter 2011). Although this research proceeds in a different domain, and focuses on cost reductions or profitability rather than productivity per se, there are clear links between such practices and the research on productivity in economics.

The popularity of process-management practices arose from widely held beliefs, influenced by Deming (1986), Ishikawa (1985), and Juran (1989), that firms can increase efficiency and quality by focusing on process improvements and adhering to systems of streamlined processes. A large body of research including case studies has focused on demonstrating how such practices—that improve organizational processes by removing wasted steps—can spur cost reductions and increase operational efficiency. In this research, firms are viewed as a set of interdependent processes that span the organization, cutting across the department "silos" in organization structure that hamper communication and efficiency in many organizations, and create wasteful duplication or costly handoffs. These systems of integrated processes not only produce the outputs for the firm's final customers (e.g., Garvin 1998), but internal downstream processes (such as manufacturing) are also viewed as the "customers" of processes upstream (such as new product development or procurement), and improvements in processes are often guided by measures of satisfaction of the organization's internal "customers."

Process-management practices are expected to reduce costs as a firm creates more efficient processes, and also improve quality, resulting in better products that drive increases in revenue (e.g., Lo, Wiengarten, Humphreys, Yeung, and Cheng 2013; Swink and Jacobs 2012; Zu, Fredendall, and Douglas 2008). Thus, improvements from these management practices are expected to lead to greater profitability, through both increases in revenue and lower costs. Several studies have found benefits for firms from implementing the best practices associated with TQM, Lean Manufacturing, ISO 9000, and Six Sigma (e.g., Easton and Jarrell 1998; Shafer and Moeller 2012; Swink and Jacobs 2012; Wruck and Jensen 1994), while other work has shown mixed or equivocal results (Samson and Terziovski 1999; Sterman, Repenning, and Kofman 1997). Although a few researchers in this field have begun to study the benefits of these practices directly on productivity (Iyer, Saranga, and Seshadri 2013; Shafer and Moeller 2012), typically the dependent variable in these studies is financial or operating performance (e.g., measures of financial performance from the firm's income statements, such as return on assets or return on sales). The primary focus on efficiency improvements as the underlying mechanisms in the link between process management and improved performance parallels the mechanisms in economics literature on innovation and productivity.

Separately, a small but growing stream of research in economics has also studied the influence of particular management practices, or constellations of management practices, on productivity. For example, Ichniowski, Shaw, and Prennushi (1997) found that specific sets of human resources practices in combination have a complementary positive effect on productivity. More recently, research has also considered the influences of more general plant management practices on productivity (e.g., Bloom and Van Reenen 2007; see also Syverson 2011 for a review). Similar to the literature on innovation and productivity, this work seeks to understand the unexplained "residual" in productivity studies, now by considering the use of different management practices across firms. Bloom and Van Reenen (2007, 2010) use survey interviews to study the specific practices that plant managers employ. These are management practices deemed "best practices" (as suggested by a leading consulting firm), and Bloom and Van

Reenen find that the greater use of these practices is associated with better firm-level performance.

Taken together, this work suggests that the use of particular management practices can improve firm-level productivity. However, this work does not consider the important effects of management practices on innovation—particularly the possibility that a focus on process improvements and adherence to best practice can actually dampen important types of innovation in firms.

12.5. THE PARADOX: MANAGEMENT PRACTICES AND INNOVATION

Although the idea that there are "best practices" that all firms can (and should) adopt to improve productivity is clearly compelling, prior research suggests it is not so straightforward. Recent research on management practices in economics and operations management has generally overlooked the idea that management practices also affect innovation, with corresponding implications for productivity. Despite the promise of specific sets of management practices for improving productivity, a paradox arises, documented in research that considers how management practices focused on process improvement or process innovations in firms can actually dampen innovation (Adler et al. 2009; Benner and Tushman 2002, 2003; see also Swink and Jacobs 2012), particularly the more novel innovations that researchers argue underlie the largely unexplained productivity growth in industries and countries. The irony is, of course, that although process-improvement practices specifically—and best practices more generally—are undertaken with the intention of improving productivity, their influences become less clear if at the same time they also dampen innovation, another key driver of productivity. Research in management, applying insights from organizational learning theory (cf. Levitt and March 1988), highlights the important trade-offs between process improvement and innovation, illuminating how increased process improvement and adherence to "best practice" focused on incremental improvement within an organization can actually "crowd out" the more novel or radical product innovation that is particularly important for firm performance and survival, and relevant to this chapter, for productivity. A full understanding of the effect of management practices on productivity therefore requires considering how management practices affect innovation.

In two papers, Benner and Tushman (2002, 2003) describe and empirically test the potential downside of process-focused programs like ISO 9000 and Six Sigma that have been widely adopted in practice. They highlight how an organization's focus on achieving the efficiency gains that are expected to arise from mapping processes, systematically improving them, and adhering to systems of processes as best practices can also drive out more novel product innovation within the same firm. Benner and Tushman (2002) argue, drawing on a large body of management and organization research, that repeatedly carrying out activities in codified systems of processes or organizational routines leads to increased proficiency and efficiency in these processes, and more incremental innovations, but at the same time, the focus on eliminating variance can also drive out the novelty in the resulting innovations (March 1991). Adherence to the improved processes and techniques spurs further exploitation of a firm's current knowledge and capabilities, which has measurable, certain benefits in the near term, but can crowd out the innovations that are more exploratory, that is, that require more distant search, risk-taking, mistakes, and experiments, and are harder to measure, but that also lead to more novel products. Moreover, the influence of process-management practices has migrated further into firms' practices, beyond manufacturing and production, to organizational areas directly responsible for innovation. Efforts to streamline the linkages between practices across a firm have spurred the application of these programs to the specific processes underlying research and product development, embodied in programs like Design for Six Sigma or ISO 9001, among others, with the aim of designing products for more efficient production (e.g., Harrington and Mathers 1997; Harry and Schroeder 2000; Hindo 2007). Thus, as these programs are implemented with the intent to further streamline firm activities and reduce costs, and as they are applied to a wider range of a firm's activities, they increasingly have ramifications for processes that underlie product innovation.

In an empirical study employing 20 years of firm-level data on ISO 9000 implementation (as a measure of process-management practices) and patenting (as a measure of innovation) in the photography and paint industries, Benner and Tushman (2002) found support for these ideas: the more that firms undertook the practices associated with the ISO 9000 process-management program, over time, the more their patenting activities shifted away from exploration (i.e., incorporating knowledge new to the firm) and toward more exploitation (i.e., incorporating knowledge already familiar to the firm). Thus, while there were more innovations (as measured by counts of patents) for firms as they increasingly adopted ISO 9000, their innovations became increasingly incremental or exploitative, building on similar knowledge the firm had used previously (as measured by the prior patents cited). These findings suggest that a concerted focus on improving productivity in a particular firm using these management practices can actually drive out exploration and novelty within the firm. The study also overcomes the weaknesses of cross-sectional studies based on survey data, as they rely on panel data on firm-year adoption of ISO 9000 (from third-party certification data) and firm-year patenting over a 20-year period, and include firm fixed effects and year controls. Thus, it is a within-firm longitudinal study, exploring the outcomes that unfolded from the pressure firms increasingly faced (from government agencies and large suppliers and buyers) to focus on process and productivity improvements by increasing the extent of their adoption of ISO 9000.

Recent notable anecdotes also underscore the tension between management practices to improve productivity and the innovation necessary for longer-term performance and survival. For example, Motorola is known for developing and widely promoting the Six Sigma program, and the company was well known for its focus on using standardized processes for many organizational activities, including manufacturing and new product development. However, Motorola's most innovative product, the RAZR mobile phone, was actually developed outside of the standard processes, because it was seen at the time as a minor product aimed at a niche market. Yet, once the RAZR was successful, a focus on incremental innovations (e.g., product extensions including RAZRs in different colors) appears to have precluded more radical, novel product innovations that might have allowed Motorola to succeed and survive in the mobile phone business. Instead, Motorola was subsequently separated into two divisions, with the mobile phone division sold first to Google, and more recently to Lenovo (Benner and Tushman 2015). Stories in the business press of Jeff Immelt at GE similarly highlight the tension of trying to spur "breakthrough innovations" for future success after many years of its well-known focus on Six Sigma and process improvement during Jack Welch's tenure as CEO (Brady 2005; Feyder 2001). Similarly, the story of Six Sigma implementation at 3M, as McNerney took the helm with his Six Sigma expertise from GE, again highlights the tension between a focus on process efficiency and product innovation. Observers believe that Six Sigma efforts nearly destroyed 3M's innovative culture (Hindo 2007). Several winners of the Malcolm Baldrige quality award (a program focused on process improvement) experienced particularly poor financial performance shortly after winning, and as Garvin (1991) notes, this gave rise to the idea that Wall Street analysts would start recommending shorting the stocks of Baldrige Award winners. The potential for a focus on efficiency and process innovation to drive out product innovation is clearly important for an individual firm's success and survival in the longer term, a concern that Abernathy raised in his 1978 book, *The Productivity Dilemma*. But this dynamic is also a potential problem for productivity growth generally, since it appears that productivity growth in the aggregate arises more from novel product innovations (e.g., Hall 2011). Thus, paradoxically, it seems that encouraging a concerted focus on management practices to improve productivity within firms might actually have a negative effect on productivity growth in the aggregate, via the intermediate effects on product innovation.

This idea is certainly worth considering in research that examines the influence of management practices and innovation on productivity. Yet, because these research streams have unfolded across disparate academic domains, the work in economics on innovation, management practices, and productivity, as well as much of the work in operations management, has not considered the potential implication of this tension:

How does the intentional pursuit of productivity improvements within a firm—utilizing specific management practices deemed "best practices"—influence novel product innovation? That is, what effect does the potential negative relationship between management practices and novel product innovation have on firm-level and aggregate productivity growth?

In the next section I consider four implications that emerge from the preceding ideas and that provide a starting point for propositions and directions for further research on this puzzle. First, I explore in more detail the findings from research in economics that are consistent with this paradox, suggesting that the effects of process innovation on productivity growth may be less positive than the effects of product innovation. I provide an alternative explanation for this largely unexplained finding. Second, I explore the importance of considering different time frames in understanding the influences of both innovation and management practices on productivity. Given the paradox described in this chapter, the immediate effects of process improvement on productivity might be positive (and captured by researchers), while longer-term effects—via the effects of management practices on innovation—might be to decrease productivity growth or even lower levels of productivity. This is also consistent with the counterintuitive findings from some of the prior research on process innovation and productivity. Third, I explore the implications of this paradox for the "selection effect" described in research in economics, specifically, the importance of industry entrants versus incumbents in explaining growth in aggregate productivity. The more that established firms are constrained in their product innovation as they heed recommendations to adopt best practices to boost within-firm productivity, the more selection and entry will explain a greater part of the observed increases in productivity. If novel product innovation is indeed a major factor in productivity growth that is observed in industries and countries, a concerted focus on process improvement and process innovation at the firm level might be a direct driver of selection dynamics. Finally, I also consider the recent research on information and communication technology (ICT) for understanding how productivity improvements arise from management practices versus innovation. This work goes further to engage research in the fields of economics, operations management, and strategic management, and has begun to make important distinctions between different management practices where ICT is applied (e.g., for improving processes versus new product innovation). These ideas parallel the dimensions of the paradox described in the preceding and provide some insights into alternative explanations as well as directions for future research.

12.6. Process Innovation and Productivity: Mixed Results and an Alternative Explanation

As noted earlier, while past research in economics has found a consistently positive link between product innovation and productivity, the relationship between process innovation and productivity growth has been ambiguous, with some studies finding no relationship and others finding a negative relationship. This is counterintuitive, since process innovation would be expected to have a clear and direct positive effect on improving efficiency and productivity. As noted earlier, scholars have explained the lack of a positive relationship by highlighting measurement challenges, plausibly arguing that one reason process innovation does not seem to lead to productivity growth in many studies arises from how product innovation and process innovation are reflected differently in the measures.

However, an alternative explanation for the findings of a non- or negative relationship between process innovation and productivity is that the more a firm engages in concerted efforts to improve operational processes and, moreover, succeeds in those efforts, the more that the firm's product innovation proceeds in more incremental, less novel ways. A reduction in novel, radical innovations dampens precisely the sort of product innovation that allows for productivity growth and that explains the observed differences in productivity across industries and countries. Thus, the more firms undertake process innovation, the more productivity growth would slow, over time, working through an intermediate influence on a firm's product innovations. The example in the introduction further illustrates this idea—that as a firm engages in concerted efforts to produce Blackberries more efficiently, it is actually less likely to create the iPhone, with its longer-term implications for economic growth. But it also likely takes time for the effects of concerted process-improvement efforts to influence product-innovation decisions and outcomes.

Thus, I hypothesize that while process-management practices and associated process innovations will increase productivity at the firm level in the short term, practices associated with process improvement, specifically intended to drive out variation, will also drive out the more novel forms of product innovation.

The more a firm engages in process improvements or process innovation, intended to improve productivity, the fewer novel or new to the firm product innovations the firm will subsequently introduce.

Given the relationship between product innovation and productivity, this suggests further that a focus on management practices specifically aimed at increasing productivity at the firm level will ultimately slow productivity growth and possibly even lower overall productivity in the aggregate. Process innovation does not necessarily always just follow product innovation as depicted in technology life cycles; product and process innovation might be pursued by firms simultaneously (Klepper 1996). However, work in management highlights the tensions that arise as firms try to pursue these very contrasting activities simultaneously, within the same organization. A large stream of research in management on "organizational ambidexterity" has aimed at examining the tensions and difficulties firms face in simultaneously pursing process improvements and novel innovations, proposing that structural or temporal separation is necessary for firms to be able to engage in both types of activities effectively (Benner and Tushman 2003; Boumgarden, Nickerson, and Zenger 2012; O'Reilly and Tushman 1997). This suggests that an important topic for future empirical research on productivity is careful consideration of the intermediate influences of best practices to improve processes on product innovation.

12.7. Now and Later: Considering Time Frames

The previous ideas suggest further that it is also important to consider time frames, that is, to distinguish between short-term and longer-term effects in understanding the influence of both management practices and innovation on productivity. While process improvement practices are likely to enhance a particular firm's productivity and efficiency in the near term, the effects of process innovation on dampening the novelty of a firm's product innovation are likely to unfold over a longer period, and therefore the potential influences on productivity are likely to fully appear over a longer time frame. The important implication of this is that a focus on operational efficiency can drive out the sort of product novelty that, over the longer term, is required for firm performance, survival, and response to major technological changes (Abernathy 1978), as well as for productivity growth in industries and countries. These ideas are consistent with—and suggest an explanation for—Huergo and Jaumandreu's (2004) findings that process innovation by firms led to immediate growth in productivity in the year the innovation was undertaken, but this effect declined over three years, such that productivity growth essentially came to a halt for firms (that were previously process innovators) that no longer innovated. These authors plausibly attributed their findings in part to the idea that process innovations are copied by the other firms in the industry, such that the initial innovators no longer have above-average productivity. However, this still leaves a puzzle – that some firms seemed to have no innovations after a process innovation for a surprisingly long time. The alternative explanation, finding some support in management research, is that as a firm focuses on process innovation, it has lower product innovation, further implying dampened future growth in productivity.

These ideas are also consistent with the important work on exploitation and exploration in management research (Levinthal and March 1993; March 1991). This work distinguishes between exploitative activities, which result in shorter-term benefits ("closer in time"), and exploration, which can spur higher costs in the near term, as firms experiment, make mistakes, and engage in costly innovation (that likely reduces their productivity), but which can also lead to substantial benefits in the longer term ("more distant in time") as firms have created the variation needed to survive in changing environments. As discussed earlier, the trade-offs between exploitation and exploration have been used to explain why exploitation tends to crowd out exploration in organizations, as managers are attracted to the shorter-term, measurable benefits of exploitation at the expense of more distant, uncertain, and potentially costly innovation and exploration.

Further, this provides some insight into the puzzle described in this chapter: process innovation and practices focused on improving processes or adhering to best practice are expected to—and likely have—a positive influence on productivity, resulting in immediately measurable benefits. But a focus on process innovation may reduce novel product innovation over time, such that over the longer term, to the extent firms have engaged in process improvement/innovation, they likely have lower productivity growth than they otherwise would, and lower productivity growth than other firms that did not engage in such practices. The longer-term effects on productivity growth would thus be expected to be greater for firms that undertake more process innovation in an earlier period.

> *A greater focus on process innovation will lead to measurable increases in firm productivity in the near term. But over a longer period, novelty in product innovation will decrease and also will trigger decreases in longer-term productivity growth, both within-firm and across-firm, as well as in the aggregate, at the level of industries and countries.*

This suggests further that a promising direction for future research would be to carefully consider these dynamics in longitudinal studies that allow for understanding how both product and process innovation unfold over time, within firm, for assessing changes within firms, as well as in the aggregate, in industries and countries.

12.8. The "Selection" Effect: Established Firms versus New Entrants

Past research has noted that productivity growth in the aggregate (industry or country) comprises both the within-firm productivity increases of existing firms, as well as the contribution to productivity from the entry of new firms or establishments (Acemoglu and Cao 2015; Bartelsman and Doms 2000; Hall 2011; Lentz and Mortenson 2008; Klepper 1996, see also Syverson 2011). Scholars have noted that productivity growth can be observed in the aggregate as more inefficient firms (or establishments) are replaced by more efficient, innovating firms (i.e., those with lower costs or better products) (e.g., Hall 2011). Prior work in economics suggests that entry—of new, more innovative and productive firms—explains part of the productivity increases in industries, in recent estimates about 25% (Acemoglu and Cao 2015; Bartelsman and Doms 2000). Relevant to this chapter, the specific management practices that established firms undertake to improve their productivity (often under pressure specifically to improve productivity or profitability), but that dampen novel product innovation, might be an additional driver underlying an observed selection effect. An increasing focus on the management practices deemed "best practices" specifically for increasing productivity is likely to be the particular means by which established firms try to enhance their productivity in practice. But the potential for process innovation as a source of productivity growth from these firms will be curtailed, both as the productivity benefits from process innovation reach a limit as other firms relatively easily adopt similar practices (Benner and Veloso 2008; Huergo and Jaumandreu 2004),[2] and, through the dynamics described in this chapter, as these process-focused firms are less able to respond to major technological changes. Research that models the selection effect has frequently employed Schumpeterian models of creative destruction, where incumbents are assumed to engage in incremental innovation while new entrants engage in radical innovation (see Acemoglu and Cao 2015). The dynamics discussed in this chapter may render this characterization more realistic—increased process innovation in established firms may make them slower and less likely to initiate or respond to major changes in technology, and may even directly encourage entry by new, innovative firms. Although major incumbent firms like IBM and AT&T have long been leaders in innovation (suggesting that incumbent firms can and do innovate), they may be less likely to do so as they focus on process improvements. As existing firms increasingly engage in process innovation with the intent to improve their operational efficiencies and productivity (in many cases, even more ironically, to address the competitive threat from new entrants through efforts to improve existing technologies to compete with new, threatening ones), they may shift the locus of innovation and productivity growth within an industry toward the faster-growing new entrants. This suggests the following proposition:

> The greater the focus on process improvement within and among established firms in an industry, the more that observed productivity increases will be due to selection, that is, the decline in productivity (and possible failure) of established firms and the entry of new firms with more novel innovations and higher productivity growth.

This suggests that a fruitful direction for research on "reallocation" or the selection effect in productivity research would be to understand the extent to which the results are driven by the growing focus of existing firms specifically on management practices (i.e., best practices) intended to improve processes and increase productivity, and the differences between existing firms and new entrants in the extent to which these practices—and more radical innovations—are undertaken.

12.9. Information and Communication Technology and Productivity: Combining Innovation and Management Practices

Recent work on the influence of ICT investments on productivity has combined ideas about the influences of both innovation and management practices on productivity, and has also engaged more with prior research across the three domains discussed in this chapter. Initially this research was spurred by the view of ICT as a general purpose technology or capital investment, that is, an innovation, driven by the underlying idea that computerization in firms will generally have a positive effect on their productivity (e.g., Brynjolfsson and Hitt 2003). But in studying the productivity benefits of ICT (as a form of innovation in firms), researchers have also considered the complementary management practices (i.e., that have positive interactive effects with ICT investments) on their effects on productivity.

Some work in this stream has viewed the benefits of ICT mainly through its influence on process improvement. For example, Brynjolfsson and Hitt (2003) proposed that an underlying mechanism for a positive effect of ICT on growth in multifactor productivity is the benefits of computerization in enabling improvements in production processes. "Computers may affect the multifactor productivity growth of the firms that use them by changing the production process itself . . . the act of computerizing a business process or collection of processes" (794). Similar to other work on ICT, they also highlight the potential complementary relationships between investments in computerization, along with other management practices (such as "new work systems, organizational redesign, and business process reengineering", 793). Kleis, Nault, and Dexter (2014) similarly focus on ICT's role in process improvement, exploring how innovation influences ICT, as an input in a production model.

In a few studies (e.g., Tambe, Brynjolfsson, and Hitt 2012), the mechanisms underlying productivity from ICT investments have shifted beyond thinking about computerization used specifically for enabling or improving production processes, to the link between ICT and product innovation, incorporating arguments about how ICT facilitates the external search for information used for developing novel products. Like other work in the research stream on ICT, this work also features complementarities between the uses of ICT and other organizational characteristics or practices. For instance, Tambe et al. (2012) specifically study the complementarities between ICT investment, decentralization, and "external focus," and find that the three variables together are associated with improved product innovation capabilities, and that a three-way complementarity among them is associated with significantly higher productivity. Similarly, Kleis, Chwelos, Ramirez, and Cockburn (2012) distinguish between product and process innovation, focusing their study specifically on the use of ICT in the knowledge creation underlying product innovation. These authors also identify complementary practices involved in product innovation that are enabled by ICT: improving the management of innovation knowledge, innovation production (through IT-based methods for design, simulation, testing, prototyping), and innovation collaboration.

Thus, research on ICT highlights two general possible sources of productivity improvement from ICT, which echo the two different types of activities and the paradox described in this chapter: (1) ICT applied to enable and streamline an organization's processes with the intent of improving productivity, and (2) ICT used to make information more available and broaden the search for information (i.e., scanning the external operating environment or searching for information incorporated in product innovations)[3] (Kleis, Nault, and Dexter 2014; Tambe et al. 2012). ICT research, where ICT is viewed as a general-purpose technology that enables the particular management practices under study, also can help illuminate the specific practices and possible mechanisms underlying the effects of both product and process innovation on productivity. Understanding how information and communication technologies are specifically used in firms (i.e., whether they are used to implement more efficient production processes or to search for novel new product ideas) matters a great deal both in understanding the effects of these investments on productivity and in further providing related insights into the influence of different management practices on productivity.

Work by Bloom, Garicano, Sadun, and Van Reenen (2014) also distinguishes between ICT uses and practices, between improvements in "information technology" versus "communication technology." They find different effects of these different applications of ICT on organizational characteristics and structure, in essence, that improvements in information technology are associated with greater decision-making autonomy by lower-level plant managers and workers, whereas improvements in communication technology are associated with more centralization and dampened decision-making autonomy at lower organizational levels. Although their study does not assess the influence of ICT directly on measures of productivity, the implication is that effects of ICT on these characteristics of firm or establishment decision-making are likely to have further effects on productivity. They suggest further that understanding the outcomes of ICT investment requires going beyond measuring hardware investments, to the associated software investments by organizations (i.e., the specific use of the hardware). One example is the use of ICT for Enterprise Resource Planning (ERP) systems. Bloom et al. (2014, 2860) note that "ERP is the generic name for software systems that integrate several data sources and processes of an organization into a unified system." While Bloom et al. focus on the increased data and information availability associated with ERP system adoption, the other important function of ERP systems is to integrate and further standardize processes in organizations. These dual uses of ERP systems echo the tension and paradox described in this chapter: To the extent that ERP systems enable organizational routinization through standardized processes, these systems may lead to increased productivity in the short term, but may also lead to dampened productivity by decreasing organizational flexibility and search for novel innovations. Moreover, like the influence of process-management practices, the impact of ERP systems on routinization of organizational process extends far beyond production processes to areas of new product development. Thus, a plausible alternative explanation for Bloom et al.'s findings is that it is the routinization of decision-making processes and not additional information that allows a greater number of decisions (capital investments, hiring, etc.) to be made by lower-level management after improvements in information technology through ERP. Routinizing the decisions simply increases the number of decisions that can be made by lower-level managers, but instead of increased autonomy, this occurs through routinizing types of decisions that have been pre-approved at a higher level; lower-level managers are not actually granted increased decision-making autonomy.

Thus, the uses of ICT described in the recent literature align closely with the topics of this chapter—management practices, that is, the organizational processes that underlie organizational activities and are used to improve productivity, and innovation (i.e., the new, novel, or radical products a firm produces). We would thus expect different findings in research that focuses on ICT applied to process innovation versus research focused on ICT as an enabler of information, applied to product innovation and search for knowledge.

> When ICT is used for enabling search for technologies and solutions, it is likely to be a driver of an increase in novelty in product innovation and therefore increased long-term productivity within-firm and aggregate productivity (at the industry or country level). When ICT is applied mainly for standardizing organizational procedures and activities, it will result in an increase in firm-level productivity in the short term, but a decrease in the novelty of a firm's product innovations and a decrease in productivity longer-term, both within-firm and in the aggregate.

The work on ICT, by proposing and showing that ICT influences both innovation and management practices, thus provides a context for theorizing and empirically testing the possible productivity outcomes from both innovation and management practices separately and in combination, as well as more insight into the enablers or constraints on both product and process innovations in organizations.

12.10. Discussion

This chapter explores the relationships between and among innovation, management practices, and productivity. I have combined work from three separate streams of research that have unfolded in disparate fields and not conversed much with each other. Research from economics has shown that firms' innovation (particularly product innovation) drives increases in total factor productivity in countries and industries. Separately, research from operations management has examined firm-level outcomes associated with management practices that are specifically aimed at improving the efficiency of operating processes and firm performance. Recent work in economics has also begun to explore how particular management "best practices" affect firm performance and productivity. While it seems compelling to label management practices aimed at improving productivity "best practices," a separate stream of research from management suggests that the relationship between management practices and productivity may not be as straightforward as this suggests. Research drawing on organizational learning theory highlights the potential for the management practices (that firms employ to improve productivity) to increase incremental innovations but actually crowd out more novel product innovations.

These ideas suggest a clear paradox—that by focusing directly on increasing productivity through management practices, firms can potentially dampen the more novel innovation that might be a driver of their longer-term productivity, as well as aggregate productivity growth in industries and countries. Concerns about a "productivity dilemma" are not new—they have been discussed in management research since Abernathy's influential 1978 book, and have more recently been studied in the context of the popular process-management best practices promoted by academics and consultants (Benner and Tushman 2003). A large literature in management on organizational ambidexterity aims at further understanding this tension and the ways that firms can balance between efficiently producing this year's technologies while still pursuing new innovations in next year's technologies.

I further have outlined several insights that arise from combining these three disparate streams of research, suggesting areas for future research to better understand the relationships among and between innovation, management practices, and productivity. The implications are consistent with—and in some cases help explain—findings from prior work in economics, for example the different outcomes associated with product versus process innovation. I also discuss the importance of considering different time frames for assessing the outcomes of process versus product innovation, as well as further study of the selection effect (i.e., the importance of new entrants versus established incumbents) in productivity increases in industries, as potentially fruitful ways to further understand the implications of the paradox raised in this chapter. Finally, I have reviewed the research on ICT and productivity, focusing in particular on the two mechanisms by which ICT is expected to influence productivity in past research, to further illuminate the process/innovation/productivity dilemma and describe avenues for future research to address and better incorporate and address this puzzle in future research.

It seems that future research would benefit from more conversation between these streams of research. With economists' increasing use of firm- and establishment-level data and increasing interest in the role of management and management practices in explaining heterogeneity across firms, more engagement with research in management seems fruitful. Researchers in strategic management have long been interested in questions about factors that influence heterogeneity in firm resources and performance, both over time within firms, as well as across firms. In such research the dependent variable is typically profit at the firm level, rather than productivity, but the analyses have long been at the firm level.[4]

Our prior understandings, for example, about how particular best practices can be appropriate and beneficial in the short term but can dampen innovation and flexibility, or the general understanding that there are unlikely to be any universal best practices, seem important for this new work aiming to assess the influences of best practices on firm outcomes. It is potentially useful to understand the contingencies that underpin whether best practices are likely to be beneficial. One example is that adherence to sets of standardized practices is likely to be more appropriate and less harmful in industries characterized by slow or incremental change. The tensions between process improvement for productivity and innovation might be lessened in environments that are relatively stable compared to those undergoing more rapid technological changes. Second, the research on ambidexterity in management research suggests that structural separation of activities focused on exploitation from those focused on exploration can help firms better balance these contrasting types of activities. Relevant to the increasing use of micro-level data in economics, a focus on productivity improvement through process innovation at the plant level might not be harmful, provided it is separated from other activities outside of manufacturing and production, limiting the ability of these practices to influence more radical product innovations.

While microdata have been extremely useful for unpacking the link between firm-level productivity and productivity in the aggregate, as well as for observing substantial cross-firm heterogeneity within industries, it does not as easily allow for understanding, at the firm level, the relationship between productivity-improving activities and innovation. Innovation—particularly in the form of R&D—is typically a firm-level activity, conducted in areas of the firm outside of the manufacturing plants (Bartelsman and Doms 2000).

Finally, an important implication from this work is that pressures to improve productivity within-firm in established firms, through adoption of particular management practices, might drive a shift in the locus of productivity growth in industries and countries, away from established firms and toward innovative new entrants. This may occur simply because new innovative firms are as yet unburdened by pressures to adopt best practices to improve productivity.

Notes

1. The term "disruptive innovation" is also a type of innovation in past research. It has been used mainly in work by Clay Christensen (see Christensen and Bower 1996; Christensen 1997) to describe a specific type of innovation, introduced by industry newcomers in a lower-price/lower-quality end of the market not served by the industry's incumbent firms. Over time, the entrant gains expertise and is able to directly challenge the incumbents in their higher-quality segments of the market. An example from Christensen's work is the disk drive industry, where entrants making newer, smaller, and less functional generations of disk drives were first ignored by the leading incumbent firms in disk drives, but ultimately displaced them.
2. Such practices are more subject to imitation than product innovation, since they are less likely to be patented or have IP protection.
3. Another source of productivity arising from ICT is the general productivity increases in the ICT industry itself. For example, Venturini (2015) considers two "channels" or mechanisms through which ICT may influence total factor productivity: connectivity between firms for more efficient exchange of more information, and the spillovers of the R&D knowledge from ICT-producing firms. The focus of this chapter is on the relationship between ICT and productivity when ICT influences management practices and innovation in firms outside of the ICT industry.
4. See recent work by Grifell-Tatjé and Lovell (2015) for explanations of the relationships between productivity, profitability, and profit.

References

Acemoglu, D., and D. Cao, 2015. "Innovation by Entrants and Incumbents." *Journal of Economic Theory* 157: 255–294.

Abernathy, W. J. 1978. *The Productivity Dilemma.* Baltimore, MD: Johns Hopkins University Press.

Abernathy, W. J., and J. M. Utterback. 1978. "Patterns of Industrial Innovation." *Technology Review* 80(7): 40–47.

Adler, P., M. Benner, D. Brunner, P. MacDuffie, E. Osono, B. Staats, H. Takeuchi, M. L. Tushman, and S. G. Winter. 2009. "Perspectives on the Productivity Dilemma." *Journal of Operations Management* 27: 99–113.

Balasubramanian, N., and J. Sivadasan. 2011. "What Happens When Firms Patent? New Evidence from U.S. Economic Census Data." *Review of Economics and Statistics* 93(1): 126–146.

Bartelsman, E. J., and M. Doms. 2000. "Understanding Productivity: Lessons from Longitudinal Microdata." *Journal of Economic Literature* 38(3): 569–594.

Belderbos, R., M. Carree, and B. Lokshin. 2004. "Cooperative R&D and Firm Performance." *Research Policy* 33: 1477–1492.

Benner, M. J. 2010. "Securities Analysts and Incumbent Response to Radical Technological Change." *Organization Science* 21(1): 42–62.

Benner, M. J., and M. Tushman. 2002. "Process Management and Technological Innovation: A Longitudinal Study of the Photography and Paint Industries." *Administrative Science Quarterly* 47: 676–706.

Benner, M. J., and M. L. Tushman. 2003. "Exploitation, Exploration, and Process Management: The Productivity Dilemma Revisited." *Academy of Management Review* 28(2): 238–256.

Benner, M. J., and M. Tushman. 2015. "Reflections on the 2013 Decade Award: 'Exploitation Exploration and Process Management: The Productivity Dilemma Revisited' Ten Years Later." *Academy of Management Review* 40(4): 497–514.

Benner, M. J., and F. M. Veloso. 2008. "ISO 9000 Practices and Financial Performance: A Technology Coherence Perspective." *Journal of Operations Management* 26: 611–629.

Bernard, A. B., S. J. Redding, and P. K. Schott. 2010. "Multiple-Product Firms and Product Switching." *American Economic Review* 100(1): 70–97.

Bloom, N., L. Garicano, R. Sadun, and J. Van Reenen. 2014. "The Distinct Effect of Information Technology and Communication Technology on Firm Organization." *Management Science* 60(12): 2859–2885.

Bloom, N., and J. Van Reenen. 2007. "Measuring and Explaining Management Practices across Firms and Countries." *The Quarterly Journal of Economics* 122(4): 1351–1408.

Boumgarden, P., J. Nickerson, and T. Zenger. 2012. "Sailing into the Wind: Exploring the Relationships among Ambidexterity, Vacillation, and Organizational Performance." *Strategic Management Journal* 33(6): 587–610.

Brady, D. 2005. "The Immelt Revolution." *Business Week*, March 27, https://www.bloomberg.com/news/articles/2005-03-27/the-immelt-revolution.

Brynjolfsson, E., and L. M. Hitt. 2003. "Computing Productivity: Firm-Level Evidence." *The Review of Economics and Statistics* 85(4): 793–808.

Cassiman, B., E. Golovko, and E. Martinez-Ros. 2010. "Innovation, Exports, and Productivity." *International Journal of Industrial Organization* 28(4): 372–376.

Christensen, C. M., and J. L. Bower. 1996. "Customer Power, Strategic Investment, and the Failure of Leading Firms." *Strategic Management Journal* 17: 197–218.

Christensen, C. M. 1997. *The Innovator's Dilemma: When New Technologies Cause Great Firms to Fail*. Boston: Harvard Business School Press.

Crepon, B., E. Duguet, and J. Mairesse. 1998. "Research, Innovation, and Productivity: An Econometric Analysis at the Firm Level." *Economics of Innovation and New Technology* 7(2): 115–158.

Deming, E. W. 1986. *Out of Crisis*. Cambridge, MA: MIT Press.

Done, A. C. Voss, N. G. Rytter. 2011. "Best Practice Interventions: Short-Term Impact and Long-Term Outcomes." *Journal of Operations Management* 29: 500–513.

Easton, G. S., and S. L. Jarrell. 1998. "The Effects of Total Quality Management on Corporate Performance: An Empirical Investigation." *Journal of Business* 71: 253–307.

Feyder, S. 2001. "3M to Use Favorite GE Quality Program: Six Sigma Adoption to Be Companywide." *Minneapolis Star Tribune*, January 25, 1D.

Foster, L., J. Haltiwanger, and C. Syverson. 2008. "Reallocation, Firm Turnover, and Efficiency: Selection on Productivity or Profitability?" *American Economic Review* 98(1): 394–425.

Garvin, D. A. 1991. "How the Baldrige Award Really Works." *Harvard Business Review* 69(6): 80–93.

Garvin, D. A. 1998. "The Processes of Organization and Management." *Sloan Management Review* 39(4): 33–50.

Geroski, P. 1989. "Innovation and Productivity Growth." *The Review of Economics and Statistics* 71(4): 572–578.

Grifell- Tatjé, E., and C. A. K. Lovell. 2015. *Productivity Accounting: The Economics of Business Performance*. New York: Cambridge University Press.

Griliches, Z. 1979. "Issues in Assessing the Contribution of Research & Development to Productivity Growth." *Bell Journal of Economics* 10(1): 92–116.

Griliches, Z. 1996. "The Discovery of the Residual: A Historical Note." *Journal of Economic Literature* 34(3): 1324–1330.

Griliches, Z. 1998. *R&D and Productivity: The Econometric Evidence*. Chicago: Chicago University Press.

Hall, B. H. 2011. "Innovation and Productivity." *Nordic Economic Policy Review* 2: 167–204.

Hall, B. H., F. Lotti, and J. Mairesse. 2008. "R&D, Innovation, and Productivity: New Evidence from Italian Manufacturing Microdata." *Industrial and Corporate Change* 17: 813–839.

Harrington, H. J., and D. D. Mathers. 1997. *ISO 9000 and Beyond: From Compliance to Performance Improvement*. New York: McGraw Hill.

Harry, M. J., and R. Schroeder. 2000. *Six Sigma: The Breakthrough Management Strategy Revolutionizing the World's Top Corporations*. New York: Currency.

Henderson, R. M., and K. B. Clark. 1990. "Architectural Innovation: The Reconfiguration of Existing Product Technologies and the Failure of Established Firms." *Administrative Science Quarterly* 35: 9–30.

Hindo, B. 2007. "At 3M a Struggle Between Efficiency and Creativity." *Businessweek*, June 10. http://www.bloomberg.com/bw/stories/2007-06-10/at-3m-a-struggle-between-efficiency-and-creativity.

Huergo, E., and J. Jaumandreu. 2004. "Firms' Age, Process Innovation and Productivity Growth." *International Journal of Industrial Organization* 22: 541–559.

Ichniowski, C., K. Shaw, and G. Prennushi. 1997. "The Effects of Human Resources Management Practices on Productivity: A Study of Steel Finishing Lines." *The American Economic Review* 87(3): 291–313.

Ishikawa, K. 1985. *What Is Total Quality Control? The Japanese Way*. Englewood Cliffs, NJ: Prentice Hall.

Iyer, A., H. Saranga, and S. Seshadri. 2013. "Effect of Quality Management Systems and Total Quality Management on Productivity Before and After: Empirical Evidence from the Indian Auto Component Industry." *Production and Operations Management* 22(2): 283–301.

Juran, J. 1989. *Juran on Leadership for Quality*. New York: Free Press.

Kleis, L., P. Chwelos, R. V. Ramirez, and I. Cockburn. 2012. "Information Technology and Intangible Output: The Impact of IT Investment on Innovation Productivity." *Information Systems Research* 23(1): 42–59.

Kleis, L., B. R. Nault, and A. S. Dexter. 2014. "Producing Synergy: Innovation, IT, and Productivity." *Decision Sciences* 45(5): 939–969.

Klepper, S. 1996. "Entry, Exit, Growth, and Innovation over the Product Life Cycle." *American Economic Review* 86(3): 562–583.

Landes, D. 1983. *Revolution in Time: Clocks and the Making of the Modern World.* Cambridge, MA: Harvard University Press.

Lentz, R., and D. T. Mortensen. 2008. "An Empirical Model of Growth Through Product Innovation." *Econometrica* 76(6): 1317–1373.

Levinthal, D. A., and J. G. March. 1993. "The Myopia of Learning." *Strategic Management Journal* 14: 95–112.

Levitt, B., and J. G. March. 1988. "Organizational Learning." *Annual Review of Sociology* 14: 319–340.

Linderman, K., R. G. Schroeder, S. Zaheer, and A. S. Choo. 2003. "Six Sigma: A Goal-Theoretic Perspective." *Journal of Operations Management* 21: 193–203.

Lo, C. K. Y., F. Wiengarten, P. Humphreys, A. C. L. Yeung, and T. C. E. Cheng. 2013. "The Impact of Contextual Factors on the Efficacy of ISO 9000 Adoption." *Journal of Operations Management* 31: 229–235.

Loof, H., and A. Heshmati. 2006. "On the Relationship Between Innovation and Performance: A Sensitivity Analysis." *Economics of Innovation and New Technology* 15: 317–344.

March, J. 1991. "Exploration and Exploitation in Organizational Learning." *Organization Science* 2: 71–87.

Mohnen, P., and B. H. Hall. 2013. "Innovation and Productivity: An Update." *Eurasian Business Review* 3(1): 47–65.

Rosenkopf, L., and A. Nerkar. 2001. "Beyond local search: Boundary-Spanning, Exploration, and Impact in the Optical Disk Industry." *Strategic Management Journal* 22: 287–306.

Samson, D., and M. Terziovski. 1999. "The Relationship Between Total Quality Management Practices and Operational Performance." *Journal of Operations Management* 17: 393–409.

Schroeder, R. G., K. Linderman, C. Liedtke, and A. S. Choo. 2008. "Six Sigma: Definition and Underlying Theory." *Journal of Operations Management* 26: 536–554.

Shafer, S. M., and S. B. Moeller. 2012. "The Effects of Six Sigma on Corporate Performance: An Empirical Investigation." *Journal of Operations Management* 30: 521–532.

Solow, R. M. 1957. "Technical Change and the Aggregate Production Function." *The Review of Economics and Statistics.* 39(3): 312–320

Sterman, J. D., N. P. Repenning, and F. Kofman. 1997. "Unanticipated Side Effects of Successful Quality Programs: Exploring a Paradox of Organizational Improvement." *Management Science* 43: 503–521.

Swink, M., and B. W. Jacobs. 2012. *Journal of Operations Management* 30: 437–453.

Syverson, C. 2011. "What Determines Productivity?" *Journal of Economic Literature* 49(2): 326–365.

Tambe, P., L. M. Hitt, and E. Brynjolfsson. 2012. "The Extroverted Firm: How External Information Practices Affect Innovation and Productivity." *Management Science* 58(5): 843–859.

Tripsas, M., and G. Gavetti. 2000. "Capabilities, Cognition, and Inertia: Evidence from Digital Imaging." *Strategic Management Journal* 21: 1147–1161.

Tushman, M.L. and P. Anderson. 1986. "Technological Discontinuities and Organizational Environments." *Administrative Science Quarterly* 31: 439–465.

Van Leeuwen, G., and L. Klomp. 2006. "On the Contribution of Innovation to Multi-Factor Productivity Growth." *Economics of Innovation and New Technology* 15: 367–390.

Venturini, F. 2015. "The Modern Drivers of Productivity." *Research Policy* 44: 357–359.

Wruck, K., and M. Jensen. 1994. "Science, Specific Knowledge and Total Quality Management." *Journal of Accounting and Economics* 18: 247–287.

Zu, X., L. D. Fredendall, and T. J. Douglas. 2008. "The Evolving Theory of Quality Management: The Role of Six Sigma." *Journal of Operations Management* 26: 630–650.

CHAPTER 13

....

INTERNATIONALIZATION, INNOVATION, AND PRODUCTIVITY

....

BRUNO CASSIMAN AND ELENA GOLOVKO

13.1. INTRODUCTION

....

INTERNATIONAL economics has emphasized the role of trade—imports and exports—as an important source of productivity growth of economies. The role of exporting in promoting economic well-being of countries has been well acknowledged. Exports facilitate the transfer of knowledge and ideas across countries; at the same time, faster productivity growth allows economies to increase the flow of exports (Bernard and Jensen 2004). Importing intermediate inputs is also considered an important channel for international technology diffusion. Imports augment a country's productivity by giving access to foreign goods, and particularly foreign technologies (Keller 2004). With the increasing availability of firm-level data, research started to investigate the relationship between trade and productivity at the firm or plant level. As Salomon and Shaver (2005b, 432) correctly mention, "for the most part, however, firms engage in trade—not industries or nations. Therefore, the inferences from the more macro level might be misleading in guiding firm strategies."

In this chapter, we take the perspective of the firm and review empirical evidence on the relationship between internationalization, innovation, and productivity at the firm level. A number of empirical regularities, or stylized facts, on firms' international exposure through trade and productivity were established, holding across different countries and industries (for a review, see, e.g., Bartelsman and Doms 2000, or De Loecker and Goldberg 2014). There is substantial heterogeneity in the productivity levels among firms, with exporting firms being significantly more productive than non-exporting ones. Early empirical research focused primarily on understanding the positive relationship between export activity and firm productivity. On the one hand, more productive firms have been shown to self-select into export markets (e.g., Bernard and Jensen 1999, 2004). On the other hand, the learning by exporting effect has been documented where export activity brings further improvements in productivity (Atkin, Khandelwal and Osman 2017; De Loecker 2007; Van Biesebroeck 2005).

Similarly, a strong positive association is documented for firm productivity levels and importing activities (Bernard, Jensen, Redding, and Schott 2012). Empirical studies testing the relationship between imports and productivity find strong support for the selection process of more productive firms into imports (Amiti and Konings 2007; Kasahara and Rodrigue 2008). The evidence of the reverse effect of import activity on firm productivity is mixed. A number of studies document a positive and significant effect of imports on firm productivity levels (e.g., Augier, Cadot, and Dovis 2013). Others fail to find any significant impact of importing on firm productivity (Liu and Buck 2007; Vogel and Wagner 2010). Finally, exporting and importing activities are found to be significantly positively correlated, pointing at the fact that most firms in international trade tend to engage in both import and export activities (e.g., Aristei, Castellani, and Franco 2013). Two-way traders also consistently exhibit the highest productivity levels and growth (Castellani, Serti, and Tomasi 2010; Kasahara and Lapham 2013; Muûls and Pisu 2009), suggesting that the performance advantages of trading over nontrading firms can be partially attributed to firms that both import and export (Bernard, Jensen, Redding, and Schott 2012).

Recent research has begun to examine the link between international trade and productivity in more detail, introducing innovation activity as an important explanatory variable in the productivity-exports association. Innovation—in particular, product innovation—has been shown to positively affect the decision of a firm to become an exporter (Basile 2001; Cassiman, Golovko, and Martínez-Ros 2010). Product innovation can also serve as a productivity-enhancing investment that allows firms to enter the export market afterward (Cassiman and Golovko 2011). Moreover, research has indicated that export and innovation decisions can be actually jointly determined and can lead to future productivity growth of new exporters (Aw, Roberts, and Xu 2011; Bustos 2011; Lileeva and Trefler 2010).

In this chapter, we focus on the complex relationship between internationalization strategies (i.e., import and export activities) and innovation behavior of firms and link them to productivity as a measure of firm performance. We bring together the existing empirical evidence on the relationship between international trade, innovation, and productivity, and provide a comprehensive overview of these links. In particular, we focus on the relationship between imports, innovation, and exports and highlight a more explicit dynamic relation between these strategic decisions of firms. We discuss the role of imports and innovation as sources of higher productivity that might lead firms to enter the export markets in the future. Using the panel of Spanish manufacturing firms during 1991–2009, we test the proposed links empirically. We find evidence consistent with innovation activities leading to import and consequently export entry. We also document a positive link between exports and next-period productivity consistent with prior studies; yet only firms that combine both product innovation and imports exhibit higher productivity, pointing to the potential complementary between these activities. In conclusion, we indicate several avenues to advance this research agenda.

13.2. Internationalization, Innovation, and Productivity

13.2.1. Exporting, Innovation, and Productivity

13.2.1.1. *Exports-Productivity Link*

Empirical research in international trade has a long tradition of examining the relationship between export activities and firm productivity. Trading firms differ substantially from firms that only serve their domestic market on a number of characteristics. In particular, exporting firms are characterized by a higher productivity (e.g., Bernard, Jensen, Redding, and Schott 2007). On the one hand, this positive link is explained through a selection mechanism, whereby the more productive firms enter into export markets. Firms with initially higher productivity levels may have comparative advantages and are more likely to overcome the difficulties in starting to trade internationally, such as sunk entry costs, compared to less efficient firms in the domestic market. On the other hand, there is a possibility of learning by exporting. The underlying explanation is that by trading, firms may learn from their foreign contacts in the export markets, thereby adopting new production technologies and developing new products, and enhancing their productivity level. While both explanations are plausible, the learning by exporting hypothesis has received limited empirical support. The general finding for developed markets is that exporters already show a higher productivity than non-exporters *before* taking up exports, and no significant productivity advantages are observed for continuous exporters over time. The examples of studies documenting the self-selection part of the causal link between exports and productivity are Clerides, Lach, and Tybout (1998); Bernard and Jensen (1999, 2004); and Delgado, Fariñas, and Ruano (2002). The notable exceptions are Blalock and Gertler (2004), who document a significant increase in productivity following the initiation of exporting for Indonesian firms; De Loecker (2007), who finds that export entrants become more productive once they start exporting for a sample of Slovenian firms; Van Biesebroeck (2005), who finds evidence of exports increasing firm productivity in a sample of sub-Saharan African firms; and Atkin, Khandelwal and Osman (2017), who convinsingly show that exporters improve their productivity after and because they start exports.

13.2.1.2. *Innovation and Selection into Exporting*

Such observed heterogeneity in productivity that precedes the entry into the export markets raises an important question about the sources of higher productivity of future exporters. How do firms obtain higher productivity levels that allow them to enter the export market, effectively setting off the internationalization process? Innovation activity is argued to be an important factor determining a firms' decision to begin exporting. In his seminal work, Vernon (1966, 1979) proposes the product cycle hypothesis, which explains the internationalization process of products and firms. He eventually argues that firms, in particular small to medium-sized enterprises (SMEs), move from home-based product innovation to exports and ultimately foreign direct investment (FDI), building on opportunities they encounter in the home markets. In the initial phase, the firm creates new products using the home-based resources and opportunities. As demand for a new product develops elsewhere, the firm starts exporting this product to similar product markets. With the continuing growth in international demand, the firm makes direct investments abroad to set up its own production facilities. In this way, the firm with product innovation is likely to start moving into exports to exploit its market power in foreign markets with a product of potentially superior quality (Hirsch and Bijaoui 1985; Hitt, Hoskisson, and Kim 1997). Additionally, investments in product innovation in preparation for exporting enable firms to achieve greater ability to meet the demands of the foreign customers in international markets, thus making exports potentially more profitable for a firm (Zahra and Covin 1994). In such a way, product innovation increases the potential benefits from export activities, thus making exports more attractive. Accordingly, Golovko and Valentini (2011) show that product innovation and export decisions are complementary activities in their effect on firm growth.

On the other hand, innovation may decrease the costs of adopting exports. Cassiman and Golovko (2011) show that innovation may actually be at the roots of superior productivity of future exporters and explain the self-selection of more productive firms into exports. In this way, innovation may reduce the burden of export-related costs. Research on the determinants of productivity growth suggests that firm-specific variations in demand, rather than firm technical efficiency, are the main factor explaining productivity increases (Foster, Haltiwanger, and Syverson 2008). This implies that different innovation activities might influence productivity levels and growth differentially. More specifically, product innovation might be related more closely to firm-specific demand variations, while process innovation is likely to affect technical efficiency. Consequently, product innovation is expected to affect measured productivity more, and thus entry into exports (Cassiman, Golovko, and Martínez-Ros 2010).

The effect of innovation activity on the decision of a firm to start exporting has been supported by a large number of empirical studies (see, e.g., Basile 2001; Becker and Egger 2013; Bernard and Jensen 2004; Cassiman, Golovko, and Martínez-Ros 2010; Cassiman and Martínez-Ros 2007; Roper and Love 2002). Basile (2001), for a sample of Italian manufacturing firms, shows that firms introducing product and/or process innovations either through research and development (R&D) or through investments in new capital are more likely to export. Bernard and Jensen (2004) find that firms switching primary *Standard Industrial Classification (SIC)* code—which could indicate new product introductions—significantly increase the probability of entering the export markets. Furthermore, Cassiman and Martinez-Ros (2007) find a strong positive effect of product—but not process—innovation on the decision of a firm to export. Becker and Egger (2013) show the importance of product innovation relative to process innovation in determining a firm's export propensity for German firms. Empirical evidence also indicates the existence of the indirect channel through which product innovation may affect export decisions. Successful product innovation increases firm productivity and leads to the entry into the export market (Cassiman and Golovko 2011). The latter finding is in line with the documented self-selection of more productive firms into exports.

13.2.1.3. *Innovation and Learning by Exporting*

Research has also emphasized potential learning outcomes associated with exports that may lead to improved innovation performance. Attempting to explain the controversial results for learning by exporting in productivity studies, this literature highlights the advantages of innovation output measures for learning by exporting as compared to firm productivity. New technologies or information about new products acquired abroad are more likely to show up in innovation output measures than in productivity indicators; for example, there may be temporal issues in using productivity as a measure of learning (Salomon and Shaver 2005b). It may take some time before the technological information acquired abroad is incorporated into the production function of a firm to translate into productivity growth. Thus, innovation output might be a less noisy measure of learning by exporting than productivity indicators. Theoretically, such positive effect of exports on innovation is again related to (a) more intense competition in the foreign markets compared to home markets, and particularly to (b) knowledge spillovers coming from technologically sophisticated foreign partners, namely, buyers, suppliers and competitors (Silva, Afonso, and Africano 2012). Interacting with carriers of valuable knowledge abroad (e.g., leading customers or competitors) allows firms to tap into new knowledge that is not available in their home countries. Once it is transferred back home, it may be used in innovation production of the exporting firm, resulting in improved innovation performance.

The hypothesized reverse effect of exporting activity on innovation output, however, received mixed empirical support, as in the case with productivity. Alvarez and Robertson (2004) document positive association between exporting and the probability of innovating both in product and process. Salomon and Shaver (2005b) find that a firm's export activity is positively associated with the ex-post increase in the number of product innovations and patent applications for Spanish firms. Analogously, Filipescu, Prashantham, Rialp, and Rialp (2013) document a positive effect of export activity on the number of product innovations and the likelihood of innovating in process in a sample of Spanish manufacturing firms. Using a sample of the UK enterprises, Criscuolo, Haskel, and Slaughter (2010) find that globally engaged firms generate more innovations, either product or process, which may further result in higher productivity explaining the export-productivity association. On the other hand, Girma, Görg, and Hanley (2008), using the samples of UK and Irish firms, find that while exporting seems to stimulate R&D activity in the case of Irish firms, there is no strong evidence for direct learning by exporting effects for UK exporters. MacGarvie (2006) adopts a more direct measure of technology transfer through exporting—patent citation data—and examines a sample of French firms, looking at the relationship between international trade and technological knowledge diffusion measured by patent citations. The findings are that exporting firms do not make more citations to patents from the countries with which the firms trade, as compared to non-exporters. Moreover, exporters do not increase the number of citations compared with similar non-exporting firms after entering export markets.

The inconclusive empirical evidence on the learning effects of exports on innovation (and productivity) might suggest that we should look for moderating factors that can shape the ability of firms to tap into foreign market knowledge as well as the way this knowledge is profitably exploited. Recent work acknowledging the heterogeneity among firms investigates such boundary conditions that may explain the heterogeneity in learning effects in terms of innovation output. These factors could be at the country (Salomon 2006a), industry (Salomon and Jin 2008), or firm level (Golovko and Valentini 2014; Salomon and Jin 2010). More specifically, the positive effect of exporting may depend on whether a firm exports to more technologically developed versus less technologically developed markets, with exporting to developed markets leading to higher innovation performance (Salomon 2006b). The realized innovation benefits may also depend on the absorptive capacity of firms approximated by firm's relative technological capabilities—technological leaders are shown to benefit more in terms of innovation once they become exporters (Salomon and Jin 2010). The differences in learning by exporting patterns across firms may also stem from differences in innovation strategies prior to the export entry. For instance, firm size may influence the incentives of firms to invest in product or process innovation, thus leading to "purposive" learning by exporting (Golovko and Valentini 2014). Larger firms are more likely to innovate in process once they become exporters, while SMEs tend to pursue product innovation after the export entry.

13.2.1.4. *Complementarity of Innovation and Exports*

Finally, a recent research stream suggests that the decision to start exporting and the decision to innovate may actually be made jointly and may be complementary for future productivity growth of new entrants (Aw and Batra 1998; Aw, Roberts, and Xu 2011; Bustos 2011; Lileeva and Trefler 2010; Van Beveren and Vandenbussche 2010). In particular, the fact that export entry is often associated with higher innovation output is precisely the consequence of the complementarity between these two activities for growth (Golovko and Valentini 2011). Lileeva and Trefler (2010) argue that for firms with lower productivity, investing in innovation is justifiable only if it is accompanied by larger sales that come with exporting. Lower foreign tariffs would induce these firms not only to export, but also to simultaneously engage in product innovation and to adopt advanced manufacturing technologies to increase their productivity. Higher-productivity firms, however, will start exporting without additional investments in innovation. For a sample of Canadian plants that were driven to export to the US market because of tariff cuts, they find support for this hypothesis. Similarly, for a sample of Argentinian firms, Bustos (2011) shows that trade liberalization inducing firms to export also induces these firms to invest in technology upgrading due to increases in export revenues. It is thus possible that the observed association between exports and innovation performance is not merely a selection of more innovative firms into exports or a pure learning by exporting outcome, but also suggests purposeful investments that firms make precisely in relation with their decision to enter the export markets.

13.2.2. Importing, Innovation, and Productivity

13.2.2.1. *Imports-Productivity Link*

While most of the international trade literature has concentrated on exports, much less attention has been focused on imports (i.e., internationalization on the input side). Recent research on imports documents a positive and significant link between import activities of firms and productivity. Similar to studies on exporting, literature indicates the presence of the selection mechanism behind the imports-productivity association. Importing activity entails sunk costs related to the process of sourcing from abroad, such as contract-specific investments or costs of transferring the embedded technology (Altomonte, Aquilante, Békés, and Ottaviano 2013). Firms with ex-ante higher productivity can bear these costs and find it profitable to start importing. Empirical studies on firm outsourcing activities and productivity find consistent evidence on the self-selection into foreign outsourcing (i.e., importing intermediate products), as well as offshoring (Fariñas, López, and Martín-Marcos 2014; Fariñas and Martín-Marcos 2010; Kohler and Smolka 2014; Kohler and Smolka 2012; Tomiura 2007). For Spanish firms, Fariñas and Martín-Marcos (2010) and Fariñas, López, and Martín-Marcos (2014) show that firms that undertake outsourcing activities abroad (i.e., import intermediate goods from foreign suppliers) are ex-ante more productive compared to firms that do not engage into outsourcing. Analogously, Kohler and Smolka (2012, 2014) find evidence for selection of more productive firms into foreign outsourcing activities. Tomiura (2007) shows that although firms engaged in outsouring are on average less productive than exporters or firms with FDI, they are still ex-ante more productive than purely domestic firms, thereby confirming productivity selection for a sample of Japanese firms.

A potentially more interesting question is whether imports can trigger "learning," leading to productivity benefits for importing firms, analogously to the learning by exporting hypothesis. Theoretically, the effect of imports on productivity can be realized through a number of channels. First, productivity can increase with the increase in the number of varieties imported, because imported inputs may have a potentially higher price-adjusted quality, and they can be imperfect substitutes for domestic inputs (Halpern, Koren, and Szeidl 2015). Thus, by importing new intermediate good varieties and thereby expanding the set of inputs used in the production process, firms reach better complementarity in production (Bas and Strauss-Kahn 2014). Halpern, Koren, and Szeidl (2015) examine such an effect on productivity for Hungarian firms and find that combining imperfectly substitutable foreign and domestic varieties is responsible for the most part of productivity gains from imports (about 60% of observed productivity increase), with the rest attributed to the quality effects. In line with their findings, Goldberg, Khandelwal, Pavcnik, and Topalova (2010) document the positive effect of the expansion in the variety of imported intermediate inputs due to tariff reduction on the product scope of Indian firms. Similarly, Bas and Strauss-Kahn (2014) show that an increase in the set of imported input varieties significantly increases the number of varieties the firm exports, with the effect running through the productivity increase reached by better complementarity of inputs.

Second, potential positive changes in productivity can be related to better technology embedded in the imported inputs, and higher-quality machinery (Belderbos, Van Roy, and Duvivier 2013; Lööf and Andersson 2010; Veugelers and Cassiman 2004), which suggests the mechanism analogous to the one proposed by learning by exporting studies. Imports may serve as a channel for technological knowledge diffusion, leading to learning, and consequently to higher productivity. Accordingly, Veugelers and Cassiman (2004) find that firms active on the international technology market are also more likely to be active in the domestic technology market, implying that direct and indirect productivity enhancements in the local economy would be generated through these firms' access to the international technology markets. Belderbos, Van Roy, and Duvivier (2013) do find these productivity enhancements for the case of Belgian firms. Lööf and Andersson (2010), focusing on imports as a channel for embodied technical change and technology diffusion, find that Swedish firms that import a higher fraction of imports from R&D–intensive and technologically advanced countries have higher productivity.

Despite empirical support for a number of mechanisms behind the imports-productivity relationship, empirical studies that directly associate imports with post-entry productivity report mixed results. A number of studies document a positive and significant effect of imports on firm productivity levels (Amiti and Konings 2007; Augier, Cadot, and Dovis 2013; Kasahara and Rodrigue 2008). Alternatively, Liu and Buck (2007) and Vogel and Wagner (2010) find no evidence for the impact of imports on post-entry productivity.

13.2.2.2. *Imports, Exports, Innovation, and Productivity*

The productivity increases associated with technology-diffusion mechanisms suggest an important role of innovation in explaining the imports-productivity association. As firms import higher-quality inputs, new materials and components, they may be able to transform them in higher-quality outputs while developing new and better products. Consequently, we observe productivity increase associated with innovation activities. A number of studies provide evidence on the positive impact of imports on innovation output. Using patent citations, MacGarvie (2006) shows that the inventions of importers cite significantly more foreign patents from countries of imports compared to non-importers. Goldberg, Khandelwal, Pavcnik, and Topalova (2010) document that the growth in imports due to the reduction of import tariffs positively affects the propensity to introduce new products for domestic firms. Alvarez and Robertson (2004) argue that in the context of trade liberalization, the increasing access to imports of intermediate inputs will positively influence technological innovation because importing firms are likely to absorb and adopt new technologies incorporated in imported goods. For Mexican firms, they show that importing intermediate inputs is associated with the adoption of new technologies.

The positive effect of imports on productivity may also suggest that imports serve as productivity-enhancing investment, facilitating future export entry. Export and import activities are found to be strongly correlated, that is, firms tend to engage in both activities simultaneously (e.g., Aristei, Castellani, and Franco 2013; Bernard, Jensen, Redding, and Schott 2012). The underlying mechanism implies that by adopting an import strategy, firms might experience positive changes in innovation performance due to learning by importing, which in turn enhance productivity and make exports viable. Empirical studies report some evidence consistent with a particular succession of adoption decisions starting from importing to innovation and finally exporting (Aristei, Castellani, and Franco 2013; Damijan and Kostevc 2015). Alternatively, Altomonte, Aquilante, Békés, and Ottaviano (2013) find that firms that adopt exports as a mode of internationalization use R&D activities and imports as alternative strategies for sourcing new inputs and creating new products. Thus, R&D and imports as source of better-quality inputs are substitutes for the export decision (Altomonte, Aquilante, Békés, and Ottaviano 2013).

Overall, existing evidence on firms' trade activities and innovation decisions suggests a complex set of relationships between exports, imports, and innovation. Figure 13.1 maps the links between firm internationalization, innovation, and productivity, as documented by empirical studies. Innovation—in particular, product innovation—is positively related with the firm's export decision through a direct demand expansion effect (1). In its turn, exporting may facilitate the diffusion of new technological information not available in the home markets, leading to learning and thus more innovations (2). Such "learning" may also occur as a result of importing intermediate products, suggesting the positive effect of imports on the decision of a firm to innovate and on productivity (3). Additionally, export and import decisions are

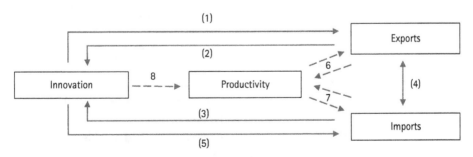

FIGURE 13.1. Internationalization and innovation activities.

highly correlated, suggesting the eventual joint adoption of these internationalization strategies (4). Being in essence a performance measure, productivity intervenes into the picture by (a) identifying a performance threshold needed to engage into exports or imports activities, and (b) measuring the performance effects of these activities. Links (6) and (7) identify the observed export-productivity and import-productivity associations, while link (8) reflects the positive effect of (product) innovation on firm productivity.

Given the large number of empirical studies on the trade-productivity link, we understand relatively well the requirements and the immediate consequences of firm export and import decisions in terms of productivity measures of performance. We still lack clear causal mechanisms that relate firm decisions and their subsequent decisions to internationalize (export and/or import). Firm decision to innovate has been identified by research as an important antecedent of export activities. We also have support (although with mixed results) for innovation being an outcome of exports and imports activities. Yet, we need to better understand the dynamic process that relates firm decisions to invest in innovation, import, or export and that explains the observed export-innovation and import-innovation associations.

Existing empirical evidence identifies a particular dynamic path going from imports to more innovation and leading to export decision (3)–(1). If we abstract from the trade liberalization context, this raises an important question about why firms initiate importing in the first place. Little is known about the determinants of the firm decision to become an importer. We argue that innovation is not just an outcome (or even a byproduct) of importing that is used as a channel for technology diffusion, as prior research suggests. Firms may intentionally start importing in search of new inputs needed for their innovation processes. Such possibility of proactive behavior on the part of the firm suggests that the decision to innovate may precede the decision to import, or that these decisions may be made jointly, resulting in improved productivity and allowing firms to start exporting. The path (5)–(3)–(1) of Figure 13.1 identifies the proposed mechanism. In what follows we conduct an empirical analysis that intends to clarify the relationship between import, innovation, and export decisions of firms. We also relate outcomes of these decisions to firm productivity as a measure of performance.

13.2.3. Internationalization and Innovation by Spanish Firms

The data for the empirical analysis come from the firm-level annual survey (ESEE) of Spanish manufacturing firms for the period 1991–2009. The project is conducted by the Fundación Empresa Pública with financial support of the Spanish Ministry of Science and Technology. The information collected each year is consistent with the information in the previous years. The data include the population of Spanish manufacturing firms with 200 or more employees. It also contains a stratified sample of small firms comprising 4% of the population of small firms with more than 10 and less than 200 employees. Small firms that exit the original sample during the sampling period are replaced by firms with similar characteristics drawn from the population.

We choose to focus on SMEs, that is, firms that had less than 200 employees in 1991. We do so for a number of reasons. SMEs, unlike large enterprises, are likely to have resource constraints, which makes the internationalization process challenging for them. Export and import activities as internationalization strategies are particularly important for these firms, as those involve comparatively lower levels of resource commitment and risk than FDI (Leonidou and Katsikeas 1996; Lu and Beamish 2006). In our sample of SMEs, few firms actually have FDI. Only about 0.3% of the firms report FDI, compared to approximately 48% performing export and import activities. Moreover, innovation (product innovation in particular) plays an important role in the internationalization process of SMEs. Successful product innovation is shown to increase the likelihood of a firm to start exporting and to positively affect firm productivity levels (Cassiman, Golovko, and Martínez-Ros 2010). On the contrary, product innovation may not be as important in driving the export decision for larger firms, as these firm likely passed the early internationalization stage and are for the most part experienced exporters and importers. About 91% of large firms in the sample export and about 92% of these firms engage in import activities. The original samples of SMEs includes 1,183 firms in 1991 and 1,550 firms in 2009 from 20 distinct industries (Table 13.1). Due to missing values, the resulting sample is an unbalanced panel with 22,185 firm-year observations during the period 1991–2009.

We are interested in assessing the relationship between import and export activities and firm innovation output. For each firm and for every year, we know whether a firm exported, imported, or innovated in product or process. Our main variables of interest are the following: (a) *import*—a dummy variable that equals 1 if a firm imported in year t, and 0 otherwise; (b) *export*—a dummy variable that equals 1 if a firm exported in year t, and 0 otherwise; (c) *product innovation*—a dummy variable that equals 1 if a firm reported product innovation occurring in year t, and 0 otherwise; (d) *process innovation*—a dummy variable that equals 1 if a firm reported process innovation occurring in year t, and 0 otherwise.

Our empirical strategy is the following. We focus on importing as a baseline activity and analyze the export and innovation behavior of firms in relation to their import decisions. Empirically, we split our sample into four subsamples, depending on the firm import status during the 1991–2009 period. We define subsamples in the following way. Always importing firms are firms that imported during the entire sample period, non-importers are those firms that did not perform any importing, and "switchers" are firms that changed their importing status during 1991–2009. Among the switching firms we make a distinction between "entrants" and "exiters." Entrants into importing are those firms that changed their importing status from non-importers to importers during 1991–2009. We distinguish between "strict" entrants and "switching" entrants depending on whether the entry occurred once or multiple times. Finally, exiters are those firms that were importers in 1991 but exited importing at some point during the sample period.

Table 13.1 Industry Breakdown

Industry	Number of Firms-Year Observations
Meat products	637
Food and tobacco	2,208
Beverages	355
Textiles	2,340
Leather and footwear	924
Wood and wood products	809
Paper	640
Publishing and printing	1,292
Chemical products	1,109
Plastic and rubber products	1,247
Non-metal mineral products	1,613
Metallurgy	423
Metallic products	2,804
Machinery and equipment	1,335
Office machinery and computing	526
Electronics and electronic equipment	833
Autos and motor vehicles industry	601
Other transport equipment	353
Furniture	1,415
Miscellaneous manufacturing	642
Total	22,106

Table 13.2 summarizes the distribution of firms in the sample according to their import status. About 68% of firms in the sample engage in importing activities. Approximately 29% of these importing firms are continuous importers, while 35% of firms are entrants changing their import status from non-importers to importers during 1990–2009. About 22% of the entrants continue to import after the entry ("strict" entrants), suggesting that import activity is rather persistent over time. About 31% of firms never imported during the sample period.

Table 13.3 presents the summary statistics of relevant firm-level variables across these subsamples. Continuous importers and non-importers differ significantly in size (Table 13.3, columns 1–2). Consistent with prior findings, importers are also significantly more likely to perform exporting activities, to engage in outsourcing, and to be foreign owned. Innovation output variables (R&D/product/process innovation frequencies, R&D intensity, and number of product innovations) are also significantly different for these two groups. Importers invest more intensely in R&D and innovate more often than

Table 13.2 Import Status of Firms

	Number of Firms–Year Observations
Importing firms	15,095 (68.28%)
Continuous importers	6,333 (28.65%)
Entrants into imports	7,743 (35.02%)
Entered once ("strict" entrants)	4,894 (22.14%)
Entered twice	1,942 (8.79%)
Entered more than twice	907 (4.10%)
Exiters from imports (no re-entry)	1,019 (4.61%)
Never importing firms	7,011 (31.72%)
Total	22,106

Table 13.3 Summary Statistics for the Four Subsamples of Firms Based on Import Status

	Continuous Importers	Never Importing Firms	Switchers Enter	Switchers Exit
	1	2	3	4
Number of employees	76.04 (57.8)	23.95 (23.6)	44.9 (43.2)	42.15 (39.2)
Import status (0/1)	1	0	0.50 (0.49)	0.46 (0.49)
Import intensity (scaled by sales, %)	16.26 (15.7)	0	3.66 (8.5)	3.63 (7.76)
Export status (0/1)	0.82 (0.38)	0.15 (0.35)	0.52 (0.49)	0.43 (0.49)
Export intensity (scaled by sales, %)	23.6 (26.2)	2.7 (11.3)	11.2 (21.2)	9.32 (19.1)
Outsourcing status (0/1)	0.48 (0.49)	0.25 (0.43)	0.40 (0.49)	0.30 (0.45)
Foreign capital, %	19.04 (37.3)	0.54 (6.7)	4.45 (19.1)	4.61 (18.9)
R&D status (0/1)	0.42 (0.49)	0.06 (0.24)	0.19 (0.39)	0.13 (0.34)
R&D intensity (scaled by sales, %)	0.92 (2.34)	0.13 (0.97)	0.51 (2.5)	0.24 (1.5)
Process innovation status (0/1)	0.33 (0.47)	0.18 (0.39)	0.27 (0.44)	0.20 (0.40)
Product innovation status (0/1)	0.27 (0.44)	0.07 (0.26)	0.18 (0.39)	0.13 (0.34)
Product innovation number	2.58 (15.1)	0.46 (4.6)	2.32 (22.4)	0.69 (3.2)
Import technology status (0/1)	0.08 (0.28)	0.000 (0.02)	0.02 (0.13)	0.01 (0.13)
Number of firms–year observations	6,333	7,011	7,743	1,019

non-importers, both in process and product. Column 3 shows the summary statistics for the firms that entered imports during 1991–2009. These firms display figures lying between those of importers and non-importers. This is to be expected since these firms are in transition between the non-importing and importing groups. Firms entering into imports perform better in terms of innovation activities also compared to exiting firms (column 4), showing significantly higher frequencies of innovation and R&D investment decisions.

We proceed by looking for the simple empirical patterns associating import, export, and innovation decisions. Table 13.4A shows the transition probabilities for the different combinations of past and present export status. More than 90% of firms remain in the same state (continuous exporters and non-exporters). About 7.5% of non-exporters enter the export market in the next period. We would like to understand the transition from non-exporters to exporters and associate it with the import status of firms. Table 13.4B shows the effect of imports on the transition probability from non-exporting to exporting. About 17% of importers make this transition, compared to about 7.5% for the unconditional case. Tables 13.5A and 13.5B and Tables 13.6A and 13.6B provide the same statistics for the product and process innovation variables. About 7% and 13% of firms with no product and process innovation at time $(t - 1)$ become innovators in product and process, respectively, in the next period. The percentage of firms starting innovating while being importers increases to 9% and 15% for product and process innovation, respectively. Product and process innovators are also more likely to continue innovating

Table 13.4A Transition Probabilities, Exports

		Export (*t*)	
		0	1
Export (*t* – 1)	0	92.54	**7.45**
	1	5.93	94.06

Table 13.4B Transition Probabilities, Exports Conditional on Import Status

			Export (*t*)	
			0	1
Export (*t* – 1)	0	Import (*t* – 1) 0	95.74	4.25
		1	83.24	**16.75**
	1	Import (*t* – 1) 0	12.68	87.31
		1	3.68	96.31

Table 13.5A Transition Probabilities, Product Innovation

		Product Innovation (t)	
		0	1
Product innovation ($t-1$)	0	92.97	**7.02**
	1	38.14	61.85

Table 13.5B Transition Probabilities, Product Innovation Conditional on Import Status

			Product Innovation (t)	
			0	1
Product innovation ($t-1$)	0	Import ($t-1$) 0	94.95	5.04
		1	90.59	**9.40**
	1	Import ($t-1$) 0	49.40	50.59
		1	33.21	66.78

if at the same time they are importing (61% versus 67% and 58% versus 62% of firms for product and process innovation, respectively). Overall, Tables 13.4–13.6 suggest that import status is strongly associated with both the decisions to export and innovate.

We proceed by focusing on the subsample of "strict" entrants into imports. This subsample is of particular importance if we want to evaluate the effect of import on export and innovation activities: we can observe changes in export and innovation behavior that are associated with the change in import status. Specifically, we examine whether importers differ significantly from non-importers in their export and innovation behavior, and we trace longitudinally the innovation and export decisions of entrants—that is, firms that start importing—to assess the potential relationship with imports.

Table 13.7 presents the results of the test for equality of means for innovation and export frequencies for the subsample of entrants into imports before and after the entry took place. First, we compare the firms at time ($t-2$) and time (t), where ($t-2$) corresponds to two years before entry, and time (t) to the year of entry into imports. Second, we do the same comparison at time ($t-2$) and time ($t+2$), where ($t-2$) corresponds to two years before, and ($t+2$)—to two years after the entry into imports.

Overall, we observe an increase in the innovation proportions for both product and process innovation. Importing is associated with significant increase in product- as well as process-innovation frequency at the year of entry. For the time window two years before to two years after entry, however, the increase in innovation frequencies is not

Table 13.6A Transition Probabilities, Process Innovation

		Process Innovation (t)	
		0	1
Process innovation ($t-1$)	0	86.98	**13.01**
	1	41.82	58.17

Table 13.6B Transition Probabilities, Process Innovation Conditional on Import Status

			Process Innovation (t)	
			0	1
Process innovation ($t-1$)	0	Import ($t-1$) 0	89.12	10.87
		1	84.48	**15.51**
	1	Import ($t-1$) 0	48.14	51.85
		1	37.63	62.36

Table 13.7 Differences in Means in Innovation and Export Propensity for the Group of Entrant Firms before and after Entering Imports

	Difference in Means	
	2 years before to year of entry	2 years before to 2 years after
Export (0/1)	0.11***	0.12***
Product innovation (0/1)	0.03*	0.00
Process innovation (0/1)	0.04*	0.00

*, **, *** are significantly different from zero at the 10%, 5%, or 1% level, respectively.

statistically significant. Concerning export activity, the difference between pre-entry and post-entry export frequency is highly significant for both time windows.

To take into account other variables that may influence firm innovation and export decisions, we conduct regression analysis. We compare the subsample of "strict" entrants into importing with the subsample of never importing firms and estimate random effects linear probability models assessing firms' propensity to innovate in product/process and export:

$$Y_{it} = \sum_{j=-3}^{3} \gamma_j P_{ij} + \beta' X_{it} + \alpha_i + e_{it},$$

where Y_{it} stands for product innovation, process innovation, and export decisions, respectively; $P_{i,-3}, \dots, P_{i,3}$ are the dummy variables that equal 1 in the moment $(t-3), \dots t, \dots (t+3)$ respectively, and moments $(t-3), \dots (t+3)$ are years before/after the entry into imports; the vector X_{it} denotes other firm characteristics influencing innovation and export decisions.

We include size, percentage of foreign capital, R&D intensity, year, and industry effects as relevant determinants of the decisions to export and innovate. R&D investments as an input in innovative effort can foster technological innovation (Salomon and Shaver 2005a). Specifically, we expect R&D expenditures normalized on firm sales (*R&D intensity*) to positively affect the innovation output. Firm size (*size*) measured as the logarithm of sales stands as an important control variable that may affect both export and innovation decisions (Bernard and Jensen 1999). Being a part of a foreign company may affect the innovation strategy of a firm compared to its purely domestic counterparts. It might also facilitate the process of becoming an exporter (Basile 2001). We include a percentage of foreign capital that controls for the presence of foreign ownership in the capital structure of the firm (*foreign capital*). The vectors of industry and year dummies are inserted to control for the industry heterogeneity and macroeconomic conditions. Table 13.8 presents the results of the estimation.

For the innovation variables, the increase in product innovation frequency is observed already one year before starting importing, with the most pronounced effect at the year of entry into imports (Table 13.8, column 1). Firms exhibit a 5% increase in the probability to innovate in product prior to becoming importers in the next year. In its turn, becoming an importer is associated with almost 6% increase in the probability of introducing product innovation in the year of entry into imports. With respect to process innovation, the results indicate significant differences between non-importers and new importers around the entry time, suggesting that process innovation adoption accompanies import entry. The likelihood of process innovation is about 8% higher for the future importers compared to non-importing firms two years and one year before import entry. The new importers tend to have about 6% higher probability of having process innovation at the moment of entry. Further, we observe a positive significant difference in export adoption at the year of starting imports, with the stable effect lasting for the coming three years. New entrants are about 6% more likely to export compared

Table 13.8 Random Effects Linear Probability Model

	Product Innovation	Process Innovation	Export
	1	2	3
$P_{-3}(t-3)$	−0.009 (0.02)	0.006 (0.02)	−0.049** (0.01)
$P_{-2}(t-2)$	0.01 (0.01)	0.08*** (0.02)	−0.01 (0.01)
$P_{-1}(t-1)$	0.05*** (0.01)	0.08*** (0.01)	−0.01 (0.01)
$P_0(t0)$	0.057*** (0.01)	0.06*** (0.01)	0.06*** (0.01)
$P_1(t+1)$	0.00 (0.01)	0.04** (0.01)	0.05*** (0.01)
$P_2(t+2)$	−0.00 (0.01)	0.05** (0.02)	0.06*** (0.01)
$P_3(t+3)$	−0.03 (0.01)	0.03 (0.02)	0.06*** (0.01)
Size	0.02*** (0.001)	0.05*** (0.005)	0.10*** (0.005)
Foreign capital, %	0.0005** (0.0002)	−0.0007* (.0003)	0.001*** (0.0002)
R&D intensity	0.018*** (0.001)	0.012*** (0.002)	0.002* (0.001)
Intercept	−0.23*** (0.06)	−0.58*** (0.09)	−1.10*** (0.09)
Industry, time effects	included	included	included
Number of observations	11,905	11,905	11,905

*, **, *** are significantly different from zero at the 10%, 5%, or 1% level, respectively.

to non-importers at the year of entry. In contrast, in years preceding import entry, new entrants are less likely to become exporters compared to similar non-importers.

The results in Table 13.8 suggest that importing SMEs are more prone to invest in product and process innovation than non-importers already before entry into imports. These findings are consistent with the joint adoption of innovation and import activities, suggesting that imports are needed for both product and process innovations. In addition, process innovation frequency increases even after the entry into imports, pointing at possible additional benefits that new importers get in terms of new production processes. The results for the exports variable suggest that SMEs are more likely to start exporting once they become importers, indicating that the decision to export may follow import entry.

Finally, we relate the firm internationalization (export and import) and innovation decisions to performance by estimating the model with productivity as a dependent variable.[1] We include firm physical capital (measured as the logarithm of stock of tangible assets) and labor (measured as the logarithm of the number of employees in a given year) to account for the differences in output that can be attributed to the increase in capital and labor inputs. The independent variables are export, import, and innovation decisions made by firms in a previous year. Sets of industry and year dummies are included as standard controls. We estimate a random effects panel data model using the subsamples of non-importers and firms entering into imports. Table 13.9 lists the results of the regression.

Table 13.9 Productivity Regression, Random Effects Model

	1	2
Import $(t-1)$	0.07*** (0.01)	
Product innovation $(t-1)$	−0.001 (0.01)	
Import and product innovation $(t-1)$		0.049* (0.02)
No import and product innovation $(t-1)$		0.01 (0.02)
Import and no product innovation $(t-1)$		0.08*** (0.01)
Process innovation $(t-1)$	0.02* (0.01)	0.02* (0.01)
Export $(t-1)$	0.07*** (0.01)	0.07*** (0.01)
Capital	0.006*** (0.001)	0.006*** (0.001)
Size	0.99*** (0.01)	0.99*** (0.01)
Foreign capital, %	0.002*** (0.00)	0.002*** (0.00)
Intercept	10.13*** (0.10)	10.12*** (0.10)
Industry and time effects	included	included
Number of observations	9,710	9,710

*, **, *** are significantly different from zero at the 10%, 5%, or 1% level, respectively.

The results in column 1 show that both import and export activities in a previous year are positively associated with the current productivity levels. The same is true for the process innovation variable. The coefficient of product innovation suggests that product innovation is not significantly related to the productivity in the next period. If exclusive combinations of product innovation and importing are used, the results show that combining product innovation and imports is positively associated with productivity, as well as just being an importer. However, these coefficients are not significantly different, suggesting the positive and significant effect of imports and not product innovation on productivity. Having only product innovation is not significantly associated with productivity (column 2).

Overall, our empirical results support the hypothesis that innovation and import decisions may be jointly determined. We find evidence of importing activity being significantly associated with both product and process innovation activity. Moreover, simple regression analysis suggests a particular timing for innovation and import decisions—entrants into import activity tend to innovate more often, in both product and process, *shortly before* starting importing, compared to never importing firms. The results are also in line with the hypothesized internationalization path with exports following import activity. Our findings suggest that export and import decisions are significantly positively associated, and export frequency increases right *after* SMEs adopt import activity. Therefore, we find some empirical support for the path (5)–(3)–(1) on Figure 13.1. We also document the positive effect of internationalization and innovation activities on firm productivity, measured as log of value added, in line with prior findings on internationalization-productivity association.

13.3. DISCUSSION AND CONCLUSIONS

In this chapter, we have provided an overview of the existing literature on the relationships between firm internationalization and innovation behavior, linking these decisions to productivity as a firm performance measure. The review of the empirical findings shows a complex dynamic interaction between export, import, and innovation decisions. By innovating, firms can enter new markets with novel products or products of better quality, thus making future exports more successful. At the same time, exporting can promote knowledge diffusion from abroad, resulting in enhanced innovation performance. Imports can also serve as a conduit for technology diffusion, facilitating learning and consequently making firms innovate more.

We argue for a need to better understand an interrelation between exports, imports, and innovation and propose a particular mechanism that may underlie these links. Innovation—product innovation in particular—may trigger firms to start importing in search for novel inputs, leading to even more innovation and productivity enhancements, which in turn facilitate export entry. Our empirical analysis is consistent with the proposed path, also highlighting the performance effects of combining export, import, and innovation.

Based on the overview and our empirical results, we indicate several research areas that need further development. In particular, we still know very little on the interaction between import and innovation strategies and their role as productivity-enhancing investments potentially leading to future exporting. In line with some prior empirical findings, our results indicate that imports and innovations seem to precede the entry of firms into the export markets. Import, innovation, and export investments also identify the most productive firms in our sample, which may suggest a complementarity between imports, exports, and innovation for productivity. Research should focus on explaining the mechanisms that might underlie the complex dynamic relationship between imports, innovation, and exports and testing these mechanisms empirically. A related question that deserves attention is the joint effect of import, innovation, and export activities on firm performance and potential complementarities that can be realized.

Another underexplored topic is related to the factors that determine the decision of firms to engage in import activities. Using the panel of Spanish firms during 1991–2009, we provide preliminary evidence on the interplay between import and innovation decisions. Our findings suggest that firms tend to pursue both product and process innovation before or simultaneously with becoming importers. Thus, the decisions to import and innovate might be made jointly, suggesting that firms make decisions to internationalize, and import in particular, in accordance with their specific needs related to their innovation strategy. In other words, firms may proactively search for new inputs needed for their innovation processes, which leads to import decisions. Our explanation does not exclude the possibility of "learning" by importing, but it highlights the importance of a firm's agency in making decisions on internationalization. More research is needed on the drivers of a firm's decision to become an importer.

Furthermore, we find differences in product and process innovation behavior associated with the import entry. Product innovation and process innovation also seem to differ in their effects on productivity, with product innovation having an effect only if accompanied by imports. Differential roles of product versus process innovation in the import-export-productivity nexus should be a topic for future research.

Finally, further research should focus on the boundary conditions—or moderating factors—that can shape the ability of firms to learn from international trade activities and profitably exploit the new knowledge. Learning by trading appears to be an important mechanism in the internationalization-innovation circle. Recent work acknowledging the heterogeneity among firms has begun to focus on factors that may explain the heterogeneity in the learning by exporting effect on innovation and productivity. Exploring the contingencies in learning by trade, and in particular learning-by-importing, can constitute a profitable avenue for future research. Examples of such contingency factors could be origins of imports or the type of importing performed by firms (importing intermediate products versus final goods).

In conclusion, we need to better understand the dynamic process that relates firm decisions to invest in innovation, import, or export, as those activities likely determine future growth trajectories and performance of firms. We also believe that a better understanding of the connection between firm innovation decisions and internationalization of its activities is necessary for improving public policies aimed at stimulating firm internationalization and innovation decisions. For instance, if import and innovation activities are a source of productivity growth leading to export entry, then policies aimed at promoting imports and innovation, and product innovation in particular, might be more effective than direct export promotions, at least for firms "at risk" for importing and innovating. The key policy issue then becomes which type of investment to leverage.

NOTE

1. To measure performance, we use productivity calculated as the logarithm of firm value added. Value added is computed by subtracting expenditures for raw materials, consumables, and services from the firms' sales. We use the classical production function introduced by Griliches (1986) of the form $Y_{it+1} = A^{\alpha} K_{it}^{\gamma} L_{it}^{\lambda}$ with Y representing the firm's output (value added), K being a firm's physical capital, calculated as the log of firm stock of tangible assets, and L representing labor measured by the log number of employees in a given year. We take natural logarithms to obtain the linear form of the production function.

REFERENCES

Altomonte, C., T. Aquilante, G. Békés, and G. I. Ottaviano. 2013. :Internationalization and Innovation of Firms: Evidence and Policy." *Economic Policy* 28(76): 663–700.

Alvarez, R., and R. Robertson. 2004. "Exposure to Foreign Markets and Plant-Level Innovation: Evidence from Chile and Mexico." *The Journal of International Trade and Economic Development* 13(1): 57–87.

Amiti, M., and J. Konings. 2007. "Trade Liberalization, Intermediate Inputs, and Productivity: Evidence from Indonesia." *The American Economic Review* 97(5): 1611–1638.

Aristei, D., D. Castellani, and C. Franco. 2013. "Firms' Exporting and Importing Activities: Is There a Two-Way Relationship?" *Review of World Economics* 149(1): 55–84.

Atkin, D., A.K. Khandelwal and A. Osman. 2017. "Exporting and Firm Performance: Evidence from a Randomized Experiment" *The Quartely Journal of Economics* 132(2): 551–615.

Augier, P., O. Cadot, and M. Dovis. 2013. "Imports and TFP at the Firm Level: The Role of Absorptive Capacity." *Canadian Journal of Economics/Revue canadienne d'économique* 46(3): 956–981.

Aw, B. Y., and G. Batra. 1998. "Technological Capability and Firm Efficiency in Taiwan (China)." *The World Bank Economic Review* 12(1): 59–79.

Aw, B. Y., M. J. Roberts, and D. Y. Xu. 2011. "R&D Investment, Exporting, and Productivity Dynamics." *American Economic Review* 101(4): 1312–1344.

Bartelsman, E. J., and M. Doms. 2000. "Understanding Productivity: Lessons from Longitudinal Microdata." *Journal of Economic Literature* 38(3): 569–594.

Bas, M., and V. Strauss-Kahn. 2014. "Does Importing More Inputs Raise Exports? Firm-Level Evidence from France." *Review of World Economics* 150(2): 241–275.

Basile, R. 2001. "Export behaviour of Italian Manufacturing Firms over the Nineties: The Role of Innovation." *Research Policy* 30(8): 1185–1201.

Becker, S. O., and P.H. Egger. 2013. "Endogenous product versus Process Innovation and a Firm's Propensity to Export." *Empirical Economics* 44(1): 329–354.

Belderbos, R., V. Van Roy, and F. Duvivier, F. 2013. "International and Domestic Technology Transfers and Productivity Growth: Firm Level Evidence." *Industrial and Corporate Change* 22(1): 1–32.

Bernard, A. B., and J. B. Jensen. 1999. "Exceptional Exporter Performance: Cause, Effect, or Both?" *Journal of International Economics* 47(1): 1–25.

Bernard, A. B., and J. B. Jensen. 2004. "Exporting and Productivity in the USA." *Oxford Review of Economic Policy* 20(3): 343–357.

Bernard, A. B., and J. B. Jensen. 2004. "Why Some Firms Export." *Review of Economics and Statistics* 86(2): 561–569.

Bernard, A. B., J. B. Jensen, S. J. Redding, and P. K. Schott. 2012. "The Empirics of Firm Heterogeneity and International Trade." *Annual Review of Economics* 4(1): 283–313.

Bernard, A. B., J. B. Jensen, S. J. Redding, and P. K. Schott. 2007. "Firms in International Trade." *The Journal of Economic Perspectives* 21(3): 105–130.

Blalock, G., and P. J. Gertler. 2004. "Learning from Exporting Revisited in a Less Developed Setting." *Journal of Development Economics* 75(2): 397–416.

Bustos, P. 2011. "Trade Liberalization, Exports, and Technology Upgrading: Evidence on the Impact of Mercosur on Argentinian Firms." *The American Economic Review* 101(1): 304–340.

Cassiman, B., and E. Golovko. 2011. "Innovation and Internationalization Through Exports." *Journal of International Bussiness Studies* 42(1): 56–75.

Cassiman, B., E. Golovko, and E. Martínez-Ros. 2010. "Innovation, Exports and Productivity." *International Journal of Industrial Organization* 28(4): 372–376.

Cassiman, B., and E. Martinez-Ros. 2007. "Product Innovation and Exports." *Evidence from Spanish Manufacturing, IESE Business School.* https://www.researchgate.net/publication/255435821_Product_Innovation_and_Exports

Castellani, D., F. Serti, and C. Tomasi. 2010. "Firms in International Trade: Importers' and Exporters' Heterogeneity in Italian Manufacturing Industry." *World Economy* 33(3): 424–457.

Clerides, S. K., S. Lach, and J. R. Tybout. 1998. "Is Learning by Exporting Important? Micro-Dynamic Evidence from Colombia, Mexico, and Morocco." *The Quarterly Journal of Economics* 113(3): 903.

Criscuolo, C., J. E. Haskel, and M. J. Slaughter. 2010. "Global Engagement and the Innovation Activities of Firms." *International Journal of Industrial Organization* 28(2): 191–202.

Damijan, J. P., and Č. Kostevc. 2015. "Learning from Trade Through Innovation." *Oxford Bulletin of Economics and Statistics* 77(3): 408–436.

De Loecker, J. 2007. "Do Exports Generate Higher Productivity? Evidence from Slovenia." *Journal of International Economics* 73(1): 69–98.

De Loecker, J., and P. K. Goldberg. 2014. "Firm Performance in a Global Market." *Annual Review of Economics* 6(1): 201–227.

Delgado, M. A., J. C. Fariñas, and S. Ruano. 2002. "Firm Productivity and Export Markets: A Non-Parametric Approach." *Journal of International Economics* 57(2): 397–422.

Fariñas, J. C., A. López, and A. Martín-Marcos. 2014. "Assessing the Impact of Domestic Outsourcing and Offshoring on Productivity at the Firm Level." *Applied Economics* 46(15): 1814–1828.

Fariñas, J. C., and A. Martín-Marcos. 2010. "Foreign Sourcing and Productivity: Evidence at the Firm Level." *World Economy* 33(3): 482–506.

Filipescu, D. A., S. Prashantham, A. Rialp, and J. Rialp. 2013. "Technological Innovation and Exports: Unpacking Their Reciprocal Causality." *Journal of International Marketing* 21(1): 23–38.

Foster, L., J. Haltiwanger, and C. Syverson. 2008. "Reallocation, Firm Turnover, and Efficiency: Selection on Productivity or Profitability?" *American Economic Review* 98(1): 394–425.

Girma, S., H. Görg, and Λ. Hanley. 2008. "R&D and Exporting: A Comparison of British and Irish Firms." *Review of World Economics* 144(4): 750–773.

Goldberg, P. K., A. K. Khandelwal, N. Pavcnik, and P. Topalova. 2010. "Imported Intermediate Inputs and Domestic Product Growth: Evidence from India." *The Quarterly Journal of Economics* 125(4): 1727–1767.

Golovko, E., and G. Valentini. 2011. "Exploring the Complementarity Between Innovation and Export for SMEs' Growth." *Journal of International Bussiness Studies* 42(3): 362–380.

Golovko, E., and G. Valentini. 2014. "Selective Learning-by-Exporting: Firm Size and Product versus Process Innovation." *Global Strategy Journal* 4(3): 161–180.

Griliches, Z. 1986. "Productivity, R&D, and the Basic Research at the Firm Level in the 1970's." *American Economic Review* 76(1): 141–154.

Halpern, L., M. Koren, and A. Szeidl. 2015. "Imported Inputs and Productivity." *American Economic Review* 105(12): 3660–3703.

Hirsch, S., and I. Bijaoui. 1985. "R&D Intensity and Export Performance: A Micro View." *Weltwirtschaftliches Archiv* 121(2): 238–251.

Hitt, M. A., R. E. Hoskisson, and H. Kim. 1997. "International Diversification: Effects on Innovation and Firm Performance in Product-Diversified Firms." *Academy of Management Journal* 40(4): 767–798.

Kasahara, H., and B. Lapham. 2013. "Productivity and the Decision to Import and Export: Theory and Evidence." *Journal of International Economics* 89(2): 297–316.

Kasahara, H., and J. Rodrigue. 2008. "Does the Use of Imported Intermediates Increase Productivity? Plant-Level Evidence." *Journal of Development Economics* 87(1): 106–118.

Keller, W. 2004. "International Technology Diffusion." *Journal of Economic Literature* 42(3): 752–782.

Kohler, W., and M. Smolka. 2012. "Global Sourcing: Evidence from Spanish Firm-Level Data." Ch.4, p. 139–193 in *Quantitative Analysis of Newly Evolving Patterns of International Trade: Fragmentation, Offshoring of Activities, and Vertical Intra-Industry Trade*. World Scientific Publishing Co,. Pte. Ltd.

Kohler, W., and M. Smolka. 2014. "Global Sourcing and Firm Selection." *Economics Letters* 124(3): 411–415.

Leonidou, L. C., and C. S. Katsikeas. 1996. "The Export Development Process: An Integrative Review of Empirical Models." *Journal of International Business Studies* 27(3): 517–551.

Lileeva, A., and D. Trefler. 2010. "Improved Access to Foreign Markets Raises Plant-Level Productivity . . . For Some Plants." *The Quarterly Journal of Economics* 125(3): 1051–1099.

Liu, X., and T. Buck. 2007. "Innovation Performance and Channels for International Technology Spillovers: Evidence from Chinese High-Tech Industries." *Research Policy* 36(3): 355–366.

Lööf, H., and M. Andersson. 2010. "Imports, Productivity and Origin Markets: The Role of Knowledge-Intensive Economies." *The World Economy* 33(3): 458–481.

Lu, J. W., and P. W. Beamish. 2006. "SME Internationalization and Performance: Growth vs. Profitability." *Journal of International Entrepreneurship* 4(1): 27–48.

MacGarvie, M. 2006. "Do Firms Learn from International Trade?" *Review of Economics and Statistics* 88(1): 46–60.

Muûls, M., and M. Pisu. 2009. "Imports and Exports at the Level of the Firm: Evidence from Belgium." *World Economy* 32(5): 692–734.

Roper, S., and J. H. Love. 2002. "Innovation and Export Performance: Evidence from the UK and German Manufacturing Plants." *Research Policy* 31(7): 1087–1102.

Salomon, R. 2006a. *Learning from Exporting: New Insights, New Perspectives*. Cheltenham, UK; Northampton, MA: Edward Elgar.

Salomon, R. 2006b. "Spillovers to Foreign Market Participants: Assessing the Impact of Export Strategies on Innovative Productivity." *Strategic Organization* 4(2): 135–164.

Salomon, R., and B. Jin. 2008. "Does Knowledge Spill to Leaders or Laggards? Exploring Industry Heterogeneity in Learning by Exporting." *Journal of International Business Studies* 39(1): 132–150.

Salomon, R., and B. Jin. 2010. "Do Leading or Lagging Firms Learn More from Exporting?" *Strategic Management Journal* 31(10): 1088–1113.

Salomon, R., and J. M. Shaver. 2005a. "Export and Domestic Sales: Their Interrelationship and Determinants." *Strategic Management Journal* 26(9): 855–871.

Salomon, R., and J. M. Shaver. 2005b. "Learning by Exporting: New Insights from Examining Firm Innovation." *Journal of Economics & Management Strategy* 14(2): 431–460.

Silva, A., O. Afonso, and A. P. Africano. 2012. "Learning-by-Exporting: What We Know and What We Would Like to Know." *The International Trade Journal* 26(3): 255–288.

Tomiura, E. 2007. "Foreign Outsourcing, Exporting, and FDI: A Productivity Comparison at the Firm Level." *Journal of International Economics* 72(1): 113–127.

Van Beveren, I., and H. Vandenbussche. 2010. "Product and Process Innovation and Firms' Decision to Export." *Journal of Economic Policy Reform* 13(1): 3–24.

Van Biesebroeck, J. 2005. "Exporting Raises Productivity in Sub-Saharan African Manufacturing Firms." *Journal of International Economics* 67: 373–391.

Vernon, R. 1966. "International Investment and International Trade in the Product Cycle." *The Quarterly Journal of Economics* 80(2): 190–207.

Vernon, R. 1979. "The Product Cycle Hypothesis in a New International Environment." *Oxford Bulletin of Economics and Statistics* 41(4): 255–267.

Veugelers, R., and B. Cassiman. 2004. "Foreign Subsidiaries as a Channel of International Technology Diffusion: Some Direct Firm Level Evidence from Belgium." *European Economic Review* 48(2): 455–476.

Vogel, A., and J. Wagner. 2010. "Higher Productivity in Importing German Manufacturing Firms: Self-Selection, Learning from Importing, or Both?" *Review of World Economics* 145(4): 641–665.

Zahra, S. A., and J. G. Covin. 1994. "Domestic and International Competitive Focus, Technology Strategy and Company Performance: An Empirical Analysis." *Technology Analysis & Strategic Management* 6(1): 39–54.

CHAPTER 14

EFFECT OF INTERNATIONAL
COMPETITION ON FIRM
PRODUCTIVITY AND
MARKET POWER

JAN DE LOECKER AND
JOHANNES VAN BIESEBROECK

14.1. INTRODUCTION

A large literature studies the effect of international trade on firm performance.[1] A wide
range of performance measures and different ways of international integration have
been investigated. In this overview we intend to focus on just two methodological issues.
We provide only a partial coverage of the literature, highlighting representative studies
that illustrate the main points we want to make.

The first point we emphasize is that it is imperative to study two aspects of firm
performance—productive efficiency and market power—in an integrated framework.
If all product and factor markets are perfectly competitive, productivity estimates are
direct measures of efficiency and they can be studied on their own. Prices equal marginal costs, and market power is irrelevant. However, it is hard to deny that perfect competition is the exception. Market power, for example due to product differentiation, is
ubiquitous. As emphasized by Katayama, Lu, and Tybout (2009) and De Loecker and
Goldberg (2014), this leads to firm-level variation in prices and makes it much harder
to determine the meaning of any productivity change as conventionally measured (i.e.,
capturing the variation in sales not explained by input use). In a domestic context,
Foster, Haltiwanger, and Syverson (2008) illustrate explicitly that revenue-based total
factor productivity (TFP) is not a good measure of productive efficiency if firms have
market power.

Our focus in this chapter is on correctly decomposing the standard recovered residual of a production function into cost, markups, and efficiency. Ignoring the different components of measured productivity can lead to misleading conclusions of how competition—trade liberalization in particular—affects firms and economies as a whole. Rather than measuring productivity as a residual, the methods we review tend to put enough structure on the problem to identify firm-level marginal costs directly. Given sufficient data, changes in marginal cost can be decomposed into changes in efficiency or input prices. However, the level of technical efficiency tends to be less relevant for differentiated products. Knowing what to produce is at least as important as how to produce it.

In most of the chapter we do not discuss productivity explicitly in great detail, but that is a deliberate choice. The primitives of the model are firm-level technical efficiency and demand, and two market-level variables: input prices and the strength of competition. Once one has recovered these, it is possible to construct marginal costs and the optimal price-cost margin, which in turn determine sales, productivity, and everything else. Rather than estimating productivity directly, we consider it a specific performance measure that might be interesting for some purposes, but not a primitive of the model. As different estimation approaches for productivity often recover different functions of the primitives, a focus on productivity will often hamper comparability of results across studies rather than facilitate it.

Our second point is that trade liberalization, by enlarging the relevant market, has the potential to increase competition. Whether it *actually* has this effect, and in which cases such effects are strongest, is not well understood. Holmes and Schmitz (2010) and De Loecker and Goldberg (2014) survey evidence of the impact of competition on productivity, respectively domestic and foreign competition, but they focus specifically on cases where it is unambiguous that an exogenous change has raised the extent of competition.

Especially in the case of geographic market boundaries, it is natural to consider the strength of competition along a continuous spectrum. A change taking place sufficiently far away will have no effect, but the threshold distance will vary by context. Trade policy changes can have similar effects as lowering of transport costs and therefore naturally influence whether products belong to the same market or not.

The effect of international integration is not always clear-cut. Tariff reductions will only affect a firm if its product competes with the products subject to those tariffs. The relevant market definition, both in terms of product characteristics and geographical distance, is not always known. It is not even necessarily constant over time as, for example, a change in technology or transportation costs can implicitly lead to entry of products. Moreover, competition can be itself endogenous to policy. We are concerned with a situation where trade liberalization, broadly defined, has the potential to affect the competition firms face, but where one still needs to verify whether it *actually* does.

The two issues, the impact of market power on the interpretation of productivity and the impact of trade on competition, are related even beyond measurement. Empirical studies have emphasized that trade liberalization raises average productivity by raising the minimum productivity threshold for survival, and by inducing reallocation of resources toward more productive producers. However, incorporating market power also changes the theoretical gains from trade. In a situation with heterogeneous firms and variable markups, the net effect on welfare crucially depends on which firms take advantage of the export possibilities and which firms see the largest increase in competition due to imports. Arkolakis, Costinot, Donaldson, and Rodriguez-Clare (2018) show that adding a pro-competitive effect in the Arkolakis, Costinot, and Rodriguez-Clare (2012) framework lowers welfare gains from trade, while in the oligopoly model of Edmond, Midrigan, and Xu (2015) the effect goes the other way.

Traditionally, the industrial organization (IO) literature has focused on market power questions, often imposing constant marginal costs on the analysis. In contrast, the trade literature has by and large interpreted observed productivity growth as greater efficiency, which is only valid under perfect or monopolistic competition. The remainder of this chapter illustrates that the two approaches are complementary and that several studies have already blended insights from the two literatures.

In the remainder of the chapter we discuss, in turn, three approaches to estimating the extent of market power. To highlight the different assumptions the alternative approaches make with respect to market definition, we first discuss this briefly in section 14.2. Then, in section 14.3, we discuss the dominant IO framework that starts from a well-defined demand system. In section 14.4 we discuss an alternative approach that exploits the zero-profit condition governing equilibrium market entry and exit. In section 14.5 we discuss the production-side approach that relies on input choices and refrains from specifying the relevant market upfront. Section 14.6 closes with a few concluding remarks and avenues for further research.

14.2. Market Definition

Defining the relevant market has been at the forefront of the IO literature on estimating and analyzing market power. The development of flexible models of consumer demand was in part to help determine the relevant market. In particular, products belong to the same market, in a geographical or product-space sense, if consumers consider them to be good substitutes and therefore have non-zero cross-price elasticities. We can use an estimated demand system to investigate these elasticities, but the estimates themselves are inherently conditional on a particular sample of products. Therefore it is indispensable to conduct some robustness analyses.

Defining the market is also critical when studying market structure more generally, as variation in the number of firms in a market is one aspect of the strength of competition. To avoid problems associated with at least partly integrated markets or with imports and exports, a range of applications study local service markets where markets can be straightforwardly segmented geographically; see, for example, the studies by Bresnahan and Reiss (1991), Syverson (2004), and Schaumans and Verboven (2015), which we discuss in the following.

The IO approach of clearly delineating markets is in contrast to the international trade literature, where the gains from integration are a central research theme. Lowering trade barriers or reducing transportation costs enlarges the market and can impact the competitive pressure on firms. It implies that the market definition itself can be endogenous to a change in the economic environment. In practice, however, empirical work in trade has also relied on an implicit market definition. A set of producers operating in an industry, as classified by statistical agencies, are pooled together and national boundaries are considered as discrete market barriers.

The literature on exchange rate pass-through has taken a different approach and it is precisely interested in the extent to which markets are segmented or integrated (see Goldberg and Knetter 1997 for a survey of this approach). In particular, price and cost variation across markets (typically countries) in response to exchange-rate shocks is used to infer the degree of segmentation across markets.

The production-side approach we propose does not require one to commit to a specific market definition to study the effects of competition on firm performance. It allows for the usual productivity effects, but also for additional effects from competition on price-cost markups. The method does, however, crucially rely on the ability to pool firms and products that produce with a common production technology. To identify the extent of market power an individual firm has, we need to measure the output elasticity of a variable input at the observed combination of output and inputs. To recover this, we specify a flexible production technology and estimate this using a sample of firms actually employing this technology. Once we have estimates of productivity and market power, we can relate these to changes in competition, for example as triggered by trade policy changes.

14.3. Estimating Competition from the Demand Side

In this section we describe the so-called demand approach to analyze the impact of competition, be it domestic or international in nature, on firm performance. As mentioned before, we always consider firm performance to include not only technical efficiency, but also marginal cost of production and the ability to mark up costs, which are components of the usual productivity measures. A first step in this type of analysis is to estimate demand, which we review first. Studies of the impact of international competition have, in a second step, supplemented the estimated demand system with a behavioral assumption on market competition to perform counterfactual simulations of trade policies, which we review next. The existing literature focuses mostly on price effects and markups, but given that marginal costs and counterfactual market shares are recovered, other types of analysis are possible. We review some extensions in the third subsection and revisit potential applications that are more directly linked to the productivity literature as an avenue for future research at the end of this chapter.

14.3.1. The Standard Framework: Discrete Choice Demand

Many applications in the field of industrial organization require knowledge about firms' own and cross-price elasticities. Berry (1994) sets out a powerful framework of how to estimate flexible elasticities in differentiated goods markets with many products using only aggregate, product-level information: quantities, prices, and other characteristics. It starts from a random indirect utility function that is a function of observable product characteristics, including price, as well as idiosyncratic consumer-specific tastes. Assuming that consumer-level tastes are distributed according to an extreme value distribution, choice probabilities can be aggregated over consumers to obtain an explicit expression for the market shares of all products.

The application in Berry, Levinsohn, and Pakes (1995) for the US automobile market uses a random coefficients demand system that incorporates consumer heterogeneity in the valuation of product characteristics. The results demonstrate that even with tightly parameterized preferences that can be estimated using only market-level data, the discrete choice model can still generate relatively flexible substitution patterns between products. Demand curves are continuous at the market level and incorporate the intuitive feature that substitution is stronger between products that are similar in characteristics space.

In principle, the demand model can be estimated without any supply restrictions. The supply side of the market can help mitigate the price endogeneity, as firms are likely to set prices taking into account unobservable product quality that enters the residual of the demand curve. Berry, Levinsohn, and Pakes (1995) use the characteristics of competing products to construct instruments for price. In order to increase estimation precision, they supplement the demand system with a set of first-order conditions derived from profit-maximizing price-setting behavior and a Nash equilibrium assumption. Firms take into account how each price they set influences sales of all their own products, as well as the strategic responses of other firms.[2]

In addition to relying on an explicit supply model to calculate markups, it allows for counterfactual analysis by changing a primitive of the model. An important application is in merger analysis, where the effect of a potential merger on the market equilibrium is predicted ex ante. Using an explicit behavior assumption, one can recover the product-level marginal costs that are consistent with the estimated-demand model and the observed prices. A merger affects the equilibrium because the merging firms have an incentive to raise prices, as their multi-product price-setting behavior now takes into account demand-stealing over an increased set of own-products. Firms not party to the merger are also likely to raise prices in response, as prices tend to be strategic complements. Possible efficiency gains from the merger can readily be incorporated in the analysis as lower marginal costs for the directly affected firms.

The entire analysis starts from a well-defined product market, populated by a set of consumers with stable preferences. Different behavioral assumptions directly imply different strengths of competition. Assuming that firms behave as oligopolists leads to a prediction of positive price-cost markups, while assuming price-taking behavior directly relates marginal costs to the observed prices. The Cournot assumption of quantity competition leads to a positive markup even for homogenous products, while the Bertrand assumption of price competition requires some product differentiation before prices can exceed marginal costs. The product-level marginal costs that are backed out as primitives of the model will depend on the specific behavioral assumption used as well as the particular functional-form assumptions.

In another application to the automobile industry, Bresnahan (1987) jointly estimates demand and marginal cost parameters under different assumptions for the mode of competition. One criterion to assess the appropriateness of alternative assumptions is to use a non-nested test to compare the fit with the data. An alternative criterion is to estimate the model separately for each year and verify which sequence of market conduct assumptions leads to the most stable set of parameters. His results indicate that parameter estimates for demand and marginal cost, the primitives of the model, are very similar in all three years if one derives the first-order conditions assuming monopoly pricing in 1954 and 1956, but Bertrand-Nash pricing in 1955. The data thus suggest that a collusive arrangement in the industry broke down for a single year when firms' behavior is well explained by a change to oligopoly pricing with stable preferences and production technologies.

A difficulty is that it is not straightforward to model the mode of competition as varying in a continuous fashion with a parameter to be estimated. An older literature in IO considered conjectural variation games, but Corts (1999) illustrated that in a more general dynamic context a range of competitive situations is consistent with the same value of the conduct parameter. Nevertheless, Genesove and Mullin (1998) show that with a freely varying conduct parameter their model leads to price-cost markups in line with those obtained directly from marginal costs, which are observable in their application to the sugar refining industry. They further show that the marginal costs one can back out of a fully specified structural model are sensitive to the particular behavioral assumption used to derive the firms' first-order conditions. They are, however, not very sensitive to the functional-form assumption of the demand system.

From a purely empirical standpoint, one would gauge the competitiveness of a market by the average prevailing price-cost margin. But unless one is willing to take accounting data at face value, which Genesove and Mullin (1998) argue is valid in some (rare) situations, one already needs to make a behavioral assumption to recover marginal costs, as outlined earlier. Even if demand were estimated separately, different assumptions on the mode of competition will lead to different price-cost markups and different conclusions.

In practice, the literature has by and large adopted the flexible assumption of a Nash equilibrium in prices for strategically behaving multi-product firms. This particular "mode of competition" or "behavioral assumption" can accommodate markets with different levels of competitiveness by varying the distance between goods in product space. More price sensitive consumers, higher cross-price elasticities, and less concentrated ownership of products will all increase the elasticity of a firm's residual demand and in turn will lower equilibrium price-cost markups.

14.3.2. Evaluating Trade Policy Using Counterfactual Simulations

The preceding framework has been used to evaluate the economic impact of trade policies or to study other questions of interest to the trade literature. Any change in a primitive of the model will influence the strength of competition that each firm faces as the observed equilibrium is supported by the intersection of best-response functions of all market participants. To predict the likely effects of a policy change, researchers calculate a counterfactual market equilibrium that again leads to a situation no firm unilaterally wants to deviate from.

To accomplish this, the estimated demand model is supplemented with an explicitly specified behavioral model that generates a system of first-order conditions, one for each firm. The most common assumption is that firms set prices according to a multiproduct Bertrand pricing game. The observed market shares and prices then imply a set of marginal costs for which the data are consistent with profit maximization given the assumed behavior. After changing a primitive (e.g., the tariff wedge incurred by imports from one country), re-solving the system of first-order conditions leads to a new equilibrium price vector for all products, which in turn implies a new set of market shares.

A wide range of trade policies has already been evaluated in this framework. The automobile industry has been the proving ground, as it fits the assumption of an oligopolistic market structure and has rich data that are widely available. The most straightforward application is a unilateral reduction in import tariffs, which lowers the relevant marginal cost that firms take into account when determining the profit-maximizing prices for their goods on an export market. Tovar (2012) studies the welfare effects of such a tariff reduction on the Colombian automobile market. The model predicts large benefits, around $3,000 per car purchaser, arising mostly due to greater variety.

Other studies have looked at the same question in the context of the establishment of a Preferential Trade Area. Brambilla (2005) studies the Customs Union between Argentina and Brazil; Park and Rhee (2014) study two Free Trade Agreements (FTA) from the Korean perspective, one with the United States and one with the European Union; Gao, Van Biesebroeck, and Verboven (2014) study FTAs between Canada and several potential FTA partners, including the European Union, Japan, Korea, and China.

The impact of the voluntary export restraints (VER) that Japanese firms agreed to on their US and EU exports are a variation on this theme. Goldberg (1995) introduces VERs into the importers' first-order conditions through a Lagrange multiplier on aggregate Japanese imports.[3] Berry, Levinsohn, and Pakes (1999) model the VERs as a specific tariff on the targeted imports. In both cases, they amount to an implicit tax on Japanese cars. The average impact on marginal cost can be estimated using a sample period that includes years when this type of protectionism was in place and years when it was not. As the fully specified structural model provides information on consumer welfare, domestic firm profit, and government revenue, it can be used to evaluate whether the imposition of VERs was a welfare-improving US policy or not.

Still focusing on the automobile market, Fershtman and Gandal (1998) study the effect of the Arab boycott on the Israeli market. In this case, the counterfactual, post-boycott equilibrium is not characterized by different marginal costs, but by the removal of Japanese and Korean car models from the market. Goldberg and Verboven (2001) use the same framework to study international price dispersion in the European car market. Exploiting the fully specified structural model, they can simply eliminate one potential explanation for the observed cross-country price differentials and calculate how much prices are predicted to change.

In other differentiated goods industries, Irwin and Pavcnik (2004) evaluate the impact of the 1992 US-EU agreement that limited subsidies in the global market for large passenger airplanes. They show that the observed price change in the market equilibrium, an Airbus-Boeing duopoly, is similar to what would be expected from a 5% increase in marginal cost. Kitano and Ohashi (2009) assess to what extent the strong recovery of Harley-Davidson in the US motorcycle market could be explained by the safeguard provisions applied by the United States. A counterfactual simulation of the likely effect of the US imposition of temporary tariff protection of 45% suggests that this alone cannot explain much of the sales boost, as consumers perceive Japanese motorcycles to be rather poor substitutes.

A few studies use the discrete choice-demand framework to study gains from trade more generally. Friberg and Ganslandt (2006) do this in the context of simultaneous imports and exports of bottled water by Sweden. They use the random utility model implied by their estimated demand system to quantify the value of increased product variety, a first source of welfare gains. The welfare gains from a second source, the pro-competitive impact of imports on domestic prices, is computed in a counterfactual simulation that eliminates all imports from the market. They find that the benefits through these two channels outweigh any plausible resource cost from international trade. Sheu (2014) investigates the same question in the Indian printer market. Following its entry into the World Trade Organziation (WTO) and the gradual elimination of an import tariff of 20%, the country experienced a large increase in imports. The relative importance of three possible factors that could boost welfare—lower price, higher quality, and greater variety—are assessed without a counterfactual analysis. She finds that higher quality of imports was the most important channel for welfare gains from trade.[4]

Khandelwal (2010) also does not perform a counterfactual simulation, but uses the residuals from the estimated demand system as proxies for product quality, in line with the structural interpretation of Berry (1994). The novelty is that he uses only widely available product-level trade information and the Armington assumption—which implies products are (only) horizontally differentiated by their country of origin—to estimate the demand system. He considers imports from each country as a different product variety, defining products as the interactions of all categories in the 10-digit harmonized system (HS) classification with countries. He then estimates demand for a large number of "markets," pooling all "products" in a 4-digit HS category. The results highlight that these product markets vary substantially in their scope for quality differentiation.

Gao, Van Biesebroeck, and Verboven (2014) use similarly estimated demand systems for several product markets to evaluate the impact of an FTA between Canada and potential partners. Rather than perform counterfactual simulations in each market, they calculate the marginal effect of tariff reductions on consumer surplus, domestic profits, and government revenue. They use the estimated demand systems, but perform a partial equilibrium analysis, calculating only first-round effects from the initial price reductions of affected imports. For the automobile industry, the most important category of differentiated goods by import volume, they compare the predicted welfare effects using both approaches. With only a few exceptions, the sources of welfare gains from different FTAs are estimated to be remarkably similar to the full-fledged counterfactual simulation using detailed product information and the partial equilibrium calculation using trade data.

14.3.3. Possible Extensions

14.3.3.1. *Reallocation*

In the trade literature there has been a lot of theoretical work, starting with Melitz (2003), showing that the reallocation of market share from less to more productive firms boosts aggregate welfare. In the setup of Arkolakis, Costinot, and Rodriguez-Clare (2012), this type of market share reallocation and the utility gains from increased product variety are the primary channels through which trade raises aggregate welfare.

Existing empirical exercises (see, e.g., Pavcnik 2002 and Eslava, Haltiwanger, Kugler, and Kugler 2004) have evaluated the impact of trade policy on aggregate productivity through a reallocation of market share toward more productive firms. A thorny issue is that measures of productivity confound *productive efficiency* and *market power*. This is an inherent problem since researchers rely on (deflated) sales to proxy for output, which except in the case of price-taking firms or homogenous products leaves price variation unaccounted for and therefore captured by the productivity residual. Collard-Wexler and De Loecker (2015) illustrates that the results from such a reallocation analysis are extremely sensitive to whether one controls for price variation, in both output and input prices, or not. Even though the underlying mechanism—the alignment of productivity to market shares—is characterized incorrectly, it is important to note that the lack of producer-level price data does not invalidate the aggregate (say industry-wide) productivity effects.

If one were to calculate a counterfactual equilibrium along the lines described in the previous section, it would be straightforward to isolate the effects of reallocation on the strength of competition in a market. Such a calculation generates a full vector of new prices and market shares for all active firms. The effect of reallocation on the sector's average price-cost margin, a weighted average of the product-level margins, can be readily computed in this framework. Moreover, one can decompose the aggregate change into a change in product-level markups and a change due to shifting weights in the aggregation. Even if the marginal cost of each product remains unchanged after a trade policy change, the average marginal cost among active firms or products is likely to change due to differences in product weights.[5]

It is not hard to predict what the expected effect of a tariff reduction should be. Highly productive foreign producers have low intrinsic marginal costs, but import tariffs inflate the relevant, landed marginal cost on their export markets. This form of protectionism depresses their market share and diminishes the strength of competition for domestic firms that can charge higher prices. Heterogeneous firm models of trade predict that the most productive foreign firms will enter export markets first. Lowering tariffs will thus reallocate market share away from less productive (domestic) firms to more productive imports. The magnitude of this effect can easily be investigated using a counterfactual simulation of a new market equilibrium under the assumption of a reduced import tariff.

14.3.3.2. *Productivity Effects*

The preceding framework can provide a direct estimate of the effect of any trade policy change on the price-cost margin. If marginal costs are assumed to be constant over time or to vary only idiosyncratically, only market-power effects are possible. The average cost in a sector can change due to weighting, but firm-level or product-level changes do not contribute to aggregate welfare.

Another strand of the trade literature has found important productivity effects of domestic trade liberalization. Amiti and Konings (2007) show that lower input tariffs raise firm-level TFP in Indonesia. De Loecker, Goldberg, Khandelwal, and Pavcnik (2016) show that in India a similar effect on TFP should not be interpreted as higher efficiency, but rather as incomplete pass-through of input price reductions. Brandt, Van Biesebroeck, Wang, and Zhang (2017) show for China that even controlling for input tariffs and price changes, lower output tariffs did lead to higher productivity. They argue that state-owned firms in particular were forced to increase efficiency to avoid bankruptcy in the face of stronger import competition.

In the methodological framework outlined in this section, a particular behavioral assumption has to be used in a counterfactual simulation, but one can already impose it at the estimation stage. Jointly estimating the demand and supply sides would increase estimation efficiency and guarantee that the demand estimates are consistent with profit maximization (i.e., generate an own price absolute elasticity of at least one). In addition, it allows one to recover how marginal costs vary with observable variables. For example, Berry, Levinsohn, and Pakes (1995) and Bresnahan (1987) include input factor prices in the functional form specification of marginal costs.

When price effects of a potential merger are calculated in a merger analysis that precedes the actual merger, one can include a direct effect of the merger on marginal costs. Such an exercise can reveal, for example, the amount of efficiency gain needed to avoid price increases following a merger. One could similarly include import tariffs directly in the marginal cost specification to incorporate potential productivity gains from trade liberalization in the model. Such a specification can provide some sensitivity analysis on the predicted effects of trade liberalization if one has outside information on likely efficiency effects.

The studies reviewed in section 14.3.2 calculate the counterfactual equilibrium assuming that marginal production costs stayed constant. As a result, any productivity effects have to be due to changes in output prices. When the industry is observed both before and after the policy change, it would be straightforward to back out marginal costs for each product-year observation from the first-order conditions using unchanged behavior but incorporating the primitive that changed. In a second step, one could then verify whether there is a systematic relationship between these costs and the policy change. This approach would be similar in spirit to studies that regress productivity on policy changes, but have the advantage of controlling for changed price-cost margins.

If such effects on marginal costs are present, one could even incorporate them in the model. For example, when evaluating the impact of VERs, Goldberg (1995) and Berry, Levinsohn, and Pakes (1999) recover a parameter that captures the implicit tax on Japanese vehicles that such a trade policy implies. Importantly, this parameter is identified assuming unchanged production costs. If policy changes influence efficiency, as for example the learning-by-exporting literature suggests, one should allow for such effects in the model when performing a counterfactual exercise.[6]

A few studies have already followed this approach. Aw, Roberts, and Xu (2011) allow for a direct efficiency-enhancing effect of export activity on a firm's marginal cost, through its impact on productivity, in line with the learning-by-exporting hypothesis. They do this in a dynamic model where forward-looking firms make both innovation and exporting decisions, but one could also incorporate this in a static model where exporting decisions are exogenous. Hashmi and Van Biesebroeck (2016) investigate the two-way impact of competition on innovation. They allow for higher product quality to boost demand, but the same variable also enters their specification for the marginal production cost.

14.4. ESTIMATING COMPETITION FROM PRODUCT ENTRY

In this section we focus more specifically on the extensive margin, the entry of either firms or products. Opening up to international competition is expected not only to impact firm's intensive margins of operation (like sales, efficiency, etc.), but will also affect the incentives to enter or exit the market, or introduce or drop products. Given that such investments will also impact a firm's organization, product portfolio, and most likely even its cost of production, their effects will thus again show up in standard measures of revenue-based productivity (TFPR). We discuss a common approach in IO that relies on equilibrium entry patterns, and we draw the analogy to theoretical models in international trade that evaluate the effect of trade liberalization on welfare, typically measured by aggregate (revenue) productivity. In the extensions, we discuss studies that imply an effect of trade-driven market expansion on measured productivity through its impact on innovation incentives, product introductions, and product prices.

14.4.1. The Standard Framework: Geographically Isolated Markets

One shortcoming of the demand-side approach is the absence of endogenous entry and exit of products or firms. A trade policy that forces some products from the market can still be evaluated (see, e.g., Fershtman and Gandal 1998), but one has to specify exogenously which products exit. How firms decide to enter or exit a market is not modeled in the static framework, but this is likely to be an important feature of many trade policies, in particular of trade liberalization. Alternatively, product characteristics may respond to trade liberalization as well, which further complicates such an approach.

A separate strand of the IO literature estimates the strength of competition in an industry solely by exploiting equilibrium patterns of product entry. It avoids explicit functional form assumptions on demand, only specifying that we observe a market-scale factor that is proportional to aggregate demand. The seminal application of Bresnahan and Reiss (1991) specifies the demand for a homogenous good by a representative consumer as $d(Z, P_N)$ and multiplies this with the number of consumers $S(Y)$ to obtain the aggregate market demand Q. The vectors Z and Y denote demographic variables affecting market demand. The price P_N is indexed by the number of active firms N as firms are expected to set prices taking into account the number of competitors they face.[7]

With these minimal assumptions, one can learn about the strength of competition in a particular industry simply by comparing the number of active competitors in geographically isolated local markets of different size. In equilibrium, firms will enter as long as they make positive profits. If competition depresses prices, and thus price-cost margins, there will exist a market size threshold S_N that is minimally needed for the Nth entrant to just break even. The following zero profit condition pins down the market size threshold S_N at which the Nth entrant just breaks even:

$$\pi_N = \left[P_N - c\left(\frac{Q}{N}, W\right) \right] d_N \frac{S_N}{N} - F_N = 0. \tag{14.1}$$

By observing many localized markets that vary in size and number of entrants, a series of thresholds $\{S_1, S_2, \ldots, S_{N_{max}}\}$ can be estimated.

In general, both the average variable cost $c(.)$, which is allowed to vary with local factor prices W, as well as fixed entry cost F_N, could vary across entrants or with the scale of production. To distinguish such variation from the dependency of the price on the number of competitors, one needs to observe prices or quantities or make behavioral assumptions (e.g., assuming the most efficient firms enter first).

In the absence of firm heterogeneity in technology or costs, the model assumes a constant and uniform marginal cost per unit, and the impact of competition can be uncovered directly from the pattern of market size thresholds $s_N = S_N / N$. This series of thresholds, one for each N, indicate how many consumers per firm are needed in a market in order for all N active firms to avoid losses. The ratio of successive thresholds provides a one-to-one mapping of the ratios of variable profits per consumer:

$$\frac{s_{N+1}}{s_N} = \frac{(P_N - c)d_N}{(P_{N+1} - c)d_{N+1}}. \tag{14.2}$$

If the number of active firms N rises less than proportionately with the market size S, it indicates that the price-cost margin falls if additional firms compete in a market. More customers are needed per firm in order for the marginal entrant still to be able to recover its fixed costs. Such a situation will be characterized by $s_{N+1} / s_N > 1$. As prices gradually converge to marginal costs with increased competition, as happens for example in the Cournot case, the ratio of thresholds converges to one. The relationship between N and S becomes a proportional relationship as price-cost margins do not fall anymore with N.

The strength of competition is thus an industry feature that can be identified by observing the same industry in a series of separate markets, for example in geographically isolated local markets. One measure of market competitiveness would be the number of firms needed for the s_{N+1} / s_N ratio to become insignificantly different from unity. For a given number of firms, the slope of the N-S relationship is a direct measure of the strength (or the lack) of competition. Once the relationship is proportional and the threshold ratio has converged to unity, market power has been exhausted.

An important caveat is that the preceding relationship is identified from variation in the number of active firms across markets of different size, which is interpreted as variation in the price-cost margins. The framework does not allow one to distinguish between perfect competition and perfect collusion, as the level of profitability is not identified. In either case, the markup would not vary with the number of active firms in the market. Moreover, a monopolistically competitive market with horizontal product differentiation would only look different from perfect competition if the residual demand that each firm faces has a variable elasticity. The case of a constant elasticity of substitution (CES) demand at the firm level would be indistinguishable from perfect competition, irrespective of whether the elasticity of substitution is 1 or 10. While the price-cost margin would be lower for higher elasticities, the crucial feature is that in both cases it would not respond to the number of active firms.

While evaluating the competitiveness of a market is straightforward once the size thresholds are obtained, estimating the shape of the variable profit function is not so straightforward. Econometric estimation is complicated if one allows firms' entry decisions to depend on the unobservables in the variable profit equation. This seems a plausible empirical feature, but given that each firm's equilibrium strategy in a dynamic entry game depends on the actions of other firms, correlation between unobservables gives rises to an endogeneity problem. Bresnahan and Reiss (1990) discuss identification strategies.

Syverson (2004) exploits a similar idea, but instead of varying the total market size, he compares markets that differ in the density of consumers. He studies the market for ready-mix concrete, where competition is highly localized (spatially) as firms face a physical limit on how far they can ship their final product. As a result, denser markets can support more firms, even conditional on total market size. Comparing regions with different densities implies a similar type of exogenous variation in the number of competitors as comparing geographically isolated markets of different size. Moreover, higher density makes it easier for consumers to switch between producers. It raises product substitutability and further lowers equilibrium price-cost margins.

To evaluate the extent of competition in an industry, Syverson (2004) does not compare the number of active firms to some absolute measure of market density. Instead, he assumes that firms differ in productivity such that the zero-profit condition implies a minimum productivity level a firm needs to attain to be able to operate profitably. In denser markets, more firms will enter and their products will be better substitutes. They will compete more fiercely, lowering price-cost margins and raising the productivity threshold needed for survival. On average, the selection of surviving firms is more stringent in denser markets, and the minimum as well as the average productivity levels will be higher.

14.4.2. Effect of Trade Policy on the Number of Competitors

This type of comparative statics is similar to the way theoretical models of international trade evaluate the impact of trade on an economy. The market equilibrium is first solved in an autarky situation. The effect of trade is then investigated by comparing it to a situation where the home and foreign markets are merged in a free trade equilibrium with a larger global market. A similar comparison can be achieved by decreasing trade barriers from infinity to zero, which even allows for a comparison with intermediate situations, as trade barriers can be varied continuously.

In the homogenous firms literature, following Krugman (1979), an increase in the relevant market size following trade integration is shown to raise output per firm. Due to scale economies in production—constant marginal costs with a fixed cost—the average cost per unit falls. As firms produce on the elastic portion of demand, it induces them to lower prices, which raises the real wage and thus welfare. For general demand curves, at the higher output the price elasticity tends to be lower and markups higher. This is a consequence of the higher output and will only offset the output and welfare gains partially, not overturn them.

Much of the subsequent literature, especially once firm heterogeneity was introduced, has assumed monopolistic competition, constant marginal costs, and CES preferences, see Arkolakis, Costinot, and Rodriguez-Clare (2012). This severely limits possible adjustment channels following trade opening. In particular, price-cost margins do not adjust when the number of firms increases, nor does firm-level productivity. Melitz (2003) stresses a different, general equilibrium effect of increased aggregate sales in the open economy case. As firms expand output by exporting, they bid up the wage rate, forcing less productive firms to exit. Even though firm-specific productivity is constant, greater selectivity raises the average productivity of surviving firms and redistributes labor input toward more productive uses (as in Syverson 2004). Such a market outcome could also be characterized as more competitive, even in the absence of any effect on price-cost margins, as sales are increasingly concentrated in more efficient firms.

Melitz and Ottaviano (2008) use a similar setup, but with quadratic preferences for consumer demand, which generates price-cost markups that decline when the market enlarges and more firms compete. As a result, trade liberalization now has an additional pro-competitive effect on the prices of surviving firms. At the same time, however, the elimination of low-productivity firms from the market reallocates market share toward highly productive survivors. These firms produce further down on their demand curve and will optimally set a higher price-cost margin. Market selection thus raises the average markup over all active firms and this is a drag on aggregate welfare gains, as highlighted by Arkolakis et al. (2018).

Eckel and Neary (2010) further generalize this setup by introducing multi-product firms. Consumers again have quadratic preferences over all product varieties, but firms now endogenously decide their product scope. Their marginal costs are lowest for their "core" product and rise if they adapt varieties to better serve consumers with horizontally differentiated tastes. Globalization, which is modeled directly as an increase in market size, raises total output but has opposite effects on high- and low-cost varieties. The increased competition that accompanies the larger market size leads to a contraction in the production of high-cost varieties, some of which will even be discontinued. For low-cost varieties the market expansion effect dominates and their production expands. This raises firm-level productivity, as firms focus on their core competences, but also raises the average price-cost margin as low-cost, high-margin varieties are more likely to survive. The impact of the increase in market size on the total number of active firms is ambiguous and depends on the substitutability of products.

Other studies have used different assumptions on market demand and production technology to study the behavior of multi-product firms. However, they mostly compare only theoretical predictions for the autarky and free trade equilibria. The few studies that provide empirical evidence illustrate equilibrium patterns of exporting and product churn, but do not compare directly the number of active firms in markets of different size.

14.4.3. Extensions

14.4.3.1. *Market Expansion*

The trade context seems well suited to apply the Bresnahan and Reiss (1991) framework for identifying the strength of competition, but to our knowledge this has never been done (yet). From each country's perspective, a lowering of the trade barriers its firms face overseas is akin to a market expansion. Lileeva and Trefler (2010) have shown that a decline in US import tariffs increased the productivity of Canadian firms, especially for intermediately productive firms for which the incentive to make productivity-enhancing investments—in order to boost productivity enough and make it as an exporter—is likely to have increased the most following the change in US trade policy. One could similarly study whether such a change increased the number of viable Canadian firms and in turn the competitiveness in the market.

However, in the context of differentiated goods markets, which is the dominant framework in international trade, it is imperative to take into account that product entry can expand the relevant market size. Schaumans and Verboven (2015) demonstrate that the minimum market size needed for an additional firm to be viable can decrease with the number of firms if market expansion, due to product variety, dominates the decrease in price-cost margins due to increased competition. This is a likely outcome in the CES demand case, which is a popular assumption in the theoretical trade literature. Profit margins do not respond at all to entry, while the love-of-variety built into the utility function leads to higher per capita sales when product variety increases. As a result, the market increment needed to recover fixed costs falls with the aggregate market size. Discrete choice demand specifications have a similar property as new products take away some market share from the outside good and directly expand the market.[8]

Ignoring this channel leads to an underestimate of the impact of the number of firms on the strength of competition. It also leads some theoretical trade models to predict that the overall number of active firms, the sum of home and foreign firms, increases as we move from autarky to free trade, even though the global market size is unchanged and firms compete more directly. In other cases this is merely a possibility if the effect of competition on price does not outweigh the beneficial effects from product variety (see, e.g., Eckel and Neary 2010).

Schaumans and Verboven (2015) illustrate how to correct for this effect when constructing the ratio of successive market thresholds. Their approach requires information on the total revenue per customer in each market. This allows for market expansion, even holding the number of customers in a market (i.e., the potential market size) fixed.

Together with the number of active firms, it can be used to estimate an equation for the average revenue per firm as a function of the market size. On export markets, this type of information is directly observable, but it might not be readily available on a firm's domestic market.

14.4.3.2. *Integrating Supply and Demand*

Abstracting from the need to correct for market expansion, the Melitz and Ottaviano (2008) study bridges the approaches in Berry, Levinsohn, and Pakes (1995) and Bresnahan and Reiss (1991). It features a demand function with varying elasticity, and trade policy directly affects markups. However, competition is monopolistically competitive, which precludes strategic responses. Moreover, as in most of the trade literature, products are only differentiated horizontally and symmetrically. An exogenous productivity draw for each firm fixes its profitability without any real scope for firm decisions. Greater competition following trade liberalization will force some products from the market, but a zero profit condition for marginal firms is all that is needed to pin down market participants.

This is a natural assumption in the Bresnahan and Reiss (1991) or Schaumans and Verboven (2015) framework, but a more flexible demand system would allow for richer forms of differentiation. A few studies connect the two literatures even more closely. They use a more flexible demand system and supplement the model with supply responses. For example, Thomas (2011) conducts a counterfactual analysis to evaluate the loss in variable profits if some laundry detergent variants would be eliminated from the market. Her results suggest that fixed costs of keeping a product in the market have to be extremely small to rationalize firm behavior. Goettler and Gordon (2011) and Eizenberg (2014) study new product introductions in the semi-conductor and computer industries and the competitive interactions this entails. However, as product introduction is a dynamic decision, the estimation becomes exceedingly complicated.

Dynamic considerations of product entry will also influence pricing in models with market power. Even the mere threat of new product entry can already change current behavior. In a context of international trade, Holmes and Schmitz (2001) and Salvo (2010) provide evidence that firms with market power sometimes practice limit pricing to keep out potential foreign competitors.

Similar dynamic considerations apply to the impact of trade policy. It can, for example, generate a different response to temporary versus permanent forms of trade protection. A large literature has shown that firms benefiting from import tariffs tend to have lower productivity, presumably because they face lower incentives to make productivity-enhancing investments (see Brandt et al. 2017 for an overview). However, Konings and Vandenbussche (2008) find the opposite for firms that benefit from temporary trade safeguard protections. They argue that firms will behave differently if they know the import protection will end in the near future. Firms can use temporarily elevated sales and variable profits to take actions that boost productivity and prepare for the expected future competition.

14.5. ESTIMATING COMPETITION FROM THE PRODUCTION SIDE

In this section we discuss the so-called production approach to investigate the impact of trade liberalization on firm performance. While this approach delivers an estimate of markups and thus, via price data, an estimate of marginal costs, the standard variable of interest, productivity, is immediately subsumed in this measure. In the absence of variation in input prices and scale effects, variation in marginal costs equals variation in technical efficiency. We highlight that two separate literatures—the trade liberalization-productivity literature on the one hand, and the international pass-through literature on the other hand—are highly interconnected. It is imperative to study both efficiency and price effects jointly in any analysis of productivity in a context where firms might have some market power.

14.5.1. Identifying Market Power at the Firm Level

Let's now turn back to our original question. We want to know whether greater (international) competition affects firm performance. In terms of performance, we consider both productive efficiency and profitability, as measured by markups.

Increased global competition, say through trade liberalization, has the potential to affect any producer. However, the extent to which a firm is affected by an exogenous change to its operating environment depends on a few factors. The first is whether the change in the operating environment is a cost or demand shock, or both. Second, the degree of substitutability across products of the affected industry will play an important role. A reduction of import tariffs on Japanese cars in the United States will affect other car producers differentially, depending on the substitution patterns across brands and models.

While we might expect a policy change to have a competitive effect on the industry, the effect is likely to vary considerably across producers. The production approach to estimating markups and marginal cost is a natural way to allow for such continuous and heterogeneous effects of competition on firm performance.

In the Bresnahan and Reiss (1991) framework, we inferred from a less than proportional increase in the number of firms with market size that the price-cost margins must have declined with the number of active firms, giving each firm a harder time to recover fixed costs. If price-cost margins were observable, we could investigate this directly by regressing them on variables that influence the relevant market size, for example trade barriers.

In the structure-conduct-performance paradigm in the IO literature, it was customary to take markup information directly from company accounts. Nickell (1996) is a recent example, treating the Lerner index as directly observable, and the work by

Tybout and Westbrook (1995) is a comparable example from the trade literature. The study by Genesove and Mullin (1998) uses such information to evaluate the demand-side approach to recover price-cost margins.

As an alternative, De Loecker and Warzynski (2012) propose a methodology to recover the firm-specific price-cost margin ($\mu \equiv P/MC$), as the ratio of the physical output elasticity a firm faces when changing a variable input, say material inputs and intermediates (M), and the corresponding revenue share of that input, that is,

$$\mu \equiv \frac{P}{MC} = \frac{\theta^M}{s_M},$$ (14.3)

with $\theta^M \equiv \dfrac{\partial \ln Q}{\partial \ln M}$ and $s_M = \dfrac{WM}{PQ}$.[9] W is the price of input M. If output prices are directly observed, this approach generates estimates of marginal costs as well.

The intuition is as follows. Holding other inputs constant, a competitive firm will expand its use of input M until the revenue share of M equals the output elasticity, which is naturally declining in M. If a firm does not increase M all the way until equality holds, but prefers to produce a lower quantity and raise the output price instead, it indicates that the firm is able to exercise market power and charge a price above marginal cost.

Importantly, deviations from perfect competition complicate the identification and estimation of the production technology in the absence of firm-specific output price information. Using deflated revenue rather than actual output level as a dependent variable in the production function inflates the output elasticities. Klette and Griliches (1996) and De Loecker (2011) show how a demand assumption can be used to recover the underlying production function parameters.

Recent work has used data on prices to estimate physical production functions (see Foster, Haltiwanger, and Syverson 2008). De Loecker et al. (2016) further show that an analog problem arises on the input side. If firms produce differentiated products, they are likely to rely on differentiated inputs as well, and therefore input prices will also vary across producers. They propose a methodology to estimate (multi-product) physical production function where input price variation, conditional on geography and exogenous factors, stems from quality variation across products and producers.

The production approach has its own limitations, of course. The main one is the need to flexibly identify the shape of technology. In the Cobb-Douglas case, all variation in input shares is interpreted as market power, which would be unreasonable. On the positive side, there has been a tremendous amount of work on the estimation of production functions in a wide range of industries and countries. The output elasticity estimates can be subjected to a wide range of robustness checks varying the model specification and estimation procedure. Results from the demand-side approach can in principle be subjected to a similar robustness analysis by varying the mode of competition and the functional form of demand, but there is a tendency in the empirical IO literature to stick with the standard assumption of static Nash in prices and a linear random utility specification.

In recent work, De Loecker and Scott (2016) compare markups obtained from the production and demand approach for the US beer industry. Both approaches yield very similar average markups for different brewers. This suggests that one can rely on either the demand or production approach, depending on the data availability and the particular research question.

14.5.2. Effect of Trade on Productivity and Market Power

Some studies have investigated the impact of trade liberalization—tariff reductions— on domestic market power. Examples of such analysis are De Loecker et al. (2016) for India, Brandt et al. (2017) for China, and De Loecker, Fuss, and Van Biesebroeck (2014) for Belgium. In the latter application, not only were tariff changes exploited as exogenous changes in the extent of foreign competition, but also the proximity to the border interacted with relative wage evolutions between Belgium and its neighbors.

Some studies have looked at the price-cost margins of exporters in both the cross section and in the time series (see, e.g., De Loecker and Warzynski 2012; Garcia Marin and Voigtländer 2013). From a reduced form regression to describe the equilibrium relationship between markups and a firm's export status, they conclude that exporters tend to have higher markups and that markups increase following export market entry. The challenge in this literature is to identify the mechanism and the causality behind this correlation. Export entry is clearly not an exogenous event, and additional structure is needed for causal inference, such as an export selection equation in Van Biesebroeck (2005) or a matching algorithm in De Loecker (2007).

To get at the causal effect of international competition on firm performance, De Loecker et al. (2016) study the impact of the extensive and unexpected trade reforms in India on markups, marginal cost, and prices. They do not use productivity itself as a dependent variable, but note that marginal cost will combine the effect of production efficiency and input prices. They run separate regressions for all three dependent variables and follow Amiti and Konings (2007), allowing for separate effects from tariffs on final products (output tariffs, τ^O) and tariffs on inputs (input tariffs, τ^I). Brandt et al. (2017) perform a similar analysis investigating the impact of Chinese tariff reductions around the time of WTO entry. Due to data limitations, they use markups and productivity at the firm rather than the product level and prices at the sector level.

The price regression does not contain any estimated variables, and both studies find that output prices decline with tariffs. At the same time, De Loecker et al. (2016) find a very strong relationship between input tariffs and marginal costs. Naturally, as input prices fall, this has a direct downward impact on firms' marginal cost of production.

The same input tariff decline also impacts markups. All things equal, it is found to raise markups in India, indicating that cost savings are not fully passed on to consumers in the form of lower final product prices. In the case of China, this effect is only present for younger firms, not for (mostly state-owned) incumbents. The approach taken in these studies underscores the benefits of not committing to a particular demand system and a mode of competition. One can relate markups to the exogenous change in trade protection in a flexible way, and verify whether this affected the competitive pressure faced by domestic producers.[10]

14.5.3. Extensions Based on the Pass-Through Literature

14.5.3.1. *Generalizing the Markup Formula*

The identification of the firm's price-cost margin in equation (14.3) is related to the way the pass-through literature exploits imperfect price adjustments to infer market power and the (residual) demand elasticity. In some situations, researchers have access to marginal cost information or to a large component of it. For example, the wholesale price of gasoline is a good proxy for a gasoline station's marginal cost. Observing that a firm does not adjust the retail price in line with the wholesale price is an indication of potential market power.

We now make the relationship between these two approaches more explicit. In particular, we illustrate that the market-power formula used in the production approach can be derived from the standard practice in the pass-through literature. In the process we derive a formula to estimate markups that generalizes De Loecker and Warzynski (2012).

Under constant returns to scale, Verboven (2012) characterizes the pass-through rate as

$$\rho = \frac{dP}{dMC} = \frac{\epsilon_W}{s_M}. \tag{14.4}$$

It is the ratio of the input price elasticity $\epsilon_W = \dfrac{\partial \ln P}{\partial \ln W}$ to the share of total expenditure on input M in total revenue $\dfrac{WM}{PQ}$. Under variable return to scale, the expression generalizes to

$$\rho = \frac{\epsilon_W}{s_M} \frac{1}{\epsilon_M} \tag{14.5}$$

with ϵ_M the input demand with respect to output, that is, the percentage increase in the input demand for each percentage increase in output $\dfrac{\partial \ln M^*}{\partial \ln Q}$.

We can rewrite expression (14.5) as

$$\frac{\rho}{\epsilon_W} = \frac{\dfrac{dP}{dMC}}{\dfrac{\partial \ln P}{\partial \ln W}} = \frac{\dfrac{\partial \ln Q}{\partial \ln M}}{s_M},$$

which reveals the same right-hand side as in equation (14.3).[11] Finally, using the pass-through coefficient ρ we can write the markup as follows:[12]

$$\mu = \frac{\dfrac{\partial \ln Q}{\partial \ln M} \dfrac{\partial \ln MC}{\partial \ln W}}{s_M}. \tag{14.6}$$

The additional term in the numerator reflects that the elasticity of the marginal costs with respect to the input price can differ from unity. It generalizes equation (14.3) to situations where the input price varies with input use, for example due to the market power a firm has on its input markets, or due to nonlinear input prices such as bulk discounting.[13]

14.5.3.2. *Interpreting Two-Step Productivity Regressions*

The pass-through literature has developed independently from the production-side approach to measuring market power. While the two literatures tend to ask different questions and rely on different data sources, they are both influenced by the same underlying mechanism for how variation in the cost of production (including variation in efficiency) shows up in variation in output prices. As production functions are usually estimated using deflated sales and deflated input expenditures, a regression that uses TFP as a dependent variable will only in special cases recover the impact on firm-level efficiency.

To illustrate this, we start from the production function in (14.7), where q denotes output and x denotes the vector of inputs, $x = \{l, m, k\}$ labor, intermediate inputs, and capital, respectively, and productivity (ω), and β is the vector of output elasticities. We rewrite the production function as

$$q_{it} = \sum_x \beta_x x_{it} + \omega_{it} \tag{14.7}$$

to reflect the practice of using deflated variables in empirical work. The price variable p_{it} is defined as the difference between the firm-level price and the average price for the industry at time t. In revenue terms, the production function becomes

$$\underbrace{q_{it} + p_{it}}_{\tilde{q}_{it}} = \sum_x \beta_x \underbrace{(x_{it} + \omega_{it}^x)}_{\tilde{x}_{it}} + \underbrace{\omega_{it} + p_{it} - \sum_x \beta_x \omega_{it}^x}_{TFP_{it}} \tag{14.8}$$

where ω^x denotes the similarly deflated input price of input x. Lowercase variables indicate logarithms, except for TFP, which represents productivity in logarithms, as usual. For simplicity, we limit ourselves to the constant returns to scale case, that is, $\sum_x \beta_x = 1$.

As an example, consider a regression that attempts to identify the impact of trade liberalization (measured through lower tariffs τ), on productivity. Using Δ to denote the year-on-year change for

$$\Delta p = \gamma_0 + \gamma_1 \Delta \omega^x + \epsilon^p \tag{14.9}$$

$$\Delta TFP = \alpha_0 + \alpha_1 \Delta \tau + \epsilon^\omega. \tag{14.10}$$

To focus on the particular mechanism of interest, consider a local industry using imported inputs. An example would be a local construction industry that relies on imported steel. Let the industry only be subject to an input tariff reduction, which directly translates into an equal change in the input price of materials, such that $\Delta \tau = \Delta w^M$. Our interest is in the interpretation of the coefficient on the input tariff in the productivity regression:

$$\alpha_1 = \frac{\partial E(TFP)}{\partial \tau}. \tag{14.11}$$

In the trade literature, this parameter is supposed to measure the productivity effects of a tariff reduction.[14] However, under the preceding assumptions, the estimate $\widehat{\alpha}_1$ equals

$$\widehat{\alpha}_1 = \frac{\partial E(\Delta \omega)}{\partial \Delta \tau} + \frac{\partial E(\Delta p)}{\partial \Delta w^M} - \beta_M. \tag{14.12}$$

We can write the difference between the estimate and the true efficiency effect in terms of the pass-through parameter $\tilde{\rho}$, introduced earlier,[15] as follows:

$$\widehat{\alpha}_1 - \frac{\partial E(\Delta \omega)}{\partial \Delta \tau} = \tilde{\rho} \times s_M - \beta_M.$$

The extent to which we get a biased estimate of the efficiency response varies by the extent of market power a firm has. Under perfect competition, $\tilde{\rho} = 1$ and $s_M = \beta_M$ such that the right-hand side is zero and $\widehat{\alpha}_1$ correctly identifies the efficiency effect. Under monopolistic competition and CES demand, it holds that $\tilde{\rho} = 1$ and $\beta_M = s_M \bar{\mu}$, with $\bar{\mu}$ the constant markup. As a result, the bias equals $s_M(1 - \bar{\mu}) < 0$ and $\widehat{\alpha}_1$ underestimates the true efficiency effect. In an oligopolistic industry with downward-sloping demand, $\tilde{\rho} \neq 1$ and $\beta_M = s_M \bar{\mu}$, such that there will be a bias but it cannot be signed in general.

Using the same equation (14.10) in a different situation where inputs are sourced locally, but $\Delta \tau$ represents a reduction in the output tariff, the estimated response in the productivity regression amounts to

$$\widehat{\alpha}_1 = \frac{\partial E(\Delta \omega)}{\partial \Delta \tau^o} + \frac{\partial E(\Delta p)}{\partial \Delta \tau^o}. \tag{14.14}$$

The second term is now a competition effect. As output tariffs fall, all things equal, domestic firms face a lower residual demand. They might adjust to this different situation by taking actions to raise their efficiency level, which will be captured by the first term, but this is likely to take some time. If firms have any market power they will also adjust their prices. Effects from equation (14.9) will thus spill over on the estimates in equation (14.10). The extent of price adjustment will depend on the nature of competition and on the substitutability between foreign and domestic products, as analyzed in the demand-side literature.

While these effects are illustrated under a variety of simplifying assumptions, the result is general. The estimated effect of increased globalization on productivity will in general be a combination of an actual efficiency response,[16] imperfect pass-through of cost changes in prices, and an impact of competition on output prices.

The setting we used to discuss the different effects is not the dominant one in the trade literature. Traditionally, the impact of trade liberalization on TFP is mainly viewed as efficiency-enhancing, for example leading to a reduction in X-inefficiency. Implicitly, the first terms in equations (14.12) and (14.14) are considered the most important. If all markets were perfectly competitive, this would be warranted, but absent that assumption there is little direct evidence for a strong efficiency impact.

14.6. Concluding Remarks

In this chapter we highlighted that standard measures of productivity capture not only physical efficiency, but also market power, and variation in output and input prices. As this conflation of effects is largely driven by data constraints that are not likely to be resolved any time soon, we need to study issues like the impact of trade liberalization in a coherent framework that allows for both efficiency and price (be it output or input) responses to increased competition.

This chapter has presented a somewhat different view on what has been a long and heavily researched topic in applied economics. Rather than reviewing the many studies that regress revenue-based measures of TFP on trade policy or trade intensity variables, we discussed how common empirical approaches in the IO literature (on demand estimation and entry) and theoretical models in international trade can inform empirical researchers on trade-induced firm-level changes that are likely to end up in measured productivity. We also discussed a recently developed framework to estimate markups (and its components, marginal cost and productivity) from micro production data, and how in particular it can be used to study the impact of increased competition on firm performance, and thus productivity.

Future research can, and we feel should, further explore the relationship among the various measures of firm performance in one integrated and internally consistent framework. The access to micro data covering a panel of producers across a variety of industries and countries, paired with recent advances in the estimation of production functions and market power, can help accomplish this.

More specifically, a first important avenue for future work would be to study the role of imported intermediate inputs or the location of economic activity (i.e., firm entry) as alternative ways in which international competition affects the domestic economy. Some work is already proceeding in this area, but the interaction between efficiency and market power tends to be ignored. This is problematic, as firms can use higher-quality (imported) inputs or favorable locations to differentiate themselves and increase or gain market power.

Endogenous productivity responses to trade liberalization in the context of imperfectly competitive product and input markets is another topic that is currently underresearched. Several studies measure the size of the effect on productivity, but identifying the firm responses that accomplish the measured change is equally important. Here again, the distinction between changes in prices and efficiency as alternative ways to improve price-cost margins is highly relevant.

In the previous section we highlighted the potential biases or difficulty in interpreting point estimates when one regresses revenue-based measures of productivity on policy variables, such as tariffs. The first two methods, starting from the demand side or the extensive margin, aim to recover marginal costs directly. Relating these cost estimates to policy variables avoids conflating efficiency effects of international competition with price effects. Katayama, Lu, and Tybout (2009) highlights that these cost estimates are quite different from productivity, but it would be useful as well to know how they have responded to exogenous changes in competition, such as following trade liberalizations.

A final research avenue we believe to be promising is to study the distinction between local and global competition. Researchers have often used tariff changes or measures of foreign direct investment (FDI) as exogenous and directly observable indications of a change in the strength of competition that firms face. It leaves open the question of whether domestic or international competition has similar effects. Perhaps competition is highly localized, and increasing the geographical distance from other firms gradually reduces competitive pressure. However, it is also possible that competition is disrupted by administrative barriers, such as national borders or free trade zones, and competitive effects change discretely at that point. Whether the effect of distance grows continuously or discretely, it is even unclear whether it is the distance from consumers to the location of production, or to the location of firm headquarters or sales offices, that matters most.

We end with the observation that market definition has received less attention that it deserves in the context of international competition. In many cases, the statistical classification that comes with the data, as developed by statistical agencies, also determines the market definition used. Such ad hoc classification of industries become even more problematic when the importance of market power is considered explicitly. The production approach does not suffer from such a data constraint, but instead requires one to group firms based on similarities in production technology—very much like the demand approach requires one to group the set of products considered part of the relevant market.

Notes

1. The authors thank Tim Bresnahan, Penny Goldberg, and Frank Verboven for conversations on the topic.
2. Reynaert and Verboven (2014) take derivatives of the entire set of first-order conditions to obtain optimal instruments for the price.
3. It implies that all Japanese firms internalize the constraint they face on their joint exports, something that is not implausible given the important coordinating role played by the Japanese Ministry of International Trade and Industry (MITI).
4. This contrasts with the finding for the Colombian car market in Tovar (2012), which stressed the importance of increased variety.
5. Katayama, Lu, and Tybout (2009) provides a nice illustration of this approach in a different context, namely to evaluate the productivity gap between exporters and non-exporters.
6. This mirrors the critique in De Loecker (2013), who argues that models failing to find evidence for learning-by-exporting effects often do not allow for the existence of such effects in their specification of the productivity evolution.
7. The per capita demand and market size shifters Z and Y generate additional variation in aggregate demand, but they are not crucial to the identification strategy.
8. See Berry and Waldfogel (1999) for an application to entry in the US radio market.
9. Note that the sum of revenue shares over all inputs will not sum to one if a firm has market power, as total revenue (PQ) will exceed total cost.
10. In fact, with long enough panels we can in theory evaluate this for an individual producer, or at least for a narrow subset of producers. For example, Brandt et al. (2017) find a differential impact of the same foreign competition shock on incumbents and more recently entered firms.
11. When equation (14.3) is used in practice, the input share is adjusted for idiosyncratic productivity shocks.
12. We use that $\rho = \dfrac{\partial P}{\partial MC} = \dfrac{\partial P}{\partial W} \bigg/ \dfrac{\partial MC}{\partial W} = \dfrac{\partial \ln P}{\partial \ln W} * \dfrac{P}{MC} \bigg/ \dfrac{\partial \ln MC}{\partial \ln W}$
13. See also Appendix D in De Loecker et al. (2016).
14. See De Loecker (2011) for more details on this so-called two-stage approach in the productivity literature and Pavcnik (2002) for a well-known example.
15. Note that in equation (14.4) ρ is defined in absolute terms—the change in price with marginal costs—while we here use the log-change or percentage pass-through $\tilde{\rho}$ (recall that in our notation).
16. In principle this includes both changes in X-inefficiency and the result of investments in new technology and better products, but the latter channels further complicate the identification and estimation of productivity; see Aw, Roberts, and Xu (2011) and De Loecker (2012) for endogenous productivity processes.

References

Amiti, M., and J. Konings. 2007. "Trade Liberalization, Intermediate Inputs and Productivity: Evidence from Indonesia." *American Economic Review* 97(5): 1611–1638.

Arkolakis, C., A. Costinot, D. Donaldson, and A. Rodriguez-Clare. 2018. "The Elusive Procompetitive Effects of Trade." *Review of Economic Studies*, forthcoming.

Arkolakis, C., A. Costinot, and A. Rodriguez-Clare. 2012. "New Trade Models, Same Old Gains?" *American Economic Review* 102(1): 94–130.

Aw, B. Y., M. J. Roberts, and D. Y. Xu. 2011. "R&D Investment, Exporting, and Productivity Dynamics." *American Economic Review* 101(4): 1312–1344.

Berry, S. 1994. "Estimating Discrete Choice Models of Product Differentiation." *RAND Journal of Economics* 25(2): 242–262.

Berry, S., J. Levinsohn, and A. Pakes. 1995. "Automobile Prices in Market Equilibrium." *Econometrica* 63(4): 841–890.

Berry, S., J. Levinsohn, and A. Pakes. 1999. "Voluntary Export Restraints on Automobiles: Evaluating a Strategic Trade Policy." *American Economic Review* 89(3): 400–430.

Berry, S. T., and J. Waldfogel. 1999. "Free Entry and Social Inefficiency in radio Broadcasting." *RAND Journal of Economics* 30(3): 397–420.

Brambilla, I. 2005. "A Customs Union with Multinational Firms: The Automobile Market in Argentina and Brazil." NBER Working Paper No. 11745.

Brandt, L., J. Van Biesebroeck, L. Wang, and Y. Zhang. 2017. "WTO Accession and Performance of Chinese Manufacturing Firms." *American Economic Review* 107(9): 2784–2820.

Bresnahan, T. F. 1987. "Competition and Collusion in the American Automobile Oligopoly: The 1955 Price War." *Journal of Industrial Economics* 35(4): 457–482.

Bresnahan, T. F., and P. C. Reiss. 1990. "Entry in Monopoly Markets." *Review of Economic Studies* 57(4): 531–553.

Bresnahan, T. F., and P. C. Reiss. 1991. "Entry and Competition in Concentrated Markets." *Journal of Political Economy* 99(5): 977–1009.

Collard-Wexler, A., and J. De Loecker. 2015. "Reallocation and Technology: Evidence from the US Steel Industry." *American Economic Review* 105(1): 131–171.

Corts, K. S. 1999. "Conduct Parameters and the Measurement of Market Power." *Journal of Econometrics* 88: 227–250.

De Loecker, J. 2007. "Do Exports Generate Higher Productivity? Evidence from Slovenia." *Journal of International Economics* 73(1): 69–98.

De Loecker, J. 2011. "Product Differentiation, Multiproduct firms, and Estimating the Impact of Trade Liberalization on Productivity." *Econometrica* 79(5): 1407–1451.

De Loecker, J. 2013. "Detecting Learning by Exporting." *American Economic Journal: Microeconomics* 5(3): 1–21.

De Loecker, J., C. Fuss, and J. Van Biesebroeck. 2014. "International Competition and Firm Performance: Evidence from Belgium." National Bank of Belgium Working Paper No. 269.

De Loecker, J., and P. K. Goldberg. 2014. "Firm Performance in a Global Market." *Annual Review of Economics* 6(1): 201–227.

De Loecker, J., P. K. Goldberg, A. K. Khandelwal, and N. Pavcnik. 2016. "Prices, Markups and Trade Reform." *Econometrica* 84(2): 445–510.

De Loecker, J., and P. T. Scott. 2016. "Estimating Market Power: Evidence from the US Beer Industry". NBER Working Paper No. 22957.

De Loecker, J., and F. Warzynski. 2012. "Markups and Firm-Level Export Status." *American Economic Review* 102(6): 2437–2471.

Eckel, C., and J. P. Neary. 2010. "Multiproduct Firms and Flexible Manufacturing in the Global Economy." *Review of Economic Studies* 77(1): 188–217.

Edmond, C., V. Midrigan, and D. Y. Xu. 2015. "Competition, Markups, and the Gains from International Trade." *American Economic Review* 105(3): 3183–3221.

Eizenberg, A. 2014. "Upstream Innovation and Product Variety in the U.S. Home PC Market." *Review of Economic Studies* 81(3): 1003–1045.

Eslava, M., J. Haltiwanger, A. Kugler, and M. Kugler. 2004. "The Effects of Structural Reforms on Productivity and Profitability Enhancing Reallocation: Evidence from Colombia." *Journal of Development Economics* 75: 333–371.

Fershtman, C., and N. Gandal. 1998. "The Effect of the Arab Boycott on Israel: The Automobile Market." *RAND Journal of Economics* 29(1): 193–214.

Foster, L., J. Haltiwanger, and C. Syverson. 2008. "Reallocation, Firm Turnover, and Efficiency: Selection on Productivity or Profitability?" *American Economic Review* 98(1): 394–425.

Friberg, R., and M. Ganslandt. 2006. "An Empirical Assessment of the Welfare Effects of Reciprocal Dumping." *Journal of International Economics* 70(1): 1–24.

Gao, H., J. Van Biesebroeck, and F. Verboven. 2014. "Strategic Trade Liberalization." KU Leuven Working Paper.

Garcia Marin, A., and N. Voigtländer. 2013. "Exporting and Plant-Level Efficiency Gains: It's in the Measure." NBER Working Paper No. 19033.

Genesove, D., and W. P. Mullin. 1998. "Testing Static Oligopoly Models: Conduct and Cost in the Sugar Industry, 1890–1914." *RAND Journal of Economics* 29(2): 355–377.

Goettler, R. L., and B. R. Gordon. 2011. "Does AMD Spur Intel to Innovate More?" *Journal of Political Economy* 119(6): 1141–1200.

Goldberg, P. K. 1995. "Product Differentiation and Oligopoly in International Markets: The Case of the U.S. Automobile Industry." *Econometrica* 63(4): 891–951.

Goldberg, P. K., and M. M. Knetter. 1997. "Goods Prices and Exchange Rates: What Have We Learned?" *Journal of Economic Literature* 35(3): 1243–1272.

Goldberg, P. K., and F. Verboven. 2001. "The Evolution of Price Dispersion in the European Car Market." *Review of Economic Studies* 68(4): 811–848.

Hashmi, A. R., and J. Van Biesebroeck. 2016. "The Relationship Between Market Structure and Innovation in Industry Equilibrium: A Case Study of the Global Automobile Industry." *Review of Economics and Statistics* 98(1): 192–208.

Holmes, T. J., and J. A. Schmitz. 2001. "Competition at Work: Railroads vs. Monopoly in the U.S. Shipping Industry." *Federal Reserve Bank of Minneapolis Quarterly Review* 25(2): 3–29.

Holmes, T. J., and J. A. Schmitz. 2010. "Competition and Productivity: A Review of Evidence." *Annual Review of Economics* 2: 619–642.

Irwin, D. A., and N. Pavcnik. 2004. "Airbus versus Boeing Revisited: International Competition in the Aircraft Market." *Journal of International Economics* 64(2): 223–245.

Katayama, H., S. Lu, and J. R. Tybout. 2009. "Firm-Level Productivity Studies: Illusions and a Solution." *International Journal of Industrial Organization* 27(3): 403–413.

Khandelwal, A. 2010. "The Long and Short (of) Quality Ladders." *Review of Economic Studies* 77(4): 1450–1476.

Kitano, T., and H. Ohashi. 2009. "Did US Safeguards Resuscitate Harley-Davidson in the 1980s?" *Journal of International Economics* 79(2): 189–197.

Klette, T. J., and Z. Griliches. 1996. "The Inconsistency of Common Scale Estimators When Output Prices Are Unobserved and Endogenous." *Journal of Applied Econometrics* 11(4): 343–361.

Konings, J., and H. Vandenbussche. 2008. "Heterogeneous Responses of Firms to Trade Protection." *Journal of International Economics* 76(2): 371–383.

Krugman, P. R. 1979. "Increasing Returns, Monopolistic Competition, and International Trade." *Journal of International Economics* 9(4): 469–479.

Lileeva, A., and D. Trefler. 2010. "Improved Access to Foreign Markets Raises Plant-Level Productivity . . . for Some Plants." *Quarterly Journal of Economics* 125(3): 1051–1099.

Melitz, M. J. 2003. "The Impact of Trade on Intra-Industry Reallocations and Aggregate Industry Productivity." *Econometrica* 71(6): 1695–1725.

Melitz, M. J., and G. I. P. Ottaviano. 2008. "Market Size, Trade, and Productivity." *Review of Economic Studies* 75(1): 295–316.

Nickell, S. J. 1996. "Competition and Corporate Performance." *Journal of Political Economy* 104(4): 724–746.

Park, M., and H. Rhee. 2014. "Effects of FTA Provisions on the Market Structure of the Korean Automobile Industry." *Review of Industrial Organization* 45(1): 39–58.

Pavcnik, N. 2002. "Trade Liberalization, Exit, and Productivity Improvement: Evidence from Chilean Plants." *Review of Economic Studies* 69(1): 245–276.

Reynaert, M., and F. Verboven. 2014. "Improving the Performance of Random Coefficients Demand Models: The Role of Optimal Instruments." *Journal of Econometrics* 179(1): 83–98.

Salvo, A. 2010. "Inferring Market Power under the Threat of Entry: The Case of the Brazilian Cement Industry." *RAND Journal of Economics* 41(2): 326–350.

Schaumans, C., and F. Verboven. 2015. "Entry and Competition in Differentiated Products Markets." *Review of Economics and Statistics* 97(1): 195–209.

Sheu, G. 2014. "Price, Quality, and Variety: Measuring the Gains from Trade in Differentiated Products." *American Economic Journal: Applied Economics* 6(4): 66–89.

Syverson, C. 2004. "Market Structure and Productivity: A Concrete Example." *Journal of Political Economy* 112(6): 1181–1222.

Thomas, C. 2011. "Too Many Products: Decentralized Decision Making in Multinational Firms." *American Economic Journal: Microeconomics* 3(1): 280–306.

Tovar, J. 2012. "Consumers Welfare and Trade Liberalization: Evidence from the Car Industry in Colombia." *World Development* 40(4): 808–820.

Tybout, J. R., and M. D. Westbrook. 1995. "Trade Liberalization and the Dimensions of Efficiency Change in Mexican Manufacturing Industries." *Journal of International Economics* 39: 53–78.

Van Biesebroeck, J. 2005. "Exporting Raises Productivity in Sub-Saharan African Manufacturing Firms." *Journal of International Economics* 67(2): 373–391.

Verboven, F. 2012. "Competition Analysis: Models and Tools." Mimeo. https://sites.google.com/site/frankverbo/manuscript.

CHAPTER 15

EFFICIENCY MEASURES IN REGULATED INDUSTRIES

History, Outstanding Challenges, and Emerging Solutions

LAURENS CHERCHYE, BRAM DE ROCK,
ANTONIO ESTACHE, AND MARIJN VERSCHELDE

15.1. INTRODUCTION

THIS chapter summarizes the evolution of the use of efficiency measures, and of their various dimensions, in efforts to improve the identification of the potential drivers of changes in productivity performance in regulated public services.[1] The concern for total factor productivity (TFP) has been central to the regulation of these services. The multiple layers of decision-making in regulated sectors and many interactions between regulators, operators, and other stakeholders demand an ability to unbundle TFP into its various efficiency drivers. A regulator cannot blame an operator for an inefficiency that is beyond its direct control. For instance, when salaries are set at the country level, without consideration for sector-specific characteristics, an operator can do little to improve productivity losses linked to this driver of allocative (in)efficiency. Or, in the case of credit rationing constraining long-term financing possibilities, similar distortions beyond the control of the operator appear. Consideration by the regulator of the need for subsidies or guarantees to restore allocative and dynamic efficiency, rather than cursing the operator, is then appropriate. For any margin for improvement in efficiency that is within the direct control of an operator, there is clearly little reason for a regulator not to be demanding with this operator.

This review of the evolution of the regulatory uses of productivity and efficiency concepts starts in the mid-1980s. We conclude with the current state of the art as being developed by academics in response to practical difficulties. Many relate to resisting information asymmetries in the design and implementation of regulatory policies. As of 2015, some of the main recent methodological improvements are indeed those that reduce the data requirements or limit the imposition of assumptions, while being rooted in a sound economic performance framework. This chapter shows that there are still research paths to explore, in order to get these conceptual improvements to meet the policy needs and constraints in regulated industries. To contribute to this research, we suggest a more structural approach to productivity analysis and, in particular, efficiency measurement (see section 15.5).

Our focus is on regulated activities, in particular infrastructure services. In this policy area, policymakers and academics saw some of the best opportunities to make the most of productivity analysis and its unbundling into various efficiency measures. However, their policy use is part of a much broader interest that started in the early 1980s. Many countries began then to favor market based approaches and developed a concern for performance assessments. This switch in policy emphasis triggered a growing academic contribution to the debates on the scope for productivity gains across a wide range of policy areas, including trade, labor, and financial markets more notably.

It is in that context that efficiency and productivity measures became a goal. Countries were adopting, or being forced to adopt, many of the reforms that eventually ended up characterizing the "Washington Consensus."[2] For instance, increased competition as a way to increase allocative and cost efficiency became a central focus of the policy agenda of a majority of Organisation for Economic Co-operation and Development (OECD) countries and many developing economies interacting with the International Monetary Fund (IMF) and/or the World Bank.

This is why the chapter starts with a few words on the major liberalization experience in the world in the last 30 years or so. Across policy areas, liberalization started to aim at cutting costs.[3] Many of the political speeches at the time also included an explicit promise to improve resource allocation, stimulate investments, and ultimately work in the interest of contemporary and future consumers. Measuring performance was becoming, often only implicitly, crucial to ensure the accountability for the political promises being made.

Infrastructure is a particularly interesting sector to consider, because its reforms went one step further. The adoption of price caps installed an explicit link between prices, on the one hand, and productivity and various specific types of efficiency measures, on the other hand. Price cap regulation was born as an alternative to traditional rate-of-return regulation for the telecom sector to give an explicit incentive to service providers to cut costs.[4] Its distinguishing feature is the requirement of a performance measure to be set in advance that is explicitly used to set a maximum allowed growth path for the average price for a specific product or service. This performance measure was explicitly quantitative, and this quantification was anchored in specific measures of efficiency, which had to be the outcome of an explicit policy choice. No other liberalization had made this link that formal. In the process, productivity and efficiency were no longer only a goal, they were also becoming a tool.[5]

The instrument pushed regulators toward an active and transparent performance monitoring role. Until then, the monitoring role of authorities was relatively passive, since it largely consisted of a validation of expenditure bills by the operators.[6] With the need to measure performance quantitatively, regulators were expected to take a much more active role in measurement. The new role for regulators implied collecting data on costs and production at an unprecedented level of detail. They also needed to engage in debates with the operators to choose the right methodology for assessing costs, production, or revenue functions in environments in which cost accounting rules were still quite partial and subject to relatively strong arbitrary cost allocation rules (see, e.g., Campos et al. 2003).

Over the years, though, the use of the productivity and efficiency concepts has evolved. The original price caps have often evolved into hybrid regimes. These regimes now include a significant share of costs enjoying automatic pass-through rules, which reduces the incentives that operators face to improve their overall efficiency performance. These changes have reduced the risks operators are facing and hence their expected returns on investment. In some countries such as the United Kingdom, the Netherlands, Norway, and Sweden, the regulatory toolkit anchored in performance measures has been diversified to include systematic benchmarking of performance (see the discussion by Agrell and Bogetoft in Chapter 16 of this *Handbook*).

Over time, it has become clearer that the adoption of these measures as a tool would not be evenly distributed across sectors and countries. They are much more common in the energy and the telecom sector and, in addition, they are a lot more common in Anglo-Saxon, Northern European, and Latin American countries. Moreover, the access to data by academics to allow independent assessments is still often limited, which clearly suggests that there is scope for a reform that obliges governments to provide evidence on the performance of the firms they supervise or regulate.

There is, however, enough diversity in experiences and enough evidence on the evolution of the policy use of productivity and efficiency measures to identify successes and recurring concerns, and to discuss possible solutions to these concerns. Academics have significantly improved their understanding of the policy challenges over the years. Much of the current research aims at identifying research paths to come up with quantitative performance evaluations that are of direct use for policymaking. This may be why there is so much emphasis on research that focuses on solutions in the context of seriously limited access to information.

The remainder of the chapter is organized as follows. Section 15.2 summarizes the historical drivers for the craving for liberalization. This sets the stage for a discussion how productivity-level measurement and its decompositions have become so central in the performance assessment of key public services. Section 15.3 discusses how productivity and efficiency measures have become both a goal and a tool in some sectors. Section 15.4 offers a short survey of the many conceptual and empirical issues that the more technical literature has been arguing about in the last few years, and that are relevant in the context of regulated industries. Section 15.5 makes the case for a switch to a structural approach to performance measurement in policy areas as a solution to many of the issues surveyed in this chapter. Section 15.6 concludes.

15.2. EVOLUTION OF THE MEASUREMENT OF PRODUCTIVITY AND EFFICIENCY

The most talked about reforms in policy circles have tended to be those conducted in areas aiming at achieving macroeconomic transformations. The liberalization of international trade and capital flows were at the top of the neoclassical policy recipes built into the Washington Consensus. Their main purpose was to induce major structural economic changes, which would increase the overall productivity of the economy as well as the performance of key public services. The expected improvements had to be measured ex ante to make the case for reform and also ex post to assess the extent to which the promises were achieved.

The diversity of approaches to make the case ex ante is too broad to be discussed here. Most of these ex ante assessments focused on cost savings, as a proxy for productivity improvements. But there were many other ways in which the ex ante assessment of potential performance gains came across in the literature and in the policy debates. They ranged from detailed assessments of changes in TFP during partial liberalization episodes in the context of specific case studies (see, e.g., Krueger 1978, 1984), to computable general equilibrium models used to track the cross sectoral indirect effects in the 1980s (see, e.g., Dervis et al. 1989). In addition, there were assessments of counterfactuals frequently anchored in sophisticated accounting approaches (see, e.g., Galal et al. 1994). Many based the counterfactual on econometric studies, which were later discredited for suffering from (what we know now) significant technical limitations (see, e.g., Dollar 1992; Edwards 1998).

The global message emerging during the 1980s and 1990s, in spite of the diversity of assessment methods, was that performance had improved or would improve with the changes, whether measured in terms of TFP or in terms of cost efficiency. It had been largely coherent initially, but this only lasted for a while. Many of these results started to be questioned during the first decade of the 2000s. The initial enthusiasm for the performance gains to be achieved was increasingly being seen as excessive. New research was showing that the early reform experiences had not always been as effective in delivering TFP or cost-efficiency gains, nor was it as equitable as expected for specific countries (see, e.g., Chisari et al. 1999; Estache et al. 2001; Rodrik 1995, 2006). Moreover, in an environment in which technological change was progressing rapidly and included an exceptionally fast global dissemination of knowledge, markets failed more often than initially anticipated to share the gains from progress. These market failures were frequently the outcome of a reluctance of regulators to reduce the incentives that firms would have to further invest in technological improvements without access to an associated rent. Further, the issue was that regulators did not have the processes and tools to come up with fair distributions of the gains. This resulted in efficiency-equity trade-offs that were more real than anticipated by the early research. In turn, it begged for a more careful assessment of the various sources of efficiency changes.

The discussion during the 2000s reflected the fact that the initial models had not internalized the dynamics of optimization. It showed that many of the violations of the core efficiency (and equity) concerns should have been more appropriately addressed. In retrospect, the specific measurement of productivity and efficiency, and the use of the concepts in policy circles, had increasingly become ideological and less conceptually rigorous. Picking the right sample of country or sector studies guaranteed the conclusion in favor of or against the reform. Many papers on the impact of privatization, for instance, picked the telecom sector as a proxy for infrastructure.[7] Telecom has benefited a great deal from reforms aiming at increasing competition, but most importantly from technological change. This has not been the case for all sectors. In particular, in developing countries competition did not always deliver the efficiency gains on the expected scale. Focusing on the telecom sector was thus misleading (see, e.g., Estache et al. 2006).

These observations reflect the importance of recognizing the consequences of an overly mechanistic and narrow use of efficiency concepts in policy debates. Ignoring uncertainty, data quality, data access, market specificities, or more dynamic concerns, in particular the effects of investments, influenced the quality of the analysis. Further, the inadequate assessments biased the conclusions on the efficiency payoffs of liberalization and structural reforms. It explained the difficulty of reconciling the factual evidence observed in the countries with some of the enthusiastic results that were widely disseminated in academic publications and quoted by some of the policy actors pushing for the reforms.

For many observers, it was then of course quite rational to start questioning the methods used to assess the efficiency performance in complex contexts. Technically, the problem was not just a selection bias in data choices or market definition. The evolution of the literature shows that there were also selection biases in the choice of measurement techniques. In the early years, assessments relied on large panels of country data to conduct (sometimes only implicitly) counterfactuals (see, e.g., Dollar 1992; Edwards 1998). The results were attractive to the supporters of reforms, but were not as robust as claimed because of major technical flaws.

These flaws explain why many of the early studies were eventually invalidated.[8] Recently, more suitable experimental design, better data collection efforts, and a stronger focus on the microeconomic evidence at the firm and household level are refining the analysis (see, e.g., De Loecker 2011; Asker et al. 2014). In some cases, these methodological improvements generated more precise information on performance improvements. Nevertheless, the data and methodological challenges continue to justify additional research efforts.[9] The real issue may be that research has distanced itself in many ways from policy concerns and has become increasingly focused on narrow technical contributions.

Performance measurement in infrastructure has suffered from many of these general problems since the early days of high policy impacts in the 1990s. The research started with creative ways of generating counterfactuals (see, e.g., Galal et al. 1994; Chisari et al. 1999). It then moved on to much narrower concerns, as it had done in trade, finance, or labor research. In infrastructure, the applied research focused on the generation of quantitative evidence (with a wide range of levels of sophistication) on the efficiency performance of the regulated sectors and the unbundling of the efficiency into its various components.[10] In the process, the distance between conceptual and empirical research grew. The main reason was the failure to account for the craving of policymakers to maintain information asymmetries to anchor financial and political rents. Theory is improving, but largely ignores the political economy surrounding the growing strategic use of managed information gaps by politicians.[11] For instance, in the energy sector, it is not unusual to see the efficiency gains being shared by operators and the governments. The first group enjoyed higher than needed prices and the second group received increased tax revenue in the best-case scenario, or campaign financing in a darker interpretation of the stylized facts, from the higher than needed costs authorized to producers.

Strong methodological debates between schools of thoughts (i.e., parametric vs. non-parametric) dominated many of the discussions in the major academic journals interested in efficiency measures, including the *Journal of Productivity Analysis*, the *Journal of Regulatory Economics*, and *Utilities Policy*.[12] International organizations such as the World Bank contributed to the disseminations of these applied techniques (see, e.g., Coelli et al. 2003). These allowed some of the academic research to trickle down to the practice of efficiency measures, as countries were internalizing many of the lessons of earlier mistakes or weaknesses. For instance, the well-structured debate on the measurement of productivity and efficiency organized by Dutch regulators illustrates the growing collaboration between top academic efficiency experts (T. Weyman-Jones and D. Newberry) with top regulatory experts (P. Burns) in applied policy work. This collaboration ensured a most effective transfer of knowledge and immediate internalization of the lessons of the British experience (see the Netherland Electricity Regulatory Service 2000). Agrell and Bogetoft had a similar impact in the European Nordic countries (see Chapter 16 for more details).

At this point, and despite the many improvements in the internalization of best-practice technical knowledge in applied policy work, the mutual learning is still ongoing. Academics are still trying to figure out how not to scare policymakers when trying to convince them to adopt relatively complex concepts. Even in countries at the frontier of regulatory practice, such as Australia, there is a continuous effort to raise awareness of the importance of these measures among less specialized audiences (e.g., Coelli and Lawrence 2006). However, the challenge of ensuring the dissemination of robust research in the policy arena, and its adoption in policy design, is not a minor one.

15.3. MOVING FROM MEASURES AS GOALS
TO MEASURES AS TOOLS: LEARNING
FROM INFRASTRUCTURE

Making productivity and efficiency measures general goals of policy was already quite a change in philosophy for many policymakers. Making it happen in practice proved to be quite challenging but doable. In the context of infrastructure policy, the implementation consisted of three building blocks. The first was a change in the market structure to unbundle and give opportunities to competitive segments to achieve their potential. The second was the introduction of competition for the market, when the scope for competition in the market was limited. This is where developments in auction theory during the same period made a big difference. The third was a debate on designing regulation of the residual non-competitive segments of the sector to achieve desirable efficiency improvements.

Some combination of these changes characterized the transformation of sectors such as energy, telecom, and transport. As in the previously mentioned cases, in infrastructure, the efficiency goals initially largely meant assessments of the scope for costs savings. In practice, however, the quantification of these goals often did not go much further than the focus on labor productivity or other types of partial indicators focusing on different costs drivers. The improvements to be achieved from restructuring the sector to increase competition were based on comparisons with best-practice benchmark indicators, typically used by specialized engineers and financial analysts.[13]

Frustration with the incoherencies associated with partial indicators led to a more precise concern for the measurement of productivity and, in particular, the various dimensions of efficiency.[14] This concern progressively became central to the research and the practice of regulation of public services. It was slowly turning the measurement of efficiency into a tool for reform in itself, with the adoption of regulatory regimes relying on some explicit efficiency measure. This happened because academics and policy advisors had managed to mainstream the idea that measuring performance quantitatively, and as precisely as possible, could be useful as a full component of the restructuring of the sectors. Restructuring was not only about pushing for competition, it also had to concern tracking the effectiveness of reforms, and using the limited information to incentivize the firms to better align their conduct with the interests of users.

This is today well understood in policy circles (even if not that much in political circles), but it is a relatively recent recognition. Less than 30 years ago, the information asymmetry was seen as a fact of life. Besides detailed audits, little could be done to deal with it. Old-fashioned regulation and competition policy were designed to avoid abuses in markets with imperfect competition. Performance measures were not really explicitly included in the regulatory tools. Incentives to cut costs were the outcome of negotiation between regulators and the firms, instead of the implementation of a regulatory regime anchored explicitly and mainly in efficiency concerns.

The adoption of regulation that made explicit the concerns for various efficiency dimensions in environments with asymmetric information between the agents and their principals resulted from developments in economic theory that made it to the policy arena. The very basic insights were provided by Baron and Myerson (1982). They came up with a Bayesian regulation scheme in a setting in which the regulators did not know the costs of the single product monopolist they were supervising. Their model characterized the information gap as the need for the regulator to rely on subjective probabilities for the unobservable technical efficiency potential of the service providers.

Their adverse selection model was quickly refined by Sappington (1983) to account for the possibility of ex post monitoring of costs for a multiproduct monopoly. It was further improved by Laffont and Tirole (1986) to account for the possibility of moral hazard as a driver of inefficiency. Lewis and Sappington (1988) then eventually showed that these models could also work in cases in which the source of information asymmetry was the demand side. During the following years, these theories continued to improve, by integrating the concerns for dynamics and quality for instance (see, e.g., the overview in Laffont and Tirole 1993 and, more recently, in Armstrong and Sappington 2007).

These new theoretical approaches to the optimal design of regulation pointed to five relevant facts in the context of this chapter:

(i)   Information asymmetry is a fact of life, but should not be seen as an impediment to efforts to achieve efficiency in either a static or dynamic sense (since the games between regulators and firms could be repeated).

(ii)   Efforts to measure cost efficiency, and its drivers ex post, that make full use of the limited data available render regulation more effective in stimulating performance. However, the effectiveness of these incentive schemes still depends on the size of the information asymmetry between the regulators and the firm.[15]

(iii) Since probabilities are subjective in these settings, the (to some extent ad hoc) choices of the regulator could have a significant influence on the level of performance the regulator could aim at.

(iv)   The decision to push for productivity, performance, and efficiency measurement in an information asymmetry world implies that regulators have to promise the firms the right to keep a share of the gains that is larger than what they would have enjoyed in a world of full information. This can be politically difficult to sell, which may explain why some regulators prefer to be protected by the veil of ignorance.

(v)   If regulators aim at maximizing performance, and are willing to be rational about the management of the information asymmetry, firms have to be given some flexibility to achieve their goals.

The main gap in these theories was a specific guidance to turn these lessons into an explicit mechanism that relies on data that are relatively easily available from firms.

This gap was closed with the price cap mechanism suggested by a 1983 report made by S. Littlechild to change telecom regulation in the United Kingdom. His suggestion was to link an allowed price change to changes in a price index exogenous to the regulated firm, but also to an efficiency (discount) factor set by the regulator. Although the new regulatory approach was not expected to be significantly better than rate-of-return regulation in terms of allocative efficiency, it was supposed to deliver improved technical and dynamic efficiency. In practice, the outcome also depended on other dimensions, such as the risk environment. Incentive regulation can deliver investment in new technologies and hence dynamic efficiency, as well as rate-of-return regulation, if the environment is not risky. In an unstable investment climate, however, it may deliver less dynamic efficiency than the more traditional form of regulation.

Ultimately, notwithstanding the many subtle additional dimensions (i.e., control variables) needed for assessing the expected impact of the Littechild mechanism, the idea was a very pragmatic interpretation of the lessons from theory. Many other equivalent mechanisms, demanding a specific measurement of efficiency, have since then been published.[16] But this creativity has not been able to meet all concerns or needs, since not all countries have switched to regulation schemes anchored in efficiency measures.

Even so, Table 15.1 shows a broad range of case studies to choose from, across the world and across sectors.[17] The blank cells show that cost-plus/rate-of-return regulation continues to be quite popular in specific sectors. For instance, in the railways sector, the scope for any type of incentive scheme is quite limited. Even when maximum prices or revenues are set by regulation, this is mostly done on a lasting assessment of a reasonable return, rather than on an effort to push facility owners to improve the efficient use of the facility in the interest of the network users. The energy and telecom sectors, however, have been much more willing to use the opportunities offered by the new incentive-oriented approaches to regulation. The water sector is somewhere between the two extremes. In a recent survey of 60 countries, Marques (2010) found that only about 58% had implemented some kind of explicit economic regulation. Of these, 60% adopted rate-of-return regulation. Among those adopting incentive-based regulation, 59% followed a price cap and 41% relied on explicit benchmarking techniques.

In retrospect, there has been an accumulation of evidence on the effectiveness of Littlechild's idea and on its potential and limitations in the context of specific sectors (see, e.g., the overviews in Joskow 2008, 2013 for electricity, and Sappington and Weisman 2010 for the telecom sector).[18] Most of this initial research focused on static views of efficiency and relatively mechanistic uses of these measures. The risk dimension, so relevant to developing countries, was actually picked up quite late. This is when Cowan (2002) argued the serious risk of perverse effects on dynamic efficiency, in particular in a context of uncertainty. Cowan's concern was confirmed by a large number of researchers and eventually led to the suggestion of modeling price caps through option pricing models. This suggestion remained an academic one, but the main implicit message (i.e., that the static approach was biasing the interpretation of the efficiency measurement and misleading the evaluation of the policy challenges) trickled down to policy discussions and further empirical research.

Table 15.1 Examples of Sectors in Which Incentive-Based Regulation Is Anchored in a Measurement of Efficiency Through a Price Cap or an Alternative Form of Benchmarking[a]

	Electricity	Gas	Telecom	Water and Sanitation	Airports[b]	Ports	Rail
Argentina	X	X	X	X	X	X	
Australia	X	X	X	X	X (for regional services)	X (until 2009)	X (on access charges for under rail assets)
Austria	X	X	X		X		
Brazil	X	X	X	X	X (for three of the major airports)	X	X (revenue cap for access charge on captive shippers but no incentive component)
Belgium	X		X		X		
Chile	X	X	X	X	X	X	
Czech Rep.	X	X	X				
France	X	X	X		X		
Germany	X	X	X	X	X (but not all airports)		
Hungary	X	X	X		X		
India	X		X		X (not all airports)	X	

Country						
Ireland	X	X	X		X	X
Mali	X	X	X	X		
Mexico	X	X	X		X (revenue per passenger)	X
Netherlands	X	X	X		X	
Portugal	X	X	X		X (revenue per passenger cap)	
Senegal	X	X	X		X	
Spain	X	X	X		X	
Sweden	X	X	X		X	
UK	X	X	X	X	X	X
US	X	X	X	X		

Source: Authors' compilation from multiple sources.

[a] Note that that an X simply means that at least one dimension of the sector in a country is subject to incentive-based regulation. For instance, in Belgium the wholesale electricity market is subject to a cap but the distribution still relies on a cost-plus approach.

[b] For airports, the major debate concerns whether a single- or dual-till form of regulation should be used. A single till considers all airport revenues (aeronautical and non-aeronautical) in the determination of the price cap. A dual-till system only considers aeronautical revenues. In Germany, Frankfurt relies on dual till while the United Kingdom use a single-till system, as do most Latin American airports, which adopted the British model. There are also hybrid approaches. The Brazilian airport, for instance, has a system in which non-aeronautical revenues are partially directed to lower aeronautical charges. Note also that the cap itself can be adjusted. In India, Mexico, or Portugal the cap is in terms of revenue per passenger. In China, it depends on the size of the airport.

This empirical follow-up research raised a number of measurement issues. Besides the obvious concerns with access to data and the poor quality of the data available in regulated industries, the most noted issue in policy discussions was linked to the importance of investments and other adjustment factors with intertemporal dimensions. There was a need to distinguish between operational and capital expenditures more systematically when assessing efficiency. If this distinction is not done in static models and efficiency is based on total costs, any increase in capital expenditures could be interpreted as an inefficiency and hence overestimate the efficiency factor in price regulation (see, e.g., Joskow 2008).

This concern has been documented for a sample of EU energy utilities from 1997 to 2007 by Cambini and Rondi (2010), for example. They show that the investment behavior of incentive-regulated firms can be negatively related to the level of the efficiency goal set by the regulatory authority if this goal is not adequately defined. Transitory inefficiency may be confused for operational efficiency. The impact of the confusion depends on how regulation is implemented in practice, as argued by Vogelsang (2010). Unfortunately, goal setting without consideration of intertemporal effects is still common, even if it has generated and continues to generate much academic research (e.g., from Färe and Grosskopf 1997 to Fallah-Fini et al. 2013). From a very pragmatic viewpoint, the implicit conclusion is that it is really necessary for any efficiency analyst to pay more attention to the specific characteristics of the markets being analyzed.

Summarizing, within less than 30 years, the process that transformed efficiency into both a central goal of policy and a key instrument in the effort to achieve that goal has been an opportunity to reveal a wide range of outstanding issues. These issues concern both the measurement of efficiency and the interpretation and use of these measures in policy circles. Internalizing these lessons implies a greater responsibility for those that construct and advocate the efficiency indices. It may also require a more structured approach, which deals with many of the issues raised in the preceding in a transparent and systematic way. This approach must be able to deal with the major empirical challenges analysts often face. This is the focus of the next two sections.

15.4. DEALING WITH EMPIRICAL CHALLENGES

Table 15.2 summarizes the research on the most recurring types of empirical issues identified by practitioners. It shows that, over 30 years after the beginning of the discussions on how to measure efficiency for regulatory decisions, the modeling of production processes continues to be an area of contemporary interest in both the operations research and economic literature.

In particular, Table 15.2 shows the main empirical issues that resulted in significant divides between the regression-based economics literature (i.e., the parametric school

Table 15.2 How the Literature on Efficiency Measurement Deals with Major Informational Problems

Empirical Issues		Noisy Data	Input Choice with Unobserved Productivity Variation	Multiproduct Firms	Unobserved Prices	Unknown Functional Forms
Established wisdom	*Economic literature*		*(Semi-)parametric regression framework:* Olley and Pakes (1996), Levinsohn and Petrin (2003), Ackerberg et al. (2015), and Wooldridge (2009)		*Nonparametric framework:* Afriat (1972), Hanoch and Rothschild (1972), Diewert and Parkan (1983), and Varian (1984)	
	Operations research			*Data envelopment analysis:* Charnes et al. (1978)		
Recent challenges to wisdom	*Economic literature*		*Semi-parametric regression framework for multi-product firms:* Foster et al. (2008), Bernard et al. (2010, 2011), De Loecker (2011) and De Loecker et al. (2016)			
	Operations research			*Nonparametric multi-output framework with output-specific technology sets:* Cherchye et al. (2008, 2013, 2014a)		

Note: This review is partial and does not deal with much of what can be done with stochastic frontier analysis (SFA) when data constraints are not a problem. See Fried et al. (2008) and Coelli et al. (2005) for overviews in those contexts.

of thoughts) and the deterministic optimization-based operation research (OR) literature (the nonparametric school of thought).[19] It shows that the main sources of the divide are also some of the main empirical concerns that need to be tackled by any analyst
in the field:

(i)   The common necessity to rely on noisy data.
(ii) The difficulty of linking input choices to unobserved productivity variations.
(iii) The necessity of dealing with the multiproduct nature of firms in a way that
      recognizes the relation of the different production processes, each with their
      own scale and scope economies.
(iv) The need to rely on strong assumptions on prices in environments in which
      prices are more often negotiated confidentially rather than set in the market.
(v)   The need to rely on functional form assumptions simply because the real pro-
      duction processes are kept confidential.

Each source of divide leads to a preferred ranking between econometric and OR
approaches. Noisy data are quite common in environments in which cost accounting
is partially subjective, which is a recurrent issue in regulated industries. The problem is
standardly assumed away in the nonparametric OR literature, but it is allowed for by default in any regression-based analysis.[20] An additional significant difference between the
two main approaches is in the concern for endogeneity. The OR literature has been quite
silent in recent decades about this issue occurring if input choices of firms are based
on an unobserved productivity component. The problem, however, can be dealt with
in various ways, including through (semi-) parametric (proxy variable) approaches, as
seen in Table 15.2.

The third divide is about how to deal with the fact that multi-product firms are the
rule rather than the exception (see, e.g., Panzar and Willig 1981). On this front, the
OR literature has long had some advantage. It standardly allows for multi-output production settings and can cope with unobserved prices by the use of shadow prices.
Technically, every linear programming problem can be expressed in a primal problem
and a dual problem. Specifically, if (technical) efficiency is anchored in an identification
of the underlying optimization behavior of the producers, it can be considered as an
upper-bound approximation of the real (economic) efficiency (see also section 15.5 for
more details). For example, the linear program for technical efficiency measurement in
the input direction, for a setting with convex input sets, will turn out to be the dual to a
linear program that computes cost efficiency in terms of unobserved shadow prices (instead of observed input prices). The estimated shadow prices are those prices that minimize inefficiency, and as such we obtain an upper bound on the real economic efficiency
(which is based on the real input prices).

The econometric techniques can also deal with multiple outputs and multiple inputs
and has been used for regulated industries. It is typically done through distance function
formulations. In spite of its attractiveness, the approach tends to suffer from endogeneity
problems for many types of activities. To avoid the problem, some assumptions may be

needed, which can be quite strong for certain markets. For the input distance function, the analyst needs to assume that outputs are exogenously given. For regulated industries in which service obligations are the norm, the assumption is credible. For output distance functions, there is an equivalent assumption with respect to the exogeneity of inputs, which also can be a problem in regulated industries. Note that, despite these problems, the technique is quite widely used in regulated industries such as railways and electricity, which suggests that many analysts do not believe that the endogeneity problem is always a major issue.[21] Recently, De Loecker et al. (2016) proposed an econometric model to deal simultaneously with multiple products, product-specific pricing behavior and the endogeneity issue. To assign inputs to products, they use the assumption that the relation between inputs and products is the same for single- and multi-product firms. While this assumption is often made implicitly in revenue-based productivity analyses, it can be strong for regulated sectors.

Recent deterministic approaches deal with this subtle aspect of the modeling of the nature of the production activity; the issue of output-specific technologies and input assignment. Cherchye et al. (2008, 2013, 2014a) extended the nonparametric framework (see references in Table 15.2 for the seminal contributions) by proposing a nonparametric multi-output framework with output-specific technology sets. An interesting feature of this multi-output methodology is that it can be extended to a setting of multi-product firms, which may differ in product mix. This flexibility is an added asset of OR in many settings.

The fourth source of disagreement between the two main schools of thoughts is the challenge imposed by unobserved prices. It is a serious issue, even if the disagreement between the OR and econometrics analysts is becoming less important in practice. Until very recently, regression-based approaches neglected the particularities of multi-output production, and used industry-wide deflators to overcome the issue of absence of firm-product-level prices. Neglecting price heterogeneity across products and across firms can imply systematically biased productivity estimation, and this has been recognized by a wide range of authors (see, e.g., Klette and Griliches 1996; Foster et al. 2008). Some of the existing solutions are that products are aggregated to a single measure of firm production by, for instance, the use of a firm-level price index or a transformation function.[22] Recently, De Loecker (2011) has shown that the problem could also be addressed by including information on demand shifters into the production model, and Bernard et al. (2010, 2011) endogenized the selection of the output portfolio.

The last source of divide is the approach to the functional form specifications. It is an important one, since it can bias inference in an unknown direction. Until very recently, the regression-based productivity and efficiency literature largely ignored the potential functional misspecification bias and heavily relied on an increasingly complex parametric structure, imposed a priori. The nonparametric linear programming methodology, which is popular in the recent OR literature, can define efficiency conditions on, for instance, prices, technological change, and productivity from observed production behavior without imposing parametric structure. The most popular operationalization of this approach is data envelopment analysis (DEA), after Charnes et al. (1978). One of the main advantages of the nonparametric approach is that it requires no a priori specification of the functional relationship between the production factors, environment, and firm production, hence reducing the possibility of a functional misspecification bias.

Overall, what this discussion shows is that the economics literature emphasizes endogenizing firm choices in a noisy setting by building a (semi-)parametric framework, while the OR literature focuses on the potential functional misspecification bias, unobserved prices, and the multi-output structure of production. In a nutshell, our sense is that, for decades, the two strands of literatures have been drifting apart. Yet there are also striking similarities in the way the two approaches deal with empirical difficulties. There is, notably, a tendency of dealing with the main empirical challenges simultaneously in both strands of the literature. See De Loecker et al. (2016) and Cherchye et al. (2018) for respectively a recent regression based and a recent linear programming based example. In the former work, as discussed above, multiple products, product-specific pricing and the endogeneity issue are modeled simultaneously. In the latter work, input choice dependency on unobserved productivity variation is modeled without the a priori imposition of restrictive functional form assumptions. Therefore the empirical analyst can cherry-pick an empirical approach according to the empirical setting, rather than following a dogmatic belief in a particular strand of literature.

In practice this means that it is essential to be pragmatic rather than dogmatic in the choice of the approach, without forgetting the importance of the economics underlying the performance diagnostic. While for a vast majority of situations, a regression-based framework is most appropriate, in the next section, we argue that for regulated activities facing significant information gaps and data gaps, a constrained optimization (e.g., linear programming) framework is often more promising. The inclusion of a concern for the optimizing behavior of the actors in the diagnostic is what makes it special and less anchored in an engineering/mechanical vision of the performance diagnostic. With the benefit of significant research progress in recent years, this approach would be able to deliver a more reliable approximation of performance at the firm level, especially if recent advances to tackle empirical difficulties are being implemented.

15.5. Toward a Structural View of Performance Measurement in Regulated Industries

The ongoing debates on the proper policy use of productivity and efficiency measures, and on their proper measurement itself, reveal two more complex and growing problems. The first is a lack of systematism in the approaches taken by analysts to generate performance measures that can anchor policy decisions. As a result, there is a lot of subjectivity in the way the performance analysis is executed. This can lead to approaches that can range from careful assessments of the behavioral and optimization options of the operators, to fairly mechanical approaches aiming mostly at generating specific efficiency measures that can be used to launch a regulatory dialogue. The growing bias toward this more mechanical approach is the second problem. It reflects a certain banalization of the measurement process.

These problems suggest that there is often a missing required step in the process followed to generate an efficiency measure capable of informing the policy analysis of the performance of a regulated firm. This step has to capture the extent to which production or management decisions are influenced by (implicit or explicit) optimization behavior with predictable constraints and biases.

From an economic policy or regulatory policy perspective, it seems to us to be essential to start the performance diagnostic with an understanding of the market being assessed, of the goals of the actors involved in the market, and of the implied optimizing behavior. This is not an obvious exercise. Typically, the regulators' objectives tend to be broader than those of the regulated firm. This should matter much more to the choice of the concept of efficiency to be used in regulatory decisions than it does in practice. Today regulatory assessments conducted by sector regulators tend to be quite focused only on the concerns of the firm. Accounting for social and environmental concerns may be part of the implicit public-sector optimization behavior, but is unlikely to be a required item of the operator. Unless it is defined as part of its regulatory obligations (in which case they enter as constraints in the optimization process rather than goals). In practice, it should only make sense to focus on the actual quantification process, when this first essential step is completed. The omission of this step may be one of the most underrated issues in the practice of efficiency measurement. Many diagnostics, implicitly or explicitly, tend to focus on the operator's optimization, without much consideration of the more complex government or regulators' broader agenda.[23] We believe that a reasonable way of minimizing the risks of jumping too quickly into the empirics is to rely on a three-step process that ensures that the analyst has covered all the key dimensions:

(i) Spell out the Economic objectives of the regulated firm that are recognized by the regulatory design. This results in an objective function $f(x, y, z)$, with inputs x, outputs y and environmental variables z, that needs to be minimized or maximized. Generally, economically meaningful objectives for regulated firms can easily be translated into an objective function.

(ii) Identify the production Technology used to optimize the economic objectives. This leads to a specification of the constraints $g_1(x,y,z) \leq c_1, \ldots, g_m(x,y,z) \leq c_m$ that the regulated firm faces due to the production process and/or the objectives stemming from the government's or regulators' broader agenda.

(iii) Implement the empirical strategy, starting with a diagnostic of the range of Challenges linked to the multiple dimensions of information asymmetry.

We label the approach ETC to reflect the fact that the focus is first on the economics (E), next on the technology (T), and then only on the implementation challenges (C).

The rest of this section briefly explains how to work through each one of these three steps. As will be clear from this discussion, the current state of the art already allows for optimally tackling each separate step; that is, to allow for a correct specification of the objective function f, the constraints $g_1(x,y,z) \leq c_1, \ldots, g_m(x,y,z) \leq c_m$ and the firm's optimization program (i.e., maximize or minimize f subject to the constraints). Academic research is trying to extend the accuracy of each separate step (e.g., a more accurate description of multi-output production or integrating environmental objectives; see the following for more details). Still, the regulator could already today mainly focus on a proper combination of the existing results in order to obtain a meaningful performance analysis.

Step 1: Spelling out the economic objectives. Any efficiency analysis relevant from an economic perspective should ideally start from an explicit identification of the economic objective and market situation of the actor under evaluation. This allows a definition of efficiency as a measure of the deviation between observed behavior and behavior consistent with optimizing the economic objective. The efficiency measure then enjoys a clear economic meaning, rather than a more mechanical engineering interpretation. It anchors the policy issues in an explicit recognition that any inefficiency index is a measure of the deviation from optimizing the objective chosen, or assigned to the actor under assessment (e.g., firm, regulator, society). Ignoring this underlying optimization process leaves the efficiency measure, at best, with a partial interpretation of the performance and, at worst, without a credible economic interpretation. In both cases, it can result in biased and misleading policy conclusions.

Consider technical efficiency, which measures the production performance of a firm. This type of efficiency is the most common focus of models used in regulatory policy and public-sector performance assessments in countries with little price information due to the poor cost accounting practice. These models aim at assessing whether or not the evaluated production unit is on the technically efficient frontier of some empirical approximation of the production possibility set (i.e., the set of technologically feasible input–output combinations). The main issue with the common use of the technique is that the construction of this possibility set is conventionally motivated from an engineering perspective. This perspective relies on often strong assumptions on dimensions such as returns-to-scale or the marginal rates of input substitution/output transformation. Yet production (i.e., the transformation of costly production inputs in valuable output [both products and services]) makes economic sense only if the production process is in line with pursuing the economic objective of the firm.

In the private sector, the most frequently maintained position is that producers operate in a fully competitive market and pursue profit maximization. In the public sector, however, cost minimization for given output might often seem a more reasonable assumption, for instance, when the producer is a price taker in input markets but operates in regulated output markets (as is often the case for public agencies). In other instances, a similar argument may motivate revenue maximization as the appropriate firm objective.

It is worth stressing that specifying the specific economic objective and integrating the market constraints (e.g., price taker or setter, specified price caps or objectives, etc.) has an impact on the efficiency assessment. If this is not appropriately defined in the first step, then the next steps of the ETC-stepwise framework are of little use, as any following efficiency index, which captures deviations of the optimal behavior, will be without economic meaning and hence without much value for policymaking. However, carefully selecting the appropriate economic environment is not always so trivial and thus requires some discussion. The following is a summary of the most important ingredients.

First, the analyst needs to distinguish between short-term and long-term optimization. This is important, as some inputs are fixed in the short term and variable at the medium or long run. Moreover, in the medium or long term, the usually unknown negative or positive spillovers between sales, loyalty, and various production risks may affect the production results.

Second, the economic objective can vary over time and over products. While revenue maximization can be a short-term objective—for example to control or increase the market share of an entering firm or a new product in a highly competitive market with scale economies—it is usually not the true long-term economic objective.

Third, the economic objective can be impacted by the economic environment in which the firm operates. Price caps and specific objectives set out by the regulator, or more generally the policymaker, influence the optimization decisions of the firms.

Finally, as the firm can have a divisional structure (i.e., a horizontal, vertical, regional, or mixed divisional structure), the objective can be introduced from a cooperative or non-cooperative perspective. The "cooperative" perspective assumes that the separate divisions cooperate in order to reach the economic objective of the firm, while in the non-cooperative perspective individual divisions pursue their own economic objective. Clearly, such a setup does not automatically imply cooperation between the different divisions (see, e.g., Cherchye et al. 2014a).

Step 2: Identify the production technology used to optimally achieve the economic objective in the given economic context and introduce inefficiency as a deviation from optimal conduct. Given the economic objective and environment identified in Step 1 and the definition of economic efficiency as the spread between observed and optimal behavior, the analyst needs to define the production technology used to optimize the economic objective, regardless of the availability of data. Firms strive in a given environment to optimize the economic objective by transforming inputs, which are costly, into outputs that have a (non-)market value, and choosing the optimal pricing strategy. Defining the technological information consists thus of

(i)   identifying the inputs, outputs, and environmental variables and their relation to each other;
(ii)   identifying the input and output prices;
(iii) defining what is controllable (endogenous) and non-controllable (exogenous);
(iv)   introducing efficiency as a deviation from the optimal conduct identified in Step 1.

The first three actions are relatively well-known and common practice, the last one is less common and yet is, we believe, an essential part of the overall process. The first two actions are taken usually assuming no information asymmetry on key observables. Full information on the production technology implies that we know which inputs are used for the production of each output and which environmental variables affect the linkages between the inputs and outputs. We also know all the relevant prices and that these prices affect how the firm demands inputs and supplies outputs in the input-specific and output-specific markets to optimize the economic objective. There is no need to assume that the markets the firms are confronted with are homogeneous over the production variables. As a result, prices are best defined at the input-output-environment level.

The modeling of the production can be quite detailed and specific. The analyst can distinguish between joint (or public) inputs, subjoint inputs, and output-specific inputs. Joint inputs benefit the production of all outputs and thus imply non-rival and non-exclusive use of the inputs within the firm. Subjoint inputs also figure as joint inputs, but only for a subset of outputs. Output-specific inputs can be allocated to the production of particular outputs (e.g., by the use of an assignment factor, which represents the fraction of the input that is used to produce the particular output; see, e.g., Cherchye et al. 2013). As such, input-specific, output-specific, and environment-specific technology sets can be constructed. If a separate production technology for each output (input) is considered, interdependencies between the different technologies are accounted for through jointly used (produced) inputs (outputs) (see, e.g., Cherchye et al. 2014a, 2015 for concrete examples in the water and electricity sector). Note at this point that the functional relationship between inputs, outputs, and the environment is still unknown at this stage of an analysis. The potential need for specifying this relationship is part of Step 3 of the ETC process.

Once the basic dimensions of the production process have been identified, the analyst has to identify the extent to which the firm can have discretionary power in the level of production variables, the selection of production variables, and level of prices. Determining what is considered to be endogenous in the pursuit of optimizing the objective is key to understanding firm behavior. First, a meaningful technology defines which inputs, outputs, and environmental variables are outside the discretion of the firm and thus exogenous to the optimization of the economic objective. Second, besides the level of production variables, the firm can influence the selection of inputs (e.g., using new innovations), output portfolio (e.g., upgrading or downgrading the portfolio depending on the output market), and operating environment (e.g., firm location, off-shoring, export choices, global sourcing). As such, the technology clarifies whether the selection of production variables is endogenous to the optimization of the economic objective. Third, even if the prices are unknown, a meaningful definition of the technology requires a clear definition of which prices are endogenous to optimizing the economic objective. As prices are the result of the confrontation between supply and demand, it is in this step that information on input and output market structures should be included.

With the optimal and actual information requirements clearly identified, the analyst can now focus on the distance between the firm's performance in terms of the specified firm objective to the optimally feasible performance as a measure of the so-called economic efficiency, which includes cost efficiency, revenue efficiency, and profit efficiency. Cost efficiency is the distance between observed costs and minimal costs (for a level of output), and revenue efficiency is the distance between observed revenues and maximum revenue (for given inputs). Analogously, profit efficiency is the distance between observed profit and maximum profit. While it is natural to consider deviations from optimal conduct solely in the negative direction, this framework is general in the sense that deviations in the positive direction (e.g., caused by exogenous productivity shocks) that imply superefficient conduct are not excluded.

As a test of the relevance of the efforts conducted so far, an analyst can check if any appropriately defined technical measure of efficiency has a (dual) interpretation in terms of economic efficiency. If not, the analysis is false and without value for policymakers. Stated differently, a measured technical efficiency that does not approximate the distance between observed conduct and the conduct that optimizes the economic objective is of no use for policy.

Step 3: Tackle the empirical challenges that the analyst is confronted with, internalizing the many lessons from the limitations of older approaches. With the benefit of the theoretical approximation of the true unknown production process identified in Step 2, the analyst can now start working on its empirical approximation. In many cases, the reliability and quality of the empirical approximation heavily rely on the chosen theoretical structure. But, as discussed in the previous section, this also depends on more down-to-earth sources of concerns.

For regulated sectors, the OR framework is often likely to be the most attractive because it deals in a natural way with unknown functional forms, unobserved or imperfect price data and the many cases with significant data unavailability in panel format (in particular when this is needed to control for input choice dependency on efficiency). In this framework, as production efficiency is anchored in production (input and output) data, the regulator avoids having to deal with the concerns for confidential costs data and avoids having to rely on a functional representation of the production technology (a recurring source of conflict between regulators and operators during tariff-setting discussions, which often end with the operators enjoying the benefit of the doubt). Regulated firms tend to be reluctant to provide detailed cost data, which often depend on negotiated agreements with their suppliers. Moreover, joint costs allocated to specific activities are usually based on subjective cost-allocation rules, which distort any assessment of performance. In this context, it seems clear that relying on production data is attractive—even more so, when the ETC framework can be used to give an economic meaning to technical efficiency in terms of deviation from optimizing behavior.

Furthermore, the approach can also be easily adapted to deal with a growing range of policy concerns relevant to regulated environments, such as services obligations, congestion, or bad outputs (environmental concerns). Service obligations are particularly important in regulated industries and can lead to significant distortions in efficiency performance when these obligations involve cross subsidies, as is common in energy, rail, postal, or water services. Congestion and environmental concerns are also quite important and are growing in importance for regulated industries, even if they are often not on the agenda of the sector regulators but only on the agenda of the environmental regulators. The extent to which coordination between the various regulators works drives the effectiveness of improving the global performance of regulated firms when multiple policy objectives must be addressed.

These concerns can be included, since a link between the economics and the technology choices are relatively easy to establish and to build into the empirical tool. Service obligations simply reflect the fact that besides minimizing the input quantities, a regulator may wish to pursue specific output targets (e.g., increases of good outputs or reductions of bad outputs). This can be done by modifying the efficiency measures, to include targets without involving specific engineering assumptions on the reference technology. Congestion problems are dealt with by including them in the definition of the technology. This ensures that they are internalized by our definition of efficiency as the distance between the observed behavior and the optimum. Finally, a vast literature—referenced in Cherchye et al. (2015)—deals with the issue of including undesirable outputs into nonparametric efficiency analysis, but without reaching consensus. Existing approaches either imply additional nonverifiable production axioms, transformations that may significantly alter efficiency results or extra modeling choices. However, by suitably applying the ETC approach spelled out earlier, Cherchye et al. (2015) advocate a characterization of bad outputs in terms of their own production technologies (while allowing for interdependencies between bad and good outputs).

15.6. CONCLUDING COMMENTS

For over 30 years, theoretical and empirical academic research has been trying to improve the measures of efficiency and how they can be used in the design of regulation in environments in which information asymmetries and data quality are serious issues. This survey shows that the efforts have been quite successful in many ways. How precisely analysts can deal with real-life data and informational constraints in their efforts to measure efficiency is quite different today from what it was when regulators started measuring efficiency. Efficiency analysis is, indeed, significantly better now, and it can lead to significantly more robust results. This is the good news, but there are also some remaining caveats to keep in mind at the end of this review on the match between the theory and practice of efficiency measurement in regulated industries.

First, there is still a major informational problem. The creativity of theorists in coming up with solutions to make the most of the use of efficiency in policy decisions in a world of sustained informational asymmetries has helped. Unfortunately, it has not yet managed to offset the data and other informational challenges as much as needed to obtain fair assessments that minimize the scope of strategic use of methodological biases in policy debates (e.g., between regulators and regulated firms). Not all sectors are equally impacted by this lack of data, revealing differences in commitment to transparency across sectors. The fact that the energy and telecom sectors studies can deliver cost-efficiency estimates, while many of the ports or water sector studies need to focus on technical efficiency because cost data are not available, is quite symptomatic of the differences in leverage enjoyed by regulators across sectors.

Next, the reaction to the informational gaps has too often been to rely on a relatively mechanical approach to the assessment of efficiency. Problems are assumed away, rather than addressed in the policy use of efficiency measurement techniques. Indeed, axioms and audacious assumptions on the irrelevance of key informational issues are quite common and are not necessarily carefully tested. Yet this is what makes the difference between an engineering and an economic perspective on efficiency. Without an explicit recognition of the behavior driving the optimization process, it seems hard to design policies that factor in the behavioral distortions that influence performance. This is where the discipline imposed by the ETC approach we suggest may help, since it anchors the definition of efficiency in a structural assessment of the optimal behavior.

Ultimately, the more technical and main policy challenges are relatively well known already. It is clear that the failure to tackle challenges usually leads to abnormal rents for regulated companies. It is fair to conclude that improvements in processes and in access to information in the policy world are not as impressive as the technical improvements achieved in the academic world. This suggests that a lasting tolerance for high rents may be linked to a more complex institutional issue. Indeed, there seems to be an incentive or moral hazard problem that explains why key policymakers are not doing enough to close a gap, which is known to generate rents.

There are certainly many reasons for this lack of effort. Some of them may be linked to concerns with the participation constraints identified by the modern regulation theory—namely, the fear that firms will simply pull out if the rent does not match the risk adjusted return. But, regulatory capture, collusion, or corruption are alternative explanations for the tolerance for a lasting failure to internalize best-measurement practice (see various chapters in Rose-Ackerman and Soreide 2012 for a recent survey).

This, in turn, suggests that there may be a need to include the impact of these institutional failures in optimal policy research and practice. The sharing of performance gains is increasingly acknowledged as being just as important as their levels. The Great Recession has indeed shown the importance of these concerns in the discussions on the large rents in the financial sectors. Academics may help to close the gap. Most likely, the pressure on regulators and regulated industries for rent-sharing will continue to be strong. Research could have a significant impact if it were to propose easily implementable ways of increasing the transparency of performance achievements, as well as of the sharing of any performance change across the various stakeholders (i.e., producers, users, and taxpayers). By increasing the visibility of capture, collusion, and corruption, the productivity and efficiency research on regulated industries will manage to establish itself as a mainstream tool, rather than a technical instrument used by a minority. After all, few thought that the popular media would eventually cover (and generate reactions from nontechnical readers) about comparative labor productivity analysis, quantitative easing, or mergers and acquisitions. So, given that people spend

15%–25% of their income in these regulated industries, the hope of broad (policy) recognition of the importance of performance assessments in regulated industries should be reasonable.

NOTES

1. We are grateful to Knox Lovell and Emili Grifell-Tatje for useful comments and suggestions.
2. The term "Washington Consensus" was coined in 1990 by John Williamson to refer to a predictable set of specific recommendations made by the IMF, the World Bank, and the US Treasury Department in negotiations with developing countries in crisis. Later, it ended up referring more generally to strongly market-oriented reforms.
3. There was a strong focus on cutting the cost of subsidies, because fiscal discipline was often also part of the policy agenda when sector reforms were taking place.
4. In OECD countries, it is known as the brain child of S. Littlechild (1983), who eventually became the energy regulator, but economists in Chile argue that the specific mechanism has already been introduced in Chile prior to the 1983 Littlechild report; see, for instance, Galetovic (2008).
5. Measuring efficiency change also aimed, initially at least, at ensuring fairness in its distribution between users and operators (and sometimes taxpayers when subsidies were part of the financing equation). A given efficiency level X guaranteed consumers (and/or taxpayers), a minimum level of average tariff reduction from costs savings and a fair return to the operator. Any efficiency gain higher than this efficiency level X would become a pure rent. Any gain lower than X implied a lower-than-expected profit and revealed that either the operator was simply not very good technically at doing what it was supposed to do (adverse selection), or that it was not trying hard enough (moral hazard).
6. This perverse effect of the traditional rate-of-return or cost-plus forms of regulation is known as the Averch-Johnson effect and it translates into overinvestment in quantity and quality, which itself usually implies lower economic efficiency.
7. Megginson and Netter (2001) is one of the most widely cited papers with this bias.
8. In trade, for instance, the technical debates became quite refined but with very strong policy implications. See, e.g., Rodriguez and Rodrik (2001), Alcalá and Ciccon (2004), or Rodrik (2006).
9. Many of the problems stem from basic data constraints. For instance, productivity measures in this literature often rely on production functions in which firm-level output is approximated by sales deflated by sector-wide producer price indexes. This can bias efficiency effect assessments; see, e.g., De Loecker (2011) and De Loecker et al. (2014).
10. It also included efforts to implement the conceptual vision defended by Schleifer (1985) to push for yardstick competition, as discussed by Agrell and Bogetoft in Chapter 16 of this volume.
11. See Campos et al. (2003) for an illustration in the context of the Argentinean railways.
12. These debates are regularly synthesized in textbooks on efficiency measurements by some of the main academic contributors to the field (see, e.g., Coelli et al. 2003 and Fried et al. 2008). More recently, Grifell-Tatje and Lovell (2015) have been arguing for alternative ways of making the most of accounting data.

13. See, for instance, the report on Peru, available at http://documents.worldbank.org/curated/en/2010/12/16278203/peru-recent-economic-development-infrastructure-investing-infrastructure-engine-growth-spending-more-faster-spending-better-vol-2-

14. See, e.g., Coelli et al. (2003) for a discussion of the biases linked to partial indicators in the context of infrastructure.

15. There is a significant amount of empirical research on the interaction between optimal regulatory choices and efficiency measurement. See, e.g., Gagnepain and Ivaldi (2002a) and Dalen and Gomez-Lobo (2003) in the context of optimal contracts for bus transports, and Bogetoft (1994, 1995) and Gagnepain and Ivaldi (2002b) more generally.

16. An earlier paper by Loeb and Magat (1979) had already addressed the importance of information asymmetry in the context of regulation, but it did not generate the awareness of the importance of efficiency measurement hinted at by Baron and Myerson (1982) and its follow-ups.

17. There are many good reasons why in some countries it is quite rational not to overemphasize efficiency, in particular when institutional capacities and concerns for risks are limited. See, for instance, Estache and Wren-Lewis (2009) for a detailed discussion in the context of developing countries.

18. One of the key lessons of this empirical research is that the relative effectiveness of the incentive-based versus non-incentive-based regulation depends on a wide range of interactions with other characteristics of the firms, sectors, and countries in which they are implemented, including political and institutional dimensions.

19. One of the arguments made in the debates on the optimal approach to assess TFP in the context of regulation is that regulators may have preferences for one method or another. There is, however, no evidence of such preferences or that regulators understand better DEA than SFA. The only bias in preferences is linked to the anecdotal evidence indicating that they feel more comfortable with approaches minimizing the risks of entering into conflict with operators. In that respect, less demanding in terms of data is often more important than the specific methodological choice.

20. Note that there are errors-in-variables techniques available to allow for measurement error in a deterministic OR framework. See, for instance, Varian (1985) and Kuosmanen et al. (2007) for seminal contributions, and Daraio and Simar (2007) for an overview.

21. Note that if the regulator uses a cost benchmark, multiple outputs are incorporated naturally.

22. Diewert (1973) introduced the transformation function for two goods, and Dhyne et al. (2014) extended this to any number of goods.

23. Quite frankly, this omission is not always innocent. In principle, utilities regulators are supposed to coordinate with environmental regulators to ensure that the full sets of concerns of the policymakers are accounted for in assessing the performance. In most countries, this is only cheap talk. For instance, when an environmental regulator pushes for demand management and expects prices to be increased to reflect externalities, politicians put pressure on the sector regulator to protect the poor and the middle class from any increase in prices. Belgium, France, and Spain have all seen episodes of this sort of behavior in the last three years, resulting in a de facto underestimation of inefficiency by ignoring the costs associated with the externalities. We did not have the space to address this schizophrenia in the chapter, even if this source of dynamic inefficiency has serious societal consequences, in particular for future generations.

REFERENCES

Ackerberg, D., K. Caves, and G. Frazer. 2015. "Identification Properties of Recent Production Functions Estimators." *Econometrica* 83: 2411–2451.

Afriat, S. 1972. "Efficiency Estimation of Production Functions." *International Economic Review* 13: 568–598.

Alcalá, F., and A. Ciccon. 2004. "Trade and Productivity." *Quarterly Journal of Economics* 119: 612–645.

Armstrong, M., and D. Sappington. 2007. "Recent Developments in the Theory of Regulation." In *The Handbook of Industrial Organization*, edited by M. Armstrong and R. Porter. Amsterdam: Elsevier Science.

Asker, J., A. Collard-Wexler, and J. De Loecker. 2014. "Dynamic Inputs and Resource (Mis) Allocation." *Journal of Political Economy* 122: 1013–1063.

Baron, D., and R. Myerson. 1982. "Regulating a Monopolist with Unknown Costs." *Econometrica* 50: 911–930.

Bernard, A. B., S. J. Redding, and P. K. Schott. 2010. "Multi-Product Firms and Product Switching." *American Economic Review* 100: 70–97.

Bernard, A. B., S. J. Redding, and P. K. Schott. 2011. "Multiproduct Firms and Trade Liberalization." *The Quarterly Journal of Economics* 126: 1271–1318.

Bogetoft, P. 1994. "Incentive Efficient Production Frontiers: An Agency Perspective on DEA." *Management Science* 40: 959–968.

Bogetoft, P. 1995. "Incentives and Productivity Measurements." *International Journal of Production Economics* 39: 67–81.

Cambini, C., and L. Rondi. 2010 "Incentive Regulation and Investment: Evidence from European Energy Utilities." *Journal of Regulatory Economics* 38: 1–26.

Campos, J., A. Estache, and L. Trujillo. 2003. "Processes and Accounting Matter for Regulators: Learning from Argentina's Railways Privatization." *Journal of Network Industry* 4: 3–28.

Charnes, A., W. W. Cooper, and E. Rhodes. 1978. "Measuring the Efficiency of Decision Making Units." *European Journal of Operational Research* 2: 429–444.

Cherchye, L., T. Demuynck, B. De Rock, and M. Verschelde. 2018, "Nonparametric Identification of Unobserved Technological Heterogeneity in Production." National Bank of Belgium Working Paper Series No. 335. https://www.nbb.be/en/articles/working-paper-ndeg-335.

Cherchye, L., T. Demuynck, B. De Rock, and K. De Witte. 2014a. "Nonparametric Analysis of Multi-Output Production with Joint Inputs." *Economic Journal* 124: 735–775.

Cherchye, L., B. De Rock, B. Dierynck, F. Roodhooft, and J. Sabbe. 2013. "Opening the 'Black Box' of Efficiency Measurement: Input Allocation in Multi-Output Settings." *Operations Research* 61: 1148–1165.

Cherchye, L., B. De Rock, and F. Vermeulen. 2008. "Analyzing Cost Efficient Production Behavior under Economies of Scope: A Nonparametric Methodology." *Operations Research* 56: 204–221.

Cherchye L., B. De Rock, and B. Walheer. 2015. "Multi-Output Efficiency with Good and Bad Outputs." *European Journal of Operational Research* 240: 872–881.

Chisari, O., A. Estache, and C. Romero. 1999. "Winners and Losers from the Privatization and Regulation of Utilities: Lessons from a General Equilibrium Model of Argentina." *The World Bank Economic Review* 13: 357–378.

Coelli, T., A. Estache, S. Perelman, and L. Trujillo. 2003. "A Primer on Efficiency Measurement for Utilities and Transport Regulators." World Bank Institute Publications, The World Bank.

Coelli, T., and D. Lawrence. 2006. *Performance Measurement and Regulation of Network Utilities.* Cheltenham, UK: Edward Elgar.

Coelli T., D. S. Prasada Rao, C. O'Donnell, and G. E. Battese. 2005. *An Introduction to Efficiency and Productivity Analysis.* New York: Springer.

Cowan, S. 2002. "Price Cap Regulation." *Swedish Economic Policy Review* 9: 167–188.

Dalen, D., and A. Gómez-Lobo. 2003. "Yardsticks on the Road: Regulatory Contracts and Cost Efficiency in the Norwegian Bus Industry." *Transportation* 30: 371–386.

Daraio, C., and L. Simar. 2007. *Advanced Robust and Nonparametric Methods in Efficiency Analysis: Methodology and Applications.* New York: Springer.

De Loecker, J. 2011. "Product Differentiation, Multiproduct Firms, and Estimating the Impact of Trade Liberalization on Productivity." *Econometrica* 79: 1407–1451.

De Loecker, J., C. Fuss, and J. Van Biesebroeck. 2014. "International Competition and Firm Performance: Evidence from Belgium." National Bank of Belgium Working Paper No. 269. https://www.nbb.be/nl/authors/fuss-c-and-van-biesebroeck-j.

De Loecker, J., P. Goldberg, A. Khandelwal, and N. Pavcnik. 2016. "Prices, Markups, and Trade Reform." *Econometrica* 84: 445–510.

Dervis, K., J. de Melo, and S. Robinson. 1989. "General Equilibrium Models for Development Policy." A World Bank research publication. http://documents.worldbank.org/curated/en/1989/08/440577/general-equilibrium-models-development-policy.

Dhyne, E., A. Petrin, V. Smeets, and F. Warzynski. 2014. "Import Competition, Productivity and Multi-Product Firms." National Bank of Belgium Working Paper No. 268. https://www.nbb.be/nl/authors/smeets-v-and-warzynski-f.

Diewert, W. E. 1973. "Functional Forms for Profit and Transformation Functions." *Journal of Economic Theory* 6: 284–316.

Diewert, W. E., and C. Parkan. 1983. "Linear Programming Tests of Regularity Conditions for Production Frontiers." In *Quantitative Studies on Production and Prices*, edited by W. Eichhorn, R. Henn, K. Neumann, and R. W. Shephard. Würzburg: Physica-Verlag.

Dollar, D. 1992. "Outward-Oriented Developing Economies Really Do Grow More Rapidly: Evidence from 95 LDCs, 1976–1985." *Economic Development and Cultural Change* 40: 523–544.

Edwards, S. 1998. "Openness, Productivity and Growth: What Do We Really Know?" *Economic Journal* 108: 383–398.

Estache, A., A. Gomez-Lobo, and D. Leipziger. 2001. "Utilities Privatization and the Poor: Lessons and Evidence from Latin America." *World Development* 29: 1179–1198.

Estache, A., S. Perelman, and L. Trujillo. 2006. "Infrastructure Reform in Developing Economies: Evidence from a Survey of Efficiency Measures." In *Performance Measurement and Regulation of Network Utilities*, edited by T. Coelli and D. Lawrence. Cheltenham, UK: Edward Elgar.

Estache, A., and L. Wren-Lewis. 2009. "Towards a Theory of Regulation for Developing Countries: Following Jean-Jacques Laffont's Lead." *Journal of Economic Literature* 47: 729–770.

Fallah-Fini, S., K. Triantis, and A. L. Johnson. 2013. "Reviewing the Literature on Non-Parametric Dynamic Efficiency Measurement: State-of-the-Art." *Journal of Productivity Analysis* 41: 1–17.

Färe, R., and S. Grosskopf. 1997. "Efficiency and Productivity in Rich and Poor Countries." In *Dynamics, Economic Growth, and International Trade*, edited by B. Jensen and K. Wong. Ann Arbor: University of Michigan Press.

Foster, L., J. Haltiwanger, and C. Syverson. 2008. "Reallocation, Firm Turnover, and Efficiency: Selection on Productivity or Profitability?" *American Economic Review* 98: 394–425.

Fried, H., K. Lovell, and S. S. Schmidt. 2008. *The Measurement of Productivity Efficiency and Productivity Growth*. New York: Oxford University Press.

Gagnepain, P., and M. Ivaldi. 2002a. "Incentive Regulatory Policies: The Case of Public Transit Systems in France." *RAND Journal of Economics* 33: 605–629.

Gagnepain, P., and M. Ivaldi. 2002b. "Stochastic Frontiers and Asymmetric Information Models." *Journal of Productivity Analysis* 18: 145–159.

Galal, A., L. Jones, P. Tandon, and I. Vogelsang. 1994. *Welfare Consequences of Selling Public Enterprises*. New York: Oxford University Press.

Galetovic, A. 2008. "Comments on Di Tella, R., and A. Dyck, 'Cost Reduction, Cost Padding, and Stock Market Prices: The Chilean Experience with Price-Cap Regulation.'" *Economia* 8: 186–190.

Grifell-Tatje, E., and K. Lovell. 2015. *Productivity Accounting: The Economics of Business Performance*. New York: Cambridge University Press.

Hanoch, G., and M. Rothschild. 1972. "Testing Assumptions of Production Theory: A Nonparametric Approach." *Journal of Political Economy* 80: 256–275.

Joskow, P. 2008. "Incentive Regulation and Its Application to Electricity Networks." *Review of Network Economics* 7: 547–560.

Joskow, P. 2013. "Incentive Regulation in Theory and Practice: Electricity Distribution and Transmission Networks." In *Economic Regulation and Its Reform: What Have We Learned?*, 291–344.

Klette, T. J., and Z. Griliches. 1996. "The Inconsistency of Common Scale Estimators When Output Prices Are Unobserved and Endogenous." *Journal of Applied Econometrics* 11: 343–361.

Krueger, A. 1978. *Foreign Trade Regimes and Economic Development: Liberalization Attempts and Consequences*. New York: National Bureau of Economic Research.

Krueger, A. 1984. "Trade Policies in Developing Countries," In *Handbook of International Economics*, Vol. I, edited by R.W. Jones and P. B. Kenen. Amsterdam: North Holland.

Kuosmanen, T., T. Post, and S. Scholtes. 2007 "Non-Parametric Tests of Productive Efficiency with Errors-in-Variables." *Journal of Econometrics* 136: 131–162.

Laffont, J.-J., and J. Tirole. 1986. "Using Cost Observation to Regulate Firms." *Journal of Political Economy* 94: 614–641.

Laffont, J.-J., and J. Tirole. 1993. *A Theory of Incentives in Procurement and Regulation*. Cambridge, MA: MIT Press.

Levinsohn, J., and A. Petrin. 2003. "Estimating Production Functions Using Inputs to Control for Unobservables." *Review of Economic Studies* 70: 317–341.

Lewis, T. R., and D. Sappington. 1988. "Regulating a Monopolist with Unknown Demand and Cost Functions." *Rand Journal of Economics* 19: 438–457.

Littlechild, S. 1983. "Regulation of British Telecommunications Profitability." Report to the Secretary of State. London: Department of Industry.

Loeb M., and W. Magat. 1979. "A Decentralized Method for Utility Regulation." *Journal of Law and Economics* 22: 399–404.

Marques R. 2010. *Regulation of Water and Wastewater Services: An International Comparison.* London: International Water Association.

Megginson, W. L., and J. M. Netter. 2001. "From State to Market: A Survey of Empirical Studies on Privatization." *Journal of Economic Literature* 39: 321–389.

Netherlands Electricity Regulatory Service. 2000. "Choice of Model and Availability of Data for the Efficiency Analysis of Dutch Network and Supply Businesses in the Electricity Sector Background Report Accompanying 'Guidelines for Price Cap Regulation in the Dutch Electricity Sector.'" https://www.frontier-economics.com/documents/2014/06/efficiency-analysis-of-dutch-network-frontier-paper.pdf.

Olley, G. S., and A. Pakes. 1996. "The Dynamics of Productivity in the Telecommunications Equipment Industry." *Econometrica* 64: 1263–1297.

Panzar, J. C., and R. D. Willig. 1981. "Economies of Scope." *American Economic Review* 71: 268–272.

Rodriguez, F., and D. Rodrik. 2001. "Trade Policy and Economic Growth: A Skeptic's Guide to the Cross-National Literature," In *NBER Macroeconomics Annual 2000*, edited by Ben S. Bernanke and Kenneth Rogoff. Cambridge, MA: MIT Press.

Rodrik, D. 1995. "Trade and Industrial Policy Reform." In *Handbook of Development Economics*, Vol. III, edited by J. R. Behrman and T. N. Srinivasan. Amsterdam: North Holland.

Rodrik, D. 2006. "Goodbye Washington Consensus, Hello Washington Confusion? A Review of the World Bank's 'Economic Growth in the 1990s: Learning from a Decade of Reform.'" *Journal of Economic Literature* 44: 973–987.

Rose-Ackerman, S., and T. Soreide. 2012. *The International Handbook of Anti-Corruption Economics*, Vol. II. Cheltenham, UK: Edward Elgar.

Sappington, D. 1983. "Optimal Regulation of a Multiproduct Monopoly with Unknown Technological Capabilities." *Bell Journal of Economics* 14: 453–463.

Sappington, D., and D. Weisman. 2010. "Price Cap Regulation: What Have We Learned from 25 Years of Experience in the Telecommunications Industry?" *Journal of Regulatory Economics* 38: 227–257.

Schleifer, A. 1985. "A Theory of Yardstick Competition." *Rand Journal of Economics* 16(3): 319–327.

Varian, H. R. 1984. "The Non-Parametric Approach to Production Analysis." *Econometrica* 52: 579–598.

Varian, H. R. 1985. "Non-Parametric Tests of Optimizing Behavior with Measurement Error." *Journal of Econometrics* 30: 445–458.

Vogelsang, I. 2010. "Incentive Regulation, Investments and Technological Change." CESifo Working Paper No. 2964, Munich. https://ideas.repec.org/p/ces/ceswps/_2964.html.

Wooldridge, J. M. 2009. "On Estimating Firm-Level Production Functions Using Proxy Variables to Control for Unobservables." *Economics Letters* 104: 112–114.

CHAPTER 16

......

THEORY, TECHNIQUES, AND APPLICATIONS OF REGULATORY BENCHMARKING AND PRODUCTIVITY ANALYSIS

......

PER J. AGRELL AND PETER BOGETOFT

16.1. INTRODUCTION

......

A number of different regulatory regimes have been applied to regulate natural monopolies: rate-of-return regulation (Vickers and Yarrow 1991), cost-plus regulation (Beesley 1997), revenue caps (Beesley and Littlechild 1983), and yardstick competition (Shleifer 1985). Chapter 15 by Chercheye et al. in this volume discusses more in detail the particular considerations related to the choice of regulatory mechanism. In this context, it suffices to recall the historical coincidence between demand (infrastructure deregulation in North America, Latin America, and Europe, surge for accountability for public management in general) and supply (rapid development of frontier analysis methods[1]), software implementations,[2] and the theory behind its use in regulation.[3] Although a large literature on econometric estimations for energy production already existed, the interest in infrastructure provision (transmission via the so-called transmission systems operators [TSOs] and distribution via the so-called distribution system operators [DSOs]) was partially inspired by national regulators, such as the early work in New Zealand (Wyatt, Brown, Caragata, Duncan, and Giles 1989), the seminal data envelopment analysis (DEA) work in Norway (Førsund and Kittelsen 1998; Kittelsen 1993), structural work in Canada (Littlechild and Yatchew 2002), and the integrated studies in Sweden (Agrell and Bogetoft 2000; Hjalmarsson and Veiderpass 1992). These studies were developed in the lapse of five years (1995–2000) of applications of frontier analysis techniques in 10 countries (Jamash and Pollitt 2000).

The objectives behind the implementations were different, from initially relatively open, learning-oriented approaches (e.g., the light-handed regulation in Sweden, 2000–2003) toward full-fledged frontier yardstick systems (e.g., in Germany from 2008). The development was partially driven in parallel by the regulatory refinements. The predominant regime during the first phase of deregulation was high-powered regulation, such as CPI-X,[4] for example in countries such as England (cf. Pollitt 1995). Agrell, Bogetoft, and Tind (2005) summarize some shortcomings of the CPI-X model, such as the risk of bankruptcy for a low cap and the risk of excessive informational rents for a too generous cap. Initially, such as in Littlechild (1983), the X was seen as an ad hoc discretionary parameter, basically the outcome of a bargaining process between the regulator and the firm(s). With the massive adoption of incentive regulation for large jurisdictions with hundreds of operators, this

Table 16.1 Some European Regulation Regimes and Cost Function Methodologies for Electricity DSOs and TSOs

Country	Regime	Method DSO	Method TSO
Austria	Revenue cap	DEA-MOLS(nat)	DEA(int)*
Belgium[20]	Revenue cap	DEA(nat)*	DEA(int)
Denmark	Revenue cap	MOLS(nat)	DEA(int)
Estonia	Revenue cap	MOLS(nat)	DEA(int)*
Finland	Revenue cap	StoNED(nat)	DEA(int)
France	Cost recovery	Ad hoc	DEA(int)*
Germany	Revenue cap	DEA-SFA(nat) best-of	DEA(int)
Great Britain	Revenue cap	MOLS(nat)	DEA(int)*
Greece	Cost recovery	-	DEA(int)*
Hungary	Price cap	Ad hoc	Ad hoc
Iceland	Revenue cap	Ad hoc DEA(int)*	DEA(int)
Ireland	Price cap	Ad hoc	Ad hoc
Italy	Revenue cap(opex)	Ad hoc	DEA(int)*
Lithuania	Price cap	Ad hoc	DEA(int)*
Luxemburg	Cost recovery	Ad hoc	DEA(int)*
Netherlands	Yardstick	MOLS(nat)	DEA(int)
Norway	Yardstick	DEA(nat)	DEA(int)
Portugal	Revenue cap	SFA(nat)	DEA(int)
Spain	Revenue cap	Engineering	DEA(int)*
Slovenia	Price cap	DEA(nat)	-
Sweden	Rate-of-return	Ad hoc DEA(nat)	DEA(int)*
Switzerland	Cost recovery[21]	Ad hoc DEA(nat)*	-

Participation in benchmarking at a nat[ional] or int[ernational] level without direct implementation in regulation is denoted by *.

approach was revealed to be infeasible, and regulators looked for reliable methods to determine the productivity parameter. In the years 2000–2010 the methods evolved from simple Ordinary Least Squares (OLS), total factor productivity (TFP), building block methods, engineering cost models to DEA[5], stochastic frontier analysis (SFA),[6] and hybrid approaches.

The features of the nonparametric models (absence of technical a priori assumptions, internal cautious estimation of the production possibility space) contributed to their popularity among regulators. Table 16.1 gives a summary of the benchmarking methodologies used for electricity DSOs in 22 European countries (Haney and Pollitt 2009) with our updates for the period after 2008.

Some countries, like Spain and previously Sweden until 2006, have chosen to rely on technical engineering norms, sometimes referred to as ideal networks, in an attempt to identify not only *relative* best practice, but *absolute* technological possibilities. Most countries rely on some revenue cap model and have derived general productivity and individual inefficiencies using benchmarking tools like DEA and SFA. It is important to note that DEA, in particular for the transmission operations, has a widespread application throughout Europe, primarily through studies such as e^3GRID[7] that is described in section 16.5. However, as indicated in Table 16.1 by an asterisk in the column, many of the countries use DEA to inform regulatory rulings, but without direct link to the regulation. Nevertheless, regulatory benchmarking is not just another application for neophytes of frontier analysis. In the following section we will briefly summarize some of the main prerequisites for an effective development and use of frontier analysis in economic regulation.

16.2. PREREQUISITES FOR REGULATORY BENCHMARKING

The frontier analysis methods provide sound empirical estimates for the cost function so as to inform regulatory proceedings, including tariff reviews, monitoring of cost and investment development, as well as productivity development in the sector. The type of estimates most usually used are cost-efficiency metrics, based on either best-practice (frontier) or quantile/average practice estimates. Since economic regulation is a judicial process that can be challenged in court if subject to bias or undue process, the objectives of the method choice are not only the *estimation accuracy in expectation* but also, at least as much, the *transparency and replicability of the estimation process* itself. The objectives for frontier estimates concern both the efficiency model and the estimation robustness.

16.2.1. Relevance

For the efficiency model to be acceptable, the scope must be relevant to the data-generation process, in particular the absence or presence of stochastic data as inputs or outputs in relation to the type of model chosen.[8] Second, the model scope must adequately reflect *multi-output services* unless they are perfectly correlated.[9] Third, the model specification must assure *structural comparability* in order to enable the determination of a homogeneous reference set. In practice, this requirement means that the data collection and variable specification should be defined such that it is neutral to different accounting reporting standards, financial policies, and nonregulated businesses. Finally, the choice of method must be compatible with the role assigned to the cost norm in the overall regulatory framework.

16.2.2. Activity Analysis

Any quantitative modeling and measurement of a nontrivial multi-output production process require a careful understanding of the activities involved. This step implies a painstakingly long review of the activities undertaken by regulatory obligation, the activities that are autonomously decided by the firm but that contribute to the regulated output and the activities undertaken that are not under regulation. An example of this process across international electricity distributors is given in Agrell and Bogetoft (2010). Failure to correctly analyze the production process will naturally result in incommensurate data and a structurally heterogeneous reference set.

16.2.3. Data Harmonization

When a clear understanding of the scope of the benchmarked activity has been established, the analyst must carefully reflect upon the data to be collected and harmonized. In regulatory settings, the regulator normally has the authority to collect any relevant data from the firm, but the level of detail and consequent cost of collection should be judged against the value they bring to the model. A particular trap is to collect large amounts of data based on implicit or evolving standards that later are revised or challenged. Ambiguous data definitions make modeling difficult or impossible, decrease the value and trust in the results, and jeopardize future repetitions of the process. In international benchmarking projects, such as Edvardsen and Førsund (2003) for electricity DSOs and Agrell and Bogetoft (2009, 2014) for electricity TSOs, the data harmonization also entails ongoing adjustments of labor costs, construction costs, land prices, currencies, outsourcing, activation policies, equipment standards, and maintenance requirements.

16.2.4. Repeatability

Benchmarking for use in regulatory regimes poses strict and very specific constraints on the process of development, parameterization, and calculation, whereas scientific research in economics and econometrics may advance through discretionary investigations, open experiments of alternative specifications, and ad hoc definition of technology and reference sets, depending on the specific research objectives pursued. A study advancing a new methodological development may use a regulatory data set for illustration without spending time on the exact relevance of the underlying model and the interpretation of the conclusions. However, since the act of economic regulation is an intervention supported by national (and European) law, leading to direct economic consequences for the owners of the firm, not only the final model, but also the process leading to it, must be transparent, documented, and justified in the sense of the supporting legal framework. As seen from the applications in this chapter, the technical level of the development may render this requirement particularly challenging. Nevertheless, the lack of documentation or justification for even the slightest methodological choices may lead to judicial recourse against the model.[10] Naturally, the process concerns for this repeatability are even higher for the actual data validation, the outlier detection, and the final calculations. In practice, strict protocols for how data are transmitted and validated are defined prior to any processing. The use of programing code or R-scripts (cf. Bogetoft and Otto 2010) has proven to be instrumental in achieving this repeatability and to enforce endogenous choices of parameters for outlier detection, for example. In international projects (Agrell and Bogetoft 2009; Agrell, Bogetoft, and Trinkner 2016; Consentec Sumicsid, Frontier Economics 2013), with confidential data, the repeatability may have to be endorsed through third-party auditing of data, process, and calculations, since the national regulators may not have authority to share certain firm-level data.

16.2.5. Structural Robustness

The previous section provided process robustness, meaning that identical estimates should result from a repetition of the process using different software, advisors, and analysts. The assumptions involved in the estimation should be a minimal set of cautiously determined parameters. The avoidance of technical parameters increases procedural reliability (i.e., variability due to interpersonal differences in skills, methodological assessment, and nonverifiable assertions). The modeling choices enhancing robustness can be called *structural robustness*. The avoidance of technical or subjective parameters or assumptions, such absence of functional form in nonparametric models, or the endogenization of weight restrictions (if used, see section 16.5) are examples of structural choices. The three most important areas of structural robustness concern (i) reference set determination (controlling for heterogeneity); (ii) scale assumptions; and (iii) incorrect scope for the activities by the firms. As noted earlier under activity analysis and data harmonization, the initial phases of a benchmarking are extremely important to achieve structural robustness.

16.2.6. Behavioral Robustness

Given that regulatory benchmarking is preannounced, documented, and often repeated, the relevant robustness must also take into account *behavioral* dimensions associated with strategic action from the players. Starting with the firm's legal actions,[11] the observable outcome is data errors leading to incorrect estimates of the firm-level efficiency and potentially of the frontier cost curve. If the strategic intention is low, the source of the misreporting may simply be inadequate information systems, misinterpreted data definitions, or errors in information processing by the firm. Many errors of these types are easily detectable in automated data validation procedures or by comparing, for example, deviations from average values from similar firms. The firm may also misreport intentionally, resulting from either *collusion* or *maverick reporting*. In a collusive setting, the firm has pre-arranged its reporting with a set of colluding firms so as to strategically increase the frontier cost curve. Collusion allows firms to behave as merged entities, manipulating the frontier toward which all firms are measured. Under collusive behavior, aggregated data are correct but disaggregated data are infeasible. The results from a yardstick model in Tangeras (2002) show that when regulated firms realize that they are played out against each other, they take precautionary measures to collude. However, the anticipation of results in a nonparametric model is much more complex than in a single-parameter bid-rigging process, making side payments costly and risky. Thus, a proper choice of method enforces the robustness against collusion.

16.3. Theory Behind DEA-Based Regulation

In this section, we provide a summary of the theoretical foundation for DEA-based incentive regulation. To the best of our knowledge, there is no similar theory linking SFA explicitly with incentive regulation.

The connection between DEA and the formal literature on games was first suggested by Banker (1980) and Banker, Charnes, Cooper, and Clarke (1989). Linkage with the formal performance evaluation and motivation literature, most notably the agency theory and related regulation and mechanism design literature, has subsequently been the subject of a series of papers, including Agrell and Bogetoft (2001); Agrell, Bogetoft, and Tind (2005); Bogetoft (1994a, 1994b, 1995, 1997, 2000); Bogetoft and Hougaard (2003); Bogetoft and Nielsen (2008); Dalen (1996); Dalen and Gomez-Lobo (1997, 2001); Førsund and Kittelsen (1998); Resende (2002); Sheriff (2001); Thanassoulis (2000); and Wunsch (1995). In the following we will highlight some of these results.

16.3.1. Framework

The basic problem addressed in this line of research is the following. Assume that a principal (regulator) having access to cost data spends x^k and obtains in return an output vector y^k from each of K agents (firms, DSOs, TSOs)

$$\left(x^k, y^k\right), \quad k = 1, \ldots, K \tag{16.1}$$

Based on this, what can the principal reasonably ask the agents to do in the future, and how should she motivate and compensate them to do so? The answer to these questions depends on the *organizational context* and in particular on the technological, informational, and preferential assumptions of the parties.

The relevance of DEA is in general related to situations in which the principal faces considerable *uncertainty about the technology*. In a single-input multiple-output cost setting, the principal may know that the cost function is increasing and convex, but otherwise have no a priori information about the cost structure.

The general case empowers agents to take *private actions*, which the principal cannot observe. The action could be to reduce costs or to decrease the quality of the work done. This leads to a usual *moral hazard problem* since the principal and the agents may conflict as to which actions the agents should take. The conventional setting depicts the agents as effort averse, tempted to rely on their good luck and to explain possibly poor performance as the result of unfavorable circumstances.

In some models, we also consider the possibility that the agents have *superior information* about the working conditions before contracting with the principal. A network operator may have good information about the primary cost drivers for network extension costs in his network, while the regulator may have at best average cost data for the same investments. This leads to the classical *adverse selection problem* where an agent will try to extract information rents by claiming to be working under less favorable conditions.

16.3.2. Interests and Decisions

It is common to assume that the principal is risk neutral and that the agents are either risk averse or risk neutral. The principal's aim is to minimize the costs of inducing the agents to take the desired (hidden) actions in the relevant (hidden) circumstances. Hence, the principal seeks to induce efficient production and to limit the incentive rents the agent can capture since actions and information are hidden. An agent's aim is usually to maximize the utility from payment minus the disutility from private effort.

In the combined moral hazard and adverse selection models, we usually make a simplifying assumption about the structure of the agent's trade-offs between effort and payment. We assume that the aim of any agent is to maximize a weighted sum of profit and slack:

$$U\left(y^k, B^k\right) = \left(B^k - x^k\right) - \rho\left(x^k - c\left(y^k\right)\right) \tag{16.2}$$

where y^k is the outputs produced, B^k is the payment received, slack is a measure of the extent to which actual input x^k exceeds the minimal possible $c\left(y^k\right)$, and $\rho^k \in (0,1)$ is the relative value of slack. Note that we here use $c\left(y^k\right)$ as the minimal possible cost of producing y^k and x^k as the actual costs used. In this model, input is one-dimensional, and technical efficiency is effectively cost efficiency.

We will rely on these assumptions in the following, but we realize that, although widely used in the literature, they constitute a stylized caricature of intra-organizational decision-making and conflict resolution. This is not satisfactory and is in sharp contrast to the nuanced production description that techniques like DEA enable.

To derive regulation and incentive schemes with a more sound theoretical basis, we need to know more about what goes on inside the black box of the firm. Only then can we study, in more detail, the combined use of incentive regulation and regulation by rights and obligations that are used in practice, and only in this way can we make valid statements about the speed and path of improvements that a new performance-based scheme may foster. The recent idea of *rational inefficiency* discussed in Asmild, Bogetoft, and Hougaard (2009, 2013), Bogetoft and Andersen (2009), Bogetoft, Fare, and Grosskopf (2009), and Bogetoft and Hougaard (2003) is an attempt to provide a more nuanced view of the preferences involved in the selection of multidimensional production plans and slack elements. A discussion of this, however, is beyond the scope of this chapter.

16.3.3. Superefficiency in Incentive Schemes

One of the first lessons from the incentive perspective is that the traditional efficiency scores are not useful. They give all agents on the relative efficient frontier a score of unity. This severely limits the ability to give high-powered incentives. The Farrell measures can give incentives to match others, but not to surpass the norm and push out the frontier. Combining this with the multidimensional characteristics of the typical DEA model and thereby with the ability to be special in different ways, the *Nash equilibria (NE)* that can be implemented using the traditional efficiency measure will often involve minimal effort and maximal slack.

Figure 16.1 illustrates this. Here we observe two agents (operators) initially operating at the frontier. We assume further that the cost (effort) to the agents is proportional to

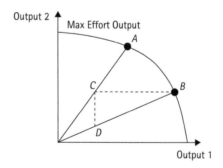

FIGURE 16.1. Nash equilibria under Farrell incentives.

From Bogetoft and Otto (2011) and Bogetoft (2012).

the length of the production vectors and that payment is decreasing in the output efficiency score F,

$$F^k > \tilde{F}^k \Rightarrow B^k\left(F^k\right) \ge B^k\left(\tilde{F}^k\right) \tag{16.3}$$

such that maximal payment is received when a firm is efficient with a score of $F = 1$. Operator 1 notes that reducing the output from A to C would yield the same reward at lower effort (i.e., a higher surplus). Clearly, A is therefore not the best response to the regulation. In a second reaction to the contraction by Operator 1, Operator 2 could move from the initial B to an easier life in D, again reducing private costs of effort without affecting its payment. It is easy to see that the successive contraction would lead to a regression approaching zero output at maximum benefit.

This somewhat discouraging outcome can easily be remedied by making the payment decrease in the super-efficiency rather than in the usual output efficiency. In Figure 16.1, the output-based super-efficiency for Operator 1 in A is approximately 0.6, but if the payment is sufficiently decreasing in the output-based super-efficiency measure F^{SUP}, it would not pay to reduce the effort. Specifically, it does not pay to reduce the effort if the marginal reduction in payment exceeds the marginal decease in the cost of effort.

More generally, one can support the implementation of most plans using super-efficiency, even so-called nondominated NE as first demonstrated in Bogetoft (1995).

16.3.4. Incentives with Individual Noise

Another fundamental result concerns a pure moral hazard context with ex post evaluations of the performance of the firms when there is

- considerable technological uncertainty a priori,
- risk aversion, and
- individual uncertainty (noise) in the firms' performance.

Technological uncertainty is represented by a large class of a priori possible technologies (e.g., the set of production functions that are increasing and concave, or the set of functions that are increasing). One may now ask whether the DEA frontier is sufficient to write an optimal contract, that is, when

$$B^{*K}\left(y^k\right) = B^K\left(x^k, y^k, C^{DEA}\left(y^k \middle| x^{-k}, y^{-k}\right)\right) \tag{16.4}$$

where $B^{*k}\left(y^k\right)$ is the optimal compensation and $C^{DEA}\left(y^k \middle| x^{-k}, y^{-k}\right)$ is the DEA estimated cost frontier based on all firms except firm k

$$C^{DEA}\left(y \middle| x^{-k}, y^{-k}\right) = \min\left\{ x \middle| x \ge \sum_{j \ne k} \lambda^j x^j, y \le \sum_{j \ne k} \lambda^j y^j, \quad \lambda \in \Lambda \right\}. \tag{16.5}$$

where Λ denotes the domain for the convex multipliers determining the returns to scale (see, e.g., Agrell and Tind 2001). This is the case where optimal relative performance evaluations can be made by comparing the performance of a given firm against the DEA best-practice frontier, estimated from the performance of the other firms.

The individual uncertainty is modeled through a non-observable, independent random variable ε^k from some distribution f:

$$y^k = \pi\left(x^k\right) - \varepsilon^k \tag{16.6}$$

where $\pi\left(x^k\right)$ is the mapping from inputs x^k to the frontier in the output space. It turns out that (i) DEA frontiers support optimal contracts when the distribution f of the individual noise terms is exponential or truncated, and that (ii) DEA frontiers, based on large samples, support optimal contracts when noise is monotonic, in the sense that small noise terms ε^k are more likely than large noise terms (cf. Bogetoft 1994a, 1994b). Hence, even when we have individual noise elements and not just structural uncertainty, which intuitively seems to favor DEA, DEA-based contracts will be optimal for special distributional assumptions and for general assumptions, if the sample is sufficiently large.

16.3.5. Incentives with Adverse Selection

Another set of results concerns combined adverse selection and moral hazard problems with

- considerable asymmetric information about the technology,
- risk-neutral firms, or
- firms seeking to maximize profit $+ \rho$ slack utility.

The firms are supposed to have superior technological information. In the extreme case, they know the underlying true cost function[12] with certainty, while the regulator only knows the general nature of the cost function. Thus, the regulator may know that there are fixed unit costs of the different outputs, but not the exact unit cost because it is the firm's private information. Alternative assumptions may be made about the information available to the regulator. We may assume, for example, that the regulator only knows that the cost function is increasing and convex.

The optimal solution in this case depends on whether the actual costs (i.e., the minimal possible cost plus the slack introduced by the firm) can or cannot be verified and therefore contracted upon.

If the actual costs x cannot be contracted upon, the optimal solution is to use

$$B^{*k}\left(y^k\right) = b^k + C^{DEA}\left(y^k \middle| x^{-k}, y^{-k}\right), \tag{16.7}$$

that is, the optimal compensation equals a lump sum payment plus the DEA estimated cost norm ex ante. The size of the lump sum payment b^k depends on the firm's alternatives (i.e., its reservation profit).

If, instead, we assume that the actual costs of the firm can be contracted upon, the optimal reimbursement scheme becomes

$$B^{*k}\left(x^k,y^k\right)=b^k+x^k+\rho^k\left(C^{DEA}\left(y^k\middle|x^{-k},y^{-k}\right)-x^k\right) \tag{16.8}$$

as demonstrated in Bogetoft (1997, 2000). This shows that the optimal compensation equals a lump sum payment plus actual costs plus a fraction ρ^k of the DEA estimated cost savings. The structure of this payment scheme can be interpreted as a *DEA-based yardstick model*: Using the realized performances of the other firms, the regulator creates a cost yardstick against which the regulated firm is evaluated. The regulated firm is allowed to keep a fraction ρ of its saving compared to the yardstick costs as its effective compensation.

These results provide an incentive rationale for using DEA-based revenue cap and yardstick competition systems in contexts where the regulator faces considerable uncertainty about the underlying cost structure. Note that the performance of the other firms can, in both cases, be interpreted as either historical data, as it is generally used in the revenue cap regulation, or as actual data, as is the idea in the ex post yardstick regulation regime. Departing from the normative use that we outline here, Blázquez-Gómez and Grifell-Tatjé (2011) use the formulation in (16.8) ex post to evaluate rent appropriation and the social welfare orientation of the regulation of electricity distribution networks in Spain.

16.3.6. Dynamic Incentives

In the previous section, we considered incentives for a single period based on historical or current information. Dynamic cases with multiple periods are more complicated since they give rise to new issues such as

- the possibility of accumulating and using new information from one or more firms,
- the need to avoid the ratchet effect (i.e., deliberate sub-performance in early periods to avoid facing too tough standards in the future), and
- the possibility of technical progress (or regress).

The structure of the optimal dynamic scheme is similar to the ones developed in the preceding, as demonstrated in Agrell, Bogetoft, and Tind (2005, 2005). Thus, the optimal revenue cap for a firm is determined by a DEA-based yardstick norm. Assuming verifiable actual costs, and taking into account the generation of new information, the ratchet effect and the possible technical progress, the optimal scheme becomes

$$B_t^{*k}\left(x_t^k,y_t^k\right)=b_t^k+x_t^k+\rho^k\left(C^{DEA}\left(y_t^k\middle|x_{1-t}^{-k},y_{1-t}^{-k}\right)-x_t^k\right) \tag{16.9}$$

where $C^{DEA}\left(y_t^k \middle| x_{1-t}^{-k}, y_{1-t}^{-k}\right)$ is the DEA-based cost norm that uses all the information from the other firms generated in periods 1 through t. By relying only on information from the other firms in setting the norm, we avoid the ratchet effect, and by relying on all previous performances, we presume that there is no technical regress.

Of course, the dynamic case can be further extended, for example by including incentives to innovate and to share innovative practices. Also, it could be extended to situations where the catch-up capacity is somewhat constrained such that immediate catch-up, as it is assumed here, is avoided.

16.4. Model Development Process

The development of a regulatory benchmarking model is a considerable task due to the diversity of the operators involved and the economic consequences that the models may have. The most important steps in model development are the following:

Initial data cleaning: Data collection for regulation starts far before the modeling since no econometric work can be made on incorrect data. In particular, activity analysis (subsection 16.2.2) and data definition are of primary importance in this respect.

Choice of variable harmonizations: Choice of accounting standards, cost-allocation rules, in/out of scope rules, assets definitions, operating standards, and so on, were necessary to ensure a good data set from operators with different internal practices, as discussed in subsection 16.2.3.

Choice of variable aggregations: The dimensionality of the parameter space may be too high for the model (e.g., types of assets, services, and environmental characteristics). An important step here is to find relevant aggregation rules and parameters, like interest and inflation rates, or industry-relevant weights using, for example, engineering analysis, to create aggregate variables. The validity of the aggregation must be verified and the sensitivity with respect to alternative aggregation rules should be documented.

Average model specification: The final model specification for a frontier cost model should also be valid in an average cost model setting, in particular for purposes of documentation and explanation (subsection 16.2.4). In particular, nonparametric models should also be documented using standard regression tools to enable comparisons, although the interpretation of the variability for deterministic variables is different.

Frontier model estimations: The relevant DEA and/or SFA models should be estimated, evaluated, and tested on full-scale data. The starting point are the cost drivers derived at the model specification stage, but the role and significance of these cost drivers should be examined in the frontier models with and without the use of outlier detection mechanisms.

Model validation: Extensive second-stage analyses should be undertaken to see if any of the omitted variables should be included. The second-stage analyses are typically done using graphical inspection, nonparametric (Kruskal-Wallis) tests for ordinal differences, and truncated regression (Tobit regressions) for cardinal variables. Using the Kruskal-Wallis method, we tested, for example, whether there was an impact on (i) asset age, (ii) the geographical location of the operator, and (iii) the impact of economies of scope from in water, district heating, gas, or telecommunication activities. We also tested a series of alternative variables related to cables, connections and meters, substations and transformers, towers, energies delivered, peak flows, decentralized generation, injection points, population changes, soil types, height differences, urbanization, areas, and so on.

Iterations: Model development is not a linear process, but rather an iterative one. During the frontier model estimation, for example, one may identify extreme observations that have resulted from data error not captured by the initial data cleaning or the econometric analyses, and which may lead to renewed data collection and data corrections. This makes it necessary to redo most steps in an iterative manner. The nonlinear nature of model development constitutes a particular challenge in a regulatory setting where the soundness and details of the process must be documented to allow opposing parties to challenge the regulation in the courtroom (see subsections 2.4 and 2.5). In practice, this calls for a clear estimation strategy and project management skills, as in any strategic process.

16.5. Application: International Electricity Transmission Benchmarking

The Council for European Energy Regulators commissioned studies of the cost efficiency of electricity transmission system operators in 2009[13] and in 2012.[14] In the following, we provide some detail for the most recent study, performed by the authors together with consultants from Frontier Economics, Consentec, and Sumicsid. In all, 18 countries participated, with 22 TSOs, each contributing data and participating in the project workshops, lasting from September 2012 to July 2013 (see Agrell and Bogetoft 2014).

16.5.1. Data Harmonization

By default, electricity TSOs are heterogeneous in terms of their internal structure, task provision, and financial accounting system. The assets involved are either acquired throughout a long horizon, or relatively recently through an unbundling process with the creation of an opening balance from assets sold by one or several incumbents. Since one of the prerequisites for a regulatory benchmarking is a commensurate reference set of cost observations, an activity-based accounting approach must be used. Based on earlier work and standards (Agrell and Bogetoft 2009), seven core functions are defined in terms of cost accounting: *market facilitation* (management cost for and/or interventions on electricity exchanges); *system operations* (maintenance of the real-time energy balance, congestion management, and ancillary services such as disturbance reserves and voltage support); *grid planning* (planning and drafting of grid expansion and network installations involving the internal and/or external human and technical resources, including access to technical consultants, legal advice, communication advisors, and possible interaction with governmental agencies for pre-approval granting); *grid construction* (tendering for construction and procurement of material, interactions, monitoring and coordination of contractors or own staff performing ground preparation, disassembly of potential incumbent installations, and recovery of land and material); *grid maintenance* (preventive and reactive service of assets, the staffing of facilities, and the incremental replacement of degraded or faulty equipment); *administration* (administrative support and associated costs, including the non-activated salaries, goods and services paid for, central and decentralized administration of human resources, finance, legal services, public relations, communication, organizational development, strategy, auditing, IT, and general management); and *grid financing* (long-term financing of the assets through equity and debt).

Thus, a reliable cost-efficiency model for regulatory use must limit its scope to the "wire-company" functions: construction, maintenance, and administration, correcting for local factor prices and capital costs when comparing individual performance (see Agrell and Bogetoft 2014).

16.5.2. Variable Specification

Data are collected for all TSOs i for all assets by asset type j and investment year t, A_{ijt}. For each asset type, relative real investment prices w_j are obtained from an engineering team. To avoid distortions due to accounting depreciation patterns, all investments are transformed to real annuities using standardized asset life times by type of assets, T_j years. Since investment data are aggregated by year, a weighted investment life time $\tilde{T}_{it}$ is calculated for each TSO i and year t.

$$\tilde{T}_{it} = \sum_j \left\{ \frac{T_j w_j \left(A_{ijt} - A_{ij,t-1} \right)}{\sum_j w_j \left(A_{ijt} - A_{ij,t-1} \right)} \right\} \tag{16.10}$$

where A_{ijt} is the number of assets of type j in TSO i in year t, and w_j is the weight or relative price of asset type j.

The annuity factor α transforms lumpy investment patterns into smooth capital expenditure in real terms.

$$\alpha_{it} = r \left(1 - \left(1 + r \right)^{-\tilde{T}_{it}} \right)^{-1} \tag{16.11}$$

where r is the interest rate.

The operating expenditure (opex) for each TSO i in year t is calculated as the sum of nonstaff costs V_{it}^{N} and labor-cost-adjusted staff costs V_{it}^{S}, all in real terms and in EUR.

$$VC_{it} = \left(V_{it}^{N} + V_{it}^{S} L_{it} \right) PI_{it} \xi_{it} \qquad (16.12)$$

where PI_{it} is the inflation adjustment for the country of TSO i from year t to the reference year, and ξ_{it} is the exchange rate factor from the currency of TSO i to EUR in the reference year.

The capital expenditure (capex) is defined as the sum of real investment annuities,

$$FC_{it} = \xi it \sum_{k=1}^{t} I_{ik} PI_{ik} \alpha_{ik}, \qquad (16.13)$$

where I_{ik} is the gross investment of TSO i in year k in local currency, PI_{ik} is the inflation adjustment for the country of TSO i from year k to the reference year, and ξ_{it} is the exchange rate factor from the currency of TSO i to EUR in the reference year. The input variable is total expenditure (TOTEX) for each TSO i at year t, here simply defined as the sum of OPEX and CAPEX, that is,

$$TOTEX_{it} = VC_{it} + FC_{it}. \qquad (16.14)$$

The main output variable is a proxy for the grid provision task, the normalized grid NG[15]. In Frontier Economics, Sumicsid, and Consentec (2013), power-system engineers estimated a system of 2,169 relative weights for opex v and capex w spanning over assets organized in nine groups (lines, cables, transformers, etc.) and four categories (voltage, power, cross-section, short-circuit current). The operating cost depends not only on the assets younger than the standard techno-economic life time, but also on all assets that are in use in year k of type j for TSO i, here denoted a_{ijk}. The relative real operating cost for assets of type j is denoted v_{j}. The grid output in terms of opex NGV is then defined from a weighted set of assets in use, where R_{v} can be used as a scaling constant to transform the relative units of the grid measure to, for instance, current average prices in a common currency.

$$NGV_{it} = R_{v} \sum_{j} v_{j} a_{ijk} \qquad (16.15)$$

The normalized grid capex NGF is defined as a weighted sum of capex-active (younger than T_{j}) assets using real annuities, possibly calibrated using a constant R_{f} to obtain a unit value comparable to, for example, average capex.

$$NGF_{it} = R_{f} \sum_{k=1}^{t} \sum_{j} w_{j} A_{ijk} \alpha_{ik} \qquad (16.16)$$

Note that $a_{ijk} \geq A_{ijk}$ for all i, j, k. Finally, the normalized grid totex is the sum of opex and capex, analogously to the costs.

$$NG_{it} = NGF_{it} + NGV_{it} \qquad (16.17)$$

In principle, NG is denominated in the base unit for the relative weights (here 1 circuit-km of double circuit 300kV overhead lines), but using the constants R_v and R_f the average costs of the reference unit can be used to obtain, for example, EUR as the unit of measurement.

16.5.3. Model Specification

The conventional consumer price index (CPI) was chosen as inflation adjustor due to data availability, but alternative inflators were tested. The final model specification is presented in Table 16.2 from Agrell and Bogetoft (2014). A large set of environmental parameters was collected, from which were retained *DenseArea* as the total area (in km²) of highest population density in EUROSTAT as a proxy for density-induced operating-cost increase, and *AngleLineSum*, the totex-weighted line length of angular towers, as a proxy for the extra costs induced by routing complexity (infrastructure, topology, urban sprawl).

After extensive model specification tests using various cost function approaches, a final cost function in log-linear functional form was found and documented in Table 16.3. As seen, the coefficients with expected signs are strongly significant both in normal OLS and in robust OLS. The model has a high explanatory value, is not subject to heteroscedasticity (*p*-value for Breusch-Pagan test 0.097) and the multicollinearity is low (maximum variance influence factor, VIF 8.3 ≤ 10).

As the sum of the coefficients in the loglin cost function is less than unity, the cost function exhibits nondecreasing returns to scale, which is used in the DEA model below.

Table 16.2 Model Parameters, Final Model Electricity TSO (2012)

Variable	Definition	units
Input		
TOTEX	Total expenditure (standardized)	EUR
Outputs		
NG	Normalized grid size	ref.units
DenseArea	Service area with population density above 100 pers/km²	km²
AngleLineSum	Totex-weighted line length of angular towers	km

LV = low voltage; MV = medium voltage; HV = high voltage.

Table 16.3 Results for TOTEX Cost Model (2012), OLS and Robust OLS

	OLS	Robust OLS
$\log(_{NG})$	0.554***	0.475***
	(0.096)	(0.052)
$\log(^D_{enseAre}{}^a)$	0.117***	0.137***
	(0.011)	(0.009)
$\log(^A_{ngleLineSu}{}^m)$	0.217***	0.284***
	(0.083)	(0.040)
Constant	9.233***	9.477***
	(0.516)	(0.338)

Observations 102

Adjusted R^2 0.912

Residual Std. Error 0.351 ($df = 98$)

F Statistic 349.668*** ($df = 3; 98$)

$^*p < 0.1; ^{**}p < 0.05; ^{***}p < 0.01.$

Source: Agrell and P. Bogetoft (2009).

16.5.4. Weight Restrictions in DEA

As seen from the parametric results, the main cost driver is the normalized grid, complemented by the two environmental proxies. To avoid nonsensical nonparametric results in DEA, a restriction for the dual weight is defined as cones around the preceding coefficients, equivalent to confidence intervals around the estimation. This procedure assures that the marginal costs are comparable to those of the average firm.

16.5.5. Capex Break

One of the primary obstacles for international benchmarking, mentioned already by Jamash and Pollitt (2000), is the issue of heterogeneity in capital formation and valuation. In addition to the previously mentioned data harmonization techniques, the *capex break* method was invented in Agrell and Bogetoft (2014) to address the problem of heterogeneous initial asset values. The idea behind the method is that an opening balance, representing a large part of the controllable benchmarked cost, may reflect exogenous conditions (political, social, or economic considerations at the time of unbundling) beyond the realm of the TSO management. Assume that a TSO i has an opening balance determined exogenously in period G, where $1 \ll G < t$ (short investment stream). The only available evidence of the ratio of capex to normalized grid capex is for the period following the opening balance, that is, $G+1,\ldots,t$. Capex break then uses this observed ratio η as a replacement of the actual capex resulting from the opening balance.

$$\eta_i = \frac{FC_{it} + FC_{iG}}{NGF_{it} + NGF_{iG}} \quad (16.18)$$

The capex-break total expenditure, TC_{it}^b in the following, replaces the original totex TC_{it} only if two conditions apply: (i) TSO i is a peer to at least one other TSO in the reference set, and (ii) TSO i has a short investment stream $G \gg 1$.

$$TC_{it}^b = \eta_i NGF_{iG} - FC_{iG} + TC_{it} \quad (16.19)$$

16.5.6. Static Results

Some static results for 2011 for 21 participating TSOs[16] are given in Table 16.4. The primary DEA model is defined for nondecreasing returns to scale (NDRS), using 50% weight restrictions (wr = 100), excluding outliers and applying capex break for efficient peers with incomplete investment streams. The average (cost) efficiency E is 86% for 2011, the minimum is 59%, and eight TSOs are considered fully cost efficient, four of which are identified as outliers by the procedures for dominance and superefficiency discussed in Agrell and Niknazar (2014). Two TSO were subject to the capex-break procedure, since they initially appear as peers with an incomplete investment stream. Both TSO are considered as cost efficient, but their position relative to the reference set is adjusted to take into account the post-opening investment ratio. The scale efficiency (SE) is low (86%) prior to the removal of outliers, when it increases to 97%. Indeed, without any other corrections for weight restrictions and outliers, under constant returns to scale, the average efficiency is only 78%, suggesting that the large range of size variation in the sample[17] comes at a cost in terms of efficiency. Sensitivity analysis

Table 16.4 Static Results (2011), $n = 21$

Metric	Mean	St. Dev.	Pctl(25)	Pctl(75)	# $E = 1$	# Outliers
$E(crs)$	0.78	0.152	0.656	0.949	3	n.a.
$E(ndrs)$	0.91	0.112	0.837	1.00	10	n.a.
$E(ndrs, wr = 100, ex.out)$	0.88	0.099	0.822	0.948	8	4
$E(ndrs, wr = 50, ex.out)$	0.86	0.103	0.805	0.941	8	4
$E(ndrs, wr = 0, ex.out)$	0.85	0.105	0.787	0.933	7	4
SE	0.86	0.116	0.767	0.956	3	n.a.
$SE(ex.out)$	0.97	0.038	0.945	1.000	9	4

was also made with 100% weight restriction ($wr = 100$), meaning that the relative prices from the preceding OLS run were doubled in the constraints.

16.6. Application: Norwegian Network Regulation

The Norwegian electricity network operators (transmission, regional transmission, and distribution) are unbundled from generation and retail since 1991. Until 1996 the DSOs were regulated using a rate of return regulation, from 1997–2006 a DEA-based revenue cap was used, and since 2007, a DEA-based yardstick model has been in use (cf. Agrell and Bogetoft 2010).

16.6.1. DEA-Based Yardstick Regulation

In 2007 the Norwegian regulator for electricity DSOs, the Norwegian Water Resources and Energy Directorate (NVE), moved from an ex ante revenue cap regulation to a DEA-based yardstick competition regime as in (16.8) with $\rho = 0.6$.

More specifically, the Norwegian revenue cap is determined as

$$B_t^k = 0.4 x_t^k + 0.6 C_{t-2}^{DEA}\left(y_{t-2}^k\right) + IA_t^k \qquad (16.20)$$

where B_t^k is the revenue cap for operator k in year t, $C_{t-2}^{DEA}\left(y_{t-2}^k\right)$ is the DEA-based cost norm based on data from year $t - 2$, and IA_t^k is the investment addition to take into account the new investments in year t. The actual costs (single input) x_t^k are calculated as

$$x_t^k = \left(VC_{t-2}^k + QC_t^k\right)\frac{CPI_t}{CPI_{t-2}} + pNL_t^k + DE_{t-2}^k + rI_{t-2}^k \qquad (16.21)$$

where QC is quality compensation by firm k to consumers as a consequence of lost load, CPI is the consumer price index, NL is the network losses in MWh, p is the price of lost energy, DE_{t-2}^k is annual depreciation in year $t - 2$, I_{t-2}^k is the capital basis for k in year $t - 2$, and r is the interest rate on capital set by the regulator.

The cost function C^{DEA} is calculated in two steps. The main calculation is a DEA CRS model with eight cost drivers covering lines, net stations, delivered energy, numbers of ordinary and vacation users, forests, snow, and coastal climate conditions. The second stage is a regression-based correction based on environmental conditions, decentralized power generation, and number of coastal islands in the concession area.

NVE has internationally been a pioneer in the design of model-based regulation of electricity DSOs. The implementation of a yardstick-based regime can be seen as a natural next step in the attempt to mimic a competitive situation in a natural monopoly industry. Still, the transition from a well-established revenue cap system required careful planning. One challenge was to convince the industry that a yardstick regime is less risky than an ex ante revenue cap system. The latter enables the companies to predict the future allowed income several years in advance. At first this may seem to be a convincing advantage, but since the reassurance does not include the cost side (except for the use of a more or less arbitrary inflation adjustment), it actually does not protect the operator's profit, which should be the main concern for the owners. The yardstick regime offers more protection to sector-wide cost shocks since technological progress and costs are estimated directly using the newest possible data. Another challenge was to calibrate the transition to avoid dramatic changes for individual firms moving from one regulatory regime to another.

16.6.2. Structural Efficiency

The structural properties of the energy industry (firm scale, scope, ownership) may be more important than the details of the regulatory reimbursement schemes. At the same time, the incumbent regulatory regime may have an impact on the structural adjustment, both directly if the regulators refuse to approve structural changes, and indirectly if the payment plans make socially attractive changes unprofitable for the individual firms.

A good example of these problems is the question of how to treat mergers. The issue is far from hypothetical, as the European energy sector has gone through a significant merger wave since 2005. The regulatory regime is not neutral to mergers. When payments are correlated with cost efficiency, the payment plans will tend to discourage mergers in convex models, though they might lead to more outputs being produced with fewer inputs. NVE handles this by calculating the mix or harmony effect in the DEA merger model first proposed in Bogetoft and Wang (2005), and by compensating a merged firm for the extra requirements corresponding to this effect.

At the same time, mergers will tend to affect the performance evaluation basis and may lead to more rents to the firms because the cost norm becomes less demanding by leaving fewer observations in the data set. The regulator, who considers allowing a merger, must therefore trade off the gains from improved costs to the firms with the losses from a shrinking information basis. The latter is the regulatory equivalent of the negative market effects in a merger case in a nonregulated sector.

16.6.3. Merger Analysis

In the rest of this section, we will show how the structural development in Norway has led to efficiency gains. To do this, we rely on data from the DSOs from 1995 to 2004. We will show also how ex ante evaluation of potential gains relate to the realized gains ex post. This serves to validate the merger analysis approach from Bogetoft and Wang (2005).

To do so, we recall the framework introduced in subsection 16.3.1 with the difference that the input variable x^k is now a vector of physical quantities rather than, as before, an aggregate cost scalar. Further, we assume that among the previous K operators there are M operators (horizontally) merging into a single unit. Naturally, the regulator as well as the firm will need to anticipate the effects of this merger with respect to *learning* (technical efficiency), *harmony* (scope or mix), and *size* (scale). As we will see, the decomposition in Bogetoft and Wang (2005) enables both an ex ante and an ex post evaluation of the effects.

A measure of the potential *overall gains* from the merger is now

$$E^M = \min\left\{\theta\sum_{k\in M} x^k \,\middle|\, \sum_{k\in M} x^k \geq \sum_j \lambda^j x^j, \sum_{k\in M} y^k \leq \sum_j \lambda^j y^j, \quad \lambda\in\Lambda\right\} \tag{16.22}$$

We see that E^M is the input-based technical efficiency score of the merged unit in the technology T. If $E^M < 1$, the merger produces savings, for instance through scale or scope advantages. On the other hand, if $E^M > 1$, the merger is socially costly (e.g., due to scale disadvantages).

The score E^M does not take into account the catch-up of technical inefficiency by potentially technically inefficient units in the merger. To adjust the overall merger gains for the learning effect, we can project the original firms to the production possibility frontier and use the projected plans as the basis for evaluating the remaining potential gains from the merger. Thus, we project (x^k, y^k) onto $(E^k x^k, y^k)$ for all $k \in M$, where E^k is the standard input efficiency score for the kth firm, and use these to calculate the *adjusted overall gains* E^{*M} from the merger:

$$E^{*M} = \min\left\{\theta\sum_{k\in M} E^k x^k \,\middle|\, \sum_j \lambda^j x^j, \sum_{k\in M} y^k \leq \sum_j \lambda^j y^j, \quad \lambda\in\Lambda\right\} \tag{16.23}$$

Expression (16.23) has two effects. First, the mix changes since it combines the output mixes of the merged firms. In addition, the scale changes since the merged firm is the sum of the original firms.

If we set

$$L^M = \frac{E^M}{E^{*M}}, \tag{16.24}$$

we get $E^M = L^M \cdot E^{*M}$, where the *learning effect* $L^M \in [0,1]$ indicates what can be saved by individual technical-efficiency adjustments for the different firms in M.

The *harmony gains* H^M are derived from the potential average input reduction in the production of the average output:

$$H^M = \min\left\{\delta\frac{\sum_{k\in M} E^k x^k}{|M|} \,\middle|\, \geq \sum_j \lambda^j x^j, \frac{\sum_{k\in M} y^k}{|M|} \leq \sum_j \lambda^j y^j, \quad \lambda\in\Lambda\right\} \tag{16.25}$$

The use of averaging controls for scale effects. Thus, H^M is driven by the change in mix for the average scale of the original merging firms. However, it assumes that the firms in M are not too different in initial scale. If the scale differs considerably within M, the interpretation may be ambiguous.

The *size effects* S^M are captured by asking how much could have been saved by operating at full rather than average scale:

$$S^M = \min_{\xi} \left\{ \xi H^M \sum_{k \in M} E^k x^k \geq \sum_j \lambda^j x^j, \sum_{k \in M} y^k \leq \sum_j \lambda^j y^j, \quad \lambda \in \Lambda \right\}. \qquad (16.26)$$

The rescaling is advantageous, $S^M < 1$, if we have economies of scale, and costly, $S^M > 1$, if there are diseconomies of scale (e.g., congestion and information costs).

Using the preceding notions of learning L, harmony H, and size S effects, we get the *basic merger decomposition*

$$E^M = L^M \cdot H^M \cdot S^M = L^M E^{*M}. \qquad (16.27)$$

The learning or technical efficiency measure L^M captures what can be gained by making the individual firms efficient. The remaining potential savings, E^{*M}, are created by the harmony or scope effect H^M and the size or scale effect S^M.

We note that the merger analysis requires only an estimate of the technology T. It is therefore not restricted to DEA-based analysis, although most applications have indeed used DEA. We note also that the preceding merger analysis is purely technical and therefore works without access to any prices on the input or output side. Needless to say, in many applications, there will only be a single input, costs, and all the technical efficiency measures behind the learning, harmony, and size measures will then be cost-efficiency measures.

The analysis in the rest of this section is based on the work in Agrell, Bogetoft, and Grammeltvedt (2015). The model in Table 16.5 from Agrell and Bogetoft (2004) corresponds to the one used by NVE during the period (Førsund and Kittelsen 1998)

16.6.4. Data

Our data are an unbalanced panel of Norwegian electricity DSO covering the years 1995–2004; see Table 16.6 for summary statistics. In total, 42 mergers among 86 firms occurred in 1995–2004, bringing the number of operators from 198 in 1995 to 130 in 2004. The data are the actual submitted reports from the DSOs to NVE, audited in several steps and used for economic regulation. The relatively low average size[18] indicates that the sample contains a majority of small companies. In terms of the structural development, the average firm size increases over time, while the median is decreasing. This indicates that the restructuring process has led to a few relatively large companies while the majority of the companies in the sample remain very small.

Table 16.5 Model Parameters, NVE Model DSO

Variable	Definition	Units (kNOK = 1,000 Norwegian crowns)
Inputs		
LABEX	Labor cost	kNOK
CAPEX	Cost of capital and depreciation	kNOK
LOSEX	Cost of energy losses	kNOK
SERVEX	Cost of goods and services	kNOK
Outputs		
CUSTOMERS	Number of customers	#
ENERGY	Energy delivered	MWh
LINES LV	Low voltage overhead lines	Km
LINES HV	High voltage overhead lines	Km

Table 16.6 Averages (1995–2004) for All Non–Merged and Merged DSOs

	All DSOs	Non-Merged DSOs	Merged DSOs
Year	1995–2004	2004	2004
n	198	112	18
LABEX	38	25	120
SERVEX	17,483	12,077	102,594
LOSEX	23,450	17,600	121,684
CAPEX	151,027	94,722	732,929
CUSTOMERS	14,555	9,241	79,382
ENERGY	396	253	2,268
LINES HV	1,074	787	5,094
LINES LV	526	449	2,015

16.6.5. Motivations and Objectives

As pointed out in section 16.1, there are two main reasons why companies merge: strategic reasons related to the possibility of gaining market power, and production economic reasons related to learning, harmony, and scale effects. For regulated monopolies, such as the Norwegian DSOs, the strategic aspects of mergers are connected to the possibility of playing the regulation, either by exploiting the way the regulated income or prices are set, or by expanding into other, usually unregulated, activities. The production economic reasons for merging are connected to the possibility of realizing higher short-, or long-run returns by exploiting the scale and scope properties in the industry. Horizontal expansions or mergers with other types of companies in some cases also can be motivated by the possibility of realizing other synergies, for instance between different types of network transportation systems like water, natural gas, and so on.

16.6.6. Ex Ante Gains

We decompose the potential effects of the actual 42 mergers ex ante into the technical efficiency or learning (L) effect (i.e., what the companies might gain from adjusting to best practice at an individual level), the scope (H) effect (i.e., what can be gained from a more efficient output and input mix), and the scale (S) effect (i.e., what can be gained from improved scale economies). Specifically, we evaluate a given merger in the technology as it looked the last year before the merger.

In Table 16.7 we see that the mergers indeed offer positive effects, on average (100 − 84.53)% = 15.47% for total expenditure (TOTEX). In more detail, the overall effect is primarily driven by learning effects (technical efficiency gains) amounting to 13.15% of the realized potential. A subvector model projecting the savings in the direction of LABEX and SERVEX (operating expenditure, OPEX) in Table 16.7 confirms this conclusion; the potential savings are even higher for this part of the costs (24.32%), where learning effects (L) correspond to 20.67%. The scope effects are relatively weak, 2.84% for TOTEX and 4.51% for OPEX. Compared to previous studies of gains from mergers (and reallocations) in other industries, these scope effects are relatively small (cf. Bogetoft and Wang 2005). One possible explanation may be that the electricity distribution technology is quite linear (i.e., that the isoquants do not have much curvature) (Agrell and Bogetoft 2004). Interestingly, the scale effects are on average negligible, −0.17% for TOTEX and 0.10% for OPEX. Facing a relatively linear technology, at least for operators

Table 16.7 Merger Gains ex ante, All Mergers (1995–2004), $n = 42$

Metric [%]	TOTEX	OPEX
E	84.53	75.68
E^*	97.36	95.52
L	86.85	79.33
H	97.16	95.49
S	100.17	99.90

with over 6,000 customers (Agrell and Bogetoft 2004), this may likely be a bias effect of the DEA estimates for the fewer and larger units.

This suggests that a priori the operators may identify opportunities for opportunistic actions, that is, initiating mergers that are attractive, not for cost-saving reasons, but for revenue-increasing purposes. Another important strategic motive behind mergers may be the possibility of gaining a larger share of the electricity retail market, either through associated firms or as default supplier. For most companies this is important, as the dominating or default supplier on average supplies more than 75% of all customers in an area. By including information about the ownership structure and operations of the merging firms, we find that 32 of the 42 mergers during the period (77%) indeed involved at least one firm associated with retail or both generation and retail. Anecdotal evidence shows that the value of information from final clients, opportunities to influence the type of metering devices selected, and the human resource aspects were intangible values taken into account by the retailer-generators while considering mergers of the distribution business.

16.6.7. Ex Post Gains

The profile of the merging firms is clear from Table 16.8. The merged companies deliver about 60% of the energy to about 60% of the customers using less than 50% of the line length, especially the high voltage lines. This suggests that the mergers are happening in the more densely populated regions of the country, which is also confirmed by detailed data reviews. Given that the mergers occur between adjacent[19] concession areas, this also supports the hypothesis that the economies of density may explain the realized

Table 16.8 Shares of Inputs and Outputs (1995 and 2004) for Merging DSOs

	Pre-merger	Post-merger	Difference
Year	1995	2004	1995–2004
n	86	18	
LABEX	53.0%	42.3%	−10.7%
SERVEX	50.3%	55.4%	5.2%
LOSEX	56.0%	59.1%	3.1%
CAPEX	58.0%	57.7%	−0.3%
CUSTOMERS	60.4%	60.3%	−0.1%
ENERGY	61.1%	61.4%	0.3%
LINES LV	53.1%	52.8%	−0.3%
LINES HV	43.8%	44.7%	0.9%

gains in operating cost. However, the most striking effect is, of course, that the merging firms reduce their share of the sector labor cost from 53% to 42% at virtually constant output level. The merging firms increase the outsourcing of services (up 5.2%), but the overall cost impact is positive (i.e., costs fall). The ex ante estimation of the overall efficiency of the mergers was 83.1% (pooled); the actual outcome is 88.4% (pooled).

16.7. SUMMARY

State-of-the-art benchmarking methods, and in particular DEA and SFA, have become well-established and informative tools for economic regulation. DEA and to some extent also SFA are now routinely used by European regulators to set reasonable revenue caps for energy transmission and distribution system operators. In this chapter, we have shared three types of insights on the theme of regulatory benchmarking.

First, we have outlined some of the particular objectives, constraints, and opportunities that frontier analysis faces in regulatory applications. The importance of endogenous parameterization, rigorous documentation, and cautiousness in the interpretation of results deserve to be mentioned in this regard.

Second, we have summarized the modern agency theory foundations for frontier-based regulation, leading to convenient yardstick-regulation formulations for both static (incumbent inefficiency) and dynamic (productivity gains) regulation regimes.

Third, we have shown three real applications of regulatory benchmarking on electricity networks, demonstrating different aspects of the theory and the techniques described. In Germany from 2007, the application to a large data set under particular economic and political pressure from the operators led to enhancements of the procedural robustness analysis, deploying systematic outlier detection and improving the traceability and replicability of the model development in general. In the international transmission system benchmarkings (2005, 2009, 2012), the challenge was focused on variable aggregation and data harmonization of a rich data set for few operators. This inspired the development of the correction method for opening balances and the systematic approach to functional activity analysis, as well as the endogenous weight restriction model. The fact that the model has withstood judicial recourse in the Netherlands shows that international regulatory benchmarking is both feasible and useful in actual practice. Finally, the Norwegian application showcases a jurisdiction that always has been on the forefront in frontier-based regulation. In 2007 Norway adopted a yardstick regime of the type developed in theory section of this chapter, with DEA as the key method. However, our analysis focuses on an original feature in the regulation where DEA is used not only to estimate ex post cost efficiency by operator, but moreover to ex ante estimate the gains from changes in industrial structure through horizontal mergers. Our results here show that indeed their estimates are relatively accurate and fair, in addition to bringing part of the gains to the consumers.

A fascinating area for future research, regulatory benchmarking still offers many technical problems awaiting more rigorous analysis. Some immediate issues concern the integration of frontier results in regulatory mechanisms that are periodic in nature, for instance the expected catch-up period for identified inefficiencies in operating and capital expenditure. Another issue concerns the incentive power itself, attached to a model residual and to actual cost, and potentially dependent on the fit to the actual data and the uncertainty. Finally, the current practice of hybrid methods combining DEA and SFA deserve more analysis beyond the pragmatic judicial viewpoint. Able and driven researchers devoting their energy to regulatory models may be awarded by unprecedented access to high-quality data and the opportunity to test advanced techniques, as well as the well-being procured by servicing society at large through the mitigation of market failures in the interests of consumers and firms alike.

Notes

1. In particular, data envelopment analysis, DEA (Charnes, Cooper, and Rhodes 1978).
2. Cf. the review of the proprietary codes OnFront, DEAP, and others in Barr (2004), the open-source R package Benchmarking in Bogetoft and Otto (2010), and spreadsheet solutions in, e.g., Zhu (2014).
3. See section 16.3 and the seminal works Agrell, Bogetoft, and Tind (2002) and Bogetoft (1994a, 1994b, 1995, 1997, 2000).
4. A classical revenue cap is defined in real terms, i.e., inflation (measured by consumer price index CPI or the retail price index RPI), is passed through to the consumers, and involves an imposed individual and/or collective efficiency improvement term X. The individual requirements are typically based on an analysis of a firm's cost efficiency, while the collective requirement is a measure of the industry-wide productively development. Given an opening revenue R_0, the formula for the revenue in a successive year becomes $R_1 = R_0 (CPI_1 - X)$. In addition, real implementations also contain volume and quality adjustment factors (cf. Agrell, Bogetoft, and Tind 2005).
5. Productivity analysis is used in Agrell and Grifell-Tatjé (2016) to show the risk of flawed models, illustrated by the failing engineering cost model in Sweden.
6. For seminal papers on stochastic frontier analysis (SFA), cf. e.g., Aigner, Lovell, and Schmidt (1977); and Battese and Coelli (1992).
7. Economic Efficiency analysis of Electricity GRIDs (e^3GRID), Agrell and Bogetoft (2009).
8. E.g., capacity investment and maintenance costs may be correlated to climatic conditions. Using annual realizations of climatic events in a model is equivalent to transforming it to a stochastic model. However, the causality with investments is not driven by annual realizations, but the expected climatic conditions, which can be used in a deterministic model.
9. E.g., distribution of electricity at high- and low-voltage levels are two different services. If only one variable is used, operators with relatively higher/lower incidence of high-voltage to low-voltage delivery will be penalized/rewarded.
10. In 2010–2011, Bundesnetzagentur in Germany faced over 180 written questions on the model development and specifications, including detailed requests to document the exact criteria and stage in the process leading to the choice among potentially multi-collinear

parameters, the normalization parameter for the heteroskedasticity control, intermediate results for linearity, etc.

11. We abstract from intentional illegal reporting, fraud, and forgery, punishable by law.
12. We use the name cost function even if we do not have input prices. The cost function in this case is simply a mapping from outputs to costs in, e.g., USD.
13. See Agrell and Bogetoft (2009).
14. See Sumicsid ,Frontier Economics, and Consentec (2013).
15. The use of asset variables as proxy for grid provision was suggested already in Neuberg (1977) and was used by Kumbhakar and Hjalmarsson (1998) for electricity distribution.
16. Two TSOs were excluded from the participation by delivering inconsistent (1 TSO) or no data (1 TSO) for analysis.
17. The ratio of NG_{2011} between the largest and smallest TSO is 156!
18. The median number of customers is even smaller: less than 6,000 customers per DSO.
19. One exception is found.
20. Under reforms (2013) delegating the DSO regulation to three regional regulators from 2015.
21. Under reform (2012).

References

Agrell, P. J., and P. Bogetoft. 2000. *Ekonomisk nätbesiktning. Final report STEM.* Technical report, Sumicsid, Eskilstuna, Sweden. In Swedish.

Agrell, P. J., and P. Bogetoft. 2001. "Should Health Regulators Use DEA?" In *Coordinacion e Incentivos en Sanidad*, edited by E. G. Fidalgo, et al., 133–154. Asociasion de Economia de la Salud. Barcelona, Spain.

Agrell, P. J., and P. Bogetoft. 2004. "NVE Network Cost Efficiency Model." Technical report, Norwegian Energy Directorate NVE.

Agrell, P J., and P. Bogetoft. 2009. "International Benchmarking of Electricity Transmission System Operators: e3gridpProject." Final report. Commissioned by the Council of European Energy Regulators (CEER), SUMICSID.

Agrell, P. J., and P. Bogetoft. 2010. "Harmonizing the Nordic Regulation of Electricity Distribution." In *Energy, Natural Resources and Environmental Economics*, edited by M. Bjorndal, E. Bjorndal, and M. Ronneqvist, 293–316. Berlin: Springer.

Agrell, P. J., and P. Bogetoft. 2014. "International Benchmarking of Electricity Transmission System Operators." In *European Energy Market (EEM), 2014 11th International Conference on the European Energy Market* , 1–5. IEEE.

Agrell, P. J., P. Bogetoft, and T. E. Grammeltvedt. "The Efficiency of the Regulation for Horizontal Mergers among Electricity Distribution Operators in Norway." In *European Energy Market (EEM), 2015 12th International Conference on the European Energy Market*, 1–5. IEEE.

Agrell, P. J., P. Bogetoft, and J. Tind. 2002. "Incentive Plans for Productive Efficiency, Innovation and Learning." *International Journal of Production Economics* 78: 1–11.

Agrell, P. J., P. Bogetoft, and J. Tind. 2005. "DEA and Dynamic Yardstick Competition in Scandinavian Electricity Distribution." *Journal of Productivity Analysis* 23: 173–201.

Agrell, P. J., P. Bogetoft, and U. Trinkner. 2016. "Benchmarking European Gas Transmission System Operators: Project e2gas." Final report commissioned by CEER, Sumicsid Group and Swiss Economics.

Agrell, P. J. and E. Grifell-Tatjé. 2016. "A Dynamic Model for Firm-Response to Non-Credible Incentive Regulation Regimes." *Energy Policy* 90: 287–299.

Agrell, P. J., and P. Niknazar. 2014. "Structural and Behavioral Robustness in Applied Best-Practice Regulation." *Socio-Economic Planning Sciences* 48(1): 89–103.

Agrell, P J., and J. Tind. 2001. "A Dual Approach to Non-Convex Frontier Models." *Journal of Productivity Analysis* 16: 129–147.

Aigner, D. J., C. A. K. Lovell, and P. Schmidt. 1977. "Formulation and Estimation of Stochastic Frontier Production Function Models." *Journal of Econometrics*, 6: 21–37.

Asmild, M., P. Bogetoft, and J. L. Hougaard. 2009. "Rationalising DEA Estimated Inefficiencies." *Journal of Business Economics* 4: 81–86.

Asmild, M., P. Bogetoft, and J. L. Hougaard. 2013. "Rationalizing Inefficiency: Staff Utilization in Branches of a Large Canadian Bank." *Omega* 41: 80–87.

Banker, R. D. 1980. "A Game Theoretic Approach to Measuring Efficiency." *European Journal of Operational Research* 5: 262–268.

Banker, R. D., A. Charnes, W. W. Cooper, and R. Clarke. 1989. "Constrained Game Formulations and Interpretations for Data Envelopment Analysis." *European Journal of Operational Research* 40: 299–308.

Barr, R. S. 2004. DEA Software Tools and Technology, Chapter 18, 539–566. In W. Cooper, L. Seiford, and J. Zhu (Eds.), *Handbook on Data Envelopment Analysis*. Berlin: Springer.

Battese, G. E., and T. J. Coelli. 1992. "Frontier Production Functions, Technical Efficiency and Panel Data: With Application to Paddy Farmers in India." *Journal of Productivity Analysis* 3: 153–169.

Beesley, M. E. 1997. *Privatization, Regulation and Deregulation*, 2nd edition. London: Routledge.

Beesley, M. E., and S. C. Littlechild. 1983. "Privatisation: Principles, Problems and Priorities." *Lloyds Bank Review* 149: 1–20.

Blázquez-Gómez, L., and E. Grifell-Tatjé. 2011. "Evaluating the Regulator: Winners and Losers in the Regulation of Spanish Electricity Distribution." *Energy Economics* 33(5): 807–815.

Bogetoft, P. 1994a. "Incentive Efficient Production Frontiers: An Agency Perspective on DEA." *Management Science* 40: 959–968.

Bogetoft, P. 1994b. *Non-Cooperative Planning Theory*. Berlin: Springer-Verlag.

Bogetoft, P. 1995. "Incentives and Productivity Measurements." *International Journal of Production Economics* 39: 67–81.

Bogetoft, P. 1997. "DEA-Based Yardstick Competition: The Optimality of Best Practice Regulation." *Annals of Operations Research* 73: 277–298.

Bogetoft, P. 2000. "DEA and Activity Planning under Asymmetric Information." *Journal of Productivity Analysis* 13: 7–48.

Bogetoft, P. 2012. *Performance Benchmarking: Measuring and Managing Performance*. New York: Springer.

Bogetoft, P., and J. Andersen. 2009. "Rational Inefficiency in Fishery." *Journal of Business Economics* 4: 63–79.

Bogetoft, P., R. Fare, and S. Grosskopf. 2009. "Rationalizing (In)Efficiency Through Price Coordination. *Journal of Business Economics* 4: 81–86.

Bogetoft, P., and J. L. Hougaard. 2003. "Rational Inefficiencies." *Journal of Productivity Analysis* 20: 243–271.

Bogetoft, P., and K. Nielsen. 2008. "DEA Based Auctions." *European Journal of Operational Research* 184: 685–700.

Bogetoft, P., and L. Otto. 2011. *Benchmarking with DEA, SFA, and R*. New York: Springer.

Bogetoft, P., and L. Otto. 2010. "Benchmark Package." Technical report.

Bogetoft, P., and D. Wang. 2005. "Estimating the Potential Gains from Mergers." *Journal of Productivity Analysis* 23: 145–171.

Bowlin, W. F. 1997. "A Proposal for Designing Employment Contracts for Government Managers." *Socio-Economic Planning Sciences* 31: 205–216.

Charnes, A., W. W. Cooper, and E. Rhodes. 1978. "Measuring the Efficiency of Decision Making Units." *European Journal of Operational Research* 2: 429–444.

Dalen, D. M. 1996. "Strategic Responses to Relative Evaluation of Bureaus: Implication for Bureaucratic Slack." *Journal of Productivity Analysis* 7: 29–39.

Dalen, D. M., and A. Gomez-Lobo. 1997. "Estimating Cost Functions in Regulated Industries under Asymmetric Information." *European Economic Review* 31: 935–942.

Dalen, D. M., and A. Gomez-Lobo. 2001. "Yardstick on the Road: Regulatory Contracts and Cost Efficiency in the Norwegian Bus Industry." Technical report, Norwegian School of Management.

Edvardsen, D. F., and F. R. Førsund. 2003. "International Benchmarking of Electricity Distribution Utilities." *Resource and Energy Economics* 25(4): 353–371.

Førsund, F. R., and S.A.C. Kittelsen. 1998. "Productivity Development of Norwegian Electricity Distribution Utilities." *Resource and Energy Economics* 20: 207–224.

Frontier Economics, Sumicsid, and Consentec. 2013. "E3grid 2012: European TSO Benchmarking Study." Final report commissioned by the Council of the European Energy Regulators (CEER), Frontier Economics and Sumicsid and Consentec.

Haney, A. B., and M. G. Pollitt. 2009. "Efficiency Analysis of Energy Networks: An International Survey of Regulators." *Energy Policy* 37(12): 5814–5830.

Hjalmarsson, L., and A. Veiderpass. 1992. "Efficiency and Ownership in Swedish Electricity Retail Distribution." *Journal of Productivity Analysis* 3(1): 7–23.

Jamash, T., and M. Pollitt. 2000. "Benchmarking and Regulation: International Electricity Experience." *Utilities Policy* 9(3): 107–130.

Kittelsen, S. 1993. "Stepwise DEA: Choosing Variables for Measuring Technical Efficiency In Norwegian Electricity Distribution." Memorandum 6: 93, Oslo University.

Kumbhakar, S. C., and L. Hjalmarsson. 1998. "Relative Performance of Public and Private Ownership under Yardstick Competition: Electricity Retail Distribution." *European Economic Review* 42(1): 97–122.

Littlechild, S. C. 1983. "Regulation of British Telecommunications' Profitability: Report to the Secretary of State." Technical report, Department of Industry, London.

Littlechild, S. C., and A. Yatchew. 2002. "Hydro One Transmission and Distribution: Should They Remain Combined or Be Separated." Report to the Electricity Distributors Association, May 6.

Neuberg, L. G. 1977. "Two Issues in the Municipal Ownership of Electric Power Distribution Systems." *The Bell Journal of Economics* 8(1): 303–323.

Pollitt, M. G. 1995. *Ownership and Performance in Electric Utilities: The International Evidence on Privatization and Efficiency*. Oxford Institute for Energy Studies. Oxford: Oxford University Press.

Resende, M. 2002. "Relative Efficiency Measurement and Prospects for Yardstick Competition in Brazilian Electricity Distribution." *Energy Policy* 30(8): 637–647.

Sheriff, G. 2001. "Using Data Envelopment Analysis to Design Contracts under Asymmetric Information." Technical report, University of Maryland.

Shleifer, A. 1985. "A Theory of Yardstick Competition." *Rand Journal of Economics* 16: 319–327.

Sumicsid, Frontier Economics, and Consentec. 2013. "E3grid2012: European TSO Benchmarking Study." Final report commissioned by the Council of European Energy Regulators (CEER), SUMICSID Group, Frontier Economics, Consentec.

Tangeras, T. P. 2002. "Collusion-Proof Yardstick Competition." *Journal of Public Economics* 83(2): 231–254.

Thanassoulis, E. 2000. "DEA and Its Use in the Regulation of Water Companies." *European Journal of Operational Research* 127: 1–13.

Vickers, J., and G. Yarrow. 1991. "Economic Perspectives on Privatization." *The Journal of Economic Perspectives* 5(2): 82.

Wunsch, P. 1995. "Peer Comparison and Regulation: An Application to Urban Mass Transit Firms in Europe." PhD thesis, Department of Economics, Université Catholique de Louvain.

Wyatt, N. S., M. R. Brown, P. J. Caragata, A. J. Duncan, and D. E. A. Giles (eds). 1989. "Performance Measures and Economies of Scale in the New Zealand Electricity Distribution System." Ministry of Energy, Wellington, New Zealand.

Zhu, J. 2014. *Quantitative Models for Performance Evaluation and Benchmarking: Data Envelopment Analysis with Spreadsheets*, Vol. 213. Berlin: Springer.

PART IV

....

MACROECONOMIC STUDIES

....

CHAPTER 17

···

PRODUCTIVITY AND WELFARE PERFORMANCE IN THE PUBLIC SECTOR

···

MATHIEU LEFEBVRE, SERGIO PERELMAN,
AND PIERRE PESTIEAU

17.1. INTRODUCTION

IN both developed and less developed countries, one can speak of a crisis of the public sector.[1] The main charge is that it is costly for what it delivers—costly at the revenue level (tax distortion, compliance cost) and at the spending level (more could be produced with less); costly or at least costlier than would be the private sector. Even though this particular charge is rarely supported by hard evidence, it has to be taken seriously because of its impact on both policymakers and public opinion. The purpose of this chapter is to address the question of whether we can measure the productivity of the public sector, a question that is very general and terribly ambitious. Consequently we will narrow it down by dealing with it in two stages.

In the first stage we consider the public sector as a set of production units that use a number of resources within a particular institutional and geographical setting and produce a number of outputs, both quantitative and qualitative. Those outputs are related to the objectives that have been assigned to the production unit by the principal authority in charge (i.e., the government). If the principal were a private firm, the objective assigned to the manager would be simply to maximize profit. However, with public firms or sectors there are multiple objectives.

For example, in the case of health care or education, maximizing the number of QALYS (years of life adjusted for quality) or the aggregate amount of human capital, respectively, is not sufficient. Equity considerations are also among the objectives of health and education policy. Within such a setting, the productivity is going to be defined in terms of productive efficiency, and to measure it, we will use the efficiency frontier technique. Admittedly, productive efficiency is just a part of an overall efficiency analysis. It has two advantages: it can be measured, and its achievement is a necessary condition for any other type of efficiency. Its main drawback, however, is that it is based on a comparison among a number of rather similar production units from which a best-practice frontier is constructed. Such a comparative approach leads to relative measures, and its quality depends on the quality of the observation units. There exists a large number of efficiency studies concerned with the public sector. Some focus exclusively on public units; others compare public and private units. We will present a small sample of these studies, whose characteristic is that even the best of them do not use the ideal data due to lack of availability. In particular, qualitative evidence is missing for both outcomes and inputs. Under the hard reality that data are insufficient, if not missing, the question is whether or not some productivity studies make sense.

Whereas in the preceding studies there is a quite good relation between the outputs and the inputs, when we move up to an aggregate level the link is not clear anymore. For example, public spending in health is not related to the quality of health, for at least two reasons: health depends more on factors such as lifestyle habits or the climate than on spending, and spending can be higher where it is needed, namely in areas of poor health. For this reason, when dealing with the public sector as a whole, we prefer to restrict our analysis to the quality of outcomes and not to the more or less efficient relation between resources used and outcomes. The problem becomes one of aggregation of outcome indicators. In this chapter, we illustrate our point by evaluating the performance of the European welfare states. We use the data envelopment analysis (DEA) technique with a unitary input. This technique gives different weights to each indicator and each decision unit, in this case each national welfare state. So doing, we expect that the weight given to a partial indicator and to a specific country reflects the importance that this country gives to this indicator. We thus meet the concern of political scientists that different welfare states can have different priorities.[2] This approach, which has been labeled *benefit of the doubt* by Cherchye et al. (2007a), was proposed by Melyn and Moesen (1991) and Lovell et al. (1995) as an alternative way to measure countries' macroeconomic performance and was used, among others, by Cherchye et al. (2004) and Coelli et al. (2010) to measure the performance of European welfare states.[3]

Accordingly, in the last section of this chapter we update Coelli et al. (2010) using five normalized outcomes indicators—which concern poverty, inequality, unemployment, education, and health—for the 28 European Union member-states, 15 historical members (EU-15) and 13 newcomers (EU-13), over the period 2005–2012. We compare the results obtained using identical weights, an average social protection index (SPI), and the DEA *benefit of the doubt* approach, either without imposing constraints on outcome weights, or by imposing 10% minimum weights on each of them. As expected, some countries' rankings vary dramatically depending on the weighting approach (SPI, unconstrained, or constrained DEA). Nevertheless, when we analyze the dynamics of performance over the 2005–2012 period, a test of the *mean reversion hypothesis* confirms that countries with lower performance grew faster. Unfortunately, this is a necessary but not a sufficient condition for convergence, and the tests we perform indicate that convergence in welfare states' performance among the EU-28 members is not yet achieved.

To sum up the spirit of this chapter, we believe that the study of the productivity of the public sector should comprise two parts: an evaluation of the productive efficiency of its components, and an assessment of its achievements as a whole. The next two sections are devoted to these two parts.

17.2. EFFICIENCY MEASURES OF PUBLIC FIRMS AND SERVICES

There is a long tradition of efficiency measurement in the public sector, and a wide number of studies report the results of productivity comparisons concerning public firms and services. As we will illustrate here with some examples—railways transportation, waste collection by municipalities, secondary education, and health care—there exists a gap between the ideal data needed for such assessments and the data used in the economic literature. On the one hand, there are the restrictions imposed by data availability—mainly sample size limitations, small number of units, and short periods—that constrain the number of dimensions that could be taken into account simultaneously, independently of the methodology used. On the other hand, it is difficult to identify and to measure accurately the final outcomes—those that justify the public nature of the firm or the activity, including quality dimensions. Reliable qualitative information on outputs is often missing. Also relevant quality features of inputs, as well as information on the environmental conditions in which these firms operate, are often neglected. We are interested in these deviations from the ideal data. Our goal is to present a list of variables for a few examples that in our view would be the ideal dimensions to consider, assuming no data restriction. We rely on Pestieau (2009) for the description of ideal data.

Furthermore, the objectives assigned by governments and regulatory agencies to public firms and public services are multidimensional. Other than technical efficiency and allocative (price) efficiency, they often include macroeconomic (growth and employment) and distributive (equity) targets.[4] Most of the literature covered focuses only on efficiency without considering prices, costs minimization or profit maximization, or macroeconomic and distributive targets. There are, however, some rare exceptions.

17.2.1. Railway Transportation

Our first example is productive efficiency in public railway transportation. The list of variables presented in Table 17.1 assumes no data availability restrictions. Besides output quantities, number of passengers, journey length and tons of freight transported, we include quality indicators: comfort, reliability of delivery, and punctuality. Equity of access

Table 17.1 Measures of Productivity in Railway Activity

	Ideal Data	(i)	(ii)	(iii)	(iv)	(v)	(vi)	(vii)
Outputs	Passenger kilometers	+	+	+	+	+	+	+
	Trains' comfort and punctuality	−	−	−	−	−	−	−
	Freight tons and kilometers (bulk, containers, etc.)	+	+	+	+	+	+	+
	Delivery quality and punctuality	−	−	−	−	−	−	−
	Equity of access	−	−	−	−	−	−	−
	Passenger per seat	−	−	+	−	−	+	+
Inputs	Labor (disaggregated)	~	+	+	+	~	+	+
	Equipment (disaggregated by type)	~	−	+	+	~	+	+
	Quality of equipment	−	−	−	−	−	−	−
	Tracks (length)	+	+	+	+	+	+	+
	Quality of tracks	−	−	−	−	~	−	−
	Energy (sources)	~	−	−	−	−	−	−
Environment	Geography, stage length	−	−	+	−	+	+	+
	Autonomy	−	+	−	−	+	−	−
	Competition or contestability	−	+	−	+	+	+	+
	Price discrimination	−	−	−	−	−	−	−
	Community service obligation	−	−	−	−	−	−	−
Observations	Large number companies (countries)	50	12	20	27	23	16	23
	Long period (years)	13	23	1	5	7	20	8

Note: + = yes; ~ = more or less; − = unavailable.

Recent studies: (i) Farsi, Filippini and Greene (2005); (ii) Friebel, Ivaldi and Vibes (2008); (iii) Yu and Lin (2008); (iv) Growitsch and Wetzel (2009); (v) Asmild, Holvad, Hougaard, and Kronborg (2009); (vi) Cantos, Pastor, and Serrano (2010); and (vii) Cantos, Pastor and Serrano (2012).

is also a key dimension: How accessible is railway transportation to different categories of the population (e.g., distinguished by income and location)? Which are the types of inputs used in production: (i) staff skills and experience; (ii) type and quality of equipment; (iii) length and quality of tracks; and (iv) different sources of energy? In our view, all these dimensions are relevant and would be considered in a benchmark study.

Furthermore, given the nature of the activity, railway companies operate, by definition, in different geographical areas and national institutional environments. Therefore, other than geographical characteristics (e.g., average stage length and population density), it is crucial to have information on railway sector regulations (e.g., autonomy of management, degree of competition, market contestability). Last but not least, we want to know if they are subject to community service obligations and, perhaps, to constraints regarding price discrimination.

Over the last decade, several studies were published on European railway productivity. The aim of most of them was to analyze the effects of the European Commission railway deregulation policy, launched in the early 1990s. The main objectives of this reform, as summarized by Friebel et al. (2008), were (a) to unbundle infrastructure from operations; (b) to create independent regulatory institutions; and (c) to open access to the railway markets for competitors. Most European countries slowly introduced these reforms, and this provided an opportunity to make efficiency comparisons among them, particularly between vertically integrated and still unbundled companies. With the exception of Farsi et al. (2005), who study the productivity of Swiss regional and local railway networks, and Yu and Lin (2008), who compare European railway productivity in 2002, the studies surveyed in Table 17.1 use panel data to draw conclusions pertaining to the effect of the ongoing deregulation process in the European Union. In Table 17.1, as well as in the following tables in this section, we use different signs to indicate that a particular dimension—output, input, or environmental (nondiscretionary) variables—is taken into account ("+ = yes") or not ("– = no") according to the ideal data, or either if it is considered but not completely ("~ = more or less").

Undoubtedly among the potential consequences of the reform, transportation quality and equity of access are key issues, as well as quality of track and of equipment. However, as we show in Table 17.1, none of these dimensions was taken into consideration in the reviewed studies. Farsi et al. (2005) estimate cost efficiency of 50 subsidized railways in Switzerland using alternative parametric approaches. They show the importance of taking into account firms' heterogeneity in stochastic frontier analysis (SFA). They rely on duality theory and, for this purpose, use input prices instead of quantities ("~" in Table 17.1). Friebel et al. (2008) estimate technical efficiency and productivity growth of 13 European railways using a linear structural relations (LISREL) model. As for the other studies of European national railways presented here, data for countries with unbundled systems were previously aggregated across all railway companies (infrastructure and operations) operating within a country. Yu and Lin (2008) use a multi-activity DEA approach to compute the technical efficiency and effectiveness of 20 European railways in 2002, including seven Eastern European railways.[5] Growitsch and Wetzel (2009) estimate economies of scope, for integrated versus unbundled railway companies, using

DEA and data of 27 European railways over the period 2000–2004. Asmild et al. (2009) address also the effect of reforms on European railway efficiency using a multidirectional DEA approach. This approach allows them to compute, separately, staff and material purchases (OPEX less staff expenditures) cost efficiency and to compare them across Europe, taking into account competition, contestability, and the companies'autonomy. Cantos et al. (2010) compute technical efficiency, technical change, and productivity growth using DEA, while Cantos et al. (2012) compare DEA and SFA results. In both cases, the authors test the influence of vertical integration versus unbundled railways, controlling simultaneously for population density.

Summing up, none of the studies surveyed here considers outputs and inputs quality dimensions. Moreover, none of them controls for the potential role on railway outcomes, eventually played, by two particular institutional features: price discrimination and community service obligations.

17.2.2. Waste Collection

In most countries around the world, waste collection is a public service whose responsibility falls on local authorities, municipalities in the majority of cases. In Table 17.2 we present the ideal data that should be considered in the model. On the output side, we expect to find garbage collected in tons and by type, the service coverage and the quality, the scores reflecting environment protection (like the percentage of waste recycling), air and water quality, and depletion of nonrenewable resources.[6] On the input side, the choice of variables will depend on the unit characteristics. For instance, for the firms that manage waste collection at the municipal level, it would be possible to use information on physical inputs, like labor and equipment, but only if they correspond exactly to the same area for which the outputs are observed. Given the increasing organizational complexity of waste collection, which implies high specialization and economies of scale, most municipalities outsource these activities. In this case, the input is represented by one variable, the total cost paid by the municipality for waste collection and treatment, which includes direct cost plus outsourcing. Finally, as for the other analyzed public services, environmental (nondiscretionary) factors must be taken into consideration. The distance to landfill and the collection frequency are two other variables in relation to the geography and population density. Also the age structure and the sociodemographic characteristics of the population must be considered, especially when they vary dramatically across municipalities. Moreover, as mentioned before, outsourcing is unavoidable in most cases for municipalities, and is therefore potentially a way to improve the services offered and to benefit from economies of scale. In the same line of reasoning, the way municipalities price waste collection—weight-based, pay-per-bag, poll tax, and so on—may influence the waste-production behavior of the population.

In Table 17.2 we survey the dimensions considered by authors in some recent studies, selected here for illustration purposes. Worthington and Dollery (2001) measure cost efficiency in domestic waste management among New South Wales municipalities

Table 17.2 Measures of Productivity in Waste Collection

	Ideal Data	(i)	(ii)	(iii)	(iv)	(v)	(vi)
Outputs	Garbage collected (types and quantities)	~	~	+	+	+	+
	Recycling rate	+	–	+	–	–	–
	Service coverage and quality	~	–	–	–	–	–
	Environment (air and water quality)	–	–	–	–	–	–
Inputs	Labor	–	+	+	–	–	–
	Equipment (disaggregated by type)	–	+	+	–	–	–
	Cost (OPEX and CAPEX)	+	–	+	+	+	+
Environment	Geography (distance landfill, frequency delivery)	+	~	+	–	–	–
	Demography (population density, age)	+	+	+	+	+	–
	Socioeconomic characteristics	–	+	+	+	+	–
	Public–private delivery, outsourcing	–	–	+	+	–	–
	Pricing (weight-based, pay-per-bag, etc.)	–	–	–	+	+	+
Observations	Large number of municipalities (operators)	103	113	29	299	293	272
	Long period (years)	1	1	1	1	1	11

Notes: + = yes; ~ = more or less; – = unavailable.

Recent studies: (i) Worthington and Dollery (2001); (ii) García-Sánchez (2008); (iii) Marques and Simões (2009); (iv) De Jaeger, Eyckmans, Rogge, and Van Puyenbroeck (2011); (v) Rogge and De Jaeger (2013); (vi) De Jaeger and Rogge (2013).

using DEA. Their study has the particularity to work with a large sample and to take into account the recycling rate and municipalities' geographic and demographic dimensions. García-Sánchez (2008, 329) analyzed the efficiency of waste collection in Spanish municipalities with more than 50,000 inhabitants which ". . . are obliged by law to provide the same solid waste services. . . ." The author computes DEA efficiencies using output and inputs quantities and in a second stage tests the effect of nondiscretionary factors, including socio-economic dimensions. Marques and Simões (2009) study the effect of incentive regulation on the efficiency of 29 Portuguese waste management operators in 2005. For this purpose, they first compute a two-output (tons collected and tons recycled) two-input (OPEX and CAPEX) DEA model and, in a second stage, analyze the effect of nondiscretionary variables, among them the institutional framework (private vs. public and regulatory schemes). It is interesting to note that the authors report a detailed list of performance indicators, which includes quality of service and environmental sustainability. This list is published every year by the regulatory agency (Institute for the Regulation of Water and Solid Waste, IRAR), as part of a so-called sunshine regulation. This kind of information is also part of our ideal data. Unfortunately, Marques and Simões decided to not include them in the analysis, because ". . . they are defined by legislation with high sanctions for non-compliance with laws and regulations" (2009, 193).

Finally, we include in Table 17.2 three recent studies in which the authors study the effect of waste-reducing policies on waste collection and treatment costs of nearly 300 municipalities in Flanders, Belgium. Particularly, these studies make the distinction among outputs according to waste types: green, packaging, bulky, residual, and EPR (extended producer responsibility: batteries, car tires, electrical equipment, etc.). De Jaeger et al. (2011) compute a DEA model with total costs as input and then test the effect of demographic and socioeconomic nondiscretionary variables, controlling for institutional differences such as weight-based pricing, cooperation agreement, and outsourcing. Rogge and De Jaeger (2013) use slightly similar updated information but rely on a shared input DEA model that allows computing partial cost efficiency for different waste types. Finally, De Jaeger and Rogge (2013) compute Malmquist productivity indices for the period 1998–2008. The results show that, contrary to expectations, weight-based pricing municipalities did not perform worse in terms of cost efficiency than those with a pay-per-bag system.

In summary, recent productivity studies on waste collection consider garbage composition, total costs paid by municipalities, and most nondiscretionary dimensions. They generally fail to include quality of service and environment sustainability indicators.

17.2.3. Secondary Education

In Table 17.3, we illustrate what would be the ideal data to study education productivity and, for this purpose, we have chosen secondary education. What are the objectives of the government (national or local) on educational matters? It is reasonable to expect

Table 17.3 Measures of Productivity in Education, at the Secondary Level

	Ideal Data	(i)	(ii)	(iii)	(iv)	(v)
Outputs	Acquired skills: reading, maths, science	+	+	+	+	+
	: foreign languages	–	–	–	+	–
	Scores' dispersion	–	–	+	–	+
	Direct employability	–	–	–	–	–
	Indirect employability (through college)	–	–	–	–	–
Inputs	Teachers: number	+	+	+	~	+
	: quality (skills)	–	–	+	–	+
	Administrative staff	–	–	+	~	+
	Building, equipment	–	~	–	~	+
	Skills at the end of the primary education	–	–	+	–	+
Environment	Autonomy / Responsibility	–	–	–	–	+
	Spatial distribution of schools	–	–	–	+	+
	Socioeconomic characteristics	–	+	+	–	+
	Family background	+	~	–	–	+
	Unemployment rate, economic growth	~	–	–	~	+
	Pedagogical techniques or innovations	–	–	–	+	+
Observations	Large number of units: countries, districts	25	29	310		39
	: schools				119	n.r.
	Long period (years)	1	1	1	1	1

Notes: + = yes; ~ = more or less; – = unavailable; n.r. = not reported.

Recent studies: (i) Afonso and St. Aubyn (2006a); (ii) Sutherland, Price, and Gonand (2009); (iii) Grosskopf, Hayes, Taylor, and Weber (1997); (iv) Haelermans and De Witte (2012); (v) Wößmann (2003).

high skills in reading comprehension, as well as in mathematics, sciences, and foreign languages. Given that students come from different backgrounds, we need indicators on not only average scores, but also scores' dispersion. Moreover, the capacity to find employment or access to higher education matters, too.

On the input side there are two possible views: physical or financial. The physical inputs are number and quality of teachers, administrative staff, the building, and other educational materials. Alternatively, one can look at overall public spending. In such cases there are two steps embodied: the first step from the financial spending to physical inputs, where inputs prices matter, and the second step from inputs to outputs. Therefore, using financial spending as input implies, as a potential shortcut, a source of bias in productivity comparisons. Finally, the skills acquired by students at the end of primary school would be ideally included as an input of secondary education.

The environmental variables that must be considered vary with the level of aggregation: country, district, or school. In a within-country comparison, one has the advantage of dealing with the same institutional and cultural setting, but a number of other dimensions matter, above all the socioeconomic environment: income inequality, unemployment, and population size and density. Also, family background and peer group characteristics are important. A between-country comparison is expected to include institutional variables such as political decentralization (schools' autonomy), competition of private schools, and educational system (mobility of students, selectivity, pedagogical techniques, etc.).

In the literature we find best-practice comparisons between countries, between districts within a country, and between schools, either within or across countries or districts. Most international comparative studies rely on data collected at the student level either by the Organisation for Economic Co-operation and Development (OECD) Program for International Student Assessment (PISA) or by the International Association for the Evaluation of Educational Achievement (IEA) Trends in International Mathematics and Science Study (TIMSS).

In Table 17.3 we present the list of outputs, inputs, and environmental variables used in a selected number of studies. Afonso and St. Aubyn (2006a) use PISA data aggregated by country in international comparisons. As expected, given the small number of observations (25 countries), the number of variables taken into account is reduced to a strict minimum. Sutherland et al. (2009) compare education efficiency in OECD countries using PISA, but relying on disaggregated data at the school level. This allows them to take into account simultaneously the family and socioeconomic background, as well as a proxy of capital (computer availability). Both studies also report the results of cost-efficiency comparisons at the national level using information on educational expenditures. Besides the difficulty to estimate accurately the real cost of education, there is evidence from Hanushek's (1997) survey of near 400 studies on US education that "there is not a strong or consistent relationship between student performance and school resources, at least after variations in family inputs are taken into account" (141). This is not surprising given the objectives of welfare states concerning education, which are not merely to maximize the average scores and expected earnings, but the overall distribution (equity). This is the reason why family background and socioeconomic environment play a key role in many studies.

In Table 17.3 we report the variables used by Grosskopf et al. (1997) to compare the productivity of 310 educational districts in Texas. For this purpose the authors use a parametric indirect distance function approach, which considers the scores obtained by students in previous levels of education. As inputs, other than schoolteachers, they consider three staff categories: administration, support, and teacher aides. Haelermans and De Witte (2012) compare 119 schools' productivity in the Netherlands, looking for the impact of educational innovations. They use a nonparametric conditional (order-m) approach, which allows for controlling schools' heterogeneity, mainly localization.

Unfortunately, given data limitations, school inputs are represented by a unique variable: expenses per student. Finally, Wößmann (2003) used probably the largest international data set available, 39 countries and more than 260,000 students who participated in the TIMMS study in 1994–1995. The author estimates an education production function using parametric models, ordinary and weighted least squares to identify the main drivers of education performances. We have chosen this study as an illustration that ideal data are not an unattainable goal, at least for input and environmental variables. In addition to the ones indicated in Table 17.3, Wößmann (2003) includes several variables controlling for teachers' influence, school responsibility, parents' role, and students' incentives.

To summarize, all these studies use data on students' acquired skills and on the number of teachers, but only two cases, Grosskopf et al. (1997) and Wößmann (2003), use data on output inequality (scores' dispersion), on teachers' quality, and, even more important, on students' skills at the end of the primary school. Moreover, none of the studies in Table 17.3 considers information on the courses followed by the students after high school, the degree of employability, or the pursuit of higher education. Such information is obviously difficult to obtain.

17.2.4. Health Care

Assuming perfect data availability, we would like to use data reflecting how patients expected lifetime and health status increase as a consequence of health care use. At the same time, as indicated in Table 17.4, we would like to consider as output the quality of the care delivered. We are interested in not only the efficiency of medical treatment, but also in the way this is delivered. Using individual data, it would be possible to compute for these variables average values and inequality indicators (distribution).

On the input side, we would consider the number and the quality of physicians, nurses, and hospitals, and how these inputs are distributed among the population and geographical terms. Furthermore, total social spending is a potential substitute of physical and qualitative input variables when the information on inputs is sparse or not reliable.

Environmental factors play a crucial role on health care delivered. Other than the age structure of the population, individual lifestyle factors like smoking, poor diet, or lack of physical activity matter. Institutions may also have an important role, for example the share of prevention in total care expenditures, the importance of the private health sector and private health insurance, copayment by patients, and so on. Our expectation is that most of the necessary information might be available, even if not in the exact desired form.

Before turning to a few recent cross-country comparative studies, the first study in Table 17.4, Crémieux et al. (1999), deals with Canadian provinces and is not interested by the measurement of productivity, but by the estimation of an average health care production function. We selected this study because it illustrates very well that collecting

Table 17.4 Measures of Productivity in Health Care Public Systems

	Ideal Data	(i)	(ii)	(iii)	(iv)	(v)	(vi)	(vii)	(viii)
Outputs	Incremental life time (average, distribution)	~	~	~	~	~	~	~	~
	Incremental health status (average, distribution)	~	−	~	~	~	−	−	−
	Quality of care (average, distribution)	−	−	−	−	−	−	−	−
Inputs	Physicians (speciality, quality, distribution)	~	−	~	~	~	~	~	−
	Nurses (speciality, quality, distribution)	−	−	~	~	−	−	~	−
	Hospitals (speciality, quality, distribution)	−	−	~	~	−	~	~	~
	Social expenditure (public and private)	+	~	~	~	−	−	−	+
Environment	Age structure, population density	+	−	~	~	−	−	−	+
	Socioeconomic characteristics	+	~	~	~	−	−	−	+
	Individual lifestyle: physical exercise, diet, etc.	+	−	−	−	−	−	−	−
	Ratio of curative to preventive care	−	−	−	−	−	−	−	−
	Role of the private sector	−	−	−	+	−	−	−	−
	Copayment by patients, private insurance	~	−	−	−	−	−	−	−
Observations	Large number of units: countries, provinces	10	191	191	191	191	10	24	30
	Long period (years)	15	5	5	5	5	15	1	1

Notes: + = yes; ~ = more or less; − = unavailable.

Recent studies: (i) Crémieux, Ouellette, and Pilon (1999); (ii) Evans, Tandon, Murray, and Lauer (2000); (iii) Tandon, Murray, Lauer, and Evans (2001); (iv) Greene (2004); (v) Lauer, Lovell, Murray, and Evans (2004); (vi) Färe, Grosskopf, Lindgren, and Poullier (1997); (vii) Afonso and St. Aubyn (2006b); (viii) Joumard, André, Nicq, and Chatal (2008).

ideal data is not an impossible task, at least for the 10 Canadian provinces over the period 1978–1992. The authors use information on health care outputs and inputs, together with detailed information on population socioeconomic composition and on individuals' behavior.

The other studies presented in Table 17.4 deal with cross-country health care data compiled either by the World Health Organization (WHO) or by OECD. Evans et al. (2000) and Tandon et al. (2001) used as health outputs, respectively, the "disability-adjusted life expectancy" (DALE) measure and a composite measure, which considers five dimensions: DALE, health inequality, responsiveness-level, responsiveness-distribution, and fair-financing.[7] Both studies deal with WHO data on 191 countries over the 1993–1997 period and DEA methodology. Two inputs are considered: total health expenditure (public plus private), and average educational attainment in the adult population.

The results of these studies, also reported in *The World Health Report 2000* (WHO, 2000), generated some debate, and other studies were undertaken using the same WHO data file.[8] Two of them are included in Table 17.4. First, Greene (2004) estimates stochastic frontiers using alternative approaches, which take into account countries' heterogeneity and several environmental (nondiscretionary) variables, such as income inequality, population density, and the percentage of health care paid by the government. Second, Lauer et al. (2004) estimate health care systems' performance assuming five different outputs, in fact, those included in the composite output measure used by Tandon et al. (2001), but taken separately. The particularity of the DEA approach used by Lauer et al. (2004) is that, rather than considering the five different outputs separately, it assumes an identical (equal to 1.0) input for all countries. It is the so-called *benefit of the doubt* model introduced by Melyn and Moesen (1991) and Lovell et al. (1995), which we adopt in the following section to measure the performance of the welfare state in European Union countries.

Finally, we include in Table 17.4 three other studies, Färe et al. (1997), Afonso and St. Aubyn (2006b), and Joumard et al. (2008), which used OECD data on health care for industrialized countries. Färe et al. (1997) compute Malmquist productivity indices for 10 countries over the period 1974–1989. The outcome of health care is represented by life expectancy of women at age 40 and the reciprocal of the infant mortality rate. Inputs are the number of physicians and care beds per capita. Afonso and St. Aubyn (2006b) computed technical efficiency of 25 countries in 2002 using the free disposal hull (FDH) approach. In their study the health care production function is specified with two outputs, infant survival rate and life expectancy, and three inputs, the number of doctors, nurses, and beds, respectively. In a recent study, Spinks and Hollingsworth (2009) recognized that "the OECD health dataset provides one of the best cross-country sources of comparative data available"; however, they also underline pitfalls in the data, mainly "the lack of an objective measure of quality of life," like additional quality-adjusted life years (QALYs), and a "measure of country-based environmental status." A study by Joumard et al. (2008) partially answered these criticisms by including on the input side a lifestyle variable and a proxy for the economic, social, and cultural status of the population. Finally, for reasons now discussed, the level of aggregation of some of these studies is highly questionable.

Summing up, none of the comparative studies of public health care systems surveyed here considers all the output-input dimensions of the ideal data. Moreover, when an output or an input is included, in most cases the authors are led to neglect the qualitative and distributional dimensions, due to lack of data. And even worse, there are the environmental (nondiscretionary) factors, in particular data on institutional issues like copayment by patients, or the ratio of curative to preventive care, which are not considered.

17.3. THE WELFARE STATE PERFORMANCE IN THE EUROPEAN UNION

In the previous section we have seen that many components of the public sector can be submitted to the test of best practices and that such exercise is useful to improve its overall efficiency. It is, however, tempting to try to evaluate the performance of the public sector as a whole, neglecting input constraints. In this section we illustrate this by showing estimates of the performance of European public sectors. We have chosen to limit our analysis to that of the welfare state, which is the most important subset of the public sector. We have two reasons for this: the availability of data, and a rather good consensus as to the objectives that the welfare state is supposed to pursue and according to which its performance can be assessed.

The objectives of traditional European welfare states are first, poverty alleviation and inequality reduction, and second, protection against life-cycle risks such as unemployment, ill health, and lack of education. Recently the European Union has adopted new means of governance based on voluntary cooperation that aims at achieving some kind of convergence in the field of social inclusion. This approach is known as the Open Method of Coordination (OMC) and it rests on benchmarking and sharing of best practice. Thanks to the OMC, various comparable and regularly updated indicators have been developed for the appraisal of social protection policies in the 28 European Union country members. The aim is to allow countries to know how well they are performing relative to the other countries.

In this section we focus on five of the most commonly used indicators, which concern poverty, inequality, unemployment, education, and health. The definitions of the indicators that we use are presented in Table 17.5. The first four indicators, poverty (POV), inequality (INE), unemployment (UNE), and early school leavers (EDU), are such that we want them as low as possible, while life expectancy (EXP) is the only "positive" indicator.[9] The five indicators we are using here cover the most relevant concerns of a modern welfare state, and their choice is determined by its objectives.[10] They also reflect aspects that people who want to enlarge the concept of gross domestic product

Table 17.5 Indicators of Social Protection

	Definition
POV:	*At-risk-of-poverty rate* after social transfers as defined as the share of persons with an equivalized disposable income below the risk-of-poverty threshold, which is set at 60% of the national median equivalized disposable income (after social transfers).
INE:	*Inequality* of income distribution as defined as the ratio of total income received by the 20% of the population with the highest income (top quintile) to that received by the 20% of the population with the lowest income (lowest quintile). Income must be understood as equivalized disposable income.
UNE:	*Long-term unemployed* (12 months or longer) as a share of the total active population harmonized with national monthly unemployment estimates.
EXP:	*Life expectancy* as the number of years a person may be expected to live, starting at age 0.
EDU:	*Early school leavers* as the percentage of the population aged 18–24 with at most lower secondary education and not in further education or training.

Source: The five indicators are taken from the Eurostat Database on Population and Social Conditions. (2014).

(GDP) to better measure social welfare generally take into account, for example the classical measurable economic welfare (MEW) developed by Nordhaus and Tobin (1972), and more recently revisited by Stiglitz et al. (2009) and by the OECD (2014).

These indicators for the 28 European Union member-states are available for the eight-year period from 2005 to 2012. Table 17.6 lists the values for the year 2012.[11] As shown in Table 17.6, countries are not good or bad in all respects, and it is difficult to make global comparisons. We are unable to confidently say that a country is doing better than another country unless all five indicators in the country are better than (or equal to) those in the other country. This is possible in a few cases, for example Austria is doing better than Bulgaria in the five indicators, but it is not the norm. To address this issue we wish to obtain a performance index of the welfare state, so that we can say which country is actually doing better than the others. This is of course not without making choices regarding the methods we shall use, and this is the purpose of this section.

To obtain one performance index that summarizes the information contained in the five given indicators, we have to make methodological choices. First, the indicators should be converted so that they are comparable; this is the case of the indicators where a higher value is bad. Second, we should decide how to aggregate the five indicators retained here. Should we use a linear aggregation function (as for the Human Development Index, HDI before 2010), or should we rely on more sophisticated techniques, as presented earlier? If we use a simple average of the five indicators, they need to be scaled so that they are measured with the same unit. Finally, we could allocate weights to each of the five indicators in the aggregation process. Should these weights vary across indicators? Furthermore, should these weights vary across countries? And, could they take extreme values, like zero?

Table 17.6 Indicators of Social Protection (2012)

Region and Country		POV	INE	UNE	EXP	EDU
EU–15		15.9	4.8	4.7	81.2	12.1
Austria	AT	14.4	4.2	1.1	81.1	7.6
Belgium	BE	15.0	3.9	3.4	80.5	12.0
Denmark	DK	13.1	4.5	2.1	80.2	9.1
Finland	FI	13.2	3.7	1.6	80.7	8.9
France	FR	14.1	4.5	4.1	82.1	11.6
Germany	DE	16.1	4.3	2.5	81.0	10.6
Greece	EL	23.1	6.6	14.4	80.7	11.4
Ireland	IE	15.2	4.5	9.1	80.9	9.7
Italy	IT	19.4	5.5	5.7	82.4	17.6
Luxembourg	LU	15.1	4.1	1.6	81.5	8.1
The Netherlands	NL	10.1	3.6	1.8	81.2	8.8
Portugal	PT	17.9	5.8	7.7	80.6	20.8
Spain	ES	22.2	7.2	11.1	82.5	24.9
Sweden	SE	14.1	3.7	1.5	81.8	7.5
United Kingdom	UK	16.2	5.4	2.7	81.0	13.6
EU–13		16.7	4.9	5.6	76.9	9.9
Bulgaria	BG	21.2	6.1	6.8	74.4	12.5
Croatia	HR	20.5	5.4	10.3	77.3	4.2
Cyprus	CY	14.7	4.7	3.6	81.1	11.4
Czech Republic	CZ	9.6	3.5	3.0	78.1	5.5
Estonia	EE	17.5	5.4	5.5	76.7	10.5
Hungary	HU	14.0	4.0	4.9	75.3	11.5
Latvia	LV	19.2	6.5	7.8	74.1	10.6
Lithuania	LT	18.6	5.3	6.6	74.1	6.5
Malta	MT	15.1	3.9	3.0	80.9	22.6
Poland	PL	17.1	4.9	4.1	76.9	5.7
Romania	RO	22.6	6.3	3.2	74.5	17.4
Slovakia	SK	13.2	3.7	9.4	76.3	5.3
Slovenia	SI	13.5	3.4	4.3	80.3	4.4
EU–28		16.3	4.8	5.1	79.2	11.1

In what follows we address these questions by presenting successively three indices of the performance of the European welfare states. Starting from a simple linear aggregation index, we then present two estimations based on best-practice frontier techniques: on the one hand, the original DEA approach, which allows for free choice of output weights, with the only condition of non-negativity; and, on the other hand, a DEA that allows for imposing minimum constraints on the weights assigned to each output.[12]

At this point it is important to stress that if we assume that these five indicators, as well as the aggregate indicator, measure the actual outcomes of the welfare state (what we call its performance), it would be interesting to also measure the true contribution of social protection to that performance and hence to evaluate to what extent the welfare state, with its financial and regulatory means, gets close to the best-practice frontier. We argue that this exercise, which in production theory amounts to the measurement of productive efficiency, is highly questionable at this level of aggregation.

Henceforth when we compare the performance of the welfare state across countries, we do not intend to explain it by social spending. We realize that many factors may explain differences in performance. First, the welfare state is not restricted to spending, but includes also a battery of regulatory measures (minimum wage, tax expenditures, safety rules, etc.) that contribute to protecting people against lifetime risks and to alleviating poverty. Second, contextual factors, such as family structure, culture, and climate, may explain educational or health outcomes as much as anything else. This is why we limit our exercise to what we call performance assessment and argue against any efficiency/productivity analysis.

17.3.1. Scaling

The first task is to normalize the five variables, not only to make them comparable, but also to include them in a simple linear aggregation index. Indeed, the five indicators listed in Table 17.5 are measured in different units. In the original *Human Development Report* (HDR, 1990), three composite indicators (health, education, and income) are used to derive a Human Development Index (HDI). The authors suggest scaling these indicators so that they lie between 0 and 1, where the bounds are set to reflect minimum and maximum targets. Thus we propose a simple scaling so that the *n*-th indicator (e.g., life expectancy) of the *i*-th country should be scaled using

$$x_{ni}^* = \frac{x_{ni} - \min_k \{x_{nk}\}}{\max_k \{x_{nk}\} - \min_k \{x_{nk}\}}, \tag{17.1}$$

so that for each indicator the highest score is 1 and the lowest is 0. For "negative" indicators, such as unemployment, where "more is bad", one alternatively uses

$$x_{ni}^* = \frac{\max_k \{x_{nk}\} - x_{ni}}{\max_k \{x_{nk}\} - \min_k \{x_{nk}\}}, \tag{17.2}$$

so that the country with the lowest rate of unemployment will receive a score of 1, and the one with the highest rate of unemployment will receive 0. This is not the only way of scaling indicators, and the results may be dependent on the chosen method. Coelli et al. (2010) compare several scaling methods and show that the results are impacted, although marginally, by the approach adopted.

Table 17.7 shows the five normalized indicators for our sample of 28 countries in 2012. We purposely distinguish between the 15 historical members of the European

Table 17.7 Normalized Indicators: EU–28 (2012)

Region and Country		POV	INE	UNE	EXP	EDU
EU-15		0.587	0.659	0.698	0.884	0.761
Austria	AT	0.674	0.783	0.957	0.875	0.890
Belgium	BE	0.640	0.848	0.791	0.825	0.766
Denmark	DK	0.747	0.717	0.885	0.800	0.847
Finland	FI	0.742	0.891	0.921	0.842	0.853
France	FR	0.691	0.717	0.741	0.958	0.777
Germany	DE	0.579	0.761	0.856	0.867	0.805
Greece	EL	0.185	0.261	0.000	0.842	0.782
Ireland	IE	0.629	0.717	0.381	0.858	0.831
Italy	IT	0.393	0.500	0.626	0.983	0.607
Luxembourg	LU	0.635	0.804	0.921	0.908	0.876
The Netherlands	NL	0.916	0.913	0.906	0.883	0.856
Portugal	PT	0.478	0.435	0.482	0.833	0.517
Spain	ES	0.236	0.130	0.237	0.992	0.401
Sweden	SE	0.691	0.891	0.928	0.933	0.893
United Kingdom	UK	0.573	0.522	0.842	0.867	0.720
EU-13		0.546	0.640	0.635	0.527	0.826
Bulgaria	BG	0.292	0.370	0.547	0.317	0.751
Croatia	HR	0.331	0.522	0.295	0.558	0.986
Cyprus	CY	0.657	0.674	0.777	0.875	0.782
Czech Republic	CZ	0.944	0.935	0.820	0.625	0.949
Estonia	EE	0.500	0.522	0.640	0.508	0.808
Hungary	HU	0.697	0.826	0.683	0.392	0.780
Latvia	LV	0.404	0.283	0.475	0.292	0.805
Lithuania	LT	0.438	0.543	0.561	0.292	0.921
Malta	MT	0.635	0.848	0.820	0.858	0.466
Poland	PL	0.522	0.630	0.741	0.525	0.944
Romania	RO	0.213	0.326	0.806	0.325	0.613
Slovakia	SK	0.742	0.891	0.360	0.475	0.955
Slovenia	SI	0.725	0.957	0.727	0.808	0.980
EU-28		0.568	0.651	0.669	0.718	0.791

Note: Normalized within the 0 to 1.0 scale over the entire period (2005–2012).

Union (hereafter EU-15) and the 13 more recent newcomers (EU-13). For normalization purposes, we take the minimum and the maximum values out of the all sample period 2005–2012 such that these extreme values can be observed at different times. Nearly all the extreme (maximum and minimum) values of the five indicators correspond to the years before 2012. The only exception is the highest unemployment rate over the period, reached by Greece in 2012.

17.3.2. Measuring Performance

On the basis of the five scaled indicators, we want to obtain an overall assessment of the welfare state performance. One option is to follow the HDI method discussed above and to calculate the raw arithmetic average of the five indicators. We call it the social protection index: $SPI_i = 1/5\sum_{n=1}^{5} x_{ni}^*$. Table 17.8 reports the indicators as well as the rank of each country in 2012. As it appears, we have at the top the Nordic countries, plus Austria, the Netherlands, and Luxembourg. But we also have new entrants countries (EU-13) doing quite well, like Slovenia or the Czech Republic, which are at the top. At the bottom, we find Bulgaria, Greece, Latvia, Romania, and Spain.

However, this summation of partial indicators is quite arbitrary and does not completely respond to the estimation problems we raised earlier. In particular, there is no reason to grant each indicator the same weight. In fact, weights could change across indicators and across countries to account for the fact that different countries have different priorities. Indeed, some countries may give more weight to employment than to income equality, and other countries may give more weight to poverty than to education. One possible solution to this problem is to use the DEA approach. As seen in the previous section, DEA is traditionally used to measure the technical efficiency scores of firms. In the case of the production of social protection by a welfare state, we could conceptualize a production process where each country is a "firm" that uses government resources to produce social outputs such as reduced unemployment and longer life expectancies. We do not follow this path, but we will assume that each country has one "government" and further one unit of input, and that it produces the five outputs discussed earlier.

As indicated in the introductory section, this approach is known in the literature as the *benefit of the doubt* weighting approach. It was often applied to compare the performance of production units—countries, public services, farms, and so on—as an alternative composite indicator of performance, one that takes into consideration idiosyncratic units' behavior. More concretely, the DEA *benefit of the doubt* scores reported on Table 17.8, called here *unconstrained DEA*, are computed under the assumption that each unit is compared to the others under the most favorable situation. In other words, each unit freely chooses the bundle of weights which maximize its weighted sum of indicators.

A number of observations can be made from the unconstrained DEA scores and rankings reported on Table 17.8.[13] First, we note that approximately 30% of the sample

Table 17.8 SPI and DEA Performance Index: EU–28 (2012)

Region and Country		SPI Index	SPI Rank	Unconstrained DEA Score	Unconstrained DEA Rank	Constrained DEA Score	Constrained DEA Rank
EU–15		0.718	–	0.964	–	0.866	–
Austria	AT	0.836	6	1.000	1	0.986	5
Belgium	BE	0.774	10	0.935	19	0.905	12
Denmark	DK	0.799	8	0.961	14	0.942	9
Finland	FI	0.850	4	0.997	10	0.981	6
France	FR	0.777	9	1.000	1	0.960	8
Germany	DE	0.773	11	0.935	19	0.918	10
Greece	EL	0.414	27	0.908	22	0.440	28
Ireland	IE	0.683	16	0.934	20	0.841	17
Italy	IT	0.622	19	1.000	1	0.841	17
Luxembourg	LU	0.829	7	0.987	11	0.969	7
The Netherlands	NL	0.895	1	1.000	1	1.000	1
Portugal	PT	0.549	22	0.874	24	0.758	22
Spain	ES	0.399	28	1.000	1	0.574	27
Sweden	SE	0.867	2	1.000	1	1.000	1
United Kingdom	UK	0.705	14	0.933	21	0.872	15
EU–13		0.635	–	0.924		0.816	–
Bulgaria	BG	0.455	25	0.790	28	0.653	25
Croatia	HR	0.538	23	1.000	1	0.756	23
Cyprus	CY	0.753	12	0.938	17	0.912	11
Czech Republic	CZ	0.855	3	1.000	1	1.000	1
Estonia	EE	0.596	20	0.853	26	0.784	20
Hungary	HU	0.675	17	0.889	23	0.823	19
Latvia	LV	0.452	26	0.838	27	0.658	24
Lithuania	LT	0.551	21	0.944	16	0.767	21
Malta	MT	0.725	13	0.947	15	0.877	14
Poland	PL	0.672	18	0.977	13	0.879	13
Romania	RO	0.457	24	0.859	25	0.634	26
Slovakia	SK	0.684	15	0.981	12	0.864	16
Slovenia	SI	0.839	5	1.000	1	1.000	1
EU–28		0.680	–	0.946	–	0.843	–

receives a DEA efficiency score of 1 (indicating that they are fully efficient). This is not unusual in a DEA analysis where the number of dimensions (variables) is large relative to the number of observations. Second, the average DEA score is 0.946 versus the mean SPI score of 0.680. The DEA scores tend to be higher because of the unlimited freedom to choose outcomes' weight compared with SPI uniform weights assumption. Third, the DEA rankings are "broadly similar" to the SPI rankings. However, a few countries do experience dramatic changes, such as Italy, Spain, and Croatia, which are ranked 19, 28, and 23, respectively, under SPI but are found to be fully efficient in the DEA results.

There are two primary reasons why we observe differences between the rankings in DEA versus the SPI. First, the SPI allocates an equal weight of 1/5 to each indicator, while in the DEA method the weights used can vary across the five indicators. They are determined by the slope of the production possibility frontier that is constructed using the linear programming methods. Second, the implicit weights (or shadow prices) in DEA can also vary from country to country because the slope of the frontier can differ for different output (indicator) mixes.

We use the shadow price information from the dual DEA linear programming to obtain the implicit weights assigned to each country indicator. These weights and their means for year 2012 are given in Table 17.9. The first thing we note is that the poverty (POV) and inequality (INE) indicators are given, in average for the whole sample EU-28, a fairly small weight, while life expectancy (EXP) and education (EDU) indicators are given a weight much larger than 0.3. These results suggest that the uniform weights of 0.2 (used in the SPI) understate the effort needed to improve health and education outcomes versus reducing inequality and poverty. Nevertheless, when we observe more in details the results for EU-15 and EU-13, we remark that huge differences appear. Several EU-15 members, mainly Italy, Portugal and Spain, assign the highest weight (higher than 0.9) to life expectancy, while several EU-13 countries, among them Croatia, Latvia, and Lithuania, do the same with education. In each case, these countries take advantage of their outstanding performances in these respective domains (see Tables 17.6 and 17.7).

Summing up, SPI and unconstrained DEA correspond to two aggregation techniques. Many attempts have then been made in the DEA literature to improve the implicit weighting procedure. They mainly consist in the inclusion of additional weight restrictions on the DEA linear program or, in other words, in restricting implicit rates of substitution (transformation) between outputs. Allen et al. (1997) and Cherchye et al. (2007a) summarized the approaches proposed in the literature, which in most cases rely on the role of experts' value judgments.[14] An interesting illustration of the use of experts' judgments in a *benefit of the doubt* DEA setting is the study on health performances of 191 WHO countries members by Lauer et al. (2004), mentioned earlier. In the case analyzed here, the performance of EU welfare states, unfortunately we do not have access to experts' value judgments. Hence we decided to adopt the same weight restriction for our five indicators. We now present the DEA results obtained assuming equal minimum weights thresholds. For illustration purposes, we have chosen a minimum

Table 17.9 Weights by Country: Unconstrained DEA, EU–28 (2012)

Region and Country		POV	INE	UNE	EXP	EDU
EU–15		0.080	0.073	0.235	0.519	0.093
Austria	AT	0.013	0.015	0.845	0.054	0.073
Belgium	BE	0.000	0.663	0.000	0.337	0.000
Denmark	DK	0.135	0.000	0.481	0.000	0.384
Finland	FI	0.045	0.189	0.766	0.000	0.000
France	FR	0.120	0.005	0.004	0.856	0.015
Germany	DE	0.000	0.000	0.141	0.859	0.000
Greece	EL	0.000	0.000	0.000	0.832	0.168
Ireland	IE	0.000	0.000	0.000	0.419	0.581
Italy	IT	0.003	0.021	0.028	0.918	0.031
Luxembourg	LU	0.000	0.000	0.672	0.328	0.000
The Netherlands	NL	0.798	0.001	0.066	0.083	0.052
Portugal	PT	0.050	0.000	0.000	0.950	0.000
Spain	ES	0.002	0.000	0.000	0.995	0.002
Sweden	SE	0.028	0.201	0.383	0.295	0.093
United Kingdom	UK	0.000	0.000	0.139	0.861	0.000
EU–13		0.038	0.154	0.132	0.089	0.587
Bulgaria	BG	0.000	0.000	0.010	0.000	0.990
Croatia	HR	0.001	0.001	0.002	0.004	0.992
Cyprus	CY	0.144	0.000	0.000	0.716	0.140
Czech Republic	CZ	0.235	0.024	0.051	0.042	0.648
Estonia	EE	0.000	0.000	0.214	0.000	0.786
Hungary	HU	0.000	0.835	0.165	0.000	0.000
Latvia	LV	0.000	0.000	0.008	0.000	0.992
Lithuania	LT	0.000	0.000	0.008	0.000	0.992
Malta	MT	0.000	0.655	0.000	0.345	0.000
Poland	PL	0.000	0.000	0.212	0.000	0.788
Romania	RO	0.000	0.000	1.000	0.000	0.000
Slovakia	SK	0.102	0.000	0.000	0.000	0.898
Slovenia	SI	0.007	0.488	0.045	0.056	0.405
EU–28		0.060	0.111	0.187	0.320	0.322

threshold of 0.10 for each of the five outcome indicators, which by construction implies a maximum weight threshold of 0.60 for each of them.

The results reported in the last columns of Table 17.8 were obtained imposing *absolute weight restrictions*;[15] that is, instead of imposing restrictions on shadow prices, these are imposed on indicators' virtual proportions (Wong and Beasley 1990). More concretely, each output is assumed to have a weight not lower than 0.10, as indicated before.

Clearly the DEA scores obtained under weight restrictions are either equal or lower than those obtained under unconstrained DEA (Pedraja-Chaparro et al. 1997). In Table 17.8 we observe that four countries, Czech Republic, The Netherlands, Slovenia, and Sweden, keep their position on the frontier in 2012, while several others suffer a sharp performance drop, accompanied in some cases by dramatic loss in rank position, like Croatia, Greece, Italy, and Spain. Finally, many other countries, including Belgium, Cyprus, Denmark, and Germany, dramatically improved their rank, even if their performance diminished in absolute terms.

Average constrained DEA scores (0.843) are, as expected, located between unconstrained DEA (0.946) and SPI (0.680) scores, but are closer to the former. On the contrary, individual countries' performances are highly correlated between constrained DEA and SPI (0.982 Spearman correlation) when compared with correlation between constrained and unconstrained DEA (0.606 Spearman correlation).

A look at the detailed weights obtained under constrained DEA in Table 17.10 shows that for a majority of countries and indicators the minimum weight constraints (0.10) are binding in 2012. Moreover, for more than half of countries one of the indicators reaches the maximum potential weight, 0.60, while the four others receive the minimum weight threshold. If we compare the average weights for the EU-15, EU-13, and EU-28 in Tables 17.9 and 17.10, it appears that in most cases the weights computed under unconstrained and constrained DEA are very close, with life expectancy (EXP) highly weighted by former European Union members (EU-15) and education (EDU) by the new EU-13 entrants. The only exceptions are the POV (at-risk-of-poverty-rate) indicator, whose weight doubles from 0.060 to 0.120 for EU-28, and the EXP indicator, whose weight increases from 0.089 to 0.169 for EU-13.

17.3.3. Welfare Performance Dynamics and Convergence

The data we used in the previous sections are available for EU-28 since 2005; thus it is interesting to see whether we observe specific trends and particularly convergence toward welfare state performance among the EU countries, the aim of the OMC strategy. For this purpose, we compute year-by-year performance indices—SPI and constrained DEA—and their rate of change using the 2005–2012 normalized indicators. In the case of SPI, its rate of change (SPIC) corresponds to performance growth, while for the DEA score it represents changes in distances to the frontier (relative performance) over time. In order to estimate performance growth in the case of the DEA indicator, we compute Malmquist decomposable indices of *performance change* (PC), following Cherchye et al. (2007b). These indices are the sum of two components: the change in relative performance, known as the *catching-up* (CU) component, and the change at the frontier level themselves, labeled the *environmental change* (EC) component by Cherchye et al. (2007b).[16]

Table 17.10 Outcomes' Weights by Country: Constrained DEA, EU-28 (2012)

Region and Country		POV	INE	UNE	EXP	EDU
EU-15		0.123	0.106	0.186	0.427	0.158
Austria	AT	0.100	0.100	0.600	0.100	0.100
Belgium	BE	0.100	0.185	0.100	0.515	0.100
Denmark	DK	0.100	0.100	0.248	0.100	0.452
Finland	FI	0.100	0.100	0.600	0.100	0.100
France	FR	0.100	0.100	0.100	0.600	0.100
Germany	DE	0.100	0.100	0.100	0.600	0.100
Greece	EL	0.100	0.100	0.100	0.600	0.100
Ireland	IE	0.100	0.100	0.100	0.165	0.535
Italy	IT	0.100	0.100	0.100	0.600	0.100
Luxembourg	LU	0.100	0.100	0.197	0.503	0.100
The Netherlands	NL	0.450	0.102	0.141	0.157	0.151
Portugal	PT	0.100	0.100	0.100	0.600	0.100
Spain	ES	0.100	0.100	0.100	0.600	0.100
Sweden	SE	0.101	0.104	0.108	0.562	0.125
United Kingdom	UK	0.100	0.100	0.100	0.600	0.100
EU-13		0.115	0.138	0.144	0.169	0.434
Bulgaria	BG	0.100	0.100	0.100	0.100	0.600
Croatia	HR	0.100	0.100	0.100	0.100	0.600
Cyprus	CY	0.114	0.100	0.100	0.586	0.100
Czech Republic	CZ	0.261	0.103	0.108	0.103	0.425
Estonia	EE	0.100	0.100	0.132	0.100	0.568
Hungary	HU	0.100	0.392	0.100	0.100	0.308
Latvia	LV	0.100	0.100	0.100	0.100	0.600
Lithuania	LT	0.100	0.100	0.100	0.100	0.600
Malta	MT	0.100	0.197	0.100	0.503	0.100
Poland	PL	0.100	0.100	0.128	0.100	0.572
Romania	RO	0.100	0.100	0.600	0.100	0.100
Slovakia	SK	0.118	0.100	0.100	0.100	0.582
Slovenia	SI	0.104	0.196	0.102	0.108	0.489
EU-28		0.120	0.121	0.167	0.307	0.286

The average results by year and by country are reported in Tables 17.11 and 17.12, respectively. It is interesting to note that for both the SPI and the constrained DEA, the average rate of performance change for the EU-28 over the whole period is positive and similar, 0.5% for SPIC and 0.4% for PC. In other words, welfare state performances

Table 17.11 Dynamic Performance Change

Country	SPIC (%)	Constrained DEA		
		CU (%)	EC (%)	PC (%)
EU15	−0.1	0.1	0.1	0.2
2005–2006	1.2	2.4	−1.5	0.9
2006–2007	1.3	−1.0	2.1	1.1
2007–2008	1.2	2.3	−1.7	0.6
2008–2009	0.1	2.0	−1.6	0.4
2009–2010	−1.2	−1.2	1.2	0.0
2011–2012	−2.4	−3.6	2.2	−1.5
EU13	1.2	1.9	−1.3	0.6
2005–2006	1.6	0.7	−0.6	0.1
2006–2007	3.4	−0.9	2.8	1.8
2007–2008	3.3	7.9	−5.4	2.1
2008–2009	0.4	0.9	−0.9	0.0
2009–2010	−2.4	1.7	−1.9	−0.2
2010–2011	0.9	1.8	−1.7	0.1
2011–2012	1.2	1.3	−0.9	0.3
EU28	0.5	1.0	−0.5	0.4
2005–2006	1.4	1.6	−1.1	0.5
2006–2007	2.3	−0.9	2.4	1.4
2007–2008	2.2	4.9	−3.4	1.3
2008–2009	0.2	1.5	−1.3	0.2
2009–2010	−1.8	0.1	−0.2	−0.1
2010–2011	0.1	1.0	−0.9	0.1
2011–2012	−0.8	−1.4	0.8	−0.6

increased by a half percentage point every year in average over the 2005–2012 period. Moreover, looking in detail at Table 17.11, we observe that SPIC and PC growth rates are in most cases worse after the financial crisis than before: null and negative growth rates are only observed from 2008–2009 on. Otherwise, several differences appear in the results across methods and between EU-15 and EU-13 member-states. For instance, EU-15 performed less well than EU-13 members, in average, both under SPIC (−0.1% vs. 1.2%) and constrained DEA (0.2% vs. 0.6%). When we analyze the components of performance change, catching-up (CU), and environmental change (EC), a clear case appears for EU-13 with a positive catching-up growth rate (CU = 1.9%) and a simultaneous decrease at the frontier level (EC = −1.3% in average for the entire period).

Table 17.12 Performance Change by Country (2005–2012 Mean)

Country		SPIC (%)	Constrained DEA CU (%)	EC (%)	PC (%)
EU-15		0.1	0.1	0.1	0.2
Austria	AT	-0.1	0.1	-0.1	0.0
Belgium	BE	0.8	0.6	0.2	0.7
Denmark	DK	-0.7	-0.6	-0.2	-0.8
Finland	FI	0.4	0.4	-0.3	0.1
France	FR	-0.1	0.6	0.2	0.8
Germany	DE	0.5	0.8	-0.1	0.7
Greece	EL	-4.9	-7.4	5.6	-2.3
Ireland	IE	0.2	0.3	-0.2	0.0
Italy	IT	0.6	0.7	0.1	0.9
Luxembourg	LU	0.5	0.5	-0.3	0.1
The Netherlands	NL	1.4	1.2	-0.5	0.7
Portugal	PT	5.0	7.9	-4.1	3.4
Spain	ES	-4.6	-3.1	2.5	-0.6
Sweden	SE	-0.6	0.0	-0.3	-0.4
United Kingdom	UK	1.0	1.0	-0.9	0.1
EU-13		1.2	1.9	-1.3	0.6
Bulgaria	BG	-3.3	-1.0	-0.8	-1.7
Croatia	HR	-1.5	-1.4	0.9	-0.6
Cyprus	CY	0.9	0.6	-0.5	0.1
Czech Republic	CZ	1.3	0.6	0.1	0.7
Estonia	EE	2.4	2.2	-1.1	1.1
Hungary	HU	0.3	1.0	-0.6	0.3
Latvia	LV	1.3	5.3	-3.6	1.5
Lithuania	LT	3.3	5.2	-3.4	1.7
Malta	MT	1.6	2.6	-1.0	1.5
Poland	PL	6.2	4.1	-2.0	2.1
Romania	RO	0.9	3.4	-3.2	0.0
Slovakia	SK	1.9	2.3	-1.3	1.0
Slovenia	SI	0.3	0.0	0.2	0.2
EU-28		0.5	1.0	-0.5	0.4

To be complete, Table 17.12 reports the results by country. For several countries both methodologies give similar results, for some of them positive SPIC and PC (e.g., Belgium, Portugal, and Slovenia), for others negative (e.g., Denmark and Bulgaria). Only France presents results of opposite sign, with a negative performance rate of change under SPI, but positive under constrained DEA. Overall the correlation between both indicators is high (0.964 Pearson correlation).

To test convergence in performance among EU countries, we perform two different tests, following Lichtenberg (1994). First, we test the *mean-reversion hypothesis*, that is, the hypothesis that countries with the lowest level of performance at period $t - 1$ grow at a highest rate in period t. For this purpose we run a simple OLS model with the logarithm of the performance score change in time t as dependent variable, and as explanatory variable the performance score at time $t - 1$. This test is a necessary but not a sufficient condition for convergence; therefore we run the test of convergence suggested by Lichtenberg (1994). The results of these tests applied to the performance scores changes (SPIC, PC, and CU) are reported in Table 17.13.

Looking first at the results corresponding to the change in performance scores SPIC and PC, we observe that the mean-reversion hypothesis is verified for the two indicators. In both cases the coefficient β associated with lagged performance has a negative and statistically significant value. Moreover, β takes a similar absolute value, −0.037 and −0.042 for the SPI and constrained DEA, respectively. In other words, countries with the lowest performance score improved their welfare state performance faster.

The test for convergence is straightforward. It is simply based on the ratio $R^2/(1+\beta)^2$ computed using the OLS estimated parameters.[17] As demonstrated by Lichtenberg (1994), this ratio is equivalent to a test on the ratio of variances between periods, the variance in $t - 1$ over the variance in t. For convergence, the expected result is that this ratio must be higher and significantly different from 1.0. The results reported in Table 17.1 are in both cases slightly higher than 1.0 (SPI = 1.005 and constrained DEA = 1.036), but none of them is significantly different from 1.0.

The second section of Table 17.13 reports the results of mean-reversion hypothesis and convergence test for the catching-up effects (CU) computed under constrained DEA. As for performance growth, the mean-reversion hypothesis is verified. The β coefficient is negative and statistically different from zero. The test on ratio $R^2/(1+\beta)^2$ shows higher values than for PC (1.054), but not sufficiently to validate convergence.

Finally, at the bottom of Table 17.13 are reported the results of a test of unequal variances between performance scores in 2005 and 2012. The ratio, in logarithmic form, indicates a value higher than 1.0 for constrained DEA (1.39). As expected, performance variance declines among the EU-28 countries. However, it was not enough to pass the convergence test. In this case, as well as for the ratio of variances corresponding to SPIC (1.01), these values are statistically nonsignificant.

Summing up, the results reported here confirm the observations made in Table 17.8. We do not observe convergence in performance among the countries, unlike Coelli et al. (2010). There are mainly two reasons. The first one comes from the fact that the

Table 17.13 Mean–Reversion Hypothesis and Convergence Test

Variables and Tests	SPI	Constrained DEA
Performance change		
OLS model – Mean-reversion hypothesis		
Dependent variable	$\log[SPIC(t)]$	$\log[PC(t)]$
Explanatory variable		
$\log[SPI(t-1)]$ (β)	-0.042^{*}	–
(std)	(0.020)	
$\log[DEA(t-1)]$ (β)	–	-0.037^{*}
(std)		(0.016)
R^2	0.922	0.975
Test of convergence		
$R^2/(1+\beta)^2$ (*F*-test)	1.005 [n–s]	1.036 [n–s]
Catching-up		
OLS model – Mean-reversion hypothesis		
Dependent variable	–	$\log[CU(t)]$
Explanatory variable		
$\log[DEA(t-1)]$ (β)	–	-0.101^{**}
(std)	–	(0.027)
R^2	–	0.852
Test of convergence		
$R^2/(1+\beta)^2$ (*F*-test)	–	1.054 [n–s]
Test of convergence based on the ratio of variances (2005/2012)		
	$Var[\log SPI(t)]$	$Var[\log DEA(t)]$
2005	0.0604	0.0538
2012	0.0600	0.0386
Ratio (*F*-test)	1.01 [n–s]	1.39 [n–s]

Notes: * and ** significant at 5% and 1%, respectively; [n–s] nonsignificant. The OLS regressions run using the whole sample (196 observations). R^2 computed from OLS model with $\log[PS(t)]$ as dependent variable and $\log[PS(t-1)]$ as explanatory variable. By construction, both models give identical values for the β coefficient.

sample we use is much more limited in terms of time: 2005–2012 versus 1995–2006. A second reason for this result is the economic crisis that started in 2007 and had direct consequences on social protection budgets in many countries.

17.3.4. Measuring Efficiency with or without Inputs

Finally, if we would like to compare these results with those presented in traditional measures of production efficiency of public services or public utilities from section 17.2, we should gather data on both outputs and inputs to construct a best-practice frontier. We showed earlier that even though it is difficult to meet the ideal data requirement, this approach is very useful and could be used when at least sufficient data are available and there exists an underlying identified technology. For example, measuring the efficiency of railway companies with this approach makes sense. Railways transport people and commodities (hopefully with comfort and punctuality), using a certain number of identifiable inputs.

When dealing with the public sector as a whole and more particularly social protection, we can easily identify its missions: social inclusion in terms of housing, education, health, work, and consumption. Yet, it is difficult to relate indicators pertaining to these missions (e.g., our five indicators) to specific inputs. A number of studies use social spending as the only input, but one has to realize that for most indicators of inclusion, social spending explains little. For example, it is well known that, for health and education, factors such as diet and family support are often just as important as public spending. This does not mean that public spending in health and in education is worth nothing; it just means that it is part of a complex process in which other factors play a crucial and complementary role.

Another reason why using social spending as the input of our five indicators is not appropriate comes from the fact that social spending as measured by international organizations is not a good measure of real spending. It does not include subsidies and tax breaks awarded to schemes such as mandatory private pensions or health care, and it includes taxes paid on social transfers.[18]

All this does not mean that the financing side of the public sector does not matter. It is always important to make sure that wastes are minimized, but wastes cannot be measured at such an aggregate level. It is difficult to think of a well-defined technology that "produces" social indicators with given inputs. To evaluate the efficiency slacks of the public sector, it is desirable to analyze micro-components of the welfare states, such as schools, hospitals, public agencies, public institution, railways, and so on, such as the studies we presented in the previous section. At the macro level, one should stop short of measuring technical inefficiency and restrict oneself to performance ranking.

To use the analogy of a classroom, it makes sense to rank students according to how they perform in a series of exams. Admittedly, we can question the quality of tests or the weights used in adding marks from different fields. Yet in general there is little discussion as to the grading of students. At the same time, we know that these students may face different "environmental conditions" that can affect their ability to perform. For example, if we have two students ranked number 1 and 2 and if the latter is forced to work at night to help ailing parents or to commute a long way from home, it is possible that he can be considered as more deserving or meritorious than the number 1, whose material and family conditions are ideal. This being said, there exists no ranking of students according to merit. The concept of "merit" is indeed too controversial. By the same token, we should not attempt to assess the "merit" of social protection systems or the public sector as a whole.

17.4. CONCLUSIONS

The purpose of this chapter was to present some guidelines as to the question of measuring and assessing the performance of the public sector. We believe that such measurement is unavoidable for two reasons. First, people constantly question the role of the public sector as a whole or of its components on the basis of questionable indicators. Second, a good measure can induce governments or public firms that are not performing to get closer to the best-practice frontier.

We began with the issue of whether or not we have to limit ourselves to a simple performance comparison, or if we can conduct an efficiency study. We have argued that efficiency evaluations can be conducted for components of the public sector when sufficient data are available and there exists a production technology link between resources used and outcomes achieved. When dealing with the overall welfare state or large aggregates such as the health or the education sector, we deliberately restrict ourselves to performance comparisons, that is, comparisons based only on the outcomes of these sectors. The reason is simple: in those instances, the link between public spending and outcomes is not clear and does not reveal a clear-cut production technology. More concretely, key factors that can affect performance are missing. For example, diet can impact health, and family can influence education, and yet it is difficult to quantify the roles of diet and of family.

We have presented an overview of recent productive efficiency studies in four areas: railways, waste collection, schools, and hospitals. For each of these areas we contrast what we call the ideal set of data with the one that is actually used by researchers. Not surprisingly, the qualitative data are consistently missing. This weakens the recommendations that can be drawn from these studies and should induce public authorities to further invest in qualitative data collection.

We then turn to the assessment of the performance of 28 European Union country members. The fact that even with a synthetic measure of performance the Nordic countries lead the pack is not surprising. Nor is it surprising to see that some Mediterranean countries, Greece and Portugal, and most new entrants (EU-13) are not doing well. It is interesting to see that with such a comprehensive concept, Anglo-Saxon welfare states,

Ireland and the United Kingdom, do as well as the Continental welfare states such as Belgium and Germany, and that the Czech Republic and Slovenia are among the best performers.

Finally, we turned to the convergence issue. Contrary to Coelli et al. (2010), we did not find a clear-cut process of convergence. This can be explained by the fact that here we deal with EU-28 and not just EU-15 and that the period is not only much shorter but also includes crisis years. It will be interesting to redo this exercise in several years when a longer time series is available.

NOTES

1. The authors are grateful to the editors and to Humberto Brea for insightful comments and suggestions on previous versions of this chapter. Sergio Perelman acknowledges financial support from the Belgian Fund for Scientific Research—FNRS (FRFC 14603726—"Beyond Incentive Regulation").

2. See, e.g., Esping-Andersen (1990).

3. The *benefit of the doubt* approach has been also applied to other fields, for example to measure the performance of European internal market dynamics (Cherchye et al. 2007b); farms sustainability (Reig-Martínez et al. 2011); citizen satisfaction with police services (Verschelde and Rogge 2012); citizens well-being (Reig-Martínez 2013); or in the case of undesirable outputs (Zanella et al. 2015).

4. As stated by Pestieau and Tulkens (1993), even if these objectives are not always completely compatible, there is one dimension, technical efficiency, that does not impede the achievement of the others.

5. The authors make in this way the distinction between railways' "efficiency," measured with outputs corresponding to the supplied capacity (seats-km and tons-km supplied) and "effectiveness," with outputs corresponding to effective demand (seats-km and tons-km transported).

6. For a detailed presentation of environmental effects of waste collection and treatment, see Emery et al. (2007).

7. For a detailed presentation of these indicators, see Gakidou et al. (2000).

8. Particularly a paper by Williams (2001) generated the debate on the performance measurement presented in WHO (2000).

9. The data are provided by the EU member-states within the OMC (see Eurostat database on Population and Social Conditions, 2014). They deal with key dimensions of individual well-being, and are comparable across countries. It is difficult to find better data for the purpose at hand. This being said, we realize that they can be perfected. There is some discontinuity in the series of inequality and poverty indicators. In addition, one could argue that life expectancy in good health is likely to be preferred to life expectancy at birth, or an absolute measure of poverty might be better than a relative measure that is too closely related to income inequality. But for the time being, these alternatives do not exist.

10. The five indicators belong to the series of 10 indicators chosen by EU members as representative of economic and social policy targets fixed by the 2000 Lisbon Agenda, the so-called "Laeken indicators" (Council of the European Union, 2001).

11. Coelli et al. (2010) study the performance of social protection in the EU-15 over the period 1995–2006. This section can be viewed as an extension of this paper, which was coauthored by Mathieu Lefebvre and Pierre Pestieau, two of the authors of this chapter.

12. See Cherchye et al. (2004), who use the DEA in a setting close to this one.

13. In order to perform DEA computations, we rescaled the five output indicators between 0.1 and 1.0, instead of 0.0 to 1.0. The main reason is to avoid zero outputs and then allow constrained share weights DEA computations. The DEA efficiency scores reported here do not take into account slacks; therefore they are invariant to this simple units measurement change in scaling, as has been proved by Lovell and Pastor (1995).

14. There are, however, some exceptions. For instance, Anderson et al. (2011) introduce a *benefit of the doubt* index which by construction will be bounded in both sides with only relying on two assumptions: non-decreasing and quasi-concave with respect to indicators; also Reig-Martínez et al. (2011) and Reig-Martínez (2013) apply a *benefit of the doubt* index in combination with a multi-criteria decision method (DEA-MCDM), which allows building a full rank of all observations in the sample, including the most efficient.

15. For a survey of weight restriction in DEA, see Pedraja-Chaparro et al. (1997), and for a survey on weight restriction in a DEA *benefit of the doubt* context, see Cherchye et al. (2007a).

16. This component represents the *technological progress* in the productivity measurement literature (Färe et al. 1994). In the performance measurement framework, Cherchye et al. (2007b, 770) postulate that this component "reflects a more favourable policy environment."

17. To perform this test, the R^2 corresponds to the OLS model with log $[DEA(t)]$ as dependent variable and log $[DEA(t-1)]$ as explanatory variable. By construction, the β coefficient and the other results are identical.

18. See Adema et al. (2011) for the definition of gross and net social spending.

References

Adema, W., P. Fron, and M. Ladaique. 2011. "Is the European Welfare State Really More Expensive? Indicators on Social Spending, 1980–2012; and a Manual to the OECD Social Expenditure Database (SOCX)." OECD Social, Employment and Migration Working Papers No. 124, OECD Publishing. doi: 10.1787/5kg2d2d4pbf0-en.

Afonso, A., and M. St. Aubyn. 2006a. "Cross-Country Efficiency of Secondary Education Provision: A Semi-Parametric Analysis with Non-Discretionary Inputs." *Economic Modeling* 23(3): 476–491.

Afonso, A., and M. St. Aubyn. 2006b. "Non-Parametric Approaches to Education and Health Efficiency in OECD Countries." *Journal of Applied Economics* 8(2): 227–246.

Allen, R., A. D. Athanassopoulos, R. G. Dyson, and E. Thanassoulis. 1997. "Weight Restrictions and Value Judgements in DEA: Evolution, Development and Future Directions." *Annals of Operations Research* 73: 13–34.

Anderson, G., I. Crawford, and A. Leicester. 2011. "Welfare Rankings from Multivariate Data, a Nonparametric Approach." *Journal of Public Economics* 95: 247–252.

Asmild, M., T. Holvad, J. L. Hougaard, and D. Kronborg. 2009. "Railway Reforms: Do They Influence Operating Efficiency?" *Transportation* 36: 617–638.

Cantos, P., J. M. Pastor, and L. Serrano. 2010. "Vertical and Horizontal Separation in the European Railway Sector and Its Effects on Productivity." *Journal of Transport Economics and Policy* 44: 139–160.

Cantos, P., J. M. Pastor, and L. Serrano. 2012. "Evaluating European Railway Deregulation Using Different Approaches." *Transport Policy* 24: 67–72.

Cherchye, L., W. Moesen, N. Rogge, and T. Van Puyenbroeck. 2007a. "An Introduction to Benefit of the Doubt Composite Indicators." *Social Indicators Research* 82: 111–145.

Cherchye, L., C. A. K. Lovell, W. Moesen, and T. Van Puyenbroeck. 2007b. "One Market, One Number? A Composite Indicator Assessment of EU Internal Market Dynamics." *European Economic Review* 51: 749–779.

Cherchye, L., W. Moesen, and T. Van Puyenbroeck. 2004. "Legitimely Diverse, Yet Comparable: On Synthesizing Social Inclusion Performance in the EU." *Journal of Common Market Studies* 42(5): 919–955.

Coelli, T. J., L. Mathieu, and P. Pestieau. 2010. "Performance in the European Union." *CESIfo Economic Studies* 56(2): 300–322.

Council of the European Union. 2001. "Report on Indicators in the Field of Poverty and Social Exclusion." http://www.consilium.europa.eu/uedocs/cms_data/docs/pressdata/en/misc/DOC.68841.pdf.

Crémieux, P. Y., P. Ouellette, and C. Pilon. 1999. "Health Care Spending as Determinants of Health Outcomes." *Health Economics* 8: 627–639.

De Jaeger, S., J. Eyckmans, N. Rogge, and T. Van Puyenbroeck. 2011. "Wasteful Waste-Reducing Policies? The Impact of Waste Reduction Policy Instruments on Collection and Processing Costs of Municipal Solid Waste." *Waste Management* 31: 1429–1440.

De Jaeger, S., and N. Rogge. 2013. "Waste Pricing Policies and Cost-Efficiency in Municipal Waste Services: The Case of Flanders." *Waste Management & Research* 31(7): 751–758.

Emery, A., A. Davies, A. Griffiths, and K. Williams. 2007. "Environmental and Economic Modelling: A Case Study of Municipal Solid Waste Management Scenarios in Wales." *Resources Conservation & Recycling* 49: 244–263.

Esping-Andersen, G. 1990. *The Three Worlds of Welfare Capitalism*. Princeton, NJ: Princeton University Press.

Eurostat. 2014. *Database on Population and Social Conditions*. (http://ec.europa.eu/eurostat/data/database).

Evans, D., A. Tandon, C. J. L. Murray, and J. A. Lauer. 2000. "The Comparative Efficiency of National Health Systems in Producing Health: An Analysis of 191 Countries." WHO GPE Discussion Paper Series 29, Geneva. http://www.who.int/healthinfo/paper29.pdf.

Färe, R., S. Grosskopf, M. Norris, and Z. Zhang. 1994. "Productivity Growth, Technical Progress and Efficiency Change in Industrialized Countries." *American Economic Review* 84: 66–83.

Färe, R., S. Grosskopf, B. Lindgren, and J. P. Poullier. 1997. "Productivity Growth on Health-Care Delivery." *Medical Care* 35(4): 354–366.

Farsi, M., M. Filippini, and W. Greene. 2005. "Efficiency Measurement in Network Industries: Application to the Swiss Railways Companies." *Journal of Regulatory Economics* 28(1): 69–90.

Friebel, G., M. Ivaldi, and C. Vibes. 2008. "Railway (De)Regulation: A European Efficiency Comparison." *Economica* 77: 77–91.

Gakidou, E., C. J. L. Murray, and J. Frenk. 2000. "Measuring Preferences on Health System Performance Assessment." WHO EIP/GPE Discussion Paper Series 20, Geneva. http://www.who.int/healthinfo/paper20.pdf.

García-Sánchez, I. M. 2008. "The Performance of Spanish Solid Waste Collection." *Waste Management & Research* 26: 327–336.

Greene, W. 2004. "Distinguishing Between Heterogeneity and Inefficiency: Stochastic Frontier Analysis of the World Health Organization's Panel Data on National Health Care Systems." *Health Economics* 13: 959–980.

Grosskopf, S., K. J. Hayes, L. L. Taylor, and W. L. Weber. 1997. "Budget-Constrained Frontier Measures of Fiscal Equality and Efficiency in Schooling." *Review of Economics and Statistics* 79(1): 116–124.

Growitsch, C., and H. Wetzel. 2009. "Testing for Economies of Scope in European Railways: An Efficiency Analysis." *Journal of Transport Economics and Policy* 43(1): 1–24.

Haelermans, C., and K. De Witte. 2012. "The Role of Innovations in Secondary School Performance: Evidence from a Conditional Efficiency Model." *European Journal of Operational Research* 223(2): 541–549.

Hanushek, E. 1997. "Assessing the Effects of School Resources on Student Performance: An Update." *Education Evaluation and Policy Analysis* 19(2): 141–164.

HDR. 1990. *Human Development Report 1990: Concepts and Measurement of Human Development*. United Nations Development Programme. New York: Oxford University Press.

Joumard, I., C. André, C. Nicq, and O. Chatal. 2008. "Health Status Determinants: Lifestyle, Environment, Health Care Resources and Efficiency." OECD Economics Department Working Papers No. 627, OECD Publishing. doi: 10.1787/240858500130.

Lauer, J. A., C. A. K. Lovell, C. J. L. Murray, and D. Evans. 2004. "World Health System Performance Revisited: The Impact of Varying the Relative Importance of Health System Goals." *BMC Health Services Research* 4: 19. doi: 10.1186/1472-6963-4-19.

Lichtenberg, F. R. 1994 "Testing the Convergence Hypothesis." *The Review of Economics and Statistics* 76(3): 576–579.

Lovell, C. A. K., and J. T. Pastor. 1995. "Units Invariant and Translation Invariant DEA Models." *Operational Research Letters* 18: 147–151.

Lovell, C. A. K., J. T. Pastor, and J. A. Turner. 1995. "Measuring Macroeconomic Performance in the OECD: A Comparison of European and Non-European Countries." *European Journal of Operational Research* 87: 507–518.

Marques, R. C., and P. Simões. 2009. "Incentive Regulation and Performance Measurement of the Portuguese Solid Waste Management Services." *Waste Management and Research* 27: 188–196.

Melyn, W., and W. Moesen. 1991. "Towards a Synthetic Indicator of Macroeconomic Performance: Unequal Weighting When Limited Information Is Available." Public Economics Research Paper No. 17, Katholieke Universiteit Leuven, Belgium.

Nordhaus, W. D., and J. Tobin. 1972. "Is Growth Obsolete?" *Economic Growth* 96. New York: National Bureau of Economic Research.

OECD. 2014. *All on board: Making Inclusive Growth Happen*. Paris: OECD. doi: http://dx.doi.org/10.1787/9789264218512-en.

Pedraja-Chaparro, F., J. Salinas-Jiménez, and P. Smith. 1997. "On the Role of Weight Restrictions in Data Envelopment Analysis." *Journal of Productivity Analysis* 8: 215–230.

Pestieau, P., and H. Tulkens. 1993. "Assessing and Explaining the Performance of Public Enterprise." *FinanzArchiv* 50: 293–323.

Pestieau, P. 2009. "Assessing the Performance of the Public Sector." *Annals of Public and Cooperative Economy* 80: 133–161.

Reig-Martínez, E. 2013. "Social and Economic Wellbeing in Europe and the Mediterranean Basin: Building an Enlarged Human Development Indicator." *Social Indicators Research* 111–112: 527–547.

Reig-Martínez, E., J. Gómez-Limón, and A. J. Picazo-Tadeo. 2011. "Ranking Farms with a Composite Indicator of Sustainability." *Agricultural Economics* 42: 561–575.

Rogge, N., and S. De Jaeger. 2013. "Measuring and Explaining the Cost Efficiency of Municipal Solid Waste Collection and Processing Services." *Omega* 41: 653–664.

Spinks, J., and B. Hollinsgsworth. 2009. "Cross-Country Comparisons of Technical Efficiency of Health Production: A Demonstration of Pitfalls." *Applied Economics* 41: 417–427.

Stiglitz, J., A. Sen, and J.-P. Fitoussi. 2009. "The Measurement of Economic Performance and Social Progress Revisited." OFCE, No. 2009-33. http://www.ofce.sciences-po.fr/pdf/dtravail/ WP2009-33.pdf.

Sutherland, D., R. Price, and F. Gonand. 2009. "Improving Public Spending Efficiency in Primary and Secondary Education." *OECD Journal: Economic Studies* 1: 1–30.

Tandon A., C. J. L. Murray, J. A. Lauer, and D. Evans. 2001. "Measuring Overall Health System Performance for 191 Countries." WHO GPE Discussion Paper Series 30, Geneva. http:// www.who.int/healthinfo/paper30.pdf.

Verschelde, M., and N. Rogge. 2012. "An Environment-Adjusted Evaluation of Citizen Satisfaction with Local Police Effectiveness: Evidence from a Conditional Data Envelopment Analysis Approach." *European Journal of Operational Research* 223(1): 214–225.

WHO. 2000. *The World Health Report 2000. Health Systems: Improving Performance.* Geneva: World Health Organization.

Williams, A. 2001. "Science or Marketing at WHO? A Commentary on World Health 2000." *Health Economics* 10: 93–100.

Wong, Y.-H. B., and J. E. Beasley. 1990. "Restricting Weight Flexibility in Data Envelopment Analysis." *The Journal of the Operational Research Society* 41(9): 829–835.

Worthington, A., and B. E. Dollery. 2001. "Measuring Efficiency in Local Government: An Analysis of New South Wales Municipalities' Domestic Waste Management Function." *Policy Studies Journal* 29(2): 232–249.

Wößmann, L. 2003. "Schooling Resources, Educational Institutions and Student Performance: The International Evidence." *Oxford Bulletin of Economics and Statistics* 65(2): 117–170.

Yu, M. N., and T. J. Lin. 2008. "Efficiency and Effectiveness in Railway Performance Using a Multi-Activity Network DEA Model." *Omega* 36: 1005–1017.

Zanella, A., A. S. Camanho, and T. G. Dias. 2015. "Undesirable Outputs and Weighting Schemes in Composite Indicators Based on Data Envelopment Analysis." *European Journal of Operational Research* 245: 517–530.

CHAPTER 18

....

MEASURING PRODUCTIVITY DISPERSION

....

ERIC J. BARTELSMAN AND ZOLTAN WOLF

18.1. INTRODUCTION

....

HETEROGENEITY in productivity or the efficiency of producers has long been recognized in the academic literature, but traditionally was considered more of a hindrance that needed to be massaged away in analysis, rather than an important feature of economic life requiring theoretical and empirical analysis.[1] Marshall (1920) introduced the notion of a "representative firm" in his "Principles" in order to analyze equilibrium in production. Robbins (1928) notes that Marshall mainly introduced the concept in order to simplify analysis. Robbins then goes on to argue that the construct of the representative firm is not needed for analysis of economic equilibrium and actually may be misleading (Robbins 1928; p.399): "The whole conception, it may be suggested, is open to the general criticism that it cloaks the essential heterogeneity of productive factors—in particular the heterogeneity of managerial ability—just at that point at which it is most desirable to exhibit it most vividly."

Notwithstanding the contribution of Robbins, much of the theoretical work in general equilibrium theory and also in macro theory of business cycles and growth continued to use the representative firm until recently. By contrast, ensuing empirical research eschewed the representative firm (e.g., Farrell 1957; Salter 1960), but did not have theoretical explanations for how productivity differences could coexist. Leibenstein (1966) contrasted deviations from efficiency as described by micro theory (allocative inefficiency), with differences in efficiency across otherwise similar production units. By giving a name to the gap from the most productive firm, "X-inefficiency," Liebenstein may have provided an appealing narrative, but did not satisfy the theoretician's desire for placing the phenomenon in the framework of cost minimization (e.g., Stigler 1976). However, following Stigler's critique and reply (Leibenstein 1978), the path had opened up for future researchers to work on building a framework to understand why productivity dispersion across firms exists and even may be compatible with optimizing behavior in output and input markets.

The explanations generally require some curvature in the profit function of a producer that prevents the most productive firm from selling to all customers in the market. Mechanisms include frictions in the adjustment of factors and the entry and exit of plants, and distortions that drive wedges in the forces pushing toward the equalization of marginal products across plants. Early models of heterogeneous producers that support productivity dispersion in equilibrium are given by Lucas (1978) and Hopenhayn (1992). Other relevant theoretical contributions point the way toward understanding how dispersion may shed light on the measurement of output and inputs (e.g., De Loecker 2011), on frictions in optimization (e.g., Cooper and Haltiwanger 2006), and on distortions to the functioning of markets (e.g., Brown et al. 2016; Hsieh and Klenow 2009). This chapter will provide some guidelines on how to measure productivity dispersion and place it into context of the models.

The recipes given in this chapter for measuring and analyzing dispersion of productivity use longitudinal firm- or plant-level data as collected by statistical agencies in annual production surveys. These data underlie much of the empirical literature reviewed by Bartelsman and Doms (2000) and Syverson (2011). Further, similar data sets are now being explored in empirical studies of productivity, innovation, employment, and trade, for example by the Eurostat ESSNet projects (Bartelsman et al. 2018a), the Organisation for Economic Co-operation and Development (OECD) DynEmp project (Criscuolo et al. 2014), and the European Central Bank CompNet project (Lopez-Garcia and di Mauro 2015). Using these data, the research finds that productivity differences across establishments indeed are large and persistent in all countries, industries, and time periods reviewed.

Dispersion is important as a measure of heterogeneity and also because it is relevant for business dynamism and growth. The role of dispersion for business dynamism and growth has been explored extensively in the context of the relationship between productivity, growth, and reallocation dynamics. A number of papers found that more productive plants are more likely to grow and less likely to exit (recent examples include Foster et al. 2017; Foster et al. 2016a). Another area of application is the frontier literature, which postulates that the technology and practices of the most productive plants, or frontier plants, are adapted by other establishments (e.g., Acemoglu et al. 2006; Bartelsman et al. 2015). In this view, growth is sourced either from innovative activity at the frontier or from the adjustment of nonfrontier establishments, in which they adopt frontier behavior. Yet another area of inquiry is related to the interpretation of dispersion in revenue productivity. Based on the insights in Hsieh and Klenow (2009)—that under certain assumptions about technology and demand, dispersion in productivity reflects market distortions—dispersion in a particular revenue productivity measure has been used to create indicators of misallocation (a recent example is Foster et al. 2016b).

The remainder of the chapter is organized as follows. Before defining productivity and its measures, we start with a theoretical discussion on productivity dispersion. The next section will discuss measurement of productivity at the plant level and will place the simple measures of productivity used in the literature on dispersion in the context of more sophisticated measures discussed in this *Handbook*. Next, some recipes will be provided for computing dispersion measures, taking into account sensitivity to measurement errors. The chapter then will conclude with a review of some evidence on productivity dispersion in a wide variety of industries and countries, as well as thoughts about a model that endogenizes productivity dispersion.

18.2. WHAT IS PRODUCTIVITY DISPERSION?

Assume we have an indicator of productivity, ω_{it}, of a production unit i in time period t, that measures how much more, or less, output (in log-points) is produced per unit of input than at some "reference" production unit. This measure of productivity, for a single firm, plant, or decision-making unit, is the basic building block for cross-sectional measures of dispersion (at time t). Dispersion is related to the "width" of the productivity distribution and thus has the same dimensionality as the underlying measure. The empirical distribution of productivity built up from the ω_{it} s that are derived from observed data is the result of our statistical methodology in collecting the data and the computational methods of computing productivity, as well as the result of economic processes driven by decisions made at production units and the interactions between economic agents in input and output markets. Finally, dispersion in productivity can reflect idiosyncracies in the processes driving creation of knowledge and production technology.

In this section we will provide some theoretical background into the drivers of the empirical measure of productivity dispersion. We start with a discussion of statistical issues. Next, we look at two sides of the economic process driving dispersion. First, we look at factors that drive dispersion across firms in their ability to produce output given inputs (i.e., at a certain level of productivity). Second, we look at processes in input and output markets that reallocate inputs and select production units and thus jointly shape the observed productivity distribution. Because of its importance as the building block for measuring dispersion, a separate section is devoted to computation of the relative productivity of a production unit, ω_{it}.

18.2.1. Statistical Issues

Dispersion in productivity is some measure of the distribution of productivity, for example the second moment. The use of the terms *measure, distribution,* and *moment* bring on thoughts about probability and statistics, and possibly about sampling and measurement error. In this section we disentangle statistical issues from the economic phenomenon that we are trying to measure.

From probability theory, we can understand a probability space to consist of a sample space, a set of events, and a function mapping events to a probability. Interpretation of the (empirical) productivity distribution depends on what we think the underlying process is through which outcomes are drawn from the sample space, and how we think about the relationship between events and the available data. For example, we could think of the outcome of NT observations from a longitudinal panel of N firms and T years as being independent draws from a particular sample space and probability mapping.[2] Given the sample size, we could then place error bounds on estimates of the standard error of the probability distribution. Under these assumptions, the interpretation of dispersion of productivity is clear. However, the underlying assumptions may not hold, and deviations require differing interpretations.

To start, the observations may not be independently drawn from the same distribution. This can easily be tested, for example by testing for the equality of the "within" (over time-series dimension) estimate of the standard error with the "between" (over cross-sectional dimension) estimate (see later discussion for details). To our knowledge, the empirical evidence shows that the standard error of the productivity measures across firms in an industry is much larger than the standard deviation of productivity at the firm-level (on average across firms) over time. To distinguish between the two dimensions, we will call the second moment over the cross-section *dispersion* and call the second moment over the time-series of productivity (growth) *volatility*.[3]

Volatility of productivity likely has different "causes" than dispersion of productivity and also plays a distinct role in different types of analysis. In the current macroeconomic literature there is a large interest in the volatility of productivity. Standard business cycle models are often driven by exogenous productivity shocks (e.g., Smets and Wouters 2007). Further, a new literature on uncertainty shocks is pointing to the ex ante uncertainty that firms face about future operating conditions when making investment decisions (e.g., Bloom 2009). In some empirical applications, sometimes the volatility is calibrated using evidence from cross-section dispersion, which to our view is not appropriate. Of course, optimal forecasts of future volatility may contain information derived from a cross section of historical volatilities (see, e.g., Senga 2015). For the remainder of this chapter, we will focus on measures of dispersion rather than on volatility. However, we will address the possibility of cyclicality of productivity dispersion and its causes and implications.

Another issue in understanding the distribution of productivity relates to how the observations derive from a data-generating process. If the data set is a census of all existing firms, then the underlying interpretation of a statistical sampling from a probability distribution does not make sense.[4] In this case, and absent pure measurement error, the estimate of dispersion of productivity across firms in an industry should not be considered a random variable, but rather an actual measure without confidence bounds.

Even with census data, the dispersion measure becomes a random variable if one makes another interpretation of the probability space (or data-generating function). For example, firms may get a (persistent) draw from a probability distribution at entry. In this case, the observations on productivity of firms by entry-cohort could provide information on the underlying (time-varying) distribution from which a firm's productivity is drawn. Other possibilities include measurement error in outputs and inputs that are the underlying cause of dispersion in observed productivity. In the section on empirical dispersion measures, we will provide an overview of the types of data-generating processes that may be underlying observed productivity dispersion.

18.2.2. Economic Issues

In this section we adapt the framework of Syverson (2011) to discuss factors that affect ω_{it}, or the (relative) efficiency. Syverson distinguishes factors that operate "within" firms, or things that firms can do to change their (relative) productivity over time, and "between" factors, or things beyond a firm's control that alter a firm's relative productivity. In the following, we provide a brief overview from the recent literature to most of Syverson's factors. We exclude the factor of market competition from this list, as we see that as one of the factors that shapes the observed dispersion through allocation and selection mechanisms.

An easy way to think about, or model, heterogeneity in productivity across firms in an industry is to assume that firms receive a random draw from some underlying distribution of productivity. An interpretation of this could be that a firm has a manager or owner whose quality is random, as in Lucas (1978). The success of management may reflect differences in individual skill or the quality of practices (coordination, allocation of the labor force, etc.). Less is known about how managers actually allocate their own time, incentivize their workers, or manage relationships outside the firm. Existing papers in this context typically focused on single-industry or single-firm data, which is not surprising because these inquiries require very detailed information.[5] A nice example of this work can be found in Bloom et al. (2016) or Bushnell and Wolfram (2009). Also, the quality of management could affect the productivity of a firm over time, leading to persistence in the effect of an initial good draw. Lazear (2000) and Ichniowski and Shaw (2003) investigate management practices such as pay-for-performance schemes, work teams, cross-training, and routinized labor-management communication in forming productivity.

Rather than assuming a random draw to (a persistent component) of productivity, firms can undertake explicit actions that result in heterogeneous productivity across firms. In a simple version, firms pay a fixed (entry) fee to receive a draw from a productivity distribution (as in Hopenhayn 1992). Alternatively, firms could undertake investment in research and development (R&D), or other intangible capital. A large literature exist on the effects of IT investment on productivity (dispersion). For example, Bartelsman et al. (2017) show how use of broadband Internet is correlated with the dispersion of productivity across firms in an industry.

The literature also provides mechanisms that alter the relative position of firms in the productivity distribution, either through explicit firm decisions or through external effects such as knowledge spillovers. Bartelsman et al. (2008) analyze push-and-pull effects, where productivity spillovers from frontier knowledge can contribute to changes in relative productivity. Some key papers are Moretti (2004), who looks at the role of skilled workers to benefit from spillovers, and Bloom et al. (2013), who look at positive knowledge spillovers as well as business stealing effects. This last idea ties in with our next section, where we look at how interactions between agents in markets may affect the observed distribution of productivity.

The market environment for inputs and outputs conditions the decisions made by producers that can influence their productivity, as described in the preceding. The market environment also shapes the allocation of inputs across firms and the share of production and sales of each firm in the market. Competition will drive market shares toward more efficient producers, shrinking relatively high-cost firms/plants and opening up room for more efficient producers. Intra-market competition has been studied in many papers. Syverson (2004) looks at the ready-mix concrete industry (homogenous product, substitutability, etc.). International trade is another area where competition can be productivity enhancing, partly through changes in dispersion (see, e.g., Eaton and Kortum 2002; Melitz 2003; Wagner 2007). In many firm-level trade models, opening up to trade increases the "threshold" productivity below which firms exit the market, thereby reducing dispersion.

18.3. PRODUCTIVITY MEASUREMENT

Productivity is simply a measure of output per unit of input. With a single homogeneous output and a single homogeneous input, productivity is a cardinal number with dimensionality units of output per unit of input. With multiple inputs or output, or when inputs or outputs are not strictly homogeneous across firms or over time, typical index number issues arise. The approach then is to either define an index that meets certain desirable properties (axiomatic approach) or that can be derived from a theoretical model (see Diewert and Nakamura 2003). A productivity index then is defined as productivity relative to some reference level, for example relative to a base period of the same production unit, or relative to some other production unit. In the frontier approach, productivity of a firm is measured relative to the frontier of production possibilities (see, e.g., Chapters 2 and 4 in this *Handbook*). Essentially, productivity is a distance measure. The distribution of productivity across firms or over time should be interpreted as showing the distribution across all production units of the distance in terms of productivity between that observation and some fixed reference observation. More generally, in the empirical literature on plant-level productivity, it is customary to sweep out industry and time effects, so the productivity observations show the distance relative to the industry- and time-specific average.

Using a rather generic notation (see, e.g., Fried et al. 2008), which we will detail later as needed, production takes place by transforming a vector of inputs $\mathbf{x} \in \mathbb{R}_k^+$ into a vector of outputs $\mathbf{y} \in \mathbb{R}^+_m$, with + and m aligned. This transformation takes place through a production function that defines transformation as $T(\mathbf{x}, \mathbf{y}) = 0$. Using this style of notation, one can define the inputs requirement set $S(\mathbf{y})$ with all feasible input vectors $\mathbf{x}$ that can achieve a certain output $\mathbf{y}$ (with free disposal). One can also define an isoquant

$$I(\mathbf{y}) = \{\mathbf{x} : \mathbf{x} \in S(\mathbf{y}) \text{ and } \theta\mathbf{x} \notin S(\mathbf{y}) \text{ if } 0 \le \theta < 1\}$$

(or more stringently an efficient subset in case the isoquant is not strictly convex) showing the boundary of the input requirements for the given output. If one can scale down the inputs usage along a ray to the origin (in the positive orthant in input space), then the input is not technically efficient. The scalar ($\theta < 1$) needed to scale the input to the technically efficient frontier is called the *measure of technical inefficiency*. The measure of technical efficiency is then given by $\Omega(\mathbf{y}, \mathbf{x}) = \min\{\theta : \theta\mathbf{x} \in S(\mathbf{y})\}$. A geometrically similar discussion can be made to give the distance between the output actually produced at input $\mathbf{x}$ and the technically efficient output given by the isoquant on which $\mathbf{x}$ lies.

Figure 18.1 illustrates the productivity and efficiency concepts. Starting with the narrative of frontier firms and inefficient firms, an inefficient firm using aggregate inputs $F(\mathbf{x}) = F(x_1, x_2)$ could produce higher output given its input quantities. The arrow on the left panel represents the input efficiency measure, which says given output $\mathbf{y}$, what fraction of the inputs would be needed if the firm were operating efficiently. The Farrell input efficiency measure is the ratio of the norm of the ray input vectors $\theta = |\mathbf{x}'| / |\mathbf{x}|$.[6] The horizontal arrow on the right panel shows the reduction in the aggregate input index in order to achieve efficient production.[7] Assuming scalar output, the vertical arrow on the right panel shows that the output inefficiency measure of this firm is $y' / y = \Omega' / \Omega = \theta_y$, namely, given the input vector $\mathbf{x}$, how much less is produced than the frontier firm could have produced with these inputs.

In empirical studies using business survey data, it generally is the case that output is a scalar, y. Assume production (with free disposal) takes place according to $y \le F(\mathbf{x}; \beta)$,

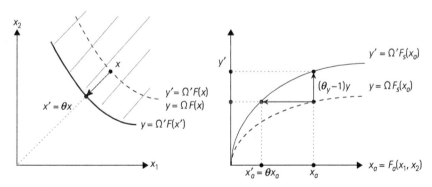

FIGURE 18.1. Productivity concepts. Left panel: input inefficiency; right panel: input and output efficiency.

where F is an appropriately redefined input aggregator, derived from the transformation function T noted earlier, with estimable parameters β. This can be rewritten as $y = F(\mathbf{x}; \beta)\Omega$, where $\Omega \leq 1$ is a Farrell-type measure of inefficiency. Productivity is thus essentially the ratio of output to aggregated inputs,

$$\Omega = y / F(\mathbf{x}; \beta)$$

Measurement of productivity depends on measurement of output and inputs. It also depends on specification and parameterization of the production (or input aggregator) function F and finally depends on the assumptions about the nature of the error or residual term in estimation or computation (see the review of Hulten 2001). We will address those issues most relevant to generating productivity dispersion measures from firm-level or plant-level longitudinal data.

18.3.1. Measurement of Outputs and Inputs

18.3.1.1. *From Observed Data to Outputs and Inputs*

A number of measurement issues need to be considered when one wants to construct productivity measures from observable data. Survey data typically record annual flows of expenses or income in currency units. The standard empirical approach is to deflate revenues or intermediate input purchases using industry-level deflators, owing to lack of product-level or firm-level prices. One consequence of this procedure is that in the presence of product differentiation the effect of heterogenous product prices is ignored. As will be discussed later in an overview of "revenue" and "quantity" total factor productivity (TFPR and TFPQ) measures, recent research has started to analyze the effects of (lack of) firm-level prices on productivity and dispersion.

Nominal output measurement generally starts with nominal sales, as recorded in firm-level survey (or register-based) data. When considering production as a physical transformation of material inputs, using capital and labor, often goods purchased for resale are subtracted from nominal sales to get a measure of output or production.[8] Sometimes data on resales are not available, but the measures for nominal output, value added, and intermediate purchases should be consistent, so that goods purchased for retail are either included in both output and intermediates, or are excluded from both. Nominal value added is then measured as output minus intermediates.

Labor input is usually measured as the number of employees or full-time equivalent (FTE) employees. If feasible, allowance should be made for work done by proprietors or unpaid family members. Often this can be proxied by adding one worker to every firm in the data set. Heterogeneity in worker quality can affect productivity measures. Sometimes wage expenditures are used as a proxy for quality-adjusted FTE, reflecting the view that this variable captures changes in the skill composition or the quality of the plant's labor force. Recent empirical work with linked employer–employee data, together with assumptions on matching/sorting between workers and firms, has made progress in parsing out firm-level productivity from worker heterogeneity (see, e.g., Lentz and Mortensen 2005).

Proper productivity measurement requires quality-adjusted capital service flows. This is quite difficult to measure. Survey and census data usually contain information only on the book value of the capital stock. Following procedures outlined by OECD (2009), researchers often use book values deflated by an industry-level investment deflator to proxy for capital. If firm- or plant-level investment is observable, then researchers apply some variant of the perpetual inventory method (PIM). PIM is a recursive procedure in which a deflated value of current investment is cumulated on the depreciated capital stock. Both approaches have drawbacks. First, deflated book values might be poor approximations of replacement values. Next, accumulated deflated investment may deviate from quality-adjusted service flows, which is the appropriate concept for capital input in production functions. One reason for this is a lack of proper deflators and/or lack of composition of investment that results in the proxy for capital input to be heterogeneous across plants. Further, the PIM requires an estimate of the initial capital stock, as well as estimates of depreciation by asset type at the firm level, which are not observed.

18.3.1.2. *Omitted-Price Bias: Physical Productivity (TFPQ) and Revenue Productivity (TFPR)*

Firm-level datasets rarely contain information on plant-level output prices and/or quantities. To obtain a plant-level output measure from nominal sales, a typical method in the empirical literature is to deflate sales using industry-level deflators. The resulting productivity index is a revenue-based indicator. Only under the assumption that the output of the industry is homogenous does TFPR calculated in this manner correctly measure productivity in quantities or physical productivity (TFPQ), and therefore technological differences across firms. If this assumption fails because products are differentiated or firms exercise market power, additional biases may result because the error term includes the effect of product prices.[9] Analogous arguments can be made about the effects of unobserved input prices because most firm-level surveys record only the total cost of inputs and not their quantities. These issues are well understood in the literature; the interpretation of alternative revenue productivity measures that emerge from various estimation procedures have become important, especially in light of the insights in Hsieh and Klenow (2009). Keeping this in mind, we will focus on the consequences that omitted output prices may have on measuring productivity dispersion.

The difference between TFPR and TFPQ impacts the interpretation of results. Klette and Griliches (1996) show that if firms operate in an imperfectly competitive environment with heterogenous product prices, iso-elastic demand, and Cobb-Douglas technology, scale estimates from these regressions of deflated sales should be considered as a mixture of the true scale elasticity and demand parameters. The basic insight is the following. If a firm experiences a negative cost shock, or equivalently a positive productivity shock, it can increase its market share by undercutting its competitor's price. Such negative correlation between productivity and prices is a result of downward sloping demand. Since the increase in output is larger than the increase in sales, replacing output with revenue as the dependent variable in a least-squares regression implies that the coefficients are downward-biased estimates of the true elasticities. This also implies the dispersion of revenue productivity is smaller than that of physical productivity or efficiency. Foster et al. (2008) and Foster et al. (2017) offer empirical evidence supporting this finding. They also highlight that demand shocks exhibit high dispersion relative to physical productivity dispersion. As such, dispersion in TFPR likely reflects both dispersion in TFPQ and in demand shocks.[10]

As mentioned earlier, not accounting for product (and price) heterogeneity within industries affects productivity estimates. In the absence of data on plant-level prices and/or quantities, earlier research used the following approach addressing this issue. Assuming some structure about demand, firm-specific product prices can be substituted out from the revenue equation. Studies differ along these assumptions and have used different variables to control for firm-level prices, but it is common to assume that the firm's residual demand is iso-elastic, and that it is determined by aggregate demand and the firms' market share, which in turn is determined by the substitution effect across products within the industry. This demand structure, together with Cobb-Douglas technology, though admittedly restrictive, has the analytical advantage that it implies a closed-form solution for TFPR, regardless of assumptions about returns to scale (see Foster et al. 2016b for details). In addition, the revenue function will include a measure of industry-level output, or aggregate demand, implying that the joint estimation of demand parameters and revenue function coefficients allows the identification of factor elasticities and returns to scale. Obtaining factor elasticities in this framework is straightforward: one has to rescale the revenue elasticities and TFPR using the markup, where the markup is estimated jointly with revenue elasticities and TFPR. If our data contain information on prices and/or quantities, then combining such a demand system with a production function also allows us to identify TFPQ shocks at the plant level.[11]

18.3.1.3. *Output: Gross Output or Value Added*

Firms produce output using the primary inputs of capital and labor, as well as purchased materials and services. Nonetheless, in more macro-based literature, productivity often is measured on the basis of value added, starting with the work of Cobb and Douglas (1928). This approach can be motivated by the fact that in the overall economy, aggregate final demand equals aggregate value added, giving a value-added based productivity measure an intuitive interpretation. Basu and Fernald (2002) show conditions under which changes in a slightly modified aggregate value-added-based Solow residual actually measure changes in welfare, even when measured productivity and technology differ owing to various market distortions. Under perfect competition and constant returns to scale, the rate of change of value-added-based productivity is a valid measure of technical progress. Bruno (1978) provides conditions for the existence of a value-added production function, and conditions when value-added-based marginal products correctly measure true marginal products.[12]

In aggregating from the firm level to the aggregate level, Basu et al. (2009), using results from Basu and Fernald (2002), show a decomposition of growth of the aggregate Solow residual into terms related to growth in aggregate primary inputs, reallocation terms, and aggregate change in technology. In this aggregation, a switch is made from viewing aggregate value added as a sum of growth in final demands by product, into a sum of growth in income earned on primary factors (value added here equals gross output minus intermediate purchases) across producers. In aggregation, and abstracting from price changes, the divisia weights differ between the two, namely shares of final demand and shares in primary factor income, respectively. The latter does not have an obvious theoretical foundation.

Instead, in a productivity aggregation framework developed by Domar (1961) and expanded by Hulten (1978), an economy is viewed as a collection of firms that make products (commodities) using primary inputs and purchased commodities, and sell the products to other producers and to final demand. Within this framework, the definition of productivity and the manner in which to aggregate now depends on the level from which one is aggregating and the level to which one is aggregating. For a production unit at any level of aggregation, productivity growth is defined as growth of *net output*, or product sold to agents outside the production unit, minus (cost-share weighted) growth in primary inputs and products purchased from agents outside the production unit. In aggregation, the *Domar-weight* is the share of net output of the production unit divided by the net output of the unit to which one is aggregating. The sum of these weights is larger than one.

For example, in aggregating firm-level productivity to productivity of the (closed economy) as a whole, one defines output of a firm as total production minus own-product used in production as net output and nonprimary inputs as inputs purchased from outside the firm. For most firms, these equal gross output and intermediate input, respectively, but at farms or energy-mining firms a significant share of firm production is "produced and consumed" and needs to be netted out. For the firm level, a net-output productivity measure thus is appropriate, but in practice will equal the gross output productivity measure. In aggregation, the net output of the "whole economy" equals the sum of all firms' net output minus the sum of all purchased inputs, in other words aggregate final demand or value added. In this case, the aggregation weights to sum each firms' productivity growth to compute aggregate productivity growth is given by firm-level gross output divided by aggregate value added.

In an equivalent manner, one can aggregate firm productivity to the industry level, or industry-level productivity to total private nonfinancial sector, by appropriately defining net output productivity for the disaggregated units, and using Domar-weights computed by dividing net output of a disaggregate unit to net output of the unit to which one is aggregating. Corrado et al. (2007) provide a convenient notation that displays the generic properties of such aggregation, as well as expanding the concepts to include imports and exports.

Turning to productivity dispersion measures, one can in principle compute the dispersion of value-added-based productivity across firms in an industry. Nonetheless, even if the separability conditions needed for the value-added production function hold, gross output may be preferable because there is a market with supply and demand for output, while no market for value added exists. And, it is precisely for understanding the dynamics of such markets that productivity dispersion is interesting. With representative firms, dispersion in either value added or gross output productivity would not exist. Empirically, choosing value added instead of gross output as the dependent variable has a large effect on within-industry dispersion measures. Tables 18.2 and 18.3 offer evidence that value-added-based dispersion is much larger than output-based dispersion. This is not surprising if one considers that, to a first approximation, value-added productivity is equal to gross output productivity times the reciprocal of the share of value added in gross output.

18.3.2. Estimating the Input Aggregator

As described earlier, we can compute TFP as the ratio of output to weighted inputs, with weights as estimated in the empirical production function literature.

$$Y_{it} = K_{it}^{\beta_K} L_{it}^{\beta_L} E_{it}^{\beta_E} M_{it}^{\beta_M} \Omega_{it} \tag{18.1}$$

where Y, K, L, E and M denote output, capital stock, labor, energy, and material inputs, respectively. i and t index plants and time periods, and the βs denote the elasticity of Q with respect to factor inputs. It is then straightforward to define TFP as a ratio of output and an index of inputs $\text{TFP} \equiv \Omega_{it} = Y_{it} / (K_{it}^{\hat{\beta}_K} L_{it}^{\hat{\beta}_L} E_{it}^{\hat{\beta}_E} M_{it}^{\hat{\beta}_M})$. The input index is a weighted average of primary-input factors where the βs are the estimated elasticities of output with respect to the appropriate input factor. A few issues are relevant in estimation of the production function or input aggregator. We start with the issue of endogeneity of a firm's factor input decisions in response to firm productivity, and discuss semi-parametric and parametric estimation methods. We also consider growth accounting methods to aggregate inputs and generate residuals, and finally refer to nonparametric data envelopment analysis (DEA)–type methods for computing productivity.

18.3.2.1. *Endogeneity of Input Decisions*

The following section briefly revisits estimation issues. Some of them have been analyzed in great detail in the literature, others were investigated more recently. Since productivity estimation requires elasticities in order to be able to calculate the weighted input index and compute productivity, we will use the terms *production function* and *productivity* interchangeably.

Perhaps the most extensively analyzed econometric issue is the endogeneity of production factors and unobserved TFP. As first pointed out by Marschak and Andrews (1944), least-squares-based production function estimates are rendered biased because plants consider their productivity in input decisions, but plant-level TFP is unobserved to the econometrician and therefore TFP is incorporated in the error term. Parametric and semi-parametric methods were developed in order to control for the variation in unobserved TFP. Parametric approaches such as instrumental variables techniques or stochastic frontiers do not explicitly control for the effects of unobserved TFP. Instead they rely on assumptions about the time series properties of plant-level productivity and apply data transformations to remove its effect from the estimating equation.[13] The aforementioned methods are all projection-based in the sense that regression techniques are used to estimate elasticities and calculate the productivity residual. Other methods, (cost-share-based techniques or growth accounting [GA] after the seminal work of Solow 1956) calculate productivity directly from data relying on first-order conditions derived from either profit maximization or cost minimization. Since GA is a nonstochastic method and therefore projection-based procedures cannot be used, the aforementioned endogeneity issue is irrelevant. However, other types of specification error do emerge if the first-order conditions are violated, for example if firms face frictions in adjusting inputs. Nevertheless, their popularity provides justification to include a short description for completeness.

18.3.2.2. *Semi-Parametric Estimation*

The original idea of using firm-level proxies in production function estimation was developed in Olley and Pakes (1996) (OP hereafter) in order to analyze the dynamics of the US telecommunications equipment industry. OP take account of the previously mentioned endogeneity problem by including an investment proxy in the estimation process. Assuming that investment is a monotonic and increasing function of productivity and that productivity is the only unobserved state variable, including investment in the estimation as a proxy for unobserved TFP developments allows the variation in investment to be used to infer plant-level TFP shocks. The algorithm consists of two steps. The first step provides consistent OLS estimates of variable input elasticities because the proxy controls for plant-level TFP shocks during the estimation procedure. The coefficient of capital is identified in the second step by forming moment conditions using the innovation component of TFP and lagged capital values.[14]

OP use the firm-level time series of investment to proxy for unobserved productivity. There is ample evidence that plant-level investment is lumpy. Lumpiness means that bursts of investment activity are followed by inactive periods where observed net investment is zero. It is a consequence of the presence of non-convexities in capital adjustment. Unfortunately, observations with zero investment are not informative for inferring productivity and are dropped, which may negatively affect precision if truncation significantly decreases sample size. In addition, OP works only if we observe both entrants and exiters.[15] In order to eliminate the efficiency loss caused by dropping zero-investment observations, Levinsohn and Petrin (2003) (LP hereafter) advocate the use of intermediate input cost or electricity instead of investment. LP discuss the conditions that must hold if the intermediate input is to be used as a proxy. The basis of the argument is that if intermediate inputs are less costly to adjust than investment, they are likely to respond more to productivity shocks. This is especially relevant in the presence of non-convexities in capital adjustment. LP also highlight that firms almost always report positive use of these variables in their data, implying that truncation due to zero proxy values is less severe.

The identifying assumptions regarding the timing of plants' input decisions have been criticized by Ackerberg et al. (2015) (ACF). ACF highlight that the optimal labor allocation is also a deterministic function of TFP and therefore the elasticity of labor is not identified. They propose a hybrid approach and offer structural assumptions on the timing of decisions concerning firms' input choices. They approach the identification problem by applying a two-step procedure that estimates all the elasticities in the second stage. Wooldridge (2009) proposed to circumvent the identification problem by estimating all the coefficients in a single generalized method of moments (GMM) step and using earlier outcomes of both capital and variable inputs as instrumental variables. His approach is advantageous because it is robust to the ACF critique and because the efficiency loss due to two-step estimation is eliminated.

18.3.2.3. *Parametric Estimation (IV, GMM)*

Although instrumental variable (IV) techniques are used within semi-parametric approaches, we mention IV-based methods separately because these estimate the parameters of the production function without the help of specific assumptions about firms' input decisions. At the heart of IV techniques is a general error components model developed by Blundell and Bond (2000). TFP is decomposed into a firm-fixed effect and autoregressive term, which allows for firm-specific dynamics in productivity. Blundell and Bond (2000) address the endogeneity issue by differencing the estimating equation. Under the error components assumption, differencing removes the firm-fixed effect and also controls for the dynamic effects of the autoregressive component. Obtaining the innovation in the output residual in this manner supports the construction of moment conditions that can be used to consistently estimate the parameters of the production function in a single step.[16] We note that while instrumental variable methods are attractive in principle, they are not commonly used given the lack of plausible and strong instruments on a wide scale basis to cover all industries over all time periods (see Griliches and Mairesse 1998 and Blundell and Bond 2000 for more details).

18.3.2.4. *Cost-Share-Based Methods, or Growth Accounting*

A frequently used nonstochastic computation method is growth accounting (GA). A typical version of GA exploits the first-order condition of a decision problem where the plant minimizes production costs given output and input prices. The first-order condition of this problem is used to rewrite elasticities as respective shares of input factors in the plant's total cost. Some of the advantages of this method include the possibility to allow for plant-level heterogeneity in elasticities,[17] easy implementation, and that it is flexible about the exact shape of the production technology. Further, available

Monte-Carlo evidence suggests that it is accurate if the data are not subject to much measurement error (see Van Biesebroeck 2007 for details). As mentioned at the beginning of this section, GA is free of statistical problems related to endogeneity and the sensitivity of estimates to sample size. In another version of GA, first-order conditions are derived from profit maximization. In this case, output elasticities are obtained as the revenue share of input costs. Using the cost share of total costs rather than of total value has the advantage that we do not require the assumption of perfect competition. This implies that another advantage of the GA-based factor elasticities using cost shares of total costs is that they are robust to alternative demand structures. As we will discuss later, this consideration becomes important if output prices are not observed in the data.

One might argue that the first-order conditions underlying this method are unlikely to hold at all points in time at plant-level. This means the elasticity estimates and the implied productivity numbers may be biased if the first-order conditions are violated. A case in point is when input markets are subject to frictions that prevent plants from adjusting labor and capital instantaneously, especially in the presence of non-convex costs. In such cases, the validity of first-order condition becomes critical. These issues are relevant for measurement purposes because the available empirical evidence suggests that the adjustment of input factors at the plant level is subject to frictions (see Bloom 2009; Cooper and Haltiwanger 2006), implying that first-order conditions are unlikely to hold for every plant in every industry and time period. It is more reasonable to expect that they hold on average across establishments and/or over time. Therefore, it is common to impose constant elasticities across plants in the same industry and/or over time. We also note that most of the alternative estimation methods assume common factor elasticities over time within the same industry.

18.3.2.5. *Hybrid Approaches*

Other papers combine elements of growth accounting with other approaches, which usually involves using a first-order condition together with regression techniques. Martin (2008) is a recent example where a first-order condition is combined with the control function approach. The basic insight is that under profit maximization and imperfect competition, the output price is given by a constant markup over marginal cost. As a consequence, elasticities of fully flexible inputs are obtained as a scalar multiple of the revenue share of input costs, where the multiplier is proportional to the revenue markup. For quasi-fixed inputs like capital, we should not expect the first-order condition to hold whenever a shock hits the firm because capital adjustment is subject to non-convexities. Martin (2008) proposes to subtract from revenues what he calls "an index of variable input usage." Then, eliminating prices from the modified revenue equation using the assumed demand structure, the revenue-elasticity of the fixed input can be written as a function of the scale elasticity and the elasticity of demand, similarly to the preceding discussion. To obtain the true coefficient of the fixed input, a control function approach is applied, but including lagged firm-level net revenues to control for unobserved TFP. Martin (2008) provides conditions under which variable revenues are monotone in TFPR.

18.3.3. Relative Productivity

In the previous description, productivity $(\widehat{\Omega}_{it})$ is a ratio of output divided by an estimated or computed input aggregator. If we denote our index of relative (log) productivity by $\omega_{it} \equiv \widehat{\omega}_{it} - \widehat{\omega}_{0}$, where $\widehat{\omega}_{it}$ is the log of productivity and $\widehat{\omega}_{0}$ is the reference measure, then the difference between two observations $\omega_{it} - \omega_{js}$ is consistent with the distance view: $\omega_{it} - \omega_{js} = \widehat{\omega}_{it} - \widehat{\omega}_{js}$.[18] The choice of reference productivity $\widehat{\omega}_{0}$ thus is not relevant per se for the dispersion measure. However, in practice, the estimated or computed residual $\widehat{\omega}_{it}$ will vary across methods with different reference productivity when the estimated or computed aggregator $F(\mathbf{x}; \widehat{\beta})$ differs. Foster et al. (2017) demonstrate that empirical differences across the estimated input aggregators often imply numerical differences in both $\widehat{\omega}_{it}$ and its dispersion. Foster et al. (2017) report average dispersion from productivity distributions for 50 industries where dispersion varies between 0.24 and 0.40.[19] This range reflects nontrivial differences across estimation methods. However, all methods yield results suggesting large productivity differences across establishments. Thus for individual industries, cross-method variation in dispersion methods may be larger.

18.3.3.1. *Stochastic Frontiers*

In stochastic frontier production functions, the residuals are relative to a frontier firm and thus fit into the narrative of "X-inefficiency" of Leibenstein (1966). This approach, in the spirit of the production frontiers in Farrell (1957), was first developed by Aigner et al. (1977) or Meeusen and van Den Broeck (1977). The main assumption underlying this approach is that residuals can be decomposed into two components with known distributional properties. The first component, labeled "efficiency," is assumed to follow a truncated, or one-sided, distribution. The second component is "measurement error" and hence is assumed to be symmetrically distributed around the frontier. This component is considered to occur through random fluctuations outside of the firm's control. To identify the two error processes, one must make assumptions regarding independence between the two, and that both are iid across observations. More important, the two-sided error must come from a symmetric distribution with mean zero. Usually normal, $N(0, \sigma)$ and half-normal, $N^{+}(\mu, \sigma_{+})$ distributions are chosen, with error parameters estimated along with production function parameters. Loosely speaking, any skewness in errors is attributed to inefficiency, while the symmetric part can either be measurement error or across-firm (and time) heterogeneity in productivity.

For the purpose of measuring across-firm dispersion of productivity, one starts with the residuals from a production function estimation. From stochastic frontier estimation, the estimated residual consists of two components, $\hat{\omega}_{it} = \hat{v}_{it} + \hat{\epsilon}_{it}$. In the frontier literature, only one component measures productivity, but we do not want to impose this interpretation, and consider ω_{it} as the building block for dispersion measures. In analysis, one can try to find a way to parse out what proportion of the dispersion can be attributed to measurement error.

In this sense, dispersion of the productivity distributions from production function versus stochastic frontier estimation will differ only owing to different parameter estimates, $\hat{\beta}$, resulting from the different estimation procedures. While Foster et al. (2017) offer evidence that the productivity ranking across firms and dispersion results are affected by the estimation method in the context of regression-based techniques and cost-share-based procedures, there is not much evidence to date on how these results compare to frontier methods. The available evidence is presented in the next section.

18.4. Dispersion Measures

Let $\hat{\omega}_{it} = \ln Y_{it} - \ln F(x_{i,t} \hat{\beta})$ denote the log productivity level for establishment (firm or decision-making unit) i in time t.[20] The basic building block for our dispersion measure is the log of productivity relative to a reference measure, as described in section 18.3.3, namely $\omega_{it} \equiv \hat{\omega}_{it} - \hat{\omega}_0$, where $\hat{\omega}_0$ is the reference measure.

Dispersion is related to the "width" of the productivity distribution, and generally is measured using the standard deviation (σ) or the interquartile range (iqr) measure, and thus has the same dimensionality as the underlying measure. In practice, quantile-based measures such as the interquartile or -decile range are usually preferable because they are robust to outliers. The two measures are given by

$$iqr_t(\omega_{it}) = p_{75}(\omega_{it}) - p_{25}(\omega_{it}) \tag{18.2}$$

and

$$\sigma_t(\omega_{it}) = \left(\frac{1}{N_t} \sum_i (\omega_{it} - \bar{\omega}_t)^2 \right)^{1/2}. \tag{18.3}$$

A time series of dispersion, either standard deviation, σ_t or interquartile range, iqr_t, can be computed for any grouping of firms for which comparing productivity levels makes sense. In practice, estimation of input aggregators and firm-level productivity is done at the most detailed level of industry disaggregation for which enough firms are available.[21]

As mentioned in section 18.2.1, other second moments of the empirical distribution on ω_{it} can be considered; for example, for each firm we can compute the standard deviation of the productivity measures over time, $\sigma_i(\omega_{it}) = \left(\frac{1}{T_i} \sum_t (\omega_{it} - \bar{\omega}_i)^2 \right)^{1/2}$, and we can call this volatility. Industry volatility could then be computed as a (size-weighted) average of firm-level volatility of firms in the industry.

Consider the following two-step procedure. First calculate iqr_{jt} for each industry j and time period t. Next, compute the average across the $j = 1 \dots J$ industries for each t as $\overline{iqr}_t = \frac{1}{J} \Sigma_j iqr_{jt}$ and over time as $\overline{\overline{iqr}} = \frac{1}{T} \Sigma_t \overline{iqr}_t$. In this approach, each industry- and time-specific iqr_{jt} is assigned equal weight. Since industries often differ in terms of the number of plant-year observations, it is reasonable to apply a weighting scheme that accounts for such differences. For example, Foster et al. (2017) report weighted average dispersion measures in manufacturing industries where the weights are based on the number of plant-year observations in industries. This approach amounts to pooling normalized establishment-level productivity measures ω_{it} from all j and t and calculating dispersion in a single step. In our notation, their approach can be illustrated by re-indexing establishments and industries. In each t, the index of establishments is defined as $s_t = (1 \dots N_{1t}, 1 \dots N_{2t}, \dots, 1 \dots N_{jt}, \dots, 1 \dots N_{Jt})$, and the following vector shows indices used in the weighted average formula: $s = (s_1, s_2, \dots, s_T)$. Assuming the panel of industries is balanced, the pooled distribution has $\Sigma_{t=1}^{T} \Sigma_{j-1}^{J} N_{jt}$ observations in total, and more populous industries will be represented according to their frequency weight $\dfrac{\Sigma_{t=1}^{T} N_{jt}}{\Sigma_{t=1}^{T} \Sigma_{j-1}^{J} N_{jt}}$. In this notation, $iqr(\omega_s) = p_{75}(\omega_s) - p_{25}(\omega_s)$ is equivalent to calculating the frequency-weighted average of the industry- and time-specific dispersion measures iqr_{jt}. This approach reflects the view that the different realizations of plant-specific productivity processes are outcomes of the same data-generating process and does not distinguish between the concepts of time-series volatility and cross-section dispersion. Such a procedure is appropriate in situations when time-series volatility is dwarfed by differences across plants, as is overwhelmingly the case in empirical micro datasets.

18.4.1. Empirical Evidence

The majority of previous studies focused on within-country differences across industries or sectors (see Syverson 2011 for a survey of the literature from the past decade). The main conclusion from these studies is that productivity differences across establishments are large, even within narrowly defined industries. This chapter adds another important dimension to the evidence: we compare measures also across European countries and the United States. Results on US industries are taken from Foster et al. (2017), while European dispersion statistics are based on our own calculations using data from Bartelsman et al. (2018a) and Lopez-Garcia and di Mauro (2015).

Although both the EU and US results are based on individual producers, a few qualifications are in order when comparing the results. First, US data on inputs and outputs are defined at the establishment level, while the unit of observation is a "firm" in European countries, namely the smallest production unit with independent accounting data. Second, the European data are available both for samples of firms where the number of employees is greater than 20 and for samples including all firms, while the results in Foster et al. (2017) are computed excluding the smallest, single-unit establishments. Third, Foster et al. (2017) use the 50 most populous manufacturing industries for estimation reasons. In contrast, the two European data sets are comprehensive in industry composition. We want to highlight that the European data allows us to estimate dispersion also in services, which is an important contribution because typical empirical data sets used in the literature contain information only on manufacturing firms.

Fourth, it is worth mentioning that although dispersion results are reported at the country level, the underlying dispersion measures are generated at a different industry detail. US results were drawn from four-digit industries, while European data, especially for small countries, allows calculations only within two-digit industries. This difference highlights an important trade-off that most researchers encounter in empirical productivity research. On the one hand, it is essential to assume some degree of homogeneity in production function coefficients in order to be able to estimate them using statistical methods. This consideration implies that it may be useful to pool industries if the narrowest industries do not have sufficient number of observations. On the other hand, possible differences in establishment-level production technology that are uncontrolled for in the estimation process affect coefficients and therefore dispersion results. For the purposes of this chapter, we assume that all characteristics relevant for productivity estimation are subsumed in production function parameters.

Fifth, we mention that differences in statistical practices across countries likely influence comparisons of dispersion measures. In recent research, Foster et al. (2017) find that dispersion measures are larger when controlling for the degree of imputed data in the sample used for computation. White et al. (forthcoming) use classification and regression trees (CART)-based methods, to estimate the empirical effects of imputation and find that underlying dispersion may be higher. No exploration has yet taken place on the differences in imputation methods across the samples in the European Union, and their effects on measured dispersion.[22]

Finally, a related issue is how dispersion measures can be made less sensitive to measurement error. In practice, outliers affect measured dispersion via two channels. First, they may affect elasticity estimates if the homogeneity assumptions about elasticities are not consistent with the data, that is, if the observations used to estimate elasticities are not derived from the same production technology. Second, extreme $\hat{\omega}_{it}$-observations directly generate large dispersion measures. In order to reduce sensitivity to outliers, observations in the United States are filtered by output-to-capital and output-to-labor ratios using the so-called Chebyshev method. In the European Union, outliers are first filtered by trimming the 1% tails of residuals from Cobb-Douglas production functions, with final productivity estimation done on the trimmed sample.

With these considerations in mind, we now turn to empirical results. The main finding is that estimated dispersion is qualitatively similar across countries, sectors, and estimation methods, namely the difference in measured productivity within-industry is always large. For example, the first two columns in Tables 18.1 and 18.2 show that the interquartile range (IQR) of value-added based TFP varies between about 0.5 and 1.0 in

European manufacturing industries. The comparable estimate from the United States is approximately 0.7; see the first entry in Table 18.3. IQR measures in services fall in the range between 0.52 and 1.23 in European countries (column 5 in Tables 18.1 and 18.2)—suggesting that there is nontrivial heterogeneity across sectors. Unfortunately, we do not have results from US service industries.

Results vary also across estimation methods; see the differences in dispersion statistics across Tables 18.1 and 18.2 and the differences across the rows of Table 18.3. The entries in Table 18.1 are based on productivity measures, which are estimated using the method proposed by Wooldridge (2009). The closest candidate for comparison with US results is LP(VA) in Table 18.3, which denotes the procedure proposed in Levinsohn and Petrin (2003) with value added as the dependent variable. Although the econometric procedure used in LP(VA) and Wooldridge (2009) are not identical, LP(VA)-based results in the United States are comparable to column 1 in Table 18.1 in the sense that the estimating equation contains the same regressand and regressors. Comparing the entries in column 1 across Tables 18.1 and 18.2 for Finland, France, Germany, and Italy shows that the estimation method may generate nontrivial differences in dispersion measures. A similar conclusion holds for US results, as well (see Table 18.3).

Table 18.2 shows results based on productivity measures that are estimated using Solow residuals or GA. The table presents variants where the dependent variable is either value added (columns 1–2 and 5–6) or gross output (columns 4–5 and 7–8). Comparing the entries in column 1 to those in column 3 suggests that gross-output-based productivity

Table 18.1 Dispersion in (Log) TFP, European Union (ECB) (2002–2012)

| | Manufacturing | | | | Services | | | |
| | IQR | | SD | | IQR | | SD | |
	ALL	20+	ALL	20+	ALL	20+	ALL	20+
Belgium	0.72	0.52	0.55	0.41	0.72	0.51	0.56	0.40
Estonia	0.93	0.65	0.64	0.50	1.09	0.87	0.70	0.60
Finland	0.66	0.52	0.51	0.46	0.65	0.40	0.51	0.35
France	0.49	0.48	0.39	0.38	0.52	0.48	0.43	0.38
Germany	0.68	0.66	0.48	0.51	0.73	0.64	0.56	0.52
Italy	0.64	0.55	0.48	0.45	0.70	0.56	0.52	0.44
Latvia	0.98	0.83	0.61	0.60	1.23	0.78	0.80	0.59
Poland		0.82		0.63		0.87		0.73
Portugal	0.67	0.61	0.53	0.50	0.86	0.65	0.62	0.51
Slovakia		0.75		0.62		1.02		0.74
Slovenia	0.80	0.58	0.56	0.46	0.87	0.79	0.65	0.58
Spain	0.72	0.65	0.53	0.54	0.77	0.59	0.57	0.49

Log TFP (VA-based) calculated using LP (Wooldridge). Full sample of firms (ALL) or sample of firms with 20 or more employees (20+).

Source: Calculated from CompNet Descriptives File; see Lopez-Garcia et al. (2015).

Table 18.2 Dispersion in (Log) TFP, European Union (Eurostat) (2001–2010)

| | Manufacturing | | | | Services | | | |
| | GO | | VA | | GO | | VA | |
	ALL	CO	ALL	CO	ALL	CO	ALL	CO
Austria	0.56	0.52	0.20	0.19	0.76	0.75	0.38	0.38
Denmark	0.58	0.57	0.25	0.24	0.73	0.72	0.34	0.33
Finland	0.70	0.67	0.36	0.33	0.81	0.78	0.48	0.45
France	0.55	0.53	0.25	0.25	0.62	0.61	0.39	0.37
Germany	0.47	0.47	0.19	0.19	0.51	0.51	0.22	0.22
Italy	0.86	0.83	0.40	0.35	1.04	1.00	0.52	0.46
Netherlands	0.56	0.56	0.24	0.24	0.72	0.71	0.38	0.37
Norway	0.80	0.79	0.38	0.37	0.96	0.94	0.51	0.50
Poland	1.01	0.99	0.55	0.52	1.18	1.15	0.96	0.93
Sweden	0.70	0.70	0.40	0.39	0.84	0.83	0.60	0.59
United Kingdom	0.76	0.74	0.45	0.43	0.98	0.96	0.60	0.58

Solow Residual measures of productivity, value added based or gross output based. Full sample of firms (ALL), or continuing firms (CO).

Source: Calculated from ESSNet; see Bartelsman et al. (2018).

Table 18.3 Descriptive Statistics of TFP Distributions in US Manufacturing Industries (1972–2010)

	IQR	SD
LP(VA)	0.68	0.57
LP(Q, GR)	0.29	0.31
GA(Q)	0.24	0.22
WLPM(Q)	0.40	1.88

LP(VA): using value added as the dependent variable; LP(Q,GR): using revenues as the dependent variable and grid search procedure for numerical optimization.

Source: Foster et al. (2017).

measures are less dispersed than value-added-based ones in European manufacturing industries. The relationship is similar in services. US results confirm this finding: the LP(VA)-row of Table 18.3 shows that value-added-based dispersion is significantly larger than other, output-based measures. This empirical finding has been established by earlier studies in the United States (see Foster et al. 2017 for more details).

An interesting cross-country comparison emerges if we contrast the entries in column 3 of Table 18.2 with GA(Q) in Table 18.3. GA-based dispersion in revenue-productivity in US manufacturing industries (0.24) is closest to that in Germany (0.19), Austria (0.20), The Netherands (0.24), Denmark (0.25), and France (0.25).[23] Comparing numbers across the restricted and unrestricted European samples in Table 18.1 and the United States implies that excluding smaller plants (EU) or industries (US) is likely to yield smaller productivity dispersion. This finding suggests that restricting the scope of the estimation sample generally implies smaller dispersion.

A further comparison can be made of estimates for European and US manufacturing dispersion in column 3 of Table 18.2 and Table 18.3, respectively. The estimates imply that the plant at the 75th percentile of the productivity distribution in the average European industry generates between 20% and 55% more revenue using the same amount of inputs than the plant at the 25th percentile. This range varies between 24% and 40% in US manufacturing, depending on the estimation method. As we will show, the variation in dispersion may be significant along a variety of dimensions such as industries, sectors, countries, time, and estimation methods. We therefore find it remarkable that these measures are comparable in magnitude and that they all suggest that cross-plant differences in productivity are sizable.

The differences we have seen so far in these tables are country specific. However, dispersion also varies across industries and time. Explaining such variation is beyond the scope of this chapter, but the dispersion underlying the entries in our tables warrants further analysis that should explore the properties of the dispersion distribution in more detail. The existence of comparable data across countries, industries, and time of within-industry dispersion in productivity will allow for empirical explorations into correlates related to policy, institutions, and technology. Recently, several studies attempted to exploit and explain the within-country variation in dispersion. In perhaps the most popular area of application, cross-country differences in the dispersion of revenue productivity measures are associated with the degree of misallocation (see Bartelsman et al. 2013; Foster et al. 2016b; Hsieh and Klenow 2009).

We conduct a simple analysis of variance by regressing a dispersion measure on country, industry, and time effects for both the CompNet (ECB) and the ESSNet (Eurostat) panels. Table 18.4 shows the analysis of variance results for the standard deviation of TFP and the interquartile range. The main findings are the following. Country and industry fixed effects are invariably significant; they explain close to two-thirds of the variance of the standard deviation of productivity or interquartile range of productivity (see columns 1 and 3). The explanatory power of these factors is similar in the upper and lower part of the support of the productivity distribution (columns 2–3 and 5–6). The contribution of time effects is relatively small, and some preliminary analysis of the time effects does not show a clear cyclical pattern.

Our data allow us to shed more light on the potential determinants of differences in dispersion. Instead of regressing dispersion measures only on country, industry, and time dummies, we add an indicator of interest to the regression. This approach is not meant to identify an exogenous effect of an explanatory indicator. Instead, the partial correlation estimated through the regression is a useful starting point in dissecting the high explanatory power of country- and industry-fixed effects. One indicator of interest

Table 18.4 Variance Decomposition of Dispersion Measures

	ESSNet Data			CompNet Data		
	SD	P90-mean	mean-P10	SD	P90-mean	mean-P10
Country	43.4	44.9	162.7	29.6	28.8	249.3
Industry	41.2	17.1	80.4	32.8	26.4	148.4
Time	.7	.8	2.6	1.1	.9	12.6
Num. Obs.	1,964	1,949	1,948	6,288	6,288	6,288
Total SSQ	122.1	82.0	364.6	102.7	92.2	570.0

Source: Calculated from ESSNet and CompNet Data. Data described in Bartelsman et al. (2018) and Lopez-Garcia et al. (2015).

is the possible differences in the phase of the business cycle, which can be measured using the output-gap. This may be relevant because earlier evidence suggests that dispersion in US manufacturing appears countercyclical (see the findings in Kehrig 2015, for example). While we did not find clear cyclical patterns in the time component of the variance decomposition, further analysis may reveal how exogenous shifts in demand may affect industry dispersion. Another, largely unexplored, area that may be relevant for dispersion is related to the differences in country- or industry-specific regulations. For example, employment protection, trade regulations, and financial conditions all have been seen to affect firm and input factor dynamics. In order to understand the link to productivity dispersion, further theoretical and empirical work seems justified in this context.

In the following we show results from a simple exercise to estimate the correlation between an indicator of technology use and dispersion. As suggested in Bartelsman et al. (2016), the intensity with which broadband Internet is used by firms in an industry is seen to be correlated with dispersion. This implies that indicators of innovation and technology intensity could control for differences in the industry-specific technology mix. We show some evidence on this from the Eurostat data that include information on technology use by firms. The results of this analysis are shown in Table 18.5. Each row displays the coefficient and t-statistic of each indicator in a regression of dispersion on the indicator and on country, industry, and time fixed effects. Our results suggest that faster growth in European industries is associated with smaller dispersion, a finding consistent with earlier results on US data in Kehrig (2015). Various indicators of technology use are positively correlated with dispersion, suggesting that more innovative/ tech-using industries are also more likely to be dispersed. This result is consistent with the mechanism in which entrepreneurial innovation entails more experimentation, thereby increasing productivity dispersion compared to sectors with less innovation. This mechanism and its empirical consequences are analyzed in Foster et al (2017b), who look at the relationship between innovative activity, entry, productivity dispersion and growth. Alternatively, sectors facing large shocks in business conditions that affect measured productivity may use information and communications–related technology to reduce adjustment frictions (see Gal 2017).

Table 18.5 Correlates of Productivity Dispersion

	ESSNet Data	
	Coef	t-stat
Industry growth	−.04	6.4
Human capital intensity	.75	10.6
IT human capital	.65	6.1
Process innovation	.08	2.4
Product innovation	.13	4.2
Organization innovation	.12	3.0
New product turnover	.20	2.9
Broadband intensity	.11	2.8
Pct ICT intensive firms	.14	2.8
Supply chain integration	−.10	2.0

Notes: Each row presents the coefficient for the indicator from a regression of the standard deviation of TFP on country, industry, and time fixed effects and the indicator. Data from ESSNet (where number of firms underlying observation > 40). The explanatory variables are indicators from the Community Innovation Survey and the ICT Use Survey that have been linked to firm-level data. Data described in Bartelsman et al. (2018).

18.5. CONCLUSION AND RESEARCH AGENDA

This chapter provides an overview of the methods currently used to construct measures of productivity dispersion using data from large, comprehensive, samples of plants or firms. In particular, the chapter draws from work done in the European Union, funded by Eurostat through the ESSNet programs[24] and by the European Central Bank's Competitiveness Network, and from work done with the Annual Survey of Manufactures and the Census of Manufactures at the US Census Bureau. The chapter further provides a comparison of estimates of productivity dispersion for different methods and for a selection of countries. Evidence also is provided on some of the correlates of productivity dispersion. Disentangling causes of productivity dispersion remains difficult and requires modeling of causes and effects, as well as empirical strategies to identify the underlying mechanisms.

The empirically observed dispersion of productivity has been an awkward fact for models of production with representative firms or for models where resources always are allocated optimally. In section 18.2, a discussion is presented of different ways in which to understand the existence of productivity dispersion. To start, many forms of measurement error could contribute to observed dispersion. Next, decisions made by firms that alter their productivity are a source of dispersion, as long as some form of friction is preventing instantaneous allocation of resources to the firm with the highest productivity. Finally, forces of selection and allocation tend to reduce dispersion, but may be held back by policy distortions, or by frictions in "taste and technology" (i.e., consumer learning, informational frictions, or search-and-matching processes).

Much work remains to be done to understand productivity dispersion. For example, the early attempt of Hsieh and Klenow (2009) to use observed dispersion as an indicator of misallocation of resources has run into criticism (e.g., Bartelsman et al. 2013; Bartelsman et al. 2018b; Brown et al. 2016; Foster et al. 2016b). The link between dispersion and misallocation hinges on the assumption of constant returns to scale, but also breaks down with alternative measures of revenue productivity or with alternate interpretations of estimated distortions. Further, careful measurement of dispersion in different sets of countries, industries, or time periods clearly places question marks on a simple monotonic relationship between productivity dispersion and misallocation.

The research agenda can be broken down into different themes. More work needs to be done to improve basic measurement of the underlying inputs and outputs. Linking the business surveys on production with information on the skills and education of each employee per firm, or with surveys on capital investment by type and quality, or with information on technology use or management quality, could all improve measurement of productivity. Similarly, information on the product markets and customers could help disentangle price, quality, and markups, further improving the measure of productivity. The effect of better measurement of productivity on the magnitude of dispersion across producers in an industry remains an empirical matter.

The econometric aspects of productivity measurement attract much research, as witnessed by many of the contributions to this *Handbook*. Some improvements in estimation, for example in disentangling productivity and markups, are generally expected to reduce measured dispersion (e.g., entrants may seem to have low productivity, thereby increasing dispersion, but this effect disappears once their lower-than-average markups are properly accounted for). On the other hand, accounting for statistical issues such as the presence of item nonresponse and imputation may increase dispersion.

Theoretical and empirical explorations into the sources of firm-level productivity evolution are an equally interesting area. Much work has already taken place here, for example following two disparate strands of work as described in Comin and Mulani (2009) and Acemoglu et al. (2013). Research should be partial equilibrium in nature, in the sense that it should try to isolate the sources driving (heterogeneous) productivity at the plant or firm level from market forces that select firms and allocate resources and market shares.

Beyond identifying isolated factors that drive dispersion, more work needs to be done on the implications of using heterogenous firm models in dynamic general equilibrium frameworks. These models should simultaneously take into account firm decisions that affect (future) productivity and market outcomes relating to allocation of input and output. The parameters of such models can be informed through calibration with moments from firm-level data sets, or can be estimated through methods of indirect inference (see, e.g., Dridi et al. 2007; Gouriéroux et al. 2010).

As measures of productivity dispersion are becoming available for researchers, systematic empirical explorations into correlates of dispersion can be made to understand how dispersion can vary across sectors, countries, or time. A recent example in this area is Kehrig (2015), who explores the differential effect that market selection mechanisms may have on dispersion over the business cycle. Another direction is taken by Brown et al. (2016), who take a theoretical and empirical look at the role of adjustment frictions on measured dispersion. The simple example given in this chapter, relating productivity dispersion in a country-industry-time panel to fixed effects and factors that vary across country or industry, could be the basis of a line of empirical literature.

This chapter serves as a guide to aid researchers in building up comparable measures of dispersion of productivity for a large set of countries, industries, and time periods. Our hope is that the availability of such data, together with research along the lines sketched in the preceding, will increase our understanding of the effect of statistical quality and methodological choices on measures of dispersion. The areas of economics where such measures can be important are wide, ranging from dynamic macro models of business cycles and growth to structural micro models of firm behavior and market outcomes. The next iteration of the *Handbook* likely will be able to host a more mature chapter on productivity dispersion, with more questions answered than asked.

NOTES

1. The authors would like to thank two referees for comments and suggestions, Bert Balk for providing guidance at an early stage of the project, and the numerous colleagues and collaborators at the European Central Bank, EuroStat, US Bureau of the Census, and many National Statistical Agencies and Central Banks in the European Union. Bartelsman would like to thank the ECB research visitor program for support under contract 24591/R/ 2012. This chapter has directly or indirectly made use of confidential firm-level data in accordance with all appropriate rules and regulations, and all published results meet relevant disclosure rules. The findings and opinions expressed in this chapter are the authors' alone and do not reflect policy of the US Census Bureau, the ECB, Eurostat, or any other agency involved.

2. Alternatively, in the empirical literature one often speaks of a "data generating process," that is, events that occur through which the outcome data are generated.

3. In general, one needs to take care of heteroskedasticity in measuring volatility: in practice, firm-level productivity is highly persistent, and an error variance should be estimated using, e.g., an auto-regressive process.

4. One could consider that all existing firms represent a draw from a distribution of firm distributions that could have existed in alternative "worlds." When analyzing within-industry distributions of firms, sample selection can be an issue even with full census data. For example, the draw of all observed firms in one country, or time period, could differ from that in another location or era because the economic environment prevents certain types of firms from entering or results in rapid death (before observation) of other types.

5. A recent effort to collect more detailed data from US manufacturers is through the Managerial and Organizational Practices Survey of the US Census Bureau, https://www.census.gov/mcd/mops.

6. We are abstracting from efficiency in factor mix. Given input prices, we can decompose the inefficiency of the original point **x** into technical and allocative inefficiency.

7. We have defined a scalar aggregate input index by splitting the production function such that $F(\mathbf{x}) = F_s(F_a(\mathbf{x}))$ and $x_a = F_a(\mathbf{x})$ and $F_a(.)$ exhibits constant returns to scale. Note that we have drawn $f_s()$ to have decreasing returns to aggregate input. Under constant returns, the input efficiency measure is the reciprocal of the output efficiency measure.

8. In our empirical section we will address the relevance of this issue, as well as the more fundamental distinction between gross output and value added measures of production.

9. While there are studies in which the chosen data set allows either to calculate quantity directly or to infer the effect of prices, these analyses are usually restricted to a small set of industries or even a single industry. Recent examples from this literature are Collard-Wexler and De Loecker (2014); Foster et al. (2008); Martin (2008); Syverson (2004).

10. In addition to differences in plants' efficiency levels and variation in product prices, other factors are potentially important contributors to TFPR dispersion. Hsieh and Klenow (2009) highlight the role of distortions in generating dispersion in TFPR. Bartelsman et al. (2013) emphasize the role of frictions such as overhead factor costs. Asker et al. (2014) explore the role of adjustment frictions in generating dispersion in TFPR.

11. Using data on product quotas to control for product-specific demand shocks at the plant level, De Loecker (2011) follows this thread and combines a demand system with a production function in order to recover estimates of TFPQ, since output quantities are unobserved in his data. The approach follows the line of thought of earlier papers and is extended to a case when plants produce a variety of products. In terms of empirical implementation, the main difference relative to the single-output case is that a weighted average of demand-specific aggregate-deflated revenues is included, instead of the total revenues in the industry.

12. Bruno (1978) explores the question of under what conditions double-deflated value added results in a production function where the partial derivatives will correctly measure the marginal productivities of production factors. Such a production function exists if the intermediate input satisfies one of three conditions: (1) it is used in fixed proportion to gross output; (2) the relative price of the intermediate inputs to value added remains constant; (3) the gross output production function is functionally separable into the intermediate and primary inputs.

13. The basic papers are Blundell and Bond (2000); Griliches and Mairesse (1998).

14. A more general point about proxy methods is related to polynomial approximations. Proxy methods use polynomials at two points of the estimation algorithm. First, a polynomial of the state variables and the proxy is included in the first step to approximate unobserved productivity. Second, to determine the expected component of TFP, its estimated value is projected on a polynomial expansion of its past values. This step is supported by a Markovian assumption about plant-level TFP. The innovation obtained in this approximation is used to construct a moment condition in order to estimate the elasticity of capital. While polynomial series provide flexible approximations, the higher order terms are also likely to exacerbate measurement error present in microdata.

15. OP focus on the period between the early 1970s and the mid-1980s in the telecommunications equipment industry. During this period, the industry saw large changes in the

size of plants and significant entry and exit. Therefore they model plants' entry and exit decisions that depend on productivity and control for these effects in the estimation procedure. This may be an important feature of the approach in cases where the data is subject to nonrandomness. The findings in Foster et al. (2017) suggest that controlling for the effect of selection may have an effect on dispersion estimates.

16. Blundell and Bond (2000) provide two sets of moment conditions. The first set is based on the orthogonality of $t-3$ levels of input factors and current-period differences of output residuals. The second set is constructed using $t-2$ levels of input factors and current period levels of the output residuals.

17. In terms of empirical results, this assumption comes at a cost. Foster et al. (2017) offer indirect evidence suggesting that plant-level shares are likely to be noisier than industry-level shares.

18. This measure also is consistent with the set of index number properties proposed in Diewert and Nakamura (2003).

19. The range is given for dispersion of gross-output-based productivity. As discussed later, dispersion for value-added-based productivity is substantially higher.

20. The possible specifications for the input aggregator $F()$ are described in the previous section.

21. There is a trade-off here: estimation of production functions at a higher level of aggregation may introduce noise in the productivity estimates owing to imposition of common output elasticities across firms while they actually differ, but given precision of the productivity estimates, addition of more firms for computation of dispersion increases precision. In Tables 18.1 and 18.2 for EU countries, we require at least 50 firms in the industry. In calculations using data from US manufacturing, a selection is made of the 50 four-digit industries with the highest number of plant-year observations. The average number of plants (over time) in these industries varies between 400 and 3,900.

22. While the production data used the EU exercises based on the Structural Business Statistics surveys in each country, some countries enrich the data with information from official registers, for example on payroll tax or value added tax, and do partial imputation for missing fields.

23. WLP(Q) in Table 18.3 shows results obtained by the method described in Wooldridge (2009), but using output as the dependent variable. Therefore, the results are not directly comparable to the results in Table 18.1. However, earlier results in Foster et al. (2017) suggest that recalculating Table 18.1 using output as the dependent variable would imply larger dispersion. Moreover, existing Monte-Carlo evidence in Foster et al. (2017) shows that the standard error of dispersion statistics implied by proxy methods may be large, especially when using the procedure proposed by Wooldridge (2009). This is an indication that appropriate caution is needed because these estimation methods seem to be more sensitive to sample size.

24. ESSLimit, ESSLait.

References

Acemoglu, D., P. Aghion, and F. Zilibotti. 2006. "Distance to Frontier, Selection, and Economic Growth." *Journal of the European Economic Association* 4(1): 37–74.

Acemoglu, Daron, Ufuk Akcigit, Nicholas Bloom, and William Kerr. 2013. "Innovation, Reallocation and Growth." Center for Economic Studies, US Census Bureau Working Paper 13-23.

Ackerberg, Daniel A., Kevin Caves, and Garth Frazer. 2015. "Identification Properties of Recent Production Function Estimators." *Econometrica* 83(6): 2411–2451.

Aigner, Dennis, C. A. Knox Lovell, and Peter Schmidt. 1977. "Formulation and Estimation of Stochastic Frontier Production Function Models." *Journal of Econometrics* 6(1): 21–37.

Asker, John, Allan Collard-Wexler, and Jan De Loecker. 2014. "Dynamic Inputs and Resource (Mis)Allocation." *Journal of Political Economy* 122(5): 1013–1063.

Bartelsman, Eric, Sabien Dobbelaere, and Bettina Peters. 2015. "Allocation of Human Capital and Innovation at the Frontier: Firm-Level Evidence on Germany and the Netherlands." *Industrial and Corporate Change* 24(5): 875–949.

Bartelsman, Eric J., and Mark Doms. 2000. "Understanding Productivity: Lessons from Longitudinal Microdata." *Journal of Economic Literature* 38(3): 569–594.

Bartelsman, Eric J., Eva Hagsten, and Michael Polder. (2018a). "Micro Moments Database for Cross-Country Analysis of ICT, Innovation, and Economic Outcomes." *Journal of Economic and Management Strategy* 27(3).

Bartelsman, Eric J., Jonathan Haskel, and Ralf Martin. 2008. "Distance to Which Frontier? Evidence on Productivity Convergence from International Firm-Level Data." CEPR Discussion Paper Series, DP7032.

Bartelsman, Eric J., Paloma Lopez-Garcia, and Giorgio Presidente. 2018b. "Cyclical and Stuctural Variation in Resource Reallocation: Evidence for Europe. Tinbergen Institute Discussion Paper 18-070/VI.

Bartelsman, Eric J., Pieter A. Gautier, and Joris De Wind. 2016. "Employment Protection, Technology Choice, and Worker Allocation." *International Economic Review* 57(3): 787–826.

Bartelsman, Eric, John Haltiwanger, and Stefano Scarpetta. 2013. "Cross-Country Differences in Productivity: The Role of Allocation and Selection." *American Economic Review* 103(1): 305–334.

Bartelsman, Eric, George van Leeuwen, and Michael Polder. 2017. "CDM Using a Cross-country Micro Moments Database." *Economics of Innovation and New Technology* 26(1–2): 168–182.

Basu, Susanto, and John G. Fernald. 2002. "Aggregate Productivity and Aggregate Technology." *European Economic Review* 46(6): 963–991.

Basu, Susanto, Luigi Pascali, Fabio Schiantarelli, and Luis Serven. 2009. "Productivity, Welfare and Reallocation: Theory and Firm-Level Evidence." National Bureau of Economic Research Working Paper No. 15579.

Bloom, Nicholas. 2009. "The Impact of Uncertainty Shocks." *Econometrica* 77(3): 623–685.

Bloom, Nicholas, Raffaella Sadun, and John Van Reenen. 2016. "Management as a Technology?" Stanford University Graduate School of Business Research Paper 16–27, Stanford, CA.

Bloom, Nicholas, Mark Schankerman, and John Van Reenen. 2013. "Identifying Technology Spillovers and Product Market Rivalry." *Econometrica* 81: 1347–1393.

Blundell, R., and S. Bond. 2000. "GMM Estimation with Persistent Panel Data: An Application to Production Functions." *Econometric Reviews* 19(3): 321–340.

Brown, J. David, Emin Dinlersoz, and John S. Earle. 2016. "Does Higher Productivity Dispersion Imply Greater Misallocation? A Theoretical and Empirical Analysis." Center for Economic Studies, US Census Bureau Working Paper No. 16-42.

Bruno, Michael. 1978. "Duality, Intermediate Inputs and Value-Added." In *Production Economics: A Dual Approach to Theory and Applications*, Vol. 2, edited by Melvyn Fuss and Daniel McFadden, Chapter III, 3–16. Amsterdam: North Holland.

Bushnell, James B., and Catherine D. Wolfram. 2009. "The Guy at the Controls: Labor Quality and Power Plant Efficiency." In *International Differences in the Business Practices and Productivity of Firms*, edited by Richard B. Freeman and Kathryn L. Shaw, 79–102. Chicago; London: University of Chicago Press.

Cobb, Charles W., and Paul H. Douglas. 1928. "A Theory of Production." *American Economic Review* 18(1): 139–165.

Collard-Wexler, Allan, and Jan De Loecker. 2014. "Reallocation and Technology: Evidence from the US Steel Industry." *American Economic Review* 105(1): 131–171.

Comin, Diego, and Sunil Mulani. 2009. "A Theory of Growth and Volatility at the Aggregate and Firm Level." *Journal of Monetary Economics* 56(8): 1023–1042.

Cooper, Russell W., and John C. Haltiwanger. 2006. "On the Nature of Capital Adjustment Costs." *The Review of Economic Studies* 73(3): 611–633.

Corrado, Carol, Paul Lengermann, Eric J. Bartelsman, and J. Joseph Beaulieu. 2007. "Sectoral Productivity in the United States: Recent Developments and the Role of IT." *German Economic Review* 8(2): 188–210.

Criscuolo, Chiara, Peter Gal, and Carlo Menon. 2014. "The Dynamics of Employment Growth." OECD Science, Technology and Industry Policy Papers 14.De Loecker, Jan. 2011. "Recovering Markups from Production Data." *International Journal of Industrial Organization* 29(3): 350–355.

Diewert, W. Erwin, and Alice O. Nakamura. 2003. "Index Number Concepts, Measures and Decompositions of Productivity Growth." *Journal of Productivity Analysis*, 19(2–3): 127–159.Domar, Evsey D. 1961. "On the Measurement of Technological Change." *The Economic Journal* 71(284): 709–729.

Dridi, Ramdan, Alain Guay, and Eric Renault. 2007. "Indirect Inference and Calibration of Dynamic Stochastic General Equilibrium Models." *Journal of Econometrics* 136(2): 397–430.

Eaton, Jonathan, and Samuel Kortum. 2002. "Technology, Geography, and Trade." *Econometrica* 70(5): 1741–1779.

Farrell, M. J. 1957. "The Measurement of Productive Efficiency." *Journal of the Royal Statistical Society, Series A (General)* 120(3): 253–290.

Foster, Lucia, Cheryl Grim, and John Haltiwanger. 2016a. "Reallocation in the Great Recession: Cleansing or Not?" *Journal of Labor Economics* 34(S1): S293–S331.

Foster, Lucia, Cheryl Grim, John Haltiwanger, and Zoltan Wolf. 2017a. "Macro and Micro Dynamics of Productivity: From Devilish Details to Insights." National Bureau of Economic Research, Working Paper Series no. 23666.

Foster, Lucia, Cheryl Grim, John Haltiwanger, and Zoltan Wolf. 2017b. "Innovation, Productivity Dispersion, and Productivity Growth." National Bureau of Economic Research Working Paper Series No. 24420.

Foster, Lucia, Cheryl Grim, John Haltiwanger, and Zoltan Wolf. 2016b. "Firm-Level Dispersion in Productivity: Is the Devil in the Details?" *American Economic Review* 106(5): 95–98.

Foster, Lucia, John Haltiwanger, and Chad Syverson. 2008. "Reallocation, Firm Turnover, and Efficiency: Selection on Productivity or Profitability?" *American Economic Review* 98(1): 394–425.

Fried, Harold O., C. A. Knox Lovell, and Shelton S. Schmidt. 2008. *The Measurement of Productive Efficiency and Productivity Growth.* Oxford: Oxford University Press.

Gal, Peter N. 2017. "How Does Demand Volatility Encourage ICT Use?" In *Essays on the Role of Frictions for Firms, Sectors and the Macroeconomy*, edited by Peter N. Gal, 53–78. PhD dissertation, Vrije Universiteit Amsterdam.

Gouriéroux, Christian, Peter C. B. Phillips, and Jun Yu. 2010. "Indirect inference for Dynamic Panel Models." *Journal of Econometrics* 157(1): 68–77.

Griliches, Z., and J. Mairesse. 1998. "Production Functions: The Search for Identification." In *Econometrics and Economic Theory in the Twentieth Century: The Ragnar Frisch Centennial Symposium*, edited by Steinar Strom, 169–203. Cambridge: Cambridge University Press.

Hopenhayn, Hugo A. 1992. "Entry, Exit, and Firm Dynamics in Long Run Equilibrium." *Econometrica* 60(5): 1127–1150.

Hsieh, Chang-Tai, and Peter J. Klenow. 2009. "Misallocation and Manufacturing TFP in China and India." *Quarterly Journal of Economics* 124(4): 1403–1448.

Hulten, Charles R. 1978. "Growth Accounting with Intermediate Inputs." *The Review of Economic Studies* 45(3): 511–518.

Hulten, Charles R. 2001. "Total Factor Productivity: A Short Biography." In *New Developments in Productivity Analysis*, Vol. 63 of *NBER Conference on Research in Income and Wealth*, edited by Edwin R. Dean, Charles R. Hulten, and Michael J. Harper, 1–54. Chicago: University of Chicago Press.

Ichniowski, Casey, and Kathryn Shaw. 2003. "Beyond Incentive Pay: Insiders Estimates of the Value of Complementary Human Resource Management Practices." *Journal of Economic Perspectives* 17(1): 155–180.

Kehrig, Matthias. 2015. "The Cyclical Nature of the Productivity Distribution." Social Science Research Network SSRN Scholarly Paper ID 1854401, Rochester, NY.

Klette, Tor Jakob, and Zvi Griliches. 1996. "The Inconsistency of Common Scale Estimators When Output Prices Are Unobserved and Endogenous." *Journal of Applied Econometrics* 11(4): 343–362.

Lazear, Edward P. 2000. "The Power of Incentives." *American Economic Review* 90(2): 410–414.

Leibenstein, Harvey. 1966. "Allocative Efficiency vs. 'X-Efficiency.'" *American Economic Review* 56(3): 392–415.

Leibenstein, Harvey. 1978. "X-Inefficiency Xists: Reply to an Xorcist." *American Economic Review* 68(1): 203–211.

Lentz, Rasmus, and Dale T. Mortensen. 2005. "Productivity Growth and Worker Reallocation." *International Economic Review* 46(3): 731–749.

Levinsohn, James, and Amil Petrin. 2003. "Estimating Production Functions Using Inputs to Control for Unobservables." *The Review of Economic Studies* 70(2): 317–341.

Lopez-Garcia, Paloma, and Filippo di Mauro. 2015. "Assessing European Competitiveness: The New CompNet Micro-Based Database." European Central Bank Working Paper Series 1764.

Lucas, Robert E. 1978. "Size Distribution of Business Firms." *Bell Journal of Economics* 9(2): 508–523.

Marschak, Jacob, and William H. Andrews. 1944. "Random Simultaneous Equations and the Theory of Production." *Econometrica* 12(3–4): 143–205.

Marshall, Alfred. 1920. *Principles of Economics.* Revised ed. London: Macmillan.

Martin, Ralf. 2008. "Productivity Dispersion, Competition and Productivity Measurement." PhD dissertation, London School of Economics.

Meeusen, Wim, and Julien van Den Broeck. 1977. "Efficiency Estimation from Cobb-Douglas Production Functions with Composed Error." *International Economic Review* 18(2): 435–444.

Melitz, Marc J. 2003. "The Impact of Trade on Intra-Industry Reallocations and Aggregate Industry Productivity." *Econometrica* 71(6): 1695–1725.

Moretti, Enrico. 2004. "Workers' Education, Spillovers, and Productivity: Evidence from Plant-Level Production Functions." *American Economic Review* 94(3): 656–690.

OECD. 2009. *Measuring Capital: OECD Manual.* Paris: OECD.

Olley, G. Steven, and Ariel Pakes. 1996. "The Dynamics of Productivity in the Telecommunications Equipment Industry." *Econometrica* 64(6): 1263–1297.

Robbins, Lionel. 1928. "The Representative Firm." *The Economic Journal* 38(151): 387–404.

Salter, W. E. G. 1960. *Productivity and Technical Change.* Cambridge: Cambridge University Press.

Senga, Tatsuro. 2015. "A New Look at Uncertainty Shocks: Imperfect Information and Misallocation." Queen Mary University of London, School of Economics and Finance Working Paper 763.

Smets, Frank, and Rafael Wouters. 2007. "Shocks and Frictions in US Business Cycles: A Bayesian DSGE Approach." *American Economic Review* 97(3): 586–606.

Solow, Robert M. 1956. "A Contribution to the Theory of Economic Growth." *Quarterly Journal of Economics* 70(1): 65–94.

Stigler, George J. 1976. "The Xistence of X-Efficiency." *American Economic Review* 66(1): 213–216.

Syverson, Chad. 2004. "Product Substitutability and Productivity Dispersion." *Review of Economics and Statistics* 86(2): 534–550.

Syverson, Chad. 2011. "What Determines Productivity?" *Journal of Economic Literature* 49(2): 326–65.

Van Biesebroeck, Johannes. 2007. "Robustness of Productivity Estimates." *Journal of Industrial Economics* 55(3): 529–569.

Wagner, Joachim. 2007. "Exports and Productivity: A Survey of the Evidence from Firm-level Data." *World Economy* 30(1): 60–82.

White, T. Kirk, Jerome P. Reiter, and Amil Petrin. forthcoming. "Imputation in U.S. Manufacturing Data and Its Implications for Productivity Dispersion." *The Review of Economics and Statistics.* https://doi.org/10.1162/REST_a_00678

Wooldridge, Jeffrey M. 2009. "On Estimating Firm-Level Production Functions Using Proxy Variables to Control for Unobservables." *Economics Letters* 104(3): 112–114.

CHAPTER 19

....

DECOMPOSING VALUE-ADDED GROWTH INTO EXPLANATORY FACTORS

....

W. ERWIN DIEWERT AND KEVIN J. FOX

19.1. INTRODUCTION

....

UNDERSTANDING sources of economic growth has long been of interest to academics and policymakers.[1] A better understanding of the determinants of value-added growth can provide insights into the potential for policies to address inefficiencies and a deeper understanding of the drivers of productivity, a topic of heightened recent interest given the slowdown in productivity growth across many developed countries (see, e.g., Byrne, Fernald, and Reinsdorf 2016; Gordon 2016; Mokyr, Vickers, and Ziebarth 2015; and Syverson 2016).

While there has been much attention to growth at the aggregate economy level, there has less at the sectoral level. To address this, we derive exact decompositions of nominal value-added growth for sectors of an economy into explanatory factors, and illustrate these using data for the US corporate nonfinancial and the US noncorporate nonfinancial sectors, 1960–2014.

We take the explanatory factors of value-added growth in a sector to be as follows:

- efficiency changes;
- changes in output prices;
- changes in primary inputs;
- changes in input prices;
- technical progress; and
- returns to scale.

We start by decomposing value-added growth in a single production sector into these components, before considering the relationship with aggregate (across sector) value-added growth. In order to implement our decomposition, an estimate of the sector's best-practice technology for the two periods under consideration is required. This could be obtained using econometric techniques or nonparametric frontier modeling, such as data envelopment analysis (DEA)–type techniques (see, e.g., Charnes and Cooper 1985; Färe, Grosskopf, and Lovell 1985). We do not make any of the convexity assumptions that are typical in this literature, and instead use the free disposal hull (FDH) approach of Tulkens (1993) and his coauthors (see also Diewert and Fox 2014, 2016a).

During recessions, it seems unlikely that production units are operating on their production frontiers (fixed capital stock components cannot be readily reduced in the light of reduced output demands) and thus it is important for a growth accounting methodology to allow for technical and allocative inefficiency. Our methodological approach does this. It has the advantages that it does not involve any econometric estimation, and involves only observable data on input and output prices and quantities for the sector. Thus it is simple enough to be implemented by statistical agencies.

Another positive feature of our approach is that it rules out technical regress, which is a problematic concept for a broad range of economic models (see, e.g., Aiyar, Dalgaard, and Moav 2008; Diewert and Fox 2016b). A consequence of ruling out technical regress is that when there is a recession, for example, the loss of efficiency is gross loss of efficiency less any technical progress that occurs during recession years. Hence, in this case, estimates of efficiency losses may be offset by technical progress, and what is measured as efficiency change is the net effect.

The rest of the chapter is organized as follows. The core methodology is explained in the following section, where we introduce the *cost-constrained value-added function* that is used throughout. In section 19.3, the method for decomposing value-added growth into our six components for each sector is derived. Section 19.4 describes our nonparametric approach to obtaining empirical estimates for the best practice cost-constrained value-added functions, which allows us to decompose total factor productivity (TFP) growth for a sector into explanatory components. Using our data on two major sectors of the US economy, sections 19.5 and 19.6 provide empirical applications of the approach, with the results shedding light on sources of value added and productivity growth for the United States over a 55-year period. Section 19.7 $w \equiv [w_1, \ldots, w_N] \gg 0_N$ presents results from one solution to the problem of aggregating over sectors, drawing on the results of Diewert and Fox (2016c), and section 19.8 concludes.

19.2. The Cost-Constrained Value-Added Function for a Sector

Suppose that a sector produces M net outputs,[2] $y \equiv [y_1, \ldots, y_M]$, using N primary inputs $x \equiv [x_1, \ldots, x_N] \geq 0_N$, while facing the strictly positive vector of net output prices

$p \equiv \left[p_1, ..., p_M \right] \gg 0_M$ and the strictly positive vector of input prices . The value of primary inputs used by the sector during period t is then $w \cdot x \equiv \Sigma_{n=1}^N w_n x_n$. Denote the period t *production possibilities set* for the sector by S^t.[3] Define the sector's *period t cost-constrained value-added function, Rt(p, w, x)* as follows:[4]

$$R^t \left(p, w, x \right) \equiv \max_{y,z} \left\{ p \cdot y : \left(y, z \right) \in S^t; \ w \cdot z \leq w \cdot z \right\}. \tag{19.1}$$

If (y^*, z^*) solves the constrained maximization problem defined by (19.1), then sectoral value added $p \cdot y$ is maximized subject to the constraints that (y, z) is a feasible production vector, and primary input expenditure $w \cdot z$ is equal to or less than "observed" primary input expenditure $w \cdot x$. Thus if the sector faces the prices $p^t \gg 0_M$ and $w^t \gg 0_N$ during period t and (y^t, x^t) is the sector's observed production vector, then production will be *value-added efficient* if the observed value added, $p^t \cdot y^t$, is equal to the optimal value added, $R^t(p^t, w^t, x^t)$. However, production may not be efficient, and so the following inequality will hold:

$$p^t \cdot y^t \leq R^t \left(p^t, w^t, x^t \right). \tag{19.2}$$

Following the example of Balk (1998, 143), we define the *value-added* or *net-revenue efficiency* of the sector during period t, e^t, as follows:

$$e^t \equiv p^t \cdot y^t / R^t \left(p^t, w^t, x^t \right) \leq 1 \tag{19.3}$$

where the inequality in (19.3) follows from (19.2). Thus if $e^t = 1$, then production is allocatively efficient in period t, and if $e^t < 1$, then production for the sector during period t is allocatively inefficient. Note that the preceding definition of value-added efficiency is a net revenue counterpart to Farrell's (1957, 255) cost-based measure of *overall efficiency* in the DEA context, which combined his measures of technical and (cost) allocative efficiency. DEA. or *data envelopment analysis*, is the term used by Charnes and Cooper (1985) and their coworkers to denote an area of analysis that is called the nonparametric approach to production theory,[5] or the measurement of the efficiency of production[6] by economists.

The cost-constrained value-added function has some interesting mathematical properties. For fixed w and x, $R^t(p, w, x)$ is a convex and linearly homogeneous function of p.[7] For fixed p and w, $R^t(p, w, x)$ is nondecreasing in x. If S^t is a convex set, then $R^t(p, w, x)$ is also concave in x. For fixed p and x, $R^t(p, w, x)$ is homogeneous of degree o in w.

It is possible to gain more insight into the properties of R^t if we introduce the sector's *period t value-added function* $\Pi^t(p, x)$. Thus for $p \gg 0_M$ and $x \geq 0_N$, define $\Pi^t(p, x)$ as follows:[8]

$$\Pi^t(p, x) \equiv \max_y \left\{ p \cdot y : (y, x) \in S^t \right\}. \tag{19.4}$$

Using definitions (19.1) and (19.4), it can be seen that the cost-constrained value-added function $R^t(p, w, x)$ has the following representation:

$$R^t\left(p, w, x\right) \equiv \max_{y,z}\left\{p\cdot y : \left(y, z\right)\in S^t; \ w\cdot z \leq w\cdot x;\right\}$$
$$= \max_z\left\{\Pi^t\left(p, z\right) : w\cdot z \leq w\cdot x; \ z\geq 0_N\right\}. \tag{19.5}$$

Holding p constant, we can define the period t *"utility" function* $f^t\left(z\right)\equiv \Pi^t\left(p, z\right)$ and the second maximization problem in (19.5) becomes the following "utility" maximization problem:

$$\max_z\left\{f^t\left(z\right) : w\cdot z \leq w\cdot x; \ z\geq 0_N\right\} \tag{19.6}$$

where $w\times x$ is the consumer's "income." For u in the range of $\Pi^t(p, z)$ over the set of non-negative z vectors and for $w \gg 0_N$, we can define the *cost function* $C^t(u, w)$ that corresponds to $f^t(z)$ as follows:[9]

$$C^t\left(u, w\right) \equiv \min_z\left\{w\cdot z : f^t\left(z\right) \geq u; \ z\geq 0_N\right\} = \min_z\left\{w\cdot z : \Pi^t\left(p, z\right) \geq u; \ z\geq 0_N\right\}.(19.7)$$

If $\Pi^t(p, z)$ increases as all components of z increase, then $C^t(u, w)$ will be increasing in u and we can solve the following maximization problem for a unique u^*:

$$\max_u\left\{u : C^t\left(u, w\right) \leq w\cdot x\right\}. \tag{19.8}$$

Using the solution to (19.8), we will have the following solution for the maximization problem that defines $R^t(p, w, x)$:

$$R^t\left(p, w, x\right) = u^* \tag{19.9}$$

with $C^t\left(u^*, w\right) = w\cdot x$.

The preceding formulae simplify considerably if S^t is a cone, so that production is subject to constant returns to scale. If S^t is a cone, then $\Pi^t(p, z)$ is linearly homogeneous in z and hence, so is $f^t\left(z\right)\equiv \Pi^t\left(p, z\right)$. Define the unit cost function c^t that corresponds to f^t as follows:[10]

$$c^t\left(w, p\right) \equiv \min_z\left\{w\cdot z : \Pi^t\left(p, z\right) \geq 1; \ z\geq 0_N\right\}. \tag{19.10}$$

The total cost function, $C^t(u, w) = C^t(u, w, p)$, is now equal to $uc^t(w, p)$ and the solution to (19.8) is the following u^*:

$$u^* = R^t\left(p, w, x\right) \equiv w\cdot x / c^t\left(w, p\right). \tag{19.11}$$

19.3. Decomposing Value-Added Growth for a Sector into Explanatory Factors

We assume that we can observe the net outputs and inputs used by the sector or production unit for two consecutive periods, say period $t-1$ and t. The observed net output and input vectors for the two periods are denoted by $y^{t-1}, y^t, x^{t-1} \gg 0_N$ and $x^t \gg 0_N$. The observed output and input price vectors are the strictly positive vectors p^{t-1}, p^t, w^{t-1}, and w^t. We also assume that $p^i \cdot y^j > 0$ and $w^i \cdot x^j > 0$ for $i = t-1, t$ and $j = t-1, t$. Our task in this section is to decompose (one plus) the growth in observed nominal value added over the two periods, $p^t \cdot y^t / p^{t-1} \cdot y^{t-1}$, into explanatory growth factors.

One of the explanatory factors will be the *growth in the value-added efficiency* of the sector or production unit. In the previous section, we defined the period t value added efficiency as $e^t \equiv p^t \cdot y^t / R^t\left(p^t, w^t, x^t\right)$. Define the corresponding period $t-1$ efficiency as $e^{t-1} \equiv p^{t-1} \cdot y^{t-1} / R^{t-1}\left(p^{t-1}, w^{t-1}, x^{t-1}\right)$. Given the preceding definitions of value-added efficiency in periods $t-1$ and t, we can define an index of the *change in value-added efficiency* ε^t for the sector over the two periods as follows:

$$\varepsilon^t \equiv e^t / e^{t-1} = \left[p^t \cdot y^t / R^t\left(p^t, w^t, x^t\right)\right] \Big/ \left[p^{t-1} \cdot y^{t-1} / R^{t-1}\left(p^{t-1}, w^{t-1}, x^{t-1}\right)\right]. \quad (9.12)$$

Thus if $\varepsilon^t > 1$, then value-added efficiency has *improved* going from period $t-1$ to t, whereas it has *fallen* if $\varepsilon^t < 1$.

Notice that the cost-constrained value-added function for the production unit in period t, $R^t(p, w, x)$, depends on four sets of variables:

- The time period t and this index t serves to indicate that the period t technology set S^t is used to define the period t value-added function;
- The vector of net output prices p that the production unit faces;
- The vector of primary input prices w that the production unit faces and
- The vector of primary inputs x which is available for use by the production unit during period t.

At this point, we will follow the methodology that is used in the economic approach to index number theory that originated with Konüs (1939) and Allen (1949), and we will use the value-added function to define various *families of indexes* that vary only *one* of the four sets of variables, t, p, w and x, between the two periods under consideration and hold constant the other sets of variables.[11]

Our first family of factors that explain sectoral value added growth is a family of *net output price indexes*, $\alpha(p^{t-1}, p^t, x, t)$:

$$\alpha(p^{t-1}, p^t, w, x, s) \equiv R^s\left(p^t, w, x\right) \Big/ R^s(p^{t-1}, w, x). \quad (19.13)$$

Thus the net output price index $\alpha(p^{t-1}, p^t, w, x, s)$ defined by (19.13) is equal to the (hypothetical) cost-constrained value-added $R^s(p^t, w, x)$ generated by the best-practice technology of period s while facing the period t net output prices p^t and the reference primary input prices w and using the reference primary input vector x, divided by the cost-constrained value-added $R^s(p^{t-1}, w, x)$ generated by the best-practice technology of period s while facing the period $t-1$ net output prices p^{t-1} and the reference primary input prices w and using the same reference primary input vector x. Thus for each choice of technology (i.e., s could equal $t-1$ or t) and for each choice of reference vectors of input prices w and quantities x, we obtain a possibly different net output price index.

Following the example of Konüs (1939) in his analysis of the true cost of living index, it is natural to single out two special cases of the family of net output price indexes defined by (19.13): one choice where we use the period $t-1$ technology and set the reference input prices and quantities equal to the period $t-1$ input prices and quantities w^{t-1} and x^{t-1} (which gives rise to a *Laspeyres-type net output price index*), and another choice where we use the period t technology and set the reference input prices and quantities equal to the period t prices and quantities w^t and x^t (which gives rise to a *Paasche-type net output price index*). We define these special cases α_L^t and α_P^t as follows:

$$\alpha_L^t \equiv \alpha(p^{t-1}, p^t, w^{t-1}, x^{t-1}, t-1) \equiv R^{t-1}\left(p^t, w^{t-1}, x^{t-1}\right)\Big/R^{t-1}\left(p^{t-1}, w^{t-1}, x^{t-1}\right); \quad (19.14)$$

$$\alpha_P^t \equiv \alpha(p^{t-1}, p^t, w^t, x^t, t) \equiv R^t\left(p^t, w^t, x^t\right)\Big/R^t\left(p^{t-1}, w^t, x^t\right). \quad (19.15)$$

Since both output price indexes, α_L^t and α_P^t, are equally representative, a single estimate of net output price change should be set equal to a symmetric average of these two estimates. We choose the geometric mean as our preferred symmetric average and thus our preferred overall measure of net output price growth is the following overall *net output price index, α^t:*[12]

$$\alpha^t \equiv \left[\alpha_L^t \alpha_P^t\right]^{1/2}. \quad (19.16)$$

Our second family of factors that explain value-added growth is a family of *input quantity indexes, $\beta(x^{t-1}, x^t, w)$:*

$$\beta(x^{t-1}, x^t, w) \equiv w \cdot x^t / w \cdot x^{t-1}. \quad (19.17)$$

The input quantity index $\beta(x^{t-1}, x^t, w)$ defined by (19.17) is equal to a ratio of simple linear aggregates of the observed input vectors for periods $t-1$ and t, x^{t-1} and x^t, where we use the vector of strictly positive input prices $w \gg 0_N$ as weights. We note that this family of input quantity indexes does not use the cost-constrained value-added function. An alternative definition for a family of input quantity indexes that uses the cost-restricted value-added function for period s and reference vectors p and w is $\beta^*\left(x^{t-1}, x^t, p, w, s\right) \equiv R^s\left(p^s, w^s, x^t\right)\Big/R^s\left(p^s, w^s, x^{t-1}\right).$[13]

If the period s technology set is a cone, then using (19.11), it can be seen that $\beta^*\left(x^{t-1}, x^t, p, w, s\right) = w \cdot x^t / w \cdot x^{t-1} = \beta\left(x^{t-1}, x^t, w\right)$. In the general case where the period s technology is not a cone, the input growth measure $\beta^*(x^{t-1}, x^t, p, w, s)$ will also incorporate the effects of nonconstant returns to scale. In this general case, it seems preferable to isolate the effects of non-constant returns to scale and the use of the simple input quantity indexes defined by (19.17) will allow us to do this, as will be seen in the following.

It is natural to single out two special cases of the family of input quantity indexes defined by (19.17): one choice where we use the period t–1 input prices w^t, which gives rise to the *Laspeyres input quantity index* $\beta_L{}^t$ and another choice where we set the reference input prices equal to w^t (which gives rise to the *Paasche input quantity index* $\beta_P{}^t$. Thus define these special cases $\beta_L{}^t$ and $\beta_P{}^t$ as follows:

$$\beta_L{}^t \equiv w^{t-1} \cdot x^t / w^{t-1} \cdot x^{t-1};$$ (19.18)

$$\beta_P{}^t \equiv w^t \cdot x^t / w^t \cdot x^{t-1}.$$ (19.19)

Since both input quantity indexes, $\beta_L{}^t$ and $\beta_P{}^t$, are equally representative, a single estimate of input quantity change should be set equal to a symmetric average of these two estimates. We choose the geometric mean as our preferred symmetric average, and thus our preferred overall measure of input quantity growth is the following overall *input quantity index*, β^t:[13]

$$\beta^t \equiv \left[\beta_L{}^t \beta_P{}^t\right]^{1/2}.$$ (19.20)

Our next family of indexes will measure the effects on cost-constrained value-added of a change in input prices going from period t–1 to t. We consider a family of measures of the relative change in cost-constrained value-added of the form $R^s(p, w^t, x)/R^s(p, w^{t-1}, x)$. Since $R^s(p, w, x)$ is homogeneous of degree 0 in the components of w, it can be seen that we cannot interpret $R^s(p, w^t, x)/R^s(p, w^{t-1}, x)$ as an input price index. If there is only one primary input, $R^s(p, w^t, x)/R^s(p, w^{t-1}, x)$ is identically equal to unity, and this measure of input price change will be independent of changes in the price of the single input. It is best to interpret $R^s(p, w^t, x)/R^s(p, w^{t-1}, x)$ as measuring the effects on cost-constrained value-added of a change in the relative proportions of primary inputs used in production or in the *mix* of inputs used in production that is induced by a change in relative input prices when there is more than one primary input. Thus define the family of *input mix indexes* $\gamma(w^{t-1}, w^t, p, x, s)$ as follows:[14]

$$\gamma\left(w^{t-1}, w^t, p, x, s\right) \equiv R^s\left(p, w^t, x\right) \big/ R^s\left(p, w^{t-1}, x\right).$$ (19.21)

As usual, we will consider two special cases of the preceding family of input mix indexes, a Laspeyres case and a Paasche case. However, the Laspeyres case $\gamma_{LPP}{}^t$ will use the period t cost-constrained value-added function and the period t–1 reference vectors

pt^{-1} and x^{t-1}, while the Paasche case $\gamma_{PLL}{}^t$ will use the use the period $t{-}1$ cost-constrained value-added function and the period t reference vectors p^t and x^t:

$$\gamma_{LPP}{}^t \equiv \gamma\left(w^{t-1}, w^t, p^{t-1}, x^t, t\right) \equiv R^t\left(p^{t-1}, w^t, x^t\right)\big/ R^t\left(p^{t-1}, w^{t-1}, x^t\right); \quad (19.22)$$

$$\gamma_{PLL}{}^t \equiv \gamma\left(w^{t-1}, w^t, p^t, x^{t-1}, t-1\right) \equiv R^{t-1}\left(p^t, w^t, x^{t-1}\right)\big/ R^{t-1}\left(p^t, w^{t-1}, x^{t-1}\right). \quad (19.23)$$

The reason for these rather odd-looking choices for reference vectors will be justified later in more detail but, basically, we make these choices in order to have value-added growth decompositions into explanatory factors that are exact without making restrictive assumptions on the technology sets.

As usual, the preceding two indexes are equally representative, and so it is natural to take an average of these two measures. We choose the geometric mean as our preferred symmetric average, and thus our preferred overall measure of input mix change is the following overall *input mix index*, γ^t:

$$\gamma^t \equiv \left[\gamma_{LPP}{}^t \gamma_{PLL}{}^t\right]^{1/2}. \quad (19.24)$$

We turn now to the effects on cost-constrained value-added due to the effects of technical progress; that is, as time marches on, new techniques are developed that allow increased net outputs using the same inputs or that allow the same net outputs to be produced by fewer inputs. Thus we use the cost-constrained value-added function in order to define a family of *technical progress indexes* going from period $t{-}1$ to t, $\tau(p, w, x)$, for reference vectors of output and input prices, p and w, and a reference vector of input quantities x as follows:[15]

$$\tau\left(t-1, t, p, w, x\right) \equiv R^t\left(p, w, x\right)\big/ R^{t-1}\left(p, w, x\right). \quad (19.25)$$

Technical progress measures are usually defined in terms of upward shifts in production functions or outward shifts of production possibilities sets due to the discovery of new techniques or managerial innovations over time. If there is positive technical progress going from period $t{-}1$ to t, then $R^t(p, w, x)$ will be greater than $R^{t-1}(p, w, x)$ and hence $\tau(p, w, x)$ will be greater than one and this measure of technical progress is equal to the proportional increase in value added that results from the expansion of the underlying best-practice technology sets due to the passage of time. For each choice of reference vectors of output and input prices, p and w, and reference vector of input quantities x, we obtain a possibly different measure of technical progress.

Again, we will consider two special cases of the preceding family of technical progress indexes, a Laspeyres case and a Paasche case. However, the Laspeyres case $\tau_L{}^t$ will use the period t input vector x^t as the reference input vector and the period $t{-}1$ reference output and input price vectors p^{t-1} and w^{t-1}, while the Paasche case $\tau_P{}^t$ will use the use the period t–1 input vector x^{t-1} as the reference input and the period t reference output and input price vectors p^t and w^t:

$$\tau_L^{\ t} \equiv \tau\!\left(t-1, t, \ p^{t-1}, \ w^{t-1}, \ x^t\right) \equiv R^t\!\left(p^{t-1}, w^{t-1}, x^t\right)/R^{t-1}\!\left(p^{t-1}, w^{t-1}, x^t\right). \quad (19.26)$$

$$\tau_P^{\ t} \equiv \tau(t-1, t, \ p^t, \ w^t, \ x^{t-1}) \equiv R^t(p^t, w^t, x^{t-1})/R^{t-1}(p^t, w^t, x^{t-1}). \quad (19.27)$$

Using (19.11), recall that if the reference technologies in periods t and t–1 are cones, then we have $R^t(p,w,x) = w \cdot x/c^t\!\left(w, p\right)$ and $R^{t-1}\!\left(p,w,x\right) = w \times x/c^{t-1}\!\left(w, p\right)$. Thus in the case where the reference technology is subject to constant returns to scale, $\tau_L^{\ t} \equiv \tau(t-1, t, p^{t-1}, w^{t-1}, x^t)$ turns out to be independent of x^t, and $\tau_P^{\ t} \equiv \tau(t-1, t, p^t, w^t, x^{t-1})$ turns out to be independent of x^{t-1}. These "mixed" indexes of technical progress are then true Laspeyres and Paasche type indexes.

We have one more family of indexes to define, and that is a family of returns-to-scale measures. Our measures are analogous to the global measures of returns to scale that were introduced by Diewert (2014, 62) using cost functions. Here we will use the cost-restricted value-added function in place of the cost function. Our returns to scale measure will be a measure of output growth divided by input growth from period t–1 to t, but the technology is held constant when we compute the output growth measure. Our measure of input growth will be $w \cdot x^t/w \cdot x^{t-1}$ where w is a positive vector of reference input prices. Now pick positive reference price vector p that will value our M net outputs. If we hold the technology constant at period t–1 levels, our measure of output growth will be $R^{t-1}\!\left(p,w,x^t\right)/R^{t-1}(p,w,x^{t-1})$. If we hold the technology constant at period t levels, our measure of output growth will be $R^t\!\left(p,w,x^t\right)/R^t(p,w,x^{t-1})$. Thus for the reference technology set indexed by s (equal to t–1 or t) and reference price vectors p and w, define the family of *returns-to-scale measures* $\delta(x^{t-1}, x^t, p, w, s)$ as follows:

$$\delta\!\left(x^{t-1}, x^t, p, w, s\right) \equiv \left[R^s\!\left(p,w,x^t\right)/R^s\!\left(p,w,x^{t-1}\right)\right]\!\Big/\!\left[w \cdot x^t / w \cdot x^{t-1}\right]. \quad (19.28)$$

We define the Laspeyres and Paasche special cases of (19.28):

$$\delta_L^{\ t} \equiv \delta\!\left(x^{t-1}, x^t, p^{t-1}, w^{t-1}, t-1\right) \equiv \\ \left[R^{t-1}\!\left(p^{t-1}, w^{t-1}, x^t\right)/R^{t-1}\!\left(p^{t-1}, w^{t-1}, x^{t-1}\right)\right]\!\Big/\!\left[w^{t-1} \cdot x^t / w^{t-1} \cdot x^{t-1}\right]; \quad (19.29)$$

$$\delta_P^{\ t} \equiv \delta(x^{t-1}, x^t, p^t, w^t, t) \equiv \left[R^t\!\left(p^t, w^t, x^t\right)/R^t\!\left(p^t, w^t, x^{t-1}\right)\right]\!\Big/\!\left[w^t \cdot x^t / w^t \cdot x^{t-1}\right]. \quad (19.30)$$

In the case where the period t–1 reference production possibilities set S^{t-1} is a cone, so that production is subject to constant returns to scale, then using (19.11), it can be seen that $\delta_L^{\ t}$ is equal to 1 and if S^t is a cone, then $\delta_P^{\ t}$ defined by (19.30) is also equal to 1.

Our preferred measure of returns to scale to be used in empirical applications is the geometric mean of the preceding special cases:

$$\delta^t \equiv \left[\delta_L^{\ t} \delta_P^{\ t} \right]^{1/2}. \tag{19.31}$$

We are now in a position to decompose (one plus) the growth in value added for the production unit going from period t–1 to t as the product of six explanatory growth factors:

- The change in cost-constrained value-added efficiency over the two periods; that is, $\varepsilon^t \equiv e^t / e^{t-1}$ defined by (19.12) above;
- Growth (or changes) in net output prices; that is, a factor of the form $\alpha(p^{t-1}, p^t, w, x, s)$ defined earlier by (19.13);
- Growth (or changes) in input quantities; that is, a factor of the form $\beta(x^{t-1}, x^t, w)$ defined by (19.17);
- Growth (or changes) in input prices; that is, an input mix index of the form $\gamma(w^{t-1}, w^t, p, x, s)$ defined by (19.21);
- Changes due to technical progress; that is, a factor of the form $\tau(t-1, t, p, w, x)$ defined by (19.25) and
- A returns-to-scale measure $\delta(x^{t-1}, x^t, p, w, s)$ of the type defined by (19.28).

Straightforward algebra using the preceding definitions shows that we have the following exact decompositions of the observed value-added ratio going from period t–1 to t into explanatory factors of the preceding type:[16]

$$p^t \cdot y^t / p^{t-1} \cdot y^{t-1} = \varepsilon^t \alpha_P^{\ t} \beta_L^{\ t} \gamma_{LPP}^{\ t} \delta_L^{\ t} \tau_L^{\ t}; \tag{19.32}$$

$$p^t \cdot y^t / p^{t-1} \cdot y^{t-1} = \varepsilon^t \alpha_L^{\ t} \beta_P^{\ t} \gamma_{PLL}^{\ t} \delta_P^{\ t} \tau_P^{\ t}. \tag{19.33}$$

Now multiply the preceding decompositions together and take the geometric mean of both sides of the resulting equation. Using the preceding definitions, it can be seen that we obtain the following *exact decomposition of value-added growth into the product of six explanatory growth factors:*[17]

$$p^t \cdot y^t / p^{t-1} \cdot y^{t-1} = \varepsilon^t \alpha^t \beta^t \gamma^t \delta^t \tau^t. \tag{19.34}$$

If the reference technology exhibits constant returns to scale in periods t–1 and t, then $\delta_L^{\ t} = \delta_P^{\ t} = \delta^t = 1$ and the returns-to-scale factors drop out of the decompositions on the right-hand sides of (19.32)–(19.34).

TFP growth for the production unit under consideration going from period t–1 to t can be defined (following Jorgenson and Griliches 1967) as an index of output growth divided by an index of input growth. An appropriate index of output growth is the value-added ratio divided by the value added price index α^t. An appropriate index of input growth is β^t. Thus define the *period t TFP growth rate*, $TFPG^t$, for the production unit as follows:[18]

$$TFPG^t \equiv \left\{ \left[p^t \cdot y^t / p^{t-1} \cdot y^{t-1} \right] / \alpha^t \right\} \Big/ \beta^t = \varepsilon^t \gamma^t \delta^t \tau^t \qquad (19.35)$$

where the last equality in (19.35) follows from (19.34). Thus in general, period t TFP growth is equal to the product of period t value-added efficiency change ε^t, a period t input mix index γ^t (which typically will be small in magnitude), period t technical progress τ^t, and period t returns to scale for the best-practice technology δ^t. If the reference best-practice technologies are subject to constant returns to scale, then the returns to scale term is identically equal to 1 and drops out of the decomposition given by (19.35).

We follow the example of Kohli (1990) and obtain a levels decomposition for the observed level of nominal value added in period t, $p^t \cdot y^t$, relative to its observed value in period 1, $p^1 \cdot y^1$. We assume that we have price and quantity data for the primary inputs used and net outputs produced by the production unit (p^t, w^t, y^t, x^t) for periods $t = 1,$ $2, \ldots, T$. We also assume that we have estimates for the cost-constrained value-added functions, $R^t(p, w, x)$, that correspond to the best-practice technology sets S^t for $t = 1,$ $2, \ldots, T$. Thus for $t = 2, 3, \ldots, T$, we can calculate the period-to-period growth factors ε^t, $\alpha^t, \beta^t, \gamma^t, \tau^t$, and δ^t. Define the cumulated explanatory variables as follows:

$$E^1 \equiv 1; \ A^1 \equiv 1; \ B^1 \equiv 1; \ C^1 \equiv 1; \ D^1 \equiv 1; \ T^1 \equiv 1. \qquad (19.36)$$

For $t = 2, 3, \ldots, T$, define the preceding variables recursively as follows:

$$E^t \equiv \varepsilon^t E^{t-1}; \ A^t \equiv \alpha^t A^{t-1}; \ B^t \equiv \beta^t B^{t-1}; \ C^t \equiv \gamma^t C^{t-1}; \ D^t \equiv \delta^t D^{t-1}; \ T^t \equiv \tau^t T^{t-1}. \qquad (19.37)$$

Using the preceding definitions and (19.34), it can be seen that we have the following *levels decomposition* for the level of period t observed value added relative to its period 1 level:

$$p^t \cdot y^t / p^1 \cdot y^1 = A^t B^t C^t D^t E^t T^t; \quad t = 2, \ldots, T. \qquad (19.38)$$

Define the level of TFP during period t, TFP^t, as follows:

$$TFP^1 \equiv 1; \ \text{for } t = 2, \ldots, T, \ \text{define } TFP^t \equiv \left(TFPG^t \right)\left(TFP^{t-1} \right) \qquad (19.39)$$

where $TFPG^t$ is defined by (19.35) for $t = 2, \ldots, T$. Using (19.35)–(19.39), it can be seen that we have the following *levels decomposition for TFP* using the cumulated explanatory factors defined by (19.36) and (19.37):

$$TFP^t = \left[p^t \cdot y^t / p^1 \cdot y^1 \right] \Big/ \left[A^t B^t \right] = C^t D^t E^t T^t; \quad t = 2, \ldots, T. \qquad (19.40)$$

In the following section, we explain a practical method for obtaining estimates for the cost-constrained value-added function for a sector.

19.4. A NONPARAMETRIC APPROXIMATION TO THE COST-CONSTRAINED VALUE-ADDED FUNCTION

We assume that (y^t, x^t) is the production unit's observed net output and primary input vector, respectively, where $x^t > 0_N$ and the observed vector of net output and primary input prices is (p^t, w^t), with $p^t \gg 0_M$ and $w^t \gg 0_N$ for $t = 1, 2, \ldots, T$.[19] We assume that the production unit's period t production possibilities set S^t is the conical free disposal hull of the period t actual production vector and past production vectors that are in our sample of time series observations for the unit.[20] Using this assumption, for strictly positive price vectors p and w and non-negative input quantity vector x, we define the *period t cost-constrained value-added function* $R^t(p, w, x)$ for the production unit as follows:

$$
\begin{aligned}
R^t\left(p, w, x\right) &\equiv \max_{y,z}\left\{p \cdot y \ : \ w \cdot z \le w \cdot x \ ; \ \left(y, z\right) \in S^t\right\} \\
&\ge \max_\lambda \left\{p \cdot \lambda y^s \ : \ w \cdot \lambda x^s \le w \cdot x; \ \lambda \ge 0\right\} \text{ since } (\lambda y^s, \lambda x^s) \in S^t \text{ for all } \lambda \ge 0 \\
&= \max_\lambda \left\{\lambda p \cdot y^s \ : \ \lambda w \cdot x^s \le w \cdot x; \ \lambda \ge 0\right\} \\
&= \left(w \cdot x \,/\, w \cdot x^s\right) p \cdot y^s .
\end{aligned}
\tag{19.41}
$$

The inequality in (19.41) will hold for all $s = 1, 2, \ldots, t$. Thus we have:

$$
R^t\left(p, w, x\right) \ge \max_s \left\{p \cdot y^s w \cdot x \,/\, w \cdot x^s : s = 1, 2, \ldots, t\right\}.
\tag{19.42}
$$

The rays $(\lambda y^s, \lambda x^s) \in S^t$ for $\lambda \ge 0$ generate the efficient points in the set S^t so the strict inequality in (19.42) cannot hold and so we have:

$$
\begin{aligned}
R^t\left(p, w, x\right) &\equiv \max_{y,z}\left\{p \cdot y \ : \ w \cdot z \le w \cdot x \ ; \ \left(y, z\right) \in S^t\right\} \\
&= \max_s \left\{p \cdot y^s w \cdot x \,/\, w \cdot x^s : s = 1, 2, \ldots, t\right\} \\
&= \max_{\lambda_1, \ldots, \lambda_t} \left\{ \begin{array}{l} p \cdot \left(\Sigma_{s=1}^{t} y^s \lambda_s\right); \ w \cdot \left(\Sigma_{s=1}^{t} x^s \lambda_s\right) \\ \le w \cdot x \ ; \lambda_1 \ge 0, \ldots, \lambda_t \ge 0 \end{array} \right\}
\end{aligned}
\tag{19.43}
$$

where the last line in (19.43) follows from the fact that the solution to the linear programming problem is an extreme point and thus its solution is equal to the second line in (19.43). Thus all three equalities in (19.43) can serve to define $R^t(p, w, x)$. Our assumption that all inner products of the form $p \cdot y^s$ and $w \cdot x^s$ are positive rules out the possibility of a $\lambda_s = 0$ solution to the third line in (19.43). The last expression in (19.43) can be used to show that when we assume constant returns to scale for our nonparametric representation for S^t, the resulting $R^t(p, w, x)$ is linear and nondecreasing in x, is convex and linearly homogeneous in p, and is homogeneous of degree 0 in w.

If t numbers, $\mu_1, \ldots, \mu_t$ are all positive, then it can be seen that $\max_s \{\mu_s : s = 1, \ldots, t\} = 1/\min_s \{1/\mu_s : s = 1, \ldots, t\}$. Using this equality and (19.43), it can be seen that we can rewrite $R^t(p, w, x)$ as follows:

$$
\begin{aligned}
R^t\left(p,\ w,\ x\right) &= w \cdot x\ \max_s\left\{p \cdot y^s\ /\ w \cdot x^s\ :\ s = 1, 2, ..., t\right\} \\
&= w \cdot x\ /\ \min_s\left\{w \cdot x^s\ /\ p \cdot y^s\ :\ s = 1, 2, ..., t\right\} \qquad (19.44) \\
&= w \cdot x\ /\ c^t\left(w, p\right)
\end{aligned}
$$

where we define the *period t nonparametric unit cost function* $c^t(w, p)$ as follows:

$$
c^t\left(w, p\right) \equiv \min_s\left\{w \cdot x^s / p \cdot y^s\ :\ s = 1, 2, ..., t\right\}. \qquad (19.45)
$$

Thus we have an explicit functional form for the unit cost function $c^t(w, p)$ that was defined earlier by (19.10). It can be seen that $c^t(w, p)$ defined by (19.45) is a linear nondecreasing function of w (and hence is linearly homogeneous and concave in w, which is a necessary property for unit cost functions) and is convex and homogeneous of degree minus one in p.

From (19.43) we can see that our cost-constrained value-added function defined by (19.41) (which did not involve the unit cost function) does in fact conform to equation (19.11), which we used to simplify our explanatory factors when we had technology sets that were cones.

Now we are in a position to apply the decompositions of value-added growth (19.34), of TFP growth (19.35), and for the level of TFP (19.40), using the specific functional form for a sector's cost-constrained value-added function defined by (19.43). However, with the assumption of constant returns to scale in production, the returns-to-scale growth factor δ^t is identically equal to one, and so this factor vanishes from the decompositions of value-added and TFP growth defined by (19.34) and (19.35). The levels return-to-scale growth factor D^t in (19.40) is also identically equal to one and hence vanishes from the decomposition (19.40).

In the following two sections, we apply our decomposition to two major sectors of the US economy, the corporate nonfinancial sector and the noncorporate nonfinancial sector, respectively.

19.5. The US Corporate Nonfinancial Sector, 1960–2014

The US Bureau of Economic Analysis (BEA), in conjunction with the Bureau of Labor Statistics (BLS) and the Board of Governors of the Federal Reserve, has developed a new set of production accounts (the Integrated Macroeconomic Accounts, or IMA) for two major private sectors of the US economy: the corporate nonfinancial sector and the noncorporate nonfinancial sector. The Balance Sheet Accounts in the IMA cover the years 1960–2014 but do not provide a decomposition of output, input, and asset values into price and quantity components. Diewert and Fox (2016a) provided such a decomposition, and we will use their data in this study.

In this section, we will use their output and input data for the US corporate nonfinancial sector (which we denote as Sector 1) for the 55 years of 1960–2014. The year t output y^{1t} is real value added,[21] and the corresponding year t value-added deflator is denoted as p^{1t}. The 10 inputs used by this sector are labor and the services of nine types of asset.[22] The output and input data are listed in Appendix A of Diewert and Fox (2016b). The year t input vector for this sector is $x^{1t} \equiv \left[x_1^{1t}, x_2^{1t}, ..., x_{10}^{1t} \right]$ where x_1^{1t} is year t labor input measured in billions of 1960 dollars and $x_2^{1t}, ..., x_{10}^{1t}$ are capital service inputs measured in billions of 1960 capital stock dollars. The corresponding year t input price vector for Sector 1 is $w^{1t} \equiv \left[w_1^{1t}, w_2^{1t}, ..., w_{10}^{1t} \right]$ for $t = 1960, ..., 2014$.

Our year t technology set for Sector 1, S^{1t}, is defined as the free disposal cone spanned by the observed output and input vectors for the sector up to and including the year t observation. However, as was shown in the previous section, the free disposal cone can be replaced by the convex free disposal cone spanned by previous observations. For convenience, we label the years 1960–2014 as years 1–55 in definitions (19.46)–(19.50) in the following. Thus S^{1t} is defined as follows:

$$S^{1t} \equiv \left\{ (y, x) : \ y \leq \Sigma_{s=1}^{t} y^{1s} \lambda_s; \ x \geq \Sigma_{s=1}^{t} x^{1s} \lambda_s; \lambda_1 \geq 0, \ ..., \lambda_s \geq 0 \right\}; \ t = 1, ..., 55. \qquad (19.46)$$

We adapt definition (19.43) of section 19.4 to the present situation and define the *Sector 1 year t cost-constrained value-added function* $R^{1t}(p, w, x)$ for $p > 0$, $w \gg 0_{10}$ and $x \gg 0_{10}$ as follows:

$$
\begin{aligned}
R^{1t}(p, w, x) &\equiv \max_{y, z} \left\{ py : \ (y, z) \in S^{1t}; \ w \cdot z \leq w \cdot x \right\} \quad t = 1, ..., 55 \\
&= \max_{\lambda_1, ..., \lambda_t} \left\{ p\left(\Sigma_{s=1}^{t} y^{1s} \lambda_s \right); w \cdot \left(\Sigma_{s=1}^{t} x^{1s} \lambda_s \right) \leq w \cdot x; \lambda_1 \geq 0, ..., \lambda_t \geq 0 \right\} \\
&= \max_s \left\{ py^{1s} w \cdot x / w \cdot x^{1s} : \ s = 1, 2, ..., t \right\} \\
&= w \cdot x \ \max_s \left\{ py^{1s} / w \cdot x^{1s} : \ s = 1, 2, ..., t \right\}.
\end{aligned}
\qquad (19.47)
$$

Using the cost-constrained value-added functions defined by (19.47), we can readily calculate the Sector 1 counterparts to the year t generic value-added growth decompositions (19.32)–(19.33) that we derived earlier in section 19.3. Using our present notation for the Sector 1 prices and quantities, these decompositions can be written as follows for $t = 2, ..., 55$:[23]

$$v^{1t} / v^{1, t-1} = p^{1t} y^{1t} / p^{1, t-1} y^{1, t-1} = \varepsilon^{1t} \alpha_P^{1t} \beta_L^{1t} \gamma_{LPP}^{1t} \tau_L^{1t}; \qquad (19.48)$$

$$v^{1t} / v^{1, t-1} = \varepsilon^{1t} \alpha_L^{1t} \beta_P^{1t} \gamma_{PLL}^{1t} \tau_P^{1t}; \qquad (19.49)$$

$$v^{1t} / v^{1, t-1} = \varepsilon^{1t} \alpha^{1t} \beta^{1t} \gamma^{1t} \tau^{1t}. \qquad (19.50)$$

As in section 19.3, we define year t TFP growth for Sector 1 as value-added growth divided by output price growth α^{1t} times input quantity growth β^{1t}:

$$TFPG^{1t} \equiv [v^{1t}/v^{1,t-1}]/[\alpha^{1t}\beta^{1t}] = \varepsilon^{1t}\gamma^{1t}\tau^{1t}; \quad t=1961,\ldots,2014. \tag{19.51}$$

Since we have only a single value-added output, $\alpha^{1t} \equiv p^{1t}/p^{1,t-1}$ can be interpreted as a Fisher output price index and $[v^{1t}/v^{1,t-1}]/\alpha^{1t}$ can be interpreted as a Fisher output quantity index going from year $t-1$ to year t. β^{1t} is the Fisher input quantity index going from year $t-1$ to year t. Thus $TFPG^{1t}$ is equal to a conventional Fisher productivity growth index in this one output case.

The (one plus) growth factors for our Sector 1 that appear in the decomposition given by (19.51) are listed in Table 19.1. In addition, we list the cost-constrained value-added efficiency levels e^{1t} that are the Sector 1 counterparts to the e^t defined by (19.3).

Table 19.1 US Corporate Nonfinancial Value–Added Growth $v^{1t}/v^{1,t-1}$, Output Price Growth a^{1t}, Input Quantity Growth β^{1t}, TFP Growth $TFPG^{1t}$, Value–Added Efficiency Growth ε^{1t}, Input Mix Growth Factors γ^{1t}, Technical Progress Growth Factors τ^{1t}, and Value–Added Efficiency Factors e^{1t}

Year t	$v^{1t}/v^{1,t-1}$	a^{1t}	β^{1t}	$TFPG^{1t}$	ε^{1t}	γ^{1t}	τ^{1t}	e^{1t}
1961	1.02696	1.00305	1.00469	1.01906	1.00000	1.00000	1.01906	1.00000
1962	1.09170	1.00647	1.03460	1.04841	1.00000	1.00000	1.04842	1.00000
1963	1.06692	1.00495	1.02435	1.03642	1.00000	1.00000	1.03641	1.00000
1964	1.08005	1.00921	1.02752	1.04153	1.00000	1.00000	1.04154	1.00000
1965	1.10313	1.01758	1.04519	1.03721	1.00000	1.00000	1.03722	1.00000
1966	1.10528	1.02920	1.05110	1.02171	1.00000	1.00000	1.02172	1.00000
1967	1.05161	1.02232	1.02739	1.00123	1.00000	1.00000	1.00123	1.00000
1968	1.09790	1.03102	1.03470	1.02914	1.00000	1.00000	1.02914	1.00000
1969	1.08381	1.04212	1.04058	0.99944	0.99950	0.99994	1.00000	0.99950
1970	1.02816	1.03715	0.99899	0.99233	0.99337	0.99894	1.00000	0.99287
1971	1.07692	1.03612	1.00738	1.03176	1.00718	1.00006	1.02436	1.00000
1972	1.11407	1.03557	1.04114	1.03330	1.00000	1.00000	1.03330	1.00000
1973	1.12293	1.05864	1.04779	1.01236	1.00000	1.00000	1.01235	1.00000
1974	1.08158	1.09825	1.01129	0.97383	0.97416	0.99966	1.00000	0.97416
1975	1.08256	1.09815	0.98241	1.00345	1.00312	1.00035	1.00000	0.97720
1976	1.13447	1.04863	1.03550	1.04476	1.02333	1.00061	1.02032	1.00000
1977	1.13447	1.05665	1.04253	1.02985	1.00000	1.00000	1.02985	1.00000
1978	1.14104	1.07144	1.05167	1.01263	1.00000	1.00000	1.01262	1.00000
1979	1.11671	1.08202	1.03863	0.99368	0.99367	1.00001	1.00000	0.99367

(continued)

Table 19.1 Continued

Year t	$v^{1t}/v^{1,t-1}$	α^{1t}	β^{1t}	$TFPG^{1t}$	ε^{1t}	γ^{1t}	τ^{1t}	e^{1t}
1980	1.08280	1.09350	1.00423	0.98604	0.98644	0.99960	1.00000	0.98019
1981	1.13011	1.08602	1.01929	1.02090	1.02021	1.00019	1.00048	1.00000
1982	1.03636	1.05950	0.98579	0.99226	0.99289	0.99937	1.00000	0.99289
1983	1.06824	1.01840	1.01903	1.02936	1.00716	1.00019	1.02185	1.00000
1984	1.12268	1.03086	1.04890	1.03830	1.00000	1.00000	1.03830	1.00000
1985	1.06489	1.01773	1.02518	1.02064	1.00000	1.00000	1.02064	1.00000
1986	1.04040	1.01396	1.01493	1.01098	1.00000	1.00000	1.01099	1.00000
1987	1.07299	1.01895	1.02831	1.02405	1.00000	1.00000	1.02404	1.00000
1988	1.08863	1.02562	1.02632	1.03421	1.00000	1.00000	1.03422	1.00000
1989	1.04995	1.03037	1.02506	0.99409	0.99408	1.00002	1.00000	0.99408
1990	1.04513	1.03022	1.00733	1.00709	1.00596	1.00003	1.00108	1.00000
1991	1.01671	1.02198	0.98427	1.01074	1.00000	1.00000	1.01073	1.00000
1992	1.04361	1.01273	1.00954	1.02075	1.00000	1.00000	1.02077	1.00000
1993	1.04598	1.02083	1.02097	1.00359	1.00000	1.00000	1.00360	1.00000
1994	1.07768	1.01521	1.03256	1.02806	1.00000	1.00000	1.02807	1.00000
1995	1.06258	1.01365	1.03237	1.01541	1.00000	1.00000	1.01541	1.00000
1996	1.06562	1.00663	1.02243	1.03537	1.00000	1.00000	1.03538	1.00000
1997	1.07519	1.00793	1.03774	1.02794	1.00000	1.00000	1.02795	1.00000
1998	1.05955	1.00264	1.02397	1.03203	1.00000	1.00000	1.03204	1.00000
1999	1.06140	1.00662	1.03224	1.02149	1.00000	1.00000	1.02148	1.00000
2000	1.06697	1.01154	1.02730	1.02676	1.00000	1.00000	1.02677	1.00000
2001	0.99271	1.01425	0.98433	0.99434	0.99529	0.99905	1.00000	0.99529
2002	1.00792	0.99938	0.98456	1.02437	1.00473	0.99999	1.01955	1.00000
2003	1.03213	1.01016	0.99016	1.03190	1.00000	1.00000	1.03189	1.00000
2004	1.06661	1.02069	1.00978	1.03488	1.00000	1.00000	1.03488	1.00000
2005	1.06847	1.03438	1.01215	1.02056	1.00000	1.00000	1.02057	1.00000
2006	1.07032	1.03063	1.01851	1.01964	1.00000	1.00000	1.01964	1.00000
2007	1.03033	1.02012	1.01042	0.99959	0.99969	0.99991	1.00000	0.99969
2008	1.00803	1.02121	0.99622	0.99084	0.99113	0.99970	1.00000	0.99082
2009	0.94412	1.01625	0.95309	0.97475	0.97620	0.99851	1.00000	0.96724
2010	1.05625	1.00079	1.00150	1.05384	1.03387	1.00112	1.01818	1.00000
2011	1.04785	1.02221	1.02168	1.00332	1.00000	1.00000	1.00332	1.00000
2012	1.05777	1.01674	1.02335	1.01661	1.00000	1.00000	1.01660	1.00000
2013	1.03693	1.00644	1.02162	1.00849	1.00000	1.00000	1.00849	1.00000
2014	1.04003	1.00803	1.02686	1.00476	1.00000	1.00000	1.00476	1.00000
Mean	1.06620	1.02880	1.01910	1.01700	1.00000	0.99995	1.01700	0.99736

Table 19.2 US Corporate Nonfinancial Value-Added Year t Levels $v^{1t}/v^{1,1960}$, Output Price Levels A^{1t}, Input Quantity Levels B^{1t}, TFP Levels TFP^{1t}, Input Mix Levels C^{1t}, Value-Added Efficiency Levels E^{1t}, and Technical Progress Levels T^{1t} Where All Levels Are Relative to 1960

Year t	$v^{1t}/v^{1,1960}$	A^{1t}	B^{1t}	TFP^{1t}	C^{1t}	E^{1t}	T^{1t}
1960	1.00000	1.00000	1.00000	1.00000	1.00000	1.00000	1.00000
1961	1.02696	1.00305	1.00469	1.01906	1.00000	1.00000	1.01906
1962	1.12113	1.00954	1.03945	1.06839	1.00000	1.00000	1.06840
1963	1.19615	1.01454	1.06476	1.10730	1.00000	1.00000	1.10730
1964	1.29190	1.02388	1.09407	1.15329	1.00000	1.00000	1.15330
1965	1.42514	1.04188	1.14350	1.19620	1.00000	1.00000	1.19622
1966	1.57518	1.07230	1.20194	1.22217	1.00000	1.00000	1.22220
1967	1.65648	1.09623	1.23486	1.22368	1.00000	1.00000	1.22370
1968	1.81864	1.13024	1.27771	1.25934	1.00000	1.00000	1.25937
1969	1.97106	1.17785	1.32956	1.25864	0.99994	0.99950	1.25937
1970	2.02656	1.22161	1.32822	1.24899	0.99888	0.99287	1.25937
1971	2.18245	1.26574	1.33802	1.28866	0.99894	1.00000	1.29004
1972	2.43141	1.31076	1.39306	1.33157	0.99894	1.00000	1.33300
1973	2.73032	1.38762	1.45963	1.34803	0.99894	1.00000	1.34947
1974	2.95307	1.52395	1.47611	1.31275	0.99860	0.97416	1.34947
1975	3.19687	1.67352	1.45016	1.31728	0.99894	0.97720	1.34947
1976	3.62675	1.75491	1.50164	1.37625	0.99955	1.00000	1.37689
1977	4.11443	1.85432	1.56550	1.41733	0.99955	1.00000	1.41799
1978	4.69473	1.98679	1.64640	1.43524	0.99955	1.00000	1.43590
1979	5.24266	2.14974	1.70999	1.42617	0.99956	0.99367	1.43590
1980	5.67676	2.35075	1.71722	1.40627	0.99916	0.98019	1.43590
1981	6.41535	2.55297	1.75035	1.43566	0.99935	1.00000	1.43659
1982	6.64861	2.70487	1.72548	1.42454	0.99872	0.99289	1.43659
1983	7.10233	2.75464	1.75831	1.46636	0.99891	1.00000	1.46798
1984	7.97366	2.83966	1.84429	1.52252	0.99891	1.00000	1.52421
1985	8.49111	2.89001	1.89073	1.55395	0.99891	1.00000	1.55567
1986	8.83418	2.93035	1.91896	1.57102	0.99891	1.00000	1.57276
1987	9.47898	2.98587	1.97328	1.60880	0.99891	1.00000	1.61057
1988	10.31908	3.06238	2.02521	1.66384	0.99891	1.00000	1.66569
1989	10.83452	3.15539	2.07596	1.65401	0.99893	0.99408	1.66569
1990	11.32345	3.25074	2.09118	1.66573	0.99896	1.00000	1.66748
1991	11.51263	3.32219	2.05828	1.68363	0.99896	1.00000	1.68537
1992	12.01468	3.36449	2.07791	1.71857	0.99896	1.00000	1.72038

(continued)

Table 19.2 Continued

Year t	$v^{1t}/v^{1,1960}$	A^{1t}	B^{1t}	TFP^{1t}	C^{1t}	E^{1t}	T^{1t}
1993	12.56706	3.43456	2.12149	1.72473	0.99896	1.00000	1.72656
1994	13.54323	3.48679	2.19055	1.77314	0.99896	1.00000	1.77502
1995	14.39079	3.53437	2.26146	1.80046	0.99896	1.00000	1.80238
1996	15.33507	3.55779	2.31219	1.86415	0.99896	1.00000	1.86615
1997	16.48815	3.58599	2.39946	1.91624	0.99896	1.00000	1.91830
1998	17.47003	3.59545	2.45697	1.97761	0.99896	1.00000	1.97976
1999	18.54264	3.61926	2.53617	2.02010	0.99896	1.00000	2.02229
2000	19.78448	3.66103	2.60542	2.07417	0.99896	1.00000	2.07642
2001	19.64021	3.71320	2.56459	2.06243	0.99802	0.99529	2.07642
2002	19.79580	3.71089	2.52498	2.11269	0.99801	1.00000	2.11702
2003	20.43174	3.74861	2.50013	2.18008	0.99801	1.00000	2.18453
2004	21.79279	3.82615	2.52457	2.25612	0.99801	1.00000	2.26072
2005	23.28502	3.95768	2.55525	2.30252	0.99801	1.00000	2.30721
2006	24.92242	4.07891	2.60254	2.34773	0.99801	1.00000	2.35252
2007	25.67843	4.16098	2.62966	2.34678	0.99791	0.99969	2.35252
2008	25.88458	4.24922	2.61973	2.32528	0.99762	0.99082	2.35252
2009	24.43813	4.31825	2.49684	2.26658	0.99613	0.96724	2.35252
2010	25.81284	4.32164	2.50058	2.38861	0.99725	1.00000	2.39529
2011	27.04786	4.41763	2.55480	2.39655	0.99725	1.00000	2.40323
2012	28.61031	4.49159	2.61446	2.43635	0.99725	1.00000	2.44312
2013	29.66699	4.52053	2.67099	2.45703	0.99725	1.00000	2.46386
2014	30.85463	4.55684	2.74273	2.46873	0.99725	1.00000	2.47559

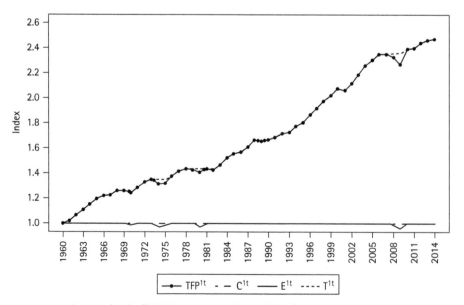

FIGURE 19.1. Sector 1 level of TFP, input mix, value added efficiency, and technology.

It can be verified that the TFP growth decomposition defined by (19.51) holds; that is, for each year t, nonparametric TFP growth $TFPG^t$ equals the product of value-added efficiency growth ε^{1t} times the year t input mix growth factor γ^{1t} times the year t technical progress measure τ^{1t}. It can be seen that the input mix factors are all very close to one. It also can be seen that when value-added efficiency in year t, e^{1t}, is less than one, then the year t technical progress measure τ^{1t} always equals one, so that there is no technical progress in years where the value-added efficiency is less than one. Our nonparametric measure of technical progress τ^{1t} is always equal to or greater than one; that is, our measure never indicates technological regress. Another important empirical regularity emerges from Table 19.1: since the input mix growth factors γ^{1t} are always very close to one, then when the year t value-added efficiency growth factor ε^t is equal to one, our nonparametric measure of TFP growth, $TFPG^t$, is virtually equal to our year t measure of technical progress τ^{1t}. Finally, the last row of Table 19.1 lists the arithmetic averages of the various growth factors. It can be seen that the arithmetic average rate of TFP growth (and of technical progress) for Sector 1 is 1.70% per year, which is a very high average rate of TFP growth over 55 years.

To conclude this section, apply the definitions (19.37)–(19.40) to Sector 1 in order to obtain the following levels decomposition for TFP in year t relative to the year 1960, TFP^{1t}:

$$TFP^{1t} = \left[v^{1t} / v^{1,1960} \right] \bigg/ \left[A^{1t} B^{1t} \right] = C^{1t} E^{1t} T^{1t}; \quad t = 1960, \ldots, 2014. \qquad (19.52)$$

Table 19.2 lists the various levels that appear in (19.52). We note that the returns to scale level for Sector 1 in year t relative to 1960, D^{1t}, is identically equal to one and so it does not appear in the decomposition defined by (19.52).

Note that the final level of TFP in 2014, 2.46873, is slightly less than the level of technology in 2014, which is 2.47559. This small difference is explained by the fact that the cumulative input mix level, 0.99725, is slightly less than one in 2014. We plot TFP^{1t}, C^{1t}, E^{1t} and T^{1t} for Sector 1 in Figure 19.1.

It can be seen that there was a substantial decline in value-added efficiency over the years 2006–2009 and, in fact, TFP has grown at a slower than average rate since 2006. The level of TFP also fell in the 1974, 1979, 1982, 1989, and 2001 recessions when efficiency growth dipped below one. However, on the whole, TFP growth in the US corporate nonfinancial sector has been satisfactory.

We turn now to an analysis of the performance of the US noncorporate nonfinancial Sector.

19.6. THE US NONCORPORATE NONFINANCIAL SECTOR, 1960–2014

In this section, we use the Diewert and Fox (2016b) output and input data for the US noncorporate nonfinancial sector (which we denote as Sector 2) for the 55 years of 1960–2014. The year t output y^{2t} is real value added for this sector, and the corresponding year t value-added deflator is denoted as p^{2t}. The 15 inputs used by this sector are labor and the services of 14 types of asset.[24] The output and input data are listed in Appendix A of Diewert and Fox (2016b). The year t input vector for this sector is $x^{2t} \equiv \left[x_1^{2t}, x_2^{2t}, ..., x_{15}^{2t} \right]$ where x_1^{2t} is year t labor input measured in billions of 1960 dollars and $x_2^{2t}, ..., x_{15}^{2t}$ are capital service inputs measured in billions of 1960 capital stock dollars. The corresponding year t input price vector for sector 2 is $w^{2t} \equiv \left[w_1^{2t}, w_2^{2t}, ..., w_{15}^{2t} \right]$ for $t = 1960, ..., 2014$.

Our year t technology set for Sector 2, S^{2t}, is defined in an analogous manner as for Sector 1 in (19.46), as the free disposal cone spanned by the observed output and input vectors up to and including the year t observation. We adapt definition (19.46) to the present situation and the *Sector 2 year t cost-constrained value-added function* $R^{2t}(p,w,x)$ for $p > 0, w \gg 0_{15}$ and $x \gg 0_{15}$ can be written as follows:

$$R^{2t}\left(p, w, x \right) = w \cdot x \ \max_s \left\{ p y^{2s} / w \cdot x^{2s} : s = 1, 2, ..., t \right\}. \qquad t = 1, ..., 55 \quad (19.53)$$

Using the cost-constrained value-added functions defined by (19.53), we can readily calculate the Sector 2 counterparts to the year t generic value-added growth decompositions (19.32)–(19.33) that we derived in section 19.3. Using our present notation for the Sector 2 prices and quantities, these decompositions can be written in the same manner as (19.48)–(19.50) except that the superscript 2 replaces the superscript 1. As in section 19.3, we define year t TFP growth for Sector 2 as value-added growth divided by output price growth α^{2t} times input quantity growth β^{2t}, which leads to the following year t decomposition of TFP growth for Sector 2:[25]

$$TFPG^{2t} \equiv \left[v^{2t} / v^{2,t-1} \right] / \left[\alpha^{2t} \beta^{2t} \right] = \varepsilon^{2t} \gamma^{2t} \tau^{2t}; \quad t = 1961, ..., 2014. \qquad (19.54)$$

Since we have only a single value-added output, $\alpha^{2t} \equiv p^{2t} / p^{2,t-1}$ can be interpreted as a Fisher output price index and $[v^{2t} / v^{2,t-1}] / \alpha^{2t}$ can be interpreted as a Fisher output quantity index going from year $t-1$ to year t. β^{2t} is the Fisher input quantity index going from year $t-1$ to year t for Sector 2. Thus $TFPG^{2t}$ is equal to a conventional Fisher productivity growth index in this one output case.

The growth factors for our Sector 2 that appear in the decomposition given by (19.54) are listed in Table 19.3. In addition, we list the cost-constrained value-added efficiency levels e^{2t} that are the Sector 2 counterparts to the e^t defined by (3).

It can be verified that the TFP growth decomposition defined by (19.54) holds; that is, for each year t, nonparametric TFP growth in Sector 2, $TFPG^{2t}$, equals the product of value-added efficiency growth ε^{2t} times the year t input mix growth factor γ^{2t} times the year t technical progress measure τ^{2t}. The arithmetic average rate of TFP growth for Sector 2 was 1.26% per year, which is well below the 1.70% per year rate of TFP growth for Sector 1, but is still quite good. As was the case with Sector 1, the Sector 2 input mix growth factors are all close to one and hence are not a significant determinant of TFP growth for the noncorporate nonfinancial sector of the US economy. Again, we see that when

Table 19.3 US Noncorporate Nonfinancial Value–Added Growth $v^{2t}/v^{2,t-1}$, Output Price Growth α^{2t}, Input Quantity Growth β^{2t}, TFP Growth $TFPG^{2t}$, Value–Added Efficiency Growth Factors ε^{2t}, Input Mix Growth Factors γ^{2t}, Technical Progress Growth Factors τ^{2t}, and Value–Added Efficiency Factors e^{2t}

Year t	$v^{2t}/v^{2,t-1}$	α^{2t}	β^{2t}	$TFPG^{2t}$	ε^{2t}	γ^{2t}	τ^{2t}	e^{2t}
1961	1.02611	1.01608	0.98336	1.02696	1.00000	1.00000	1.02695	1.00000
1962	1.03628	1.01432	0.99047	1.03148	1.00000	1.00000	1.03149	1.00000
1963	1.02537	1.01138	0.98980	1.02428	1.00000	1.00000	1.02426	1.00000
1964	1.05036	1.01681	1.00129	1.03166	1.00000	1.00000	1.03169	1.00000
1965	1.05693	1.01991	0.99748	1.03891	1.00000	1.00000	1.03889	1.00000
1966	1.06541	1.03070	1.00046	1.03319	1.00000	1.00000	1.03320	1.00000
1967	1.02600	1.03158	0.99474	0.99984	1.00000	0.99976	1.00003	1.00000
1968	1.05414	1.04532	0.99242	1.01614	1.00000	1.00000	1.01619	1.00000
1969	1.05337	1.04377	1.00590	1.00327	1.00000	1.00000	1.00330	1.00000
1970	1.03555	1.03923	0.99661	0.99986	1.00000	0.99959	1.00023	1.00000
1971	1.05931	1.04708	0.99649	1.01525	1.00000	1.00000	1.01529	1.00000
1972	1.10456	1.04810	1.01373	1.03960	1.00000	1.00000	1.03965	1.00000
1973	1.16895	1.04374	1.03526	1.08181	1.00000	1.00000	1.08176	1.00000
1974	1.05229	1.09421	1.02312	0.93996	0.94041	0.99956	1.00000	0.94041
1975	1.07140	1.10309	0.99317	0.97796	0.97815	0.99985	1.00000	0.91986
1976	1.09366	1.08706	1.00684	0.99924	0.99895	1.00030	1.00000	0.91889
1977	1.09102	1.08397	1.01453	0.99208	0.99188	1.00024	1.00000	0.91143
1978	1.13298	1.07146	1.02691	1.02970	1.02912	1.00063	1.00000	0.93797
1979	1.11623	1.11798	1.02918	0.97012	0.97030	0.99984	1.00000	0.91011
1980	1.05125	1.06681	1.01524	0.97062	0.97138	0.99923	1.00000	0.88406
1981	1.08929	1.09691	1.00518	0.98793	0.98828	0.99960	1.00000	0.87370
1982	1.04364	1.06451	1.00908	0.97157	0.97353	0.99798	1.00000	0.85057
1983	1.05757	1.07541	1.01796	0.96606	0.96782	0.99826	1.00000	0.82319
1984	1.15730	1.01282	1.02387	1.11602	1.11439	1.00148	1.00000	0.91736
1985	1.07921	1.04855	1.01081	1.01823	1.01809	1.00017	1.00000	0.93396
1986	1.05984	1.01768	1.01298	1.02808	1.03079	0.99734	1.00000	0.96272
1987	1.04901	1.04904	1.01400	0.98616	0.98582	1.00038	1.00000	0.94906
1988	1.08921	1.04848	1.01531	1.02319	1.02319	1.00004	1.00000	0.97107
1989	1.06461	1.05355	1.02123	0.98950	0.99138	0.99813	1.00000	0.96269
1990	1.04318	1.04174	1.01110	0.99039	0.99286	0.99751	1.00000	0.95582
1991	1.00925	1.04153	1.00458	0.96459	0.96850	0.99596	1.00000	0.92571
1992	1.06726	1.01569	0.98668	1.06495	1.06571	0.99930	1.00000	0.98654

(continued)

Table 19.3 Continued

Year t	$v^{2t}/v^{2,t-1}$	α^{2t}	β^{2t}	$TFPG^{2t}$	ε^{2t}	γ^{2t}	τ^{2t}	e^{2t}
1993	1.03876	1.02356	1.02364	0.99141	0.99190	0.99947	1.00000	0.97855
1994	1.05278	1.01154	1.01235	1.02807	1.02192	0.99940	1.00665	1.00000
1995	1.04291	1.04735	1.00941	0.98649	0.98648	0.99999	1.00000	0.98648
1996	1.07813	1.05142	1.00882	1.01645	1.01370	0.99997	1.00272	1.00000
1997	1.06300	1.03341	1.01934	1.00912	1.00000	1.00000	1.00916	1.00000
1998	1.08134	1.02197	1.00929	1.04836	1.00000	1.00000	1.04834	1.00000
1999	1.06748	1.01844	1.00857	1.03925	1.00000	1.00000	1.03922	1.00000
2000	1.08263	1.05231	1.01848	1.01015	1.00000	1.00000	1.01012	1.00000
2001	1.15232	1.04426	1.08093	1.02086	1.00000	1.00000	1.02087	1.00000
2002	1.04271	1.00449	1.01851	1.01918	1.00000	1.00000	1.01918	1.00000
2003	1.05478	1.00840	1.02963	1.01589	1.00000	1.00000	1.01587	1.00000
2004	1.08508	1.01994	1.03304	1.02984	1.00000	1.00000	1.02985	1.00000
2005	1.06903	1.02104	1.03269	1.01386	1.00000	1.00000	1.01387	1.00000
2006	1.09790	1.01809	1.03878	1.03814	1.00000	1.00000	1.03815	1.00000
2007	1.02757	1.02451	1.02994	0.97382	0.97366	1.00015	1.00000	0.97366
2008	1.05018	1.00395	1.00167	1.04431	1.02705	0.99990	1.01689	1.00000
2009	0.93797	0.98063	0.98224	0.97379	0.97479	0.99898	1.00000	0.97479
2010	1.03208	1.03383	0.99483	1.00349	1.00318	1.00033	1.00000	0.97788
2011	1.08243	1.01786	1.00189	1.06143	1.02262	1.00079	1.03713	1.00000
2012	1.05758	1.02064	1.01541	1.02047	1.00000	1.00000	1.02049	1.00000
2013	1.03553	1.02191	1.01072	1.00258	1.00000	1.00000	1.00261	1.00000
2014	1.04452	1.02358	1.01703	1.00338	1.00000	1.00000	1.00340	1.00000
Mean	1.06400	1.03890	1.01180	1.01260	0.99971	1.00030	1.01250	0.97086

the year t efficiency factor e^{2t} is below one, then the year t rate of technological change τ^{2t} is equal to one. Moreover, the rate of technological change τ^{2t} is always greater than or equal to one. What is very surprising is the very large number of years where value-added efficiency e^{2t} is below unity, indicating that Sector 2 is operating well within the production frontier during those years.[26] The mean level of the value-added efficiency factors is equal to 0.97086. Compare this very low average level of efficiency with the corresponding average level of efficiency for Sector 1, which was 0.99736.[27] Nevertheless, we see that the average rate of TFP growth for Sector 2 was 1.26% per year, which is very close to the average rate of technical progress for Sector 2, which was 1.25% per year.

To conclude this section, we apply definitions (19.37)–(19.40) to our present Sector 2 in order to obtain the following levels decomposition for TFP in year t relative to the year 1960, $TFP^{2t} \equiv [v^{2t}/v^{2,1960}]/[A^{2t}B^{2t}] = C^{2t}E^{2t}T^{2t}$. Table 19.4 lists these cumulative explanatory factors.

Table 19.4 US Noncorporate Nonfinancial Value-Added Year t Levels $v^{2t}/v^{2,1960}$, Output Price Levels A^{2t}, Input Quantity Levels B^{2t}, TFP Levels TFP^{2t}, Input Mix Levels C^{2t}, Value-Added Efficiency Levels E^{2t}, and Technical Progress Levels T^{2t} Where All Levels Are Relative to 1960

Year t	$v^{2t}/v^{2,1960}$	A^{2t}	B^{2t}	TFP^{2t}	C^{2t}	E^{2t}	T^{2t}
1960	1.00000	1.00000	1.00000	1.00000	1.00000	1.00000	1.00000
1961	1.02611	1.01608	0.98336	1.02696	1.00000	1.00000	1.02695
1962	1.06334	1.03063	0.97399	1.05928	1.00000	1.00000	1.05930
1963	1.09031	1.04236	0.96406	1.08500	1.00000	1.00000	1.08499
1964	1.14522	1.05988	0.96531	1.11935	1.00000	1.00000	1.11938
1965	1.21041	1.08098	0.96288	1.16291	1.00000	1.00000	1.16291
1966	1.28958	1.11417	0.96332	1.20151	1.00000	1.00000	1.20152
1967	1.32310	1.14936	0.95825	1.20132	0.99976	1.00000	1.20156
1968	1.39474	1.20145	0.95099	1.22070	0.99976	1.00000	1.22102
1969	1.46917	1.25404	0.95660	1.22470	0.99976	1.00000	1.22505
1970	1.52140	1.30323	0.95336	1.22452	0.99935	1.00000	1.22532
1971	1.61164	1.36458	0.95001	1.24320	0.99935	1.00000	1.24406
1972	1.78014	1.43021	0.96305	1.29243	0.99935	1.00000	1.29339
1973	2.08089	1.49277	0.99701	1.39816	0.99935	1.00000	1.39913
1974	2.18970	1.63340	1.02006	1.31422	0.99891	0.94041	1.39913
1975	2.34606	1.80178	1.01309	1.28526	0.99877	0.91986	1.39913
1976	2.56580	1.95864	1.02002	1.28428	0.99906	0.91889	1.39913
1977	2.79932	2.12311	1.03484	1.27411	0.99930	0.91143	1.39913
1978	3.17157	2.27483	1.06269	1.31196	0.99993	0.93797	1.39913
1979	3.54018	2.54321	1.09370	1.27276	0.99977	0.91011	1.39913
1980	3.72163	2.71313	1.11037	1.23536	0.99900	0.88406	1.39913
1981	4.05393	2.97606	1.11613	1.22045	0.99861	0.87370	1.39913
1982	4.23086	3.16805	1.12627	1.18576	0.99659	0.85057	1.39913
1983	4.47442	3.40696	1.14649	1.14551	0.99485	0.82319	1.39913
1984	5.17824	3.45063	1.17385	1.27841	0.99632	0.91736	1.39913
1985	5.58841	3.61816	1.18655	1.30171	0.99649	0.93396	1.39913
1986	5.92280	3.68213	1.20195	1.33826	0.99385	0.96272	1.39913
1987	6.21307	3.86270	1.21878	1.31974	0.99422	0.94906	1.39913
1988	6.76733	4.04995	1.23744	1.35034	0.99426	0.97107	1.39913
1989	7.20459	4.26681	1.26371	1.33616	0.99240	0.96269	1.39913
1990	7.51567	4.44489	1.27773	1.32333	0.98993	0.95582	1.39913
1991	7.58523	4.62950	1.28359	1.27647	0.98593	0.92571	1.39913
1992	8.09540	4.70216	1.26649	1.35937	0.98524	0.98654	1.39913

(continued)

Table 19.4 Continued

Year t	$v^{2t}/v^{2,1960}$	A^{2t}	B^{2t}	TFP^{2t}	C^{2t}	E^{2t}	T^{2t}
1993	8.40916	4.81293	1.29644	1.34770	0.98472	0.97855	1.39913
1994	8.85297	4.86845	1.31245	1.38553	0.98413	1.00000	1.40844
1995	9.23288	5.09895	1.32480	1.36681	0.98412	0.98648	1.40844
1996	9.95424	5.36112	1.33647	1.38929	0.98410	1.00000	1.41227
1997	10.58131	5.54023	1.36232	1.40195	0.98410	1.00000	1.42521
1998	11.44201	5.66193	1.37498	1.46974	0.98410	1.00000	1.49411
1999	12.21415	5.76635	1.38676	1.52743	0.98410	1.00000	1.55271
2000	13.22343	6.06797	1.41238	1.54294	0.98410	1.00000	1.56842
2001	15.23758	6.33652	1.52669	1.57512	0.98410	1.00000	1.60115
2002	15.88833	6.36495	1.55495	1.60534	0.98410	1.00000	1.63186
2003	16.75867	6.41842	1.60103	1.63085	0.98410	1.00000	1.65776
2004	18.18448	6.54641	1.65393	1.67950	0.98410	1.00000	1.70725
2005	19.43982	6.68416	1.70799	1.70279	0.98410	1.00000	1.73094
2006	21.34295	6.80506	1.77422	1.76773	0.98410	1.00000	1.79697
2007	21.93133	6.97187	1.82734	1.72145	0.98425	0.97366	1.79697
2008	23.03184	6.99939	1.83040	1.79772	0.98415	1.00000	1.82732
2009	21.60307	6.86380	1.79789	1.75060	0.98315	0.97479	1.82732
2010	22.29602	7.09602	1.78859	1.75672	0.98347	0.97788	1.82732
2011	24.13380	7.22277	1.79196	1.86463	0.98424	1.00000	1.89516
2012	25.52348	7.37188	1.81957	1.90280	0.98424	1.00000	1.93399
2013	26.43038	7.53339	1.83908	1.90771	0.98424	1.00000	1.93904
2014	27.60715	7.71100	1.87039	1.91416	0.98424	1.00000	1.94563

Note that the final level of TFP for Sector 2 in 2014, 1.91416, is somewhat less than the level of technology in 2014, which is 1.94563. This small difference is explained by the fact that the cumulative input mix level, 0.98424, is 1.5% less than one in 2014.[28] Note also that the final level of TFP in Sector 2, 1.91416, is much lower than the final level of TFP for Sector 1, which is 2.46873. We plot TFP^{2t}, C^{2t}, E^{2t} and T^{2t} for Sector 2 in Figure 19.2.

It can be seen that the loss of value-added efficiency in Sector 2 was massive over the 20 years of 1974–1993 and this loss of efficiency dragged down the level of Sector 2 TFP over these years. However, TFP growth resumed in 1994 and was excellent until 2006, when TFP growth again stalled with the exception of two good years of growth in 2011 and 2012.

It can be seen that our nonparametric methodology provides a useful supplement to traditional index number methods for calculating TFP growth. It illustrates the adverse influence of recessions when output falls, but inputs cannot be adjusted optimally due to

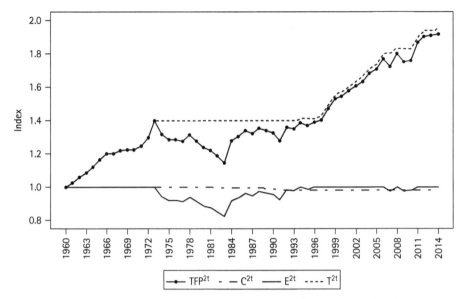

FIGURE 19.2. Sector 2 level of TFP, input mix, value added efficiency, and technology.

the fixity of many capital stock (and labor) components of aggregate input. Under these circumstances, production takes place in the interior of the production possibilities set and for Sector 2, the resulting waste of resources was substantial.[29]

We now consider the problem of how to decompose aggregate (across sectors) value added into explanatory factors.

19.7. AGGREGATION OVER SECTORS: WEIGHTED AVERAGE APPROACH

Diewert and Fox (2016c) considered different ways to go between sectoral and a higher level of aggregation decompositions, in particular, a *sectoral weighted average approach* and an *aggregate cost-constrained value-added approach*. The first method is a "bottom-up" approach, while the second method is a "top-down" approach. Diewert and Fox found that both methods produced results that approximated each other very closely. Drawing on the material of the previous sections, we present here a summary of the results from the "bottom-up" approach. This uses weighted averages of the sectoral decompositions to provide an approximate decomposition into explanatory components at the aggregate level.

Define *period t aggregate value added* v^t as the sum of the period t sectoral value added for each sector, $v^t \equiv v^{1t} + v^{2t}$. Then define the *period t share of aggregate value added for sector k* as $s^{kt} \equiv v^{kt}/v^t$, for $k = 1, 2$. Diewert and Fox (2016c) showed that, using the year t sector k explanatory growth factors, $\alpha_{kt}, \beta_{kt}, \gamma_{kt}, \varepsilon_{kt}$, and τ_{kt}, that are listed in Tables 19.1

and 19.3, we can write the following approximate decomposition of the (logarithm of the) aggregate value-added ratio between periods $t-1$ and t:

$$
\begin{aligned}
\ln v^t / v^{t-1} &\approx \sum_{k=1}^{2} (1/2)\left(s^{kt} + s^{k,t-1}\right) \ln\left(v^{kt} / v^{k,t-1}\right) \\
&= \sum_{k=1}^{2} (1/2)\left(s^{kt} + s^{k,t-1}\right) \ln\left(\alpha^{kt} \beta^{kt} \gamma^{kt} \varepsilon^{kt} \tau^{kt}\right) \\
&= \ln \alpha^{t\cdot} + \ln \beta^{t\cdot} + \ln \gamma^{t\cdot} + \ln \varepsilon^{t\cdot} + \ln \tau^{t\cdot},
\end{aligned}
\tag{19.55}
$$

using (19.50) where the terms in the last line of (19.55) are defined as follows:

$$
\ln \alpha^{t\cdot} \equiv \sum_{k=1}^{2} (1/2)\left(s^{kt} + s^{k,t-1}\right) \ln \alpha^{kt};
\tag{19.56}
$$

$$
\ln \beta^{t\cdot} \equiv \sum_{k=1}^{2} (1/2)\left(s^{kt} + s^{k,t-1}\right) \ln \beta^{kt};
\tag{19.57}
$$

$$
\ln \gamma^{t\cdot} \equiv \sum_{k=1}^{2} (1/2)(s^{kt} + s^{k,t-1}) \ln \gamma^{kt};
\tag{19.58}
$$

$$
\ln \varepsilon^{t\cdot} \equiv \sum_{k=1}^{2} (1/2)\left(s^{kt} + s^{k,t-1}\right) \ln \varepsilon^{kt};
\tag{19.59}
$$

$$
\ln \tau^{t\cdot} \equiv \sum_{k=1}^{2} (1/2)\left(s^{kt} + s^{k,t-1}\right) \ln \tau^{kt}.
\tag{19.60}
$$

Period t aggregate TFP growth, TFPG^t, can then be defined as aggregate real value-added growth divided by aggregate primary input growth:

$$
TFPG^t \equiv [v^t / v^{t-1}] / \alpha^{t\cdot} \beta^{t\cdot} \approx \gamma^{t\cdot} \varepsilon^{t\cdot} \tau^{t\cdot}; \quad t = 2,\dots,T
\tag{19.61}
$$

where the approximate equality in (19.61) follows from the approximate equality (19.55). Thus (19.61) provides an approximate decomposition of aggregate (one plus) TFP growth into the product of various aggregate explanatory growth factors (mix effects, returns to scale effects, cost-constrained value-added efficiency effects, and technical progress effects). Using definitions (19.37)–(19.40) applied to aggregate value added, we obtain the following levels decomposition for approximate aggregate TFP in year t relative to the year 1960, $TFP^{t\cdot}$:

$$
TFP^{t\cdot} = \left[v^t / v^{1960}\right] / [A^{t\cdot} B^{t\cdot}] \approx C^{t\cdot} E^{t\cdot} T^{t\cdot}; \quad t = 1960,\dots,2014.
\tag{19.62}
$$

The growth decomposition components that appear in (19.61) are listed in Table 19.5, with the arithmetic means of the growth rates over the 54 years of 1961–2014 listed in the last row. The average rate of aggregate TFP growth over these years was 1.60% per year, which is equal to the average rate of technical progress. There was no technical progress growth for eight of the years: 1974, 1975, 1979, 1980, 1982, 1989, 2007, and 2009. For these years, the rate of growth of value-added efficiency was below unity, and this translated into negative rates of TFP growth. The aggregate approximate input mix growth factors, the $\gamma^{t\cdot}$, are all very close to unity. The approximate equality in (19.61) was very close to being an equality, with the absolute value of the difference between $TFPG^t$ and $\gamma^{t\cdot} \varepsilon^{t\cdot} \tau^{t\cdot}$ always less than 0.00003, and a mean difference of –0.0000034.

In Figure 19.3, we plot $TFP^{t\cdot}$, and the explanatory factor $TFP^{t\cdot}s$ $C^{t\cdot}$, $E^{t\cdot}$, and $T^{t\cdot}$, which appear in (19.62). Since Sector 1 is almost three times as big as Sector 2, it can be seen

Table 19.5 US Aggregate Nonfinancial Value–Added Growth v^t/v^{t-1}, Output Price Growth α^t, Input Quantity Growth β^t, TFP Growth $TFPG^t$, Input Mix Growth Factors γ^t, Value–Added Efficiency Growth Factors ε^t, Technical Progress Growth Factors τ^t, and Sector 1 Shares of Aggregate Value Added s^{1t}

Year t	v^t/v^{t-1}	α^t	β^t	$TFPG^t$	γ^t	ε^t	τ^t	s^{1t}
1960	1.00000	1.00000	1.00000	1.00000	1.00000	1.00000	1.00000	0.70438
1961	1.02671	1.00688	0.99834	1.02139	1.00000	1.00000	1.02139	0.70455
1962	1.07533	1.00874	1.02160	1.04347	1.00000	1.00000	1.04348	0.71528
1963	1.05509	1.00675	1.01453	1.03300	1.00000	1.00000	1.03298	0.72330
1964	1.07183	1.01129	1.02027	1.03882	1.00000	1.00000	1.03883	0.72884
1965	1.09060	1.01820	1.03223	1.03766	1.00000	1.00000	1.03767	0.73721
1966	1.09480	1.02959	1.03773	1.02468	1.00000	1.00000	1.02468	0.74427
1967	1.04506	1.02466	1.01902	1.00088	0.99994	1.00000	1.00093	0.74893
1968	1.08691	1.03454	1.02408	1.02592	1.00000	1.00000	1.02592	0.75650
1969	1.07640	1.04252	1.03212	1.00037	0.99995	0.99962	1.00079	0.76171
1970	1.02992	1.03765	0.99842	0.99412	0.99910	0.99495	1.00005	0.76041
1971	1.07270	1.03872	1.00478	1.02781	1.00005	1.00547	1.02219	0.76340
1972	1.11182	1.03851	1.03461	1.03478	1.00000	1.00000	1.03479	0.76495
1973	1.13375	1.05506	1.04479	1.02851	1.00000	1.00000	1.02850	0.75765
1974	1.07448	1.09728	1.01411	0.96559	0.99964	0.96596	1.00000	0.76265
1975	1.07991	1.09932	0.98494	0.99737	1.00023	0.99716	1.00000	0.76452
1976	1.12486	1.05743	1.02877	1.03402	1.00054	1.01762	1.01556	0.77105
1977	1.12452	1.06275	1.03615	1.02121	1.00005	0.99816	1.02304	0.77788
1978	1.13925	1.07144	1.04613	1.01639	1.00014	1.00638	1.00981	0.77910
1979	1.11660	1.08986	1.03654	0.98843	0.99997	0.98846	1.00000	0.77917
1980	1.07583	1.08762	1.00662	0.98266	0.99952	0.98313	1.00000	0.78422
1981	1.12130	1.08833	1.01627	1.01380	1.00006	1.01333	1.00038	0.79038
1982	1.03789	1.06055	0.99064	0.98787	0.99908	0.98879	1.00000	0.78922
1983	1.06599	1.03011	1.01881	1.01573	0.99978	0.99877	1.01722	0.79088
1984	1.12992	1.02702	1.04355	1.05428	1.00031	1.02319	1.03007	0.78581
1985	1.06796	1.02429	1.02207	1.02012	1.00004	1.00387	1.01616	0.78356
1986	1.04461	1.01477	1.01450	1.01469	0.99942	1.00663	1.00858	0.78040
1987	1.06772	1.02543	1.02518	1.01568	1.00008	0.99690	1.01876	0.78425
1988	1.08876	1.03051	1.02393	1.03182	1.00001	1.00496	1.02674	0.78416
1989	1.05311	1.03536	1.02423	0.99309	0.99961	0.99349	1.00000	0.78180
1990	1.04470	1.03272	1.00815	1.00343	0.99948	1.00309	1.00084	0.78212
1991	1.01508	1.02620	0.98865	1.00053	0.99912	0.99307	1.00839	0.78337

(continued)

Table 19.4 Continued

Year t	v^t/v^{t-1}	α^t	β^t	$TFPG^t$	γ^t	ε^t	τ^t	s^{1t}
1992	1.04873	1.01338	1.00450	1.03025	0.99985	1.01401	1.01619	0.77955
1993	1.04439	1.02143	1.02156	1.00090	0.99988	0.99821	1.00281	0.78074
1994	1.07222	1.01441	1.02813	1.02806	0.99987	1.00472	1.02338	0.78471
1995	1.05835	1.02076	1.02742	1.00915	1.00000	0.99710	1.01210	0.78785
1996	1.06827	1.01601	1.01951	1.03131	0.99999	1.00290	1.02833	0.78589
1997	1.07258	1.01331	1.03379	1.02390	1.00000	1.00000	1.02392	0.78781
1998	1.06417	1.00674	1.02081	1.03549	1.00000	1.00000	1.03551	0.78438
1999	1.06271	1.00916	1.02708	1.02530	1.00000	1.00000	1.02529	0.78342
2000	1.07036	1.02028	1.02537	1.02312	1.00000	1.00000	1.02312	0.78093
2001	1.02768	1.02115	1.00598	1.00042	0.99927	0.99638	1.00481	0.75436
2002	1.01647	1.00065	0.99290	1.02307	0.99999	1.00355	1.01946	0.74802
2003	1.03784	1.00971	1.00004	1.02781	1.00000	1.00000	1.02780	0.74391
2004	1.07134	1.02050	1.01572	1.03357	1.00000	1.00000	1.03358	0.74062
2005	1.06862	1.03090	1.01744	1.01881	1.00000	1.00000	1.01883	0.74052
2006	1.07748	1.02733	1.02378	1.02445	1.00000	1.00000	1.02446	0.73560
2007	1.02960	1.02128	1.01554	0.99272	0.99997	0.99275	1.00000	0.73612
2008	1.01915	1.01656	0.99768	1.00489	0.99975	1.00063	1.00450	0.72809
2009	0.94245	1.00646	0.96091	0.97449	0.99864	0.97582	1.00000	0.72938
2010	1.04971	1.00955	0.99971	1.04008	1.00091	1.02554	1.01327	0.73393
2011	1.05705	1.02104	1.01631	1.01865	1.00021	1.00604	1.01231	0.72754
2012	1.05772	1.01780	1.02118	1.01766	1.00000	1.00000	1.01766	0.72758
2013	1.03655	1.01063	1.01864	1.00688	1.00000	1.00000	1.00689	0.72784
2014	1.04125	1.01225	1.02417	1.00438	1.00000	1.00000	1.00439	0.72699
Mean	1.06550	1.03100	1.01720	1.01600	0.99990	1.00000	1.01600	0.76069

that the overall aggregate results are closer to the Sector 1 results. In particular, the huge value-added inefficiency results that showed up in Sector 2 are no longer so huge in the aggregate results. However, inefficiency effects that are a result of recessions still show up as significant determinants of TFP at the aggregate level.

It can be seen that the input mix is not important in explaining US nonfinancial private sector TFP growth over the period 1960–2014. The most important explanatory factor is the level of technical progress, but during recession years the level of value-added efficiency plays an important role. Also noteworthy is the very high rate of TFP growth for the nonfinancial sector over this long period: the geometric average rate of TFP growth was 1.583% per year.

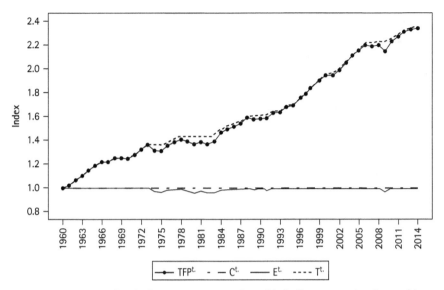

FIGURE 19.3. Aggregate level of TFP, input mix, value added efficiency, technology, and returns to scale.

19.8. CONCLUSION

We have derived decompositions of nominal value-added growth (and TFP growth) for individual sectors into explanatory factors. Starting with Denison (1962), various authors have presented decompositions of either aggregate labor productivity growth or TFP growth into sectoral explanatory factors by manipulating the index number formulae that are used to define the relevant aggregate.[30] The approach taken here relied instead on the economic approach to index number theory that started with Konüs (1939).

Rather than using the consumer's expenditure function in order to define various economic indexes, we used the sectoral cost-constrained value-added function, $R^t(p, w, x)$, as the basic building block in our approach. This function depends on four sets of variables: t (indicating which technology set is in scope), the output price vector p, the primary input price vector w, and the primary input quantity vector x. Ratios of the cost-constrained value-added functions were used to define various explanatory "economic" indexes where three of the four sets of variables are held constant in the numerator and denominator and the remaining variable changes from a period $t-1$ level in the denominator to a period t level in the numerator.

With the goal of decomposing value-added growth into a product of economic indexes, we operationalized our approach by assuming that an adequate approximation to a period t technology set can be obtained by taking the conical free disposal hull of past quantity observations for the sector under consideration. With a single output, we found that our approach generated estimates of TFP growth that are identical to standard index number estimates of TFP growth.

A main advantage of our approach is that our new nonparametric measure of technical progress never indicates technical regress. During recessions, value-added efficiency drops below unity and depresses TFP growth. For our US data set, TFP growth is well explained as the product of value-added efficiency growth times the rate of technical progress. For the US noncorporate nonfinancial sector, we found that the cost of recessions was particularly high.

Implementation of the decompositions can provide key insights into the drivers of economic growth at a detailed sectoral level. Hence, we believe that they will provide new insights into the sources of economic growth. Our decompositions may also indicate data mismeasurement problems that can then be addressed by statistical agencies.

NOTES

1. The authors thank Knox Lovell, Robin Sickles, Marcel Timmer, and seminar participants at the US Bureau of Economic Analysis for helpful comments. The first author gratefully acknowledges the financial support of the SSHRC of Canada, and both authors gratefully acknowledge the financial support of the Australian Research Council (DP150100830).

2. Let $(y, x) \in S^t$ where $y = [y_1, \ldots, y_M]$ and $x \equiv [x_1, \ldots, x_N] \geq 0_N$. If $y_m > 0$, then the sector produces the mth net output during period t while if $y_m < 0$, then the sector uses the mth net output as an intermediate input.

3. We assume that S^t satisfies the following regularity conditions: (i) S^t is a closed set; (ii) for every $x \geq 0_N$, $(0_M, x) \in S^t$; (iii) if $(y, x) \in S^t$ and $y^* \leq y$, then $(y^*, x) \in S^t$ (free disposability of net outputs); (iv) if $(y, x) \in S^t$ and $x^* \geq x$, then $(y, x^*) \in S^t$ (free disposability of primary inputs); (v) if $x \geq 0_N$ and $(y, x) \in S^t$, then $y \leq b(x)$ where the upper bounding vector b can depend on x (bounded primary inputs implies bounded from above net outputs). When applying our methodology, we will need somewhat stronger conditions that will imply that the cost-constrained value-added function is *positive* when evaluated at observed data points.

4. Note that $R^t(p, w, x)$ is well defined even if there are increasing returns to scale in production; i.e., the constraint $w \cdot z \leq w \cdot x$ leads to a finite value for $R^t(p, w, x)$. The cost-constrained value-added function is analogous to Diewert's (1983, 1086) *balance of trade restricted value-added function* and Diewert and Morrison's (1986, 669) *domestic sales function*. However, the basic idea can be traced back to Shephard's (1974) *maximal return function*, Fisher and Shell's (1998, 48) *cost-restricted sales function* and Balk's (2003, 34) *indirect revenue function*. See also Färe, Grosskopf, and Lovell (1992, 286) and Färe and Primont (1994, 203) on Shephard's formulation. Shephard, Fisher and Shell, and Balk defined their functions as $IR^t\left(p, w, c\right) \equiv \max_{y,z}\left\{p \cdot y : w \cdot z \leq c ; \left(y, z\right) \in S^t\right\}$ where $c > 0$ is a scalar cost constraint. It can be seen that our cost-constrained value-added function replaces c in the above definition by $w \cdot x$, a difference that will be important in forming our input indexes and hence our value-added decompositions. Another difference is that our y vector is a net output vector; i.e., some components of y can be negative. Excluding Diewert and Morrison (1986) and Diewert (1983), the other authors required that y be non-negative. This makes a difference to our analysis. Also, our regularity conditions are weaker than the ones that are usually used.

5. See Diewert and Mendoza (2007); Diewert and Parkan (1983); Hanoch and Rothschild (1972); Varian (1984).

6. See Afriat (1972); Balk (1998, 2003); Coelli, Rao, and Battese (1997); Färe, Grosskopf, and Lovell (1985); Färe and Lovell (1978); Farrell (1957).

7. A version of Hotelling's Lemma also holds for $R^t(p, w, x)$. Suppose y^*, x^* is a solution to the constrained maximization problem that defines $R^t(p^*, w^*, x^*)$ and $\nabla_p R^t\left(p^*, w^*, x^*\right)$ exists. Then $y^* = \nabla_p R^t\left(p^*, w^*, x^*\right)$. See Diewert and Morrison (1986, 670) for the analogous properties for their sales function.

8. This function is known as the GDP function or the national product function in the international trade literature; see Feenstra (2004, 76); Kohli (1978, 1990); and Woodland (1982). It is known as the gross, restricted, or variable profit function in the duality literature; see Diewert (1973, 1974); Gorman (1968); and McFadden (1978). Sato (1976) called it a value-added function. It was introduced into the economics literature by Samuelson (1953). We use the cost-constrained value-added function as our basic building block in this chapter, rather than the conceptually simpler GDP function because the cost-constrained value-added function allows us to deal with technologies that exhibit global increasing returns to scale.

9. Of course, $f^t(z)$ should be denoted as $f^t(z, p)$, and $C^t(u, w)$ should be denoted as $C^t(u, w, p)$.

10. $c^t(w, p)$ will be linearly homogeneous and concave in w for fixed p and it will be homogeneous of degree minus one in p for fixed w. If $\Pi^t(p, z)$ is increasing in p_m, then $c^t(w, p)$ will be decreasing in p_m.

11. The theory that follows is largely adapted from Diewert (1980a, 455–461; 1983, 1054–1076; 2014); Diewert and Morrison (1986); Kohli (1990); Fox and Kohli (1998); and the IMF, ILO, OECD, UN, and the World Bank (2004, 455–456). This approach to the net output quantity and input price indexes is an adaptation of the earlier work on theoretical price and quantity indexes by Konüs (1939); Allen (1949); Fisher and Shell (1972, 1998); Samuelson and Swamy (1974); Archibald (1977); and Balk (1998).

12. Choosing the geometric mean leads to a measure of net output price inflation that satisfies the time reversal test; i.e., the resulting index has the property that it is equal to the reciprocal of the corresponding index that measures price change going backward in time rather than forward in time; see Diewert (1997) and Diewert and Fox (2017) on this point.

13. The counterpart to this family of input quantity indexes was defined by Sato (1976, 438) and Diewert (1980a, 456) using value-added functions (i.e., the functions $\Pi^s(p, x)$) with the assumption that there was no technical progress between the two periods being compared.

14. It would be more accurate to say that $\gamma(w^{t-1}, w^t, p, x, s)$ represents the hypothetical proportional change in cost-constrained value added for the period s reference technology due to the effects of a change in the input price vector from w^{t-1} to w^t when facing the reference net output prices p and the reference vector of inputs x. Thus we shorten this description to say that γ is an "input mix index". If there is only one primary input, then since $R^s(p, w, x)$ is homogeneous of degree 0 in w, it can be seen that

$$\gamma(w^{t-1}, w^t, p, x, s) \equiv R^s\left(p, w^t, x\right) / R^s(p, w^{t-1}, x) = \left[\left(w_1^t\right)^0 R^s\left(p, 1, x\right)\right] \Big/ \left[\left(w_1^{t-1}\right)^0 R^s\left(p, 1, x\right)\right] = 1 ;$$ i.e., if

there is only one primary input, then the input mix index is identically equal to 1. For alternative mix definitions, see Balk (2001) and Diewert (2014, 62).

15. This family of technical progress measures was defined by Diewert and Morrison (1986, 662) using the value-added function $\Pi^t(p, x)$. A special case of the family was defined earlier by Diewert (1983, 1063). Balk (1998, 99) also used this definition, and Balk (1998, 58), following the example of Salter (1960), also used the joint cost function to define a similar family of technical progress indexes.

16. Diewert (2011) obtained decompositions of cost growth analogous to (19.32) and (19.33) under the assumption that the production unit was cost efficient in each period.

17. Balk (2003, 9–10) introduced the term "profitability" to describe the period t ratio of revenue to cost π^t but he considered this concept earlier; see Balk (1998, 66) for historical references. Diewert and Nakamura (2003, 129) described the same concept by the term "margin." If we divide both sides of (19.34) through by (one plus) the rate of cost growth, $w^t \cdot x^t / w^{t-1} \cdot x^{t-1}$, we obtain an expression for (one plus) the rate of growth of profitability, π^t / π^{t-1}, which will equal $\varepsilon^t \alpha^t \gamma^t \delta^t \tau^t / \beta^{t*}$ where β^{t*} is the Fisher ideal input price index that matches up with the Fisher ideal input quantity index β^t; i.e., $\beta^t \beta^{t*} = w^t \cdot x^t / w^{t-1} \cdot x^{t-1}$. This decomposition of profitability growth can be compared to the alternative profitability growth decompositions obtained by Balk (2003, 22); Diewert and Nakamura (2003); O'Donnell (2010, 531); and Diewert (2014, 63). Our present decomposition of profitability is closest to that derived by Diewert. The problem with Diewert's decomposition is that his measure of returns to scale combined returns to scale with mix effects.

18. There are similar decompositions for TFP growth using just quantity data and Malmquist gross output and input indexes; see Diewert and Fox (2014, 2017). For additional decompositions of TFP growth using both price and quantity data, see Balk (1998, 2001, 2003); Caves, Christensen, and Diewert (1982); Diewert and Fox (2008, 2010); Diewert and Morrison (1986); and Kohli (1990). However, we believe that our present decomposition is the most comprehensive decomposition of TFP growth into explanatory factors that makes use of observable price and quantity data for both outputs and inputs.

19. We also assume that $p^s \cdot y^t > 0$ for $s = 1, \ldots, T$ and $t = 1, \ldots, T$. This will ensure that all of our explanatory factors are strictly positive.

20. Diewert (1980b, 264) suggested that the convex, conical, free disposal hull of past and current production vectors be used as an approximation to the period t technology set S^t when measuring TFP growth. Tulkens (1993, 201–206), Tulkens and Vanden Eeckaut (1995a, 1995b), and Diewert and Fox (2014, 2017) dropped the convexity and constant returns to scale assumptions and used free disposal hulls of past and current production vectors to represent the period t technology sets. In this chapter, we also drop the convexity assumption but maintain the free disposal and constant returns to scale assumptions. We also follow Diewert and Parkan (1983, 153–157) and Balk (2003, 37) in introducing price data into the computations.

21. There is only a single value-added output for this sector. The published data for this sector did not allow Diewert and Fox (2016a) to decompose real value added into gross output and intermediate input components.

22. The nine types of asset used in this sector and the corresponding input numbers are as follows: 2 = Equipment; 3 = Intellectual property products; 4 = Nonresidential structures; 5 = Residential structures; 6 = Residential land; 7 = Farmland; 8 = Commercial land; 9 = Beginning of year inventory stocks; and 10 = Beginning of the year real holdings of currency and deposits. The prices are user costs that use predicted asset inflation rates rather than ex post inflation rates, but balancing rates of return were used that make the value of input in each year equal to the corresponding value of output.

23. Since our Sector 1 technology sets are cones, our returns to scale explanatory factors are all equal to unity; i.e., $\delta_L^{1t} = \delta_P^{1t} = \delta^{1t} = 1$ for $t = 2, \ldots, 55$. Thus these explanatory factors do not appear in the decompositions (19.48)–(19.50). Since there is only one output for Sector 1, we have $\alpha_L^{1t} = \alpha_P^{1t} = \alpha^{1t} = p^{1t} / p^{1,t-1}$.

24. The 14 types of asset used in this sector and the corresponding input numbers are as follows: 2 = Equipment held by sole proprietors; 3 = Equipment held by partners; 4 = Equipment held by cooperatives; 5 = Intellectual property products held by sole proprietors; 6 = Intellectual property products held by partners; 7 = Nonresidential structures held by sole proprietors; 8 = Nonresidential structures held by partners; 9 = Nonresidential structures held by cooperatives; ; 10 = Residential structures held by the noncorporate nonfinancial sector; 11 = Residential land held by the noncorporate nonfinancial sector; 12 = Farmland held by the noncorporate nonfinancial sector; 13 = Commercial land held by noncorporate nonfinancial sector; 14 = Beginning of the year inventories held by the noncorporate nonfinancial sector and 15 = Beginning of the year real holdings of currency and deposits by noncorporate nonfinancial sector.

25. The returns to scale measures δ^{2t} for Sector 2 are all equal to one and thus these growth factors do not appear in (19.53).

26. Recall that as we our approach rules out technical regress, loss of efficiency is gross loss of efficiency less any technical progress that occurs during recession years. Hence estimates of efficiency loss are a bit too low in magnitude, and our estimates of technical progress are biased downward.

27. The efficiency level e^{2t} was below unity for the years 1974–1993, 1995, 2007, 2009, and 2010, which is a total of 24 years. A possible explanation for the long stretch of inefficient years 1974–1993 is that Sector 2 uses a high proportion of structures and land to produce its net outputs, and there may have been a boom in these investments prior to 1974. Once the recession of 1974 occurred, these relatively fixed inputs could not be contracted in line with the net outputs produced by this sector, leading to the long string of inefficient years. An alternative explanation is that there are measurement errors in our data for Sector 2.

28. For most observations, γ^{2t} is only slightly less than one. But over time, the product of these γ^{2t} cumulate to 0.984, which is significantly below one.

29. We note that our empirical results in this section and the previous one, which use the cost-restricted value-added function, are very similar to our previous results for these sectors in Diewert and Fox (2016b), which used a cost function approach. However, our previous approach relied on the fact that we had only a single output in each sector. Our present approach is preferred if there are many sectoral net outputs.

30. See for example, Balk (2014, 2015, 2016); Diewert (2015, 2016); Dumagan (2013); Tang and Wang (2004).

References

Afriat, S. N. 1972. "Efficiency Estimation of Production Function." *International Economic Review* 13: 568–598.

Aiyar, S., C.-J. Dalgaard, and O. Moav. 2008. "Technological Progress and Regress in Pre-industrial Times." *Journal of Economic Growth* 13: 125–144.

Allen, R. D. G. 1949. "The Economic Theory of Index Numbers." *Economica* 16: 197–203.

Archibald, R. B. 1977. "On the Theory of Industrial Price Measurement: Output Price Indexes." *Annals of Economic and Social Measurement* 6: 57–62.

Balk, B. M. 1998. *Industrial Price, Quantity and Productivity Indexes.* Boston: Kluwer Academic.

Balk, B. M. 2001. "Scale Efficiency and Productivity Change." *Journal of Productivity Analysis* 15: 159–183.

Balk, B. M. 2003. "The Residual: On Monitoring and Benchmarking Firms, Industries and Economies with Respect to Productivity." *Journal of Productivity Analysis* 20: 5–47.

Balk, B. M. 2014. "Dissecting Aggregate Labour and Output Productivity Change." *Journal of Productivity Analysis* 42: 35–43.

Balk, B. M. 2015. "Measuring and Relating Aggregate and Subaggregate Total Factor Productivity Change Without Neoclassical Assumptions." *Statistica Neerlandica* 69: 21–48.

Balk, B. M. 2016. "The Dynamics of Productivity Change: A Review of the Bottom-up Approach." In *Productivity and Efficiency Analysis*, edited by W. H. Greene, L. Khalaf, R. C. Sickles, M. Veall, and M.-C. Voia, 15–49. New York: Springer Cham Heidelberg.

Byrne, D., J. Fernald, and M. Reinsdorf. 2016. "Does the United States Have a Productivity Slowdown or a Measurement Problem?" In *Brookings Papers on Economic Activity: Spring 2016*, edited by J. Eberly and J. Stock, 109–157. Washington, DC: Brookings Institution.

Caves, D. W., L. R. Christensen, and W. E. Diewert. 1982. "The Economic Theory of Index Numbers and the Measurement of Input, Output and Productivity." *Econometrica* 50: 1393–1414.

Charnes, A., and W. W. Cooper. 1985. "Preface to Topics in Data Envelopment Analysis." *Annals of Operations Research* 2: 59–94.

Coelli, T., D. S. P. Rao, and G. Battese. 1997. *An Introduction to Efficiency and Productivity Analysis*. Boston: Kluwer Academic.

Denison, E. F. 1962. *The Sources of Economic Growth in the United States and the Alternatives Before Us*. New York: Committee for Economic Development.

Diewert, W. E. 1973. "Functional Forms for Profit and Transformation Functions." *Journal of Economic Theory* 6: 284–316.

Diewert, W. E. 1974. "Applications of Duality Theory." In *Frontiers of Quantitative Economics*, edited by M. D. Intriligator and D. A. Kendrick, Vol. II, 106–171. Amsterdam: North Holland.

Diewert, W. E. 1976. "Exact and Superlative Index Numbers." *Journal of Econometrics* 4: 114–145.

Diewert, W. E. 1980a. "Aggregation Problems in the Measurement of Capital." In *The Measurement of Capital*, edited by D. Usher, 433–528. Chicago: University of Chicago Press.

Diewert, W. E. 1980b. "Capital and the Theory of Productivity Measurement." *American Economic Review* 70: 260–267.

Diewert, W. E. 1983. "The Theory of the Output Price Index and the Measurement of Real Output Change." In *Price Level Measurement*, edited by W. E. Diewert and C. Montmarquette, 1049–1113. Ottawa: Statistics Canada.

Diewert, W. E. 1997. "Commentary on Mathew D. Shapiro and David W. Wilcox: Alternative Strategies for Aggregating Prices in the CPI." *The Federal Reserve Bank of St. Louis Review* 79(3): 127–137.

Diewert, W. E. 2011. "Measuring Productivity in the Public Sector: Some Conceptual Problems." *Journal of Productivity Analysis* 36: 177–191.

Diewert, W. E. 2014. "Decompositions of Profitability Change Using Cost Functions." *Journal of Econometrics* 183: 58–66.

Diewert, W. E. 2015. "Decompositions of Productivity Growth into Sectoral Effects." *Journal of Productivity Analysis* 43: 367–387.

Diewert, W. E. 2016. "Decompositions of Productivity Growth into Sectoral Effects: Some Puzzles Explained." In *Productivity and Efficiency Analysis*, edited by W. H. Greene, L. Khalaf, R. C. Sickles, M. Veall, and M.-C. Voia, 1–14. New York: Springer Cham Heidelberg.

Diewert, W. E., and K. J. Fox. 2008. "On the Estimation of Returns to Scale, Technical Progress and Monopolistic Markups." *Journal of Econometrics* 145: 174–193.

Diewert, W. E., and K. J. Fox. 2010. "Malmquist and Törnqvist Productivity Indexes: Returns to Scale and Technical Progress with Imperfect Competition." *Journal of Economics* 101(1): 73–95.

Diewert, W. E., and K. J. Fox. 2014. "Reference Technology Sets, Free Disposal Hulls and Productivity Decompositions." *Economics Letters* 122: 238–242.

Diewert, W. E., and K. J. Fox. 2016a. "Alternative User Costs, Rates of Return and TFP Growth Rates for the US Nonfinancial Corporate and Noncorporate Business Sectors: 1960–2014." Discussion Paper 16–03, Vancouver School of Economics, University of British Columbia. http://econ.sites.olt.ubc.ca/files/2016/06/pdf_paper_erwin-diewert-16-03AlternativeUserCostsetc.pdf (accessed December 22, 2016).

Diewert, W. E., and K. J. Fox. 2016b. "A Decomposition of U.S. Business Sector TFP Growth into Technical Progress and Cost Efficiency Components." Discussion Paper 16-04, Vancouver School of Economics, University of British Columbia. http://econ.sites.olt.ubc.ca/files/2016/06/pdf_paper_erwin-diewert-16-04DecompUSBusinessetc.pdf (accessed December 22, 2016).

Diewert, W. E., and K. J. Fox. 2016c. "Decomposing Value Added Growth over Sectors into Explanatory Factors." Discussion Paper 16-07, Vancouver School of Economics, University of British Columbia. http://econ.sites.olt.ubc.ca/files/2016/09/pdf_paper_erwin-diewert-16-07-DecomposingValue.pdf (accessed December 22, 2016).

Diewert, W. E., and K. J. Fox. 2017. "Decomposing Productivity Indexes into Explanatory Factors." *European Journal of Operational Research* 256: 275–291.

Diewert, W. E., and N. F. Mendoza. 2007. "The Le Chatelier Principle in Data Envelopment Analysis." In *Aggregation, Efficiency, and Measurement*, edited by Rolf Färe, Shawna Grosskopf, and Daniel Primont, 63–82. New York: Springer.

Diewert, W. E., and C. J. Morrison. 1986. "Adjusting Output and Productivity Indexes for Changes in the Terms of Trade." *The Economic Journal* 96: 659–679.

Diewert, W. E., and A. O. Nakamura. 2003. "Index Number Concepts, Measures and Decompositions of Productivity Growth." *Journal of Productivity Analysis* 19: 127–159.

Diewert, W. E., and C. Parkan. 1983. "Linear Programming Tests of Regularity Conditions for Production Functions." In *Quantitative Studies on Production and Prices*, edited by W. Eichhorn, R. Henn, K. Neumann, and R. W. Shephard, 131–158. Vienna: Physica Verlag.

Dumagan, J. C. 2013. "A Generalized Exactly Additive Decomposition of Aggregate Labor Productivity Growth." *Review of Income and Wealth* 59: 157–168.

Färe, R., and C. A. K. Lovell. 1978. "Measuring the Technical Efficiency of Production." *Journal of Economic Theory* 19: 150–162.

Färe, R., S. Grosskopf, and C. A. K. Lovell. 1985. *The Measurement of Efficiency of Production*. Boston: Kluwer-Nijhoff.

Färe, R., S. Grosskopf, and C. A. K. Lovell. 1992. "Indirect Productivity Measurement." *Journal of Productivity Analysis* 2: 283–298.

Färe, R., and D. Primont. 1994. "The Unification of Ronald W. Shephard's Duality Theory." *Journal of Economics* 60: 199–207.

Farrell, M. J. 1957. "The Measurement of Production Efficiency." *Journal of the Royal Statistical Society, Series A* 120: 253–278.

Feenstra, R. C. 2004. *Advanced International Trade: Theory and Evidence*. Princeton NJ: Princeton University Press.

Fisher, F. M., and K. Shell. 1972. "The Pure Theory of the National Output Deflator." In *The Economic Theory of Price Indexes*, 49–113. New York: Academic Press.

Fisher, F. M., and K. Shell. 1998. *Economic Analysis of Production Price Indexes.* New York: Cambridge University Press.

Fox, K .J., and U. Kohli. 1998. "GDP Growth, Terms of Trade Effects and Total Factor Productivity." *Journal of International Trade and Economic Development* 7: 87–110.

Gordon, R. 2016. *The Rise and Fall of American Growth: The U.S. Standard of Living since the Civil War.* Princeton, NJ: Princeton University Press.

Gorman, W. M. 1968. "Measuring the Quantities of Fixed Factors." In *Value, Capital and Growth: Papers in Honour of Sir John Hicks*, edited by J. N. Wolfe, 141–172. Chicago: Aldine Press.

Hanoch, G., and M. Rothschild. 1972. "Testing the Assumptions of Production Theory: A Nonparametric Approach." *Journal of Political Economy* 80: 256–275.

IMF, ILO, OECD, UN, and the World Bank. 2004. *Producer Price Index Manual: Theory and Practice.* Washington, DC: International Monetary Fund.

Jorgenson, D. W., and Z. Griliches. 1967. "The Explanation of Productivity Change." *Review of Economic Studies* 34: 249–283.

Kohli, U. 1978. "A Gross National Product Function and the Derived Demand for Imports and Supply of Exports." *Canadian Journal of Economics* 11: 167–182.

Kohli, U. 1990. "Growth Accounting in the Open Economy: Parametric and Nonparametric Estimates." *Journal of Economic and Social Measurement* 16: 125–136.

Konüs, A. A. 1939. "The Problem of the True Index of the Cost of Living." *Econometrica* 7: 10–29.

McFadden, D. 1978. "Cost, Revenue and Profit Functions." In *Production Economics: A Dual Approach to Theory and Applications*, Vol. 1, edited by M. Fuss and D. McFadden, 3–109. Amsterdam: North Holland.

Mokyr, J., C. Vickers, and N. L. Ziebarth. 2015. "The History of Technological Anxiety and the Future of Economic Growth: Is This Time Different?" *Journal of Economic Perspectives* 29(3): 31–50.

O'Donnell, C. J. 2010. "Measuring and Decomposing Agricultural Productivity and Profitability Change." *Australian Journal of Agricultural and Resource Economics* 54(4): 527–560.

Salter, W. E. G. 1960. *Productivity and Technical Change.* Cambridge: Cambridge University Press.

Samuelson, P. A. 1953. "Prices of Factors and Goods in General Equilibrium." *Review of Economic Studies* 21: 1–20.

Samuelson, P. A., and S. Swamy. 1974. "Invariant Economic Index Numbers and Canonical Duality: Survey and Synthesis." *American Economic Review* 64: 566–593.

Sato, K. 1976. "The Meaning and Measurement of the Real Value Added Index." *Review of Economics and Statistics* 58: 434–442.

Shephard, R. W. 1974. *Indirect Production Functions.* Meisenheim Am Glan: Verlag Anton Hain.

Syverson, C. 2016. "Challenges to Mismeasurement Explanations for the U.S. Productivity Slowdown." NBER Working Paper No. 21974.

Tang, J., and W. Wang. 2004. "Sources of Aggregate Labour Productivity Growth in Canada and the United States." *Canadian Journal of Economics* 37: 421–444.

Tulkens, H. 1993. "On FDH Efficiency Analysis: Some Methodological Issues and Application to Retail Banking, Courts, and Urban Transit." *Journal of Productivity Analysis* 4: 183–210.

Tulkens, H., and P. Vanden Eeckaut. 1995a. "Non-Frontier Measures of Efficiency, Progress and Regress for Time Series Data." *International Journal of Production Economics* 39: 83–97.

Tulkens, H., and P. Vanden Eeckaut. 1995b. "Nonparametric Efficiency, Progress and Regress Measures for Panel Data: Methodological Aspects." *European Journal of Operational Research* 80: 474–499.

Varian, H. R. 1984. "The Nonparametric Approach to Production Analysis." *Econometrica* 52: 579–597.

Woodland, A. D. 1982. *International Trade and Resource Allocation*. Amsterdam: North Holland.

CHAPTER 20

THE WORLD KLEMS INITIATIVE

Measuring Productivity at the Industry Level

DALE W. JORGENSON

20.1. INTRODUCTION

THE World KLEMS Initiative was established at the First World KLEMS Conference at Harvard University in August 2010.[1] The purpose of this Initiative was to generate industry-level data on outputs, inputs, and productivity. Productivity is defined as output per unit of all inputs. The inputs consist of the primary factors of production—capital (K) and labor (L)—and the intermediate inputs of energy (E), materials (M), and services (S). The acronym KLEMS describes these inputs. Industry-level data have been proved to be indispensable for analyzing the sources of economic growth for countries around the world.

International productivity comparisons are the second focus of industry-level productivity research. Productivity gaps between two countries are defined in terms of differences in productivity levels. These differences are measured by linking the productivity levels for each country by purchasing power parities (PPPs) for inputs and outputs. As an example, the PPP for Japan and the United States is defined as the price in Japan, expressed in yen, relative to the price in the United States, expressed in dollars. Purchasing power parities can be defined in this way for commodities, industries, or aggregates like gross domestic product (GDP). Productivity gaps are essential for assessing competitive advantage and designing strategies for economic growth.

We review productivity measurement at the industry level in section 20.2. The landmark EU (European Union) KLEMS study was initiated in 2003 and completed in 2008. This study provided industry-level data sets for the countries of the European Union. These data have proved to be invaluable for analyzing the slowdown in European economic growth. The EU KLEMS study also included data for Australia, Canada, Japan,

Korea, and the United States. These data have been widely used for international comparisons between European countries and the leading industrialized countries of Asia and North America.

Regional organizations—LA KLEMS in Latin America and Asia KLEMS in Asia—have joined the European Union in supporting industry-level research on productivity. The Latin American affiliate of the World KLEMS Initiative, LA KLEMS, was established in 2009 at the Economic Commission for Latin American and the Caribbean (ECLAC) in Santiago, Chile. The Asian affiliate, Asia KLEMS, was founded at the Asian Development Bank Institute (ADBI) in Tokyo in 2010. The regional organizations have stimulated the development of industry-level productivity measures for the emerging economies of Asia and Latin America, such as Brazil, China, and India, as well as measures for the advanced economies of Asia, Europe, and North America.

In section 20.3 we present the KLEMS framework for productivity measurement for a single country. Development of this framework within the national accounts has the important advantage that official measures can be generated at regular intervals in a standardized format.[2] The production account in current prices contains nominal outputs and incomes, while the production account in constant prices provides real outputs and inputs, as well as productivity. Paul Schreyer's (2001) *OECD Productivity Manual* provided methods for productivity measurement within the national accounts.

A key feature of the KLEMS framework is a *constant quality index of labor input* that combines hours worked for different types of labor inputs by using labor compensation per hour as weights. Similarly, a *constant quality index of capital input* deals with the heterogeneity among capital services by using rental prices of these services as weights. Schreyer's (2009) Organisation for Economic Co-operation and Developent (OECD) Manual, *Measuring Capital*, presented methods for measuring capital services. Finally, inputs of energy, materials, and services are generated from a time series of input–output tables in current and constant prices.

In 2008 the Advisory Committee on Measuring Innovation in the 21st Century to the US Secretary of Commerce recommended that productivity data be incorporated into the US national accounts. This was successfully completed by the Bureau of Economic Analysis (BEA), the agency responsible for the US national accounts, and the Bureau of Labor Statistics (BLS), the agency that produces industry-level measures of productivity for the United States. Susan Fleck, Steven Rosenthal, Matthew Russell, Erich Strassner, and Lisa Usher (2014) published an integrated BEA/BLS industry-level production account for the United States for 1998–2009 in Jorgenson, Landefeld, and Schreyer (2014).

In section 20.4 we illustrate the KLEMS methodology for a single country by summarizing the industry-level productivity data for the United States for the period 1947–2012 compiled by Jorgenson, Ho, and Samuels (2016). We analyze the sources of US economic growth for three broad periods: the Postwar Recovery of 1947–1973, the Big Slump of 1973–1995, following the energy crisis of 1973, and the period of Growth and Recession, 1995–2012. To provide more detail on the period of Growth and Recession, we analyze the sources of growth for the subperiods 1995–2000, 2000–2007, and 2007–2012—the Investment Boom, the Jobless Recovery, and the Great Recession.

In section 20.5 we introduce the KLEMS framework for international comparisons by presenting price-level indices and productivity gaps. The price-level index is an indicator of international competitiveness, often expressed as over- or undervaluation of currencies. A specific example is the over- or undervaluation of the Japanese yen relative to the US dollar. The price-level index for Japan and the United States compares market exchange rates with PPPs for the GDP.

The productivity gaps between Japan and the United States are indicators of the relative efficiency of two countries in transforming inputs into outputs. To measure these productivity gaps, we first construct comparable measures of productivity. We then link the US and Japanese outputs and inputs at the industry level by means of PPPs. As an illustration, the US productivity data presented in section 20.4 for 1947–2012 have been linked to comparable Japanese productivity data for 1955–2012 by Jorgenson, Nomura, and Samuels (2016).

The international comparisons between Japan and the United States presented in section 20.6 are based on industry-level PPPs. These comparisons provide important information on the valuation of the Japanese yen relative to the US dollar. The yen was undervalued from 1955 until the Plaza Accord of 1985. This enabled Japan to achieve a high level of international competitiveness, despite a large productivity gap with the United States. Since 1985 the yen has been overvalued, relative to the dollar, reaching a peak in 1995 that greatly undermined Japanese competitiveness. The yen finally achieved PPP with the dollar only in 2015, restoring Japanese international competitiveness after several years of monetary policies based on quantitative easing by the Bank of Japan.

The large productivity gap between Japan and the United States that existed in 1955 gradually closed until the end of the "bubble economy" in Japanese real estate in 1991. Since that time, Japanese productivity has been stagnant, while productivity in the United States has continued to rise. The widening productivity gap can be traced to a relatively small number of industrial sectors in Japan, mainly in trade and services, but also including agriculture. Productivity gaps for Japanese manufacturing industries have remained relatively small. This has created opportunities for formulating a Japanese growth strategy based on stimulating productivity growth in the lagging industrial sectors. Section 20.7 presents our conclusions.

20.2. Development of World KLEMS

The EU KLEMS study provided industry-level data sets on the sources of growth for the EU member countries.[3] These data have found widespread application in analyzing the slowdown in European economic growth before the financial and fiscal crisis. The initial data sets and results were presented at the EU KLEMS Conference in Groningen, The Netherlands, in June 2008.[4] Marcel P. Timmer, Robert Inklaar, Mary O'Mahony, and Bart van Ark (2010) summarized the data and analyzed the sources of economic growth in Europe in their book, *Economic Growth in Europe: A Comparative Industry Perspective*.

20.2.1. Economic Growth in Europe

The EU KLEMS project also included data sets for Australia, Canada, Japan, Korea, and the United States. In their book, *Industrial Productivity in Europe*, Matilde Mas and Robert Stehrer (2012) presented international comparisons within Europe and between Europe and the advanced economies in Asia and North America. As European policymakers have focused their attention on the revival of economic growth, international comparisons of the sources of growth have become essential for analyzing the impacts of changes in economic policy.

The EU KLEMS project identified Europe's failure to develop a knowledge economy as the most important explanation of the slowdown in European economic growth. Development of a knowledge economy will require investments in human capital, information technology, and intellectual property. An important policy implication is that extension of the single market to the service industries, which are particularly intensive in the use of information technology, will be essential for removing barriers to the growth of a knowledge economy in Europe.

A new phase of the EU KLEMS project was initiated by van Ark and Kirsten Jager (2017). An initial report by Jager (2016) includes annual data for 1995–2014 for 10 countries of the European Union, including the four European members of the G7: France, Germany, Italy, and the United Kingdom.[5] The report by Jager (2016) includes a list of EU KLEMS estimates, beginning with the original EU KLEMS study conducted during 2003–2008. The final report by Jager (2017) includes data for all 28 members of the European Union for the period 1995–2015 and comparable data for Japan and the United States. The new EU KLEMS project was supported by the Economic and Financial Affairs Council of the European Commission.

The Second World KLEMS Conference was held at Harvard University on August 2012. The conference included reports on recent progress in the development of industry-level data sets, as well as extensions and applications.[6] Regional organizations in Asia and Latin America joined the European Union in supporting research on industry-level data. With growing recognition of the importance of these data, successful efforts have been made to extend the KLEMS framework to emerging and transition economies, such as Brazil, China, and India.

The Latin American affiliate of the World-KLEMS Initiative, LA KLEMS, was established in December 2009 at a conference at ECLAC, the Economic Commission for Latin America and the Caribbean, in Santiago, Chile. This affiliate was coordinated by ECLAC and included seven research organizations in four leading Latin American countries—Argentina, Brazil, Chile, and Mexico.[7] Mario Cimoli, Andre Hofman, and Nanno Mulder (2010) summarized the results of the initial phase of the LA KLEMS project in their book, *Innovation and Economic Development*. A second phase of the project was recently established under the sponsorship of the Inter-American Development Bank in Washington, D.C., in October 2016. This involves the Latin American countries of the original LA KLEMS project and a number of additional countries.[8]

A detailed report on Mexico KLEMS was published in 2013 by INEGI, the National Institute of Statistics and Geography. This was presented in an international seminar at the Instituto Techologico Autonoma de Mexico (ITAM) in Mexico City on October 2013.[9] Mexico KLEMS includes industry-level productivity data for 1990–2014 that is integrated with the Mexican national accounts. This database is updated annually.[10] A very important finding is that productivity has not grown in Mexico since 1990. Periods of positive economic growth have been offset by the negative impacts of the Mexican sovereign debt crisis of 1995, the US dot-com crash in 2000, and the US financial and economic crisis of 2007–2009.

Asia KLEMS, the Asian affiliate of the World KLEMS Initiative, was founded in December 2010, and the first Asia KLEMS Conference was held at the Asian Development Bank Institute in Tokyo in July 2011.[11] Asia KLEMS includes the Japan Industrial Productivity database,[12] the Korea Industrial Productivity database,[13] and the China Industrial Productivity database.[14] Industry-level data have been assembled for Taiwan, and work is underway to develop similar data for Malaysia. These databases were discussed at the Second Asia KLEMS Conference, held at the Bank of Korea in Seoul in August 2013, the Third Asia KLEMS Conference, held at the Chung-Hua Research Institution in Taipei, Taiwan, in August 2015, and the Fourth Asia KLEMS Conference, held at Hitotsubashi University in Kunitachi, Japan, in July 2017 and the Research Institute of Economy, Trade, and Industry in Tokyo in August 2017.[15]

Kyoji Fukao (2012, 2013) has employed the Japan Industrial Productivity database in analyzing the slowdown in productivity growth in Japan after 1991, now extending beyond the "Two Lost Decades." The initial downturn followed the collapse of the "bubble" in Japanese real estate prices in 1991. A brief revival of productivity growth after 2000 ended with the sharp decline in Japanese exports in 2008–2009. This followed the rapid appreciation of the Japanese yen, relative to the US dollar. When the Bank of Japan failed to respond to the adoption of a monetary policy of quantitative easing by the US Federal Reserve, Japan experienced a much more severe downturn in productivity growth and a larger decline in output than the United States.

The Third World KLEMS Conference was held in Tokyo in May 2014.[16] This conference discussed industry-level data sets for more than 40 countries, including participants in the three regional organizations that make up the World KLEMS Initiative—EU KLEMS in Europe, LA KLEMS in Latin America, and Asia KLEMS in Asia. In addition, the conference considered research on linking data for 40 countries through the World Input-Output Database (WIOD).[17] An important theme of the conference was the extension of the measurement of capital inputs to include intangible assets such as human capital and intellectual property.

Linked data sets are especially valuable in analyzing the development of global value chains in Asia, North America, and Europe. For this purpose, international trade can be decomposed into trade by the tasks that contribute to value added at each link of the value chain. Trade in commodities involves "double-counting" of intermediate goods as products pass through the value chain. Bart Los, Timmer, and Gaaitzen J. de Vries (2015) showed that regional value chains are merging into global value chains involving all the major countries in the world.[18]

The Third World KLEMS Conference included reports on new industry-level data sets for India and Russia. Russia KLEMS was developed by Timmer and Ilya Voskoboynikov (2016) and was released in July 2013 by the Laboratory for Research in Inflation and Growth at the Higher School of Economics in Moscow.[19] Russia's recovery from the sharp economic downturn that followed the dissolution of the Soviet Union and the transition to a market economy has been impressive. Surprisingly, increases in productivity growth widely anticipated by observers inside and outside Russia have characterized only the service industries, which were underdeveloped under central planning. Mining industries have attracted large investments, but these have not been accompanied by gains in efficiency. The collapse in world oil prices poses an important challenge for the future growth of the Russian economy.

The India KLEMS database was released in July 2014 by the Reserve Bank of India,[20] shortly after the Third World KLEMS Conference in Tokyo. This database covers 26 industries for the period 1980–2011. Beginning in the 1980s, liberalization of the Indian economy resulted in a gradual and sustained acceleration in economic growth. The most surprising feature of this acceleration has been the stagnant share of manufacturing and the rapid growth in the share of services. Given the shrinking share of agriculture and the size of the Indian agricultural labor force, another surprise is that growth of capital input has been the most important source of growth in manufacturing and services, as well as more recently in agriculture.

The Fourth World KLEMS Conference was held in Madrid in May 2016. Many of the important contributions are published in a Special Issue of the *International Productivity Monitor*, edited by Dale W. Jorgenson (2017). These include reports from the regional organisations in the World KLEMS Initiative – European Union (EU) KLEMS, Latin America (LA) KLEMS, and Asia KLEMS. The conference also included papers on investments in intangible and human capital, prices of information and communications technology equipment and services, and global value chains. Updated data sets for ten major European countries are presented by van Ark and Jaeger (2017). The emerging picture of the European economy reveals little evidence of a recovery from the Great Recession.

20.3. The KLEMS Framework for Productivity Measurement

Jorgenson, Frank M. Gollop, and Barbara M. Fraumeni (1987) constructed the first data set containing annual time series data on outputs, inputs of capital, labor, and intermediate goods, and productivity for all the industries in the US economy. This study provided the model for the methods of economy-wide and industry-level productivity measurement presented in Schreyer's (2001) OECD Manual, *Measuring Productivity*. The hallmarks of these methods are constant quality indices of capital and labor services at the industry level and indices of energy, materials, and services inputs constructed from a time series of input-output tables.

Jorgenson, Mun S. Ho, and Kevin J. Stiroh (2005) updated the US data set and revised it to include investment in information technology (IT). This required new data on the production of hardware, telecommunications equipment, and software, as well as inputs of IT capital services. The new data set has demonstrated the importance of industry-level productivity growth in understanding the US Investment Boom of the 1990s. Jorgenson, Ho, and Stiroh (2005) provided the framework for the new data and for the international comparisons of Europe, Japan, and the United States presented by Jorgenson (2009).

The key idea underlying a *constant quality index of labor input* is to capture the heterogeneity of different types of labor inputs in measuring the quantity of labor input. Hours worked for each type of labor input are combined into a constant quality index of labor input, using labor compensation per hour as weights. Constant quality indices of labor input for the United States at the industry level are discussed in detail by Jorgenson, Ho, and Stiroh (2005, 201–290).

Similarly, a *constant quality index of capital input* deals with the heterogeneity among different types of capital inputs. These capital inputs are combined into a constant quality index, using rental prices of the inputs as weights, rather than the asset prices used in measuring capital stocks. This makes it possible to incorporate differences among asset-specific inflation rates that are particularly important in analyzing the impact of investments in information technology, as well as differences in depreciation rates and tax treatments for different assets. Constant quality indices of capital input for the United States at the industry level are presented by Jorgenson, Ho, and Stiroh (2005, 147–200).

The KLEMS framework for productivity measurement incorporates a time series of input–output tables in current and constant prices. Estimates of intermediate inputs of energy, materials, and services are generated from these tables. Details on the construction of the time series of input–output tables and estimates of intermediate inputs are presented by Jorgenson, Ho, and Stiroh (2005, 87–146).

Jorgenson and Steven Landefeld (2006) developed a new architecture for the US national income and product accounts (NIPAs) that includes prices and quantities of capital services for all productive assets in the US economy. This was published in a volume on the new architecture by Jorgenson, Landefeld, and Nordhaus (2006). The incorporation of the price and quantity of capital services into the United Nations *System of National Accounts 2008* (2009) was approved by the United Nations Statistical Commission at its February–March 2007 meeting. Schreyer, then head of national accounts at the OECD, prepared an OECD Manual, *Measuring Capital*, published in

2009. This provides detailed recommendations on methods for the construction of prices and quantities of capital services.

In Chapter 20 of the United Nations (2009, 415) *System of National Accounts 2008*, estimates of capital services are described as follows: "By associating these estimates with the standard breakdown of value added, the contribution of labor and capital to production can be portrayed in a form ready for use in the analysis of productivity in a way entirely consistent with the accounts of the System." The prototype system of US national accounts presented by Jorgenson and Landefeld (2006) is consistent with the OECD Manual *Measuring Productivity*, the United Nations *System of National Accounts 2008*, and the OECD Manual *Measuring Capital*.

The new architecture for the US national accounts was endorsed by the Advisory Committee on Measuring Innovation in the 21st Century Economy to the US Secretary of Commerce:[21]

> The proposed new "architecture" for the NIPAs would consist of a set of income statements, balance sheets, flow of funds statements, and productivity estimates for the entire economy and by sector that are more accurate and internally consistent. The new architecture will make the NIPAs much more relevant to today's technology-driven and globalizing economy and will facilitate the publication of much more detailed and reliable estimates of innovation's contribution to productivity growth.

In response to the Advisory Committee's recommendations, the BEA and the BLS produced an initial set of multifactor productivity estimates integrated with the NIPAs. Data on capital and labor inputs are provided by the BLS. The results are reported by Michael Harper, Brent Moulton, Steven Rosenthal, and David Wasshausen (2009).[22] This is a critical step in implementing the new architecture. The omission of productivity statistics from the NIPAs and *System of National Accounts 1993* has been a serious barrier to analyzing the sources of economic growth.

Reflecting the international consensus on productivity measurement at the industry level, the Advisory Committee on Measuring Innovation in the 21st Century Economy to the US Secretary of Commerce (2008, 7) recommended that the Bureau of Economic Analysis (BEA) should

> [d]evelop annual, industry-level measures of total factor productivity by restructuring the NIPAs to create a more complete and consistent set of accounts integrated with data from other statistical agencies to allow for the consistent estimation of the contribution of innovation to economic growth.

In December 2011 the Bureau of Economic Analysis (BEA) released a new industry-level data set. This integrated three separate industry programs—benchmark input–output tables released every five years, annual input–output tables, and gross domestic product by industry, also released annually. The input–output tables provide data on the output side of the national accounts, along with intermediate inputs in current and constant prices. The BEA's industry-level data set is described in more detail by Nicole M. Mayerhauser and Erich H. Strassner (2010).

The BEA's annual input–output data were employed in the industry-level production accounts presented by Susan Fleck, Rosenthal, Matthew Russell, Strassner, and Lisa Usher (2014) in their paper for the Second World KLEMS Conference, "A Prototype BEA/BLS Industry-Level Production Account for the United States." The paper covers the period 1998–2009 for the 65 industrial sectors used in the NIPAs. The capital and labor input are provided by the BLS, while the data on output and intermediate inputs are generated by the BEA. This paper was published in a second volume on the new architecture for the US national accounts, edited by Jorgenson, Landefeld, and Schreyer (2014).

Stefanie H. McCulla, Alyssa E. Holdren, and Shelly Smith (2013) have summarized the 2013 benchmark revision of the NIPAs. A particularly significant innovation is the addition of intellectual property products, such as research and development and entertainment, artistic, and literary originals. Investment in intellectual property is treated symmetrically with other types of capital expenditures. Intellectual property products are included in the national product and the capital services generated by these products are included in the national income. Donald D. Kim, Strassner, and Wasshausen (2014) discuss the 2014 benchmark revision of the industry accounts, including the incorporation of intellectual property.

The 2014 benchmark revision of the US industry accounts is incorporated into the paper by Rosenthal, Matthew Russell, Samuels, Strassner, and Lisa Usher (2016), "Integrated Industry-Level Production Account for the United States: Intellectual Property Products and the 2007 NAICS." The paper covers the period 1997–2012 for the 65 industrial sectors used in the NIPAs. The capital and labor inputs are provided by the BLS, while output and intermediate inputs are generated by the BEA.[23] This paper was presented at the Third World KLEMS Conference and has been published in a volume edited by Jorgenson, Fukao, and Timmer (2016).

20.4. INDUSTRY-LEVEL PRODUCTION ACCOUNT FOR THE UNITED STATES, 1947–2012

Jorgenson and Schreyer (2013) have shown how to integrate a complete system of production accounts at the industry level into the United Nations *System of National Accounts 2008*. To illustrate the application of these accounts, we summarize the industry-level production account for the United States for 1947–2012 presented by Jorgenson, Ho, and Samuels (2016) at the Third World KLEMS Conference published as Chapter 2 of the volume *The World Economy: Growth or Stagnation?* edited by Jorgenson, Fukao, and Timmer (2016). The lengthy time series is especially valuable in comparing recent changes in the sources of economic growth with long-term trends.

The NAICS industry classification includes the industries identified by Jorgenson, Ho, and Samuels (2016) as IT-producing industries, namely, computers and electronic products, and two IT-services industries, information and data processing and computer systems design. Jorgenson, Ho, and Samuels (2016) have classified industries as IT-using if the intensity of IT capital input is greater than the median for all US industries that do not produce IT equipment, software, or services. All other industries are classified as non-IT.

Value added in the IT-producing industries during 1947–2012 is only 2.5% of the US economy. Value added in the IT-using industries is about 47.5% and the remaining 50% is in the non-IT industries. The IT-using industries are mainly in trade and services, and most manufacturing industries are in the non-IT sector. The NAICS industry classification provides much more detail on services and trade, especially the industries that are intensive users of IT. We begin by discussing the results for the IT-producing sectors, now defined to include the two IT-service sectors.

Figure 20.1 shows a steady increase in the share of IT-producing industries in the growth of value added since 1947. This is paralleled by a decline in the contribution of the non-IT industries, while the share of IT-using industries remained relatively constant through 1995. Figure 20.2 decomposes the growth of value added for the period 1995–2012. The contributions of the IT-producing and IT-using industries peaked during the Investment Boom of 1995–2000 and have declined since then. The contribution of the non-IT industries also declined substantially. Figure 20.3 gives the contributions to value added for the 65 individual industries over the period 1947–2012.

The growth rate of aggregate productivity includes a weighted average of industry productivity growth rates, using an ingenious weighting scheme originated by Domar (1961). In the Domar weighting scheme, the productivity growth rate of each industry is weighted by the ratio of the industry's gross output to aggregate value added.

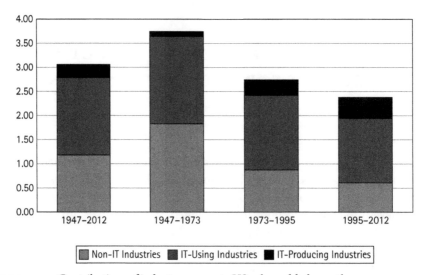

FIGURE 20.1. Contributions of industry groups to US value-added growth, 1947–2012.

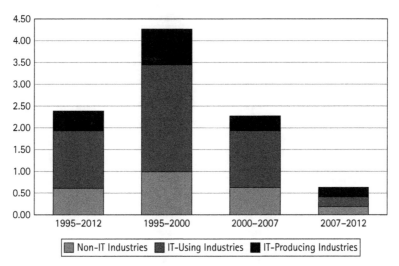

FIGURE 20.2. Contributions of industry groups to US value-added growth, 1995–2012.

A distinctive feature of Domar weights is that they sum to more than one, reflecting the fact that an increase in the growth of the industry's productivity has two effects. The first is a direct effect on the industry's output, and the second an indirect effect via the output delivered to other industries as intermediate inputs.

The rate of growth of aggregate productivity also depends on the reallocations of capital and labor inputs among industries. The aggregate productivity growth rate exceeds the weighted sum of industry productivity growth rates when these reallocations are positive. This occurs when capital and labor inputs are paid different prices in different industries, and industries with higher prices have more rapid input growth rates. Aggregate capital and labor inputs then grow more rapidly than weighted averages of industry capital and labor input growth rates, so that the reallocations are positive. When industries with lower prices for inputs grow more rapidly, the reallocations are negative.

Figure 20.4 shows that the contributions of IT-producing, IT-using, and non-IT industries to aggregate productivity growth are similar in magnitude for the period 1947–2012. The non-IT industries greatly predominated in the growth of value added during the Postwar Recovery, 1947–1973, but this contribution became negative after 1973. The contribution of IT-producing industries was relatively small during this Postwar Recovery, but became the predominant source of growth during the Long Slump, 1973–1995, and increased considerably during the period of Growth and Recession of 1995–2012.

The IT-using industries contributed substantially to US economic growth during the Postwar Recovery, but this contribution disappeared during the Long Slump, 1973–1995, before reviving after 1995. The reallocation of capital input made a small but positive contribution to growth of the US economy for the period 1947–2012 and for each of the subperiods. The contribution of reallocation of labor input was negligible for the period as a whole. During the Long Slump and the period of Growth and Recession, the contribution of the reallocation of labor input was slightly negative.

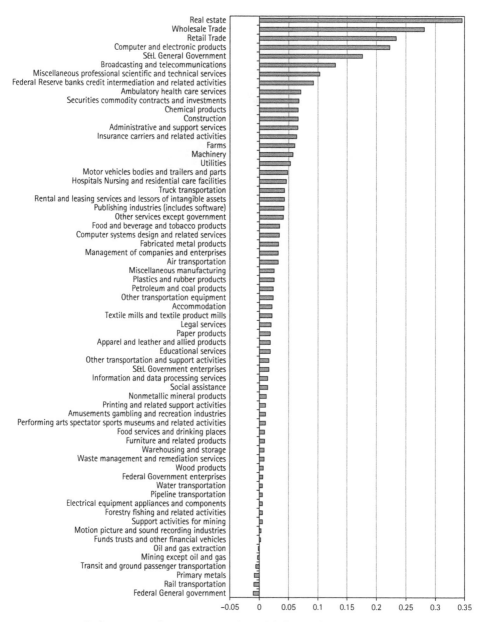

FIGURE 20.3. Industry contributions to US value-added growth, 1947–2012.

Considering the period 1995–2012 in more detail in Figure 20.5, the IT-producing industries predominated as a source of productivity growth during the period as a whole. The contribution of these industries remained substantial during each of subperiods—1995–2000, 2000–2007, and 2007–2012—despite the strong contraction of economic activity during the Great Recession of 2007–2009. The contribution of the IT-using industries was slightly greater than that of the IT-producing industries during the period of Jobless Growth, but dropped to nearly zero during the Great Recession. The non-IT industries

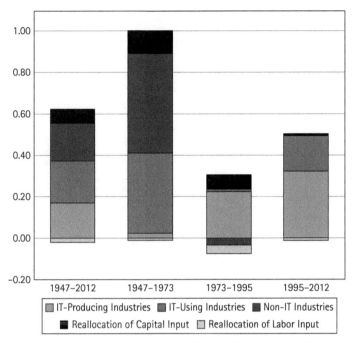

FIGURE 20.4. Contributions of industry groups to US productivity growth, 1947–2012.

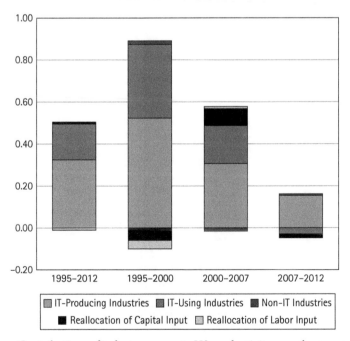

FIGURE 20.5. Contributions of industry groups to US productivity growth, 1995–2012.

contributed positively to productivity growth during the Investment Boom of 1995–2000, but these contributions were almost negligible during the Jobless Recovery and became substantially negative during the Great Recession. The contributions of reallocations of capital and labor inputs were not markedly different from historical averages.

Figure 20.6 gives the contributions of each of the 65 industries to productivity growth for the period 1947–2012. Wholesale and retail trade, farms, computer and peripheral

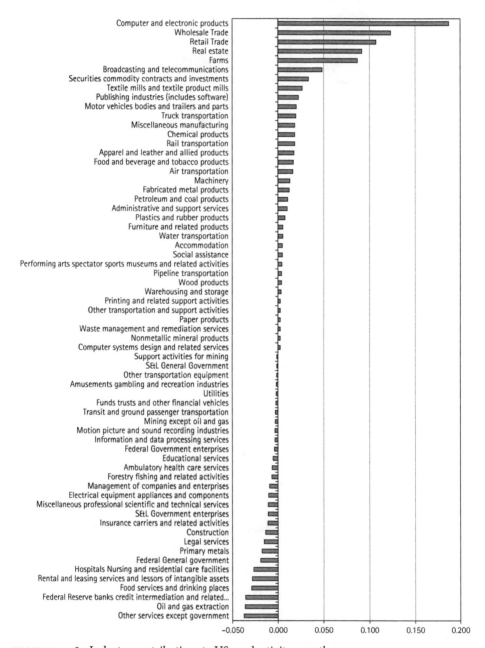

FIGURE 20.6. Industry contributions to US productivity growth, 1947–2012.

equipment, and semiconductors and other electronic components were among the leading contributors to US productivity growth during the postwar period. About half the 65 industries made negative contributions to aggregate productivity growth. These include non-market services, such as health, education, and general government, as well as resource industries affected by resource depletion, such as oil and gas extraction and mining. Other negative contributions reflect the growth of barriers to resource mobility in product and factor markets due, in some cases, to more stringent government regulations.

The price of an asset is transformed into the price of capital input by the *cost of capital*, introduced by Jorgenson (1963). The cost of capital includes the nominal rate of return, the rate of depreciation, and the rate of capital loss due to declining prices. The distinctive characteristics of IT prices—high rates of price decline and high rates of depreciation—imply that cost of capital for IT capital input is very large relative to the cost of capital for the price of non-IT capital input.

The contributions of college-educated and non-college-educated workers to US economic growth are given by the relative shares of these workers in the value of output, multiplied by the growth rates of their labor input. Personnel with a college degree or higher level of education correspond closely with "knowledge workers" who deal with information. Of course, not every knowledge worker is college educated, and not every college graduate is a knowledge worker.

All the sources of economic growth contributed to the US growth resurgence during the 1995–2000 Investment Boom represented in Figure 20.8, relative to the Long Slump of 1973–1995 in Figure 20.7. Jorgenson, Ho, and Stiroh (2005) have analyzed the sources of the US growth resurgence in greater detail. After the dot-com crash in 2000, the

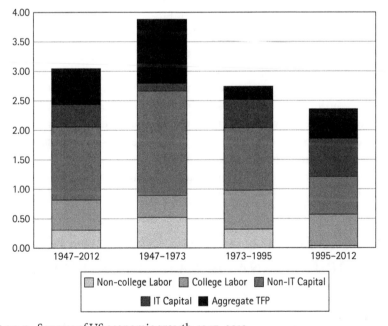

FIGURE 20.7. Sources of US economic growth, 1947–2012.

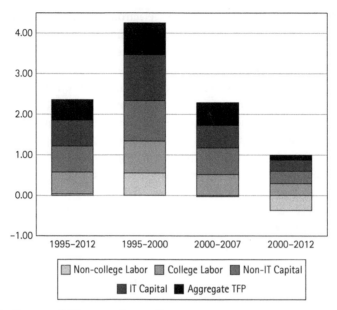

FIGURE 20.8. Sources of US economic growth, 1995–2012.

overall growth rate of the US economy dropped to well below the long-term average of 1947–2012. The contribution of investment also declined below the long-term average, but the shift from non-IT to IT capital input continued. Jorgenson, Ho, and Stiroh (2008) argue that the rapid pace of US economic growth after 1995 was not sustainable.

The contribution of labor input dropped precipitously during the period of Growth and Recession, accounting for most of the decline in US economic growth during the Jobless Recovery. The contribution to growth by college-educated workers continued at a reduced rate, but that of non-college workers was negative. The most remarkable feature of the Jobless Recovery was the continued growth in productivity, indicating a continuing surge of innovation.

Both IT and non-IT investment continued to contribute substantially to US economic growth during the Great Recession period after 2007. Productivity growth became negative, reflecting a widening gap between actual and potential growth of output. The contribution of college-educated workers remained positive and substantial, while the contribution of non-college-educated workers became strongly negative. These trends represent increased rates of substitution of capital for labor and college-educated workers for non-college-educated workers.

20.5. THE KLEMS FRAMEWORK
FOR INTERNATIONAL COMPARISONS

We introduce the framework for international comparisons with a brief discussion of the two basic concepts, the price level index and the productivity gap. The price level index is defined as the ratio of the PPP to the market exchange rate; PPP represents the price of a commodity in Japan, expressed in yen, relative to the price in the United States, expressed in dollars. By comparing this relative price with the market exchange rate of the yen and the dollar, we obtain the price barrier faced by Japanese producers in competing with their American counterparts in international markets.

As a specific illustration, the PPP of a unit of the GDP in Japan and the United States in 2005 was 124.9 yen per dollar, while the market exchange rate was 110.2 yen per dollar. The price level index was 1.13, so that the yen was overvalued relative to the dollar by 13%. Firms located in Japan had to overcome a 13% price disadvantage in international markets to compete with US producers. This provides a quantitative measure of the international competitiveness of Japan and the United States in 2005.

Jorgenson, Nomura, and Samuels (2016) give estimates of price level indices for 36 industries in Japan and the United States. These estimates are derived from detailed PPPs for 174 products, constructed within the framework of a bilateral Japan-US input–output table for 2005 by Nomura and Miyagawa (2015). Jorgenson, Nomura, and Samuels (2016) develop price-level indices for capital stock and capital services for 33 types of capital assets, including research and development, land, and inventories. Finally, they develop price-level indices for 1,680 categories of labor inputs, cross-classified by gender (2), age (6), education attainment (4), and industry (35) categories. The detailed price-level indices are used to construct prices for outputs and the KLEMS inputs of the 36 industries—capital (K), labor (L), energy (E), materials (M), and services (S).

Price level indices between Japan and the United States have real counterparts in the productivity gaps between the two countries. At the economy-wide level, total factor productivity (TFP) is defined as the GDP divided by the total of capital and labor inputs. This can be distinguished from labor productivity, the ratio of GDP to labor input, or capital productivity, the ratio of GDP to capital input. The productivity gap reflects the difference between the levels of TFP and captures the relative efficiency of production in the two countries.

We trace the Japan-US productivity gap to its sources at the industry level by comparing industry-level production accounts for Japan and the United States that employ similar national accounting concepts. The US production account presented insSection 20.4 was developed by Jorgenson, Ho, and Samuels (2016), who extended the estimates of Jorgenson, Ho, and Stiroh (2005) backward to 1947 and forward to 2012. Jorgenson, Nomura, and Samuels (2016) extended the Japanese production account presented by Jorgenson and Nomura (2007) backward to 1955 and forward to 2012.

The convergence of Japanese economy to US levels of productivity has been analyzed in a number of earlier studies—Jorgenson, Kuroda, and Nishimizu (1987), Jorgenson and Kuroda (1990), van Ark and Pilat (1993), Kuroda and Nomura (1999), Nomura (2004), and Cameron (2005), as well as Jorgenson and Nomura (2007). The productivity gap between Japan and the United States is defined as the difference between unity and the ratio of levels of TFP in the two countries. For example, in 1955, three years after Japan regained sovereignty at the end of the Allied occupation in 1952, Japan's TFP was 45.4% of the US level, so that the productivity gap between the two economies was 54.6%.

Japanese GDP grew at double-digit rates for a decade and a half, beginning in 1955. This rapid growth is often associated with the "income-doubling" plan of Prime Minister Hayato Ikeda. Ikeda took office in 1960 and immediately announced a plan to double Japanese incomes during the decade 1960–1970. The growth rate of Japanese GDP averaged more than 10% per year from 1955 to 1970, considerably more than the income-doubling growth rate of 7%. The growth of TFP contributed about 40% of this growth in output, while growth of capital and labor inputs contributed around 60%.

The oil price shock of 1973 slowed Japanese growth, but Japanese GDP doubled more than three times between 1955 and 1991. The growth of TFP accounted for a little under a third of this, while growth of capital and labor inputs accounted for slightly more than two-thirds. US economic growth averaged less than half the Japanese growth rate from 1955 to 1991. Japanese TFP grew at 2.46% per year until 1991, while annual US TFP growth averaged only 0.46%. In 1991 Japanese TFP reached 92.9% of the US level, leaving a productivity gap of 7.1%.

The collapse in Japanese real estate prices ended the "bubble economy" in 1991 and ushered in a period of much slower growth, often called the Lost Decade. The Japanese growth rate plummeted to only 0.70% per year during 1991–2012, less than a tenth of the growth rate during 1955–1991. US economic growth continued at 2.71% during 1991–2012, including the IT investment boom of 1995–2000, when the growth rate rose to 4.40% per year. After 1991, Japanese TFP was almost unchanged, falling at 0.05% per year, while US TFP continued to grow at 0.53%. By 2012, the Japan-US productivity gap had widened to 17.3%, the level of the early 1980s.

Hamada and Okada (2009) have employed price-level indices to analyze the monetary and international factors behind Japan's Lost Decade. The Lost Decade is discussed in much greater detail by Hamada, Kashyap, and Weinstein (2010), Iwata (2011), and Fukao (2013). The Lost Decade of the 1990s in Japan was followed by a brief revival in economic growth. The Great Recession of 2007–2009 in the United States was transmitted to Japan by a sharp appreciation of the yen in response to quantitative easing by the Federal Reserve. This led to a downturn in Japan that was more severe than in any of the other major industrialized countries, providing the setting for a renewed focus on economic growth by the government of Prime Minister Shinzo Abe in 2012 under the rubric of "Abenomics."

20.6. INDUSTRY-LEVEL PRODUCTION ACCOUNTS FOR JAPAN AND THE UNITED STATES

We estimate PPPs for GDP in Japan and the United States in 2005 from industry-level PPPs for gross output, factor inputs of capital and labor, and intermediate inputs of energy, materials, and services. The PPP for GDP is an index of the industry-level PPPs for value added, weighted by average industry shares of value added in the two countries. Similarly, the PPPs for factor inputs and intermediate inputs by industry are defined as indices of PPPs for these inputs at the elementary level, using average industry shares as weights. Taking estimates of the PPPs for 2005 as a benchmark, we derive time-series estimates of the PPPs by extending the benchmark back to 1955 and forward to 2012, using time-series data on prices for outputs and inputs.

Table 20.1 presents our estimates of PPPs and price level indices (PLIs) for Japan relative to the United States. Figure 20.9 represents the long-term trends of PPPs for output and inputs.[24] The yen-dollar exchange rate is represented as a shadow in Figure 20.9. If the PPP is higher than the exchange rate, the Japanese price is higher than the US price. Through the mid-1970s the Japanese price for output (GDP) was lower than the US price. The Japanese prices of inputs of capital, labor, energy, materials, and services (KLEMS), except for energy, were lower than the US prices as well.

Lower input prices, especially the price of labor input (only 17% of the US level in 1955), provided a source of international competitiveness for Japanese products from the 1950s until the middle of 1970s. During this period the PPP for materials was quite stable and the rise of the PPP for services was nearly proportional to the rise in the PPP for output. The PPPs for capital and labor inputs increased much more rapidly than the PPP for output. With the rise in the price of labor and the yen appreciation in the 1970s, Japan's competitiveness in international markets eroded substantially.

By 1985 the yen was undervalued by 13%, based on our estimate of the price level index (PLI) for GDP. After the Plaza Accord of 1985, the rapid strengthening of the yen reversed this relationship, leading to an overvaluation of the yen by 28% in 1990. The revaluation of the yen continued through 1995, leading to a huge overvaluation of 75%. At that time the price of labor input was 54% higher in Japan, which posed a formidable barrier to Japanese products in international markets.

Japanese policymakers required more than a decade to deal with the overvaluation of the yen that followed the Plaza Accord. This was accomplished through domestic deflation, with a modest devaluation of the yen. The PLI for GDP in Japan, relative to the United States, declined by 4.64% annually through 2007 from the peak attained in 1995. The decline in the PPP for GDP of 2.77% per year was the result of modest inflation in the United States of 1.92% and deflation in Japan of 0.85%. In addition, the yen-dollar exchange rate depreciated by 1.87% per year.

Although the market exchange rate of the yen approached the PPP for GDP in 2007, the yen appreciated sharply due to quantitative easing by the Federal Reserve in response to the financial crisis in the United States. In November 2011 the market exchange rate reached 75.5 yen per dollar, the highest level since World War II. By 2012 the price level index for GDP was 34.5% higher in Japan. In response to quantitative easing by the Bank of Japan, the yen sharply declined, reaching 119.6 yen per dollar as of the end of February 2015. This is well below the estimate of the PPP for GDP of 107.3 in 2012 and restored Japanese international competitiveness.

Table 20.1 PPPs and Price Level Indices for Output and KLEMS

	1955	1960	1965	1970	1975	1980	1985	1990	1995	2000	2005	2010	2012
Output (GDP)	210.2	215.1	237.0	247.3	279.4	247.3	206.8	185.1	164.3	146.3	124.9	114.0	107.3
Capital	166.6	235.7	217.9	291.2	222.4	227.2	207.9	194.4	145.7	141.9	125.0	112.7	103.2
Labor	60.7	66.2	101.5	123.6	200.2	178.4	153.3	147.7	144.6	114.1	90.4	79.2	75.4
Energy	627.4	625.1	618.9	581.6	600.6	521.3	461.1	308.9	271.9	231.1	169.1	151.3	143.8
Material	270.8	254.3	259.3	255.3	255.8	218.8	193.6	154.3	135.5	128.3	112.3	100.1	93.1
Service	175.2	168.3	197.4	206.4	259.7	246.3	205.6	181.7	163.0	142.5	122.6	108.4	103.3
GDP-expenditure based	–	170.6	204.1	226.0	266.0	245.6	206.9	189.2	174.5	155.0	129.6	111.6	104.6
Exchange Rate	360.0	360.0	360.0	360.0	296.8	226.8	238.5	144.8	94.1	107.8	110.2	87.8	79.8
PLIs (Price Level Indices) Output (GDP)	0.58	0.60	0.66	0.69	0.94	1.09	0.87	1.28	1.75	1.36	1.13	1.30	1.34
Capital	0.53	0.74	0.68	0.90	0.83	1.09	0.93	1.40	1.59	1.32	1.14	1.29	1.30
Labor	0.17	0.18	0.28	0.34	0.67	0.79	0.64	1.02	1.54	1.06	0.82	0.90	0.95
Energy	1.74	1.74	1.72	1.62	2.02	2.30	1.93	2.13	2.89	2.14	1.53	1.72	1.80
Material	0.75	0.71	0.72	0.71	0.86	0.97	0.81	1.07	1.44	1.19	1.02	1.14	1.17
Service	0.49	0.47	0.55	0.57	0.88	1.09	0.86	1.25	1.73	1.32	1.11	1.24	1.29

Note: The PPP for GDP-output based is defined as a translog index of industry-level PPPs for value added, which is calculated by a double deflation method. The PLIs are defined as the ratio of PPPs to the annual average exchange rate (Tokyo Market Interbank Rate). The PPP and exchange rate are defined by Japanese yen/US dollar. The PPP for GDP-expenditure based is the estimate by Eurostat–OECD.

(Japanese Yen/US Dollar)

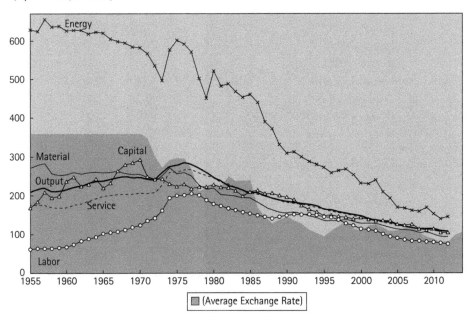

FIGURE 20.9. Japan-US purchasing power parities for output and KLEMS inputs, 1955–2012.

Figure 20.10 gives the contribution of individual industries to the price level index for GDP. For example, the Japanese wholesale and retail industry has the largest contribution to the PLI for GDP. By contrast, Japan's medical care sector in services and motor vehicles and primary metal sectors in manufacturing contributed negatively to the PLI for GDP. All three of these industries are highly competitive with their US counterparts.

Table 20.2 summarizes the productivity gaps between Japan and the United States. This table compares output, output per capita, input per capita, and TFP for the two countries over the period 1955–2012. Differences in output per capita can be decomposed into differences in input per capita and differences in TFP. For example, Japanese GDP was 26.3% of the US level in 2012. GDP per capita in Japan was 64.6% of the US level, while Japanese input per capita was 78.1% and Japanese TFP was 82.7%.

Differences in input per capita in Table 20.2 result from differences in capital and labor inputs. In 1955 Japanese labor input per capita was 60.6% of the US level. The gap of 39.4% was the result of the lower quality of labor in Japan, reaching only 57.6% of the US level. After 1970 the lower quality of Japanese labor was largely offset by longer hours worked per capita, 39.1% longer than the U.S. level in 1970. Subsequently, Japan reduced hours worked per capita and improved labor quality, reducing the gap in labor quality to around 10.0% in 2010.[25]

The level of Japanese capital input per capita remains significantly below the US level, presenting a striking contrast to labor input. In 1955 Japanese capital input per capita was only 17.3% of the US level, but rapidly rising levels of investment in Japan reduced

FIGURE 20.10.   Industry contributions to the Japan-US price level index, 2005.

the gap to 46.3% by 1973. The gap continued to close, and Japanese capital input per capita reached 79.4% of the US level in 1995. The US investment boom of the late 1990s widened the gap to 29.1% in 2000 and 36.3% in 2012, while an investment slump in Japan followed the collapse of the bubble economy.

Table 20.2 Volume Level Indices of Output and Inputs and Productivity Level Indices

	1955	1960	1965	1970	1975	1980	1985	1990	1995	2000	2005	2010	2012
Output	0.084	0.125	0.172	0.259	0.302	0.328	0.348	0.381	0.372	0.316	0.289	0.272	0.263
Output per capita	0.155	0.239	0.336	0.508	0.583	0.637	0.684	0.770	0.790	0.703	0.668	0.657	0.646
Input per capita	0.341	0.431	0.563	0.694	0.780	0.789	0.797	0.843	0.886	0.803	0.781	0.788	0.781
Capital input per capita	0.173	0.215	0.334	0.443	0.574	0.607	0.619	0.704	0.794	0.709	0.649	0.638	0.637
Capital stock per capita	0.319	0.380	0.502	0.616	0.727	0.792	0.816	0.853	0.928	0.932	0.919	0.916	0.909
Capital quality	0.541	0.566	0.664	0.719	0.790	0.766	0.758	0.825	0.855	0.761	0.706	0.696	0.701
Labor input per capita	0.606	0.789	0.866	0.988	0.999	0.987	1.002	1.001	0.993	0.919	0.949	0.987	0.970
Hours worked per capita	1.051	1.288	1.308	1.391	1.298	1.225	1.210	1.172	1.150	1.042	1.061	1.097	1.090
Labor quality	0.576	0.612	0.662	0.711	0.770	0.805	0.828	0.854	0.864	0.882	0.895	0.900	0.890
TFP	0.454	0.555	0.597	0.732	0.748	0.808	0.858	0.912	0.892	0.876	0.855	0.833	0.827
Average labor productivity	0.147	0.186	0.257	0.365	0.449	0.520	0.565	0.657	0.686	0.675	0.629	0.599	0.593
Average capital productivity	0.895	1.112	1.008	1.146	1.017	1.051	1.105	1.093	0.995	0.991	1.029	1.030	1.014

Note: All figures present the level indices (Japan/US) in each period. See Jorgenson, Nomura, and Samuels (2016, 486), Table 13.2.

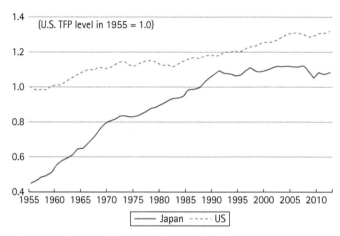

FIGURE 20.11. Japan and US total factor productivity levels, 1955–2012.

The estimates of input per capita by Jorgenson and Nomura (2007) have been revised downward by Jorgenson, Nomura, and Samuels (2016) and productivity gaps have been revised upward. The Japan-US gap for TFP in 1955 was 54.6%. This gradually declined over the following 36 years and reached a low of 7.1% in 1991, as shown in Figure 20.11. Table 20.3 presents the sources of economic growth in Japan and the United States for 1955–2012. The growth rate of TFP in Japan was 2.46% per year from 1955 to 1991, but became slightly negative after 1991, averaging –0.05. By comparison, the growth rate of TFP in the United States was 0.46 per year during 1955–1991 and 0.53% after 1991.

Figure 20.12 presents Japan-US gaps in TFP in manufacturing and non-manufacturing sectors for the period 1955–2012. In 1955 both gaps were very large. The TFP gap for manufacturing disappeared by 1980,[26] and the overall TFP gap reflected the lower TFP in non-manufacturing. Japanese manufacturing productivity relative to the United States peaked at 103.8 in 1991 and deteriorated afterward, leaving a current gap that is almost negligible. The gap for non-manufacturing also contracted from 1955 to 1991, when the gap reached 8.9%, but expanded until the end of the period in 2012.

Figure 20.13 presents the contributions of each industry to the overall TFP gap for the two countries. Industries are ordered by their contributions to the TFP gap. The contribution of each industry to the aggregate TFP gap uses the Domar weights we have described in section 20.4. Note that TFP gaps for public administration and household sectors are zero by definition, since the outputs of these industries consist entirely of total inputs.

In 2005, Japanese productivity exceeded that in the United States for 12 of 36 industries, led by medical care. This industry made a contribution to Japanese TFP, relative to the United States, of 4.1 percentage points. This reflects the higher output price of medical care services in the United States, shown in Figure 20.10. Other domestically oriented industries in Japan, such as wholesale and retail trade, other services, finance and insurance, construction, electricity and gas, and real estate, have much lower

Table 20.3 Sources of Economic Growth in Japan and the United States

	1955–1960	1960–1965	1965–1970	1970–1975	1975–1980	1980–1985	1985–1990	1990–1995	1995–2000	2000–2005	2005–2010	2010–2012	1955–1991	1991–2012
Japan														
Output	10.45	11.16	11.97	5.82	4.97	4.45	5.33	2.00	1.14	0.96	-0.23	0.34	7.67	0.70
Capital input	3.56	6.46	5.62	4.46	1.97	1.66	2.82	2.00	0.79	0.50	0.43	0.16	3.79	0.73
IT capital	0.09	0.17	0.21	0.23	0.13	0.19	0.37	0.22	0.37	0.46	0.30	0.16	0.20	0.32
(of which quality)	0.00	0.01	0.00	-0.01	0.00	0.01	-0.02	0.00	0.02	0.05	0.02	-0.04	0.00	0.02
Non-IT capital	3.47	6.29	5.41	4.23	1.85	1.48	2.45	1.77	0.42	0.04	0.13	0.00	3.59	0.40
(of which quality)	0.83	1.95	1.21	1.33	0.12	0.32	1.31	0.74	-0.21	-0.02	-0.02	0.13	1.04	-0.02
Labor input	2.68	1.66	2.01	0.67	1.42	1.00	0.86	0.09	-0.17	0.07	-0.06	0.17	1.42	0.02
(of which quality)	0.94	1.02	0.72	1.08	0.78	0.56	0.47	0.36	0.38	0.35	0.33	0.02	0.78	0.33
TFP	4.22	3.03	4.34	0.70	1.58	1.79	1.65	-0.09	0.53	0.39	-0.60	0.00	2.46	-0.05
Agriculture	0.63	-0.10	-0.31	0.03	-0.12	0.09	0.04	-0.07	0.06	-0.07	0.01	0.03	0.03	-0.01
IT-manufacturing	0.08	0.13	0.15	0.15	0.22	0.17	0.28	0.12	0.35	0.29	0.10	-0.03	0.17	0.19
Motor vehicle	0.17	0.11	0.27	0.04	0.24	-0.03	0.07	-0.04	0.00	0.09	-0.05	-0.05	0.12	-0.01
Other manufacturing	1.77	1.86	2.24	0.10	0.73	0.78	0.48	-0.02	0.07	0.00	-0.24	-0.37	1.12	-0.11
Communications	0.15	0.16	0.07	0.07	-0.02	0.05	0.08	0.07	0.10	0.01	0.02	0.07	0.08	0.05
Trade	0.73	1.05	0.88	0.23	0.70	0.02	0.64	0.66	-0.07	0.29	-0.39	0.04	0.62	0.06
Finance and insurance	-0.05	0.29	0.24	0.20	0.23	0.15	0.29	-0.18	0.18	0.10	-0.19	-0.12	0.18	-0.02
Other services	0.73	-0.47	0.81	-0.12	-0.40	0.56	-0.22	-0.63	-0.17	0.15	0.44	-0.20	0.13	-0.20

(continued)

Table 20.3 Continued

	1955–1960	1960–1965	1965–1970	1970–1975	1975–1980	1980–1985	1985–1990	1990–1995	1995–2000	2000–2005	2005–2010	2010–2012	1955–1991	1991–2012
United States														
Output	2.51	4.78	3.74	2.74	3.31	3.29	3.51	2.47	4.40	2.79	0.96	2.12	3.33	2.71
Capital input	2.00	2.30	2.79	2.10	1.92	1.83	1.98	1.44	2.40	1.78	1.04	0.69	2.11	1.59
IT capital	0.05	0.11	0.16	0.16	0.29	0.42	0.48	0.51	1.02	0.56	0.36	0.21	0.24	0.58
(of which quality)	−0.09	0.14	0.05	0.04	0.09	0.14	0.14	0.16	0.29	0.14	0.07	0.03	0.07	0.15
Non-IT capital	1.95	2.19	2.63	1.94	1.63	1.41	1.50	0.93	1.38	1.22	0.68	0.48	1.87	1.00
(of which quality)	0.59	0.26	0.42	0.51	0.35	0.35	0.53	0.24	0.49	0.53	0.12	−0.02	0.42	0.32
Labor input	0.31	0.92	0.67	0.37	1.38	0.86	1.11	0.65	1.12	0.15	−0.01	1.04	0.76	0.59
(of which quality)	0.28	0.24	0.02	0.20	0.21	0.22	0.13	0.21	0.14	0.20	0.27	0.28	0.19	0.21
TFP	0.20	1.55	0.28	0.27	0.01	0.60	0.41	0.38	0.89	0.86	−0.07	0.39	0.46	0.53
Agriculture	0.12	0.04	0.03	0.02	−0.05	0.24	0.05	−0.01	0.07	0.02	0.00	−0.08	0.06	0.01
IT-manufacturing	−0.03	0.09	0.07	0.14	0.20	0.21	0.20	0.28	0.52	0.19	0.15	0.03	0.13	0.26
Motor vehicle	−0.04	0.12	−0.07	0.01	−0.03	0.05	−0.03	0.05	0.01	0.05	0.01	0.06	0.00	0.03
Other manufacturing	−0.14	0.60	0.15	−0.10	−0.01	0.26	0.16	0.04	0.03	0.14	−0.08	−0.08	0.12	0.02
Communications	0.00	0.05	0.02	0.04	0.14	−0.02	0.04	0.00	−0.02	0.11	0.01	−0.02	0.04	0.03
Trade	0.13	0.23	0.14	0.38	−0.08	0.34	0.15	0.21	0.48	0.21	−0.12	−0.07	0.19	0.16
Finance and insurance	0.00	−0.05	−0.09	−0.06	0.12	−0.17	−0.03	−0.02	0.12	0.08	−0.04	−0.01	−0.04	0.03
Other services	0.16	0.48	0.03	−0.15	−0.27	−0.31	−0.12	−0.17	−0.31	0.05	0.01	0.56	−0.04	−0.02

Note: All figures present the average annual growth rates in each period.

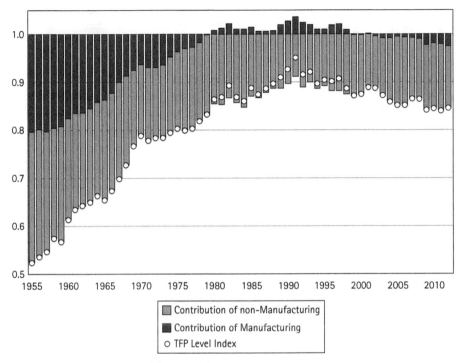

FIGURE 20.12. Japan-US total factor productivity gaps, 1955–2012.

productivity levels than their US counterparts and made negative contributions of 16.7% to the overall TFP gap in 2005.

The productivity level of the agriculture, forestry, and fishery industry is only a little more than half the level of its US counterpart. Not all of this gap can be traced to differences in the small scale of Japanese farms or differences in the fertility of land between the two countries. One of the targets for the growth strategy proposed by the Abe administration is to reform Japanese agricultural cooperatives. These organizations contribute substantially to the higher costs of Japanese agricultural products and the lower productivity of Japanese agriculture.

20.7. CONCLUSIONS

We conclude that industry-level data sets on productivity and economic growth have been very valuable in analyzing the sources of economic growth for countries in Asia, Europe, and North and South America. Beginning with the EU KLEMS study completed in 2008, industry-level data sets have been compiled for more than 40 countries. These include the advanced economies of the European Union, as well as Australia, Canada, Korea, Japan, and the United States.

FIGURE 20.13. Industry contributions to the Japan-US total factor productivity gap, 2005.

The Latin American regional affiliate of the World KLEMS Initiative, LA KLEMS, has generated data sets for the emerging economies of Argentina, Brazil, Chile, Columbia, and Mexico. The Asian affiliate, Asia KLEMS, includes data sets for the China and India, the two largest of the world's emerging economies, as well as Japan, Korea, and Taiwan. Finally, an industry-level data set has been constructed for Russia at the Higher School of Economics in Moscow.

Industry-level production accounts are now prepared on a regular basis by national statistical agencies in Australia, Canada, Denmark, Finland, Italy, Mexico, The Netherlands, Sweden, and the United Kingdom, as well as the United States.[27] These accounts provide current information about the growth of outputs, inputs, and productivity at the industry level and can be used in international comparisons of patterns of structural change like those presented by Jorgenson and Timmer (2011). The World KLEMS Initiative has made it possible to extend these comparisons to countries around the world, including important emerging and transition economies.

The KLEMS framework for productivity measurement is employed in analyzing the sources of growth of the United States in section 20.3 and making international comparisons between the United States and Japan in section 20.5. Industry-level data for the United States shows that replication of established technologies explains by far the largest proportion of US economic growth. Replication takes place through the augmentation of the labor force and the accumulation of capital. International productivity comparisons reveal similar patterns for the world economy, its major regions, and leading industrialized, developing, and emerging economies.[28] Studies are now underway to extend these comparisons to the countries included in the World KLEMS Initiative.

Innovation is defined as the growth in output that is not explained by the growth of input. In the KLEMS framework this is measured by productivity growth. Innovation is far more challenging than replication of established technologies and is subject to much greater risk. The diffusion of successful innovation requires substantial financial commitments. These fund the investments that replace outdated products and processes and establish new organizational structures, systems, and business models. Innovation accounts for a relatively modest part of US economic growth, but this is vital for maintaining gains in the US standard of living in the long run.

Second, international comparisons of productivity levels are very promising for the analysis of sources of international competitiveness and the formulation of strategies for economic growth. In section 20.6 we present international comparisons of productivity levels between Japan and the United States based on industry-level PPPs. These provide important information on the undervaluation and overvaluation of the Japanese yen relative to the US dollar.

The yen was undervalued, relative to the dollar, for three decades from 1955 until 1985, when the Plaza Accord produced an upward revaluation of the yen. Japan remained internationally competitive, despite a large productivity gap with the United States. The yen has been overvalued since 1985, relative to the dollar, reaching a peak in 1995 and greatly undercutting Japanese international competitiveness. After several years of monetary easing by the Bank of Japan, the yen achieved PPP with the dollar in 2015 and restored Japan's international competitiveness.

A large productivity gap between Japan and the United States existed in 1955, but gradually closed until the collapse of Japanese real estate prices that signaled the end of the "bubble economy" in 1991. Japanese productivity has remained stagnant since that time, while US productivity has continued to grow. The widening productivity gap between Japan and the United States can be traced to a relatively small number of trade and service sectors in Japan, but also includes agriculture. The contribution of manufacturing sectors to the productivity gap remains relatively small. We recommend formulating a growth strategy for Japan that will stimulate productivity growth in the Japan's lagging industrial sectors.[29]

Japan's highly competitive manufacturing industries should find new opportunities in both international and domestic markets under the devaluation of the yen by the Bank of Japan. Efforts to improve Japanese productivity should focus on industries in trade and services that are protected from international competition. Agriculture will require structural reform followed by an opening to trade.

Our overall conclusion is that the World KLEMS Initiative has been very successful in promoting the development of industry-level data sets on productivity and economic growth for economies around the world. These data have been incorporated into the official national accounts for a number of countries and have been documented by the OECD and the United Nations. These data have been used extensively in analyzing the sources of economic growth and the opportunities for promoting growth. International comparisons of productivity are far more challenging and require industry-level PPPs. These comparisons are potentially very valuable in analyzing international competitiveness and formulating growth strategies in a highly competitive international environment.

Notes

1. For the program and participants, see http://www.worldklems.net/conference1.htm
2. The World KLEMS website presents data sets in a common format for many of the participating countries. See http://www.worldklems.net/data.htm
3. The available data are posted on the EU KLEMS website: http://www.euklems.net/eukNACE2.shtml The EU KLEMS data set will be updated with support from the Directorate General of Economic and Financial Affairs (DG-ECFIN) of the European Commission. See http://www.google.com/url?sa=t&rct=j&q=&esrc=s&source=web&cd=6&ved=0ahUKEwiTxKfch87NAhULFz4KHfHiAwMQFghCMAU&url=http%3A%2F%2Fscholar.harvard.edu%2Ffiles%2Fjorgenson%2Ffiles%2F6.2.pptx%3Fm%3D1464016998&usg=AFQjCNHJVM1YtRqOinlstZJPt6Pke5JJ5A
4. For the program and participants, see http://www.euklems.net/conference.html
5. Kirsten Jager (2016) *EU KLEMS Productivity and Growth Accounts: Statistical Module, ESA 2010, and ISIC Rev. IV Industry Classification*. (Brussels: The Conference Board, December). See: http://euklems.net/index.html

6. The conference program and presentations are available at http://www.worldklems.net/conference2.htm

7. Information about LA KLEMS is available on the project website: http://www.cepal.org/la-klems/noticias/paginas/9/40269/Triptico_LA_KLEMS.pdf.

8. Regional Integration Project, *LA KLEMS: Economic Growth and Productivity in Latin America* (Washington, DC: Inter-American Development Bank, October). See http://www.iadb.org/en/topics/regional-integration/project-information,3072.html?id=RG-T2867.

9. For the program and participants, see http://www.inegi.org.mx/eventos/2013/contabilidad_mexico/presentacion.aspx.

10. See, for example, http://www.inegi.org.mx/est/contenidos/proyectos/cn/ptf/.

11. For the program and participants, see http://asiaklems.net/conferences/conferences.asp. Asia KLEMS was preceded by International Comparison of Productivity among Asian Countries (ICPAC). The results were reported by Jorgenson, Kuroda, and Motohashi (2007).

12. http://www.rieti.go.jp/en/database/JIP2014/index.html.

13. https://www.kpc.or.kr/eng/Productivity/kip.asp.

14. http://www.rieti.go.jp/en/database/CIP2015/index.html.

15. For the programs and participants, see http://asiaklems.net/conferences/conferences.asp. http://hias.ad.hit-u.ac.jp/wp-content/uploads/2017/05/4th-AsiaKLEMS_Agenda-20170521.pdf.

16. http://www.worldklems.net/conference3.htm.

17. http://www.wiod.org/new_site/home.htm.

18. The World Input-Output Database has been updated through 2014 with support from the Directorate General of Economic and Financial Affairs (DG-ECFIN) of the European Commission. See http://scholar.harvard.edu/files/jorgenson/files/6.4_timmer_gvcs2.pdf.

19. See: http://www.hse.ru/en/org/hse/expert/lipier/ruklems.

20. https://rbidocs.rbi.org.in/rdocs/PublicationReport/Pdfs/EPGIKLEMS110614.pdf. Details about the Research Team and the preparation of the Report are presented in the Foreward, pp. A–C.

21. The Advisory Committee was established on December 6, 2007, with 10 members from the business community, including Carl Schramm, president and CEO of the Kauffman Foundation and chair of the Committee. The Committee also had five academic members, including Jorgenson. The Advisory Committee met on February 22 and September 12, 2007, to discuss its recommendations. The final report was released on January 18, 2008.

22. The most recent data set is available at http://www.bea.gov/national/integrated_prod.htm.

23. For current data, see http://www.bea.gov/industry/index.htm.

24. Our estimates of PPP for GDP are based on outputs, while the Eurostat-OECD PPPs presented in Table 20.1 are based on expenditures. Although the two PPP estimates are nearly identical in 2012, our output-based estimates are higher through the beginning of the 1970s and lower in the 1990s and 2000s.

25. By comparison with Jorgenson and Nomura (2007), the PPPs for labor were revised upward, reflecting the shift of the base year from 1990 to 2005 and the revision of Japanese data. Nomura and Shirane (2014) treat full-time, part-time, and temporary employees separately. The PPP for labor was revised upward from 105.0 to 114.1 yen per dollar in 2000. This revision reduced the volume and quality level indices for labor, although the volume

level index for hours worked was not affected. The downward revision in the volume of labor increased the level index for TFP.

26. Cameron (2005) analyzes the convergence of Japan's manufacturing productivity to the US level and estimates the difference in TFP between Japan and the United States in 1989 as 91.3. Our estimate is 102.2 in the same year. The main source the difference is that he used the PPP estimates from Jorgenson and Nomura (2007). Our new estimates are revised upward considerably relative to Jorgenson and Nomura (2007).

27. See the statistical data bases presented in the World KLEMS website: http://www. worldklems.net/data.htm.

28. See Jorgenson and Vu (2013).

29. More details on recommendations for Japan's growth strategy are presented by Jorgenson (2016): http://scholar.harvard.edu/files/jorgenson/files/16_0316_jpec.pdf.

References

Advisory Committee on Measuring Innovation in the 21st Century Economy. 2008. *Innovation Measurement: Tracking the State of Innovation in the American Economy.* Washington, DC: US Department of Commerce, January.

Cameron, Gavin. 2005. "The Sun Also Rises: Productivity Convergence between Japan and the USA." *Journal of Economic Growth* 10(4): 387–408.

Cimoli, Mario, Andre Hofman, and Nanno Mulder (eds.). 2010. *Innovation and Economic Development.* Northampton, MA: Edward Elgar.

Domar, Evsey. 1961. "On the Measurement of Technological Change." *Economic Journal* 71(284): 709–729.

Fleck, Susan, Steven Rosenthal, Matthew Russell, Erich Strassner, and Lisa Usher. 2014. "A Prototype BEA/BLS Industry-Level Production Account for the United States." In *Measuring Economic Stability and Progress*, edited by Dale W. Jorgenson, J. Steven Landefeld, and Paul Schreyer, 323–372. Chicago: University of Chicago Press.

Fukao, Kyoji. 2012. *Japan's Economy and the Lost Two Decades.* Tokyo: Nikkei Publishing (in Japanese).

Fukao, Kyoji. 2013. "Explaining Japan's Unproductive Two Decades." *Asian Economic Policy Review* 8(2): 193–213.

Hamada, Koichi, Anil K. Kashyap, and David E. Weinstein (eds.). 2010. *Japan's Bubble, Deflation, and Long-term Stagnation.* Cambridge, MA: MIT Press.

Hamada, Koichi, and Yasushi Okada. 2009. "Monetary and International Factors behind Japan's Lost Decade." *Journal of the Japanese and International Economies,* 23(2): 200–219.

Harper, Michael, Brent Moulton, Steven Rosenthal, and David Wasshausen. 2009. "Integrated GDP-Productivity Accounts." *American Economic Review* 99(2): 74–79.

INEGI (National Institute of Statistics and Geography). 2013. *Sistema de Cuentas Nacionales de Mexico: Productividad Total de los Factores, 1990–2011.* Aguascalientes, Mexico: INEGI (in Spanish).

Iwata, Kazumasa (ed.). 2011. *The Japanese Economy and Macroeconomic Policies from the Beginnings of the Bubble to the Overcoming of Deflation—What Did We Learn?* Tokyo: Saiki Printing (in Japanese).

Kirsten Jager. 2016. *EU KLEMS Productivity and Growth Accounts: Statistical Module, ESA 2010, and ISIC Rev. IV Industry Classification* (Brussels: The Conference Board, December).

Kirsten Jager. 2017. *EU KLEMS Growth and Productivity Accounts, 2017 Release – Description of Methodology and General Notes* (Brussels: The Conference Board, September).

Jorgenson, Dale W. 1963. "Capital Theory and Investment Behavior." *American Economic Review* 53(2): 247–259.

Jorgenson, Dale W. (ed.). 2009. *The Economics of Productivity.* Northampton, MA: Edward Elgar.

Jorgenson, Dale W. 2016. "A Productivity Revolution and Japan's Re-Vitalization." Tokyo: Presentation to the Japan Center for Economic Research, March.

Jorgenson. Dale W. (ed.). 2017. "Special Issue from the Fourth World KLEMS Conference," *International Productivity Monitor,* Number 33, Fall.

Jorgenson, Dale W., Kyoji Fukao, and Marcel P. Timmer (eds.). 2016. *The World Economy: Growth or Stagnation?* Cambridge: Cambridge University Press.

Jorgenson, Dale W., Frank M. Gollop, and Barbara M. Fraumeni. 1987. *Productivity and U.S. Economic Growth.* Cambridge, MA: Harvard University Press.

Jorgenson, Dale W., Mun S. Ho, and Jon D. Samuels. 2016. "U.S. Economic Growth—Retrospect and Prospect: Lessons from a Prototype Industry-Level Productivity Account for the United States, 1947–2012." In *The World Economy: Growth or Stagnation?* edited by Dale W. Jorgenson, Kyoji Fukao, and Marcel P. Timmer, 34–69. Cambridge: Cambridge University Press.

Jorgenson, Dale W., Mun S. Ho, and Kevin J. Stiroh. 2005. *Information Technology and the American Growth Resurgence.* Cambridge, MA: MIT Press.

Jorgenson, Dale W., and Masahiro Kuroda. 1990. "Productivity and International Competitiveness in Japan and the United States, 1960–1985." In *Productivity Growth in Japan and the United States,* edited by C. R. Hulten, 29–55. Chicago: University of Chicago Press.

Jorgenson, Dale W., Masahiro Kuroda, and Kazuyuki Motohashi (eds.). 2007. *Productivity in Asia.* Northampton, MA: Edward Elgar.

Jorgenson, Dale W., Masahiro Kuroda, and Mieko Nishimizu. 1987. "Japan-U.S. Industry-Level Productivity Comparison, 1960–1979." *Journal of the Japanese and International Economies* 1: 1–30.

Jorgenson, Dale W., and J. Steven Landefeld. 2006. "Blueprint for an Expanded and Integrated U.S. National Accounts: Review, Assessment, and Next Steps." In *A New Architecture for the U.S. National Accounts,* edited by Dale W. Jorgenson, J. Steven Landefeld, and William D. Nordhaus, 13–112. Chicago: University of Chicago Press.

Jorgenson, Dale W., J. Steven Landefeld, and William D. Nordhaus (eds.). 2006. *A New Architecture for the U.S. National Accounts.* Chicago: University of Chicago Press.

Jorgenson, Dale W., J. Steven Landefeld, and Paul Schreyer (eds.). 2014. *Measuring Economic Stability and Progress.* Chicago: University of Chicago Press.

Jorgenson, Dale W., and Koji Nomura. 2007. "The Industry Origins of the Japan-US Productivity Gap." *Economic System Research* 19(3): 315–341.

Jorgenson, Dale W., Koji Nomura, and Jon D. Samuels. 2016. "A Half-Century of Trans-Pacific Competition: Price Level Indices and Productivity Gaps for Japanese and U.S. Industries, 1955–2012." In *The World Economy: Growth or Stagnation?* edited by Dale W. Jorgenson, Kyoji Fukao, and Marcel P. Timmer, 469–507. Cambridge: Cambridge University Press.

Jorgenson, Dale W., and Paul Schreyer. 2013. "Industry-Level Productivity Measurement and the 2008 System of National Accounts." *Review of Income and Wealth* 58(4): 185–211.

Jorgenson, Dale W., and Marcel P. Timmer. 2011. "Structural Change in Advanced Nations: A New Set of Stylized Facts." *Scandinavian Economic Journal* 113(1): 1–29.

Jorgenson, Dale W., and Khuong M. Vu. 2013. "Emergence of the New Economic Order: Economic Growth in the G7 and the G20." *Journal of Policy Modeling* 35(3): 389–399.

Los, Bart, Marcel P. Timmer, and Gaaitzen J. de Vries. 2015. "How Global Are Global Value Chains? A New Approach to Measure International Fragmentation." *Journal of Regional Science* 55(1): 66–92.

Kim, Donald D., Erich H. Strassner, and David B. Wasshausen. 2014. "Industry Economic Accounts: Results of the Comprehensive Revision Revised Statistics for 1997–2012." *Survey of Current Business* 94(2): 1–18.

Kuroda, Masahiro, and Koji Nomura. 1999. "Productivity Comparison and International Competitiveness." *Journal of Applied Input-Output Analysis* 5: 1–37.

Mas, Matilde, and Robert Stehrer (eds.) 2012. *Industrial Productivity in Europe*. Northampton, MA: Edward Elgar.

Mayerhauser, Nicole M., and Erich H. Strassner. 2010. "Preview of the Comprehensive Revision of the Annual Industry Accounts: Changes in Definitions, Classification, and Statistical Methods." *Survey of Current Business* 90(3): 21–34.

McCulla, Stephanie H., Alyssa E. Holdren, and Shelly Smith. 2013. "Improved Estimates of the National Income and Product Accounts: Results of the 2013 Comprehensive Revision." *Survey of Current Business* 93(9): 14–45.

Nomura, Koji. 2004. *Measurement of Capital and Productivity in Japan*. Tokyo: Keio University Press (in Japanese).

Nomura, Koji, and Kozo Miyagawa. 2015. "The Japan-US Price Level Index for Industry Outputs." RIETI Discussion Paper Series 15-E-059, May, Research Institute for Economy, Trade, and Industry.

Nomura, Koji, and Hiroshi Shirane. 2014. "Measurement of Quality-Adjusted Labor Input in Japan, 1955–2012." KEO Discussion Paper No.133, Keio University, December (in Japanese).

Reserve Bank of India. 2014. *Estimates of Productivity Growth for the Indian Economy*. Mumbai: Reserve Bank of India.

Rosenthal, Steven, Matthew Russell, Jon D. Samuels, Erich H. Strassner, and Lisa Usher. 2016. "Integrated Industry-Level Production Account for the United States: Intellectual Property Products and the 2007 NAICS." In *The World Economy: Growth or Stagnation?* edited by Dale W. Jorgenson, Kyoji Fukao, and Marcel P. Timmer, 377–428. Cambridge: Cambridge University Press..

Schreyer, Paul. 2001. *OECD Manual: Measuring Productivity: Measurement of Aggregate and Industry-Level Productivity Growth*. Paris: Organisation for Economic Co-operation and Development.

Schreyer, Paul. 2009. *OECD Manual: Measuring Capital*. Paris: Organisation for Economic Co-operation and Development.

Timmer, Marcel P., Robert Inklaar, Mary O'Mahony, and Bart van Ark. 2010. *Economic Growth in Europe: A Comparative Industry Perspective*. Cambridge: Cambridge University Press, 2010.

Timmer, Marcel P., and Ilya Voskoboynikov. 2016. "Is Mining Fueling Long-Run Growth in Russia: Industry Productivity Trends since 1995." In *The World Economy: Growth or Stagnation?* edited by Dale W. Jorgenson, Kyoji Fukao, and Marcel P. Timmer, 281–318. Cambridge: Cambridge University Press.

United Nations, Commission of the European Communities, International Monetary Fund, Organisation for Economic Co-operation and Development, and World Bank. 2009. *System of National Accounts 2008*. New York: United Nations.

United Nations, Commission of the European Communities, International Monetary Fund, Organisation for Economic Co-operation and Development, and World Bank. 1993. *System of National Accounts 1993*. New York, United Nations.

van Ark, Bart, and Dirk Pilat. 1993. "Productivity Levels in Germany, Japan, and the United States: Differences and Causes." *Brookings Papers on Economic Activity, Microeconomics* 2: 1–48.

van Ark, Bart, and Kirsten Jager. 2017. "Recent Trends in Europe's Output and Productivity Growth Performance at the Sector Level, 2002-2015. In "Special Issue from the Fourth World KLEMS Conference," *International Productivity Monitor*, edited by Dale W. Jorgenson, Number 33, Fall.

CHAPTER 21

PRODUCTIVITY AND SUBSTITUTION PATTERNS IN GLOBAL VALUE CHAINS

MARCEL P. TIMMER AND XIANJIA YE

21.1. INTRODUCTION

THE increasing fragmentation of production processes is posing new challenges to the analysis and measurement of productivity. Traditional approaches focus on firms, industries, or countries as the unit of analysis. In this chapter we argue that studies of global value chains (GVCs) are needed in situations where production is highly fragmented across firms and geographical borders. Due to improvements in information and telecommunication technologies, production processes increasingly fragment across borders in order to gain access to cheap resources, both natural and human, as well as to acquire customer market entrance. This process was boosted in the first decade of the 2000s as major emerging economies like China and India opened up borders and became integrated into the world economy. As a result, today a production process of a good typically consists of a set of different activities in various stages of production, which can be carried out in many places around the world. For example, an iPad is designed in California, United States, but is assembled in Shenzen, China, on the basis of more than a hundred components manufactured around the world, with logistics handled by a Hong Kong firm. This is referred to as global value chain (GVC) production.

The emergence of GVCs raises many new questions, and its analysis requires novel methodologies and data. In this chapter we will review the conceptual and empirical issues that arise in analyzing productivity in the context of international production fragmentation. We discuss how patterns of substitution and productivity growth can be measured in such chains and illustrate this by empirical exercises using new data from the World Input-Output Database (WIOD). To this end, we will build upon the standard toolkit of production analysis, known as the KLEMS approach. In their classical study of the US economy Jorgenson, Gollop and Fraumeni (1987) introduced this approach, which is built around the concept of a gross output production function with two groups of factor inputs—capital (K) and labor (L)—and three groups of intermediate inputs—energy (E), materials (M), and services (S). This approach offers useful insights into the changes in efficiency with which the inputs are being used in the production process of the industry (or firm) as measured by productivity growth. It also offers the conceptual framework to analyze econometrically the various substitution elasticities between inputs, as well as possible biases in productivity change. The KLEMS approach has become a standard tool in the applied economist's toolkit (see, e.g., Jorgenson, Chapter 20 in this *Handbook*).

However, modeling and measuring patterns of substitution and productivity growth at the industry (or firm) level has become both more difficult and less meaningful. With increased outsourcing and offshoring, the share of the industry value added in gross output is declining such that analyses based on industry value added have to rely on strong assumptions of separability. Conditions that are jointly necessary and sufficient for the existence of sectoral value-added functions are typically rejected, and intermediate inputs should be treated symmetrically with factor inputs (Diewert and Wales 1995; Jorgenson, Gollop, and Fraumeni 1987). As ratios of intermediate input to gross output continue to increase, the robustness of the standard approach becomes increasingly dependent on proper price measurement of intermediate inputs. However, tracking prices of intermediate inputs is challenging, in particular when they are imported and/or contain intangible characteristics (Houseman and Mandel 2015).

In this chapter we outline how the existing KLEMS methodology can be modified to analyze GVC production and what type of data would be needed. We argue that in order to understand trends in productivity and technical change in global production, one needs to go beyond the traditional analysis of separate industries (or firms) and to focus on a set of discrete activities in distinct locations, which altogether form a GVC.. Unfortunately, our official statistical systems are not well equipped to identify the emergence and existence of these global production chains. We outline an approximation method to derive cost shares in GVCs, based on a linear system of cost equations rooted in the input-output approach introduced by Leontief (1936, 1949). Simply put, the production function G in the KLEMS approach is given by

Gross output of industry = G (factor inputs in industry, intermediate inputs).

Instead, we will analyze a production function F where final output is produced based on factor inputs only, including both domestic as well as foreign factors:

Final output of product = F (factor inputs in all industries domestically and abroad)

Basically, in this approach the flow of intermediate inputs will be traced to the ultimate factor usage such that the production function of a final good can be written in terms of factor inputs only. These factor inputs are located in the industry where the last stage of production takes place, as well as in other industries contributing in earlier stages of production. These can be other domestic industries, as wel as industries abroad. This opens up the possibility of studying the various substitutions of factor inputs and the possible biased nature of technical change.[1]

This GVC modeling approach will allow us to focus on three important issues. First is the increasing importance of intangible capital: GVC production entails not only a flow of goods and materials, but also of information, technology, and managerial knowledge. It not only includes physical production processes, but also the full set of activities both in the pre- and post-production phases. This comprises for example research and development, software, design, branding, finance, logistics, after-sales services, and system integration activities. Recent case studies of electronic products such as the Nokia smartphone (Ali-Yrkkö, Rouvinen, Seppälä, and Ylä-Anttila, 2011; Ali-Yrkkö and Rouvinen, 2015) and the iPod and laptops (Dedrick et al. 2010) suggest that it is especially in these activities that most value is added. With international production, however, it has become more difficult to trace the profits for these capital assets. Due to, among other factors, transfer pricing and shifting of accounting profits, analyses of a single firm or industry might be inadequate. For example, a multinational might record its profits in a production facility abroad so that an analysis on domestic data will not reveal the importance of its capital inputs. This can only be accounted for in an analysis of cost shares of all factors of production used in any stage of production. Using this approach, Timmer et al. (2014) and Wen et al. (2017) have shown that compensation for capital assets has been increasing, in particular in emerging economies.

Second, and related to the first issue, there is mounting evidence that suggests that advanced countries are increasingly specializing in skill- and capital-intensive activities within GVCs, more popularly described as a process of turning into "headquarter economies." This indicates that, together with fragmentation, the nature of production processes is changing: a firm or industry can no longer be characterized by its outputs (the products it is selling), but only by what it does in terms of activities. Production fragmentation goes hand in hand with functional specialization across firms, regions, and countries, and this needs to be studied in a coherent framework with explicit modeling of inter-industry linkages.

Third, there is renewed interest in a possible factor bias in technological change in order to explain the widespread polarization within the labor market that characterizes advanced nations today. According to the "routinization hypothesis" put forward by Autor, Levy, and Murnane (2003), information technology capital complements highly educated workers engaged in abstract tasks, substitutes for moderately educated workers performing routine tasks, and has little effect on less-skilled workers performing manual and services tasks. At the same time, routine tasks are also often offshored, so the effects of increasing imported intermediates and factor bias in productivity may be observationally equivalent when only using data on domestic factor use.

More generally, increasing international production fragmentation limits our understanding of the substitution and complementarity of various inputs in the production process, and the measurement of possible biases in technical change. Rather than studying this from the perspective of individual firms, industries, or countries, one needs an approach in which the various stages of production are analyzed together.

The remainder of this chapter is organized as follows. In section 21.2, we outline the concept of GVCs using a linear system of cost equations rooted in the input–output approach introduced by Leontief (1936). Using this framework, we can derive the cost shares and total factor requirements of a sector's (final) output employing the so-called Leontief inverse. We model producer behavior through a translog production function, and construct corresponding index numbers of output and input growth. Productivity growth is measured by the rate of decline in the total (direct and indirect) labor and capital requirements in the production of a good, weighted by their cost shares. In section 21.3 an illustrative empirical example is given based on an analysis of the GVC production of German automobiles. In section 21.4 we apply our approach to a broad set of products and analyze trends in the factor cost shares in 240 GVCs of manufacturing goods. We show how the cost shares of capital and high-skilled labor are rapidly increasing, while the cost shares of medium- and in particular low-skilled labor are rapidly declining between 1995 and 2007. In section 21.5 we econometrically estimate the unknown parameters of the translog function to analyze the possible causes for the changes in factor shares in GVCs. A system of cost equations is estimated to measure substitution elasticities and possible factor biases in productivity change. Section 21.6 concludes, emphasizing the approximate nature of the GVC approach and stressing the need for new data collection efforts in order to better understand the causes and consequences of fragmenting production processes.

21.2. FRAMEWORK TO ANALYZE GLOBAL VALUE CHAIN PRODUCTION

In this section we introduce a framework for measuring factor cost shares and productivity in global value chains (GVCs). We start outlining our general approach and clarify some of the terminology used. In subsection 21.2.2 we provide a more technical exposition of the framework.

21.2.1. General Approach and Terminology

A global value chain of a product is a description of all the factor inputs needed for its production, taking into account all phases of production. As such, it can be viewed as a special case of vertically integrated production (Williamson 1971), characterized by the fact that production stages are carried out in at least two countries. The coordination of the various stages can be done within a multinational corporation, or it can be market mediated through arms-length transactions. Typically, it has a governance mode that lies within these two extremes (Antras and Yeaple 2014). Baldwin and Venables (2013) introduced the concepts of "snakes" and "spiders" as two archetypal configurations of production systems. The snake refers to a production chain organized as a sequence of production stages, whereas the spider refers to an assembly-type process on the basis of delivered components and parts. Of course, actual production systems are composed of a combination of various types. Our method measures the value added in each activity in the process, irrespective of its position in the network. It is important to stress that our approach refers not only to the physical production process, but also to the full set of activities both in the pre- and post-production phases, including research and development (R&D), software, design, branding, finance, logistics, after-sales services, and system integration. Therefore Timmer et al. (2014) propose using the term "global value chains" to distinguish this approach from studies of "global supply chains" or "international production chains" that typically refer only to the physical production stages.

To analyze vertical integrated production we rely on a standard methodology that allows for a decomposition of the value of a final product into the value added by all factors (labor and capital) in any country that is involved in its production process. This decomposition method is rooted in the analysis introduced by Leontief (1936) in which the modeling of input–output (IO) structures of industries is central. The IO structure of an industry indicates the amount and type of intermediate inputs needed in the production of one unit of output, so that one can trace the gross output in all stages of production that is needed to produce one unit of final demand. To see this, take the example of car production in Germany. Demand for German cars will in the first instance raise the output of the German car industry. But production in this industry relies on car parts and components that are produced elsewhere, such as engines, braking systems, car bodies, paint, seat upholstery, or window screens, as well as energy, and various business services such as logistics, transport, marketing, and financial services. These intermediate goods and services need to be produced as well, thus raising output in the industries delivering these, say the German business services industry, the Czech braking systems industry, and the Indian textile industry. In turn, this will raise output in industries delivering intermediates to these industries, and so on. These indirect contributions from both manufacturing and non-manufacturing sectors will be explicitly accounted for through the modeling of input–output linkages across sectors. When we know the gross output flows associated with a particular level of final demand, we can derive the value added by multiplying these flows with the value-added to gross-output ratio for each industry. By construction, the sum of value added across all industries involved in production will be equal to the value of the final demand. Following the same logic, one can also trace the number of workers that are directly and indirectly involved in GVC production, or the amount of capital.

21.2.2. Technical Exposition

This section gives a mathematical exposition of our measurement framework, grounded in the older literature on input–output accounting with multiple regions, going back in particular to work by Miller (1966), and surveyed by Millar and Blair (2009). The usefulness of the input–output approach has recently been rediscovered by scholars of vertical specialiation in trade such as in Johnson and Noguera (2012), Koopman, Wang, and Wei (2014) and Los, Timmer, and de Vries (2016). We start with the fundamental input–output identity and use this to derive an expression for the factor cost shares in the production of final products. Output in each country-sector is produced using domestic production factors and intermediate inputs, which may be sourced domestically or from foreign suppliers. Output may be used to satisfy final demand (either at home or abroad) or used as intermediate input in production (either at home or abroad as well). To track the shipments of intermediate and final goods within and across countries, it is necessary to define source and destination country-sectors. For a particular product, we define i as the source country, j as the destination country, s as the source sector, and t as the destination sector. Each country-sector produces one good such that there are SN products. We use the term *country-sector* to denote a sector in a country, such as the French chemicals sector or the German transport equipment sector. We use the term "good", but this may refer to a physical product as well as a service. Although we will apply annual data in our empirical analysis, time subscripts are left out in the following discussion for ease of exposition.

Product markets clear, so the quantity of a good produced in a particular country-sector must equal the quantities of this goodused domestically and abroad. This condition can be written as

$$y_i(s) = \sum_j f_{ij}(s) + \sum_j \sum_t m_{ij}(s,t)$$

(21.1)

where $y_i(s)$ is the output in sector s of country i, $f_{ij}(s)$ the products shipped from this sector for final use in any country j, and $m_{ij}(s,t)$ the products shipped from this sector for intermediate use by sector t in country j. Note that the use of products can be at home (in case $i = j$) or abroad ($i \neq j$). Using matrix algebra, the market clearing conditions for each of the SN goods can be combined to form a compact global input–output system. Let $\mathbf{y}$ be the vector of production of dimension (SN x 1), which is obtained by stacking output levels in each country-sector. Define $\mathbf{f}$ as the vector of dimension (SN x 1) that is constructed by stacking world demand for final output from each country-sector $f_i(s)$. World final demand is the summation of demand from any country, such that $f_i(s) = \Sigma_j f_{ij}(s)$. We further define a global intermediate input coefficients matrix $\mathbf{A}$ of dimension (SN x SN). The elements $a_{ij}(s,t) = m_{ij}(s,t)/y_j(t)$ describe the output from sector s in country i used as intermediate input by sector t in country j, expressed as a ratio of output in the latter sector. Columns in the matrix $\mathbf{A}$ describe how the goods of each country-sector are produced using a combination of various intermediate products, both domestic and foreign.

Using this we can rewrite the stacked SN market-clearing conditions from (21.1) in compact form as $\mathbf{y} = \mathbf{f} + \mathbf{A}\mathbf{y}$. Rearranging, we arrive at the fundamental input–output identity:

$$\mathbf{y} = (\mathbf{I} - \mathbf{A})^{-1}\mathbf{f} \tag{21.2}$$

where $\mathbf{I}$ is an (SN x SN) identity matrix with ones on the diagonal and zeros elsewhere. The matrix $(\mathbf{I} - \mathbf{A})^{-1}$ is famously known as the Leontief inverse. The element in row m and column n of this matrix gives the total production of sector m needed for production of one unit of final output of product n. To see this, let $\mathbf{z}_n$ be a column vector with the nth element representing a euro of global consumption of goods from country-sector n, while all the remaining elements are zero. The production of $\mathbf{z}_n$ requires intermediate inputs given by $\mathbf{A}\mathbf{z}_n$. In turn, the production of these intermediates requires the use of other intermediates given by $\mathbf{A}^2\mathbf{z}_n$, and so on. As a result, the increase in output in each sector is given by the sum of all direct and indirect effects $\sum_{k=0}^{\infty} \mathbf{A}^k \mathbf{z}_n$. This geometric series converges (under mild conditions) to $(\mathbf{I} - \mathbf{A})^{-1} \mathbf{z}_n$.

Using the Leontief inverse, we can derive the total factor requirements of a unit of final output by netting out all intermediate input flows. Let us define $l_i(s)$ as the labor per unit of gross output in sector s in country i and create the row-vector l containing these "direct" labor coefficients, and similarly for capital coefficients k. Then the total (direct plus indirect) labor and capital requirements per unit of final output can be derived as

$$\Lambda = \hat{\imath}(\mathbf{I} - \mathbf{A})^{-1} \quad \text{and} \quad K = \hat{k}(\mathbf{I} - \mathbf{A})^{-1} \tag{21.3}$$

in which a hat-symbol indicates a diagonal matrix with the elements of the vector on the diagonal. Λ is the matrix of dimension (SN x SN) with an element (i, j) indicating the amount of labor in country-sector j needed in the production of one unit of final output by country-sector i, referred to as the total labor coefficient, and similarly for the matrix of capital inputs K.

Due to the linearity of the system, these total factor requirements have the useful property that when multiplied with the actual levels of final demand $\mathbf{f}$, they sum up to the overall quantity of labor and capital available in each country-sector. As such, this approach provides an exhaustive accounting decomposition of global final demand such that all production factors in the world are accounted for.

Using these total factor requirements matrices, we can define factor cost shares in a GVC of a final product. At this point, we first need to define prices of output and factor inputs. Let $\mathbf{p}$ be a (row) vector of output prices for products from each country-sector, $\mathbf{w}$ the (row) vector of hourly wage rates, and $\mathbf{r}$ the (row) vector of profit rates. The profit rate is derived as a residual such that capital compensation (the profit rate times the quantity of capital) plus labor compensation (wage times hours worked) equals gross value added. We allow output and factor input prices to differ across sectors and countries. Value added in a country-sector is defined in the standard way as gross output value (at basic prices) minus the cost of intermediate inputs (at purchasers' prices)[2] or $\mathbf{p(I-A)}$. As profit rates are measured residually such that wages and profits exhaust value added for each country-sector, the following accounting identity holds:

$$\mathbf{p(I-A) = w\hat{\imath} + r\hat{k}} \tag{21.4}$$

Post-multiplying both sides of (21.4) with the inverse of (I – A) and substituting from (21.3), we arrive at an important result: the output price of a final product (from a given country-sector) can be rewritten as a linear combination of the prices of all factors that were directly *and indirectly* needed in its production, or

$$\mathbf{p = w\Lambda + rK} \tag{21.5}$$

with Λ and $\mathbf{K}$ the matrices with total labor and capital coefficients. The identity in equation (21.5) forms the basis for deriving cost shares of labor and capital in the GVC of a particular product. Multiplying the left- and right-hand side by final output quantity, the share of wage and capital costs in total costs is generated for each final product. Through appropriate selection of elements in the matrices Λ and $\mathbf{K}$, one may trace the country-sector origins of these factor costs. We will use this decomposition in the next section to investigate the shifting factor shares in GVCs of manufacturing products.

The cost shares and quantities derived in the preceding can also be used to measure total factor productivity (TFP) growth in the production of a final good (following Wolff 1994). The consolidated data provide the opportunity to use the standard approach in growth accounting in measuring TFP, assuming a final output production function with arguments based on total (direct and indirect) labor and capital used. Let F be a translog production function for a final product j: $f_j = F_j(\lambda_j, \kappa_j, T)$ where λ_j the column vector of total labor requirements for producing one unit of good j from Λ and similarly κ_j a column of $\mathbf{K}$. Under the standard assumptions of constant returns to scale and perfectly competitive input markets, we can define productivity growth π in the GVC of product j by the weighted rate of decline of its total labor and capital requirements:

$$\frac{\partial \pi_j}{\partial t} \equiv -\alpha_j^L \frac{\partial \ln \lambda_j}{\partial t} - \alpha_j^K \frac{\partial \ln \kappa_j}{\partial t} \tag{21.6}$$

where $\partial \ln \lambda_j / \partial t$ is a (column) vector containing the differentials of the logarithms of all elements in λ_j. The weights are given by α_j^L, a (row) vector of value shares with elements reflecting the costs of labor from all country-sectors used in the production of one unit of product j, and similarly for the capital value shares given in α_j^K. Summed over all contributing sectors and countries, the elements in α_j^L add up to the labor share in final output of j, and similarly for capital. As all factor inputs are accounted for, the labor and capital share add up to unity. Since productivity growth rates are measured over discrete time periods rather than instantaneously, the average value shares over the sample period can be used to measure productivity, generating the so-called Tornqvist-Divisia productivity index (see Jorgenson et al. 1987). The productivity measure in (21.6) essentially shows the rate of productivity growth in the composite sector producing good j if all the sectors that contributed directly or indirectly to sector j's final output were fully integrated.[3]

At this point, it is instructive to compare the GVC productivity measure to the more traditional measure used in growth accounting studies in the KLEMS tradition. The main point to notice is that in standard applications only one stage of production is analyzed. It relates the output of a sector (firm) to the inputs used by this sector (firm) consisting of the factor inputs in the sector (firm) itself and intermediate inputs produced elsewhere. The direct factor requirements, as well as the value shares, are now expressed in value added of the sector, not final output of the product as in (21.6). The traditional productivity measure thus reflects only changes in direct factor requirements instead of the total requirements. This is a valid measure of the rate of productivity growth in the case when technical change only affects factor inputs in a single domestic stage of production, and when the prices of intermediate inputs are well measured; that is, any decline in the factor requirements in upstream sectors will be translated into a lower price for intermediates used by sectors downstream. Only in that case can the price of value added be properly measured through separate deflation of gross output and all intermediate inputs, also known as double deflation.

However, double deflation is becoming increasingly difficult as production fragmentation progresses. There is increasing doubt about the reliability of price indices for imported intermediates due to the practice of intra-firm transfer pricing and, more generally, inadequate statistical systems to monitor prices of imports (see Houseman et al. 2011). A particular instance of this is the measurement of intangible service flows, such as the use of knowledge, disembodied technology, brand names, and software. Intangibles are becoming increasingly important in production (e.g., Atalay et al. 2014),[4] but so far their measurement is elusive (see Corrado et al. 2012 for pioneering attempts). For example, Foxconn in China is producing iPhones using intangible designs and technology from Apple. These services are typically not recorded in production and trade statistics, so any study of the productivity of the Chinese or the US electronics industry is seriously hampered. The attribution of productivity growth to either industry will crucially depend on the measurement of intermediate inputs and their prices. In fact, this reflects a more general issue of attribution of productivity growth across industries when intermediate input prices are not well measured. Triplett (1996) has forcefully shown that in the case of measuring productivity in the US production of computers, the use of alternative quality-adjusted prices leads to radically different assessments of the location of productivity, which may be in the computer industry itself, or in the semi-conductor industry that delivers the main inputs to the computer industry, or even further back in the chain, namely the manufacturing of semi-conductor machinery. The same situation arises when production is fragmented across countries, adding to the measurement problem. The GVC approach, based on an integrated assessment, will thus provide a useful alternative to measure productivity growth in modern integrated production systems.

21.3. AN ILLUSTRATIVE EXAMPLE: GLOBAL VALUE CHAIN PRODUCTION OF GERMAN AUTOMOBILES

In this section, we illustrate our GVC methodology by analyzing the production of German cars. Throughout this chapter we will use data from the World Input-Output database (WIOD). This database provides data for 40 countries, as well as for the rest-of-the-world region such that all inputs can be accounted for (see Timmer et al. 2015). We decompose the value of output of all final products delivered by the German transport equipment industry (NACE rev. 1 industries 34 and 35)—in short, "German cars." This includes the value added in the last stage of production, which will take place in Germany by definition, but also the value added by all other activities in the chain, which take place anywhere in the world. To decompose value added in production, we make use of Leontief's decomposition method outlined in section 21.2 and given in equation (21.5).

Table 21.1 indicates the geographical origin of the value added in production of German cars in 1995 and in 2008. It reveals striking developments. Between 1995 and 2008, the share of domestic value added decreased rapidly from 79% to 66% of the value of a German car. Conversely, foreign value increased from 21% to 34%. With the new availability of cheap and relatively skilled labor, firms from Germany relocated parts of the production process to Eastern Europe. At the same time, the industry quickly

Table 21.1 Value Added Shares in Final Output of Automotives Finalized in Germany (%)

Generated in	1995	2008	Change
Germany	78.9	66.0	−12.8
Eastern Europe	1.3	4.3	3.0
Other European Union	11.9	14.3	2.4
NAFTA	2.5	3.1	0.6
East Asia	2.1	4.3	2.2
Other	3.3	8.0	4.7
Total	100.0	100.0	

Notes: Decomposition of final output of the transport equipment manufacturing industry in Germany (ISIC rev. 3 industries 34 and 35) based on equation (21.5). Eastern Europe refers to countries that joined the EU as of January 1, 2004. East Asia refers to China, Japan, South Korea, and Taiwan. Numbers may not sum due to rounding.

Source: Authors' calculations based on WIOD (2013 release).

globalized by sourcing more and more from outside Europe. Countries outside Europe actually accounted for more than half of the increase in foreign value added.

With additional information on the quantity of factors used in each country, we can provide a growth accounting decomposition of the growth rate of final output of German automotives using equation (21.6). Data on workers are measured by the number of hours, classified on the basis of educational attainment levels as defined in the International Standard Classification of Education (ISCED): low-skilled (ISCED categories 1 and 2), medium-skilled (ISCED 3 and 4), and high-skilled (ISCED 5 and 6). Capital stock volumes are measured on the basis of capital stocks of reproducible assets as covered in national account statistics following the SNA 2008 (thus including physical assets, software, and R&D, but excluding other intangibles), measured at 1995 constant price. Capital income is derived as gross value added minus labor income.

The results are shown in Table 21.2: final output volumes of German automotives increased by 59 log points over the period 1995–2007.[5] This was mainly due to increases in the use of capital, both domestically and abroad, together accounting for almost half of the increase in final output. The number of workers employed in production

Table 21.2 Growth Accounting for Vertical Production of Automotives from Germany

	Cost shares (%)		Quantities (1995 = 1)		Contribution to Final Output Growth	
	1995	2007	1995	2007	log pts	%
Factors in Germany						
Low-skilled labor	7.3	4.5	1.00	1.05	0.3	0.5
Medium-skilled labor	34.5	24.7	1.00	1.18	4.8	8.2
High-skilled labor	16.4	15.8	1.00	1.44	5.8	9.8
Capital	20.7	22.7	1.00	1.84	13.3	22.4
Factors outside Germany						
Low-skilled labor	4.0	3.8	1.00	1.99	2.7	4.5
Medium-skilled labor	6.1	8.6	1.00	2.05	5.3	8.9
High-skilled labor	2.8	5.3	1.00	3.02	4.5	7.5
Capital	8.3	14.5	1.00	2.57	10.8	18.2
Total factor productivity			1.00	1.13	11.8	20.0
Final output	100.0	100.0	1.00	1.81	59.2	100.0

Note and source: Authors' calculations based on equations (21.5) and (21.6) using data from WIOD (2013 release). The shares and volumes for foreign factors are based summations across 39 countries and the rest-of-the-world region. Capital growth is proxied by growth in capital stocks. Input quantities are set to 1 in 1995. Growth rates are in logs. Numbers may not add due to rounding.

increased as well, both within Germany and abroad, with higher growth rates for more skilled workers. Growth in workers in Germany contributed to 19% of final output growth, and workers abroad contributed another 21%. Note that although the number of high-skilled workers located abroad increased much faster than the number of German high-skilled workers, their contribution to final output growth is much less. This follows from the assumption of perfect competition in factor markets in the KLEMS approach such that the lower wages of foreign workers are presumed to reflect lower quality compared to German workers. While this might be true for higher-skilled workers, this can reasonably be doubted for less skilled workers. Integration of labor markets across countries is still incomplete such that wage differentials are not necessarily arbitraged away. Obviously, the potential cost saving was a main determinant for firms' decision to offshore. Econometric estimation of output elasticities (as done later on in this chapter) provides a way to arrive at estimates of marginal productivity. Capital input was growing fast, both within Germany and abroad. The cost share of domestic capital even rose, whereas labor shares declined, and it contributed 22% to final output growth for the period 1995–2007. Capital abroad grew even faster, but given its lower cost share contributed 18%. Productivity growth is derived as a residual, as in equation (21.6). It corresponds to an annual rate of 0.99% and is shown to contribute 20% of final output growth over this period.

Has productivity growth mainly took place within Germany, or did it affect all production factors in the chain? To answer this question, we may compare productivity growth in the last stage with productivity growth in the entire GVC. Productivity in the last stage can be computed by subtracting growth in factor inputs from growth in real value added in the German car industry. Factor inputs are weighted by their cost shares, and real value added should be derived using the double deflation method based on final output and intermediate input prices.[6] Annual productivity growth thus derived is a high 2.62%. Under the assumption that intermediate input prices have been well measured and the GVC production is separable in the last-stage factor inputs, one can derive the part of productivity growth due to the last stage by multiplying productivity growth rate in last stage by the ratio of last-stage value added to final output.[7] Averaged over the period, this ratio was 0.28, so 0.73 (= 2.62 x 0.28) percentage points out of 0.99% GVC productivity growth was realized in the German car industry, and the remainder of 0.26 in other industries in the GVC. However, as mentioned, the validity of this decomposition analysis depends heavily on the quality of the intermediate input deflator.

21.4. FACTOR INCOME SHARES IN MANUFACTURING GLOBAL VALUE CHAINS

In this section we extend the analysis and provide factor cost share measures for a wide set of manufacturing goods. We denote these goods by the term *manufactures*.

Production systems of manufactures are highly prone to international fragmentation, as activities have a high degree of international contestability: they can be undertaken in any country with little variation in quality. It is important to note that GVCs of manufactures do not coincide with all activities in the manufacturing sector, or with all activities that are internationally contestable. Some activities in the manufacturing sector are geared toward the production of intermediates for final non-manufacturing products and are not part of manufactures GVCs. On the other hand, GVCs of manufactures also includes value added outside the manufacturing sector, such as business services, transport, communication, and finance, and in raw materials production. These indirect contributions will be explicitly accounted for through the modeling of input-output linkages across sectors.

To start, we first illustrate the pervasiveness of the production fragmentation process. This includes domestic as well as international outsourcing. The former predates the latter: since the 1970s a steady process of outsourcing has taken place in advanced economies. In order to benefit from economies of scale and specialization, manufacturing firms outsourced non-core activities such as cleaning, catering, accounting, and other administrative back-office activities to other firms, often in the services industries.[8] More recent is the trend of international production fragmentation of services as well as manufacturing activities (see, e.g.. Feenstra 1998 for an overview).

Figure 21.1 provides trends in fragmentation in the production of manufactures. Product GVCs are identified by the country-industry of completion, and we have data for 240 manufacturing product chains: 12 groups of final manufacturing goods completed in 20 advanced countries, including 14 advanced EU economies (Austria, Belgium, Denmark, Finland, France, Germany, Greece, Ireland, Italy, Netherlands, Portugal, Spain, Sweden, and the United Kingdom) and six non-European economies (Australia, Canada, Japan, South Korea, Taiwan, and the United States). In Figure 21.1A, we provide a Kernel density plot of the share of last-stage production in GVC output. This share is defined as the value added to the product in the industry of completion as a ratio of the final output of the product.[9] Already in 1995 only around 36% (unweighted average) value was added in the last stage, and this has further declined to 34% in 2007. In Figure 21.1B, we document the international fragmentation trend ("offshoring"), adding the value-added contributions by domestic industries in earlier stages of production to the value added by the industry of completion. By definition, these shares of domestic value added in GVC output will be higher than the last-stage shares only, but the trend is even clearer: the (unweighted) average foreign share rose from 24.7% to 30.0%. For 84.5% of the product chains, the foreign value-added share has increased, indicating the pervasiveness of international fragmentation.[10]

Anecdotal evidence suggests that the factor content of the offshored activities might be different from the activities that remain onshore. For example, activities offshored to low-wage countries are typically low-skilled labor intensive. This will be reflected in

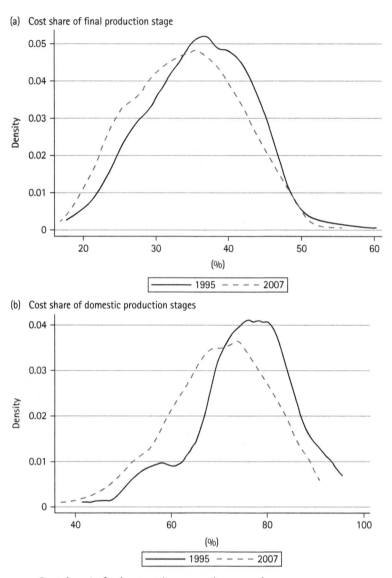

FIGURE 21.1. Cost share in final output (in percent), 1995 and 2007.

changes in the factor cost shares in GVCs that are plotted in Figure 21.2. For each factor, we show on the horizontal axis the cost share in 1995 and on the vertical axis the share in 2008. Points above the 45-degree line indicate GVCs in which the factor has increased its share. It illustrates some clear major trends: cost shares of capital (and in particular, high-skilled labor) are increasing in many chains, while the cost shares of low-skilled labor are decreasing (see also Timmer et al. 2014). Capital captures around 36.7% of cost share in the value chain on average, increasing from 35.3% in 1995 to 38.7% in 2007 (un-weighted average). Remember that capital income is derived as a residual and defined

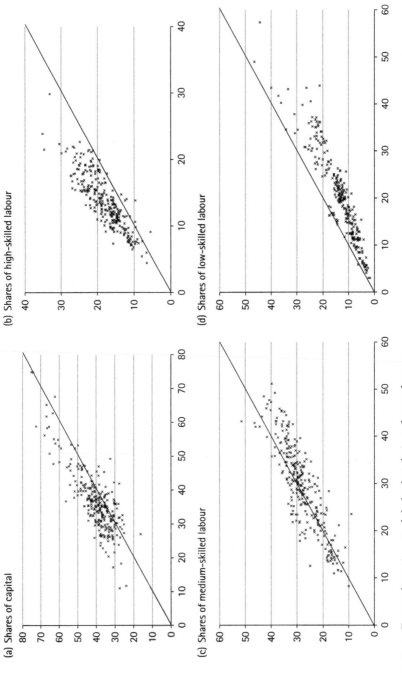

FIGURE 21.2. Factor shares in 240 global value chains of manufactures.

as gross value added minus labor income. It thus represents remuneration for capital in the broadest sense, including physical capital (such as machinery and buildings), land (including mineral resources), intangible capital (such as software and R&D, but also patents and trademarks), and financial capital. The share of high-skilled workers income increased as well and even more than the capital share, on average by 4.6% percentage points The value-added share of medium-skilled labor declined by 1.4, and low-skilled workers by a hefty 6.7 percentage points.

21.5. PATTERNS OF SUBSTITUTION AND PRODUCTIVITY GROWTH IN GLOBAL VALUE CHAINS

What might explain the trends in factor income shares in global production of manufacturing goods? To this end we will employ an econometric framework to estimate parameters in the GVC production function to investigate the impact of substitution elasticities and possible biases in productivity on the distribution of the value of output.[11] Following Christensen, Jorgenson, and Lau (1973), it is assumed that the product cost-functions can be approximated by a translog function, which is twice differentiable, linearly homogenous, and concave in factor prices. For a particular product, it is given by (product subscripts are omitted throughout for ease of presentation)

$$\ln C\left(\boldsymbol{p}_t, t\right) = \alpha + \sum_{i \in F} \beta_i \ln p_{it} + \frac{1}{2} \sum_{j \in F} \sum_{i \in F} \gamma_{ij} \ln p_{it} \ln p_{jt} + \beta_T t + \sum_{i \in F} \gamma_{iT} t \ln p_{it} + \frac{1}{2} \gamma_{TT} t^2 \quad (21.7)$$

where C represents variable cost per unit of output and is a function of prices p_i for factors i ($i \in F$, F refers to the set of factors) and time. The parameters γ_{ij} will provide information on the factor demand elasticities, while β_T represents the speed of Hicks-neutral technological change. The parameter γ_{iT} indicates a trend of productivity growth that complements factor i if positive, or substitutes when negative. γ_{TT} indicates the acceleration in productivity growth. If cost-minimization is assumed, Shephard's lemma can be used to derive the well-known factor cost-share (S) equation for a factor i:

$$S_{it} = \beta_i + \sum_{j \in F} \gamma_{ij} \ln p_{jt} + \gamma_{iT} t \quad (21.8)$$

As discussed in Jorgenson, Gollop, and Fraumeni (1987, Chapter 7), under necessary conditions for producer equilibrium the cost share of each input is equal to the elasticity of output with respect to that input. One can then define so-called share elasticities with respect to prices as the derivative of the value share with respect to the (log) of factor prices. These elasticities can be employed to derive the implications of patterns of substitution for the relative distribution of the value of output among the factor inputs. This is captured by the second term on the right-hand side. Similarly, one can define the bias of productivity growth with respect to a particular factor quantity as the derivative of the value share with respect to time. If the bias is positive for a factor, the corresponding value share increases over time. If it is negative, the value share decreases with time. This is captured by the last term on the right-hand side.

To estimate this system, we further impose constant returns to scale to simplify and other standard restrictions on the parameters in order to have a valid cost-function system. Constant returns to scale requires that the cost function is linearly homogenous in factor prices, which implies $\Sigma_{i \in F} \beta_i = 1$, and $\Sigma_{j \in F} \gamma_{ij} = 0$ for any i. Without loss of generality, we also impose symmetry such that $\gamma_{ij} = \gamma_{ji}$. Finally, the summation of the cost shares of all factors by definition equals to one such that $\Sigma_{i \in F} \gamma_{iT} = 0$. Given the cross restrictions in the share equations, we can improve the efficiency of parameter estimates by estimating in a simultaneous equation system. Berndt (1991) shows that this restricted equation system can be estimated by first dropping one cost-share equation and transforming the other equations accordingly. The cost-share equation for capital is dropped, and this choice is arbitrary as it does not affect the estimates since we iterate using Zellner's method (using ISUR).[12]

We estimate the model with country-fixed as well as product-fixed effects using annual data (1995–2007) for 240 product GVCs. Both sets of dummies jointly show significance at a high level, and a Hausman test clearly rejects the pooled regression. Before one can start interpreting the results, it is necessary to check whether the estimated cost function is consistent with economic theory and cost-minimization behavior. Cost functions are well behaved if they are quasi-concave. This implies that the so-called Hessian matrix of second-order derivatives with respect to factor prices must be negative semi-definite. A test for this is rather complex, and Diewert and Wales (1987) provide a simpler alternative: namely, whether the Hessian matrix $(H - \text{Diag}(s) + ss')$ is negative semi-definite, where H refers to the symmetric matrix containing all γ_{ij} of factors, and s is a column vector of cost shares of each factor. The eigenvalues of this matrix should be evaluated for each observation, and it is unlikely that negative semi-definity holds for all observations. Nevertheless, we have checked the quasi-concavity for each observation, and only 150 out of 3,116 observations have positive eigenvalue, which suggests that the Hessian matrix associated with the estimated translog cost function is negative semi-definite in most of the cases.[13] Production functions for GVCs thus generally appear to be consistent with economic theory and cost-minimization behavior.

Given the strong changes in relative prices, it is also interesting to investigate the elasticities of substitution and price elasticities of factor demand. The coefficients γ_{ij} in system (21.8) are the second-order derivatives with respect to factor prices. A positive γ_{ij} can be roughly interpreted as a net substitution between factor i and j, since it means that a price increase of factor j would increase the cost share paid to factor i, which implies that the usage of i must have increased. Formally, the relationship between the γ parameters and substitution elasticities between factors i and j (σ_{ij}) can be given by the so-called Morishima elasticities of substitution. Compared to the more well-known Allen-Uzawa (partial) elasticities, the Morishima elasticities have superior characteristics, particularly in cases with more than two inputs, in particular, they can beasymmetric (see Blackorby and Russell 1989). The cross-price elasticity of demand of factor i with respect to price of j (ε_{ij}) is given by

$$\varepsilon_{ij} = \frac{\gamma_{ij}}{s_i} + s_j \text{ (for } i \neq j) \quad \text{and} \quad \varepsilon_{ii} = \frac{\gamma_{ii}}{s_i} + s_i - 1. \tag{21.9}$$

Then the Morishima elasticities of substitution are given by

$$\sigma_{ij} = \varepsilon_{ji} - \varepsilon_{ii}. \tag{21.10}$$

As is clear from these definitions, elasticities depend on the actual cost shares and can vary across observations. We follow common practice and evaluate the elasticities on the basis of simple average cost shares across all observations. Results are given in Table 21.3 with price elasticities (at left) and elasticities of substitution between each factor (at right). The implied own-price elasticities are negative for all factors, as expected given the concavity of the cost functions, and are strongest for unskilled labor, while weakest for capital. For low-skilled labor, the self-price elasticity is as low as −0.66, which means that 1% decrease in the wage of a low-skilled worker corresponds to a 0.66% increase in the number of low-skilled hours worked in the value chain. This elasticity suggests that the rapid decline in the price of low-skilled work will only have a modest impact on its cost share. Indeed, the majority of the falling cost share is attributable to the low-skill saving nature of productivity growth, as shown in the following.

Table 21.3 Factor Demand Elasticities in Manufacturing Global Value Chains

	Implied Price Elasticity				Implied Elasticity of Substitution			
	w_L	w_M	w_H	r	L	M	H	K
L	−0.661	0.366	0.153	0.143	−	0.868	0.814	0.726
M	0.207	−0.443	0.127	0.109	0.808	−	0.668	0.531
H	0.153	0.225	−0.450	0.072	0.603	0.577	−	0.483
K	0.065	0.089	0.033	−0.187	0.329	0.296	0.259	−

Note: The elasticities are based on equations (21.9) and (21.10) in main text using parameters estimated in system of cost equations given in (21.8) based on annual data for 240 manufacturing GVCs, with ISUR including country and product group dummies. R^2 for each equation 0.9478 (L); 0.9243 (M); 0.8740 (H). w refers to wages of high-skilled labor (H), medium-skilled labor (M), low-skilled labor (L) and r to the price capital (K). Elasticities are evaluated at the simple average cost

Also interesting are the elasticities of substitution between the various factor inputs given in the right-hand part of the table. All elasticities are below one, suggesting that the four factor inputs are complements in global production of manufacturing products. Most notable is the low substitution elasticities of capital with all labor types. Capital appears to be particularly complementary to high-skilled workers, but there is also a strong complementarity to medium-skilled and low-skilled labor.

Another determinant of the factor share change is the possible factor-saving or factor-augmenting nature of technological change, which is captured by interactions with a linear time trend, γ_{iT}, in the specification. There is no a priori reason to assume that the effects are linear, and hence we follow Baltagi and Griffin (1988), who proposed a more general index approach in which the time trend t is replaced by year dummies using the first year as base. For a factor i, $\gamma_{it}t$ is replaced by $\Sigma_{t=2}^{12} \lambda_{it}D_t$ where D_t are year dummies. The parameter restrictions $\Sigma_{i\in F}\gamma_{iT} = 0$ are subsequently replaced by $\Sigma_{i\in F}\lambda_{it} = 0$ for all t. The results for the year dummies can be found in Table 21.4, accumulating from the beginning year. A strong bias is found for each factor. On average, productivity growth in GVCs of manufactures was saving on low- and medium-skilled labor, while using on high-skilled labor and capital. For low- and high-skilled labor, the accumulated factor biases are highly significantly different from 0 throughout the period. Accumulated factor bias is significant for capital in all years except the first two. For medium-skilled labor only, the bias in technical change is initially insignificant, but significant after 2004.

Using the estimates of the substitution elasticities and factor biases, we can use equation (21.8) to decompose the change in factor income shares shown in the previous section. The results are given in Table 21.5 and show that the model provides generally a good prediction for the average change in cost share of each factor. The effect of the factor bias in productivity growth strongly dominates the effects of factor price changes. Factor prices of low-skilled labor have declined on average 1% annually relative to capital, and about 2% relative to high-skilled labor, but this can explain only a little of the great decline in the low-skill cost share, which instead is driven by biased technological change. The substitution effects are strongest in the case of capital. Capital prices declined relative to medium- and high-skilled worker wages, which should lead to a decline in its cost share of 1.48. But strong capital using productivity growth pushed up its share by 4.43, more than counteracting the price effects (see Reijnders et al, 2016, for more).

21.6. CONCLUDING REMARKS

Production systems have evolved from a one-stage process taking place in a single location to a multi-stage process involving multiple locations in various countries. This is posing new challenges to analyses of factor incomes, substitution, and productivity growth. The canonical KLEMS modeling framework (as in Jorgenson et al. 1987) needs

Table 21.4. Estimates of factor bias in productivity growth in manufactures GVCs

	1996	1997	1998	1999	2000	2001	2002	2003	2004	2005	2006	2007
γ_{LT}	−0.0073	−0.0160	−0.0240	−0.0301	−0.0362	−0.0400	−0.0476	−0.0379	−0.0553	−0.0593	−0.0626	−0.0650
	0.0018	*0.0018*	*0.0018*	*0.0018*	*0.0018*	*0.0018*	*0.0018*	*0.0018*	*0.0019*	*0.0019*	*0.0019*	*0.0019*
γ_{MT}	−0.0004	0.0023	0.0002	−0.0023	−0.0022	−0.0049	−0.0072	−0.0122	−0.0047	−0.0110	−0.0180	−0.0208
	0.0019	*0.0019*	*0.0019*	*0.0019*	*0.0019*	*0.0019*	*0.0020*	*0.0019*	*0.0020*	*0.0020*	*0.0021*	*0.0021*
γ_{HT}	0.0042	0.0083	0.0129	0.0150	0.0196	0.0235	0.0255	0.0262	0.0342	0.0363	0.0376	0.0369
	0.0015	*0.0015*	*0.0015*	*0.0015*	*0.0015*	*0.0015*	*0.0016*	*0.0015*	*0.0016*	*0.0016*	*0.0016*	*0.0017*
γ_{KT}	*0.0034*	*0.0053*	*0.0109*	*0.0174*	*0.0189*	*0.0215*	*0.0293*	*0.0239*	*0.0258*	*0.0340*	*0.0430*	*0.0489*
	0.0026	*0.0026*	*0.0026*	*0.0026*	*0.0026*	*0.0026*	*0.0026*	*0.0026*	*0.0026*	*0.0026*	*0.0026*	*0.0027*

Note: Accumulation of estimates on year-dummies in system of cost share equations, see Table 21.3. Subscripts refer to high-skilled labor (H), medium-skilled labor (M), low-skilled labor (L) and Capital (K). Parameters involving K are implicitly derived using the parameter restrictions discussed in the main text. Standard errors are given below. Values that are not significant at 1% level are in italics.

Table 21.5 Explaining the changes in average cost shares in manufacturing GVCs

| | Actual Change in Cost Share | Predicted Cost Share Changes | Due to Change in Relative Prices of | | | | Tech Bias |
			Low-Skilled Labor	Medium-Skilled Labor	High-Skilled Labor	Sum of Price Effects	
LS	-6.67	-6.50	-0.38	0.17	-0.04	-0.24	-6.26
MS	-1.37	-1.31	-0.15	1.17	-0.20	0.82	-2.13
HS	4.64	4.86	0.03	-0.18	1.05	0.89	3.96
K	3.39	2.95	0.49	-1.16	-0.81	-1.48	4.43

Note: Change in cost over 1995–2007, averaged over 240 manufacturing GVCs. Predictions based on cost equations model; see Tables 21.3 and 21.4 for elasticities and factor bias in productivity. Relative wages are the wage rate relative to capital return.

to be amended, as it provides few insights into the effects of changing production linkages across industries and countries. Its central concept is a single firm or industry in one-stage production. Moreover, its empirical validity depends crucially on the tracking of prices and quantities of intermediate goods and services flowing across plants and borders. With low value-added to gross-output ratios, the accurate measurement of prices of intermediates becomes paramount to the measurement of productivity. These are increasingly hard to measure due to the practice of transfer pricing within multinational enterprises, the difficulty of pricing the flow of intangibles, as well as an inadequate statistical system to track the prices of intermediates when quality is improving.[14]

An approach using global value chains as the unit of observation offers an alternative approach toward a framework to study the important but elusive characteristics of modern production systems. In this chapter we introduced the GVC accounting approach as a complement to the traditional KLEMS type of analyses. Apart from being conceptually appealing, the GVC accounting approach bypasses some of the empirical problems that confront traditional analyses. We have defined cost shares, factor substitution, and productivity growth in GVC production, providing a structural foundation in Leontief's input–output model. We showed that these measures can be empirically implemented using synthetic input–output tables and that the results offer new insights into the nature of today's global production systems.

It should be emphasized, however, that the outlined GVC approach serves only as a first attempt. Arguably, the input–output model derives its popularity from the clear intuition of its measures in the case of "snake" production systems, where industries produce only one output and deliver to only one industry. But in the case of joint production and multiple-product output, it has to rely on strong (linear) proportionality assumptions in allocating the use of inputs. And although the accounting model is relatively straightforward, it is clear that the validity of the findings relies heavily on the quality of the database used. Data can, and needs, to be improved in many dimensions. For example, the WIOD is a prototype database developed mainly to provide a proof-of-concept, and it is up to the statistical community to bring international input-output tables into the realm of official statistics. Recently, the UNECE published its *Guide to Measuring Global Production* (UNECE, 2015), and the development work done by the OECD in its Trade-in-Vale-Added project is a step in the right direction.Ways forward would involve bringing information from establishment surveys into extended supply and use tables. In the longer term this would entail common business registers across countries and new data collections on value-chains beyond counterparty transactions.

Firm-level studies are needed for a better understanding of substitution and productivity in international production systems. Unfortunately, there is very little direct detailed information on plant-to-plant transactions in multiple stages of production. Given firms' secrecy or even ignorance about their own position in global production chains, this situation will not easily improve without major new data-collection efforts. Recent new data sources based on value-added tax data provide fresh evidence on firms' interactions at the transaction level (see Bernard et al. 2015 for an example) and provide an interesting avenue for further research.

A particular appealing avenue for new analysis of GVCs is the socalled "task-based approach" simultaneously arising in the literature on international trade and in labor economics. The task approach centers around a mapping from factor inputs to tasks, and then from tasks to output, so as to provide a structure on the possible substitution between labor and capital, both at home and abroad. Acemoglu and Autor (2011) outline a general framework that revolves around differences in the comparative advantages of factors in carrying out tasks: some workers are relatively better at performing certain tasks. Substitution of skills across tasks is possible, such that there is an endogenous mapping from workers to tasks depending solely on labor supplies and the comparative advantages of the various labor skill types. Capital may compete with labor in the supply of certain tasks such as routine activities. International specialization arises naturally as skilled workers in advanced countries have a comparative advantage in headquarter activities, while less skilled workers in emerging economies have a comparative advantage in carrying out low-tech activities like assembly, testing, and packaging (de Vries et al., 2018). It highlights that income distributions are determined by the interplay of technological change and global trading of labour and capital services. Combining the task approach with the empirical tools developed in the venerable KLEMS tradition is a fruitful avenue for future research.

NOTES

1. It is important to note that production fragmentation does not invalidate analysis of the welfare contribution of productivity change in sectors using the standard KLEMS growth accounting framework. The contribution of productivity growth in a sector to aggregate welfare in the country is well-defined in a setting with intermediate inputs (see, e.g., Hulten 1978), provided intermediate input prices are well measured.

2. For ease of exposition, we assume here that there is only one price for the output of each country-sector, and this price is paid by all intermediate and final users. This assumption is loosened up in the empirical application later.

3. Analyses of productivity in vertically integrated chains harks back to the work by Pasinetti (1977); see also Wolff (1994) and ten Raa and Wolff (2001). Gu and Yan (2017) provide a recent empirical application.

4. In a study of US multinational firms, they find that vertical ownership is not primarily used to facilitate transfers of goods along the production chain, as is often presumed: roughly one-half of upstream plants report no shipments to their firms' downstream units. Instead, an acquired plant begins to resemble the acquiring firm along multiple other dimensions, such as production technologies and sales destination. This is consistent with the hypothesis that vertical integration promotes efficient intra-firm transfers of intangible inputs rather than of goods.

5. The data in WIOD are in current US$. The volume growth rate is based on constant prices in euros, using the official exchange rate and the gross output deflator of German transport equipment manufacturing as deflators.

6. Note that conceptually, the figures should refer to inputs related to the production of final output of the industry, and not to overall output and all factor inputs used in the industry,

as part of output may be used as intermediate input elsewhere. Empirically, however, the latter approach will be equivalent to the former, as there are no separate data on production of final and intermediate products in the industry. Production technologies are assumed to be the same.

7. Again, in the data at hand, this ratio is equivalent to the value-added–gross-output ratio of the industry.

8. Ten Raa and Wolff (2001) analyzed the impact of services outsourcing on manufacturing productivity. Services input used by manufacturing industries is reduced into their constituent elements of material inputs, using an input–output technique akin to the one described in the preceding. They find that outsourcing of sluggish services can account up to one-fifth of the US manufacturing productivity recovery in the 1980s.

9. Note that this share is sensitive to the level of industry detail in the data. With higher industry detail, the shares will be lower by definition, and in the limit reflect plant (or firm) shares.

10. Los et al. (2015) investigated the regional origin of foreign value added, focusing on three regional trading blocs: Europe, NAFTA, and East Asia. They found that value added originating from outside the region to which the country-of-completion belongs is growing faster than the value added from within the region. This is suggesting a transition from production systems that were mainly regional to more extensive networks that are truly global. They also find that this tendency was only briefly interrupted by the financial crisis in 2008.

11. This section relies on results described in full in Reijnders, Timmer, and Ye (2016).

12. The simultaneous equation system can be estimated via Zellner's seemingly unrelated regression (SUR), either in one-step or using iterated SUR (ISUR). The one-step SUR combines multiple equations into one stack form, and the stack form is estimated via ordinary least square (OLS), while the iterated method is equivalent to maximum likelihood (ML) estimates. We use the latter, and although it might not always converge, it did in all our applications. Also, it appeared to be empirically close to the one-step SUR.

13. Typically, an even simpler method is used in the literature by investigating the eigenvalues evaluated at the simple average of the cost shares. Doing this, we find that all eigenvalues are non-positive (−0.1875, −0.1164, −0.0807, 0), which satisfies the requirement.

14. See Houseman and Mandel (2015) for an overview of the problems in the measurement of globalized production.

References

Acemoglu, Daron, and David H. Autor. 2011. "Skills, Tasks and Technologies: Implications for Employment and Earnings." In *Handbook of Labor Economics*, Vol.4B, edited by David Card and Orley Ashenfelter, 1043–1171. Amsterdam: Elsevier.

Ali-Yrkkö, Jyrki, Petri Rouvinen, Timo Seppälä, and Pekka Ylä-Anttila. 2011. "Who Captures Value in Global Supply Chains? Case NOKIA N95 Smartphone." *Journal of Industry, Competition and Trade* 11(3): 263–278.

Ali-Yrkkö, Jyrki, and Petri Rouvinen. 2015. "Slicing Up Global Value Chains: A Micro View." *Journal of Industry, Competition and Trade* 15(1): 69–85.

Antràs, Pol, and Stephen R Yeaple. 2014. "Multinational Firms and the Structure of International Trade." *Handbook of International Economics* 4: 55–130.

Atalay, Enghin, Ali Hortaçsu, and Chad Syverson. 2014. "Vertical Integration and Input Flows." *American Economic Review* 104(4): 1120–1148.

Autor, David H, Frank Levy, and Richard J. Murnane. 2003. "The Skill Content of Recent Technological Change: An Empirical Exploration." *The Quarterly Journal of Economics* 118 (4): 1279–1333.

Baldwin, Richard, and Anthony J. Venables. 2013. "Spiders and Snakes: Offshoring and Agglomeration in the Global Economy." *Journal of International Economics* 90(2): 245–254.

Baltagi, Badi H., and James M. Griffin. 1988. "A General Index of Technical Change." *Journal of Political Economy* 96(1): 20–41.

Bernard, A., Andreas Moxnes, and Yukiko U. Saito. 2015. "Production Networks, Geography and Firm Performance." NBER Working Paper No. 21082, National Bureau of Economic Research.

Berndt, E. 1991. *The Practice of Econometrics: Classic and Contemporary*. Reading, MA: Addison-Wesley.

Blackorby, Charles, and R. Robert Russell. 1989. "Will the Real Elasticity of Substitution Please Stand Up? (A Comparison of the Allen/Uzawa and Morishima Elasticities)." *The American Economic Review* 79(4): 882–888.

Chen, Wen, Bart Los and Marcel P. Timmer (2017), "Measuring intangible capital income in goods production: a global value chain approach", paper presented NBER-CRIW conference "Measuring and Accounting for Innovation in the 21st Century", Washington, March 10-11, 2017.

Christensen, Laurits R., Dale Jorgenson, and Lawrence J. Lau. 1973. "Transcendental Logarithmic Production Frontiers." *The Review of Economics and Statistics* 55(1): 28–45.

Corrado, Carol, Jonathan Haskel, Cecilia Jona-Lasinio, and Massimiliano Iommi (2012). "Intangible Capital and Growth in Advanced Economies: Measurement Methods and Comparative Results." CEPR Discussion Paper No. 9061.

Dedrick, Jason, Kenneth L. Kraemer, and Greg Linden. 2010. "Who Profits from Innovation in Global Value Chains? A Study of the iPod and Notebook PCs." *Industrial and Corporate Change* 19(1): 81–116.

De Vries, Gaaitzen J., Sébastien Miroudot and Marcel P. Timmer (2018), "Measuring Functional Specialization in Trade", mimeo University of Groningen.

Diewert, Walter E., and Terence J. Wales. 1987. "Flexible Functional Forms and Global Curvature Conditions." *Econometrica* 55(1): 43–68.

Diewert, W. E., and T. J. Wales. 1995. "Flexible Functional Forms and Tests of Homogeneous Separability." *Journal of Econometrics* 67(2): 259–302.

Feenstra, Robert C. 1998. "Integration of Trade and Disintegration of Production in the Global Economy." *Journal of Economic Perspectives* 12(4): 31–50.

Gu, Wulong and Beiling Yan 2017, "Productivity Growth and International Competitiveness." *Review of Income and Wealth*, 63: S113–S133

Houseman, Susan, Christopher Kurz, Paul Lengermann, and Benjamin Mandel. 2011. "Offshoring Bias in U.S. Manufacturing." *Journal of Economic Perspectives* 25(2): 111–132.

Houseman, S. N., and M. Mandel (eds.). 2015. *Measuring Globalization: Better Trade Statistics for Better Policy*, Vols. 1 and 2. Kalamazoo, MI: W. E. Upjohn Institute.

Hulten, Charles R. 1978. "Growth Accounting with Intermediate Inputs." *Review of Economic Studies* 45(3): 511–518.

Johnson, R. C., and G. Noguera. 2012. "Accounting for Intermediates: Production Sharing and Trade in Value Added." *Journal of International Economics* 86(2): 224–236.

Jorgenson, D. W., F. M. Gollop, and B. Fraumeni. 1987. *Productivity and U.S. Economic Growth.* Amsterdam: North Holland.

Koopman, Robert, Zhi Wang, and Shang-Jin Wei. 2014. "Tracing Value-Added and Double Counting in Gross Exports." *American Economic Review* 104(2): 459–494

Leontief, W. 1936. "Quantitative Input–Output Relations in the Economic System of the United States." *Review of Economics and Statistics* 18(3): 105–125.

Leontief, W. (1949). "Structural matrices of national economies". *Econometrica*: 273–282.

Los, B., M. P. Timmer, and G. J. de Vries. (2015), "How Global Are Global Value Chains? A New Approach to Measure International Fragmentation." *Journal of Regional Science* 55(1): 66–92.

Los, B., M. P. Timmer, and G. J. de Vries. 2016. "Tracing Value-Added and Double Counting in Gross Exports: Comment." *American Economic Review* 106(7): 1958–1966.

Miller, Ronald E. 1966. "Interregional Feedbacks in Input-Output Models: Some Preliminary Results." *Papers of the Regional Science Association* 17: 105–125.

Miller, R. E., and P. D. Blair. 2009. *Input–Output Analysis: Foundations and Extensions.* Cambridge: Cambridge University Press.

Pasinetti, Luigi L. 1977. *Lectures on the Theory of Production.* London: Macmillan.

Reijnders, L. S. M., M. P. Timmer, and X. Ye. 2016. "Offshoring, Biased Technical Change and Labour Demand: New Evidence from Global Value Chains." GGDC Research Memorandum No. 164, University of Groningen.

Ten Raa, Thijs, and Edward Wolff. 2001. "Outsourcing of Services and the Productivity Recovery in U.S. Manufacturing in the 1980s and 1990s." *Journal of Productivity Analysis* 16(2): 149–165.

Timmer, M. P., E. Dietzenbacher, B. Los, R. Stehrer, and G. J. de Vries. 2015. "An Illustrated User Guide to the World Input-Output Database: The Case of Global Automotive Production." *Review of International Economics* 23(3): 575–605.

Timmer, M. P., A. A. Erumban, B. Los, R. Stehrer, and G. J. de Vries. 2014. "Slicing Up Global Value Chains." *Journal of Economic Perspectives* 28(2): 99–118.

Triplett, Jack E. 1996. "High-Tech Industry Productivity and Hedonic Price Indices." In *OECD Proceedings Industry Productivity: International Comparisons and Measurement Issues*, 119–142. Paris: OECD.

UNECE (2015). *Guide to Measuring Global Production.* New York and Geneva: United Nations.

Williamson, O. E. 1971. "The Vertical Integration of Production: Market Failure Considerations." *The American Economic Review*, 61(2): 112–123.

Wolff, Edward N. 1994. "Productivity Measurement within an Input-Output Framework." *Regional Science and Urban Economics* 24(1): 75–92.

CHAPTER 22

....

THE INDUSTRY SOURCES OF PRODUCTIVITY GROWTH AND CONVERGENCE

....

ROBERT INKLAAR

22.1. INTRODUCTION

....

THE analysis of productivity at the industry level stands at the midway point between economy-wide and firm-level analyses. On the firm-level end of the spectrum, the survey by Syverson (2011) on "what determines productivity" is devoted to studies of the role of, for instance, management practices, competition, trade, innovation, and resource allocation, which are addressed most convincingly at the firm level. On the economy-wide end of the spectrum, aggregate productivity can shed light on, for instance, the sources of growth (Fernald and Jones 2014) or cross-country income differences (Caselli 2005). So what role is there for an industry perspective?

I would argue that a particular advantage of the industry level over the firm level is that it can deliver a more comprehensive and an international comparative perspective. In other words, a main advantage of industry-level analysis over firm-level analysis is that data can be drawn from National Accounts—which are publicly available—and that the output of all industries together add up to gross domestic product (GDP). In contrast, in firm-level studies, the manufacturing sector is heavily overrepresented, which limits the extent to which outcomes can be generalized.[1] Similarly, high-quality firm-level data, which cover a comprehensive set of firms and can be used to trace entry and exit, are typically confidential and cannot be easily used in an international comparative perspective.[2] Another challenge at the firm level is that, for almost any analysis, important pieces of information are not available at that level of detail. For instance, an industrial survey may provide information on firm revenues, but not on the prices charged (Foster, Haltiwanger and Syverson 2008). Similarly, information about the skill level of employees is also typically collected through household, rather than enterprise surveys.[3] Industry identifiers, though, are usually part of all such surveys, which means that industry-level analysis can typically draw on a greater variety of data items.

Economy-wide analysis likewise has important shortcomings, which are best illustrated with the debate about the acceleration of US productivity growth, starting in 1995 and the comparison with Europe.[4] In the United States, the debate was between Jorgenson and Stiroh (2000) and Oliner and Sichel (2000), who argued that there had been a substantial change in the US productivity growth pattern, while Gordon (2000) argued that the increase in productivity growth was highly localized in information technology (IT) production. This was not resolved until the more detailed work of Jorgenson, Ho, and Stiroh (2005) showed that increases in productivity growth were also apparent in many industries that used information and communications technology (ICT) intensively.[5] Similarly, when comparing Europe and the United States, Timmer and van Ark (2005) showed that the EU-US growth gap could be explained by differences in the importance of the IT production sector, while van Ark, O'Mahony, and Timmer (2008) could later show that this aggregate picture concealed a large difference in productivity growth in the (ICT-intensive) market services.

This is not to say that industry-level analysis is without shortcomings. Just as economy-wide data can conceal important industry-level differences, so can industry data obscure differences in productivity across firms, as Chapter 18 of this *Handbook* illustrates. Another problem is measurement of industry output. One reason why many firm-level studies focus on manufacturing is that their production process is understood more clearly than that of many services, and we can more easily measure the price of their output. In services, more careful modeling and surveying are typically needed, and progress in this area is highly uneven across countries and industries.[6] Finally, in a globalizing world where different stages of production are fragmented across borders, the concept of a domestic industry becomes less relevant. As a result, the same industry may engage in very different activities in different countries. For example, the electronics industry in the United States will include design of the iPhone, while the same industry in China focuses on assembly of the iPhone. A more in-depth discussion of this problem is beyond the scope of this chapter, but is taken up in Chapter 21 of this volume.

This discussion suggests that the analysis of productivity at the industry level should be done where its strengths are greatest or the weaknesses of the alternatives make it the best choice. In the remainder of this chapter, I will present three examples of such applications. First, I will analyze the industry sources of transatlantic productivity growth differences, to examine whether the findings of van Ark et al. (2008) still hold in the face of data revisions and the more turbulent macroeconomic backdrop of the financial crisis. Second, for a broader set of countries, I will trace the industry origins of changes in aggregate cross-country productivity dispersion. One important question is whether the manufacturing sector is somehow special as a source of convergence, as suggested by the work of Rodrik (2013). Third, I examine to what extent the varied patterns of industry productivity growth and convergence can be explained using factors that play a role in determining productivity. This extends the analysis of Inklaar, Timmer, and van Ark (2008) and McMorrow, Röger, and Turrini (2010) to a broader set of countries and a more recent period.[7]

22.2. THE TRANSATLANTIC PRODUCTIVITY GROWTH GAP

The growth experience of Europe relative to the United States since World War II can be characterized in two phases, namely a rapid convergence in GDP per hour worked from 1950 until the mid-1990s, followed by a period of divergence. Figure 22.1 illustrates this by plotting GDP per hour worked for the EU-15 (i.e., the 15 member-states of the European Union until 2004), relative to the United States. Also shown in the chart is GDP per capita, which has been fairly stable in relative terms since the early 1970s. The difference between the evolution in GDP per hour and GDP per capita is due to differences in hours worked per capita, which in general will reflect differences in labor market outcomes and different preferences for leisure.

The relative decline in GDP per hour worked is substantial: after peaking at 87% in 1995, the level in 2013 stood at only 78%, a relative level comparable to the early 1980s. This relative decline has been fairly constant over this 18-year period, suggesting a

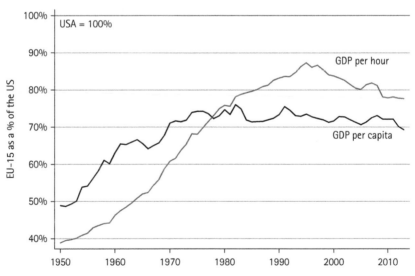

FIGURE 22.1. GDP per hour worked and GDP per capita in the EU-15 relative to the United States, 1950–2013.

Notes: EU-15 refers to the 15 member countries of the European Union until 2004: Austria, Belgium, Denmark, Finland, France, Germany, Greece Ireland, Italy, Luxembourg, Netherlands, Portugal, Spain, Sweden, United Kingdom.

Source: The Conference Board Total Economy Database™, January 2014, http://www.tcb.org/data/economydatabase/.

persistent source of growth differences. Moreover, the relative decline has been widespread across the EU-15: 13 of the 15 countries had a lower level of GDP per hour worked relative to the United States in 2013 than in 1995 (the exceptions were Ireland and Sweden).

At this economy-wide level of analysis, we can go one step further and assess whether differences in growth of GDP per hour worked are due to differences in the growth contribution from other inputs. For this, we rely on the growth accounting decomposition provided in the Total Economy Database of The Conference Board:

$$\Delta \ln Y_{it} = \overline{\alpha}_{it} \Delta \ln L_{it} + \left(1 - \overline{\alpha}_{it}\right) \Delta \ln K_{it} + \Delta \ln A_{it}, \qquad (22.1)$$

where Y is GDP in country i at t, α is the share of labor income in GDP, the upper-bar denotes a two-period average, L is labor input, K is capital input, and A is total factor productivity (TFP). The labor input index is based on data on hours worked by workers with different levels of educational attainment, giving greater weight to workers that earn higher wages and thus (are assumed to) have a higher marginal product. Similarly, the index for capital input is based on data for different capital assets, notably ICT assets and non-ICT assets—buildings, transport equipment, and other machinery. Here, too, the assumption is made that assets with higher marginal costs—like ICT assets, which depreciate rapidly and show falling prices over time—have higher marginal products. As detailed in Jorgenson (2005) and Hulten (2010), equating marginal products to marginal costs means assuming that firms are cost-minimizing price-takers in factor markets. Furthermore, under the assumption of perfect competition in output markets, income shares equal output elasticities.[8]

To relate the growth accounting decomposition to the pattern in Figure 22.1, equation (22.1) can be rewritten in terms of labor productivity:

$$\Delta \ln \left(Y_{it} / H_{it}\right) = \overline{\alpha}_{it} \Delta \ln \left(L_{it} / H_{it}\right) + \left(1 - \overline{\alpha}_{it}\right) \Delta \ln \left(K / H_{it}\right) + \Delta \ln A_{it}, \qquad (22.2)$$

where H is the total number of hours worked. From this equation, we can see that differences in labor productivity growth may be accounted for by differences in the pace of change in labor composition, $\Delta \ln \left(L_{it} / H_{it}\right)$, differences in the rate of capital deepening, $\Delta \ln \left(K / H_{it}\right)$, or differences in TFP growth, $\Delta \ln A_{it}$.

Figure 22.2 shows the development of TFP in the EU-15 and the United States since 1990, indexed to 1995 = 1. As the figure shows, TFP has grown by more than 10% in the United States over the period since 1995, while EU TFP was barely higher in 2013 than in 1995. In other words, the decline in Europe's relative labor productivity level from Figure 22.1 can be fully accounted for by lower TFP growth in Europe than in the United States. Indeed, the correlation between the relative changes in labor productivity and the relative changes in TFP is close to one. But what this actually says is that we do not really know what is behind the difference in labor productivity growth, since differences in the pace of change in labor composition or differences in capital deepening have no (overall) explanatory power. For individual countries within the EU-15, the TFP growth pattern is more mixed than the labor productivity growth pattern—with Austria, Finland, and

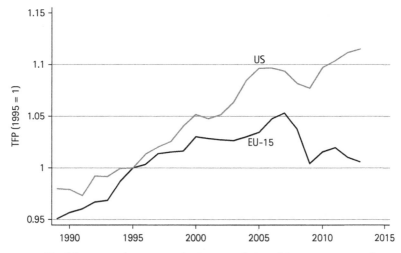

FIGURE 22.2. Total factor productivity in the EU-15 and United States, 1989–2013 (1995 = 1).

Notes: EU-15 refers to the 15 member countries of the European Union until 2004: Austria, Belgium, Denmark, Finland, France, Germany, Greece, Ireland, Italy, Luxembourg, Netherlands, Portugal, Spain, Sweden, United Kingdom.

Source: The Conference Board Total Economy Database™, January 2014, http://www.tcb.org/data/economydatabase/.

Germany showing similar TFP growth as the United States, and Ireland and Sweden showing somewhat faster growth—but the United States has a clear growth advantage over the other 10 EU countries.

To advance our understanding of these growth differences, we turn to an industry-level breakdown of total economy TFP growth. Note that this should be seen more as a diagnostic than an explanatory device: merely comparing growth in specific industries or groups of industries will not reveal *why* growth is faster. However, it can be helpful in suggesting where to look. For instance, if the United States has a TFP growth advantage in industries that use ICT intensively, then the more specific question becomes why US firms are able to better use this technology to increase their productivity, for instance through better "people management" practices (Bloom, Sadun, and van Reenen 2012).

It is not straightforward, though, to gain a detailed industry perspective, as it requires not only the type of information that is regularly found in country National Accounts, on the value added, investments, and total employment of industries, but also data on the skill composition of the workforce and the asset composition of investment. Though collecting such data is feasible for numerous countries,[9] it is much harder to achieve comprehensive and up-to-date country coverage. For the analysis here, I use the 2012 version of the EU KLEMS database,[10] which includes data for the United States and for 10 of the EU-15 countries (representing 93% of EU-15 GDP), and covers the period through 2009 for all countries. Industry TFP growth is computed using an analogous growth accounting approach, as in equation (22.1), so industry TFP growth is equal to growth in industry value added minus cost-share-weighted growth of industry labor input and capital input. A helpful consequence of this is that we can decompose overall TFP growth into contributions by industries or groups of industries with comparable features. Specifically, aggregate TFP growth can be written as

$$\Delta \ln A_{it} = \sum_j \bar{v}_{ijt} \Delta \ln A_{ijt},\qquad(22.3)$$

where $\Delta \ln A_{ijt}$ is the growth of TFP in industry j (in country i at time t) and v is the value-added share of industry j, $v_{ijt} = V_{ijt}/\Sigma_j V_{ijt}$ with V denoting value added at current prices and the upper bar indicating a two-period average. The same equation can be used to compute TFP growth for groups of industries.

Table 22.1 compares the TFP growth experience of the EU-10 and the United States between 1995 and 2009 for major industry groups. Note that, as Figure 22.2 shows, using 2009 as the final year of the comparison (a necessity given the coverage of EU KLEMS) is relatively flattering, as a larger growth gap has opened up in more recent years. In addition to average growth, the table shows the average value-added share of each group and the contribution to market economy TFP growth.

Table 22.1 The Industry Composition of TFP Growth in the EU–10 and the United States, Average 1995–2009 (in %)

	TFP Growth		Share		Contribution	
	EU-10	US	EU-10	US	EU-10	US
Total economy	0.0	0.3	100	100		
Market economy	0.3	0.6	59	67	0.3	0.6
ICT production	2.8	5.9	7	7	0.3	0.6
Goods-producing industries	0.2	−0.4	21	20	0.1	−0.1
Market services	−0.3	0.2	31	40	−0.1	0.1
Distribution and trade	0.3	1.2	15	16	0.1	0.3
Finance and business services	−0.8	−0.5	12	18	−0.2	−0.1
Personal services	−0.7	−0.9	4	6	−0.1	−0.1

Notes: EU-10 incudes Austria, Belgium, Finland, France, Germany, Italy, Netherlands, Spain, Sweden, and the United Kingdom. The share is the share in total economy value added. The growth contributions in the final columns are computed using equation (22.3). ICT production includes electronics manufacturing and information and communication services. Goods-producing industries include agriculture, mining, manufacturing (excluding electronics), utilities, and construction. The market economy includes all industries except government, health, education, for which output measurement is more challenging and likely more heterogeneous across countries, and real estate, for which output growth is equal to input growth for much of the industry.

Sources: Computations based on EU KLEMS database; see O'Mahony and Timmer (2009) and www.euklems.net.

Table 22.1 shows that the growth differential between the EU-10 and the United States for the market economy matches the growth differential for the total economy over the 1995–2009 period, with US TFP growing at twice the rate of the EU-10. The subsequent rows replicate the industry breakdown of van Ark et al. (2008): the production of ICT goods and services, goods-producing industries, and market services. Market services, in turn, are further split into distribution and trade industries, finance and business services, and personal services. The final two columns, which show the contribution of each industry grouping to market economy TFP growth, shows that the contributions from ICT production exactly match the aggregate growth. In other words, the net contribution of all industries other than ICT production is zero. Furthermore, the larger contribution from ICT production in the United States can be traced to faster TFP growth, not a larger ICT sector.[11]

Despite a net difference of zero, the table does point to some similarities and differences compared with earlier analyses. Most important, TFP growth in goods-producing industries in the EU-10 is positive, while TFP declined in the United States. This can mostly be traced to TFP declines in construction, but also to slower TFP growth in manufacturing outside ICT production. Conversely, the United States had a clear TFP growth advantage in market services, mostly because of faster TFP growth in distribution and trade. This has often been linked to the intensity with which this sector uses ICT, as in Stiroh (2002) and Jorgenson et al. (2005). However, the fact that finance and business services show an overall negative contribution, despite ICT-use being most intensive in that sector, suggests the limitations of that view. Furthermore, the earlier focus on growth differences in market services (e.g., Inklaar et al. 2008) still seems relevant with today's numbers, but some of the US productivity growth advantage in this sector has disappeared over time. In part, this is due to the period chosen, with the earlier analysis based on data for the 1995–2004 period. But data revisions play an important role as well: in Inklaar et al. (2008), US TFP growth in market services was an annual average of 1.3%, but based on the current vintage of productivity data, growth only averaged 0.8% between 1995 and 2004.

22.2.1. Summing Up

This section on the transatlantic productivity growth gap has illustrated some of the strengths, but also the limitations of industry-level analysis for the diagnosis of aggregate growth differences. When specific industries are particularly dynamic, which has clearly been the case for the ICT production sector, it is important to isolate its role from that of other industries. Ever since the early studies of the US productivity growth resurgence (e.g., Gordon 2000; Jorgenson and Stiroh 2000; Oliner and Sichel 2000), it has been clear that the ICT sector has played a notable role, and it has also long been clear that the growth benefits from this sector have been smaller in Europe (Timmer et al. 2010). Some of the other diagnoses have been subject to greater variability over time, though. The role of ICT use seemed at one point to be quite important, suggesting possible productivity spillovers from this technology. But the fact that in finance and business services, among the most ICT-intensive industries of the economy, US TFP growth has been revised from strongly positive to clearly negative suggests that caution is in order.[12] This is even more pressing when making international growth comparisons, since price and volume measurement practices differ considerably across countries (Inklaar et al. 2008).

22.3. THE INDUSTRY SOURCES OF CONVERGENCE

Recent literature has focused on the role of industry productivity in shaping cross-country income differences and the importance of structural change for aggregate outcomes.[13] However, most studies in this area give a comprehensive coverage of industries only for Organisation for Economic Co-operation and Development (OECD) countries. This begs the question of whether rich-country results are applicable to emerging economies as well. Alternatively, studies covers a wide range of countries, but only for a specific sector of the economy, such as agriculture or manufacturing.[14] This begs the question of whether a specific sector truly plays an exceptional role in explaining cross-country differences in economic performance. In particular, the recent work of Rodrik (2013) suggests that productivity in manufacturing converges across countries, regardless of country factors (i.e., unconditional convergence). In this section, I will give a comprehensive accounting of changes in market economy productivity dispersion into the role of several major sectors of the economy for 38 economies that span much of the development spectrum.

22.3.1. Methodology

The crucial input for the analysis of convergence consists of estimates of relative industry productivity. Though there are clear parallels between the comparison of productivity growth over time and productivity levels across countries, there are sufficient differences in methodology and data to warrant further discussion. Here I give an overview, drawing on the more detailed exposition in Inklaar and Diewert (2016).

To analyze the degree of convergence toward the productivity frontier, it is necessary to measure output and input levels that are comparable across countries and over time. It is also useful to have measures that are invariant to the choice of a reference point—that is, a single country and year that act as a basis for comparison for all other countries and years. Finally, it is useful to have a methodology that is based on an economic approach to production theory. Such an approach was developed by Caves, Christensen, and Diewert (1982a) (hereafter CCD), but their approach has a significant limitation. Their approach relies on the distance function methodology for aggregating inputs and outputs that can be traced back to Malmquist (1953), which they further developed (CCD 1982a). The problem is that this distance function methodology does not allow us to compare real GDP or real value added across countries, as that methodology requires a strict separation of outputs and inputs. Net output aggregates based on distance function techniques do not work if the output aggregate includes intermediate inputs or imports. In this section, we show how this problem can be addressed in a production theory framework by using the methodology that was developed by Diewert and Morrison (1986), drawing also on the techniques used by CCD.

We give a brief explanation of the methodology developed by Diewert and Morrison (1986) for a comparison of real outputs, inputs, and productivity levels across two time periods or two production units in the same industry. Consider a set of production units that produce a vector of M net outputs,[15] $y \equiv \left[y_1, \ldots, y_M \right]$, using a non-negative vector of N primary inputs, $x \equiv \left[x_i, \ldots, x_N \right]$. Let the feasible set of net outputs and primary inputs for production unit i be denoted by S^i for $i = 1, \ldots, I$. It is assumed that each S^i is a closed convex cone in R^{M+N} so that production is subject to constant returns to scale for each production unit. For each strictly positive net-output price vector $p \equiv \left[p_1, \ldots, p_M \right] \gg 0_M$ and each strictly positive primary-input vector $x \gg 0_N$, define the *value added function* or *GDP function* for production unit k, $g^i \left(p, x \right)$, as follows:

$$g^i \left(p, x \right) \equiv \max_{y} \left\{ \sum_{m=1}^{M} p_m y_m : \left(y, x \right) \in S^i \right\}; \quad i = 1, \ldots, I. \tag{22.4}$$

These value-added functions g^i provide a dual representation of the technology sets S^i under our assumptions on the technology sets. Finally, Diewert and Morrison assume specific functional forms for the value-added functions g^i defined by (22.1): they assumed that each value-added function has a translog functional form. Armed with these assumptions, Diewert and Morrison (1986, 661–665) were able to construct output, input, and productivity levels between any two production units using the economic approach to index number theory and Törnqvist-Theil (1967, 136–137) output price and input quantity indexes.

Given this starting, we can detail the methodology for comparing industry productivity level across countries and over time. We assume that there are four sets of basic data, each for $k = 1, \ldots, K$ countries and $t = 1, \ldots, T$ years. (i) The *value of net output m* in country k in domestic currency during period t is v_{ktm} for $m = 1, \ldots, M$. Thus there are M net output commodities, and if $v_{ktm} < 0$, commodity m is used as an input by country k in period t. (ii) The *price or purchasing power parity (PPP, in domestic currency)* for net output m in country k for time period t is $p_{ktm} > 0$. These output prices or PPPs are prices that use the same unit of measurement for the same commodity across countries. (iii) The *value of primary input n* in country k in domestic currency during period t is $V_{ktn} > 0$ for $n = 1, \ldots, N$. (iv) The *price or PPP (in domestic currency)* for primary input n in country k for time period t is $w_{ktn} > 0$ for $n = 1, \ldots, N$.

Given the preceding primary data sets, we can construct implicit output and input quantities for each country and each time period. Define the *implicit quantity* (or volume) y_{ktm} of net output as $y_{ktm} \equiv v_{ktm} / p_{ktm}$ and define the *implicit quantity* (or volume) x_{ktn} of primary inputs as $x_{ktn} \equiv V_{ktn} / w_{ktn}$. Define the *total value added* in domestic currency for country k in period t, v_{kt}, and the *total value of primary inputs* for country k in period t, V_{kt}, by summing over net outputs and inputs:[16]

$$v_{kt} \equiv \sum_{m=1}^{M} v_{ktm}; V_{kt} \equiv \sum_{n=1}^{N} V_{ktn}; \quad k=1,...,K; \quad t=1,...,T. \tag{22.5}$$

In what follows, we will make use of *value-added output shares* $s_{ktm} \equiv v_{ktm} / v_{kt}$ and *primary-input cost shares* $S_{ktm} \equiv V_{ktn} / V_{kt}$.

Define the (strictly positive) net output price vector for country k in period t as $p_{kt} \equiv [p_{kt1}, ..., p_{ktM}]$ and the corresponding net output quantity vector as $y_{kt} \equiv [y_{kt1}, ..., y_{ktM}]$. Then under our assumptions on technology and behavior, Diewert and Morrison (1986, 665) have showed that the aggregate price of real value added in country k in period t relative to the aggregate price of real value added in country j in period s, $P_{kt/js}$, is equal to the Törnqvist-Theil output price index $P_T(p_{js}, p_{kt}, y_{js}, y_{kt})$; that is,

$$P_{kt/js} \equiv P_T\left(p_{js}, p_{kt}, y_{js}, y_{kt}\right) \equiv \exp\left[\sum_{m=1}^{M} \frac{1}{2}\left(s_{jsm} + s_{ktm}\right)\ln\left(p_{ktm} / p_{jsm}\right)\right] \tag{22.6}$$

Diewert and Morrison (1986, 665) also indicated that the corresponding implicit quantity index, $Y_{kt/js}$, provides a good estimator of the ratio of real value added in country k in period t relative to the real value added of country j in period s; that is, we have

$$Y_{kt/js} \equiv \left[v_{kt} / v_{js}\right] / P_T\left(p_{js}, p_{kt}, y_{js}, y_{kt}\right). \tag{22.7}$$

Obviously, we could pick a country and a time period (say period 1 and country 1) and treat this production unit as a numeraire unit and measure the GDP output prices and quantities of other observations relative to this numeraire unit. This would lead to a sequence of aggregate prices, $P_{kt/11}$, and quantities, $Y_{kt/11}$. However, we could just as easily pick country 2 in period 1 as the numeraire country, and this would lead to the sequence of country PPPs and real value added of $P_{kt/21}$ and $Y_{kt/21}$. Unfortunately, $P_{kt/21}$ will not, in general, be proportional to $P_{kt/11}$ and $Y_{kt/21}$ will not be proportional to $Y_{kt/11}$; that is, the results will depend on the choice of the numeraire country. CCD solved this numeraire dependence problem by averaging over all possible choices of the numeraire observation. Following this strategy, we use the Diewert-Morrison PPPs as the basic bilateral building blocks, rather than the CCD bilateral choice of index number formula, which did not allow for negative net outputs. Thus define the *geometric mean of all the PPP parities* for country k in time period t relative to all possible choices j, s of the base country, P_{kt^*} as follows:

$$P_{kt^*} \equiv \left[\prod_{j=1}^{K}\prod_{s=1}^{T} P_{kt/js}\right]^{\frac{1}{KT}}. \tag{22.8}$$

It is usually convenient to pick out the country with the largest economy (say country 1) in period 1 and form a set of normalized aggregate output PPPs that compare the PPPs defined by (22.9) or (22.11) to the PPP for country 1 in period 1. Thus we define our final set of *value-added output deflators, P_{kt},* as follows:

$$P_{kt} \equiv P_{kt^*} / P_{11^*}.$$ (22.9)

The final set of *real value-added estimates* Y_{kt} that are comparable across time and space is defined by deflating each country's nominal value added by the PPPs defined by (22.9):[17]

$$Y_{kt} \equiv \left[v_{kt} / P_{kt} \right].$$ (22.10)

We next turn our attention to the problems associated with measuring real primary input across countries. Define the (strictly positive) *input quantity vector* as $x_{kt} \equiv \left[x_{kt1}, \ldots, x_{ktN} \right]$ and the corresponding *input price vector* as $w_{kt} \equiv \left[w_{kt1}, \ldots, w_{ktN} \right]$. Then under our assumptions on technology and behavior, Diewert and Morrison (1986, 665) showed that the aggregate quantity of primary input in country k in period t relative to the aggregate quantity of primary input in country j in period s, $X_{kt/js}$, is equal to the Törnqvist-Theil input quantity index $Q_T\left(w_{js}, w_{kt}, x_{js}, x_{kt}\right)$; that is, we have

$$X_{kt/js} \equiv Q_T\left(w_{js}, w_{kt}, x_{js}, x_{kt}\right) \equiv \exp\left[\sum_{n=1}^{N} \frac{1}{2}\left(S_{jsn} + S_{ktn}\right)\ln\left(x_{ktn}/x_{jsn}\right)\right].$$ (22.11)

As was the case with the construction of output aggregates, there are KT different choices of a base country, and so we follow the same strategy of taking a geometric average of these alternative choices of a base observation. Thus define X_{kt^*} as

$$X_{kt^*} \equiv \left[\prod_{j=1}^{K}\prod_{s=1}^{T} X_{kt/js}\right]^{\frac{1}{KT}}.$$ (22.12)

We follow the same convention as on the output side to define a set of *input-quantity aggregates, X_{kt}* relative to country 1 in year 1 as[18]

$$X_{kt} \equiv V_{11} X_{kt^*} / X_{11^*}.$$ (22.13)

Diewert and Morrison (1986, 663) showed that under their assumptions, a theoretical productivity index[19] between the production unit k at period t relative to the production unit j at period s, $\Gamma_{kt/js}$, was equal to the output ratio $Y_{kt/js}$ defined by (22.7) divided by the input ratio $X_{kt/js}$ defined by (22.11); that is, we have

$$\Gamma_{kt/js} \equiv Y_{kt/js} / X_{kt/js}.$$ (22.14)

As before, the bilateral productivity indexes defined by (22.14) are not transitive, and so they are made transitive by defining the ratio of the productivity of country k in period t to the geometric mean of all country TFP levels over all years, Γ_{kt^*}, as follows:[20]

$$\Gamma_{kt^*} \equiv \left[\prod_{j=1}^{K} \prod_{s=1}^{T} \Gamma_{kt/js} \right]^{\frac{1}{KT}} = Y_{kt^*} / X_{kt^*}. \tag{22.15}$$

The Γ_{kt^*} are analogs to the translog *multilateral productivity indexes* defined by CCD (1982a, 81). Again, for ease of interpretation, we replace the productivity levels defined by (11.22) by the following *normalized productivity levels* Γ_{kt}:

$$\Gamma_{kt} \equiv \left[Y_{kt^*} / X_{kt^*} \right] / \left[Y_{11^*} / X_{11^*} \right] = Y_{kt} / X_{kt}, \tag{22.16}$$

where Y_{kt} is defined by (22.10) and X_{kt} is defined by (22.13); that is, the KT normalized TFP levels, Γ_{kt}, defined by (22.16) are equal to the corresponding normalized output level Y_{kt} divided by the corresponding normalized input level X_{kt}.

This completes the exposition of our methodology for making cross-country comparisons of output, input, and productivity using the economic approach to index number theory when the output aggregate contains intermediate inputs. To determine whether the degree to which productivity levels differ, it is useful to, first, consider how to measure the level of "world" productivity[21] in each time period t. We define the world productivity level at time period t as the ratio of world output to world input, thus requiring a definition of world output and input. The multilateral output indexes, Y_{kt} defined by (22.10), are comparable across countries and time periods. Hence, it is meaningful to add them up to obtain aggregate measures of real output. Thus define *world output*, Y_t, as follows:

$$Y_t \equiv \sum_{k=1}^{K} Y_{kt}. \tag{22.17}$$

In a similar fashion, *world input*, X_t, is defined as the sum of the multilateral input aggregates X_{kt} defined by (22.13):

$$X_t \equiv \sum_{k=1}^{K} X_{kt}. \tag{22.18}$$

Define the country k share of world real input during period t, ω_{kt}, as

$$\omega_{kt} \equiv X_{kt} / \sum_{j=1}^{K} X_{jt}. \tag{22.19}$$

Finally, the level of *world productivity*, Γ_t, is defined as the ratio of world output to input. It is then straightforward to show that Γ_t is equal to an input-share-weighted average of the multilateral productivity indexes Γ_{kt} over all countries k for time period t:

$$\Gamma_t \equiv Y_t / X_t = \sum_{k=1}^{K} \omega_{kt} \Gamma_{kt}. \tag{22.20}$$

To assess the degree of convergence, I consider the dispersion of country productivity levels around world productivity levels. This is more commonly known as σ

-convergence (see Lichtenberg 1994 and Barro 2015). This can be seen as the productivity counterpart to measures of cross-country income inequality (Milanovic 2012), showing to what extent productivity levels are becoming more similar over time. We define the following input-weighted measure of productivity dispersion as

$$\sigma_t \equiv \left[\sum_{k=1}^{K} \omega_{kt} \ln\left(\Gamma_{kt} / \Gamma_t\right)^2 \right]^{1/2}.$$
(22.21)

Note that Γ_{kt}/Γ_t is the ratio of the productivity level of country k in period t to world average level of productivity in period t. If all country productivity levels are the same in period t, each Γ_{kt} will be equal to Γ_t and σ_t will be equal to 0; that is, there is complete productivity convergence.

22.3.2. Data

The approach to estimating industry productivity levels discussed in the previous section requires data on the input–output structure of each country over time and data on relative prices that can be used to infer relative industry output prices and input prices. For information on country input–output structures, I make use of the World Input-Output Database (WIOD). This is a source of harmonized input–output tables, covering 35 industries and 40 countries for the period 1995–2011. For our analysis, we omit Luxembourg and Indonesia due to data challenges. Still, the remaining 38 countries represent two-thirds of the world population and over 80% of world GDP and span much of the development spectrum, from India to the United States.

The construction and features of the WIOD are described in detail in Timmer, Dietzenbacher, Los, Stehrer, and de Vries (2015). The WIOD is constructed based on national supply and use tables (SUTs), combined with time series data from country National Accounts to ensure consistency with trends in industry output and overall economic activity. Importantly for analysis of global value chains, the SUTs are combined with data on trade in goods and services. This way, it is possible to distinguish the composition of intermediate inputs not only in terms of *what* products are used, but also *where* these products are produced and, in many cases, imported from. For the purposes of this chapter, though, this level of detail is not necessary, as only a distinction between domestically produced and imported intermediate inputs (from any country) is needed. Still, the fact that much effort has gone into harmonizing the industrial classifications across countries makes the WIOD ideally suited for this type of cross-country analysis.

The input–output data from WIOD include the net output and factor input values, the v_{ktm} and V_{ktn}. We additionally need information on relative prices to allow for comparisons of output and factor inputs, that is, the p_{ktm} and w_{ktn}. In part, these are drawn from the Socio-Economic Accounts (SEA) of WIOD. These provide information on the labor compensation and number of hours worked by workers who are high-skilled, medium-skilled, and low-skilled (based on their level of education) as well as on capital stocks.[22]

For computing prices of industry output (and hence domestically produced intermediate inputs), relative prices for consumption and investment are used. Consumption and investment prices are from the International Comparison Program (ICP), run by the World Bank, and we use the three surveys covering a global sample of countries that were done in the 1995–2011 period, namely for 1996, 2005, and 2011.[23] We use the most detailed publicly available data from each of these years and map consumption and investment categories to industries. Aggregating across expenditure categories is done using the CCD index. ICP prices are based on surveys of purchaser prices rather than producer prices, which means that differences in product taxes and distribution margins would lead to a bias in industry output prices. I therefore use tax and margin data from WIOD to adjust the ICP prices.[24] For years not covered by ICP survey data, we use industry deflators to interpolate (for, say, 2007) or extrapolate (e.g., 1995) relative prices, as in Feenstra, Inklaar and Timmer (2015).

For three of the services industries—government, health, and education—the ICP prices do not reflect the prices paid by purchasers of these services, since public provision or funding makes output prices hard or even impossible to observe. Instead, ICP aims to measure input prices (see Heston 2013). In our framework, this implies equal productivity levels across countries since relative "output" prices equal relative input prices. These industries are therefore excluded when analyzing productivity differences over time, just as they were in the previous section on growth differences. Similarly, the real estate industry is excluded, as (for the most part) its output is the imputed rental cost of owner-occupied housing, and the "private households with employed persons" industry is excluded as its dominant (sometimes only) input is labor (as well as incomplete coverage across countries). The remaining set of 30 industries will be referred to as the market economy.

In contrast to other industries, there is direct data on producer prices in agriculture, from the Food and Agricultural Organization (FAO). These have been widely used in studying productivity in agriculture, typically based on the relative prices estimated by Rao (1993).[25] For this analysis, I collected prices and production quantities for crops and livestock directly from FAO and aggregated these to overall agriculture relative output prices for each year using the CCD index.

The relative price of capital—estimated using equation (22.8)—requires data on investment prices, for which ICP prices can be used directly. The required rate of return is taken as the lending rate, taken from the International Monetary Fund (IMF) International Financial Statistics; the depreciation rates are from Penn World Table version 8.1, which provides country-level average depreciation rates in each year; and the investment price change is from WIOD. One drawback is that relative investment prices cover only fixed reproducible assets, thus omitting land. This omission can be particularly relevant for agriculture, so I also computed relative productivity using the procedure of Vollrath (2009). The results for cross-country differences in agricultural productivity over time are qualitatively similar to those presented in the following.

22.3.3. Results

To frame the context of the sectorial analysis, Figure 22.3 presents the trend in market economy productivity dispersion across the set of 38 countries covered in the analysis. As discussed earlier, the market economy refers to the aggregate of all industries except government, health and education, real estate, and households. Each country's (log) productivity level is multiplied by the share of factor inputs to give greater weight to (e.g.) China and less to (e.g.) Cyprus; see equation (2.21). The figure shows a substantial and fairly steady decline in the standard deviation, so that in 2011 it is 37% lower than it was in 1995.

Aggregate convergence is also found if weighting is omitted (−21%). Furthermore, the 38% decline in Figure 22.1 is both economically substantial and, using the T^3 test of Carree and Klomp (1997), statistically significant at the 10% level. Figure 22.3 also shows that the finding of convergence is a fairly continuous process, so the subsequent comparison will be done by comparing the dispersion in 2011 to that in 1995. Aggregate convergence is due in part to rapidly rising productivity levels in China (increasing from 18% to 40% of the 1995 US level) and India (39% to 45%). However, big increases in productivity are also seen in Turkey (38% to 49%) and in Central and Eastern Europe, in countries like Estonia (27% to 39%) and Poland (30% to 64%).

To analyze the sectorial pattern of convergence and how these contribute to aggregate convergence, I split the market economy into a traded and non-traded sector, where the traded sector encompasses agriculture, mining, and manufacturing, and the non-traded sector covers utilities, construction, and (market) services. Alternatively, I consider a split into the more traditional major sectors, distinguishing agriculture, manufacturing,

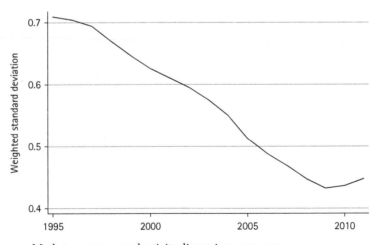

FIGURE 22.3. Market economy productivity dispersion, 1995–2011.

Notes: Productivity dispersion is measured as the standard deviation of log productivity levels, weighted using the share of each country in global factor inputs. Market economy covers all industries except government, health, education, real estate, and households.

Table 22.2 Productivity Dispersion in 1995 and 2011
             by Main Sectors

	1995	2011	% Change	
Market economy	0.709	0.448	−37	*
Traded sector	1.144	0.871	−24	*
Non-traded sector	0.373	0.347	−7	
Agriculture	0.822	0.703	−14	
Manufacturing	1.161	0.920	−21	
Market services	0.437	0.413	−5	
Other goods	0.328	0.233	−29	*

Notes: Table reports the standard deviation of log productivity levels, weighted using country shares in factor inputs.

* indicates that the indicated change is significant at the 10% level according to the T^3 test of Carree and Klomp (1997).

market services (transport, distribution, communication, hotels and restaurants, finance and business services), and other goods (mining, utilities, and construction). Table 22.2 summarizes this analysis and shows that productivity convergence is driven primarily by convergence in the traded sector. The major sector distinction shows that manufacturing and other goods showed notable convergence, with smaller declines in dispersion in agriculture and, particularly, market services.

Convergence analyses for OECD countries have typically shown that productivity in services converges more rapidly than manufacturing productivity; this was the main result of Bernard and Jones (1996), and van Biesebroeck (2009) has similar findings. In contrast, the study of manufacturing productivity for a much broader set of countries by Rodrik (2013) showed clear evidence of convergence. The results in Table 22.2 suggest that the convergence of productivity in services in OECD countries is specific to that group of countries or to the time period, rather than a more general result.[26] The sizable productivity dispersion in agriculture is consistent with the broader literature (e.g., Caselli 2005) and the relative lack of convergence in this sector shows that this large dispersion is a persistent factor.

22.3.4. Summing Up

Compared with the earlier analysis of the transatlantic growth gap, which came in a line of studies of industry productivity growth, this industry perspective on productivity convergence is a much less well-trodden path. As before, the analysis here plays, in part, a diagnostic role: Which industries are driving aggregate productivity convergence in this sample of countries? However, by confirming the result of Rodrik (2013) that manufacturing plays an important role in aggregate convergence, this analysis increases support for policies that aim to strengthen the role of manufacturing in the economy.

22.4. Determinants of Productivity Growth and Convergence

Given an increased understanding of the role of different sectors in aggregate convergence, it is useful to find potential determinants of productivity growth and, ideally, to better understand why convergence is stronger in some sectors and industries than in others. The differences in convergence shown in Table 22.2 are magnified when analyzing individual industries or countries. In the median industry, productivity dispersion decreased by 21%, similar to the market economy rate, but productivity dispersion in the textiles and wearing apparel industry decreased by 58%, while productivity dispersion in air transport increased by 24%. Indeed, 6 out of 30 industries showed divergence rather than convergence. Also, countries that show larger increases in their aggregate relative productivity levels tend to have more industries with increasing productivity levels, but the correlation is low at 0.09. This raises the question of what could be driving these differences.

To answer this question, I use the following general model used broadly in the "Schumpeterian" growth literature (Aghion et al. 2014):[27]

$$\Delta \ln\left(\frac{A_{ict}}{A_{ict-1}}\right) = \beta_1 \ln\left(\frac{A_{ict-1}}{A^F_{it-1}}\right) + \beta_2 X_{ict-1} + \beta_3 X_{ict-1} \times \ln\left(\frac{A_{ict-1}}{A^F_{it-1}}\right) + \eta_{ic} + \eta_t + \epsilon_{ict}. \quad (22.22)$$

In this equation, productivity growth for industry i in country c from year $t-1$ to year t is explained using the proximity to the productivity frontier—the productivity level in country c relative to the productivity level of the country with the highest productivity level at $t-1$, explanatory variable X and an interaction between X and the proximity to the productivity frontier.[28] In addition, a full set of country-industry dummies and year dummies is included. We would expect a negative coefficient for β_1, since a greater proximity to the productivity frontier implies fewer opportunities to achieve productivity growth by imitating frontier technologies.

The main interest is in coefficient β_3. If this coefficient is significantly different from zero, it implies that variable X has a different effect on productivity growth depending on the proximity to the productivity frontier. So, for example, Griffith et al. (2004) find that in countries that are closer to the frontier, research and development (R&D) spending contributes less to productivity growth, indicating that R&D spending helps both innovation (pushing out the frontier) and imitation (catching up to the frontier).

Table 22.3 Potential Determinants of Productivity Growth

Variable	Definition	Effect on Convergence	Source
High-skilled	The share of university-educated workers in total hours worked	− (Vandenbussche et al. 2006)	WIOD, SEA
High-tech M	Industry imports of intermediate inputs of chemicals, machinery, electronics, and transport equipment as a share of industry gross output	+ (Keller, 2004)	WIOD
R&D	Business enterprise research and development expenditure as a share of industry gross output	+ (Griffith et al. 2004)	OECD, Eurostat
FDI	Stock of inward foreign direct investment as a share of gross output	+ (Keller, 2004)	OECD, Eurostat
Lerner	Ratio of price over marginal cost	+ (Aghion et al. 2014)	INDICSER database

Note: WIOD, see www.wiod.org; INDICSER, see www.indicser.com. The (hypothesized) effect on convergence is positive if a higher value would lead to faster growth in industries that are farther from the frontier (or slower growth in industries close to the frontier).

Table 22.3 defines and describes the set of X-variables that are considered in the analysis. The first is the share of hours worked by high-skilled workers which, according to Vandenbussche et al. (2006), should contribute positively to productivity growth only in settings of close proximity to the frontier since more high-skilled workers would stimulate the rate of innovation.[29] The second is the share of high-tech imports. As the survey of Keller (2004) discusses, imports of more advanced inputs are an important source of technology transfer, so these imports would be expected to have a greater impact on productivity growth for industries that are farther from the productivity frontier.[30] Note that "high-tech" uses the OECD definition of high and medium-high technology industries. The third variable is R&D, which according to Griffith et al. (2004) would have a greater impact in industries farther from the productivity frontier since R&D helps both innovation and imitation. The fourth variable is foreign direct investment (FDI), which—again—following Keller (2004) could be a source of foreign technology and thus help growth in industries more distant from the frontier.[31] The final variable is the Lerner index, or price-cost margin, where a higher Lerner index implies less intensive competition. As discussed in Aghion et al. (2014), fiercer competition (so a lower Lerner index) would be particularly beneficial for industries close to the frontier, as those industries rely more on innovation for growth and (unless competition turns too cut-throat) competition is beneficial for growth.[32]

Given these predictions, equation (22.11) can be estimated for each of the variables of interest. As indicated in the equation, the regressions include dummies for each country/industry pair to account for unobserved heterogeneity and year dummies to account for common shocks. In addition, I use two further lags of the explanatory variables (so at $t-2$ and $t-3$) as instruments in a two-step Generalized Method of Moments procedure to reduce endogeneity concerns. Though more truly exogenous variables, such as the introduction of the European Single Market Program exploited by Griffith et al. (2010), would be preferable, these are typically hard to find. Finally, standard errors are clustered by country-industry pair to allow for correlation of errors within each cross-section.

Table 22.4 shows the results of the analysis. The first row shows industries that are closer to the productivity frontier grow less rapidly, though in the more limited samples for R&D (mostly manufacturing and omitting some emerging economies) and FDI (omitting some emerging economies) these are less significant. In the final column, the coefficient is not significantly different from zero and the sample covers only eight European economies after 2002. Turning to the explanatory variables, the table shows that high-tech imports, R&D, and FDI have a significant positive effect on productivity growth. This is a useful confirmation of the literature in these areas. Furthermore, given that high-tech imports and R&D are more important in manufacturing, and even more

Table 22.4 Explaining Productivity Growth and Convergence: Regression Results

	(1)	(2)	(3)	(4)	(5)
	High-Skilled	High-Tech M	R&D	FDI	Lerner
Proximity to the frontier	−0.0279***	−0.0334***	−0.0174*	−0.0185*	0.0369
	(0.00765)	(0.00755)	(0.00957)	(0.0108)	(0.0310)
Explanatory variable	−0.00123	0.162***	0.852***	0.00259**	−0.101
	(0.0386)	(0.0582)	(0.329)	(0.00103)	(0.201)
Interaction	−0.0276	0.0663	−0.478	−0.00283	−0.279
	(0.0338)	(0.0430)	(0.395)	(0.00254)	(0.216)
Observations	13,435	13,435	5,676	4,398	1,955
Overid. restrictions	0.727	0.404	0.129	0.197	0.0482

Notes: Each column represents a separate regression explaining productivity growth using the proximity to the productivity frontier, the explanatory variable that is identified in the column header and an interaction between the proximity to the frontier and the explanatory variable; see also equation (22.8) for the specification and Table 22.3 for definitions of the explanatory variables. Each regression includes country-industry dummies and year dummies and two lagged values of the independent variables are used as instruments in a two-step GMM procedure. Standard errors, clustered by country-industry pair, are in parentheses. "Overid. restrictions" gives the p-value of the Hansen J statistic on the overidentifying restrictions of all instruments.

*** $p < 0.01$, ** $p < 0.05$, * $p < 0.1$.

so in ICT manufacturing, these factors will clearly be important, whether in trying to close the transatlantic growth gap (Ortega-Argilés, 2012) or more broadly. However, these effects do not vary depending on the proximity to the productivity frontier. In fact, none of the interaction coefficients is significantly different from zero, thus failing to contribute to our understanding of why some industries show faster convergence than others.

If the results had shown that a particular variable had a stronger effect on productivity growth for industries farther from the frontier, this would have been clear evidence that this variable enhances the rate of convergence. A more indirect way would be if that variable has a direct effect on productivity growth and takes on higher values in industries farther from the frontier. The high-tech import share is negatively correlated with the proximity to the frontier but at −0.04, the relationship is weak. In contrast, R&D intensity is positively correlated with proximity to the frontier and, at 0.11, this relationship is somewhat stronger. So, if anything, the high-tech import share is a force of convergence, while R&D would lead to divergence. However, it is unclear whether these correlations have systematic drivers or are a coincidence.

To establish the robustness of the results in Table 22.4, I have considered that the industry proximity to the frontier could be measured with error and that, due to the persistence in this variable, this is not adequately addressed by using lagged values of industry proximity. In the first sensitivity analysis, I therefore use two lagged values of the aggregate proximity to the productivity frontier as instruments for industry proximity to the frontier. These are clearly weaker instruments, as indicated by first-stage F-statistics, and the pattern of results is the same.

In the second sensitivity analysis, I run the regressions for major sectors (i.e., subsets of industries, rather than all industries together). Specifically, I run regressions for manufacturing, market services and other goods (including agriculture, as well as mining, utilities, and construction). This provides some evidence that the impact of FDI varies with proximity to the frontier, but it is unclear why FDI would have a stronger effect on productivity growth when an industry is close to the productivity frontier in manufacturing and other goods production, but a weaker effect in market services.

22.4.1. Summing Up

The aim of this section was to establish why some industries show more rapid growth and convergence than others by testing whether a variety of variables have an effect on productivity growth and whether this effect differs in industries that are more distant from the productivity frontier. While some variables—R&D, FDI, and high-tech imports intensity—were indeed significantly related to productivity growth, others—high-skilled workers and competition—were not. More important, none of the variables showed a significantly different effect on productivity growth depending on the proximity to the productivity frontier.

So where should one look to better understand productivity convergence? It could be that the specification chosen here is not appropriate; for instance, it could be that learning takes place in proportion to actual trade or investment between specific countries (e.g., Keller 2004) instead of a common rate of learning from the frontier industry. Beyond that, a first set of alternative candidates are sector- or industry-specific regulations, such as import tariffs and other trade restrictions (e.g., Lileeva and Trefler 2010) or barriers to entry (Nicoletti and Scarpetta 2003). Other candidates are macro-level variables whose effects differ across industries, such as financial development (Rajan and Zingales 1998), infrastructure (Fernald 1999), or labor market institutions (Bassanini, Nunziata, and Venn 2009). A third possibility would be that a variable considered here has a different effect depending on some other variable that is related to, but not perfectly correlated with, (industry) productivity. For example, Alfaro et al. (2010) find that FDI has a larger effect on productivity in countries with a greater level of financial development.

22.5. DISCUSSION AND CONCLUSIONS

This chapter started with the question in which settings, industry-level productivity analysis has added value in the face of growing body of firm-level studies and academic and policy interest in economy-wide results. The aim of the three illustrations presented in this chapter has been to showcase not only some of strengths, but also the limitations, of industry-level productivity analysis. In terms of strengths, there is a clear role for industry-level analysis in diagnosing why overall (productivity) growth is faster in some countries than in others. As shown in the discussion of the transatlantic productivity growth, one may find that overall productivity growth is faster in one country than in another, but this can be for a multitude of reasons. And since firm-level analysis is typically not able to cover a considerable number of countries in a single study and because firm-level analysis typically does not cover all areas of the economy, industry-level analysis is the next best thing. In the case of productivity growth differences between the European Union and the United States, this showed that the United States gets most of its growth advantage for more rapid growth in the ICT production sector, but also that the productivity growth benefits from ICT use in the United States are less impressive or even absent compared to earlier vintages of the data. The other result is that distribution and trade is a sector where the European Union lags behind. This is an area where EU policy to strengthen the internal market may play an important role, as unified distribution systems and fewer restrictions on cross-border activity could lead to higher productivity. Though this is speculative, such a result can focus the attention of researchers and policymakers.

Similarly, in the broader cross-country setting, I strengthened the finding of Rodrik (2013) that convergence in manufacturing is a powerful force. My analysis has shown that this sector has made a clear contribution to the overall convergence of productivity among 38 major emerging and advanced economies. Finally, the analysis of the determinants of productivity growth has shown (again) the importance of R&D, FDI, and high-tech imports in fostering productivity growth. However, these play no systematic role in helping or hindering the pace of convergence. This means there is still a clear role for systematic industry-level analysis to better understand why, for example, manufacturing productivity converges and what governments may do to speed this process along.

On the limitations side, the analysis of productivity growth in the European Union and the United States has shown how some growth differences have not proven robust to changing times and measurement practices. Especially in the area of financial and business services, it has long been known that measurement of prices, and thus productivity, is challenging. Furthermore, cross-country differences in measurement can confound cross-country comparisons. This can be a reason to stay away from such sectors in research, but the fact that these services industries represent a large and growing part of economic activity should, in my view, be a spur to improve our state of knowledge and measurement.

So what may be learned from future industry-level research, and how? Especially for understanding growth in services industries, the industry level remains a relevant platform—judging in part by the absence of much firm-level research in this area. Furthermore, this is also the area where some of the newer "sources of growth" may originate, as the source of "intangible assets," such as new financial products, brand equity, and organization capital (Corrado and Hulten 2010). Understanding whether and how such assets contribute to growth requires a better understanding of these activities and how innovation takes place in, for example, management consulting. Beyond that, more careful consideration of how the regulatory environment has an impact on different industries in different countries remains important, especially in relation to policymakers.

NOTES

1. Though this bias is weaker than it used to be; see, for example, Foster, Haltiwanger, and Krizan (2006) with a micro-level perspective on productivity in retail trade; Adamopoulos and Restuccia (2014) on farm size and productivity; or Chandra, Finkelstein, Sacarny, and Syverson (2016) on productivity dispersion in hospitals.
2. The work of Hsieh and Klenow (2009) and Bartelsman, Haltiwanger, and Scarpetta (2013) are notable exceptions.
3. Linked employer-employee data, as used in, e.g., Utar (2014), are an important exception.
4. See also Ortega-Argilés (2012) for a survey on the transatlantic productivity (growth) gap.
5. To be precise, this refers to changes in the pace of total factor productivity growth; Stiroh (2002) had shown a similar result for labor productivity growth in ICT-intensive industries. See also Chapter 3 of this volume for additional analyses of US data.
6. See, e.g., Inklaar et al. (2008) or Inklaar and Wang (2011) specifically on measuring real output of banks.
7. The second and third application draw heavily on Inklaar (2015).

8. Though even when these conditions are not satisfied, aggregate TFP growth can be meaningful in tracking consumer welfare; see Basu, Pascali, Schiantarelli, and Servén (2014).

9. Data on the skill composition of the workforce can be typically be collected from household surveys, while a breakdown of industry investment by type of asset can be available either from detailed tabulations by statistical agencies or estimates by researchers based on additional surveys.

10. See O'Mahony and Timmer (2009) and Timmer, Inklaar, O'Mahony, and van Ark (2010) for a detailed description of the data, and see www.euklems.net for the data.

11. And even within the ICT production sector, the share of ICT manufacturing and ICT services are comparable, though in the United States the semiconductor industry is much more important and concentrated in products that have generated most TFP growth since 1995.

12. In the March 2007 version of the EU KLEMS database, the finance and business services industry showed an annual average TFP growth of 0.9 percent between 1995 and 2004. These numbers are from the *SIC*-based data set; the data set based off the newer NAICS industry classification system showed growth of 0.5 % for the finance and business services industry. In the March 2008 release, growth for the 1995–2004 period had declined to –0.2%. The data in the March 2013 release, used here, show growth for the 1995–2004 period of –0.7%. These revisions are primarily due to differences in value-added growth in more recent vintages of the GDP-by-industry accounts of the US Bureau of Economic Analysis.

13. See, e.g., Restuccia, Yang, and Zhu (2008), Vollrath (2009), Herrendorf and Valentinyi (2012), Lagakos and Waugh (2013), and Gollin, Lagakos, and Waugh (2014) on industry productivity differences; on structural change, see, e.g., Duarte and Restuccia (2010), McMillan and Rodrik (2011), and Herrendorf, Rogerson, and Valentinyi (2014).

14. See, e.g., Bernard and Jones (1996), Inklaar and Timmer (2009), and van Biesebroeck (2009) on industry-level convergence across OECD countries. See, e.g., Restuccia, Yang, and Zhu (2008), Vollrath (2009), and Gollin, Lagakos, and Waugh (2014) on the role of agricultural productivity; and see Rodrik (2013) on manufacturing.

15. If $y_m > 0$, then net output m is an output and y_m denotes the production of this commodity; if $y_m < 0$, then net output m is an intermediate input and y_m denotes the negative of the amount of this input that is used by the production unit.

16. Assuming that $v_{kt} = V_{kt}$ so that the data are consistent with the constant returns to scale assumption required for implementing the Diewert-Morrison methodology.

17. Note that equations (22.12) and (22.13) imply that $P_{11} = 1$ and $Y_{11} = v_{11}$.

18. Note that our normalizations will imply that $Y_{11} = X_{11} = v_{11} = V_{11}$.

19. Index number methods for computing productivity go back to Jorgenson and Griliches (1967).

20. $Y_{kt^*} \equiv v_{kt} \Big/ \left\{ P_{kt^*} \left[\Pi_{j=1}^{K} \Pi_{s=1}^{T} v_{js} \right]^{\frac{1}{KT}} \right\}.$

21. "World" productivity here means the productivity of the aggregate of the productivity levels of the K countries in the sample for each time period t.

22. Capital compensation is determined as value added minus labor compensation. Aggregate compensation and employment data from PWT are used to extrapolate data from the final year covered in the Socio-Economic Accounts to 2011; note that this extrapolation is only used to update cost shares, not for estimating industry productivity growth.

23. See World Bank (2008) for the description of the 2005 survey and results, and World Bank (2014) for the 2011 results.
24. See Inklaar and Timmer (2014) for more details on the mapping procedure and the adjustment for taxes and distribution margins.
25. Studies using these data are, e.g., Caselli (2005), Vollrath (2009), and Restuccia et al. (2008).
26. See, e.g., Inklaar et al. (2008) on diverging productivity growth patterns in market services across Europe and the United States after 1995.
27. See also, e.g., Inklaar et al. (2008) and McMorrow et al. (2010) for applications of this model to the setting of industry productivity growth in Europe.
28. In contrast to the "transatlantic growth gap" section, industry productivity growth here is (1) computed based on gross output rather than value added; and (2) relies on data from the WIOD's Socio-Economic Accounts (SEA), rather than EU KLEMS, to increase country coverage. The main difference between these two sources is that the SEA capital input variable is not based on the capital services concept, whereby assets with different marginal costs are weighted differently, but rather are based on a capital stock concept.
29. The work by Ang et al. (2011) shows that the results of Vandenbussche et al. (2006) are relevant not only for high-income but also for middle-income countries.
30. See also Cameron, Proudman, and Redding (2005).
31. See also Alfaro, Chanda, Kalemli-Ozcan, and Sayek (2010), Bloom, Sadun, and van Reenen (2012), and Cipollina, Giovannetti, Pietrovit, and Pozzolo (2012) with various perspectives on the role of FDI for productivity.
32. See also Griffith, Harrison, and Simpson (2010) for an industry-level analysis.

References

Adamopoulos, Tasso, and Diego Restuccia. 2014. "The Size Distribution of Farms and International Productivity Differences." *American Economic Review* 104(6): 1667–1697.

Aghion, Philippe, Ufuk Akcigit, and Peter Howitt. 2014. "What Do We Learn from Schumpeterian Growth Theory?" In *Handbook of Economic Growth*, edited by Philippe Aghion and Steven N. Durlauf, Vol. 2B, 515–563. Philadelphia: Elsevier.

Alfaro, Laura, Areendam Chanda, Sebnem Kalemli-Ozcan, and Selin Sayek. 2010. "Does Foreign Direct Investment Promote Growth? Exploring the Role of Financial Markets on Linkages." *Journal of Development Economics* 91: 242–256.

Ang, James B., Jakob B. Madsen, and Md. Rabiul Islam. 2011. "The Effects of Human Capital Composition on Technological Convergence." *Journal of Macroeconomics* 33: 405–476.

Barro, Robert J. (2015). "Convergence and Modernisation" *Economic Journal* 125: 911–942.

Bartelsman, Eric J., John Haltiwanger, and Stefano Scarpetta. 2013. "Cross-Country Differences in Productivity: The Role of Allocation and Selection." *American Economic Review* 103(1): 305–334.

Bassanini, Andrea, Luca Nunziata, and Danielle Venn. 2009. "Job Protection Legislation and Productivity Growth in OECD Countries." *Economic Policy* 24(58): 349–402.

Basu, Susanto, Luigi Pascali, Fabio Schiantarelli, and Luis Servén. 2014. "Productivity, Welfare and Reallocation: Theory and Firm-Level Evidence." NBER Working Paper No. 15579. http://www.nber.org/papers/w15579.

Bernard, Andrew B., and Charles I. Jones. 1996. "Comparing Apples to Oranges: Productivity Convergence and Measurement across Industries and Countries." *American Economic Review* 86(5): 1216–1238.

Bloom, Nicholas, Rafaela Sadun, and John van Reenen. 2012. "Americans Do IT Better: US Multinationals and the Productivity Miracle." *American Economic Review* 102(1): 167–201.

Cameron, Gavin, James Proudman, and Stephen Redding. 2005. "Technological Convergence, R&D, Trade and Productivity Growth." *European Economic Review* 49: 775–807.

Carree, Martin, and Luuk Klomp. 1997. "Testing the Convergence Hypothesis: A Comment." *Review of Economics and Statistics* 79: 683–686.

Caselli, Francesco. 2005. "Accounting for Cross-Country Income Differences." In *Handbook of Economic Growth*, edited by Philippe Aghion and Steven N. Durlauf, 679–741. Amsterdam: North-Holland.

Caves, Douglas W., Laurits R. Christensen, and W. Erwin Diewert. 1982a. "Multilateral Comparisons of Output, Input and Productivity Using Superlative Index Numbers." *Economic Journal* 92: 73–86.

Caves, Douglas W., Laurits R. Christensen, and W. Erwin Diewert. 1982b. "The Economic Theory of Index Numbers and the Measurement of Input, Output, and Productivity." *Econometrica* 50: 1392–1414.

Christensen, Laurits R., Dale W. Jorgenson, and Lawrence Lau. 1971. "Conjugate Duality and the Transcendental Logarithmic Production Function." *Econometrica* 39: 255–256.

Chandra, Amitabh, Amy Finkelstein, Adam Sacarny, and Chad Syverson. 2016. "Healthcare Exceptionalism? Productivity and Allocation in the U.S. Healthcare Sector." *American Economic Review* 106(8): 2110–2144.

Cipollina, Maria, Giorgia Giovannetti, Filomena Pietrovito, and Alberto F. Pozzolo. 2012. "FDI and Growth: What Cross-Country Industry Data Say." *The World Economy* 35(11): 1599–1629.

Corrado, Carol A., and Charles R. Hulten. 2010. "How Do You Measure a 'Technological Revolution'?" *American Economic Review: Papers & Proceedings* 100(3): 99–104.

Diewert, W. Erwin, and Catherine J. Morrison. 1986. "Adjusting Output and Productivity Indexes for Changes in the Terms of Trade." *Economic Journal* 96: 659–679.

Duarte, Margarida, and Diego Restuccia. 2010. "The Role of the Structural Transformation in Aggregate Productivity." *Quarterly Journal of Economics* 125(1): 129–173.

Feenstra, Robert C., and John Romalis. 2014. "International Prices and Endogenous Quality." *Quarterly Journal of Economics* 129(2): 477–527.

Feenstra, Robert C., Robert Inklaar, and Marcel P. Timmer. (2015). "The Next Generation of the Penn World Table." *American Economic Review* 105(10): 3150–3382.

Fernald, John G. 1999. "Roads to Prosperity? Assessing the Link Between Public Capital and Productivity." *American Economic Review* 89(3): 619–638.

Fernald, John G., and Charles I. Jones. 2014. "The Future of U.S. Economic Growth." *American Economic Review* 104(5): 44–49.

Foster, Lucia, John Haltiwanger, and C. J. Krizan. 2006. "Market Selection, Reallocation, and Restructuring in the U.S. Retail Trade Sector in the 1990s." *Review of Economics and Statistics* 88(4): 748–758.

Foster, Lucia, John Haltiwanger, and Chad Syverson. 2008. "Reallocation, Firm Turnover, and Efficiency: Selection on Productivity or Profitability?" *American Economic Review* 98(1): 394–425.

Gollin, Douglas, David Lagakos, and Michael E. Waugh. 2014. "The Agricultural Productivity Gap." *Quarterly Journal of Economics* 129(2): 939–993.

Gordon, Robert J. 2000. "Does the "New Economy" Measure up to the Great Inventions of the Past?" *Journal of Economic Perspectives* 14(4): 49–74.

Griffith, Rachel, Rupert Harrison, and Helen Simpson. 2010. "Product Market Reform and Innovation in the EU." *Scandinavian Journal of Economics* 112(2): 389–415.

Griffith, Rachel, Stephen Redding, and John van Reenen. 2004. "Mapping the Two Faces of R&D: Productivity Growth in a Panel of OECD Industries." *Review of Economics and Statistics* 86(4): 883–895.

Herrendorf, Berthold, and Ákos Valentinyi. 2012. "Which Sectors Make Poor Countries So Unproductive?" *Journal of the European Economic Association* 10(2): 323–341.

Herrendorf, Berthold, Richard Rogerson, and Ákos Valentinyi. 2014. "Growth and Structural Transformation." In *Handbook of Economic Growth*, edited by Philippe Aghion and Steven N. Durlauf, Vol. 2B, 855–941. Amsterdam: Elsevier.

Heston, Alan. 2013. "Government Services: Productivity Adjustments," In *Measuring the Real Size of the World Economy*, edited by the World Bank. 413–440.Washington, DC: World Bank.

Hsieh, Chang-Tai, and Peter J. Klenow. 2009. "Misallocation and Manufacturing TFP in China and India." *Quarterly Journal of Economics* 124(4): 1403–1448.

Hulten, Charles R. 2010. "Growth Accounting." In *Handbook of the Economics of Innovation*, edited by Bronwyn H. Hall and Nathan Rosenberg, Vol. 2, 987–1031. Amsterdam: Elsevier/North Holland.

Inklaar, Robert. 2015. "Searching for Convergence and Its Causes: An Industry Perspective." In *The World Economy: Growth or Stagnation?*, edited by Dale W. Jorgenson, Kyoji Fukao, and Marcel P. Timmer, 508–534. Cambridge: Cambridge University Press.

Inklaar, Robert, and W. Erwin Diewert. 2016. "Measuring Industry Productivity and Cross-Country Convergence." *Journal of Econometrics* 191(2): 426–433.

Inklaar, Robert, and Marcel P. Timmer. 2009. "Productivity Convergence across Industries and Countries: The Importance of Theory-Based Measurement." *Macroeconomic Dynamics* 13(S2): 218–240.

Inklaar, Robert, and Marcel P. Timmer. 2014. "The Relative Price of Services." *Review of Income and Wealth* 60(4): 727–746.

Inklaar, Robert, Marcel P. Timmer, and Bart van Ark. 2008. "Market Services Productivity across Europe and the US." *Economic Policy* 23(53): 139–194.

Inklaar, Robert, and J. Christina Wang. 2011. "Real Output of Bank Services: What Counts Is What Banks Do, Not What They Own." *Economica* 80(317): 96–117.

Jorgenson, Dale W. 2005. "Accounting for Growth in the Information Age." In *Handbook of Economic Growth*, edited by Phillipe Aghion and Steven N. Durlauf, Vol. 1A, 743–815. Amsterdam: Elsevier/North Holland.

Jorgenson, Dale W., and Zvi Griliches. 1967. "The Explanation of Productivity Change." *Review of Economic Studies* 34: 249–283.

Jorgenson, Dale W., Mun S. Ho, and Kevin J. Stiroh. 2005. *Information Technology and the American Growth Resurgence*. Cambridge, MA: MIT Press.

Jorgenson, Dale W., and Kevin J. Stiroh. 2000. "Raising the Speed Limit: US Economic Growth in the Information Age." *Brookings Papers on Economic Activity* 1: 125–211.

Keller, Wolfgang. 2004. "International Technology Diffusion." *Journal of Economic Literature* XLII: 752–782.

Lagakos, David, and Michael E. Waugh. 2013. "Selection, Agriculture, and Cross-Country Productivity Differences." *American Economic Review* 103(2): 948–980.

Lichtenberg, Frank R. 1994. "Testing the Convergence Hypothesis." *Review of Economics and Statistics* 76(3): 576–579.

Lileeva, Alla, and Daniel Trefler. 2010. "Improved Access to Foreign Markets Raises Plant-Level Productivity . . . for Some Plants." *Quarterly Journal of Economics* 125(3): 1051–1099.

Malmquist, Sten (1953), "Index Numbers and Indifference Surfaces", *Trabajos de Estastistica* 4, 209–242.

McMillan, Margaret S., and Dani Rodrik. 2011. "Globalization, Structural Change and Productivity Growth." In *Making Globalization Socially Sustainable*, edited by Mark Bachetta and Marion Jansen, 49–84. Geneva: International Labor Organization.

McMorrow, Kieran, Werner Röger, and Alessandro Turrini. 2010. "Determinants of TFP Growth: A Close Look at Industries Driving the EU-US TFP Gap." *Structural Change and Economic Dynamics* 21: 165–180.

Milanovic, Branko. 2012. "Global Inequality Recalculated and Updated: The Effect of New PPP Estimates on Global Inequality and 2005 Estimates." *Journal of Economic Inequality* 10: 1–18.

Nicoletti, Giuseppe, and Stefano Scarpetta. 2003. "Regulation, Productivity and Growth: OECD Evidence." *Economic Policy* 18(36): 9–72.

Oliner, Stephen D., and Daniel E. Sichel. 2000. "The Resurgence of Growth in the Late 1990s: Is Information Technology the Story?" *Journal of Economic Perspectives* 14(4): 3–22.

O'Mahony, Mary, and Marcel P. Timmer. 2009. "Output, Input and Productivity Measures at the Industry Level: The EU KLEMS Database." *Economic Journal* 119: F374–F403.

Ortega-Argilés, Raquel. 2012. "The Transatlantic Productivity Gap: A Survey of the Main Causes." *Journal of Economic Surveys* 26(3): 395–419.

Rajan, Raghuram G., and Luigi Zingales. 1998. "Financial Dependence and Growth." *American Economic Review* 88(3): 559–586.

Rao, D. S. Prasada. 1993. "Intercountry Comparisons of Agricultural Output and Productivity." FAO Economic and Social Development Paper No. 112. http://www.fao.org/fileadmin/templates/ess/ess_test_folder/World_Census_Agriculture/Publications/FAO_ESDP/ESDP_112_Intercountry_comparisons_of_agricultural_output_and_productivity.pdf.

Restuccia, Diego, Dennis Tao Yang, and Xiaodung Zhu. 2008. "Agriculture and Aggregate Productivity: A Quantitative Cross-Country Analysis." *Journal of Monetary Economics* 55: 234–250.

Rodrik, Dani. 2013. "Unconditional Convergence in Manufacturing." *Quarterly Journal of Economics* 128(1): 165–204.

Stiroh, Kevin J. 2002. "Information Technology and the US Productivity Revival: What Do The Industry Data Say?" *American Economic Review* 92(5): 1559–1576.

Syverson, Chad. 2011. "What Determines Productivity?" *Journal of Economic Literature* 49(2): 326–365.

Theil, Henri. 1967. *Economics and Information Theory*. Amsterdam: North Holland.

Timmer, Marcel P., Erik Dietzenbacher, Bart Los, Robert Stehrer, and Gaaitzen J. de Vries. 2015. "An Illustrated Guide to the World Input-Output Database: The Case of Global Automotive Production." *Review of International Economics* 23: 575–605.

Timmer, Marcel P., and Bart van Ark. 2005. "Does Information and Communication Technology Drive EU-US Productivity Growth Differentials?" *Oxford Economic Papers* 57: 693–716.

Timmer, Marcel P., Robert Inklaar, Mary O'Mahony, and Bart van Ark. 2010. *Economic Growth in Europe: A Comparative Industry Perspective*. Cambridge: Cambridge University Press.

Utar, Hale. 2014 "When the Floodgates Open: 'Northern' Firms' Response to Removal of Trade Quotas on Chinese Goods." *American Economic Journal: Applied Economics* 6(4): 226–250.

van Ark, Bart, Mary O'Mahony, and Marcel P. Timmer. 2008. "The Productivity Gap Between Europe and the United States: Trends and Causes." *Journal of Economic Perspectives* 22: 25–44.

Van Biesebroeck, Johannes. 2009. "Disaggregate Productivity Comparisons: Sectoral Convergence in OECD Countries." *Journal of Productivity Analysis* 32: 63–79.

Vandenbussche, Jérôme, Philippe Aghion, and Costas Meghir. 2006. "Growth, Distance to Frontier and Composition of Human Capital." *Journal of Economic Growth* 11: 97–127.

Vollrath, Dietrich. 2009. "How Important Are Dual Economy Effects for Aggregate Productivity?" *Journal of Development Economics* 88(2): 325–334.

World Bank. 2008. *Global Purchasing Power Parities and Real Expenditures: 2005 International Comparison Program.* Washington, DC: World Bank.

World Bank. 2014. *Purchasing Power Parities and the Real Size of World Economies: A Comprehensive Report of the 2011 International Comparison Program.* Washington, DC: World Bank.

CHAPTER 23

......

PRODUCTIVITY AND ECONOMIC DEVELOPMENT

......

HAK K. PYO

23.1. INTRODUCTION

THE title of this chapter was revised from "Productivity and Economic Growth" to "Productivity and Economic Development" to reflect two recent trends in growth and development literature after the proliferation of new growth theory. One trend is reflected in Bardhan (1995), who argues that notwithstanding popular impressions to the contrary, the advances made thus far in the new literature on growth theory (over and above its discovery, with great fanfare, of some of the insights of the old development literature) have barely scratched the surface. He further argues that while new emphasis on fixed costs and non-convexities in the process of introduction of new goods and technologies is important, these fixed costs actually go far beyond the ordinary setup costs in a developing country. He proposes devoting more attention to the organizational-institutional issues and distributive conflicts in the development process, which are less amenable to neat formalization. Bardhan's proposal was followed up by Rodrik (2003), Isaksson et al. (2005), and Acemoglu and Robinson (2012), who searched for deeper determinants of productivity growth, such as institutions and social capital, in addition to technology and human capital. The other trend is to link productivity growth and development with distribution of income and wealth, which is by nature a development issue rather than a growth issue. Alesina and Perotti (1996) and Barro (2000) had initiated the search for the relationship between inequality and growth. It was followed by literature on pro-poor growth, such as Ravallion and Chen (2003) and the Swedish International Development Cooperation Agency (SIDA) (2006), and inclusive growth, such as Commission on Growth and Development (2008) and World Bank (2008). This line of research on pro-poor growth and inclusive growth has been accelerated after the global financial crisis in the form of wage-led growth theories in

Lavoie and Stockhammer (2012) and empirical researches such as Hein and Tarassow (2010) and Onaran and Galanis (2012).

As Isaksson et al. (2005) point out, any international organization dealing with economic development is concerned with the question of how to generate per capita growth. This is not because growth is synonymous with economic development. However, if it did not have the backdrop of per capita growth, neither sizable nor long-term development could be possible. Isaksson et al. (2005, 2) further point out that growth comes from the conjunction of, on the one hand, the accumulation of endowments, and, on the other, productivity gains. Looking at a cross-country variation of income per worker, empirical studies find that the majority of the differences in level and most of the differences in growth rate can be explained by differences in productivity (the rest being attributable to differences in physical and human capital). In Organisation for Economic Co-operation and Development (OECD) countries, productivity gains contribute to about half of growth. In developing countries, too, productivity is an important component of growth. Admittedly, in the first stage of development, productivity is not nearly as important as accumulation. Yet, it is far from negligible. In short, growth at the intensive margin is limited by productivity gains at the extensive margin.

Acemoglu (2008, 768–769) argues that economic development is intimately linked to economic growth, but it may require different, even specialized, models that do not focus only on balanced growth and the orderly growth behavior captured by the neoclassical and endogenous technology models. He distinguishes between structural change, such as changes in the composition of production and employment, and structural transformation, such as changes in the organization and efficiency of production accompanying the process of development. Noting that the current growth literature is far from a satisfactory framework, he emphasizes the development of a unified theoretical framework for understanding the process of development and an approach that can make contact with and benefit from the wealth of evidence collected by the empirical development literature (Acemoglu 2008, 695).

After the global financial crisis in 2007–2008, the productivity growth in major advanced countries has continued to decline, and income and wealth inequality has worsened, as observed by Piketty (2014a) and Milanovic (2012, 2016). Piketty (2014a), after extensive examination of historical data on income and wealth in advanced countries, has initiated research on the trend in global inequality and has concluded that the history of the distribution of wealth has always been deeply political and thus cannot be reduced to purely economic mechanisms, and that the dynamics of wealth distribution reveal powerful mechanisms pushing alternately toward convergence and divergence. Milanovic (2016), after examining the household income panel data set across the world by Lakner and Milanovic (2015) has shown a so-called elephant curve describing how much richer each part of the global income distribution of 2008 was compared to the same part of the distribution in 1988. It shows a very strong income growth for the global middle class (for example, China) and the global top 1%, but a stagnation of incomes over a 20-year period (1988–2008) by the lower middle class of the rich world (US and

UK). This is linked to the political economy of the Great Britain's Brexit and the heated debate on the shrinking middle class in the US presidential race in 2016.

In what follows in section 23.2, we review the literature on productivity and development following the first trend, which is the theoretical and empirical searches for determinants of productivity for development beyond the endogenous growth theory. Section 23.3 reviews the second trend in development literature, which focuses on the distribution of income and wealth that results from productivity and development. We also examine how productivity growth and growth rate is related to capital/income ratio and inequality of income and wealth in the long-run steady-state growth path of a capitalist economy. Section 23.4 summarizes the discussions on inclusive development and the debate on income-led growth versus profit-led growth and country narratives. The last section (23.5) summarizes important research outcomes and analytics since the new growth theory and reviews future research topics on productivity and development.

23.2. PRODUCTIVITY AND DEVELOPMENT AFTER NEW GROWTH THEORY

Rodrik (2003), in his introduction to the book *In Search of Prosperity: Analytic Narratives on Economic Growth*, observes the spectacular gap in incomes between the world's rich and poor nations; he notes that the starting points for all these countries were not so far apart prior to the Industrial Revolution and that these disparities must be attributed almost entirely to differences in long-term growth rates of per capita income. He concludes that the difference in productivity growth almost determines the fate of countries' development. He argues that both conventional growth models and new endogenous growth models have been increasingly replaced with attempts to shed light on the diversity of experience with economic growth. One new trend after the new growth theory is to search for deeper determinants of income growth in addition to endogenous determinants such as factor endowments and productivity. He defines such determinants as partly endogenous determinants, such as trade and institutions, and exogenous determinants, such as geography. The search for deeper determinants means an increasing trend to rely on determinants for economic development beyond per capita income growth. He distinguishes between the "proximate" and "deep" determinants of growth and defines factor endowments and productivity as endogenous proximate determinants for income generation. The deeper determinants are geography (which relates to a country's physical location), trade regime (which is the country's integration with world markets), and institutions such as property rights, regulatory structures, and the judiciary and bureaucratic capacity. He then categorizes trade and institutions as partly endogenous factors coevolving with economic performance and the country's policy choices, and identifies geography as the only exogenous factor. He also notes that moderate changes in country-specific circumstances (policies and institutional arrangements) can produce discontinuous changes in economic performances, setting off virtuous or vicious cycles. He takes China and India during the last two decades as examples of the virtuous cycle that have gone through remarkable transformations. The stagnation of the Philippines and Bolivia in the 1980s and the very sharp divergence in the performance of the former socialist economies are the examples of the vicious cycle.

Griliches (1998), who pioneered the search for new determinants in productivity growth, found that econometric studies underestimated the full contribution of research and development (R&D), especially since it is difficult to trace its spillover effects. He argued that a recent study found a significant contribution of R&D to productivity growth in the largest US manufacturing corporations, and a larger role for basic research and a smaller one for federally financed R&D expenditures than is implied by their relative importance in total R&D expenditures. In the little time that he had before passing away in 1999, Griliches had made three points on perspectives on the sources of productive growth. The first point is that there are several productivity-enhancing activities, such as general education, specific training, health investments, and R&D, that are not included in national accounts. The second point is that longer-term productivity growth comes from the discovery of new resources, the creation of new knowledge in science and industrial R&D labs, the diffusion of knowledge and technology, and the elimination of various legal and social barriers to efficiency. The third point concerns the measurement of the production and dissemination of information and new knowledge and science, which are intangible by nature.

After an extensive historical review of development in productivity and economic growth, Jorgenson (1990, 90) concludes,

> We do not have to go all the way back to Adam Smith to appreciate benefits of a division of labor. Accountants can design systems that are adapted to modeling, econometricians can develop models based on consistent systems of accounts and sound conceptualization, and theorists can choose a level of abstraction appropriate to applications in accounting and econometric modeling. [. . .] The view of economic growth that is now coming into focus is very different from the picture based on Douglas's fateful abstraction of the aggregate production function. While this new perspective represents important scientific progress, additional challenges are constantly emerging, even in this much studied area. The research opportunities that have been created are more than sufficient to utilize the combined talents of a legion of national accountants, econometricians, and economic theorists for the next half century and beyond.

The Solow (1957) decomposition of output growth by changes of observable inputs and the residual has served as the standard measurement of total factor productivity (TFP) since it avoids restrictive assumptions regarding the production technology, statistical models, or econometric specifications. However, due to the fact that the capital stock is basically unobservable, it must be imputed from the unknown initial conditions and the cumulated past investments, even after assuming the retirement pattern, depreciations, and capacity utilization. While the perpetual inventory method (PIM) has been widely used as the standard capital measurement for the OECD and national accounting agencies in practice, the measurement error in capital became more serious for developing and transition countries, as noted by Ward (1976), and for new types of capital such R&D, information and communications technology (ICT), and intangible and public capital, as noted by Triplett (1999). For these reasons, there were alternative measurements of capital and TFP proposed by Dadkhah and Zahedi (1986), Young (1995), Pyo (2008) as reviewed in OECD (2009), and Burda and Severgnini (2014).

On the empirical research side, the relationship between productivity and economic growth and development has been centered on the OECD countries. However, Deininger and Squire (1998), Rodrik (2003), Kraay (2004), and Isaksson et al. (2005) are a few studies dealing with non-OECD countries for income inequality, country reports, and analytic narratives on economic growth. Isaksson et al. (2005, 3–4) argue that productivity is key to raising living standards, to poverty reduction, and to a sound environment, and they summarize the role of productivity in development as follows:

> Without productivity growth there would be no social advancement. From a welfare point of view, the economy would tend to a situation such that the utility of the increment of income would be offset by the disutility of the increment of efforts. In other words, without productivity gains, one hand would give away all the welfare that the other receives. Without productivity gains there cannot be welfare gains. Yet, it must be admitted that productivity gains are only the wherewithal to welfare improvement. Economic mechanisms may offer a productivity outcome and propose a distribution between consumers (by way of price reductions) and factors connected to production (by way of remuneration of their services). But how this distribution will actually occur, and how effectively it will be directed to welfare improvement, is another story. Here, it is the interplay of socio-political processes that will have the last word.

While the new growth theory has provided a theoretical ground for the search for new sources of growth, the development and proliferation of ICT has created a new dimension on productivity and development on a worldwide scale. The development of ICT industries was made after the post-1973 productivity slowdown in the United States and Europe.

According to the US Department of Labor, Bureau of Labor Statistics (1998), multi-factor productivity (MFP) and labor productivity of the United States grew at the rate of 1.9% and 2.9%, respectively, between 1948 and 1973. But there was a marked productivity slowdown after 1973 to the growth rate of 0.2% and 1.1%, respectively. Triplett (1999) notes that similar slowdowns have been observed in most of the industrialized economies of the OECD. He observes that in 1997, investment in information-processing equipment accounted for about 34% of producer durable equipment investment, which is more than the share of industrial machinery (22%). Then in 1987, Solow's aphorism followed: "You can see the computer age everywhere but in the productivity statistics." This is called the Solow paradox: Why has US output not grown faster as investment in computers grows rapidly and widely? Triplett (1999) summarizes seven explanations for the paradox:

(1) Computers and information-processing equipment are a relatively small share of gross domestic product (GDP) and of the capital stock.
(2) Government hedonic price indexes for computers fall "too fast" and therefore, measured real computer output growth is also "too fast."
(3) The outputs of heavy users of information technology such as finance and insurance are poorly measured.
(4) Some of what computers do, such as consumption on the job, convenience, better user-interface, and so forth, are not counted in economic statistics.
(5) The productivity implications of a new technology are only visible with a long lag, like the diffusion of electricity.
(6) Computers are not as productive as one thinks, and computer and software design has taken a wrong turn.
(7) There is no paradox: some economists are counting innovations and new products on an arithmetic scale, when they should count on a logarithmic scale.

Triplett (1999) argues that the post-1973 productivity slowdown may have something to do with the supposed recent shift from a goods economy to a services economy—from an economy where information was less abundant and less costly to an "information economy." The fifth explanation of the long-lag hypothesis of a new technology seems the most persuasive one.

Krueger (1993) finds that the increased inequality in income and earnings distributions in the United States between workers who use computers and workers who do not is connected with the growth of computers. On the other hand, there is an alternative view that computers which substitute for human capital are reducing the demand for skill in jobs. We have to ask ourselves what happened to the ICT investments in non-OECD countries and whether we observe the same Solow paradox and a digital divide. Researchers on ICT contributions such as Jorgenson and Vu (2005) and Fukao et al. (2012) and those on intangible assets (such as R&D, intellectual property rights, and business rights) such as Corrado et al. (2009), Miyagawa and Shoich (2013), and Chun et. al.(2016) have initiated studies on the significant impacts of ICT and intangible investments on growth and development of not only OECD countries, but also some non-OECD countries on a limited scale. The issue of digital divide within a country and between the rich nations and the poor nations has sparked research on productivity and inequality and inclusive development, such as the report of Commission on Growth and Development (2008). The prolonged economic recovery after the global financial crisis in 2007–2008 and the stagnation in world economy in the subsequent post-crisis period have provoked a debate on income-led growth versus profit-led growth.

Isaksson et al. (2005, 2) stress that development could be possible without growth. A modicum of development could be implemented without any growth, by the mere rearrangement of available resources. Accumulation fuels growth by putting more inputs at work in the economy. Productivity gains enhance the ability of economic agents to transform these inputs into output. Without productivity gains, growth would be subject to the physical limitations imposed by demography and the supply of natural resources, and to the limitation that the savings rate places on the growth of capital equipment. With productivity, these constraints are no longer binding. In OECD countries, productivity gains contribute to about half of growth. In developing countries, too, productivity is an important component of growth. Beyer and Vergara (2002) have calculated that about two-thirds of the variance in growth rates observed among 107 countries between 1980 and 2000 is due to variations in the rate of TFP growth.

Lucas (1988) offers an ingenious rule of thumb to concretize what growth can do for development: an economy (country) that grows at the rate g sees its income per capita double after $70/g$ years. Doubling income per capita is not development, but it means a lot of resources for development. A growth rate of 1% would make that contribution available in 70 years; with 4%, a little less than 18 years is needed. Productivity being one of the sources of growth, it is clear that productivity enhancement translates into a higher g. This is why anyone interested in development would value any contribution, however modest, that productivity could make to growth. Moreover, part of the growth that apparently comes from accumulation should actually be ascribed to productivity (high productivity will probably determine an increase of output, hence of savings and capital formation). Anyway, in the long run, accumulation meets the limits set by its very success. The supply of labor loses elasticity, and the law of diminishing returns to capital sets in. It is then the turn of productivity to take the driver's seat. An indicator of how productivity actually drives the economy is the extent to which productivity explains the variations of economic growth among countries. In other words, it is the rate of TFP growth that determines whether there will be a bad or a good period of economic growth. Productivity, in sum, is a facet of growth. At the end of the day, to study productivity is much the same as to study growth, which spurs development.

23.3. ANALYTICS ON PRODUCTIVITY AND DEVELOPMENT WITH INEQUALITY

One of the remarkable contributions of the new growth theory to understanding development is the fact that it has opened up the avenue and enlarged the scope for examining the relationship between productivity and development. One of the factors limiting the economy's transformation that often has been secondary in the standard growth literature is the distribution of income and wealth. In this context, we review two lines of research on the relationship between productivity and development considering inequality in income and wealth as a major cause of development traps.

One line of research is pioneered by Piketty (2014a), who observes from historical data in advanced economies and emerging market economies a strong tendency toward a rise in inequality on the distribution of wealth and income, which limits a sustainable healthy capitalist development. He proposes a progressive income tax and a wealth tax to avoid inheritance capitalism, and he argues that the only exit from destructive capitalist development is to increase productivity and fertility. The other line of research is to find the clues for avoiding falling into development traps in the tradition of the neoclassical growth model, but highlighting a range of issues that are often secondary in the study of growth analysis. Jones (2015) revisits the issue of income and wealth inequality in the context of macroeconomic theories linking the Pareto distribution more explicitly to the Piketty propositions. Milanovic (2012, 2016) re-examines global inequality in the context of globalization. Acemoglu (2008, 758–764) introduces several models focusing on the link between various aspects of development and inequality. He introduces the models of class conflicts, credit market imperfections, and human capital to explain how different aspects of developmental problems can promote inequality and how inequality interacts with these development traps. In what follows, we review both of these lines of research.

23.3.1. Historical Observations on Inequality and Development

Piketty (2014a, 47–49) defines "national wealth" or "national capital" (K) as the total market value of everything owned by the residents and government of a given country at a given point in time, provided that it can be traded on some market. Therefore, it excludes human capital but includes "immaterial" (or intangible) capital, such as patents and other intellectual property, stock market capitalization of corporate reputation and trademarks, and so on. National capital is composed of domestic capital and net foreign capital. It is also composed of physical capital and financial capital. National capital also uses net concept, and therefore it is mostly composed of physical assets because the financial assets are netted out by financial liabilities. He defines the share of capital income from the following accounting identity:

$$\alpha = r \times K / Y = r \times \beta \tag{23.1}$$

where α is the share of capital income and β is the capital/income ratio. The capital/income ratio (β) is related to the share of income from capital in national income (α) and is a measure of how intensely capitalistic the society in question is. It should be noted that the capital/income ratio is the reciprocal of income/capital ratio that measures partial productivity of capital. In other words, the rising capital/income ratio implies the falling productivity of capital and the "U-shaped curve" of capital/income ratio is identical to the inversely U-shaped curve of income/capital ratio. Therefore, if the rising capital/income ratio matters, then the falling income/capital ratio also matters. In short, the divergence in wealth distribution implies declining capital productivity.

Since the formula (23.1) is a pure accounting identity, it can be applied to all societies in all periods of history, by definition. It should nevertheless be regarded as a simple, transparent relationship among the three most important concepts for analyzing the capitalist system: the capital/income ratio, the share of capital in income, and the rate of return on capital. The formula tells us nothing about the subtleties of how these three variables are determined, but tells us how to relate these three variables for framing discussion. It also tells us that these three variables are not independent but are linked by one identity, and therefore, the degree of freedom is not three but two.

Piketty (2014a) observes the "U-shaped curve" of the capital/income ratio historically through time from US (1910–2010), European (Germany, France, and Britain for the period 1870–2010), and world data (1870–2010). He notes that the very high level of private wealth in Europe in the late nineteenth century hovered around six or seven years of national income. Then the ratio fell sharply to the level of two or three in response to the shocks of the period 1914–1945. The return of high capital/income ratios was observed from 1950 on, and now the ratio reaches five or six years of national income in both Britain and France. Piketty projects the world capital/income ratio might reach 700% by the end of the twenty-first century. He argues that the return of high capital/income ratios over the past few decades can be explained in large part by the return to a regime of relatively slow growth. Piketty (2014a, 170) starts at the beginning of his book simply explaining the dynamics of the capital/income ratio, but moves on in Part Three to explaining how it is related to the question of wealth distribution. He argues that the rising capital/income ratio signals rising inequality of income and wealth because capital income is more unequally distributed than labor income, so that rising capital growth due to inheritance relative to stagnant income growth has made the inequality of income and wealth worse.

Piketty (2014a, 166–168) demonstrates that avoiding excessive inequality through maintaining lower capital/income ratio is essential to maintaining positive growth in productivity and a sustainable capitalist development. He shows that in the long run, the capital/income ratio (β) is related to the savings rate (s) and the growth rate (g) according to the following formula, which he calls the second fundamental law of capitalism.

$$\beta = s / g \qquad (23.2)$$

Piketty's own derivation, based on a basic mathematical equation describing wealth accumulation, is available on his website as "Technical Appendix" (Piketty 2014b). The other alternative derivation is available in Pyo (2015), who uses the neoclassical growth models like Solow (1956), and Barro and Sala-i-Martin (2004).

Piketty (2014a, 227–228) notes this last expression of the second fundamental law of capitalism, which is the application of the first and the second fundamental laws to Marx's principle of infinite accumulation: capitalists accumulate ever increasing quantities of capital, which ultimately leads to a falling rate of return on capital and eventually to their own downfall. He argues that it is equivalent to consider the dynamic law $\beta = s / g$ in the special case where the growth rate g is zero or very close to zero. Piketty (2014a, 25) shows that the return of high capital/income ratios over the past few decades can be explained in large part by the return to a regime of relatively slow growth. In slowly growing economies, past wealth naturally takes on disproportionate importance because it takes only a small flow of new savings to increase the stock of wealth steadily and substantially. If, moreover, the rate of return on capital remains significantly above the growth rate for an extended period of time, then the risk of divergence in the distribution of wealth is very high. He shows that the long-run growth rate of economy depends on productivity growth (v) and population growth (n). He argues that in the long run the only exit from the destructive forces of infinite accumulation of capital in an economy without population growth is to maintain positive productivity growth. The second fundamental law of capitalism is thus related to the long-run issue of the relationship between productivity and development with consideration of inequality. He proposes a progressive income tax and a wealth tax to avoid inheritance capitalism, and he argues that the only exit from destructive capitalist development is to increase productivity and fertility.

23.3.2. Inequality and Development in the Neoclassical Tradition

While the Piketty propositions have been interpreted in the preceding subsection by relying on the neoclassical models of Solow and Phelps, they are rooted in a non-neoclassical European tradition of long-run historical empirical studies, rather than mechanics of growth models. There has been a large flow of literature which demonstrates that the relationship between inequality and development can be investigated within the tradition of neoclassical growth models.

Jones (2015) revisits the issue of income and wealth inequality in the context of macroeconomic theories linking the Pareto distribution more explicitly to the Piketty propositions. Jones (2015, 38–39) notes that whether changes in the parameters in this genre can explain the large changes in wealth inequality that we see in the data is an open question in the context of general equilibrium. He argues that all the parameters considered in Piketty (2014a) could be endogenous. For example, the economy's growth rate (g) or the rate of wealth tax can be subject to change by variations in interest rates and the fraction of wealth to be consumed depending on the rate of time preference and the death rate of the economy. He concludes that Piketty is right to highlight the link between $r - g$ and top wealth inequality, but this partial equilibrium reasoning can be easily wiped out by a general equilibrium standpoint. He further argues that these research ideas are relatively new, and the empirical evidence needed to sort out such details is not yet available. The familiar formula derived from a neoclassical model of growth for the steady-state capital-output ratio $\left(k_t / y_t \right)$ based on Solow (1956) is as follows:

$$k_t / y_t = s / \left(n + v + \delta \right). \tag{23.3}$$

Since Piketty treats capital as wealth and assumes that depreciation rate (δ) converges to zero in the long-run, we have

$$k_t / y_t = s / (n + v).$$ (23.4)

Jones (2015) links more formally the Pareto inequality measure to Piketty's second law of capitalism and points out that the depreciation rate (δ) in the denominator of the Solow expression (23.3) pertains to the ratio of reproducible capital—machines, buildings, and highways—and therefore is not strictly comparable to Piketty's capital, which includes land. He argues that a slowing growth rate of aggregate GDP in recent decades and in the future could contribute to a rise in the capital-output ratio, but the quantitative magnitude of these effects is significantly mitigated by taking depreciation into account and, therefore, should not be exaggerated. On Piketty's conjecture that the elasticity of substitution between capital and labor may be greater than one, as opposed to equaling one in the Cobb-Douglas case, Jones (2005) agrees with the conjecture, noting that the capital share and capital-output ratio have moved together, at least over the long swing of history, as depicted in his Figures 4 (40) and 5 (41). But he is hesitant to make a definite conclusion because the land was included in the definition of Piketty's capital and empirical evidence on this elasticity is inconclusive, as demonstrated in Karabarbounis and Neiman (2013), Krusell and Smith (2014), and Oberfield and Raval (2014).

Milanovic (2012, 2016) follows up the issue of global inequality and its socio-political implications in world development by examining Lakner-Milanovic's (2015) World Panel Income Distribution (LM-WPID) data for 1988–2008 at five-year intervals. According to the so-called elephant curve, which depicts change in real income between 1988 and 2008 at various percentiles of global income distribution (calculated in 2005 international dollars), there are two groups, the top 1% group of national and global income distributions and the middle classes of emerging market economies such as China, India, Indonesia, and Brazil, who are the big winners of the two decades of globalization. The biggest loser groups are the very poorest 5% and the group between the 75th and 90th percentile of the global income distribution, whose real income gains were essentially nil. The group may be called a global upper-middle class, which includes many from former Communist countries and Latin America, as well as those citizens of rich countries whose incomes have stagnated. This may have served as the background of the recent changes in the political economy of Great Britain's exit decision from European Union and the Trump candidacy in the US presidential election.

The impact of institutions and distributional conflict on long-run development has been studied and summarized in Acemoglu (2008, Chapter 22) within the tradition of neoclassical growth models. The major difference of the neoclassical distributional conflict model from the Piketty propositions is that while the latter starts from observing the rising inequality from historical data of major advanced nations, the former starts from considering a neoclassical growth model with institutions and distributional conflicts among themselves. In other words, the inequality of income and wealth has been endogenized. The process of economic development involves a complex transformation of the economy, which may include the changes in the structure of production and major social changes, such as demographic transition, migration, urbanization, organizational change, among others. A less-developed economy can be characterized as an economy that is in the interior of its production possibility set or which has been subject to severe market failures (Acemoglu 2008, 725). Low productivity and inefficiencies in such an economy limit various dimensions of structural transformations and keep the economy stuck in development traps.

Acemoglu and Robinson (2000, 2006) and Acemoglu (2006; 2008, Chapter 22) have introduced how inequality and inefficiencies can be set up in a neoclassical model of distributional conflict based on the political economy approach. They began by searching for the relationship between inequality and development in the context of institutional differences among both advanced economies and developing economies. Institutional differences are defined as differences in a broad cluster of social arrangements, including security of property rights, writing contracts to facilitate economic transactions, the entry and exit barrier of firms, the socially imposed costs and barriers facing individual investments in human capital, and incentives of politicians to provide public goods. They have posed the question as to why some societies choose institutions that do not encourage growth and equity and that block technological and economic progress. They model both social conflict and commitment problems in their political economy approach by considering three social groups (workers, entrepreneurs, and the elite who make the political decisions in an oligarchic system) in order to trace tractable aggregation of political preferences of individuals. The derived propositions of the model demonstrate how the elite's preferences over policies translate into preferences over economic institutions. When the elite prefer to commit to lower taxes, this can lead to the emergence of economic institutions that provide greater security of property rights. On the other hand, the factor price manipulation or the political replacement effects may also induce the elite to choose arrangements that block technology adoption or more generally reduce the productivity of competing groups and enlarge the inequality of income and wealth among different groups. Acemoglu (2008, 817) shows that, holding average productivity constant, a decline in the productivity of the median entrepreneur (voter) leads to greater distortionary taxation. Since higher taxes correspond to lower output and the larger gap between the mean and the median of the productivity distribution can be viewed as a measure of inequality, this result suggests a political mechanism by which greater inequality may translate into higher distortions and lower output, providing a link between inequality and distortionary taxation.

Multiple mechanisms in the context of the distribution of income on human capital have been examined by several studies. Galor and Zeira (1993) have examined the effect of inequality and credit market imperfection on human capital. Defining the behavior of the human capital of a single individual without any general equilibrium interactions as the Markov process, they show the possibility of the presence of poverty traps in multiple steady states in the development process of an economy with a high degree of inequality and an imperfect capital market. Depending on the fraction of the economy that starts with initial human capital below a certain threshold level, any fraction of the population may end up at the low level of human capital. The greater this fraction is, the poorer is the economy. The inequality of income and wealth affects individuals who are below the threshold level and, therefore, are unable to invest in human capital accumulation. It also influences the long-run income level of the economy, implying that the inequality of income and wealth leads the economy to lower output and growth. While models with multiple equilibria exhibit indeterminacy, models with multiple steady states avoid indeterminacy and show a unique equilibrium and provide a framework for potential development traps and the importance of initial conditions in determining where the economy will end up, as discussed in Krugman (1991) and Matsuyama (1992). Banerjee and Newman (1993) have examined the issue in the context of inequality on occupational choice. Aghion and Bolton (1997) and Piketty (1997) have dealt with the interaction between inequality and entrepreneurial investments. Loury (1981), Tamura (1991), Benabou (1996), Durlauf (1996), Fernandez and Rogerson (1996), Glomm and Ravikumar (1992), and Acemoglu (1998) have presented dynamic models of inequality and its interactions with efficiency.

23.3.3. Empirical Studies on Inequality and Development

The empirical cross-country studies were carried out to provide an answer regarding the relationship between productivity and inequality. When we measure productivity as per capita income for an aggregate economy, the relationship between productivity growth and inequality is transformed into that between per capita income growth and inequality. In fact, Acemoglu (2008, 146) demonstrates the similarity between estimated labor-productivity differences from the Trefler (1993) approach and calibrated productivity differences from the Hall-Jones (1999) approach based on the Cobb-Douglas specification. Even though productivity and per capita income are not the same concept, empirical findings on the relationship between per capita income and inequality are followed by findings equivalent to those on the relationship between productivity and inequality.

The empirical cross-country literature suggests that growth has neither a positive nor a negative effect on inequality, and that the impact of inequality on growth is ambiguous. These results do not imply the absence of links when looking at a specific policy or a specific country. Lopez (2004b) surveys the empirical literature and concludes that macroeconomic stability related to inflation, as well as education and infrastructure-related policies, seem to be win-win or "super pro-poor" policies that have both a positive effect on growth and a negative effect on inequality. Moreover, asset inequality rather than income inequality may matter for growth outcomes. Deininger and Squire (1998) use land distribution as a proxy for asset inequality and show that high asset inequality has a significant negative effect on growth. Controlling for initial asset inequality, Birdsall and Londono (1997) show that income inequality does not seem to play a role in expanding growth outcomes. The cross-country literature on both growth and pro-poor growth has been criticized for not giving enough guidance to policymakers. Much of the so-called pro-poor growth agenda has been focusing on aggregated income and poverty statistics, measuring to what extent growth was reducing poverty, and analyzing whether (and why) poverty was reduced in an absolute or relative sense.

From the beginning of the 2000s, however, a new wave of literature emerged, focusing on the importance of the context and ex ante analysis of constraints to future economic development. Several cross-country studies have shown that growth determinants are highly dependent on not only initial conditions such as levels of income, poverty, and asset inequality, but also a host of other factors such as geography, demography, governance, politics, social considerations, and the set of existing policies. These differ not only between countries, but also over time within the same country. One key example of the post-1990s literature is the volume *Economic Growth in the 1990s: Learning from a Decade of Reform* (World Bank 2005). It concludes that although the necessary fundamentals for growth, such as a stable macroeconomic environment, enforcement of property rights, openness to trade, and effective government, are key factors in the growth process, they are not the whole story. This work and the work of the Growth Commission highlight the diverse ways in which the fundamentals can interact with policies and institutional setups in different country contexts.

So far, empirical findings on the effect of productivity growth identified by per capita income growth on inequality have been mixed and inconclusive. The findings include Ravallion and Chen (1997), Deininger and Squire (1998), Easterly (1999), and Dollar and Kraay (2002). The impact of inequality on growth was also ambiguous. Alesina and Rodrik (1994), Person and Tabellini (1994), and Perotti (1996) find a negative relationship, while Li and Zhou (1998), Forbes (2000), and Banerjee and Duflo (2003) find a positive relationship, and Barro (2000) and Lopez (2004a) find no relationship. In addition, asset inequality, rather than income inequality, might affect growth outcomes. Deininger and Squire (1998), who used land distribution as a proxy for asset inequality, has shown that high asset inequality has a significant negative effect on growth. On the other hand, Saint-Paul and Verdier (1993) show that higher inequality can promote growth if tax revenues are invested in human capital accumulation. Birdsall and Londono (1997) show that income inequality does not affect growth outcome, controlling for initial inequality in asset distribution. More recent empirical papers on inequality and growth include Eicher and Turnovsky (2000), OECD (2008, 2011), Ostry, Berg, and Tsangarides (2014), and van der Weide and Milanovic (2014).

Acemoglu (2008) concludes, after a review of TFP accounting, regression analysis, and calibration based on the Solow model, that technology (productivity in the model) is the main source of economic growth over time and cross-country differences in prosperity and inequality. He also argues that what the Solow model makes us focus on—physical capital, human capital, and technology (productivity)—are proximate causes of economic growth in cross-country differences. However, there are other factors that make some countries more abundant in physical capital, human capital, and technology. He refers to these as the fundamental causes of differences in prosperity, such as geography, demography, and institutions. He argues that while the proximate causes are essential to understand the mechanics of economic growth, the fundamental causes are also essential to understand why some societies make choices that lead them to low physical capital, low human capital, and inefficient technology (productivity) and thus to relative poverty. In the following section, we address with these fundamental causes that affect the relationship between productivity and development.

23.4. INCLUSIVE DEVELOPMENT AND INCOME-LED GROWTH

23.4.1. Inclusive Growth and Poverty Reduction

The rising inequality through time in income and wealth distribution and the slow pace of the growth in the global economy have invited the debate on the cause of unequal growth. One line of research on this issue is a debate on inclusive growth and development initiated by international development organizations such as the World Bank (2008) and OECD (2008). Ianchovichina and Lundstrom (2009) state that rapid and sustained poverty reduction requires inclusive growth that allows people to contribute to and benefit from economic growth. Rapid pace of growth is unquestionably necessary for substantial poverty reduction, but for this growth to be sustainable in the long run, it should be broad-based across sectors and should not omit a small part of a country's labor force and all residents outside the labor force.

This definition of inclusive growth implies a direct link between the macro and micro determinants of growth. The micro dimension captures the importance of structural transformation for economic diversification and competition, including creative destruction of jobs and firms. The inclusive growth definition is in line with the absolute definition of pro-poor growth, but not the relative definition. Under the absolute definition, growth is considered to be pro-poor as long as poor people benefit in absolute terms, as reflected in some agreed measure of poverty (Ravallion and Chen 2003). In contrast, in the relative definition, growth is "pro-poor" if and only if the incomes of poor people grow faster than those of the population as a whole (i.e., inequality declines). However, while absolute pro-poor growth can be the result of direct income redistribution schemes, for growth to be inclusive, productivity must be improved and new employment opportunities created. In short, inclusive growth is about enlarging the size of the economy, rather than redistributing resources, and about raising the pace of growth, while leveling the playing field for investment and increasing productive employment opportunities.

We often find that inclusive growth refers to both the pace and pattern of growth, which are considered interlinked, and therefore need to be addressed together. The idea that both the pace and pattern of growth are critical for achieving a high, sustainable growth record, as well as poverty reduction, is consistent with the findings in the "Growth Report: Strategies for Sustained Growth and Inclusive Development" (Commission on

Growth and Development 2008). The commission notes that inclusiveness—a concept that encompasses equity, equality of opportunity, and protection in market and employment transitions—is an essential ingredient of any successful growth strategy. The Commission considers systematic inequality of opportunity "toxic," as it will derail the growth process through political channels or conflict. Here we emphasize the idea of equality of opportunity in terms of access to markets, resources, and an unbiased regulatory environment for businesses and individuals.

Ianchovichina and Lundstrom (2009) further argue that by focusing on inequality, the relative definition could lead to suboptimal outcomes for both poor and non-poor households. For example, a society attempting to achieve pro-poor growth under the relative definition would favor an outcome characterized by average income growth of 2% where the income of poor households grew by 3%, over an outcome where average growth was 6%, but the incomes of poor households grew by only 4%. While the distributional pattern of growth favors poor households in the first scenario, both poor and non-poor households are better off in the second scenario. There is broad recognition that when poverty reduction is the objective, then the absolute definition of pro-poor growth is the most relevant (DFID 2004). Using the absolute definition, the aim is to increase the rate of growth to achieve the greatest pace of poverty reduction. They conclude that policies for inclusive growth are an important component of most government strategies for sustainable growth. For instance, a country that has grown rapidly over a decade but has not seen substantial reduction in poverty rates may need to focus specifically on the inclusiveness of its growth strategy (i.e., on the equality of opportunity for individuals and firms). Other examples can be drawn from resource-rich countries. Extractive industries usually do not employ much labor, and the non-resource sectors typically suffer contractions associated with Dutch disease effects during boom periods. These cases may call for analysis of constraints to broad-based growth with a particular emphasis on the non-resource sectors in the economy. Moreover, in countries starting at a very low income level and low growth, an inclusive growth approach would be very close to an approach for speeding up the pace of growth, as the main focus should be on getting the fundamentals for growth right.

A high pace of growth over extended periods of time is a necessary and often the main contributing factor in reducing poverty, as found by a sizable body of literature, including Deininger and Squire (1998), Ravallion (2001), White and Anderson (2001), Dollar and Kraay (2002), and Bourguignon (2003). In a frequently cited cross-country study, Kraay (2004) shows that growth in average incomes explains 70% of the variation in poverty reduction (as measured by the headcount ratio) in the short run, and as much as 97% in the long run. Most of the remainder of the variation in poverty reduction is accounted for by changes in the distribution, with only a negligible share attributed to differences in the growth elasticity of poverty. Lopez and Servén (2006) suggest that for a given inequality level, the poorer the country is, the more important is the growth component in explaining poverty reduction. Sustained, high growth rates and poverty reduction, however, can be realized only when the sources of growth are expanding, and an increasing share of the labor force is included in the growth process in an efficient way. From a static point of view, growth associated with progressive distributional changes will have a greater impact in reducing poverty than growth that leaves distribution unchanged. Evidence in White and Anderson (2001) suggests that in a significant number of cases (around a quarter), distribution has been as important as growth in explaining the income growth of the poor. Some policies may have a positive effect on both growth and inequality.

23.4.2. Wage-Led Growth versus Profit-Led Growth

Inclusive growth and development literature confirms that it all depends on where we find the sources of growth. The global financial crisis of 2007–2008 and the stagnation in most of the developed nations has invited a debate on income-led growth which includes both wage income and non-wage income such as welfare transfer income and profit-led growth. The International Labour Organization (ILO) (2008) reports that the rising inequality of income from wage disparity is the primary cause of lower growth rates in both developed economies and developing economies. Lavoie and Stockhammer (2012), using the model of Kalecki (1971), proposed the need to switch from profit-led growth to wage-led growth. Berg and Tobin (2011) provided the case study of Brazil, which had switched from export-led and commodity-driven growth to promoting domestic consumption and investment. The government of Brazil has tried to compensate for loss of export earnings due to the sudden decline of export demand by a series of income-led growth policies protecting wage levels and social security policies and reducing taxes, and indeed, they have been successful in achieving these policy goals.

Blecker (1989, 2011) and Bhaduri and Marglin (1990) have examined the effects of changes in income distribution on net exports. It is usually argued that an increase in real wages will have a negative impact on the trade balance through a profit squeeze in which profit margins are compressed between domestic costs, on the one side, and foreign competition, on the other. But an increase in real wages may not have a negative effect on net exports if producers and exporters decide to reduce their profit margins.

The wage-led policy will have an impact on not only aggregate demand, but also on aggregate supply. Increases in wage growth may have a positive effect on productivity growth, if either firms react by increasing productivity-enhancing investments in order to maintain competitiveness, or if workers' contribution to the production process improves, which is the so-called efficiency wage hypothesis that has been accepted by the empirical study in Krassoi and Stanley (2009). Aghion, Caroli, and Garcia-Penalosa (1999) present possible positive supply-side effects of higher wages and lower inequality and point out that income and wealth inequality makes investment more difficult when it is combined with capital market imperfections.

The proponents of wage-led growth argue that the declining share of wage income and the increasing share of capital income, as documented in International Monetary Fund (IMF) (2007), Atkinson, Piketty, and Saez (2011), OECD (2011), and Piketty (2014a), have been the major cause of stagnation in the global economy. While mainstream explanations point out technological changes as the main determinant of income inequality and agree with IMF (2007) and European Commission (2007) in admitting that globalization has had negative effects on the wage share in advanced economies, ILO (2008), Jayadev (2008), and Hein and Mundt (2012) point out that welfare state retrenchment and financialization have suppressed wages. In advancing their proposition, proponents of wage-led policy rely on the Kaldor-Verdoorn law in Kaldor (1957), which claims that there is positive relation between the growth rates of GDP and the growth rate of labor productivity. It suggests that demand-led growth will have an impact on the supply components of growth. McCombie (2002, 106) reports that a one percentage point addition to the growth rate of output will generate a 0.3–0.6 percentage point increase (the Verdoorn coefficient) in the growth rate of labor productivity. It is consistent with the estimates by Storm and Naastepad (2008) and Hein and Tarassow (2010), which find a similar range around 0.30 for European countries (1960–2007 data) but a lower range for the United Kingdom and the United States, between 0.1 and 0.25. Marquetti (2004) has found, however, that while real wages Granger-cause productivity, the reverse is not true. Onaran and Galanis (2012) report the effects of a national and global one percentage point increase in the profit share on the GDP share of the components of aggregate demand (consumption share, investment share, and net export share) and find all negative coefficients on consumption share and all positive coefficients on investment and net export share for 24 major economies including the United States, China, and Euro area 12 (12 West European Member States of the euro area). They also report all negative coefficients for the effect of simultaneous worldwide increase in profit share on aggregate demand, except China (1.115) and Australia (0.172), which suggests that the global simultaneous increase in profit share could have benefited resource-rich countries.

While there is ongoing debate on wage-led growth versus profit-led growth, the priority should be given to the characteristics of the economy and its stage of development. Wage-led policy cannot be applied to all levels of economies unless they have a sizable domestic market. For small open economies, the loss of export earnings cannot be readily substituted by lifting up domestic consumption and investment. They may have to search for other export markets, new technological development, and profit-led growth by destructive creation. Wage-led or income-led growth policy can be an alternative to profit-led growth policy at the time of external shocks if the economy in question has a relatively large share of domestic absorption. The opposite is true if the economy in question has a relatively large export and import sector. The reckless reliance on wage-led growth could invite a zero-sum game among economic agents and may lose incentives for creatively destructive entrepreneurial spirits.

23.4.3. Country Narratives on Productivity and Development

Rodrik (2003) provides country narratives on the relationship between productivity and development. The country narratives on Australia, India, and Botswana take a longer historical perspective on economic growth and social development. It also contains the narratives of six countries (Vietnam, the Phillippines, Indonesia, India, Mauritius and Venezuela) and two transition economies in Eastern Europe (Poland and Romania).

The country narratives on China, Bolivia, and Mexico are analyzed in the context of institutional development. The case of Pakistan highlights a case of growth without social development to remind us that economic growth is not all that matters. Acemoglu and Robinson (2012) distinguish inclusive political institutions and inclusive economic institutions from extractive institutions.

Isaksson et al. (2005) document several country studies. They have noted that the Asian region has performed well in terms of physical capital accumulation, even though there is an interesting difference between China and South Korea, on the one hand, and Indonesia, on the other. The former used domestic capital in funding investment, while the latter funded investment with foreign capital, which became much more vulnerable at the time of the Asian financial crisis. They note that income and wealth inequality in Latin America remains a big problem and impedes equal access to education and hence has impeded TFP growth. In Chile, privatization has been successful because it ensured the abolishment of state-protected monopolies. In Mexico, it was less successful because its goals were not to increase competition, but rather to maximize state income. In Argentina, it was less successful because its goals were not to reduce state-owned companies' inefficiency. Even though there were substantial increases in their profitability and operating efficiency after the privatization of nonfinancial enterprises, privatization in Argentina was met by rising unpopularity because the benefits of privatization were not transferred to consumers, thus limiting the social benefits generated by privatization. Privatization in Argentina resulted in massive layoffs, reducing employment in former state enterprises by 40% and increasing tariffs for consumer services such as basic telephone services, without substantial quality improvements such as passenger railway services.

All countries included in the study, except Brazil, experienced problems with privatization, the main one being the shift from state to private monopoly, in which competition cannot play its role. In case of Brazil, since the 1990s the government has been adopting initiatives to increase competition in domestic markets by freeing firms and markets from controls introduced during the import-substitution industrialization (ISI) phase, and by strengthening competition agencies. A first set of measures was implemented by the Federal Deregulation Program. Another set of measures was aimed at strengthening antitrust and consumer protection policies. Other measures focused on the elimination of legal restrictions limiting entry into several nontradable sectors. The end of the high inflation era in mid-1994 exposed the deficiencies of bank supervision in Brazil, and triggered a process of reform that has produced better and more stringent regulation, particularly regarding minimum capital requirements. Isaksson et al. (2005, 38–39) notes that it was in infrastructure that regulatory reform in Brazil was most significant. Infrastructure regulation started to change in the early 1990s, but the first critical steps were taken in 1995, when a Concessions Law was approved and the constitution was amended to end public monopolies in telecom and pipeline gas distribution and to discontinue the restrictions to foreign entry in some key sectors, in particular electricity generation.

In Tanzania, with its many state-owned enterprises, privatization has clearly led to higher TFP. It was argued that the legacy of apartheid had a strong lingering effect on productivity by creating a dual economy: one that is highly developed, where firms use modern technology, and one that is characterized by high poverty, unemployment, and underemployment. This situation was thought to negatively impact TFP growth by, for example, increasing social tensions. In Morocco, although a competition law has been introduced, there are still many barriers to the entry of both foreign and domestic investments. Hence, it seems that competition efforts have been undermined.

Isaksson et al. (2005, 39–40, 95) has quoted from Pyo (2000, 2005) and has discussed the case of South Korea as follows. At early stages of development, intense efforts to ensure 100% primary education are certainly justified. Human capital accumulation need not be biased toward higher skills. The effort made by South Korea in the 1960s to fully enroll the population in primary education was the fundamental cause of South Korea's exemplary growth, as argued in Pyo (2005). Following Young (1995) and Pyo (2005), it would seem that the Asian "Tigers," in general, owe much of their success to state intervention in a timely expansion of primary and secondary education of high quality. In terms of industrial policy, the South Korean government's aim has been to keep the degree of (monopolistic) competition high but controlled, as evidenced by a gradual lowering of entry barriers over time. The government has worked hard to maintain a competitive market environment. Although the economy is dominated by a few large firms, these firms compete fiercely among one another. Pyo (2000) shows that the government has deliberately introduced limited competition by lowering entry barriers over time and by monitoring market failures by major conglomerates in order to maximize the efficient use of limited resources. In other words, the government has played the role of competition promoter and supervisor through government-controlled banks, which are part of quasi-internal organization. In this regard, the system has promoted monopolistic competition across industries. That is why one observes a larger number of automobile manufacturers, telecommunication equipment producers, and mobile phone companies in South Korea than one normally observes in many developing countries or smaller advanced countries.

Other case studies for productivity in Asia are included in Jorgenson, Kuroda, and Motohashi (2007), who include estimation of TFP and growth accounting for Japan, United States, China, South Korea, and Taiwan, with purchasing power parities and international productivity comparison among these five countries. The contribution of information technology to economic growth has been documented in Pyo, Rhee, and Ha (2008) and Rhee and Pyo (2010) for Korea and Fukao et al. (2012) for Japan and Korea, and the contribution of intangible assets to industrial productivity growth of Japan and Korea has been analyzed by Miyagawa and Shoichi (2013) and Chun et al. (2016).

23.5. Summary and Future Productivity Research for Development

This chapter was intended to review both theoretical and empirical researches on productivity and development after the emergence of new endogenous growth theory, which emphasized the role of technology and human capital. The first development we revisited is the search for deeper determinants for productivity growth, such as that by Rodrik (2003) and Isaksson et al. (2005). The search resulted in finding the importance of institutions, in addition to human capital, as a deep determinant for productivity growth and poverty reduction. The second development is a renewed interest on growth and inequality. We have revisited recent studies on this issue, including Piketty (2014a). We have outlined analytics of growth inequality based on two fundamental laws of capitalism by revisiting Piketty's derivations and interpretations of two fundamental laws of capitalism. We have also revisited the golden rule of accumulation and have arrived at the conclusion, derived from Piketty, that the only exit from the contradicting downfall of capitalism is to find a positive growth of technology and productivity. The third development is the search for pro-poor growth and inclusive growth to explain the possibility of poverty reduction and path to development. We have outlined two important inclusive growth analytics: one by Hausmann, Rodrik, and Velasco (2005), who developed a heuristic approach based on the Keynes-Ramsey rule with balanced growth of consumption and investment equations to identify the most binding constraint to growth; and the other by SIDA (2006), which blends the diagnostic approach with different techniques to answer questions about trends, constraints to, and sources of sustainable, broad-based growth. Since the main instrument for a sustainable and inclusive growth is assumed to be productive employment, inclusive growth and development are naturally linked with wage-led growth and income-led growth, initiated by ILO. While there is ongoing debate on wage-led growth versus profit-led growth, the priority should be given to the characteristics of the economy and its stage of development. Wage-led growth policy can be an alternative to profit-led growth policy at the time of external shocks if the economy in question has a relatively large share of domestic absorption. The opposite is true if the economy in question has a relatively large export-and-import sector. The reckless reliance on wage-led growth could invite a zero-sum game among economic agents and may lose incentives for creatively destructive entrepreneurial spirits.

For priorities and directions for future productivity research, Schreyer (2014) identifies important data gaps related to nonproduced, nonfinancial assets, such as land and sub-soil assets, health and education sectors, and intellectual property that is developed in one country but used in many. Sichel (2014) adds to this list the high-tech sector as a priority area for future productivity research. Fixler (2014) identifies health, education, and financial services as hard-to-measure services given the difficulty of measuring prices and output in these sectors. He also lists land and natural resources with the increased attention to the environment and factory-less goods manufacturing due to the globalization and fragmentation of production processes. Fraumeni (2014) also lists intangible capital and adds management practices and human capital as priority areas for future productivity research. van Ark (2014) lists intangible assets as well, but adds the impact of innovation and the gap between firm-level measures and industry-level measures of productivity to the list of priority areas of future productivity research. These priority areas are equally and at times more important in developing nations than in developed nations, and the difficulty of measuring human capital, intangible capital, land and natural resources, and service outputs and prices in developing nations becomes compounded because of the lack of institutional environment. But at the same time, these areas are potentially important areas for the future productivity growth of developing nations.

On the productivity study from the econometric side, the use of panel data in spatial productivity spillover models is noteworthy because it has potential to be applied to regional data and international data. Schmidt and Sickles (1984) initiated the use of panel data in frontier production models. Lee and Pyo (2007) estimated a stochastic frontier protection model with Korean industry-panel data. Anselin (1988), Le Sage and Pace (2009), and Elhorst (2014) have introduced spatial econometric models. Holtz-Eakin and Schwartz (1995) have applied a spatial productivity spillover model to public infrastructure, and Pereira and Andraz (2013) have applied the model to public infrastructure investment using an international survey data. Glass, Kenjegalieva, and Sickles (2013) have applied a spatial econometric model to analyze US cities' congestion management. These spatial econometric models have a great deal of potential to be applied to international technology spillovers and the spatial correlations of pollution across borders.

Acemoglu (2008, 769) notes that there is now a large literature on empirical development economics—documenting the extent of credit market imperfections, the impact of inequality on human capital investments and occupation choices, the process of social change, and various other market failures in less-developed economies—which suggests the combination of theoretical models of economic growth. He further notes that by and large, this literature is about market failures in less-developed economies and sometimes focuses on how these market failures can be rectified and that the standard models of economic growth do not feature these market failures. He points to a fruitful area for future research as the combination of theoretical models of economic growth and development (that pay attention to market failures) with the rich empirical evidence on the incidence, characterization, and costs of these market failures. He concludes that this combination can focus on the essence of development economics—the question of why some countries are less developed, how they can grow more rapidly, and how they can jump-start the process of structural transformation necessary for economic development.

References

Acemoglu, D. 1998. "Why Do New Technologies Complement Skills? Directed Technical Change and Wage Inequality." *Quarterly Journal of Economics* 113: 1055–1089.

Acemoglu, D. 2006. "Modeling Inefficient Institutions." In *Advances in Economic Theory, Proceedings of World Congress 2005*, edited by Richard Blundell, Whitney Newey, and Torsten Persson, 341–380. Cambridge: Cambridge University Press.

Acemoglu, D. 2008. *Introduction to Modern Economic Growth*. Princeton, NJ: Princeton University Press.

Acemoglu, D., and J. A. Robinson. 2000. "Why Did the West Extend the Franchise? Democracy, Inequality, and Growth in Historical Perspective." *The Quarterly Journal of Economics* 115(4): 1167–1199.

Acemoglu, D., and J. A. Robinson. 2006. "Persistence of Power, Elites and Institutions." *American Economic Review* 98(1): 267–293.

Acemoglu, D., and J. A. Robinson. 2012. *Why Nations Fail: The Origins of Power, Prosperity and Poverty*. New York: Crown Business.

Aghion, P., and P. Bolton. 1997. "A Theory of Trickle-Down Growth and Development." *Review of Economic Studies* 64(2): 151–172.

Aghion, P., E. Caroli, and C. Garcia-Penalosa. 1999. "Inequality and Economic Growth: The Perspective of the New Growth Theories." *Journal of Economic Literature* 37(4): 1615–1660.

Alesina, A., and R. Perotti. 1996. "Income Distribution, Political Instability, and Investment." *European Economic Review* 40(6): 1203–1228.

Alesina, A., and D. Rodrik. 1994. "Distributive Politics and Economic Growth." *Quarterly Journal of Economics* 109(2): 465–490.

Anselin, L. 1988. *Spatial Econometrics: Methods and Models*. Dordrecht: Springer.

Atkinson, A. B., T. Piketty, and E. Saez. 2011. "Top Incomes in the Long Run of History." *Journal of Economic Literature* 49(1): 3–71.

Banerjee, A. V., and A. F. Newman. 1993. "Occupational Choice and the Process of Development." *Journal of Political Economy* 101(2): 274–298.

Banerjee, A. V., and E. Duflo. 2003. "Inequality and Growth: What Can the Data Say." *Journal of Economic Growth* 8: 267–299.

Bardhan, P. 1995. "The Contributions of Endogenous Growth Theory to the Analysis of Development Problems: An Assessment." In *Handbook of Development Economics*, Vol. 3, 2983–2998. Amsterdam: North Holland.

Barro, R. J. 2000. "Inequality and Growth in a Panel of Countries." *Journal of Economic Growth* 5(1): 5–32.

Barro, R. J., and X. Sala-i-Martin. 2004. *Economic Growth*. Cambridge, MA: MIT Press.

Benabou, R. 1996. "Inequality and Growth." In *NBER Macroeconomics Annual 1996*, Vol. 11, 11–92. National Bureau of Economic Research. Cambridge, MA: MIT Press.

Berg, J., and S. Tobin. 2011. "Income-Led Growth as a Crisis Response: Lessons from Brazil." Paper presented at research conference on *Key Lessons from the Crisis and Way Forward*, International Labour Office, Geneva. http://www.ilo.org/wcmsp5/groups/public/---dgreports/---inst/documents/genericdocument/wcms_192380.pdf.

Beyer, H., and R. Vergara. 2002. "Productivity and Economic Growth: The Case of Chile." Central Bank of Chile, Working Paper No. 174. http://citeseerx.ist.psu.edu/viewdoc/download?doi=10.1.1.487.8619&rep=rep1&type=pdf.

Bhaduri, A., and S. Marglin. 1990. "Unemployment and the Real Wage: The Economic Basis for Contesting Political Ideologies." *Cambridge Journal of Economics* 14(4): 375–393.

Birdsall, N., and J. Londono. 1997. "Asset Inequality Matters: An Assessment of the World Bank's Approach to Poverty Reduction." *American Economic Review Papers and Proceeding* 87(2): 32–37.

Blecker, R. A. 1989. "International Competition, Income Distribution and Economic Growth." *Cambridge Journal of Economics* 13(3): 395–412.

Blecker, R. A. 2011. "Open Economy Models of Distribution and Growth." Working Paper 2010-03, American University, Department of Economics. http://citeseerx.ist.psu.edu/viewdoc/download?doi=10.1.1.617.5092&rep=rep1&type=pdf.

Bourguignon, F. 2003. "The Growth Elasticity of Poverty Reduction: Explaining Heterogeneity across Countries and Time Periods." DELTA Working Paper 2002-03, DELTA (Ecole Normale Supérieure). http://siteresources.worldbank.org/INTPGI/Resources/342674-1206111890151/13565_32322_growth_elasticity.pdf.

Burda, M. C., and B. Severgnini. 2014. "Solow Residuals Without Capital Stocks." *Journal of Development Economics* 109(C): 154–171.

Chun, H., T. Miyagawa, H. Pyo, and T. Konomi. 2016. "Do Intangibles Contribute to Productivity Growth in East Asian Countries? Evidence from Japan and Korea." In *The World Economy: Growth or Stagnation?* edited by D. Jorgenson, K. Fukao, and M. Timmer, 1–27. Cambridge: Cambridge University Press.

Commission on Growth and Development. 2008. "Growth Report: Strategies for Sustained Growth and Inclusive Development." The World Bank, Washington, DC. http://www.sgb.gov.tr/EADD%20alma%20Platformu/E%C4%9Fitim%20Faaliyetleri/Murat%20%C3%9C%C3%A7er%20%C3%87al%C4%B1%C5%9Fma%20Dosyas%C4%B1/Reading%20List/Growth%20and%20Employment/The%20Growth%20Report%20Strategies%20for%20Sustained%20Growth%20and%20Inclusive%20Development,%20Michael%20Spence%20Lecture.pdf.

Corrado, C., H. Charles, and D. Sichel. 2009. "Intangible Capital and U.S. Economic Growth." *Review of Income and Wealth* 55(3): 661–685.

Dadkhah, K. M., and F. Zahedi. 1986. "Simultaneous Estimation of Production Functions and Capital Stocks for Developing Countries." *The Review of Economics and Statistics* 68(3): 443–451.

Deininger, K., and L. Squire. 1998. "New Ways of Looking at Old Issues: Inequality and Growth." *Journal of Development Economics* 57(2): 259–287.

DFID. 2004. "What Is Pro-Poor Growth and Why Do We Need to Know." Pro-Poor Growth Briefing Note 1, Department for International Development, London.

Dollar, D., and A. Kraay. 2002. "Growth Is Good for the Poor." *Journal of Economic Growth* 7: 195–225.

Durlauf, S. N. 1996. "A Theory of Persistent Income Inequality." *Journal of Economic Growth* 1: 75–94.

Easterly, W. 1999. "Life during Growth." *Journal of Economic Growth* 4(3): 239–275.

Eicher, T., and S. J. Turnovsky. 2000. "Scale, Congestion and Growth." *Economica* 67(267): 325–346.

Elhorst, J. P. 2014. *Spatial Econometrics: From Cross-Sectional Data to Spatial Panels.* London: Springer.

European Commission. 2007. "The Labour Income Share in the European Union." In *Employment in Europe 2007*, edited by Directorate-General for Employment, Social Affairs and Equal Opportunities, 237–272. Brussels.

Fernandez, R., and R. Rogerson. 1996. "Income Distribution, Communities, and the Quality of Public Education." *The Quarterly Journal of Economics* 111(1): 135–164.

Fixler, D. 2014. "Priorities and Directions for Future Productivity Research: A BEA Perspective." *International Productivity Monitor* 27: 10–13.

Forbes, K. J. 2000. "A Reassessment of the Relationship Between Inequality and Growth." *American Economic Review* 90(4): 869–887.

Fukao, K., T. Miyagawa, H. Pyo, and K. Rhee. 2012. "Estimates of Total Factor Productivity, the Contribution of ICT, and Resource Reallocation Effects in Japan and Korea." In *Industrial Productivity in Europe: Growth and Crisis*, edited by Matilde Mas and Robert Stehrer, 264–305. Northampton, MA: Edward Elgar.

Fraumeni, B. M. 2014. "Frontiers and Opportunities in Productivity Research." *International Productivity Monitor* 27: 20–21.

Galor, O., and J. Zeira. 1993. "Income Distribution and Macroeconomics." *The Review of Economic Studies* 60(1): 35–52.

Glass, A. J., K. Kenjegalieva, and R. Sickles. 2013. "How Efficiently Do US Cities Manage Roadway Congestion?" *Journal of Productivity Analysis* 40(3): 407–428.

Glomm, G., and B. Ravikumar. 1992. "Public vs. Private Investment in Human Capital: Endogenous Growth and Income Inequality." *Journal of Political Economy* 100: 818–834.

Griliches, Z. 1998. *R&D and Productivity: The Econometric Evidence*. Chicago: University of Chicago Press.

Hall, R. E., and C. I. Jones. 1999. "Why Do Some Countries Produce So Much More Output per Worker Than Others?" *Quarterly Journal of Economics* 114: 83–116.

Hausmann, R., D. Rodrik, and A. Velasco. 2005. *Growth Diagnostics*. Cambridge, MA: John F. Kennedy School of Government. http://www6.iadb.org/WMSFiles/products/research/files/pubS-852.pdf.

Hein, E., and M. Mundt. 2012. "Financialisation and the Requirements and Potentials for Wage-led Recovery: A Review Focusing on the G20." ILO Working Papers, Conditions of Work and Employment Series No. 37.

Hein, E., and A. Tarassow. 2010. "Distribution, Aggregate Demand and Productivity Growth: Theory and Empirical Results for Six OECD Countries Based on a Post-Kaleckian Model." *Cambridge Journal of Economics* 34(4): 727–754.

Holtz-Eakin, D., and A. E. Schwartz. 1995. "Spatial Productivity Spillovers from Public Infrastructure: Evidence from State Highways." *International Tax and Public Finance* 2(3): 459–468.

Ianchovichina, E., and S. Lundstrom. 2009. "Inclusive Growth Analytics: Framework and Application." Policy Research Working Paper No. 4851, Economic Policy and Debt Department, Economic Policy Division, The World Bank, Washington, DC. http://documents.worldbank.org/curated/en/771771468180864543/pdf/WPS4851.pdf.

International Labour Office. 2008. *Income Inequalities in the Age of Financial Globalization*. World of Work Report. Geneva: ILO.

International Monetary Fund. 2007. "Globalization and Inequality, World Economic Outlook." https://www.imf.org/external/pubs/ft/weo/2007/02/pdf/text.pdf.

Isaksson, A., T. H. Ng, and G. Robyn. 2005. *Productivity in Developing Countries: Trends and Policies*. Vienna: United Nations Industrial Development Organization.

Jayadev, A. 2008. "The Class Content of Preferences Towards Anti-inflation and Anti-Unemployment Policies." *International Review of Applied Economics* 22(2): 161–172.

Jones, Charles I. 2005. "Pareto and Piketty: The Macroeconomics of Top Income and Wealth Inequality." *The Journal of Economic Perspectives* 29(1): 29–46.

Jorgenson, D. 1990. "Productivity and Economic Growth." In *Fifty Years of Economic Measurement, Studies in Income and Wealth*, Vol. 54, edited by E. Berndt and J. Triplett, 1–98. Chicago: University of Chicago Press.

Jorgenson, D., M. Kuroda, and K. Motohashi (eds.). 2007. *Productivity in Asia, Economic Growth and Competitiveness*. Cheltenham, UK: Edward Elgar.

Jorgenson, D. W., and K. Vu. 2005. "Information Technology and the World Economy." *Scandinavian Journal of Economics* 107(4): 631–650.

Kaldor, N. 1957. "A Model of Economic Growth." *The Economic Journal* 67(268): 591–624.

Kalecki, M. 1971. *Selected Essays in the Dynamics of the Capitalist Economy*. Cambridge: Cambridge University Press.

Karabarbounis, L., and B. Neiman. 2013. "The Global Decline of the Labor Share." *Quarterly Journal of Economics* 129(1): 61–103.

Kraay, A. 2004. "When Is Growth Pro-Poor? Cross-Country Evidence." IMF Working Paper 4- 47, International Monetary Fund, Washington, DC. https://www.imf.org/external/pubs/ft/wp/2004/wp0447.pdf.

Krassoi, P. E., and T. D. Stanley. 2009. "Efficiency Wages, Productivity and Simultaneity: A Meta-Regression Analysis." *Journal of Labor Research* 30(3): 262–268.

Krueger, A. B. 1993. "How Computers Have Changed the Wage Structure: Evidence from Microdata, 1984–1989." *Quarterly Journal of Economics* 108: 33–60.

Krugman, P. 1991. "Increasing Returns and Economic Geography." *Journal of Political Economy* 99: 483–499.

Krusell, Per, and Tony Smith. 2014. "Is Piketty's "Second Law of Capitalism' Fundamental?" October 21. http://aida.wss.yale.edu/smith/piketty1.pdf.

Lakner, C., and B. Milanovic. 2015. "Global Income Distribution: From the Fall of Berlin Wall to the Great Recession." *The World Bank Economic Review* 30(2): 203–232.

Lavoie, M., and E. Stockhammer. 2012. "Wage-Led Growth: Concept, Theories and Policies." ILO Working Papers, Conditions of Work and Employment Series No. 41. http://www.ilo.org/wcmsp5/groups/public/---ed_protect/---protrav/---travail/documents/publication/wcms_192507.pdf.

Lee, Y., and H. Pyo. 2007. "Productivity Growth and Patterns of Efficiency Changes in Korean Economy: Stochastic Frontier Approach with Industry-Panel Data." *Seoul Journal of Economics* 20(1): 23–58.

Le Sage, J., and R. K. Pace. 2009. *Introduction to Spatial Econometrics*. Boca Raton, FL: Chapman and Hall/CRC.

Li, H., and H. Zhou. 1998. "Income Inequality Is Not Harmful for Growth: Theory and Evidence." *Review of Development Economics* 2(3): 318–334.

Lopez, H. 2004a. "Pro Growth, Pro Poor: Is There a Trade Off?" Working Paper WPS3378. World Bank. Washington, DC. http://siteresources.worldbank.org/INTPGI/Resources/15040_WBSWP3378.pdf.

Lopez, H. 2004b. "Pro-Poor Growth: A Review of What We Know (and of What We Don't). Mimeo. World Bank. http://eldis.org/vfile/upload/1/document/0708/DOC17880.pdf.

Lopez, H., and L. Serven. 2006. "A Normal Relationship? Poverty, Growth and Inequaility" Policy Research Working Paper, no. WPS 38114, Washington DC, World Bank.

Loury, G. C. 1981. "Intergenerational Transfers and the Distribution of Earnings." *Econometrica* 49(4): 834–867.

Lucas, R. E., Jr. 1988. "On the Mechanics of Economic Development." *Journal of Monetary Economics* 22: 3–42.

Marquetti, A. 2004. "Do Rising Real Wages Increase the Rate of Labor-Saving Technical Change? Some Econometric Evidence." *Metroeconomica* 55(4): 432–441.

Matsuyama, K. 1992. "Agricultural Productivity, Comparative Advantage, and Economic Growth." *Journal of Economic Theory* 58(2): 317–334.

McCombie, J. 2002. "Increasing Returns and the Verdoorn Law from a Kaldorian Perspective." In *Productivity Growth and Economic Performance: Essays on Verdoorn' Law*, edited by J. McCombie, M. Pugno, and B. Soro, 64–114. Basingstoke, UK: Palgrave Macmillan.

Miyagawa, T., and H. Shoichi. 2013. "Estimates of Intangible Investment by Industry and Productivity Growth in Japan." *Japanese Economic Review* 64(1): 42–72.

Milanovic, Branco. 2012. "Global Inequality, From Class to Location, from Proletarians to Migrants." *Global Policy* 3(2): 125–134.

Milanovic, Branco. 2016. *Global Inequality: A New Approach for the Age of Globalization*. Cambridge, MA: Harvard University Press.

Oberfield, Ezra, and Devesh Raval. 2014. "Micro Data and Macro Technology." August 29. https://sites.google.com/site/ezraoberfield/CESAggregation.pdf.

OECD. 2008. *Growing Unequal? Income Distribution and Poverty in OECD Countries*. Paris: OECD.

OECD. 2009. *Measuring Capital-OECD Manual 2009*, 2nd edition. Paris: OECD.

OECD. 2011. *Growing Income Inequality in OECD Countries: What Drives It and How Can Policy Tackle it?* Paris: OECD.

Onaran, Ö., and G. Galanis. 2012. "Is Aggregate Demand Wage-Led or Profit-Led? National and Global Effects." ILO Working Paper No. 478623, International Labour Organization. http://www.robinson.cam.ac.uk/postkeynesian/downloads/soas12/ZN080612.pdf.

Ostry, J. D., A. Berg, and C. G. Tsangarides. 2014. "Redistribution, Inequality, and Growth." IMF Staff Discussion Note, SDN/14/02, International Monetary Fund. http://www.redproteccionsocial.org/sites/default/files/redistribution_inequality_and_growth.pdf.

Pereira, A. M., and J. M. Andraz. 2013. "On the Economic Effects of Public Infrastructure Investment: A Survey of the International Evidence." *Journal of Economic Development* 38(4): 1–37.

Perotti, R. 1996. "Growth, Income Distribution and Democracy." *Journal of Economic Growth* 1: 149–187.

Persson T., and G. Tabellini, 1994. "Is Inequality Harmful for Growth?" *The American Economic Review* 84(3): 600–621.

Piketty, T. 1997. "The Dynamics of the Wealth Distribution and the Interest Rate with Credit Rationing." *Review of Economic Studies* 64(2): 173–189.

Piketty, T. 2014a. *Capital in the Twenty-First Century*. Cambridge, MA: The Belknap Press of Harvard University Press.

Piketty, T. 2014b. "Technical Appendix" to *Capital in the Twenty-First Century*. http://piketty.pse.ens.fr/files/capital21c/en/Piketty2014TechnicalAppendix.pdf.

Pyo, H. 2005. *Productivity Performance in Developing Countries: Country Case Studies, Republic of Korea*. Vienna: United Nations Industrial Development Organization.

Pyo, II. 2000. "Excess Competition, Moral Hazard, and Industrial Trauma in Korea (1997–1998)." In *The Aftermath of the Asian Crisis*, edited by U. Dadush, D. Dasgupta, and M. Uzan, 13–26. Cheltenham, UK: Edward Elgar.

Pyo, H. 2008. "The Estimation of Industry-Level of Capital Stock for Emerging-Market and Transition Economies." Paper presented at the *2008 World Congress on National Accounts and Economic Performance Measures for Nations*, Washington, DC.

Pyo, H. K. 2015. "A Test of the Piketty Propositions Using Historical Data in the Republic of Korea." *The Korean Economic Forum* 8(1): 45–81.

Pyo, H., K. Rhee, and B. Ha. 2008. "Estimates of Labor and Total Factor Productivity by 72 industries in Korea (1970-2003)." In *Productivity Measurement, and Analysis*. Paris: OECD.

Ravallion, M. 2001. "Growth, Inequality and Poverty: Looking Beyond Averages." *World Development* 29(11): 1803–1815.

Ravallion, M., and S. Chen. 1997. "What Can New Survey Data Tell Us about Recent Changes in Distribution and Poverty?" *The World Bank Economic Review* 11(2): 357–382.

Ravallion, M., and S. Chen. 2003. "Measuring Pro-Poor Growth." *Economics Letters* 78: 93–99.

Rodrik, D. (ed.). 2003. *In Search of Prosperity: Analytic Narratives on Economic Growth*. Princeton, NJ: Princeton University Press.

Saint-Paul, G., and T. Verdier. 1993. "Education, Democracy and Growth." *Journal of Development Economics* 42: 399–407.

Schmidt, P., and R. C. Sickles. 1984. "Production Frontiers and Panel Data." *Journal of Business and Economic Statistics* 2(4): 367–374.

Schreyer, P. 2014. "Priorities and Directions for Future Productivity Research: An OECD Perspective." *International Productivity Monitor* 27: 7–9.

Sichel, D. 2014. "Priorities and Directions for Future Productivity Research: Health Care, Intangible Capital and High-Tech." *International Productivity Monitor* 27: 14–16.

SIDA. 2006. "Integrated Economic Analysis for Pro-Poor Growth: A Methodological Approach." Method Document. Stockholm: The Swedish International Development Cooperation Agency. http://www.sida.se/contentassets/4e5f543f34c2466b9850f9cf232143eb/integrated-economic-analysis-for-pro-poor-growth_1397.pdf.

Solow, R. M. 1956. "A Contribution to the Theory of Economic Growth." *The Quarterly Journal of Economics* 70(1): 65–94.

Solow, R. M. 1957. "Technical Change and the Aggregate Production Function." *Review of Economics and Statistics* 39: 312–320.

Storm, S., and C. W. M. Naastepad. 2008. "Why Labour Market Deregulation May Raise Unemployment." *International Review of Applied Economics* 22(5): 527–544.

Tamura, R. 1991. "Income Convergence in an Endogenous Growth Model." *Journal of Political Economy* 99: 522–540.

Trefler, D. 1993. "International Factor Price Differences: Leontief Was Right!" *Journal of Political Economy* 101: 961–987.

Triplett, J. E. 1999. "The Solow Productivity Paradox: What Do Computers Do to Productivity?" *Canadian Journal of Economics* 32(2): 309–334.

US Department of Labor. 1998. *Multifactor Productivity Trends, 1995 and 1996: Private Business, Private Nonfarm Business, and Manufacturing.* Washington, DC: Bureau of Labor Statistics.

van Ark, B. 2014. "Priorities and Directions for Future Productivity Research: The Need for Historical Perspective." *International Productivity Monitor* 27: 17–19.

van der Weide, R., and B. Milanovic. 2014. "Inequality Is Bad for Growth of the Poor (But Not for That of the Rich)." Policy Research Working Paper 6963, World Bank Group.

Ward, M. 1976. "Problems of Measuring Capital in Less Developed Countries." *The Review of Income and Wealth* 22(3): 207–221.

White, H., and E. Anderson. 2001. "Growth vs. Redistribution: Does the Pattern of Growth Matter?" *Development Policy Review* 19(3): 167–289.

World Bank. 2005. *Economic Growth in the 1990s: Learning from a Decade of Reform.* Washington, DC: World Bank.

World Bank. 2008. *Growth Report: Strategies for Sustained Growth and Inclusive Development.* Commission on Growth and Development. Washington, DC: World Bank.

Young, A. 1995. "The Tyranny of Numbers: Confronting the Statistical Realities of the East Asian Growth Experience." *Quarterly Journal of Economics* 110(3): 641–680.

CHAPTER 24

THE PRODUCTIVITY
OF NATIONS

OLEG BADUNENKO, DANIEL J. HENDERSON,
AND VALENTIN ZELENYUK

24.1. INTRODUCTION

THIS chapter concerns the patterns and sources of the growth of labor productivity of nations, with a focus on the preceding half-century.[1] The hallmarks of this review are threefold. First, by *patterns* we mean changes over time of economic performance for single economies and for all economies jointly. Second, while the economic growth and convergence literatures discuss several economic measures, such as aggregate output, aggregate output per capita, or aggregate labor productivity, we focus on the latter. Specifically, we focus our review on a simple, yet commonly used measure of productivity, namely labor productivity. It is one of the most intuitive indicators of national economic performance since it plainly tells how much a nation produces per unit of labor, given its endowment of other inputs (e.g., capital) and available technology. We will discuss relevant studies whose subject is either growth of labor productivity or other types of productivity change measures, such as a Malmquist productivity index. Third, we discuss long-run tendencies and forces behind the growth of labor productivity, and we pay special attention to the shift over time of the worldwide distribution of labor productivity levels. We will primarily focus on studies that used frontier methods via the so-called data envelopment analysis estimator, yet also briefly mention other popular methods.[2]

In recent years, there has been a re-emergence of the interest in economic growth. Research on national economic performance may be divided into two main strands. One group is seeking to determine the sources of economic growth. Within this group, several approaches are used in studies trying to explain why growth rates of per capita or per unit of labor output differ (Fagerberg 1988). The outdated descriptive analysis of why productivity growth rates differ between countries—typically referred to as "catch-up" analysis—was ascribing differences in productivity levels to various events, such as wars, and so on (Maddison 1984). In these studies, productivity differences are thought of as technological gaps, which less-developed economies fill by imitating the technology of more advanced economies, thus "catching up" to leading economies. The major limitation of "catch-up" analysis is that it does not explain structural changes in leading economies (i.e., those that experience large growth rates, the existence of those that catch up), and it does not anticipate changes in leadership (Abramovitz 1986).

Two other popular approaches are "level-accounting" and "growth-accounting" analyses. The former splits aggregate output into components; the latter relates the growth of aggregate output and the growth of its components using national accounts. Abramovitz (1956) was first to perform "growth-accounting" analysis for the United States. He measured labor services in man-hours and total volume of capital as land, structures, producers' durable equipment, inventories, and net foreign claims. He used net national product as aggregate output. Over two time periods (1869–1878 and 1944–1953), the author compared growth in aggregate output per capita to the combined growth of per capita labor and capital inputs, weighted proportionally to the base period incomes going to labor and property, respectively. He found that only a small part of net national product growth could be explained by growth in resources (or inputs). Abramovitz (1956) therefore came to the conclusion that almost the entire increase of net national product growth must be contributed to growth of resources productivity. "Growth accounting" analysis studied this unexplained part, which after the seminal work of Solow (1957) was dubbed the "Solow residual" and routinely was attributed as a measure of technological change.[3] In the common case with two inputs (capital and labor) and constant returns to scale, the Solow residual is the difference between the growth rate of labor productivity and the growth rate of capital per unit of labor, the latter being weighted by the fraction of output used to rent capital, known as the capital share (Barro and Sala-i-Martin 2004).

Solow (1957) also initiated a regression-based strand of studies trying to explain why growth rates differ. His study inspired a voluminous literature of econometric applications of cross-country production functions. Chenery (1986) summarized this literature, emphasizing that the Solow-type econometric approach to explaining differences in growth rates of labor productivity is of little help when the sample includes less-developed and semi-industrialized economies along with developed ones. Chenery termed such situations "disequilibrium growth" and attributed it to the fact that equilibrium conditions of the neoclassical theory—at the heart of the Solow (1957) approach—are not fulfilled for nonindustrialized countries. Most important, countries differ by the degree to which they satisfy the assumptions of the underlying model (returns to scale, resource allocation, perfect competition). Chenery also pointed out that a production function approach can account for different types of disequilibria by adding variables that reveal these disequilibria (see Chenery 1986, 27–31).

The second group studies whether growth rates of labor productivity of national economies converge or polarize over time. The premise that relatively poor and slow-growing economies have the potential to grow faster than more developed economies has not been uniformly confirmed. On the one hand, growth rates of labor productivity (Baumol 1986) or output per capita weighted by population (Sala-i-Martin 2006) tended to equalize. On the other hand, growth rates of labor productivity for narrow samples (De Long 1988) and output per capita for a large cross-section of countries (Pritchett 1997; Sala-i-Martin 1996)[4] failed to converge. Since the factors of production flew to already developed sectors of economies and rich countries (Easterly and Levine 2001), this suggested even more indication of the divergence of national economies in terms of level and growth of output per capita. Starting from the 1960s, there was a weak tendency for the initially rich economies to grow faster than the poor (Barro and Sala-i-Martin 1992). The consequence of this tendency was that in terms of labor productivity, economies of the world appeared to form two clubs, the poor and the rich (Quah 1996, 1997). The worldwide labor productivity distribution had been transforming from having one mode in the 1960s to being bimodal sometime during 1960–2000.

Previous analyses of sources and convergence of growth rates of labor productivity neglected the fact that economies utilize their productive capacities differently. Largely inspired by the works of Caves, Christensen, and Diewert (1982) and Färe, Grosskopf, Norris, and Zhang (1994b), the next generation of growth studies were taking the potential inefficiency of production into account. A new twist in this generation was made by Kumar and Russell (2002), who inspired a literature that combined a version of the Malmquist productivity index decomposition with distributional analysis to analyze sources and evolution of the growth of labor productivity, taking changes in technology, efficiency, and factors of production into consideration. This next generation of the growth literature (Henderson and Russell 2005; Badunenko, Henderson, and Zelenyuk 2008; Badunenko and Romero-Ávila 2013; Isaksson, Sickles, and Shang 2016; Duygun, Isaksson, Hao, and Sickles 2016) presented statistically supported evidence to explain many of the stylized views about differences in the productive performance of national economies.[5]

In what follows, we briefly describe some of the key methods and empirical evidence for the analysis of economic growth since the 1960s. Due to space limitations, we consider a subsample of the voluminous literature, and we are likely missing some interesting papers. The purpose of this review, however, is to provide an overview of the major findings that shaped the understanding of productivity growth patterns over half a century, with some remarks on directions for future research. The rest of the chapter is structured as follows. Section 24.2 reviews work on proximate causes of economic growth and describes the shift of interest from mere comparison of growth rates of labor productivity across countries to the analysis of the transformation of the entire labor productivity distribution. Section 24.3 introduces decompositions of Malmquist productivity indices and labor productivity. The core of this chapter is section 24.4, which summarizes empirical work on sources of productivity growth and the evolution of the worldwide distribution of productivity, most importantly the increased dispersion and the transformation over time from a unimodal to a bimodal distribution within a production frontier framework. Section 24.5 makes concluding remarks and a glimpse into possible future directions.

24.2. Early Works on Economic Growth and Convergence of Labor Productivity

24.2.1. From Within- to Cross-Country Analysis of Sources of Labor Productivity Growth

Under a set of relatively restrictive conditions, Solow (1957) showed how to distinguish between movements of the production function from movements along it in an analysis of labor productivity growth. He was the first to decompose labor productivity into components attributable to technical change and increased use of capital. Using US data from 1909–1949, he found that technological progress was on average approximately neutral and that technological change accounted for 87% of US productivity growth.

Since the work of Solow (1957), the empirical analysis of economic growth and its sources trended toward the top of the macroeconomics research agenda. The focus of empirical macroeconomists, however, shifted from looking at national economies in isolation to cross-country analyses. One of the triggers was the fact that during the post–World War II period, the growth of real national income per worker in eight European countries, with the exception of the United Kingdom, was larger than that of the United States (see Denison 1967, 18, Table 2-2). In an analysis of sources of national income growth rates for eight European countries and the United States during 1950–1962, Denison also found that the sources vary by place and time period. While there was no clear answer to the principal driver of the economies, the author identified advances of knowledge, nonresidential structures and equipment, and economies of scale as the sources contributing most to national income per worker growth for the majority of the nine investigated countries.

Following the Solow model, cross-country income difference and economic growth were attributed to improvements in technology, investment in physical capital, and accumulation of human capital. These causes, while vital, are only proximate causes of economic growth (Acemoglu 2009). The real challenge is to investigate the fundamental causes of differences in income and economic growth, that is, why some nations are not sufficiently improving technology, investing in physical capital and accumulating human capital (Acemoglu 2009; Weil 2014). Hall and Jones (1999) for example, found that variables attributable to physical and human capital only partially explained variation of output per worker across countries, while differences in "social infrastructure" (e.g., institutions and government policies) had the largest effect on the variation of economic development. Given the importance of differences in total factor productivity (TFP) for explaining cross-country differences in output per worker (see, e.g., Hall and Jones 1999), Hsieh and Klenow (2009) analyzed the causes of TFP differences. They found that physical capital and labor misallocation at the micro level significantly shrunk aggregate TFP, an argument also put forward by Chenery (1986). Other fundamental causes of productivity and economic growth considered in the literature are cultural and geographical idiosyncrasies (Acemoglu 2009).

24.2.2. Evolution of Growth Rates of Labor Productivity

Abramovitz (1986) expanded the macroeconomics research agenda by considering the question of whether growth rates of national economies converge. Convergence studies concentrated on two types of convergence. In the analysis of absolute β-convergence, researchers looked to the sign and significance of the coefficient β in a Baumol (1986) type cross-country regression:

$$\begin{aligned} \text{Growth rate of output per unit of labor (from } b \text{ to } c) = \\ \alpha + \beta \log(\text{Output per unit of labor in } b) + u, \end{aligned} \tag{24.1}$$

where b and c denote the base period and current period, respectively, and u is the disturbance term. The notion of σ-convergence, which focuses on the reduction in the dispersion of labor productivity over time, goes back at least to Easterlin (1960) and Borts and Stein (1964) (Sala-i-Martin 1996). β-convergence is a necessary, but not a sufficient condition for the existence of σ-convergence (Sala-i-Martin 1996). Conditional β-convergence is an extended version of absolute β-convergence, where structural characteristics of countries are taken into account as conditional variables are added to the convergence regression (24.1). It was noted that a negative β in a Baumol type regression does not necessarily imply convergence (see Bliss 2000 for discussion of Galton's Fallacy).

In one of the earliest examinations of long-run economic growth of gross domestic product (GDP) per worker, Baumol (1986) confirms the convergence phenomenon for eight industrialized countries during 1870–1979. Going beyond the ex post chosen sample of countries that are now rich and that have successfully developed yields different results. Using the same variables as Baumol (1986), De Long (1988) found that in a wider sample of 22 nations, rather than exhibiting a tendency to converge in terms of GDP per worker, some of the poorest countries have not been growing faster than rich ones. The argument of De Long is that Baumol's findings are not informative, since those economies that have not converged, but that were rich back in 1870, have been excluded from the analysis, which only considered economies that belonged to what Baumol termed the "convergence club" nations. De Long concluded that such a finding of convergence cannot be trusted because the sample suffers from selection bias.

In the mid-1980s, data on internationally comparable macroeconomic variables compiled by Heston and Summers (1988) from the real national accounts facilitated analyses of an even wider samples of countries. Mankiw, Romer, and Weil (1992) confirmed previous results of unconditional convergence[6] of incomes per worker across rich countries (OECD) from 1960–1985. However, there appeared to be no tendency for the poor economies to perform better than rich ones in a wider sample of countries, and the gap between the poor and the rich was not narrowing. Abramovitz (1986) seconds that convergence may take place only within a group of economies. Pritchett (1997) advocates divergence between developed and developing countries, although he concludes that growth rates of GDP per capita in developed economies appeared to converge. In contrast to Pritchett (1997), Sala-i-Martin (2006) argues that if population-weights are used, income per capita tends to converge during 1970–2000 for a wider sample, including African, Asian, Latin American, and former Soviet Union economies.

Divergence in a wider sample and convergence within smaller and relatively homogeneous samples required full reconsideration of the approach to study the evolution of growth rates. Quah (1996) introduced alternative models of distribution dynamics to study whether poor economies catch up. These models hinge on the observation that there emerge groups of rich and poor, while a middle-income group vanishes. Standard deviations or any other moment of the cross-sectional distribution, as well as relation of growth rates and per capita levels, which lie at the heart of β- and σ-convergence, cannot adequately explain growth dynamics leading to such twin-peakedness. A combination of β- and σ-convergence is not satisfactory either (see Quah 1997).

Since then, a segment of the convergence literature explicitly focused on the shape of the distribution, more specifically on the observation that the world is moving from a unimodal labor productivity distribution toward a bimodal distribution, the so-called twin-peaks distribution.[7] Jones (1997) centered his attention on the shape of the production function, allowing him to investigate the dynamics of income per capita. The author found that economies above the 50th percentile of the income distribution were expected to "catch up" or even overtake the United States, while economies below the 50th percentile were predicted to remain very close to where they are. Jones (1997) thus reaffirmed previous findings that there is divergence of per capita income at the bottom, while there is convergence at the top of per capita income distribution.

More recently, Andrews et al. (2015) consider national and global productivity frontiers. In their work, national frontiers using micro-level data are formed by choosing the 10 most productive firms by country, industry, and year, while the global frontier is formed by the 100 top productivity performers. In a related work, the Organisation for Economic Co-operation and Development (OECD 2016) reports considerable divergence between the productivity performance of global frontier firms—whose growth remained stable over time and who are more capital and patent-intensive, have larger sales, and are more profitable—and the rest, "non-frontier" firms. From their results, one can see that at the micro level, there is the same tendency as at the macro level: the building of two groups (see, for example, OECD 2016, 17–18, for a discussion). Using a different approach, Inklaar and Diewert (2016) use a similar best-practice concept to analyze industry convergence by considering what can be termed "E-convergence" of multilateral productivity. E measures the gap between the actual world productivity and the potential level of world productivity in a given time period. If the productivity of each nation is at the potential level, E equals one, indicating 100% efficiency in terms of the world productivity frontier. The dynamics of E over time tells us about shifts away or toward convergence of productivity to best practice.[8]

The frameworks involving β- and σ-convergence concepts cannot adequately investigate bimodalism in labor productivity distribution. One challenge in reconciling "convergence clubs" and bimodality notions is that bimodality could be a consequence of club convergence, but not vice versa, since members can move across clubs. Emergence and persistence of bimodality require revisiting the approaches to analyze the evolution of growth rates.

A major drawback of many of the studies we have mentioned in this section, and other studies in the same vein, was that they assumed that economies were producing at their full potential. Market failures, poor legal systems, weak institutions, market power, over-regulation, or other reasons lead many national economies to be technically inefficient, in the sense of being below the world technological frontier. The investigation of efficiency changes as a source of economic growth is important for at least two reasons. First, the efficiency of countries relative to the best practice may change over time. If this change is neglected, its effect on economic growth will be picked by other proximate causes of economic growth, which will be then estimated with a bias. Second, as will be discussed in this chapter, efficiency change (improvement or deterioration) is not a fundamental, but rather a proximate cause of economic growth. In the late 1990s and early 2000s, it was becoming *the* force behind emergence of a second (higher) mode of the labor productivity distribution. Hence finding reasons that are preventing nations from improving efficiency becomes a new challenge in the economic growth literature. The relatively new strand of the literature analyzes the growth patterns accounting for inefficiency, thus bringing together the macroeconomic and production frontier literatures (the latter being based on the pioneering work of Farrell 1957), to which we move next.

24.3. A Nonparametric Construction of Worldwide Technology and Technical Efficiency

24.3.1. Data Envelopment Analysis

Nonparametric production-frontier methods, based on envelopment of input and output quantity data in the "smallest" or "tightest fitting" convex and free disposal and possibly conical hulls, have been extensively employed over the last several decades in many areas of economics (e.g., manufacturing, agriculture, and finance). The principal objective of these methods has been to construct efficiency scores for a given decision-making unit (DMU). While traditionally a DMU is a unit such as a firm or an agency, here it is a country-year observation.

Consider a production process in which multiple inputs produce multiple outputs. If vector $x = (x_1,...,x_N)$ denotes N non-negative inputs, and vector $y = (y_1,..., y_M)$ denotes M non-negative outputs, the production technology in the period t can be characterized by a set T^t, broadly defined as

$$T^t = \{(x, y) : y \text{ are producible from } x \text{ in period } t\}. \tag{24.2}$$

The true technology set T^t is typically not observed in practice and is usually approximated with the help of activity analysis models and is operationalized or estimated via the linear-programming technique, for example as

$$\widehat{T}^{t, \text{CRS}} = \{(x, y) : \sum_{j=1}^{n} z_j y_{jm}^t \geq y_m, \quad m = 1,...,M,$$

$$\sum_{j=1}^{n} z_j x_{jq}^t \leq x_q, \quad q = 1,...,N, \tag{24.3}$$

$$z_j \geq 0, \quad j = 1,...,n\},$$

where $x^t = \langle x_i^t \rangle_{i=1}^n$ and $y^t = \langle y_i^t \rangle_{i=1}^n$, $x_i^t = (x_{i1}^t,...,x_{iN}^t)$ and $y_i^t = (y_{i1}^t,..., y_{iM}^t)$ denote data vectors of N inputs and M outputs for country i, $(i = 1, ..., n)$, in time period t, and vector $z = (z_1, ..., z_n)$ denotes the intensity variables that help "envelop" the data with the smallest convex free disposal cone. Since no parametric assumptions are imposed, the estimator in (24.3) is referred to as a nonparametric estimator of technology set T^t, which satisfies constant returns to scale (CRS), free disposability, and convexity. The roots of this approach go back to at least Farrell (1957) and Afriat (1972), and especially Charnes, Cooper, and Rhodes (1978), who branded this approach as data envelopment analysis (DEA hereafter).[9]

The upper boundary of the technology set T^t defines the (technology) frontier for that period t. How far a given country is from the frontier is referred to as its technical efficiency. Popular measures of technical efficiency for countries are conventional radial Debreu-Farrell measures of output-oriented technical efficiency, hereafter OTE (Debreu 1951; Farrell 1957), defined for a point (x_i, y_i) as

$$OTE(x_i, y_i \mid T^t) = \max\{\theta_i : (x_i, \theta_i y_i) \in T^t\}. \tag{24.4}$$

Intuitively, OTE measures the degree of necessary (equi-proportional) expansion of all outputs to move a country with allocation for a point (x_i, y_i) to technology frontier T^t, while keeping inputs and technology fixed for the particular period t. The true T^t in

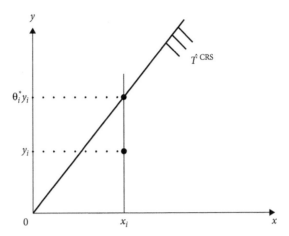

FIGURE 24.1. Output measure of technical efficiency.

(24.4) is unobserved, and replacing it with its DEA estimate in (24.3), gives the DEA estimator of this efficiency measure, formulated as

$$\widehat{OTE}\left(x_i, y_i \mid \widehat{\mathcal{T}}^{t,\mathrm{CRS}}\right) = \max \theta_i$$

$$\text{s.t.} \quad \sum_{j=1}^{n} z_j y_{jm}^t \geq y_{im} \theta_i, \quad m = 1, \dots, M,$$

$$\sum_{j=1}^{n} z_j x_{jq}^t \leq x_{iq}, \quad q = 1, \dots, N, \tag{24.5}$$

$$z_j \geq 0, \quad j = 1, \dots, n,$$

$$\theta_i \geq 0.$$

Figure 24.1 illustrates an output-based measure of technical efficiency in a hypothetical one-input-one-output production technology. The DMU (x_i, y_i) is inefficient as it is below the frontier. Given its input x_i it could have produced output $\theta_i^* y_i$ were it to exploit the technology, where θ_i^* is the optimal value of θ_i obtained from (24.5). For ease of interpretation, efficiency score is typically calculated as the reciprocal of the Debreu-Farrell measure, $1/\theta_i^*$, multiplied by 100 to obtain a percentage interpretation.

24.3.2. Malmquist Productivity Index

A Malmquist productivity index (MPI hereafter) is a theoretical index that measures the changes in productivity, allowing for various useful decompositions of sources of the changes and allowing for multi-input–multi-output production technologies.[10] It makes use of Shephard's distance functions, which are reciprocals of the Debreu-Farrell measure of technical efficiency (Färe, Grosskopf, and Lovell 1994a). Output-based MPI from time period b to time period c for country i is defined as the following (see Caves, Christensen, and Diewert, 1982):

$$
MPI_i^{bc} = \left[\frac{OTE\left(x_i^b, y_i^b \mid T^{b,\text{CRS}}\right)}{OTE\left(x_i^c, y_i^c \mid T^{b,\text{CRS}}\right)} \times \frac{OTE\left(x_i^b, y_i^b \mid T^{c,\text{CRS}}\right)}{OTE\left(x_i^c, y_i^c \mid T^{c,\text{CRS}}\right)} \right]^{1/2},
$$

where $OTE\left(x_i^b, y_i^b \mid T^{c,\text{CRS}}\right)$ is the Debreu-Farrell measure calculated for country i observed in time period b relative to the frontier in time period c for technology that satisfies CRS, free disposability and convexity. This index of productivity change for country i can be decomposed as

$$
MPI_i^{bc} = \frac{OTE\left(x_i^b, y_i^b \mid T^{b,\text{CRS}}\right)}{OTE\left(x_i^c, y_i^c \mid T^{c,\text{CRS}}\right)}
$$

$$
\times \left[\frac{OTE\left(x_i^c, y_i^c \mid T^{c,\text{CRS}}\right)}{OTE\left(x_i^c, y_i^c \mid T^{b,\text{CRS}}\right)} \times \frac{OTE\left(x_i^b, y_i^b \mid T^{c,\text{CRS}}\right)}{OTE\left(x_i^b, y_i^b \mid T^{b,\text{CRS}}\right)} \right]^{1/2}. \tag{24.6}
$$

$$
\equiv EFF_i^{bc} \times TECH_i^{bc},
$$

where EFF_i^{bc} and $TECH_i^{bc}$ are components attributable to a change in efficiency and change in technology, respectively. If $EFF_i^{bc} \gtreqless 1$, contribution of change in efficiency to productivity change from time-period b to time period c was positive/zero/negative for country i. If $TECH_i^{bc} \gtreqless 1$, this implies respectively that for country i, technical progress/stagnation/regress has occurred between periods b and c. The empirical estimates of EFF_i^{bc} and $TECH_i^{bc}$ provide a way to quantify what is sometimes referred to as economic catching up (or falling behind) and forging ahead—the concepts inspired by Abramovitz (1986).

The decomposition in (24.6) is a theoretical concept. The MPI, as well as components EFF and $TECH$, are unobserved and must be estimated, for example, with DEA, as described earlier, to obtain an empirical version of (24.6), given by

$$
\widehat{MPI}_i^{bc} = \widehat{EFF}_i^{bc} \times \widehat{TECH}_i^{bc}. \tag{24.7}
$$

Figure 24.2 demonstrates the decomposition of $\widehat{MPI}_i^{bc}$ in the one-input–one-output case, the movement from (x_b, y_b) to (x_c, y_c).[11] Denote $\bar{y}_c^b = \widehat{OTE}\left(x_c, y_c \mid \widehat{T}^{b,\text{CRS}}\right) \times y_c$ as the potential output in time period c given the estimated technology in time period b. The first term in (24.7) represents the estimated "catching up," or how much closer a given country is to the production frontier over time, that is, the movement of $\bar{y}_b^b / y_b$ to $\bar{y}_c^c / y_c$. The second term in (24.7) measures shifts in the frontier, from $\widehat{T}^{b,\text{CRS}}$ to $\widehat{T}^{c,\text{CRS}}$, in the region of input–output space occupied by a given country, and is thus referred to as technical change.

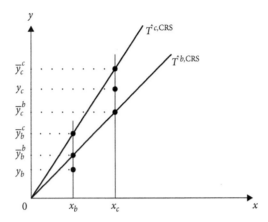

FIGURE 24.2. Output-based Malmquist productivity index MPI.

Source: Replication of Figure 1 in Färe, Grosskopf, Norris and Zhang (1994b).

The MPI decomposition is akin to "growth accounting." It is based on production theory axioms, thus potentially not contradicting economic growth theory. It decomposes an index of productivity change, which relates to the earlier discussion of productivity sources, with the advantage that it takes potential inefficiencies into account and addresses modeling issues raised by Bernard and Jones (1996). The MPI decomposition in (24.6) imposes CRS, implying that larger economies do not have scale advantage over smaller economies.[12] If they perform better, it is due to adopting better technology and/or being more efficient. Färe, Grosskopf, Norris, and Zhang (1994b) were among the first to use the MPI decomposition in (24.7) to study productivity change and its sources at the macro level. Early empirical study using productivity measurement include, among others, Färe, Grosskopf, Lindgren, and Roos (1989, 1994) (see Färe, Grosskopf, and Lovell 1994a, 239, for historical remarks).

24.3.3. Labor Productivity Decomposition

Kumar and Russell (2002) decomposed growth of labor productivity into factors attributable to changes in efficiency, technological change, and physical capital deepening. The authors assume that worldwide technology exists, and they model it with three macroeconomic variables: aggregate output (Y), labor (L), and physical capital (K) as inputs. They estimated the worldwide technology frontier using DEA, allowing for the measurement of the efficiency of countries. To be consistent with the notation of Kumar and Russell (2002), we let $y = Y / L$ and $k = K / L$ denote labor productivity and capital per unit of labor and drop subscript i for simplicity.[13] Further, denote $\bar{y}_b(k_b)$ as a potential labor productivity in time period b using capital intensity of time period b. Denote $\bar{y}_c(k_c)$ as a potential labor productivity in time period c using capital intensity of time period c. By definition, $y_b \times \widehat{OTE}_b = \bar{y}_b(k_b)$ and $y_c \times \widehat{OTE}_c = \bar{y}_c(k_c)$, where $\widehat{OTE}_b$ and

$\widehat{OTE_c}$ are the values of the estimated efficiency scores in the respective periods, as calculated in equation (24.5). Therefore,

$$\frac{y_c}{y_b} = \frac{\widehat{OTE_b}}{\widehat{OTE_c}} \times \frac{\bar{y}_c(k_c)}{\bar{y}_b(k_b)}. \tag{24.8}$$

By multiplying the numerator and denominator by potential labor productivity at current period capital intensity using base period technology, we obtain

$$\frac{y_c}{y_b} = \frac{\widehat{OTE_b}}{\widehat{OTE_c}} \times \frac{\bar{y}_c(k_c)}{\bar{y}_b(k_c)} \times \frac{\bar{y}_b(k_c)}{\bar{y}_b(k_b)}. \tag{24.9}$$

Alternatively, by multiplying the numerator and denominator by potential labor productivity at base period capital intensity using current period technology, we obtain

$$\frac{y_c}{y_b} = \frac{\widehat{OTE_b}}{\widehat{OTE_c}} \times \frac{\bar{y}_c(k_b)}{\bar{y}_b(k_b)} \times \frac{\bar{y}_c(k_c)}{\bar{y}_c(k_b)}. \tag{24.10}$$

As described in more detail in Henderson and Russell (2005), these identities decompose the growth of labor productivity in the two periods into changes in efficiency, technology changes, and changes in the capital-labor ratio. As shown in Figure 24.3, the decomposition in (24.9) measures technological change by the shift in the frontier in the output direction at the current-period capital-labor ratios, whereas the decomposition in (24.10) measures technological change by the shift in the frontier in the output direction at base-period capital-labor ratios. Similarly, (24.9) measures the effect of physical capital deepening along the base-period frontier, whereas (24.10) measures the effect of physical capital deepening along the current-period frontier.

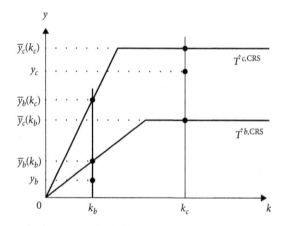

FIGURE 24.3. Tripartite decomposition of labor productivity.

Source: Replication of the Figure 3 in Kumar and Russell (2002).

The choice between (24.9) and (24.10) is arbitrary. Kumar and Russell (2002) found that while the results for many countries differed, the basic results of their study stayed the same when employing either path. They eventually report the "Fisher Ideal" approach (Persons 1921), simply by taking geometric averages of the two measures. This results in the following decomposition of primary interest:

$$
\frac{y_c}{y_b} = \frac{\widehat{OTE_b}}{\widehat{OTE_c}} \times \left(\frac{\bar{y}_c(k_c)}{\bar{y}_b(k_c)} \times \frac{\bar{y}_c(k_b)}{\bar{y}_b(k_b)} \right)^{1/2} \times \left(\frac{\bar{y}_b(k_c)}{\bar{y}_b(k_b)} \times \frac{\bar{y}_c(k_c)}{\bar{y}_c(k_b)} \right)^{1/2}
$$

$$
\equiv \widehat{EFF}^{bc} \times \widehat{TECH}^{bc} \times \widehat{KLACC}^{bc},
$$

(24.11)

where the $\widehat{KLACC}^{bc}$ term represents a contribution to labor productivity growth between time period b and time period c, attributable to change in capital per unit of labor.[14] Note that the components are country specific. We omit the country index for simplicity. The major difference between the approaches of Färe, Grosskopf, Norris, and Zhang (1994b) and Kumar and Russell (2002) therefore is distinguishing movements along the frontier as a separate source of the transition of point (k_b, y_b) to point (k_c, y_c). What is of great importance about MPI and labor productivity decompositions is that they introduce an additional, previously neglected by the virtue of the Solow model, proximate cause of growth (i.e., the efficiency change). Decompositions illustrate that efficiency change has an effect on labor productivity growth, which is direct, and is not channeled through other proximate causes such as changes in technology and physical capital deepening.

24.4. Empirical Analysis of Growth and the Evolution of Labor Productivity Using a Production Frontier Approach

In this section, we review some of the cross-country empirical studies of growth and convergence of labor productivity that used a production frontier framework.

24.4.1. Data Used in Cross-Country Studies

One of the factors behind the emergence of the voluminous cross-country analyses was the availability of data, which allowed making real international quantity comparison both between countries and over time (Feenstra et al. 2015; Heston and Summers 1988). These data were compiled from the Real National Accounts, better known as the Penn World Tables (PWT hereafter).[15] These data are used by numerous authors analyzing growth patterns of labor productivity and therefore deserve some description.

Table 24.1 Summary Statistics of Macroeconomic Variables for 57 Countries Used in Kumar and Russell (2002)

Variable	sd	min	p25	mean	p50	p75	max
1965							
Y	313.4	1.2	6.4	110.5	26.2	65.3	2263.5
K	199.2	0.1	4.4	74.8	16.4	55.1	1412.7
L	29.5	0.1	1.4	11.5	3.4	8.8	204.2
1990							
Y	658.2	3.4	15.3	266.0	70.1	194.8	4520.2
K	689.3	0.3	13.0	283.0	60.5	201.9	4266.2
L	46.9	0.1	2.6	17.8	4.7	13.2	331.9

Following the definition used by PWT, Y and K are measured in billions of US dollars at prices of 1985, L is measured in millions of workers (census definition based on economically active population; data from International Labor Organization); sd, min, mean, and max denote the sample standard deviation, the sample minimum, the sample arithmetic mean, and sample maximum, respectively; p# denotes the #[th] sample percentile.

Färe, Grosskopf, Norris, and Zhang (1994b), Kumar and Russell (2002), and Henderson and Russell (2005) used PWT, Mark 5, to obtain macroeconomic variables as follows: aggregate output Y is real GDP, obtained by multiplying chain-index of real GDP (RGDPCH) by population (POP) and aggregate inputs; capital stock K and employment L are retrieved from capital stock per worker and real GDP per worker (KAPW and RGDPW). Note that the PWT converts GDP at national prices to US dollars, making them comparable across countries. Real GDP and the capital stock are measured in billions of US dollars, using prices of 1985 as a benchmark. Productivity is aggregate labor productivity. Färe, Grosskopf, Norris, and Zhang (1994b) used a sample of 17 OECD countries over the period 1979–1988. Kumar and Russell (2002) and Henderson and Russell (2005) used a wider sample of 57 and 52 countries, respectively, including OECD as well as African, Asian, and Latin American nations for 1965–1990. Basic summary statistics for the data used in Kumar and Russell (2002) are given in Table 24.1. We will describe and mention the sources of variables used in other studies as they are discussed.

24.4.2. Färe, Grosskopf, Norris, and Zhang (1994b) Cross-Country Analysis of a Malmquist Productivity Index

In one of the most cited works in the area, Färe, Grosskopf, Norris, and Zhang (1994b) used DEA to nonparametrically estimate production frontier for industrialized countries, assuming that the technology can be characterized via three macroeconomic variables—aggregate output, labor, and physical capital as inputs—and compare each of the countries in their sample to that frontier. The purpose of their study was to construct the MPI between 1979 and 1988 and perform analysis of productivity change by decomposing the MPI as in (24.6). *Inter alia*, the authors found that over the period 1979–1988, US productivity was higher than average, mainly due to technical change. Interestingly, Japan was found to benefit the most of the industrialized countries from catching up to the world production frontier. By and large, this study, together with Caves et al. (1982), inspired a whole new stream of literature that used MPI and its decomposition in general, and for macroeconomic growth analysis in particular, and we discuss some recent studies in the following.

24.4.3. Labor Productivity Growth and Its Decomposition

Convergence in income is closely related to productivity growth (Färe, Grosskopf, Norris, and Zhang, 1994b). Bernard and Jones (1996) argued that the analysis of convergence should focus more carefully on technology, for example by allowing economies to accumulate technology at different rates. Addressing this issue, Kumar and Russell (2002) were the first to put two strands of literatures together: macroeconomic convergence and production frontiers. Their starting point was the stylized fact that during 1965–1990, the countries became divided into two groups, the rich and the poor (Quah 1996, 1997). It must be noted that neither Quah nor Kumar and Russell tested if multimodality were actually present in 1990. Henderson, Parmeter, and Russell (2008) applied calibrated Silverman and Dip tests for multimodality to test worldwide labor productivity distribution and found that it was during the period 1960–2000 that the multimodality of the labor productivity distribution was either present or emerged. Figure 24.4, showing distributions of labor productivity in 1965 and 1990,[16] indicated

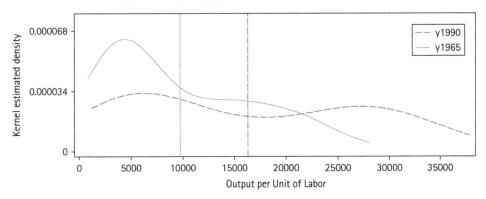

FIGURE 24.4. Distributions of labor productivity, 1965 and 1990.

The vertical green solid line represents the mean of labor productivity in 1965.
The vertical blue dotted line represents the mean of labor productivity in 1990.

Source: Replication of the Figure 1 in Kumar and Russell (2002).

that the distribution of labor productivity shifted from being unimodal in 1965 to bi-modal in 1990.[17] The main interest of Kumar and Russell (2002) thus lied in studying the forces behind the emergence of apparent bimodality in the labor productivity distribution, a phenomenon routinely referred to starting from the work of Quah (1996) as "two-club" or "twin-peak" convergence.[18]

Among the key findings of Kumar and Russell (2002) was that over the period 1965–1990, labor productivity increased by 75% on average, being primarily driven by physical capital deepening, about 60%, while change in technology and efficiency changes contributed only about 5% each to this growth.[19] Kumar and Russell also used the decomposition (24.11) to analyze the evolution of the worldwide distribution of productivity, most importantly, the transformation over time from a unimodal to a bimodal distribution. Figure 24.5 suggests that physical capital deepening was primarily responsible for the change in the shape of the distribution. Neither change in efficiency nor technical change contributed to shifting the distribution of labor productivity. Here we use the same data and the bootstrapped version of the Li (1996) test to distinguish the component (set of components) that contributes to overall changes in the distribution of labor productivity.[20] Table 24.2 presents the results of the bootstrapped test of equality of distributions. The distributions of labor productivity in 1965 and 1990 are statistically different. Neither efficiency change (panel a of figure 24.5) nor technological change

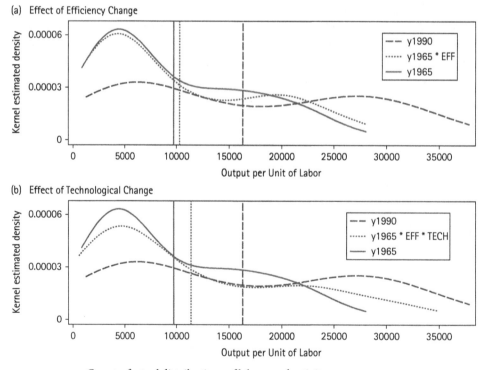

FIGURE 24.5. Counterfactual distributions of labor productivity.

Source: A replication of Figure 9 in Kumar and Russell (2002).

Table 24.2 Distribution Hypothesis Tests (p-Values):
A Replication of the Results of Table 3
in Kumar and Russell (2002)

H_0: Distributions Are Equal H_i: Distributions Are Not Equal	Bootstrap p-Value
$g(y_{1990})$ vs. $f(y_{1965})$	0.0022
$g(y_{1990})$ vs. $f(y_{1965} \times EFF)$	0.0074
$g(y_{1990})$ vs. $f(y_{1965} \times TECH)$	0.0366
$g(y_{1990})$ vs. $f(y_{1965} \times KLACC)$	0.3688
$g(y_{1990})$ vs. $f(y_{1965} \times EFF \times TECH)$	0.0502
$g(y_{1990})$ vs. $f(y_{1965} \times EFF \times KLACC)$	0.4012
$g(y_{1990})$ vs. $f(y_{1965} \times TECH \times KLACC)$	0.8780

Notes: We employed the bootstrapped Li (1996) tests with 5,000
bootstrap replications and the Sheather and Jones (1991) bandwidth.

Table 24.3 Mean Percentage Change of the Tripartite Decomposition Indices
for Kumar and Russell (2002) Sample: A Replication of the Last Rows
of Table A1 and B1 in Badunenko, Henderson, and Zelenyuk (2008)

Time Period	Labor Productivity Change	$(EFF-1)\times100$	$(TECH-1)\times100$	$(KLACC-1)\times100$
1992–2000	13.2	−3.2	7.3	9.0
1965–2000	88.9	−9.7	13.3	84.7

alone can make the 1965 distribution closer to that of 1990. They can do so only in combination with physical capital deepening (panel b of Figure 24.5). What is remarkable,
though, is that physical capital deepening alone statistically shifts the distribution of
labor productivity between 1965 and 1990.

Badunenko, Henderson, and Zelenyuk (2008) updated the Kumar and Russell study
by considering a more recent time period, 1992–2000, and using a wider sample (approximately 50%) that includes 22 transitional countries. They discovered an apparent structural change in the growth process in the 1990s. By comparing the 1992–2000 results to
the 1965–2000 results, Badunenko, Henderson, and Zelenyuk (2008) concluded that the
major fall in efficiency and rise in technology components happened during the final
decade (Table 24.3). The predominant contribution of physical capital deepening therefore was before 1990. Figure 24.6, a replication of Figure 6 in Badunenko, Henderson,
and Zelenyuk (2008) shows that technological change (panel a of figure 24.6) made

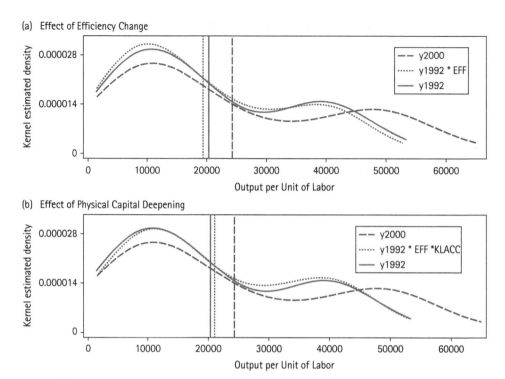

(a) Effect of Efficiency Change

(b) Effect of Physical Capital Deepening

FIGURE 24.6. Counterfactual distributions of labor productivity.

Source: A replication of Figure 6 in Badunenko, Henderson, and Zelenyuk (2008).

Table 24.4 Distribution Hypothesis Tests (*p*-Values): A Replication of Results of Table 4 in Badunenko, Henderson, and Zelenyuk (2008)

H_0: Distributions Are Equal H_1: Distributions Are Not Equal	Bootstrap *p*-Value
$g(y_{2000})$ vs. $f(y_{1992})$	0.0824
$g(y_{2000})$ vs. $f(y_{1992} \times EFF)$	0.0504
$g(y_{2000})$ vs. $f(y_{1992} \times TECH)$	0.9786
$g(y_{2000})$ vs. $f(y_{1992} \times KLACC)$	0.0754
$g(y_{2000})$ vs. $f(y_{1992} \times EFF \times TECH)$	0.9722
$g(y_{2000})$ vs. $f(y_{1992} \times EFF \times KLACC)$	0.0576
$g(y_{2000})$ vs. $f(y_{1992} \times TECH \times KLACC)$	0.8601

Notes: We employed the bootstrapped Li (1996) tests with 5,000 bootstrap replications and the Sheather and Jones (1991) bandwidth.

most countries richer. Table 24.4 confirms that it is technological change that shifted the labor productivity of 1992 to that of 2000. Neither efficiency change nor physical capital deepening alone, or in combination (panel b of figure 24.6), was responsible for the shift in the sample of countries and the periods they considered.

24.4.3.1. *Role of Human Capital*

Human capital and its growth were identified by empirical growth researchers to be an important source of differences in growth patterns of nations. This motivated Henderson and Russell (2005) to incorporate human capital into the Kumar and Russell framework.[21] They adopted a standard approach in the literature (e.g., Hall and Jones, 1999; Klenow and Bils, 2000; Lucas, Jr., 1988) and assumed that human capital entered the technology as a multiplicative augmentation of physical labor input. This labor-augmenting human capital specification reflects the idea that human capital captures the "efficiency units of labor" embedded in raw labor (see Weil 2014). This allowed Henderson and Russell (2005) to decompose labor productivity growth into four components, including human capital deepening (see Henderson and Russell 2005, 1178–1880, for details),

$$\frac{y_c}{y_b} \equiv \widehat{EFF}^{bc} \times \widehat{TECH}^{bc} \times \widehat{KLACC}^{bc} \times \widehat{HLACC}^{bc}, \qquad (24.12)$$

where the $\widehat{HLACC}^{bc}$ term represents a contribution to labor productivity growth between time period b and time period c, attributable to human capital deepening.[22] The authors also constructed the worldwide technology that precluded technological implosion (Diewert 1980) by including past observations in current-period frontier estimation.

By accounting for human capital, Henderson and Russell (2005) showed that compared to Kumar and Russell (2002), the mean contribution of physical capital deepening decreased from 58% to 40%. Meanwhile, 16% of productivity growth on average was explained by human capital deepening (Table 24.5). They also argued that roughly one-third of the growth of productivity attributed to physical capital deepening by Kumar and Russell (2002) was in fact attributable to human capital deepening.

Table 24.5 Mean Percentage Change of Tripartite and Quadripartite Decomposition Indices, 1965–1990: A Replication of Two Last Rows of Table 3 in Henderson and Russell (2005)

Decomposition	Labor Productivity change	$(EFF-1)$ ×100	$(TECH-1)$ ×100	$(KLACC-1)$ ×100	$(HLACC-1)$ ×100
Tripartite	78.6	3.9	9.6	58.0	
Quadripartite	78.6	0.7	7.1	40.5	16.6

Moreover, Henderson and Russell (2005) confirm that both growth and bimodal polarization are driven by physical capital deepening to a large extent. Specifically, physical capital deepening alone (panel a of figure 24.7) did not change the shape of the labor productivity distribution from unimodal to bimodal (Figure 24.7). It did so only in combination with technological change or human capital deepening (panels b and c of figure 24.7). The joint contribution of physical capital deepening and human capital deepening in Henderson and Russell (2005) is essentially the contribution of physical capital deepening in Kumar and Russell (2002).

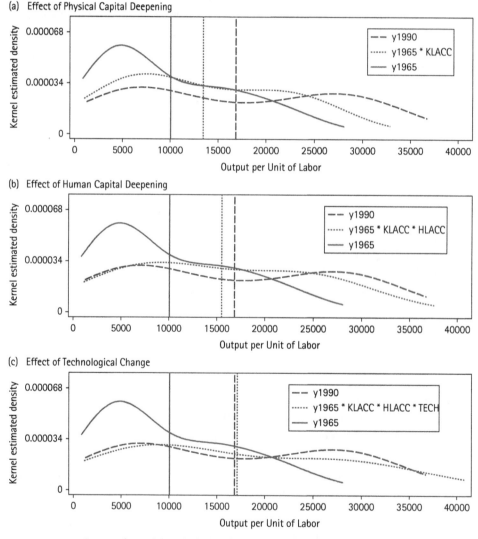

FIGURE 24.7. Counterfactual distributions of labor productivity.

Source: A replication of Figure 10 in Henderson and Russell (2005).

Table 24.6 contains the results of the bootstrapped Li (1996) test for equality of the counterfactual distributions and the actual 1990 distribution. Table 24.7 contains the results of the Silverman (1981) multimodality test to statistically assess which component (or set of components) causes bimodality in the 1990 productivity distribution. Physical capital deepening does not play the dominant role in the overall change in the distribution between 1965 and 1990. Only in combination with technological change or human capital deepening—but not when it is combined with efficiency changes—does physical capital deepening transform the distribution to be bimodal. The hypothesis that the 1990 distribution has one mode is rejected at the 1% significance level. None of the components alone can account for the emergence of bimodality in the distribution at even the 5% significance level. Efficiency changes, in combination with physical capital deepening or human capital deepening, indicate the emergence of bimodalism. Without efficiency changes and physical capital deepening, or efficiency changes and human capital deepening, technical change does not add to the transformation of the 1965 productivity distribution from unimodal to bimodal in 1990.

Table 24.6 Distribution Hypothesis Tests (p-Values): A Replication of the Results of Table 7 in Henderson and Russell (2005)

H_0: Distributions Are Equal H_1: Distributions Are Not Equal	Bootstrap p-Value
$g(y_{1990})$ vs. $f(y_{1965})$	0.0036
$g(y_{1990})$ vs. $f(y_{1965} \times EFF)$	0.0024
$g(y_{1990})$ vs. $f(y_{1965} \times TECH)$	0.0266
$g(y_{1990})$ vs. $f(y_{1965} \times KLACC)$	0.0664
$g(y_{1990})$ vs. $f(y_{1965} \times HLACC)$	0.0348
$g(y_{1990})$ vs. $f(y_{1965} \times EFF \times TECH)$	0.0094
$g(y_{1990})$ vs. $f(y_{1965} \times EFF \times KLACC)$	0.0118
$g(y_{1990})$ vs. $f(y_{1965} \times EFF \times HLACC)$	0.0042
$g(y_{1990})$ vs. $f(y_{1965} \times TECH \times KLACC)$	0.9348
$g(y_{1990})$ vs. $f(y_{1965} \times TECH \times HLACC)$	0.0700
$g(y_{1990})$ vs. $f(y_{1965} \times KLACC \times HLACC)$	0.5156
$g(y_{1990})$ vs. $f(y_{1965} \times EFF \times TECH \times KLACC)$	0.4782
$g(y_{1990})$ vs. $f(y_{1965} \times EFF \times TECH \times HLACC)$	0.2314
$g(y_{1990})$ vs. $f(y_{1965} \times EFF \times KLACC \times HLACC)$	0.0634
$g(y_{1990})$ vs. $f(y_{1965} \times TECH \times KLACC \times HLACC)$	0.8830

Notes: We employed the bootstrapped Li (1996) tests with 5,000 bootstrap replications and the Sheather and Jones (1991) bandwidth.

Table 24.7 Modality Tests (p-Values): A Replication
of the Results of Table 6 in Henderson and
Russell (2005)

H_0: Distribution Has One Mode	Bootstrap
H_1: Distribution Has More Than One Mode	p-Value
$f(y_{1965})$	0.458
$f(y_{1990})$	0.010
$f(y_{1965} \times EFF)$	0.091
$f(y_{1965} \times TECH)$	0.839
$f(y_{1965} \times KLACC)$	0.097
$f(y_{1965} \times HLACC)$	0.338
$f(y_{1965} \times EFF \times TECH)$	0.155
$f(y_{1965} \times EFF \times KLACC)$	0.020
$f(y_{1965} \times EFF \times HLACC)$	0.042
$f(y_{1965} \times TECH \times KLACC)$	0.072
$f(y_{1965} \times TECH \times HLACC)$	0.663
$f(y_{1965} \times KLACC \times HLACC)$	0.076
$f(y_{1965} \times EFF \times TECH \times KLACC)$	0.030
$f(y_{1965} \times EFF \times TECH \times HLACC)$	0.218
$f(y_{1965} \times EFF \times KLACC \times HLACC)$	0.000
$f(y_{1965} \times TECH \times KLACC \times HLACC)$	0.149

Notes: We employed the bootstrapped Li (1996) tests with 5,000 bootstrap
replications and the Sheather and Jones (1991) bandwidth.

In a more recent study, Badunenko, Henderson, and Russell (2013) use the Henderson and Russell decomposition and data for 1965–2007[23] to provide new findings on the causes of polarization (the emergence of bimodality) and divergence (increased variance) of the world productivity distribution. The deterioration of efficiency in the 1990s documented in Badunenko, Henderson, and Zelenyuk (2008) continued to an extent that efficiency change has become the unique driver of the emergence of a second mode. This suggests that economies operating at low capital-labor ratios were lagging behind those with high capital intensity, and most of the benefits of technical progress accrued to rich countries that pushed the technological frontier forward.

24.4.3.2. *Preliminary Summary*

The reader of this chapter might have noticed by now that the conclusions about sources of productivity change, as well as driving forces behind the shift and transformation of the distribution of productivity levels, vary with decomposition and time period. In particular, several interesting observations are worth summarizing here before going further.

First, irrespective of the decomposition, physical capital deepening seems to be the major proximate cause of productivity growth during 1965–1990. This holds true whether the original sample of 57 nations or the wider sample of 98 nations is considered. However, the magnitude of this cause abates by about a third once productivity decomposition accounts for human capital. Moreover, although physical capital deepening remains the strongest force, human capital deepening is a very important cause of productivity growth. Furthermore, physical capital deepening, together with efficiency change, was responsible for the transformation of the cross-country distribution of productivity levels from being unimodal in 1965 to bimodal in 1990. On the other hand, neither technological change nor human capital deepening, nor their combination, made the 1965 distribution bimodal.

Second, while the predominant contribution of physical capital deepening to productivity growth was before 1990, the 1990s seem to have brought about structural change in the growth process, where technological change started to play a more prominent role (in a statistical sense). Moreover, efficiency change became a more substantial contributor to the growth of productivity.

Third, during the first decade of this century, efficiency changes solidified as a unique driver of the emergence of a second (higher) mode. Technological change and human capital deepening were also significant factors explaining this change in the distribution (most notably the emergence of an even longer right-hand tail).

Finally, the reviewed studies indicate that the time period matters for conclusions. This is encouraging since it helps mark the structural changes in growth patterns.

24.4.4. Growth and Convergence of Labor Productivity at the Regional Level

In addition to studies that look at performance of national economies, numerous studies have investigated performance and within-country convergence of regions. Here we list several examples.

Henderson, Tochkov, and Badunenko (2007) analyzed growth pattern across Chinese provinces. The distribution of labor productivity was found to be multimodal. Over the period 1978–2000, physical capital deepening was the major driving force behind the growth performance of Chinese provinces, and it contributed the most to the shift of the labor productivity distribution, whereas minimal technological progress and human capital deepening were key factors responsible for regional disparities in China.

Delgado-Rodríguez and Álvarez Ayuso (2008) first performed the Kumar and Russell and MPI decompositions analysis for 15 EU member-states, which comprised the integrated European economy over the time period 1980–2001, and then related the components to initial labor productivity level and private, public, and human capital in a panel data setting. Physical capital deepening played the leading role in labor productivity growth throughout, followed by technological improvements in the 1990s. The authors found that in the middle and the end of the observed time period, less productive economies tended to grow faster than more productive counterparts, supporting the convergence of EU member-states.

Badunenko and Tochkov (2010) compared regional growth and convergence in China, Russia, and India over the period 1993–2000 and showed that largely wealthy regions drove the overall growth in all three countries. The physical capital deepening was the major determinant of regional growth in China and India. In Russia, the regional growth was mainly due to technological change, while physical capital deepening impeded labor productivity growth.

Enflo and Hjertstrand (2009) investigated Western European regional productivity growth and convergence. The authors found that most of the 69 regions in five different countries had fallen behind the production frontier and that physical capital deepening prevented convergence in labor productivity.

Badunenko and Romero-Ávila (2014) found that physical capital deepening was the primary contributor to productivity growth of Spanish regions during 1980–2003, closely followed by human capital deepening and technological change. They also found evidence that many regions fell behind the production frontier, and higher efficiency losses exhibited by rich regions in fact drove productivity convergence.

24.4.5. Statistical Inference

Earlier studies that use nonparametric production frontier measurement have largely ignored the issue of statistical inference when identifying the sources of labor productivity growth. Indeed, the individual and average components found in these papers are point estimates obtained relative to the finite sample DEA estimate of the true and unobserved frontier.

Using the finite sample estimate implies that the efficiency scores and consequently the components of MPI decomposition are subject to sampling variation of the estimated frontier. Simar and Wilson (1999) developed bootstrap methods to provide statistical inference regarding MPI and its components. Jeon and Sickles (2004) extended it for bootstrapping the Malmquist-Luenberger productivity index and its components in OECD and Asian economies, while taking explicit account of environmental waste byproducts.

Meanwhile, Henderson and Zelenyuk (2007) used several statistical methods for inference on efficiency scores and convergence of national economies, further extending the framework of Kumar and Russell (2002) and Henderson and Russell (2005). One of the novelties of their approach was to allow for a group-wise heterogeneous data-generating process: they assumed that while countries share the same global frontier, the distribution of efficiencies might differ between some groups, such as developed and developing countries. Specifically, the authors first performed a smooth bootstrap to correct for small-sample bias of efficiency estimates in the sample of countries used in Henderson and Russell (2005). Interestingly, such correction of the bias suggested that most countries experienced substantially greater inefficiency than previously reported. For example, the average efficiency dropped from 63% to 53%, and more so for some countries. Indeed, some surprisingly frontier-defining countries from earlier studies, such as Sierra Leone, appeared with more plausible levels of inefficiency (70% rather than 100%). The second bootstrap-based procedure the authors deployed was for testing distributions of DEA-estimated efficiency, due to Simar and Zelenyuk (2006). Here, the authors concluded that the distributions of efficiencies were statistically and substantially different between groups (developed vs. developing countries) in any considered time periods, yet those distributions did not change significantly over time for any particular group they considered. The third bootstrap-based procedure the authors used was for inference on aggregate (weighted) efficiency scores, due to Simar and Zelenyuk (2007), to allow for an adequate account of the economic weights (in terms of relative GDP) of countries whose efficiency scores were aggregated into a group efficiency. With this procedure, the authors concluded that the developed countries were significantly and substantially more efficient than the developing countries, in both considered periods (1965 and 1990). Moreover, they also found some evidence for what they called "efficiency convergence," both for the entire sample and within each group.

Recently, Daskovska et al. (2010) extended the bootstrapping methods for MPI further, to account for possible temporal correlation in the data for constructing prediction intervals of the MPI. The authors first consider MPI decomposition where components possess the circularity property, that is, $I^{t,t+2} = I^{t,t+1} \times I^{t+1,t+2}, \forall t$ (Pastor and Lovell 2007). Then they introduce a dynamic procedure for forecasting MPI. Finally, inference on the forecasted MPI was made by extending the smoothed bootstrap procedure in Simar and Wilson (1999) for the sample of industrialized economies used in Färe, Grosskopf, Norris, and Zhang (1994b).

More recently, Badunenko, Henderson, and Houssa (2014) made use of the bootstrap method in Simar and Wilson (1999) to provide statistical inference regarding the growth components of the Henderson and Russell (2005) quadripartite decomposition to analyze the sources of growth in Africa for the period 1970–2007, using data on 35 African countries.[24] On average (Table 24.8), physical capital deepening seemed to be the largest factor behind growth (contribution of 67%), followed by human capital deepening (60%). However, considering statistical inference, physical capital deepening

Table 24.8 Mean Percentage Change of Quadripartite Decomposition Indices in African Countries, 1970–2007: A Replication of Table 2 in Badunenko, Henderson, and Houssa (2014)

Group	Productivity change	$(EFF-1)$ ×100	$(TECH-1)$ ×100	$(KLACC-1)$ ×100	$(HLACC-1)$ ×100
Mean	54.18	−38.21	1.53	67.35	**60.19**

Bold implies significance at 1% level.

was not statistically different from 0, even at the 10% level of significance, while human capital deepening was statistically significant at the 1% level. Badunenko, Henderson, and Houssa (2014) showed that ignoring statistical inference leads to falsely concluding that physical capital deepening was a major economic engine in Africa when it was not (see Pritchett 2000, for discussion of the effect of capital on growth). For other regions of the world, physical capital deepening was a large and significant contributor to productivity growth elsewhere, but not in Africa.

24.4.6. Growth and Convergence of Labor Productivity Using Stochastic Frontier Methods

In this review, we have chosen to focus mostly on DEA-based approaches to analyze productivity growth and its convergence. However, we acknowledge that economic growth within a production frontier framework can also be analyzed using a stochastic frontier approach (SFA). We therefore mention a few key studies in this vein.

The first work to note in the area is due to Hultberg, Nadiri, and Sickles (1999), who proposed a dynamic model that considers technology diffusion and possible inefficiency caused by institutional rigidities. Applying the model to a total of 40 countries in three regions, Europe, Latin America, and East Asia, the authors found that difference of a leader nation in terms of labor productivity was a significant source of growth during the period 1960–1985, which can be interpreted as realizing the catching-up potential described in Abramovitz (1986).

In a related and follow-up study, Hultberg, Nadiri, and Sickles (2004) argued that technology transfer from a leading economy affects followers' productivity growth in manufacturing sectors in particular, and GDP in general. They also analyzed the catch-up in labor productivity across manufacturing sectors and GDP for 16 OECD nations for the period 1960–1985. *Inter alia*, they found that catch-up rates are underestimated in aggregate studies due to failure to account for heterogeneity of technology levels, and that institutional factors such as bureaucratic efficiency are important determinants of the estimated catch-up rates.

Meanwhile, Kumbhakar and Wang (2005) suggested decomposing TFP growth into technical change, technological catch-up, and scale-related components of TFP growth using a stochastic frontier panel data model. One important contribution of the authors is that their specification accounts for country-specific effects, which, as econometric analysis suggests, are present. Ignoring heterogeneity tends to underestimate the catch-up rate (see also Hultberg, Nadiri, and Sickles 2004) and overestimate technical regress. For 82 countries over the period 1960–1987, they estimated the annual average decline in TFP to be about 1.5% (approximately 33% over 27 years). Moreover, their method attributed this drop to technological regress of about 3.1% per year and movement away from optimal scale by 2.5% annually (approximately 57% and 49% over the whole period, respectively). They also concluded that countries got closer to the production frontier on average by 4.2% per year (approximately 203% over the entire time period).

Recently, Sickles, Hao, and Shang (2014) performed model averaging using various weighting schemes in the TFP decomposition framework for Asian economies for the time period 1980–2000. They found that the TFP changed annually by 1.56% over 31 years, which was driven by technological change of 1.63% and was hindered by deteriorating technical efficiency of 0.07% per annum.

Most recently, Sickles, Hao, and Shang (2016) consider the period 1960–2010 for 24 OECD countries and revisited the decomposition of the TFP index into components attributable to technical change and catch-up, using a different approach. Specifically, they consider three competing stochastic panel data models, and then, instead of choosing the best, they combine estimates by weighting them using the method proposed in Hansen (2007).[25] Sickles, Hao, and Shang (2016) find that the annual TFP growth of 1.13% (approximately 75% over 50 years) occurred mostly due to technological progress of 1.04% per year (approximately 67% over 50 years). Meanwhile, they concluded that catch-up comprised only 0.09% per year, or approximately 4.6% over 50 years. Other studies of productivity measurement making use of model averaging approaches include Isaksson, Sickles, and Shang (2016) and Duygun, Isaksson, Hao, and Sickles (2016). For more discussions and details, see Chapter 16 of Sickles and Zelenyuk (2017).

Finally, a concomitant stream of literature worth mentioning here—as the one that has yet to realize its potential for analyzing cross-country productivity change and its decompositions—delves into the theory and estimation of dynamic adjustments in an SFA framework. This important segment of literature goes back at least to Chang and Stefanou (1988), Luh and Stefanou (1991), and Sickles and Streitwieser (1998), and was revisited more recently by Silva and Stefanou (2003, 2007), Rungsuriyawiboon and Stefanou (2007), Lansink, Stefanou, and Serra (2015), and Silva, Lansink, and Stefanou (2015). See Chapter 16 of Sickles and Zelenyuk (2017) for further details on dynamic modeling.

24.5. Concluding Remarks and Future Directions

Measuring productivity and understanding the patterns of its growth is important for connecting a number of macroeconomic trends, such as current and potential income levels, poverty, wage determination, social stability, and so on. Estimating productivity growth and its sources is not an easy task. Models of differences in the performance of national economies depend on assumptions about (the changes in) macroeconomic behavior, such as saving rates and technology. Many such approaches exist, and the results depend upon the method applied and the sample period under investigation.

As is true for virtually any study, the results of the reviewed studies may need to be taken with a grain of salt. First, the decompositions put forward in the literature are not necessarily unique, and should labor productivity or MPI be broken down differently, different conclusions might follow (see discussions in Ray and Desli 1997, and Färe, Grosskopf, Norris, and Zhang 1997). Second, the levels of aggregation of variables typically used in cross-country and regional comparisons hide growth patterns at the industry level, where technical change and its dissemination might play a more important role than it does at the aggregate level. Third, average performance is an important benchmark, and additional and valuable insights can be gained from using aggregate productivity measures where averaging of individual scores is done with weighting, where weights account for the economic importance of each individual (Henderson and Zelenyuk, 2007; Mayer and Zelenyuk, 2014; Simar and Zelenyuk, 2007; Zelenyuk, 2006). Fourth, as Badunenko, Henderson, and Houssa (2014) note, the significance of the components is paramount for making conclusions that are useful for policymakers. Most important, the temporal correlation present in the data needs to be taken into account for making consistent statistical inference. Kneip, Simar, and Wilson (2015) suggest a method for making inference about mean efficiency levels. A natural extension would be to adopt this method to provide inference regarding the mean of components of the growth decomposition. Moreover, testing for the structure of the technology, such as returns to scale or convexity, cannot be neglected when analyzing differences in growth based on production frontiers (Kneip, Simar, and Wilson, 2016). Fifth, Alam and Sickles (2000) developed a time-series methodology to link efficiency, convergence, and cointegration measures, while Ahn and Sickles (2000) consider a frontier model in which firm-specific technical inefficiency levels are autoregressive (applied to the US airline industry). These interesting methodologies can be applied to the cross-country analysis as well, thus adding novelty to the stream of literature we focus on.

Furthermore, while the current literature we have focused on here provides interesting insights about differences in the productivity of nations, many important aspects have been left out and naturally call for further research. Other important aspects include proper accounting of dynamic adjustments (e.g., Silva et al. 2015), accounting for the problem of the uneven process of technological diffusion (Andrews et al. 2015; OECD 2016), and accounting for the influence of information and communications technology (ICT) and e-commerce (especially due to "Googlization" and various Internet-based social networks), which have been among the key engines of the recent developments of nations, yet are rarely considered directly in productivity studies.[26] Finally, the suggested components of growth are proximate causes.[27] To better understand the patterns of growth, the fundamental causes should gain more attention. Mastromarco and Simar (2015), for example, use a nonparametric two-step approach on conditional efficiencies to investigate how foreign direct investment (FDI) and time affect the process of catching up. Each of these issues suggests possible areas for fruitful future research.

Notes

1. GDP is usually used to measure the total output or total income of a country, although some studies argue that GNP is a more appropriate measure Abramovitz 1956; Solow 1957).

2. This review complements Sickles, Hao, and Shang (2015), which mainly focused on the regression-based approaches to productivity measurement.

3. Note that growth accounting is a mere accounting decomposition; it is not used to identify the sources of growth (Barro and Sala-i-Martin, 2004).

4. However, Sala-i-Martin (1996) found that growth rates of labor productivity converged for the subsample of OECD countries, the states within the United States, the prefectures of Japan, and regions within several European countries.

5. Sickles, Hao, and Shang (2014, 2016) considered a model-averaging approach using various weighting schemes in the TFP decomposition framework.

6. Sala-i-Martin (1996) calls this type of convergence absolute β- convergence.

7. Henderson, Parmeter, and Russell (2008) showed that twin-peakedness of labor productivity distribution was present throughout or emerged during 1960–2000.

8. Also see Henderson and Zelenyuk (2007) for a related discussion and about testing of efficiency convergence.

9. Other assumptions (non-CRS technology, weak disposability of inputs or outputs, non-convexity, etc.) can also be imposed. For more details see Färe, Grosskopf, and Lovell (1994a) and Sickles and Zelenyuk (2017).

10. The MPI was introduced by Caves, Christensen, and Diewert (1982), and was inspired by related ideas of Malmquist (1953), who dealt with price and quantity indexes based on input distance functions (see Lovell 2003).

11. Here and in what follows, we reproduce figures and tables as close as possible to the original studies using publicly available data.

12. Starting from Solow (1957), CRS is habitually assumed in growth and convergence studies.

13. Note that in previous section y denoted an output vector. Starting from Section 24.3.3, y is labor productivity.

14. The old notation for this component in the literature is $KACC$, which might be incorrectly interpreted as capital accumulation, while in fact it is component indicating (the contribution to labor productivity change from) changes in capital per unit of labor rather than total capital. We therefore hope the addition of L to the old notation will limit confusion. Also note that if $KLACC$ indicates an increase (i.e., $KLACC > 1$), it is interpreted as a positive impact on labor productivity due to physical capital deepening (i.e., due to an increase of capital per unit of labor).

15. PWT have seen many updates; the most recent version (9.0 as of this writing) can be downloaded from http://dx.doi.org/10.15141/S5J01T.

16. The sample of 57 countries described in section 24.4.1 were used to produce this figure.

17. This and other replicated figures are very close to those in the original papers, but may not be exact (e.g., potentially different bandwidth parameters for the kernel density estimates).

18. Also see Zelenyuk (2014), for a related discussion of multi-peak distributions of labor productivity for developed countries, and testing in the growth accounting context.

19. The contributions are not additive, mainly because the contributions are averages of contributions, rather than contributions of the averages. Percent individual contributions are also not additive since they are calculated as an index minus 1 times 100.

20. Kumar and Russell (2002) used the Li (1996) test with asymptotic critical values. Briefly, the idea of the Li (1996) test is the following: if f and g are two distributions, this statistic tests the null hypothesis $H_0 : f(x) = g(x)$ for all x , against the alternative $H_1 : f(x) \neq g(x)$ for some x.

21. Henderson and Russell (2005) used Barro and Lee (2001) education data and the Psacharopoulos (1994) survey of wage equations evaluating returns to education and followed Hall and Jones (1999) to construct human capital. Data on output, capital stock, and labor came from PWT, Mark 5. The data set includes 52 countries, 5 fewer than the Kumar and Russell (2002) data set, because data on human capital were not available for some countries.

22. Note a slight change in notation relative to the previous literature: we added L (use $HLACC$ instead of $HACC$), to emphasize the way human capital is accounted for in the model—as a multiplicative augmentation of L (see Henderson and Russell, 2005, for details).

23. The data on 98 economies for output, capital stock, and labor came from PWT, Version 6.3, and for human capital, Badunenko, Henderson, and Russell (2013) used Barro and Lee (2013) education data.

24. Badunenko, Henderson, and Houssa (2014) follow Simar and Wilson (1999) and use a smoothed bootstrap, where the assumption that the density of efficiency scores is independent of the distributions of inputs and outputs needs to be maintained. This assumption can be confirmed using a test of independence (Wilson 2003). For the sample of 35 African countries in Badunenko, Henderson and Houssa (2014), the null hypothesis of independence was not rejected.

25. A similar approach was suggested by Sickles (2005) for efficiency estimation of panel data.

26. For related discussion, e.g., see Brynjolfsson and Hitt (2000); Jorgenson (2001); Zelenyuk (2014).

27. Exception in this line of research is Badunenko and Romero-Ávila (2013), who investigate the role of changes in financial system, quality of institutions, and legal environment in labor productivity growth.

References

Abramovitz, Moses. 1956. "Resource and Output Trends in the United States since 1870." *American Economic Review* 46: 5–23.

Abramovitz, Moses. 1986. "Catching Up, Forging Ahead, and Falling Behind." *Journal of Economic History* 46(2): 385–406.

Acemoglu, Daron. 2009. *Introduction to Modern Economic Growth*. Princeton, NJ: Princeton University Press.

Afriat, Sidney N. 1972. "Efficiency Estimation of Production Functions," *International Economic Review* 13(3): 568–598.

Ahn, Seung C., and Robin C. Sickles. 2000. "Estimation of Long-Run Inefficiency Levels: A Dynamic Frontier Approach." *Econometric Reviews* 19(4): 461–492.

Alam, Ila M. Semenick, and Robin C. Sickles. 2000. "Time Series Analysis of Deregulatory Dynamics and Technical Efficiency: The Case of the U.S. Airline Industry." *International Economic Review* 41(1): 203–218.

Andrews, Dan, Chiara Criscuolo, and Peter N. Gal. 2015. "Frontier Firms, Technology Diffusion and Public Policy: Micro Evidence from OECD Countries." OECD Productivity Working Paper No. 02. http://dx.doi.org/10.1787/5jrql2q2jj7b-en.

Badunenko, Oleg, Daniel J. Henderson, and Romain Houssa. 2014. "Significant Drivers of Growth in Africa." *Journal of Productivity Analysis* 42(3): 339–354.

Badunenko, Oleg, Daniel J. Henderson, and R. Robert Russell. 2013. "Polarization of the Worldwide Distribution of Productivity." *Journal of Productivity Analysis* 40(2): 153–171.

Badunenko, Oleg, Daniel J. Henderson, and Valentin Zelenyuk. 2008. "Technological Change and Transition: Relative Contributions to Worldwide Growth During the 1990s." *Oxford Bulletin of Economics and Statistics* 70(4): 461–492.

Badunenko, Oleg, and Diego Romero-Ávila. 2013. "Financial Development and the Sources of Growth and Convergence." *International Economic Review* 54(2): 629–663.

Badunenko, Oleg, and Diego Romero-Ávila. 2014. "Productivity Growth across Spanish Regions and Industries: A Production-Frontier Approach." *Regional Studies* 48(7): 1242–1262.

Badunenko, Oleg, and Kiril Tochkov. 2010. "Soaring Dragons, Roaring Tigers, Growling Bears." *Economics of Transition* 18(3): 539–570.

Barro, Robert J., and Jong-Wha Lee. 2001. "International Data on Educational Attainment: Updates and Implications." *Oxford Economic Papers* 53(3): 541–563.

Barro, Robert J., and Jong-Wha Lee. 2013. "A New Data Set of Educational Attainment in the World, 1950–2010." *Journal of Development Economics* 104: 184–198.

Barro, Robert J., and Xavier Sala-i-Martin. 1992. "Convergence." *Journal of Political Economy* 100(2): 407–443.

Barro, Robert J., and Xavier X. Sala-i-Martin. 2004. *Economic Growth.* Cambridge, MA: MIT Press.

Baumol, William J. 1986. "Productivity Growth, Convergence, and Welfare: What the Long-Run Data Show." *American Economic Review* 76(5): 1072–1085.

Bernard, Andrew B., and Charles I. Jones. 1996. "Productivity Across Industries and Countries: Time Series Theory and Evidence." *The Review of Economics and Statistics* 78(1): 135–146.

Bliss, Christopher. 2000. "Galton's Fallacy and Economic Convergence: A Reply to Cannon and Duck." *Oxford Economic Papers* 52(2): 420–422.

Borts, George H., and Jerome L. Stein. 1964. *Economic Growth in a Free Market.* New York: Columbia University Press.

Brynjolfsson, Erik, and Lorin M. Hitt. 2000. "Beyond Computation: Information Technology, Organizational Transformation and Business Performance." *Journal of Economic Perspectives* 14(4): 23–48.

Caves, Douglas W., Laurits R. Christensen, and W. Erwin Diewert. 1982. "The Economic Theory of Index Numbers and the Measurement of Input, Output, and Productivity." *Econometrica* 50: 1393–1414.

Chang, Ching-Cheng, and Spiro E. Stefanou. 1988. "Specification and Estimation of Asymmetric Adjustment Rates for Quasi-Fixed Factors of Production." *Journal of Economic Dynamics and Control* 12(1): 145–151.

Charnes, A., W. W. Cooper, and E. Rhodes. 1978. "Measuring the Efficiency of Decision Making Units." *European Journal of Operational Research* 2(6): 429–444.

Chenery, Hollis B. 1986. "Growth and Transformation." In *Industrialisation and Growth: A Comparative Study*, edited by Hollis B. Chenery, S. Robinson, and Moshe Syrquin, 13–36. Oxford: Oxford University Press.

Daskovska, Alexandra, Léopold Simar, and Sébastien Van Bellegem. 2010. "Forecasting the Malmquist Productivity Index." *Journal of Productivity Analysis* 33(2): 97–107.

De Long, J. Bradford. 1988. "Productivity Growth, Convergence, and Welfare: Comment." *American Economic Review* 78(5): 1138–1154.

Debreu, Gerard. 1951. "The Coefficient of Resource Utilization." *Econometrica* 19: 273–292.

Delgado-Rodríguez, Ma Jesús, and Immaculada Álvarez Ayuso. 2008. "Economic Growth and Convergence of EU Member States: An Empirical Investigation." *Review of Development Economics* 12(3): 486–497.

Denison, Edward F. 1967. *Why Growth Rates Differ*. Washington, DC: The Brookings Institution.

Diewert, W. Erwin. 1980. "Capital and the Theory of Productivity Measurement." *The American Economic Review* 70(2): 260–267.

Duygun, Meryem, Anders Isaksson, Jiaqi Hao, and Robin C. Sickles. 2017. "World Productivity Growth: A Model Averaging Approach." *Pacific Economic Review* 22(4): 587–619.

Easterlin, Richard A. 1960. "Regional Growth of Income: Long-Run Tendencies, 1880–1950" in *Population Redistribution and Economic Growth, United States, 1870–1950*, Vol. II: *Analyses of Economic Change*, edited by Simon Kuznets, Ann Ratner Miller, and Richard A. Easterlin, 141–181. Philadelphia: American Philosophical Society.

Easterly, William, and Ross Levine. 2001. "It's Not Factor Accumulation: Stylized Facts and Growth Models." *The World Bank Economic Review* 15(2): 177–219.

Enflo, Kerstin, and Per Hjertstrand. 2009. "Relative Sources of European Regional Productivity Convergence: A Bootstrap Frontier Approach." *Regional Studies* 43(5): 643–659.

Fagerberg, Jan. 1988. "Why Growth Rates Differ." In *Technical Change and Economic Theory*, edited by Giovanni Dosi, Christopher Freeman, Richard Nelson, Gerald Silverberg, and Luc Soete, 432–457. London: Pinter.

Färe, Rolf, Shawna Grosskopf, B. Lindgren, and P. Roos. [1989] 1994. "Productivity Developments in Swedish Hospital: A Malmquist Output Index Approach." In *Data Envelopment Analysis: Theory, Methodology and Applications*, edited by A. Charnes, W. W. Cooper, A. Lewin, and L. Seiford, 679–741. Boston: Kluwer Academic.

Färe, Rolf, Shawna Grosskopf, and C. A. Knox Lovell. 1994a. *Production Frontiers*. Cambridge: Cambridge University Press.

Färe, Rolf, Shawna Grosskopf, Mary Norris, and Zhongyang Zhang. 1994b. "Productivity Growth, Technical Progress, and Efficiency Change in Industrialized Countries." *American Economic Review* 84(1): 66–83.

Färe, Rolf, Shawna Grosskopf, Mary Norris, and Zhongyang Zhang. 1997. "Productivity Growth, Technical Progress, and Efficiency Change in Industrialized Countries: Reply." *American Economic Review* 87(5): 1040–1044.

Farrell, Michael J. 1957. "The Measurement of Productive Efficiency." *Journal of the Royal Statistical Society. Series A (General)* 120(3): 253–290.

Feenstra, Robert C., Robert Inklaar, and Marcel P. Timmer. 2010. "The Next Generation of the Penn World Table." *American Economic Review* 105(10): 3150–3182.

Hall, Robert E., and Charles I. Jones. 1999. "Why Do Some Countries Produce So Much More Output per Worker Than Others?" *Quarterly Journal of Economics* 114(1): 83–116.

Hansen, Bruce E. 2007. "Least Squares Model Averaging." *Econometrica* 75(4): 1175–1189.

Henderson, Daniel J., Christopher F. Parmeter, and R. Robert Russell. 2008. "Modes, Weighted Modes, and Calibrated Modes: Evidence of Clustering Using Modality Tests." *Journal of Applied Econometrics* 23(5): 607–638.

Henderson, Daniel J., and R. Robert Russell. 2005. "Human Capital and Convergence: A Production-Frontier Approach." *International Economic Review* 46(4): 1167–1205.

Henderson, Daniel J., Kiril Tochkov, and Oleg Badunenko. 2007. "A Drive up the Capital Coast? Contributions to Post-Reform Growth Across Chinese Provinces." *Journal of Macroeconomics* 29(3): 569–594.

Henderson, Daniel J., and Valentin Zelenyuk. 2007. "Testing for (Efficiency) Catching-up." *Southern Economic Journal* 73(4): 1003–1019.

Heston, Alan, and Robert Summers. 1988. "A New Set of International Comparisons of Real Product and Price Levels Estimates for 130 Countries, 1950–1985." *Review of Income and Wealth* 34: 1–25.

Hsieh, Chang-Tai, and Peter J. Klenow. 2009. "Misallocation and Manufacturing TFP in China and India." *The Quarterly Journal of Economics* 124(4): 1403–1448.

Hultberg, Patrick T., M. Ishaq Nadiri, and Robin C. Sickles. 1999. "An International Comparison of Technology Adoption and Efficiency: A Dynamic Panel Model." *Annals of Economics and Statistics* 55–56: 449–474.

Hultberg, Patrick T., M. Ishaq Nadiri, and Robin C. Sickles. 2004. "Cross-Country Catch-Up in the Manufacturing Sector: Impacts of Heterogeneity on Convergence and Technology Adoption." *Empirical Economics* 29(4): 753–768.

Inklaar, Robert, and W. Erwin Diewert. 2016. "Measuring Industry Productivity and Cross-Country Convergence." *Journal of Econometrics* 191(2): 426–433.

Isaksson, Anders, Robin C. Sickles, and Chenjun Shang. 2016. "Non-Structural Analysis of World Productivity Growth: A Model Averaging Approach." Mimeo, Department of Economics, Rice University.

Jeon, Byung M., and Robin C. Sickles. 2004. "The Role of Environmental Factors in Growth Accounting: A Nonparametric Analysis." *Journal of Applied Econometrics* 19(5): 567–591.

Jones, Charles I. 1997. "Convergence Revisited." *Journal of Economic Growth* 2(2): 131–153.

Jorgenson, Dale W. 2001. "Information Technology and the U.S. Economy/" *American Economic Review* 91(1): 1–32.

Klenow, Peter J., and Mark Bils. 2000. "Does Schooling Cause Growth?" *American Economic Review* 90(5): 1160–1183.

Kneip, Alois, Léopold Simar, and Paul W. Wilson. 2015. "When Bias Kills the Variance: Central Limit Theorems for DEA and FDH Efficiency Scores." *Econometric Theory* 31(02): 394–422.

Kneip, Alois, Léopold Simar, and Paul W. Wilson. 2016. "Testing Hypotheses in Nonparametric Models of Production." *Journal of Business & Economic Statistics* 34(3): 435–456.

Kumar, Subodh, and R. Robert Russell. 2002. "Technological Change, Technological Catch-up, and Capital Deepening: Relative Contributions to Growth and Convergence." *American Economic Review* 92(3): 527–548.

Kumbhakar, Subal C., and Hung-Jen Wang. 2005. "Estimation of Growth Convergence Using a Stochastic Production Frontier Approach." *Economics Letters* 88(3): 300–305.

Lansink, Alfons Oude, Spiro E. Stefanou, and Teresa Serra. 2015. "Primal and Dual Dynamic Luenberger Productivity Indicators,." *European Journal of Operational Research* 241(2): 555–563.

Li, Qi. 1996. "Nonparametric Testing of Closeness Between Two Unknown Distribution Functions." *Econometric Reviews* 15: 261–274.

Lovell, C. A. Knox. 2003. "The Decomposition of Malmquist Productivity Indexes." *Journal of Productivity Analysis* 20(3): 437–458.

Lucas, R. E., Jr. 1988. "On the Mechanics of Economic Development." *Journal of Monetary Economics* 22(1): 3–42.

Luh, Yir-Hueih, and Spiro E. Stefanou. 1991. "Productivity Growth in U.S. Agriculture under Dynamic Adjustment." *American Journal of Agricultural Economics* 73(4): 1116–1125.

Maddison, Angus. 1984. "Comparative Analysis of the Productivity Situation in the Advanced Capitalist Countries." In *International Comparisons of Productivity and Causes of the Slowdown*, edited by John W. Kendrick, 59–92. Cambridge: Ballinger.

Malmquist, Sten. 1953. "Index Numbers and Indifference Surfaces." *Trabajos de Estadistica* 504(2): 209–242.

Mankiw, N. Gregory, David Romer, and David N. Weil. 1992. "A Contribution to the Empirics of Economic Growth." *Quarterly Journal of Economics* 107(2): 407–437.

Mastromarco, Camilla, and Léopold Simar. 2015. "Effect of FDI and Time on Catching Up: New Insights from a Conditional Nonparametric Frontier Analysis." *Journal of Applied Econometrics* 30(5): 826–847.

Mayer, Andreas, and Valentin Zelenyuk. 2014. "Aggregation of Malmquist Productivity Indexes Allowing for Reallocation of Resources." *European Journal of Operational Research* 238(3): 774–785.

OECD. 2016. *The Productivity-Inclusiveness Nexus*. Paris: OECD. doi: http://dx.doi.org/10.1787/9789264258303-en.

Pastor, Jesús T., and C. A. Knox Lovell. 2007. "Circularity of the Malmquist Productivity Index," *Economic Theory* 33(3): 591–599.

Persons, Warren M. 1921. "Fisher's Formula for Index Numbers." *The Review of Economics and Statistics* 3(5): 103–113.

Pritchett, Lant. 1997. "Divergence, Big Time." *Journal of Economic Perspectives* 11(3): 3–17.

Pritchett, Lant. 2000. "The Tyranny of Concepts: CUDIE (Cumulated, Depreciated, Investment Effort) Is Not Capital." *Journal of Economic Growth* 5(4): 361–84.

Psacharopoulos, George. 1994. "Returns to Investment in Education: A Global Update." *World Development* 22: 1325–1343.

Quah, Danny. 1996. "Twin Peaks: Growth and Convergence in Models of Distribution Dynamics." *Economic Journal* 106(437): 1045–1055.

Quah, Danny. 1997. "Empirics for Growth and Distribution: Stratification, Polarization, and Convergence Clubs." *Journal of Economic Growth* 2(1): 27–59.

Ray, Subhash C., and Evangelia Desli. 1997. "Productivity Growth, Technical Progress, and Efficiency Change in Industrialized Countries: Comment." *American Economic Review* 87(5): 1033–1039.

Rungsuriyawiboon, Supawat, and Spiro E. Stefanou. 2007. "Dynamic Efficiency Estimation: An Application to U.S. Electric Utilities." *Journal of Business & Economic Statistics* 25: 226–238.

Sala-i-Martin, Xavier X. 1996. "The Classical Approach to Convergence Analysis," *Economic Journal* 106(437): 1019–1036.

Sala-i-Martin, Xavier X. 2006. "The World Distribution of Income: Falling Poverty and . . . Convergence, Period." *Quarterly Journal of Economics* CXXI(2): 351–397.

Sheather, Simon J., and Michael C. Jones. 1991. "A Reliable Data Based Bandwidth Selection Method for Kernel Density Estimation." *Journal of Royal Statistical Society, Series B* 53: 683–990.

Sickles, Robin C. 2005. "Panel Estimators and the Identification of Firm-Specific Efficiency Levels in Parametric, Semiparametric and Nonparametric Settings." *Journal of Econometrics* 126(2): 305–334.

Sickles, Robin C., Jiaqi Hao, and Chenjun Shang. 2014. "Panel Data and Productivity Measurement: An Analysis of Asian Productivity Trends." *Journal of Chinese Economic and Business Studies* 12(3): 211–231.

Sickles, Robin C., Jiaqi Hao, and Chenjun Shang. 2015. "Panel Data and Productivity Measurement." In *The Oxford Handbook of Panel Data*, edited by Badi H. Baltagi, 517–547. Oxford: Oxford University Press, 2015.

Sickles, Robin C., Jiaqi Hao, and Chenjun Shang, 2016. "Productivity Measurement, Model Averaging, and World Trends in Growth and Inequality." In *Productivity and Efficiency Analysis*, edited by William H. Greene, Lynda Khalaf, Robin C. Sickles, Michael Veall, and Marcel-Cristian Voia, 305–323. London: Springer.

Sickles, Robin C., and Mary L. Streitwieser. 1998. "An Analysis of Technology, Productivity, and Regulatory Distortion in the Interstate Natural Gas Transmission Industry: 1977–1985." *Journal of Applied Econometrics* 13(4): 377–395.

Sickles, Robin C., and Valentin Zelenyuk. 2018. *Measurement of Productivity and Efficiency: Theory and Practice*. Cambridge: Cambridge University Press.

Silva, Elvira, Alfons Oude Lansink, and Spiro E. Stefanou. 2015. "The Adjustment-Cost Model of the Firm: Duality and Productive Efficiency." *International Journal of Production Economics* 168(C): 245–256.

Silva, Elvira, and Spiro E. Stefanou. 2003. "Nonparametric Dynamic Production Analysis and the Theory of Cost." *Journal of Productivity Analysis* 19(1): 5–32.

Silva, Elvira, and Spiro E. Stefanou. 2007. "Dynamic Efficiency Measurement: Theory and Application." *American Journal of Agricultural Economics* 89(2): 398–419.

Silverman, Bernard W. 1981. "Using Kernel Density Estimates to Investigate Multimodality." *Journal of the Royal Statistical Society, Series B* 43: 97–99.

Simar, Léopold, and Paul W. Wilson. 1999. "Estimating and Bootstrapping Malmquist Indices." *European Journal of Operational Research* 115(3): 459–471.

Simar, Léopold, and Valentin Zelenyuk. 2006. "On Testing Equality of Distributions of Technical Efficiency Scores." *Econometric Reviews* 25(4): 497–522.

Simar, Léopold, and Valentin Zelenyuk. 2007. "Statistical Inference for Aggregates of Farrell-Type Efficiencies." *Journal of Applied Econometrics* 22(7): 1367–1394.

Solow, Robert M. 1957. "Technical Change and the Aggregate Production Function." *The Review of Economics and Statistics* 39(3): 312–320.

Weil, David N. 2014. *Economic Growth*, 3rd edition. New York: Routledge.

Wilson, Paul W. 2003. "Testing Independence in Models of Productive Efficiency." *Journal of Productivity Analysis* 20: 361–390.

Zelenyuk, Valentin. 2006. "Aggregation of Malmquist Productivity Indexes." *European Journal of Operational Research* 174(2): 1076–1086.

Zelenyuk, Valentin. 2014. "Testing Significance of Contributions in Growth Accounting, with Application to Testing ICT Impact on Labor Productivity of Developed Countries." *International Journal of Business and Economics* 13(2): 115–126.

Author Index

Subject Index